Price $36.00

TENNESSEE STATISTICAL ABSTRACT 1994/95

Betty B. Vickers, Editor

Vickie C. Cunningham, Assistant Editor

Center for Business and Economic Research
College of Business Administration
The University of Tennessee, Knoxville

November 1994

129664

Fifteenth Edition, November 1994
Library of Congress Catalogue No. 68-66499

SUGGESTED CITATION
The University of Tennessee, Knoxville
Center for Business and Economic Research
Tennessee Statistical Abstract 1994/95
Knoxville, Tennessee, 1994

Cover Photo: Hawkins County Courthouse, Rogersville, TN. Photo courtesy of Randy Ball Photography. The Hawkins County Courthouse is the oldest courthouse in the state.

UT Authorization No. E01-1490-004-95

ISBN 0–940191–18–0

1994/95 TENNESSEE STATISTICAL ABSTRACT
PROJECT STAFF

Betty B. Vickers, *Research Associate, and Editor, TSA*

Vickie C. Cunningham, *Research Associate, and Assistant Editor, TSA*

Jeanne P. McDonald, *Managing Editor of Publications*

Joan M. Snoderly, *Associate Editor of Publications*

Lynn J. Landry, *Publications Coordinator*

Patricia A. Hunley, *Word Processing Group Supervisor*

Julia C. Elkins, *Word Processing Specialist*

Patricia D. Flynn, *Word Processing Specialist*

Stacy M. Diorio, *Student Assistant*

Raymond D. Easley, *Student Assistant*

INTRODUCTION: NOTE FOR DATA USERS

The *Tennessee Statistical Abstract* attempts to provide, in a single convenient reference, the most useful available current data as well as some historical time-series data. These data are also available on IBM compatible 3-1/2" floppy diskettes in LOTUS 1-2-3.™ (LOTUS 1-2-3™ is a trademark of LOTUS Development Corporation. IBM® is a registered trademark of International Business Machines, Inc.) Every effort is made to insure the accuracy of the data. Responsibility for errors in reproduction of data or in calculations, however, is assumed by the Center for Business and Economic Research.

The user is urged to read carefully the chapter prefaces and any footnotes accompanying the tables. Those who employ these data for research or for purposes where the choice of statistics must be defended should become familiar with the methodology and computation of the relevant data. Data may have been collected either by a census–a "complete" count of the population of interest–or by a sample survey. Methods of sampling will vary, affecting the validity of the information for various uses. Specialized information on the methodology behind the data cannot be included in the *Abstract*, but the source notes at the end of each table will lead the reader to that information.

Much of the value of the *Abstract* lies in its many references to other sources of information. There are 25 libraries in Tennessee, designated as federal depository libraries, which house a variety of federal publications and have reference staffs to assist in locating information. In addition, the Bureau of the Census has designated a Tennessee State Data Center, a joint project of the Tennessee State Planning Office, Nashville, and the Center for Business and Economic Research, The University of Tennessee, Knoxville. The State Data Center, 16 affiliate data centers, and a census depository library (in addition to the federal depository libraries, a list of which follows) maintain for public use a collection of all census publications relating to Tennessee.

Every effort has been made to provide *Abstract* users with the most complete data collection possible. Often space requirements limit the detail provided for counties and municipalities. For example, Table 2.4 is also available for counties, but the amount of detail published was limited to that given in Table 2.13. Full detail at the sub-state level is available upon request for these and other data. Occasionally data are not available on certain topics or for state or sub-state areas. The cost of collecting and processing data for specialized concerns and small geographic areas is often prohibitive. Also, data are not provided for a subject until expressed interest demands it, or, where concepts and interest exist, there may be no appropriate agency to represent the interests and establish data collection. New data are incorporated into the *Abstract* as collected, and substitutions are made when appropriate. We solicit your suggestions about other sources, as well as areas about which you wish to have more detailed information.

PREFACE

The *1994/95 Tennessee Statistical Abstract* is the fifteenth published by the Center for Business and Economic Research (CBER) since publication began in 1969. Although publication of the *Abstract* requires considerable effort, we feel that it provides better access to these data than answering individual requests. In each of the nineteen data areas, we have tried to provide answers to users' most frequent data needs. The publication is facilitated both by your purchase and by CBER's continued commitment to support informed decison-making in Tennessee.

The *Abstract* is also available on IBM® compatible 3-1/2" floppy diskettes in LOTUS 1-2-3™ (version 2.01) format. The price of the entire volume is $75.00, or $20.00 for single chapters. Although technological advancement and private and public sector data initiatives provide access to an ever-increasing supply of data, barriers to informed decision-making remain.

First, the availability of data in electronic media excludes many data users either because they do not have the technical equipment or user knowledge to access these data or because the existence of the data is veiled by the medium. Published indexes to electronically disseminated information should be readily available to data users. A statistical abstract serves as an index to both published and unpublished data and data sources. Secondly, the imposition of user fees either by the public or the private sector excludes both the casual data user and those who cannot afford the purchase price. Although arguments for recovering the costs of value-added services have merit, these charges should not prohibit access to public data. Finally, the abundance of data engenders an "information-poor" class, because a data user must deal with a multitude of different measurements for each data item and is often hindered in the selection of the best measure by the absence of collection dates, methodology, or source.

The necessity for maintaining standards in data presentation, whether electronic or print, underscores the importance of compendia such as the *Statistical Abstract of the United States* and state counterparts like the *Tennessee Statistical Abstract*. Unless agencies such as ours assume lead responsibility for accessing, compiling, and publishing statistical information, standards may fall victim to indiscriminate accessibility.

Numerous federal, state, and private publications were used in compiling this volume, and source documentation has been made as complete as possible. The chapter prefaces and the source notes following each table provide valuable direction to the user who wishes to obtain additional information. All data users should be aware of the inherent limitations of data of all kinds and are urged to read the "Notes for Data Users" on page iv.

In this *1994/95 Tennessee Statistical Abstract*, data are given primarily for 1991 and 1992 for the state of Tennessee, its Metropolitan Statistical Areas, counties, and, where data are available and space permits, for towns. Also presented are comparisons between Tennessee and other southeastern states. The reporting lag is the time required by the collecting agencies to accumulate and process the data.

The *Tennessee Statistical Abstract* is produced from a CBER research database, and thus, the price reflects only the cost of publication. We need your feedback on content, your repeated purchase of annual editions, and your recommendation to other potential users. We encourage the placement of a standing order. Use either the card enclosed for this purpose or contact the Center for Business and Economic Research, College of Business Administration, The University of Tennessee, Knoxville, Tennessee, 37996-4170, (615) 974-5441.

Compiling the *Tennessee Statistical Abstract* is a task that requires a variety of talents ranging from graphic arts to statistical detective work, sophisticated computer programming and desktop publishing skills, and editorial judgment. Each CBER staff member and student assistant gave countless hours in the attempt to insure that the *Abstract* is as useful and accurate as possible. The list of those contributing to the *1994/95 Tennessee Statistical Abstract* may be found on page iii. We are grateful for their dedication, patience, and cooperation. Special thanks go to Pene Gilmore, Computer Resources Group, CBER, for her continued assistance and guidance in building and monitoring the *Abstract* database. We also appreciate the work of Will Fontanez, cartographer, The University of Tennessee, Department of Geography, for creation of the county maps. Tennessee state government personnel, too numerous to list individually, have been generous in providing data and answering questions; and finally, the reference and government documents staffs of the UTK Library have provided assistance in locating materials throughout this research effort.

David A. Hake, *Director*
Betty B. Vickers, *Research Associate*

Center for Business and Economic Research
College of Business Administration
The University of Tennessee, Knoxville
Knoxville, Tennessee

TABLE OF CONTENTS

Chapter   Page

LIST OF FIGURES

Figure   Page

LIST OF FIGURES (Continued)

TENNESSEE STATE DATA CENTER

Tennessee State Planning Office, 309 John Sevier Building, 500 Charlotte Avenue, Nashville, TN 37219, (615) 741-1676

Center for Business and Economic Research, Suite 100, Glocker Business Administration Building, The University of Tennessee, Knoxville, TN 37996-4170, (615) 974-6080

EAST TENNESSEE DATA RESOURCES

Federal Depository Libraries

E. W. King Library, King College, Bristol, TN 37620, (615) 968-1187

Sherrod Library, East Tennessee State University, P. O. Box 22450A, Johnson City, TN 37614-0002, (615) 929-4337

Carson-Newman College Library, Russell Avenue, Jefferson City, TN 37760, (615) 475-9061

Lawson-McGhee Public Library, 500 Church Street, SW, Knoxville, TN 37902-2505 (615) 544-5750

The University of Tennessee Law Library, College of Law, 1505 W. Cumberland, Knoxville, TN 37996-1800, (615) 974-4381

John C. Hodges Library, The University of Tennessee at Knoxville, Knoxville, TN 37996-1000, (615) 974-4127

U.S. TVA Technical Library, 1101 Market Street, Chattanooga, TN 37402, (615) 751-4913

Cleveland State Community College Library, P. O. Box 3570, Cleveland, TN 37320-3570, (615) 472-7141

Chattanooga-Hamilton County Bicentennial Library, 1001 Broad Street, Chattanooga, TN 37402-2652, (615) 757-5310

Jesse Ball DuPont Library, University of the South, Sewanee, TN 37375-4005, (615) 598-5931

Census Depository Library

J. Fred Johnson Memorial Library, Broad and New Streets, Kingsport, TN 37660-4292, (615) 229-9465

State Data Center Affiliates

First Tennessee-Virginia Development District, 207 North Boone Street, Johnson City, TN 37601, (615) 928-0224

East Tennessee Development District, Westwood Building, 5616 Kingston Pike, P. O. Box 19806, Knoxville, TN 37939-2806, (615) 584-8553

Southeast Tennessee Development District, 216 West 8th Street, Suite 300, Chattanooga, TN 37402, (615) 266-5781

Oak Ridge Public Library, Civic Center, Oak Ridge, TN 37830, (615) 483-6386

Knoxville/Knox County Metropolitan Planning Commission, Suite 403, 400 Main Avenue, Knoxville, TN 37902-2476, (615) 521-2500

MIDDLE TENNESSEE DATA RESOURCES

Federal Depository Libraries

University Library, Tennessee Technological University, P. O. Box 5066, Cookeville, TN 38505, (615) 372-3408

Andrew L. Todd Library, Middle Tennessee State University, P. O. Box 13, Murfreesboro, TN 37132, (615) 898-2772

Public Library of Nashville and Davidson County, 8th Avenue N. and Union, Nashville, TN 37203-3585, (615) 259-6004

Fisk University Library, 17th Avenue N., Nashville, TN 37208-3051, (615) 329-8641

Brown-Daniel Library, Tennessee State University, 3500 J. Merritt Blvd., Nashville, TN 37209-1561, (615) 320-3682

Vanderbilt Law Library, College of Law, Nashville, TN 37240, (615) 322-2568

Vanderbilt University Library, 419 21st Avenue S., Nashville, TN 37240-0007, (615) 322-7100

Felix G. Woodward Library, Austin Peay State University, Clarksville, TN 37044, (615) 648-7618

Tennessee State Library and Archives, State Library Division, 403 7th Avenue N., Nashville, TN 37219, (615) 741-2451

John W. Finney Memorial Library, Columbia State Community College, P. O. Box 1315, Columbia, TN 38401, (615) 388-0120

State Data Center Affiliates

Upper Cumberland Development District, 1225 Burgess Falls Road, Cookeville, TN 38506-4194, (615) 432-4111

Greater Nashville Regional Council, 7th Floor Stahlman Building, Box 233, 211 Union Street, Nashville, TN 37201, (615) 862-8828

South Central Tennessee Development District, P. O. Box 1346, Columbia, TN 38402-1346, (615) 381-2040

Department of Economic and Community Development, 8th Floor, Rachel Jackson Building, Nashville, TN 37219, (615) 741-1995

WEST TENNESSEE DATA RESOURCES

Federal Depository Libraries

Paul Meek Library, The University of Tennessee at Martin, Martin, TN 38238-5047, (901) 587-7060

Luther L. Gobbel Library, Lambuth College, Lambuth Blvd., Jackson, TN 38301-5296, (901) 425 2500

Memphis and Shelby County Public Library and Information Center, 1850 Peabody Avenue, Memphis, TN 38104-4025, (901) 725-8855

Cecil C. Humphreys School of Law Library, Memphis State University, Memphis, TN 38152, (901) 678-2426

Regional Depository and State Data Center Affiliate

John W. Brister Library, Memphis State University, Memphis, TN 38152, (901) 678-2206

State Data Center Affiliates

Northwest Tennessee Development District, 124 Weldon Street, P. O. Box 63, Martin, TN 38237, (901) 587-4215

Southwest Tennessee Development District, 27 Conrad Drive, Siute 150, Jackson, TN 38305, (901) 668-7112

Library, The University of Tennessee at Martin, Martin, TN 38238, (901) 587-7065

Memphis Delta Development District, 157 Poplar Avenue, B150, Memphis, TN 38103, (901) 576-4610

Bureau for Business and Economic Research, Memphis State University, Memphis, TN 38152, (901) 678-2281

Memphis and Shelby County Office of Planning and Development, City Hall, 125 N. Main Street, Memphis, TN 38103, (901) 576-6610

FIGURE 0.1
Counties, Metropolitan Areas, and Selected Places

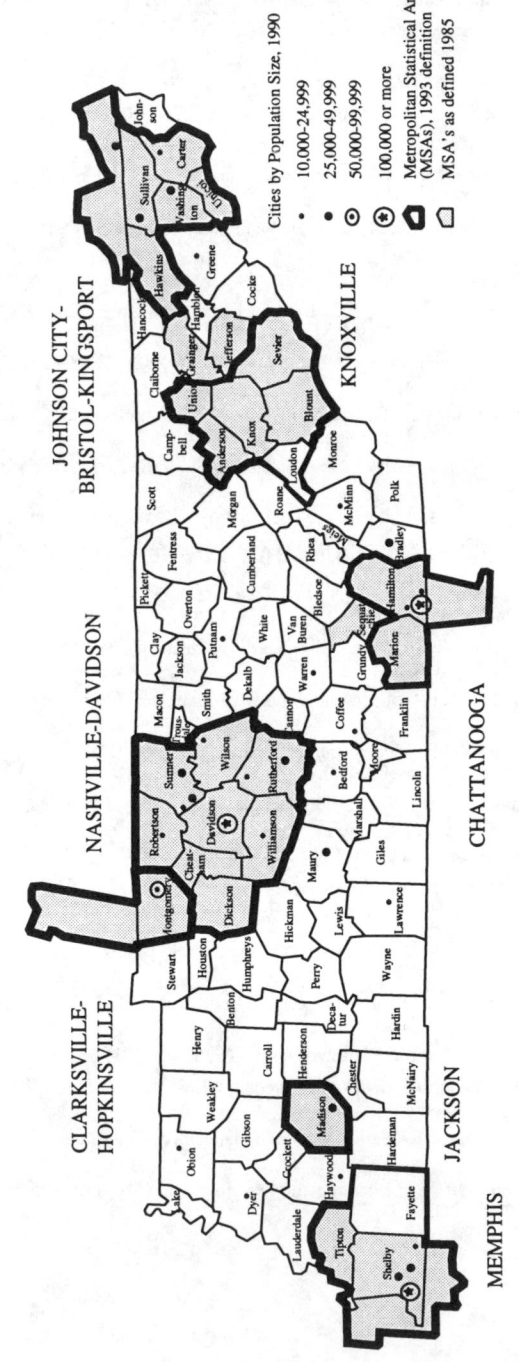

Note: Areas outlined in bold represent newly defined Metropolitan Statistical Areas; shaded areas represent MSA boundaries used for the 1987 Economic Censuses.

Source: U.S. Department of Commerce, Bureau of the Census, *Census of Population: 1990*, and U.S. Office of Management and Budget, Bulletin No. 9–17, June 30, 1993.

Since its beginning in 1790, the decennial census has provided the only data which count and describe all individuals and households in the United States. Details of age, race, income, education, ancestry, language, family and household characteristics, employment and other facts are available from the 1990 Census for areas as small as a group of city blocks. Although most printed data are reported for counties, places, and county subdivisions, information for smaller geographic units is readily accessible using CD-ROM (compact disc - read only memory). Moreover, greater detail in each subject area is also available on computer tape or CD-ROM. In fact, many of the tables included in this chapter were prepared from the Summary Tape File 3A CD-ROM.

In addition to describing how we live and providing for reapportionment, decennial census data also provide benchmarks for intercensal population estimates and numerous other data series. Population estimates for Tennessee and its counties are reported annually. These are produced by the Bureau of the Census in cooperation with the Tennessee State Planning Office and published in *Current Population Reports*. Estimates for 1992 are given in Tables 1.7 and 1.8.

County population estimates also provide the means to estimate the population of Metropolitan Statistical Areas (MSA). Such areas are aggregates of whole counties, including their rural areas, which meet established criteria of population density and economic integration with a large central city. Recent revisions to the Tennessee MSAs emphasize that when time series MSA data are used, one should determine whether the geographic areas are consistent. Although some tables in this *Abstract* employ the 1985 MSA designations, most data describe the MSAs as designated by the Office of Management and Budget, effective June 30, 1993. Table 1.7 provides comparable population data for these areas from 1950 to 1992 using the June 1993 definition. Current MSA boundaries as well as geographic changes in Tennessee MSAs from 1985 to 1993 are shown in Figure 0.1.

In addition to details of the population according to age, race and household size, several specific population groups are described in this chapter. Military veterans residing in Tennessee on April 1, 1990 are detailed by their periods of military service, and county populations are reported by veteran, nonveteran and active military status. Populations living in group quarters are identified by type of quarters such as military, college dormitories, prisons and nursing homes. Immigrants and other foreign-born populations are described by publications issued by the U.S. Department of Commerce, Bureau of the Census, and also by the U.S. Department of Justice, Immigration and Naturalization Service. These data provide a broad understanding of the population of Tennessee.

1. POPULATION

TABLE OF CONTENTS

TABLE OF CONTENTS
(Continued)

1. POPULATION

TABLE 1.1-- URBAN AND RURAL POPULATION, TENNESSEE, 1790-1990, DECENNIAL CENSUS YEARS

Year	Total	Urban	Rural	Urban as percent of total	Rural as percent of total
1990	4,877,185	2,969,948	1,907,237	60.9	39.1
1980	4,591,120	2,773,573	1,817,547	60.4	39.6
1970	3,926,018	2,318,458	1,605,229	59.1	40.9
1960	3,567,089	1,864,828	1,702,261	52.3	47.7
1950	3,291,718	1,452,602	1,839,116	44.1	55.9
1940	2,915,841	1,027,206	1,888,635	35.2	64.8
1930	2,616,556	896,538	1,720,018	34.3	65.7
1920	2,337,885	611,226	1,726,659	26.1	73.9
1910	2,184,789	441,045	1,743,744	20.2	79.8
1900	2,020,616	326,639	1,693,977	16.2	83.8
1890	1,767,518	238,394	1,529,124	13.5	86.5
1880	1,542,359	115,984	1,426,375	7.5	92.5
1870	1,258,520	94,237	1,164,283	7.5	92.5
1860	1,109,801	46,541	1,063,260	4.2	95.8
1850	1,002,717	21,983	980,734	2.2	97.8
1840	829,210	6,929	822,281	0.8	99.2
1830	681,904	5,566	676,338	0.8	99.2
1820	422,823	0	422,823	0.0	100.0
1810	261,727	0	261,727	0.0	100.0
1800	105,602	0	105,602	0.0	100.0
1790	35,691	0	35,691	0.0	100.0

Note: 1790 population is that of territory south of the Ohio River, including area now constituting parts of Mississippi, Alabama, and Georgia. Definition of urban population before 1950: All persons living in incorporated places of 2,500 or more inhabitants and in areas (usually minor civil divisions) classified as urban under special rules relating to population size and density.

Current definition of urban population:

1) All persons living in places of 2,500 or more inhabitants but excluding those in rural portions of extended cities.

2) All persons living in any territory within urbanized areas.

Source: U.S. Department of Commerce, Bureau of the Census, *1990 Census of Population, General Population Characteristics, Tennessee*, and earlier editions.

TABLE 1.2-- POPULATION AND PERCENT CHANGE, TENNESSEE AND UNITED STATES, 1790-1990, DECENNIAL CENSUS YEARS

	Population		Percent increase in each decade		Tennessee as a
Year	Tennessee	United States	Tennessee	United States	percent of U.S.
1990	4,877,185	248,709,873	6.2	9.8	2.0
1980	4,591,120	226,545,805	16.9	11.4	2.0
1970	3,926,018	203,302,031	10.0	13.3	1.9
1960	3,567,089	179,323,175	8.4	19.0	2.0
1950	3,291,718	150,697,361	12.9	14.5	2.2
1940	2,915,841	131,669,275	11.4	7.2	2.2
1930	2,616,556	122,775,046	11.9	16.1	2.1
1920	2,337,885	105,710,620	7.0	14.9	2.2
1910	2,184,789	91,972,266	8.1	21.0	2.4
1900	2,020,616	75,995,575	14.3	20.7	2.7
1890	1,767,518	62,947,714	14.6	25.5	2.8
1880	1,542,359	50,155,783	22.6	26.0	3.1
1870	1,258,520	39,818,449	13.4	26.6	3.2
1860	1,109,801	31,443,321	10.7	35.6	3.5
1850	1,002,717	23,191,876	20.9	35.9	4.3
1840	829,210	17,069,453	21.6	32.7	4.9
1830	681,904	12,866,020	61.3	33.5	5.3
1820	422,823	9,638,453	61.6	33.1	4.4
1810	261,727	7,239,881	147.8	36.4	3.6
1800	105,602	5,308,483	195.9	35.1	2.0
1790	35,691	3,929,214	(X)	(X)	0.9

Note: United States includes Alaska and Hawaii beginning in 1960. Data are as of April 1.
(X) Not applicable.
Source: U.S. Department of Commerce, Bureau of the Census, *1990 Census of Population, General Population Characteristics, United States*, and earlier editions.

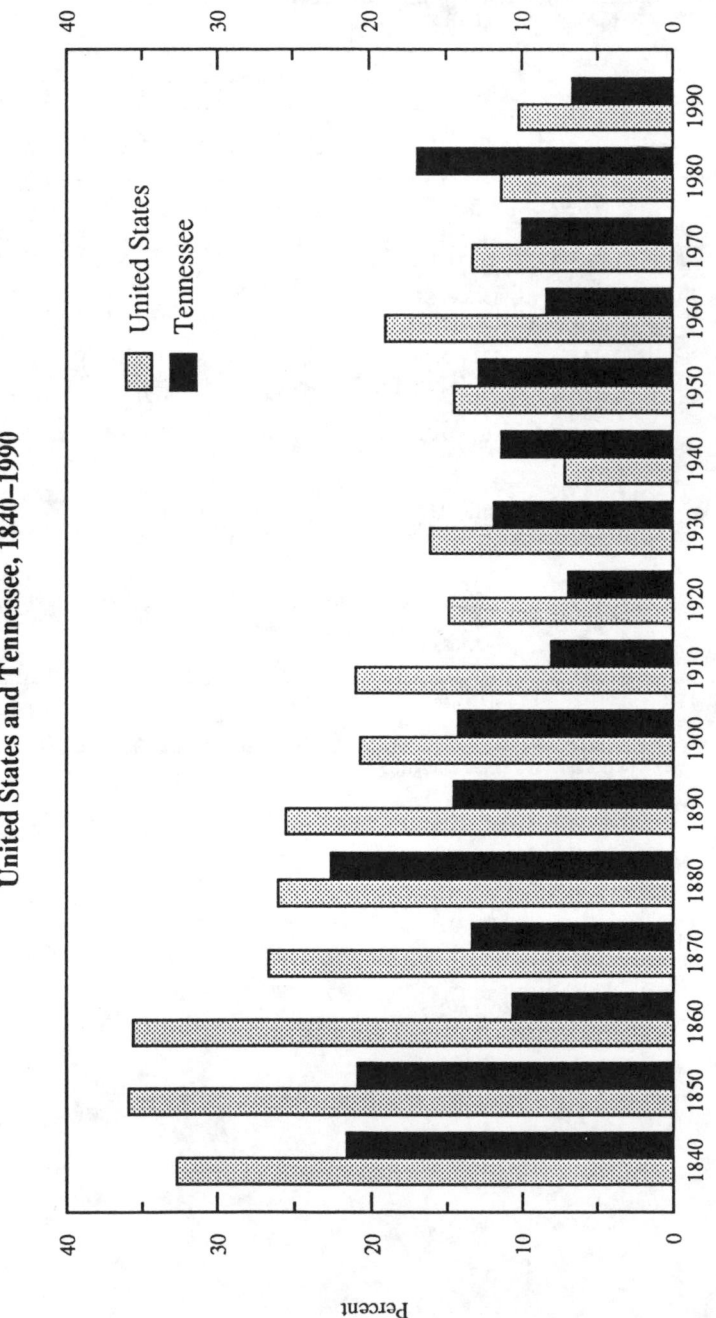

FIGURE 1.1
Percent Change in Population Between Census Years
United States and Tennessee, 1840–1990

Note: Percentages were computed by the Center for Business and Economic Research.
Source: U.S. Department of Commerce, Bureau of the Census, direct correspondence; and *1990 Census of Population, General Population Characteristics, Tennessee* and earlier editions.

TABLE 1.3-- POPULATION BY AGE, BY RACE, AND BY SEX, TENNESSEE, 1990

Age group	Total		White		Black		American Indian, Eskimo or Aleut		Asian or Pacific Islander		Other races	
	Male	Female	Male	Female	Male	Female	Male	Female	Male	Female	Male	Female
Total (all ages)	2,348,928	2,528,257	1,962,430	2,085,638	360,861	417,174	5,078	4,961	15,319	16,520	5,240	3,964
Under 1	29,879	28,174	23,205	21,797	6,343	6,063	40	44	186	185	105	85
1-2	72,335	68,902	55,487	52,563	15,888	15,411	141	131	574	534	245	263
3-4	68,499	65,626	53,201	50,771	14,410	13,979	136	122	533	540	219	214
5	34,355	32,693	26,850	25,456	7,061	6,794	58	58	267	286	119	99
6	33,683	32,227	26,361	25,158	6,871	6,627	75	59	279	289	97	94
7-9	105,151	99,259	82,456	77,278	21,385	20,707	213	207	824	808	273	259
10-11	71,500	68,062	55,550	52,585	15,067	14,667	172	156	556	516	155	138
12-13	69,178	65,950	54,610	51,870	13,733	13,350	150	136	522	489	163	105
14	33,290	31,118	26,303	24,401	6,611	6,322	65	65	244	265	67	65
15	34,720	33,126	27,501	26,156	6,833	6,549	70	78	246	271	70	72
16	35,395	33,291	27,993	26,149	6,972	6,685	77	69	284	333	69	55
17	36,317	33,874	28,694	26,803	7,199	6,648	95	70	271	282	58	71
18	38,876	36,903	31,018	28,966	7,267	7,473	90	80	352	302	149	82
19	43,072	40,992	34,715	32,409	7,692	8,109	104	83	343	284	218	107
20	39,523	39,582	31,970	31,546	6,934	7,578	98	74	349	303	172	81
21	36,977	36,754	29,930	29,427	6,394	6,908	91	63	371	281	191	75
22-24	106,950	108,026	87,272	86,164	17,953	20,517	267	219	972	842	486	284
25-29	197,983	204,994	164,078	165,619	31,126	36,865	451	417	1,613	1,612	715	481
30-34	198,835	210,509	165,754	169,768	30,494	37,998	464	502	1,526	1,809	597	432
35-39	188,331	197,996	158,659	161,757	27,442	33,662	496	494	1,341	1,775	393	308
40-44	173,786	180,875	150,543	153,295	21,405	25,419	442	420	1,157	1,534	239	207
45-49	140,241	146,312	124,181	126,549	14,649	18,350	355	330	897	969	159	114
50-54	115,412	124,245	102,281	107,276	12,121	15,987	256	256	648	636	106	90
55-59	103,714	117,238	92,320	101,612	10,750	14,851	223	235	361	497	60	43
60-61	39,773	45,694	35,510	39,841	4,077	5,604	65	67	107	163	14	19
62-64	58,504	69,666	52,181	60,803	6,067	8,520	93	102	140	209	23	32
65-69	88,550	112,436	78,933	98,659	9,288	13,415	138	131	155	203	36	28
70-74	64,921	91,516	57,521	80,270	7,230	10,965	66	106	90	147	14	28
75-79	46,459	76,080	40,717	66,435	5,628	9,469	45	80	59	80	10	16
80-84	26,646	53,416	23,055	46,839	3,519	6,461	30	45	32	45	10	9
85 and over	16,073	42,721	13,581	37,416	2,452	5,221	12	45	20	31	8	8

Source: U.S. Department of Commerce, Bureau of the Census, 1990 Census of Population and Housing, Summary Tape File 1A, Tennessee.

TABLE 1.4-- RESIDENT POPULATION, BY AGE AND BY SEX, TENNESSEE, 1980–1992

Year	All ages	Under 5 years	5 to 24 years	25 to 44 years	45 to 64 years	65 years or more	Median age
1992							
Female	2,603	172	698	815	530	389	35.4
Male	2,421	181	724	780	484	252	32.8
1991							
Female	2,568	169	693	812	511	383	35.2
Male	2,386	177	720	777	466	247	32.5
1990[a]							
Female	2,528	166	693	793	502	374	34.8
Male	2,349	174	721	758	455	242	32.1
1989							
Female	2,517	164	698	787	499	370	34.5
Male	2,338	172	723	752	452	239	31.8
1988							
Female	2,500	160	704	777	494	364	34.2
Male	2,323	168	730	743	446	236	31.5
1987							
Female	2,480	157	708	769	488	358	33.9
Male	2,303	166	732	735	438	233	31.2
1986							
Female	2,457	157	715	751	482	351	33.6
Male	2,282	165	739	718	431	229	30.8
1985							
Female	2,443	158	726	735	481	345	33.2
Male	2,272	166	749	703	429	225	30.4
1984							
Female	2,428	160	734	717	478	338	32.8
Male	2,259	168	757	687	425	221	30.0
1983							
Female	2,413	162	742	701	476	332	32.5
Male	2,247	170	764	672	422	218	29.7
1982							
Female	2,405	162	754	687	476	325	32.1
Male	2,241	171	776	658	421	215	29.4
1981							
Female	2,394	162	765	672	477	318	31.8
Male	2,234	171	787	644	421	212	29.1
1980[a]							
Female	2,375	159	776	653	477	310	31.4
Male	2,217	167	798	625	419	208	28.7

a. As of April 1; other years are as of July 1.

Source: U.S. Department of Commerce, Bureau of the Census, Current Population Reports P25-1106, *State Population Estimates by Age and Sex: 1980 to 1992.*

TABLE 1.5-- VETERANS, BY PERIOD OF MILITARY SERVICE, TENNESSEE, 1990

Period of military service	Veterans
May 1975 or later only	59,357
September 1980 or later only	36,566
With less than 2 years of service	6,560
With 2 or more years of service	30,006
May 1975 to August 1980 only	22,791
Both, May 1975 to August 1980 and September 1980 or later	5,784
Vietnam era, no Korean conflict nor World War II	154,757
Vietnam era and Korean conflict, no World War II	7,874
Vietnam era, Korean conflict, and World War II	4,556
February 1955 to July 1964 only	58,195
Korean conflict, no Vietnam era nor World War II	71,222
Korean conflict and World War II, no Vietnam era	10,792
World War II, no Korean conflict nor Vietnam era	154,130
World War I	1,142
Other service	3,914

Source: U.S. Department of Commerce, Bureau of the Census, *1990 Census of Population and Housing, Summary Tape File 3A, Tennessee.*

TABLE 1.6-- PERSONS NATURALIZED, BY FORMER NATIONALITY, TENNESSEE AND UNITED STATES, FISCAL YEARS, 1980–1992, SELECTED YEARS

Country of birth	Tennessee							United States						
	1992	1991	1990	1989	1988	1987	1980	1992	1991	1990	1989	1988	1987	1980
All countries	979	1,043	1,002	1,015	1,004	911	490	240,252	308,058	270,101	233,777	242,063	227,008	157,938
Cambodia	n.a.	29	33	21	n.a.	n.a.	n.a.	n.a.	4,786	3,525	3,234	n.a.	n.a.	n.a.
China	24	40	50	41	24	24	51	13,488	16,783	13,563	11,664	10,509	9,208	12,524
Colombia	10	9	10	6	12	7	n.a.	6,439	5,513	5,540	4,736	5,021	4,006	n.a.
Cuba	3	9	4	6	6	8	9	7,763	9,554	10,291	9,514	11,228	6,738	12,717
Dominican Republic	2	3	3	1	0	0	n.a.	8,464	6,368	5,984	6,454	5,842	4,257	n.a.
Guyana	3	4	11	4	n.a.	n.a.	n.a.	4,717	4,436	4,306	3,654	n.a.	n.a.	n.a.
Haiti	1	3	1	1	n.a.	n.a.	n.a.	3,993	4,436	5,009	3,692	n.a.	n.a.	n.a.
India	104	104	69	112	85	77	51	13,413	12,961	11,499	9,833	9,983	8,659	6,552
Iran	58	78	51	36	40	48	n.a.	6,778	10,411	5,973	4,485	4,970	4,277	n.a.
Israel	n.a.	n.a.	n.a.	n.a.	n.a.	n.a.	4	n.a.	n.a.	n.a.	n.a.	n.a.	n.a.	1,280
Italy	n.a.	12	8	7	8	8	2	n.a.	n.a.	n.a.	n.a.	n.a.	n.a.	5,410
Jamaica	3	n.a.	n.a.	n.a.	n.a.	n.a.	1	6,765	6,838	6,762	6,455	6,441	5,196	5,840
Korea	61	62	69	80	95	86	81	8,297	12,266	10,500	11,301	13,012	14,233	14,703
Laos	n.a.	n.a.	n.a.	70	77	92	n.a.	n.a.	n.a.	n.a.	3,463	3,480	3,159	n.a.
Mexico	19	20	12	13	12	6	8	12,880	22,066	17,564	18,520	22,085	21,999	9,341
Pakistan	14	n.a.	n.a.	n.a.	n.a.	n.a.	n.a.	3,350	n.a.	n.a.	n.a.	n.a.	n.a.	n.a.
Philippines	64	66	60	74	71	66	45	28,579	33,714	25,936	24,802	24,580	25,296	17,683
Poland	12	11	15	21	1	2	1	4,681	5,493	5,972	5,002	n.a.	n.a.	1,996
Portugal	n.a.	n.a.	n.a.	n.a.	30	16	0	n.a.	n.a.	n.a.	n.a.	3,236	3,518	3,631
Taiwan	40	29	24	51	3	12	n.a.	6,408	10,876	6,895	5,779	5,716	4,033	n.a.
U.S.S.R.	n.a.	n.a.	n.a.	n.a.	n.a.	n.a.	n.a.	n.a.	n.a.	n.a.	n.a.	5,304	7,276	n.a.
United Kingdom	52	41	36	57	53	41	25	7,800	9,935	8,286	7,865	7,042	7,102	7,282
Vietnam	63	76	71	74	80	88	n.a.	18,357	29,603	22,027	19,357	21,636	25,469	n.a.
Yugoslavia	n.a.	n.a.	n.a.	n.a.	n.a.	n.a.	4	n.a.	n.a.	n.a.	n.a.	n.a.	n.a.	2,021

Note: Totals include detail not shown separately.

n.a. not available.

1. Before 1982, China includes Formosa (Taiwan). Beginning in 1982, China includes mainland China only.

Source: U.S. Department of Justice, Immigration and Naturalization Service, Statistical Yearbook of the Immigration and Naturalization Service, 1992, and earlier editions.

TABLE 1.7-- POPULATION, METROPOLITAN STATISTICAL AREAS, 1950–1990, DECENNIAL CENSUS
YEARS AND 1992 ESTIMATES

MSA and counties	1992	1990	1980	1970	1960	1950
Chattanooga Tennessee: Hamilton, Marion Georgia: Catoosa, Dade, Walker	430,848	424,347	417,838	364,526	333,972	289,483
Clarksville-Hopkinsville Tennessee: Montgomery Kentucky: Christian	178,155	169,439	150,220	118,945	112,549	86,545
Jackson Madison	80,230	77,982	74,546	65,774	60,655	60,128
Johnson City-Kingsport-Bristol Tennessee: Carter, Hawkins, Sullivan, Unicoi, Washington Virginia: Scott, Washington, Bristol City[1]	444,625	436,047	433,638	373,591	347,132	324,976
Knoxville Anderson, Blount, Knox, Loudon, Sevier, Union	610,482	585,960	546,488	461,916	424,586	392,332
Memphis Tennessee: Fayette, Shelby, Tipton Arkansas: Crittenden Mississippi: DeSoto	1,033,813	1,007,306	938,777	856,795	751,615	611,493
Nashville-Davidson Cheatham, Davidson, Dickson, Robertson, Rutherford, Sumner, Williamson, Wilson	1,023,315	985,026	850,505	699,271	596,865	501,608

Note: Metropolitan Statistical Areas as defined by the Office of Management and Budget, June 30, 1993. Data are
revised to provide population for comparable land areas.
1. In Virginia the cities are independent of counties.
Source: U.S. Department of Commerce, Bureau of the Census, direct correspondence; *1990 Census of Population,
General Population Characteristics, Tennessee*, and earlier editions.

1. POPULATION

TABLE 1.8-- POPULATION, TENNESSEE AND COUNTIES, AS OF JULY 1, 1992

County	1992	1991^r	1990	Change, 1990–92 Number	Change, 1990–92 Percent
Anderson	70,525	69,282	68,250	2,275	3.3
Bedford	31,738	31,053	30,411	1,327	4.4
Benton	15,073	14,829	14,524	549	3.8
Bledsoe	9,779	9,726	9,669	110	1.1
Blount	90,403	88,404	85,969	4,434	5.2
Bradley	75,934	74,933	73,712	2,222	3.0
Campbell	35,656	35,391	35,079	577	1.6
Cannon	10,756	10,630	10,467	289	2.8
Carroll	27,641	27,665	27,514	127	0.5
Carter	52,029	51,810	51,505	524	1.0
Cheatham	28,795	28,007	27,140	1,655	6.1
Chester	12,961	12,869	12,819	142	1.1
Claiborne	27,079	26,645	26,137	942	3.6
Clay	7,226	7,194	7,238	-12	-0.2
Cocke	29,490	29,282	29,141	349	1.2
Coffee	41,641	41,097	40,339	1,302	3.2
Crockett	13,286	13,400	13,378	-92	-0.7
Cumberland	36,743	36,042	34,736	2,007	5.8
Davidson	517,798	512,893	510,784	7,014	1.4
Decatur	10,393	10,448	10,472	-79	-0.8
DeKalb	14,637	14,498	14,360	277	1.9
Dickson	36,509	35,881	35,061	1,448	4.1
Dyer	34,847	34,839	34,854	-7	0.0
Fayette	25,995	25,775	25,559	436	1.7
Fentress	14,916	14,776	14,669	247	1.7
Franklin	35,301	35,115	34,725	576	1.7
Gibson	46,392	46,316	46,315	77	0.2
Giles	26,667	26,296	25,741	926	3.6
Grainger	17,766	17,485	17,095	671	3.9
Greene	57,243	56,539	55,853	1,390	2.5
Grundy	13,475	13,436	13,362	113	0.8
Hamblen	51,657	50,804	50,480	1,177	2.3
Hamilton	288,637	287,509	285,536	3,101	1.1
Hancock	6,725	6,631	6,739	-14	-0.2
Hardeman	23,770	23,517	23,377	393	1.7
Hardin	23,508	23,239	22,633	875	3.9
Hawkins	45,955	45,296	44,565	1,390	3.1
Haywood	19,474	19,441	19,437	37	0.2
Henderson	22,136	21,891	21,844	292	1.3
Henry	28,323	28,037	27,888	435	1.6
Hickman	17,579	17,274	16,754	825	4.9
Houston	7,177	7,046	7,018	159	2.3
Humphreys	15,864	15,791	15,795	69	0.4
Jackson	9,107	9,187	9,297	-190	-2.0
Jefferson	34,770	33,949	33,016	1,754	5.3
Johnson	15,209	15,013	13,766	1,443	10.5
Knox	347,583	341,956	335,749	11,834	3.5
Lake	7,304	7,083	7,129	175	2.5
Lauderdale	23,639	23,503	23,491	148	0.6
Lawrence	36,436	35,934	35,303	1,133	3.2
Lewis	9,820	9,602	9,247	573	6.2
Lincoln	28,451	28,326	28,157	294	1.0

TABLE 1.8-- POPULATION, TENNESSEE AND COUNTIES, AS OF JULY 1, 1992 (Continued)

County	1992	1991ʳ	1990	Change, 1990–92 Number	Change, 1990–92 Percent
Loudon	33,242	32,259	31,255	1,987	6.4
McMinn	43,552	42,818	42,383	1,169	2.8
McNairy	22,563	22,632	22,422	141	0.6
Macon	16,343	16,119	15,906	437	2.7
Madison	80,230	79,011	77,982	2,248	2.9
Marion	25,297	25,130	24,860	437	1.8
Marshall	22,974	22,469	21,539	1,435	6.7
Maury	59,740	58,131	54,812	4,928	9.0
Meigs	8,412	8,261	8,033	379	4.7
Monroe	31,376	30,900	30,541	835	2.7
Montgomery	109,992	103,137	100,498	9,494	9.4
Moore	4,906	4,824	4,721	185	3.9
Morgan	17,714	17,417	17,300	414	2.4
Obion	31,558	31,694	31,717	-159	-0.5
Overton	17,809	17,772	17,636	173	1.0
Perry	6,825	6,746	6,612	213	3.2
Pickett	4,554	4,532	4,548	6	0.1
Polk	13,903	13,769	13,643	260	1.9
Putnam	53,162	52,238	51,373	1,789	3.5
Rhea	25,270	24,717	24,344	926	3.8
Roane	48,094	47,731	47,227	867	1.8
Robertson	43,745	42,710	41,494	2,251	5.4
Rutherford	128,731	124,113	118,570	10,161	8.6
Scott	18,836	18,590	18,358	478	2.6
Sequatchie	9,186	9,020	8,863	323	3.6
Sevier	54,670	53,125	51,043	3,627	7.1
Shelby	844,847	835,985	826,330	18,517	2.2
Smith	14,407	14,336	14,143	264	1.9
Stewart	10,144	9,645	9,479	665	7.0
Sullivan	146,676	144,976	143,596	3,080	2.1
Sumner	107,937	105,499	103,281	4,656	4.5
Tipton	39,221	38,525	37,568	1,653	4.4
Trousdale	5,949	5,935	5,920	29	0.5
Unicoi	16,791	16,551	16,549	242	1.5
Union	14,059	13,957	13,694	365	2.7
Van Buren	4,891	4,903	4,846	45	0.9
Warren	33,479	33,440	32,992	487	1.5
Washington	94,934	93,935	92,315	2,619	2.8
Wayne	15,204	14,134	13,935	1,269	9.1
Weakley	31,931	31,987	31,972	-41	-0.1
White	20,490	20,309	20,090	400	2.0
Williamson	88,640	85,161	81,021	7,619	9.4
Wilson	71,160	69,667	67,675	3,485	5.1
TENNESSEE	5,025,261	4,952,395	4,877,185	148,076	3.0

r revised.
Source: U.S. Department of Commerce, Bureau of the Census, direct correspondence.

1.   POPULATION

TABLE 1.9-- TOTAL POPULATION, TENNESSEE AND COUNTIES, 1950-1990, DECENNIAL CENSUS
YEARS

County	1990	1980	1970	1960	1950	Change, 1980-1990 Number	%
Anderson	68,250	67,346	60,300	60,032	59,407	904	1.3
Bedford	30,411	27,916	25,039	23,150	23,627	2,495	8.9
Benton	14,524	14,901	12,126	10,662	11,495	-377	-2.5
Bledsoe	9,669	9,478	7,643	7,811	8,561	191	2.0
Blount	85,969	77,770	63,744	57,525	54,691	8,199	10.5
Bradley	73,712	67,547	50,686	38,324	32,338	6,165	9.1
Campbell	35,079	34,923	26,045	27,936	34,369	156	0.4
Cannon	10,467	10,234	8,467	8,537	9,174	233	2.3
Carroll	27,514	28,285	25,741	23,476	26,553	-771	-2.7
Carter	51,505	50,205	43,259	41,578	42,432	1,300	2.6
Cheatham	27,140	21,616	13,199	9,428	9,167	5,524	25.6
Chester	12,819	12,727	9,927	9,569	11,149	92	0.7
Claibome	26,137	24,595	19,420	19,067	24,788	1,542	6.3
Clay	7,238	7,676	6,624	7,289	8,701	-438	-5.7
Cocke	29,141	28,792	25,283	23,390	22,991	349	1.2
Coffee	40,339	38,311	32,572	28,603	23,049	2,028	5.3
Crockett	13,378	14,941	14,402	14,594	16,624	-1,563	-10.5
Cumberland	34,736	28,676	20,733	19,135	18,877	6,060	21.1
Davidson	510,784	477,811	447,877	399,743	321,758	32,973	6.9
Decatur	10,472	10,857	9,457	8,324	9,442	-385	-3.5
DeKalb	14,360	13,589	11,151	10,774	11,680	771	5.7
Dickson	35,061	30,037	21,977	18,839	18,805	5,024	16.7
Dyer	34,854	34,663	30,427	29,537	33,473	191	0.6
Fayette	25,559	25,305	22,692	24,577	27,535	254	1.0
Fentress	14,669	14,826	12,593	13,288	14,917	-157	-1.1
Franklin	34,725	31,983	27,289	25,528	25,431	2,742	8.6
Gibson	46,315	49,467	47,871	44,699	48,132	-3,152	-6.4
Giles	25,741	24,625	22,138	22,410	26,961	1,116	4.5
Grainger	17,095	16,751	13,948	12,506	13,086	344	2.1
Greene	55,853	54,422	47,630	42,163	41,048	1,431	2.6
Grundy	13,362	13,787	10,631	11,512	12,558	-425	-3.1
Hamblen	50,480	49,300	38,696	33,092	23,976	1,180	2.4
Hamilton	285,536	287,643	255,077	237,905	208,255	-2,107	-0.7
Hancock	6,739	6,887	6,719	7,757	9,116	-148	-2.1
Hardeman	23,377	23,873	22,435	21,517	23,311	-496	-2.1
Hardin	22,633	22,280	18,212	17,397	16,908	353	1.6
Hawkins	44,565	43,751	33,757	30,468	30,494	814	1.9
Haywood	19,437	20,318	19,596	23,393	26,212	-881	-4.3
Henderson	21,844	21,390	17,360	16,115	17,173	454	2.1
Henry	27,888	28,656	23,749	22,275	23,828	-768	-2.7
Hickman	16,754	15,151	12,096	11,862	13,353	1,603	10.6
Houston	7,018	6,871	5,853	4,794	5,318	147	2.1
Humphreys	15,795	15,957	13,560	11,511	11,030	-162	-1.0
Jackson	9,297	9,398	8,141	9,233	12,348	-101	-1.1
Jefferson	33,016	31,284	24,940	21,493	19,667	1,732	5.5
Johnson	13,766	13,745	11,569	10,765	12,278	21	0.2
Knox	335,749	319,694	276,293	250,523	223,007	16,055	5.0
Lake	7,129	7,455	8,074	9,572	11,655	-326	-4.4
Lauderdale	23,491	24,555	20,271	21,844	25,047	-1,064	-4.3
Lawrence	35,303	34,110	29,097	28,049	28,818	1,193	3.5

14

TABLE 1.9-- TOTAL POPULATION, TENNESSEE AND COUNTIES, 1950–1990, DECENNIAL CENSUS
YEARS (Continued)

County	1990	1980	1970	1960	1950	Change, 1980–1990 Number	%
Lewis	9,247	9,700	6,761	6,269	6,078	-453	-4.7
Lincoln	28,157	26,483	24,318	23,829	25,624	1,674	6.3
Loudon	31,255	28,553	24,266	23,757	23,182	2,702	9.5
McMinn	42,383	41,878	35,462	33,662	32,024	505	1.2
McNairy	22,422	22,525	18,369	18,085	20,390	-103	-0.5
Macon	15,906	15,700	12,315	12,197	13,599	206	1.3
Madison	77,982	74,546	65,774	60,655	60,128	3,436	4.6
Marion	24,860	24,416	20,577	21,036	20,520	444	1.8
Marshall	21,539	19,698	17,319	16,859	17,768	1,841	9.3
Maury	54,812	51,095	44,028	41,699	40,368	3,717	7.3
Meigs	8,033	7,431	5,219	5,160	6,080	602	8.1
Monroe	30,541	28,700	23,475	23,316	24,513	1,841	6.4
Montgomery	100,498	83,342	62,721	55,645	44,186	17,156	20.6
Moore	4,721	4,510	3,568	3,454	3,948	211	4.7
Morgan	17,300	16,604	13,619	14,304	15,727	696	4.2
Obion	31,717	32,781	30,247	26,957	29,056	-1,064	-3.2
Overton	17,636	17,575	14,866	14,661	17,566	61	0.3
Perry	6,612	6,111	5,238	5,273	6,462	501	8.2
Pickett	4,548	4,358	3,774	4,431	5,093	190	4.4
Polk	13,643	13,602	11,669	12,160	14,074	41	0.3
Putnam	51,373	47,690	35,487	29,236	29,869	3,683	7.7
Rhea	24,344	24,235	17,202	15,863	16,041	109	0.4
Roane	47,227	48,425	38,881	39,133	31,665	-1,198	-2.5
Robertson	41,494	37,021	29,102	27,335	27,024	4,473	12.1
Rutherford	118,570	84,058	59,428	52,368	40,696	34,512	41.1
Scott	18,358	19,259	14,762	15,413	17,362	-901	-4.7
Sequatchie	8,863	8,605	6,331	5,915	5,685	258	3.0
Sevier	51,043	41,418	28,241	24,251	23,375	9,625	23.2
Shelby	826,330	777,113	722,111	627,019	482,393	49,217	6.3
Smith	14,143	14,935	12,509	12,059	14,098	-792	-5.3
Stewart	9,479	8,665	7,319	7,851	9,175	814	9.4
Sullivan	143,596	143,968	127,329	114,139	95,063	-372	-0.3
Sumner	103,281	85,790	56,266	36,217	33,533	17,491	20.4
Tipton	37,568	32,930	28,001	28,564	29,782	4,638	14.1
Trousdale	5,920	6,137	5,155	4,914	5,520	-217	-3.5
Unicoi	16,549	16,362	15,254	15,082	15,886	187	1.1
Union	13,694	11,707	9,072	8,498	8,670	1,987	17.0
Van Buren	4,846	4,728	3,758	3,671	3,985	118	2.5
Warren	32,992	32,653	26,972	23,102	22,271	339	1.0
Washington	92,315	88,755	73,924	64,832	59,971	3,560	4.0
Wayne	13,935	13,946	12,365	11,908	13,864	-11	-0.1
Weakley	31,972	32,896	28,827	24,227	27,962	-924	-2.8
White	20,090	19,567	16,329	15,577	16,204	523	2.7
Williamson	81,021	58,108	34,423	25,267	24,307	22,913	39.4
Wilson	67,675	56,064	36,999	27,668	26,318	11,611	20.7
TENNESSEE	4,877,185	4,591,023	3,926,018	3,567,089	3,291,718	286,162	6.2

Source: U.S. Department of Commerce, Bureau of the Census, *1990 Census of Population, General Population
Characteristics,Tennessee*, and *1980 Census of Population, Number of Inhabitants, Tennessee*, and earlier
editions.

FIGURE 1.2

Percent Change in Population, Counties, 1980–1990

(Tennessee percent change = 6.2)

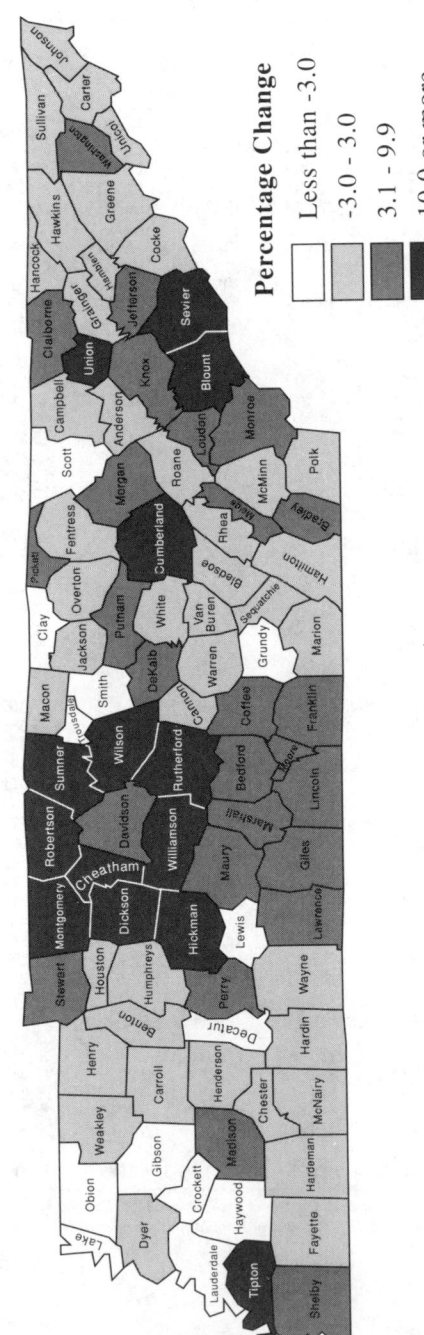

Percentage Change

☐ Less than -3.0

▨ -3.0 - 3.0

▨ 3.1 - 9.9

■ 10.0 or more

Source: U.S. Department of Commerce, Bureau of the Census, direct correspondence.

TABLE 1.10--VETERAN STATUS, BY AGE, TENNESSEE AND COUNTIES, 1990

County	Armed Forces	Persons 16 to 64 years		Persons 65 years and over	
		Civilian		Civilian	
		Veteran	Nonveteran	Veteran	Nonveteran
Anderson	64	6,345	36,873	2,524	7,967
Bedford	5	2,402	16,604	896	3,628
Benton	17	1,187	7,785	548	2,053
Bledsoe	0	731	5,794	217	944
Blount	219	8,353	47,573	2,718	9,888
Bradley	34	6,159	43,379	1,913	6,255
Campbell	12	2,519	19,637	1,008	4,148
Cannon	16	652	5,893	304	1,291
Carroll	24	2,011	14,740	934	3,993
Carter	5	4,672	29,066	1,767	6,051
Cheatham	9	2,332	15,754	560	1,719
Chester	18	884	7,339	320	1,568
Claiborne	24	1,513	15,408	516	2,882
Clay	0	552	4,018	228	946
Cocke	10	2,129	17,170	627	3,118
Coffee	173	3,633	21,667	1,342	4,269
Crockett	16	657	7,273	354	2,187
Cumberland	0	3,059	18,495	1,684	4,424
Davidson	772	41,687	304,454	13,104	46,131
Decatur	4	702	5,714	344	1,636
DeKalb	3	745	8,292	356	1,922
Dickson	20	2,800	19,468	947	3,404
Dyer	46	2,406	19,345	865	4,349
Fayette	9	1,651	13,794	589	2,731
Fentress	15	1,014	8,396	431	1,545
Franklin	130	3,037	19,081	1,128	3,870
Gibson	39	3,339	24,710	1,425	7,097
Giles	9	2,051	13,861	758	3,418
Grainger	0	1,064	10,129	392	1,814
Greene	16	4,654	32,349	1,514	6,221
Grundy	8	817	7,364	382	1,533
Hamblen	19	4,248	29,837	1,299	4,773
Hamilton	206	25,114	161,162	8,938	29,321
Hancock	0	282	3,892	163	895
Hardeman	9	1,338	12,783	559	2,777
Hardin	0	1,568	12,668	712	2,782
Hawkins	32	3,938	25,577	1,252	4,611
Haywood	16	986	10,450	410	2,596
Henderson	7	1,362	12,321	599	2,707
Henry	28	2,214	14,584	1,309	4,179
Hickman	12	1,521	9,343	435	1,938
Houston	9	596	3,699	258	988
Humphreys	51	1,513	8,467	492	1,785
Jackson	0	601	5,261	254	1,344
Jefferson	29	2,987	19,420	956	3,444
Johnson	17	1,056	7,667	454	1,812
Knox	290	28,765	197,596	9,809	32,863
Lake	0	534	4,186	176	879
Lauderdale	19	1,313	12,877	530	2,984
Lawrence	16	2,425	19,411	984	4,234

17

TABLE 1.10--VETERAN STATUS, BY AGE, TENNESSEE AND COUNTIES, 1990 (Continued)

County	Armed Forces	Persons 16 to 64 years		Persons 65 years and over	
		Civilian		Civilian	
		Veteran	Nonveteran	Veteran	Nonveteran
Lewis	10	639	5,037	268	1,128
Lincoln	20	2,139	15,465	783	3,602
Loudon	14	2,836	17,383	960	3,596
McMinn	26	3,457	23,935	1,080	4,928
McNairy	17	1,946	12,061	680	2,902
Macon	20	779	9,275	279	2,026
Madison	124	5,655	43,193	2,088	8,646
Marion	24	1,853	14,212	618	2,476
Marshall	5	1,671	11,796	544	2,725
Maury	26	4,512	30,279	1,313	5,934
Meigs	7	644	4,639	240	745
Monroe	11	1,954	17,718	931	3,253
Montgomery	13,079	10,563	45,064	1,854	6,080
Moore	10	341	2,690	140	510
Morgan	6	1,543	9,820	449	1,585
Obion	45	2,572	17,416	939	4,007
Overton	15	1,285	9,909	608	2,111
Perry	0	366	3,685	192	903
Pickett	0	350	2,442	131	642
Polk	16	1,045	7,808	419	1,545
Putnam	51	3,760	31,031	1,475	5,183
Rhea	12	2,082	13,514	785	2,675
Roane	64	5,039	25,425	1,765	5,288
Robertson	49	3,462	22,726	1,023	3,999
Rutherford	195	10,194	69,848	2,383	7,611
Scott	2	1,208	10,204	458	1,742
Sequatchie	23	714	5,009	266	820
Sevier	39	4,391	29,512	1,488	4,920
Shelby	9,651	65,462	462,082	19,419	66,734
Smith	22	900	7,827	362	1,886
Stewart	72	1,014	4,911	389	1,260
Sullivan	94	13,806	81,083	4,519	15,986
Sumner	117	9,089	58,293	2,161	8,332
Tipton	498	2,831	19,833	780	3,249
Trousdale	5	323	3,336	154	847
Unicoi	21	1,588	9,019	617	2,223
Union	10	938	7,930	246	1,265
Van Buren	9	379	2,768	102	487
Warren	65	2,290	18,491	958	3,878
Washington	121	8,730	52,789	3,077	9,825
Wayne	15	828	7,911	392	1,662
Weakley	45	1,876	18,662	920	4,224
White	7	1,466	11,125	766	2,478
Williamson	45	6,793	46,375	1,715	4,992
Wilson	76	5,991	38,515	1,281	5,246
TENNESSEE	27,260	399,422	2,754,672	132,301	486,070

Source: U.S. Department of Commerce, Bureau of the Census, *1990 Census of Population and Housing, Summary Tape File 3A, Tennessee.*

TABLE 1.11--POPULATION, BY AGE, TENNESSEE AND COUNTIES, 1990

Age	Anderson	Bedford	Benton	Bledsoe	Blount	Bradley	Campbell	Cannon
TOTAL	68,250	30,411	14,524	9,669	85,969	73,712	35,079	10,467
Under 1 year	757	310	148	97	957	791	401	120
1 and 2 years	1,757	889	326	249	2,123	1,979	923	262
3 and 4 years	1,692	844	337	227	2,199	1,949	898	276
5 years	913	374	182	118	1,011	965	412	159
6 years	940	405	161	109	1,088	938	440	142
7 to 9 years	2,760	1,301	586	372	3,275	2,915	1,478	462
10 and 11 years	1,895	904	394	278	2,315	2,152	1,087	297
12 and 13 years	1,917	915	364	309	2,147	2,232	1,077	330
14 years	872	422	217	97	1,035	1,015	524	133
15 years	897	453	193	120	1,169	1,105	567	155
16 years	922	449	200	166	1,170	1,104	579	145
17 years	1,012	449	232	226	1,173	1,103	617	156
18 years	909	442	173	175	1,275	1,246	584	134
19 years	895	460	198	139	1,273	1,406	541	133
20 years	835	442	174	109	1,245	1,346	488	147
21 years	803	371	174	125	1,139	1,189	476	153
22 to 24 years	2,467	1,208	527	410	3,455	3,487	1,424	419
25 to 29 years	4,857	2,303	973	855	6,617	6,107	2,482	768
30 to 34 years	5,391	2,320	1,011	811	6,832	6,059	2,517	782
35 to 39 years	5,351	2,162	966	811	6,960	5,686	2,508	727
40 to 44 years	5,109	2,123	1,037	739	6,751	5,475	2,462	696
45 to 49 years	4,264	1,853	866	569	5,631	4,808	2,168	614
50 to 54 years	3,546	1,534	847	522	4,553	3,882	1,886	572
55 to 59 years	3,388	1,486	814	441	4,016	3,455	1,710	616
60 and 61 years	1,369	579	336	186	1,546	1,291	675	180
62 to 64 years	2,247	877	491	248	2,406	1,856	995	294
65 to 69 years	3,693	1,400	834	388	4,116	2,748	1,668	452
70 to 74 years	2,738	1,151	640	285	3,369	2,070	1,299	427
75 to 79 years	2,019	904	517	210	2,549	1,587	1,100	346
80 to 84 years	1,260	628	359	167	1,495	1,114	643	220
85 years and over	775	453	247	111	1,079	652	450	150

19

TABLE 1.11--POPULATION, BY AGE, TENNESSEE AND COUNTIES, 1990 (Continued)

Age	Carroll	Carter	Cheatham	Chester	Claiborne	Clay	Cocke	Coffee
TOTAL	27,514	51,505	27,140	12,819	26,137	7,238	29,141	40,339
Under 1 year	281	470	390	142	243	63	300	477
1 and 2 years	720	1,233	860	343	687	150	676	1,153
3 and 4 years	706	1,236	836	334	680	178	738	1,141
5 years	354	607	437	151	350	89	367	597
6 years	333	559	383	155	347	85	376	575
7 to 9 years	1,118	1,855	1,340	493	1,129	280	1,114	1,772
10 and 11 years	758	1,334	841	356	776	199	808	1,228
12 and 13 years	777	1,277	871	372	773	206	826	1,186
14 years	361	624	425	154	366	114	427	537
15 years	357	697	397	182	424	118	416	564
16 years	400	707	389	173	480	94	458	591
17 years	366	790	437	159	413	98	478	558
18 years	403	787	373	324	429	103	486	569
19 years	452	930	346	399	482	110	428	546
20 years	382	931	338	357	409	79	437	509
21 years	364	804	346	345	410	98	412	487
22 to 24 years	1,015	2,203	1,006	610	1,171	299	1,223	1,517
25 to 29 years	1,942	3,961	2,435	875	1,898	556	2,192	3,078
30 to 34 years	1,827	3,826	2,626	863	2,001	483	2,336	3,113
35 to 39 years	1,796	3,774	2,447	835	2,034	518	2,191	2,937
40 to 44 years	1,902	3,800	2,143	850	1,950	496	2,211	2,733
45 to 49 years	1,683	3,316	1,712	665	1,573	475	1,856	2,404
50 to 54 years	1,401	2,838	1,384	623	1,344	426	1,645	2,226
55 to 59 years	1,415	2,555	1,105	570	1,240	377	1,550	2,134
60 and 61 years	573	991	423	230	452	151	580	880
62 to 64 years	882	1,576	578	342	678	219	860	1,203
65 to 69 years	1,433	2,460	744	583	1,188	367	1,169	1,921
70 to 74 years	1,289	2,012	610	465	836	297	963	1,467
75 to 79 years	1,007	1,654	456	392	672	239	808	1,040
80 to 84 years	713	1,014	268	273	385	152	484	698
85 years and over	504	684	194	204	317	119	326	498

TABLE 1.11--POPULATION, BY AGE, TENNESSEE AND COUNTIES, 1990 (Continued)

Age	Crockett	Cumberland	Davidson	Decatur	DeKalb	Dickson	Dyer	Fayette
TOTAL	13,378	34,736	510,784	10,472	14,360	35,061	34,854	25,559
Under 1 year	165	377	6,480	107	175	468	458	299
1 and 2 years	292	862	15,440	232	331	1,092	936	853
3 and 4 years	382	869	14,023	204	363	1,051	932	844
5 years	183	461	6,668	121	167	515	484	379
6 years	185	463	6,644	144	177	550	538	390
7 to 9 years	554	1,282	19,378	378	578	1,579	1,519	1,300
10 and 11 years	395	902	12,659	303	431	1,103	1,007	896
12 and 13 years	351	897	11,677	307	399	1,136	984	880
14 years	179	453	5,562	144	210	475	529	427
15 years	192	506	5,760	132	200	518	500	469
16 years	178	534	5,996	164	215	565	498	461
17 years	201	515	6,254	156	216	524	522	443
18 years	170	479	7,550	129	186	496	514	397
19 years	195	493	9,154	136	204	549	548	352
20 years	147	452	8,681	160	189	502	510	321
21 years	132	437	8,328	126	196	412	457	309
22 to 24 years	500	1,237	25,822	382	566	1,475	1,428	966
25 to 29 years	1,032	2,485	53,527	683	1,062	2,797	2,667	1,865
30 to 34 years	1,008	2,500	50,513	705	991	2,899	2,732	2,017
35 to 39 years	921	2,342	43,354	734	1,055	2,548	2,540	1,841
40 to 44 years	809	2,311	35,819	680	976	2,487	2,533	1,675
45 to 49 years	809	1,938	27,251	657	896	2,063	2,099	1,395
50 to 54 years	676	1,851	22,908	594	802	1,790	1,701	1,240
55 to 59 years	591	1,882	21,242	539	731	1,624	1,527	1,175
60 and 61 years	256	829	8,543	203	305	585	587	411
62 to 64 years	334	1,271	12,322	372	461	875	896	634
65 to 69 years	681	2,189	19,022	591	716	1,331	1,552	964
70 to 74 years	645	1,570	14,709	500	579	1,098	1,252	861
75 to 79 years	565	1,133	11,611	417	498	901	1,164	678
80 to 84 years	397	699	7,860	277	278	630	718	499
85 years and over	253	517	6,027	195	207	423	522	318

TABLE 1.11--POPULATION, BY AGE, TENNESSEE AND COUNTIES, 1990 (Continued)

Age	Fentress	Franklin	Gibson	Giles	Grainger	Greene	Grundy	Hamblen
TOTAL	14,669	34,725	46,315	25,741	17,095	55,853	13,362	50,480
Under 1 year	151	381	479	303	177	571	176	516
1 and 2 years	374	883	1,203	712	426	1,330	310	1,335
3 and 4 years	373	920	1,168	709	425	1,302	375	1,267
5 years	202	444	629	345	248	702	165	685
6 years	188	430	623	356	193	648	203	642
7 to 9 years	664	1,420	1,852	1,064	682	2,099	602	1,940
10 and 11 years	446	1,002	1,330	726	467	1,500	494	1,292
12 and 13 years	448	1,015	1,273	739	487	1,443	454	1,399
14 years	228	439	589	337	278	748	232	647
15 years	235	516	603	389	266	837	239	746
16 years	236	546	628	359	260	797	238	796
17 years	284	534	674	390	262	820	230	817
18 years	224	633	663	407	261	817	235	840
19 years	256	705	689	471	271	857	216	811
20 years	208	572	604	392	289	817	203	745
21 years	198	580	533	319	229	760	181	666
22 to 24 years	605	1,252	1,706	967	746	2,259	501	2,201
25 to 29 years	1,063	2,400	3,329	1,814	1,281	4,202	914	3,934
30 to 34 years	1,031	2,650	3,282	1,855	1,384	4,229	958	3,886
35 to 39 years	1,086	2,610	3,126	1,779	1,255	4,136	912	3,732
40 to 44 years	1,126	2,356	3,047	1,779	1,246	4,278	893	3,895
45 to 49 years	938	2,149	2,660	1,637	1,104	3,622	833	3,579
50 to 54 years	776	1,791	2,305	1,371	978	3,374	732	2,964
55 to 59 years	698	1,752	2,374	1,202	864	3,079	580	2,755
60 and 61 years	260	684	942	455	322	1,123	222	924
62 to 64 years	395	1,063	1,488	708	488	1,768	349	1,430
65 to 69 years	643	1,615	2,455	1,259	690	2,498	594	2,148
70 to 74 years	517	1,280	2,197	1,059	564	1,974	502	1,580
75 to 79 years	410	1,013	1,856	856	461	1,593	375	1,139
80 to 84 years	249	666	1,166	597	295	965	242	675
85 years and over	157	424	842	385	196	705	202	494

TABLE 1.11--POPULATION, BY AGE, TENNESSEE AND COUNTIES, 1990 (Continued)

Age	Hamilton	Hancock	Hardeman	Hardin	Hawkins	Haywood	Henderson	Henry
TOTAL	285,536	6,739	23,377	22,633	44,565	19,437	21,844	27,888
Under 1 year	3,380	48	290	262	480	247	232	293
1 and 2 years	7,976	186	745	623	1,091	574	570	665
3 and 4 years	7,590	178	737	550	1,095	546	550	636
5 years	3,748	98	345	295	580	295	283	311
6 years	3,648	110	353	312	570	276	270	339
7 to 9 years	11,421	280	1,090	880	1,723	1,024	945	1,112
10 and 11 years	8,006	221	782	686	1,215	715	691	794
12 and 13 years	7,720	195	838	682	1,174	705	640	776
14 years	3,656	98	364	311	599	337	346	352
15 years	3,911	87	410	355	674	318	301	339
16 years	3,912	102	325	345	663	327	313	393
17 years	4,042	98	342	351	730	274	311	361
18 years	4,226	109	360	339	691	297	313	369
19 years	4,568	79	336	306	660	281	298	371
20 years	4,349	94	296	318	627	246	269	320
21 years	4,145	79	304	270	570	255	271	284
22 to 24 years	11,989	288	948	882	1,883	763	833	902
25 to 29 years	22,147	485	1,801	1,534	3,476	1,399	1,655	1,845
30 to 34 years	23,652	527	1,773	1,579	3,540	1,479	1,632	1,951
35 to 39 years	22,942	472	1,680	1,661	3,408	1,493	1,574	1,819
40 to 44 years	21,698	427	1,550	1,573	3,397	1,173	1,575	1,896
45 to 49 years	16,990	393	1,196	1,412	3,013	902	1,304	1,626
50 to 54 years	14,201	349	1,041	1,198	2,563	831	1,088	1,502
55 to 59 years	13,785	358	1,053	1,155	2,195	856	1,184	1,495
60 and 61 years	5,507	133	446	504	834	294	441	638
62 to 64 years	7,991	187	633	736	1,225	524	657	1,015
65 to 69 years	12,362	333	1,039	1,079	1,935	766	1,063	1,687
70 to 74 years	9,544	280	812	882	1,484	782	808	1,416
75 to 79 years	7,434	217	664	704	1,190	650	695	1,133
80 to 84 years	5,140	154	459	486	770	454	431	722
85 years and over	3,856	74	365	363	510	354	301	526

TABLE 1.11--POPULATION, BY AGE, TENNESSEE AND COUNTIES, 1990 (Continued)

Age	Hickman	Houston	Humphreys	Jackson	Jefferson	Johnson	Knox	Lake
TOTAL	16,754	7,018	15,795	9,297	33,016	13,766	335,749	7,129
Under 1 year	179	59	169	92	309	130	3,624	70
1 and 2 years	457	183	421	225	745	307	9,209	186
3 and 4 years	426	178	399	200	742	350	8,593	143
5 years	217	81	178	88	344	139	4,284	71
6 years	195	80	207	99	394	157	4,155	72
7 to 9 years	659	280	679	354	1,170	486	12,709	254
10 and 11 years	467	198	494	236	761	372	8,350	181
12 and 13 years	471	198	481	272	839	403	7,934	190
14 years	228	105	218	136	442	195	3,871	101
15 years	233	102	240	138	450	214	4,069	92
16 years	249	116	241	132	514	227	4,088	103
17 years	238	111	244	142	528	211	4,226	102
18 years	239	104	219	121	666	194	5,525	96
19 years	228	100	212	120	801	208	7,010	109
20 years	217	93	205	120	750	175	6,842	123
21 years	207	71	188	110	642	186	6,450	150
22 to 24 years	657	242	549	384	1,429	524	16,785	399
25 to 29 years	1,381	469	1,027	633	2,400	930	28,850	623
30 to 34 years	1,441	471	1,200	664	2,398	968	29,174	604
35 to 39 years	1,304	490	1,203	698	2,292	974	27,521	558
40 to 44 years	1,249	461	1,083	669	2,356	1,035	24,596	481
45 to 49 years	1,008	413	1,030	562	2,233	919	19,433	366
50 to 54 years	907	398	904	511	1,972	802	15,962	360
55 to 59 years	801	415	849	507	1,812	700	14,799	343
60 and 61 years	300	137	323	180	688	284	5,903	117
62 to 64 years	461	215	539	306	940	410	9,097	180
65 to 69 years	777	375	774	491	1,448	671	14,117	328
70 to 74 years	633	319	600	404	1,170	576	10,701	229
75 to 79 years	463	256	445	322	858	478	8,337	235
80 to 84 years	285	162	274	228	521	298	5,492	143
85 years and over	177	136	200	153	402	243	4,043	120

TABLE 1.11--POPULATION, BY AGE, TENNESSEE AND COUNTIES, 1990 (Continued)

Age	Lauderdale	Lawrence	Lewis	Lincoln	Loudon	McMinn	McNairy	Macon
TOTAL	23,491	35,303	9,247	28,157	31,255	42,383	22,422	15,906
Under 1 year	293	441	102	346	308	485	229	201
1 and 2 years	716	1,133	261	761	826	1,040	581	428
3 and 4 years	677	979	258	743	817	1,058	521	454
5 years	349	516	131	425	382	539	303	232
6 years	377	487	134	385	398	531	260	214
7 to 9 years	1,119	1,561	422	1,152	1,164	1,765	913	687
10 and 11 years	799	1,047	301	849	816	1,234	673	467
12 and 13 years	714	1,021	294	780	837	1,217	712	443
14 years	362	457	137	387	419	606	325	231
15 years	382	527	145	353	455	612	299	205
16 years	313	505	146	417	443	638	346	222
17 years	302	541	148	382	467	649	341	240
18 years	316	510	140	416	435	666	285	222
19 years	359	526	140	410	397	651	289	235
20 years	340	510	125	392	409	630	261	241
21 years	307	500	124	335	405	558	253	227
22 to 24 years	996	1,493	333	1,088	1,238	1,688	791	682
25 to 29 years	1,953	2,715	675	2,058	2,206	3,136	1,547	1,228
30 to 34 years	1,901	2,618	663	2,184	2,531	3,322	1,606	1,218
35 to 39 years	1,653	2,383	656	1,983	2,380	3,072	1,572	1,148
40 to 44 years	1,480	2,310	658	1,904	2,375	3,042	1,619	1,119
45 to 49 years	1,264	2,075	531	1,668	2,025	2,704	1,481	995
50 to 54 years	1,087	1,866	441	1,529	1,711	2,327	1,241	763
55 to 59 years	974	1,732	439	1,430	1,655	2,129	1,160	789
60 and 61 years	381	661	163	567	659	791	482	268
62 to 64 years	553	983	284	845	944	1,220	717	442
65 to 69 years	986	1,607	434	1,407	1,515	1,991	1,055	778
70 to 74 years	899	1,368	341	1,104	1,202	1,510	921	585
75 to 79 years	789	1,069	309	928	921	1,191	760	454
80 to 84 years	467	668	191	530	534	795	498	293
85 years and over	383	494	121	399	381	586	381	195

TABLE 1.11--POPULATION, BY AGE, TENNESSEE AND COUNTIES, 1990 (Continued)

Age	Madison	Marion	Marshall	Maury	Meigs	Monroe	Montgomery	Moore
TOTAL	77,982	24,860	21,539	54,812	8,033	30,541	100,498	4,721
Under 1 year	952	288	264	680	73	335	1,557	49
1 and 2 years	2,357	676	550	1,604	189	851	3,779	112
3 and 4 years	2,199	679	560	1,591	199	772	3,345	110
5 years	1,104	320	300	779	112	406	1,529	62
6 years	1,133	341	280	757	108	378	1,492	54
7 to 9 years	3,503	1,073	922	2,457	311	1,209	4,397	208
10 and 11 years	2,412	772	667	1,734	247	922	2,785	154
12 and 13 years	2,360	774	664	1,687	269	942	2,615	149
14 years	1,090	379	298	776	112	440	1,212	72
15 years	1,048	404	325	733	126	495	1,299	74
16 years	1,091	397	289	748	143	474	1,356	82
17 years	1,076	424	335	732	108	507	1,267	77
18 years	1,275	401	304	815	142	547	1,597	77
19 years	1,547	378	318	720	127	594	2,346	70
20 years	1,424	326	276	732	114	511	2,415	58
21 years	1,192	313	266	672	125	427	2,430	53
22 to 24 years	3,253	978	875	2,165	343	1,221	7,060	170
25 to 29 years	6,169	1,876	1,628	4,315	596	2,176	10,996	314
30 to 34 years	6,426	1,981	1,693	4,666	569	2,237	9,141	354
35 to 39 years	6,093	1,921	1,638	4,434	624	2,187	7,789	360
40 to 44 years	5,479	1,839	1,532	3,960	669	2,265	6,447	348
45 to 49 years	4,129	1,604	1,323	3,085	544	2,031	4,690	344
50 to 54 years	3,347	1,312	999	2,638	456	1,601	3,977	264
55 to 59 years	3,239	1,262	980	2,547	360	1,464	3,785	221
60 and 61 years	1,262	469	380	1,036	143	503	1,363	101
62 to 64 years	2,059	638	606	1,495	239	857	1,858	144
65 to 69 years	3,201	1,000	1,037	2,264	359	1,365	2,737	210
70 to 74 years	2,649	736	850	1,846	254	1,110	2,026	175
75 to 79 years	2,113	601	628	1,525	156	854	1,490	142
80 to 84 years	1,573	436	441	940	123	483	1,002	68
85 years and over	1,227	262	311	679	93	377	716	45

TABLE 1.11--POPULATION, BY AGE, TENNESSEE AND COUNTIES, 1990 (Continued)

Age	Morgan	Obion	Overton	Perry	Pickett	Polk	Putnam	Rhea
TOTAL	17,300	31,717	17,636	6,612	4,548	13,643	51,373	24,344
Under 1 year	195	329	169	78	35	143	560	249
1 and 2 years	439	766	414	177	127	330	1,266	640
3 and 4 years	432	758	435	204	132	314	1,234	615
5 years	255	409	209	81	51	160	606	325
6 years	220	411	215	94	54	129	643	342
7 to 9 years	723	1,208	717	245	183	468	1,908	1,010
10 and 11 years	556	957	497	181	143	424	1,279	726
12 and 13 years	497	951	504	197	128	419	1,269	696
14 years	258	493	266	100	66	188	566	352
15 years	294	485	252	103	63	212	641	377
16 years	309	540	292	96	70	252	636	372
17 years	284	530	272	104	65	255	637	454
18 years	264	514	287	73	55	212	1,133	423
19 years	271	454	243	89	51	213	1,635	447
20 years	257	452	233	66	57	197	1,437	400
21 years	228	442	239	88	44	185	1,364	358
22 to 24 years	741	1,190	722	219	169	562	3,102	978
25 to 29 years	1,499	2,131	1,204	430	304	938	4,072	1,712
30 to 34 years	1,461	2,323	1,260	438	296	962	3,766	1,826
35 to 39 years	1,411	2,435	1,241	434	335	985	3,570	1,711
40 to 44 years	1,285	2,268	1,334	483	290	1,000	3,488	1,798
45 to 49 years	1,015	1,984	1,088	405	270	948	2,958	1,568
50 to 54 years	855	1,707	1,026	351	266	792	2,394	1,245
55 to 59 years	794	1,599	923	395	283	703	2,265	1,132
60 and 61 years	298	554	356	160	87	259	905	449
62 to 64 years	425	891	519	226	151	429	1,376	665
65 to 69 years	647	1,409	860	361	226	640	2,094	1,083
70 to 74 years	521	1,292	693	252	188	501	1,716	885
75 to 79 years	413	1,094	544	219	164	421	1,330	718
80 to 84 years	261	633	361	157	109	243	883	481
85 years and over	192	508	261	106	86	159	640	307

TABLE 1.11--POPULATION, BY AGE, TENNESSEE AND COUNTIES, 1990 (Continued)

Age	Roane	Robertson	Rutherford	Scott	Sequatchie	Sevier	Shelby	Smith
TOTAL	47,227	41,494	118,570	18,358	8,863	51,043	826,330	14,143
Under 1 year	453	576	1,524	228	93	537	11,433	151
1 and 2 years	1,119	1,358	3,862	543	256	1,304	28,673	412
3 and 4 years	1,094	1,233	3,548	510	223	1,273	26,439	378
5 years	605	660	1,783	266	110	643	13,001	195
6 years	584	652	1,805	277	97	655	12,523	197
7 to 9 years	1,814	1,942	5,634	894	394	2,047	38,466	622
10 and 11 years	1,267	1,325	3,557	676	271	1,451	25,506	413
12 and 13 years	1,405	1,231	3,425	693	288	1,380	23,483	393
14 years	675	613	1,599	317	142	656	11,166	176
15 years	669	577	1,721	339	130	744	11,852	195
16 years	711	570	1,606	316	141	786	11,751	182
17 years	711	648	1,709	322	141	733	12,014	225
18 years	742	552	2,072	277	151	713	13,577	180
19 years	684	554	2,739	257	167	742	15,020	178
20 years	609	519	2,850	294	138	726	13,814	167
21 years	544	477	2,529	278	121	623	12,626	176
22 to 24 years	1,624	1,535	6,599	777	340	2,013	38,204	551
25 to 29 years	3,096	3,412	11,287	1,422	684	4,012	74,151	1,132
30 to 34 years	3,423	3,683	11,125	1,365	700	4,173	75,269	1,107
35 to 39 years	3,711	3,339	9,940	1,303	728	4,197	69,858	1,021
40 to 44 years	3,501	2,940	8,415	1,293	662	3,876	59,423	975
45 to 49 years	3,112	2,312	6,334	1,100	542	3,368	43,302	826
50 to 54 years	2,748	2,064	5,041	889	488	2,947	35,052	681
55 to 59 years	2,608	1,974	4,173	767	397	2,628	31,983	693
60 and 61 years	1,028	695	1,476	284	144	1,014	12,516	287
62 to 64 years	1,635	998	2,206	471	229	1,394	18,893	382
65 to 69 years	2,611	1,588	3,357	718	310	2,270	28,911	633
70 to 74 years	1,775	1,250	2,564	548	270	1,678	21,585	601
75 to 79 years	1,251	1,004	1,886	427	236	1,171	16,484	453
80 to 84 years	839	663	1,248	286	177	731	10,965	328
85 years and over	579	550	956	221	93	558	8,390	233

TABLE 1.11--POPULATION, BY AGE, TENNESSEE AND COUNTIES, 1990 (Continued)

Age	Stewart	Sullivan	Sumner	Tipton	Trousdale	Unicoi	Union	Van Buren
TOTAL	9,479	143,596	103,281	37,568	5,920	16,549	13,694	4,846
Under 1 year	75	1,457	1,286	520	62	154	183	54
1 and 2 years	209	3,523	3,028	1,376	134	386	408	126
3 and 4 years	200	3,422	2,938	1,318	146	332	363	137
5 years	124	1,667	1,597	657	72	203	200	75
6 years	101	1,622	1,563	596	84	195	173	58
7 to 9 years	360	5,252	4,927	1,972	259	589	653	221
10 and 11 years	237	3,583	3,310	1,293	181	395	440	170
12 and 13 years	268	3,648	3,261	1,322	168	412	412	168
14 years	131	1,796	1,529	630	87	212	212	54
15 years	154	1,974	1,651	641	70	227	228	66
16 years	124	2,098	1,682	578	73	243	203	73
17 years	123	2,212	1,676	584	85	249	194	71
18 years	131	2,105	1,486	537	79	236	195	75
19 years	136	2,115	1,505	541	99	230	208	78
20 years	97	1,974	1,401	534	72	227	213	74
21 years	95	1,974	1,259	493	73	189	176	58
22 to 24 years	364	5,739	3,923	1,513	217	591	650	190
25 to 29 years	628	10,343	8,064	3,117	413	1,220	1,131	377
30 to 34 years	666	11,024	8,664	3,136	472	1,255	1,193	393
35 to 39 years	698	11,049	8,844	2,875	425	1,246	998	359
40 to 44 years	661	10,982	8,363	2,554	438	1,155	1,016	377
45 to 49 years	592	9,926	7,059	2,139	339	1,044	844	269
50 to 54 years	556	8,386	5,448	1,673	312	891	730	260
55 to 59 years	552	7,623	4,501	1,524	285	910	646	246
60 and 61 years	220	3,069	1,583	553	116	346	214	75
62 to 64 years	328	4,532	2,268	835	166	572	300	153
65 to 69 years	561	7,369	3,465	1,258	320	910	476	196
70 to 74 years	380	5,230	2,683	1,030	236	729	379	151
75 to 79 years	345	3,938	2,063	864	200	533	328	120
80 to 84 years	230	2,374	1,292	545	134	345	186	75
85 years and over	133	1,590	962	360	103	323	142	47

TABLE 1.11--POPULATION, BY AGE, TENNESSEE AND COUNTIES, 1990 (Continued)

Age	Warren	Washington	Wayne	Weakley	White	Williamson	Wilson	TENNESSEE
TOTAL	32,992	92,315	13,935	31,972	20,090	81,021	67,675	4,877,185
Under 1 year	375	876	192	350	225	958	836	58,053
1 and 2 years	878	2,305	384	783	509	2,497	2,037	141,237
3 and 4 years	862	2,123	338	696	505	2,578	1,992	134,125
5 years	454	1,136	199	404	241	1,302	1,028	67,048
6 years	441	1,053	202	393	252	1,314	989	65,910
7 to 9 years	1,432	3,343	555	1,218	792	4,205	3,287	204,410
10 and 11 years	981	2,199	429	850	571	2,815	2,256	139,562
12 and 13 years	954	2,327	445	811	583	2,762	2,164	135,128
14 years	480	1,120	189	365	260	1,291	957	64,408
15 years	476	1,236	185	376	277	1,299	995	67,846
16 years	485	1,164	232	398	271	1,274	1,000	68,686
17 years	476	1,203	226	393	318	1,263	998	70,191
18 years	465	1,526	232	748	274	1,055	981	75,779
19 years	500	2,028	175	1,100	269	942	955	84,064
20 years	472	1,924	204	927	275	823	844	79,105
21 years	447	1,809	204	851	271	816	766	73,731
22 to 24 years	1,312	4,484	557	1,681	791	2,356	2,397	214,976
25 to 29 years	2,495	7,334	1,043	2,317	1,423	5,196	5,193	402,977
30 to 34 years	2,520	7,489	1,009	2,209	1,441	7,043	6,052	409,344
35 to 39 years	2,406	7,090	952	2,035	1,422	8,009	6,044	386,327
40 to 44 years	2,363	6,789	987	1,950	1,453	8,200	5,690	354,661
45 to 49 years	1,990	5,524	852	1,665	1,256	5,871	4,671	286,553
50 to 54 years	1,718	4,625	776	1,501	1,068	4,311	3,626	239,657
55 to 59 years	1,633	4,280	671	1,422	1,091	3,407	2,884	220,952
60 and 61 years	678	1,738	245	523	401	1,173	970	85,467
62 to 64 years	915	2,697	398	867	615	1,574	1,454	128,170
65 to 69 years	1,525	4,306	669	1,456	998	2,304	2,152	200,986
70 to 74 years	1,179	3,103	510	1,261	847	1,625	1,754	156,437
75 to 79 years	910	2,463	413	1,129	679	1,264	1,294	122,539
80 to 84 years	670	1,638	262	687	417	840	855	80,062
85 years and over	500	1,383	200	606	295	654	554	58,794

Source: U.S. Department of Commerce, Bureau of the Census, *1990 Census of Population and Housing, Summary Tape File 1A, Tennessee.*

TABLE 1.12--POPULATION, BY RACE, TENNESSEE AND COUNTIES, 1990

County	Total	White	Black	American Indian, Eskimo or Aleut	Asian or Pacific Islander	Other
Anderson	68,250	64,615	2,763	243	547	82
Bedford	30,411	27,097	3,068	36	147	63
Benton	14,524	14,109	345	23	31	16
Bledsoe	9,669	9,242	375	42	3	7
Blount	85,969	82,503	2,783	195	409	79
Bradley	73,712	70,132	2,900	200	232	248
Campbell	35,079	34,727	130	175	41	6
Cannon	10,467	10,236	186	15	14	16
Carroll	27,514	24,303	3,138	35	10	28
Carter	51,505	50,763	456	91	144	51
Cheatham	27,140	26,460	534	84	36	26
Chester	12,819	11,355	1,412	20	22	10
Claiborne	26,137	25,701	250	56	112	18
Clay	7,238	7,103	116	11	3	5
Cocke	29,141	28,398	613	78	31	21
Coffee	40,339	38,459	1,493	84	251	52
Crockett	13,378	11,097	2,252	9	9	11
Cumberland	34,736	34,475	42	137	49	33
Davidson	510,784	381,740	119,273	1,162	7,081	1,528
Decatur	10,472	10,000	417	23	21	11
DeKalb	14,360	14,074	215	19	12	40
Dickson	35,061	33,145	1,744	68	71	33
Dyer	34,854	30,541	4,145	64	63	41
Fayette	25,559	14,204	11,295	33	15	12
Fentress	14,669	14,636	2	10	18	3
Franklin	34,725	32,425	2,095	55	95	55
Gibson	46,315	37,237	8,944	37	61	36
Giles	25,741	22,184	3,405	57	61	34
Grainger	17,095	16,939	102	42	8	4
Greene	55,853	54,440	1,223	89	70	31
Grundy	13,362	13,294	19	28	6	15
Hamblen	50,480	47,891	2,323	85	128	53
Hamilton	285,536	227,413	54,477	585	2,479	582
Hancock	6,739	6,596	122	18	1	2
Hardeman	23,377	14,536	8,748	20	62	11
Hardin	22,633	21,539	997	34	37	26
Hawkins	44,565	43,664	741	78	59	23
Haywood	19,437	9,676	9,651	24	19	67
Henderson	21,844	19,982	1,816	20	19	7
Henry	27,888	24,955	2,813	50	54	16
Hickman	16,754	15,831	859	40	8	16
Houston	7,018	6,725	268	12	5	8
Humphreys	15,795	15,175	551	26	32	11
Jackson	9,297	9,247	7	19	19	5
Jefferson	33,016	31,937	930	75	41	33
Johnson	13,766	13,668	61	14	14	9
Knox	335,749	301,421	29,603	797	3,327	601
Lake	7,129	5,418	1,702	4	2	3
Lauderdale	23,491	16,007	7,303	127	20	34
Lawrence	35,303	34,666	482	59	73	23
Lewis	9,247	9,082	119	26	7	13
Lincoln	28,157	25,583	2,422	38	64	50

31

TABLE 1.12--POPULATION, BY RACE, TENNESSEE AND COUNTIES, 1990 (Continued)

County	Total	White	Black	American Indian, Eskimo or Aleut	Asian or Pacific Islander	Other
Loudon	31,255	30,732	400	52	50	21
McMinn	42,383	40,085	2,051	96	121	30
McNairy	22,422	20,918	1,432	21	40	11
Macon	15,906	15,810	44	35	10	7
Madison	77,982	53,423	24,170	66	253	70
Marion	24,860	23,749	1,035	36	32	8
Marshall	21,539	19,536	1,909	24	53	17
Maury	54,812	45,868	8,607	79	157	101
Meigs	8,033	7,884	118	28	2	1
Monroe	30,541	29,561	833	48	71	28
Montgomery	100,498	79,118	17,872	394	1,831	1,283
Moore	4,721	4,536	174	8	2	1
Morgan	17,300	16,957	265	46	25	7
Obion	31,717	28,324	3,256	47	48	42
Overton	17,636	17,582	30	10	4	10
Perry	6,612	6,470	119	8	7	8
Pickett	4,548	4,542	0	4	2	0
Polk	13,643	13,571	0	25	42	5
Putnam	51,373	49,878	873	79	457	86
Rhea	24,344	23,571	581	62	53	77
Roane	47,227	45,444	1,456	95	191	41
Robertson	41,494	36,802	4,555	63	43	31
Rutherford	118,570	105,740	10,678	234	1,706	212
Scott	18,358	18,263	5	67	13	10
Sequatchie	8,863	8,851	2	4	5	1
Sevier	51,043	50,462	216	130	203	32
Shelby	826,330	455,063	360,083	1,468	7,740	1,976
Smith	14,143	13,626	459	36	13	9
Stewart	9,479	9,294	96	56	26	7
Sullivan	143,596	140,076	2,562	372	485	101
Sumner	103,281	97,073	5,562	195	347	104
Tipton	37,568	28,436	8,852	114	100	66
Trousdale	5,920	5,040	853	14	8	5
Unicoi	16,549	16,488	3	11	14	33
Union	13,694	13,658	3	23	5	5
Van Buren	4,846	4,823	5	16	0	2
Warren	32,992	31,511	1,131	51	119	180
Washington	92,315	88,409	3,275	155	378	98
Wayne	13,935	13,762	137	17	10	9
Weakley	31,972	29,368	2,222	39	277	66
White	20,090	19,654	378	24	25	9
Williamson	81,021	74,903	5,396	130	469	123
Wilson	67,675	62,561	4,607	185	259	63
TENNESSEE	4,877,185	4,048,068	778,035	10,039	31,839	9,204

Source: U.S. Department of Commerce, Bureau of the Census, *1990 Census of Population, General Population Characteristics, Tennessee*.

TABLE 1.13--POPULATION, BY SEX, TENNESSEE AND COUNTIES, 1990

County	Total Persons	Male	Female	County	Total Persons	Male	Female
Anderson	68,250	32,534	35,716	Lewis	9,247	4,520	4,727
Bedford	30,411	14,750	15,661	Lincoln	28,157	13,581	14,576
Benton	14,524	6,879	7,645	Loudon	31,255	15,058	16,197
Bledsoe	9,669	5,263	4,406	McMinn	42,383	20,224	22,159
Blount	85,969	41,279	44,690	McNairy	22,422	10,819	11,603
Bradley	73,712	35,531	38,181	Macon	15,906	7,736	8,170
Campbell	35,079	16,733	18,346	Madison	77,982	36,746	41,236
Cannon	10,467	5,105	5,362	Marion	24,860	12,118	12,742
Carroll	27,514	13,221	14,293	Marshall	21,539	10,408	11,131
Carter	51,505	24,875	26,630	Maury	54,812	26,245	28,567
Cheatham	27,140	13,580	13,560	Meigs	8,033	4,044	3,989
Chester	12,819	6,123	6,696	Monroe	30,541	14,839	15,702
Claiborne	26,137	12,666	13,471	Montgomery	100,498	51,503	48,995
Clay	7,238	3,567	3,671	Moore	4,721	2,350	2,371
Cocke	29,141	14,035	15,106	Morgan	17,300	9,112	8,188
Coffee	40,339	19,445	20,894	Obion	31,717	15,161	16,556
Crockett	13,378	6,369	7,009	Overton	17,636	8,669	8,967
Cumberland	34,736	16,805	17,931	Perry	6,612	3,247	3,365
Davidson	510,784	242,492	268,292	Pickett	4,548	2,223	2,325
Decatur	10,472	5,045	5,427	Polk	13,643	6,725	6,918
DeKalb	14,360	6,854	7,506	Putnam	51,373	25,197	26,176
Dickson	35,061	17,025	18,036	Rhea	24,344	11,748	12,596
Dyer	34,854	16,504	18,350	Roane	47,227	22,744	24,483
Fayette	25,559	12,449	13,110	Robertson	41,494	20,323	21,171
Fentress	14,669	7,172	7,497	Rutherford	118,570	58,373	60,197
Franklin	34,725	17,073	17,652	Scott	18,358	8,944	9,414
Gibson	46,315	21,714	24,601	Sequatchie	8,863	4,383	4,480
Giles	25,741	12,427	13,314	Sevier	51,043	24,838	26,205
Grainger	17,095	8,473	8,622	Shelby	826,330	393,614	432,716
Greene	55,853	27,026	28,827	Smith	14,143	6,842	7,301
Grundy	13,362	6,460	6,902	Stewart	9,479	4,675	4,804
Hamblen	50,480	24,319	26,161	Sullivan	143,596	68,886	74,710
Hamilton	285,536	134,764	150,772	Sumner	103,281	50,567	52,714
Hancock	6,739	3,320	3,419	Tipton	37,568	18,331	19,237
Hardeman	23,377	11,239	12,138	Trousdale	5,920	2,873	3,047
Hardin	22,633	10,923	11,710	Unicoi	16,549	7,915	8,634
Hawkins	44,565	21,752	22,813	Union	13,694	6,767	6,927
Haywood	19,437	9,106	10,331	Van Buren	4,846	2,398	2,448
Henderson	21,844	10,512	11,332	Warren	32,992	15,900	17,092
Henry	27,888	13,370	14,518	Washington	92,315	44,658	47,657
Hickman	16,754	8,622	8,132	Wayne	13,935	6,822	7,113
Houston	7,018	3,402	3,616	Weakley	31,972	15,312	16,660
Humphreys	15,795	7,756	8,039	White	20,090	9,710	10,380
Jackson	9,297	4,525	4,772	Williamson	81,021	39,817	41,204
Jefferson	33,016	16,136	16,880	Wilson	67,675	33,417	34,258
Johnson	13,766	6,826	6,940	TENNESSEE	4,877,185	2,348,928	2,528,257
Knox	335,749	160,367	175,382				
Lake	7,129	3,808	3,321				
Lauderdale	23,491	11,376	12,115				
Lawrence	35,303	16,949	18,354				

Source: U.S. Department of Commerce, Bureau of the Census, *1990 Census of Population and Housing, 1990: Summary Tape File 1A, Tennessee.*

1.   **POPULATION**

TABLE 1.14--NUMBER OF HOUSEHOLDS AND AVERAGE POPULATION PER HOUSEHOLD,
TENNESSEE AND COUNTIES, 1980 AND 1990

County	Number of households		Change, 1980 to 1990		Average population per household	
	1990	1980	Number	%	1990	1980
Anderson	27,384	24,616	2,768	11.2	2.47	2.70
Bedford	11,608	9,943	1,665	16.7	2.59	2.77
Benton	5,784	5,577	207	3.7	2.46	2.64
Bledsoe	3,261	2,979	282	9.5	2.64	2.88
Blount	33,624	28,177	5,447	19.3	2.51	2.72
Bradley	27,604	23,026	4,578	19.9	2.61	2.87
Campbell	13,150	12,087	1,063	8.8	2.65	2.88
Cannon	3,980	3,625	355	9.8	2.60	2.80
Carroll	10,727	10,321	406	3.9	2.50	2.70
Carter	20,189	17,868	2,321	13.0	2.49	2.76
Cheatham	9,515	7,063	2,452	34.7	2.82	3.04
Chester	4,558	4,210	348	8.3	2.59	2.75
Claiborne	9,629	8,295	1,334	16.1	2.65	2.91
Clay	2,855	2,731	124	4.5	2.51	2.79
Cocke	11,191	10,154	1,037	10.2	2.58	2.83
Coffee	15,500	13,649	1,851	13.6	2.57	2.77
Crockett	5,183	5,380	-197	-3.7	2.53	2.76
Cumberland	13,426	9,887	3,539	35.8	2.55	2.88
Davidson	207,530	177,737	29,793	16.8	2.36	2.58
Decatur	4,216	4,081	135	3.3	2.45	2.64
DeKalb	5,696	4,956	740	14.9	2.50	2.72
Dickson	13,019	10,468	2,551	24.4	2.65	2.85
Dyer	13,617	12,696	921	7.3	2.52	2.71
Fayette	8,453	7,431	1,022	13.8	2.97	3.35
Fentress	5,511	5,027	484	9.6	2.64	2.94
Franklin	12,660	10,792	1,868	17.3	2.64	2.87
Gibson	18,361	18,202	159	0.9	2.48	2.69
Giles	9,832	8,825	1,007	11.4	2.58	2.75
Grainger	6,394	5,694	700	12.3	2.64	2.92
Greene	21,482	19,157	2,325	12.1	2.52	2.76
Grundy	4,784	4,510	274	6.1	2.75	3.05
Hamblen	19,429	17,257	2,172	12.6	2.56	2.84
Hamilton	111,799	103,319	8,480	8.2	2.50	2.71
Hancock	2,484	2,351	133	5.7	2.65	2.93
Hardeman	8,276	7,623	653	8.6	2.73	3.00
Hardin	8,726	7,970	756	9.5	2.56	2.77
Hawkins	17,167	15,288	1,879	12.3	2.58	2.86
Haywood	7,014	6,513	501	7.7	2.74	3.10
Henderson	8,527	7,686	841	10.9	2.54	2.76
Henry	11,362	10,914	448	4.1	2.42	2.60
Hickman	5,976	5,094	882	17.3	2.63	2.84
Houston	2,683	2,410	273	11.3	2.55	2.83
Humphreys	6,063	5,634	429	7.6	2.56	2.82
Jackson	3,642	3,363	279	8.3	2.52	2.78
Jefferson	12,329	10,623	1,706	16.1	2.55	2.81
Johnson	5,406	4,840	566	11.7	2.52	2.83
Knox	133,639	117,951	15,688	13.3	2.42	2.61
Lake	2,418	2,575	-157	-6.1	2.50	2.84
Lauderdale	8,423	8,281	142	1.7	2.68	2.86
Lawrence	13,338	11,867	1,471	12.4	2.62	2.85

34

TABLE 1.14--NUMBER OF HOUSEHOLDS AND AVERAGE POPULATION PER HOUSEHOLD,
TENNESSEE AND COUNTIES, 1980 AND 1990 (Continued)

County	Number of households				Average population per household	
	1990	1980	Change, 1980 to 1990		1990	1980
			Number	%		
Lewis	3,533	3,055	478	15.6	2.58	2.84
Lincoln	10,881	9,533	1,348	14.1	2.57	2.75
Loudon	12,155	10,289	1,866	18.1	2.54	2.75
McMinn	16,351	14,727	1,624	11.0	2.55	2.81
McNairy	8,834	8,179	655	8.0	2.51	2.73
Macon	6,159	5,645	514	9.1	2.57	2.75
Madison	29,609	26,713	2,896	10.8	2.55	2.71
Marion	9,215	8,270	945	11.4	2.67	2.93
Marshall	8,268	7,144	1,124	15.7	2.57	2.72
Maury	20,608	18,180	2,428	13.4	2.62	2.78
Meigs	2,996	2,520	476	18.9	2.64	2.95
Monroe	11,363	9,637	1,726	17.9	2.63	2.93
Montgomery	34,345	27,198	7,147	26.3	2.72	2.87
Moore	1,734	1,534	200	13.0	2.72	2.94
Morgan	5,841	5,389	452	8.4	2.74	3.00
Obion	12,412	12,079	333	2.8	2.53	2.70
Overton	6,734	6,122	612	10.0	2.59	2.85
Perry	2,512	2,240	272	12.1	2.57	2.71
Pickett	1,786	1,542	244	15.8	2.52	2.82
Polk	5,092	4,607	485	10.5	2.66	2.95
Putnam	19,753	16,706	3,047	18.2	2.45	2.65
Rhea	9,185	8,285	900	10.9	2.57	2.85
Roane	18,453	17,078	1,375	8.1	2.53	2.82
Robertson	14,801	12,532	2,269	18.1	2.77	2.93
Rutherford	42,118	28,002	14,116	50.4	2.69	2.84
Scott	6,534	6,200	334	5.4	2.78	3.09
Sequatchie	3,287	2,891	396	13.7	2.67	2.93
Sevier	19,520	14,741	4,779	32.4	2.58	2.79
Shelby	303,571	269,186	34,385	12.8	2.65	2.81
Smith	5,358	5,392	-34	-0.6	2.61	2.76
Stewart	3,678	3,104	574	18.5	2.53	2.79
Sullivan	56,729	52,022	4,707	9.0	2.49	2.75
Sumner	36,850	28,557	8,293	29.0	2.77	2.99
Tipton	13,033	10,778	2,255	20.9	2.86	3.04
Trousdale	2,261	2,227	34	1.5	2.56	2.73
Unicoi	6,621	5,948	673	11.3	2.46	2.74
Union	4,932	3,947	985	25.0	2.75	2.96
Van Buren	1,799	1,590	209	13.1	2.69	2.97
Warren	12,681	11,869	812	6.8	2.57	2.74
Washington	35,823	31,191	4,632	14.9	2.45	2.71
Wayne	5,174	4,792	382	8.0	2.65	2.88
Weakley	11,992	11,567	425	3.7	2.47	2.60
White	7,722	6,988	734	10.5	2.57	2.78
Williamson	27,928	18,723	9,205	49.2	2.88	3.08
Wilson	24,070	18,863	5,207	27.6	2.79	2.94
TENNESSEE	1,853,725	1,618,505	235,220	14.5	2.56	2.77

Source: U.S. Department of Commerce, Bureau of the Census, *1990 Census of Population, General Population Characteristics, Tennessee.*

TABLE 1.15--GROUP QUARTERS POPULATION BY TYPE, TENNESSEE AND COUNTIES, 1990

County	Total	Noninstitutional residents			Institutional residents		
		Total [1]	Military quarters	College dormitories	Total [1]	Correctional institutions	Nursing homes
Anderson	655	77	0	0	578	78	444
Bedford	380	37	0	0	343	69	274
Benton	269	41	0	0	228	30	198
Bledsoe	1,061	10	0	0	1,051	822	50
Blount	1,506	462	0	407	1,044	116	741
Bradley	1,669	1,130	0	1,058	539	0	519
Campbell	296	11	0	0	285	31	254
Cannon	111	0	0	0	111	15	96
Carroll	654	266	0	197	388	46	342
Carter	1,280	531	0	503	749	263	438
Cheatham	300	120	0	0	180	65	99
Chester	1,028	841	0	831	187	16	171
Claiborne	604	394	0	365	210	26	184
Clay	80	9	0	0	71	9	62
Cocke	301	31	0	0	270	56	190
Coffee	484	32	2	0	452	131	301
Crockett	275	0	0	0	275	23	252
Cumberland	529	0	0	0	529	33	476
Davidson	21,095	10,778	0	9,384	10,317	4,687	3,331
Decatur	142	0	0	0	142	22	118
DeKalb	123	17	0	15	106	15	86
Dickson	529	140	0	0	389	60	271
Dyer	511	37	0	0	474	163	303
Fayette	449	13	0	0	436	60	203
Fentress	110	0	0	0	110	14	96
Franklin	1,296	982	0	967	314	33	251
Gibson	747	103	0	0	644	107	537
Giles	405	200	0	178	205	28	177
Grainger	183	37	0	0	146	16	130
Greene	1,678	951	0	128	727	141	521
Grundy	205	12	0	0	193	11	182
Hamblen	730	205	0	129	525	143	360
Hamilton	6,492	2,870	0	2,462	3,622	749	2,204
Hancock	168	0	0	0	168	121	47
Hardeman	788	18	0	0	770	49	187
Hardin	283	20	0	16	263	42	221
Hawkins	333	34	0	0	299	35	264
Haywood	197	138	0	0	59	55	4
Henderson	214	2	0	0	212	37	175
Henry	432	44	0	0	388	57	331
Hickman	1,039	0	0	0	1,039	840	161
Houston	176	13	0	0	163	12	151
Humphreys	244	134	0	0	110	38	68
Jackson	121	2	0	0	119	10	109
Jefferson	1,601	1,156	0	1,074	445	144	301
Johnson	157	12	0	0	145	28	117
Knox	12,349	9,061	0	7,766	3,288	758	1,765
Lake	1,072	21	0	0	1,051	883	168
Lauderdale	893	9	0	0	884	641	243
Lawrence	311	9	0	0	302	35	267

TABLE 1.15--GROUP QUARTERS POPULATION BY TYPE, TENNESSEE AND COUNTIES, 1990
(Continued)

County	Total	Noninstitutional residents			Institutional residents		
		Total [1]	Military quarters	College dormitories	Total [1]	Correctional institutions	Nursing homes
Lewis	149	13	0	0	136	11	116
Lincoln	247	8	0	0	239	58	181
Loudon	329	0	0	0	329	38	291
McMinn	673	227	0	227	446	70	376
McNairy	242	0	0	0	242	17	225
Macon	89	33	0	0	56	16	40
Madison	2,467	1,626	0	1,422	841	140	693
Marion	215	10	0	0	205	29	161
Marshall	291	62	0	0	229	43	177
Maury	739	51	0	0	688	68	529
Meigs	112	0	0	0	112	17	95
Monroe	601	284	0	284	317	64	240
Montgomery	6,982	6,510	5,516	962	472	0	426
Moore	7	0	0	0	7	7	0
Morgan	1,289	0	0	0	1,289	1,153	124
Obion	318	20	0	0	298	45	253
Overton	201	9	0	0	192	29	163
Perry	152	0	0	0	152	4	93
Pickett	54	5	0	0	49	1	48
Polk	105	0	0	0	105	27	78
Putnam	2,954	2,420	0	2,385	534	59	432
Rhea	706	296	0	289	410	45	365
Roane	480	46	0	0	434	53	381
Robertson	449	0	0	0	449	63	353
Rutherford	5,198	3,743	0	3,483	1,455	237	742
Scott	169	0	0	0	169	20	149
Sequatchie	85	0	0	0	85	12	67
Sevier	649	67	0	0	582	89	327
Shelby	23,245	11,065	5,608	4,366	12,180	5,847	4,370
Smith	145	11	0	0	134	14	120
Stewart	184	89	0	0	95	7	88
Sullivan	2,147	796	0	362	1,351	364	875
Sumner	1,216	579	0	63	637	179	454
Tipton	267	0	0	0	267	58	209
Trousdale	125	25	0	0	100	10	90
Unicoi	231	11	0	0	220	42	178
Union	121	31	0	0	90	14	76
Van Buren	5	0	0	0	5	5	0
Warren	395	14	0	0	381	78	284
Washington	4,424	2,407	0	2,318	2,017	139	1,469
Wayne	226	22	0	0	204	42	154
Weakley	2,403	1,924	0	1,924	479	26	422
White	210	18	0	0	192	28	164
Williamson	713	14	0	0	699	149	464
Wilson	565	294	0	118	271	55	210
TENNESSEE	129,129	63,740	11,126	43,683	65,389	21,335	35,192

1. Includes categories not shown separately.

Source: U.S. Department of Commerce, Bureau of the Census, *1990 Census of Population and Housing, Summary Tape File 1A, Tennessee.*

TABLE 1.16--LAND AREA, POPULATION DENSITY, AND POPULATION LIVING IN URBAN AND
RURAL AREAS, TENNESSEE AND COUNTIES, 1990

County	Land area (square miles)	Popu- lation per square mile	Population		Percent of total population	
			Urban	Rural	Urban	Rural
Anderson	337.5	202.2	36,022	32,228	52.8	47.2
Bedford	473.7	64.2	14,049	16,362	46.2	53.8
Benton	394.8	36.8	3,643	10,881	25.1	74.9
Bledsoe	406.3	23.8	0	9,669	0.0	100.0
Blount	558.6	153.9	44,394	41,575	51.6	48.4
Bradley	328.8	224.2	40,975	32,737	55.6	44.4
Campbell	480.1	73.1	7,192	27,887	20.5	79.5
Cannon	265.7	39.4	0	10,467	0.0	100.0
Carroll	599.1	45.9	9,058	18,456	32.9	67.1
Carter	341.1	151.0	26,128	25,377	50.7	49.3
Cheatham	302.7	89.7	2,552	24,588	9.4	90.6
Chester	288.5	44.4	4,760	8,059	37.1	62.9
Claiborne	434.3	60.2	2,657	23,480	10.2	89.8
Clay	236.1	30.7	0	7,238	0.0	100.0
Cocke	434.4	67.1	7,123	22,018	24.4	75.6
Coffee	428.9	94.1	23,467	16,872	58.2	41.8
Crockett	265.3	50.4	0	13,378	0.0	100.0
Cumberland	681.6	51.0	6,930	27,806	20.0	80.0
Davidson	502.3	1,016.9	505,786	4,998	99.0	1.0
Decatur -	333.9	31.4	0	10,472	0.0	100.0
DeKalb	304.6	47.1	3,791	10,569	26.4	73.6
Dickson	489.9	71.6	8,791	26,270	25.1	74.9
Dyer	510.6	68.3	18,832	16,022	54.0	46.0
Fayette	704.5	36.3	0	25,559	0.0	100.0
Fentress	498.7	29.4	0	14,669	0.0	100.0
Franklin	553.1	62.8	7,308	27,417	21.0	79.0
Gibson	602.7	76.8	21,982	24,333	47.5	52.5
Giles	611.0	42.1	7,895	17,846	30.7	69.3
Grainger	280.4	61.0	0	17,095	0.0	100.0
Greene	621.8	89.8	13,532	42,321	24.2	75.8
Grundy	360.6	37.1	0	13,362	0.0	100.0
Hamblen	161.0	313.5	21,385	29,095	42.4	57.6
Hamilton	542.5	526.3	250,761	34,775	87.8	12.2
Hancock	222.3	30.3	0	6,739	0.0	100.0
Hardeman	667.6	35.0	5,969	17,408	25.5	74.5
Hardin	577.9	39.2	6,547	16,086	28.9	71.1
Hawkins	486.7	91.6	16,039	28,526	36.0	64.0
Haywood	533.2	36.5	10,019	9,418	51.5	48.5
Henderson	520.1	42.0	5,810	16,034	26.6	73.4
Henry	561.8	49.6	9,447	18,441	33.9	66.1
Hickman	612.7	27.3	3,616	13,138	21.6	78.4
Houston	200.2	35.1	0	7,018	0.0	100.0
Humphreys	532.2	29.7	3,925	11,870	24.8	75.2
Jackson	308.9	30.1	0	9,297	0.0	100.0
Jefferson	273.8	120.6	5,494	27,522	16.6	83.4
Johnson	298.5	46.1	0	13,766	0.0	100.0
Knox	508.5	660.3	261,720	74,029	78.0	22.0
Lake	163.4	43.6	0	7,129	0.0	100.0
Lauderdale	470.5	49.9	6,188	17,303	26.3	73.7
Lawrence	617.2	57.2	10,412	24,891	29.5	70.5

TABLE 1.16--LAND AREA, POPULATION DENSITY, AND POPULATION LIVING IN URBAN AND
RURAL AREAS, TENNESSEE AND COUNTIES, 1990 (Continued)

County	Land area (square miles)	Population per square mile	Population		Percent of total population	
			Urban	Rural	Urban	Rural
Lewis	282.1	32.8	3,760	5,487	40.7	59.3
Lincoln	570.3	49.4	6,921	21,236	24.6	75.4
Loudon	228.6	136.7	10,441	20,814	33.4	66.6
McMinn	430.3	98.5	15,881	26,502	37.5	62.5
McNairy	560.1	40.0	3,838	18,584	17.1	82.9
Macon	307.1	51.8	3,641	12,265	22.9	77.1
Madison	557.1	140.0	53,048	24,934	68.0	32.0
Marion	499.8	49.7	6,075	18,785	24.4	75.6
Marshall	375.4	57.4	9,879	11,660	45.9	54.1
Maury	612.9	89.4	32,422	22,390	59.2	40.8
Meigs	194.9	41.2	0	8,033	0.0	100.0
Monroe	635.2	48.1	8,087	22,454	26.5	73.5
Montgomery	539.2	186.4	75,857	24,641	75.5	24.5
Moore	129.2	36.5	714	4,007	15.1	84.9
Morgan	522.1	33.1	51	17,249	0.3	99.7
Obion	544.9	58.2	13,201	18,516	41.6	58.4
Overton	433.4	40.7	3,809	13,827	21.6	78.4
Perry	414.9	15.9	0	6,612	0.0	100.0
Pickett	162.9	27.9	0	4,548	0.0	100.0
Polk	435.1	31.4	0	13,643	0.0	100.0
Putnam	401.0	128.1	24,303	27,070	47.3	52.7
Rhea	315.9	77.1	5,671	18,673	23.3	76.7
Roane	361.0	130.8	20,209	27,018	42.8	57.2
Robertson	476.5	87.1	15,824	25,670	38.1	61.9
Rutherford	619.0	191.6	65,963	52,607	55.6	44.4
Scott	532.1	34.5	3,502	14,856	19.1	80.9
Sequatchie	265.9	33.3	3,731	5,132	42.1	57.9
Sevier	592.3	86.2	18,726	32,317	36.7	63.3
Shelby	754.9	1,094.6	793,545	32,785	96.0	4.0
Smith	314.4	45.0	0	14,143	0.0	100.0
Stewart	457.7	20.7	0	9,479	0.0	100.0
Sullivan	413.0	347.7	103,352	40,244	72.0	28.0
Sumner	529.4	195.1	63,644	39,637	61.6	38.4
Tipton	459.4	81.8	7,487	30,081	19.9	80.1
Trousdale	114.2	51.8	0	5,920	0.0	100.0
Unicoi	186.1	88.9	5,015	11,534	30.3	69.7
Union	223.6	61.2	0	13,694	0.0	100.0
Van Buren	273.5	17.7	0	4,846	0.0	100.0
Warren	432.7	76.2	11,194	21,798	33.9	66.1
Washington	326.2	283.0	61,474	30,841	66.6	33.4
Wayne	734.0	19.0	0	13,935	0.0	100.0
Weakley	580.3	55.1	8,775	23,197	27.4	72.6
White	376.7	53.3	4,681	15,409	23.3	76.7
Williamson	582.7	139.0	40,551	40,470	50.0	50.0
Wilson	570.6	118.6	30,477	37,198	45.0	55.0
TENNESSEE	41,219.2	118.3	2,969,948	1,907,237	60.9	39.1

Note: Urban population includes all persons living in urbanized areas and in places of 2,500 or more inhabitants
  outside urbanized areas. Rural population is all population not classified as urban.

Source: U.S. Department of Commerce, Bureau of the Census, *Census of Population and Housing, 1990:*
  Summary Tape File 1A, Tennessee.

TABLE 1.17--LOCATION AND POPULATION, INCORPORATED PLACES, 1960-1990, DECENNIAL
CENSUS YEARS

Incorporated place	County	1990	1980	1970	1960	Percent change 1980-1990
Adams	Robertson	587	600	458	(X)	-2.2
Adamsville	McNairy	1,745	1,453	1,344	1,046	20.1
Alamo	Crockett	2,426	2,615	2,499	1,665	-7.2
Alcoa	Blount	6,400	6,870	7,739	6,395	-6.8
Alexandria	DeKalb	730	689	680	599	6.0
Algood	Putnam	2,399	2,406	1,808	886	-0.3
Allardt	Fentress	609	654	610	(X)	-6.9
Altamont	Grundy	679	679	546	552	0.0
Ardmore	Giles	866	835	601	195	3.7
Arlington	Shelby	1,541	1,778	1,349	620	-13.3
Ashland City	Cheatham	2,552	2,329	2,027	1,400	9.6
Athens	McMinn	12,054	12,080	11,790	12,103	-0.2
Atoka	Tipton	659	691	446	357	-4.6
Atwood	Carroll	1,066	1,143	937	461	-6.7
Auburntown	Cannon	240	204	213	256	17.6
Baileyton[1]	Greene	309	333	258	206	-7.2
Baneberry[1]	Jefferson	218	12	(X)	(X)	(X)
Bartlett	Shelby	26,989	18,691[a]	1,150	508	44.4
Baxter	Putnam	1,289	1,411	1,229	853	-8.6
Beersheba Springs	Grundy	596	643	560	577	-7.3
Bell Buckle	Bedford	326	450	393	318	-27.6
Belle Meade	Davidson	2,839	3,182	2,933	3,082	-10.8
Bells	Crockett	1,643	1,571	1,474	1,232	4.6
Benton	Polk	992	1,115	749	638	-11.0
Berry Hill	Davidson	802	1,113	1,517	1,551	-27.9
Bethel Springs	McNairy	755	873	781	533	-13.5
Big Sandy	Benton	505	650	539	492	-22.3
Blaine	Grainger	1,326	1,147	(X)	(X)	15.6
Bluff City	Sullivan	1,390	1,121	985	948	24.0
Bolivar	Hardeman	5,969	6,597	6,674	3,338	-9.5
Braden	Fayette	354	293	(X)	(X)	20.8
Bradford	Gibson	1,154	1,146	968	763	0.7
Brentwood	Williamson	16,392	10,701	4,099	(X)	53.2
Brighton	Tipton	717	976	952	652	-26.5
Bristol	Sullivan	23,421	23,986	20,064	17,582	-2.4
Brownsville	Haywood	10,019	9,307	7,011	5,424	7.7
Bruceton	Carroll	1,586	1,579	1,450	1,158	0.4
Bulls Gap	Hawkins	659	821	774	682	-19.7
Burlison	Tipton	394	386	397	(X)	2.1
Burns	Dickson	1,127	777	456	386	45.0
Byrdstown	Pickett	998	884	582	613	12.9
Calhoun	McMinn	552	590	624	(X)	-6.4
Camden	Benton	3,643	3,586	3,052	2,774	1.6
Carthage	Smith	2,386	2,672	2,491	2,021	-10.7
Caryville	Campbell	1,751	2,039	648	(X)	-14.1
Cedar Hill	Robertson	347	420	355	(X)	-17.4
Celina	Clay	1,493	1,580	1,370	1,228	-5.5
Centertown	Warren	332	300	181	169	10.7
Centerville	Hickman	3,616	2,824	2,592	1,678	28.0
Chapel Hill	Marshall	833	861	752	630	-3.3
Charleston	Bradley	653	756	792	764	-13.6
Charlotte	Dickson	854	788	610	551	8.4
Chattanooga	Hamilton	152,466	169,514[a]	119,923	130,009	-10.1

TABLE 1.17--LOCATION AND POPULATION, INCORPORATED PLACES, 1960-1990, DECENNIAL
CENSUS YEARS (Continued)

Incorporated place	County	1990	1980	1970	1960	Percent change 1980-1990
Church Hill	Hawkins	4,834	4,110	2,822	769	17.6
Clarksburg	Carroll	321	400	349	(X)	-19.8
Clarksville	Montgomery	75,494	60,591	31,719	22,021	24.6
Cleveland	Bradley	30,354	26,415	21,446	16,196	14.9
Clifton	Wayne	620	773	737	708	-19.8
Clinton	Anderson	8,972	7,790 [a]	4,794	4,943	15.2
Coalmont	Grundy	813	625	518	458	30.1
Collegedale	Hamilton	5,048	4,607	3,031	(X)	9.6
Collierville	Shelby	14,427	7,839	3,651	2,020	84.0
Collinwood	Wayne	1,014	1,064	922	596	-4.7
Columbia	Maury	28,583	26,570 [a]	21,471	17,624	7.6
Cookeville	Putnam	21,744	21,604 [a]	14,403	7,805	0.6
Copperhill	Polk	362	418	563	631	-13.4
Cornersville	Marshall	683	722	655	314	-5.4
Cottage Grove	Henry	85	117	119	130	-27.4
Covington	Tipton	7,487	6,065	5,801	5,298	23.4
Cowan	Franklin	1,738	1,790	1,772	1,979	-2.9
Crab Orchard	Cumberland	876	1,065	(X)	(X)	-17.7
Cross Plains	Robertson	1,025	655	(X)	(X)	56.5
Crossville	Cumberland	6,930	6,394	5,381	4,668	8.4
Crump	Hardin	2,028	(X)	(X)	(X)	(X)
Cumberland City	Stewart	319	276	416	314	15.6
Cumberland Gap	Claiborne	210	263	231	291	-20.2
Dandridge	Jefferson	1,540	1,383	1,270	829	11.4
Dayton	Rhea	5,671	5,582 [a]	4,361	3,500	1.6
Decatur	Meigs	1,361	1,069	698	681	27.3
Decaturville	Decatur	879	1,004	958	571	-12.5
Decherd	Franklin	2,196	2,233	2,148	1,704	-1.7
Dickson	Dickson	8,791	7,040	5,665	5,028	24.9
Dover	Stewart	1,341	1,197	1,179	736	12.0
Dowelltown	DeKalb	308	341	329	279	-9.7
Doyle	White	345	344	446	(X)	0.3
Dresden	Weakley	2,488	2,256	1,939	1,510	10.3
Ducktown	Polk	421	583	562	741	-27.8
Dunlap	Sequatchie	3,731	3,681	1,672	1,488	1.4
Dyer	Gibson	2,204	2,442	2,501	1,909	-9.7
Dyersburg	Dyer	16,317	15,856	14,523	12,499	2.9
Eagleville	Rutherford	462	444	437	363	4.1
East Ridge	Hamilton	21,101	21,236	21,799	19,570	-0.6
Eastview	McNairy	563	552	423	(X)	2.0
Elizabethton	Carter	11,931	12,431	12,269	10,896	-4.0
Elkton	Giles	448	540	341	199	-17.0
Englewood	McMinn	1,611	1,840	1,878	1,574	-12.4
Enville	McNairy-Chester	211	287	228	250	-26.5
Erin	Houston	1,586	1,614	1,165	1,097	-1.7
Erwin	Unicoi	5,015	5,283	4,715	3,210	-5.1
Estill Springs	Franklin	1,408	1,324	919	734	6.3
Ethridge	Lawrence	565	548	(X)	(X)	3.1
Etowah	McMinn	3,815	3,898	3,736	3,223	-2.1
Fairview	Williamson	4,210	3,648	1,630	1,017	15.4
Farragut	Knox	12,793	6,279	(X)	(X)	103.7
Fayetteville	Lincoln	6,921	7,651 [a]	7,691	6,804	-9.5
Finger	McNairy	279	245	(X)	(X)	13.9

41

POPULATION

TABLE 1.17--LOCATION AND POPULATION, INCORPORATED PLACES, 1960–1990, DECENNIAL
CENSUS YEARS (Continued)

Incorporated place	County	1990	1980	1970	1960	Percent change 1980–1990
Forest Hills	Davidson	4,231	4,516	4,255	2,101	-6.3
Franklin	Williamson	20,098	13,424 [a]	9,497	6,977	49.7
Friendship	Crockett	467	763	441	399	-38.8
Friendsville	Blount	792	694	575	606	14.1
Gadsden	Crockett	561	683	523	222	-17.9
Gainesboro	Jackson	1,002	1,119	1,101	1,021	-10.5
Gallatin	Sumner	18,794	17,191	13,253	7,901	9.3
Gallaway	Fayette	762	804	304	(X)	-5.2
Garland	Tipton	194	301	292	168	-35.5
Gates	Lauderdale	608	729	523	291	-16.6
Gatlinburg	Sevier	3,417	3,500	2,329	1,764	-2.4
Germantown	Shelby	32,893	22,722 [a]	3,474	1,104	44.8
Gibson	Gibson	281	458	302	297	-38.6
Gilt Edge	Tipton	447	404	406	(X)	10.6
Gleason	Weakley	1,402	1,335	1,314	900	5.0
Goodlettsville	Davidson-Sumner	11,219	8,327	6,168	3,163	34.7
Gordonsville	Smith	891	893	601	249	-0.2
Grand Junction	Hardeman	365	366	427	446	-0.3
Graysville	Rhea	1,301	1,380	951	838	-5.7
Greenback	Loudon	611	546	318	285	11.9
Greenbrier	Robertson	2,873	3,180	2,279	1,238	-9.7
Greeneville	Greene	13,532	14,097	13,722	11,759	-4.0
Greenfield	Weakley	2,105	2,109	2,050	1,779	-0.2
Gruetli-Laager	Grundy	1,810	2,021	(X)	(X)	-10.4
Guys	McNairy	497	486	(X)	(X)	2.3
Halls	Lauderdale	2,431	2,444	2,323	1,890	-0.5
Harriman	Roane	7,119	8,303	8,734	5,931	-14.3
Hartsville	Trousdale	2,188	2,674	2,243	1,712	-18.2
Henderson	Chester	4,760	4,449	3,581	2,691	7.0
Hendersonville	Sumner	32,188	26,561	412	(X)	21.2
Henning	Lauderdale	802	638	605	466	25.7
Henry	Henry	317	295	302	178	7.5
Hickory Valley	Hardeman	159	252	180	179	-36.9
Hohenwald	Lewis	3,760	3,922	3,385	2,194	-4.1
Hollow Rock	Carroll	902	955	722	568	-5.5
Hornbeak	Obion	445	452	418	307	-1.5
Hornsby	Hardeman	313	401	212	228	-21.9
Humboldt	Gibson	9,651	10,209	10,066	8,482	-5.5
Huntingdon	Carroll	4,180	4,345	3,661	2,119	-3.8
Huntland	Franklin	885	983	849	500	-10.0
Huntsville	Scott	660	519	337	(X)	27.2
Iron City	Lawrence-Wayne	402	482	504	(X)	-16.6
Jacksboro	Campbell	1,568	1,722	689	(X)	-8.9
Jackson	Madison	48,949	49,258 [a]	39,996	34,376	-0.6
Jamestown	Fentress	1,862	2,364	1,899	1,727	-21.2
Jasper	Marion	2,780	2,633	2,009	1,450	5.6
Jefferson City	Jefferson	5,494	5,639 [a]	5,124	4,550	-2.6
Jellico	Campbell	2,447	2,798	2,235	2,210	-12.5
Johnson City[2]	Carter-Washington	49,381	45,642 [a]	33,770	31,187	8.2
Jonesborough	Washington	3,091	2,829	1,510	1,148	9.3
Kenton	Gibson-Obion	1,366	1,551	1,439	1,095	-11.9

42

TABLE 1.17--LOCATION AND POPULATION, INCORPORATED PLACES, 1960–1990, DECENNIAL
CENSUS YEARS (Continued)

Incorporated place	County	1990	1980	1970	1960	Percent change 1980–1990
Kimball	Marion	1,243	1,220	807	(X)	1.9
Kingsport	Hawkins-Sullivan	36,365	32,027	31,938	26,314	13.5
Kingston	Roane	4,552	4,561	4,142	2,010	-0.2
Kingston Springs	Cheatham	1,529	1,017	312	(X)	50.3
Knoxville	Knox	165,121	175,045	174,587	111,827	-5.7
Lafayette	Macon	3,641	3,808	2,583	1,590	-4.4
LaFollette	Campbell	7,192	8,198	6,902	6,204	-12.3
LaGrange	Fayette	167	185	213	217	-9.7
Lake City	Anderson	2,166	2,335	1,923	1,914	-7.2
Lakeland	Shelby	1,204	612	(X)	(X)	96.7
Lakesite	Hamilton	732	651	(X)	(X)	12.4
Lakewood	Davidson	2,009	2,325	2,282	1,896	-13.6
LaVergne	Rutherford	7,499	5,793 [a]	(X)	(X)	29.4
Lawrenceburg	Lawrence	10,412	10,184	8,889	8,042	2.2
Lebanon	Wilson	15,208	13,004 [a]	12,492	10,512	16.9
Lenoir City	Loudon	6,147	5,505 [a]	5,324	4,979	11.7
Lewisburg	Marshall	9,879	8,760	7,207	6,338	12.8
Lexington	Henderson	5,810	5,934	5,024	3,943	-2.1
Liberty	DeKalb	391	365	332	293	7.1
Linden	Perry	1,099	1,087	1,062	1,086	1.1
Livingston	Overton	3,809	3,372	3,050	2,817	13.0
Lobelville	Perry	830	993	773	449	-16.4
Lookout Mountain	Hamilton	1,901	1,886	1,741	1,817	0.8
Loretto	Lawrence	1,515	1,612	1,375	929	-6.0
Loudon	Loudon	4,026	4,199	3,728	3,812	-4.1
Luttrell	Union	812	962	819	(X)	-15.6
Lynchburg	Moore	4,721	4,510	538	396	4.7
Lynnville	Giles	344	383	327	362	-10.2
McEwen	Humphreys	1,442	1,352	1,237	979	6.7
McKenzie[3]	Carroll-Henry-Weakley	5,168	5,405	4,873	3,780	-4.4
McLemoresville	Carroll	280	311	328	285	-10.0
McMinnville	Warren	11,194	11,227 [a]	10,662	9,013	-0.3
Madisonville	Monroe	3,033	2,884	2,614	1,812	5.2
Manchester	Coffee	7,709	7,250	6,208	3,930	6.3
Martin	Weakley	8,600	8,898	7,781	4,750	-3.3
Maryville	Blount	19,208	17,480	13,808	10,348	9.9
Mason	Tipton	337	471	443	407	-28.5
Maury City	Crockett	782	989	813	624	-20.9
Maynardville	Union	1,298	924	702	620	40.5
Medina	Gibson	658	687	755	722	-4.2
Medon	Madison	137	169	136	97	-18.9
Memphis	Shelby	610,337	646,170 [a]	623,988	497,524	-5.5
Michie	McNairy	677	530	377	(X)	27.7
Middleton	Hardeman	536	596	654	461	-10.1
Milan	Gibson	7,512	8,083	7,313	5,208	-7.1
Milledgeville	Hardin-Chester-McNairy	279	392	349	(X)	-28.8
Millersville	Sumner	2,575	1,415	(X)	(X)	82.0
Millington	Shelby	17,866	20,236	21,177	6,059	-11.7
Minor Hill	Giles	372	564	315	(X)	-34.0

43

1. POPULATION

TABLE 1.17--LOCATION AND POPULATION, INCORPORATED PLACES, 1960–1990, DECENNIAL
CENSUS YEARS (Continued)

Incorporated place	County	1990	1980	1970	1960	Percent change 1980–1990
Mitchellville	Sumner	193	209	177	184	-7.7
Monteagle	Marion-Grundy	1,138	1,126	934	(X)	1.1
Monterey	Putnam	2,559	2,610	2,351	2,069	-2.0
Morrison	Warren	570	587	379	294	-2.9
Morristown	Hamblen	21,385	21,422 [a]	20,318	21,267	-0.2
Moscow	Fayette	384	499	448	368	-23.0
Mosheim	Greene	1,451	1,539	(X)	(X)	-5.7
Mount Carmel	Hawkins	4,082	3,764	2,821	(X)	8.4
Mount Juliet	Wilson	5,389	2,879	(X)	(X)	87.2
Mount Pleasant	Maury	4,278	3,891	3,530	2,921	9.9
Mountain City	Johnson	2,169	2,125	1,883	1,379	2.1
Munford	Tipton	2,326	2,336	1,281	1,014	-0.4
Murfreesboro	Rutherford	44,922	32,845	26,360	18,991	36.8
Nashville [4]	Davidson	487,973	455,651	426,029	154,563	7.1
New Hope	Marion	854	681	(X)	(X)	25.4
New Johnsonville	Humphreys	1,643	1,824	970	559	-9.9
New Market	Jefferson	1,086	1,216	(X)	(X)	-10.7
New Tazewell	Claiborne	1,864	1,677	1,192	768	11.2
Newbern	Dyer	2,515	2,794	2,124	1,695	-10.0
Newport	Cocke	7,123	7,580	7,328	6,448	-6.0
Niota	McMinn	745	765	629	679	-2.6
Normandy	Bedford	118	118	122	119	0.0
Norris	Anderson	1,303	1,374	1,359	1,389	-5.2
Oak Hill	Davidson	4,301	4,609	4,645	4,490	-6.7
Oak Ridge	Anderson-Roane	27,310	27,662	28,319	27,169	-1.3
Oakdale	Morgan	268	323	376	470	-17.0
Oakland	Fayette	392	472	353	306	-16.9
Obion	Obion	1,241	1,282	1,010	1,097	-3.2
Oliver Springs	Anderson-Morgan-Roane	3,433	3,659	3,405	1,163	-6.2
Oneida	Scott	3,502	4,271 [a]	2,602	2,480	-18.0
Orlinda	Robertson	469	382	347	(X)	22.8
Orme	Marion	150	181	122	171	-17.1
Palmer	Grundy	769	1,027	898	1,069	-25.1
Paris	Henry	9,332	10,728	9,892	9,325	-13.0
Parker's Crossroads	Henderson	161	186	(X)	(X)	-13.4
Parrottsville	Cocke	121	118	115	91	2.5
Parsons	Decatur	2,033	2,422	2,167	1,859	-16.1
Pegram	Cheatham	1,371	1,081	(X)	(X)	26.8
Petersburg	Lincoln-Marshall	514	681	463	423	-24.5
Philadelphia	Loudon	463	507	554	(X)	-8.7
Pigeon Forge	Sevier	3,027	1,822	1,361	(X)	66.1
Pikeville	Bledsoe	1,771	2,085	1,454	951	-15.1
Piperton	Fayette	612	746	(X)	(X)	-18.0
Pittman Center	Sevier	478	488	(X)	(X)	-2.0
Pleasant Hill	Cumberland	494	371	293	267	33.2
Portland	Sumner	5,165	4,030	2,872	2,424	28.2
Powell's Crossroads	Marion	1,098	918	(X)	(X)	19.6
Pulaski	Giles	7,895	7,184	6,989	6,616	9.9
Puryear	Henry	592	624	458	408	-5.1

TABLE 1.17--LOCATION AND POPULATION, INCORPORATED PLACES, 1960–1990, DECENNIAL
CENSUS YEARS (Continued)

Incorporated place	County	1990	1980	1970	1960	Percent change 1980–1990
Ramer	McNairy	337	429	347	358	-21.4
Red Bank	Hamilton	12,322	13,129	12,715	10,777	-6.1
Red Boiling Springs	Macon	905	1,173	726	597	-22.8
Rickman	Overton	n.a.	798	(X)	(X)	(X)
Ridgely	Lake	1,775	1,932	1,657	1,464	-8.1
Ridgeside	Hamilton	400	417	458	448	-4.1
Ridgetop	Davidson-Robertson	1,132	1,225	858	372	-7.6
Ripley	Lauderdale	6,188	6,366	4,794	3,782	-2.8
Rives	Obion	344	386	385	291	-10.9
Rockford	Blount	646	567	(X)	(X)	13.9
Rockwood	Roane	5,348	5,695 [a]	5,259	5,345	-6.1
Rogersville	Hawkins	4,149	4,368	4,076	3,121	-5.0
Rossville	Fayette	291	379	410	183	-23.2
Rutherford	Gibson	1,303	1,378	1,385	983	-5.4
Rutledge	Grainger	903	1,058	863	793	-14.7
St. Joseph	Lawrence	789	897	637	547	-12.0
Saltillo	Hardin	383	434	423	397	-11.8
Samburg	Obion	374	465	463	451	-19.6
Sardis	Henderson	305	301	350	274	1.3
Saulsbury	Hardeman	106	156	156	141	-32.1
Savannah	Hardin	6,547	6,992	5,576	4,315	-6.4
Scotts Hill	Henderson-Decatur	594	668	548	298	-11.1
Selmer	McNairy	3,838	3,979	3,495	1,897	-3.5
Sevierville	Sevier	7,178	5,444	2,661	2,890	31.9
Sharon	Weakley	1,047	1,134	1,188	966	-7.7
Shelbyville	Bedford	14,049	13,530	12,262	10,466	3.8
Signal Mountain	Hamilton	7,034	5,818	4,839	3,413	20.9
Silerton	Hardeman-Chester	59	100	88	84	-41.0
Slayden	Dickson	111	69	95	101	60.9
Smithville	DeKalb	3,791	3,839	2,997	2,348	-1.3
Smyrna	Rutherford	13,647	9,441 [a]	5,698	3,612	44.6
Sneedville	Hancock	1,446	1,110	874	799	30.3
Soddy-Daisy	Hamilton	8,240	8,388	7,569	(X)	-1.8
Somerville	Fayette	2,047	2,264	1,816	1,820	-9.6
South Carthage	Smith	851	1,004	859	(X)	-15.2
South Fulton	Obion	2,688	2,980	3,122	2,512	-9.8
South Pittsburg	Marion	3,295	3,636	3,613	4,130	-9.4
Sparta	White	4,681	4,864	4,930	4,510	-3.8
Spencer	Van Buren	1,125	1,126	1,179	870	-0.1
Spring City	Rhea	2,199	1,951	1,756	1,800	12.7
Spring Hill	Williamson-Maury	1,464	989	685	689	48.0
Springfield	Robertson	11,227	10,814	9,720	9,221	3.8
Stanton	Haywood	487	540	372	458	-9.8
Stantonville	McNairy	264	271	296	(X)	-2.6
Surgoinsville	Hawkins	1,499	1,536	1,285	1,132	-2.4
Sweetwater	Monroe	5,066	5,175	4,340	4,145	-2.1
Tazewell	Claiborne	2,150	2,090	1,860	1,264	2.9
Tellico Plains	Monroe	657	698	773	794	-5.9
Tennessee Ridge	Houston	1,271	1,325	664	324	-4.1

TABLE 1.17--LOCATION AND POPULATION, INCORPORATED PLACES, 1960–1990, DECENNIAL
CENSUS YEARS (Continued)

Incorporated place	County	1990	1980	1970	1960	Percent change 1980–1990
Tiptonville	Lake	2,149	2,438	2,407	2,068	-11.9
Toone	Hardeman	279	355	200	202	-21.4
Townsend	Blount	329	351	267	283	-6.3
Tracy City	Grundy	1,556	1,434	1,388	1,577	8.5
Trenton	Gibson	4,836	4,601	4,226	4,225	5.1
Trezevant	Carroll	874	921	877	944	-5.1
Trimble	Dyer-Obion	694	722	675	581	-3.9
Troy	Obion	1,047	1,093	826	587	-4.2
Tullahoma	Coffee-Franklin	16,761	15,800	15,311	12,242	6.1
Tusculum	Greene	1,918	2,190	1,180	1,433	-12.4
Union City	Obion	10,513	10,436	11,925	8,837	0.7
Vanleer	Dickson	369	401	320	234	-8.0
Viola	Warren	123	149	193	206	-17.4
Vonore	Monroe	605	528	524	(X)	14.6
Walden	Hamilton	1,523	1,293	(X)	(X)	17.8
Wartburg	Morgan	932	761	541	(X)	22.5
Wartrace	Bedford	494	540	616	545	-8.5
Watauga	Carter	389	376	314	(X)	3.5
Watertown	Wilson	1,250	1,300	1,061	919	-3.8
Waverly	Humphreys	3,925	4,405	3,794	2,891	-10.9
Waynesboro	Wayne	1,824	2,109	1,983	1,343	-13.5
Westmoreland	Sumner	1,726	1,754	1,423	865	-1.6
White Bluff	Dickson	1,988	2,055	1,163	486	-3.3
White House	Robertson-Sumner	2,987	2,225	(X)	(X)	34.2
White Pine	Jefferson	1,771	1,900	1,532	1,035	-6.8
Whiteville	Hardeman	1,050	1,270	992	757	-17.3
Whitwell	Marion	1,622	1,783	1,669	1,857	-9.0
Williston	Fayette	427	395	(X)	(X)	8.1
Winchester	Franklin	6,305	6,099 [a]	5,256	4,760	3.4
Winfield[1]	Scott	564	470	(X)	(X)	(X)
Woodbury	Cannon	2,287	2,160	1,725	1,562	5.9
Woodland Mills	Obion	398	526	396	(X)	-24.3
Yorkville	Gibson	347	272	243	(X)	27.6

Note: Population is as counted in each Decennial Census year. No provision has been made for comparable land areas. Growth by annexation is reflected in the data.

(X) Not applicable.

1. City not incorporated in 1980.

2. Beginning in 1980 includes Carter County.

3. Beginning in 1980 includes Henry County.

4. Beginning in 1970 includes metro Nashville-Davidson. 1990 population for Nashville was derived by subtracting population of other wholly Davidson County cities and that portion of the population of Goodlettsville and Ridgetop that were located in Davidson County in 1980.

a. Changes in the 1980 base population figures are the result of census corrections or annexations.

Source: U.S. Department of Commerce, Bureau of the Census, *Census of Population and Housing, 1990: Summary Tape File 1A, Tennessee*; and *1980 Census of Population, Number of Inhabitants, Tennessee*, and earlier editions.

TABLE 1.18--LAND AREA, POPULATION, AND AGE CHARACTERISTICS, SOUTHEASTERN STATES
AND UNITED STATES, 1990

State	Land area (square miles)	Total population (1,000)	Population per square mile	Percent Under 5 years of age	Percent 5 to 17 years of age	Percent 65 years of age or older
TENNESSEE	41,220	4,877	118.3	6.8	18.1	12.7
Alabama	50,750	4,041	79.6	7.0	19.2	12.9
Arkansas	52,075	2,351	45.1	7.0	19.4	14.9
Florida	53,997	12,938	239.6	6.6	15.6	18.3
Georgia	57,919	6,478	111.9	7.6	19.0	10.1
Kentucky	39,732	3,685	92.8	6.8	19.1	12.7
Louisiana	43,566	4,220	96.9	7.9	21.2	11.1
Mississippi	46,914	2,573	54.9	7.6	21.4	12.5
North Carolina	48,718	6,629	136.1	6.9	17.3	12.1
South Carolina	30,111	3,487	115.8	7.4	19.0	11.4
Virginia	39,598	6,187	156.3	7.2	17.2	10.7
West Virginia	24,087	1,793	74.5	5.9	18.8	15.0
UNITED STATES	3,536,342	248,710	70.3	7.6	18.1	12.5

Note: Percentages computed by the Center for Business and Economic Research.
Source: U.S. Department of Commerce, Bureau of the Census, *Statistical Abstract of the United States, 1992.*

POPULATION

TABLE 1.19--POPULATION AND PERCENT OF U.S. POPULATION, SOUTHEASTERN STATES AND
UNITED STATES, 1960–1990, DECENNIAL CENSUS YEARS

	1990			1980		
State	Population	Decen- nial percent change	Percent of U.S. popu- lation [1]	Population	Decen- nial percent change	Percent of U.S. popu- lation [1]
TENNESSEE	4,877,185	6.2	2.0	4,591,120	16.9	2.0
Alabama	4,040,587	3.8	1.6	3,893,888	13.1	1.7
Arkansas	2,350,725	2.8	0.9	2,286,435	18.9	1.0
Florida	12,937,926	32.7	5.2	9,746,324	43.5	4.3
Georgia	6,478,216	18.6	2.6	5,463,105	19.1	2.4
Kentucky	3,685,296	0.7	1.5	3,660,777	13.7	1.6
Louisiana	4,219,973	0.3	1.7	4,205,900	15.4	1.9
Mississippi	2,573,216	2.1	1.0	2,520,638	13.7	1.1
North Carolina	6,628,637	12.7	2.7	5,881,766	15.7	2.6
South Carolina	3,486,703	11.7	1.4	3,121,820	20.5	1.4
Virginia	6,187,358	15.7	2.5	5,346,818	14.9	2.4
West Virginia	1,793,477	-8.0	0.7	1,949,644	11.8	0.9
UNITED STATES	248,709,873	9.8	100.0	226,545,805	11.4	100.0

	1970			1960		
State	Population	Decen- nial percent change	Percent of U.S. popu- lation [1]	Population	Decen- nial percent change	Percent of U.S. popu- lation [1]
TENNESSEE	3,926,018	10.1	1.9	3,567,089	8.4	2.0
Alabama	3,444,354	5.4	1.7	3,266,740	6.7	1.8
Arkansas	1,923,322	7.7	0.9	1,786,272	-6.5	1.0
Florida	6,791,418	37.2	3.3	4,951,560	78.7	2.8
Georgia	4,587,930	16.4	2.3	3,943,116	14.5	2.2
Kentucky	3,220,711	6.0	1.6	3,038,156	3.2	1.7
Louisiana	3,644,637	12.0	1.8	3,257,022	21.4	1.8
Mississippi	2,216,994	1.8	1.1	2,178,141	0.0	1.2
North Carolina	5,084,411	11.6	2.5	4,556,155	12.2	2.5
South Carolina	2,590,713	8.7	1.3	2,382,594	12.5	1.3
Virginia	4,651,448	17.3	2.3	3,966,949	19.5	2.2
West Virginia	1,744,237	-6.2	0.9	1,860,421	-7.2	1.0
UNITED STATES	203,302,031	11.4	100.0	179,323,175	18.5	100.0

1. Percentages computed by the Center for Business and Economic Research.

Source: U.S. Department of Commerce, Bureau of the Census, *1990 Census of Population, General Population
Characteristics, United States*; *1980 Census of Population, Number of Inhabitants, United States Summary*, and
earlier editions.

TABLE 1.20--POPULATION AND COMPONENTS OF CHANGE, SOUTHEASTERN STATES, 1980-1992, SELECTED YEARS [In thousands]

State	Population					
	1992ʳ	1991ʳ	1990	1989ʳ	1988ʳ	1980
TENNESSEE	5,024	4,953	4,877	4,854	4,822	4,591
Alabama	4,136	4,091	4,041	4,030	4,024	3,894
Arkansas	2,399	2,373	2,351	2,346	2,343	2,286
Florida	13,488	13,267	12,938	12,638	12,306	9,746
Georgia	6,751	6,623	6,478	6,411	6,316	5,463
Kentucky	3,755	3,713	3,685	3,677	3,680	3,661
Louisiana	4,287	4,254	4,220	4,253	4,289	4,206
Mississippi	2,614	2,593	2,573	2,574	2,580	2,521
North Carolina	6,843	6,736	6,629	6,565	6,481	5,882
South Carolina	3,603	3,560	3,487	3,457	3,412	3,122
Virginia	6,377	6,280	6,187	6,120	6,037	5,347
West Virginia	1,812	1,803	1,793	1,807	1,830	1,950

	Change April 1, 1990 to July 1, 1992					
				Components of change		
					Net movement from abroad	
	Net change		Natural increase	International migration	Federal U.S. citizen	Residual change [1]
	Number	%				
TENNESSEE	147	3.0	64	7	3	73
Alabama	95	2.4	52	6	3	34
Arkansas	48	2.0	25	3	1	19
Florida	550	4.2	137	90	11	310
Georgia	273	4.2	132	13	7	121
Kentucky	69	1.9	42	5	3	19
Louisiana	67	1.6	78	14	3	-28
Mississippi	41	1.6	41	3	2	-4
North Carolina	214	3.2	101	9	11	93
South Carolina	117	3.3	63	5	6	43
Virginia	190	3.1	115	28	16	30
West Virginia	19	1.0	7	2	0	10

Note: 1990 and 1980 population is as of April 1. Population estimates for intercensal years are as of July 1. Estimates for 1991 and 1992 were derived by combining results of the Medicare Change Method for 65 years and older population with estimates of the under 65 population produced by the Federal Tax Returns Method. Estimates for the 1980s are consistent with 1980 census counts and 1990 census modified counts.
r revised.
1. The bulk of the residual change component is internal (domestic) net migration, though we have no reliable way to quantify it. The residual change figure is also affected by any inaccuracies in input data or variations in implementing the estimating method.
Source: U.S. Department of Commerce, Bureau of the Census, Current Population Reports P25-1106, *State Population Estimates by Age and Sex: 1980 to 1992.*

TABLE 1.21--FOREIGN BORN AND NATIVE POPULATION, SOUTHEASTERN STATES AND UNITED STATES, 1990

State	Total native	Total foreign born		Persons under 18 years Foreign born			Persons 18 years and over Foreign born		
		Naturalized	Not a citizen	Native	Naturalized	Not a citizen	Native	Naturalized	Not a citizen
TENNESSEE	4,818,071	26,591	32,523	1,209,842	1,144	4,670	3,608,229	25,447	27,853
Alabama	3,997,054	21,391	22,142	1,056,536	655	2,810	2,940,518	20,736	19,332
Arkansas	2,325,858	12,121	12,746	619,090	485	1,693	1,706,768	11,636	11,053
Florida	11,275,325	713,505	949,096	2,719,752	18,635	126,113	8,555,573	694,870	822,983
Georgia	6,305,090	67,390	105,736	1,711,773	3,159	15,718	4,593,317	64,231	90,018
Kentucky	3,651,177	15,890	18,229	952,733	445	2,440	2,698,444	15,445	15,789
Louisiana	4,132,566	38,082	49,325	1,220,483	1,622	7,172	2,912,083	36,460	42,153
Mississippi	2,552,833	9,514	10,869	745,485	336	1,550	1,807,348	9,178	9,319
North Carolina	6,513,560	49,616	65,461	1,598,431	1,610	8,452	4,915,129	48,006	57,009
South Carolina	3,436,739	25,411	24,553	918,315	758	2,975	2,518,424	24,653	21,578
Virginia	5,875,549	125,653	186,156	1,471,761	4,979	27,587	4,403,788	120,674	158,569
West Virginia	1,777,765	9,276	6,436	443,398	180	628	1,334,367	9,096	5,808
UNITED STATES	228,942,557	7,996,998	11,770,318	61,514,084	340,034	1,752,426	167,428,473	7,656,964	10,017,892

Source: U.S. Department of Commerce, Bureau of the Census, *Census and You*, December 1992.

TABLE 1.22.--PERSONS NATURALIZED, BY STATE OF RESIDENCE, SOUTHEASTERN STATES AND UNITED STATES, 1970-1992, SELECTED YEARS

State	1992	1991	1990	1989	1988	1987	1986	1985	1980	1975	1970
TENNESSEE	979	1,043	1,002	1,015	1,004	911	1,033	846	490	482	351
Alabama	598	798	590	653	646	506	664	609	414	357	393
Arkansas	380	413	388	374	417	540	605	456	163	135	82
Florida	21,129	23,281	22,978	14,216	15,589	8,041	20,366	10,362	11,417	10,576	11,556
Georgia	2,299	3,414	2,952	3,235	2,104	1,856	1,834	1,804	985	853	873
Kentucky	567	338	514	572	438	630	675	910	199	347	313
Louisiana	1,709	1,145	1,882	1,847	2,115	1,406	2,575	2,490	772	652	828
Mississippi	315	300	301	423	259	239	381	432	189	238	176
North Carolina	2,172	1,856	1,362	1,644	1,609	1,208	1,702	1,626	1,057	693	598
South Carolina	670	713	761	1,028	1,112	484	558	1,289	419	409	334
Virginia	4,662	5,353	5,606	6,799	5,000	3,335	4,892	5,147	1,653	2,207	1,509
West Virginia	137	261	176	199	267	241	235	278	281	178	118
UNITED STATES	240,252	308,058	270,101	233,777	242,063	227,008	280,623	244,717	157,938	141,537	110,399

Note: United States total includes territories.

Source: U.S. Department of Justice, Immigration and Naturalization Service, *Statistical Yearbook of the Immigration and Naturalization Service, 1992*, and earlier editions.

TABLE 1.23--METROPOLITAN AND NONMETROPOLITAN AREA POPULATION, SOUTHEASTERN STATES AND UNITED STATES, 1970, 1980 AND 1990

	Metropolitan area population							Nonmetropolitan area population						
	Total (1,000)			Percent change		Percent of state		Total (1,000)			Percent change		Percent of state	
State	1990	1980	1970	1980–1990	1970–1980	1990	1980	1990	1980	1970	1980–1990	1970–1980	1990	1980
TENNESSEE	3,195	2,946	2,630	8.4	12.0	65.5	64.2	1,682	1,645	1,296	2.3	26.9	34.5	35.8
Alabama	2,710	2,560	2,274	5.8	12.6	67.1	65.7	1,331	1,334	1,171	-0.2	13.9	32.9	34.3
Arkansas	1,040	963	730	8.0	31.9	44.2	42.1	1,311	1,323	1,193	-0.9	10.9	55.8	57.9
Florida	12,023	9,039	6,213	33.0	45.5	92.9	92.7	915	708	578	29.1	22.5	7.1	7.3
Georgia	4,331	3,489	2,807	24.2	24.3	66.9	63.9	2,147	1,974	1,781	8.7	10.8	33.1	36.1
Kentucky	1,755	1,710	1,550	2.6	10.3	47.6	46.7	1,930	1,950	1,671	-1.0	16.7	52.4	53.3
Louisiana	3,101	3,074	2,439	0.9	26.0	73.5	73.1	1,119	1,132	1,205	-1.1	-6.1	26.5	26.9
Mississippi	776	716	564	8.3	27.0	30.1	28.4	1,798	1,805	1,653	-0.4	9.2	69.9	71.6
North Carolina	4,325	3,713	2,755	16.5	34.8	65.2	63.2	2,304	2,167	2,330	6.3	-7.0	34.8	36.8
South Carolina	2,423	2,114	1,504	14.6	40.6	69.5	67.8	1,064	1,006	1,087	5.7	-7.5	30.5	32.2
Virginia	4,773	3,966	3,279	20.4	21.0	77.1	74.2	1,414	1,381	1,373	2.4	0.6	22.9	25.8
West Virginia	748	796	683	-6.0	16.5	41.7	40.8	1,045	1,155	1,061	-9.5	8.9	58.3	59.2
UNITED STATES	197,467	176,663	156,085	11.6	13.2	79.4	78.0	49,879	51,243	47,217	2.7	8.5	20.6	22.0

Note: Metropolitan refers to 250 metropolitan statistical areas and 18 consolidated metropolitan statistical areas as defined by U.S. Office of Management and Budget, December 31, 1992; nonmetropolitan is the area outside metropolitan areas.

Source: U.S. Department of Commerce, Bureau of the Census, *Statistical Abstract of the United States, 1993.*

TABLE 1.24--RESIDENT POPULATION, BY RACE AND HISPANIC ORIGIN, SOUTHEASTERN STATES AND UNITED STATES, 1990 [In thousands, except percent]

State	Total[1]	White		Black		American Indian, Eskimo, Aleut		Asian, Pacific Islander		Hispanic origin[2]	
		Number	Percent	Number	Percent	Number	Percent	Number	Percent	Number	Percent
TENNESSEE	4,877	4,048	83.0	778	16.0	10	0.2	32	0.7	33	0.7
Alabama	4,041	2,976	73.6	1,021	25.3	17	0.4	22	0.5	25	0.6
Arkansas	2,351	1,945	82.7	374	15.9	13	0.5	13	0.5	20	0.8
Florida	12,938	10,749	83.1	1,760	13.6	36	0.3	154	1.2	1,574	12.2
Georgia	6,478	4,600	71.0	1,747	27.0	13	0.2	76	1.2	109	1.7
Kentucky	3,685	3,392	92.0	263	7.1	6	0.2	18	0.5	22	0.6
Louisiana	4,220	2,839	67.3	1,299	30.8	19	0.4	41	1.0	93	2.2
Mississippi	2,573	1,633	63.5	915	35.6	9	0.3	13	0.5	16	0.6
North Carolina	6,629	5,008	75.6	1,456	22.0	80	1.2	52	0.8	77	1.2
South Carolina	3,487	2,407	69.0	1,040	29.8	8	0.2	22	0.6	31	0.9
Virginia	6,187	4,792	77.4	1,163	18.8	15	0.2	159	2.6	160	2.6
West Virginia	1,793	1,726	96.2	56	3.1	2	0.1	7	0.4	8	0.5
UNITED STATES	248,710	199,686	80.3	29,986	12.1	1,959	0.8	7,274	2.9	22,354	9.0

1. Includes other races, not shown separately.
2. Persons of Hispanic origin may be of any race.

Source: U.S. Department of Commerce, Bureau of the Census, *Statistical Abstract of the United States, 1991.*

TABLE 1.25--NUMBER OF HOUSEHOLDS AND PERSONS PER HOUSEHOLD, SOUTHEASTERN
STATES AND UNITED STATES, 1980 AND 1990

	Households			Persons per household	
	Number (1,000)		Percent change		
State	1990	1980	1980–90	1990	1980
TENNESSEE	1,854	1,619	14.5	2.56	2.77
Alabama	1,507	1,342	12.3	2.62	2.84
Arkansas	891	816	9.2	2.57	2.74
Florida	5,135	3,744	37.1	2.46	2.55
Georgia	2,367	1,872	26.4	2.66	2.84
Kentucky	1,380	1,263	9.2	2.60	2.82
Louisiana	1,499	1,412	6.2	2.74	2.91
Mississippi	911	827	10.2	2.75	2.97
North Carolina	2,517	2,043	23.2	2.54	2.78
South Carolina	1,258	1,030	22.1	2.68	2.93
Virginia	2,292	1,863	23.0	2.61	2.77
West Virginia	689	686	0.3	2.55	2.79
UNITED STATES	91,947	80,390	14.4	2.63	2.75

Source: U.S. Department of Commerce, Bureau of the Census, *Statistical Abstract of the United States, 1991.*

The measure most commonly used as a gauge of the United States' economy is gross national product, or GNP, defined as the market value of all goods and services produced over a given period of time. Tables 2.1 and 2.2 present analogous information for Tennessee. Tennessee gross state product (GSP) information, formerly estimated by the Center for Business and Economic Research, is now estimated biennially by the U.S. Department of Commerce, Bureau of Economic Analysis (BEA). These estimates are part of a consistent series for all states in the U.S.

Personal income is also estimated by BEA for counties, states, regions, and the nation. Income is estimated for geographic areas, both as a place of work–wages, salary, and proprietors' income paid there, and as a place of residence–total income of all persons residing there, including dividends, rents, and transfer payments. Summary data are published in the April and August issues of the *Survey of Current Business*. Detailed data are published periodically in regional volumes of *Local Area Personal Income*; but perhaps the best source of these data is the REIS CD-ROM available from BEA [tel: (202)–606-9900]. Transfer payments, formerly found in this chapter, are now reported in Chapter 18.

"Money income," another measurement of wealth (or poverty), is reported for counties and cities as per capita amounts, family income and household income. "Money income," the only measure of income reported for cities, differs from "personal income" in the following respects: money income is measured before the deduction of personal contributions for social insurance, and it excludes imputed income, lump-sum payments other than those received as part of earnings, income received by quasi-individuals, certain in-kind payments such as medicaid, medicare, and food stamps and employer contributions to private welfare and pension funds. "Money income" includes–and "personal income" excludes–income from private pensions and annuities and interpersonal transfers, such as child support.

The Consumer Price Index (CPI) is used to measure changes in the cost of living for any specific location over a selected period of time. Though some 27 cities have a consumer price index specific to them, no index is computed specifically for Tennessee or any of its cities. The most commonly used measure is the U.S. City Average. Indexes are issued in monthly news releases by the Bureau of Labor Statistics (BLS), and published in *Monthly Labor Review* as well as in the *Survey of Current Business* and most newspapers. Beginning with 1978, data are reported for "All Urban Consumers" (CPI-U) as well as "Wage Earners and Clerical Workers" (CPI-W). CPI-W covers only about 32 percent of the population, but CPI-U covers 80 percent of all noninstitutional civilian population and includes professional, managerial, and technical workers, the self-employed, short-term workers, the unemployed, retirees, and others not in the labor force, in addition to wage earners and clerical workers.

2. INCOME AND PRICES

TABLE OF CONTENTS

56

TABLE OF CONTENTS
(Continued)

TABLE 2.1– GROSS STATE PRODUCT, BY SECTOR, AND PERCENTAGE CHANGE, TENNESSEE, 1980–1991 [In millions of current dollars]

Sector	1991	1990ʳ	1989ʳ	1988ʳ	1987ʳ	1986ʳ	1985ʳ	1984ʳ	1983ʳ	1982ʳ	1981ʳ	1980ʳ
GROSS STATE PRODUCT	100,804	95,234	91,598	86,501	80,781	73,370	67,892	63,315	56,287	51,623	50,135	45,077
Percentage change	5.85	3.97	5.89	7.08	10.10	8.07	7.23	12.49	9.03	2.97	11.22	7.00
Mining	310	354	351	365	350	334	350	374	355	389	410	376
Percentage change	-12.43	0.85	-3.84	4.29	4.79	-4.57	-6.42	5.35	-8.74	-5.12	9.04	8.99
Construction	3,587	3,698	3,763	3,691	3,579	3,336	2,840	2,519	2,087	1,999	1,940	1,980
Percentage change	-3.00	-1.73	1.95	3.13	7.28	17.46	12.74	20.70	4.40	3.04	-2.02	-0.95
Manufacturing	23,678	22,478	22,363	20,755	19,403	17,493	16,569	16,151	14,743	13,154	13,515	11,787
Percentage change	5.34	0.51	7.75	6.97	10.92	5.58	2.59	9.55	12.08	-2.67	14.66	3.98
Durable goods	11,269	10,654	10,990	10,200	9,647	8,803	8,185	8,073	6,473	5,672	6,190	5,336
Percentage change	5.77	-3.06	7.75	5.73	9.59	7.55	1.39	24.72	14.12	-8.37	16.00	1.75
Nondurable goods	12,409	11,824	11,372	10,555	9,756	8,690	8,384	8,078	8,270	7,482	7,326	6,450
Percentage change	4.95	3.97	7.74	8.19	12.27	3.65	3.79	-2.32	10.53	2.13	13.58	5.86
Wholesale trade	7,209	6,850	6,573	6,250	5,886	5,454	5,037	4,697	4,096	3,908	3,877	3,588
Percentage change	5.24	4.21	5.17	6.18	7.92	8.28	7.24	14.67	4.81	0.80	8.05	4.73
Retail trade	11,351	10,702	10,378	9,925	9,305	8,702	8,073	7,382	6,401	5,744	5,282	4,815
Percentage change	6.06	3.12	4.56	6.66	6.93	7.79	9.36	15.33	11.44	8.75	9.70	5.59
Services	18,096	16,923	15,497	13,967	12,686	11,497	10,366	9,349	8,101	7,328	6,611	5,841
Percentage change	6.93	9.20	10.95	10.10	10.34	10.91	10.88	15.41	10.55	10.85	13.18	13.95
Finance, insurance, and real estate	14,519	13,540	13,119	12,495	11,770	10,820	9,644	8,817	7,987	7,171	6,806	6,101
Percentage change	7.23	3.21	4.99	6.16	8.78	12.19	9.38	10.39	11.38	5.36	11.56	12.01
Transportation, communication and public utilities	7,638	7,036	6,952	7,039	6,519	5,703	5,222	4,873	4,340	3,803	3,701	3,351
Percentage change	8.56	1.21	-1.24	7.98	14.31	9.21	7.16	12.28	14.12	2.76	10.44	6.41
Government	12,857	12,155	11,201	10,665	10,007	8,923	8,531	7,757	7,238	6,804	6,645	6,181
Percentage change	5.78	8.52	5.03	6.58	12.15	4.60	9.98	7.17	6.38	2.39	7.51	9.96

TABLE 2.1-- GROSS STATE PRODUCT, BY SECTOR, AND PERCENTAGE CHANGE, TENNESSEE, 1980-1991 [In millions of current dollars] (Continued)

Sector	1991	1990^r	1989^r	1988^r	1987^r	1986^r	1985^r	1984^r	1983^r	1982^r	1981^r	1980^r
Federal civilian	4,487	4,160	3,768	3,663	3,501	3,155	3,051	2,716	2,569	2,419	2,426	2,274
Percentage change	7.86	10.40	2.87	4.63	10.97	3.41	12.33	5.72	6.20	-0.29	6.68	12.13
Federal military	658	638	587	566	546	514	519	486	440	433	381	325
Percentage change	3.13	8.69	3.71	3.66	6.23	-0.96	6.79	10.45	1.62	13.65	17.23	16.07
State and local	7,712	7,356	6,846	6,436	5,960	5,253	4,961	4,555	4,228	3,952	3,839	3,581
Percentage change	4.84	7.45	6.37	7.99	13.46	5.89	8.91	7.73	6.98	2.94	7.20	8.09
Agriculture	1,558	1,498	1,401	1,347	1,276	1,108	1,258	1,395	938	1,322	1,348	1,056
Percentage change	4.01	6.92	4.01	5.56	15.16	-11.92	-9.82	48.72	-29.05	-1.93	27.65	-5.71
Farms	1,231	1,209	1,153	1,101	1,019	914	1,058	1,200	762	1,168	1,212	938
Percentage change	1.82	4.86	4.72	8.05	11.49	-13.61	-11.83	57.48	-34.76	-3.63	29.21	-7.04
Agricultural services, forestry, fisheries	327	290	248	247	257	194	200	195	176	154	136	118
Percentage change	12.76	16.94	0.40	-3.89	32.47	-3.00	2.56	10.80	14.29	13.24	15.25	6.31
PER CAPITA GROSS STATE PRODUCT (dollars)	20,355	19,470	18,869	17,935	16,887	15,481	14,397	13,508	12,079	11,111	10,834	9,794
Percentage change	4.54	3.19	5.21	6.20	9.08	7.53	6.58	11.83	8.71	2.56	10.62	5.38

r revised.

Source: U.S. Department of Commerce, Bureau of Economic Analysis, direct correspondence.

FIGURE 2.1
Tennessee Gross State Product and Percent Change, 1980–1991

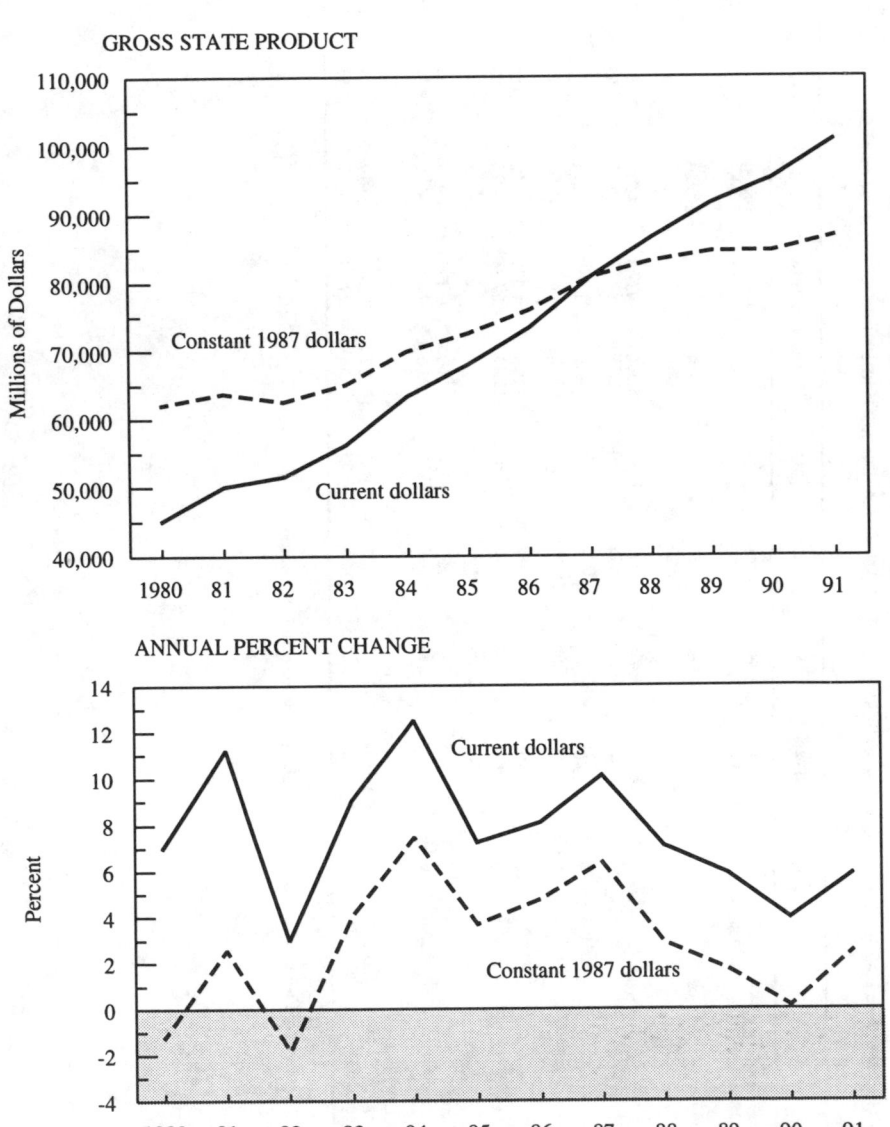

GROSS STATE PRODUCT

ANNUAL PERCENT CHANGE

Source: U.S. Department of Commerce, Bureau of Economic Analysis, *United States Department of Commerce News*, August 1994.

TABLE 2.2.– GROSS STATE PRODUCT, BY SECTOR, AND PERCENTAGE CHANGE, TENNESSEE, 1980–1991 [In millions of 1987 dollars]

Sector	1991	1990ᴿ	1989ᶠ	1988ᶠ	1987ᶠ	1986ᶠ	1985ᶠ	1984ᴿ	1983ᶠ	1982ᶠ	1981ᴿ	1980ᶠ
GROSS STATE PRODUCT	86,763	84,644	84,532	83,105	80,781	75,961	72,507	69,942	65,098	62,560	63,730	62,127
Percentage change	2.50	0.13	1.72	2.88	6.35	4.76	3.67	7.44	4.06	-1.84	2.58	-1.23
Mining	332	364	360	372	350	338	313	326	289	286	295	310
Percentage change	-8.79	1.11	-3.23	6.29	3.55	7.99	-3.99	12.80	1.05	-3.05	-4.84	-3.13
Construction	3,123	3,237	3,399	3,433	3,579	3,455	3,312	2,982	2,573	2,547	2,620	2,853
Percentage change	-3.52	-4.77	-0.99	-4.08	3.59	4.32	11.07	15.90	1.02	-2.79	-8.17	-11.09
Manufacturing	21,148	20,486	20,712	20,017	19,403	17,398	16,851	16,565	15,705	14,495	15,431	14,501
Percentage change	3.23	-1.09	3.47	3.16	11.52	3.25	1.73	5.48	8.35	-6.07	6.41	-5.08
Durable goods	10,622	10,078	10,522	10,066	9,647	8,657	8,164	8,073	6,549	5,931	6,896	6,428
Percentage change	5.40	-4.22	4.53	4.34	11.44	6.04	1.13	23.27	10.42	-13.99	7.28	-6.88
Nondurable goods	10,526	10,408	10,190	9,951	9,756	8,741	8,687	8,492	9,156	8,564	8,535	8,073
Percentage change	1.13	2.14	2.40	2.00	11.61	0.62	2.30	-7.25	6.91	0.34	5.72	-3.58
Wholesale trade	6,272	6,029	6,066	5,880	5,886	5,757	4,973	4,716	4,107	3,938	3,784	3,567
Percentage change	4.03	-0.61	3.16	-0.10	2.24	15.77	5.45	14.83	4.29	4.07	6.08	-5.08
Retail trade	10,115	9,921	9,995	9,883	9,305	9,420	8,702	8,124	7,277	6,750	6,483	6,300
Percentage change	1.96	-0.74	1.13	6.21	-1.22	8.25	7.11	11.64	7.81	4.12	2.90	-3.76
Services	14,317	14,098	13,767	13,104	12,686	12,133	11,530	11,002	10,156	9,857	9,758	9,477
Percentage change	1.55	2.40	5.06	3.29	4.56	5.23	4.80	8.33	3.03	1.01	2.97	3.27
Finance, insurance and real estate	12,237	11,951	12,231	12,188	11,770	11,299	11,000	10,899	10,313	10,374	10,415	10,103
Percentage change	2.39	-2.29	0.35	3.55	4.17	2.72	0.93	5.68	-0.59	-0.39	3.09	3.37
Transportation, communication and public utilities	7,377	6,808	6,705	6,824	6,519	5,665	5,283	5,158	4,692	4,168	4,242	4,282
Percentage change	8.36	1.54	-1.74	4.68	15.08	7.23	2.42	9.93	12.57	-1.74	-0.93	-2.24
Government	10,447	10,473	10,127	10,143	10,007	9,353	9,326	8,994	8,962	8,896	9,503	9,747
Percentage change	-0.25	3.42	-0.16	1.36	6.99	0.29	3.69	0.36	0.74	-6.39	-2.50	2.17

TABLE 2.2-- GROSS STATE PRODUCT, BY SECTOR, AND PERCENTAGE CHANGE, TENNESSEE, 1980–1991 [In millions of 1987 dollars] (Continued)

Sector	1991	1990f	1989f	1988f	1987f	1986f	1985f	1984f	1983f	1982f	1981r	1980f
Federal civilian	3,621	3,639	3,440	3,507	3,501	3,300	3,271	3,096	3,132	3,062	3,379	3,595
Percentage change	-0.49	5.78	-1.91	0.17	6.09	0.89	5.65	-1.15	2.29	-9.38	-6.01	5.02
Federal military	539	556	537	543	546	531	552	541	509	523	506	487
Percentage change	-3.06	3.54	-1.10	-0.55	2.82	-3.80	2.03	6.29	-2.68	3.36	3.90	4.73
State and local	6,286	6,277	6,149	6,094	5,960	5,521	5,504	5,357	5,321	5,311	5,618	5,665
Percentage change	0.14	2.08	0.90	2.25	7.95	0.31	2.74	0.68	0.19	-5.46	-0.83	0.21
Agriculture	1,395	1,277	1,169	1,261	1,276	1,143	1,218	1,175	1,023	1,249	1,199	988
Percentage change	9.24	9.24	-7.30	-1.18	11.64	-6.16	3.66	14.86	-18.09	4.17	21.36	7.27
Farms	1,099	1,017	941	1,029	1,019	934	1,012	965	832	1,080	1,055	852
Percentage change	8.06	8.08	-8.55	0.98	9.10	-7.71	4.87	15.99	-22.96	2.37	23.83	7.85
Agricultural services, forestry, fisheries	296	260	228	233	257	209	205	210	192	170	145	135
Percentage change	13.85	14.04	-2.15	-9.34	22.97	1.95	-2.38	9.38	12.94	17.24	7.41	2.27
PER CAPITA GROSS STATE PRODUCT (dollars)	17,519	17,305	17,413	17,231	16,887	16,028	15,375	14,922	13,970	13,465	13,772	13,498
Percentage change	1.24	-0.62	1.06	2.03	5.36	4.24	3.04	6.82	3.75	-2.23	2.03	-2.72

r revised.

Source: U.S. Department of Commerce, Bureau of Economic Analysis, direct correspondence.

TABLE 2.3-- PER CAPITA PERSONAL INCOME, TENNESSEE, 1929-1993, SELECTED YEARS

Year	Per capita personal income	Percent of U.S.[1]	Percent change[2]
1993	$18,415	88.6	4.5
1992[r]	17,622	87.5	6.9
1991[r]	16,489	85.9	3.7
1990[r]	15,903	85.2	5.5
1989[r]	15,074	85.2	6.4
1988	14,161	85.2	6.6
1987	13,286	84.9	6.6
1986	12,467	83.6	10.8
1985	11,252	81.0	5.6
1984	10,651	81.2	9.2
1983	9,752	80.6	5.9
1982	9,206	80.2	4.5
1981	8,810	80.5	9.7
1980	8,030	81.0	8.6
1979	7,392	81.8	10.5
1978	6,692	82.3	12.5
1977	5,948	81.5	9.0
1976	5,457	82.0	10.8
1975	4,924	81.1	6.7
1974	4,615	81.8	8.9
1973	4,236	81.7	13.1
1972	3,745	80.3	10.3
1971	3,396	79.1	7.8
1970	3,151	77.8	52.4
1965	2,067	74.6	31.2
1960	1,575	71.1	21.3
1955	1,298	69.3	27.8
1950	1,016	68.1	11.6
1945	910	74.3	170.0
1940	337	57.2	28.1
1935	263	55.6	-30.4
1929	378	54.2	(a)

Note: These data represent more current revisions to personal income and differ slightly from detail shown in Table 2.4.

r revised.

1. Computed by the Center for Business and Economic Research.

2. Computed by the Center for Business and Economic Research for five-year periods prior to 1970 except for the period 1929-1935.

a. Personal income was not estimated for years prior to 1929.

Source: U.S. Department of Commerce, Bureau of Economic Analysis, *United States Department of Commerce News*, August 1994; and *Survey of Current Business*, August issues.

TABLE 2.4-- PERSONAL INCOME BY MAJOR SOURCE, TENNESSEE, 1987–1992 [In thousands of dollars]

Source	1992	1991[r]	1990[r]	1989[r]	1988[r]	1987[r]
INCOME BY PLACE OF RESIDENCE						
Total personal income	88,816,292	81,831,284	77,785,887	73,177,495	68,378,781	63,690,979
Nonfarm personal income	88,238,974	81,379,697	77,373,824	72,771,041	68,015,705	63,381,872
Farm income[1]	577,318	451,587	412,063	406,454	363,076	309,107
Population (thousands)[2]	5,025	4,952	4,891	4,855	4,823	4,784
Per capita personal income (dollars)	17,674	16,524	15,903	15,074	14,177	13,315
Derivation of total personal income						
Earnings by place of work	66,584,396	61,076,462	58,392,711	55,195,242	51,899,843	48,287,265
Less: personal cont. for social insur.[3]	4,296,113	4,006,091	3,731,627	3,391,604	3,264,509	2,819,051
Plus: adjustment for residence	-629,810	-681,452	-694,794	-662,258	-626,190	-597,877
Equals: net earn. by place of residence[4]	61,658,473	56,388,919	53,966,290	51,141,380	48,009,144	44,870,337
Plus: dividends, interest, and rent[4]	11,507,366	11,404,340	11,412,247	10,862,994	9,631,518	8,810,605
Plus: transfer payments	15,650,453	14,038,025	12,407,350	11,173,121	10,738,119	10,010,037
EARNINGS BY PLACE OF WORK						
Components of earnings						
Wages and salaries	52,649,041	48,639,180	46,781,269	44,233,121	41,796,446	38,783,436
Other labor income[5]	6,037,520	5,420,572	4,904,074	4,470,300	4,071,799	3,696,169
Proprietors' income[5]	7,897,835	7,016,710	6,707,368	6,491,821	6,031,598	5,807,660
Farm	449,749	319,430	276,891	289,423	254,245	212,690
Nonfarm	7,448,086	6,697,280	6,430,477	6,202,398	5,777,353	5,594,970
Earnings by industry						
Farm	577,318	451,587	412,063	406,454	363,076	309,107
Nonfarm	66,007,078	60,624,875	57,980,648	54,788,788	51,536,767	47,978,158
Private	56,542,610	51,439,855	49,120,859	46,602,398	43,677,863	40,668,136
Ag. serv., for., fish., and other[6]	268,913	256,805	226,388	190,318	184,099	193,147
Agricultural services	264,992	252,556	220,591	183,630	176,311	178,704
Forestry, fisheries, and other[6]	3,921	4,249	5,797	6,688	7,788	14,443
Forestry	4,471	4,694	6,146	7,242	5,516	12,549
Fisheries	-550	-445	-349	-554	2,272	1,894
Mining	190,785	192,731	215,149	214,570	208,751	151,965
Coal mining	43,891	51,412	73,116	76,407	80,143	78,828
Oil and gas extraction	13,452	11,419	7,849	7,720	12,916	10,926
Metal mining	34,566	32,430	32,217	31,274	27,593	25,999
Nonmetallic minerals, except fuels	98,876	97,470	101,967	99,169	88,099	36,212
Construction	3,511,702	3,154,537	3,271,040	3,329,888	3,272,842	3,186,237
General building contractors	1,004,345	829,270	862,622	900,489	1,004,768	999,356

TABLE 2.4-- PERSONAL INCOME BY MAJOR SOURCE, TENNESSEE, 1987–1992 [In thousands of dollars] (Continued)

Source	1992	1991	1990F	1989F	1988F	1987F
Heavy construction contractors	413,086	399,311	431,549	430,860	414,357	419,670
Special trade contractors	2,094,271	1,925,956	1,976,869	1,998,539	1,853,717	1,767,211
Manufacturing	16,045,650	14,637,018	14,110,870	13,627,104	12,789,251	11,985,126
Nondurable goods	7,589,921	6,985,929	6,742,322	6,436,562	6,070,809	5,705,291
Food and kindred products	1,186,354	1,110,286	1,096,320	1,039,496	1,019,086	965,133
Textile mill products	487,377	443,231	435,848	433,482	418,093	430,863
Apparel and other textile products	996,508	924,986	902,668	875,828	843,530	792,268
Paper and allied products	871,866	796,105	741,966	704,768	641,664	581,693
Printing and publishing	1,046,809	965,214	940,016	884,047	813,328	717,459
Chemicals and allied products	1,762,773	1,684,195	1,584,087	1,467,171	1,381,515	1,362,252
Petroleum and coal products	33,032	33,955	31,813	32,103	30,031	30,752
Tobacco manufactures	52,366	41,504	48,246	41,988	43,023	40,455
Rubber and misc. plastic products	1,003,225	848,058	820,105	807,841	735,574	642,674
Leather and leather products	149,611	138,395	141,253	149,838	144,965	141,742
Durable goods	8,455,729	7,651,089	7,368,548	7,190,542	6,718,442	6,279,835
Lumber and wood products	480,470	444,260	439,258	441,740	438,766	411,409
Furniture and fixtures	632,273	550,701	537,868	520,688	480,537	457,095
Primary metal industries	603,796	567,948	567,738	551,368	530,285	480,897
Fabricated metal products	1,402,867	1,340,475	1,319,811	1,258,711	1,157,251	1,058,869
Machinery, except electrical	1,184,023	1,111,830	1,117,445	1,144,421	1,066,244	985,886
Electric and electronic equipment	1,108,832	999,969	979,546	1,025,473	945,707	865,344
Trans. equip. excl. motor vehicles	397,800	405,306	422,453	415,393	429,428	478,348
Motor vehicles and equipment	1,473,228	1,163,031	915,242	746,169	668,002	591,990
Stone, clay, and glass products	476,208	426,070	444,230	448,120	453,984	440,766
Instruments and related products	351,132	339,037	313,057	295,781	268,560	233,319
Misc. manufacturing industries	345,100	302,462	311,900	342,678	279,678	275,912
Transportation and public utilities	4,585,878	4,291,260	4,081,927	3,805,197	3,554,596	3,349,324
Railroad transportation	295,646	280,550	273,994	285,179	290,080	281,155
Trucking and warehousing	1,642,404	1,504,825	1,481,375	1,377,704	1,304,110	1,230,006
Water transportation	(D)	(D)	(D)	(D)	39,942	31,210
Other transportation	(D)	(D)	(D)	(D)	1,002,733	891,864
Local & interurban passenger transit	120,589	109,244	100,781	98,134	87,369	91,022
Transportation by air	1,171,931	1,098,750	1,020,995	931,158	809,143	708,045
Pipelines, except natural gas	(D)	(D)	(D)	(D)	1,724	1,604
Transportation services	147,588	135,912	120,498	118,664	104,497	91,193
Communication	875,205	864,489	820,664	752,518	732,844	737,483
Electric, gas, and sanitary services	268,665	236,934	210,580	191,129	184,887	177,606
Wholesale trade	4,383,803	4,099,802	3,904,300	3,713,853	3,530,055	3,299,991
Retail trade	7,116,956	6,492,681	6,233,264	5,961,823	5,782,482	5,405,859

TABLE 2.4-- PERSONAL INCOME BY MAJOR SOURCE, TENNESSEE, 1987-1992 [In thousands of dollars] (Continued)

Source	1992	1991[r]	1990[f]	1989[f]	1988[f]	1987[f]
Building materials and garden equipment	403,455	362,856	345,319	377,746	362,677	349,418
General merchandise stores	820,428	758,821	749,688	693,255	649,555	602,140
Food stores	1,045,544	982,220	946,001	920,078	878,206	808,456
Automotive dealers & service stations	1,247,304	1,121,741	1,053,260	1,045,085	1,111,829	1,017,358
Apparel and accessory stores	372,145	341,435	311,945	284,775	279,948	270,951
Home furniture and furnishings stores	378,939	351,909	395,822	387,286	368,770	352,198
Eating and drinking places	1,794,989	1,589,169	1,415,798	1,278,270	1,238,338	1,160,944
Miscellaneous retail	1,054,152	984,530	1,015,431	975,328	893,159	844,394
Finance, insurance, and real estate	3,487,129	3,187,289	3,000,504	2,902,412	2,816,256	2,669,282
Depository & non-dep. credit institutions	1,195,073	1,098,951	1,038,495	1,011,894	986,066	926,480
Other finance, insur., & real estate	2,292,056	2,088,338	1,962,009	1,890,518	1,830,190	1,742,802
Security & commodity brokers & serv.	370,645	302,757	239,445	234,357	262,952	278,511
Insurance carriers	759,585	716,132	696,953	629,495	590,245	577,475
Insurance agents, brokers, & services	549,123	519,076	515,219	475,830	466,357	404,715
Real estate	473,957	431,666	418,448	434,815	368,731	327,993
Holding & other investment companies	138,746	118,707	91,944	116,021	141,905	166,573
Services	16,951,794	15,127,732	14,077,417	12,857,233	11,539,531	10,427,205
Hotels and other lodging places	625,404	606,336	643,426	605,699	533,621	534,298
Personal services	653,563	610,265	609,528	614,065	610,001	569,881
Private households	149,153	134,367	138,074	134,995	130,086	125,145
Business services	2,568,306	2,214,688	2,116,371	1,868,184	1,615,859	1,990,045
Auto repair, services, and garages	461,189	424,514	401,601	408,086	401,655	378,350
Miscellaneous repair services	229,982	206,459	210,569	197,420	187,097	171,641
Amusement and recreation services	844,679	772,835	640,449	492,018	457,190	362,103
Motion pictures	108,705	97,646	94,382	81,487	68,988	40,062
Health services	6,819,247	5,985,386	5,458,983	4,930,628	4,414,730	3,944,729
Legal services	834,965	767,640	724,296	676,994	616,950	551,173
Educational services	635,912	593,168	476,691	442,259	412,311	368,351
Social services	288,886	254,461	226,088	195,620	168,429	150,620
Museums, botanical, zoological gardens	21,176	16,491	14,884	12,645	10,804	5,086
Membership organizations	584,896	553,841	540,824	523,141	482,228	439,283
Engineering and management services[7]	2,054,667	1,824,458	1,713,871	1,602,544	1,380,992	n.a.
Miscellaneous services	71,064	65,177	67,380	71,448	48,590	796,438
Government and government enterprises	9,464,468	9,185,020	8,859,789	8,186,390	7,858,904	7,310,022
Federal, civilian	2,280,528	2,289,577	2,251,268	2,022,105	2,108,601	1,934,842
Military	447,632	448,360	434,654	402,674	391,109	383,528
State and local	6,736,308	6,447,083	6,173,867	5,761,611	5,359,194	4,991,652

Notes on following page.

TABLE 2.4– PERSONAL INCOME BY MAJOR SOURCE, TENNESSEE, 1987–1992 [In thousands of dollars] (Continued)

Note: Industry detail for 1988 and later are based on the 1987 SIC. Data for 1987 are based on the 1972 SIC.

(D) Not shown to avoid disclosure of confidential information.

n.a. not available for this year.

r revised.

1. Farm income consists of proprietors' net farm income, the wages of hired farm labor, the pay-in-kind of hired farm labor, and the salaries of officers of corporate farms.
2. Census Bureau midyear population estimates. Estimates for 1990–92 reflect state and county population estimates available as of February 1994.
3. Personal contributions for social insurance are included in earnings by type and industry but excluded from personal income.
4. Includes the capital consumption adjustment for rental income of persons.
5. Includes the inventory valuation and capital consumption adjustments.
6. "Other" consists of the wages and salaries of U.S. residents employed by international organizations and foreign embassies and consulates in the United States.
7. This category is new under the 1987 Standard Industrial Classification; therefore estimates prior to 1988 do not exist.

Source: U.S. Department of Commerce, Bureau of Economic Analysis, Regional Economic Measurement Division, *Regional Economic Information System 1969–1992* CD-ROM.

TABLE 2.5— PER CAPITA EARNINGS, PROPERTY INCOME, AND TRANSFER PAYMENTS, AND PERCENT OF TOTAL PERSONAL INCOME, TENNESSEE AND METROPOLITAN STATISTICAL AREAS, 1992

Metropolitan Statistical Area	Earnings			Property income			Transfer payments		
	Per capita ($)	Percent of total personal income	Percent change 1991–92	Per capita ($)	Percent of total personal income	Percent change 1991–92	Per capita ($)	Percent of total personal income	Percent change 1991–92
TENNESSEE	12,270	69.4	9.3	2,290	13.0	0.9	3,114	17.6	11.5
Chattanooga	12,129	67.8	6.7	2,606	14.6	1.4	3,161	17.7	10.5
Clarksville-Hopkinsville	10,294	72.0	18.7	1,445	10.1	1.1	2,553	17.9	10.3
Jackson	12,002	69.2	11.3	2,144	12.4	0.9	3,200	18.4	10.9
Johnson City-Kingsport-Bristol	10,945	67.4	7.4	2,189	13.5	0.6	3,099	19.1	10.7
Knoxville	12,790	69.6	9.4	2,580	14.1	0.9	2,993	16.3	11.0
Memphis	13,755	70.5	7.3	2,332	11.9	0.8	3,431	17.6	12.2
Nashville-Davidson	15,133	73.6	10.9	2,772	13.5	1.0	2,665	13.0	11.4

Source: U.S. Department of Commerce, Bureau of Economic Analysis, Regional Economic Measurement Division, *Regional Economic Information System 1969–1992 CD-ROM.*

TABLE 2.6-- PERSONAL INCOME BY MAJOR SOURCE, CHATTANOOGA METROPOLITAN STATISTICAL AREA, 1987-1992 [In thousands of dollars]

Source	1992	1991	1990[f]	1989[f]	1988[f]	1987[f]
INCOME BY PLACE OF RESIDENCE						
Total personal income	7,710,061	7,237,386	7,038,996	6,619,757	6,238,830	5,793,374
Nonfarm personal income	7,689,638	7,219,130	7,023,814	6,603,757	6,228,415	5,785,826
Farm income[1]	20,423	18,256	15,182	16,000	10,415	7,548
Population (thousands)[2]	431	428	425	423	420	417
Per capita personal income (dollars)	17,895	16,906	16,572	15,664	14,850	13,896
Derivation of total personal income						
Earnings by place of work	5,708,365	5,363,976	5,242,100	4,963,722	4,780,709	4,435,097
Less: personal cont. for social insur.[3]	366,696	349,116	333,016	306,564	299,164	261,008
Plus: adjustment for residence	-116,304	-116,690	-112,517	-120,967	-119,007	-112,953
Equals: net earn. by place of residence[4]	5,225,365	4,898,170	4,796,567	4,536,191	4,362,538	4,061,136
Plus: dividends, interest, and rent[4]	1,122,771	1,107,231	1,149,905	1,091,942	923,486	831,212
Plus: transfer payments	1,361,925	1,231,985	1,092,524	991,624	952,806	901,026
EARNINGS BY PLACE OF WORK						
Components of earnings						
Wages and salaries	4,641,234	4,397,809	4,324,978	4,102,004	3,979,097	3,688,642
Other labor income	509,182	468,011	434,496	401,006	371,665	338,845
Proprietors' income[5]	557,949	498,156	482,626	460,712	429,947	407,610
Farm	18,122	15,707	12,551	13,695	8,241	5,599
Nonfarm	539,827	482,449	470,075	447,017	421,706	402,011
Earnings by industry						
Farm	20,423	18,256	15,182	16,000	10,415	7,548
Nonfarm	5,687,942	5,345,720	5,226,918	4,947,722	4,770,294	4,427,549
Private	4,678,745	4,349,754	4,250,715	4,056,718	3,850,309	3,599,402
Ag. serv., for., fish., and other[6]	13,613e	(D)	13,675	11,407	12,223	12,482
Agricultural services	12,902e	(D)	13,025	(D)	(D)	(D)
Forestry, fisheries, and other[6]	722	946	650	637e	925e	1,298e
Forestry	875	1,080	769	789	501	(D)
Fisheries	-153	-134	-119	-148e	424e	(D)
Mining	17,935e	3,458	13,655	12,508	15,709	16,484
Coal mining	4,600	733	2,359	(D)	(D)	(D)
Oil and gas extraction	(D)	(D)	(D)	(D)	(D)	(D)
Metal mining	(L)	(L)	(D)	(L)	(L)	(L)
Nonmetallic minerals, except fuels	(D)	(D)	(D)	(D)	(D)	(D)
Construction	284,829	270,195	278,984	288,112	299,290	276,717
General building contractors	72,817	69,254	71,472e	74,195e	85,149	84,073
Heavy construction contractors	24,890	21,802	19,424e	23,483e	28,461	29,318

TABLE 2.6— PERSONAL INCOME BY MAJOR SOURCE, CHATTANOOGA METROPOLITAN STATISTICAL AREA, 1987–1992 [In thousands of dollars] (Continued)

Source	1992	1991	1990[f]	1989[f]	1988[f]	1987[f]
Special trade contractors	187,122	179,139	186,606	186,230	185,680	163,326
Manufacturing	1,324,115	1,231,033	1,239,339	1,211,401	1,166,834	1,089,827
Nondurable goods	802,001	752,739	736,100	716,589	683,795	643,415
Food and kindred products	201,340	186,294	178,190	178,433	171,799	155,420
Textile mill products	268,382	260,798	256,850	249,092	235,020	228,450
Apparel and other textile products	18,122	(D)	18,561	(D)	(D)	9,978
Paper and allied products	(D)	(D)	(D)	(D)	(D)	(D)
Printing and publishing	66,769	61,729	57,041	56,181	52,796	46,655
Chemicals and allied products	127,331	134,393	136,775	122,535	119,867	115,768
Petroleum and coal products	213	430	369	338	0	2,577
Tobacco manufactures						
Rubber and misc. plastic products	15,682	12,607	10,229	(D)	15,241	18,247
Leather and leather products	8,001	5,537	5,780	5,597	6,569	6,359
Durable goods	522,114	478,294	503,239	494,812	483,039	446,412
Lumber and wood products	13,153	(D)	(D)	(D)	(D)	(D)
Furniture and fixtures	(D)	12,990	13,176	13,409	13,406	10,593
Primary metal industries	122,968	101,198	104,801	111,369	107,960	99,197
Fabricated metal products	112,011	111,354	123,649	116,398	115,957	102,057
Machinery, except electrical	90,364	80,681	84,699	80,122	71,583	63,725
Electric and electronic equipment	(D)	(D)	(D)	(D)	(D)	(D)
Trans. equip. excl. motor vehicles	(D)	(D)	(D)	(D)	(D)	(D)
Motor vehicles and equipment	27,267	22,110	24,164	22,439	38,378	41,023
Stone, clay, and glass products	(D)	19,855	18,122	16,436	14,972	15,734
Instruments and related products	17,789	16,933	20,346	15,376	18,865	17,105
Misc. manufacturing industries						
Transportation and public utilities	285,466	283,207	286,304	277,056	264,416	268,720
Railroad transportation	53,347	51,358	46,775	45,725	46,466	46,042
Trucking and warehousing	113,296	(D)	(D)	(D)	(D)	119,024
Water transportation	(D)	(D)	(D)	(D)	3,053	2,797
Other transportation	(D)	(D)	(D)	(D)	25,555	25,735
Local & interurban passenger transit	10,536	9,301	8,678	9,131	8,525	9,585
Transportation by air	4,695	4,931	7,326	7,396	8,791	8,941
Pipelines, except natural gas	(D)	(D)	(D)	(D)	1,724	1,604
Transportation services	8,181	8,131	7,483	8,307	6,542	5,605
Communication	57,291	57,389	53,986	49,464	51,602	51,527
Electric, gas, and sanitary services	(D)	(D)	23,442	21,657	21,020	20,403
Wholesale trade	372,614	356,978	358,352	346,480	324,892	307,804
Retail trade	625,278	573,974	569,118	541,721	526,749	478,012
Building materials and garden equipment	(D)	29,908	23,764	30,978	26,780	25,106
General merchandise stores	(D)	57,806	(D)	(D)	47,735	42,359
Food stores	(D)	93,778	98,035	91,783	82,023	66,073

TABLE 2.6-- PERSONAL INCOME BY MAJOR SOURCE, CHATTANOOGA METROPOLITAN STATISTICAL AREA, 1987–1992 [In thousands of dollars] (Continued)

Source	1992	1991	1990f	1989f	1988f	1987f
Automotive dealers & service stations	94,368	86,488	78,866	80,185	90,687	82,887
Apparel and accessory stores	27,418	26,150	21,227	19,972	18,759	17,988
Home furniture and furnishings stores	30,270	27,886	28,068 e	28,286 e	27,455 e	25,661 e
Eating and drinking places	168,276 e	153,302 e	152,777 e	137,332 e	134,524 e	125,524
Miscellaneous retail	102,503	97,076	105,234	98,726	89,747	85,013
Finance, insurance, and real estate	408,196	388,731	362,185	340,306	325,458	313,645
Depository & non-dep. credit institutions	(D)	(D)	69,032 e	69,948 e	64,744 e	(D)
Other finance, insur., & real estate	317,157 e	302,018 e	282,553 e	261,885 e	251,986 e	239,422 e
Security & commodity brokers & serv.	11,704	8,512	7,095	7,691	8,831	10,374
Insurance carriers	219,099 e	200,417 e	184,721 e	168,944 e	159,404 e	162,280 e
Insurance agents, brokers, & services	41,951 e	50,140	48,299	44,224	44,086	37,499
Real estate	43,053	37,791 e	35,978	36,221 e	29,478 e	24,900 e
Holding & other investment companies	2,915 e	6,602 e	8,002 e	5,876 e	10,883 e	10,051
Services	1,345,263	1,215,120	1,129,103	1,027,727	914,738	835,711
Hotels and other lodging places	24,949	24,203	25,726 e	26,697 e	24,882 e	(D)
Personal services	84,058	87,365	84,822	82,324	78,674	72,859
Private households	(D)	8,773	9,005	8,969	8,809	8,629
Business services	249,844	212,410	199,169	169,690	131,349	153,151
Auto repair, services, and garages	40,753	34,210	32,839	34,677	32,517	32,407
Miscellaneous repair services	23,624	21,485	22,316	19,879	18,329	17,282
Amusement and recreation services	30,897	28,697	25,427	21,288	20,270	18,208
Motion pictures	6,635 e	6,389 e	7,736 e	6,694 e	4,995	3,218 e
Health services	545,592	479,211	442,431	386,123	349,021	307,047
Legal services	88,790	83,202	78,197	71,940	67,119	60,279
Educational services	(D)	(D)	(D)	(D)	(D)	(D)
Social services	25,611 e	24,304 e	20,404 e	17,778 e	15,378 e	12,990 e
Museums, botanical, zoological gardens	(D)	966	947	797	695	(D)
Membership organizations	47,939	45,569	45,508	45,093	42,441	38,528
Engineering and management services7	125,117	122,169	100,524	101,754	91,174	n.a.
Miscellaneous services	5,776	5,462	4,838	5,858	3,727	62,534
Government and government enterprises	1,009,197	995,966	976,203	891,004	919,985	828,147
Federal, civilian	378,335	391,064	398,290	356,951	415,330	368,564
Military	17,624	16,705	16,716	15,307	14,974	14,268
State and local	613,238	588,197	561,197	518,746	489,681	445,315

See Table 2.4 for notes.

e. The estimate shown here constitutes the major portion of the true estimate.

(L) Less than $50,000. Estimates are included in totals.

Source: U.S. Department of Commerce, Bureau of Economic Analysis, Regional Economic Measurement Division, *Regional Economic Information System 1969–1992* CD-ROM.

TABLE 2.7.– PERSONAL INCOME BY MAJOR SOURCE, CLARKSVILLE-HOPKINSVILLE METROPOLITAN STATISTICAL AREA, 1987–1992
[In thousands of dollars]

Source	1992	1991	1990[r]	1989[r]	1988[r]	1987[r]
INCOME BY PLACE OF RESIDENCE						
Total personal income	2,546,810	2,212,389	2,060,082	2,025,066	1,885,412	1,786,740
Nonfarm personal income	2,505,318	2,189,178	2,036,875	1,997,516	1,865,757	1,765,946
Farm income[1]	41,492	23,211	23,207	27,550	19,655	20,794
Population (thousands)[2]	178	169	170	167	165	162
Per capita personal income (dollars)	14,295	13,066	12,091	12,096	11,430	11,001
Derivation of total personal income						
Earnings by place of work	1,973,854	1,619,837	1,505,902	1,511,840	1,427,975	1,361,264
Less: personal cont. for social insur.[3]	111,761	95,147	87,723	86,771	82,231	73,202
Plus: adjustment for residence	-27,740	20,687	20,676	13,712	11,452	6,141
Equals: net earn. by place of residence	1,834,353	1,545,377	1,438,855	1,438,781	1,357,196	1,294,203
Plus: dividends, interest, and rent[4]	257,557	254,692	256,961	258,491	220,625	204,699
Plus: transfer payments	454,900	412,320	364,266	327,794	307,591	287,838
EARNINGS BY PLACE OF WORK						
Components of earnings						
Wages and salaries	1,661,885	1,359,256	1,262,972	1,275,199	1,213,187	1,157,369
Other labor income	128,607	111,128	99,364	88,613	79,074	72,151
Proprietors' income[5]	183,362	149,453	143,566	148,028	135,714	131,744
Farm	37,009	18,563	18,457	23,436	15,845	17,421
Nonfarm	146,353	130,890	125,109	124,592	119,869	114,323
Earnings by industry						
Farm	41,492	23,211	23,207	27,550	19,655	20,794
Nonfarm	1,932,362	1,596,626	1,482,695	1,484,290	1,408,320	1,340,470
Private	959,534	847,289	810,995	779,447	737,990	696,264
Ag. serv., for., fish., and other[6]	4,433	4,222	3,480	3,060	3,575	3,619
Agricultural services	(D)	4,014	3,467	3,035	3,594	3,558
Forestry, fisheries, and other[6]	(D)	208	(L)	(L)	(L)	61
Forestry	(D)	(D)	(L)	(L)	(L)	(L)
Fisheries	(L)	(D)	(L)	(L)	(L)	(L)
Mining	8,102	7,931	6,726	7,133	6,040	324
Coal mining	5,152	(D)	(D)	4,297	3,720	(D)
Oil and gas extraction	(D)	165	(D)	(D)	(D)	(D)
Metal mining	621	(D)	400	609	561	443
Nonmetallic minerals, except fuels	(D)	(D)	(D)	(D)	(D)	(D)
Construction	67,440	57,009	59,463	60,401	62,413	61,930
General building contractors	14,446	11,260	12,361	12,185	16,140	16,338
Heavy construction contractors	10,749	8,924	9,291	10,685	9,707	10,162

TABLE 2.7– PERSONAL INCOME BY MAJOR SOURCE, CLARKSVILLE-HOPKINSVILLE METROPOLITAN STATISTICAL AREA, 1987–1992
[In thousands of dollars] (Continued)

Source	1992	1991	1990[F]	1989[F]	1988[F]	1987[F]
Special trade contractors	42,245	36,825	37,811	37,531	36,566	35,430
Manufacturing	307,899	277,233	277,273	266,211	237,673	228,413
Nondurable goods	118,764	108,433	108,923	115,792	106,094	104,107
Food and kindred products	(D)	(D)	(D)	(D)	(D)	(D)
Textile mill products	(D)	(D)	(D)	1,984	(D)	(D)
Apparel and other textile products	23,789[e]	19,758[e]	(D)	(D)	(D)	(D)
Paper and allied products	(D)	(D)	(D)	(D)	(D)	(D)
Printing and publishing	(D)	(D)	(D)	(D)	(D)	(D)
Chemicals and allied products	(D)	1,765	(D)	23,719[e]	(D)	21,233[e]
Petroleum and coal products	3,459	2,987	2,633	(D)	2,423	(D)
Tobacco manufactures	1,693	1,201	(D)	2,931	(D)	5,708[e]
Rubber and misc. plastic products	(D)	(D)	(D)	(D)	(D)	(D)
Leather and leather products	(D)	(D)	(D)	(D)	(D)	(D)
Durable goods	189,135	168,800	168,350	150,419	131,579	124,306
Lumber and wood products	9,434	9,162	8,093	8,079	7,453	6,901
Furniture and fixtures	(D)	(D)	(D)	(D)	(D)	(D)
Primary metal industries	(D)	(D)	(D)	(D)	(D)	(D)
Fabricated metal products	12,896	10,951	12,446	11,494	10,739	10,661
Machinery, except electrical	(D)	(D)	(D)	(D)	(D)	(D)
Electric and electronic equipment	(D)	(D)	(D)	(D)	(D)	(D)
Trans. equip. excl. motor vehicles	(D)	(D)	(D)	(D)	(D)	(D)
Motor vehicles and equipment	(D)	(D)	(D)	(D)	(D)	(D)
Stone, clay, and glass products	9,894	5,417	4,208	3,612	3,758	(D)
Instruments and related products	0	0	0	0	0	0
Misc. manufacturing industries	(D)	(D)	(D)	(D)	(D)	(D)
Transportation and public utilities	52,143	42,419	40,431	37,299	35,557	36,079
Railroad transportation	613	600	648	734	912	(D)
Trucking and warehousing	(D)	17,962	16,777	13,981	11,957	12,059
Water transportation	(D)	(D)	(D)	(D)	(D)	(D)
Other transportation	(D)	(D)	(D)	(D)	(D)	(D)
Local & interurban passenger transit	978	(D)	(D)	(D)	(D)	1,637
Transportation by air	(D)	(D)	(D)	(D)	(D)	426[e]
Pipelines, except natural gas	0	0	0	0	0	0
Transportation services	493	356	325	329	303	337
Communication	17,788	16,475	15,761	15,804	16,327	16,348
Electric, gas, and sanitary services	(D)	5,756	5,492	5,315	5,041	5,027
Wholesale trade	53,924	48,363	48,032	46,766	44,944	40,733
Retail trade	179,221	159,744	146,962	143,161	141,197	134,493
Building materials and garden equipment	12,527	10,691	9,572	8,900	8,781	7,341
General merchandise stores	21,826	19,989	19,499	18,982	18,468	16,431
Food stores	20,664	19,077	16,534	17,349	15,333	14,466

TABLE 2.7.– PERSONAL INCOME BY MAJOR SOURCE, CLARKSVILLE-HOPKINSVILLE METROPOLITAN STATISTICAL AREA, 1987–1992
[In thousands of dollars] (Continued)

Source	1992	1991	1990[e]	1989[e]	1988[e]	1987[e]
Automotive dealers & service stations	36,782	32,688	29,919	30,601	33,477	31,641
Apparel and accessory stores	5,602	5,444	3,659	3,307	3,491	5,108
Home furniture and furnishings stores	10,507	9,282	9,907	9,601	8,840	9,358
Eating and drinking places	47,505	41,076	36,621	33,470	33,385	31,539
Miscellaneous retail	23,808	21,477	21,251	20,951	19,422	18,609
Finance, insurance, and real estate	43,944	40,264	36,985	35,178	39,212	36,302
Depository & non-dep. credit institutions	21,681	19,767	18,835	17,813	22,051	20,331
Other finance, insur., & real estate	22,263	20,497	18,150	17,365	17,161	15,971
Security & commodity brokers & serv.	(D)	(D)	(D)	(D)	(D)	(D)
Insurance carriers	4,907	(D)	(D)	(D)	(D)	(D)
Insurance agents, brokers, & services	10,033	9,241	8,484	7,840	8,401	7,763
Real estate	5,815	5,577	5,765	6,092	5,062	4,078
Holding & other investment companies	(D)	(D)	(D)	(D)	(D)	(D)
Services	242,428	210,104	191,643	180,238	167,379	154,371
Hotels and other lodging places	5,967	5,822	5,010	5,189	4,815	5,301
Personal services	13,694	12,529	12,719	12,722	13,317	12,722
Private households	5,258	4,744	4,883	4,710	4,481	4,261
Business services	28,681	23,448	23,672	20,851	19,821	19,222
Auto repair, services, and garages	13,086	10,887	10,617	11,386	12,174	11,829
Miscellaneous repair services	3,647	3,338	3,329	3,122	2,864	2,693
Amusement and recreation services	(D)	(D)	(D)	(D)	(D)	(D)
Motion pictures	312	295	(D)	(D)	(D)	(L)
Health services	108,269	91,866	81,199	75,121	66,698	59,777
Legal services	12,672	11,696	10,549	10,314	8,821	8,283
Educational services	8,660	8,426	5,299	6,062	7,429	6,505
Social services	8,371	5,357	4,163	3,371	3,135	4,041
Museums, botanical, zoological gardens	(D)	(D)	(D)	(D)	(D)	(D)
Membership organizations	13,424	12,726	12,182	11,799	10,085	9,063
Engineering and management services[7]	10,920	10,321	10,145	9,174	7,759	n.a.
Miscellaneous services	857	792	(D)	(D)	(D)	7,093
Government and government enterprises	972,828	749,337	671,700	704,843	670,330	644,206
Federal, civilian	132,824	124,485	110,698	92,876	85,864	84,052
Military	642,009	438,701	388,484	455,621	442,089	429,885
State and local	197,995	186,151	172,518	156,346	142,377	130,269

See Table 2.4 for notes.

e. The estimate shown here constitutes the major portion of the true estimate.

(L) Less than $50,000. Estimates are included in totals.

Source: U.S. Department of Commerce, Bureau of Economic Analysis, Regional Economic Measurement Division, *Regional Economic Information System 1969–1992* CD-ROM.

TABLE 2.8– PERSONAL INCOME BY MAJOR SOURCE, JACKSON METROPOLITAN STATISTICAL AREA, 1987–1992 [In thousands of dollars]

Source	1992	1991	1990[f]	1989[f]	1988[f]	1987[f]
INCOME BY PLACE OF RESIDENCE						
Total personal income	1,391,200	1,266,712	1,205,516	1,098,046	1,031,106	964,095
Nonfarm personal income	1,379,782	1,257,537	1,200,819	1,093,065	1,023,748	953,502
Farm income[1]	11,418	9,175	4,697	4,981	7,358	10,593
Population (thousands)[2]	80	79	78	78	78	77
Per capita personal income (dollars)	17,340	16,032	15,418	14,108	13,286	12,472
Derivation of total personal income						
Earnings by place of work	1,190,653	1,069,851	1,022,974	947,584	872,977	812,246
Less: personal cont. for social insur.[3]	74,328	68,134	63,655	57,378	54,033	46,220
Plus: adjustment for residence	-153,729	-136,999	-133,570	-126,649	-116,216	-111,689
Equals: net earn. by place of residence	962,596	864,718	825,749	763,557	702,728	654,337
Plus: dividends, interest, and rent[4]	171,981	170,513	173,912	147,823	148,114	140,236
Plus: transfer payments	256,623	231,481	205,855	186,666	180,264	169,522
EARNINGS BY PLACE OF WORK						
Components of earnings						
Wages and salaries	971,112	877,631	846,516	781,866	721,274	665,144
Other labor income	112,559	97,894	89,197	79,891	72,686	66,737
Proprietors' income[5]	106,982	94,326	87,261	85,827	79,017	80,365
Farm	9,263	6,944	2,413	3,005	5,516	8,960
Nonfarm	97,719	87,382	84,848	82,822	73,501	71,405
Earnings by industry						
Farm	11,418	9,175	4,697	4,981	7,358	10,593
Nonfarm	1,179,235	1,060,676	1,018,277	942,603	865,619	801,653
Private	964,761	864,338	828,816	780,188	715,177	662,483
Ag. serv., for., fish., and other[6]	2,900	(D)	2,779	2,645	2,410	2,493
Agricultural services	2,906	(D)	2,782	2,631	2,370	2,419
Forestry, fisheries, and other[6]	(L)	(L)	(L)	(L)	(L)	74
Forestry	(L)	(L)	(L)	(D)	(L)	60
Fisheries	(L)	(L)	(L)	(D)	(D)	(L)
Mining	1,065	(D)	818	863	652	430
Coal mining	293	267	254	277	(D)	(L)
Oil and gas extraction	(D)	119	(D)	(D)	(L)	(D)
Metal mining	0	0	0	0	(D)	0
Nonmetallic minerals, except fuels	(D)	(D)	(D)	(D)	0	(D)
Construction	91,504	84,997	88,340	89,888	69,537	60,621
General building contractors	23,353	22,110	24,013	20,873	16,886	16,125
Heavy construction contractors	19,000	18,271	19,439	17,694	14,936	14,158

TABLE 2.8– PERSONAL INCOME BY MAJOR SOURCE, JACKSON METROPOLITAN STATISTICAL AREA, 1987–1992 [In thousands of dollars] (Continued)

Source	1992	1991	1990^f	1989^f	1988^f	1987^f
Special trade contractors	49,151	44,616	44,888	51,321	37,715	30,338
Manufacturing	298,378	257,249	257,756	248,850	235,947	231,777
Nondurable goods	111,787	106,151	107,412	106,397	98,564	94,713
Food and kindred products	66,624	65,640	71,531	68,027	62,435	61,654
Textile mill products	(D)	(D)	(D)	(D)	(D)	(D)
Apparel and other textile products	4,629	(D)	(D)	(D)	(D)	(D)
Paper and allied products	17,100	16,670	14,575	13,942	12,386	8,927
Printing and publishing	12,673	11,338	10,358	9,467	8,553	7,390
Chemicals and allied products	(D)	3,091	3,531	3,309	3,096	2,176
Petroleum and coal products	213	181	158	138	(D)	(D)
Tobacco manufactures	0	0	0	0	0	0
Rubber and misc. plastic products	7,241	4,476	3,031	2,962	2,408	1,671
Leather and leather products	0	0	0	0	0	0
Durable goods	186,591	151,098	150,344	142,453	137,383	137,064
Lumber and wood products	21,932	18,920	20,175	21,029	23,121	22,902
Furniture and fixtures	(D)	2,891	(D)	(D)	(D)	(D)
Primary metal industries	38,513	32,312	32,175	26,857	(D)	(D)
Fabricated metal products	12,800	11,016	10,343	11,559	4,105	7,484
Machinery, except electrical	55,237	52,358	52,164	47,984	35,329	26,122
Electric and electronic equipment	(D)	1,276	1,149	1,551	3,871	(D)
Trans. equip. excl. motor vehicles	(D)	(D)	(D)	(D)	(D)	(D)
Motor vehicles and equipment	21,331	18,822	(D)	(D)	(D)	(D)
Stone, clay, and glass products	(D)	(D)	(D)	(D)	(D)	27,323
Instruments and related products	(D)	(D)	(D)	(D)	819	661
Misc. manufacturing industries	731	709	710	834	527	477
Transportation and public utilities	61,198	59,124	56,482	46,582	47,711	45,187
Railroad transportation	7,893	7,208	7,602	8,412	8,664	8,443
Trucking and warehousing	31,780	30,849	28,451	18,210	19,186	15,948
Water transportation	0	0	0	0	0	0
Other transportation	(D)	2,293	1,884	2,869	2,795	2,788
Local & interurban passenger transit	222	264	(D)	(D)	(D)	(D)
Transportation by air	0	96	(D)	(D)	(D)	(D)
Pipelines, except natural gas	0	0	0	0	0	0
Transportation services	2,137	1,933	1,532	2,586	2,505	2,509
Communication	19,058	18,713	18,485	17,004	16,880	17,718
Electric, gas, and sanitary services	(D)	61	60	87	186	290
Wholesale trade	60,268	58,377	51,493	42,953	40,506	37,876
Retail trade	129,274	118,407	110,998	110,652	104,993	90,098
Building materials and garden equipment	9,159	7,592	6,712	6,610	6,274	5,081
General merchandise stores	18,274	16,541	16,624	15,400	14,787	11,693
Food stores	14,432	13,094	13,270	14,104	12,098	11,263

TABLE 2.8-- PERSONAL INCOME BY MAJOR SOURCE, JACKSON METROPOLITAN STATISTICAL AREA, 1987-1992 [In thousands of dollars] (Continued)

Source	1992	1991	1990ᶠ	1989ᶠ	1988ᶠ	1987ᶠ
Automotive dealers & service stations	21,083	19,417	18,074	18,395	17,768	16,655
Apparel and accessory stores	5,312	5,701	4,799	4,600	5,171	4,677
Home furniture and furnishings stores	7,238	6,771	6,750	7,487	6,913	6,553
Eating and drinking places	24,181	22,741	21,434	21,695	20,009	19,026
Miscellaneous retail	29,595	26,550	23,335	22,361	21,973	15,150
Finance, insurance, and real estate	37,928	35,898	35,440	32,637	31,823	31,467
Depository & non-dep. credit institutions	15,258	13,793	14,743	13,810	(D)	15,723
Other finance, insur., & real estate	22,670	22,105	20,697	18,827	(D)	15,744
Security & commodity brokers & serv.	(D)	742	753	1,732	(D)	(D)
Insurance carriers	11,103	10,739	9,432	6,555	6,633	(D)
Insurance agents, brokers, & services	5,937	6,145	6,235	5,945	5,349	5,641
Real estate	4,123	3,673	3,817	4,306	2,365	2,331
Holding & other investment companies	(D)	806	460	289	467	929
Services	282,246	246,107	224,710	205,118	181,598	162,534
Hotels and other lodging places	9,853	10,170	9,307	8,045	6,581	6,152
Personal services	10,835	9,564	7,677	8,000	7,714	7,970
Private households	2,224	2,003	2,060	1,945	1,811	1,679
Business services	41,453	31,405	28,914	27,304	20,462	17,649
Auto repair, services, and garages	7,602	7,309	6,710	6,929	6,609	6,838
Miscellaneous repair services	4,765	4,329	5,192	4,913	5,530	4,753
Amusement and recreation services	6,846	6,018	6,029	4,826	4,265	2,720
Motion pictures	708	629	837	760	646	132
Health services	138,472	121,155	109,198	97,806	87,439	79,431
Legal services	13,737	12,259	10,929	10,070	9,281	8,236
Educational services	16,822	15,899	15,328	13,880	12,382	11,377
Social services	4,445	3,743	3,825	3,492	2,931	2,623
Museums, botanical, zoological gardens	0	0	0	0	0	0
Membership organizations	9,548	9,067	8,810	8,350	8,439	7,399
Engineering and management services[7]	14,452	12,112	9,437	8,317	7,189	n.a.
Miscellaneous services	484	445	457	481	319	5,575
Government and government enterprises	214,474	196,338	189,461	162,415	150,442	139,170
Federal, civilian	23,036	21,670	20,033	18,739	18,489	15,244
Military	3,108	3,078	3,073	2,719	2,628	2,504
State and local	188,330	171,590	166,355	140,957	129,325	121,422

See Table 2.4 for notes.

(L) Less than $50,000. Estimates are included in totals.

Source: U.S. Department of Commerce, Bureau of Economic Analysis, Regional Economic Measurement Division, *Regional Economic Information System 1969–1992 CD-ROM.*

TABLE 2.9-- PERSONAL INCOME BY MAJOR SOURCE, JOHNSON CITY-KINGSPORT-BRISTOL METROPOLITAN STATISTICAL AREA, 1987-1992
[In thousands of dollars]

Source	1992	1991	1990[f]	1989[r]	1988[r]	1987[f]
INCOME BY PLACE OF RESIDENCE						
Total personal income	7,217,251	6,743,729	6,420,855	5,924,894	5,547,900	5,185,378
Nonfarm personal income	7,173,308	6,702,383	6,383,385	5,896,950	5,530,913	5,170,813
Farm income[1]	43,943	41,346	37,470	27,944	16,987	14,565
Population (thousands)[2]	445	440	437	437	437	437
Per capita personal income (dollars)	16,232	15,313	14,699	13,575	12,693	11,865
Derivation of total personal income						
Earnings by place of work	5,118,626	4,772,337	4,548,086	4,221,230	3,953,202	3,695,259
Less: personal cont. for social insur.[3]	341,016	322,863	300,035	268,277	254,787	220,776
Plus: adjustment for residence	88,537	82,673	87,745	75,006	66,601	60,725
Equals: net earn. by place of residence	4,866,147	4,532,147	4,335,796	4,027,959	3,765,016	3,535,208
Plus: dividends, interest, and rent[4]	973,126	966,993	965,624	876,973	812,274	744,203
Plus: transfer payments	1,377,978	1,244,589	1,119,435	1,019,962	970,610	905,967
EARNINGS BY PLACE OF WORK						
Components of earnings						
Wages and salaries	4,156,248	3,897,269	3,729,502	3,467,158	3,255,107	3,039,457
Other labor income	499,227	456,211	413,757	373,678	340,412	306,613
Proprietors' income[5]	463,151	418,857	404,827	380,394	357,683	349,189
Farm	34,151	31,165	27,131	18,984	8,618	7,164
Nonfarm	429,000	387,692	377,696	361,410	349,065	342,025
Earnings by industry						
Farm	43,943	41,346	37,470	27,944	16,987	14,565
Nonfarm	5,074,683	4,730,991	4,510,616	4,193,286	3,936,215	3,680,694
Private	4,414,033	4,104,436	3,913,923	3,635,793	3,410,982	3,183,002
Ag. serv., for., fish., and other[6]	(D)	(D)	12,858	11,386	11,135	11,743
Agricultural services	(D)	(D)	12,591	11,071	11,018	11,157
Forestry, fisheries, and other[6]	270	315	267	315	117	586
Forestry	159	205	177	247	(L)	532
Fisheries	111	110	90	68	92	54
Mining	(D)	(D)	9,529	9,529	11,483	7,067
Coal mining	923	964	(D)	(D)	(D)	(D)
Oil and gas extraction	(D)	(D)	(D)	(D)	(D)	(D)
Metal mining	(L)	(L)	(L)	(L)	(L)	(L)
Nonmetallic minerals, except fuels	(D)	(D)	(D)	(D)	(D)	(D)
Construction	282,128	257,868	230,414	216,587	207,486	192,387
General building contractors	113,262[e]	108,073[e]	86,908[e]	77,811[e]	80,503[e]	72,117[e]
Heavy construction contractors	31,663[e]	27,575[e]	24,112[e]	23,959[e]	21,639[e]	19,925[e]

TABLE 2.9-- PERSONAL INCOME BY MAJOR SOURCE, JOHNSON CITY-KINGSPORT-BRISTOL METROPOLITAN STATISTICAL AREA, 1987-1992
[In thousands of dollars] (Continued)

Source	1992	1991	1990[f]	1989[f]	1988[f]	1987[f]
Special trade contractors	134,350	120,272	117,474	113,064	103,455	98,575
Manufacturing	1,821,209	1,729,253	1,683,154	1,592,367	1,511,722	1,437,157
Nondurable goods	1,136,746	1,086,516	1,042,103	976,413	924,421	890,052
Food and kindred products	38,370[e]	39,482[e]	(D)	49,503[e]	(D)	(D)
Textile mill products	(D)	(D)	(D)	(D)	(D)	(D)
Apparel and other textile products	(D)	(D)	(D)	(D)	(D)	48,049[e]
Paper and allied products	(D)	(D)	(D)	(D)	(D)	(D)
Printing and publishing	126,535[e]	122,665[e]	120,518[e]	(D)	(D)	(D)
Chemicals and allied products	(D)	683,534[e]	(D)	(D)	(D)	(D)
Petroleum and coal products	163	151	673	(D)	478[e]	604
Tobacco manufactures	(D)	0	0	0	(D)	0
Rubber and misc. plastic products	(D)	(D)	(D)	(D)	(D)	(D)
Leather and leather products	(D)	(D)	(D)	(D)	(D)	(D)
Durable goods	684,463	642,737	641,051	615,954	587,301	547,105
Lumber and wood products	27,290	21,987	23,892	19,351	18,672	17,176
Furniture and fixtures	(D)	(D)	(D)	(D)	(D)	(D)
Primary metal industries	(D)	(D)	(D)	(D)	(D)	(D)
Fabricated metal products	(D)	(D)	(D)	(D)	(D)	(D)
Machinery, except electrical	(D)	(D)	(D)	(D)	(D)	(D)
Electric and electronic equipment	(D)	(D)	(D)	(D)	(D)	(D)
Trans. equip. excl. motor vehicles	73,234[e]	(D)	(D)	(D)	(D)	(D)
Motor vehicles and equipment	(D)	(D)	(D)	(D)	(D)	(D)
Stone, clay, and glass products	(D)	(D)	(D)	(D)	(D)	(D)
Instruments and related products	(D)	(D)	(D)	(D)	(D)	(D)
Misc. manufacturing industries	(D)	(D)	(D)	(D)	(D)	(D)
Transportation and public utilities	232,289	213,509	206,444	198,275	190,528	182,470
Railroad transportation	26,498[e]	24,395[e]	23,984	23,090	22,807	20,468
Trucking and warehousing	87,962	70,445	71,510	67,861	63,912	(D)
Water transportation	(D)	(D)	(D)	(D)	(D)	(D)
Other transportation	(D)	(D)	(D)	(D)	(D)	(D)
Local & interurban passenger transit	(D)	5,242	(D)	(D)	(D)	(D)
Transportation by air	3,498[e]	3,765[e]	3,398[e]	3,593[e]	3,938[e]	4,550[e]
Pipelines, except natural gas	0	0	0	0	0	0
Transportation services	4,274	(D)	(D)	(D)	2,633	2,438
Communication	(D)	(D)	78,118[e]	(D)	73,859[e]	(D)
Electric, gas, and sanitary services	247,096	252,049	234,721	206,786	191,711	183,499
Wholesale trade	530,509	490,414	481,468	453,535	432,231	401,704
Retail trade	(D)	(D)	(D)	(D)	(D)	(D)
Building materials and garden equipment	32,778	29,774	26,387[e]	28,479	26,630	24,555
General merchandise stores	71,109[e]	61,756[e]	61,511[e]	55,807[e]	51,399[e]	46,062[e]

TABLE 2.9-- PERSONAL INCOME BY MAJOR SOURCE, JOHNSON CITY-KINGSPORT-BRISTOL METROPOLITAN STATISTICAL AREA, 1987–1992

[In thousands of dollars] (Continued)

Source	1992	1991	1990[r]	1989[r]	1988[r]	1987[r]
Food stores	77,690	72,607	74,994	70,375	61,959	59,328
Automotive dealers & service stations	97,542	94,081	88,599	84,708	87,152	78,728
Apparel and accessory stores	21,781ᵉ	20,624ᵉ	19,630	17,919ᵉ	16,906ᵉ	17,110ᵉ
Home furniture and furnishings stores	26,482	25,171	31,381	32,308	31,354	29,809
Eating and drinking places	131,088	120,507	110,042	96,817	95,435	87,480
Miscellaneous retail	71,801	65,632	68,060	66,531	60,809	58,118
Finance, insurance, and real estate	163,481	147,172	142,719	132,130	119,210	110,816
Depository & non-dep. credit institutions	59,743ᵉ	51,146ᵉ	52,398ᵉ	(D)	(D)	(D)
Other finance, insur., & real estate	94,637ᵉ	86,892ᵉ	81,650ᵉ	(D)	(D)	60,827ᵉ
Security & commodity brokers & serv.	(D)	(D)	(D)	(D)	(D)	5,677
Insurance carriers	(D)	(D)	(D)	(D)	(D)	(D)
Insurance agents, brokers, & services	23,858	23,496	22,924ᵉ	21,412	22,412	18,956
Real estate	18,079	15,345ᵉ	15,741	(D)	8,258	5,969
Holding & other investment companies	(D)	(D)	(D)	(D)	(D)	(D)
Services	1,110,937	989,110	912,616	815,198	735,476	656,159
Hotels and other lodging places	16,652ᵉ	(D)	14,572ᵉ	14,159ᵉ	(D)	15,174ᵉ
Personal services	51,051	47,051	46,912	42,477	41,662	38,953
Private households	9,798	8,825	9,056	8,699	8,223	7,566ᵉ
Business services	119,107	105,182	92,787	89,573	81,763	81,999
Auto repair, services, and garages	23,400ᵉ	22,067ᵉ	20,806	19,877	21,890	22,641
Miscellaneous repair services	16,247	13,770	15,689	13,608	12,745	11,424
Amusement and recreation services	29,356	26,792	21,952ᵉ	16,099	16,238	12,114ᵉ
Motion pictures	5,693ᵉ	5,204ᵉ	(D)	(D)	(D)	(D)
Health services	606,422	526,095	469,815	410,500	367,236	329,598
Legal services	42,894	39,867	41,257	38,246	37,751	33,541
Educational services	(D)	(D)	23,981	(D)	(D)	(D)
Social services	21,979ᵉ	19,453ᵉ	16,138ᵉ	13,798ᵉ	12,722ᵉ	10,628ᵉ
Museums, botanical, zoological gardens	(D)	(D)	(D)	(D)	(D)	(D)
Membership organizations	42,755	41,058	40,368	39,940	37,733	34,628
Engineering and management services[7]	91,789	85,136	87,743	75,029	56,598	n.a.
Miscellaneous services	6,358ᵉ	5,110ᵉ	(D)	(D)	2,706	36,552
Government and government enterprises	660,650	626,555	596,693	557,493	525,233	497,692
Federal, civilian	138,208	127,249	116,240	107,523	107,568	100,905
Military	17,893	17,571	17,526	15,729	15,508	14,558
State and local	504,549	481,735	462,927	434,241	402,157	382,229

See Table 2.4 for notes.

e. The estimate shown here constitutes the major portion of the true estimate.

(L) Less than $50,000. Estimates are included in totals.

Source: U.S. Department of Commerce, Bureau of Economic Analysis, Regional Economic Measurement Division, *Regional Economic Information System 1969–1992* CD-ROM.

TABLE 2.10—PERSONAL INCOME BY MAJOR SOURCE, KNOXVILLE METROPOLITAN STATISTICAL AREA, 1987–1992 [In thousands of dollars]

Source	1992	1991	1990[r]	1989[r]	1988[r]	1987[r]
INCOME BY PLACE OF RESIDENCE						
Total personal income	11,210,975	10,345,551	9,699,487	9,104,108	8,648,524	7,972,283
Nonfarm personal income	11,191,176	10,328,997	9,680,774	9,088,231	8,635,981	7,956,413
Farm income[1]	19,799	16,554	18,713	15,877	12,543	15,870
Population (thousands)[2]	611	599	588	583	579	573
Per capita personal income (dollars)	18,364	17,272	16,498	15,616	14,939	13,921
Derivation of total personal income						
Earnings by place of work	8,324,954	7,612,909	7,199,111	6,840,040	6,476,874	5,910,978
Less: personal cont. for social insur.[3]	537,206	498,367	458,326	418,234	403,671	341,132
Plus: adjustment for residence	20,587	23,427	43,696	14,831	9,153	17,254
Equals: net earn. by place of residence[4]	7,808,335	7,137,969	6,784,481	6,436,657	6,082,356	5,587,100
Plus: dividends, interest, and rent[4]	1,575,230	1,560,964	1,447,056	1,339,267	1,293,008	1,185,942
Plus: transfer payments	1,827,410	1,646,618	1,467,950	1,328,184	1,273,160	1,199,241
EARNINGS BY PLACE OF WORK						
Components of earnings						
Wages and salaries	6,572,238	6,046,381	5,731,522	5,431,832	5,193,782	4,724,324
Other labor income	732,242	657,783	590,913	540,334	496,960	442,165
Proprietors' income[5]	1,020,474	908,745	876,676	867,874	786,132	744,489
Farm	5,190	1,445	3,218	2,483	(L)	4,750
Nonfarm	1,015,284	907,300	873,458	865,391	786,131	739,739
Earnings by industry						
Farm	19,799	16,554	18,713	15,877	12,543	15,870
Nonfarm	8,305,155	7,596,355	7,180,398	6,824,163	6,464,331	5,895,108
Private	7,041,916	6,364,971	6,002,473	5,717,622	5,340,784	4,834,998
Ag. serv., for., fish., and other[6]	26,513	24,424	21,199	17,440	16,161	15,769
Agricultural services	26,393	24,367	21,107	17,328	15,909	14,162^e
Forestry, fisheries, and other[6]	120	57	92	(D)	252	(D)
Forestry	178	107	(D)	(D)	(D)	(D)
Fisheries	-58	-50	42^e	-53^e	(D)	(D)
Mining	24,449	26,093	30,157	31,279	33,599	34,201
Coal mining	(D)	(D)	(D)	(D)	16,541	(D)
Oil and gas extraction	(D)	(D)	(D)	(D)	393^e	406^e
Metal mining	(D)	3,769^e	4,452^e	4,611^e	5,060^e	(D)
Nonmetallic minerals, except fuels	10,698^e	10,856^e	11,356^e	11,881^e	10,944^e	6,906^e
Construction	544,858	419,566	441,335	478,865	462,221	413,715
General building contractors	217,061^e	135,917^e	144,818^e	182,997^e	(D)	159,138^e
Heavy construction contractors	(D)	(D)	(D)	(D)	(D)	(D)

TABLE 2.10–PERSONAL INCOME BY MAJOR SOURCE, KNOXVILLE METROPOLITAN STATISTICAL AREA, 1987–1992 [In thousands of dollars] (Continued)

Source	1992	1991	1990[f]	1989[f]	1988[f]	1987[f]
Special trade contractors	247,517[e]	215,401[e]	(D)	(D)	(D)	184,466[e]
Manufacturing	1,680,302	1,578,623	1,508,851	1,470,388	1,400,932	1,295,597
Nondurable goods	534,578	476,449	456,597	445,923	453,596	428,183
Food and kindred products	86,716[e]	90,736[e]	92,811[e]	88,433[e]	86,823[e]	84,142[e]
Textile mill products	(D)	(D)	(D)	(D)	(D)	(D)
Apparel and other textile products	152,161[e]	135,759[e]	119,565[e]	124,036[e]	(D)	(D)
Paper and allied products	15,647	13,605	12,422	11,684	11,596[e]	11,387[e]
Printing and publishing	130,821[e]	111,381	108,129[e]	99,744	90,626	73,951
Chemicals and allied products	31,336[e]	38,351	(D)	31,639[e]	(D)	(D)
Petroleum and coal products	1,450[e]	(D)	1,416[e]	1,009[e]	1,265[e]	542[e]
Tobacco manufactures	0	0	0	0	0	0
Rubber and misc. plastic products	(D)	(D)	(D)	(D)	(D)	(D)
Leather and leather products	(D)	(D)	(D)	(D)	(D)	(D)
Durable goods	1,145,724	1,102,174	1,052,254	1,024,463	947,336	867,414
Lumber and wood products	46,966	44,768	44,596	42,890	44,237	39,566
Furniture and fixtures	(D)	(D)	(D)	(D)	(D)	(D)
Primary metal industries	175,384[e]	184,463	179,223[e]	171,690[e]	161,720[e]	145,968[e]
Fabricated metal products	(D)	(D)	(D)	(D)	(D)	(D)
Machinery, except electrical	73,355	68,667	70,037	71,539	63,531[e]	72,122[e]
Electric and electronic equipment	80,631[e]	71,372[e]	70,839[e]	65,775[e]	60,114[e]	61,039[e]
Trans. equip. excl. motor vehicles	(D)	(D)	(D)	(D)	(D)	(D)
Motor vehicles and equipment	(D)	(D)	(D)	(D)	(D)	(D)
Stone, clay, and glass products	(D)	(D)	(D)	(D)	(D)	(D)
Instruments and related products	87,547[e]	89,731[e]	85,018[e]	84,179[e]	75,365[e]	(D)
Misc. manufacturing industries	33,710	31,539	32,991[e]	37,826[e]	28,412[e]	27,185[e]
Transportation and public utilities	406,463	385,511	372,283	352,119	347,236	295,877
Railroad transportation	55,548	53,836	49,934	49,359	48,132	44,271[e]
Trucking and warehousing	158,447	147,686	147,027	145,924	157,738	111,313
Water transportation	(D)	(D)	(D)	(D)	(D)	(D)
Other transportation	47,808[e]	45,750[e]	(D)	(D)	(D)	34,646[e]
Local & interurban passenger transit	20,814	19,499	16,173[e]	(D)	(D)	16,158
Transportation by air	16,843[e]	16,934[e]	(D)	15,039[e]	12,179[e]	12,652[e]
Pipelines, except natural gas	0	0	(D)	(D)	0	(D)
Transportation services	10,633	9,743	8,564	7,556[e]	6,022[e]	6,178
Communication	(D)	(D)	(D)	(D)	(D)	(D)
Electric, gas, and sanitary services	(D)	(D)	95,032[e]	86,811[e]	(D)	(D)
Wholesale trade	556,126	524,769	490,815	474,406	450,470	405,880
Retail trade	886,877[e]	818,886[e]	794,130[e]	737,902[e]	709,385[e]	701,368
Building materials and garden equipment	67,230	59,380	54,724[e]	63,022	55,654[e]	50,442[e]
General merchandise stores	101,682[e]	95,934[e]	99,692[e]	92,723[e]	83,078[e]	84,630[e]
Food stores	86,286	80,397	76,068	84,551	80,292	75,285

TABLE 2.10--PERSONAL INCOME BY MAJOR SOURCE, KNOXVILLE METROPOLITAN STATISTICAL AREA, 1987-1992 [In thousands of dollars] (Continued)

Source	1992	1991	1990^r	1989^r	1988^r	1987^r
Automotive dealers & service stations	155,535	143,789	142,688	135,058	142,562	135,870
Apparel and accessory stores	63,291	54,940	46,677	32,277	29,636	26,387
Home furniture and furnishings stores	47,392^e	44,148^e	43,431^e	42,830^e	40,322^e	37,910^e
Eating and drinking places	247,625^e	228,353^e	209,213^e	193,725^e	187,107^e	163,832^e
Miscellaneous retail	170,166	159,395	155,348	136,288	122,947	112,889
Finance, insurance, and real estate	325,924	290,039	280,535	265,994	262,542	243,501
Depository & non-dep. credit institutions	121,914^e	102,982^e	108,114^e	99,759^e	(D)	93,406
Other finance, insur., & real estate	195,291^e	178,919^e	164,187^e	159,497^e	153,562^e	150,095
Security & commodity brokers & serv.	16,706^e	14,378^e	12,295^e	14,032^e	22,965^e	21,047
Insurance carriers	39,296^e	37,744^e	32,585^e	28,688^e	31,631^e	32,121^e
Insurance agents, brokers, & services	61,550	59,609	58,133	54,324	51,549	45,434
Real estate	73,838	60,629	55,619^e	58,543^e	46,067^e	36,710^e
Holding & other investment companies	(D)	(D)	(D)	5,564^e	(D)	15,811^e
Services	(D)	(D)	(D)	(D)	(D)	1,429,090
Hotels and other lodging places	114,539	104,726	99,253	98,238	90,269	89,885
Personal services	92,793	82,964	77,153	74,574	74,406	69,107
Private households	(D)	13,560	13,938	13,415	12,713	12,021
Business services	370,222	320,073	297,677	264,312	219,760	231,608
Auto repair, services, and garages	53,412	49,285	49,396	51,652	56,522	50,421
Miscellaneous repair services	29,786	26,268	25,868	23,871	21,564	20,346
Amusement and recreation services	86,664	76,414	65,147^e	53,709^e	48,954^e	41,131
Motion pictures	21,039	18,159	15,549^e	12,950^e	10,110^e	(D)
Health services	1,013,598	898,275	817,930	746,047	646,804	575,884
Legal services	152,962	140,903	133,131	126,559	105,901	90,473
Educational services	(D)	(D)	(D)	(D)	(D)	(D)
Social services	28,934	25,945	22,217^e	18,890^e	15,642^e	13,921^e
Museums, botanical, zoological gardens	3,015^e	(D)	(D)	1,729^e	1,722^e	(D)
Membership organizations	69,380	66,237	64,212	62,557	57,269	51,826
Engineering and management services[7]	395,207	(D)	(D)	(D)	(D)	n.a.
Miscellaneous services	9,540	8,927	(D)	9,699^e	(D)	(D)
Government and government enterprises	1,263,239	1,231,384	1,177,925	1,106,541	1,123,547	1,060,110
Federal, civilian	301,654	302,078	293,842	286,410	357,981	327,632
Military	26,564	26,137	26,000	22,911	22,060	21,135
State and local	935,021	903,169	858,083	797,220	743,506	711,343

See Table 2.4 for notes.

e. The estimate shown here constitutes the major portion of the true estimate.

(L) Less than $50,000. Estimates are included in totals.

Source: U.S. Department of Commerce, Bureau of Economic Analysis, *Regional Economic Information System 1969-1992* CD-ROM.

TABLE 2.11—PERSONAL INCOME BY MAJOR SOURCE, MEMPHIS METROPOLITAN STATISTICAL AREA, 1987–1992 [In thousands of dollars]

Source	1992	1991	1990[f]	1989[r]	1988[r]	1987[f]
INCOME BY PLACE OF RESIDENCE						
Total personal income	20,176,939	18,799,603	18,001,203	16,947,812	15,582,656	14,452,351
Nonfarm personal income	20,110,884	18,744,507	17,956,825	16,911,017	15,523,605	14,408,863
Farm income[1]	66,055	55,096	44,378	36,795	59,051	43,488
Population (thousands)[2]	1,034	1,021	1,010	1,002	995	983
Per capita personal income (dollars)	19,517	18,405	17,821	16,913	15,661	14,701
Derivation of total personal income						
Earnings by place of work	15,651,484	14,601,388	14,019,890	13,187,650	12,306,525	11,457,869
Less: personal cont. for social insur.[3]	1,002,066	948,704	890,140	801,411	768,895	666,336
Plus: adjustment for residence	-429,439	-405,250	-393,558	-353,250	-308,703	-306,633
Equals: net earn. by place of residence	14,219,979	13,247,434	12,736,192	12,032,989	11,228,927	10,484,900
Plus: dividends, interest, and rent[4]	2,410,497	2,392,099	2,500,774	2,445,169	2,007,962	1,818,072
Plus: transfer payments	3,546,463	3,160,070	2,764,237	2,469,654	2,345,767	2,149,379
EARNINGS BY PLACE OF WORK						
Components of earnings						
Wages and salaries	12,705,406	11,933,576	11,531,158	10,834,824	10,139,225	9,428,316
Other labor income	1,407,570	1,290,788	1,176,694	1,063,874	958,369	864,994
Proprietors' income[5]	1,538,508	1,377,024	1,312,038	1,288,952	1,208,931	1,164,559
Farm	44,525	32,036	21,289	17,086	40,948	27,765
Nonfarm	1,493,983	1,344,988	1,290,749	1,271,866	1,167,983	1,136,794
Earnings by industry						
Farm	66,055	55,096	44,378	36,795	59,051	43,488
Nonfarm	15,585,429	14,546,292	13,975,512	13,150,855	12,247,474	11,414,381
Private	13,114,177	12,110,821	11,649,658	10,992,815	10,235,041	9,524,496
Ag. serv., for., fish., and other[6]	60,488[e]	57,484[e]	50,881[e]	43,468[e]	40,616	40,117
Agricultural services	60,423[e]	57,368[e]	50,820[e]	43,395[e]	40,280	39,612
Forestry, fisheries, and other[6]	227	286	204	187	336	505
Forestry	158	214	(D)	(D)	(D)	317
Fisheries	69	72	(D)	(D)	(D)	188
Mining	(D)	6,765	5,923	6,242	1,651	(D)
Coal mining	426	391	404	388	(D)	2,267
Oil and gas extraction	1,136	744	339[e]	439	(D)	(D)
Metal mining	(D)	615	345	150	119	244
Nonmetallic minerals, except fuels	5,348	5,015	(D)	5,265	(D)	(D)
Construction	767,781	711,336	756,466	732,860	721,628	707,418
General building contractors	195,183	166,423	187,780	180,542	216,608	207,764
Heavy construction contractors	78,522	76,457	85,254	84,728	69,697	78,804

TABLE 2.11--PERSONAL INCOME BY MAJOR SOURCE, MEMPHIS METROPOLITAN STATISTICAL AREA, 1987-1992 [In thousands of dollars] (Continued)

Source	1992	1991	1990[f]	1989[f]	1988[f]	1987[f]
Special trade contractors	494,076	468,456	483,432	467,590	435,323	420,850
Manufacturing	2,287,669	2,145,253	2,074,573	1,997,671	1,834,211	1,678,309
Nondurable goods	1,369,491	1,238,130	1,187,333	1,115,600	1,051,031	975,417
Food and kindred products	284,713[e]	262,118[e]	249,295[e]	241,712[e]	243,453[e]	235,185[e]
Textile mill products	(D)	(D)	(D)	(D)	(D)	(D)
Apparel and other textile products	(D)	(D)	(D)	(D)	(D)	(D)
Paper and allied products	352,792[e]	320,175[e]	295,830[e]	284,849[e]	247,634[e]	188,541[e]
Printing and publishing	(D)	(D)	(D)	(D)	(D)	(D)
Chemicals and allied products	289,611[e]	268,708[e]	258,913[e]	245,235[e]	247,337[e]	265,231[e]
Petroleum and coal products	30,359[e]	32,097[e]	29,923[e]	22,907[e]	21,641[e]	20,789
Tobacco manufactures	23,897	15,794	(D)	(D)	(D)	(D)
Rubber and misc. plastic products	74,380	56,031[e]	52,068[e]	1,882[e]	(D)	38,033[e]
Leather and leather products	(D)	(D)	(D)	(D)	(D)	(D)
Durable goods	918,178	907,123	887,240	882,071	783,180	702,892
Lumber and wood products	58,560	60,439	64,342	74,854	72,499	67,168
Furniture and fixtures	(D)	(D)	(D)	(D)	(D)	(D)
Primary metal industries	(D)	(D)	(D)	(D)	(D)	(D)
Fabricated metal products	162,300[e]	160,660[e]	167,836[e]	156,520[e]	145,002[e]	130,431[e]
Machinery, except electrical	199,742[e]	217,090[e]	194,236[e]	226,646[e]	179,242[e]	135,174[e]
Electric and electronic equipment	139,641[e]	127,817[e]	119,120[e]	115,818[e]	103,483[e]	87,853[e]
Trans. equip. excl. motor vehicles	8,395	(D)	(D)	(D)	(D)	(D)
Motor vehicles and equipment	(D)	34,465[e]	(D)	(D)	(D)	(D)
Stone, clay, and glass products	(D)	(D)	(D)	(D)	41,277[e]	57,870[e]
Instruments and related products	107,920[e]	99,535[e]	91,619[e]	66,488[e]	61,036[e]	48,408[e]
Misc. manufacturing industries	37,429[e]	31,305[e]	34,676[e]	43,965[e]	26,827[e]	30,853[e]
Transportation and public utilities	1,927,739	1,802,683	1,718,917	1,575,317	1,411,410	1,293,807
Railroad transportation	66,618	61,291	61,306	66,518	65,611	67,056
Trucking and warehousing	(D)	(D)	(D)	(D)	367,970	335,494
Water transportation	20,361[e]	20,020[e]	19,389[e]	18,626[e]	15,583[e]	11,223[e]
Other transportation	(D)	(D)	(D)	(D)	787,739[e]	694,527[e]
Local & interurban passenger transit	37,380	35,617[e]	34,180[e]	33,531[e]	30,300	30,693[e]
Transportation by air	(D)	(D)	(D)	(D)	707,898[e]	616,102[e]
Pipelines, except natural gas	0	0	0	0	0	0
Transportation services	71,271	65,386	57,807	56,601	51,066	48,832
Communication	157,959	168,573	163,960	148,950	148,045	159,304[e]
Electric, gas, and sanitary services	34,799[e]	26,651[e]	25,117	22,582	23,628	21,849[e]
Wholesale trade	1,484,318	1,380,665	1,329,951	1,299,046	1,245,240	1,174,833
Retail trade	1,583,090	1,464,276	1,428,958	1,368,788	1,337,518	1,292,791
Building materials and garden equipment	59,307[e]	53,497[e]	48,408[e]	56,198[e]	56,703[e]	60,615[e]
General merchandise stores	150,261[e]	162,146[e]	150,504[e]	147,088[e]	144,808[e]	143,498[e]
Food stores	227,185	209,853	195,263	183,458	178,489	168,834

TABLE 2.11--PERSONAL INCOME BY MAJOR SOURCE, MEMPHIS METROPOLITAN STATISTICAL AREA, 1987-1992 [In thousands of dollars] (Continued)

Source	1992	1991	1990ᶠ	1989ᶠ	1988ᶠ	1987ᶠ
Automotive dealers & service stations	336,032	284,044	267,144	256,589	270,076	258,418
Apparel and accessory stores	95,197	84,765	81,061	77,339	76,769	73,064
Home furniture and furnishings stores	90,491	86,324	93,383	90,728	86,464	83,199
Eating and drinking places	380,148	352,212	337,829	308,825	300,283	288,438
Miscellaneous retail	236,432	223,724	235,864	234,646	211,270	210,376
Finance, insurance, and real estate	1,044,653e	934,377e	827,076e	817,546e	821,767e	782,635e
Depository & non-dep. credit institutions	353,884e	330,026e	288,534e	304,577e	300,668e	290,690e
Other finance, insur., & real estate	674,595e	588,088e	515,675e	498,335e	506,920e	485,711e
Security & commodity brokers & serv.	239,686e	184,490e	139,462e	128,411e	151,763e	170,671e
Insurance carriers	121,716e	119,170e	113,466e	107,359e	100,732e	96,739e
Insurance agents, brokers, & services	126,948	116,437	118,819	108,570	111,624	91,644
Real estate	154,730	151,425	134,708	139,364	124,610e	100,919e
Holding & other investment companies	43,405e	35,028e	26,882e	29,228e	32,938e	33,870
Services	3,927,626	3,588,843	3,439,081	3,134,554	2,801,339	2,543,381
Hotels and other lodging places	260,693e	260,079e	302,198e	267,212e	228,198e	233,808e
Personal services	150,018	134,359	138,562	127,112	126,133	118,078
Private households	53,344e	49,360	50,745	49,373	47,365	45,348
Business services	689,319	604,483	565,813	509,985	465,110	461,681
Auto repair, services, and garages	124,874	115,820	107,074	103,615	98,597	93,730
Miscellaneous repair services	57,249	52,071	55,309	48,391	45,848	42,206
Amusement and recreation services	105,961	99,594	(D)	(D)	58,648e	(D)
Motion pictures	23,637e	22,125e	20,312e	17,672e	14,937e	(D)
Health services	1,607,630	1,469,584	1,346,780	1,221,881	1,094,603	990,768
Legal services	211,672	186,892	177,040	165,175	153,260	137,254
Educational services	98,209e	94,927	85,654e	81,605e	75,985e	66,217e
Social services	67,755e	58,355e	52,915e	47,037e	40,268e	37,223e
Museums, botanical, zoological gardens	6,333	5,465	4,863	4,046	3,069	(D)
Membership organizations	124,108	119,590	119,590	113,829	103,706	94,440
Engineering and management services[7]	330,373	303,444	307,422	286,576	225,968	n.a.
Miscellaneous services	13,140	12,195	12,425	13,166	8,938	155,671
Government and government enterprises	2,471,252	2,435,471	2,325,854	2,158,040	2,012,433	1,889,885
Federal, civilian	651,447	678,305	648,236	589,390	549,622	500,235
Military	263,253	267,307	256,577	245,098	240,252	238,009
State and local	1,556,552	1,489,859	1,421,041	1,323,552	1,222,559	1,151,641

See Table 2.4 for notes.

e. The estimate shown here constitutes the major portion of the true estimate.

Source: U.S. Department of Commerce, Bureau of Economic Analysis, Regional Economic Measurement Division, *Regional Economic Information System 1969-1992* CD-ROM.

TABLE 2.12—PERSONAL INCOME BY MAJOR SOURCE, NASHVILLE-DAVIDSON METROPOLITAN STATISTICAL AREA, 1987–1992 [In thousands of dollars]

Source	1992	1991	1990[f]	1989[f]	1988[f]	1987[f]
INCOME BY PLACE OF RESIDENCE						
Total personal income	21,048,536	19,218,820	18,127,050	17,044,706	16,042,338	15,085,668
Nonfarm personal income	21,008,531	19,187,662	18,101,909	17,019,086	16,022,263	15,066,525
Farm income[1]	40,005	31,158	25,141	25,620	20,075	19,143
Population (thousands)[2]	1,023	1,004	989	974	958	944
Per capita personal income (dollars)	20,569	19,144	18,333	17,509	16,748	15,980
Derivation of total personal income						
Earnings by place of work	16,877,414	15,231,400	14,463,102	13,696,980	12,945,563	12,225,025
Less: personal cont. for social insur.[3]	1,089,835	1,000,107	924,423	834,664	813,144	714,382
Plus: adjustment for residence	-302,443	-268,874	-293,546	-283,871	-310,555	-299,737
Equals: net earn. by place of residence	15,485,136	13,962,419	13,245,133	12,578,445	11,821,864	11,210,906
Plus: dividends, interest, and rent[4]	2,836,223	2,808,374	2,717,307	2,517,194	2,338,133	2,118,001
Plus: transfer payments	2,727,177	2,448,027	2,164,610	1,949,067	1,882,341	1,756,761
EARNINGS BY PLACE OF WORK						
Components of earnings						
Wages and salaries	13,310,689	12,062,040	11,532,035	10,983,473	10,440,944	9,826,997
Other labor income	1,461,003	1,288,099	1,156,466	1,060,688	976,554	911,857
Proprietors' income[5]	2,105,722	1,881,261	1,774,601	1,652,819	1,528,065	1,486,171
Farm	27,105	17,788	11,476	13,784	9,107	9,428
Nonfarm	2,078,617	1,863,473	1,763,125	1,639,035	1,518,958	1,476,743
Earnings by industry						
Farm	40,005	31,158	25,141	25,620	20,075	19,143
Nonfarm	16,837,409	15,200,242	14,437,961	13,671,360	12,925,488	12,205,882
Private	14,876,450	13,327,381	12,628,737	11,981,071	11,335,167	10,774,714
Ag. serv., for., fish., and other[6]	(D)	52,613[e]	51,479	44,287	40,098[e]	40,204[e]
Agricultural services	(D)	52,221[e]	51,403	44,207	39,744[e]	39,479[e]
Forestry, fisheries, and other[6]	(D)	455	76	80	405	1,072
Forestry	(D)	500	111	179	(L)	726
Fisheries	(D)	(L)	(L)	-99	395	346
Mining	34,583[e]	31,086[e]	32,362	31,269	25,545[e]	
Coal mining	2,727[e]	2,728[e]	3,921[e]	2,923[e]	2,146[e]	431[e]
Oil and gas extraction	(D)	(D)	(D)	(D)	(D)	(D)
Metal mining	4,595	329	221	343	(D)	(D)
Nonmetallic minerals, except fuels	345	(D)	(D)	(D)	(D)	(D)
Construction	915,346	844,747	892,347	918,654	950,240	1,000,823
General building contractors	236,881	206,637	218,953	229,463	265,781	302,333
Heavy construction contractors	103,491	107,611	116,194	113,479	128,700	137,268

TABLE 2.12--PERSONAL INCOME BY MAJOR SOURCE, NASHVILLE-DAVIDSON METROPOLITAN STATISTICAL AREA, 1987-1992 [In thousands of dollars] (Continued)

Source	1992	1991	1990[f]	1989[f]	1988[f]	1987[f]
Special trade contractors	574,974	530,499	557,200	575,712	555,759	561,222
Manufacturing	3,093,075	2,761,156	2,651,396	2,577,434	2,452,150	2,422,586
Nondurable goods	1,210,046	1,103,833	1,055,826	1,009,797	945,213	915,515e
Food and kindred products	211,507e	198,648e	199,809e	193,182e	203,328e	191,740e
Textile mill products	60,349e	50,943e	47,961e	(D)	(D)	(D)
Apparel and other textile products	(D)	(D)	(D)	(D)	(D)	(D)
Paper and allied products	(D)	(D)	(D)	(D)	(D)	(D)
Printing and publishing	350,317e	324,199e	317,366e	295,455e	268,520e	241,524e
Chemicals and allied products	(D)	106,305	(D)	(D)	(D)	(D)
Petroleum and coal products	1,587e	1,495	1,323	1,899e	1,931e	2,612
Tobacco manufactures	24,831	20,918	(D)	(D)	(D)	(D)
Rubber and misc. plastic products	(D)	(D)	(D)	(D)	(D)	(D)
Leather and leather products	(D)	(D)	(D)	(D)	(D)	(D)
Durable goods	1,883,029	1,657,323	1,595,570	1,567,637	1,506,937	1,467,243e
Lumber and wood products	65,327	55,683	56,853	56,718	(D)	(D)
Furniture and fixtures	(D)	(D)	(D)	(D)	(D)	(D)
Primary metal industries	53,798e	51,381e	43,788e	37,746e	36,878e	31,850e
Fabricated metal products	256,591e	243,833e	223,117e	203,096e	184,887e	169,128e
Machinery, except electrical	251,191e	220,194e	226,733	212,685	192,218	154,721e
Electric and electronic equipment	(D)	(D)	(D)	(D)	(D)	(D)
Trans. equip. excl. motor vehicles	144,926e	138,196e	151,355e	140,853e	(D)	(D)
Motor vehicles and equipment	(D)	(D)	(D)	(D)	(D)	(D)
Stone, clay, and glass products	146,700e	150,244e	153,410e	170,906e	172,581e	153,902e
Instruments and related products	(D)	(D)	(D)	(D)	(D)	(D)
Misc. manufacturing industries	65,359e	(D)	(D)	(D)	(D)	(D)
Transportation and public utilities	1,138,092	1,056,402	970,417	925,215	878,440	862,101
Railroad transportation	49,021e	46,655	47,074	49,481	50,910	46,199
Trucking and warehousing	435,865	399,736	366,551	373,852	373,389	387,128
Water transportation	28,807e	(D)	(D)	(D)	(D)	(D)
Other transportation	30,138	(D)	(D)	(D)	14,186e	(D)
Local & interurban passenger transit	113,353e	106,341e	99,643e	(D)	19,879	(D)
Transportation by air	(D)	(D)	(D)	0	(D)	(D)
Pipelines, except natural gas	(D)	(D)	(D)	0	0	0
Transportation services	40,674e	37,565e	(D)	30,689	24,326	20,373
Communication	347,986e	331,630e	306,139e	273,125e	259,203e	259,580e
Electric, gas, and sanitary services	75,448e	70,469e	62,762e	59,837e	55,090e	50,740e
Wholesale trade	1,273,352	1,179,249	1,119,480	1,040,233	986,189	924,082
Retail trade	1,902,614	1,689,022	1,581,722	1,527,965	1,489,637	1,401,399
Building materials and garden equipment	(D)	77,977e	69,945e	(D)	70,108e	67,076e
General merchandise stores	248,845e	230,452e	212,567e	197,439e	183,121e	175,102e
Food stores	(D)	273,403	264,197	268,753	273,381	257,719

TABLE 2.12.--PERSONAL INCOME BY MAJOR SOURCE, NASHVILLE-DAVIDSON METROPOLITAN STATISTICAL AREA, 1987–1992 [In thousands of dollars]
(Continued)

Source	1992	1991	1990f	1989f	1988f	1987f
Automotive dealers & service stations	292,555	263,048	248,357	253,012	270,255	242,432
Apparel and accessory stores	102,105	96,696	100,175	91,882	87,911	85,599
Home furniture and furnishings stores	103,721	93,244	107,166	101,313	99,951	91,534
Eating and drinking places	533,664	436,753	349,668	313,360	291,893	281,362
Miscellaneous retail	231,926	213,159	211,473	210,709	198,058	186,906
Finance, insurance, and real estate	1,180,745	1,079,215	1,057,541	1,036,079	982,137	941,168
Depository & non-dep. credit institutions	313,164e	288,642e	279,457e	263,386e	256,378e	244,779e
Other finance, insur., & real estate	819,729e	702,341e	738,345e	731,000e	688,194e	686,752e
Security & commodity brokers & serv.	93,730	86,892	73,704e	77,095e	71,113e	69,644
Insurance carriers	311,015e	295,732e	309,373e	274,249e	249,488e	238,641e
Insurance agents, brokers, & services	221,046	198,285	195,339	181,105e	171,046	150,826e
Real estate	150,918	128,327e	139,131	147,080	130,286	131,648e
Holding & other investment companies	72,819e	52,347e	44,749e	74,302e	85,201e	99,931
Services	5,277,903	4,628,372	4,271,993	3,879,935	3,527,046	3,174,093
Hotels and other lodging places	164,439	159,283	162,908	153,504	140,498	132,889
Personal services	157,189	144,907	144,863	139,361	141,270	138,529
Private households	29,294	26,388	27,120	27,218	26,912	26,537
Business services	774,796	654,231	660,746	579,658	511,986	584,200
Auto repair, services, and garages	135,366	124,553	120,326	127,587	120,755	106,183
Miscellaneous repair services	67,080	61,184	55,397	52,098	51,487	46,681
Amusement and recreation services	508,164	466,910	375,524	283,975	257,987	207,191
Motion pictures	(D)	(D)	(D)	(D)	(D)	(D)
Health services	2,019,796	1,709,513	1,579,590	1,453,740	1,321,888	1,165,303
Legal services	247,886	232,816	215,705	200,223	184,429	167,126
Educational services	347,573	318,812	249,709	223,440	211,526	188,050
Social services	92,985	83,034	72,178	61,063	50,047	45,718
Museums, botanical, zoological gardens	6,151e	6,120e	5,764e	5,283e	4,647e	2,417e
Membership organizations	155,314	143,047	134,401	127,571	115,946	105,508
Engineering and management services[7]	515,313	444,836	413,294	393,084	345,783	n.a.
Miscellaneous services	24,081e	22,441e	23,138e	24,839e	18,890e	
Government and government enterprises	1,960,959	1,872,861	1,809,224	1,690,289	1,590,321	1,431,168
Federal, civilian	472,518	439,452	419,691	371,588	360,139	312,508
Military	58,376	56,307	54,301	48,081	45,360	43,982
State and local	1,430,065	1,377,102	1,335,232	1,270,620	1,184,822	1,074,678

See Table 2.4 for notes.

e. The estimate shown here constitutes the major portion of the true estimate.

(L) Less than $50,000. Estimates are included in totals.

Source: U.S. Department of Commerce, Bureau of Economic Analysis, Regional Economic Measurement Division, *Regional Economic Information System 1969–1992 CD-ROM.*

TABLE 2.13--TOTAL PERSONAL INCOME, RESIDENCE ADJUSTED, COUNTIES, 1970–1992, SELECTED YEARS [In millions of dollars]

County	1992	1991ʳ	1990ʳ	1989ʳ	1988ʳ	1987ʳ	1986ʳ	1985ʳ	1980ʳ	1970ʳ
Anderson	1,310.9	1,203.2	1,111.2	1,072.4	999.2	921.5	885.7	832.6	598.7	202.8
Bedford	494.8	457.7	441.6	432.4	401.3	372.2	342.6	313.1	209.6	79.5
Benton	210.2	208.0	189.4	180.8	168.1	155.2	147.2	139.2	105.7	32.1
Bledsoe	113.3	105.0	102.5	99.3	93.6	89.5	84.3	78.8	49.1	16.4
Blount	1,545.7	1,415.8	1,308.3	1,211.1	1,151.6	1,077.3	1,016.2	946.7	648.0	196.9
Bradley	1,280.9	1,172.6	1,124.6	1,079.4	982.5	904.6	833.8	773.0	494.7	159.1
Campbell	422.4	388.2	372.9	349.6	334.1	309.3	302.4	286.4	223.1	55.0
Cannon	160.7	146.1	136.6	127.9	117.1	110.6	105.8	96.5	65.5	21.0
Carroll	404.8	369.9	349.7	335.8	311.7	292.0	276.4	260.2	186.2	71.6
Carter	685.5	636.2	600.3	549.6	521.9	490.8	465.1	436.9	312.7	109.9
Cheatham	424.5	388.3	369.9	349.9	329.6	314.2	285.6	260.9	165.1	39.8
Chester	151.3	137.2	130.5	125.6	123.0	118.6	111.7	104.5	72.2	24.0
Claiborne	340.1	308.4	291.1	274.7	250.8	235.9	220.6	216.2	157.2	39.2
Clay	94.1	87.2	81.6	77.0	70.3	66.2	60.7	55.4	38.2	13.3
Cocke	395.5	354.2	328.5	300.6	277.8	258.0	238.8	223.1	166.5	56.1
Coffee	725.8	664.4	636.6	608.0	564.6	545.8	516.9	469.2	308.2	106.3
Crockett	215.0	192.4	178.3	167.9	155.7	154.0	130.3	120.1	84.7	40.7
Cumberland	486.3	445.6	430.9	399.0	363.4	349.1	320.1	289.1	181.9	47.1
Davidson	11,532.9	10,627.6	10,070.4	9,493.1	9,033.8	8,539.0	7,908.6	7,179.5	4,597.6	1,758.4
Decatur	132.4	121.6	116.0	111.8	105.3	102.8	98.9	94.1	67.0	23.4
DeKalb	224.2	205.0	191.5	177.7	180.7	168.7	152.5	136.0	91.1	27.9
Dickson	568.9	521.3	497.7	465.6	437.8	407.2	376.2	342.2	225.8	63.3
Dyer	567.6	524.6	516.9	497.2	458.6	402.0	378.8	360.5	244.0	88.5
Fayette	370.0	340.0	316.1	302.8	280.4	259.9	241.1	221.3	148.3	44.0
Fentress	184.1	167.3	150.8	143.7	131.9	121.4	116.0	107.6	70.0	22.9
Franklin	514.9	474.7	455.3	428.1	390.7	365.0	348.3	321.8	207.5	72.8
Gibson	741.6	672.1	641.0	622.1	598.7	561.5	524.4	502.2	335.4	144.4
Giles	426.0	391.6	364.6	344.2	318.8	301.8	282.4	264.7	183.9	62.0
Grainger	211.6	190.7	180.7	169.5	153.5	140.8	129.6	121.9	83.9	28.6
Greene	793.8	750.0	731.9	690.6	636.4	600.1	570.1	533.7	351.0	119.5
Grundy	156.2	146.1	137.3	134.0	121.4	114.0	113.0	105.6	82.7	22.8
Hamblen	823.8	755.2	720.9	676.3	617.7	565.9	525.9	490.6	332.1	115.0
Hamilton	5,730.4	5,385.2	5,268.0	4,946.4	4,655.0	4,294.3	3,952.3	3,656.9	2,611.0	959.2
Hancock	68.3	60.7	56.3	52.2	49.1	47.2	43.7	41.6	30.8	12.3
Hardeman	311.6	290.2	270.7	256.1	240.9	227.9	201.5	186.5	134.8	43.9
Hardin	303.0	277.2	260.2	239.6	223.6	215.5	199.4	183.5	142.3	40.1
Hawkins	678.6	626.6	590.4	532.6	502.3	468.9	416.2	391.3	261.4	82.8
Haywood	293.7	263.0	238.4	223.6	220.8	214.3	187.5	168.4	121.4	43.6
Henderson	306.8	280.4	269.7	257.4	238.9	226.3	212.9	198.2	132.9	45.8
Henry	431.1	393.9	380.7	357.8	333.9	318.2	307.2	293.0	215.4	61.3
Hickman	223.7	208.3	196.7	187.2	175.9	172.9	162.8	150.3	97.1	30.8
Houston	83.5	80.1	74.8	69.9	66.2	62.9	57.8	53.0	44.0	15.0
Humphreys	222.5	208.7	198.7	190.2	180.5	167.4	160.3	150.5	125.3	37.5
Jackson	116.5	107.1	102.1	94.7	86.5	83.5	77.3	71.1	46.0	15.5
Jefferson	490.2	453.1	431.4	405.0	363.4	337.0	312.2	292.1	201.1	60.0
Johnson	151.6	142.3	132.3	119.8	113.5	106.3	102.5	100.4	75.9	24.3
Knox	6,813.1	6,323.0	5,936.7	5,566.9	5,337.9	4,905.6	4,522.0	4,163.0	2,798.8	920.9
Lake	87.0	74.4	74.8	67.7	66.0	55.2	54.9	54.0	42.9	17.8
Lauderdale	321.7	286.3	273.7	262.5	260.9	238.6	217.7	207.1	139.0	45.9
Lawrence	553.0	508.1	464.8	422.7	395.2	373.8	353.4	333.9	244.7	71.5
Lewis	123.7	110.2	101.5	93.9	86.1	79.1	76.0	74.2	48.1	15.8
Lincoln	425.4	388.8	385.9	366.4	335.8	309.9	289.0	268.7	185.0	64.1
Loudon	517.6	478.0	456.6	431.8	399.7	370.3	340.7	313.2	214.6	66.8

TABLE 2.13--TOTAL PERSONAL INCOME, RESIDENCE ADJUSTED, COUNTIES, 1970–1992,
SELECTED YEARS [In millions of dollars] (Continued)

County	1992	1991[r]	1990[r]	1989[r]	1988[r]	1987[r]	1986[r]	1985[r]	1980[r]	1970[r]
McMinn	626.9	585.0	574.5	546.4	504.1	468.9	453.7	422.9	289.2	97.0
McNairy	315.9	292.1	282.6	269.7	254.1	236.8	218.6	207.9	135.5	41.4
Macon	222.8	201.4	189.0	174.9	165.0	156.6	144.9	132.3	94.7	32.3
Madison	1,391.2	1,266.7	1,205.5	1,098.0	1,031.1	964.1	894.4	826.5	564.4	193.8
Marion	351.1	329.9	314.6	291.8	277.8	257.7	249.9	238.0	164.7	49.7
Marshall	397.8	356.0	331.4	304.9	280.4	256.0	240.5	226.6	146.5	51.5
Maury	986.7	886.9	801.6	736.1	672.6	627.0	598.0	543.4	390.6	137.5
Meigs	106.1	97.9	94.8	86.6	82.6	77.5	72.4	68.4	47.3	11.8
Monroe	395.4	361.1	340.0	325.9	304.9	275.8	261.8	243.5	165.4	53.7
Montgomery	1,635.4	1,413.3	1,318.3	1,281.8	1,184.8	1,101.4	1,012.8	937.5	621.0	204.9
Moore	67.0	62.4	59.5	56.8	54.2	51.1	48.2	46.5	30.6	9.4
Morgan	206.8	187.5	172.9	161.3	142.0	125.8	117.3	111.4	89.2	25.6
Obion	533.0	481.7	486.2	458.1	448.0	406.2	391.7	364.6	232.6	93.7
Overton	212.3	195.3	185.7	174.9	164.5	149.3	139.0	128.9	84.7	29.6
Perry	85.8	78.3	74.8	71.9	67.0	61.8	60.2	56.7	38.0	11.9
Pickett	59.1	55.2	50.4	46.7	41.0	37.8	35.2	32.8	19.9	8.6
Polk	182.8	169.2	160.0	150.2	140.4	139.6	137.1	127.5	87.7	32.3
Putnam	850.6	784.2	745.6	725.5	670.8	603.4	556.3	506.1	321.2	89.4
Rhea	329.5	305.4	299.1	276.1	266.7	260.1	246.6	236.0	170.7	41.0
Roane	770.3	709.9	674.2	639.1	593.5	543.3	522.0	508.1	403.8	110.2
Robertson	687.4	622.9	592.3	557.6	518.2	487.8	448.1	412.5	254.6	84.6
Rutherford	2,301.1	2,046.8	1,909.3	1,787.8	1,642.6	1,557.7	1,410.4	1,244.1	667.2	158.7
Scott	223.9	206.3	196.8	183.4	174.2	157.1	156.4	146.4	106.6	28.3
Sequatchie	121.7	113.4	104.9	96.1	88.0	83.3	79.1	72.5	50.6	14.1
Sevier	861.0	779.4	750.3	696.7	645.1	591.0	540.8	489.4	300.9	75.8
Shelby	17,274.4	16,118.2	15,459.8	14,595.0	13,391.6	12,438.0	11,506.8	10,628.5	7,329.9	2,583.2
Smith	219.1	203.4	192.9	185.6	172.3	158.1	150.0	141.8	109.8	32.5
Stewart	127.0	119.3	111.0	104.9	97.4	92.8	87.2	80.5	52.3	22.5
Sullivan	2,609.9	2,458.2	2,347.6	2,144.4	2,019.2	1,887.0	1,829.4	1,711.1	1,191.1	442.5
Sumner	1,922.0	1,765.8	1,687.6	1,573.7	1,468.0	1,367.3	1,273.1	1,159.7	720.8	184.0
Tipton	590.0	542.8	507.3	457.7	434.1	400.5	361.5	333.1	231.1	71.7
Trousdale	74.3	68.0	64.9	61.7	57.5	55.3	49.9	46.9	43.5	14.7
Unicoi	248.6	230.5	220.2	205.8	191.6	176.9	168.7	154.2	110.6	41.0
Union	162.8	146.2	136.3	125.2	115.1	106.6	99.0	92.9	63.1	18.3
Van Buren	49.7	46.2	45.2	43.6	41.0	39.7	37.5	35.8	26.2	6.8
Warren	485.8	446.2	430.6	415.4	386.9	354.7	326.5	301.2	241.9	76.8
Washington	1,632.8	1,501.5	1,426.8	1,333.4	1,237.4	1,156.0	1,093.1	1,010.9	715.0	232.6
Wayne	181.9	161.5	148.6	140.5	131.7	128.7	121.8	116.5	86.9	27.5
Weakley	471.1	426.7	414.3	401.7	371.4	342.4	328.2	303.8	212.4	78.3
White	270.9	248.8	238.4	231.1	223.4	207.5	196.7	187.2	136.8	39.2
Williamson	2,317.9	2,088.5	1,900.1	1,778.8	1,643.2	1,504.8	1,346.8	1,179.5	639.9	125.2
Wilson	1,293.7	1,157.7	1,099.9	1,038.1	969.2	907.7	832.3	756.1	478.6	118.2

r revised.

Source: U.S. Department of Commerce, Bureau of Economic Analysis, Regional Economic Measurement
Division, *Regional Economic Information System 1969–1992* CD-ROM.

FIGURE 2.2

Per Capita Personal Income, Tennessee Counties, 1992

(Tennessee Per Capita Personal Income = $17,674)

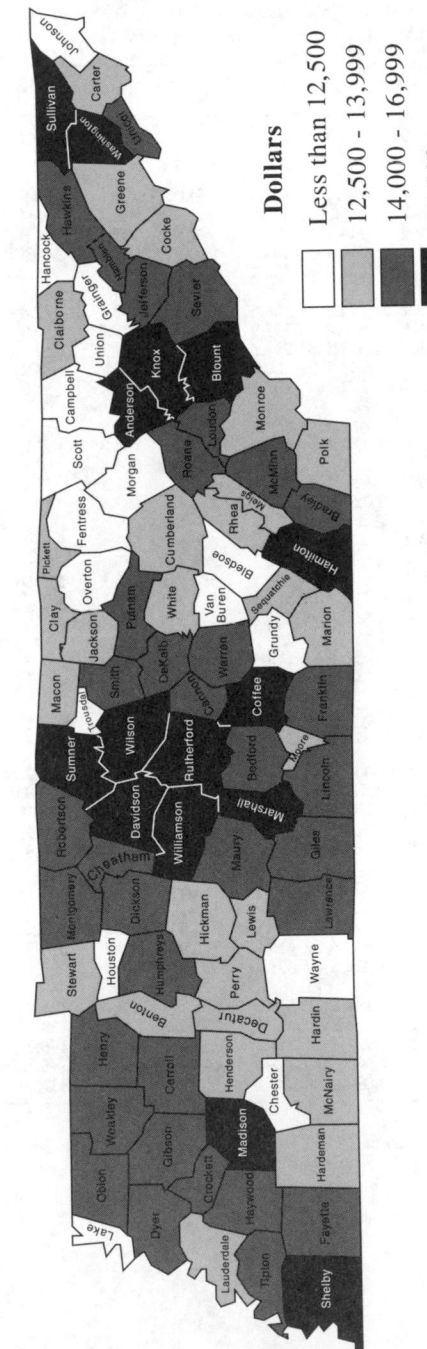

Dollars

Less than 12,500

12,500 - 13,999

14,000 - 16,999

17,000 or more

Source: U.S. Department of Commerce, Bureau of Economic Analysis, Regional Economic Measurement Division, Regional Economic Information System 1969–1992 CD-ROM.

TABLE 2.14--PER CAPITA PERSONAL INCOME, RESIDENCE ADJUSTED, TENNESSEE AND
COUNTIES, 1980-1992, SELECTED YEARS [In dollars]

County	1992	1991^r	1990^r	1989^r	1988^r	1987^r	1986^r	1985^r	1984^r	1983^r	1980^r
Anderson	18,587	17,366	16,244	15,759	14,747	13,669	13,235	12,431	11,815	10,842	8,870
Bedford	15,589	14,738	14,461	14,299	13,372	12,515	11,575	10,732	10,238	8,980	7,506
Benton	13,945	14,024	12,989	12,401	11,470	10,589	9,964	9,345	8,907	7,868	7,087
Bledsoe	11,588	10,791	10,587	10,299	9,750	9,261	8,814	8,384	7,826	6,813	5,181
Blount	17,098	16,015	15,156	14,180	13,605	12,905	12,352	11,606	11,163	10,217	8,314
Bradley	16,868	15,648	15,210	14,742	13,543	12,676	11,757	10,965	10,301	9,464	7,304
Campbell	11,846	10,969	10,604	9,943	9,478	8,797	8,466	8,027	7,873	7,385	6,375
Cannon	14,944	13,746	13,001	12,228	11,208	10,547	10,184	9,223	8,926	7,799	6,389
Carroll	14,643	13,370	12,685	12,170	11,259	10,544	9,994	9,306	9,455	8,443	6,585
Carter	13,176	12,279	11,636	10,674	10,143	9,501	9,035	8,499	8,091	7,552	6,210
Cheatham	14,743	13,863	13,541	13,139	12,704	12,449	11,779	11,105	10,393	9,356	7,624
Chester	11,673	10,663	10,171	9,795	9,593	9,162	8,775	8,185	7,824	6,931	5,688
Claiborne	12,559	11,575	11,115	10,512	9,603	9,153	8,545	8,202	7,967	7,259	6,373
Clay	13,016	12,119	11,292	10,591	9,600	9,031	8,232	7,407	6,727	6,004	4,980
Cocke	13,412	12,095	11,261	10,323	9,549	8,908	8,223	7,678	7,450	6,761	5,770
Coffee	17,429	16,166	15,722	15,116	14,095	13,693	13,019	11,908	11,128	9,823	8,002
Crockett	16,180	14,356	13,330	12,438	11,404	11,132	9,320	8,535	8,521	7,011	5,714
Cumberland	13,234	12,363	12,324	11,667	10,853	10,672	10,096	9,293	8,797	7,923	6,321
Davidson	22,273	20,721	19,700	18,688	17,920	16,966	15,955	14,670	13,517	12,205	9,618
Decatur	12,739	11,639	11,086	10,622	9,932	9,532	9,072	8,593	8,189	7,467	6,161
DeKalb	15,320	14,138	13,294	12,403	12,650	11,886	10,718	9,666	9,305	7,547	6,686
Dickson	15,583	14,528	14,108	13,478	12,932	12,326	11,647	10,908	10,012	9,119	7,496
Dyer	16,287	15,059	14,796	14,289	13,210	11,752	11,114	10,538	9,998	8,609	7,032
Fayette	14,233	13,190	12,343	11,877	11,037	10,243	9,627	8,861	8,408	7,348	5,856
Fentress	12,345	11,322	10,297	9,761	8,917	8,192	7,744	7,194	6,588	5,721	4,716
Franklin	14,586	13,518	13,085	12,402	11,412	10,767	10,308	9,670	8,925	8,078	6,477
Gibson	15,986	14,511	13,816	13,355	12,758	11,866	10,990	10,480	10,070	8,648	6,784
Giles	15,975	14,892	14,135	13,428	12,508	11,974	11,266	10,501	10,427	9,159	7,473
Grainger	11,910	10,908	10,533	9,915	8,984	8,299	7,576	7,134	6,800	6,010	5,003
Greene	13,867	13,266	13,073	12,359	11,386	10,711	10,141	9,513	8,896	8,033	6,431
Grundy	11,590	10,877	10,250	9,979	8,976	8,294	8,245	7,588	7,512	6,977	5,978
Hamblen	15,948	14,865	14,230	13,343	12,122	11,181	10,293	9,372	8,800	7,801	6,712
Hamilton	19,853	18,731	18,443	17,373	16,416	15,235	14,164	13,115	12,213	11,299	9,052
Hancock	10,150	9,147	8,344	7,729	7,255	6,883	6,496	6,056	5,683	5,041	4,466
Hardeman	13,111	12,339	11,579	10,951	10,294	9,740	8,628	8,008	7,524	6,778	5,656
Hardin	12,891	11,929	11,466	10,605	9,924	9,596	8,930	8,193	7,623	7,136	6,371
Hawkins	14,767	13,834	13,230	11,959	11,292	10,592	9,407	8,780	8,027	7,407	5,949
Haywood	15,080	13,527	12,278	11,468	11,285	10,835	9,459	8,522	7,888	6,620	5,971
Henderson	13,861	12,810	12,318	11,796	10,968	10,420	9,794	9,112	8,669	7,572	6,203
Henry	15,221	14,051	13,632	12,795	11,901	11,296	10,827	10,312	10,504	8,956	7,499
Hickman	12,728	12,057	11,667	11,252	10,673	10,673	10,104	9,511	8,802	7,707	6,393
Houston	11,640	11,369	10,672	9,992	9,500	9,067	8,436	7,721	7,506	6,733	6,380
Humphreys	14,022	13,213	12,582	12,042	11,432	10,696	10,149	9,607	9,413	8,510	7,838
Jackson	12,791	11,636	10,907	10,199	9,327	8,992	8,397	7,727	7,008	6,157	4,896
Jefferson	14,100	13,345	13,028	12,284	11,043	10,300	9,542	8,942	8,290	7,651	6,400
Johnson	9,966	9,482	9,582	8,678	8,186	7,598	7,285	7,184	6,644	6,368	5,505
Knox	19,601	18,491	17,634	16,628	16,008	14,845	13,784	12,597	11,747	10,662	8,727
Lake	11,911	10,498	10,514	9,417	9,098	7,425	7,305	7,028	6,468	5,990	5,740
Lauderdale	13,611	12,181	11,642	11,145	11,038	10,046	9,100	8,642	8,168	7,125	5,666
Lawrence	15,177	14,139	13,134	12,001	11,256	10,715	10,129	9,621	9,356	8,110	7,161
Lewis	12,592	11,475	10,918	10,107	9,207	8,440	8,065	7,726	6,787	5,803	4,916
Lincoln	14,951	13,727	13,689	13,084	12,081	11,310	10,593	9,935	9,186	8,020	6,993
Loudon	15,569	14,818	14,530	13,906	12,985	12,151	11,291	10,408	10,072	8,953	7,478

2. INCOME AND PRICES

TABLE 2.14--PER CAPITA PERSONAL INCOME, RESIDENCE ADJUSTED, TENNESSEE AND
COUNTIES, 1980-1992, SELECTED YEARS [In dollars] (Continued)

County	1992	1991[r]	1990[r]	1989[r]	1988[r]	1987[r]	1986[r]	1985[r]	1984[r]	1983[r]	1980[r]
McMinn	14,394	13,663	13,535	12,896	11,906	11,036	10,729	9,989	9,487	8,682	6,881
McNairy	13,999	12,908	12,572	12,030	11,339	10,544	9,751	9,273	8,222	7,409	5,997
Macon	13,630	12,492	11,864	11,024	10,436	9,954	9,191	8,431	8,285	7,179	5,998
Madison	17,340	16,032	15,418	14,108	13,286	12,472	11,555	10,696	10,287	9,204	7,546
Marion	13,878	13,126	12,640	11,786	11,281	10,494	10,189	9,864	8,913	8,143	6,729
Marshall	17,315	15,844	15,239	14,246	13,220	12,125	11,622	11,016	10,905	9,353	7,424
Maury	16,517	15,257	14,496	13,505	12,438	11,639	11,251	10,359	9,979	9,007	7,628
Meigs	12,611	11,852	11,709	10,890	10,529	10,099	9,583	9,199	8,820	7,988	6,350
Monroe	12,602	11,685	11,108	10,710	10,075	9,141	8,725	8,209	7,699	7,099	5,751
Montgomery	14,868	13,704	12,976	12,971	12,269	11,756	10,980	10,480	9,898	8,941	7,419
Moore	13,659	12,944	12,613	12,034	11,470	11,014	10,417	9,630	9,385	8,375	6,760
Morgan	11,675	10,763	9,974	9,379	8,332	7,387	6,984	6,752	6,517	6,529	5,343
Obion	16,889	15,199	15,309	14,386	13,995	12,545	12,078	11,149	10,660	9,069	7,089
Overton	11,920	10,992	10,510	9,916	9,324	8,476	7,957	7,312	6,858	6,080	4,814
Perry	12,579	11,612	11,270	10,929	10,259	9,628	9,397	8,710	8,600	7,662	6,199
Pickett	12,970	12,169	11,050	10,290	9,054	8,287	7,721	7,299	6,426	5,707	4,547
Polk	13,152	12,291	11,694	11,023	10,320	10,262	10,086	9,482	8,931	8,162	6,434
Putnam	16,000	15,011	14,446	14,198	13,225	12,023	11,169	10,198	9,467	8,429	6,709
Rhea	13,040	12,354	12,265	11,355	10,991	10,781	10,173	9,818	9,163	8,661	7,032
Roane	16,016	14,874	14,274	13,499	12,497	11,425	10,904	10,520	10,227	9,968	8,325
Robertson	15,714	14,584	14,202	13,598	12,849	12,276	11,585	10,871	9,974	8,565	6,851
Rutherford	17,875	16,492	15,948	15,454	14,691	14,520	13,754	12,622	11,472	10,236	7,878
Scott	11,888	11,095	10,706	9,920	9,331	8,248	8,099	7,537	7,146	6,422	5,508
Sequatchie	13,245	12,575	11,784	10,856	9,958	9,484	9,038	8,271	7,753	6,897	5,871
Sevier	15,749	14,671	14,612	13,881	13,154	12,322	11,559	10,617	10,014	8,983	7,222
Shelby	20,447	19,281	18,671	17,734	16,364	15,361	14,347	13,267	12,550	11,450	9,408
Smith	15,210	14,185	13,607	13,089	12,112	11,027	10,510	10,009	9,516	8,378	7,349
Stewart	12,524	12,371	11,697	11,120	10,400	9,985	9,435	8,725	8,141	7,047	6,027
Sullivan	17,794	16,956	16,321	14,929	14,055	13,130	12,760	11,965	11,083	10,465	8,255
Sumner	17,807	16,737	16,270	15,462	14,718	14,008	13,431	12,578	11,681	10,514	8,363
Tipton	15,044	14,090	13,393	12,333	11,898	11,221	10,356	9,748	9,206	8,415	6,993
Trousdale	12,491	11,458	10,955	10,458	9,784	9,446	8,695	8,276	8,555	7,213	7,089
Unicoi	14,808	13,926	13,313	12,415	11,541	10,700	10,097	9,206	9,031	8,486	6,744
Union	11,579	10,473	9,915	9,271	8,676	8,265	7,811	7,400	6,934	6,221	5,369
Van Buren	10,157	9,421	9,318	8,992	8,434	8,155	7,614	7,223	6,883	6,212	5,532
Warren	14,510	13,344	13,020	12,632	11,822	10,822	10,057	9,250	9,005	8,258	7,404
Washington	17,199	15,985	15,405	14,435	13,386	12,583	11,918	10,883	10,374	9,580	8,022
Wayne	11,965	11,430	10,641	10,070	9,426	9,167	8,657	8,312	8,233	7,263	6,219
Weakley	14,753	13,341	12,931	12,522	11,529	10,628	10,107	9,225	8,752	7,632	6,448
White	13,221	12,250	11,836	11,530	11,185	10,463	9,907	9,575	9,058	8,107	6,967
Williamson	26,149	24,524	23,221	22,455	21,398	20,287	18,895	17,333	15,814	14,140	10,933
Wilson	18,181	16,618	16,174	15,571	14,843	14,257	13,556	12,501	11,719	10,576	8,506
TENNESSEE	17,674	16,524	15,903	15,074	14,177	13,315	12,492	11,579	10,876	9,850	8,010

r revised.

Source: U.S. Department of Commerce, Bureau of Economic Analysis, Regional Economic Measurement
Division, *Regional Economic Information System 1969-1992* CD-ROM.

TABLE 2.15--PER CAPITA MONEY INCOME, MEDIAN FAMILY INCOME AND MEDIAN HOUSEHOLD
INCOME, TENNESSEE AND COUNTIES, 1989 [In dollars]

Counties	Per capita money income	Median family income	Median household income
Anderson	13,182	31,690	26,496
Bedford	11,311	27,891	23,613
Benton	10,046	24,181	20,382
Bledsoe	8,053	21,941	18,250
Blount	12,674	30,277	25,575
Bradley	11,768	30,372	25,678
Campbell	8,098	20,151	16,450
Cannon	9,863	27,481	22,847
Carroll	10,121	25,088	20,763
Carter	9,809	22,520	19,140
Cheatham	11,868	33,373	30,778
Chester	8,281	24,679	19,413
Claiborne	8,371	19,993	17,132
Clay	8,753	21,228	17,799
Cocke	8,574	20,644	16,818
Coffee	11,416	28,778	24,802
Crockett	10,636	24,577	20,296
Cumberland	9,782	23,498	20,474
Davidson	15,195	34,785	28,377
Decatur	9,345	22,134	17,925
DeKalb	9,570	22,956	19,388
Dickson	11,162	28,792	24,419
Dyer	11,270	28,115	22,105
Fayette	9,627	26,715	22,199
Fentress	6,927	16,405	13,924
Franklin	10,513	27,731	23,438
Gibson	10,277	25,535	20,938
Giles	10,983	26,912	22,078
Grainger	8,415	21,697	19,097
Greene	10,161	25,600	21,513
Grundy	7,227	19,555	16,425
Hamblen	11,127	27,325	23,853
Hamilton	13,619	32,185	26,523
Hancock	6,266	14,745	11,822
Hardeman	8,650	22,165	19,128
Hardin	9,654	21,812	17,719
Hawkins	10,358	26,402	21,960
Haywood	8,696	22,081	17,376
Henderson	9,564	25,507	21,099
Henry	10,423	22,753	18,891
Hickman	9,723	25,678	21,567
Houston	9,060	23,629	20,112
Humphreys	10,614	26,965	22,256
Jackson	9,159	21,834	18,081
Jefferson	10,562	26,133	22,219
Johnson	7,531	18,024	14,967
Knox	14,007	32,614	26,010
Lake	8,285	20,730	16,804
Lauderdale	8,607	22,516	18,972
Lawrence	10,094	25,197	20,842

TABLE 2.15--PER CAPITA MONEY INCOME, MEDIAN FAMILY INCOME AND MEDIAN HOUSEHOLD
INCOME, TENNESSEE AND COUNTIES, 1989 [In dollars] (Continued)

Counties	Per capita money income	Median family income	Median household income
Lewis	8,180	20,901	17,362
Lincoln	10,704	27,140	21,996
Loudon	12,006	28,712	24,258
McMinn	10,508	26,207	21,901
McNairy	9,185	22,920	18,715
Macon	10,158	22,739	19,147
Madison	11,655	29,273	23,716
Marion	9,274	24,178	20,045
Marshall	11,248	29,089	23,855
Maury	11,942	31,095	26,238
Meigs	9,237	22,605	20,181
Monroe	9,080	22,999	19,932
Montgomery	11,056	27,848	25,568
Moore	11,545	30,524	28,056
Morgan	7,722	22,163	19,280
Obion	11,096	27,448	22,344
Overton	8,622	21,586	18,293
Perry	9,260	21,782	19,039
Pickett	9,564	18,379	14,993
Polk	9,311	23,934	21,663
Putnam	11,004	27,015	21,693
Rhea	9,333	23,789	19,915
Roane	12,015	28,262	24,210
Robertson	12,077	32,341	28,687
Rutherford	12,536	36,035	30,878
Scott	7,803	18,637	15,858
Sequatchie	9,377	23,228	19,223
Sevier	10,848	26,340	23,042
Shelby	13,330	32,671	27,132
Smith	10,950	27,393	23,255
Stewart	9,935	24,497	20,802
Sullivan	12,725	30,167	25,089
Sumner	13,497	36,212	31,795
Tipton	9,796	27,389	23,860
Trousdale	9,618	23,514	20,127
Unicoi	10,727	26,283	20,536
Union	8,351	22,544	19,595
Van Buren	8,186	23,242	20,676
Warren	10,472	25,900	21,019
Washington	11,949	29,701	23,698
Wayne	8,240	21,565	18,429
Weakley	9,857	26,206	21,004
White	9,299	24,147	19,874
Williamson	19,339	48,332	43,615
Wilson	13,681	36,861	32,852
TENNESSEE	12,255	29,546	24,807

Source: U.S. Department of Commerce, Bureau of the Census, *Census of Population and Housing, 1990:
Summary Tape File 3A, Tennessee.*

TABLE 2.16—POVERTY STATUS OF FAMILIES AND PERSONS, TENNESSEE AND COUNTIES, 1989

	Anderson	Bedford	Benton	Bledsoe	Blount	Bradley	Campbell	Cannon
Total families	20,018	8,861	4,286	2,498	25,379	21,607	10,191	3,102
Below poverty level								
Number	2,299	1,143	590	408	2,530	2,432	2,280	374
% of total families	11.5	12.9	13.8	16.3	10.0	11.3	22.4	12.1
Total families with related children under 18 years	9,447	4,398	1,905	1,305	11,650	10,786	5,166	1,525
Below poverty level								
Number	1,702	771	354	232	1,728	1,658	1,680	196
% of families with related children under 18 years	18.0	17.5	18.6	17.8	14.8	15.4	32.5	12.9
Total female householder families	2,862	1,253	468	257	3,058	2,792	1,618	314
Below poverty level								
Number	1,018	490	171	94	929	893	684	99
% of total female householder families	35.6	39.1	36.5	36.6	30.4	32.0	42.3	31.5
With related children under 18 years	1,743	819	214	120	1,754	1,727	911	192
Number	853	414	132	60	761	740	561	69
% of female householder families with related children under 18 years	48.9	50.5	61.7	50.0	43.4	42.8	61.6	35.9
Total persons for whom poverty status is determined	67,535	30,012	14,255	8,605	84,354	72,059	34,688	10,325
Persons 18 years and over below poverty level	6,430	3,102	1,753	1,178	7,156	6,618	5,955	1,123
% of persons 18 years and over for whom poverty status is determined	12.5	13.9	16.0	18.4	11.0	12.2	23.1	14.4
Persons 65 years and over below poverty level	1,296	1,077	552	318	1,627	1,632	1,097	448
% of persons 65 years and over for whom poverty status is determined	12.8	24.8	23.0	28.6	13.7	20.8	22.2	29.7
Total related children under 18 years	16,050	7,658	3,264	2,187	19,359	17,677	8,812	2,546
Below poverty level								
Number	3,206	1,648	697	448	3,230	3,214	3,302	368
% of total related children under 18 years	20.0	21.5	21.4	20.5	16.7	18.2	37.5	14.5

TABLE 2.16--POVERTY STATUS OF FAMILIES AND PERSONS, TENNESSEE AND COUNTIES, 1989 (Continued)

	Carroll	Carter	Cheatham	Chester	Claiborne	Clay	Cocke	Coffee
Total families	8,225	15,075	7,741	3,480	7,639	2,137	8,554	11,786
Below poverty level								
Number	989	2,190	636	522	1,658	401	1,813	1,456
% of total families	12.0	14.5	8.2	15.0	21.7	18.8	21.2	12.4
Total families with related children under 18 years	3,908	6,920	4,294	1,623	3,875	1,029	4,223	5,886
Below poverty level								
Number	576	1,368	439	349	1,072	232	1,139	1,009
% of families with related children under 18 years	14.7	19.8	10.2	21.5	27.7	22.5	27.0	17.1
Total female householder families	1,090	1,960	757	409	971	305	1,536	1,490
Below poverty level								
Number	303	698	229	181	387	113	624	412
% of total female householder families	27.8	35.6	30.3	44.3	39.9	37.0	40.6	27.7
With related children under 18 years	638	1,034	493	206	568	181	903	1,003
Below poverty level								
Number	251	522	173	143	324	101	487	360
% of female householder families with related children under 18 years	39.3	50.5	35.1	69.4	57.0	55.8	53.9	35.9
Total persons for whom poverty status is determined	26,795	50,174	26,827	11,774	25,490	7,148	28,790	39,814
Persons 18 years and over below poverty level	3,077	6,532	2,043	1,548	4,480	1,180	4,957	4,052
% of persons 18 years and over for whom poverty status is determined	15.1	16.8	10.6	17.6	23.7	21.5	22.6	13.8
Persons 65 years and over below poverty level	1,249	1,859	401	490	1,026	426	1,345	1,208
% of persons 65 years and over for whom poverty status is determined	27.0	25.0	18.0	28.4	31.8	38.5	37.4	22.6
Total related children under 18 years	6,435	11,169	7,436	2,983	6,553	1,657	6,838	10,361
Below poverty level								
Number	1,160	2,460	832	668	2,049	454	2,294	1,990
% of total related children under 18 years	18.0	22.0	11.2	22.4	31.3	27.4	33.5	19.2

TABLE 2.16--POVERTY STATUS OF FAMILIES AND PERSONS, TENNESSEE AND COUNTIES, 1989 (Continued)

	Crockett	Cumberland	Davidson	Decatur	DeKalb	Dickson	Dyer	Fayette
Total families	3,879	10,481	132,152	3,115	4,342	10,082	9,991	6,741
Below poverty level								
Number	515	1,485	13,244	501	708	1,216	1,403	1,197
% of total families	13.3	14.2	10.0	16.1	16.3	12.1	14.0	17.8
Total families with related children under 18 years	1,846	4,767	66,246	1,376	2,040	5,345	5,198	3,767
Below poverty level								
Number	299	964	10,522	276	432	863	998	842
% of families with related children under 18 years	16.2	20.2	15.9	20.1	21.2	16.1	19.2	22.4
Total female householder families	511	1,279	29,072	377	611	1,499	1,577	1,252
Below poverty level								
Number	141	432	8,781	154	218	484	615	456
% of total female householder families	27.6	33.8	30.2	40.8	35.7	32.3	39.0	36.4
With related children under 18 years	336	821	19,332	215	329	1,072	1,046	859
Below poverty level								
Number	121	330	7,918	123	140	435	519	364
% of female householder families with related children under 18 years	36.0	40.2	41.0	57.2	42.6	40.6	49.6	42.4
Total persons for whom poverty status is determined	13,045	34,166	489,347	10,302	14,208	34,599	34,314	25,019
Persons 18 years and over below poverty level	1,668	4,133	40,973	1,561	2,102	3,443	4,135	3,691
% of persons 18 years and over for whom poverty status is determined	17.0	15.9	10.9	19.6	19.5	13.7	16.2	20.9
Persons 65 years and over below poverty level	638	1,101	8,154	614	586	1,069	1,305	909
% of persons 65 years and over for whom poverty status is determined	27.6	19.4	14.5	32.6	26.7	25.9	26.7	29.0
Total related children under 18 years	3,197	8,058	113,289	2,313	3,394	9,419	8,705	7,347
Below poverty level								
Number	623	2,003	21,965	481	786	1,820	1,882	2,308
% of total related children under 18 years	19.5	24.9	19.4	20.8	23.2	19.3	21.6	31.4

TABLE 2.16–POVERTY STATUS OF FAMILIES AND PERSONS, TENNESSEE AND COUNTIES, 1989 (Continued)

	Fentress	Franklin	Gibson	Giles	Grainger	Greene	Grundy	Hamblen
Total families	4,264	9,789	13,494	7,442	5,023	16,451	3,690	14,897
Below poverty level								
Number	1,164	1,134	1,610	967	848	2,127	775	1,659
% of total families	27.3	11.6	11.9	13.0	16.9	12.9	21.0	11.1
Total families with related children under 18 years	2,193	4,812	6,375	3,606	2,439	7,792	2,017	7,175
Below poverty level								
Number	750	745	1,054	661	517	1,273	516	1,107
% of families with related children under 18 years	34.2	15.5	16.5	18.3	21.2	16.3	25.6	15.4
Total female householder families	670	1,123	2,170	1,004	599	2,250	458	2,122
Below poverty level								
Number	277	405	637	416	198	635	210	740
% of total female householder families	41.3	36.1	29.4	41.4	33.1	28.2	45.9	34.9
With related children under 18 years	405	631	1,320	624	343	1,311	265	1,294
Below poverty level								
Number	226	335	560	368	136	466	181	627
% of female householder families with related children under 18 years	55.8	53.1	42.4	59.0	39.7	35.5	68.3	48.5
Total persons for whom poverty status is determined	14,534	33,288	45,577	25,328	16,873	54,835	13,111	49,710
Persons 18 years and over below poverty level	3,207	3,324	5,050	2,767	2,406	6,722	2,088	4,650
% of persons 18 years and over for whom poverty status is determined	29.8	13.4	14.6	14.6	18.8	15.9	22.1	12.3
Persons 65 years and over below poverty level	734	972	1,806	1,004	591	1,685	447	1,222
% of persons 65 years and over for whom poverty status is determined	38.3	20.5	22.6	25.0	28.5	23.1	25.4	21.1
Total related children under 18 years	3,763	8,381	10,840	6,348	4,044	12,350	3,646	11,771
Below poverty level								
Number	1,479	1,449	2,293	1,366	1,047	2,495	1,040	2,230
% of total related children under 18 years	39.3	17.3	21.2	21.5	25.9	20.2	28.5	18.9

TABLE 2.16--POVERTY STATUS OF FAMILIES AND PERSONS, TENNESSEE AND COUNTIES, 1989 (Continued)

	Hamilton	Hancock	Hardeman	Hardin	Hawkins	Haywood	Henderson	Henry
Total families	79,031	1,940	6,206	6,676	13,396	5,263	6,593	8,322
Below poverty level								
Number	8,047	657	1,141	1,142	1,920	1,271	837	1,199
% of total families	10.2	33.9	18.4	17.1	14.3	24.1	12.7	14.4
Total families with related children under 18 years	38,951	924	3,439	3,173	6,438	2,985	3,184	3,691
Below poverty level								
Number	6,013	392	820	657	1,260	886	472	772
% of families with related children under 18 years	15.4	42.4	23.8	20.7	19.6	29.7	14.8	20.9
Total female householder families	14,431	297	1,388	882	1,523	1,318	913	1,200
Below poverty level								
Number	4,823	160	580	398	493	601	267	476
% of total female householder families	33.4	53.9	41.8	45.1	32.4	45.6	29.2	39.7
With related children under 18 years	9,370	167	1,047	488	985	939	532	735
Below poverty level								
Number	4,056	109	533	306	411	520	223	376
% of female householder families with related children under 18 years	43.3	65.3	50.9	62.7	41.7	55.4	41.9	51.2
Total persons for whom poverty status is determined	278,587	6,560	22,576	22,301	44,193	19,297	21,592	27,457
Persons 18 years and over below poverty level	23,897	1,782	3,309	3,105	5,520	3,415	2,434	3,643
% of persons 18 years and over for whom poverty status is determined	11.3	36.6	20.7	18.5	16.4	24.9	15.0	17.1
Persons 65 years and over below poverty level	5,634	464	853	1,018	1,535	1,093	947	1,134
% of persons 65 years and over for whom poverty status is determined	15.6	45.4	28.0	31.2	27.3	36.4	30.3	21.9
Total related children under 18 years	67,621	1,686	6,548	5,484	10,393	5,546	5,385	6,184
Below poverty level								
Number	12,428	842	1,938	1,354	2,343	1,870	955	1,534
% of total related children under 18 years	18.4	49.9	29.6	24.7	22.5	33.7	17.7	24.8

TABLE 2.16--POVERTY STATUS OF FAMILIES AND PERSONS, TENNESSEE AND COUNTIES, 1989 (Continued)

	Hickman	Houston	Humphreys	Jackson	Jefferson	Johnson	Knox	Lake
Total families	4,608	2,047	4,587	2,777	9,488	4,230	91,357	1,753
Below poverty level Number	608	316	495	432	1,123	1,008	9,336	400
% of total families	13.2	15.4	10.8	15.6	11.8	23.8	10.2	22.8
Total families with related children under 18 years	2,236	966	2,152	1,233	4,242	1,981	43,633	927
Below poverty level Number	360	195	351	200	666	615	6,839	302
% of families with related children under 18 years	16.1	20.2	16.3	16.2	15.7	31.0	15.7	32.6
Total female householder families	470	253	583	376	1,005	656	15,032	324
Below poverty level Number	189	117	181	136	320	296	4,689	193
% of total female householder families	40.2	46.2	31.0	36.2	31.8	45.1	31.2	59.6
With related children under 18 years	297	163	338	172	554	375	9,001	234
Below poverty level Number	148	90	161	73	231	231	3,938	169
% of female householder families with related children under 18 years	49.8	55.2	47.6	42.4	41.7	61.6	43.8	72.2
Total persons for whom poverty status is determined	15,642	6,833	15,630	9,196	31,415	13,590	323,827	6,036
Persons 18 years and over below poverty level	1,913	920	1,493	1,448	3,491	2,731	31,840	1,067
% of persons 18 years and over for whom poverty status is determined	16.3	17.8	12.7	20.4	14.3	26.2	12.8	23.7
Persons 65 years and over below poverty level	545	315	376	524	1,008	729	6,056	229
% of persons 65 years and over for whom poverty status is determined	24.7	28.3	17.1	34.8	24.1	34.0	14.9	24.9
Total related children under 18 years	3,915	1,672	3,890	2,074	7,006	3,142	73,747	1,518
Below poverty level Number	904	354	743	376	1,230	1,140	13,447	580
% of total related children under 18 years	23.1	21.2	19.1	18.1	17.6	36.3	18.2	38.2

TABLE 2.16—POVERTY STATUS OF FAMILIES AND PERSONS, TENNESSEE AND COUNTIES, 1989 (Continued)

	Lauderdale	Lawrence	Lewis	Lincoln	Loudon	McMinn	McNairy	Macon
Total families	6,440	10,268	2,563	8,315	9,403	12,501	6,697	4,769
Below poverty level								
Number	1,196	1,287	446	888	1,002	1,784	1,076	738
% of total families	18.6	12.5	17.4	10.7	10.7	14.3	16.1	15.5
Total families with related children under 18 years	3,523	5,069	1,331	4,010	4,394	6,167	3,255	2,263
Below poverty level								
Number	779	721	289	523	663	1,221	643	425
% of families with related children under 18 years	22.1	14.2	21.7	13.0	15.1	19.8	19.8	18.8
Total female householder families	1,305	1,246	264	967	1,195	1,810	813	575
Below poverty level								
Number	572	340	128	259	324	644	317	186
% of total female householder families	43.8	27.3	48.5	26.8	27.1	35.6	39.0	32.3
With related children under 18 years	960	686	206	613	674	1,123	497	326
Below poverty level								
Number	493	265	110	214	296	579	230	161
% of female householder families with related children under 18 years	51.4	38.6	53.4	34.9	43.9	51.6	46.3	49.4
Total persons for whom poverty status is determined	22,494	34,948	9,050	27,835	30,875	41,586	22,157	15,785
Persons 18 years and over below poverty level	3,300	3,748	1,358	2,866	2,899	4,818	3,251	2,112
% of persons 18 years and over for whom poverty status is determined	20.4	14.5	20.3	13.7	12.3	15.3	19.5	17.9
Persons 65 years and over below poverty level	1,202	1,342	421	1,123	846	1,347	1,136	734
% of persons 65 years and over for whom poverty status is determined	36.5	27.1	31.7	26.5	19.6	23.7	33.5	32.4
Total related children under 18 years	6,263	9,109	2,365	6,858	7,304	10,108	5,442	3,954
Below poverty level								
Number	1,728	1,576	537	1,061	1,285	2,279	1,218	924
% of total related children under 18 years	27.6	17.3	22.7	15.5	17.6	22.5	22.4	23.4

TABLE 2.16--POVERTY STATUS OF FAMILIES AND PERSONS, TENNESSEE AND COUNTIES, 1989 (Continued)

	Madison	Marion	Marshall	Maury	Meigs	Monroe	Montgomery	Moore
Total families	21,418	7,296	6,167	15,687	2,295	8,839	27,211	1,417
Below poverty level								
Number	3,050	1,184	590	1,722	424	1,341	2,937	83
% of total families	14.2	16.2	9.6	11.0	18.5	15.2	10.8	5.9
Total families with related children under 18 years	11,317	3,869	3,122	8,140	1,161	4,424	15,250	663
Below poverty level								
Number	2,245	803	406	1,128	270	841	2,127	29
% of families with related children under 18 years	19.8	20.8	13.0	13.9	23.3	19.0	13.9	4.4
Total female householder families	4,668	942	841	2,546	275	1,175	3,869	81
Below poverty level								
Number	1,890	358	258	849	100	372	1,505	10
% of total female householder families	40.5	38.0	30.7	33.3	36.4	31.7	38.9	12.3
With related children under 18 years	3,238	588	534	1,633	160	627	2,595	28
Below poverty level								
Number	1,645	304	227	696	81	313	1,261	0
% of female householder families with related children under 18 years	50.8	51.7	42.5	42.6	50.6	49.9	48.6	0.0
Total persons for whom poverty status is determined	75,507	24,609	21,257	53,940	7,907	29,851	93,281	4,700
Persons 18 years and over below poverty level	8,220	3,147	1,879	4,900	1,241	3,602	7,451	257
% of persons 18 years and over for whom poverty status is determined	14.9	17.3	11.8	12.3	21.0	16.2	11.1	7.3
Persons 65 years and over below poverty level	2,262	804	734	1,419	264	978	1,282	113
% of persons 65 years and over for whom poverty status is determined	22.4	27.5	23.4	21.0	29.5	24.7	17.0	17.4
Total related children under 18 years	20,150	6,416	5,342	13,976	1,979	7,555	26,293	1,183
Below poverty level								
Number	4,590	1,599	884	2,210	510	1,671	4,447	49
% of total related children under 18 years	22.8	24.9	16.5	15.8	25.8	22.1	16.9	4.1

TABLE 2.16–POVERTY STATUS OF FAMILIES AND PERSONS, TENNESSEE AND COUNTIES, 1989 (Continued)

	Morgan	Obion	Overton	Perry	Pickett	Polk	Putnam	Rhea
Total families	4,628	9,267	5,274	1,927	1,385	4,011	14,029	6,976
Below poverty level								
Number	733	1,081	760	300	285	570	1,789	1,103
% of total families	15.8	11.7	14.4	15.6	20.6	14.2	12.8	15.8
Total families with related children under 18 years	2,470	4,487	2,399	909	696	1,901	6,602	3,567
Below poverty level								
Number	468	683	372	157	175	362	1,001	749
% of families with related children under 18 years	18.9	15.2	15.5	17.3	25.1	19.0	15.2	21.0
Total female householder families	662	1,273	602	203	152	402	1,589	1,049
Below poverty level								
Number	228	381	171	52	82	90	545	451
% of total female householder families	34.4	29.9	28.4	25.6	53.9	22.4	34.3	43.0
With related children under 18 years	357	725	241	110	104	216	958	717
Below poverty level								
Number	155	315	83	44	70	70	406	402
% of female householder families with related children under 18 years	43.4	43.4	34.4	40.0	67.3	32.4	42.4	56.1
Total persons for whom poverty status is determined	15,973	31,369	17,454	6,458	4,483	13,536	48,268	23,618
Persons 18 years and over below poverty level	2,165	3,333	2,203	821	783	1,628	6,064	3,016
% of persons 18 years and over for whom poverty status is determined	18.7	14.2	16.7	17.0	23.1	15.9	16.3	17.2
Persons 65 years and over below poverty level	554	1,257	815	280	270	479	1,676	746
% of persons 65 years and over for whom poverty status is determined	28.8	26.5	31.5	28.0	37.2	25.4	26.7	23.4
Total related children under 18 years	4,389	7,784	4,206	1,636	1,087	3,253	11,016	6,079
Below poverty level								
Number	1,025	1,413	907	377	332	817	1,903	1,447
% of total related children under 18 years	23.4	18.2	21.6	23.0	30.5	25.1	17.3	23.8

TABLE 2.16--POVERTY STATUS OF FAMILIES AND PERSONS, TENNESSEE AND COUNTIES, 1989 (Continued)

	Roane	Robertson	Rutherford	Scott	Sequatchie	Sevier	Shelby	Smith
Total families	14,166	11,959	31,285	5,160	2,566	15,116	213,632	4,127
Below poverty level								
Number	1,728	1,092	2,378	1,271	510	1,554	31,314	487
% of total families	12.2	9.1	7.6	24.6	19.9	10.3	14.7	11.8
Total families with related children under 18 years	6,653	6,332	17,757	2,932	1,295	7,121	119,158	1,985
Below poverty level								
Number	1,145	686	1,656	908	322	987	24,953	254
% of families with related children under 18 years	17.2	10.8	9.3	31.0	24.9	13.9	20.9	12.8
Total female householder families	1,804	1,402	3,911	755	334	1,760	56,508	408
Below poverty level								
Number	566	499	1,085	327	135	437	21,631	139
% of total female householder families	31.4	35.6	27.7	43.3	40.4	24.8	38.3	34.1
With related children under 18 years	1,073	945	2,712	493	219	980	39,706	230
Below poverty level								
Number	470	415	985	291	125	306	19,042	97
% of female householder families with related children under 18 years	43.8	43.9	36.3	59.0	57.1	31.2	48.0	42.2
Total persons for whom poverty status is determined	46,656	40,960	113,316	18,090	8,724	50,348	801,199	13,959
Persons 18 years and over below poverty level	5,246	2,935	8,745	3,242	1,395	4,696	86,858	1,500
% of persons 18 years and over for whom poverty status is determined	14.7	9.9	10.7	25.3	21.4	12.2	15.0	14.4
Persons 65 years and over below poverty level	1,406	930	1,885	588	294	1,244	16,813	581
% of persons 65 years and over for whom poverty status is determined	20.9	19.8	20.4	28.6	28.8	20.3	20.5	27.3
Total related children under 18 years	10,920	11,116	31,421	5,211	2,191	11,919	222,191	3,528
Below poverty level								
Number	2,193	1,348	3,448	1,741	607	1,894	59,385	521
% of total related children under 18 years	20.1	12.1	11.0	33.4	27.7	15.9	26.7	14.8

TABLE 2.16—POVERTY STATUS OF FAMILIES AND PERSONS, TENNESSEE AND COUNTIES, 1989 (Continued)

	Stewart	Sullivan	Sumner	Tipton	Trousdale	Unicoi	Union	Van Buren
Total families	2,860	42,468	29,758	10,496	1,738	4,914	4,132	1,446
Below poverty level								
Number	345	4,405	2,079	1,645	245	626	753	233
% of total families	12.1	10.4	7.0	15.7	14.1	12.7	18.2	16.1
Total families with related children under 18 years	1,255	19,122	16,225	6,078	871	2,139	2,145	710
Below poverty level								
Number	167	2,958	1,401	1,287	152	388	466	162
% of families with related children under 18 years	13.3	15.5	8.6	21.2	17.5	18.1	21.7	22.8
Total female householder families	223	5,213	3,312	1,714	236	632	481	187
Below poverty level								
Number	54	1,672	771	878	74	181	204	74
% of total female householder families	24.2	32.1	23.3	51.2	31.4	28.6	42.4	39.6
With related children under 18 years	116	2,939	2,111	1,164	157	280	268	104
Below poverty level								
Number	32	1,281	668	729	64	117	133	55
% of female householder families with related children under 18 years	27.6	43.6	31.6	62.6	40.8	41.8	49.6	52.9
Total persons for whom poverty status is determined	9,323	141,577	102,448	37,196	5,799	16,325	13,568	4,839
Persons 18 years and over below poverty level	1,223	13,224	6,405	4,345	750	2,021	1,973	622
% of persons 18 years and over for whom poverty status is determined	16.7	12.1	8.6	16.8	17.0	15.9	19.8	17.3
Persons 65 years and over below poverty level	381	3,138	1,898	1,033	265	649	479	174
% of persons 65 years and over for whom poverty status is determined	24.2	15.9	18.8	26.8	28.7	24.2	32.9	29.5
Total related children under 18 years	2,006	31,809	27,925	11,376	1,397	3,578	3,593	1,246
Below poverty level								
Number	307	5,830	2,854	3,095	276	736	894	307
% of total related children under 18 years	15.3	18.3	10.2	27.2	19.8	20.6	24.9	24.6

TABLE 2.16--POVERTY STATUS OF FAMILIES AND PERSONS, TENNESSEE AND COUNTIES, 1989 (Continued)

	Warren	Washington	Wayne	Weakley	White	Williamson	Wilson	TENNESSEE
Total families	9,707	25,401	4,144	8,592	5,975	23,452	19,779	1,356,342
Below poverty level								
Number	1,341	2,890	617	945	841	1,000	1,308	168,182
% of total families	13.8	11.4	14.9	11.0	14.1	4.3	6.6	12.4
Total families with related children under 18 years	4,760	11,794	2,065	4,030	2,771	13,261	10,541	687,078
Below poverty level								
Number	862	1,987	395	614	443	579	852	117,828
% of families with related children under 18 years	18.1	16.8	19.1	15.2	16.0	4.4	8.1	17.1
Total female householder families	1,231	3,719	463	1,007	713	2,250	2,190	227,322
Below poverty level								
Number	417	1,135	135	346	263	344	533	78,055
% of total female householder families	33.9	30.5	29.2	34.4	36.9	15.3	24.3	34.3
With related children under 18 years	743	2,049	244	590	401	1,312	1,400	146,258
Below poverty level								
Number	335	899	120	292	183	279	435	66,148
% of female householder families with related children under 18 years	45.1	43.9	49.2	49.5	45.6	21.3	31.1	45.2
Total persons for whom poverty status is determined	32,565	87,891	13,714	29,375	19,862	80,230	67,147	4,743,685
Persons 18 years and over below poverty level	3,789	9,503	1,793	3,339	2,504	3,194	3,936	493,412
% of persons 18 years and over for whom poverty status is determined	15.5	14.0	17.5	14.9	16.7	5.6	8.0	13.9
Persons 65 years and over below poverty level	1,149	1,953	523	1,050	821	984	1,097	122,767
% of persons 65 years and over for whom poverty status is determined	24.9	16.7	27.3	22.3	26.6	15.6	17.3	20.9
Total related children under 18 years	8,094	19,893	3,468	6,970	4,830	23,160	18,203	1,193,453
Below poverty level								
Number	1,658	4,112	768	1,187	830	1,375	1,886	247,366
% of total related children under 18 years	20.5	20.7	22.1	17.0	17.2	5.9	10.4	20.7

Notes on following page.

TABLE 2.16--POVERTY STATUS OF FAMILIES AND PERSONS, TENNESSEE AND COUNTIES, 1989 (Continued)

Note: Classification of families by poverty status varies according to family size, age and place of residence. Data for state and substate levels are available only from the decennial census. The latest data are for 1989. However, poverty thresholds are updated annually to reflect changes in the annual average Consumer Price Index and are published in *Current Population Reports*, Consumer Income, Series P-60.

Poverty thresholds for selected categories

Year	Family of four	Single person 65 and over	Two persons, householder 65 and over
1991	$13,924	$6,532	$8,241
1990	13,359	6,268	7,905
1989	12,675	5,947	7,501
1988	12,092	5,674	7,158
1987	11,612	5,447	6,872
1986	11,203	5,255	6,630
1985	10,989	5,156	6,503
1984	10,609	4,979	6,282
1983	10,178	4,775	6,023
1982	9,862	4,626	5,836
1981	9,287	4,359	5,498
1980	8,414	3,941	4,954
1979	7,412	3,479	4,390

Source: U.S. Department of Commerce, Bureau of the Census, *Census of Population and Housing, 1990: Summary Tape File 3A, Tennessee;* and *Current Population Reports,* Series P-60, No. 181, and earlier editions.

TABLE 2.17--PER CAPITA MONEY INCOME, MEDIAN FAMILY INCOME, MEDIAN HOUSEHOLD
INCOME, AND PERCENT OF PERSONS AND FAMILIES BELOW POVERTY,
MUNICIPALITIES AND CENSUS DESIGNATED PLACES, TENNESSEE, 1989

Places	Per capita income	Median family income	Median household income	Persons below poverty %	Families below poverty %
Adams	$10,202	$30,125	$22,000	11.1	7.1
Adamsville	9,846	22,316	18,316	16.2	12.7
Alamo	9,064	21,739	16,622	24.9	16.8
Alcoa	12,876	27,385	22,398	14.0	11.5
Alexandria	9,219	22,109	16,842	21.1	18.2
Algood	9,224	22,882	18,662	20.6	16.3
Allardt	11,284	21,985	19,444	17.4	13.8
Altamont	6,529	15,875	14,766	31.6	30.1
Ardmore	11,111	29,286	22,292	11.8	8.5
Arlington	8,164	33,250	30,000	8.5	5.9
Ashland City	10,270	24,335	20,372	17.4	14.2
Athens	10,286	24,179	19,259	23.3	20.5
Atoka	10,707	36,875	31,111	10.2	7.3
Atwood	10,264	27,173	24,420	14.6	11.4
Auburntown	8,921	23,750	19,063	6.2	0.0
Baileyton	9,483	21,563	19,432	22.3	17.4
Baneberry	23,172	47,188	39,688	0.0	0.0
Banner Hill CDP	9,753	26,625	16,667	21.0	12.9
Bartlett	16,080	49,013	47,346	2.3	2.1
Baxter	7,944	19,095	15,099	25.9	21.9
Beersheba Springs	6,375	14,792	12,813	27.1	24.6
Belinda City CDP	11,675	36,055	34,063	6.3	5.5
Bell Buckle	11,127	29,659	26,806	8.8	4.0
Belle Meade	66,898	135,439	125,459	3.2	3.1
Bells	10,040	21,635	17,853	20.3	15.1
Benton	8,423	20,956	17,500	30.0	22.6
Berry Hill	13,999	30,357	21,292	13.0	7.5
Bethel Springs	8,015	19,148	15,200	27.1	22.3
Big Sandy	10,066	18,026	12,083	26.8	22.5
Blaine	8,776	22,601	21,333	17.7	15.2
Bloomingdale CDP	10,338	27,202	23,573	14.3	11.6
Blountville CDP	12,088	33,917	30,268	11.1	10.1
Bluff City	10,761	27,115	23,315	14.1	8.5
Bolivar	9,927	22,067	20,129	24.5	16.2
Braden	11,431	27,917	27,500	16.6	16.7
Bradford	9,635	25,294	20,919	11.7	9.3
Brentwood	27,417	74,736	70,287	1.4	0.9
Brighton	9,694	25,625	22,333	18.5	14.4
Bristol	13,985	29,611	22,660	12.7	9.0
Brownsville	9,066	23,135	17,682	26.8	21.5
Bruceton	10,491	26,786	21,745	10.1	7.7
Bulls Gap	10,019	29,318	23,409	13.4	10.5
Burlison	9,732	23,947	19,773	18.5	17.3
Burns	11,341	27,292	23,333	15.3	12.9
Byrdstown	7,156	15,592	12,621	31.4	26.9
Calhoun	10,298	26,786	24,750	4.4	2.4
Camden	9,990	24,813	18,192	19.4	15.5
Carthage	10,773	24,464	18,470	23.4	20.2
Caryville	9,159	22,846	19,556	17.9	13.6
Cedar Hill	7,464	18,958	17,273	21.5	20.0
Celina	9,052	21,741	16,042	25.0	23.4
Centertown	12,747	29,286	28,214	9.9	8.2
Centerville	10,497	28,583	22,782	19.6	13.5
Central CDP	10,445	25,833	20,441	9.8	8.5
Chapel Hill	12,597	32,500	27,788	3.4	1.7

TABLE 2.17--PER CAPITA MONEY INCOME, MEDIAN FAMILY INCOME, MEDIAN HOUSEHOLD
INCOME, AND PERCENT OF PERSONS AND FAMILIES BELOW POVERTY,
MUNICIPALITIES AND CENSUS DESIGNATED PLACES, TENNESSEE, 1989 (Continued)

Places	Per capita income	Median family income	Median household income	Persons below poverty %	Families below poverty %
Charleston	$11,225	$29,000	$24,500	19.1	18.2
Charlotte	9,682	22,375	19,803	14.9	15.2
Chattanooga	12,332	27,487	22,197	18.2	14.4
Church Hill	11,577	29,859	25,495	15.5	13.0
Clarksburg	10,306	26,250	18,750	8.8	2.1
Clarksville	11,252	27,557	25,341	13.3	11.0
Cleveland	12,265	28,715	22,894	17.4	13.8
Clifton	8,528	24,750	18,021	13.2	9.0
Clinton	13,187	29,495	24,241	15.4	12.9
Coalmont	6,783	17,284	15,474	28.0	24.9
Collegedale	10,491	33,867	28,004	8.0	6.3
Collierville	16,529	51,682	47,517	6.6	5.4
Collinwood	8,222	21,510	18,333	15.7	13.3
Colonial Heights CDP	16,310	42,058	37,973	3.7	3.1
Columbia	12,558	31,156	25,238	14.3	11.6
Cookeville	11,852	29,465	20,646	18.9	12.2
Copperhill	11,411	23,472	17,266	15.5	13.8
Cornersville	10,361	29,821	23,125	12.5	9.5
Cottage Grove	10,602	21,250	19,375	3.1	0.0
Covington	8,812	21,984	16,565	37.0	29.4
Cowan	8,485	21,597	18,047	20.9	19.3
Crab Orchard	7,117	16,625	14,022	28.5	26.7
Cross Plains	10,174	30,652	22,917	16.3	13.9
Crossville	8,895	18,958	16,081	28.6	23.1
Crump	7,784	18,856	16,075	25.2	20.0
Cumberland City	9,157	22,083	17,500	20.8	19.6
Cumberland Gap	8,330	16,563	15,357	26.5	18.8
Dandridge	10,862	25,893	21,227	11.6	7.5
Dayton	8,946	22,857	18,355	20.8	16.9
Decatur	9,330	27,000	21,312	23.3	17.8
Decaturville	9,685	21,354	16,974	25.8	23.1
Decherd	9,328	25,757	20,472	20.0	16.0
Dickson	11,109	28,232	20,840	19.2	15.6
Dover	10,153	25,347	20,559	15.0	10.8
Dowelltown	8,057	15,208	8,810	41.3	33.0
Doyle	6,662	17,273	13,750	17.8	13.5
Dresden	10,919	25,357	18,662	14.4	10.7
Ducktown	8,432	20,179	13,295	21.1	19.2
Dunlap	8,928	20,023	17,920	24.3	21.9
Dyer	10,606	26,844	22,106	10.3	6.4
Dyersburg	11,400	25,961	20,053	22.7	18.7
Eagleton Village CDP	11,593	26,527	23,363	11.2	10.4
Eagleville	11,149	40,268	22,159	11.4	7.2
East Brainerd CDP	17,511	49,001	48,072	3.5	3.0
East Cleveland CDP	7,407	13,859	11,932	35.2	33.1
East Ridge	13,989	30,970	26,728	7.6	6.1
Eastview	10,334	25,694	22,417	14.0	9.7
Elizabethton	10,954	23,343	17,532	20.3	16.1
Elkton	10,122	35,341	26,111	13.8	11.8
Englewood	7,843	20,607	14,722	23.3	19.2
Enville	8,202	22,500	12,125	22.4	11.3
Erin	8,813	20,208	14,154	31.6	27.9
Erwin	10,948	27,352	19,194	16.0	12.9
Estill Springs	13,189	32,566	24,907	12.3	9.0
Ethridge	9,023	23,958	21,193	17.6	14.2

111

TABLE 2.17--PER CAPITA MONEY INCOME, MEDIAN FAMILY INCOME, MEDIAN HOUSEHOLD
INCOME, AND PERCENT OF PERSONS AND FAMILIES BELOW POVERTY,
MUNICIPALITIES AND CENSUS DESIGNATED PLACES, TENNESSEE, 1989 (Continued)

Places	Per capita income	Median family income	Median household income	Persons below poverty %	Families below poverty %
Etowah	$9,853	$24,176	$18,703	20.0	17.5
Fairfield Glade CDP	17,323	32,147	29,031	3.3	2.6
Fairmount CDP	15,482	41,250	34,635	6.5	6.3
Fairview	10,610	32,943	30,191	12.3	8.0
Fall Branch CDP	16,044	28,919	24,625	8.7	8.8
Farragut	22,139	62,878	60,137	1.8	1.3
Fayetteville	10,404	25,789	18,759	20.4	15.9
Finger	7,095	18,542	18,438	25.3	16.9
Forest Hills	46,767	95,453	92,795	2.4	2.3
Franklin	16,202	38,138	32,348	7.2	5.2
Friendship	9,117	19,276	17,344	18.5	14.2
Friendsville	12,070	33,750	30,000	7.9	5.5
Gadsden	11,635	32,639	28,750	6.6	5.6
Gainesboro	9,152	20,179	12,250	34.0	24.6
Gallatin	11,677	32,413	26,498	16.3	12.3
Gallaway	5,078	14,265	12,167	37.7	35.4
Garland	23,662	42,500	33,750	11.0	9.6
Gates	7,309	19,205	16,875	20.6	17.4
Gatlinburg	15,204	32,078	24,925	9.3	5.8
Germantown	28,087	71,958	69,019	1.1	1.0
Gibson	8,338	24,688	18,125	14.2	10.1
Gilt Edge	9,196	31,250	24,875	12.2	6.7
Gleason	7,903	22,321	17,372	22.9	18.1
Goodlettsville	15,576	40,271	35,483	4.8	2.8
Gordonsville	11,198	30,329	25,556	13.8	9.3
Grand Junction	9,942	23,125	17,679	21.0	8.4
Gray CDP	11,177	29,152	26,500	7.2	4.4
Graysville	8,394	22,933	20,673	21.9	20.8
Greenback	11,366	25,000	21,364	12.8	8.0
Greenbrier	12,193	32,453	30,412	5.7	4.6
Greeneville	11,429	27,034	20,066	16.6	12.7
Greenfield	9,221	24,212	18,300	20.0	16.7
Green Hill CDP	16,935	46,354	45,380	2.0	1.2
Gruetli-Laager	7,426	20,128	17,051	21.5	19.2
Guys	11,129	23,583	20,625	20.9	15.0
Halls	9,131	20,833	17,174	24.2	20.1
Halls CDP	14,109	40,852	32,864	6.2	3.9
Harriman	8,785	20,588	16,130	26.9	22.9
Harrison CDP	14,819	39,756	35,606	3.6	2.0
Harrogate-Shawanee CDP	11,166	27,663	23,458	20.4	14.4
Hartsville	8,885	22,132	16,700	21.4	16.0
Henderson	7,482	23,694	16,908	25.8	19.4
Hendersonville	16,010	41,985	38,068	4.5	3.0
Henning	6,795	16,250	14,583	33.2	31.3
Henry	6,895	16,719	17,500	23.5	22.0
Hickory Valley	8,325	19,500	18,125	21.8	12.0
Hohenwald	8,489	19,247	15,685	24.9	20.0
Hollow Rock	9,225	24,286	19,896	17.2	14.3
Hopewell CDP	13,582	35,625	30,244	9.8	7.9
Hornbeak	8,203	19,922	17,569	18.4	17.4
Hornsby	8,801	25,938	22,875	8.9	6.3
Humboldt	9,892	23,647	19,624	18.4	12.8
Hunter CDP	9,590	19,336	17,981	11.7	8.6
Huntingdon	10,044	22,153	18,750	24.6	18.8
Huntland	9,649	25,789	20,368	14.3	8.5

TABLE 2.17--PER CAPITA MONEY INCOME, MEDIAN FAMILY INCOME, MEDIAN HOUSEHOLD
INCOME, AND PERCENT OF PERSONS AND FAMILIES BELOW POVERTY,
MUNICIPALITIES AND CENSUS DESIGNATED PLACES, TENNESSEE, 1989 (Continued)

Places	Per capita income	Median family income	Median household income	Persons below poverty %	Families below poverty %
Huntsville	$8,687	$18,875	$16,625	33.6	31.6
Iron City	7,803	24,167	18,214	21.0	17.9
Jacksboro	10,501	24,758	21,318	15.2	12.0
Jackson	11,268	26,466	21,063	21.0	17.9
Jamestown	6,390	14,388	10,500	43.5	34.9
Jasper	10,653	25,408	19,203	22.4	17.7
Jefferson City	8,083	19,539	14,527	25.7	18.0
Jellico	7,274	16,427	13,642	31.7	23.5
Johnson City	13,071	31,421	23,053	17.3	11.7
Jonesborough	10,348	27,955	22,306	12.0	9.2
Karns CDP	14,075	37,429	32,596	1.3	0.0
Kenton	9,425	21,977	18,750	15.2	11.7
Kimball	9,482	25,450	20,707	16.7	13.8
Kingsport	13,825	30,279	22,750	18.1	14.3
Kingston	13,196	31,548	26,958	13.0	10.3
Kingston Springs	14,643	45,000	40,764	6.5	3.8
Knoxville	12,108	26,131	19,923	20.8	15.3
Lafayette	9,511	23,352	14,944	21.6	16.7
La Follette	7,694	17,239	12,543	33.1	29.7
La Grange	12,869	27,500	24,167	28.7	10.0
Lake City	7,634	18,676	13,526	31.6	28.6
Lakeland	20,994	48,864	42,266	2.2	0.8
Lakesite	14,735	47,000	42,000	8.3	7.4
Lakewood	12,591	30,500	21,410	7.7	4.5
La Vergne	11,543	33,634	31,250	6.8	5.7
Lawrenceburg	10,742	23,573	18,297	17.3	15.0
Lebanon	11,797	30,387	25,403	16.0	11.6
Lenoir City	9,345	22,094	18,014	21.2	16.7
Lewisburg	11,011	28,521	21,381	16.9	12.0
Lexington	10,173	23,848	20,093	20.0	14.7
Liberty	8,381	22,917	20,795	18.8	13.7
Linden	8,641	21,875	16,500	21.5	18.2
Livingston	9,166	22,089	17,769	12.8	8.8
Lobelville	10,727	25,714	19,792	13.1	10.1
Lookout Mountain	41,079	86,360	64,266	3.1	1.4
Loretto	10,425	28,357	24,048	9.3	8.1
Loudon	10,140	25,375	19,460	18.1	13.5
Luttrell	7,045	18,833	16,667	26.0	21.2
Lynchburg, Moore County	11,545	30,524	28,056	6.5	5.9
Lynnville	9,638	16,786	12,337	30.1	24.0
McEwen	10,031	25,179	18,323	19.5	15.3
McKenzie	10,006	25,786	20,638	15.2	13.1
McLemoresville	10,694	25,625	20,577	11.0	3.5
McMinnville	9,752	25,111	17,058	20.8	15.7
Madisonville	9,911	22,305	19,314	15.1	9.4
Manchester	11,054	28,453	22,514	15.2	13.2
Martin	9,447	28,917	19,258	20.3	10.5
Maryville	13,420	32,442	25,223	13.9	11.1
Mascot CDP	7,881	21,059	19,097	19.1	15.2
Mason	7,662	22,708	18,929	15.6	13.2
Maury City	7,851	19,036	17,216	18.6	15.4
Maynardville	7,522	19,141	15,842	25.6	22.7
Medina	11,261	30,000	19,250	11.0	7.3
Medon	10,698	26,250	16,250	15.9	17.6
Memphis	11,682	27,178	22,674	23.0	18.7

113

2.   **INCOME AND PRICES**

TABLE 2.17--PER CAPITA MONEY INCOME, MEDIAN FAMILY INCOME, MEDIAN HOUSEHOLD
INCOME, AND PERCENT OF PERSONS AND FAMILIES BELOW POVERTY,
MUNICIPALITIES AND CENSUS DESIGNATED PLACES, TENNESSEE, 1989 (Continued)

Places	Per capita income	Median family income	Median household income	Persons below poverty %	Families below poverty %
Michie	$8,672	$22,891	$19,167	25.2	22.0
Middleton	10,994	25,568	20,341	11.1	9.2
Middle Valley CDP	13,647	42,071	40,193	3.9	3.3
Midway CDP	9,477	25,000	19,830	14.1	11.5
Milan	10,910	24,993	20,962	18.8	13.4
Milledgeville	8,436	20,221	17,566	18.9	10.6
Millersville	10,431	27,318	24,933	14.4	12.2
Millington	9,292	25,356	23,815	11.2	10.5
Minor Hill	10,990	23,393	19,423	9.4	3.7
Mitchellville	9,577	30,750	27,708	9.6	8.8
Monteagle	8,815	20,278	16,801	26.1	19.0
Monterey	8,374	20,997	16,867	23.0	17.2
Morrison	8,608	21,250	18,750	24.0	17.6
Morristown	10,490	23,930	19,749	20.1	15.8
Moscow	10,715	23,542	19,712	14.0	14.0
Mosheim	10,181	27,703	25,233	9.9	7.5
Mountain City	9,149	17,182	13,380	31.0	25.9
Mount Carmel	12,570	36,937	28,932	6.3	3.6
Mount Juliet	14,248	44,167	40,385	4.6	3.7
Mount Pleasant	9,587	21,082	18,397	20.7	19.4
Munford	11,141	25,909	23,409	18.0	16.2
Murfreesboro	12,983	35,633	26,394	16.0	9.9
Nashville-Davidson[1]	14,490	34,009	27,821	13.4	10.4
Newbern	10,034	24,710	20,596	19.5	16.2
New Hope	10,241	26,458	22,632	14.2	13.7
New Johnsonville	12,931	34,937	32,104	9.6	8.5
New Market	10,570	25,859	23,900	12.7	10.8
Newport	9,347	19,990	15,885	28.7	24.3
New Tazewell	10,421	19,097	14,515	29.6	25.6
Niota	11,226	25,694	21,797	12.5	8.5
Nolensville CDP	14,869	46,125	44,509	1.7	0.0
Normandy	10,479	41,250	30,500	8.9	8.3
Norris	15,325	38,558	31,406	8.8	6.7
Oakdale	8,137	22,750	17,500	16.5	17.6
Oak Grove CDP	12,301	31,741	27,986	7.8	8.3
Oak Hill	31,760	65,649	55,417	2.1	0.8
Oakland	8,538	28,036	25,250	13.7	8.0
Oak Ridge	17,661	42,345	32,615	9.5	7.0
Obion	8,982	20,469	16,414	27.9	22.3
Oliver Springs	10,042	25,125	20,637	18.9	15.7
Oneida	8,959	21,778	15,437	27.9	27.2
Ooltewah CDP	15,020	31,329	26,833	11.1	8.9
Orlinda	9,714	25,694	23,500	16.6	10.4
Orme	8,036	24,167	22,917	26.3	20.5
Palmer	6,493	16,250	14,063	25.9	24.0
Paris	9,834	20,427	15,977	23.2	18.2
Parker's Cross Roads	12,075	26,563	25,938	3.0	4.4
Parrottsville	7,508	24,375	22,813	11.1	11.8
Parsons	9,127	21,628	16,696	20.1	15.5
Pegram	14,374	35,921	31,944	8.4	5.0
Petersburg	9,264	26,339	23,333	11.3	6.2
Philadelphia	9,809	23,958	18,375	20.8	18.5
Pigeon Forge	10,887	25,987	21,622	10.9	8.7
Pikeville	9,065	21,071	15,217	26.6	23.8
Pine Crest CDP	10,252	25,905	22,716	12.9	9.3

114

TABLE 2.17--PER CAPITA MONEY INCOME, MEDIAN FAMILY INCOME, MEDIAN HOUSEHOLD
INCOME, AND PERCENT OF PERSONS AND FAMILIES BELOW POVERTY,
MUNICIPALITIES AND CENSUS DESIGNATED PLACES, TENNESSEE, 1989 (Continued)

Places	Per capita income	Median family income	Median household income	Persons below poverty %	Families below poverty %
Piperton	$15,478	$38,846	$37,885	15.9	10.9
Pittman Center	12,411	31,250	24,444	12.6	7.9
Pleasant Hill	10,907	22,768	19,667	15.5	10.7
Portland	9,803	27,674	22,733	14.5	11.2
Powell CDP	13,985	40,833	31,113	7.2	4.8
Powells Crossroads	10,453	28,214	25,398	13.9	11.0
Pulaski	11,236	22,366	17,729	22.6	17.8
Puryear	9,088	26,591	20,000	17.3	13.9
Ramer	9,325	23,125	20,938	16.0	14.0
Red Bank	13,662	30,279	25,015	9.9	6.2
Red Boiling Springs	7,458	18,281	14,128	27.8	19.2
Ridgely	9,036	20,817	16,346	26.6	23.0
Ridgeside	36,476	71,983	57,036	4.8	1.7
Ridgetop	12,924	37,216	35,054	3.9	3.2
Ripley	7,963	17,500	16,116	34.4	31.0
Rives	8,704	25,500	22,083	10.4	6.5
Roan Mountain CDP	6,340	17,553	14,125	27.5	23.0
Rockford	11,817	30,417	28,036	10.1	7.4
Rockwood	9,654	23,399	17,024	23.5	15.8
Rogersville	11,528	27,500	18,049	20.4	11.4
Rossville	9,693	30,625	25,568	14.1	7.9
Rural Hill CDP	17,343	48,958	47,639	4.0	4.3
Rutherford	10,238	27,650	21,098	9.0	5.0
Rutledge	7,733	21,731	14,812	28.8	22.9
St. Joseph	8,528	22,100	19,167	15.3	15.7
Saltillo	6,906	19,583	12,000	22.3	19.4
Samburg	9,230	20,455	12,368	21.6	18.6
Sardis	8,621	19,432	14,500	21.3	18.8
Saulsbury	8,258	26,563	14,375	18.8	22.2
Savannah	10,281	20,498	15,895	26.3	21.5
Scotts Hill	9,173	21,106	14,432	23.4	21.7
Selmer	10,463	22,975	15,983	22.3	16.7
Sevierville	12,001	25,503	20,842	18.7	14.6
Sewanee CDP	8,903	32,798	25,000	10.7	4.9
Seymour CDP	12,334	33,214	31,054	5.9	4.2
Sharon	10,646	25,333	20,521	10.6	4.1
Shelbyville	10,458	25,406	20,099	19.8	16.2
Signal Mountain	23,983	60,924	49,821	1.1	1.1
Silerton	9,355	14,750	13,571	26.0	26.3
Slayden	8,558	21,563	21,250	8.4	13.2
Smithville	9,698	21,535	17,600	25.4	20.4
Smyrna	11,864	34,797	31,155	11.0	9.9
Sneedville	7,003	12,214	10,982	42.9	39.2
Soddy-Daisy	10,709	27,022	22,115	15.9	12.1
Somerville	9,194	23,088	15,255	29.8	21.4
South Carthage	9,706	25,938	19,107	22.0	15.5
South Cleveland CDP	10,556	29,556	26,858	11.4	8.6
South Fulton	11,065	25,170	22,287	12.2	9.3
South Pittsburg	9,287	23,246	18,204	25.9	20.0
Sparta	9,281	20,458	16,589	25.2	21.4
Spencer	8,578	25,250	20,208	18.5	15.9
Spring City	9,412	24,028	19,757	21.1	17.1
Springfield	11,256	27,219	21,645	19.5	17.3
Spring Hill	10,713	32,188	28,674	12.2	9.5
Spurgeon CDP	12,169	30,701	26,971	11.1	10.3

TABLE 2.17--PER CAPITA MONEY INCOME, MEDIAN FAMILY INCOME, MEDIAN HOUSEHOLD
INCOME, AND PERCENT OF PERSONS AND FAMILIES BELOW POVERTY,
MUNICIPALITIES AND CENSUS DESIGNATED PLACES, TENNESSEE, 1989 (Continued)

Places	Per capita income	Median family income	Median household income	Persons below poverty %	Families below poverty %
Stanton	$6,284	$13,594	$10,703	43.4	40.8
Stantonville	8,715	27,692	15,694	20.4	9.2
Surgoinsville	10,272	28,472	24,833	13.7	11.4
Sweetwater	10,061	24,184	19,865	16.2	12.7
Tazewell	8,372	18,929	14,980	27.3	22.5
Tellico Plains	7,141	20,846	14,904	24.4	22.4
Tennessee Ridge	9,443	23,205	21,603	17.2	15.9
Tiptonville	7,827	16,961	15,132	34.0	30.4
Toone	8,240	23,125	17,321	25.8	22.4
Townsend	10,428	18,125	16,625	15.6	9.7
Tracy City	8,607	19,883	16,760	21.6	17.4
Trenton	9,777	21,886	16,307	26.2	21.2
Trezevant	9,586	24,091	19,226	16.0	10.5
Trimble	9,952	27,917	21,429	14.5	9.5
Troy	11,049	26,875	18,654	12.1	7.3
Tullahoma	12,606	33,296	26,298	14.2	10.8
Tusculum	8,779	32,250	27,898	40.4	7.3
Union City	11,784	27,195	20,745	17.2	13.0
Vanleer	8,198	23,929	21,000	19.8	15.7
Viola	12,985	28,750	22,083	16.5	11.4
Vonore	8,484	20,486	16,354	21.5	13.5
Walden	27,007	56,221	51,118	4.4	4.2
Walnut Hill CDP	12,612	30,664	25,625	10.3	7.7
Walterhill CDP	11,749	37,391	35,469	9.9	9.7
Wartburg	8,601	18,942	14,395	26.1	21.6
Wartrace	10,806	26,875	22,115	14.5	15.4
Watauga	10,721	24,250	23,000	14.1	14.2
Watertown	9,784	23,696	19,565	17.0	14.1
Waverly	11,498	29,178	20,355	17.4	12.9
Waynesboro	9,941	22,500	16,981	14.3	11.5
Westmoreland	8,658	22,965	18,393	17.6	13.5
White Bluff	9,918	28,582	22,788	17.9	14.4
White House	12,938	36,165	32,138	6.0	5.2
White Pine	9,215	24,032	19,158	19.8	14.1
Whiteville	8,317	19,500	15,469	27.4	25.5
Whitwell	8,040	19,219	15,568	20.3	16.7
Wildwood Lake CDP	10,932	31,062	27,250	11.9	10.2
Williston	10,836	21,667	20,694	18.5	16.9
Winchester	10,159	27,083	19,836	16.2	12.6
Winfield	7,303	14,766	14,226	22.9	19.5
Woodbury	9,299	23,750	17,697	21.4	17.3
Woodland Mills	14,668	37,250	35,662	3.8	1.5
Yorkville	10,037	26,042	24,375	14.4	10.0

Note: Percent below poverty computed by Center for Business and Economic Research.
1. Nashville and that part of Davidson County not included in other municipalities.
Source: U.S. Department of Commerce, Bureau of the Census, *Census of Population and Housing, 1990:
Summary Tape File 3A, Tennessee.*

TABLE 2.18–TOTAL GROSS STATE PRODUCT, SOUTHEASTERN STATES, 1980–1991

State	1991	1990f	1989f	1988f	1987f	1986f	1985r	1984r	1983f	1982f	1981r	1980f
					Millions of 1987 dollars							
TENNESSEE	86,763	84,644	84,532	83,105	80,781	75,961	72,507	69,942	65,097	62,560	63,730	62,127
Alabama	64,049	62,987	61,904	61,084	59,545	56,935	55,363	53,473	50,469	48,388	49,318	48,530
Arkansas	35,201	34,243	33,588	33,151	32,078	31,096	30,390	30,109	27,846	26,548	27,234	26,881
Florida	217,900	216,334	213,320	205,938	197,054	185,823	176,462	167,657	155,859	143,814	142,071	136,631
Georgia	123,831	122,154	121,295	119,829	115,171	109,879	102,860	96,611	87,388	82,055	80,042	77,393
Kentucky	60,453	60,056	59,112	57,508	55,536	53,789	52,937	52,405	49,155	48,862	50,723	49,987
Louisiana	80,544	79,071	77,286	79,673	75,205	74,735	80,447	80,844	77,699	78,609	79,747	76,996
Mississippi	35,636	35,053	34,826	34,693	33,743	31,893	31,890	31,221	29,093	29,005	29,791	29,082
North Carolina	124,501	123,195	122,182	118,442	113,246	108,423	102,713	97,892	90,717	86,243	88,769	86,043
South Carolina	57,478	56,884	54,727	53,096	50,848	47,898	45,386	44,234	40,668	38,349	38,945	37,762
Virginia	122,596	123,340	122,553	118,439	113,936	108,489	102,204	97,582	91,547	87,891	88,020	85,321
West Virginia	25,909	25,768	25,243	24,874	24,086	24,193	23,739	23,724	22,692	23,313	24,001	24,270
					Millions of nominal dollars							
TENNESSEE	100,804	95,234	91,598	86,501	80,781	73,370	67,892	63,315	56,287	51,623	50,135	45,077
Alabama	73,956	70,594	67,117	63,584	59,545	55,119	52,267	48,933	44,145	40,561	39,139	35,296
Arkansas	40,561	38,376	36,424	34,356	32,078	30,179	28,852	27,898	24,490	22,710	22,221	19,873
Florida	255,129	244,527	231,022	213,937	197,054	178,536	163,508	149,726	132,811	118,130	108,887	95,851
Georgia	143,643	137,064	131,080	124,587	115,171	106,073	96,154	87,229	75,340	66,784	62,321	55,608
Kentucky	69,839	67,028	63,694	59,501	55,536	52,313	50,110	48,382	43,176	41,396	40,390	36,553
Louisiana	95,377	91,784	84,314	82,581	75,205	73,123	84,864	83,460	78,227	78,804	77,677	64,652
Mississippi	41,481	39,471	37,619	35,964	33,743	31,089	30,655	29,252	26,106	25,284	24,773	22,062
North Carolina	147,520	140,630	133,458	123,811	113,246	104,333	95,305	87,712	77,333	68,279	65,893	59,067
South Carolina	66,408	63,706	59,245	55,306	50,848	46,300	42,492	40,158	35,295	31,864	30,579	27,315
Virginia	145,189	140,362	133,465	123,518	113,936	104,457	94,745	86,890	77,557	69,775	65,130	58,037
West Virginia	29,014	28,180	26,914	25,649	24,086	23,684	23,128	22,598	20,791	20,835	20,158	18,768

r revised.

Source: U.S Department of Commerce, Bureau of Economic Analysis, *United States Department of Commerce News*, August 1994.

TABLE 2.19--PERSONAL INCOME, SOUTHEASTERN STATES, 1935-1993, SELECTED YEARS [In millions of dollars]

State	1993	1992ʳ	1991ʳ	1990ʳ	1989ʳ	1988ʳ	1987ʳ	1986ʳ	1985ʳ	1984ʳ	1983ʳ
TENNESSEE	93,894	88,553	81,659	77,786	73,177	68,379	63,691	59,201	54,605	50,979	45,900
Alabama	71,620	68,254	63,808	60,332	56,291	52,521	49,341	46,573	43,601	40,578	37,023
Arkansas	38,776	37,312	34,276	32,450	30,702	28,793	27,200	26,140	24,841	23,322	20,982
Florida	283,297	265,418	254,880	244,604	228,024	205,127	189,558	175,287	160,983	146,339	132,908
Georgia	132,832	125,116	116,891	111,406	104,184	97,819	90,312	83,967	76,713	69,878	61,326
Kentucky	64,237	61,698	57,365	54,454	50,586	46,930	44,260	42,342	40,568	39,014	35,325
Louisiana	71,252	67,831	63,944	60,228	56,369	53,911	51,015	51,140	51,288	49,386	46,639
Mississippi	38,869	36,744	34,243	32,398	30,672	28,854	27,043	25,546	24,459	23,343	21,386
North Carolina	129,790	121,880	113,445	108,339	100,010	93,560	86,328	80,253	74,243	68,706	61,161
South Carolina	61,236	58,262	55,077	52,855	47,995	45,018	41,239	38,374	36,049	33,711	30,412
Virginia	139,831	133,452	126,229	121,397	114,864	106,011	97,653	90,253	83,132	76,991	69,318
West Virginia	29,392	28,086	26,385	25,034	23,352	22,193	21,099	20,721	19,878	19,195	18,053

State	1982ʳ	1980ʳ	1975ʳ	1970ʳ	1965	1960	1955	1950	1945	1940	1935
TENNESSEE	43,043	36,868	20,838	12,381	7,849	5,632	4,434	3,367	2,616	989	737
Alabama	34,759	29,879	17,148	10,140	6,797	4,959	3,812	2,748	2,160	794	590
Arkansas	19,836	16,880	9,810	5,447	3,484	2,451	1,999	1,606	1,296	504	391
Florida	120,438	96,780	49,688	27,000	14,413	9,877	6,136	3,623	2,902	988	602
Georgia	55,840	45,832	25,816	15,534	9,540	6,561	5,078	3,644	2,705	1,042	790
Kentucky	34,518	29,507	16,813	10,136	6,491	4,843	3,836	2,871	2,062	910	729
Louisiana	45,037	36,655	18,950	11,191	7,339	5,389	4,029	2,968	2,126	850	640
Mississippi	20,503	17,352	9,854	5,757	3,709	2,636	2,122	1,661	1,303	464	365
North Carolina	56,128	47,183	27,198	16,484	10,226	7,282	5,691	4,331	2,880	1,148	897
South Carolina	28,020	23,693	13,363	7,797	4,774	3,358	2,654	1,932	1,434	581	404
Virginia	63,913	52,914	29,365	17,460	10,926	7,529	5,754	4,087	3,350	1,252	873
West Virginia	17,780	15,571	8,983	5,368	3,699	2,960	2,438	2,092	1,480	760	598

r revised.

Source: U.S. Department of Commerce, Bureau of Economic Analysis, *United States Department of Commerce News*, August 23, 1994; Regional Economic Measurement Division, *Regional Economic Information System 1969-1992 CD-ROM*; and *Survey of Current Business*, various issues.

TABLE 2.20—PER CAPITA PERSONAL INCOME, SOUTHEASTERN STATES AND UNITED STATES, 1940–1993, SELECTED YEARS [In dollars]

State	1993	1992r	1991r	1990f	1989f	1988f	1985f	1980f	1970f	1960	1950	1940
TENNESSEE	18,415	17,622	16,489	15,903	15,074	14,177	11,579	8,010	3,145	1,575	1,016	337
Alabama	17,106	16,496	15,601	14,899	13,967	13,051	10,975	7,656	2,939	1,515	899	279
Arkansas	15,994	15,584	14,458	13,779	13,085	12,289	10,674	7,371	2,822	1,370	842	258
Florida	20,710	19,686	19,203	18,785	18,043	16,666	14,181	9,835	3,944	1,974	1,289	516
Georgia	19,203	18,472	17,636	17,121	16,250	15,485	12,864	8,353	3,373	1,658	1,054	334
Kentucky	16,954	16,436	15,442	14,751	13,756	12,751	10,979	8,051	3,138	1,593	978	318
Louisiana	16,588	15,852	15,067	14,279	13,254	12,568	11,634	8,672	3,066	1,653	1,101	359
Mississippi	14,708	14,050	13,210	12,578	11,915	11,181	9,449	6,868	2,592	1,208	764	213
North Carolina	18,688	17,828	16,810	16,284	15,233	14,435	11,870	8,000	3,233	1,592	1,065	321
South Carolina	16,810	16,171	15,469	15,101	13,884	13,192	10,912	7,558	3,001	1,404	914	305
Virginia	21,544	20,870	20,074	19,543	18,768	17,558	14,544	9,857	3,747	1,889	1,233	460
West Virginia	16,148	15,542	14,665	13,964	12,926	12,124	10,424	7,972	3,073	1,597	1,043	398
SOUTHEAST	18,650	17,881	17,062	16,501	15,600	14,607	12,283	8,491	3,290	1,632	1,032	340
UNITED STATES[1]	20,781	20,131	19,199	18,667	17,690	16,610	14,155	9,940	4,047	2,216	1,492	589
Southeast as percent of U.S. per capita income	89.7	88.8	88.9	88.4	88.2	87.9	86.8	85.4	81.3	73.6	69.2	57.7

r revised.

1. Includes Alaska and Hawaii after 1960.

Source: U.S. Department of Commerce, Bureau of Economic Analysis, *United States Department of Commerce News*, August 23, 1994; *Regional Economic Measurement Division*, *Regional Economic Information System 1969–1992 CD-ROM*; and *Survey of Current Business*, various editions.

INCOME AND PRICES

TABLE 2.21--POVERTY STATUS OF PERSONS AND FAMILIES, SOUTHEASTERN STATES AND
UNITED STATES, 1959-1989 SELECTED YEARS [In thousands]

	Number below poverty level							
	Persons				Families			
State	1989	1979	1969	1959	1989	1979	1969	1959
TENNESSEE	745	736	836	1,374	168	164	186	306
Alabama	724	720	857	1,374	158	154	181	292
Arkansas	437	424	523	843	97	94	115	190
Florida	1,604	1,287	1,088	1,371	320	268	229	309
Georgia	923	884	924	1,505	198	189	192	314
Kentucky	682	626	718	1,137	163	144	159	253
Louisiana	967	765	933	1,274	213	163	188	26
Mississippi	631	587	767	1,173	137	121	154	240
North Carolina	830	840	996	1,796	180	183	211	373
South Carolina	518	500	595	1,049	111	106	119	206
Virginia	612	611	691	1,164	127	129	143	245
West Virginia	345	287	380	637	80	62	82	139
UNITED STATES	31,743	27,393	27,209	38,685	6,488	5,670	5,481	8,315

	Poverty rate (%)							
	Persons				Families			
State	1989	1979	1969	1959	1989	1979	1969	1959
TENNESSEE	15.7	16.5	21.8	39.3	12.4	13.1	18.2	34.2
Alabama	18.3	18.9	25.4	42.5	14.3	14.8	20.7	36.9
Arkansas	19.1	19.0	27.8	47.5	14.8	14.9	22.8	42.1
Florida	12.7	13.5	16.4	28.4	9.0	9.9	12.7	23.8
Georgia	14.7	16.6	20.7	39.0	11.5	13.2	16.7	33.1
Kentucky	19.0	17.6	22.9	38.3	16.0	14.6	19.2	33.6
Louisiana	23.6	18.6	26.3	39.5	19.4	15.1	21.5	34.0
Mississippi	25.2	23.9	35.4	54.5	20.2	18.7	28.9	47.9
North Carolina	13.0	14.8	20.3	40.6	9.9	11.6	16.3	34.1
South Carolina	15.4	16.6	23.9	45.4	11.9	13.1	19.0	38.0
Virginia	10.2	11.8	15.5	30.6	7.7	9.2	12.3	25.7
West Virginia	19.7	15.0	22.2	35.6	16.0	11.7	18.0	30.2
UNITED STATES	13.1	12.4	13.7	22.1	10.0	9.6	10.7	18.4

Note: See Table 2.16 for detail on poverty thresholds for 1989.

Source: U.S. Department of Commerce, Bureau of the Census, *Census of Population and Housing, 1990: Summary Tape File 3A*, individual states; and earlier censuses.

TABLE 2.22– ESTIMATED ANNUAL EXPENDITURES ON A CHILD BORN IN 1993 BY INCOME GROUP, UNITED STATES, 1993–2010 [In dollars][1]

Year	Age	Income group		
		Lowest	Middle	Highest
1993	Under 1 year	$4,960	$6,870	$10,210
1994	1 year	5,260	7,280	10,820
1995	2 years	5,570	7,720	11,470
1996	3 years	6,260	8,600	12,660
1997	4 years	6,640	9,120	13,420
1998	5 years	7,040	9,660	14,230
1999	6 years	7,830	10,580	15,250
2000	7 years	8,300	11,220	16,160
2001	8 years	8,800	11,890	17,130
2002	9 years	8,570	11,790	17,230
2003	10 years	9,080	12,500	18,270
2004	11 years	9,620	13,250	19,360
2005	12 years	11,070	14,870	21,490
2006	13 years	11,730	15,760	22,780
2007	14 years	12,430	16,710	24,150
2008	15 years	15,000	19,890	28,260
2009	16 years	15,900	21,080	29,950
2010	17 years	16,860	22,350	31,750
TOTAL[1]		$170,920	$231,140	$334,590
TOTAL [1993 dollars]		$97,710	$132,660	$192,780

Note: Estimates are for the younger child in a husband-wife family with two children for the overall United States.

1. Estimates assume an average annual inflation rate of 6 percent.

Source: U.S. Department of Agriculture, Agricultural Research Service, Family Economics Research Group, *Expenditures on a Child by Families, 1993.*

FIGURE 2.3
Consumer Price Index, Not Seasonally Adjusted, Urban Consumers,
12-Month Change, 1989–1993

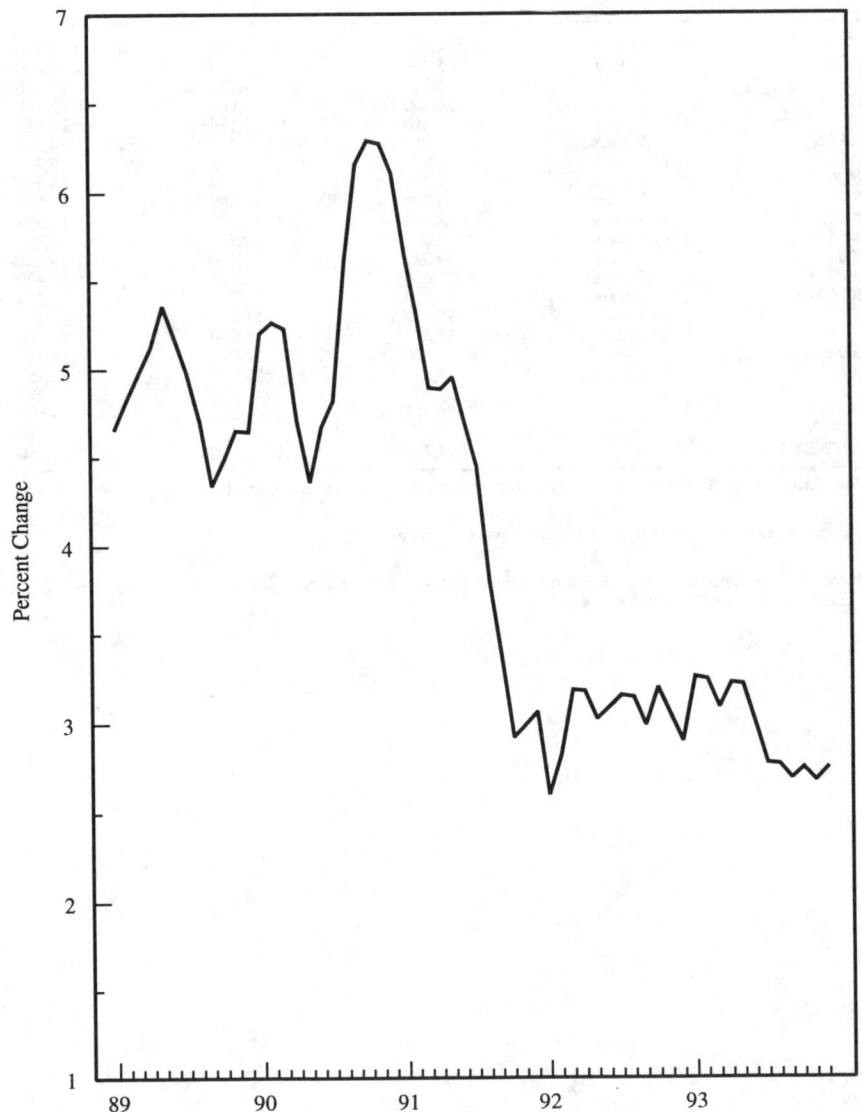

Note: Percent change is from the same month one year earlier.
Source: U.S. Department of Labor, Bureau of Labor Statistics, monthly news releases.

TABLE 2.23--CONSUMER PRICE INDEX FOR ALL URBAN CONSUMERS AND FOR URBAN WAGE EARNERS AND CLERICAL WORKERS, U.S. CITY AVERAGE, NOT SEASONALLY ADJUSTED, 1970–1993, SELECTED YEARS [1982–84=100]

Year	Jan.	Feb.	March	April	May	June	July	August	Sept.	Oct.	Nov.	Dec.	Annual average	Annual change (%)
						All urban consumers (CPI-U)								
1993	142.6	143.1	143.6	144.0	144.2	144.4	144.4	144.8	145.1	145.7	145.8	145.8	144.5	3.0
1992	138.1	138.6	139.3	139.5	139.7	140.2	140.5	140.9	141.3	141.8	142.0	141.9	140.3	3.0
1991	134.6	134.8	135.0	135.2	135.6	136.0	136.2	136.6	137.2	137.4	137.8	137.9	136.2	4.2
1990	127.4	128.0	128.7	128.9	129.2	129.9	130.4	131.6	132.7	133.5	133.8	133.8	130.7	5.4
1989	121.1	121.6	122.3	123.1	123.8	124.1	124.4	124.6	125.0	125.6	125.9	126.1	124.0	4.8
1988	115.7	116.0	116.5	117.1	117.5	118.0	118.5	119.0	119.8	120.2	120.3	120.5	118.3	4.1
1987	111.2	111.6	112.1	112.7	113.1	113.5	113.8	114.4	115.0	115.3	115.4	115.4	113.6	3.7
1986	109.6	109.3	108.8	108.6	108.9	109.5	109.5	109.7	110.2	110.3	110.4	110.5	109.6	1.9
1985	105.5	106.0	106.4	106.9	107.3	107.6	107.8	108.0	108.3	108.7	109.0	109.3	107.6	3.5
1984	101.9	102.4	102.6	103.1	103.4	103.7	104.1	104.5	105.0	105.3	105.3	105.3	103.9	4.3
1983	97.8	97.9	97.9	98.6	99.2	99.5	99.9	100.2	100.7	101.0	101.2	101.3	99.6	3.2
1982	94.3	94.6	94.5	94.9	95.8	97.0	97.5	97.7	97.9	98.2	98.0	97.6	96.5	6.1
1981	87.0	87.9	88.5	89.1	89.8	90.6	91.6	92.3	93.2	93.4	93.7	94.0	90.9	10.3
1980	77.8	78.9	80.1	81.0	81.8	82.7	82.7	83.3	84.0	84.8	85.5	86.3	82.4	13.5
1979	68.3	69.1	69.8	70.6	71.5	72.3	73.1	73.8	74.6	75.2	75.9	76.7	72.6	11.3
1978	62.5	62.9	63.4	63.9	64.5	65.2	65.7	66.0	66.5	67.1	67.4	67.7	65.2	7.6

TABLE 2.23—CONSUMER PRICE INDEX FOR ALL URBAN CONSUMERS AND FOR URBAN WAGE EARNERS AND CLERICAL WORKERS, U.S. CITY AVERAGE, NOT SEASONALLY ADJUSTED, 1970–1993, SELECTED YEARS [1982–84=100] (Continued)

Year	Jan.	Feb.	March	April	May	June	July	August	Sept.	Oct.	Nov.	Dec.	Annual average	Annual change (%)
						Urban wage earners and clerical workers (CPI-W)								
1993	140.3	140.7	141.1	141.6	141.9	142.0	142.1	142.4	142.6	143.3	143.4	143.3	142.1	2.8
1992	136.0	136.4	137.0	137.3	137.6	138.1	138.4	138.8	139.1	139.6	139.8	139.8	138.2	2.9
1991	132.8	132.8	133.0	133.3	133.8	134.1	134.3	134.6	135.2	135.4	135.8	135.9	134.3	4.0
1990	125.9	126.4	127.1	127.3	127.5	128.3	128.7	129.9	131.1	131.9	132.2	132.2	129.0	5.3
1989	119.7	120.2	120.8	121.8	122.5	122.8	123.2	123.2	123.6	124.2	124.4	124.6	122.6	4.8
1988	114.5	114.7	115.1	115.7	116.2	116.7	117.2	117.7	118.5	118.9	119.0	119.2	117.0	4.0
1987	110.0	110.5	111.0	111.6	111.9	112.4	112.7	113.3	113.8	114.1	114.3	114.2	112.5	3.6
1986	108.9	108.5	107.9	107.6	107.9	108.4	108.4	108.6	109.1	109.1	109.2	109.3	108.6	1.6
1985	104.9	105.4	105.9	106.3	106.7	107.0	107.1	107.3	107.6	107.9	108.3	108.6	106.9	3.5
1984	101.6	101.8	101.8	102.1	102.5	102.8	103.2	104.2	104.8	104.8	104.7	104.8	103.3	3.4
1983	98.1	98.1	98.4	99.0	99.5	99.8	100.1	100.5	101.0	101.2	101.2	101.2	99.8	3.0
1982	94.7	95.0	94.8	95.2	96.2	97.4	98.0	98.2	98.3	98.6	98.4	98.0	96.9	6.0
1981	87.5	88.5	89.0	89.6	90.3	91.1	92.2	92.8	93.7	93.9	94.1	94.4	91.4	10.3
1980	78.3	79.4	80.5	81.4	82.3	83.2	83.3	83.8	84.6	85.3	86.1	86.9	82.9	13.5
1979	68.7	69.5	70.3	71.1	71.9	72.8	73.7	74.4	75.1	75.7	76.4	77.2	73.1	11.4
1978	62.8	63.2	63.7	64.3	64.9	65.6	66.0	66.4	66.8	67.4	67.7	68.1	65.6	7.6
1977	58.9	59.5	59.8	60.3	60.6	61.0	61.3	61.5	61.8	61.9	62.2	62.5	60.9	6.5
1976	56.0	56.1	56.2	56.5	56.8	57.1	57.4	57.7	57.9	58.2	58.3	58.5	57.2	5.7
1975	52.4	52.8	53.0	53.2	53.5	53.9	54.5	54.7	54.9	55.3	55.6	55.8	54.1	9.2
1974	46.9	47.5	48.0	48.3	48.8	49.3	49.7	50.3	50.9	51.4	51.8	52.2	49.6	11.0
1973	42.9	43.2	43.6	43.9	44.1	44.4	44.5	45.4	45.5	45.9	46.2	46.5	44.7	6.2
1972	41.4	41.6	41.6	41.7	41.9	42.0	42.1	42.2	42.4	42.5	42.6	42.7	42.1	3.3
1971	40.0	40.1	40.2	40.4	40.6	40.8	40.9	41.0	41.0	41.1	41.2	41.3	40.7	4.3
1970	38.0	38.2	38.4	38.7	38.8	39.0	39.2	39.2	39.4	39.6	39.8	40.0	39.0	5.8

Note: Beginning with the release of data for January 1988, CPI's were shifted from the old reference base period 1967=100 to the new reference base period 1982–84=100. Factors for conversion from the old base to the new base for CPI-U AND CPI-W are .3338279 and .3357176, respectively. When multiplied by the appropriate conversion factor, the January 1988 CPI-U of 346.7 becomes 115.7 and the CPI-W of 341.0 becomes 114.5. Because of rounding effects, there may be minor differences between the final rebased index and the result obtained using the conversion factor.

Source: U.S. Department of Labor, Bureau of Labor Statistics, CPI Detailed Report, monthly.

TABLE 2.24--PURCHASING POWER OF THE CONSUMER DOLLAR AND THE CONSUMER PRICE INDEX, ANNUAL AVERAGES, 1958–1993

Year	Purchasing power (1982–84=$1.00)[1]	Consumer Price Index (1982–84=100)
1993	$0.692	144.5
1992	0.713	140.3
1991	0.734	136.2
1990	0.766	130.7
1989	0.807	124.0
1988	0.846	118.3
1987	0.880	113.6
1986	0.912	109.6
1985	0.929	107.6
1984	0.962	103.9
1983	1.004	99.6
1982	1.036	96.5
1981	1.100	90.9
1980	1.214	82.4
1979	1.377	72.6
1978	1.534	65.2
1977	1.650	60.6
1976	1.757	56.9
1975	1.859	53.8
1974	2.028	49.3
1973	2.252	44.4
1972	2.392	41.8
1971	2.469	40.5
1970	2.577	38.8
1969	2.725	36.7
1968	2.874	34.8
1967	2.994	33.4
1966	3.077	32.5
1965	3.175	31.5
1964	3.226	31.0
1963	3.268	30.6
1962	3.300	30.3
1961	3.344	29.9
1960	3.378	29.6
1959	3.425	29.2
1958	3.460	28.9

Note: The Consumer Price Index used is that for All Urban Consumers.

1. Computed by the Center for Business and Economic Research.

Source: U.S. Department of Labor, Bureau of Labor Statistics, *CPI Detailed Report*, January 1994, and earlier editions.

INCOME AND PRICES

TABLE 2.25--ANNUAL AVERAGE CONSUMER PRICE INDEX, UNITED STATES CITY AVERAGE AND SELECTED CITIES, 1993 [1982–84=100]

City	Annual average 1993	Annual average 1992	Percent change 1992 to 1993	Annual average, 1993 by commodity group	
				Food	Medical
U.S. CITY AVERAGE	144.5	140.3	3.0	140.9	201.4
Anchorage, AK	132.2	128.2	3.1	129.8	189.6
Atlanta, GA	143.4	138.5	3.5	141.2	213.0
Baltimore, MD	143.1	140.1	2.1	144.7	198.7
Boston-Lawrence-Salem-MA-NH	152.9	148.6	2.9	146.2	239.0
Buffalo-Niagara Falls, NY	142.7	137.9	3.5	138.7	172.4
Chicago-Gary-Lake County, IL-IN-WI	145.4	141.1	3.0	141.8	203.1
Cincinnati-Hamilton, OH-KY-IN	137.8	134.1	2.8	130.9	200.7
Cleveland-Akron-Lorain, OH	140.3	136.8	2.6	139.7	187.2
Dallas-Fort Worth, TX	137.3	133.9	2.5	137.5	196.8
Denver-Boulder, CO	135.8	130.3	4.2	131.5	217.9
Detroit-Ann Arbor, MI	139.6	135.9	2.7	134.5	190.9
Honolulu, HI	160.1	155.1	3.2	152.7	197.4
Houston-Galveston-Brazoria, TX	133.4	129.1	3.3	131.4	200.8
Kansas City, MO-KS	138.1	134.3	2.8	137.6	195.6
Los Angeles-Anaheim-Riverside, CA	150.3	146.5	2.6	143.1	206.6
Miami-Fort Lauderdale, FL	139.1	134.5	3.4	147.5	181.9
Milwaukee, WI	142.1	137.1	3.6	138.6	185.5
Minneapolis-St. Paul, MN-WI	139.2	135.0	3.1	145.5	193.8
New Orleans, LA	124.7	120.2	3.7	121.2	157.8
N.Y.-Northern N.J.-Long Island, NY-NJ-CT	154.5	150.0	3.0	148.7	209.1
Philadelphia-Wilmington-Trenton,PA-NJ-DE-MD	150.2	146.6	2.5	138.1	211.6
Pittsburgh-Beaver Valley, PA	139.9	136.0	2.9	135.6	196.8
Portland-Vancouver, OR-WA	144.7	139.8	3.5	133.0	186.6
St. Louis-East St. Louis, MO-IL	137.5	134.7	2.1	139.1	191.5
San Diego, CA	150.6	147.4	2.2	143.9	213.7
San Francisco-Oakland-San Jose, CA	146.3	142.5	2.7	145.9	199.1
Seattle-Tacoma, WA	142.9	139.0	2.8	142.0	193.1
Tampa-St. Petersburg-Clearwater, FL[1]	124.0	119.2	4.0	117.4	165.8
Washington, DC-MD-VA	149.3	144.7	3.2	141.5	195.3

Note: The sample used to compute the United States City Average includes 85 urban areas across the U.S., 29 of which have a Consumer Price Index specific to their area. Consumer price indexes are meant to compare price changes in a given area over time so the indexes should not be used to compare one city to another.
1. 1987=100
Source: U.S. Department of Labor, Bureau of Labor Statistics, *CPI Detailed Report*, January 1994.

TABLE 2.26—CONSUMER PRICE INDEX FOR CITIES IN THE SOUTH, BY POPULATION SIZE CLASS, 1993 [1982–84=100]

Population size	Jan.	Feb.	March	April	May	June	July	August	Sept.	Oct.	Nov.	Dec.	Annual[1] Average	Annual[1] Percent change
						All urban consumers								
SOUTH[2]	138.4	139.1	139.7	140.2	140.7	140.8	140.9	141.5	141.6	142.2	142.3	142.2	140.8	3.2
Less than 50,000	136.4	136.7	137.0	137.7	138.7	138.8	139.0	139.4	139.1	140.0	141.1	140.7	138.7	3.2
50,000–450,000	137.8	138.1	138.6	139.3	140.0	140.2	140.1	140.6	141.1	141.5	141.1	140.9	139.9	3.0
450,000–1,200,000	139.9	140.3	141.6	141.9	142.1	142.6	142.7	143.1	143.5	143.8	143.9	143.8	142.4	3.1
More than 1,200,000	138.9	139.8	140.4	140.8	141.1	141.0	141.0	142.0	141.9	142.5	142.6	142.7	141.2	3.2
						Urban wage earners and clerical workers								
SOUTH[2]	137.2	137.6	138.3	138.8	139.3	139.6	139.6	140.2	140.3	140.9	141.0	140.8	139.5	3.0
Less than 50,000	136.6	136.8	137.0	137.8	138.8	138.9	139.2	139.6	139.4	140.3	141.4	140.9	138.9	3.1
50,000–450,000	137.9	138.1	138.5	139.3	140.1	140.2	140.2	140.6	141.0	141.5	141.0	140.8	139.9	3.0
450,000–1,200,000	136.8	136.9	138.2	138.6	138.9	139.4	139.5	139.8	140.2	140.7	140.8	140.7	139.2	3.0
More than 1,200,000	137.2	138.0	138.5	138.8	139.4	139.6	139.5	140.4	140.1	141.0	141.0	141.0	139.5	3.0

Note: Indexes are not seasonally adjusted.

1. Computed by the Center for Business and Economic Research.

2. South includes Alabama, Arkansas, Delaware, District of Columbia, Florida, Georgia, Kentucky, Louisiana, Maryland, Mississippi, North Carolina, Oklahoma, South Carolina, Tennessee, Texas, Virginia, and West Virginia.

Source: U.S. Department of Labor, Bureau of Labor Statistics, *CPI Detailed Report*, monthly.

The Bureau of Labor Statistics (BLS) in the U.S. Department of Labor publishes state, regional, and national data on employment and earnings. Its monthly periodical, *Employment and Earnings*, is based on surveys taken across the U.S. The Employment Cost Index (ECI), a relatively new series first published by BLS in 1976, gives quarterly indices for national, regional, and metropolitan/nonmetropolitan areas for the civilian non-farm economy. (Private household workers and employees of the federal government are excluded.) These indices measure change in employers' costs for employee compensation over time. Therefore, the ECI does not estimate wage or compensation levels, but rather the change in levels.

Each state's department of employment security cooperates with the BLS in the provision of employment statistics for its own state. The Tennessee Department of Employment Security (TDES) is the primary source of employment data at the state and county levels. Its annual report, *Tennessee Covered Employment and Wages by Industry*, provides summary payroll data on workers covered by unemployment insurance laws. These data, collected from employers, provide a count of jobs held, detailed by major industry group. In *Annual Average Labor Force Estimates*, TDES publishes the results of sample surveys used to estimate the size of the civilian labor force, employment and unemployment rates for the state, metropolitan statistical areas, and nonmetropolitan counties. This report also details estimated nonagricultural employment or jobs by industry group. The Department of Employment Security also publishes a monthly newsletter, *The Labor Market Report*, which provides estimates of hours and earnings for manufacturing production workers (these estimates are reported in Chapter 4). In addition, the local offices of TDES can provide timely information for their areas, although they point out that even the best efforts may not be able to accurately track mobile employment such as construction crews.

The term "labor force" includes all those persons who are 16 years of age or over and classified as employed, unemployed, or members of the armed forces. Employed persons include those counted during the survey week who did any work for pay or profit or worked 15 or more hours unpaid in family enterprises and those who had jobs but were temporarily absent for noneconomic reasons. Unemployed persons are defined as those not at work during the survey week but who had attempted to find work within the previous four weeks and were still available for work. Those laid off or waiting to report to a new job within 30 days are also counted as unemployed.

Data from the *1990 Census of Population*, Equal Employment Opportunity (EEO) file provide information on total and minority employment by occupation. This chapter also includes information on mass layoffs, Department of Defense contract awards, and number and median salary of doctoral scientists and engineers.

3. EMPLOYMENT AND EARNINGS

TABLE OF CONTENTS

TABLE OF CONTENTS
(Continued)

TABLE 3.1-- EMPLOYMENT AND WAGES COVERED BY UNEMPLOYMENT INSURANCE, BY INDUSTRY, TENNESSEE, 1991

Industry	Number of employers	Average annual employment	Total wages	Average annual wages	Average premium rate	Total premiums due
TOTAL	114,368	2,068,943	$43,904,800,522	$21,220	$1.59	$205,178,223
Agriculture, forestry and fishing	1,816	13,120	176,310,087	13,438	1.85	1,819,631
Mining	320	5,463	150,147,891	27,484	2.16	976,195
Contract construction	10,563	86,447	1,960,499,898	22,678	3.30	26,513,622
Manufacturing	8,136	501,939	12,433,924,156	24,771	1.79	70,279,345
Durable goods	4,735	249,241	6,388,348,442	25,631	1.87	36,741,112
Lumber and wood products	1,106	18,489	305,532,949	16,525	1.67	2,379,134
Furniture and fixtures	351	25,885	471,549,417	18,217	1.82	3,664,387
Stone, clay, and glass products	359	13,298	362,420,408	27,253	1.54	1,636,681
Primary metal industries	178	15,142	465,629,122	30,750	1.29	1,543,700
Fabricated metal products	707	41,945	1,128,469,519	26,903	1.48	4,905,907
Machinery, except electrical	891	35,803	959,869,126	26,809	2.38	6,884,137
Electrical and electronic equipment	336	35,570	869,003,211	24,430	1.93	5,331,248
Transportation equipment	339	41,292	1,298,498,484	31,446	2.31	7,503,409
Instruments and related products	189	11,060	297,985,081	26,942	1.76	1,502,396
Miscellaneous manufacturing industries	279	10,758	229,391,125	21,322	1.67	1,390,113
Nondurable goods	3,401	252,698	6,045,575,714	23,924	1.71	33,538,233
Food and kindred products	351	37,318	946,348,670	25,359	1.56	4,511,920
Tobacco manufactures	12	1,298	32,582,586	25,102	1.97	190,078
Textile mill products	191	20,558	403,482,948	19,626	1.62	2,562,218
Apparel and other textile products	627	60,934	816,097,331	13,393	2.27	10,347,254
Paper and allied products	173	21,360	691,805,159	32,387	1.74	2,923,529
Printing and publishing	1,306	34,397	813,166,987	23,640	1.25	3,176,581
Chemical and allied products	294	39,637	1,463,770,016	36,929	0.81	2,689,007
Petroleum and coal products	38	963	30,779,537	31,962	2.77	326,209
Rubber and miscellaneous plastic products	330	27,854	727,799,005	26,129	2.24	4,953,655
Leather and leather products	79	8,378	119,743,475	14,292	3.08	1,857,782
Transportation and utilities	4,653	112,769	3,169,936,694	28,110	1.29	11,518,123
Trade	38,414	509,276	8,135,553,088	15,974	1.26	43,856,507
Wholesale trade	11,984	127,561	3,467,399,542	27,182	1.30	13,004,110
Retail trade	26,430	381,715	4,668,153,546	12,229	1.24	30,852,397
Finance, insurance, and real estate	9,262	96,402	2,486,042,081	25,788	1.00	7,420,240
Services	34,776	429,727	8,255,199,023	19,210	1.47	35,946,777
State and local government	2,008	272,012	5,730,315,040	21,066	1.15	2,118,570
State government						
Education	56	32,290	758,410,868	23,487	0.59	1,374
Other	356	44,685	997,845,431	22,330	1.95	3,493
Local government						
Education	469	92,251	1,878,682,654	20,364	0.93	276,626
Other	1,127	102,785	2,095,376,087	20,386	1.20	1,837,077
Other	4,420	41,787	1,406,872,564	33,667	1.41	4,729,213

Source: Tennessee Department of Employment Security, Research and Statistics Section, *Covered Employment and Wages by Industry, Statewide and by County, in Tennessee, 1991.*

FIGURE 3.1
Distribution of Tennessee Insured Employment and Average Weekly Wages by Sector, 1991

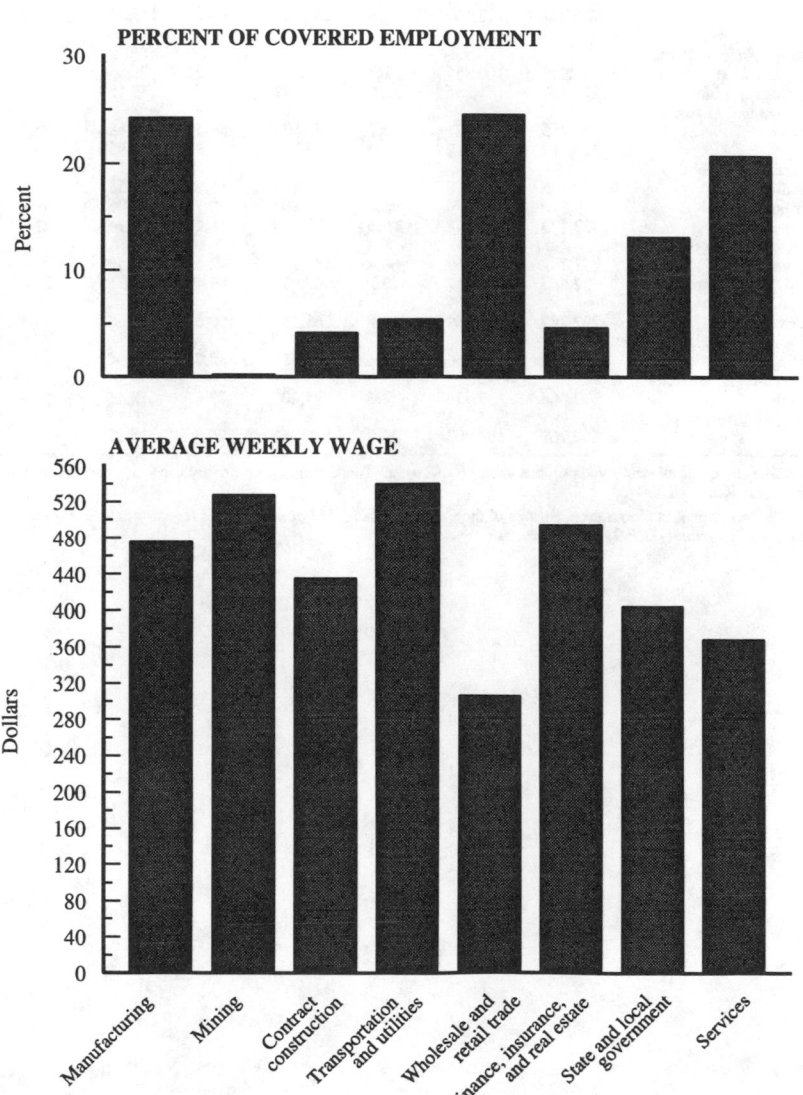

Source: Tennessee Department of Employment Security, *Tennessee Covered Employment and Wages by Industry, Statewide and by County, 1991.*

TABLE 3.2-- EMPLOYMENT, BY OCCUPATION, BY SEX, AND BY RACE, TENNESSEE, 1990

Category	Total	Female		White		Nonwhite	
		Number	%	Number	%	Number	%
TOTAL	2,405,077	1,113,147	46.3	2,041,337	84.9	363,740	15.1
Executive, administrative, and managerial	241,983	100,855	41.7	220,317	91.0	21,666	9.0
Professional specialty	277,792	154,896	55.8	244,639	88.1	33,153	11.9
Technicians and related support	79,385	40,221	50.7	68,505	86.3	10,880	13.7
Sales	283,713	141,812	50.0	254,758	89.8	28,955	10.2
Administrative support, including clerical	347,785	269,118	77.4	296,234	85.2	51,551	14.8
Private household	9,913	9,574	96.6	4,962	50.1	4,951	49.9
Protective services	37,123	5,778	15.6	28,978	78.1	8,145	21.9
Service, except protective and household	257,702	171,019	66.4	187,171	72.6	70,531	27.4
Farming, forestry, and fishing	52,647	6,912	13.1	47,090	89.4	5,557	10.6
Precision production, craft, and repair	292,782	31,869	10.9	265,214	90.6	27,568	9.4
Machine operators, assemblers, and inspectors	270,827	134,456	49.6	223,885	82.7	46,942	17.3
Transportation and material moving	112,664	9,734	8.6	94,201	83.6	18,463	16.4
Handlers, cleaners, helpers, and laborers	140,761	36,903	26.2	105,383	74.9	35,378	25.1

Note: Percentages are of all employed persons aged 16 and over. These were computed by the Center for Business and Economic Research.

Source: U.S. Department of Commerce, Bureau of the Census, *Census of Population and Housing, 1990: Equal Employment Opportunity (EEO) File, Tennessee.*

TABLE 3.3.– UNEMPLOYMENT RATE, TENNESSEE AND UNITED STATES, MONTHLY, 1980–1993, SELECTED YEARS [Not seasonally adjusted]

	Jan.	Feb.	March	April	May	June	July	August	Sept.	Oct.	Nov.	Dec.	Annual average
1993r													
Tennessee	6.4	6.1	6.1	5.8	5.5	6.4	5.9	5.7	5.2	5.2	5.3	4.6	5.7
United States	7.9	7.7	7.3	6.8	6.7	7.1	6.9	6.5	6.4	6.3	6.1	6.0	6.8
1992r													
Tennessee	7.4	7.0	6.9	6.3	6.1	6.9	6.4	6.4	5.9	5.9	6.0	5.3	6.4
United States	8.0	8.1	7.7	7.1	7.2	7.8	7.6	7.3	7.2	6.8	7.0	7.0	7.4
1991r													
Tennessee	7.0	6.9	7.0	6.7	6.3	7.2	6.9	6.7	6.2	6.3	6.4	5.9	6.6
United States	7.0	7.2	7.1	6.5	6.6	6.9	6.7	6.5	6.4	6.4	6.6	6.8	6.7
1990f													
Tennessee	5.5	5.2	5.1	4.9	4.7	5.6	5.3	5.2	5.0	5.1	5.6	5.2	5.2
United States	5.9	5.8	5.4	5.2	5.1	5.3	5.5	5.4	5.5	5.4	5.8	5.9	5.5
1989f													
Tennessee	5.9	5.5	5.4	5.0	4.7	5.6	5.3	5.2	4.7	4.7	4.9	4.3	5.1
United States	6.0	5.6	5.2	5.1	5.0	5.5	5.3	5.1	5.1	5.0	5.2	5.1	5.3
1988f													
Tennessee	6.6	6.3	6.2	5.7	5.5	6.3	5.9	5.9	5.4	5.4	5.5	4.7	5.8
United States	6.3	6.2	5.9	5.3	5.4	5.5	5.5	5.4	5.2	5.0	5.2	5.0	5.5
1987f													
Tennessee	7.8	7.4	7.3	6.8	6.5	7.3	6.6	6.5	6.0	5.9	5.9	5.3	6.6
United States	7.3	7.2	6.9	6.2	6.1	6.3	6.1	5.8	5.7	5.7	5.6	5.4	6.2
1986f													
Tennessee	8.7	8.8	8.5	8.2	7.8	8.7	8.4	8.1	7.5	7.4	7.6	6.8	8.0
United States	7.3	7.8	7.5	7.0	7.0	7.3	7.0	6.7	6.8	6.6	6.6	6.3	7.0
1985f													
Tennessee	8.5	8.5	8.2	7.9	7.5	8.4	8.2	8.1	7.6	7.7	7.9	7.3	8.0
United States	8.0	7.8	7.5	7.1	7.0	7.5	7.4	6.9	6.9	6.8	6.7	6.7	7.2
1980f													
Tennessee	6.7	6.8	6.6	6.6	6.7	8.0	8.3	7.9	7.4	7.5	7.7	7.3	7.3
United States	6.9	6.8	6.6	6.7	7.1	7.8	7.9	7.6	7.2	7.1	7.1	6.9	7.1

r revised.

Source: Tennessee Department of Employment Security, direct correspondence.

FIGURE 3.2

Unemployment Rate, Tennessee and the United States, Monthly, 1989–1993

(Not seasonally adjusted)

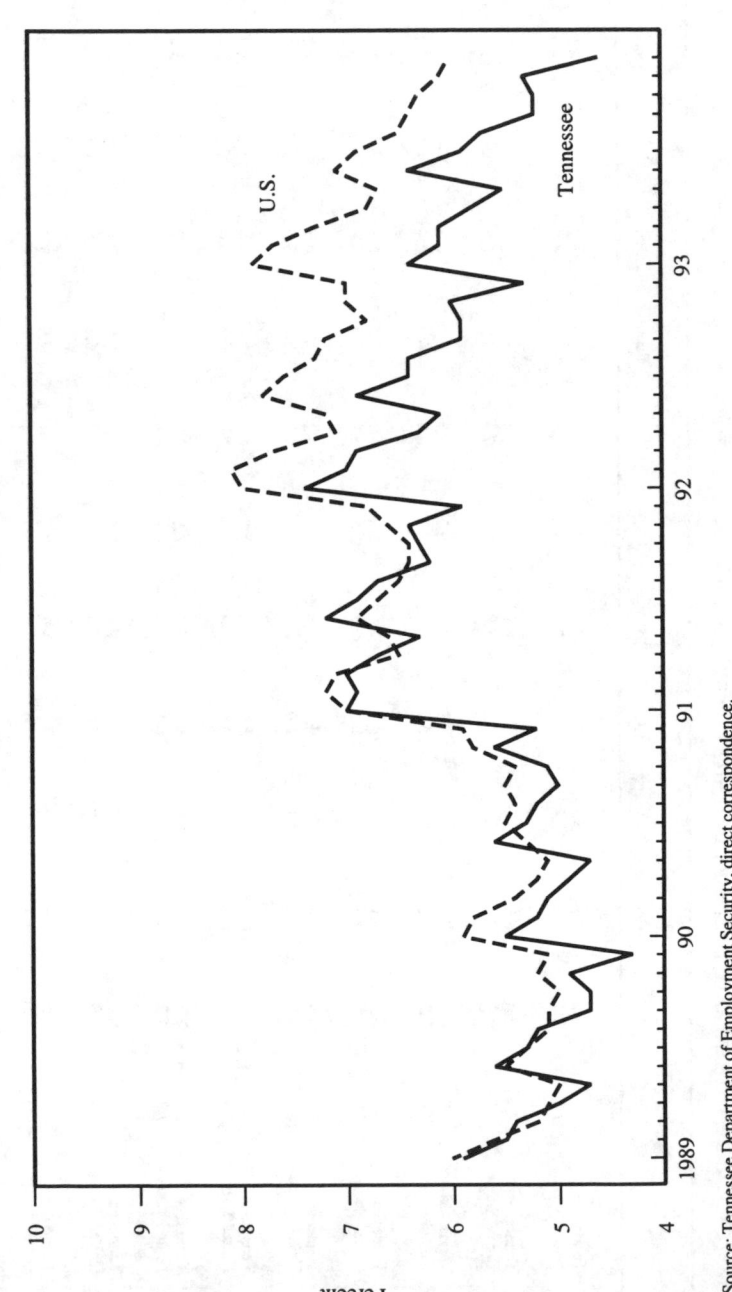

Source: Tennessee Department of Employment Security, direct correspondence.

TABLE 3.4-- FULL-TIME EQUIVALENT EMPLOYMENT AND PAYROLLS OF STATE AND LOCAL GOVERNMENTS, WITH RATES PER 10,000 POPULATION, BY FUNCTION, TENNESSEE, OCTOBER 1991

Function	State and local governments			State government only	
	Employ-ment	Employment per 10,000 population	Payroll ($1,000)	Employ-ment	Payroll ($1,000)
All functions	249,897	504.5	487,544	76,111	156,928
Education	117,800	237.8	235,643	31,187	67,511
Higher education	29,256	59.1	63,421	29,256	63,421
Instructional employees only	11,493	23.2	34,956	11,493	34,956
Elementary and secondary education	86,613	174.9	168,133	0	0
Instructional employees only	58,575	118.3	135,128	0	0
Other education	1,931	3.9	4,090	1,931	4,090
Libraries	1,091	2.2	1,639	0	0
Social services and income maintenance	43,778	88.4	81,675	20,846	41,168
Public welfare	8,671	17.5	14,874	5,054	9,878
Hospitals	26,659	53.8	50,235	10,160	19,597
Health	6,835	13.8	13,283	4,019	8,410
Social insurance administration	1,613	3.3	3,283	1,613	3,283
Transportation	12,833	25.9	21,363	4,791	9,128
Highways	11,700	23.6	18,914	4,791	9,128
Air and water transportation	1,133	2.3	2,449	0	0
Public safety	28,154	56.8	55,831	7,891	15,344
Police protection	12,361	25.0	24,556	1,524	3,470
Police officers only	9,494	19.2	19,860	938	2,484
Fire protection	5,715	11.5	13,314	0	0
Firefighters only	5,364	10.8	12,552	0	0
Corrections	10,078	20.3	17,961	6,367	11,874
Environment and housing	14,264	28.9	23,970	4,233	7,493
Natural resources	3,366	6.8	6,296	3,095	5,910
Parks and recreation	3,493	7.1	5,395	1,138	1,583
Housing and community development	2,410	4.9	4,256	0	0
Sewerage	2,116	4.3	3,922	0	0
Solid waste management	2,879	5.8	4,101	0	0
Governmental administration	13,722	27.7	28,100	4,544	10,858
Judicial and legal	4,702	9.5	10,563	1,459	4,384
Financial and other	9,020	18.2	17,537	3,085	6,474
Local utilities	10,986	22.2	25,172	0	0
Water supply	3,449	7.0	6,992	0	0
Electric power and gas supply	7,292	14.7	17,797	0	0
Public transit	245	0.5	383	0	0
Other and unallocable	7,269	14.7	14,152	2,619	5,424

Source: U.S. Department of Commerce, Bureau of the Census, *Public Employment: 1991*.

TABLE 3.5-- GOVERNMENT EMPLOYMENT, BY LEVEL OF GOVERNMENT, TENNESSEE, 1945-1991, SELECTED YEARS [In thousands of employees]

Year	All governments[1]	Federal (civilian)[2]	State	Local[3]
1991	336	56	89	191
1990	339	56	92	191
1989	332	57	88	188
1988	329	57	84	189
1987	321	58	82	181
1986	314	58	81	175
1985	307	57	79	171
1984	307	58	78	171
1983	303	58	76	168
1982	310	66	77	168
1981	319	72	75	172
1980	325	70	74	180
1979	321	68	75	177
1978	315	68	73	174
1977	293	57	74	162
1976	283	55	69	158
1975	275	53	63	159
1974	265	50	64	151
1973	263	49	61	153
1972	248	48	60	140
1971	235	46	56	133
1970	221	42	55	124
1969	217	43	51	124
1968	217	44	47	126
1967	206	42	45	119
1966	198	45	41	113
1965	187	38	37	111
1964	179	38	34	108
1963	172	38	32	102
1962	170	38	30	101
1961	160	36	28	96
1960	151	36	26	89
1959	150	39	25	86
1955	132	42	21	69
1950	114	36	17	60
1945	93	42	n.a.	n.a.

Note: Detail may not add to total due to independent rounding.

n.a. not available.

1. Employment as of October 12, except for the years 1945 and 1957. Data for these years are as of April 12.

2. The month in which federal civilian employment is enumerated has varied.

3. Statistics for local governments are estimates subject to sampling variations.

Source: U.S. Department of Commerce, Bureau of the Census, *Public Employment: 1991*, and earlier editions.

TABLE 3.6-- CIVILIAN EMPLOYMENT IN THE FEDERAL GOVERNMENT, BY SELECTED AGENCIES, TENNESSEE,1950–1990, SELECTED YEARS

Year	Total	Department of Defense	U.S. Postal Service	Veterans Administration	Other agencies
1990	56,416	7,851	13,607	7,635	27,323
1986	57,950	7,211	13,615	7,188	29,936
1982	58,200	7,300	11,700	6,500	32,700
1981	67,300	8,100	11,800	6,300	41,100
1980	71,600	7,800	12,000	6,400	45,400
1979	69,900	7,800	12,000	6,200	43,900
1978	68,000	7,800	11,800	6,100	42,300
1977	63,700	8,100	11,900	6,200	37,500
1976	51,800	7,500	11,100	5,900	27,300
1975	55,400	8,000	12,100	5,900	27,000
1974	50,300	7,900	12,000	4,700	26,100
1973	49,300	7,600	11,100	5,300	25,300
1972	48,500	7,500	11,000	5,300	24,700
1971	46,900	7,100	11,200	5,100	23,600
1970	44,800	7,400	10,900	4,600	21,800
1969	42,400	8,000	11,200	4,500	18,700
1968	40,300	7,300	11,100	4,600	17,300
1967	40,100	7,200	10,800	4,600	17,500
1966	39,300	7,200	10,700	4,500	16,900
1965	40,700	6,100	12,500	4,500	17,500
1964	38,200	6,200	9,400	4,600	17,900
1963	36,300	6,300	9,400	4,700	15,900
1962	36,400	6,600	9,400	4,700	15,700
1961	35,600	6,700	9,200	4,900	14,700
1960	34,100	6,600	9,000	4,800	13,500
1959	36,300	7,700	9,000	4,900	14,700
1958	37,500	8,500	8,800	4,800	15,400
1957	37,400	8,000	9,700	5,000	14,600
1956	37,900	9,500	8,700	5,100	14,700
1955	37,800	9,500	7,900	5,000	15,300
1954	41,200	8,700	7,900	5,200	19,400
1953	41,200	9,700	8,200	5,400	18,000
1952	44,100	10,400	8,500	5,400	19,900
1951	44,500	12,700	8,100	5,600	18,100
1950	36,300	7,900	8,200	5,700	14,500

Note: Excludes members and employees of Congress, Central Intelligence Agency, temporary Christmas help of the U.S. Postal Service, and the National Security Agency.

Source: Tax Foundation, Inc., *Facts and Figures on Government Finance, 1993*, and earlier editions; and U.S. Department of Commerce, Bureau of the Census, *Statistical Abstract of the United States, 1984*, and earlier editions.

TABLE 3.7.– NUMBER OF EMPLOYEES IN NONAGRICULTURAL ESTABLISHMENTS, BY SECTOR, TENNESSEE, 1950-1993, SELECTED YEARS
[In thousands of persons]

Sector	1993	1992	1991 r	1990	1989	1988	1987	1986	1985
Total	2,327.5	2,245.0	2,183.6	2,193.2	2,167.2	2,092.1	2,011.6	1,929.8	1,867.8
Manufacturing	528.3	514.5	502.7	520.3	524.5	511.9	497.4	490.5	492.4
Construction and mining	99.1	93.3	92.0	98.6	103.5	103.3	102.0	97.2	93.3
Transportation and public utilities	126.4	120.6	117.4	116.4	115.8	109.2	103.4	97.6	93.0
Trade	534.2	517.7	511.6	517.2	508.4	495.6	477.2	452.1	435.3
Finance, insurance, and real estate	103.7	101.0	101.6	103.1	103.4	103.2	101.4	95.4	89.4
Services	574.0	541.1	505.2	486.3	467.2	440.3	408.9	384.7	360.2
Government	361.7	356.9	353.2	351.4	344.3	328.4	321.2	312.4	304.2

Sector	1984	1983	1982	1981	1980	1975	1970	1960	1950
Total	1,812.0	1,719.0	1,703.0	1,755.4	1,746.6	1,505.7	1,327.6	925.4	759.3
Manufacturing	497.1	468.6	466.7	506.9	502.1	459.0	463.8	315.0	249.2
Construction and mining	86.2	77.5	81.4	86.2	91.3	85.5	72.4	56.0	60.7
Transportation and public utilities	89.1	83.6	84.0	86.7	86.6	70.8	66.4	55.4	59.5
Trade	413.3	389.9	380.5	379.9	379.7	320.8	257.7	193.2	161.1
Finance, insurance, and real estate	85.9	81.9	79.9	79.6	78.7	68.9	56.5	39.2	24.6
Services	344.3	323.4	313.1	304.4	291.0	229.4	184.9	120.3	93.0
Government	296.1	294.1	297.5	311.7	317.2	271.3	225.9	146.3	111.2

r revised.

Source: U.S. Department of Labor, Bureau of Labor Statistics, *Employment and Earnings*, May editions.

TABLE 3.8-- LABOR FORCE, EMPLOYMENT, AND UNEMPLOYMENT RATE, TENNESSEE AND
METROPOLITAN STATISTICAL AREAS, 1992 AND 1993

Metropolitan Statistical Area	1993			1992		
	Labor force	Employed persons	Unemploy- ment rate	Labor force	Employed persons	Unemploy- ment rate
TENNESSEE	2,500,000	2,358,000	5.7	2,454,000	2,298,000	6.4
Chattanooga	214,300	203,300	5.1	210,500	197,500	6.2
Hamilton County	144,230	137,290	4.8	141,410	133,590	5.5
Marion County	11,810	10,900	7.7	11,620	10,610	8.7
Georgia Portion	58,180	55,070	5.3	57,390	53,260	7.2
Clarksville-Hopkinsville	67,300	63,600	5.5	65,600	61,600	6.1
Montgomery County	43,880	41,360	5.7	42,830	40,090	6.4
Kentucky Portion	23,400	22,210	5.1	22,740	21,460	5.6
Jackson[1]	4,200	3,830	8.8	4,090	3,760	8.1
Johnson City-Kingsport- Bristol	219,600	207,000	5.7	217,800	204,500	6.1
Carter County	25,020	23,440	6.3	24,790	23,140	6.7
Hawkins County	21,770	20,540	5.6	21,560	20,280	5.9
Sullivan County	72,420	68,920	4.8	71,640	68,040	5.0
Unicoi County	7,930	7,170	9.6	7,900	7,080	10.4
Washington County	48,430	45,690	5.7	47,660	45,100	5.4
Virginia Portion	44,000	41,250	6.3	44,300	40,900	7.7
Knoxville	322,800	307,500	4.7	314,200	297,600	5.3
Anderson County	35,440	33,730	4.8	34,500	32,650	5.4
Blount County	45,980	43,350	5.7	44,540	41,950	5.8
Knox County	186,950	179,740	3.9	182,160	173,950	4.5
Loudon County	17,450	16,650	4.6	17,070	16,110	5.6
Sevier County	30,260	27,630	8.7	29,470	26,740	9.3
Union County	6,660	6,390	4.1	6,490	6,190	4.6
Memphis	484,900	458,600	5.4	484,200	455,700	5.9
Fayette County	11,270	10,470	7.1	11,350	10,410	8.3
Shelby County	396,410	375,180	5.4	395,450	373,080	5.7
Tipton County	17,130	16,040	6.4	17,160	15,950	7.1
Arkansas Portion	21,620	20,030	7.4	21,790	20,030	8.1
Mississippi Portion	38,490	36,870	4.2	38,470	36,230	5.8
Nashville	555,300	532,200	4.2	537,600	510,700	5.0
Cheatham County	15,100	14,570	3.5	14,690	13,980	4.8
Davidson County	285,200	273,980	3.9	276,120	262,900	4.8
Dickson County	17,960	17,070	5.0	17,470	16,380	6.2
Robertson County	22,920	21,450	6.4	22,000	20,580	6.5
Rutherford County	70,690	67,610	4.4	68,130	64,880	4.8
Sumner County	57,840	54,910	5.1	56,240	52,690	6.3
Williamson County	47,430	46,030	3.0	45,890	44,170	3.7
Wilson County	38,130	36,570	4.1	37,020	35,100	5.2

Note: Data are based on 1993 benchmark.
1. Jackson Metropolitan Statistical Area consists of Madison County.
Source: Tennessee Department of Employment Security, CPS Labor Force Estimates Summary, direct
correspondence.

TABLE 3.9.– NUMBER OF EMPLOYEES IN NONAGRICULTURAL ESTABLISHMENTS, BY SECTOR, METROPOLITAN STATISTICAL AREAS, 1980-1993, SELECTED YEARS [In thousands of jobs]

MSA and sector	1993	1992	1991 r	1990 r	1989 r	1988	1987	1986	1985	1980
CHATTANOOGA										
Total	207.6	201.7	198.8	200.1	197.7	195.6	190.3	179.7	174.9	168.7
Manufacturing	44.7	43.4	43.9	46.4	46.7	46.6	46.0	43.8	43.7	50.2
Construction and mining	7.4	7.0	n.a.	7.7	8.2	8.7	8.6	8.4	8.5	7.7
Transportation	7.3	7.4	7.8	9.0	8.6	8.6	9.0	8.7	8.3	7.3
Trade	50.9	48.4	47.5	47.4	47.4	46.6	43.9	41.2	40.1	33.0
Finance	13.5	13.3	13.3	12.9	12.4	12.6	12.0	11.1	10.5	9.6
Services	50.3	48.3	44.9	42.9	40.5	38.6	37.5	35.2	33.3	28.2
Government	33.6	34.0	34.7	33.9	33.9	34.1	33.3	31.2	30.5	32.7
MSA and sector	1993	1992	1991	1990	1989	1988	1987	1986	1985	1980
CLARKSVILLE-HOPKINSVILLE[1]										
Total	25.6	24.8	24.0	24.7	24.5	23.9	23.3	22.1	21.0	20.7
Manufacturing	6.0	6.0	5.6	6.1	5.8	5.5	5.3	4.9	4.8	6.1
Construction and mining	1.1	1.1	1.0	1.2	1.3	1.4	1.4	1.0	0.8	0.9
Transportation	1.1	1.1	1.0	1.0	1.0	1.0	0.9	0.9	0.8	0.7
Trade	6.4	6.0	5.9	5.9	5.9	5.8	5.8	5.2	4.9	4.3
Finance	1.0	1.1	1.1	1.2	1.2	1.2	1.2	1.1	1.0	0.8
Services	3.2	3.4	3.3	3.3	3.3	3.2	3.2	3.3	3.2	2.5
Government	6.8	6.2	6.0	6.0	5.9	5.8	5.8	5.7	5.5	5.4
MSA and sector	1993	1992	1991	1990	1989	1988	1987	1986	1985	1980
JACKSON										
Total	42.9	41.7	40.9	38.9	37.8	37.2	34.5	33.6	32.7	30.3
Manufacturing	9.9	9.5	9.0	8.9	8.8	8.6	8.2	8.2	8.3	8.6
Construction and mining	2.6	2.2	2.5	2.3	2.2	2.0	1.8	1.5	1.6	1.8
Transportation	1.6	1.5	1.5	1.6	1.5	1.5	1.6	1.5	1.4	1.3
Trade	9.4	9.4	9.4	8.8	8.6	8.9	7.8	7.5	7.6	6.7
Finance	1.2	1.2	1.2	1.3	1.2	1.2	1.0	1.2	1.0	1.1
Services	9.7	9.7	9.3	8.5	8.0	7.6	6.8	6.6	6.0	4.3
Government	8.5	8.1	8.0	7.4	7.4	7.3	7.3	7.1	6.8	6.5

TABLE 3.9-- NUMBER OF EMPLOYEES IN NONAGRICULTURAL ESTABLISHMENTS, BY SECTOR, METROPOLITAN STATISTICAL AREAS, 1980-1993, SELECTED YEARS [In thousands of jobs] (Continued)

MSA and sector	1993	1992	1991 r	1990 r	1989 r	1988	1987	1986	1985	1980
JOHNSON CITY-KINGSPORT-BRISTOL										
Total	184.2	181.1	175.2	174.0	168.9	163.7	159.5	154.4	151.1	136.3
Manufacturing	53.7	54.0	53.6	54.6	54.1	52.6	53.2	52.8	52.7	53.1
Construction and mining	8.3	8.3	8.2	7.5	7.4	7.4	7.0	6.3	6.2	7.3
Transportation	7.6	6.6	6.3	6.2	6.1	6.2	6.0	6.1	6.0	5.8
Trade	41.1	40.7	39.5	40.0	38.9	37.4	35.7	34.4	33.5	24.1
Finance	5.3	5.6	5.5	5.5	5.3	5.2	5.2	4.9	4.8	4.4
Services	39.9	38.9	36.9	35.2	32.7	30.7	28.7	27.0	25.3	17.1
Government	28.3	27.2	25.3	25.0	24.4	24.2	23.7	23.0	22.7	24.4

MSA and sector	1993	1992	1991 r	1990 r	1989 r	1988	1987	1986	1985	1980
KNOXVILLE[1]										
Total	295.7	285.3	271.0	266.1	262.0	259.7	251.9	242.0	235.0	195.3
Manufacturing	50.4	49.7	48.9	49.2	50.0	52.7	50.6	51.0	50.9	52.4
Construction and mining	14.6	13.0	12.3	13.8	16.2	15.3	14.3	13.7	12.9	11.1
Transportation	11.1	10.3	10.1	10.7	10.8	10.2	9.8	9.0	8.8	8.2
Trade	73.1	73.4	71.9	71.1	68.7	65.8	63.6	60.7	57.5	41.5
Finance	10.6	10.6	9.9	9.9	10.2	10.0	9.5	9.0	8.8	8.2
Services	80.5	74.9	66.7	60.5	56.2	54.8	53.4	50.1	48.8	32.4
Government	55.4	53.5	51.3	50.8	50.0	50.8	50.8	48.4	47.2	41.5

MSA and sector	1993	1992	1991 r	1990 r	1989 r	1988	1987	1986	1985	1980
MEMPHIS[2]										
Total	487.3	482.8	478.6	482.1	476.9	452.8	422.0	403.0	388.7	359.4
Manufacturing	64.9	62.8	61.8	64.4	64.9	62.2	53.6	51.8	52.2	59.6
Construction and mining	18.0	17.8	18.3	20.3	20.4	19.6	19.2	18.6	18.2	16.1
Transportation	48.7	47.6	46.9	47.2	46.9	41.6	38.8	35.5	33.3	27.5
Trade	125.3	125.3	125.2	127.1	125.8	122.0	116.3	111.2	108.2	97.1
Finance	25.1	24.8	25.0	25.1	25.6	25.2	24.2	22.9	21.9	19.8
Services	128.8	125.7	122.5	120.4	117.0	108.4	98.9	93.8	88.3	73.6
Government	76.7	78.9	78.9	77.6	76.3	73.8	71.1	69.2	66.6	65.7

TABLE 3.9— NUMBER OF EMPLOYEES IN NONAGRICULTURAL ESTABLISHMENTS, BY SECTOR, METROPOLITAN STATISTICAL AREAS, 1980–1993, SELECTED YEARS [In thousands of jobs] (Continued)

MSA and sector	1993	1992	1991 r	1990	1989	1988	1987	1986	1985	1980
NASHVILLE-DAVIDSON										
Total	540.4	514.5	500.4	501.9	497.2	490.0	476.7	456.1	434.1	360.2
Manufacturing	93.9	90.7	86.9	88.5	90.3	90.2	90.3	90.5	89.4	80.8
Construction and mining	22.3	19.9	21.0	23.8	25.8	27.5	29.6 r	28.8	26.4	18.7
Transportation	31.9	30.3	29.2	28.7	26.7	25.2	24.2	22.7	22.2	19.5
Trade	129.2	125.0	122.8	124.2	122.1	119.6	116.9 r	111.5	105.5	82.0
Finance	30.7	30.6	30.7	31.1	32.0	33.6	33.6	31.4	29.0	24.5
Services	159.7	149.3	140.2	136.6	131.7	126.5	116.4	107.0	99.1	71.9
Government	72.7	68.8	69.7	69.0	68.7	67.4	65.7	64.2	62.4	62.8

Note: For area included in each MSA beginning in 1989, see current MSA boundaries in Figure 0.1. Detail may not add to total due to independent rounding.

r revised to 1993 benchmark and current MSA boundaries.

1. Knoxville includes the counties of Knox, Anderson, Blount, and Union prior to 1983; Jefferson, Grainger and Sevier are added beginning in 1983. Clarksville includes only the Montgomery County, Tennessee portion of this MSA.

2. Because of the incorporation of data for DeSoto County, Mississippi, Memphis MSA data prior to 1988 are not comparable to later years.

Source: U.S. Department of Labor, Bureau of Labor Statistics, *Employment and Earnings*, May editions; and Tennessee Department of Employment Security, Research and Statistics Section, *Tennessee Annual Average Labor Force Estimates, 1989–1993*, and earlier editions.

TABLE 3.10--PAYROLL AND FULL-TIME EQUIVALENT EMPLOYMENT OF CITY GOVERNMENTS, BY
SELECTED FUNCTIONS, TENNESSEE CITIES WITH POPULATION OF 75,000 OR MORE,
OCTOBER 1992

City	Employment								
	Total	Education	Highways	Police	Fire	Utili- ties	Solid waste manage- ment	Parks	Govern- mental adminis- tration
Chattanooga	5,229	2,313	138	462	407	607	206	213	169
Clarksville	701	0	80	164	144	201	0	35	22
Knoxville	2,508	0	75	384	372	897	125	32	104
Memphis	22,382	11,752	156	1,942	1,450	2,945	1,421	1,298	409
Nashville-Davidson[1]	16,594	6,977	292	1,432	1,082	1,305	155	465	948

	Average October earnings[2] ($)	Payroll ($1,000)							
Chattanooga	2,449	12,397	6,054	234	1,008	957	1,761	313	390	408
Clarksville	1,943	1,353	0	121	317	284	411	0	60	51
Knoxville	2,500	6,231	0	155	883	872	2,537	194	49	233
Memphis	2,361	52,621	27,084	382	5,043	4,237	8,585	2,680	1,257	900
Nashville-Davidson[1]	2,430	40,370	19,879	606	3,314	2,877	2,060	300	875	2,222

Note: Total includes other categories not shown separately.
1. Education data are for October 1991.
2. Full-time employees only.
Source: U.S. Department of Commerce, Bureau of the Census, *City Employment: 1992.*

3. EMPLOYMENT AND EARNINGS

TABLE 3.11--NONAGRICULTURAL EMPLOYMENT, BY SECTOR, NON-MSA COUNTIES, 1993

County	Total	Manufacturing Employed	%	Construction and mining Employed	%	Transportation, communications and utilities Employed	%	Wholesale and retail trade Employed	%
Bedford	12,150	5,360	44.1	450	3.7	730	6.0	1,900	15.6
Benton	4,060	1,090	26.8	260	6.4	230	5.7	950	23.4
Bledsoe	2,190	710	32.4	40	1.8	60	2.7	190	8.7
Bradley	31,250	11,310	36.2	1,110	3.6	670	2.1	6,590	21.1
Campbell	7,630	1,650	21.6	630	8.3	150	2.0	1,800	23.6
Cannon	2,090	600	28.7	40	1.9	100	4.8	300	14.4
Carroll	10,190	4,850	47.6	120	1.2	310	3.0	1,470	14.4
Chester	3,330	1,060	31.8	200	6.0	190	5.7	470	14.1
Claiborne	7,770	3,800	48.9	140	1.8	150	1.9	1,120	14.4
Clay	2,820	1,680	59.6	20	0.7	40	1.4	170	6.0
Cocke	7,000	2,780	39.7	160	2.3	60	0.9	1,630	23.3
Coffee	20,870	5,640	27.0	630	3.0	260	1.2	4,020	19.3
Crockett	3,660	1,770	48.4	220	6.0	60	1.6	450	12.3
Cumberland	10,520	2,710	25.8	360	3.4	130	1.2	2,630	25.0
Decatur	3,490	1,330	38.1	200	5.7	170	4.9	520	14.9
DeKalb	4,750	2,400	50.5	100	2.1	80	1.7	760	16.0
Dyer	15,350	6,220	40.5	710	4.6	380	2.5	2,960	19.3
Fentress	4,360	1,670	38.3	110	2.5	50	1.1	840	19.3
Franklin	8,280	2,190	26.4	290	3.5	80	1.0	1,790	21.6
Gibson	18,260	8,350	45.7	810	4.4	420	2.3	3,070	16.8
Giles	8,810	4,200	47.7	240	2.7	190	2.2	1,620	18.4
Grainger	2,880	1,480	51.4	150	5.2	70	2.4	390	13.5
Greene	20,160	8,730	43.3	520	2.6	580	2.9	3,110	15.4
Grundy	1,710	290	17.0	40	2.3	150	8.8	310	18.1
Hamblen	26,410	14,580	55.2	550	2.1	860	3.3	3,940	14.9
Hancock	970	370	38.1	40	4.1	0	0.0	70	7.2
Hardeman	7,280	2,470	33.9	190	2.6	140	1.9	1,110	15.2
Hardin	6,460	2,390	37.0	290	4.5	230	3.6	1,440	22.3
Haywood	5,520	2,170	39.3	160	2.9	230	4.2	1,020	18.5
Henderson	7,930	4,340	54.7	110	1.4	170	2.1	1,360	17.2
Henry	11,400	4,270	37.5	500	4.4	320	2.8	2,700	23.7
Hickman	3,500	1,300	37.1	130	3.7	100	2.9	330	9.4
Houston	1,840	470	25.5	(D)	-	(D)	-	180	9.8
Humphreys	4,820	1,760	36.5	300	6.2	(D)	-	490	10.2
Jackson	1,960	870	44.4	60	3.1	70	3.6	140	7.1
Jefferson	9,890	3,170	32.1	850	8.6	570	5.8	1,920	19.4
Johnson	3,860	1,760	45.6	230	6.0	(D)	-	300	7.8
Lake	2,080	560	26.9	10	0.5	20	1.0	230	11.1
Lauderdale	7,690	3,570	46.4	120	1.6	160	2.1	1,020	13.3
Lawrence	13,480	7,420	55.0	300	2.2	390	2.9	2,120	15.7
Lewis	2,920	1,370	46.9	30	1.0	50	1.7	510	17.5
Lincoln	7,610	2,950	38.8	280	3.7	140	1.8	1,430	18.8
McMinn	18,020	8,660	48.1	740	4.1	860	4.8	2,830	15.7
McNairy	7,380	3,410	46.2	120	1.6	300	4.1	880	11.9
Macon	4,320	2,380	55.1	50	1.2	160	3.7	350	8.1
Marshall	11,140	7,070	63.5	150	1.3	180	1.6	1,350	12.1
Maury	28,030	10,950	39.1	1,040	3.7	1,250	4.5	4,890	17.4
Meigs	1,470	580	39.5	(D)	-	80	5.4	160	10.9

146

TABLE 3.11--NONAGRICULTURAL EMPLOYMENT, BY SECTOR, NON-MSA COUNTIES, 1993
(Continued)

Finance, insurance and real estate		Services		Government		
Em-ployed	%	Em-ployed	%	Em-ployed	%	County
280	2.3	1,700	14.0	1,710	14.1	Bedford
90	2.2	630	15.5	810	20.0	Benton
30	1.4	200	9.1	950	43.4	Bledsoe
720	2.3	6,760	21.6	4,000	12.8	Bradley
300	3.9	1,060	13.9	2,040	26.7	Campbell
110	5.3	400	19.1	540	25.8	Cannon
260	2.6	1,870	18.4	1,300	12.8	Carroll
(D)	-	(D)	-	470	14.1	Chester
210	2.7	1,160	14.9	1,190	15.3	Claibome
30	1.1	350	12.4	520	18.4	Clay
240	3.4	990	14.1	1,140	16.3	Cocke
660	3.2	6,440	30.9	3,180	15.2	Coffee
130	3.6	400	10.9	620	16.9	Crockett
600	5.7	2,320	22.1	1,710	16.3	Cumberland
80	2.3	570	16.3	620	17.8	Decatur
130	2.7	520	10.9	760	16.0	DeKalb
500	3.3	2,290	14.9	2,250	14.7	Dyer
120	2.8	790	18.1	770	17.7	Fentress
180	2.2	2,450	29.6	1,220	14.7	Franklin
480	2.6	2,810	15.4	2,280	12.5	Gibson
260	3.0	1,080	12.3	1,200	13.6	Giles
(D)	-	380	13.2	510	17.7	Grainger
480	2.4	3,290	16.3	3,330	16.5	Greene
40	2.3	280	16.4	590	34.5	Grundy
540	2.0	3,330	12.6	2,510	9.5	Hamblen
(D)	-	(D)	-	380	39.2	Hancock
210	2.9	1,220	16.8	1,930	26.5	Hardeman
160	2.5	560	8.7	1,390	21.5	Hardin
220	4.0	640	11.6	1,060	19.2	Haywood
210	2.6	670	8.4	1,060	13.4	Henderson
290	2.5	1,250	11.0	2,040	17.9	Henry
100	2.9	400	11.4	1,140	32.6	Hickman
(D)	-	560	30.4	490	26.6	Houston
(D)	-	410	8.5	1,520	31.5	Humphreys
40	2.0	270	13.8	500	25.5	Jackson
180	1.8	1,730	17.5	1,470	14.9	Jefferson
(D)	-	310	8.0	970	25.1	Johnson
50	2.4	260	12.5	950	45.7	Lake
220	2.9	840	10.9	1,760	22.9	Lauderdale
230	1.7	1,370	10.2	1,630	12.1	Lawrence
80	2.7	420	14.4	460	15.8	Lewis
250	3.3	780	10.2	1,760	23.1	Lincoln
480	2.7	2,120	11.8	2,290	12.7	McMinn
160	2.2	1,390	18.8	1,110	15.0	McNairy
190	4.4	450	10.4	740	17.1	Macon
180	1.6	970	8.7	1,210	10.9	Marshall
1,260	4.5	4,310	15.4	4,290	15.3	Maury
40	2.7	140	9.5	470	32.0	Meigs

TABLE 3.11--NONAGRICULTURAL EMPLOYMENT, BY SECTOR, NON-MSA COUNTIES, 1993
(Continued)

County	Total	Manufacturing		Construction and mining		Transportation, communications and utilities		Wholesale and retail trade	
		Em-ployed	%	Em-ployed	%	Em-ployed	%	Em-ployed	%
Monroe	9,470	4,380	46.3	190	2.0	200	2.1	1,680	17.7
Moore	1,360	390	28.7	(D)	-	(D)	-	60	4.4
Morgan	2,710	970	35.8	90	3.3	100	3.7	260	9.6
Obion	13,310	5,830	43.8	330	2.5	360	2.7	3,090	23.2
Overton	4,910	2,350	47.9	110	2.2	90	1.8	710	14.5
Perry	2,160	1,200	55.6	30	1.4	30	1.4	130	6.0
Pickett	1,190	610	51.3	10	0.8	20	1.7	110	9.2
Polk	2,920	1,090	37.3	10	0.3	70	2.4	340	11.6
Putnam	25,790	8,950	34.7	790	3.1	860	3.3	6,060	23.5
Rhea	9,340	4,580	49.0	110	1.2	150	1.6	1,110	11.9
Roane	15,120	6,720	44.4	270	1.8	340	2.2	2,320	15.3
Scott	5,210	1,830	35.1	370	7.1	130	2.5	870	16.7
Sequatchie	2,440	930	38.1	200	8.2	110	4.5	430	17.6
Smith	4,570	2,010	44.0	(D)	-	200	4.4	550	12.0
Stewart	2,750	700	25.5	(D)	-	(D)	-	220	8.0
Trousdale	2,360	970	41.1	(D)	-	(D)	-	550	23.3
Van Buren	1,250	820	65.6	20	1.6	20	1.6	30	2.4
Warren	13,550	6,740	49.7	380	2.8	220	1.6	2,360	17.4
Wayne	4,400	2,160	49.1	20	0.5	60	1.4	450	10.2
Weakley	13,270	3,970	29.9	260	2.0	260	2.0	2,310	17.4
White	6,290	3,540	56.3	120	1.9	150	2.4	1,130	18.0

TABLE 3.11--NONAGRICULTURAL EMPLOYMENT, BY SECTOR, NON-MSA COUNTIES, 1993
(Continued)

Finance, insurance and real estate		Services		Government		
Employed	%	Employed	%	Employed	%	County
280	3.0	1,400	14.8	1,290	13.6	Monroe
(D)	-	120	8.8	680	50.0	Moore
50	1.8	240	8.9	1,000	36.9	Morgan
470	3.5	1,660	12.5	1,550	11.6	Obion
130	2.6	530	10.8	980	20.0	Overton
40	1.9	400	18.5	330	15.3	Perry
30	2.5	120	10.1	290	24.4	Pickett
140	4.8	510	17.5	720	24.7	Polk
560	2.2	2,970	11.5	5,500	21.3	Putnam
140	1.5	1,290	13.8	1,910	20.4	Rhea
220	1.5	2,050	13.6	3,170	21.0	Roane
130	2.5	650	12.5	1,180	22.6	Scott
90	3.7	270	11.1	410	16.8	Sequatchie
170	3.7	490	10.7	720	15.8	Smith
150	5.5	(D)	-	1,420	51.6	Stewart
(D)	-	190	8.1	400	16.9	Trousdale
10	0.8	10	0.8	340	27.2	Van Buren
370	2.7	1,710	12.6	1,680	12.4	Warren
100	2.3	760	17.3	850	19.3	Wayne
260	2.0	2,790	21.0	3,390	25.5	Weakley
120	1.9	450	7.2	770	12.2	White

Note: Percentages were computed by the Center for Business and Economic Research.

(D) Withheld to avoid disclosing operations of individual companies.

Source: Tennessee Department of Employment Security, Research and Statistics Section, *Annual Averages: Labor Force and Nonagricultural Employment Estimates, 1989–1993*.

TABLE 3.12--EMPLOYMENT, BY OCCUPATION, COUNTIES, 1990

County	Total employed	Executive, administrative and managerial	Professional specialty	Technicians and related support	Sales	Administrative support, clerical	Private household
Anderson	32,313	3,316	4,957	1,806	3,332	4,414	140
Bedford	15,059	1,102	1,261	354	1,472	1,714	62
Benton	6,425	450	554	234	553	599	9
Bledsoe	3,880	203	296	58	263	377	13
Blount	41,016	3,876	4,712	1,686	5,017	5,780	97
Bradley	37,763	3,044	4,191	962	3,813	5,132	54
Campbell	13,274	844	1,090	356	1,231	1,429	22
Cannon	5,131	309	299	129	334	699	18
Carroll	12,612	689	909	402	925	1,362	52
Carter	23,850	1,778	2,371	856	2,388	2,956	61
Cheatham	14,033	1,141	1,471	489	1,402	2,486	98
Chester	5,886	416	594	100	592	878	13
Claiborne	10,724	743	951	265	811	1,109	23
Clay	3,361	169	267	87	167	286	0
Cocke	13,482	867	797	235	1,283	1,292	39
Coffee	18,765	1,751	2,061	528	2,242	2,409	98
Crockett	6,067	470	370	180	551	660	33
Cumberland	14,999	1,017	1,351	373	1,781	1,626	41
Davidson	274,858	37,235	42,155	10,917	37,657	49,995	1,173
Decatur	4,539	224	312	98	398	586	8
DeKalb	6,751	461	563	151	523	711	29
Dickson	16,962	1,424	1,531	494	1,807	2,728	58
Dyer	16,508	1,391	1,391	428	1,859	2,009	82
Fayette	11,297	767	711	288	992	1,374	67
Fentress	6,185	318	518	165	486	476	7
Franklin	16,100	1,183	1,930	424	1,453	1,922	49
Gibson	21,236	1,368	1,493	509	2,050	2,539	77
Giles	12,009	809	890	350	1,162	1,438	85
Grainger	7,731	380	376	77	625	673	21
Greene	27,745	2,009	2,573	808	2,448	2,922	89
Grundy	5,250	223	391	102	472	476	9
Hamblen	25,107	2,023	2,134	540	2,894	3,239	85
Hamilton	140,029	16,319	19,709	4,829	18,541	22,643	350
Hancock	2,165	85	148	42	128	197	12
Hardeman	9,520	565	733	204	698	1,246	23
Hardin	10,037	663	682	185	865	1,176	22
Hawkins	20,285	1,214	1,842	697	1,778	2,147	60
Haywood	8,253	513	698	169	805	759	89
Henderson	10,584	596	925	294	975	1,173	55
Henry	12,200	953	995	316	1,244	1,459	69
Hickman	7,342	578	656	150	656	817	19
Houston	2,853	164	237	75	208	255	8
Humphreys	7,073	558	518	215	665	835	14
Jackson	4,126	221	337	33	260	388	22
Jefferson	16,040	1,065	1,645	364	1,544	2,149	20
Johnson	5,860	326	346	111	477	536	5
Knox	170,840	21,093	28,283	6,715	25,027	25,745	599
Lake	2,674	124	166	37	184	237	52
Lauderdale	9,877	493	698	145	730	1,039	57
Lawrence	15,863	982	1,285	320	1,496	1,757	28

TABLE 3.12--EMPLOYMENT, BY OCCUPATION, COUNTIES, 1990 (Continued)

Protective services	Service, except protective and household	Farming, forestry and fishing	Precision production, craft and repair	Machine operators, assemblers, inspectors	Transportation and material moving	Handlers, cleaners, helpers and laborers[1]	County
670	3,547	355	4,621	2,750	1,148	1,257	Anderson
176	1,472	782	2,460	2,822	618	764	Bedford
38	790	298	1,025	1,112	445	318	Benton
104	397	363	595	780	286	145	Bledsoe
407	5,013	780	6,047	3,657	2,234	1,710	Blount
389	3,076	514	5,774	7,116	1,874	1,824	Bradley
237	1,664	235	2,557	1,878	979	752	Campbell
58	440	253	928	1,150	306	208	Cannon
145	1,079	425	1,793	3,413	865	553	Carroll
393	2,856	390	3,677	3,997	1,014	1,113	Carter
218	1,360	302	2,398	1,238	820	610	Cheatham
87	701	206	802	914	321	262	Chester
92	1,043	481	1,851	2,074	837	444	Claibome
15	296	165	484	1,030	249	146	Clay
200	2,562	389	1,868	2,502	888	560	Cocke
270	1,835	558	2,545	2,967	817	684	Coffee
32	606	501	855	1,125	421	263	Crockett
283	1,968	710	2,281	1,838	1,027	703	Cumberland
4,948	32,112	2,429	24,268	13,964	10,050	7,955	Davidson
129	334	195	640	1,137	324	154	Decatur
45	491	397	1,016	1,727	300	337	DeKalb
215	1,655	484	2,664	1,970	1,026	906	Dickson
323	1,652	573	2,222	2,929	807	842	Dyer
181	1,497	638	1,807	1,639	708	628	Fayette
45	607	284	1,075	1,414	393	397	Fentress
258	1,875	717	2,484	2,523	649	633	Franklin
244	2,150	757	3,019	5,057	1,144	829	Gibson
92	1,104	639	1,533	2,710	693	504	Giles
83	696	448	1,364	2,105	519	364	Grainger
308	2,728	1,206	4,868	5,313	1,296	1,177	Greene
96	457	389	838	1,068	420	309	Grundy
337	2,687	398	3,641	4,930	1,211	988	Hamblen
2,393	16,223	1,759	15,277	11,546	6,134	4,306	Hamilton
21	257	232	386	421	150	86	Hancock
138	1,174	345	1,325	1,931	608	530	Hardeman
131	930	405	1,494	2,285	800	399	Hardin
199	2,206	658	3,504	3,904	1,060	1,016	Hawkins
117	949	472	1,033	1,766	466	417	Haywood
112	959	325	1,586	2,519	645	420	Henderson
167	1,351	527	1,724	1,903	842	650	Henry
145	517	319	1,207	1,445	478	355	Hickman
27	324	147	633	505	132	138	Houston
183	658	288	1,251	1,103	419	366	Humphreys
55	432	215	680	933	265	285	Jackson
181	1,904	630	2,436	2,716	823	563	Jefferson
27	559	268	1,077	1,464	430	234	Johnson
2,362	19,698	1,974	17,241	10,373	6,719	5,011	Knox
184	327	174	252	646	146	145	Lake
296	991	460	1,515	2,232	617	604	Lauderdale
193	1,495	562	2,306	3,932	834	673	Lawrence

TABLE 3.12--EMPLOYMENT, BY OCCUPATION, COUNTIES, 1990 (Continued)

County	Total employed	Executive, administrative and managerial	Professional specialty	Technicians and related support	Sales	Administrative support, clerical	Private household
Lewis	4,121	157	368	119	405	394	6
Lincoln	13,796	918	1,057	407	1,479	1,558	43
Loudon	15,313	1,423	1,279	582	1,773	1,978	34
McMinn	19,898	1,375	1,610	577	1,945	2,213	87
McNairy	9,878	692	635	160	916	1,191	40
Macon	7,572	374	451	142	490	746	21
Madison	37,022	3,847	4,794	1,444	5,073	5,144	108
Marion	11,225	653	857	253	1,141	1,361	53
Marshall	10,878	759	835	296	858	1,255	23
Maury	26,761	2,260	2,643	793	2,526	3,847	154
Meigs	3,607	235	221	61	229	384	0
Monroe	13,629	680	1,007	278	1,118	1,286	35
Montgomery	40,118	3,942	4,588	1,427	5,277	5,744	191
Moore	2,463	139	256	74	156	314	6
Morgan	6,728	424	399	174	633	616	32
Obion	14,824	887	1,233	290	1,492	1,741	67
Overton	8,225	367	622	200	475	734	24
Perry	2,856	216	214	41	154	255	5
Pickett	1,969	75	140	56	184	145	0
Polk	6,153	403	387	56	396	677	2
Putnam	25,535	2,489	3,026	725	3,291	3,516	70
Rhea	10,881	737	1,017	223	810	1,134	29
Roane	21,805	1,815	2,542	957	1,939	2,765	99
Robertson	20,611	1,956	1,546	584	2,292	3,143	57
Rutherford	62,914	6,593	7,047	2,344	8,293	10,329	222
Scott	6,890	355	583	182	537	840	57
Sequatchie	4,099	269	337	124	329	493	13
Sevier	26,446	3,211	2,088	612	4,199	3,238	81
Shelby	396,513	50,349	52,887	16,226	54,117	72,500	3,019
Smith	6,703	447	456	242	555	739	13
Stewart	4,132	301	291	61	342	426	14
Sullivan	68,574	6,192	8,650	2,701	8,834	9,762	202
Sumner	53,416	6,521	5,829	1,556	7,176	8,159	144
Tipton	16,627	1,101	1,195	457	1,762	2,579	93
Trousdale	2,883	113	204	77	224	359	4
Unicoi	7,336	527	648	310	524	734	8
Union	6,124	349	194	95	594	772	9
Van Buren	2,254	104	76	25	126	175	19
Warren	16,244	1,153	1,129	353	1,626	1,760	99
Washington	45,101	4,578	6,053	1,761	6,160	6,292	151
Wayne	6,411	280	422	85	372	555	30
Weakley	15,387	1,197	1,526	396	1,300	1,899	37
White	9,545	656	593	103	840	1,039	32
Williamson	42,261	8,081	7,000	1,148	6,769	6,296	172
Wilson	35,544	4,271	3,484	1,256	4,718	5,844	92

TABLE 3.12--EMPLOYMENT, BY OCCUPATION, COUNTIES, 1990 (Continued)

Protective services	Service, except protective and household	Farming, forestry and fishing	Precision production, craft and repair	Machine operators, assemblers, inspectors	Transportation and material moving	Handlers, cleaners, helpers and laborers[1]	County
56	419	111	614	951	303	218	Lewis
175	1,267	976	2,088	2,433	779	616	Lincoln
127	1,810	517	2,237	2,082	746	725	Loudon
245	1,672	690	3,226	4,172	1,192	894	McMinn
60	703	370	1,749	2,266	676	420	McNairy
89	489	412	1,299	2,251	397	411	Macon
633	4,448	560	4,077	3,743	1,765	1,386	Madison
81	1,180	164	2,078	2,030	768	606	Marion
192	898	474	1,577	2,626	571	514	Marshall
402	2,837	722	3,874	4,095	1,517	1,091	Maury
37	440	164	656	800	201	179	Meigs
84	1,380	540	2,249	3,297	879	796	Monroe
1,006	5,400	833	4,830	3,611	1,737	1,532	Montgomery
34	264	170	303	485	134	128	Moore
428	669	140	1,300	1,153	431	329	Morgan
251	1,659	587	1,820	3,159	866	772	Obion
43	781	350	1,320	2,176	576	557	Overton
62	225	140	367	853	196	128	Perry
40	128	129	312	463	138	159	Pickett
69	454	267	1,109	1,583	393	357	Polk
278	2,884	498	3,125	3,357	1,015	1,261	Putnam
127	1,041	219	1,803	2,690	435	616	Rhea
492	2,631	412	3,428	2,879	995	851	Roane
174	1,932	986	3,229	2,566	1,273	873	Robertson
873	6,552	912	7,794	6,131	2,949	2,875	Rutherford
90	622	184	1,188	1,357	598	297	Scott
40	428	150	630	743	299	244	Sequatchie
354	3,771	511	4,008	2,241	1,113	1,019	Sevier
8,574	45,232	4,187	34,947	21,993	16,346	16,136	Shelby
57	588	338	1,140	1,256	527	345	Smith
59	434	243	691	789	268	213	Stewart
791	7,807	934	9,798	7,092	3,120	2,691	Sullivan
466	5,116	958	7,278	5,629	2,424	2,160	Sumner
325	1,888	579	2,886	1,997	840	925	Tipton
30	234	219	382	635	250	152	Trousdale
120	793	193	1,064	1,543	584	288	Unicoi
53	468	246	1,190	1,252	580	322	Union
121	172	170	368	708	126	64	Van Buren
169	1,330	1,331	2,588	3,071	1,006	629	Warren
631	5,297	960	5,388	4,303	2,069	1,458	Washington
109	498	240	957	2,025	513	325	Wayne
188	1,860	647	1,866	2,785	1,010	676	Weakley
91	772	401	1,765	2,228	601	424	White
362	3,189	1,090	3,923	1,873	1,330	1,028	Williamson
386	3,336	702	5,334	2,982	1,871	1,268	Wilson

1. Excludes laborers, except construction.

Source: U.S. Department of Commerce, Bureau of the Census, *Census of Population and Housing, 1990: Equal Employment Opportunity (EEO) File on CD-ROM.*

TABLE 3.13--NONWHITE EMPLOYMENT, BY OCCUPATION, COUNTIES, 1990

County	Total employed	Executive, administrative and managerial	Professional specialty	Technicians and related support	Sales	Administrative support, clerical	Private household
Anderson	1,574	138	271	117	80	175	26
Bedford	1,436	38	137	26	59	115	53
Benton	180	14	25	0	3	4	0
Bledsoe	63	0	6	7	0	1	2
Blount	1,409	118	116	32	153	140	0
Bradley	1,838	103	114	13	129	159	18
Campbell	167	19	8	11	14	0	0
Cannon	104	0	7	9	0	7	0
Carroll	1,477	46	49	5	29	142	31
Carter	322	0	8	10	20	27	11
Cheatham	298	22	15	16	8	20	19
Chester	546	10	33	9	34	43	0
Claibome	176	2	8	13	12	18	2
Clay	111	8	19	20	12	9	0
Cocke	305	16	0	0	15	31	10
Coffee	891	142	108	25	63	95	15
Crockett	977	33	19	15	35	57	4
Cumberland	229	7	6	0	37	22	0
Davidson	59,425	4,667	7,194	2,504	5,108	10,695	586
Decatur	164	4	11	2	18	8	3
DeKalb	73	2	3	0	2	0	0
Dickson	900	59	45	11	54	121	17
Dyer	1,626	77	88	14	98	133	45
Fayette	4,295	84	253	102	135	254	60
Fentress	7	2	2	0	0	0	0
Franklin	1,059	30	72	49	51	151	14
Gibson	3,853	117	152	73	230	223	35
Giles	1,551	55	56	44	64	98	42
Grainger	82	3	7	0	0	2	0
Greene	722	11	56	27	50	56	7
Grundy	14	0	0	0	0	0	0
Hamblen	1,072	67	37	26	70	127	24
Hamilton	23,727	1,335	2,332	710	1,879	3,513	174
Hancock	17	0	0	0	0	7	0
Hardeman	3,126	56	163	87	63	211	21
Hardin	483	34	40	17	38	40	10
Hawkins	441	25	71	44	29	55	16
Haywood	3,746	80	188	75	207	191	75
Henderson	849	26	64	23	57	51	24
Henry	1,104	54	47	38	61	59	26
Hickman	174	14	22	0	14	7	0
Houston	97	0	5	0	3	27	0
Humphreys	236	26	5	0	10	11	7
Jackson	31	0	7	0	2	0	0
Jefferson	472	29	21	2	19	54	7
Johnson	24	0	7	0	9	0	0
Knox	14,640	1,102	2,151	650	1,419	1,782	165
Lake	492	0	15	0	0	19	41
Lauderdale	2,562	80	109	25	48	104	45
Lawrence	287	11	12	9	22	16	0

TABLE 3.13--NONWHITE EMPLOYMENT, BY OCCUPATION, COUNTIES, 1990 (Continued)

Protective services	Service, except protective and household	Farming, forestry and fishing	Precision production, craft and repair	Machine operators, assemblers, inspectors	Transportation and material moving	Handlers, cleaners, helpers and laborers [1]	County
37	303	21	171	166	23	46	Anderson
30	177	49	162	387	75	128	Bedford
0	54	0	7	48	9	16	Benton
2	18	5	0	12	0	10	Bledsoe
12	363	18	106	180	48	123	Blount
20	373	37	207	478	94	93	Bradley
0	48	0	19	19	7	22	Campbell
2	21	7	19	23	0	9	Cannon
26	164	20	156	679	62	68	Carroll
0	49	15	31	118	26	7	Carter
11	44	10	37	42	41	13	Cheatham
0	133	15	67	139	22	41	Chester
5	29	13	33	22	10	9	Claiborne
0	21	0	0	20	0	2	Clay
16	43	0	88	51	20	15	Cocke
6	97	7	59	219	32	23	Coffee
0	194	86	105	314	67	48	Crockett
5	28	28	51	33	0	12	Cumberland
1,446	12,741	476	3,998	4,825	2,720	2,465	Davidson
10	23	0	10	69	4	2	Decatur
0	8	0	20	32	0	6	DeKalb
0	195	8	66	165	55	104	Dickson
56	338	34	85	464	97	97	Dyer
51	967	242	502	970	324	351	Fayette
0	0	0	0	2	0	1	Fentress
23	180	38	107	269	7	68	Franklin
23	667	140	349	1,435	201	208	Gibson
0	290	41	113	649	45	54	Giles
0	2	5	19	44	0	0	Grainger
0	116	13	90	219	9	68	Greene
0	0	0	2	7	3	2	Grundy
25	232	8	133	225	32	66	Hamblen
591	5,657	318	1,614	3,110	1,398	1,096	Hamilton
0	0	0	0	10	0	0	Hancock
45	594	69	305	1,033	212	267	Hardeman
0	35	11	54	176	20	8	Hardin
8	37	14	46	60	18	18	Hawkins
35	555	173	302	1,329	249	287	Haywood
1	135	13	88	324	14	29	Henderson
9	196	15	118	323	69	89	Henry
0	14	0	21	62	7	13	Hickman
0	17	0	5	15	7	18	Houston
13	37	10	22	59	12	24	Humphreys
0	0	18	0	4	0	0	Jackson
23	89	20	37	98	27	46	Jefferson
0	2	0	0	6	0	0	Johnson
229	3,748	99	1,093	1,317	435	450	Knox
22	98	22	25	187	22	41	Lake
22	416	49	318	982	165	199	Lauderdale
0	43	0	13	122	29	10	Lawrence

155

EMPLOYMENT AND EARNINGS

TABLE 3.13--NONWHITE EMPLOYMENT, BY OCCUPATION, COUNTIES, 1990

County	Total employed	Executive, administrative and managerial	Professional specialty	Technicians and related support	Sales	Administrative support, clerical	Private household
Lewis	41	0	14	0	0	0	0
Lincoln	1,106	2	50	31	51	46	16
Loudon	257	6	11	0	32	37	3
McMinn	939	35	54	17	39	47	26
McNairy	630	29	17	0	7	26	0
Macon	38	0	9	0	5	8	0
Madison	9,831	531	766	322	954	870	36
Marion	368	3	12	2	0	30	0
Marshall	921	33	57	22	37	83	10
Maury	3,806	114	200	98	157	329	97
Meigs	75	8	0	0	0	7	0
Monroe	348	14	17	14	11	21	5
Montgomery	6,925	406	537	131	671	865	74
Moore	117	7	0	0	6	10	0
Morgan	30	0	5	0	0	0	0
Obion	1,317	27	97	34	55	73	42
Overton	35	0	9	0	0	0	0
Perry	51	0	11	0	0	9	0
Pickett	6	0	0	0	0	0	0
Polk	23	0	13	0	0	5	0
Putnam	687	35	170	22	55	55	15
Rhea	374	1	39	18	15	44	0
Roane	806	35	32	0	65	74	9
Robertson	2,133	42	71	51	177	185	23
Rutherford	5,833	379	573	182	503	669	54
Scott	62	2	19	0	3	3	0
Sequatchie	0	0	0	0	0	0	0
Sevier	238	42	19	0	41	21	0
Shelby	154,895	10,250	14,638	4,582	14,394	26,969	2,613
Smith	241	29	15	3	0	39	0
Stewart	75	0	3	0	3	0	5
Sullivan	1,415	132	153	44	113	256	4
Sumner	2,826	110	281	35	187	345	31
Tipton	3,260	84	186	80	302	272	65
Trousdale	358	5	19	14	6	16	4
Unicoi	35	0	14	0	0	0	0
Union	4	0	0	0	0	0	0
Van Buren	6	0	0	0	0	0	0
Warren	641	4	19	0	21	18	46
Washington	1,599	149	107	109	103	194	31
Wayne	66	2	6	5	0	0	2
Weakley	905	15	26	0	97	147	9
White	182	4	21	3	5	18	11
Williamson	3,179	235	428	102	207	411	63
Wilson	2,470	130	251	99	170	269	22

TABLE 3.13--NONWHITE EMPLOYMENT, BY OCCUPATION, COUNTIES, 1990 (Continued)

Protective services	Service, except protective and household	Farming, forestry and fishing	Precision production, craft and repair	Machine operators, assemblers, inspectors	Transportation and material moving	Handlers, cleaners, helpers and laborers [1]	County
0	5	0	7	15	0	0	Lewis
38	254	22	104	303	87	102	Lincoln
0	74	0	40	26	0	28	Loudon
16	142	27	189	295	27	25	McMinn
0	93	2	83	241	61	71	McNairy
0	0	0	8	8	0	0	Macon
224	2,269	171	818	1,687	494	689	Madison
0	75	0	77	64	30	75	Marion
0	140	21	83	286	44	105	Marshall
32	814	54	283	1,153	231	244	Maury
0	14	6	17	11	4	8	Meigs
0	83	0	65	81	21	16	Monroe
202	1,637	84	624	1,074	308	312	Montgomery
0	23	17	6	29	19	0	Moore
0	5	0	14	6	0	0	Morgan
43	349	8	126	336	27	100	Obion
0	26	0	0	0	0	0	Overton
0	4	0	3	16	5	3	Perry
6	0	0	0	0	0	0	Pickett
0	0	0	0	3	2	0	Polk
2	167	8	16	95	22	25	Putnam
5	51	23	33	115	2	28	Rhea
5	184	10	120	199	25	48	Roane
39	425	113	191	568	109	139	Robertson
107	1,188	33	500	986	310	349	Rutherford
0	2	7	24	0	0	2	Scott
0	0	0	0	0	0	0	Sequatchie
0	56	5	14	27	7	6	Sevier
4,423	29,482	2,255	11,498	14,588	9,129	10,074	Shelby
3	43	12	18	55	3	21	Smith
0	16	15	16	13	3	1	Stewart
19	269	20	96	196	35	78	Sullivan
29	584	84	305	529	119	187	Sumner
41	683	113	366	663	133	272	Tipton
9	55	7	52	127	11	33	Trousdale
0	0	21	0	0	0	0	Unicoi
0	0	0	0	4	0	0	Union
0	3	0	0	3	0	0	Van Buren
0	132	42	83	178	23	75	Warren
42	349	43	107	269	55	41	Washington
0	3	2	12	27	5	2	Wayne
12	247	3	66	191	23	69	Weakley
0	34	0	9	62	0	15	White
16	531	146	274	436	210	120	Williamson
28	429	16	348	435	162	111	Wilson

1. Excludes laborers, except construction.

Source: U.S. Department of Commerce, Bureau of the Census, *Census of Population and Housing, 1990: Equal Employment Opportunity (EEO) File on CD-ROM.*

TABLE 3.14--FEMALE EMPLOYMENT, BY OCCUPATION, COUNTIES, 1990

County	Total employed	Executive, adminis- trative and managerial	Profes- sional specialty	Techni- cians and related support	Sales	Adminis- trative support, clerical	Private house- hold
Anderson	14,774	1,547	2,398	822	1,969	3,554	140
Bedford	6,837	423	786	153	758	1,412	62
Benton	2,887	198	317	131	296	427	9
Bledsoe	1,686	83	215	50	151	299	13
Blount	18,389	1,575	2,715	879	2,494	4,602	89
Bradley	17,168	1,031	2,295	418	1,952	3,880	47
Campbell	5,710	309	716	229	685	1,202	22
Cannon	2,280	141	189	89	165	568	18
Carroll	5,774	260	475	173	533	1,021	52
Carter	10,521	812	1,275	483	1,316	2,210	50
Cheatham	6,249	530	809	234	677	2,100	98
Chester	2,755	156	381	48	255	697	13
Claiborne	4,576	352	601	153	471	896	23
Clay	1,611	105	113	49	86	216	0
Cocke	6,257	300	488	131	802	1,039	39
Coffee	8,462	686	981	225	1,250	1,869	92
Crockett	2,754	168	264	109	236	545	26
Cumberland	6,620	467	876	193	882	1,313	41
Davidson	133,840	16,880	22,903	5,728	18,055	38,806	1,102
Decatur	2,051	68	177	38	213	429	8
DeKalb	3,212	158	381	73	264	543	29
Dickson	7,590	631	904	287	1,038	2,159	58
Dyer	7,629	564	819	248	1,121	1,427	78
Fayette	5,189	328	501	149	556	1,134	67
Fentress	2,873	124	323	131	293	364	7
Franklin	7,168	458	1,076	202	730	1,465	49
Gibson	10,286	634	901	279	1,047	1,993	77
Giles	5,241	333	553	156	607	1,134	85
Grainger	3,179	148	230	32	350	487	21
Greene	12,740	846	1,596	379	1,278	2,077	74
Grundy	2,186	99	262	53	234	378	9
Hamblen	11,419	657	1,250	296	1,459	2,517	85
Hamilton	65,950	6,315	10,571	2,497	8,874	17,953	347
Hancock	875	45	92	16	51	152	12
Hardeman	4,365	241	458	131	352	914	23
Hardin	4,476	234	384	113	423	847	17
Hawkins	8,490	554	1,161	495	1,145	1,616	60
Haywood	3,905	163	490	94	402	598	89
Henderson	4,975	184	604	187	526	904	55
Henry	5,502	427	532	184	636	1,188	69
Hickman	3,243	271	485	73	395	643	19
Houston	1,267	67	158	40	121	201	8
Humphreys	3,107	213	350	90	455	665	14
Jackson	1,941	142	225	20	150	295	22
Jefferson	7,274	376	911	191	812	1,619	20
Johnson	2,525	127	197	62	308	386	5
Knox	79,549	8,922	14,034	3,296	11,486	19,755	572
Lake	1,217	56	102	21	104	165	52
Lauderdale	4,661	224	430	89	407	879	57
Lawrence	7,031	393	699	196	828	1,282	28

TABLE 3.14--FEMALE EMPLOYMENT, BY OCCUPATION, COUNTIES, 1990 (Continued)

Protective services	Service, except protective and household	Farming, forestry and fishing	Precision production, craft and repair	Machine operators, assemblers, inspectors	Transportation and material moving	Handlers, cleaners, helpers and laborers [1]	County
67	2,412	55	321	1,159	114	216	Anderson
20	1,033	92	218	1,589	35	256	Bedford
9	628	34	71	678	22	67	Benton
10	292	23	79	443	0	28	Bledsoe
95	3,492	98	375	1,564	120	291	Blount
79	1,855	76	967	3,741	192	635	Bradley
19	1,169	8	134	1,077	24	116	Campbell
13	303	44	107	595	17	31	Cannon
14	825	36	195	2,005	83	102	Carroll
22	1,864	34	329	1,906	70	150	Carter
23	943	29	207	430	94	75	Cheatham
8	494	0	77	567	17	42	Chester
0	734	39	106	1,113	33	55	Claiborne
3	217	14	74	700	19	15	Clay
30	1,747	63	282	1,182	72	82	Cocke
49	1,267	59	268	1,534	58	124	Coffee
5	430	25	111	716	55	64	Crockett
21	1,330	106	191	915	65	220	Cumberland
886	19,067	326	2,587	5,034	987	1,479	Davidson
8	242	10	32	768	21	37	Decatur
0	382	46	184	1,096	12	44	DeKalb
30	1,211	63	144	809	90	166	Dickson
7	1,175	35	199	1,564	94	298	Dyer
22	1,133	67	153	909	73	97	Fayette
0	378	32	127	1,018	8	68	Fentress
22	1,293	111	222	1,374	35	131	Franklin
22	1,602	48	381	2,961	102	239	Gibson
0	784	114	101	1,217	56	101	Giles
7	508	37	125	1,127	44	63	Grainger
63	1,908	171	1,234	2,683	106	325	Greene
1	339	68	90	605	16	32	Grundy
35	1,827	61	575	2,320	65	272	Hamblen
354	10,156	335	1,539	5,313	589	1,107	Hamilton
5	185	37	55	201	15	9	Hancock
27	748	36	132	1,110	48	145	Hardeman
6	658	13	200	1,451	50	80	Hardin
42	1,553	91	281	1,240	139	113	Hawkins
16	656	20	161	1,063	25	128	Haywood
5	694	16	248	1,417	53	82	Henderson
25	940	37	311	958	52	143	Henry
18	378	61	77	734	55	34	Hickman
3	259	18	71	283	3	35	Houston
30	450	49	131	549	62	49	Humphreys
3	295	32	64	574	34	85	Jackson
38	1,335	96	268	1,427	48	133	Jefferson
2	393	0	74	906	25	40	Johnson
377	12,404	363	1,644	5,190	579	927	Knox
18	255	0	38	359	14	33	Lake
70	700	23	220	1,374	25	163	Lauderdale
16	1,164	111	199	1,871	58	186	Lawrence

159

TABLE 3.14--FEMALE EMPLOYMENT, BY OCCUPATION, COUNTIES, 1990

County	Total employed	Executive, administrative and managerial	Professional specialty	Technicians and related support	Sales	Administrative support, clerical	Private household
Lewis	1,887	85	205	56	218	309	6
Lincoln	6,154	344	537	253	734	1,226	43
Loudon	6,860	587	725	279	943	1,547	34
McMinn	8,973	611	938	227	1,035	1,698	87
McNairy	4,346	250	379	87	459	930	40
Macon	3,507	144	299	56	298	585	21
Madison	17,830	1,621	2,959	788	2,509	4,112	108
Marion	4,845	301	506	150	690	1,038	53
Marshall	4,997	275	518	157	459	955	23
Maury	12,270	937	1,563	391	1,300	3,104	154
Meigs	1,544	100	108	33	163	285	0
Monroe	6,188	279	617	193	652	980	35
Montgomery	19,961	1,766	2,901	711	3,149	4,402	191
Moore	1,128	26	143	30	74	281	6
Morgan	2,874	121	236	114	405	491	32
Obion	6,479	365	719	176	744	1,391	52
Overton	3,720	112	356	148	250	591	24
Perry	1,297	87	128	23	80	185	5
Pickett	828	31	56	28	65	123	0
Polk	2,752	199	264	41	223	512	2
Putnam	11,673	985	1,421	293	1,449	2,770	70
Rhea	4,986	338	546	87	505	913	23
Roane	9,858	776	1,181	457	1,006	2,142	94
Robertson	8,984	766	889	311	1,192	2,448	57
Rutherford	28,927	2,761	3,975	1,036	4,350	7,820	218
Scott	2,868	85	375	141	307	601	57
Sequatchie	1,799	118	209	37	123	382	13
Sevier	12,447	1,428	1,193	277	2,550	2,526	80
Shelby	193,939	21,418	30,797	7,807	26,092	54,868	2,895
Smith	2,961	199	298	136	301	566	13
Stewart	1,863	148	182	31	183	315	14
Sullivan	30,238	2,652	4,160	1,247	4,643	7,622	202
Sumner	24,202	2,706	3,357	826	3,208	6,474	144
Tipton	7,475	361	742	263	1,053	2,167	89
Trousdale	1,368	30	145	46	108	286	4
Unicoi	3,197	201	443	147	290	574	8
Union	2,564	134	142	63	328	576	9
Van Buren	1,017	46	46	12	72	116	18
Warren	7,402	556	607	207	800	1,408	99
Washington	20,459	1,902	3,189	842	3,025	4,694	145
Wayne	2,840	115	245	54	199	417	30
Weakley	7,107	512	783	221	693	1,518	37
White	4,399	200	377	51	428	839	23
Williamson	18,516	2,450	3,799	605	2,624	4,870	172
Wilson	16,013	1,702	1,985	668	2,135	4,636	92

TABLE 3.14--FEMALE EMPLOYMENT, BY OCCUPATION, COUNTIES, 1990 (Continued)

Protective services	Service, except protective and household	Farming, forestry and fishing	Precision production, craft and repair	Machine operators, assemblers, inspectors	Transportation and material moving	Handlers, cleaners, helpers and laborers [1]	County
9	318	16	45	567	6	47	Lewis
13	905	172	219	1,469	55	184	Lincoln
42	1,393	114	122	903	48	123	Loudon
26	1,251	67	556	2,146	96	235	McMinn
0	471	85	212	1,300	55	78	McNairy
0	394	38	212	1,322	53	85	Macon
90	3,115	65	354	1,635	187	287	Madison
3	859	37	120	978	22	88	Marion
10	600	45	267	1,452	67	169	Marshall
46	1,813	126	398	2,099	125	214	Maury
1	280	19	79	425	19	32	Meigs
10	1,007	65	268	1,915	68	99	Monroe
95	3,907	127	502	1,630	233	347	Montgomery
0	205	24	31	278	5	25	Moore
63	437	33	88	760	26	68	Morgan
15	1,143	32	200	1,416	69	157	Obion
9	495	45	178	1,329	40	143	Overton
5	183	18	50	503	6	24	Perry
0	107	0	34	360	0	24	Pickett
11	287	49	158	878	36	92	Polk
42	1,799	67	585	1,803	81	308	Putnam
11	684	54	201	1,481	48	95	Rhea
56	1,767	81	192	1,761	120	225	Roane
26	1,359	110	356	1,177	108	185	Robertson
136	4,012	152	780	2,629	327	731	Rutherford
1	489	22	74	677	28	11	Scott
7	302	5	30	520	7	46	Sequatchie
50	2,598	44	377	1,055	61	208	Sevier
1,899	29,757	572	3,518	9,618	1,488	3,210	Shelby
2	445	29	141	759	30	42	Smith
7	346	20	65	480	17	55	Stewart
91	5,293	148	990	2,404	283	503	Sullivan
48	3,348	132	706	2,525	281	447	Sumner
42	1,316	41	289	859	46	207	Tipton
3	197	28	75	364	34	48	Trousdale
36	508	25	162	738	22	43	Unicoi
6	337	20	101	732	32	84	Union
0	105	35	87	435	29	16	Van Buren
18	989	264	592	1,625	78	159	Warren
83	3,519	149	637	1,787	239	248	Washington
5	345	15	169	1,131	47	68	Wayne
36	1,289	50	182	1,525	99	162	Weakley
0	541	23	456	1,296	47	118	White
45	2,195	166	405	864	99	222	Williamson
35	2,202	121	627	1,427	194	189	Wilson

1. Excludes laborers, except construction.

Source: U.S. Department of Commerce, Bureau of the Census, *Census of Population and Housing, 1990: Equal Employment Opportunity (EEO) File on CD-ROM.*

FIGURE 3.3
Unemployment Rates by County, 1993
(Tennessee average = 5.7%)

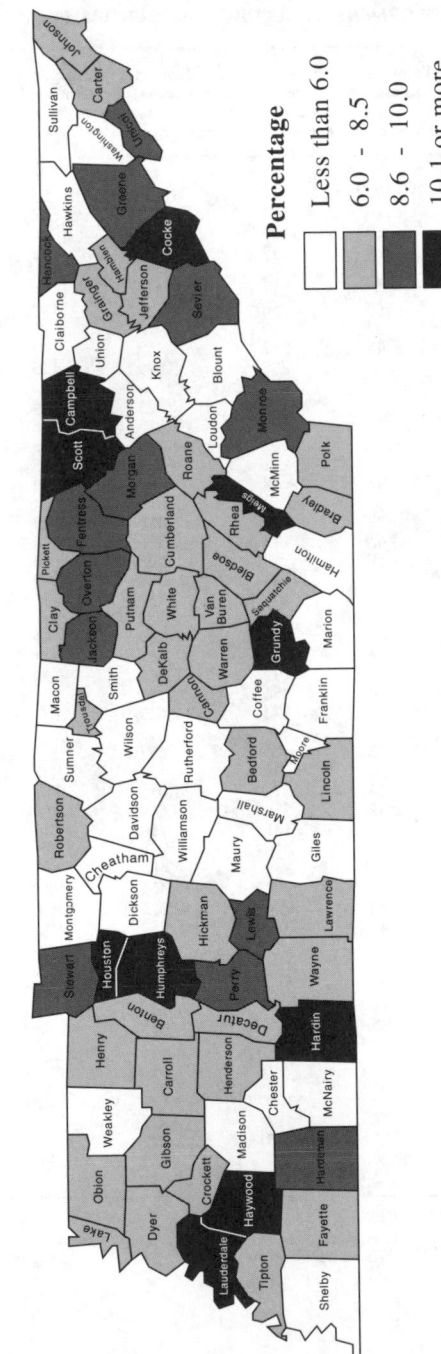

Percentage

Less than 6.0
6.0 - 8.5
8.6 - 10.0
10.1 or more

Note: Rates are benchmarked 1993.
Source: Tennessee Department of Employment Security, direct correspondence.

TABLE 3.15--LABOR FORCE, EMPLOYMENT, AND UNEMPLOYMENT RATE, TENNESSEE AND
COUNTIES, 1992 AND 1993

| County | 1993 | | | 1992ʳ | | |
	Labor force	Employed persons	Unemployment rate	Labor force	Employed persons	Unemployment rate
Anderson	35,440	33,730	4.8	34,500	32,650	5.4
Bedford	16,040	15,060	6.1	15,780	14,610	7.4
Benton	7,140	6,560	8.1	7,050	6,470	8.2
Bledsoe	3,490	3,230	7.4	3,490	3,180	8.9
Blount	45,980	43,350	5.7	44,540	41,950	5.8
Bradley	38,800	36,360	6.3	38,080	35,610	6.5
Campbell	14,180	12,720	10.3	14,830	12,870	13.2
Cannon	5,050	4,720	6.5	5,340	5,030	5.8
Carroll	13,990	13,120	6.2	13,530	12,510	7.5
Carter	25,020	23,440	6.3	24,790	23,140	6.7
Cheatham	15,100	14,570	3.5	14,690	13,980	4.8
Chester	6,490	6,200	4.5	5,990	5,650	5.7
Claiborne	11,880	11,180	5.9	11,660	10,920	6.3
Clay	3,510	3,250	7.4	3,560	3,290	7.6
Cocke	14,650	12,970	11.5	14,720	12,870	12.6
Coffee	20,470	19,280	5.8	19,480	18,280	6.2
Crockett	7,050	6,510	7.7	7,090	6,620	6.6
Cumberland	16,310	14,940	8.4	16,400	14,950	8.8
Davidson	285,200	273,980	3.9	276,120	262,900	4.8
Decatur	4,970	4,620	7.0	4,820	4,320	10.4
DeKalb	7,590	7,080	6.7	7,570	7,020	7.3
Dickson	17,960	17,070	5.0	17,470	16,380	6.2
Dyer	16,840	15,640	7.1	16,710	15,330	8.3
Fayette	11,270	10,470	7.1	11,350	10,410	8.3
Fentress	7,110	6,410	9.8	6,920	6,240	9.8
Franklin	17,080	16,140	5.5	16,320	15,300	6.3
Gibson	22,120	20,560	7.1	21,910	20,140	8.1
Giles	13,490	12,810	5.0	13,040	12,120	7.1
Grainger	8,520	7,910	7.2	8,460	7,850	7.2
Greene	27,980	25,450	9.0	28,020	24,870	11.2
Grundy	4,560	4,040	11.4	4,810	4,170	13.3
Hamblen	27,090	25,300	6.6	27,130	25,110	7.4
Hamilton	144,230	137,290	4.8	141,410	133,590	5.5
Hancock	2,260	2,040	9.7	2,330	2,140	8.2
Hardeman	9,370	8,440	9.9	9,470	8,680	8.3
Hardin	10,770	9,580	11.0	10,680	9,570	10.4
Hawkins	21,770	20,540	5.6	21,560	20,280	5.9
Haywood	8,410	7,410	11.9	8,680	7,660	11.8
Henderson	11,930	11,140	6.6	11,410	10,470	8.2
Henry	13,910	12,970	6.8	13,250	12,260	7.5
Hickman	8,030	7,420	7.6	8,150	7,490	8.1
Houston	3,170	2,810	11.4	3,160	2,740	13.3
Humphreys	7,110	6,310	11.3	6,510	5,650	13.2
Jackson	4,200	3,830	8.8	4,090	3,760	8.1
Jefferson	17,970	16,440	8.5	17,830	16,320	8.5
Johnson	7,130	6,650	6.7	6,980	6,380	8.6
Knox	186,950	179,740	3.9	182,160	173,950	4.5
Lake	2,850	2,670	6.3	2,690	2,480	7.8
Lauderdale	9,290	7,990	14.0	9,400	8,500	9.6
Lawrence	19,770	18,510	6.4	19,590	18,100	7.6

EMPLOYMENT AND EARNINGS

TABLE 3.15--LABOR FORCE, EMPLOYMENT, AND UNEMPLOYMENT RATE, TENNESSEE AND
COUNTIES, 1992 AND 1993 (Continued)

County	1993			1992^r		
	Labor force	Employed persons	Unemployment rate	Labor force	Employed persons	Unemployment rate
Lewis	4,600	4,190	8.9	4,560	4,220	7.5
Lincoln	13,860	12,910	6.9	14,270	13,390	6.2
Loudon	17,450	16,650	4.6	17,070	16,110	5.6
McMinn	20,120	18,610	7.5	20,030	18,220	9.0
McNairy	11,170	10,290	7.9	11,120	10,220	8.1
Macon	8,880	8,420	5.2	8,680	8,140	6.2
Madison	40,740	38,490	5.5	39,950	37,520	6.1
Marion	11,810	10,900	7.7	11,620	10,610	8.7
Marshall	11,900	11,340	4.7	11,610	10,910	6.0
Maury	32,850	30,930	5.8	30,880	28,370	8.1
Meigs	3,890	3,470	10.8	3,890	3,390	12.9
Monroe	15,010	13,630	9.2	13,710	12,280	10.4
Montgomery	43,880	41,360	5.7	42,830	40,090	6.4
Moore	2,750	2,650	3.6	2,630	2,510	4.6
Morgan	6,000	5,430	9.5	6,880	6,210	9.7
Obion	14,280	13,270	7.1	14,240	12,940	9.1
Overton	11,060	10,040	9.2	10,530	9,520	9.6
Perry	8,790	7,960	9.4	8,550	7,820	8.5
Pickett	2,920	2,720	6.8	2,880	2,620	9.0
Polk	2,040	1,900	6.9	2,020	1,870	7.4
Putnam	6,270	5,790	7.7	6,280	5,680	9.6
Rhea	27,130	25,430	6.3	26,800	24,990	6.8
Roane	20,600	19,140	7.1	20,250	18,590	8.2
Robertson	22,920	21,450	6.4	22,000	20,580	6.5
Rutherford	70,690	67,610	4.4	68,130	64,880	4.8
Scott	7,580	6,550	13.6	7,580	6,440	15.0
Sequatchie	4,570	4,220	7.7	4,470	4,060	9.2
Sevier	30,260	27,630	8.7	29,470	26,740	9.3
Shelby	396,410	375,180	5.4	395,450	373,080	5.7
Smith	8,350	7,920	5.1	7,830	7,350	6.1
Stewart	4,290	3,900	9.1	4,420	4,010	9.3
Sullivan	72,420	68,920	4.8	71,640	68,040	5.0
Sumner	57,840	54,910	5.1	56,240	52,690	6.3
Tipton	17,130	16,040	6.4	17,160	15,950	7.1
Trousdale	2,930	2,740	6.5	2,720	2,480	8.8
Unicoi	7,930	7,170	9.6	7,900	7,080	10.4
Union	6,660	6,390	4.1	6,490	6,190	4.6
Van Buren	2,390	2,210	7.5	2,290	2,090	8.7
Warren	18,530	17,240	7.0	17,740	16,300	8.1
Washington	48,430	45,690	5.7	47,660	45,100	5.4
Wayne	7,420	6,880	7.3	7,410	6,850	7.6
Weakley	18,460	17,770	3.7	17,730	16,880	4.8
White	9,850	9,050	8.1	9,970	9,000	9.7
Williamson	47,430	46,030	3.0	45,890	44,170	3.7
Wilson	38,130	36,570	4.1	37,020	35,100	5.2
TENNESSEE	2,500,000	2,358,000	5.7	2,454,000	2,298,000	6.4

Note: Data are based on 1993 benchmark.

r revised.

Source: Tennessee Department of Employment Security, CPS Labor Force Summary, direct correspondence.

TABLE 3.16--INSURED EMPLOYMENT AND AVERAGE WAGES, COUNTIES, 1991

County	Number of em- ployers	Annual average employ- ment	Annual average wages	Average weekly wages	Rank of average weekly wages	Taxable wages	Average premium rate [1]
Anderson	1,574	32,380	$26,887	$517	2	$220,617,642	$1.46
Bedford	634	10,856	18,675	359	29	70,810,692	1.59
Benton	329	3,816	16,465	316	52	23,077,775	1.82
Bledsoe	113	1,569	14,114	271	85	8,960,535	1.83
Blount	1,661	24,973	21,859	420	11	159,947,853	1.69
Bradley	1,494	29,905	20,410	392	19	192,894,097	1.52
Campbell	570	7,726	15,516	298	69	41,626,728	1.98
Cannon	144	2,165	14,516	279	79	13,987,028	1.41
Carroll	536	8,540	14,995	288	76	53,619,747	1.66
Carter	644	10,325	16,920	325	46	60,823,154	1.72
Cheatham	299	4,451	19,349	372	24	26,457,190	1.44
Chester	207	2,796	16,110	309	62	16,358,786	1.99
Claiborne	413	7,433	13,560	260	88	42,195,615	1.74
Clay	114	2,600	14,334	275	83	18,965,026	1.79
Cocke	440	7,252	16,803	323	47	45,274,224	2.63
Coffee	1,006	19,707	21,288	409	14	133,332,359	1.41
Crockett	258	3,612	16,176	311	58	25,684,306	2.96
Cumberland	756	9,924	15,743	302	66	59,472,166	1.88
Davidson	16,374	343,452	23,370	449	6	2,001,567,821	1.31
Decatur	255	3,043	14,422	277	80	18,979,601	2.01
DeKalb	291	4,872	16,044	308	63	31,573,219	1.61
Dickson	693	9,324	18,104	348	33	57,741,590	1.64
Dyer	833	14,294	19,279	370	25	90,589,659	1.92
Fayette	314	4,842	17,792	342	34	29,391,179	1.43
Fentress	242	3,983	12,916	248	94	25,282,459	1.87
Franklin	577	7,016	16,621	319	50	35,845,361	1.47
Gibson	1,018	16,820	17,775	341	35	110,286,458	1.95
Giles	512	8,280	18,508	355	31	54,930,238	1.51
Grainger	184	2,677	13,569	260	89	16,293,902	1.85
Greene	1,015	21,971	17,306	332	42	126,320,831	2.19
Grundy	161	1,747	12,933	248	95	8,952,287	1.51
Hamblen	1,211	27,555	19,564	376	23	180,076,408	1.67
Hamilton	7,627	144,604	21,184	407	15	911,509,456	1.42
Hancock	62	881	13,303	255	92	4,666,064	1.27
Hardeman	403	7,392	17,430	335	38	40,454,648	1.46
Hardin	479	6,696	16,623	319	51	43,464,915	2.06
Hawkins	506	10,635	22,862	439	9	68,362,365	1.37
Haywood	366	5,559	17,224	331	43	35,865,086	2.06
Henderson	421	7,589	15,846	304	65	50,118,407	1.66
Henry	691	9,510	16,838	323	48	60,046,071	1.69
Hickman	230	2,813	15,130	290	74	16,810,392	2.32
Houston	121	1,413	14,636	281	77	8,722,859	1.51
Humphreys	313	4,691	23,032	442	8	31,819,465	2.47
Jackson	89	1,690	15,960	306	64	11,301,585	1.41
Jefferson	555	9,297	17,539	337	37	56,915,689	1.70
Johnson	195	3,452	13,553	260	90	22,633,928	2.63
Knox	9,283	161,075	20,766	399	16	936,870,548	1.65
Lake	137	1,379	14,274	274	84	9,131,675	1.74
Lauderdale	379	7,311	16,323	313	55	47,312,069	1.58
Lawrence	681	12,029	18,727	360	28	85,976,681	3.87

TABLE 3.16—INSURED EMPLOYMENT AND AVERAGE WAGES, COUNTIES, 1991 (Continued)

County	Number of employers	Annual average employment	Annual average wages	Average weekly wages	Rank of average weekly wages	Taxable wages	Average premium rate[1]
Lewis	168	2,844	15,044	289	75	18,501,922	1.82
Lincoln	577	7,577	16,161	310	61	47,632,699	1.82
Loudon	554	8,432	18,670	359	30	56,190,366	1.55
McMinn	779	15,691	20,526	394	18	106,183,678	1.41
McNairy	426	6,825	15,440	296	70	45,016,386	1.86
Macon	254	4,290	15,132	291	72	31,898,940	1.93
Madison	2,156	38,128	20,525	394	17	222,930,284	1.75
Marion	368	5,599	16,190	311	59	36,368,887	1.37
Marshall	426	9,083	19,846	381	20	64,661,163	1.41
Maury	1,397	25,492	26,641	512	3	171,787,077	1.89
Meigs	78	1,534	16,411	315	54	9,730,400	2.28
Monroe	569	8,406	16,271	312	57	53,355,411	2.05
Montgomery	1,768	23,973	17,319	333	41	130,388,962	2.11
Moore	61	1,064	21,831	419	12	5,061,186	1.82
Morgan	148	2,929	17,198	330	44	17,845,626	1.70
Obion	691	13,118	21,591	415	13	88,862,208	1.35
Overton	267	4,105	14,118	271	86	27,507,013	1.58
Perry	112	1,912	16,476	316	53	13,375,876	1.48
Pickett	82	1,187	13,615	261	87	7,768,975	2.33
Polk	198	2,524	14,663	281	78	13,898,498	2.63
Putnam	1,382	25,107	17,412	334	40	149,272,039	1.72
Rhea	398	7,866	16,801	323	49	49,731,012	1.83
Roane	681	18,561	28,255	543	1	115,610,690	0.79
Robertson	657	9,836	17,074	328	45	58,332,072	1.94
Rutherford	2,256	46,001	24,425	469	5	304,829,359	1.94
Scott	302	4,945	15,754	302	67	35,784,105	2.40
Sequatchie	159	2,408	15,158	291	73	15,022,189	2.29
Sevier	1,777	20,763	14,448	277	81	137,385,115	3.03
Shelby	19,183	394,377	23,324	448	7	2,399,724,648	1.36
Smith	283	4,550	17,656	339	36	30,255,372	1.64
Stewart	121	1,705	14,374	276	82	12,073,989	1.61
Sullivan	3,042	65,926	24,678	474	4	449,332,913	1.28
Sumner	1,957	25,128	19,618	377	22	163,991,975	1.85
Tipton	570	6,934	17,458	335	39	41,795,441	1.58
Trousdale	125	1,806	13,159	253	93	11,532,856	1.69
Unicoi	239	4,253	19,197	369	26	27,472,089	1.68
Union	157	1,956	15,238	293	71	13,377,347	1.83
Van Buren	36	978	15,611	300	68	6,670,355	1.73
Warren	708	11,987	18,842	362	27	80,410,141	2.25
Washington	2,219	41,646	18,316	352	32	240,512,864	1.65
Wayne	218	3,887	13,385	257	91	27,106,188	2.11
Weakley	581	10,784	16,200	311	60	64,444,208	1.76
White	354	5,926	16,297	313	56	39,571,602	1.69
Williamson	2,511	26,554	22,363	430	10	179,618,666	1.77
Wilson	1,321	16,691	19,727	379	21	119,126,726	1.59

Note: Rankings were based on unrounded average weekly wages.

1. Average premium rate was computed by the Center for Business and Economic Research, taking total contributions as a percent of taxable wages.

Source: Tennessee Department of Employment Security, Research and Statistics Section, *Covered Employment and Wages by Industry, Statewide and by County, in Tennessee, 1991.*

FIGURE 3.4
Average Weekly Wages of Covered Employment by County, 1991
(Tennessee average = $408)

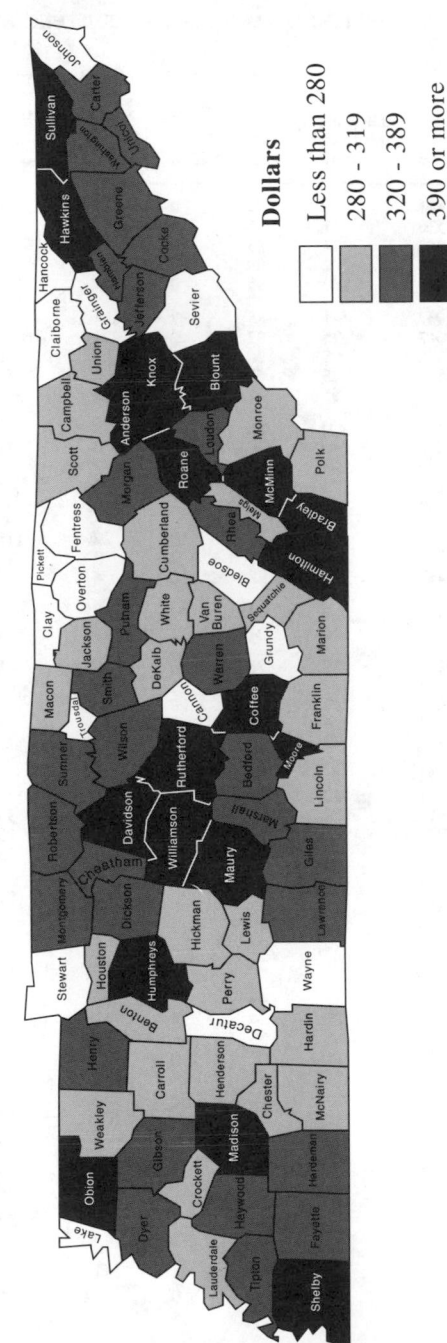

Source: Tennessee Department of Employment Security, *Tennessee Covered Employment and Wages by Industry. Statewide and by County,* 1991.

TABLE 3.17--LOCAL GOVERNMENT EMPLOYMENT, BY SELECTED FUNCTION, COUNTIES,
OCTOBER 1987

County	Total[1]	Edu-cation	Environ-ment and housing	High-ways	Public welfare	Health and hospi-tals	Fire and police	Govern-ment adminis-tration	Utilities
Anderson	2,227	1,461	92	77	0	57	182	148	104
Bedford	1,054	530	51	73	47	134	82	37	81
Benton	421	262	14	33	0	5	28	26	44
Bledsoe	273	186	2	29	0	0	8	15	2
Blount	2,711	1,333	100	95	0	744	148	84	141
Bradley	2,386	1,037	41	88	137	617	156	78	154
Campbell	1,302	642	75	92	0	293	72	35	50
Cannon	262	160	8	30	0	11	12	14	0
Carroll	792	503	28	69	0	0	59	40	57
Carter	1,372	975	51	49	4	2	103	57	100
Cheatham	628	493	0	28	68	0	5	2	5
Chester	299	201	0	10	0	0	11	27	0
Claiborne	939	569	15	34	0	229	20	15	22
Clay	238	167	2	21	0	7	8	9	1
Cocke	851	405	60	62	2	210	67	36	0
Coffee	1,337	825	91	53	0	22	118	70	112
Crockett	398	267	3	39	2	9	24	22	20
Cumberland	814	567	18	22	0	4	28	46	8
Davidson-Nashville	17,802	7,476	1,600	348	185	1,730	2,369	896	1,948
Decatur	431	215	10	24	1	98	10	16	1
DeKalb	440	235	19	26	0	0	31	20	89
Dickson	922	573	39	47	2	2	66	46	114
Dyer	1,125	646	69	68	10	0	143	55	48
Fayette	682	494	7	58	0	3	15	32	5
Fentress	431	288	12	43	1	10	20	29	14
Franklin	940	676	21	24	0	1	24	49	2
Gibson	1,538	973	80	73	4	20	149	53	104
Giles	771	458	39	63	0	16	56	35	79
Grainger	355	271	6	26	0	7	13	14	2
Greene	1,496	1,006	53	83	0	5	95	9	101
Grundy	389	292	10	24	0	0	20	17	12
Hamblen	1,309	848	77	52	0	0	130	60	95
Hamilton	12,538	4,470	894	347	813	2,942	1,257	513	665
Hancock	214	141	4	27	0	2	4	14	4
Hardeman	665	453	4	34	0	3	15	29	0
Hardin	826	478	17	49	0	170	41	35	19
Hawkins	1,448	993	33	64	10	151	48	47	48
Haywood	775	459	35	55	0	12	64	43	22
Henderson	651	389	20	45	0	5	47	33	99
Henry	1,191	508	35	68	94	264	85	41	81
Hickman	554	283	11	39	0	142	23	30	10
Houston	247	167	3	30	0	0	5	14	0
Humphreys	566	367	17	37	1	17	32	41	31
Jackson	239	149	6	25	0	0	7	17	9
Jefferson	1,220	614	25	45	5	391	42	31	43
Johnson	422	302	9	46	1	0	32	14	12
Knox	9,101	4,955	621	105	79	143	959	373	1,030
Lake	208	124	2	17	0	2	9	14	0
Lauderdale	830	497	22	56	0	74	51	37	39
Lawrence	1,086	652	61	111	0	1	78	31	97

TABLE 3.17--LOCAL GOVERNMENT EMPLOYMENT, BY SELECTED FUNCTION, COUNTIES, OCTOBER 1987 (Continued)

County	Total[1]	Edu-cation	Environ-ment and housing	High-ways	Public welfare	Health and hospi-tals	Fire and police	Govern-ment adminis-tration	Utilities
Lewis	299	171	18	40	0	6	19	26	5
Lincoln	909	503	31	64	0	112	58	25	104
Loudon	1,029	615	28	46	3	116	61	48	99
McMinn	1,395	808	78	75	5	130	92	55	81
McNairy	702	350	4	32	4	183	24	33	7
Macon	423	239	16	38	0	26	31	29	7
Madison	5,983	1,315	234	123	35	3,722	373	109	1
Marion	550	361	8	42	0	0	25	16	3
Marshall	623	363	38	37	0	13	57	40	58
Maury	1,545	161	137	105	3	698	155	96	104
Meigs	247	158	0	40	0	0	13	10	0
Monroe	841	556	31	54	1	19	65	50	34
Montgomery	3,145	1,530	97	122	39	638	297	89	222
Moore	158	108	0	18	0	5	4	9	0
Morgan	418	308	6	26	0	14	16	27	11
Obion	1,097	751	42	81	0	0	82	49	38
Overton	534	356	11	51	0	3	54	24	15
Perry	198	119	3	24	0	4	3	11	0
Pickett	173	81	0	58	0	2	6	9	0
Polk	537	278	5	18	2	144	25	16	10
Putnam	1,738	741	82	67	1	497	146	70	85
Rhea	902	532	45	45	0	131	42	44	27
Roane	1,560	830	85	59	0	245	133	61	121
Robertson	1,404	722	20	43	0	324	68	57	6
Rutherford	2,835	1,758	229	87	0	41	281	197	129
Scott	843	408	0	38	0	282	25	13	32
Sequatchie	313	229	12	23	0	0	13	24	4
Sevier	1,551	856	81	82	5	85	154	76	55
Shelby	29,104	13,340	2,575	595	1,019	572	3,732	1,791	3,440
Smith	358	240	7	30	0	5	14	19	2
Stewart	285	208	4	25	0	0	6	17	3
Sullivan	4,376	2,959	198	249	1	35	365	195	92
Sumner	3,043	1,756	141	120	1	415	254	151	117
Tipton	1,004	736	32	69	0	4	53	37	32
Trousdale	207	113	14	23	0	8	16	16	5
Unicoi	392	266	14	32	0	10	33	23	8
Union	272	188	1	30	6	2	7	23	4
Van Buren	137	81	3	22	0	0	7	11	8
Warren	1,050	649	67	37	0	106	82	41	45
Washington	2,547	1,500	206	172	13	8	223	132	174
Wayne	424	280	2	58	0	0	15	21	0
Weakley	1,027	503	43	83	138	0	68	39	87
White	534	390	7	33	0	0	10	23	5
Williamson	2,032	1,054	17	53	69	343	55	79	19
Wilson	1,505	1,031	53	58	0	0	125	95	78

Note: Data are full-time equivalent employment for all government functions.

1. Includes categories not shown separately.

Source: U.S. Department of Commerce, Bureau of the Census, *1987 Census of Governments, Public Employment, Compendium of Public Employment.*

TABLE 3.18–NUMBER AND RATE OF UNEMPLOYED AND INSURED UNEMPLOYED, SOUTHEASTERN STATES, 1988–1991

	Total unemployed								Insured unemployed							
	Number (1,000)				Rate[1]				Number (1,000)				Rate[2]			
State	1991	1990	1989	1988	1988	1989	1990	1991	1988	1989	1990	1991	1988	1989	1990	1991
TENNESSEE	160	125	121	136	5.8	5.1	5.2	6.6	39.5	41.5	51.3	63.0	2.0	2.0	2.5	3.0
Alabama	135	128	134	136	7.2	7.0	6.8	7.2	31.3	32.4	35.7	41.7	2.1	2.2	2.4	2.7
Arkansas	82	78	82	86	7.7	7.2	6.9	7.3	25.0	24.7	26.4	31.7	3.0	2.9	3.1	3.6
Florida	471	378	348	305	5.0	5.6	5.9	7.3	51.0	58.1	76.7	120.8	1.0	1.1	1.5	2.3
Georgia	158	175	177	185	5.8	5.5	5.4	5.0	36.0	39.4	46.7	66.3	1.3	1.4	1.7	2.3
Kentucky	128	103	108	134	7.9	6.2	5.8	7.4	27.9	27.3	30.6	40.6	2.2	2.1	2.3	3.0
Louisiana	137	117	151	209	10.9	7.9	6.2	7.1	42.4	36.3	30.0	35.2	3.0	2.5	2.1	2.3
Mississippi	102	88	91	96	8.4	7.8	7.5	8.6	21.8	21.9	23.4	28.2	2.6	2.5	2.7	3.2
North Carolina	198	139	119	121	3.6	3.5	4.1	5.8	38.7	41.2	56.1	80.3	1.3	1.4	1.9	2.7
South Carolina	108	81	80	76	4.5	4.7	4.7	6.2	20.6	22.9	26.9	41.0	1.5	1.6	1.9	2.8
Virginia	193	137	123	120	3.9	3.9	4.3	5.8	22.5	21.7	27.9	45.3	0.9	0.9	1.1	1.7
West Virginia	82	64	66	74	9.9	8.6	8.3	10.5	16.9	16.1	16.3	22.9	3.0	2.8	2.9	3.9

1. Total unemployment as a percent of civilian labor force.
2. Insured unemployment as a percent of average covered employment in the previous year.
Source: U.S. Department of Commerce, Bureau of the Census, *Statistical Abstract of the United States, 1993*, and earlier editions.

TABLE 3.19--CIVILIAN LABOR FORCE AND PARTICIPATION RATES, BY SEX, SOUTHEASTERN STATES AND UNITED STATES, 1991 AND 1992 [Labor force in thousands]

State	Total	Male	Female Total	Percent of labor force	Participation rate[1] Male	Participation rate[1] Female	Employed as a percent of total population[2]
				1992			
TENNESSEE	2,440	1,298	1,142	46.8	72.4	55.6	59.4
Alabama	1,937	1,052	885	45.7	71.9	53.4	57.5
Arkansas	1,149	616	533	46.4	72.6	55.4	58.9
Florida	6,553	3,495	3,058	46.7	69.7	54.8	56.8
Georgia	3,232	1,712	1,520	47.0	75.5	57.9	61.5
Kentucky	1,744	964	780	44.7	71.8	52.8	57.6
Louisiana	1,934	1,053	881	45.6	71.9	53.1	56.9
Mississippi	1,182	640	542	45.9	71.3	53.1	56.6
North Carolina	3,487	1,842	1,645	47.2	76.1	60.8	64.0
South Carolina	1,772	947	825	46.6	74.9	58.8	62.3
Virginia	3,359	1,819	1,540	45.8	79.4	63.0	66.4
West Virginia	766	445	321	41.9	66.3	43.7	48.3
UNITED STATES	126,982	69,184	57,798	45.5	75.6	57.8	61.4
				1991			
TENNESSEE	2,416	1,336	1,080	44.7	73.8	53.9	59.1
Alabama	1,894	1,040	854	45.1	71.4	51.8	56.6
Arkansas	1,118	608	510	45.6	71.3	53.6	57.4
Florida	6,431	3,432	2,999	46.6	70.6	54.6	57.6
Georgia	3,166	1,666	1,500	47.4	75.2	57.4	62.3
Kentucky	1,744	957	787	45.1	72.2	52.9	57.5
Louisiana	1,933	1,045	888	45.9	72.1	52.7	57.3
Mississippi	1,183	626	557	47.1	71.1	54.1	56.6
North Carolina	3,445	1,843	1,602	46.5	76.3	60.5	64.1
South Carolina	1,744	923	821	47.1	73.7	59.5	62.1
Virginia	3,306	1,739	1,567	47.4	78.3	64.0	66.7
West Virginia	783	457	326	41.6	67.6	44.2	49.5
UNITED STATES	125,303	68,410	56,893	45.4	75.5	57.3	61.6

Note: Data are annual averages. Rates are based on civilian noninstitutional population, 16 years and older. Detail may not add to total due to independent rounding.

1. Percent of civilian noninstitutional population of each specified group in the civilian labor force.

2. Civilian employment as a percent of civilian noninstitutional population.

Source: U.S. Department of Commerce, Bureau of the Census, *Statistical Abstract of the United States, 1993*, and earlier editions; and U.S. Department of Labor, Bureau of Labor Statistics, *Geographic Profile of Employment and Unemployment, 1980*.

TABLE 3.20--UNEMPLOYED, BY SEX, 1992, AND UNEMPLOYMENT RATE, BY SEX, 1991 AND 1992, SOUTHEASTERN STATES AND UNITED STATES

State	1992 unemployed (1,000)			Rate of unemployment[1]					
				1992			1991		
	Total	Male	Female	Total	Male	Female	Total	Male	Female
TENNESSEE	155	76	79	6.4	5.9	6.9	6.6	6.7	6.6
Alabama	142	68	74	7.3	6.5	8.3	7.2	6.8	7.6
Arkansas	83	45	38	7.2	7.2	7.2	7.3	7.2	7.5
Florida	536	286	250	8.2	8.2	8.2	7.3	7.1	7.6
Georgia	224	125	99	6.9	7.3	6.5	5.0	4.8	5.2
Kentucky	120	74	46	6.9	7.7	5.9	7.4	7.4	7.3
Louisiana	156	86	70	8.1	8.2	7.9	7.1	6.6	7.8
Mississippi	96	46	50	8.1	7.2	9.2	8.6	8.3	8.9
North Carolina	207	107	100	5.9	5.8	6.0	5.8	5.8	5.7
South Carolina	111	57	54	6.2	6.0	6.6	6.2	6.4	6.0
Virginia	213	121	92	6.4	6.7	6.0	5.8	5.7	6.0
West Virginia	86	59	27	11.3	13.3	8.5	10.5	11.5	9.1
UNITED STATES	9,384	5,379	4,005	7.4	7.8	6.9	6.7	7.0	6.3

Note: Data are annual averages for civilian noninstitutional population, 16 years and older. Detail may not add to total due to independent rounding.

1. Percent unemployed of civilian labor force in specified group.

Source: U.S. Department of Commerce, Bureau of the Census, *Statistical Abstract of the United States, 1993*, and earlier editions.

TABLE 3.21--MASS LAYOFF EVENTS, SEPARATIONS, AND INITIAL CLAIMANTS FOR
UNEMPLOYMENT INSURANCE, BY INDUSTRY, SOUTHEASTERN STATES, 1989 AND 1990

State	1990 Total Establish-ments	1990 Total Layoff events	1990 Total Separa-tions	1990 Total Initial claimants for unemployment insurance	1990 Manufacturing Establish-ments	1990 Manufacturing Layoff events	1990 Manufacturing Separa-tions	1990 Manufacturing Initial claimants for unemployment insurance
TENNESSEE	51	54	10,224	5,512	36	38	6,726	3,860
Alabama	106	121	18,386	20,636	67	76	10,986	15,315
Arkansas	31	34	6,452	8,643	28	31	6,252	8,438
Florida	125	144	51,825	26,458	44	50	11,982	10,450
Georgia	75	96	19,390	15,630	49	61	11,638	9,672
Kentucky	55	63	9,284	9,211	37	43	6,108	6,919
Louisiana	53	67	11,810	8,299	18	21	3,027	2,995
Mississippi	43	44	7,055	6,055	27	28	4,464	3,723
North Carolina	85	102	19,841	10,523	62	72	14,142	7,061
South Carolina	69	76	13,710	10,713	51	56	10,513	8,453
Virginia	72	80	10,244	13,407	43	47	7,510	9,723
West Virginia	21	25	2,505	2,235	8	8	626	584

State	1989 Total Establish-ments	1989 Total Layoff events	1989 Total Separa-tions	1989 Total Initial claimants for unemployment insurance	1989 Manufacturing Establish-ments	1989 Manufacturing Layoff events	1989 Manufacturing Separa-tions	1989 Manufacturing Initial claimants for unemployment insurance
TENNESSEE	31	33	9,641	4,088	22	24	6,145	3,120
Alabama	95	121	22,073	20,265	64	82	16,953	15,984
Arkansas	26	30	5,810	5,040	22	26	5,366	4,637
Florida	101	115	37,403	18,262	40	47	8,037	6,430
Georgia	85	100	20,270	15,278	48	51	7,407	5,822
Kentucky	60	69	14,851	12,310	42	48	10,591	9,331
Louisiana	70	90	17,361	12,501	22	30	6,374	5,184
Mississippi	36	39	5,876	4,699	24	27	3,852	3,014
North Carolina	55	66	12,644	7,785	41	46	7,363	4,353
South Carolina	43	47	7,770	6,374	28	32	5,407	4,509
Virginia	48	53	7,262	9,155	20	21	3,248	5,298
West Virginia	24	27	3,396	2,758	9	10	987	955

Source: U.S. Department of Labor, Bureau of Labor Statistics, *Mass Layoffs in 1990*, February 1992, Bulletin
2395, and earlier editions.

TABLE 3.22--STATE AND LOCAL GOVERNMENT FULL-TIME EQUIVALENT EMPLOYMENT, SOUTHEASTERN STATES, OCTOBER 1991

State	FTE employment			Number per 10,000 population		
	Total	State	Local[1]	Total	Education	Other
TENNESSEE	249,897	76,111	173,766	504.5	237.8	266.7
Alabama	232,437	81,505	150,932	568.4	279.8	288.7
Arkansas	123,132	43,320	79,812	519.1	288.1	231.0
Florida	657,460	163,450	494,010	495.2	224.2	271.0
Georgia	383,290	111,839	271,451	578.7	273.5	305.3
Kentucky	195,563	76,351	119,212	526.7	298.6	228.1
Louisiana	244,064	87,696	156,368	574.0	292.7	281.3
Mississippi	151,964	46,511	105,453	586.3	312.8	273.5
North Carolina	360,844	107,545	253,299	535.6	280.0	255.6
South Carolina	200,233	80,678	119,555	562.5	291.2	271.2
Virginia	338,478	114,134	224,344	538.5	284.5	254.0
West Virginia	91,332	33,558	57,774	507.1	295.1	212.0

Note: Detail may not add to total due to independent rounding.
1. Statistics for local governments are estimates subject to sampling variations.
Source: U.S. Department of Commerce, Bureau of the Census, *Public Employment: 1991*.

TABLE 3.23--PAID CIVILIAN EMPLOYMENT IN THE FEDERAL GOVERNMENT, SOUTHEASTERN STATES, 1988 AND 1990

State	1990			1988		
	Total (1,000)	Rate per 10,000 population[1]	Percent defense	Total (1,000)	Rate per 10,000 population[1]	Percent defense
TENNESSEE	56	114.8	13.9	57	116.4	13.0
Alabama	57	141.1	44.5	58	141.4	45.0
Arkansas	19	80.8	25.6	19	79.3	25.4
Florida	112	86.6	29.4	109	88.3	29.9
Georgia	88	135.8	41.2	88	138.8	43.4
Kentucky	35	95.0	35.4	35	93.9	37.9
Louisiana	34	80.6	25.7	34	77.1	26.7
Mississippi	24	93.3	43.6	24	91.6	43.4
North Carolina	46	69.4	33.0	46	70.9	32.9
South Carolina	32	91.8	59.0	33	95.2	60.2
Virginia	161	260.2	66.2	160	266.1	67.5
West Virginia	15	83.6	11.0	16	85.3	11.3

Note: Rate for 1990 based on April 1 resident population; rate for 1988 based on July 1 resident population.
1. Computed by the Center for Business and Economic Research.
Source: U.S. Department of Commerce, Bureau of the Census, *Statistical Abstract of the United States, 1993*, and earlier editions.

TABLE 3.24--DEPARTMENT OF DEFENSE CONTRACT AWARDS, PAYROLL CIVILIAN AND MILITARY PERSONNEL, SOUTHEASTERN STATES AND UNITED STATES, 1989-1992, SELECTED YEARS [In millions of dollars and thousands of employees]

State	Contract awards[1]			Payroll			Civilian employees			Military personnel		
	1992	1990	1989	1992	1990	1989	1992	1990	1989	1992	1990	1989
TENNESSEE	1,262	2,059	1,118	984	944	393	7.6	7.9	7.7	8.4	9.3	9.9
Alabama	1,949	1,834	1,392	2,139	2,093	1,378	26.0	26.0	25.7	17.6	18.6	21.2
Arkansas	288	306	370	703	718	336	4.5	4.9	5.2	6.6	8.7	9.0
Florida	4,995	5,166	4,452	6,277	6,003	3,246	32.3	32.4	33.8	74.8	75.0	77.8
Georgia	3,796	1,984	1,864	4,234	3,793	2,762	37.3	37.3	39.9	60.8	60.0	63.3
Kentucky	437	591	333	1,843	1,807	1,444	14.2	14.2	14.0	34.8	38.7	38.8
Louisiana	1,204	1,246	1,693	1,358	1,414	925	9.0	9.2	8.5	21.6	26.4	25.3
Mississippi	2,567	1,792	1,235	1,079	1,062	692	11.0	11.3	13.3	12.3	12.8	14.7
North Carolina	1,540	1,561	1,104	4,041	3,774	2,673	17.1	17.5	15.5	95.0	98.0	92.3
South Carolina	756	985	568	2,699	2,622	1,912	17.6	19.1	20.7	39.1	38.3	41.6
Virginia	6,571	6,781	5,897	11,157	10,507	7,634	106.3	105.2	111.7	92.3	94.0	96.2
West Virginia	83	152	163	205	206	58	1.7	1.7	2.0	0.5	0.6	0.4
UNITED STATES	112,285	124,119	119,917	99,250	96,970	66,180	899.0	911.2	964.6	1213.7	1263.4	1342.1

1. Military awards for supplies, services, and construction. Net value of contracts of over $25,000 for work in each State. Figures reflect impact of prime contracting on State distribution of defense work. Often the State in which a prime contractor is located is not the State in which the subcontracted work is done.

Source: U.S. Department of Commerce, Bureau of the Census, Statistical Abstract of the United States, 1993, and earlier editions.

TABLE 3.25—NUMBER OF DOCTORAL SCIENTISTS AND ENGINEERS AND MEDIAN ANNUAL SALARY, BY SELECTED FIELDS, SOUTHEASTERN STATES AND UNITED STATES, 1991

State	Total doctoral scientists and engineers	Engineers	Scientists							
			Total	Physical	Mathematical	Computer	Life	Environmental	Psychologists	Social
UNITED STATES										
Number	437,206	69,766	367,440	80,872	20,049	5,376	113,743	13,263	65,672	68,465
Median salary ($)	60,700	70,200	59,000	65,100	60,800	68,100	55,500	60,200	55,500	56,100
TENNESSEE										
Percent of U.S.	1.7	1.4	1.7	2.0	1.9	n.a.	1.8	1.7	1.9	1.1
Median salary ($)	55,700	64,000	54,100	60,600	52,600	(a)	48,300	(a)	60,700	54,900
Alabama										
Percent of U.S.	1.1	1.8	1.0	0.8	2.3	2.3	1.2	1.1	0.8	0.7
Median salary ($)	60,000	63,700	55,600	55,700	(a)	(a)	53,400	(a)	55,300	62,200
Arkansas										
Percent of U.S.	0.4	0.2	0.4	0.3	n.a.	n.a.	0.5	0.5	0.5	0.5
Median salary ($)	46,000	(a)	45,000	(a)	(a)	(a)	46,400	(a)	(a)	(a)
Florida										
Percent of U.S.	2.4	2.8	2.4	1.4	1.2	1.8	2.4	3.5	3.8	2.3
Median salary ($)	55,700	60,100	55,100	63,500	(a)	(a)	54,400	55,900	52,400	51,100
Georgia										
Percent of U.S.	1.8	1.5	1.9	1.2	1.9	2.7	2.6	0.7	1.9	1.6
Median salary ($)	58,100	72,100	55,300	53,400	(a)	(a)	57,400	(a)	58,700	46,200
Kentucky										
Percent of U.S.	0.8	0.5	0.9	0.6	1.8	0.1	0.8	0.8	1.1	0.9
Median salary ($)	55,500	66,600	55,000	61,400	(a)	(a)	55,000	(a)	52,300	55,600
Louisiana										
Percent of U.S.	1.1	1.2	1.1	1.1	0.8	0.7	1.5	0.9	0.7	1.0
Median salary ($)	52,800	61,700	51,100	64,500	(a)	(a)	47,400	(a)	53,200	48,500

TABLE 3.25–NUMBER OF DOCTORAL SCIENTISTS AND ENGINEERS AND MEDIAN ANNUAL SALARY, BY SELECTED FIELDS, SOUTHEASTERN STATES AND UNITED STATES, 1991 (Continued)

State	Total doctoral scientists and engineers	Engineers	Scientists							
			Total	Physical	Mathe-matical	Computer	Life	Environ-mental	Psychol-ogists	Social
Mississippi										
Percent of U.S.	0.7	0.7	0.7	0.3	0.3	0.8	1.1	0.7	0.4	0.7
Median salary ($)	48,900	56,400	48,200	(a)	(a)	(a)	46,400	(a)	(a)	48,800
North Carolina										
Percent of U.S.	2.4	1.5	2.6	2.3	2.8	3.9	3.4	1.4	2.3	1.8
Median salary ($)	57,200	68,100	55,900	61,100	51,700	(a)	58,600	(a)	53,800	50,800
South Carolina										
Percent of U.S.	1.0	1.0	1.0	0.8	2.2	n.a.	1.1	1.2	0.9	1.0
Median salary ($)	52,100	62,000	50,400	56,900	(a)	(a)	50,300	(a)	46,600	44,600
Virginia										
Percent of U.S.	3.0	3.1	3.0	2.8	5.3	3.4	1.8	4.3	3.0	4.0
Median salary ($)	65,700	70,500	63,800	72,100	67,900	(a)	55,700	62,100	66,000	61,800
West Virginia										
Percent of U.S.	0.4	0.5	0.3	0.5	0.1	n.a.	0.4	0.3	0.1	0.3
Median salary ($)	56,900	58,200	56,000	57,100	(a)	(a)	54,900	(a)	(a)	(a)

Note: Total includes categories not shown separately.

n.a. not available (no cases reported in sample).

a. No median was computed for groups with fewer than 20 individuals reporting salary.

Source: National Science Foundation, *Characteristics of Doctoral Scientists and Engineers in the U.S.: 1991.*

TABLE 3.26—EMPLOYMENT COST INDEX, PRIVATE NONFARM WORKERS, REGIONS, 1991 AND 1992 [June 1989=100]

Region	1992				Percent change Dec. 1991– Dec. 1992	1991			
	March	June	September	December		March	June	September	December
	Compensation[1]								
All private industry workers[2]	113.1	113.9	114.8	115.6	3.5	108.5	109.8	111.0	111.7
Workers, by region									
Northeast	113.9	114.5	115.5	116.4	3.5	109.4	110.6	111.7	112.5
South	112.5	113.3	114.1	114.8	3.2	108.4	109.8	110.7	111.2
Midwest	113.8	114.6	115.3	116.1	3.5	108.5	109.7	111.2	112.2
West	111.9	112.9	114.1	114.9	3.6	107.5	108.9	110.0	110.9
Workers, by area size									
Metropolitan areas	113.1	113.9	114.8	115.6	3.4	108.5	109.8	111.0	111.8
Nonmetropolitan areas	113.1	113.7	114.8	115.6	4.0	108.4	109.9	110.7	111.2
	Wages and salaries								
All private industry workers[2]	110.9	111.6	112.2	112.9	2.6	107.3	108.4	109.3	110.0
Workers, by region									
Northeast	111.7	112.2	113.0	113.7	2.5	108.3	109.4	110.3	110.9
South	110.8	111.5	112.0	112.7	2.8	107.4	108.5	109.2	109.6
Midwest	110.7	111.3	111.8	112.5	2.4	106.9	107.7	108.9	109.9
West	110.2	111.1	112.2	112.8	3.1	106.4	107.6	108.6	109.4
Workers, by area size									
Metropolitan areas	110.9	111.6	112.3	112.9	2.5	107.3	108.4	109.3	110.1
Nonmetropolitan areas	110.7	111.2	112.0	112.8	3.1	107.2	108.4	109.0	109.4

1. Compensation consists of wages, salaries, and employer cost of employee benefits.
2. The indexes for the occupation and industry groups are calculated differently from those for regions.
Source: U.S. Department of Labor, Bureau of Labor Statistics, Employment Cost Indexes and Levels 1975–93, September 1993, Bulletin 2434.

TABLE 3.27—EMPLOYER COSTS FOR EMPLOYEE COMPENSATION PER HOUR WORKED, BY MAJOR INDUSTRY AND BY OCCUPATIONAL CATEGORIES, UNITED STATES AVERAGE, MARCH 1993 [Dollars]

Compensation component	All private industry	Industry categories				Occupational categories		
		Goods-producing	Service-producing	Manufacturing	Nonmanufacturing	White-collar	Blue-collar	Service
Total	16.70	20.22	15.51	20.09	15.85	19.67	16.43	8.54
Wages and salaries	11.90	13.54	11.34	13.35	11.54	14.32	11.01	6.48
Total benefits	4.80	6.67	4.17	6.74	4.31	5.35	5.42	2.06
Paid leave	1.11	1.38	1.01	1.52	1.00	1.44	0.97	0.36
Vacation	0.54	0.72	0.48	0.78	0.48	0.69	0.50	0.18
Holiday	0.38	0.50	0.34	0.56	0.33	0.49	0.35	0.12
Sick	0.14	0.11	0.15	0.13	0.14	0.21	0.08	0.06
Other	0.05	0.05	0.05	0.06	0.05	0.06	0.04	(a)
Supplemental pay	0.42	0.67	0.34	0.71	0.35	0.44	0.56	0.12
Insurance	1.19	1.74	1.01	1.86	1.03	1.32	1.39	0.48
Life insurance	0.05	0.07	0.04	0.08	0.04	0.06	0.05	(a)
Health insurance	1.10	1.59	0.93	1.69	0.95	1.20	1.28	0.45
Sickness and accident	0.05	0.08	0.04	0.09	0.04	0.06	0.06	(a)
Retirement and savings	0.48	0.77	0.39	0.72	0.43	0.57	0.56	0.11
Pensions	0.38	0.60	0.31	0.55	0.34	0.42	0.47	0.09
Savings and thrift	0.10	0.17	0.08	0.17	0.09	0.15	0.09	(a)
Legally required[1]	1.55	1.99	1.40	1.79	1.49	1.54	1.87	0.98
Social Security	0.99	1.17	0.93	1.16	0.95	1.16	0.96	0.56
Federal unemployment insurance	0.03	0.03	0.03	0.03	0.03	0.03	0.03	0.03
State unemployment insurance	0.11	0.15	0.10	0.14	0.11	0.11	0.14	0.09
Workers' compensation	0.39	0.63	0.31	0.44	0.38	0.23	0.70	0.29
Other benefits[2]	0.04	0.12	(a)	0.14	0.02	0.04	0.07	(a)

Note: Goods-producing includes mining, construction and manufacturing; service-producing includes all other private sector industries.

a. Cost is $0.01 or less.

1. Includes railroad retirement and supplemental retirement, railroad unemployment insurance, and other legally required benefits in addition to those shown.

2. Includes severance pay and supplemental unemployment benefits.

Source: U.S. Department of Labor, Bureau of Labor Statistics, *Employment Cost Indexes and Levels, 1975–93*, September 1993, Bulletin 2434.

Nearly 23 percent of the nonagricultural jobs in Tennessee in 1993 were in manufacturing, as compared to an average of 16 percent in the U.S. Data on manufacturing–statistics on employment, payrolls, value added by manufacture, inventories, and new capital expenditures–are very important to decision-making processes in Tennessee. A major source of manufacturing industry data is the *Census of Manufactures*, compiled every five years by the U.S. Department of Commerce, Bureau of the Census. Data from the 1987 Census are included in this edition.

For most sources, industrial data are given by Standard Industrial Classification (SIC). This code provides classifications for industries where industry is defined as a number of establishments producing a single product or a closely related group of products. An establishment is classified in a particular industry if its production of a product or product group exceeds in value its production of any other product group. Data reported in this edition of the *Abstract* are classified in accordance with the *1987 Standard Industrial Classification Manual*. This revision to the SIC system affects the comparability of current industry specific data (data for 1987 to present) to data collected prior to 1987. Industry data for Tennessee and other states are made comparable by "bridge tables" published in the 1987 Census, and these have been included in this edition of the *Abstract* where possible.

Employment data for Tennessee's metropolitan areas are provided by the Tennessee Department of Employment Security in its monthly *Labor Market Report*, whose data are the most current available. In addition to providing employment by sector, it will provide estimates of weekly and hourly earnings and hours worked for production workers in selected categories.

In addition to those sources specifically concerned with manufacturing, virtually every source cited in the preface to Chapter 3 on Employment and Earnings will produce data for categories of manufacturing.

Pollution abatement expenditures are collected and published in the Census Bureau's *Current Industrial Report* series. These costs to the manufacturing process are important for a clean environment. Data are included for operating costs and capital expenditures by type of pollution.

Intercensal data for states are published in the *Annual Survey of Manufactures* (ASM). These data supplement the census data in Table 4.1 and 4.2. Export-related manufacturing data in Table 4.24 are also from the ASM. Another source of data on manufacturing establishments is *County Business Patterns*. Published annually since 1964, *County Business Patterns* is the only series that provides annual subnational data by two-, three-, and four-digit SIC levels.

TABLE OF CONTENTS

TABLE OF CONTENTS
(Continued)

TABLE 4.1– NUMBER OF MANUFACTURING ESTABLISHMENTS, EMPLOYEES, AND PRODUCTION
WORKERS, AND VALUE ADDED BY MANUFACTURE, TENNESSEE, 1899–1991,
SELECTED YEARS

Year	Total estab- lishments	Total employees	Total production workers	Value added by manufacture ($1,000)
1991	n.a.	493,000	358,200	32,499,400
1990	n.a.	503,700	369,000	30,245,000
1989	n.a.	499,600	371,600	30,648,800
1988	n.a.	493,700	366,000	28,851,500
1987	6,864	484,900	359,200	27,049,700
1986	n.a.	466,600	341,300	23,624,900
1985	n.a.	468,200	344,400	22,223,800
1984	n.a.	477,000	353,200	21,963,900
1983	n.a.	457,400	336,600	19,868,300
1982	6,417	461,600	337,500	17,841,600
1981[a]	5,753	493,583	n.a.	n.a.
1980[a]	5,739	509,694	n.a.	n.a.
1979[a]	5,765	524,443	n.a.	n.a.
1978	n.a.	509,900	389,000	14,045,800
1977	6,487	489,800	375,700	12,663,400
1976	n.a.	478,700	359,800	10,723,600
1975	n.a.	452,100	338,000	9,289,200
1974	n.a.	489,500	381,700	9,563,800
1973	n.a.	493,300	389,300	8,772,500
1972	5,647	467,400	367,000	7,662,000
1971	n.a.	444,200	346,900	6,728,900
1970	n.a.	447,900	348,200	6,297,000
1969	n.a.	456,300	360,500	5,982,100
1968	n.a.	434,100	345,100	5,542,000
1967	5,040	418,000	333,600	4,921,100
1966	n.a.	401,100	320,800	4,627,800
1965	n.a.	373,400	299,200	4,139,400
1964	n.a.	344,900	273,945	3,577,187
1963	4,787	334,900	266,969	3,299,300
1958	4,508	279,300	220,823	2,207,073
1954	4,058	267,496	214,027	1,678,786
1947	3,345	222,300	193,197	961,385
1939	2,225	152,179	131,024	318,378
1929	2,855	142,020	128,400	322,898
1919	4,426	107,725	94,564	210,201
1909	4,609	82,257	73,840	76,201
1899	3,116	49,292	45,963	38,190

n.a. not available.
a. Data are from *County Business Patterns* and do not provide direct comparison with economic census data.
Source: U.S. Department of Commerce, Bureau of the Census, *1991 Annual Survey of Manufactures, Geographic
Area Statistics*, and earlier editions; *1987 Census of Manufactures, Geographic Area Series*, Tennessee, and
earlier editions; and *County Business Patterns*, 1979–1981.

TABLE 4.2– MANUFACTURING STATISTICS, BY SECTOR, TENNESSEE, 1987 AND 1991 [Dollar amounts in millions]

Sector	1991		1987								
	Total employees (1,000)	Value added by manufacture	Number of establishments		All employees		Production workers		Value added by manufacture	Value of shipments	New capital expenditures
			Total	With 20 or more employees	Number (1,000)	Payroll	Number (1,000)	Wages			
All industries, total	493.0	$32,499.4	6,864	2,799	484.9	$9,869.2	359.2	$6,282.6	$27,049.7	$57,752.9	$1,904.7
Food and kindred products	37.4	4464.3	356	194	36.7	785.2	23.6	443.4	3342.4	8492.6	307.1
Tobacco products	n.a.	n.a.	8	8	1.3	25.4	1.0	14.1	314.9	498.0	(D)
Textile mill products	21.7	790.3	137	102	23.9	392.1	20.5	292.1	872.3	1999.6	46.1
Apparel and other textile products	52.0	1669.3	485	342	59.8	638.9	52.6	505.1	1524.2	2698.0	40.0
Lumber and wood products	15.9	469.0	831	193	17.9	259.3	15.0	191.3	612.1	1333.0	40.6
Furniture and fixtures	23.5	942.7	301	149	24.1	359.8	20.4	267.8	826.7	1648.3	34.9
Paper and allied products	21.3	1750.8	160	120	18.2	458.1	14.2	327.4	1585.8	3249.6	116.1
Printing and publishing	37.6	2057.1	1,121	237	31.2	634.8	18.8	352.5	1562.6	2442.4	104.9
Chemicals and allied products	43.0	5274.2	243	102	40.2	1158.2	23.8	597.4	3743.6	7149.0	326.4
Petroleum and coal products	n.a.	n.a.	48	9	0.9	22.6	0.6	12.2	75.8	672.4	(D)
Rubber and miscellaneous plastics products	28.3	1850.7	277	144	23.6	522.2	18.8	378.4	1593.3	3009.1	96.0
Leather and leather products	7.9	307.3	66	42	8.3	108.5	6.9	77.5	275.3	561.3	(D)
Stone, clay, and glass products	11.2	731.7	335	118	13.7	337.4	11.0	252.6	948.7	1709.6	75.5
Primary metal industries	14.5	1400.7	123	77	13.8	359.2	11.2	268.9	861.5	2659.1	144.0
Fabricated metal products	36.1	1849.8	622	292	35.4	707.8	27.7	483.4	1645.1	3272.3	82.3
Industrial machinery and equipment	37.6	2344.3	742	226	38.5	838.7	28.6	567.3	2181.7	4588.2	133.3
Electronic and other electric equipment	31.4	1808.5	236	114	31.5	621.5	25.1	433.3	1722.3	4344.3	118.6
Transportation equipment	35.5	2853.2	214	112	33.2	860.2	25.5	606.5	2264.9	5567.9	168.4
Instruments and related products	8.3	780.7	106	39	8.4	191.6	5.3	95.1	547.4	855.9	(D)
Miscellaneous manufacturing industries	11.8	624.1	290	77	11.5	198.3	8.5	116.3	548.9	1002.3	31.9
Auxiliaries	16.2	0.0	163	102	12.6	389.2	0.0	0.0	0.0	0.0	0.0

Note: Individual columns may not add to totals due to independent rounding.

(D) Withheld to avoid disclosing operations of individual companies.

n.a. not available.

Source: U.S. Department of Commerce, Bureau of the Census, 1991 Annual Survey of Manufactures, Geographic Area Statistics; and 1987 Census of Manufactures, Geographic Area Series, Tennessee.

FIGURE 4.1
Manufacturing Employment and Value Added,
Distribution by Sector, Tennessee, 1991

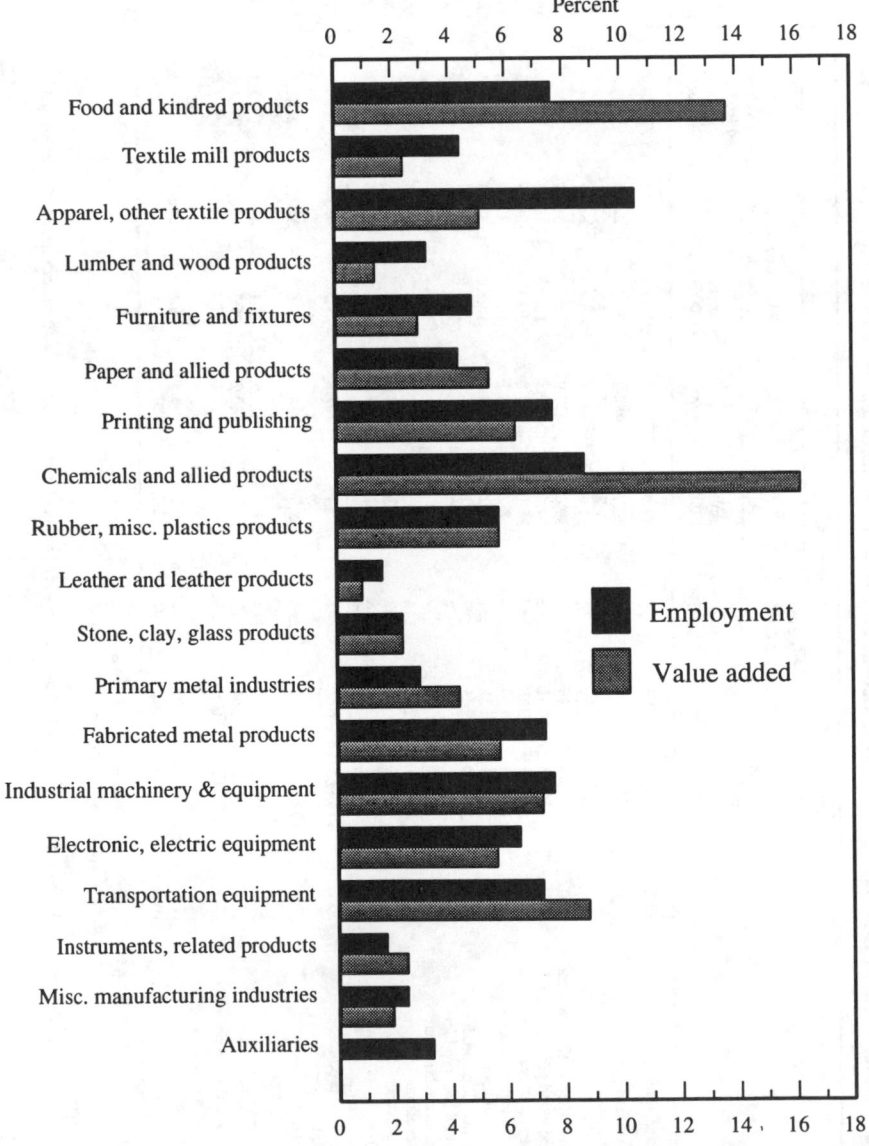

Source: U.S. Department of Commerce, Bureau of the Census, *1991 Annual Survey of Manufactures, Geographic Area Statistics.*

TABLE 4.3– NUMBER OF MANUFACTURING ESTABLISHMENTS, BY SECTOR AND BY EMPLOYMENT-SIZE CLASS, TENNESSEE, 1991

Sector	Total	Employment-size class								
		1–4	5–9	10–19	20–49	50–99	100–249	250–499	500–999	1,000 or more
All industries, total	7,375	2,289	1,103	1,066	1,106	695	663	276	129	48
Food and kindred products	322	75	29	43	48	36	48	27	14	2
Tobacco products	11	1	0	0	2	5	2	1	0	0
Textile mill products	166	29	10	15	35	18	32	16	10	1
Apparel, other textile products	527	104	36	46	83	86	110	47	12	3
Lumber and wood products	906	380	191	160	95	40	36	3	1	0
Furniture and fixtures	283	85	30	36	49	33	23	15	9	3
Paper and allied products	178	25	7	20	35	31	44	10	4	2
Printing and publishing	1,214	550	254	154	125	73	38	8	8	4
Chemicals and allied products	248	65	29	43	37	23	24	11	7	9
Petroleum and coal products	53	20	9	12	7	3	2	0	0	0
Rubber, plastics products	316	63	31	45	67	45	40	15	7	3
Leather and leather products	66	19	4	8	6	6	8	14	1	0
Stone, clay, and glass products	323	70	72	68	59	27	18	6	2	1
Primary metal industries	138	18	10	19	34	18	24	11	2	2
Fabricated metal products	647	162	98	93	131	80	54	21	6	2
Industrial machinery and equipment	839	256	140	169	143	53	41	23	9	5
Electronic and other electronic equipment	246	76	29	22	28	28	28	18	14	3
Transportation equipment	234	59	20	38	35	22	30	13	12	5
Instruments, related products	131	48	26	13	12	14	9	3	4	2
Miscellaneous manufacturing	297	130	52	41	31	14	17	9	3	0
Administrative and auxiliary	230	54	26	21	44	40	35	5	4	1

Source: U.S. Department of Commerce, Bureau of the Census, *County Business Patterns, 1991, Tennessee.*

TABLE 4.4-- AVERAGE WEEKLY HOURS AND AVERAGE WEEKLY AND HOURLY EARNINGS FOR MANUFACTURING PRODUCTION WORKERS, BY SECTOR, TENNESSEE, 1990–1993

Sector	Average weekly earnings				Average hourly earnings				Average weekly hours			
	1993	1992	1991	1990r	1993	1992	1991	1990r	1993	1992	1991	1990r
All manufacturing	$421.19	$408.60	$392.86	$368.97	$10.33	$10.13	$9.91	$9.55	40.8	40.3	39.6	38.6
Durable goods	432.51	422.59	403.51	375.43	10.65	10.45	10.33	9.99	40.6	40.4	39.0	37.6
Lumber and wood products	296.13	282.37	268.97	255.23	7.39	7.12	6.83	6.51	40.1	39.7	39.4	39.2
Furniture and fixtures	358.72	340.64	314.71	298.38	9.40	9.15	8.68	8.40	38.2	37.2	36.2	35.5
Stone, clay, and glass products	537.56	529.90	505.62	531.04	12.22	12.20	12.27	12.55	44.0	43.4	41.2	42.3
Primary metal products	481.10	510.31	505.53	507.05	11.61	12.05	12.02	11.93	41.4	42.3	42.0	42.5
Fabricated metal products	464.63	429.80	432.67	414.50	11.44	10.81	10.74	10.33	40.6	39.8	40.3	40.1
Machinery, including electric	421.88	426.83	403.48	351.69	10.29	10.06	10.01	9.41	41.0	42.5	40.3	37.4
Instruments and related products	426.46	435.30	395.88	376.34	10.58	10.54	9.88	9.19	40.3	41.3	40.0	40.9
Nondurable goods	408.90	394.25	382.13	361.97	10.00	9.79	9.51	9.12	40.9	40.3	40.2	39.7
Food and kindred products	416.92	400.07	389.64	359.27	10.06	9.78	9.45	8.78	41.3	40.9	41.2	40.9
Textile mill products	359.85	352.15	331.60	315.75	8.72	8.46	7.85	7.74	41.3	41.6	42.3	40.8
Apparel	258.39	251.78	242.95	222.04	6.64	6.64	6.57	6.11	38.9	37.9	37.0	36.3
Paper and allied products	564.67	560.64	542.48	533.20	13.01	12.83	12.26	12.10	43.4	43.7	44.2	44.0
Chemical and allied products	519.16	530.09	544.68	385.79	12.78	13.23	13.03	9.44	40.6	40.0	41.8	40.7
Rubber and plastic products	508.36	459.60	445.34	380.24	11.61	10.82	10.74	9.45	43.8	42.5	41.5	40.2
Leather and leather products	282.04	273.46	269.32	276.30	7.17	7.03	6.73	7.04	39.3	38.9	40.0	39.2

r revised.

Source: Tennessee Department of Employment Security, direct correspondence.

TABLE 4.5-- POLLUTION ABATEMENT OPERATING COSTS, BY INDUSTRY GROUP AND BY TYPE OF POLLUTION, TENNESSEE, 1991 [In millions of dollars]

| Industry group | Total gross annual cost | Payments to governmental units | | | Operating costs by form of pollutants abated | | | | |
| | | Total | Public sewage services | Solid collection and disposal | Total | Air | Water | Solid Waste | |
								Hazardous	Non-hazardous
TOTAL	420.8	49.6	39.5	10.1	371.2	92.1	144.0	60.3	74.7
Food and kindred products	(D)	(D)	(D)	3.0	(D)	(D)	(D)	(D)	(D)
Textile mill products	15.5	5.8	5.3	0.5	9.7	2.2	2.6	0.9	4.0
Lumber and wood products	8.3	2.1	0.2	1.8	6.2	1.4	0.1	0.4	4.3
Furniture and fixtures	17.0	4.5	4.3	0.3	12.5	3.0	1.8	3.0	4.7
Paper and allied products	32.8	5.6	5.5	0.1	27.2	7.2	9.3	2.3	8.3
Printing and publishing	11.1	1.0	0.6	0.4	10.1	5.1	0.8	1.3	2.9
Chemicals and allied products	185.7	4.0	3.6	0.4	181.6	30.3	94.0	35.0	22.4
Petroleum and coal products	(D)	(D)	(D)	(a)	(D)	(D)	(D)	(D)	(D)
Rubber and miscellaneous plastics products	10.6	3.4	2.3	1.1	7.2	2.0	1.4	0.8	3.1
Stone, clay, and glass products	4.7	0.5	0.4	0.1	4.3	2.0	0.6	0.3	1.3
Primary metal industries	24.5	0.8	0.7	0.1	23.6	11.8	5.4	3.2	3.2
Fabricated metal products	9.4	1.2	0.9	0.3	8.2	1.2	3.0	2.0	2.0
Industrial machinery and equipment	17.5	2.6	2.4	0.2	15.0	3.2	4.0	2.7	5.1
Electronic and other electric equipment	11.4	2.9	2.2	0.7	8.6	3.0	1.3	1.4	2.9
Transportation equipment	25.3	2.4	1.8	0.7	22.8	(D)	4.5	5.8	(D)
Miscellaneous manufacturing industries	4.1	1.1	0.8	0.2	3.0	0.6	0.2	0.5	1.7

Note: Detail may not add to total due to independent rounding. Data exclude industry group 23, apparel and other textile products, and cover only establishments with 20 or more employees. No industry is shown where pollution abatement gross annual cost is less than $1.0 million.

(D) Withheld to avoid disclosing operations of individual companies.

a. Less than $0.5 million.

Source: U.S. Department of Commerce, Bureau of the Census, *Current Industrial Reports, Pollution Abatement Costs and Expenditures, 1991.*

TABLE 4.6— POLLUTION ABATEMENT CAPITAL EXPENDITURES, BY TYPE OF POLLUTANT ABATED, TENNESSEE, 1978–1991, SELECTED YEARS [In millions of dollars]

Year	Total pollution abatement capital expenditures	Air							Water	Solid waste		
		Total[1]	Particulates	Sulfur oxides	Nitrogen oxides and carbon monoxide	Hydrocarbon volatile organic compounds	Lead	Hazardous air pollutants		Total	Hazardous	Nonhazardous
1991	139.2	95.1	38.2	(D)	11.4	21.9	(D)	2.7	28.4	15.7	6.6	9.1
1990	136.3	84.4	36.3	1.7	2.6	38.8	0.1	3.0	39.2	12.7	7.9	4.8
1989	86.1	38.4	19.0	1.6	(D)	6.7	(D)	8.0	32.8	14.9	9.1	5.8
1988	148.2	42.8	23.4	(D)	(D)	10.6	(a)	(D)	78.9	26.5	13.0	13.5
1986	118.8	40.7	18.8	1.0	1.5	8.7	(a)	5.1	53.5	24.6	16.1	8.4
1985	88.9	37.7	11.6	1.7	0.5	12.5	0.1	5.8	38.6	12.6	8.7	3.9
1984	57.4	29.7	12.3	(D)	(D)	11.3	(D)	1.8	15.6	12.0	7.7	4.3
1983	62.6	33.4	19.6	(D)	(D)	3.4	(D)	(D)	24.9	4.4	1.1	3.3
1982	112.9	71.1	42.5	6.5	9.8b	n.a.	n.a.	n.a.	32.6	9.2	n.a.	n.a.
1981	89.8	57.5	35.3	2.5	9.3b	n.a.	n.a.	n.a.	28.6	3.7	n.a.	n.a.
1980	78.7	32.6	23.0	0.6	6.7b	n.a.	n.a.	n.a.	41.1	5.0	n.a.	n.a.
1979	83.1	36.7	29.1	3.0	3.1b	n.a.	n.a.	n.a.	38.4	8.0	n.a.	n.a.
1978	79.1	41.6	35.6	2.6	2.0b	n.a.	n.a.	n.a.	29.8	7.6	n.a.	n.a.

Note: Data exclude industry 23, apparel and other textile products, and cover only establishments with 20 or more employees.

(D) Withheld to avoid disclosing operations of individual companies.

n.a. not available.

1. Total includes categories not detailed separately.

a. Less than $50,000.

b. Includes hydrocarbons.

Source: U.S. Department of Commerce, Bureau of the Census, *Current Industrial Reports, Pollution Abatement Costs and Expenditures, 1991*, and earlier editions.

TABLE 4.7.– EXPORT-RELATED MANUFACTURING SHIPMENTS AND EMPLOYMENT, TENNESSEE, 1987 [Shipments in millions of dollars and employment in thousands of jobs]

Industry	Value of shipments				Employment			
	Total export-related		Direct exports	Supporting exports	Total export-related		Direct exports	Supporting exports
	Amount	Percent of total manufacturing shipments			Amount	Percent of total manufacturing employment		
Total	7,315.4	12.7	3,567.2	3,748.2	52.2	10.8	22.1	30.1
Food and kindred products	469.4	5.5	301.9	167.5	0.8	2.2	0.3	0.5
Tobacco products	118.6	23.8	115.3	3.3	0.6	46.2	0.6	(a)
Textile mill products	153.7	7.7	54.1	99.6	1.3	5.4	0.2	1.1
Apparel and other textile products	98.8	3.7	78.6	20.2	2.0	3.3	1.5	0.5
Lumber and wood products	101.2	7.6	44.6	56.6	1.0	5.6	0.3	0.7
Furniture and fixtures	63.5	3.9	31.9	31.6	0.8	3.3	0.3	0.5
Paper and allied products	417.3	12.8	82.1	335.2	2.2	12.1	0.3	1.9
Printing and publishing	102.5	4.2	13.6	88.9	1.1	3.5	(a)	1.1
Chemicals and allied products	1,681.1	23.5	1,085.9	595.2	8.2	20.4	5.1	3.1
Petroleum and coal products	50.3	7.5	5.3	45.0	(a)	(a)	(a)	(a)
Rubber, miscellaneous plastics products	395.3	13.1	117.3	278.0	3.1	13.1	0.8	2.3
Leather and leather products	27.4	4.9	18.5	8.9	0.3	3.6	0.2	0.1
Stone, clay, and glass products	220.2	12.9	152.2	68.0	1.5	10.9	0.8	0.7
Primary metal industries	793.6	29.8	104.9	688.7	3.9	28.3	0.3	3.6
Fabricated metal products	438.6	13.4	113.1	325.5	4.6	13.0	1.1	3.5
Machinery, except electrical	587.6	12.8	300.6	287.0	6.0	15.6	3.0	3.0
Electric and electronic equipment	819.8	18.9	379.0	440.8	6.1	19.4	2.1	4.0
Transportation equipment	550.5	9.9	399.0	151.5	3.3	9.9	2.4	0.9
Instruments and related products	111.0	13.0	83.9	27.1	1.2	14.3	0.9	0.3
Miscellaneous manufacturing	114.5	11.4	84.8	29.7	1.2	10.4	0.9	0.3
Auxiliaries	0.0	0.0	0.0	0.0	2.0	16.1	0.0	2.0

a. Less than 0.05.

Source: U.S. Department of Commerce, Bureau of the Census, *Manufacturing Analytical Report Series, Exports from Manufacturing Establishments: 1987.*

TABLE 4.8– AVERAGE WEEKLY HOURS AND AVERAGE WEEKLY AND HOURLY EARNINGS FOR MANUFACTURING PRODUCTION WORKERS, METROPOLITAN STATISTICAL AREAS, 1955-1993, SELECTED YEARS [Earnings in dollars]

| | Chattanooga | | | Johnson City-Kingsport-Bristol | | | Knoxville | | | Memphis | | | Nashville-Davidson | | |
| | Earnings | | | Earnings | | | Earnings | | | Earnings | | | Earnings | | |
Year	Weekly	Hourly	Hours	Weekly	Hourly	Hours	Weekly	Hourly	Hours	Weekly	Hourly	Hours	Weekly	Hourly	Hours
1993	399.18	9.76	40.9	410.28	10.52	39.0	409.37	10.26	39.9	434.66	10.55	41.2	463.81	11.34	40.9
1992ᶠ	392.51	9.55	41.1	406.74	10.51	38.7	410.04	10.20	40.2	430.35	10.42	41.3	455.39	11.30	40.3
1991ᶠ	373.27	9.06	41.2	430.26	10.65	40.4	390.85	9.92	39.4	422.65	10.41	40.6	459.20	11.20	41.0
1990ᶠ	348.94	8.68	40.2	392.35	9.64	40.7	349.44	9.22	37.9	385.92	9.60	40.2	438.98	11.17	39.3
1989ᶠ	336.90	8.36	40.3	410.86	9.69	42.4	369.47	9.33	39.6	398.37	9.44	42.3	442.21	10.63	41.6
1988	348.30	8.10	43.0	414.42	9.44	43.9	366.79	8.99	40.8	387.23	9.09	42.6	434.72	10.45	41.6
1987	334.68	7.90	42.4	403.47	9.21	43.8	369.58	9.08	40.7	379.14	8.84	42.9	433.51	10.23	42.4
1986	320.04	7.62	42.0	396.36	9.07	43.7	352.63	8.95	39.4	377.54	8.78	43.0	378.58	9.56	39.6
1985	307.93	7.42	41.5	374.85	8.82	42.5	360.93	8.89	40.6	361.15	8.64	41.8	376.65	9.30	40.5
1984	309.86	7.36	42.1	352.49	8.44	41.8	353.76	8.80	40.2	339.49	8.26	41.1	368.74	8.95	41.2
1983	296.31	7.14	41.5	n.a.	n.a.	n.a.	358.27	8.39	40.3	324.69	7.90	41.1	338.65	8.28	40.9
1982	272.84	7.05	38.7	n.a.	n.a.	n.a.	324.24	8.40	38.6	311.22	7.80	39.9	307.72	7.87	39.1
1981	265.36	6.52	40.7	n.a.	n.a.	n.a.	296.56	7.47	39.7	302.25	7.50	40.3	298.00	7.34	40.6
1980	247.25	6.09	40.6	n.a.	n.a.	n.a.	274.51	6.88	39.9	275.77	6.86	40.2	256.89	6.52	39.4
1979	224.62	5.56	40.4	n.a.	n.a.	n.a.	260.98	6.46	40.4	250.22	6.24	40.1	237.21	5.96	39.8
1978	209.44	5.21	40.2	n.a.	n.a.	n.a.	238.58	5.92	40.3	237.55	5.88	40.4	220.70	5.49	40.2
1975	168.05	4.17	40.3	n.a.	n.a.	n.a.	176.91	4.49	39.4	187.80	4.66	40.3	163.80	4.20	39.0
1970	116.91	2.93	39.9	n.a.	n.a.	n.a.	120.87	3.06	39.5	122.31	3.02	40.5	117.20	2.93	40.0
1965	92.74	2.24	41.4	n.a.	n.a.	n.a.	96.63	2.38	40.6	97.11	2.34	41.5	92.74	2.24	41.4
1960	74.48	1.90	39.2	n.a.	n.a.	n.a.	84.38	2.12	39.8	81.81	2.01	40.7	78.58	1.95	40.3
1955	62.37	1.54	40.5	n.a.	n.a.	n.a.	69.20	1.73	40.0	69.01	1.62	42.6	n.a.	n.a.	n.a.

Note: Data are given for MSA's according to their boundaries at the time. See the "area definitions" in the source to see when area changes occurred. Memphis data exclude the DeSoto, Mississippi component. For state level data see Table 4.4.

r revised.

n.a. not available.

Source: U.S. Department of Labor, Bureau of Labor Statistics, *Employment and Earnings*, May 1994, and earlier editions; and *Employment and Earnings, States and Areas, 1939–1974*; and *Tennessee and Standard Metropolitan Statistical Areas, Employment Estimates, 1981*, and earlier editions.

TABLE 4.9-- MANUFACTURING STATISTICS, METROPOLITAN STATISTICAL AREAS, 1982 AND 1987 [Dollar amounts in millions]

MSA's	Establishments Total	Establishments With 20 or more employees	1987 Employees Number (1,000)	1987 Employees Payroll	1987 Production workers Number (1,000)	1987 Production workers Wages	1987 Value added by manufacture	1987 Value of shipments	1987 New capital expenditures	1982 Employees (1,000)	1982 Value added by manufacture
TENNESSEE	6,864	2,799	484.9	$9,869.2	359.2	$6,282.6	$27,049.7	$57,752.9	$1,904.7	461.6	$17,841.6
Chattanooga, TN-GA	644	292	44.2	887.1	32.5	559.4	2,298.7	5,744.3	178.2	45.8	1,703.2
Portion in Tennessee	498	219	32.8	693.3	23.3	418.9	1,748.5	3,783.2	124.6	37.8	1,401.7
Portion in Georgia	146	73	11.4	193.8	9.2	140.5	550.1	1,961.1	53.6	8.0	301.5
Clarksville-Hopkinsville, TN-KY	117	46	9.3	177.8	7.0	115.7	461.4	945.1	28.1	9.4	291.6
Portion in Tennessee	70	23	5.3	105.2	3.8	63.3	295.5	548.8	(D)	6.2	206.0
Portion in Kentucky	47	23	4.0	72.6	3.2	52.4	165.9	396.3	(D)	3.1	85.5
Jackson, TN	100	44	8.5	191.4	6.2	121.0	621.1	1,341.2	(D)	8.1	356.2
Johnson City-Kingsport-Bristol, TN-VA	494	199	52.8	1,243.5	36.7	754.2	3,105.8	6,594.6	318.4	52.9	2,227.4
Portion in Tennessee	383	148	43.3	1,067.9	29.9	644.0	2,691.4	5,519.2	277.7	44.0	1,875.4
Portion in Virginia	111	51	9.5	175.6	6.9	110.2	414.5	1,075.4	40.6	8.9	351.9
Knoxville, TN	796	267	48.8	1,061.0	34.2	617.8	2,621.8	5,336.3	191.7	39.3	1,625.0
Memphis, TN-MS-AR	1,178	520	60.3	1,330.8	40.1	741.9	4,114.2	9,347.3	228.2	60.5	3,026.6
Portion in Tennessee	1,033	448	52.3	1,183.5	34.5	655.7	3,734.8	8,386.6	206.5	54.3	2,780.9
Portion in Arkansas	48	20	1.9	31.5	1.4	20.6	77.5	250.1	8.4	1.8	47.4
Portion in Mississippi	97	52	6.2	115.8	4.3	65.5	302.0	710.6	13.3	4.4	198.3
Nashville-Davidson, TN	1,506	545	88.6	2,051.6	60.6	1,236.2	4,989.5	11,727.8	342.3	79.0	2,707.0

(D) Withheld to avoid disclosing operations of individual companies.

Source: U.S. Department of Commerce, Bureau of the Census, 1987 Census of Manufactures, Geographic Area Series, Tennessee, and 1982.

TABLE 4.10–MANUFACTURING STATISTICS, BY SECTOR, CHATTANOOGA METROPOLITAN STATISTICAL AREA, 1982 AND 1987 [Dollar amounts in millions]

Sector	Establishments		Employees		Production workers		Value added by manufacture	Value of shipments	New capital expenditures	1982	
	Total	With 20 or more employees	Number (1,000)	Payroll	Number (1,000)	Wages				Employees (1,000)	Value added by manufacture
All industries, total	644	292	44.2	$887.1	32.5	$559.4	$2,298.7	$5,744.3	$178.2	45.8	$1,703.2
Food and kindred products	38	21	6.6	137.0	3.6	64.7	467.9	1,232.2	56.8	5.4	341.3
Textile mill products	61	50	10.7	173.1	9.2	133.4	576.7	1,815.8	41.0	9.8	333.0
Apparel, other textile products	46	21	1.4	12.8	1.2	10.1	20.7	53.3	1.7	1.0	12.2
Lumber and wood products	40	6	0.5	6.1	0.4	4.4	17.3	33.2	0.4	0.5	12.9
Furniture and fixtures	15	9	0.5	7.7	0.5	5.5	16.9	29.3	(D)	0.6	9.6
Paper and allied products	19	15	1.6	39.8	1.3	28.9	104.2	222.8	6.9	1.4	60.5
Printing and publishing	86	20	1.9	41.0	1.1	20.6	86.2	136.4	5.1	1.6	47.8
Chemicals and allied products	39	19	3.4	99.0	2.2	53.4	272.7	668.6	25.2	5.0	274.1
Rubber and miscellaneous plastics products	18	8	0.6	11.4	0.5	7.8	34.5	71.1	2.2	0.4	17.6
Leather and leather products	11	8	0.6	6.9	0.5	4.5	13.7	38.4	0.4	0.8	21.5
Stone, clay and glass products	26	11	1.1	19.3	0.9	14.5	51.1	100.4	4.7	2.8	106.8
Primary metal industries	16	11	3.1	72.9	2.7	54.7	156.7	312.4	5.7	3.4	110.9
Fabricated metal products	62	31	3.9	91.1	2.9	61.4	187.6	334.6	5.7	6.3	190.1
Industrial machinery and equipment	85	25	2.7	57.1	2.0	35.7	96.0	209.6	4.5	2.9	80.2
Electric, electronic equipment	17	8	2.9	50.2	2.3	38.7	109.9	322.2	(D)	1.8	56.7
Transportation equipment	10	4	0.4	9.7	0.3	6.3	24.3	47.3	0.8	n.a.	n.a.
Instruments and related products	10	3	0.6	12.2	0.4	8.3	31.2	49.9	0.1	(a)	(D)
Miscellaneous manufacturing industries	23	8	0.7	9.9	0.6	5.8	24.3	44.0	(D)	0.5	12.4
Auxiliaries	17	14	0.9	29.0	0.0	0.0	0.0	0.0	0.0	1.1	0.0

Note: 1982 data were based on the 1977 SIC code with 1982 revisions. 1987 data were based on 1987 SIC code. Totals include categories not shown separately.

n.a. not available.

(D) Withheld to avoid disclosing operations of individual companies.

a. Range is from 250 to 499 employees. Actual data withheld to avoid disclosure.

Source: U.S. Department of Commerce, Bureau of the Census, 1987 Census of Manufactures, Geographic Area Series, Tennessee; and 1982.

TABLE 4.11–MANUFACTURING STATISTICS, BY SECTOR, CLARKSVILLE–HOPKINSVILLE METROPOLITAN STATISTICAL AREA, 1982 AND 1987
[Dollar amounts in millions]

| Sector | Establishments | | 1987 | | | | | | | 1982 | |
| | Total | With 20 or more employees | Employees | | Production workers | | Value added by manufacture | Value of shipments | New capital expenditures | Employees (1,000) | Value added by manufacture |
			Number (1,000)	Payroll	Number (1,000)	Wages					
All industries, total	117	46	9.3	$177.8	7.0	$115.7	$461.4	$945.1	$28.1	9.4	$291.6
Apparel, other textile products	9	4	1.5	17.6	1.4	14.8	40.5	55.0	(D)	1.2	20.2
Printing and publishing	22	6	1.1	19.1	0.8	11.8	51.4	75.1	2.3	1.1	37.9
Rubber and miscellaneous plastics products	5	3	1.0	20.5	0.9	16.4	46.0	89.5	(D)	(c)	(D)
Leather and leather products	2	1	(a)	(D)	(D)	(D)	(D)	(D)	(D)	1.3	12.5
Primary metal industries	5	4	(a)	(D)	(D)	(D)	(D)	(D)	(D)	(a)	(D)
Industrial machinery and equipment	7	2	(b)	(D)	(D)	(D)	(D)	(D)	(D)	(b)	(D)
Electronic and other electric equipment	6	4	(a)	(D)	(D)	(D)	(D)	(D)	(D)	(c)	(D)
Auxiliaries	5	4	0.5	11.6	0.0	0.0	0.0	0.0	0.0	0.5	0.0

Note: 1982 data were based on the 1977 SIC code with 1982 revisions. 1987 data were based on 1987 SIC code. Totals include categories not shown separately.

(D) Withheld to avoid disclosing figures of individual companies.

a. Range is 500–999. Actual data withheld to avoid disclosure.

b. Range is 1,000–2,499. Actual data withheld to avoid disclosure.

c. Range is 250–499. Actual data withheld to avoid disclosure.

Source: U.S. Department of Commerce, Bureau of the Census, 1987 Census of Manufactures, Geographic Area Series, Tennessee; and 1982.

TABLE 4.12–MANUFACTURING STATISTICS, BY SECTOR, JACKSON METROPOLITAN STATISTICAL AREA, 1982 AND 1987 [Dollar amounts in millions]

Sector	Establishments		1987							1982	
			Employees		Production workers						
	Total	With 20 or more employees	Number (1,000)	Payroll	Number (1,000)	Wages	Value added by manufacture	Value of shipments	New capital expenditures	Employees (1,000)	Value added by manufacture
All industries, total	100	44	8.5	$191.4	6.2	$121.0	$621.1	$1,341.2	(D)	8.1	$356.2
Food and kindred products	11	8	2.2	56.2	1.4	30.5	325.7	602.3	(D)	1.9	163.6
Textile mill products	1	1	(a)	(D)	(D)	(D)	(D)	(D)	(D)	(a)	(D)
Lumber and wood products	15	5	1.1	17.1	1.0	15.0	29.5	67.2	(D)	0.9	12.8
Paper and allied products	7	5	0.6	13.0	0.5	9.1	30.4	108.9	$1.3	0.5	21.6
Printing and publishing	14	2	(b)	(D)	(D)	(D)	(D)	(D)	(D)	n.a.	n.a.
Stone, clay and glass products	9	6	(a)	(D)	(D)	(D)	(D)	(D)	(D)	(c)	(D)
Primary metal industries	2	2	(a)	(D)	(D)	(D)	(D)	(D)	(D)	(a)	(D)
Industrial machinery and equipment	11	3	(c)	(D)	(D)	(D)	(D)	(D)	(D)	(a)	(D)
Transportation equipment	2	2	(b)	(D)	(D)	(D)	(D)	(D)	(D)	n.a.	n.a.

Note: 1982 data were based on the 1977 SIC code with 1982 revisions. 1987 data were based on 1987 SIC code. Totals include categories not shown separately.

n.a. not available.

(D) Withheld to avoid disclosing operations of individual companies.

a. Range is 500-999. Actual data withheld to avoid disclosure.

b. Range is 250-499. Actual data withheld to avoid disclosure.

c. Range is 1,000-2,499. Actual data withheld to avoid disclosure.

Source: U.S. Department of Commerce, Bureau of the Census, *1987 Census of Manufactures, Geographic Area Series, Tennessee;* and *1982.*

TABLE 4.13–MANUFACTURING STATISTICS, BY SECTOR, JOHNSON CITY-KINGSPORT-BRISTOL METROPOLITAN STATISTICAL AREA, 1982 AND 1987

[Dollar amounts in millions]

Sector	Establishments		Employees		Production workers		Value added by manufacture	Value of shipments	New capital expenditures	1982	
	Total	With 20 or more employees	Number (1,000)	Payroll	Number (1,000)	Wages				Employees (1,000)	Value added by manufacture
					1987						
All industries, total	494	199	52.8	$1,243.5	36.7	$754.2	$3,105.8	$6,594.6	$318.4	52.9	$2,227.4
Food and kindred products	26	13	2.7	50.8	1.1	17.6	130.4	337.4	3.3	2.9	127.7
Textile mill products	19	13	2.7	47.7	2.4	39.4	95.6	250.3	(D)	3.0	64.0
Apparel, other textile products	34	27	4.4	43.3	3.9	37.6	83.3	121.5	1.8	4.1	73.4
Lumber and wood products	61	10	1.2	17.2	1.0	13.2	32.6	81.5	4.1	0.9	13.8
Furniture and fixtures	12	6	(a)	(D)	(D)	(D)	(D)	(D)	(D)	0.8	15.1
Paper and allied products	12	8	1.5	50.7	1.2	39.8	97.4	217.6	(D)	1.6	74.3
Printing and publishing	79	20	4.1	85.7	3.1	61.1	198.3	323.9	17.8	4.5	136.2
Chemicals and allied products	19	12	(b)	(D)	(D)	(D)	(D)	(D)	(D)	(b)	(D)
Rubber and miscellaneous plastic products	18	9	0.9	16.8	0.7	11.6	53.1	106.2	(D)	1.0	48.3
Stone, clay and glass products	31	13	2.1	49.2	1.8	39.0	204.7	309.0	8.1	1.7	90.3
Primary metal industries	16	10	1.4	29.6	1.1	20.7	63.7	175.0	(D)	1.2	31.7
Fabricated metal products	36	15	2.5	56.9	2.1	44.3	139.0	357.8	13.1	2.8	141.0
Industrial machinery and equipment	66	19	5.1	98.5	3.0	63.7	279.3	561.4	13.7	4.7	583.2
Electronic and other electric equipment	11	9	2.5	45.7	1.9	27.8	128.3	274.9	13.5	5.3	127.7
Transportation equipment	15	6	2.9	84.7	2.3	57.6	229.8	422.8	12.6	1.0	55.7
Instruments and related products	8	4	(a)	(D)	(D)	(D)	(D)	(D)	(D)	(a)	(D)
Miscellaneous manufacturing industries	22	1	0.4	5.2	0.3	3.1	14.2	27.5	(D)	0.3	8.1
Auxiliaries	6	3	0.4	11.9	0.0	0.0	0.0	0.0	0.0	0.6	0.0

Note: 1982 data were based on the 1977 SIC code with 1982 revisions. 1987 data were based on 1987 SIC code. Totals include categories not shown separately.

n.a. not available.

(D) Withheld to avoid disclosing operations of individual companies.

a. Range is 1,000-2,499. Actual data withheld to avoid disclosure.

b. Range is 2,500 or more. Actual data withheld to avoid disclosure.

Source: U.S. Department of Commerce, Bureau of the Census, 1987 Census of Manufactures, Geographic Area Series, Tennessee; and 1982.

TABLE 4.14--MANUFACTURING STATISTICS, BY SECTOR, KNOXVILLE METROPOLITAN STATISTICAL AREA, 1982 AND 1987 [Dollar amounts in millions]

Sector	Establishments		1987 Employees		1987 Production workers		Value added by manufacture	Value of shipments	New capital expenditures	1982 Employees (1,000)	1982 Value added by manufacture
	Total	With 20 or more employees	Number (1,000)	Payroll	Number (1,000)	Wages					
All industries, total	796	267	48.8	$1,061.0	34.2	$617.8	$2,621.8	$5,336.3	$191.7	39.3	$1,625.0
Food and kindred products	43	18	3.3	58.7	1.9	30.5	183.5	487.3	10.1	3.7	183.3
Textile mill products	17	10	3.1	44.5	2.7	33.9	73.3	130.0	(D)	(c)	(D)
Apparel, other textile products	49	31	7.8	99.4	7.2	83.5	363.5	645.4	8.2	6.8	247.9
Lumber and wood products	59	17	1.4	22.8	1.0	13.4	46.0	106.9	2.0	0.7	12.2
Furniture and fixtures	47	18	1.9	26.1	1.7	20.0	48.4	102.8	(D)	0.6	11.0
Paper and allied products	9	6	(a)	(D)	(D)	(D)	(D)	(D)	(D)	(d)	(D)
Printing and publishing	153	21	2.3	42.5	1.2	19.8	114.4	165.6	5.5	2.1	79.7
Chemicals and allied products	23	6	(b)	(D)	(D)	(D)	(D)	(D)	(D)	(b)	(D)
Rubber and miscellaneous plastic products	25	14	1.6	32.4	1.2	21.9	72.4	150.7	3.0	1.4	39.3
Stone, clay and glass products	44	18	1.6	32.1	1.3	22.9	84.9	170.8	5.5	1.0	33.8
Primary metal industries	14	8	(b)	(D)	(D)	(D)	(D)	(D)	(D)	(b)	(D)
Fabricated metal products	72	31	2.5	52.5	2.0	37.1	129.2	333.1	7.5	2.0	67.0
Industrial machinery and equipment	88	19	(c)	(D)	(D)	(D)	(D)	(D)	(D)	1.8	64.5
Electronic and other electric equipment	27	9	1.4	28.9	1.1	20.1	70.3	103.3	1.6	0.6	12.5
Transportation equipment	32	16	3.5	69.8	2.7	47.9	169.5	347.8	8.5	1.9	58.7
Instruments and related products	31	11	(c)	(D)	(D)	(D)	(D)	(D)	(D)	0.7	31.8
Miscellaneous manufacturing industries	46	6	1.2	24.9	0.9	13.7	71.2	118.8	2.6	1.0	22.8
Auxiliaries	6	6	1.8	66.5	0.0	0.0	0.0	0.0	0.0	0.4	0.0

Note: 1982 data were based on the 1977 SIC code with 1982 revisions. 1987 data were based on 1987 SIC code. Totals include categories not shown separately.

(D) Withheld to avoid disclosing operations of individual companies.

a. Range is 500-999. Actual data withheld to avoid disclosure.

b. Range is 2,500 or more. Actual data withheld to avoid disclosure.

c. Range is 1,000-2,499. Actual data withheld to avoid disclosure.

d. Range is 250-499. Actual data withheld to avoid disclosure.

Source: U.S. Department of Commerce, Bureau of the Census, *1987 Census of Manufactures, Geographic Area Series, Tennessee;* and *1982.*

TABLE 4.15—MANUFACTURING STATISTICS, BY SECTOR, MEMPHIS METROPOLITAN STATISTICAL AREA, 1982 AND 1987 [Dollar amounts in millions]

| Sector | Establishments | | 1987 | | | | | | | 1982 | |
| | Total | With 20 or more employees | Employees | | Production workers | | Value added by manufacture | Value of shipments | New capital expenditures | Employees (1,000) | Value added by manufacture |
			Number (1,000)	Payroll	Number (1,000)	Wages					
All industries, total	1,178	520	60.3	$1,330.8	40.1	$741.9	$4,114.2	$9,347.3	$228.2	60.5	$3,026.6
Food and kindred products	71	48	7.0	185.3	5.1	125.1	837.1	2,278.7	73.5	8.4	600.6
Tobacco products	1	1	(a)	(D)	(D)	(D)	(D)	(D)	(D)	(a)	(D)
Textile mill products	9	6	(a)	(D)	(D)	(D)	(D)	(D)	(D)	0.5	12.0
Apparel, other textile products	38	22	1.9	23.0	1.7	16.8	51.9	105.9	1.5	2.2	55.0
Lumber and wood products	82	37	2.5	37.8	2.1	27.1	68.7	153.1	2.2	2.4	43.0
Furniture and fixtures	53	26	2.5	35.6	2.0	21.7	80.9	183.7	1.8	3.3	80.9
Paper and allied products	42	34	5.8	137.6	4.4	95.7	606.0	1,145.8	29.7	5.8	437.1
Printing and publishing	232	46	5.2	109.5	3.1	61.0	262.6	402.1	13.1	4.2	166.0
Chemicals and allied products	81	40	7.0	160.7	3.9	84.8	809.8	1,468.1	31.3	6.2	629.2
Petroleum and coal products	16	4	0.7	16.1	0.4	8.9	44.7	578.0	(D)	(b)	(D)
Rubber and miscellaneous plastic products	37	21	1.5	30.4	1.2	21.3	95.5	214.6	5.3	2.4	91.1
Stone, clay and glass products	54	25	1.8	38.8	1.5	27.7	103.1	213.9	5.0	1.2	37.7
Primary metal industries	13	10	0.9	16.9	0.7	12.6	41.1	124.9	1.7	1.0	29.7
Fabricated metal products	135	69	5.3	99.7	3.9	60.4	250.3	521.5	9.2	5.2	173.6
Industrial machinery and equipment	103	35	4.8	114.4	3.2	67.7	278.7	590.7	12.5	5.1	227.6
Electronic and other electric equipment	37	19	3.4	73.0	2.6	43.3	222.8	692.2	14.9	3.3	214.2
Transportation equipment	31	19	2.3	40.6	1.8	29.3	90.9	249.0	5.0	1.6	42.3
Instruments and related products	18	6	1.5	38.9	0.8	15.9	118.3	163.8	(D)	1.1	63.6
Miscellaneous manufacturing industries	55	15	1.6	24.0	1.3	13.9	56.4	100.1	3.1	1.6	37.3
Auxiliaries	68	36	4.0	136.0	0.0	0.0	0.0	0.0	0.0	3.4	0.0

(D) 1982 data were based on the 1977 SIC code with 1982 revisions. 1987 data were based on 1987 SIC code. Withheld to avoid disclosing operations of individual companies.
a. Range is 250–499. Actual data withheld to avoid disclosure.
b. Range is 500–999. Actual data withheld to avoid disclosure.
Source: U.S. Department of Commerce, Bureau of the Census, 1987 Census of Manufactures, Geographic Area Series, Tennessee; and 1982.

TABLE 4.16—MANUFACTURING STATISTICS, BY SECTOR, NASHVILLE-DAVIDSON METROPOLITAN STATISTICAL AREA, 1982 AND 1987
[Dollar amounts in millions]

Sector	Establishments		Employees		Production workers		Value added by manu-facture	Value of shipments	New capital expend-itures	Employees (1,000)	Value added by manu-facture
	Total	With 20 or more employees	Number (1,000)	Payroll	Number (1,000)	Wages					
										1982	
All industries, total	1,506	545	88.6	$2,051.6	60.6	$1,236.2	$4,989.5	$11,727.8	$342.3	79.0	$2,707.0
Food and kindred products	71	44	7.3	165.0	4.0	75.7	570.6	1,779.5	35.4	7.0	321.5
Tobacco products	5	5	(a)	(D)	(D)	(D)	(D)	(D)	(D)	(a)	(D)
Textile mill products	12	9	2.9	80.7	2.2	49.4	106.1	399.2	(D)	1.3	31.1
Apparel, other textile products	60	26	4.2	53.8	3.7	39.0	109.0	251.9	4.7	4.5	135.5
Lumber and wood products	98	20	2.1	34.9	1.8	26.6	98.1	225.9	9.5	1.5	38.8
Furniture and fixtures	43	22	4.2	77.5	3.3	54.3	187.1	400.6	5.5	3.9	138.2
Paper and allied products	31	16	2.1	44.3	1.6	28.3	107.8	257.2	6.6	2.2	81.7
Printing and publishing	359	88	13.0	278.8	7.1	143.0	729.4	1,147.7	43.3	11.4	378.0
Chemicals and allied products	47	8	(b)	(D)	(D)	(D)	(D)	(D)	(D)	3.7	184.1
Rubber, miscellaneous plastics products	69	27	4.5	105.4	3.4	69.2	289.9	533.1	26.4	2.9	113.3
Leather and leather products	14	7	2.2	33.9	1.5	17.3	78.1	138.0	1.7	3.7	106.3
Stone, clay and glass products	67	24	3.3	123.4	2.5	91.6	311.2	518.5	37.5	4.0	171.1
Primary metal industries	26	11	0.9	21.1	0.7	13.4	61.0	180.0	(D)	0.9	30.4
Fabricated metal products	148	74	7.2	140.9	5.3	87.5	318.2	649.5	10.1	6.5	241.6
Industrial machinery and equipment	171	51	5.1	119.7	3.8	75.3	278.5	550.7	17.8	3.4	106.6
Electronic and other electric equipment	86	28	7.4	147.5	5.9	104.0	336.6	987.7	31.3	7.2	304.4
Transportation equipment	67	34	14.3	434.6	10.6	308.0	968.9	2,942.5	84.9	8.0	188.5
Instruments and related products	17	5	0.8	15.6	0.6	10.6	21.9	41.0	(D)	0.8	14.9
Misc. manufacturing industries	62	17	2.0	33.8	1.4	19.9	80.0	151.8	3.8	0.9	30.4
Auxiliaries	44	27	3.2	102.1	0.0	0.0	0.0	0.0	0.0	4.3	0.0

Note: 1982 data were based on the 1977 SIC code with 1982 revisions. 1987 data were based on 1987 SIC code. Totals include categories not shown separately.
(D) Withheld to avoid disclosing operations of individual companies.
a. Range is 500–999. Actual data withheld to avoid disclosure.
b. Range is 1,000–2,499. Actual data withheld to avoid disclosure.
Source: U.S. Department of Commerce, Bureau of the Census, 1987 Census of Manufactures, Geographic Area Series, Tennessee; and 1982.

TABLE 4.17–MANUFACTURING EMPLOYEES AND PAYROLL, AND NUMBER OF ESTABLISHMENTS BY EMPLOYMENT–SIZE CLASS, COUNTIES, 1991

| County | Number of employees[1] | Annual payroll ($1,000) | Total | Employment–size class | | | | | | | | |
				1–4	5–9	10–19	20–49	50–99	100–249	250–499	500–999	1,000 or more
Anderson	12,035	402,992	97	31	19	10	19	5	5	5	2	1
Bedford	5,365	110,778	51	17	4	8	5	6	5	2	4	0
Benton	1,120	20,189	19	5	5	2	1	1	3	1	0	0
Bledsoe	(b)	(D)	11	5	1	4	0	0	0	1	0	0
Blount	6,646	210,243	95	30	17	20	12	8	3	1	3	1
Bradley	12,846	283,054	148	50	21	19	18	13	14	5	7	1
Campbell	1,993	29,373	42	15	4	10	4	3	5	0	1	0
Cannon	680	8,722	16	4	4	4	0	2	1	1	0	0
Carroll	3,808	64,348	48	15	6	3	9	6	6	2	0	1
Carter	3,282	63,792	41	15	7	2	8	1	5	2	0	1
Cheatham	2,155	50,161	26	11	6	3	4	1	0	0	0	1
Chester	1,201	17,360	21	5	3	3	6	1	0	3	0	0
Claiborne	3,667	53,633	40	16	6	3	2	5	4	3	1	0
Clay	1,670	23,413	14	2	3	2	1	2	3	0	1	0
Cocke	2,475	50,784	35	12	3	3	2	8	5	1	1	0
Coffee	5,898	124,514	78	15	9	13	11	15	7	6	2	0
Crockett	1,480	24,063	17	2	3	2	4	1	4	0	1	0
Cumberland	2,734	53,664	53	17	8	4	10	3	9	2	0	0
Davidson	39,113	1,120,898	874	342	129	125	138	62	41	24	9	4
Decatur	1,293	16,270	34	13	9	1	2	4	4	1	0	0
DeKalb	2,678	42,192	33	10	1	4	5	5	6	1	1	0
Dickson	2,673	56,657	51	24	3	9	5	3	3	3	1	0
Dyer	5,771	133,851	37	6	9	6	1	5	2	4	2	2
Fayette	1,954	41,016	32	10	1	9	4	3	3	1	1	0
Fentress	1,868	20,988	39	12	5	3	5	8	5	1	0	0
Franklin	1,800	30,892	40	14	5	4	7	4	4	2	0	0
Gibson	8,134	168,578	82	29	11	7	5	10	12	6	1	1
Giles	3,539	72,870	49	12	9	6	8	5	5	2	2	0
Grainger	1,233	18,239	32	15	2	5	3	1	6	0	0	0
Greene	9,448	193,459	94	24	11	10	17	16	7	5	3	1

TABLE 4.17–MANUFACTURING EMPLOYEES AND PAYROLL, AND NUMBER OF ESTABLISHMENTS BY EMPLOYMENT-SIZE CLASS, COUNTIES, 1991 (Continued)

County	Number of employees[1]	Annual payroll ($1,000)	Total	Employment-size class								
				1–4	5–9	10–19	20–49	50–99	100–249	250–499	500–999	1,000 or more
Grundy	578	4,684	18	7	4	2	1	1	3	0	0	0
Hamblen	16,163	341,435	126	26	10	14	23	17	19	9	6	2
Hamilton	32,719	803,261	499	130	74	87	78	55	55	9	7	4
Hancock	(a)	(D)	4	2	0	0	0	1	1	0	0	0
Hardeman	2,773	57,775	32	10	6	6	1	4	2	2	0	1
Hardin	2,711	57,443	60	22	8	11	5	5	6	3	0	0
Hawkins	5,928	171,746	35	5	5	8	3	2	5	3	3	1
Haywood	2,329	50,091	21	1	3	4	5	3	2	2	1	0
Henderson	3,739	68,665	41	12	8	5	4	3	4	3	2	0
Henry	3,086	57,794	68	24	6	11	12	6	5	4	0	0
Hickman	1,404	21,246	29	5	8	4	4	3	4	0	0	0
Houston	436	7,568	17	5	5	3	1	2	1	1	0	0
Humphreys	1,863	72,112	24	6	6	4	2	1	3	1	1	0
Jackson	1,073	15,689	23	8	2	2	4	5	0	2	0	0
Jefferson	3,170	55,263	55	13	8	8	14	3	6	1	2	0
Johnson	1,512	23,642	19	3	3	4	3	2	2	1	1	0
Knox	22,339	525,532	475	174	74	65	72	37	30	17	5	1
Lake	679	10,537	9	3	2	1	0	1	1	0	1	0
Lauderdale	3,814	71,680	26	5	2	2	2	3	7	4	1	0
Lawrence	5,546	115,601	67	21	14	9	7	6	7	2	0	1
Lewis	1,273	23,136	22	7	4	3	5	0	1	1	1	0
Lincoln	2,121	41,414	39	16	8	6	4	4	3	0	2	0
Loudon	3,046	70,689	41	13	7	1	6	4	7	2	1	0
McMinn	9,122	222,617	74	18	10	8	11	5	13	5	3	1
McNairy	3,023	48,399	55	18	6	6	9	8	5	2	1	0
Macon	2,175	34,616	32	12	2	3	4	3	5	3	0	0
Madison	8,988	221,423	123	24	22	15	23	16	13	5	5	0
Marion	1,514	27,119	27	10	3	2	3	5	3	1	0	0
Marshall	5,544	127,553	46	6	7	7	11	5	4	3	2	1

TABLE 4.17--MANUFACTURING EMPLOYEES AND PAYROLL, AND NUMBER OF ESTABLISHMENTS BY EMPLOYMENT-SIZE CLASS, COUNTIES, 1991
(Continued)

County	Number of employees[1]	Annual payroll ($1,000)	Total	Employment-size class								
				1-4	5-9	10-19	20-49	50-99	100-249	250-499	500-999	1,000 or more
Maury	10,557	356,160	81	25	11	9	13	11	5	5	1	1
Meigs	226	3,048	8	3	1	1	2	0	1	0	0	0
Monroe	3,291	67,596	74	21	14	9	13	7	7	3	0	0
Montgomery	5,874	130,827	71	26	7	13	6	8	4	3	3	1
Moore	(b)	(D)	8	4	0	1	0	1	2	0	0	0
Morgan	953	15,617	19	3	4	6	2	1	1	2	0	0
Obion	6,248	158,057	47	11	6	6	9	2	7	5	0	1
Overton	1,779	24,428	36	12	5	6	2	5	5	1	0	0
Perry	1,041	16,133	18	5	4	2	3	0	3	1	0	0
Pickett	513	7,244	8	1	1	0	3	1	2	0	0	0
Polk	897	18,571	22	5	6	2	4	3	1	1	0	0
Putnam	8,511	163,809	120	39	15	21	16	10	10	5	3	1
Rhea	4,296	72,149	41	12	7	3	11	1	3	1	1	2
Roane	2,290	31,370	36	15	2	2	6	5	3	2	1	0
Robertson	2,971	55,145	57	20	14	4	5	4	7	2	1	0
Rutherford	16,105	475,461	171	42	28	30	25	15	20	4	4	3
Scott	1,882	33,511	44	13	14	7	4	1	3	1	1	0
Sequatchie	816	11,766	13	3	1	1	4	2	1	1	0	0
Sevier	2,256	48,129	75	35	14	10	7	4	3	1	1	0
Shelby	49,071	1,438,444	1,030	301	152	175	186	103	80	19	9	5
Smith	1,906	34,764	20	4	3	0	0	4	8	1	0	0
Stewart	829	9,142	16	5	1	6	2	0	1	1	0	0
Sullivan	22,221	770,918	163	48	26	25	27	9	17	3	3	5
Sumner	9,619	212,974	190	55	32	27	28	22	20	2	4	0
Tipton	2,513	53,683	37	10	6	3	5	5	5	3	0	0
Trousdale	1,033	16,047	12	3	0	2	1	3	1	2	0	0
Unicoi	2,059	52,943	26	6	1	5	6	2	5	0	1	0
Union	692	13,158	15	7	0	0	3	3	2	0	0	0

TABLE 4.17--MANUFACTURING EMPLOYEES AND PAYROLL, AND NUMBER OF ESTABLISHMENTS BY EMPLOYMENT-SIZE CLASS, COUNTIES, 1991
(Continued)

County	Number of employees[1]	Annual payroll ($1,000)	Total	Employment-size class								
				1-4	5-9	10-19	20-49	50-99	100-249	250-499	500-999	1,000 or more
Van Buren	756	11,391	14	5	1	2	2	1	2	1	0	0
Warren	6,285	140,017	66	21	9	5	14	6	3	4	3	1
Washington	9,851	216,612	136	39	21	23	17	14	10	10	1	1
Wayne	2,243	37,350	27	6	2	4	4	2	6	3	0	0
Weakley	3,690	64,880	56	19	8	6	8	4	5	5	1	0
White	3,358	59,467	44	7	6	10	3	10	4	2	2	0
Williamson	5,330	131,118	123	42	25	17	19	6	8	5	1	0
Wilson	4,568	105,650	95	32	15	18	13	7	4	4	2	0

(D) Withheld to avoid disclosing operations of individual companies.
1. Number of employees for week including March 12.
a. 250-499 employees.
b. 500-999 employees.
Source: U.S. Department of Commerce, Bureau of the Census, *County Business Patterns, 1991.*

TABLE 4.18–MANUFACTURING STATISTICS, COUNTIES, 1982 AND 1987 [Dollar amounts in millions]

County	Establishments		1987							1982	
	Total	With 20 or more employees	Employees		Production workers		Value added by manu-facture	Value of shipments	New capital expend-itures	Em-ployees (1,000)	Value added by manu-facture
			Number (1,000)	Payroll	Number (1,000)	Wages					
Anderson	98	27	10.4	$301.2	5.5	$135.6	$828.0	$983.1	(D)	10.0	$637.9
Bedford	52	29	4.6	86.3	3.7	63.6	277.5	549.1	$35.4	3.7	124.5
Benton	19	8	0.8	13.4	0.7	10.5	25.9	51.6	1.1	0.6	14.2
Bledsoe	11	4	0.5	6.9	0.4	4.6	20.0	45.9	(D)	0.3	9.9
Blount	90	26	6.3	169.2	5.3	136.3	393.2	1,427.3	(D)	(D)	(D)
Bradley	138	64	13.1	245.8	9.7	154.0	864.9	1,768.9	66.4	12.4	437.4
Campbell	42	15	2.0	29.7	1.6	20.4	58.3	126.4	2.4	2.0	44.7
Cannon	17	8	(D)	(D)	(D)	(D)	(D)	(D)	(D)	(D)	(D)
Carroll	49	19	3.4	45.8	2.9	35.6	141.4	328.0	10.4	2.8	66.7
Carter	42	16	3.6	59.7	3.0	43.6	111.5	210.8	5.6	3.2	70.3
Cheatham	24	6	(D)	(D)	(D)	(D)	(D)	(D)	(D)	2.0	121.2
Chester	18	8	1.0	13.8	0.9	9.5	22.0	51.2	1.4	1.0	25.6
Claiborne	31	9	2.6	28.3	2.2	22.6	48.2	102.6	1.4	1.8	27.1
Clay	13	8	1.4	18.9	1.3	15.9	37.6	65.6	1.0	0.9	17.5
Cocke	33	16	2.5	42.4	2.1	31.1	190.7	340.8	10.8	2.5	77.2
Coffee	71	35	5.1	90.2	3.9	60.4	230.4	379.4	8.7	4.9	177.2
Crockett	17	7	(D)	(D)	(D)	(D)	(D)	(D)	(D)	1.1	34.0
Cumberland	54	21	2.8	49.8	2.2	33.0	135.1	256.7	5.4	1.7	46.9
Davidson	863	300	48.1	1,234.5	30.7	709.2	2,881.8	6,089.8	165.5	45.5	1,577.7
Decatur	24	8	1.3	16.6	0.9	11.9	30.6	45.5	0.6	1.9	24.0
DeKalb	26	15	2.0	25.5	1.7	18.3	60.1	98.9	2.3	1.6	47.1
Dickson	38	12	(D)	(D)	(D)	(D)	(D)	(D)	(D)	2.4	60.7
Dyer	39	13	4.4	93.2	3.5	64.3	275.2	511.8	11.5	3.8	141.4
Fayette	26	12	1.8	28.3	1.5	20.0	67.0	158.1	3.0	1.6	29.6
Fentress	35	16	1.7	15.3	1.5	12.9	25.8	44.7	1.0	1.5	13.7
Franklin	34	16	1.6	21.2	1.4	15.8	55.1	136.9	5.1	1.6	32.9
Gibson	72	36	8.3	157.0	6.9	113.8	395.6	843.1	18.2	7.7	234.9
Giles	41	16	3.3	63.5	2.8	50.1	190.8	338.7	7.9	4.1	181.5

TABLE 4.18—MANUFACTURING STATISTICS, COUNTIES, 1982 AND 1987 [Dollar amounts in millions] (Continued)

County	Establishments		1987							1982	
	Total	With 20 or more employees	Employees		Production workers		Value added by manufacture	Value of shipments	New capital expenditures	Employees (1,000)	Value added by manufacture
			Number (1,000)	Payroll	Number (1,000)	Wages					
Grainger	26	7	0.8	10.1	0.7	7.6	23.0	51.0	(D)	0.9	22.9
Greene	85	42	9.9	174.7	7.7	120.0	492.5	1,225.4	27.5	8.4	503.2
Grundy	16	5	0.6	4.5	0.5	3.2	7.7	10.1	0.2	0.7	5.9
Hamblen	117	66	13.2	240.4	10.2	152.1	645.1	1,366.2	46.8	11.5	336.8
Hamilton	465	204	31.0	669.2	21.8	401.1	1,691.4	3,642.0	117.9	36.1	1,352.2
Hancock	2	2	(D)	(D)	(D)	(D)	(D)	(D)	(D)	(D)	(D)
Hardeman	32	12	2.7	47.9	2.2	37.3	143.0	245.8	6.2	2.0	68.3
Hardin	55	19	3.3	53.8	2.7	40.1	198.4	411.7	7.3	2.8	104.0
Hawkins	35	13	5.2	135.9	4.1	100.2	383.4	658.2	20.8	4.2	198.1
Haywood	20	14	2.1	36.0	1.7	28.1	96.9	234.3	6.2	1.4	67.0
Henderson	31	18	3.6	54.7	3.1	42.6	164.9	482.2	7.4	3.1	80.8
Henry	55	24	3.3	57.4	2.4	38.2	122.5	293.7	6.6	3.7	132.3
Hickman	22	9	1.3	19.1	1.2	14.7	76.3	128.8	1.5	1.1	46.5
Houston	12	5	0.5	6.9	0.5	5.5	13.5	23.7	0.2	0.4	10.5
Humphreys	22	7	1.8	49.5	1.5	36.0	340.7	511.0	(D)	2.0	142.2
Jackson	26	9	1.0	14.6	0.8	11.1	28.3	52.2	1.1	1.4	39.8
Jefferson	51	20	2.6	38.9	2.1	30.0	104.3	263.0	3.1	3.0	70.4
Johnson	21	5	1.6	19.3	1.3	15.8	57.7	140.2	2.0	2.1	37.3
Knox	452	164	25.5	490.2	18.0	269.8	1,160.9	2,404.9	51.6	22.9	778.8
Lake	8	3	0.5	6.6	0.4	4.8	(a)	33.0	0.5	0.4	7.6
Lauderdale	27	19	4.7	76.0	4.2	61.2	299.2	506.7	16.0	3.6	172.5
Lawrence	57	21	5.6	95.4	4.7	77.3	254.4	659.1	(D)	4.4	116.2
Lewis	24	8	1.0	16.3	0.9	12.6	36.6	72.6	(D)	1.3	29.8
Lincoln	33	7	2.5	39.9	2.1	28.4	94.4	231.6	4.5	2.1	52.7
Loudon	37	20	2.8	58.9	2.3	45.5	226.5	458.4	26.6	2.9	133.2
McMinn	75	39	9.4	199.2	7.2	137.3	520.9	1,110.4	55.6	8.1	344.0
McNairy	51	20	3.3	44.0	2.7	32.6	120.2	207.5	7.8	3.6	113.2

TABLE 4.18–MANUFACTURING STATISTICS, COUNTIES, 1982 AND 1987 [Dollar amounts in millions] (Continued)

County	Establishments Total	With 20 or more employees	1987 Employees Number (1,000)	Payroll	Production workers Number (1,000)	Wages	Value added by manufacture	Value of shipments	New capital expenditures	1982 Employees (1,000)	Value added by manufacture
Macon	28	10	1.9	26.4	1.7	21.4	45.2	127.3	3.1	1.7	37.7
Madison	100	44	8.5	191.4	6.2	121.0	621.1	1,341.2	(D)	8.1	356.2
Marion	23	10	1.4	19.9	1.2	14.5	53.6	128.6	(D)	1.3	44.1
Marshall	44	26	5.9	106.3	4.5	67.6	339.1	714.7	39.2	4.5	154.7
Maury	77	33	5.0	106.5	4.2	82.5	217.7	639.9	19.8	5.0	241.9
Meigs	7	4	0.2	2.8	0.2	2.1	4.5	7.7	(D)	(D)	(D)
Monroe	56	25	3.6	53.8	3.1	41.6	154.6	301.3	7.1	2.5	44.5
Montgomery	70	23	5.3	105.2	3.8	63.3	295.5	548.8	(D)	6.2	206.0
Moore	7	3	(D)	(D)	(D)	(D)	(D)	(D)	(D)	(D)	(D)
Morgan	21	6	0.8	10.0	0.7	8.3	30.2	42.2	0.6	0.8	32.3
Obion	44	21	6.4	166.9	5.4	134.0	636.2	1,130.6	32.7	5.2	378.8
Overton	33	8	0.9	10.0	0.7	8.1	17.9	35.3	0.5	1.1	10.7
Perry	19	6	1.1	13.6	0.9	10.7	36.0	69.0	2.9	0.7	15.5
Pickett	10	7	0.5	3.8	0.4	3.0	4.6	10.3	(D)	0.7	8.1
Polk	18	7	(D)	(D)	(D)	(D)	(D)	(D)	(D)	(D)	(D)
Putnam	104	46	8.1	129.3	6.3	85.0	357.1	772.2	14.9	5.7	186.9
Rhea	37	20	4.9	73.4	4.4	60.2	196.3	323.5	7.9	3.7	122.0
Roane	33	14	2.9	33.3	2.5	24.7	89.6	154.9	3.3	(D)	(D)
Robertson	43	20	(D)	(D)	(D)	(D)	(D)	(D)	(D)	3.3	111.8
Rutherford	153	70	14.8	350.1	10.6	226.8	1,022.3	3,093.9	92.8	9.1	322.0
Scott	35	9	1.5	25.4	1.1	14.5	59.0	115.8	4.6	0.6	19.6
Sequatchie	10	5	0.4	4.2	0.4	3.3	3.5	12.5	(D)	0.4	5.4
Sevier	70	18	2.6	44.3	2.2	33.1	98.9	172.1	10.4	2.4	62.8
Shelby	1,005	431	50.3	1,150.6	32.9	631.5	3,582.5	8,089.0	(D)	53.0	2,732.9
Smith	13	8	1.3	20.1	1.1	14.9	64.5	183.7	5.1	1.6	33.8
Stewart	10	2	0.7	8.6	0.6	7.8	25.7	41.0	0.6	0.1	1.2
Sullivan	153	54	22.4	640.0	14.2	366.5	1,532.4	3,450.2	(D)	24.1	1,222.8
Sumner	182	68	8.8	158.6	6.9	106.2	373.1	882.3	18.6	6.8	223.6

TABLE 4.18--MANUFACTURING STATISTICS, COUNTIES, 1982 AND 1987 [Dollar amounts in millions] (Continued)

County	Establishments		1987							1982	
	Total	With 20 or more employees	Employees		Production workers		Value added by manufacture	Value of shipments	New capital expenditures	Employees (1,000)	Value added by manufacture
			Number (1,000)	Payroll	Number (1,000)	Wages					
Tipton	28	17	1.9	32.9	1.6	24.3	152.3	297.6	(D)	1.3	48.0
Trousdale	11	8	1.1	13.2	0.9	7.8	31.7	47.7	0.7	1.0	19.3
Unicoi	27	11	1.9	37.9	1.5	23.8	87.2	128.4	(D)	1.4	64.5
Union	9	5	0.5	7.2	0.4	5.5	13.4	35.0	0.2	(D)	(D)
Van Buren	11	5	0.9	10.3	0.8	7.7	13.5	35.6	0.7	0.6	8.9
Warren	58	26	5.0	95.4	4.1	72.2	289.1	533.3	9.8	5.4	235.3
Washington	126	54	10.2	194.4	7.1	109.8	576.9	1,071.5	25.3	11.2	319.8
Wayne	26	12	2.2	26.0	1.9	17.6	70.9	122.4	1.3	1.8	42.4
Weakley	48	20	3.5	50.8	2.9	37.0	96.1	225.7	13.9	3.1	61.7
White	38	22	3.4	50.7	2.9	39.0	106.6	193.2	12.7	3.0	65.5
Williamson	110	38	5.0	96.1	3.2	47.2	184.6	363.3	9.1	4.3	118.7
Wilson	93	31	5.1	95.1	4.0	64.7	224.8	566.8	29.1	5.7	171.3

(D) Withheld to avoid disclosing operations of individual companies.

a. Withheld because estimate did not meet publication standards.

Source: U.S. Department of Commerce, Bureau of the Census, 1987 Census of Manufactures, Geographic Area Series, Tennessee, and 1982.

TABLE 4.19–MANUFACTURING STATISTICS, CITIES WITH 450 OR MORE MANUFACTURING EMPLOYEES, 1982 AND 1987 [Dollar amounts in millions]

| | Establishments | | 1987 | | | | | | | 1982 | |
| | | | Employees | | Production workers | | | | | | |
City	Total	With 20 or more employees	Number (1,000)	Payroll	Number (1,000)	Wages	Value added by manufacture	Value of shipments	New capital expenditures	Employees (1,000)	Value added by manufacture
Alcoa	11	6	(D)	(D)	(D)	(D)	(D)	(D)	(D)	(D)	(D)
Athens	33	21	5.0	$94.3	3.9	$64.7	$214.7	$455.9	(D)	4.1	$124.8
Bolivar	8	5	(D)	(D)	(D)	(D)	(D)	(D)	(D)	1.1	30.0
Brentwood	38	12	1.0	26.1	0.5	10.4	33.0	60.5	$1.7	n.a.	n.a.
Bristol	55	18	6.2	147.4	3.3	74.2	488.6	749.0	(D)	(D)	(D)
Brownsville	16	12	(D)	(D)	(D)	(D)	(D)	(D)	(D)	1.4	65.9
Camden	9	4	0.5	6.0	0.4	5.2	11.2	18.2	(D)	n.a.	n.a.
Carthage	5	4	(D)	(D)	(D)	(D)	(D)	(D)	(D)	n.a.	n.a.
Centerville	8	5	(D)	(D)	(D)	(D)	(D)	(D)	(D)	(D)	(D)
Chattanooga	368	170	25.3	562.9	18.5	352.5	1,416.6	3,130.3	62.0	32.1	1,219.7
Church Hill	3	2	(D)	(D)	(D)	(D)	(D)	(D)	(D)	(D)	(D)
Clarksville	55	19	4.6	90.7	3.3	53.8	260.9	422.7	12.8	(D)	(D)
Cleveland	96	48	9.6	178.3	7.0	107.7	566.0	1,276.1	43.2	10.1	282.2
Clinton	16	6	1.7	31.8	1.4	25.4	68.2	143.1	(D)	1.7	44.8
Collegedale	8	5	(D)	(D)	(D)	(D)	(D)	(D)	(D)	(D)	(D)
Collierville	42	18	2.3	48.0	1.8	33.6	161.8	422.5	5.2	2.0	109.8
Columbia	45	20	3.7	77.9	3.2	62.8	142.1	466.2	13.0	3.1	109.0
Cookeville	81	36	6.2	106.5	4.6	64.2	328.3	601.7	13.8	5.0	177.6
Covington	21	13	(D)	(D)	(D)	(D)	(D)	(D)	(D)	(D)	(D)
Crossville	40	17	(D)	(D)	(D)	(D)	(D)	(D)	(D)	1.5	43.7
Dayton	23	13	4.4	67.4	3.9	55.3	188.0	302.8	(D)	2.7	79.5
Dickson	16	6	1.1	17.6	0.9	12.8	38.6	74.2	(D)	1.9	47.6
Dyersburg	27	6	3.3	74.5	2.7	52.9	186.3	367.5	(D)	2.8	97.1
East Ridge	17	4	0.5	7.8	0.3	3.8	11.2	23.0	(D)	n.a.	n.a.
Elizabethton	25	15	(D)	(D)	(D)	(D)	(D)	(D)	(D)	2.9	67.1
Erwin	15	5	(D)	(D)	(D)	(D)	(D)	(D)	(D)	(D)	(D)
Etowah	7	3	0.7	6.7	0.6	5.2	10.8	15.9	(D)	(D)	(D)

TABLE 4.19—MANUFACTURING STATISTICS, CITIES WITH 450 OR MORE MANUFACTURING EMPLOYEES, 1982 AND 1987 [Dollar amounts in millions]
(Continued)

City	Establishments Total	With 20 or more employees	1987 Employees Number (1,000)	Payroll	Production workers Number (1,000)	Wages	Value added by manufacture	Value of shipments	New capital expenditures	1982 Employees (1,000)	1982 Value added by manufacture
Fayetteville	23	7	2.4	39.1	2.0	27.8	92.7	228.0	(D)	2.0	51.5
Franklin	59	21	3.6	60.5	2.4	32.6	136.8	268.9	7.1	3.7	111.1
Gallatin	59	29	4.4	81.7	3.5	58.2	229.7	545.0	12.7	3.1	123.1
Goodlettsville	34	8	(D)	(D)	(D)	(D)	(D)	(D)	(D)	1.6	39.2
Greeneville	55	33	8.1	139.0	6.3	97.0	403.6	1,050.4	24.0	7.2	462.5
Harriman	7	4	2.2	22.7	1.9	17.5	55.8	96.2	(D)	2.3	71.2
Hartsville	8	6	(D)	(D)	(D)	(D)	(D)	(D)	(D)	(D)	(D)
Henderson	11	4	0.6	5.7	0.5	4.4	14.4	16.8	(D)	0.9	23.7
Hendersonville	60	11	1.5	29.2	1.1	19.3	52.7	117.7	2.4	1.6	48.6
Hohenwald	12	4	0.8	13.4	0.7	10.4	30.9	62.7	(D)	1.3	28.9
Humboldt	16	10	1.6	33.8	1.3	22.3	96.8	206.4	4.0	2.0	59.9
Huntingdon	15	5	0.9	15.6	0.8	11.7	49.6	102.5	(D)	(D)	(D)
Jackson	88	42	8.4	188.5	6.1	119.3	616.4	1,331.1	71.0	7.7	348.9
Jefferson City	10	5	0.5	6.4	0.4	5.4	20.3	46.7	(D)	n.a.	n.a.
Johnson City	82	45	9.2	175.5	6.4	100.8	532.6	981.9	22.1	8.3	262.0
Kingsport	55	21	15.0	471.2	10.0	278.2	980.7	2,572.6	(D)	17.1	570.4
Knoxville	332	112	18.6	334.7	14.0	210.0	944.8	1,957.1	41.4	17.9	625.9
Lafayette	18	8	1.4	20.0	1.2	15.7	32.3	107.5	(D)	1.4	28.7
LaFollette	22	9	(D)	(D)	(D)	(D)	(D)	(D)	(D)	0.9	20.7
LaVergne	34	16	(D)	(D)	(D)	(D)	(D)	(D)	(D)	1.5	46.2
Lawrenceburg	28	13	4.7	85.2	3.9	69.0	230.4	610.4	(D)	(D)	(D)
Lebanon	51	24	4.6	85.7	3.7	58.8	204.5	524.8	(D)	5.3	164.3
Lenoir City	14	7	1.0	19.2	0.8	14.7	66.1	96.8	(D)	1.0	31.9
Lewisburg	40	25	(D)	(D)	(D)	(D)	(D)	(D)	(D)	(D)	(D)
Lexington	21	15	3.3	50.1	2.8	39.3	155.4	468.5	(D)	2.6	75.8
Livingston	19	6	0.7	8.1	0.6	6.5	13.5	25.8	(D)	0.8	8.5

TABLE 4.19--MANUFACTURING STATISTICS, CITIES WITH 450 OR MORE MANUFACTURING EMPLOYEES, 1982 AND 1987 [Dollar amounts in millions] (Continued)

| | Establishments | | 1987 | | | | | | | 1982 | |
| | | | Employees | | Production workers | | | | | | |
City	Total	With 20 or more employees	Number (1,000)	Payroll	Number (1,000)	Wages	Value added by manufacture	Value of shipments	New capital expenditures	Em-ployees (1,000)	Value added by manufacture
Loudon	14	9	1.5	35.0	1.3	27.3	153.9	318.5	(D)	(D)	(D)
McKenzie	16	9	1.4	17.8	1.2	13.0	39.5	88.2	(D)	1.3	32.2
McMinnville	29	14	(D)	(D)	(D)	(D)	(D)	(D)	(D)	5.0	221.1
Madisonville	8	5	0.5	4.4	0.4	2.6	7.9	16.1	0.2	n.a.	n.a.
Manchester	18	8	1.8	26.4	1.5	19.7	100.1	171.1	(D)	1.8	80.8
Martin	9	4	(D)	(D)	(D)	(D)	(D)	(D)	(D)	n.a.	n.a.
Maryville	33	8	(D)	(D)	(D)	(D)	(D)	(D)	(D)	0.8	27.2
Memphis	853	369	43.4	988.5	28.1	536.9	3,138.7	6,941.7	180.2	47.1	2,324.5
Milan	18	9	2.3	42.2	1.8	27.5	114.3	397.0	8.7	1.8	76.3
Monterey	6	4	(D)	(D)	(D)	(D)	(D)	(D)	(D)	n.a.	n.a.
Morristown	93	57	(D)	(D)	(D)	(D)	(D)	(D)	(D)	(D)	(D)
Mount Carmel	3	2	(D)	(D)	(D)	(D)	(D)	(D)	(D)	(D)	(D)
Mount Pleasant	9	7	0.7	15.0	0.6	10.8	44.2	104.8	(D)	0.9	60.8
Murfreesboro	86	37	5.3	110.3	3.8	72.0	321.4	658.9	13.0	5.5	228.6
Nashville-Davidson	827	292	(D)	(D)	(D)	(D)	(D)	(D)	(D)	43.9	1,538.8
Newbern	6	3	(D)	(D)	(D)	(D)	(D)	(D)	(D)	0.8	41.6
Newport	19	13	(D)	(D)	(D)	(D)	(D)	(D)	(D)	(D)	(D)
Oak Ridge	64	17	8.5	265.7	3.9	107.9	752.6	826.8	4.5	(D)	(D)
Oneida	18	6	1.0	19.1	0.7	9.8	46.6	90.5	(D)	0.5	16.9
Paris	34	16	2.3	43.4	1.7	29.2	95.0	231.5	5.1	2.8	110.8
Portland	28	14	(D)	(D)	(D)	(D)	(D)	(D)	(D)	1.3	35.1
Pulaski	20	10	1.7	32.2	1.4	25.1	117.2	183.4	(D)	1.7	83.5
Ripley	14	9	2.6	42.4	2.2	33.0	169.1	266.2	9.4	1.5	55.0
Rockwood	9	6	(D)	(D)	(D)	(D)	(D)	(D)	(D)	(D)	(D)
Savannah	23	11	(D)	(D)	(D)	(D)	(D)	(D)	(D)	(D)	(D)
Selmer	12	7	1.3	18.0	1.1	13.9	43.5	81.0	2.9	1.9	60.9
Sevierville	29	15	2.3	40.3	1.9	30.6	89.2	150.1	(D)	1.1	27.1

TABLE 4.19–MANUFACTURING STATISTICS, CITIES WITH 450 OR MORE MANUFACTURING EMPLOYEES, 1982 AND 1987 [Dollar amounts in millions]
(Continued)

City	Establishments		1987							1982	
			Employees		Production workers						
	Total	With 20 or more employees	Number (1,000)	Payroll	Number (1,000)	Wages	Value added by manufacture	Value of shipments	New capital expenditures	Employees (1,000)	Value added by manufacture
Shelbyville	38	24	(D)	(D)	(D)	(D)	(D)	(D)	(D)	3.3	107.3
Smithville	17	11	1.6	21.3	1.3	15.1	54.0	88.3	(D)	1.3	43.3
Smyrna	18	11	(D)	(D)	(D)	(D)	(D)	(D)	(D)	1.7	34.7
South Pittsburg	11	6	1.0	14.4	0.9	11.1	32.2	79.8	(D)	1.0	20.2
Sparta	23	13	2.5	37.9	2.2	31.3	76.8	129.2	(D)	2.6	61.3
Springfield	24	15	2.8	46.5	2.0	29.9	132.9	345.1	(D)	2.7	99.4
Sweetwater	14	9	1.2	21.2	1.0	15.6	43.1	82.8	1.8	1.0	24.0
Trenton	8	5	0.5	7.4	0.4	6.5	17.9	36.9	(D)	0.9	5.2
Tullahoma	37	23	3.1	57.9	2.2	36.6	121.9	186.0	4.3	3.0	82.9
Union City	17	9	5.1	147.9	4.3	120.4	550.1	1,010.6	(D)	4.1	353.8
Winchester	13	9	(D)	(D)	(D)	(D)	(D)	(D)	(D)	(D)	(D)

n.a. not available.

(D) Withheld to avoid disclosing operations of individual companies.

Source: U.S. Department of Commerce, Bureau of the Census, 1987 Census of Manufactures, Geographic Area Series, Tennessee; and 1982.

TABLE 4.20—MANUFACTURING STATISTICS, SOUTHEASTERN STATES, 1977-1987, CENSUS YEARS

State	Total establishments			Total employees (1,000)			Total payroll ($1,000,000)			Value added by manufacture ($1,000,000)			Index of employment change 1987 (1977= 100)
	1987	1982	1977	1987	1982	1977	1987	1982	1977	1987	1982	1977	
TENNESSEE	6,864	6,417	6,487	484.9	461.6	489.8	9,869.2	7,377.7	5,218.7	27,049.7	17,841.6	12,663.4	99
Alabama	5,843	5,528	5,863	347.3	329.6	341.0	6,962.5	5,234.4	3,773.2	18,652.1	12,045.7	8,405.9	102
Arkansas	3,390	3,313	3,595	205.5	189.8	197.1	3,814.6	2,823.7	1,932.4	10,826.9	7,755.3	4,881.6	104
Florida	15,603	13,723	12,399	499.3	454.4	358.0	10,954.0	7,773.2	4,133.1	27,574.2	18,111.8	9,255.1	139
Georgia	9,187	8,535	8,623	569.9	503.2	484.7	11,933.1	7,912.2	5,124.5	33,708.1	19,212.2	12,548.8	118
Kentucky	3,693	3,502	3,548	251.6	246.6	277.5	5,865.2	4,638.8	3,452.2	18,091.7	11,819.7	9,545.7	91
Louisiana	3,816	4,107	4,276	161.4	202.0	194.8	4,175.9	4,304.2	2,682.7	16,425.8	11,754.6	9,418.3	83
Mississippi	3,318	3,126	3,289	218.9	201.7	219.4	3,827.3	2,880.8	2,061.5	10,502.6	7,824.9	5,619.3	100
North Carolina	10,995	10,134	9,954	842.4	799.1	765.3	16,293.4	11,723.5	7,518.5	47,007.4	28,510.2	18,230.6	110
South Carolina	4,534	4,205	4,229	365.8	367.4	374.2	7,323.9	5,538.6	3,804.9	19,111.9	12,216.9	8,186.1	98
Virginia	6,137	5,568	5,519	429.2	391.1	395.2	9,740.1	6,649.0	4,442.4	26,857.3	17,255.6	10,882.0	109
West Virginia	1,619	1,662	1,857	83.8	95.8	117.0	2,107.6	2,007.0	1,620.5	5,404.4	4,049.2	3,880.2	72

Note: The United States index of employment change for 1987 was 97 (1977=100).

Source: U.S. Department of Commerce, Bureau of the Census, 1987 Census of Manufactures, Geographic Area Series, individual states.

TABLE 4.21--UNION MEMBERSHIP IN MANUFACTURING, SOUTHEASTERN STATES AND UNITED STATES, 1984-1989, SELECTED YEARS

State	Manufacturing union membership (1,000)				Percent of employed[1]			
	1989	1988	1987	1984	1989	1988	1987	1984
TENNESSEE[2]	65.0	67.2	69.6	78.4	12.7	13.5	14.0	15.8
Alabama[2]	55.1	57.4	59.8	72.2	14.3	15.3	16.7	20.1
Arkansas[2]	26.3	27.3	28.4	28.6	11.2	12.0	13.0	13.4
Florida[2]	48.9	48.2	47.6	43.3	9.0	8.9	9.1	8.6
Georgia[2]	66.3	67.8	70.9	77.3	11.7	11.9	12.4	14.1
Kentucky	60.4	62.6	63.9	69.6	21.5	23.0	24.8	27.0
Louisiana	33.4	34.5	34.9	36.8	19.4	20.4	20.8	20.2
Mississippi[2]	18.4	19.0	19.8	19.0	7.6	8.1	8.8	8.7
North Carolina[2]	38.3	39.7	41.5	41.4	4.4	4.6	4.9	5.0
South Carolina[2]	11.1	11.8	13.2	14.6	2.9	3.1	3.6	3.9
Virginia[2]	50.6	52.1	53.1	48.5	11.9	12.2	12.5	11.5
West Virginia	24.4	25.7	29.1	34.9	28.1	29.8	33.6	38.1
UNITED STATES	4,603.1	4,771.1	4,883.6	5,285.9	23.8	24.9	25.8	27.3

Note: Data represent annual average, dues-paying full-time equivalent membership derived from financial records. Excludes unemployed members.
1. Employed in manufacturing.
2. Right-to-work state.
Source: U.S. Department of Commerce, Bureau of the Census, *Statistical Abstract of the United States, 1993*, and earlier editions.

TABLE 4.22--AVERAGE HOURLY EARNINGS FOR MANUFACTURING PRODUCTION WORKERS, SOUTHEASTERN STATES AND UNITED STATES, 1975-1993, SELECTED YEARS
[In dollars]

State	1993	1992[r]	1991	1990	1989	1988	1987	1986	1985	1984	1980	1975
TENNESSEE	10.33	10.13	9.92	9.55	9.22	8.96	8.78	8.58	8.29	7.93	6.08	3.93
Alabama	10.36	9.99	9.72	9.39	9.10	8.95	8.76	8.64	8.48	7.97	6.49	4.10
Arkansas	9.36	9.05	8.81	8.51	8.26	8.07	7.88	7.76	7.57	7.31	5.71	3.69
Florida	9.76	9.59	9.30	8.98	8.67	8.39	8.16	8.02	7.86	7.62	5.98	4.11
Georgia	10.08	9.86	9.56	9.17	8.87	8.65	8.49	8.35	8.10	7.58	5.77	3.80
Kentucky	11.48	11.28	11.00	10.70	10.37	10.16	10.02	9.86	9.53	9.28	7.34	4.77
Louisiana	12.66	12.19	11.86	11.61	11.13	10.94	10.90	10.60	10.43	10.06	7.74	4.88
Mississippi	9.16	8.91	8.67	8.37	8.03	7.83	7.59	7.46	7.22	6.95	5.44	3.58
North Carolina	9.80	9.49	9.19	8.79	8.42	8.12	7.84	7.54	7.29	7.01	5.37	3.52
South Carolina	9.80	9.48	9.17	8.84	8.54	8.30	8.10	7.92	7.61	7.28	5.59	3.59
Virginia	10.85	10.62	10.43	10.07	9.69	9.37	9.14	8.83	8.51	8.10	6.22	3.99
West Virginia	12.27	12.11	11.77	11.53	11.17	10.81	10.55	10.38	10.24	9.93	8.08	4.93
UNITED STATES	11.76	11.46	11.18	10.83	10.48	10.19	9.91	9.73	9.54	9.19	7.27	4.83

r revised.
Source: U.S. Department of Labor, Bureau of Labor Statistics, *Employment and Earnings*, May 1994, and earlier editions.

TABLE 4.23--NUMBER OF EMPLOYEES IN MANUFACTURING ESTABLISHMENTS, SOUTHEASTERN
STATES, 1950-1993, SELECTED YEARS [In thousands of persons]

State	1993	1992	1991	1990	1989	1988	1987	1986	1985	1984	1983
TENNESSEE	528.3	514.5	502.7	520.3	524.5	511.9	497.4	490.5	492.4	497.1	468.6
Alabama	383.3	380.7	379.3	384.5	385.6	380.6	368.8	358.6	358.1	359.8	340.9
Arkansas	243.2	237.0	233.7	232.8	231.0	226.3	219.6	211.8	209.6	213.0	200.3
Florida	484.2	482.9	492.8	522.1	537.9	539.6	531.0	517.2	514.4	501.9	464.3
Georgia	554.6	545.2	541.0	561.1	568.3	574.3	571.2	564.6	557.1	546.5	511.1
Kentucky	292.4	286.9	281.4	287.5	284.2	274.1	262.5	253.8	255.3	257.4	242.5
Louisiana	185.6	185.0	186.4	184.4	176.3	171.5	164.5	166.0	178.0	182.4	180.1
Mississippi	254.4	251.9	246.9	246.5	243.6	238.8	228.6	223.7	221.6	218.7	204.7
North Carolina	845.9	834.4	826.1	861.5	871.1	867.5	856.0	832.8	828.6	835.6	796.1
South Carolina	373.6	371.0	369.2	383.3	389.6	385.0	374.0	365.2	365.4	377.6	362.4
Virginia	404.7	407.4	412.0	426.4	429.6	427.4	428.9	424.7	423.4	421.3	403.6
West Virginia	82.9	82.2	83.2	87.5	87.8	87.0	86.2	86.8	89.5	91.5	89.8

	1982	1981	1980	1979	1978	1977	1975	1970	1965	1960	1950
TENNESSEE	466.7	506.9	502.1	524.7	526.0	507.5	459.0	463.8	386.6	315.0	249.0
Alabama	337.8	362.0	363.1	374.9	368.9	354.3	321.9	327.2	279.2	238.7	218.0
Arkansas	195.2	209.7	209.1	217.8	217.5	209.3	179.2	168.6	135.9	103.0	n.a.
Florida	456.7	472.2	456.4	443.6	415.5	380.9	339.4	322.5	252.6	207.5	103.0
Georgia	500.3	524.6	519.2	528.5	515.8	494.1	439.3	467.1	403.9	341.6	287.0
Kentucky	244.8	270.5	276.2	297.2	292.2	284.9	259.7	255.4	207.8	173.2	141.0
Louisiana	202.6	222.1	214.2	213.6	209.5	203.3	186.2	179.0	161.1	144.9	n.a.
Mississippi	203.2	220.3	221.8	235.2	235.3	230.1	201.8	182.1	153.0	120.2	87.0
North Carolina	782.2	820.7	820.0	826.8	807.2	780.9	715.5	713.0	590.6	504.5	414.0
South Carolina	364.3	390.2	391.9	399.5	391.1	380.2	339.9	340.3	293.0	244.6	210.0
Virginia	397.2	414.0	413.8	413.8	409.4	400.8	371.5	366.0	322.5	275.0	230.0
West Virginia	98.1	111.5	117.2	126.1	126.6	123.8	121.1	126.5	129.2	124.6	131.0

n.a. not available.

Source: U.S. Department of Labor, Bureau of Labor Statistics, *Employment and Earnings*, May 1994, and earlier
editions; *Handbook of Labor Statistics*, Bulletin 2340, August 1989; and *Employment and Earnings, States and
Areas, 1939-1978.*

TABLE 4.24--EXPORT STATISTICS, SOUTHEASTERN STATES AND UNITED STATES, 1986 AND 1987

State	Value of shipments ($ million)						Manufacturing employment (1,000)					
	Total		Export-related		Export shipments as percent of total		Total		Export-related		Export employment as percent of total	
	1987	1986	1987	1986	1987	1986	1987	1986	1987	1986	1987	1986
TENNESSEE	57,752.9	52,717.0	7,315.4	5,760.5	12.7	10.9	484.7	466.4	52.2	42.2	10.8	9.0
Alabama	40,901.4	36,537.2	5,832.3	4,409.9	14.3	12.1	348.5	328.9	42.0	31.7	12.1	9.6
Arkansas	25,307.6	22,131.2	3,140.2	2,343.8	12.4	10.6	205.4	193.6	22.2	17.8	10.8	9.2
Florida	56,612.7	50,322.3	8,794.7	6,215.1	15.5	12.4	498.2	479.7	77.7	52.5	15.6	10.9
Georgia	75,709.2	67,848.2	7,718.4	5,864.0	10.2	8.6	567.5	543.3	53.9	42.5	9.5	7.8
Kentucky	41,827.1	37,348.9	5,998.6	4,147.3	14.3	11.1	251.5	237.9	30.5	24.4	12.1	10.3
Louisiana	50,699.7	43,861.1	7,707.3	5,977.3	15.2	13.6	160.4	158.5	19.2	16.7	12.0	10.5
Mississippi	24,380.6	21,719.1	3,273.6	2,459.4	13.4	11.3	219.7	204.7	20.3	16.7	9.2	8.2
North Carolina	95,317.3	84,934.9	12,266.1	9,713.7	12.9	11.4	841.5	802.9	86.9	75.5	10.3	9.4
South Carolina	41,211.7	36,119.2	6,591.7	4,944.9	16.0	13.7	366.2	352.5	48.1	39.1	13.1	11.1
Virginia	51,902.1	47,346.0	6,794.0	5,083.4	13.1	10.7	426.3	406.5	46.4	38.4	10.9	9.4
West Virginia	11,560.8	10,736.2	2,550.9	2,106.7	22.1	19.6	83.8	85.9	13.8	12.4	16.5	14.4
UNITED STATES	2,475,900.9	2,260,314.6	378,796.8	294,339.5	15.3	13.0	18,900.1	18,371.2	2,770.6	2,318.2	14.7	12.6

Source: U.S. Department of Commerce, Bureau of the Census, *Manufacturing Analytical Report Series, Exports from Manufacturing Establishments: 1987*.

According to information compiled by the U.S. Bureau of the Census from data published by the U.S. Bureau of Mines and the U.S. Energy Information Administration, coal is the principal mineral produced in Tennessee, followed by stone and zinc. Also noteworthy is the fact that Tennessee leads the nation in the quantities of zinc and pyrites produced. These and other mineral statistics are available from three principal sources: the U.S. Department of Commerce, Bureau of the Census *Census of Mineral Industries*, published every five years; the U.S. Department of the Interior, Bureau of Mines, *Minerals Yearbook*, issued annually, and numerous publications of the U.S. Department of Energy, Energy Information Administration, also issued annually.

The *Geographic Area Report* from the 1987 *Census of Mineral Industries* provides information on the number of mineral establishments for each Tennessee county. These data are presented in Table 5.3. Tables featuring state and county data on the value of nonfuel mineral production are from the *Minerals Yearbook, Volume II*, and are currently available for 1988.

Data on fuel minerals are excluded from the *Minerals Yearbook* beginning in 1978. Since the establishment of the U.S. Department of Energy, Energy Information Administration (EIA) in 1977, data on the mining of fuel minerals have been detailed in EIA publications, *Coal Production, Petroleum Supply Annual*, and the *Natural Gas Annual*. An alternative source for gas data is *Gas Facts*, an annual yearbook published by the American Gas Association. Each of these publications provides data on the utilization of fuels as well as their production. However, utilization data have been reserved for Chapter 10 in order to present a complete picture of energy consumption. Therefore, the reader should turn to the Energy chapter for more information on fuel minerals.

Part of the difficulty in providing minerals data is the nature of the industry itself. Much of the production is characterized by small, independent companies, with frequent entry and exit of firms or turnover in management. The data, when they can be obtained, are not always consistent or accurate. In many cases, data for local areas must be suppressed to avoid disclosing data for any individual firm.

TABLE OF CONTENTS

FIGURE 5.1

Principal Mineral-Producing Counties in Tennessee

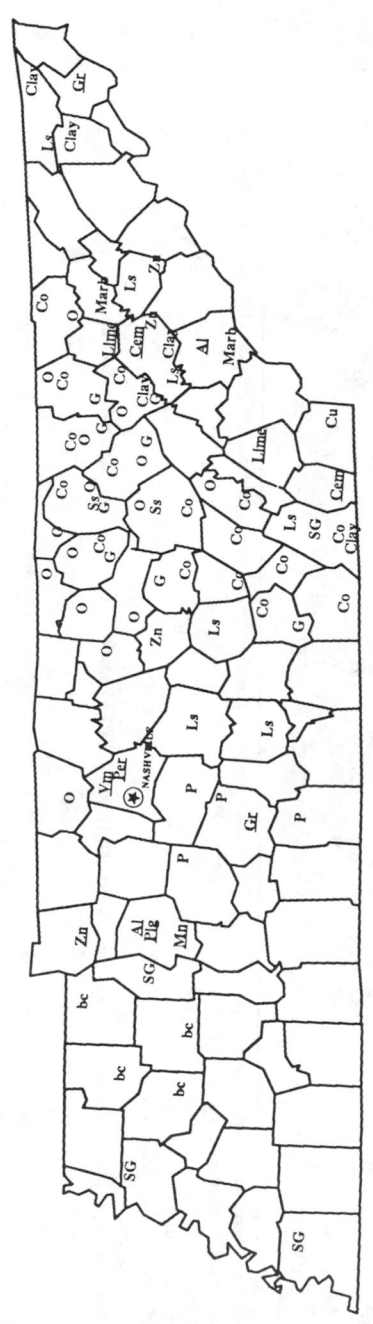

Non-fuel Minerals

Al	Aluminum plant	**Gr**	Graphite products
bc	Ball clay	**Lime**	Lime plant
Cem	Cement plant	**Ls**	Limestone
Clay	Clay	**Marb**	Marble-dimension
Cu	Copper	**Mn**	Manganese plant

P	Phosphate rock	**Ss**	Sandstone
Per	Perlite plant	**Vm**	Vermiculite plant
Pig	Titanium dioxide pigments	**Zn**	Zinc
SG	Sand and gravel	**Zn**	Zinc smelter

Fuel Minerals

Co	Coal	**G**	Natural Gas
		O	Crude Oil

Note: Underscoring represents a manufacturing operation.

Source: U.S. Department of Interior, Bureau of Mines, *Minerals Yearbook, 1985;* and Tennessee Department of Economic and Community Development, Energy Division, *Tennessee Energy Statistics Quarterly,* Fourth Quarter 1985.

TABLE 5.1.– PRODUCTION AND VALUE OF PRODUCTION OF SELECTED NON-FUEL MINERALS, TENNESSEE, 1950-1988, SELECTED YEARS

Mineral and units of measure	1988	1987	1986	1985	1980	1975	1970	1965	1960	1955	1950
Production											
Clays (1,000 short tons)[1]	1,285	1,261	1,164	1,244	1,188	1,310	1,401	1,495	1,270	1,208	787
Phosphate rock (1,000 metric tons)	(D)	(D)	1,231	1,233	1,582	2,291	3,073[a]	2,637	1,939	1,466	1,384
Sand and gravel (1,000 short tons)	6,836	7,900[e]	7,848	7,769[e]	8,921	10,909	6,715	8,193	6,293	5,137	4,153
Stone (1,000 short tons)	52,204[e]	51,409	40,706[e]	37,945	38,594	38,439	35,374	28,888	20,074	14,381[b]	7,979
Zinc, recoverable content of ores (metric tons)	119,954	115,699	102,118	104,471	111,754	83,293	118,260	122,387	91,394	40,216	35,326
Value ($1,000)											
Clays[1]	27,696	25,480	25,228	25,913	22,844	9,008	7,123	6,103	4,537	4,170	3,094
Phosphate rock	(D)	(D)	21,191	27,000	12,765	28,803	15,005	22,296	15,424	10,526	10,028
Sand and gravel	23,343	28,900	30,115	28,156[e]	24,930	22,102	10,639	10,690	7,655	5,814	4,411
Stone	235,567	227,836	177,153[e]	157,616	127,876	81,187	50,013	38,859	29,942	22,276	13,802
Zinc	159,201	106,926	85,550	92,971	92,218	64,968	36,233	35,737	23,580	9,893	10,033

Note: Production is as measured by mine shipments, sales, or marketable production (including consumption by producers). Beginning in 1985, stone excludes granite.
(D) Withheld to avoid disclosing operations of individual companies.
e estimated.
1. Excludes fuller's earth.
a. Measurement in thousand short tons.
b. Excludes granite.
Source: U.S. Department of the Interior, Bureau of Mines, *Minerals Yearbook, 1988, Volume II, Area Reports: Domestic,* and earlier editions.

TABLE 5.2-- COAL PRODUCTION AND NUMBER OF COAL MINES, BY TYPE OF MINING, AND AVERAGE MINE PRICE, TENNESSEE, 1960-1991, SELECTED YEARS [Production in thousands of short tons]

Year	Total			Underground		Surface	
	Number	Produc-tion	Average mine price ($ per short ton)	Number	Produc-tion	Number	Produc-tion
1991	51	4,203	26.74	37	3,006	14	1,197
1990	66	6,103	27.96	45	4,453	21	1,650
1988	77	6,409	26.78	54	4,613	23	1,796
1987	72	6,351	27.65	47	4,813	25	1,538
1986	75	6,749	28.00	49	5,232	26	1,516
1985	90	7,339	28.54	54	5,147	36	2,192
1984	90	7,211	28.99	55	5,196	35	2,014
1983	95	6,565	29.02	48	4,358	47	2,208
1982	105	7,287	29.49	51	4,518	54	2,769
1981	115	9,706	29.45	46	5,058	69	4,648
1980	117	9,157	27.54	54	4,682	63	4,474
1979	122	9,303	26.94	54	4,760	68	4,543
1978	231	10,032	23.21	85	4,150	146	5,882
1977	183	9,433	21.86	64	3,858	121	5,575
1976	185	9,283	16.31	75	4,428	110	4,855
1975	166	8,206	17.10	62	3,806	104	4,400
1974	125	7,541	18.02	50	3,106	75	4,435
1973	119	8,220	8.13	46	3,636	73	4,584
1972	211	11,260	7.23	108	5,866	103	5,394
1971	186	9,271	6.40	78	3,543	108	5,728
1970	203	8,236	4.90	116	4,350	87	3,886
1969	185	8,082	3.80	112	4,473	73	3,609
1968	182	8,148	3.64	114	4,624	68	3,524
1967	193	6,833	3.95	126	3,954	67	2,879
1966	203	6,308	3.77	144	3,730	59	2,578
1965	230	5,865	3.57	180	3,581	50	2,284
1964	253	5,990	3.79	199	3,664	54	2,326
1963	266	6,121	3.71	200	3,379	66	2,742
1962	353	6,214	3.63	289	3,721	64	2,493
1961	391	5,860	3.53	314	3,835	77	2,024
1960	415	5,931	3.57	332	3,939	83	1,992

Note: Data exclude mines producing less than 10,000 short tons of coal during the year.

Source: U.S. Department of Energy, Energy Information Administration, Office of Coal, Nuclear, Electric and Alternate Fuels, *Coal Production, 1991*, and earlier editions; and The Tennessee Energy Authority, *Tennessee Energy Profiles, 1960-1980*.

5.

MINING

TABLE 5.3-- NUMBER OF MINERAL ESTABLISHMENTS, BY MAJOR ACTIVITY, SELECTED
COUNTIES, 1987

County	All mineral industries	Metal mining	Coal mining	Nonmetallic minerals mining
Anderson	15	0	13	2
Bedford	1	0	0	1
Benton	4	0	0	4
Blount	3	0	0	3
Bradley	1	0	0	1
Campbell	17	0	15	2
Carter	1	0	0	1
Cheatham	1	0	0	1
Claiborne	9	0	9	0
Clay	1	0	0	1
Coffee	2	0	0	2
Cumberland	7	0	0	7
Davidson	16	1	2	13
Decatur	4	0	0	4
Dickson	2	0	0	2
Fayette	1	0	0	1
Fentress	4	0	2	2
Franklin	2	0	0	2
Gibson	1	0	0	1
Greene	2	0	0	2
Grundy	6	0	6	0
Hamblen	1	0	0	1
Hamilton	10	0	1	9
Hancock	1	0	0	1
Hardin	2	0	0	2
Hawkins	2	0	0	2
Henry	3	0	0	3
Hickman	1	0	0	1
Humphreys	1	0	0	1
Jefferson	7	5	0	2
Knox	22	1	5	16
Lincoln	2	0	1	1
Loudon	1	0	0	1
McMinn	1	0	0	1
Madison	1	0	0	1
Marion	6	0	4	2
Marshall	1	0	1	0
Maury	7	0	0	7
Meigs	1	0	0	1
Monroe	2	0	0	2
Montgomery	1	0	0	1
Moore	1	0	0	1
Morgan	8	0	8	0
Overton	1	0	0	1
Polk	2	1	0	1
Putnam	2	0	0	2
Rhea	5	0	3	2
Roane	2	0	0	2
Robertson	2	0	0	2
Rutherford	3	0	0	3
Scott	16	0	16	0
Sequatchie	15	0	14	1

TABLE 5.3-- NUMBER OF MINERAL ESTABLISHMENTS, BY MAJOR ACTIVITY, SELECTED
COUNTIES, 1987 (Continued)

County	All mineral industries	Metal mining	Coal mining	Nonmetallic minerals mining
Sevier	1	0	0	1
Shelby	6	0	0	6
Smith	1	1	0	0
Sullivan	6	0	3	3
Sumner	1	0	0	1
Tipton	2	0	0	2
Unicoi	1	0	0	1
Union	1	0	0	1
Van Buren	1	0	1	0
Warren	2	0	0	2
Washington	3	0	2	1
Weakley	2	0	0	2
White	1	0	0	1
Williamson	3	0	2	1
Wilson	1	0	0	1

Source: U.S. Department of Commerce, Bureau of the Census, *1987 Census of Mineral Industries, Geographic Area Series, East South Central States.*

TABLE 5.4-- COAL PRODUCTION AND NUMBER OF COAL MINES, BY TYPE OF MINING, AND
AVERAGE MINE PRICE, TENNESSEE AND SELECTED COUNTIES, 1991
(Production in thousands of short tons)

County	Total			Underground		Surface	
	Number	Produc-tion	Avg. mine price ($ per short ton)	Number	Produc-tion	Number	Produc-tion
Anderson	8	737	22.33	7	725	1	12
Bledsoe	1	115	(D)	0	0	1	115
Campbell	11	1,271	22.74	7	1,050	4	221
Claiborne	3	192	(D)	1	37	2	155
Fentress	1	22	(D)	0	0	1	22
Grundy	1	29	(D)	0	0	1	29
Marion	3	158	(D)	3	158	0	0
Morgan	1	106	(D)	1	106	0	0
Rhea	1	33	(D)	1	33	0	0
Scott	5	388	28.73	4	368	1	20
Sequatchie	16	1,152	27.62	13	530	3	622
TENNESSEE	51	4,203	26.74	37	3,006	14	1,197

Note: Excludes silt, culm, refuse bank, slurry dam and dredge production. Excludes mines producing less than
10,000 short tons of coal during the year.

(D) Withheld to avoid disclosing operations of individual companies.

Source: U. S. Department of Energy, Energy Information Administration, Office of Coal, Nuclear, Electric and
Alternate Fuels, *Coal Production, 1991.*

TABLE 5.5-- PRINCIPAL NON-FUEL MINERALS AND VALUE OF NON-FUEL MINERAL PRODUCTION, SOUTHEASTERN STATES, 1988

State	Value ($1,000)	Rank in U.S.	Percent of U.S. production	Principal minerals in order of value
TENNESSEE	585,649	17	1.95	Stone, zinc, cement, clays
Alabama	459,495	21	1.53	Cement, stone, lime, sand and gravel
Arkansas	306,789	29	1.02	Bromine, stone, cement, sand and gravel
Florida	1,391,881	6	4.64	Phosphate rock, stone, cement, sand and gravel
Georgia	1,373,825	7	4.58	Clays, stone, cement, sand and gravel
Kentucky	344,979	28	1.15	Lime, cement, sand and gravel, clays
Louisiana	434,536	23	1.45	Sulfur, salt, sand and gravel, stone
Mississippi	103,400	42	0.34	Sand and gravel, clays, cement, stone
North Carolina	529,434	19	1.76	Stone, phosphate rock, lithium minerals, sand and gravel
South Carolina	357,802	27	1.19	Cement, stone, clays, gold
Virginia	494,512	20	1.65	Stone, sand and gravel, cement, lime
West Virginia	127,455	39	0.42	Stone, cement, salt, sand and gravel (industrial), sand and gravel (construction)

Note: Unless otherwise noted, stone is crushed stone; sand and gravel is for construction; cement is portland; and sulfur is Frasch.

Source: U.S. Department of the Interior, Bureau of Mines, *Minerals Yearbook, 1988, Volume II, Area Reports: Domestic.*

TABLE 5.6-- VALUE OF PRODUCTION OF MINERALS,[1] SOUTHEASTERN STATES, 1930-1988, SELECTED YEARS [In thousands of dollars]

State	1988	1987	1986	1985	1980	1970	1960	1950	1940	1930
TENNESSEE	585,649	527,812	481,656	472,287	407,837	220,465	145,538	90,405	42,683	32,499
Alabama	459,495	446,643	405,216	405,915	328,633	323,245	221,802	158,975	64,998	55,462
Arkansas	306,789	264,162	263,007	256,697	286,631	225,625	159,519	119,642	37,479	34,901
Florida	1,391,881	1,346,237	1,295,153	1,559,266	1,508,754	300,042	180,286	70,717	14,854	15,484
Georgia	1,373,825	1,212,370	1,091,455	946,075	770,688	203,225	92,305	43,394	16,932	12,831
Kentucky	344,979	290,335	267,265	267,558	204,300	847,465	414,553	459,956	131,974	111,691
Louisiana	434,536	424,221	446,798	522,268	583,766	5,102,321	1,990,895	693,607	189,153	71,929
Mississippi	103,400	110,079	101,095	102,793	103,940	249,973	199,210	102,945	7,240	1,775
North Carolina	529,434	476,917	466,423	432,756	379,366	98,365	45,096	26,338	21,113	7,462
South Carolina	357,802	341,325	295,889	275,929	194,779	56,365	30,987	11,394	5,306	3,341
Virginia	494,512	461,442	393,037	381,276	305,306	374,321	208,880	137,806	50,004	34,603
West Virginia	127,455	144,021	129,809	105,409	106,286	1,285,364	722,628	829,633	329,892	290,119
TENNESSEE as percent of U.S.	1.95	2.00	2.05	2.03	1.62	0.74	0.81	0.76	0.76	0.67
SOUTHEAST as percent of U.S.	21.68	22.95	24.04	24.66	20.63	31.17	24.47	23.14	16.25	14.10

Note: Percentages computed by the Center for Business and Economic Research.

1. Beginning in 1978 fuel minerals are excluded from this data source.

Source: U.S. Department of the Interior, Bureau of Mines, *Minerals Yearbook, 1988, Volume II, Area Reports: Domestic,* and earlier editions; and *Mineral Resources of the United States, 1931, Part 1 - Metals, Summary.*

TABLE 5.7.– AVERAGE DAILY PRODUCTION, DAILY PRODUCTIVE CAPACITY, AND PERCENT UTILIZATION OF COAL MINES, BY TYPE OF MINING, SELECTED SOUTHEASTERN STATES AND UNITED STATES, 1986 [In thousands of short tons]

State	Total			Underground			Surface		
	Average daily production[1]	Daily productive capacity at end of year[2]	Percent utilization[3]	Average daily production[1]	Daily productive capacity at end of year[2]	Percent utilization[3]	Average daily production[1]	Daily productive capacity at end of year[2]	Percent utilization[3]
TENNESSEE	29	31	96.18	22	23	96.59	7	8	94.99
Alabama	107	112	95.32	57	61	93.49	49	50	97.55
Arkansas	1	(D)	(D)	0	0	0.00	1	(D)	(D)
Kentucky	718	761	94.40	413	445	92.72	305	316	96.76
Louisiana	7	(D)	(D)	0	0	0.00	7	(D)	(D)
Virginia	202	206	98.22	168	171	98.10	34	35	98.85
West Virginia	623	664	93.75	493	528	93.36	130	136	95.24
UNITED STATES	3,768	4,040	93.27	1,675	1,810	92.55	2,093	2,230	93.84

Note: Includes only those states producing significant amounts of coal; excludes silt, culm, refuse bank, slurry dam, and dredge production, and excludes mines producing less than 10,000 short tons of coal during the year.

(D) Withheld to avoid disclosing operations of individual companies.

1. Computed at the mine level by dividing the mine production by the total number of days worked at the mine during the year.

2. Maximum amount of coal that can be produced on a daily basis as reported by mining companies on government forms.

3. Computed by dividing average daily production by daily productive capacity and multiplying by 100.

Source: U.S. Department of Energy, Energy Information Administration, Office of Coal, Nuclear, Electric and Alternate Fuels, *Coal Production, 1986.*

TABLE 5.8-- RECOVERABLE COAL RESERVES AT COAL MINES, BY TYPE OF MINING, SELECTED
SOUTHEASTERN STATES AND UNITED STATES, 1991 [In millions of short tons]

	Total		Underground		Surface	
State	Recoverable coal reserves [1]	Average recovery percent [2]	Recoverable coal reserves [1]	Average recovery percent [2]	Recoverable coal reserves [1]	Average recovery percent [2]
TENNESSEE	55.7	70.88	(D)	(D)	(D)	(D)
Alabama	470.1	80.76	364.6	56.00	105.8	85.82
Arkansas	(D)	(D)	0.0	0.00	(D)	(D)
Kentucky	1,632.1	67.35	1,159.2	61.34	472.9	79.68
Louisiana	(D)	(D)	0.0	0.00	(D)	(D)
Virginia	411.8	66.12	383.2	62.39	28.6	80.07
West Virginia	2,122.1	65.10	1,742.5	59.30	379.6	78.93
UNITED STATES	21,998.5	70.14	7,105.4	60.13	14,893.1	80.71

Note: Includes only those states producing significant amounts of coal; excludes silt, culm, refuse bank, slurry
dam, and dredge production, and excludes mines producing less than 10,000 short tons of coal during the year.

(D) Withheld to avoid disclosing operations of individual companies.

1. Represents the quantity of coal that can be recovered from existing coal reserves at reporting mines.

2. Represents the percent of coal that can be recovered from coal reserves at reporting mines, averaged for all mines
in the reported geographic area.

Source: U.S. Department of Energy, Energy Information Administration, Office of Coal, Nuclear, Electric and
Alternate Fuels, *Coal Production, 1991*.

TABLE 5.9-- COAL PRODUCTION AND NUMBER OF COAL MINES, BY TYPE OF MINING, SELECTED
SOUTHEASTERN STATES AND UNITED STATES, 1991 [In thousands of short tons]

State	Total		Underground		Surface	
	Number	Production	Number	Production	Number	Production
TENNESSEE	51	4,203	37	3,006	14	1,197
Alabama	74	27,167	10	17,062	64	10,104
Arkansas	2	34	0	0	2	34
Kentucky	681	158,330	457	97,019	224	61,310
Louisiana	2	3,151	0	0	2	3,151
Virginia	266	41,811	202	34,034	64	7,777
West Virginia	566	166,935	394	119,667	172	47,277
UNITED STATES	2,394	993,486	1,255	406,344	1,139	587,143

Note: Includes only those states producing significant amounts of coal; excludes silt, culm, refuse bank, slurry
dam, and dredge production and excludes mines producing less than 10,000 short tons of coal during the year.

Source: U.S. Department of Energy, Energy Information Administration, Office of Coal, Nuclear, Electric and
Alternate Fuels, *Coal Production, 1991*.

TABLE 5.10--COAL STOCKS AT COAL MINES, SELECTED SOUTHEASTERN STATES AND UNITED
STATES, 1988 [In thousands of short tons]

State	Coal stocks at end of 1988	Coal stocks at end of 1987	Net change in coal stocks during year	Percent change in coal stocks during year
TENNESSEE	99	84	15	17.64
Alabama	2,794	2,388	406	17.01
Arkansas	2	2	0	0.00
Kentucky	4,321	4,010	311	7.76
Louisiana	0	0	0	0.00
Virginia	2,694	2,211	483	21.85
West Virginia	3,926	3,437	489	14.22
UNITED STATES	30,719	26,917	3,801	14.12

Note: Includes only those states producing significant amounts of coal; excludes silt, culm, refuse bank, slurry
dam, and dredge production and excludes mines producing less than 10,000 short tons of coal during the year.
Total may not equal sum of components due to independent rounding.

Source: U.S. Department of Energy, Energy Information Administration, Office of Coal, Nuclear, Electric and
Alternate Fuels, *Coal Production, 1988*.

TABLE 5.11–COAL MINING PRODUCTIVITY, BY TYPE OF MINING, SELECTED SOUTHEASTERN STATES AND UNITED STATES, 1991

State	Total			Underground			Surface		
	Average number of miners working daily [1]	Average number of days worked during year	Average production per miner per hour [2] (short tons)	Average number of miners working daily [1]	Average number of days worked during year	Average production per miner per hour [2] (short tons)	Average number of miners working daily [1]	Average number of days worked during year	Average production per miner per hour [2] (short tons)
TENNESSEE	1,242	218	1.88	988	215	1.72	254	223	2.45
Alabama	6,314	215	2.17	4,473	235	1.90	1,841	211	2.84
Arkansas	14	165	2.27	0	0	0.00	14	165	2.27
Kentucky	26,642	221	3.01	18,481	222	2.71	8,161	220	3.66
Louisiana	103	261	12.56	0	0	0.00	103	261	12.56
Virginia	10,055	215	2.23	8,515	218	2.12	1,540	209	2.95
West Virginia	28,310	220	3.11	22,512	219	2.83	5,798	222	4.18
UNITED STATES	120,602	224	4.09	78,050	222	2.69	42,552	228	6.38

Note: See Table 5.9 for total production, by type of mining, for the Southeastern states and United States.

1. Includes all employees engaged in production, preparation, processing, development, maintenance, repair, shop or yard work at mining operations. Excludes office workers. Includes mining operations management and all technical and engineering personnel.

2. Calculated by dividing total coal production by the total direct labor hours worked by all mine employees identified in footnote 1.

Source: U.S. Department of Energy, Energy Information Administration, Office of Coal, Nuclear, Electric and Alternate Fuels, *Coal Production, 1991*.

TABLE 5.12--COAL PRODUCTION AND AVERAGE MINE PRICE, BY DISPOSITION, SELECTED
SOUTHEASTERN STATES AND UNITED STATES, 1991

State	Total[1]		Open market[2]		Captive[3]	
	Production (1,000 short tons)	Average mine price ($ per short ton)	Production (1,000 short tons)	Average mine price ($ per short ton)	Production (1,000 short tons)	Average mine price ($ per short ton)
TENNESSEE	4,203	26.74	4,055	(D)	148	(D)
Alabama	27,167	41.14	26,455	41.11	712	42.06
Arkansas	34	(D)	34	(D)	0	0.00
Kentucky	158,330	25.45	156,666	(D)	1,664	(D)
Louisiana	3,151	(D)	410	(D)	2,741	(D)
Virginia	41,811	27.45	41,800	(D)	11	(D)
West Virginia	166,935	28.62	158,837	28.21	8,097	36.72
UNITED STATES	993,486	21.49	905,263	21.57	88,223	20.66

Note: Includes only those states producing significant amounts of coal; excludes silt, culm, refuse bank, slurry
dam, and dredge production, and excludes mines producing less than 10,000 short tons of coal during the year.
Average mine price is calculated by dividing the total f.o.b. mine value of the coal produced by the total
production.

(D) Withheld to avoid disclosing operations of individual companies.

1. Total may not equal sum of components due to independent rounding.

2. Open market includes all coal sold on the open market to other coal companies or consumers.

3. Captive includes all coal used by the producing company or sold to affiliated or parent companies.

Source: U.S. Department of Energy, Energy Information Administration, Office of Coal, Nuclear, Electric and
Alternate Fuels, *Coal Production, 1991*.

TABLE 5.13--PRODUCTION OF CRUDE OIL (INCLUDING LEASE CONDENSATE), SELECTED
SOUTHEASTERN STATES AND UNITED STATES, 1992 [In thousands of barrels]

State	Production	Daily average
TENNESSEE	501	1
Alabama	19,025	52
Arkansas	10,260	28
Florida	5,425	15
Kentucky	5,478	15
Louisiana[1]	143,075	391
Mississippi	25,182	69
Virginia	9	(a)
West Virginia	2,068	6
UNITED STATES	2,624,632	7,171

Note: Includes only those states which produce over 10,000 barrels per month.

1. Includes offshore production of 23,490 thousand barrels.

a. Less than 500 barrels.

Source: U.S. Department of Energy, Energy Information Administration, Office of Oil and Gas, *Petroleum Supply
Annual, 1992, Volume 1*.

TABLE 5.14--NUMBER OF PRODUCING GAS WELLS AND MARKETED PRODUCTION OF NATURAL
GAS, SOUTHEASTERN STATES AND UNITED STATES, 1970-1990,
SELECTED YEARS

State	Number of producing gas wells[1]							
	1990	1989	1988	1987	1986	1985	1980	1970
TENNESSEE	690	700	802	840	921	988	177	15
Alabama	2,362	1,701	1,264	1,135	1,029	863	314	2
Arkansas	2,952	2,830	2,996	2,847	2,719	2,623	1,114	1,008
Florida	0	0	0	0	0	0	0	0
Kentucky	11,713	11,248	10,777	10,366	9,747	9,285	7,984	6,913
Louisiana	16,889	16,309	14,071	15,890	15,313	16,716	16,190	9,690
Mississippi	585	543	634	775	414	710	447	325
Virginia	819	752	728	689	573	495	258	115
West Virginia	37,500	36,240	35,800	34,300	33,400	32,475	25,900	20,702
UNITED STATES	269,790	262,483	257,279	249,225	241,527	243,344	182,004	117,483

	Marketed production[2] (1,000,000 cubit feet)							
	1990	1989	1988	1987	1986	1985	1980	1970
TENNESSEE	2,067	1,900	2,100	2,707	3,464	4,686	1,241	64
Alabama	135,276	128,411	129,524	117,241	107,184	107,342	65,294	627
Arkansas	174,956	168,300	166,573	141,151	131,075	155,099	111,808	181,351
Florida	6,483	7,534	7,484	8,281	8,833	10,545	40,638	0
Kentucky	75,333	72,417	73,629	70,125	80,195	73,126	57,180	77,892
Louisiana	5,241,989	5,078,125	5,180,267	5,122,509	4,895,394	5,013,702	6,939,924	7,788,276
Mississippi	94,616	102,645	124,053	139,727	140,833	144,172	175,061	126,031
Virginia	14,774	17,935	18,424	19,223	15,427	15,041	7,812	2,805
West Virginia	178,000	198,200	182,000	160,000	135,431	144,883	156,551	242,452
UNITED STATES	18,561,596	18,095,147[r]	17,918,465[r]	17,432,901[r]	16,858,675[r]	17,197,999	20,179,724	21,920,642

r revised.

1. Data pertain only to dry gas and condensate wells. Data are as of December 31.

2. Marketed Production equals gross withdrawals less gas used for repressuring, quantities vented and flared, and
nonhydrocarbon gases removed in treating or processing operations.

Source: Energy Information Administration, *Natural Gas Annual, 1990,* and earlier editions.

TABLE 5.15--GROSS WITHDRAWALS OF NATURAL GAS, BY TYPE OF WELL, SOUTHEASTERN
STATES, 1980–1990, SELECTED YEARS [In millions of cubic feet]

State	1990 Total	Gas wells	Oil wells	1989 Total	Gas wells	Oil wells
TENNESSEE	2,067	1	2,067	1,900	(a)	1,900
Alabama[1]	186,542	181,324	5,219	180,300	174,345	5,955
Arkansas	195,404	161,148	34,256	168,300	168,300	0
Florida	7,566	0	7,566	8,773	0	8,773
Kentucky	75,333	75,333	(a)	72,417	72,417	(a)
Louisiana	5,303,485[b]	4,726,927	576,558	5,142,971[b]	4,556,530	586,441
Mississippi	200,592	180,609	19,983	199,856	184,000	15,856
Virginia	14,774	14,774	0	17,935	17,935	0
West Virginia	178,000	178,000	(a)	198,200	198,200	(a)

State	1988 Total	Gas wells	Oil wells	1980 Total	Gas wells	Oil wells
TENNESSEE	2,100	0	2,100	1,241	478	763
Alabama	175,054	168,484	6,570	111,836	105,447	6,389
Arkansas	190,678	146,898	43,780	127,696	87,994	39,702
Florida	8,407	0	8,407	46,421	0	46,421
Kentucky	73,629	73,629	0	57,180	57,180	(a)
Louisiana	5,248,205	4,607,205	641,000	7,008,489	6,417,127	591,362
Mississippi	237,180	222,539	14,640	215,105	202,711	12,394
Virginia	18,682	18,682	0	7,812	7,812	0
West Virginia	182,000	182,000	0	156,551	156,551	(a)

a. Breakdown not provided by state agency.
b. Excludes most quantities of nonhydrocarbon gases removed on leases.
1. Gas well withdrawals for 1989 and 1990 include production from coal seam methane drainage projects.
Source: Energy Information Administration, *Natural Gas Annual, 1990*, and earlier editions.

The only complete assessment of the United States' housing stock occurs in each decennial census. Characteristics of the physical structure, including plumbing and heating, are reported along with market value or rent paid, number of persons per unit, housing ownership, and the use of mobile homes as well as single- and multi-family units.

Between decennial census years, the Bureau of the Census monitors additions to the national housing stock in 17,000 permit-issuing counties and places. The sample size for this survey has been increased twice in the last ten years–from 14,000 to 16,000 in 1978 and then from 16,000 to 17,000 in 1984. These permits for housing stock additions are published in the Bureau's monthly *Construction Reports, Housing Authorized by Building Permits and Public Contracts*. Permit data are collected for approximately 25 types of residential and nonresidential structures. While the volume of such information precludes regular publication, monthly reports for specified regions are available upon request from Construction Statistics Division at the Bureau. *Construction Reports* are also published in *Housing Starts* (including new mobile homes put in place), *Characteristics of New Housing* and *One-Family Houses Sold and for Sale*. Information on the number of households and population per household is reported for Tennessee counties in Table 1.14. While these data describe the population, they also influence the housing stock.

Within Tennessee, the Tennessee Housing Development Agency (THDA) publishes annually a *Report on the Need for Housing in Tennessee*. These survey data on public and private additions to the housing stock, and prices, rents, and vacancy rates are the most comprehensive annual data available at the county level. Information on the mean and median sales price of new and existing single family homes sold are also included in this report. Because the report has not been issued since 1990, data included in this edition of the *Abstract* were provided by THDA.

Nonresidential construction information at the local level is not widely available. F. W. Dodge, McGraw-Hill, Inc., provides estimates of construction contract valuations by states; however, such data are proprietary and are published here by special permission.

Additional information on the construction industry may be found in Chapters 2 and 3. Tables 2.1 and 2.2 provide information on the construction industry's contribution to gross state product, while other tables in this chapter include personal income from construction employment. For additional information on employment and earnings, the reader should turn to Chapter 3.

TABLE OF CONTENTS

TABLE 6.1-- ESTIMATED CONSTRUCTION CONTRACT VALUATIONS, BY TYPE OF CONSTRUCTION, TENNESSEE, 1967–1992 [In thousands of dollars]

Year	Total	Nonbuilding[1]	Residential	Nonresidential
1992	5,273,000	936,000	2,717,000	1,620,000
1991[a]	4,358,000	929,000	2,055,000	1,293,000
1990	4,388,000	(b)	(b)	(b)
1989[a]	5,027,000	1,058,000	2,084,000	1,693,000
1988[a]	5,019,000	773,000	2,194,000	1,781,000
1987[a]	5,108,000	741,000	2,407,000	1,960,000
1986[a]	4,568,000	694,342	2,423,080	1,435,908
1985[a]	4,394,000	686,798	2,383,811	1,385,569
1984	4,238,431	671,176	2,160,211	1,407,044
1983	3,531,869	589,679	1,816,036	1,126,154
1982	2,541,742	520,738	1,127,555	893,449
1981	2,520,206	554,618	945,782	1,019,806
1980[a]	2,789,000	559,319	1,190,349	1,041,142
1979	4,880,482	2,425,089	1,362,367	1,093,026
1978	3,084,033	649,570	1,601,226	833,237
1977	6,219,038	4,193,985	1,291,950	733,103
1976	1,781,294	281,369	849,854	650,071
1975	1,673,873	433,454	654,531	585,888
1974	2,026,559	530,128	738,059	758,372
1973	2,219,007	333,973	1,166,880	718,154
1972	1,840,944	281,551	1,059,803	499,590
1971	1,530,737	244,116	763,896	522,725
1970	1,562,621	354,334	526,169	682,118
1969	1,480,916	520,033	494,148	466,735
1968	1,227,739	209,049	573,285	445,405
1967	1,043,884	171,761	522,278	349,845

1. Nonbuilding construction includes streets and highways, bridges, dams and reservoirs, water supply systems, etc.

a. Total has been revised; revisions for subcategories are not available.

b. Subcategory data not available for 1990.

Source: Data for 1989 and following years and revised data are from the *Statistical Abstract of the United States, 1993*; original source is F. W. Dodge, proprietary data reprinted by special permission. Reproduction or dissemination of this information is granted only by contract or prior written permission from F. W. Dodge, McGraw-Hill, Inc., 24 Hartwell Avenue, Lexington, MA 02173, (617) 863-5100.

TABLE 6.2-- PRIVATELY OWNED HOUSING UNITS AUTHORIZED BY BUILDING PERMITS,
TENNESSEE, 1969-1993

			Multifamily			
			Number of units in structure			
Year	Total[1]	Single-family	Total	2 units	3 and 4 units	5 or more units
1993	26,984	24,065	2,919	488	678	1,753
1992	23,319	21,214	2,105	342	633	1,130
1991	19,265	16,916	2,349	484	390	1,475
1990	20,194	16,373	3,821	472	332	3,017
1989	24,244	17,638	6,606	656	574	5,376
1988	27,803	19,397	8,406	666	632	7,108
1987	29,919	21,686	8,233	874	942	6,417
1986	34,356	21,607	12,749	1,708	777	10,264
1985	38,126	17,310	20,816	2,366	887	17,563
1984	36,764	13,769	22,995	3,962	1,508	17,525
1983	26,553	13,548	13,005	3,072	995	8,938
1982	14,799	7,328	7,471	1,330	838	5,303
1981	11,675	7,531	4,144	950	407	2,787
1980	19,389	12,334	7,055	1,204	577	5,274
1979	23,340	15,484	7,856	1,128	511	6,217
1978	28,611	18,947	9,664	1,274	906	7,484
1977	26,262	16,914	9,348	850	626	7,872
1976	18,906	14,436	4,470	550	293	3,627
1975	14,025	10,711	3,314	722	390	2,202
1974	17,911	10,908	7,003	740	416	5,847
1973	38,834	14,829	24,005	1,304	363	22,338
1972	45,488	17,506	27,982	1,828	611	25,543
1971	35,599	17,072	18,527	2,296	305	15,926
1970	22,499	14,157	8,342	1,148	459	6,735
1969	22,012	10,439	11,573	1,314	482	9,777

1. Excluding mobile homes.
Source: U.S. Department of Commerce, Bureau of the Census, *Current Construction Reports, Housing Authorized by Building Permits and Public Contracts, 1993*, and earlier editions.

FIGURE 6.1
Residential Building Permits in Tennessee, Private Units, 1983–1993

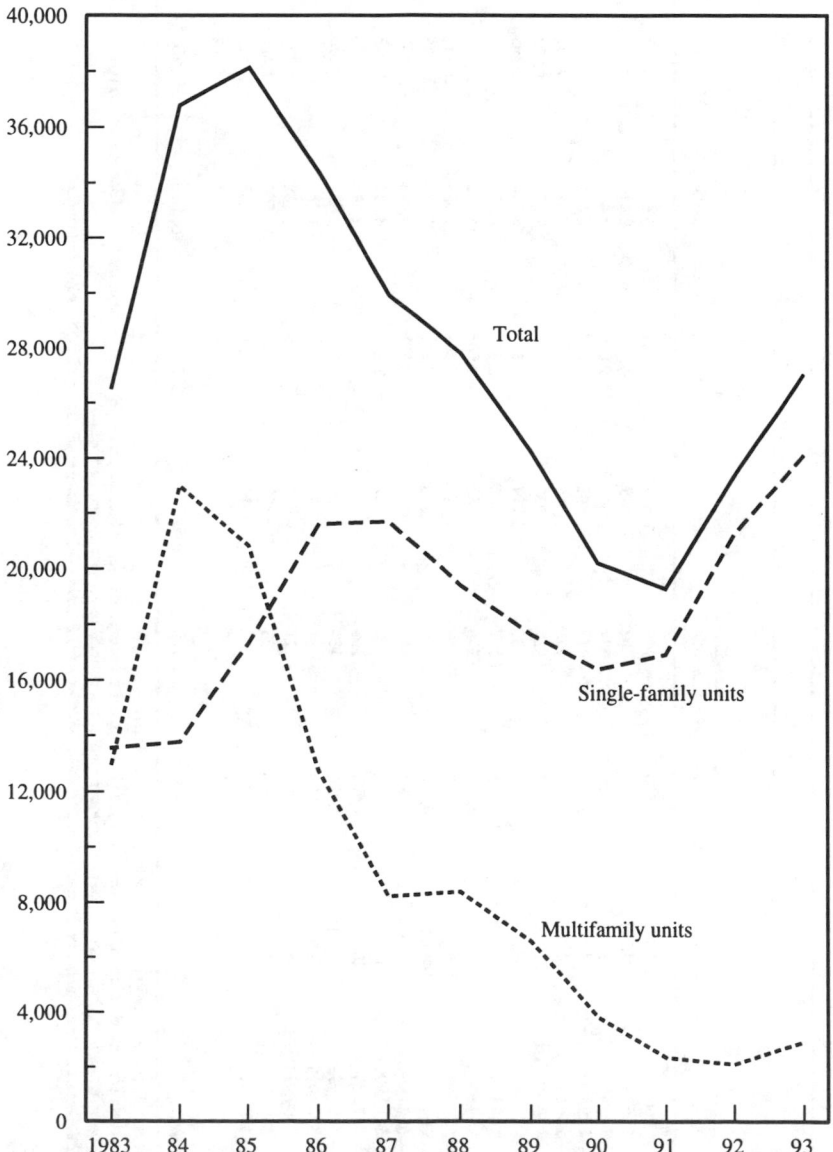

Source: U.S. Department of Commerce, Bureau of the Census, *Construction Reports: Housing Authorized by Building Permits and Public Contracts, 1991*, and earlier editions.

237

TABLE 6.3– NUMBER OF HOUSING UNITS, BY VALUE, TENNESSEE AND METROPOLITAN STATISTICAL AREAS,[1] 1990

Value[2]	TENNESSEE	Chattanooga	Clarksville-Hopkinsville	Jackson	Johnson City-Kingsport-Bristol	Knoxville	Memphis	Nashville
Less than $15,000	35,448	1,890	195	518	2,687	3,618	3,588	2,117
$15,000 – $19,999	24,531	1,402	202	619	1,959	2,676	2,814	1,447
$20,000 – $24,999	31,148	1,786	334	660	2,869	3,440	3,414	1,836
$25,000 – $29,999	38,951	2,678	483	805	3,817	4,684	4,369	2,345
$30,000 – $34,999	54,802	3,657	721	1,155	4,948	7,056	7,542	3,847
$35,000 – $39,999	61,686	4,267	938	1,225	6,066	7,635	9,390	5,390
$40,000 – $44,999	68,827	4,498	1,236	1,217	6,300	8,708	11,795	7,181
$45,000 – $49,999	63,835	4,715	1,507	1,316	5,618	8,576	12,150	8,419
$50,000 – $59,999	119,000	9,185	3,356	2,160	10,045	16,770	21,358	21,919
$60,000 – $74,999	156,706	11,509	3,962	2,937	12,161	22,657	28,451	38,081
$75,000 – $99,999	144,648	10,674	2,438	1,836	9,677	21,235	29,535	43,231
$100,000 – $124,999	55,704	3,882	553	695	3,251	7,393	13,451	17,578
$125,000 – $149,999	36,060	2,611	390	357	1,822	4,559	9,547	12,481
$150,000 – $174,999	20,628	1,670	198	193	1,113	2,543	5,066	7,793
$175,000 – $199,999	11,102	1,016	134	139	495	1,451	2,695	4,145
$200,000 – $249,999	11,511	816	61	123	558	1,489	2,907	4,667
$250,000 – $299,999	6,100	586	21	47	196	738	1,802	2,213
$300,000 – $399,999	4,524	307	23	63	135	564	1,412	1,797
$400,000 – $499,999	1,805	145	0	14	36	253	563	737
$500,000 or more	2,226	163	0	22	15	298	623	1,025
Median value[2]	$58,000	$59,600	$58,200	$52,500	$52,600	$60,000	$65,200	$75,900

1. Includes only Tennessee portions of Metropolitan Statistical Areas.
2. The value data are limited to "specified" owner-occupied housing units and exclude mobile homes, houses with a business or medical office, houses on 10 or more acres, and housing units in multi-unit buildings. One-family condominiums not in multi-unit structures are also included.

Source: U.S. Department of Commerce, Bureau of the Census, *1990 Census of Population and Housing, Summary Tape File 3A, Tennessee.*

TABLE 6.4-- NUMBER OF HOUSING UNITS, BY GROSS RENT, TENNESSEE AND METROPOLITAN STATISTICAL AREAS,[1] 1990

Gross rent[2]	TENNESSEE	Chattanooga	Clarksville-Hopkinsville	Jackson	Johnson City-Kingsport-Bristol	Knoxville	Memphis	Nashville
					Metropolitan Statistical Area			
Less than $100	22,970	1,707	228	596	1,437	2,464	4,425	5,127
$ 100 -- $ 149	34,595	2,332	415	733	2,231	4,470	5,997	5,668
$ 150 -- $ 199	29,197	1,704	415	605	2,249	3,568	5,454	3,617
$ 200 -- $ 249	43,445	2,565	776	791	4,111	5,798	7,827	4,290
$ 250 -- $ 299	58,113	4,151	1,238	1,080	5,244	9,088	10,352	6,564
$ 300 -- $ 349	66,408	5,453	2,077	1,218	5,314	9,487	13,255	11,776
$ 350 -- $ 399	68,056	5,971	2,016	1,404	3,619	9,076	15,688	17,345
$ 400 -- $ 449	62,484	5,601	1,780	1,122	2,715	7,509	15,231	20,213
$ 450 -- $ 499	47,800	3,966	1,260	747	1,568	5,114	13,368	17,184
$ 500 -- $ 549	33,560	2,457	759	476	1,176	3,352	10,001	12,666
$ 550 -- $ 599	21,555	1,363	446	221	748	2,278	6,472	8,293
$ 600 -- $ 649	13,367	863	332	155	348	1,281	4,287	5,195
$ 650 -- $ 699	8,647	538	170	91	203	953	2,666	3,513
$ 700 -- $ 749	5,546	366	58	53	140	467	1,804	2,302
$ 750 -- $ 999	10,012	598	137	95	171	1,072	3,230	4,262
$1,000 or more	3,860	320	7	30	68	323	1,204	1,781
No cash rent	39,260	2,250	934	549	3,277	5,715	4,148	5,127
Median rent, renter-occupied	$357	$367	$373	$337	$304	$341	$392	$426

1. Includes only Tennessee portions of Metropolitan Statistical Areas.
2. Gross rent is the contract rent plus the estimated average monthly cost of utilities and fuels for "specified" renter-occupied units paying cash rent. One-family houses on ten or more acres are excluded.

Source: U.S. Department of Commerce, Bureau of the Census, 1990 Census of Population and Housing, Summary Tape File 3A, Tennessee.

TABLE 6.5.– NUMBER OF HOUSING UNITS, BY TENURE AND VACANCY STATUS AND BY NUMBER OF PERSONS PER ROOM, AND MEAN NUMBER OF ROOMS PER HOUSING UNIT, COUNTIES, 1990

County	Total	Total occupied	Owner-occupied	Renter-occupied	Vacant	Occupied with 1.01 or more persons per room		Mean number of rooms per housing unit
						Number	Percent	
Anderson	29,323	27,384	19,401	7,983	1,939	568	2.07	5.5
Bedford	12,638	11,608	8,329	3,279	1,030	327	2.82	5.5
Benton	7,107	5,784	4,638	1,146	1,323	122	2.11	5.1
Bledsoe	3,771	3,261	2,568	693	510	105	3.22	5.3
Blount	36,532	33,624	25,072	8,552	2,908	483	1.44	5.6
Bradley	29,562	27,604	19,001	8,603	1,958	609	2.21	5.4
Campbell	14,817	13,150	9,709	3,441	1,667	442	3.36	5.2
Cannon	4,368	3,980	3,157	823	388	101	2.54	5.4
Carroll	11,783	10,727	8,477	2,250	1,056	251	2.34	5.5
Carter	21,779	20,189	15,410	4,779	1,590	379	1.88	5.3
Cheatham	10,297	9,515	7,910	1,605	782	293	3.08	5.5
Chester	4,944	4,558	3,529	1,029	386	113	2.48	5.4
Claiborne	10,711	9,629	7,542	2,087	1,082	273	2.84	5.3
Clay	3,340	2,855	2,324	531	485	71	2.49	5.1
Cocke	12,282	11,191	8,137	3,054	1,091	380	3.40	5.0
Coffee	16,786	15,500	10,862	4,638	1,286	329	2.12	5.6
Crockett	5,521	5,183	3,959	1,224	338	135	2.60	5.5
Cumberland	15,864	13,426	10,526	2,900	2,438	322	2.40	5.3
Davidson	229,064	207,530	111,691	95,839	21,534	5,238	2.52	5.2
Decatur	5,346	4,216	3,395	821	1,130	88	2.09	5.2
DeKalb	6,694	5,696	4,351	1,345	998	116	2.04	5.3
Dickson	14,149	13,019	9,854	3,165	1,130	356	2.73	5.5
Dyer	14,384	13,617	8,965	4,652	767	312	2.29	5.4
Fayette	9,115	8,453	6,327	2,126	662	705	8.34	5.4
Fentress	6,120	5,511	4,329	1,182	609	155	2.81	5.4

TABLE 6.5-- NUMBER OF HOUSING UNITS, BY TENURE AND VACANCY STATUS AND BY NUMBER OF PERSONS PER ROOM, AND MEAN NUMBER OF ROOMS PER HOUSING UNIT, COUNTIES, 1990 (Continued)

| County | Total | Number of housing units | | | | Occupied with 1.01 or more persons per room | | Mean number of rooms per housing unit |
		Total occupied	Owner-occupied	Renter-occupied	Vacant	Number	Percent	
Franklin	13,717	12,660	9,835	2,825	1,057	287	2.27	5.7
Gibson	19,635	18,361	13,332	5,029	1,274	422	2.30	5.4
Giles	10,828	9,832	7,175	2,657	996	255	2.59	5.4
Grainger	7,501	6,394	5,271	1,123	1,107	180	2.82	5.2
Greene	23,270	21,482	16,548	4,934	1,788	443	2.06	5.5
Grundy	5,155	4,784	3,896	888	371	210	4.39	5.2
Hamblen	20,514	19,429	14,009	5,420	1,085	400	2.06	5.5
Hamilton	122,588	111,799	71,640	40,159	10,789	2,511	2.25	5.5
Hancock	2,890	2,484	1,946	538	406	88	3.54	5.1
Hardeman	9,174	8,276	6,094	2,182	898	477	5.76	5.3
Hardin	10,275	8,726	6,750	1,976	1,549	258	2.96	5.2
Hawkins	18,779	17,167	13,236	3,931	1,612	372	2.17	5.3
Haywood	7,475	7,014	4,659	2,355	461	399	5.69	5.3
Henderson	9,278	8,527	6,799	1,728	751	147	1.72	5.4
Henry	13,774	11,362	8,692	2,670	2,412	193	1.70	5.3
Hickman	6,662	5,976	4,826	1,150	686	170	2.84	5.4
Houston	3,085	2,683	2,112	571	402	64	2.39	5.3
Humphreys	7,136	6,063	4,688	1,375	1,073	132	2.18	5.5
Jackson	4,219	3,642	2,971	671	577	81	2.22	5.2
Jefferson	14,170	12,329	9,519	2,810	1,841	254	2.06	5.3
Johnson	6,090	5,406	4,360	1,046	684	127	2.35	5.4
Knox	143,582	133,639	85,369	48,270	9,943	2,399	1.80	5.5
Lake	2,610	2,418	1,413	1,005	192	75	3.10	5.1
Lauderdale	9,343	8,423	5,636	2,787	920	400	4.75	5.2
Lawrence	14,229	13,338	10,213	3,125	891	317	2.38	5.6

TABLE 6.5-- NUMBER OF HOUSING UNITS, BY TENURE AND VACANCY STATUS AND BY NUMBER OF PERSONS PER ROOM, AND MEAN NUMBER OF ROOMS PER HOUSING UNIT, COUNTIES, 1990 (Continued)

County	Total	Total occupied	Owner-occupied	Renter-occupied	Vacant	Occupied with 1.01 or more persons per room Number	Occupied with 1.01 or more persons per room Percent	Mean number of rooms per housing unit
Lewis	3,943	3,533	2,678	855	410	103	2.92	5.3
Lincoln	11,902	10,881	7,982	2,899	1,021	246	2.26	5.5
Loudon	12,995	12,155	9,428	2,727	840	209	1.72	5.6
McMinn	17,616	16,351	12,448	3,903	1,265	319	1.95	5.5
McNairy	9,734	8,834	6,993	1,841	900	191	2.16	5.3
Macon	6,879	6,159	4,853	1,306	720	145	2.35	5.3
Madison	31,809	29,609	19,359	10,250	2,200	696	2.35	5.5
Marion	10,011	9,215	7,284	1,931	796	283	3.07	5.3
Marshall	8,909	8,268	5,851	2,417	641	201	2.43	5.5
Maury	22,286	20,608	14,225	6,383	1,678	524	2.54	5.5
Meigs	3,689	2,996	2,393	603	693	86	2.87	5.1
Monroe	12,803	11,363	9,052	2,311	1,440	333	2.93	5.3
Montgomery	37,233	34,345	20,983	13,362	2,888	1,168	3.40	5.4
Moore	1,912	1,734	1,451	283	178	32	1.85	5.8
Morgan	6,378	5,841	4,844	997	537	182	3.12	5.4
Obion	13,359	12,412	8,762	3,650	947	266	2.14	5.4
Overton	7,388	6,734	5,409	1,325	654	171	2.54	5.3
Perry	3,225	2,512	2,107	405	713	86	3.42	5.1
Pickett	2,253	1,786	1,407	379	467	42	2.35	5.0
Polk	5,659	5,092	4,220	872	567	148	2.91	5.3
Putnam	21,417	19,753	13,187	6,566	1,664	309	1.56	5.4
Rhea	10,361	9,185	6,844	2,341	1,176	209	2.28	5.3
Roane	20,334	18,453	14,102	4,351	1,881	335	1.82	5.6
Robertson	15,823	14,801	11,085	3,716	1,022	450	3.04	5.6
Rutherford	45,755	42,118	27,826	14,292	3,637	1,081	2.57	5.4

TABLE 6.5-- NUMBER OF HOUSING UNITS, BY TENURE AND VACANCY STATUS AND BY NUMBER OF PERSONS PER ROOM, AND MEAN NUMBER OF ROOMS PER HOUSING UNIT, COUNTIES, 1990 (Continued)

| County | Total | Number of housing units | | | | Occupied with 1.01 or more persons per room | | Mean number of rooms per housing unit |
		Total occupied	Owner-occupied	Renter-occupied	Vacant	Number	Percent	
Scott	7,122	6,534	4,924	1,610	588	287	4.39	5.2
Sequatchie	3,570	3,287	2,550	737	283	89	2.71	5.2
Sevier	24,166	19,520	14,803	4,717	4,646	533	2.73	5.2
Shelby	327,796	303,571	180,490	123,081	24,225	13,843	4.56	5.5
Smith	6,049	5,358	4,223	1,135	691	123	2.30	5.5
Stewart	4,384	3,678	3,032	646	706	69	1.88	5.3
Sullivan	60,623	56,729	42,530	14,199	3,894	848	1.49	5.6
Sumner	39,807	36,850	27,641	9,209	2,957	831	2.26	5.8
Tipton	14,071	13,033	9,376	3,657	1,038	598	4.59	5.4
Trousdale	2,537	2,261	1,690	571	276	66	2.92	5.3
Unicoi	7,076	6,621	5,114	1,507	455	134	2.02	5.4
Union	5,696	4,932	3,936	996	764	185	3.75	5.1
Van Buren	2,001	1,799	1,507	292	202	50	2.78	5.3
Warren	13,802	12,681	9,277	3,404	1,121	292	2.30	5.5
Washington	38,378	35,823	24,135	11,688	2,555	547	1.53	5.5
Wayne	5,741	5,174	4,328	846	567	150	2.90	5.4
Weakley	12,857	11,992	8,453	3,539	865	230	1.92	5.4
White	8,369	7,722	6,295	1,427	647	217	2.81	5.4
Williamson	29,875	27,928	22,210	5,718	1,947	453	1.62	6.6
Wilson	26,198	24,070	19,379	4,691	2,128	473	1.97	5.9

Source: U.S. Department of Commerce, Bureau of the Census, 1990 Census of Population and Housing, Summary Population and Housing Characteristics, Tennessee.

FIGURE 6.2

Median Value of Owner-Occupied Housing Units, by County, 1990
(Tennessee median value = $58,400)

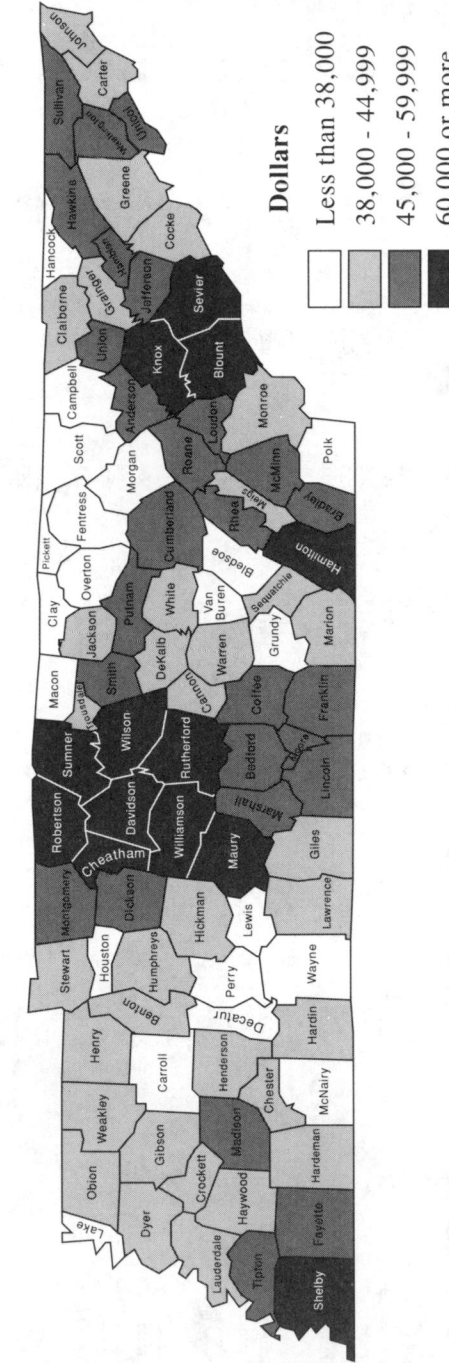

Dollars

Less than 38,000
38,000 - 44,999
45,000 - 59,999
60,000 or more

Source: U.S. Department of Commerce, Bureau of the Census, *Census of Population and Housing, Summary Population and Housing Characteristics, Tennessee.*

TABLE 6.6— HOUSING UNITS, BY TYPE, PERSONS IN HOUSEHOLDS, AND MEDIAN VALUE AND RENT OF SPECIFIED OCCUPIED HOUSING UNITS, TENNESSEE AND COUNTIES, 1990

County	Persons in households	Persons per household	Single-family	Multifamily 2 to 9 units	Multifamily 10 or more units	Mobile home or trailer	Other	Median value of owner-occupied units [2]	Median rent of renter-occupied units [3]
Anderson	67,595	2.47	20,688	3,035	2,340	3,030	230	$55,100	$262
Bedford	30,031	2.59	9,559	943	282	1,704	150	48,400	227
Benton	14,255	2.46	5,114	212	71	1,648	62	39,700	169
Bledsoe	8,608	2.65	2,795	106	67	761	42	36,000	143
Blount	84,463	2.51	27,408	3,058	1,518	4,237	311	60,200	239
Bradley	72,043	2.61	20,951	4,416	1,092	2,876	227	55,000	247
Campbell	34,783	2.65	10,727	893	427	2,626	144	37,900	174
Cannon	10,356	2.60	3,448	185	80	610	45	41,500	174
Carroll	26,860	2.50	9,151	700	16	1,823	93	35,700	170
Carter	50,225	2.49	15,278	1,946	509	3,817	229	43,800	202
Cheatham	26,840	2.82	7,679	336	108	2,082	92	64,000	281
Chester	11,791	2.59	3,887	272	67	659	59	40,200	164
Claiborne	25,533	2.65	7,963	430	91	2,092	135	41,400	164
Clay	7,158	2.51	2,428	97	38	753	24	37,100	141
Cocke	28,840	2.58	8,437	771	269	2,619	186	40,300	145
Coffee	39,855	2.57	12,118	1,745	516	2,236	171	52,800	234
Crockett	13,103	2.53	4,658	165	49	586	63	38,600	156
Cumberland	34,207	2.55	11,856	1,054	192	2,502	260	49,100	217
Davidson	489,689	2.36	129,294	40,745	53,146	3,971	1,908	76,000	359
Decatur	10,330	2.45	4,051	163	51	1,035	46	34,700	150
DeKalb	14,237	2.50	5,341	399	87	776	91	44,200	189
Dickson	34,532	2.65	10,290	1,191	376	2,168	124	54,100	257
Dyer	34,343	2.52	10,833	1,937	432	1,084	98	44,100	212
Fayette	25,110	2.97	6,672	352	149	1,803	139	51,400	137
Fentress	14,559	2.64	4,793	236	20	998	73	32,300	139
Franklin	33,429	2.64	10,969	918	77	1,598	155	48,700	210
Gibson	45,568	2.48	15,591	1,921	271	1,665	187	39,200	177
Giles	25,336	2.58	8,145	1,007	192	1,370	114	44,600	195

TABLE 6.6-- HOUSING UNITS, BY TYPE, PERSONS IN HOUSEHOLDS, AND MEDIAN VALUE AND RENT OF SPECIFIED OCCUPIED HOUSING UNITS, TENNESSEE AND COUNTIES, 1990 (Continued)

County	Persons in households	Persons per household	Single-family	Multifamily 2 to 9 units	Multifamily 10 or more units	Mobile home or trailer	Other	Median value of owner-occupied units [2]	Median rent of renter-occupied units [3]
Grainger	16,912	2.64	5,461	149	17	1,785	89	40,300	161
Greene	54,175	2.52	17,080	1,431	427	4,104	228	44,500	194
Grundy	13,157	2.75	3,743	207	10	1,134	61	29,800	155
Hamblen	49,750	2.56	15,112	2,482	661	2,093	166	51,300	210
Hamilton	279,044	2.50	81,903	20,953	12,893	5,847	992	62,000	285
Hancock	6,571	2.65	2,211	128	14	498	39	32,200	100[a]
Hardeman	22,589	2.73	6,790	402	149	1,585	248	39,200	163
Hardin	22,350	2.56	7,937	390	87	1,767	94	39,100	165
Hawkins	44,232	2.58	13,298	1,020	829	3,458	174	48,600	211
Haywood	19,240	2.74	5,961	709	125	575	105	40,400	174
Henderson	21,630	2.54	6,678	493	23	2,007	77	42,200	174
Henry	27,456	2.42	9,579	939	147	2,998	111	41,700	176
Hickman	15,715	2.63	5,038	117	165	1,285	57	43,200	199
Houston	6,842	2.55	2,310	117	46	583	29	35,300	170
Humphreys	15,551	2.56	5,231	373	73	1,354	105	43,700	198
Jackson	9,176	2.52	3,208	152	17	793	49	38,000	137
Jefferson	31,415	2.55	10,139	776	251	2,854	150	47,900	195
Johnson	13,609	2.52	4,390	295	90	1,227	88	41,300	147
Knox	323,400	2.42	96,949	17,865	19,546	7,848	1,374	63,900	272
Lake	6,057	2.50	1,950	319	22	288	31	35,100	119
Lauderdale	22,598	2.68	6,822	1,024	77	1,322	98	38,700	183
Lawrence	34,992	2.62	11,490	1,021	130	1,450	138	43,300	176
Lewis	9,098	2.58	2,839	264	9	791	40	37,200	158
Lincoln	27,910	2.57	8,884	948	216	1,705	149	47,100	189
Loudon	30,926	2.54	10,162	648	266	1,795	124	51,000	190
McMinn	41,710	2.55	13,171	1,685	176	2,382	202	45,600	192
McNairy	22,180	2.51	7,690	350	70	1,535	89	36,400	159

TABLE 6.6— HOUSING UNITS, BY TYPE, PERSONS IN HOUSEHOLDS, AND MEDIAN VALUE AND RENT OF SPECIFIED OCCUPIED HOUSING UNITS, TENNESSEE AND COUNTIES, 1990 (Continued)

| County | Persons in households | Persons per household | Type of structure[1] | | | | | Median value of owner-occupied units[2] | Median rent of renter-occupied units[3] |
| | | | Single-family | Multifamily | | Mobile home or trailer | Other | | |
				2 to 9 units	10 or more units				
Macon	15,817	2.57	5,151	329	61	1,249	89	36,600	170
Madison	75,515	2.55	22,925	5,366	1,549	1,743	226	53,500	242
Marion	24,645	2.67	7,210	453	213	2,054	81	42,600	192
Marshall	21,248	2.57	6,687	735	362	1,018	107	47,900	228
Maury	54,073	2.62	16,375	2,562	777	2,397	175	60,700	284
Meigs	7,921	2.64	2,337	123	16	1,171	42	44,200	183
Monroe	29,940	2.63	9,387	573	85	2,618	140	40,200	180
Montgomery	93,516	2.72	26,166	5,065	2,232	3,526	244	58,100	298
Moore	4,714	2.72	1,549	43	1	306	13	50,400	214
Morgan	16,011	2.74	4,790	177	18	1,313	80	37,800	165
Obion	31,399	2.53	10,036	1,555	191	1,471	106	43,500	194
Overton	17,435	2.59	5,480	269	82	1,493	64	36,700	154
Perry	6,460	2.57	2,289	99	11	792	34	35,600	158
Pickett	4,494	2.52	1,605	84	29	504	31	34,200	100[a]
Polk	13,538	2.66	4,150	152	14	1,225	118	37,800	170
Putnam	48,419	2.45	14,683	2,990	1,018	2,563	163	55,000	230
Rhea	23,638	2.57	7,157	837	79	2,198	90	45,300	207
Roane	46,747	2.53	15,174	1,407	712	2,843	198	48,700	194
Robertson	41,045	2.77	12,276	1,136	317	1,977	117	61,300	240
Rutherford	113,372	2.69	31,062	6,395	4,006	3,983	309	71,800	333
Scott	18,189	2.78	5,053	409	96	1,480	84	33,600	156
Sequatchie	8,778	2.67	2,550	156	37	785	42	39,000	183
Sevier	50,394	2.58	17,365	1,749	867	3,826	359	62,400	254
Shelby	803,085	2.65	219,124	58,048	43,390	4,082	3,152	66,500	302
Smith	13,998	2.61	4,636	381	48	913	71	45,900	175
Stewart	9,295	2.53	3,198	105	55	983	43	43,700	156
Sullivan	141,449	2.49	44,318	5,253	2,857	7,669	526	55,600	231
Sumner	102,065	2.77	30,105	3,724	2,005	3,743	230	73,900	339

TABLE 6.6– HOUSING UNITS, BY TYPE, PERSONS IN HOUSEHOLDS, AND MEDIAN VALUE AND RENT OF SPECIFIED OCCUPIED HOUSING UNITS, TENNESSEE AND COUNTIES, 1990 (Continued)

County	Persons in households	Persons per household	Single-family	Type of structure[1] Multifamily 2 to 9 units	10 or more units	Mobile home or trailer	Other	Median value of owner-occupied units[2]	Median rent of renter-occupied units[3]
Tipton	37,301	2.86	10,547	867	174	2,346	137	56,100	215
Trousdale	5,795	2.56	1,825	142	88	454	28	41,900	187
Unicoi	16,318	2.46	5,291	408	157	1,154	66	48,100	184
Union	13,573	2.75	3,865	174	39	1,534	84	45,500	181
Van Buren	4,841	2.69	1,580	69	7	324	21	33,000	132
Warren	32,597	2.57	10,480	1,410	343	1,433	136	42,200	209
Washington	87,891	2.45	25,899	5,356	2,712	4,056	355	57,300	244
Wayne	13,709	2.65	4,318	82	0	1,270	71	32,800	145
Weakley	29,569	2.47	9,500	1,257	354	1,626	120	39,800	184
White	19,880	2.57	6,546	370	79	1,297	77	40,300	180
Williamson	80,308	2.88	23,997	2,188	1,613	1,900	177	131,100	407
Wilson	67,110	2.79	20,687	1,940	409	3,006	156	82,000	310
TENNESSEE	4,748,056	2.56	1,413,523	238,928	166,172	188,517	18,927	58,400	273

1. Includes vacant-for-sale and vacant-for-rent housing units.
2. Value data are limited to owner-occupied one-family houses on less than ten acres, without a commercial establishment or medical office on the property. Mobile homes, boats, trailers, and owner-occupied non-condominium units in multifamily buildings are excluded.
3. Contract rent data are tabulated for specified renter-occupied housing units paying cash rent, and exclude one-family houses on ten acres or more.
a. The median value falls within the lower interval of an open-ended distribution. The median is shown as the upper value of the category.
Source: U.S. Department of Commerce, Bureau of the Census, *1990 Census of Population and Housing, Summary Population and Housing Characteristics, Tennessee.*

TABLE 6.7-- ESTIMATED MEDIAN AND MEAN PRICES, SINGLE FAMILY HOMES SOLD, COUNTIES, 1992

County	All sales		New homes		Existing homes	
	Median price ($)	Mean price ($)	Median price ($)	Mean price ($)	Median price ($)	Mean price ($)
Anderson	62,500	74,264	86,950	103,841	58,350	66,820
Bedford	47,000	49,364	65,500	61,230	44,000	47,210
Benton	29,000	32,353	n.a.	n.a.	29,000	32,353
Bledsoe	35,000	40,844	48,500	48,500	35,000	40,178
Blount	65,625	69,907	78,200	81,021	60,900	67,630
Bradley	54,900	59,132	56,000	59,409	54,418	59,084
Campbell	42,450	53,009	61,500	77,201	37,500	48,361
Cannon	36,400	38,227	54,550	50,520	35,000	36,364
Carroll	35,000	44,299	53,000	60,059	35,000	43,367
Carter	40,000	45,420	49,500	47,900	39,950	45,342
Cheatham	64,000	65,815	72,900	68,287	62,533	65,021
Chester	40,000	43,639	47,750	45,422	40,000	43,500
Claiborne	43,000	44,449	43,000	40,200	42,500	44,800
Clay	24,500	29,154	44,600	44,600	24,000	28,795
Cocke	34,750	38,581	53,000	56,357	33,100	37,913
Coffee	54,950	59,826	75,647	83,014	49,000	52,346
Crockett	37,000	37,013	41,500	37,000	35,000	37,015
Cumberland	52,500	61,450	57,250	56,957	52,000	62,516
Davidson	80,000	96,131	103,930	117,953	75,000	91,311
Decatur	24,717	29,884	10,000	10,000	24,758	30,266
DeKalb	48,000	50,646	48,000	46,000	46,758	51,052
Dickson	61,000	63,929	68,500	65,305	57,250	63,558
Dyer	45,000	50,791	58,850	58,075	45,000	49,840
Fayette	59,900	65,096	59,975	51,358	59,900	66,825
Fentress	27,000	32,030	33,230	35,243	27,000	31,759
Franklin	50,000	54,119	61,125	72,203	48,500	52,240
Gibson	42,000	43,915	53,000	55,182	40,500	43,011
Giles	45,000	48,313	63,600	62,255	45,000	47,173
Grainger	40,000	43,093	47,500	76,800	39,950	40,875
Greene	45,000	50,410	58,500	70,735	44,350	48,816
Grundy	27,000	32,842	n.a.	n.a.	27,000	32,842
Hamblen	50,000	55,552	69,950	72,351	48,000	53,771
Hamilton	71,500	84,155	87,350	105,899	67,900	81,478
Hancock	41,500	36,470	43,000	43,000	41,250	36,003
Hardeman	37,500	41,403	42,000	46,515	35,500	40,895
Hardin	42,125	58,721	78,000	91,040	40,000	56,196
Hawkins	53,000	60,215	64,000	70,754	47,500	57,198
Haywood	42,000	49,974	51,000	50,127	41,750	49,958
Henderson	43,500	48,199	61,950	63,170	40,000	44,872
Henry	38,500	41,892	62,500	73,377	38,000	40,851
Hickman	43,400	43,183	50,900	49,005	40,000	41,992
Houston	35,250	25,192	12,000	12,000	36,200	35,874
Humphreys	47,500	51,349	49,900	55,472	45,000	50,954
Jackson	35,000	31,128	42,000	36,206	24,512	29,266
Jefferson	48,700	52,694	26,000	37,250	49,000	55,724
Johnson	35,000	37,067	39,900	36,490	34,950	37,160
Knox	72,000	88,295	99,710	116,792	68,000	80,665
Lake	29,000	30,275	41,000	41,000	29,000	29,828
Lauderdale	35,750	39,059	50,500	51,718	35,000	37,709
Lawrence	42,500	45,587	16,755	27,536	43,000	46,188

TABLE 6.7-- ESTIMATED MEDIAN AND MEAN PRICES, SINGLE FAMILY HOMES SOLD, COUNTIES, 1992 (Continued)

County	All sales		New homes		Existing homes	
	Median price ($)	Mean price ($)	Median price ($)	Mean price ($)	Median price ($)	Mean price ($)
Lewis	36,000	39,672	44,500	47,123	33,750	38,491
Lincoln	47,000	51,985	53,750	52,336	45,000	51,948
Loudon	49,250	60,136	46,500	53,752	50,000	61,471
McMinn	43,500	50,967	48,000	52,350	42,713	50,832
McNairy	33,750	37,033	43,000	44,038	33,000	36,446
Macon	35,000	36,716	48,950	44,495	32,000	34,679
Madison	50,281	52,509	68,500	74,600	48,180	50,438
Marion	44,000	52,589	46,900	52,979	44,000	52,552
Marshall	56,500	56,802	69,000	65,195	49,850	54,543
Maury	72,000	69,455	76,950	71,440	65,000	67,990
Meigs	44,500	49,122	50,100	48,200	42,900	49,264
Monroe	38,000	41,950	15,000	24,166	38,250	42,240
Montgomery	64,325	68,591	66,250	70,813	62,000	66,777
Moore	55,000	54,476	64,010	66,755	55,000	52,657
Morgan	36,262	39,445	50,000	50,000	36,131	39,256
Obion	38,000	42,595	46,900	44,336	37,500	42,491
Overton	36,750	38,609	62,250	62,250	36,250	38,154
Perry	28,000	29,720	n.a.	n.a.	28,000	29,720
Pickett	31,600	33,518	42,500	38,350	26,500	32,265
Polk	35,000	41,271	45,800	45,000	34,000	40,864
Putnam	59,805	66,738	69,000	76,817	55,000	63,033
Rhea	50,000	52,860	62,375	60,525	50,000	52,450
Roane	56,375	67,625	50,750	65,852	56,950	67,799
Robertson	67,850	69,440	69,900	70,629	64,500	68,828
Rutherford	73,375	77,459	76,900	81,445	69,500	73,980
Scott	31,000	35,789	38,000	42,274	31,000	35,177
Sequatchie	43,880	43,613	11,000	21,626	44,539	44,882
Sevier	63,875	66,975	65,750	67,599	62,950	66,869
Shelby	79,211	93,895	n.a.	n.a.	n.a.	n.a.
Smith	44,900	43,303	53,860	49,982	41,500	42,038
Stewart	49,250	46,256	57,850	59,916	42,000	43,293
Sullivan	57,000	66,555	85,000	89,846	55,950	62,960
Sumner	75,900	89,755	81,950	98,066	74,000	87,386
Tipton	66,500	65,769	71,000	72,568	56,300	58,165
Trousdale	37,000	37,016	51,000	44,000	36,950	36,400
Unicoi	50,000	55,157	36,500	40,379	50,000	56,846
Union	40,000	41,267	48,800	50,320	39,000	40,189
Van Buren	28,750	32,800	10,000	10,000	29,000	34,000
Warren	45,350	51,549	56,750	56,918	44,325	50,466
Washington	63,000	73,235	69,000	80,512	59,950	71,259
Wayne	31,000	35,450	85,000	85,000	30,500	34,815
Weakley	33,000	39,644	82,575	87,691	32,500	38,385
White	40,000	46,140	48,000	42,889	40,000	46,531
Williamson	134,000	155,410	130,950	160,069	135,500	152,459
Wilson	84,476	91,344	86,950	88,759	83,500	92,261

n.a. not available.
Source: Tennessee Housing Development Agency, direct correspondence.

TABLE 6.8– NUMBER OF HOUSING UNITS, BY TENURE AND VACANCY STATUS AND BY NUMBER OF PERSONS PER ROOM, AND MEAN NUMBER OF ROOMS PER HOUSING UNIT, INCORPORATED AND CENSUS DESIGNATED PLACES, 1990

Place	Total	Total occupied	Owner-occupied	Renter-occupied	Vacant	Occupied with 1.01 or more persons per room		Mean number of rooms per housing unit
						Number	Percent	
Adams	236	213	167	46	23	11	5.16	5.3
Adamsville	764	706	495	211	58	8	1.13	5.3
Alamo	1,049	994	671	323	55	29	2.92	5.3
Alcoa	2,892	2,692	1,834	858	200	41	1.52	5.5
Alexandria	352	321	247	74	31	5	1.56	5.4
Algood	1,016	938	598	340	78	14	1.49	5.2
Allardt	258	244	206	38	14	0	0.00	.2
Altamont	256	232	194	38	24	14	6.03	5.2
Ardmore	355	335	243	92	20	1	0.30	5.6
Arlington	372	356	287	69	16	17	4.78	5.8
Ashland City	1,094	1,009	618	391	85	21	2.08	5.1
Athens	5,184	4,844	3,045	1,799	340	73	1.51	5.4
Atoka	259	233	174	59	26	10	4.29	5.4
Atwood	452	422	362	60	30	6	1.42	5.3
Auburntown	111	101	87	14	10	3	2.97	5.3
Baileyton	143	128	103	25	15	5	3.91	5.3
Baneberry	109	90	68	22	19	1	1.11	5.8
Banner Hill CDP	724	690	568	122	34	22	3.19	5.2
Bartlett	8,807	8,456	7,685	771	351	65	0.77	6.7
Baxter	579	527	345	182	52	19	3.61	5.2
Beersheba Springs	290	231	190	41	59	8	3.46	5.2
Belinda City CDP	707	673	551	122	34	16	2.38	5.6
Bell Buckle	142	132	98	34	10	1	0.76	6.4
Belle Meade	1,149	1,099	1,022	77	50	0	0.00	8.5
Bells	676	622	473	149	54	17	2.73	5.3

TABLE 6.8– NUMBER OF HOUSING UNITS, BY TENURE AND VACANCY STATUS AND BY NUMBER OF PERSONS PER ROOM, AND MEAN NUMBER OF ROOMS PER HOUSING UNIT, INCORPORATED AND CENSUS DESIGNATED PLACES, 1990 (Continued)

Place	Total	Number of housing units				Occupied with 1.01 or more persons per room		Mean number of rooms per housing unit
		Total occupied	Owner-occupied	Renter-occupied	Vacant	Number	Percent	
Benton	397	360	260	100	37	18	5.00	5.1
Berry Hill	475	402	149	253	73	11	2.74	4.3
Bethel Springs	348	312	256	56	36	8	2.56	5.3
Big Sandy	289	246	177	69	43	4	1.63	4.8
Blaine	505	470	378	92	35	12	2.55	5.3
Bloomingdale CDP	4,447	4,232	3,442	790	215	80	1.89	5.4
Blountville CDP	919	879	749	130	40	15	1.71	5.9
Bluff City	609	544	416	128	65	20	3.68	5.3
Bolivar	2,098	2,000	1,322	678	98	127	6.35	5.3
Braden	150	137	99	38	13	4	2.92	5.5
Bradford	503	472	378	94	31	11	2.33	5.4
Brentwood	5,514	5,276	4,903	373	238	11	0.21	8.4
Brighton	301	275	200	75	26	7	2.55	5.4
Bristol	10,403	9,745	6,455	3,290	658	132	1.35	5.6
Brownsville	3,848	3,698	2,230	1,468	150	196	5.30	5.2
Bruceton	699	640	492	148	59	7	1.09	5.6
Bulls Gap	312	271	217	54	41	2	0.74	5.4
Burlison	171	161	136	25	10	2	1.24	5.6
Burns	440	408	278	130	32	14	3.43	5.4
Byrdstown	429	390	245	145	39	5	1.28	5.1
Calhoun	219	204	179	25	15	5	2.45	5.7
Camden	1,667	1,532	1,043	489	135	22	1.44	5.4
Carthage	1,080	993	604	389	87	17	1.71	5.4
Caryville	732	677	524	153	55	16	2.36	5.4
Cedar Hill	133	126	100	26	7	6	4.76	5.3

TABLE 6.8— NUMBER OF HOUSING UNITS, BY TENURE AND VACANCY STATUS AND BY NUMBER OF PERSONS PER ROOM, AND MEAN NUMBER OF ROOMS PER HOUSING UNIT, INCORPORATED AND CENSUS DESIGNATED PLACES, 1990 (Continued)

| Place | Total | Number of housing units | | | | Occupied with 1.01 or more persons per room | | Mean number of rooms per housing unit |
		Total occupied	Owner-occupied	Renter-occupied	Vacant	Number	Percent	
Celina	685	641	436	205	44	14	2.18	5.2
Centertown	120	109	92	17	11	3	2.75	5.4
Centerville	1,604	1,481	986	495	123	26	1.76	5.4
Central CDP	1,130	1,056	807	249	74	17	1.61	5.2
Chapel Hill	346	325	271	54	21	7	2.15	5.5
Charleston	265	252	200	52	13	5	1.98	5.8
Charlotte	374	355	264	91	19	8	2.25	5.6
Chattanooga	69,601	62,177	33,721	28,456	7,424	1,770	2.85	5.1
Church Hill	2,004	1,889	1,298	591	115	26	1.38	5.4
Clarksburg	140	128	110	18	12	1	0.78	5.3
Clarksville	27,642	25,442	13,906	11,536	2,200	940	3.69	5.3
Cleveland	13,050	11,996	6,605	5,391	1,054	277	2.31	5.2
Clifton	284	240	197	43	44	6	2.50	5.5
Clinton	4,006	3,795	2,229	1,566	211	64	1.69	5.3
Coalmont	293	283	240	43	10	12	4.24	5.4
Collegedale	1,641	1,516	969	547	125	41	2.70	5.4
Collierville	4,613	4,429	3,700	729	184	114	2.57	6.6
Collinwood	440	405	312	93	35	5	1.23	5.4
Colonial Heights CDP	2,613	2,538	2,084	454	75	12	0.47	6.5
Columbia	12,142	11,267	6,906	4,361	875	261	2.32	5.4
Cookeville	9,284	8,563	4,306	4,257	721	118	1.38	5.3
Copperhill	205	174	127	47	31	1	0.57	5.4
Cornersville	307	285	229	56	22	5	1.75	5.6
Cottage Grove	42	36	32	4	6	0	0.00	5.5
Covington	2,920	2,729	1,396	1,333	191	144	5.28	5.2

TABLE 6.8-- NUMBER OF HOUSING UNITS, BY TENURE AND VACANCY STATUS AND BY NUMBER OF PERSONS PER ROOM, AND MEAN NUMBER OF ROOMS PER HOUSING UNIT, INCORPORATED AND CENSUS DESIGNATED PLACES, 1990 (Continued)

Place	Total	Total occupied	Owner-occupied	Renter-occupied	Vacant	Occupied with 1.01 or more persons per room		Mean number of rooms per housing unit
						Number	Percent	
Cowan	728	676	491	185	52	21	3.11	5.4
Crab Orchard	420	328	263	65	92	13	3.96	4.7
Cross Plains	382	355	284	71	27	14	3.94	5.6
Crossville	3,054	2,837	1,535	1,302	217	70	2.47	5.0
Crump	937	782	640	142	155	28	3.58	5.1
Cumberland City	157	131	83	48	26	1	0.76	5.2
Cumberland Gap	104	91	50	41	13	2	2.20	5.4
Dandridge	625	558	418	140	67	7	1.25	5.3
Dayton	2,306	2,129	1,236	893	177	41	1.93	5.3
Decatur	550	505	330	175	45	5	0.99	5.2
Decaturville	385	339	239	100	46	11	3.24	5.4
Decherd	913	847	590	257	66	19	2.24	5.5
Dickson	3,818	3,523	2,017	1,506	295	81	2.30	5.3
Dover	607	564	381	183	43	5	0.89	5.6
Dowelltown	151	141	106	35	10	3	2.13	5.2
Doyle	149	139	110	29	10	5	3.60	5.3
Dresden	1,102	1,031	662	369	71	24	2.33	5.4
Ducktown	214	202	144	58	12	4	1.98	5.4
Dunlap	1,501	1,417	1,003	414	84	40	2.82	5.2
Dyer	982	924	721	203	58	10	1.08	5.6
Dyersburg	7,041	6,696	3,605	3,091	345	156	2.33	5.1
Eagleton Village CDP	2,281	2,176	1,565	611	105	30	1.38	5.3
Eagleville	194	182	137	45	12	1	0.55	5.8
East Brainerd CDP	3,810	3,682	3,396	286	128	29	0.79	7.3
East Cleveland CDP	520	475	288	187	45	23	4.84	4.7

Number of housing units

TABLE 6.8— NUMBER OF HOUSING UNITS, BY TENURE AND VACANCY STATUS AND BY NUMBER OF PERSONS PER ROOM, AND MEAN NUMBER OF ROOMS PER HOUSING UNIT, INCORPORATED AND CENSUS DESIGNATED PLACES, 1990 (Continued)

| Place | Total | Number of housing units | | | | Occupied with 1.01 or more persons per room | | Mean number of rooms per housing unit |
		Total occupied	Owner-occupied	Renter-occupied	Vacant	Number	Percent	
East Ridge	9,631	9,109	5,613	3,496	522	95	1.04	5.4
Eastview	267	244	197	47	23	6	2.46	5.4
Elizabethton	5,191	4,936	3,218	1,718	255	61	1.24	5.3
Elkton	184	165	127	38	19	8	4.85	5.6
Englewood	719	669	471	198	50	18	2.69	5.2
Enville	108	94	87	7	14	3	3.19	5.4
Erin	668	613	390	223	55	14	2.28	5.2
Erwin	2,259	2,144	1,541	603	115	25	1.17	5.5
Estill Springs	605	572	465	107	33	8	1.40	5.7
Ethridge	236	219	161	58	17	6	2.74	5.5
Etowah	1,737	1,584	1,067	517	153	21	1.33	5.3
Fairfield Glade CDP	1,566	1,083	922	161	483	5	0.46	5.3
Fairmount CDP	605	541	437	104	64	11	2.03	6.3
Fairview	1,479	1,411	1,180	231	68	39	2.76	5.6
Fall Branch CDP	509	480	391	89	29	9	1.88	5.5
Farragut	4,456	4,252	3,892	360	204	12	0.28	7.9
Fayetteville	3,277	3,016	1,751	1,265	261	74	2.45	5.3
Finger	120	108	89	19	12	3	2.78	5.3
Forest Hills	1,597	1,549	1,499	50	48	2	0.13	8.8
Franklin	8,748	7,828	4,276	3,552	920	174	2.22	5.4
Friendship	210	198	155	43	12	5	2.53	5.5
Friendsville	337	301	259	42	36	8	2.66	5.6
Gadsden	214	194	165	29	20	7	3.61	5.8
Gainesboro	495	460	292	168	35	11	2.39	5.2
Gallatin	7,635	7,028	4,311	2,717	607	215	3.06	5.4

TABLE 6.8– NUMBER OF HOUSING UNITS, BY TENURE AND VACANCY STATUS AND BY NUMBER OF PERSONS PER ROOM, AND MEAN NUMBER OF ROOMS PER HOUSING UNIT, INCORPORATED AND CENSUS DESIGNATED PLACES, 1990 (Continued)

| Place | Total | Number of housing units | | | | Occupied with 1.01 or more persons per room | | Mean number of rooms per housing unit |
		Total occupied	Owner-occupied	Renter-occupied	Vacant	Number	Percent	
Gallaway	211	198	50	148	13	26	13.13	4.6
Garland	79	76	70	6	3	0	0.00	6.0
Gates	241	220	153	67	21	14	6.36	5.5
Gatlinburg	2,923	1,484	1,018	466	1,439	26	1.75	5.1
Germantown	11,131	10,713	9,597	1,116	418	36	0.34	8.1
Gibson	113	111	90	21	2	2	1.80	5.7
Gilt Edge	180	167	137	30	13	5	2.99	5.7
Gleason	583	550	406	144	33	11	2.00	5.5
Goodlettsville	4,761	4,394	2,814	1,580	367	58	1.32	5.7
Gordonsville	372	347	279	68	25	3	0.86	5.8
Grand Junction	184	160	111	49	24	4	2.50	5.8
Gray CDP	444	431	331	100	13	5	1.16	5.3
Graysville	532	483	353	130	49	13	2.69	5.2
Greenback	250	231	192	39	19	8	3.46	5.8
Greenbrier	1,111	1,053	783	270	58	32	3.04	5.6
Greeneville	6,058	5,581	3,535	2,046	477	71	1.27	5.5
Greenfield	949	891	638	253	58	20	2.24	5.5
Green Hill CDP	2,369	2,227	2,039	188	142	15	0.67	6.6
Gruetli-Laager	680	643	561	82	37	37	5.75	5.2
Guys	194	183	146	37	11	8	4.37	5.1
Halls CDP	2,539	2,467	2,040	427	72	11	0.45	6.3
Halls	1,053	975	598	377	78	44	4.51	5.1
Harriman	3,234	2,931	1,730	1,201	303	64	2.18	5.2
Harrison CDP	2,709	2,586	2,019	567	123	34	1.31	6.1
Harrogate-Shawnee CDP	1,035	951	755	196	84	24	2.52	5.7

TABLE 6.8– NUMBER OF HOUSING UNITS, BY TENURE AND VACANCY STATUS AND BY NUMBER OF PERSONS PER ROOM, AND MEAN NUMBER OF ROOMS PER HOUSING UNIT, INCORPORATED AND CENSUS DESIGNATED PLACES, 1990 (Continued)

| Place | Total | Number of housing units | | | | Occupied with 1.01 or more persons per room | | Mean number of rooms per housing unit |
		Total occupied	Owner-occupied	Renter-occupied	Vacant	Number	Percent	
Hartsville	964	878	543	335	86	28	3.19	5.2
Henderson	1,600	1,497	957	540	103	49	3.27	5.4
Hendersonville	12,472	11,441	8,330	3,111	1,031	119	1.04	6.1
Henning	316	290	171	119	26	23	7.93	5.1
Henry	132	117	79	38	15	3	2.56	5.6
Hickory Valley	69	66	48	18	3	5	7.58	5.2
Hohenwald	1,685	1,536	1,061	475	149	33	2.15	5.2
Hollow Rock	397	357	272	85	40	12	3.36	5.2
Hopewell CDP	1,016	986	656	330	30	10	1.01	5.7
Hornbeak	185	168	134	34	17	3	1.79	5.3
Hornsby	128	120	93	27	8	6	5.00	5.4
Humboldt	4,000	3,781	2,481	1,300	219	133	3.52	5.4
Hunter CDP	547	520	422	98	27	3	0.58	5.4
Huntingdon	1,790	1,664	1,196	468	126	35	2.10	5.6
Huntland	367	346	300	46	21	5	1.45	5.6
Huntsville	240	215	121	94	25	12	5.58	5.2
Iron City	161	150	134	16	11	1	0.67	5.6
Jacksboro	650	605	410	195	45	9	1.49	5.5
Jackson	20,739	19,206	10,738	8,468	1,533	485	2.53	5.3
Jamestown	904	786	375	411	118	19	2.42	4.9
Jasper	1,199	1,105	811	294	94	20	1.81	5.5
Jefferson City	2,006	1,888	951	937	118	31	1.64	5.1
Jellico	1,104	1,033	654	379	71	26	2.52	5.1
Johnson City	21,241	19,675	11,184	8,491	1,566	267	1.36	5.4
Jonesborough	1,262	1,185	806	379	77	20	1.69	5.5

TABLE 6.8-- NUMBER OF HOUSING UNITS, BY TENURE AND VACANCY STATUS AND BY NUMBER OF PERSONS PER ROOM, AND MEAN NUMBER OF ROOMS PER HOUSING UNIT, INCORPORATED AND CENSUS DESIGNATED PLACES, 1990 (Continued)

| Place | Total | Number of housing units | | | | Occupied with 1.01 or more persons per room | | Mean number of rooms per housing unit |
		Total occupied	Owner-occupied	Renter-occupied	Vacant	Number	Percent	
Karns CDP	583	569	483	86	14	5	0.88	6.0
Kenton	606	566	371	195	40	10	1.77	5.3
Kimball	507	471	369	102	36	16	3.40	5.2
Kingsport	16,742	15,629	9,832	5,797	1,113	193	1.23	5.5
Kingston	2,071	1,936	1,427	509	135	17	0.88	5.5
Kingston Springs	519	498	448	50	21	5	1.00	6.2
Knoxville	76,453	69,973	34,892	35,081	6,480	1,602	2.29	5.0
Lafayette	1,695	1,585	1,089	496	110	19	1.20	5.1
LaFollette	3,116	2,927	1,662	1,265	189	81	2.77	5.0
LaGrange	78	63	49	14	15	6	9.52	5.7
Lake City	912	857	450	407	55	21	2.45	4.8
Lakeland	475	455	423	32	20	6	1.32	6.5
Lakesite	302	254	208	46	48	1	0.39	6.2
Lakewood	853	800	561	239	53	21	2.63	5.5
LaVergne	2,810	2,580	2,109	471	230	84	3.26	5.4
Lawrenceburg	4,711	4,423	2,831	1,592	288	76	1.72	5.4
Lebanon	6,592	5,909	3,448	2,461	683	156	2.64	5.4
Lenoir City	2,734	2,569	1,594	975	165	58	2.26	5.2
Lewisburg	4,275	4,008	2,404	1,604	267	94	2.35	5.2
Lexington	2,612	2,409	1,588	821	203	34	1.41	5.4
Liberty	160	150	105	45	10	2	1.33	5.5
Linden	504	443	321	122	61	11	2.48	5.2
Livingston	1,679	1,552	1,030	522	127	33	2.13	5.3
Lobelville	387	348	279	69	39	6	1.72	5.3
Lookout Mountain	818	774	680	94	44	1	0.13	7.9

TABLE 6.8-- NUMBER OF HOUSING UNITS, BY TENURE AND VACANCY STATUS AND BY NUMBER OF PERSONS PER ROOM, AND MEAN NUMBER OF ROOMS PER HOUSING UNIT, INCORPORATED AND CENSUS DESIGNATED PLACES, 1990 (Continued)

| Place | Total | Number of housing units | | | | Occupied with 1.01 or more persons per room | | Mean number of rooms per housing unit |
		Total occupied	Owner-occupied	Renter-occupied	Vacant	Number	Percent	
Loreto	620	591	496	95	29	10	1.69	5.8
Loudon	1,832	1,712	1,118	594	120	33	1.93	5.3
Luttrell	303	278	222	56	25	21	7.55	5.2
Lynchburg	1,912	1,734	1,451	283	178	32	1.85	5.8
Lynnville	154	142	116	26	12	3	2.11	5.9
McEwen	632	601	428	173	31	11	1.83	5.4
McKenzie	2,158	1,997	1,357	640	161	45	2.25	5.4
McLemoresville	140	121	98	23	19	2	1.65	5.5
McMinnville	5,123	4,738	2,749	1,989	385	91	1.92	5.2
Madisonville	1,344	1,259	885	374	85	26	2.07	5.3
Manchester	3,330	3,047	1,907	1,140	283	77	2.53	5.4
Martin	3,104	2,941	1,508	1,433	163	39	1.33	5.2
Maryville	8,280	7,718	4,957	2,761	562	84	1.09	5.6
Mascot CDP	877	819	663	156	58	27	3.30	5.2
Mason	135	126	81	45	9	9	7.14	5.3
Maury City	311	294	223	71	17	14	4.76	5.7
Maynardville	544	500	243	257	44	21	4.20	4.8
Medina	332	308	234	74	24	1	0.32	5.4
Medon	59	57	47	10	2	1	1.75	5.5
Memphis	248,573	229,829	126,749	103,080	18,744	12,609	5.49	5.2
Michie	294	270	215	55	24	6	2.22	5.3
Middleton	247	227	162	65	20	5	2.20	5.7
Middle Valley CDP	4,297	4,108	3,533	575	189	45	1.10	6.4
Midway CDP	1,192	1,141	822	319	51	23	2.02	5.5
Milan	3,300	3,089	1,990	1,099	211	70	2.27	5.3

TABLE 6.8-- NUMBER OF HOUSING UNITS, BY TENURE AND VACANCY STATUS AND BY NUMBER OF PERSONS PER ROOM, AND MEAN NUMBER OF ROOMS PER HOUSING UNIT, INCORPORATED AND CENSUS DESIGNATED PLACES, 1990 (Continued)

Place	Total	Number of housing units				Occupied with 1.01 or more persons per room		Mean number of rooms per housing unit
		Total occupied	Owner-occupied	Renter-occupied	Vacant	Number	Percent	
Milledgeville	144	127	110	17	17	1	0.79	5.1
Millersville	1,044	969	641	328	75	56	5.78	4.9
Millington	4,440	4,168	1,392	2,776	272	175	4.20	5.0
Minor Hill	179	155	121	34	24	6	3.87	5.5
Mitchellville	81	74	63	11	7	4	5.41	5.2
Monteagle	444	408	275	133	36	10	2.45	5.1
Monterey	1,113	1,010	651	359	103	21	2.08	5.2
Morrison	251	224	152	72	27	8	3.57	5.4
Morristown	9,248	8,715	5,032	3,683	533	190	2.18	5.2
Moscow	184	163	99	64	21	3	1.84	5.1
Mosheim	586	565	463	102	21	4	0.71	5.5
Mountain City	1,050	956	556	400	94	18	1.88	5.3
Mount Carmel	1,630	1,563	1,336	227	67	12	0.77	5.7
Mount Juliet	1,926	1,832	1,655	177	94	27	1.47	6.4
Mount Pleasant	1,879	1,699	1,077	622	180	49	2.88	5.3
Munford	912	853	517	336	59	29	3.40	5.4
Murfreesboro	18,708	17,110	8,139	8,971	1,598	427	2.50	5.1
Nashville-Davidson	219,258	198,585	104,944	93,641	20,943	5,155	2.60	5.1
Newbern	1,058	1,009	602	407	49	24	2.38	5.5
New Hope	347	311	271	40	36	10	3.22	5.2
New Johnsonville	680	590	481	109	90	12	2.03	5.7
New Market	412	390	329	61	22	4	1.03	5.9
Newport	3,171	2,965	1,660	1,305	206	74	2.50	5.0
New Tazewell	785	728	433	295	57	20	2.75	5.1
Niota	344	314	224	90	30	5	1.59	5.4

TABLE 6.8– NUMBER OF HOUSING UNITS, BY TENURE AND VACANCY STATUS AND BY NUMBER OF PERSONS PER ROOM, AND MEAN NUMBER OF ROOMS PER HOUSING UNIT, INCORPORATED AND CENSUS DESIGNATED PLACES, 1990 (Continued)

| Place | Total | Number of housing units | | | | Occupied with 1.01 or more persons per room | | Mean number of rooms per housing unit |
		Total occupied	Owner-occupied	Renter-occupied	Vacant	Number	Percent	
Nolensville CDP	537	517	473	44	20	9	1.74	6.4
Normandy	45	42	36	6	3	2	4.76	5.9
Norris	622	581	423	158	41	5	0.86	5.9
Oakdale	111	97	74	23	14	4	4.12	5.4
Oak Grove CDP	1,456	1,348	901	447	108	15	1.11	5.3
Oak Hill	1,788	1,729	1,570	159	59	2	0.12	7.8
Oakland	134	130	108	22	4	12	9.23	5.7
Oak Ridge	12,694	11,763	7,824	3,939	931	159	1.35	5.8
Obion	536	503	356	147	33	19	3.78	5.4
Oliver Springs	1,385	1,309	1,006	303	76	31	2.37	5.5
Oneida	1,506	1,425	808	617	81	28	1.96	5.3
Ooltewah CDP	1,847	1,728	1,388	340	119	35	2.03	5.8
Orlinda	200	184	158	26	16	2	1.09	5.8
Orme	52	48	42	6	4	3	6.25	5.0
Palmer	298	284	267	17	14	6	2.11	5.2
Paris	4,538	4,214	2,662	1,552	324	56	1.33	5.2
Parker's Crossroads	69	64	50	14	5	2	3.13	5.5
Parrotsville	44	42	29	13	2	1	2.38	6.1
Parsons	928	838	572	266	90	6	0.72	5.4
Pegram	535	485	404	81	50	9	1.86	5.6
Petersburg	237	213	166	47	24	3	1.41	5.8
Philadelphia	196	185	154	31	11	2	1.08	5.4
Pigeon Forge	1,371	1,195	807	388	176	30	2.51	5.2
Pikeville	802	719	429	290	83	15	2.09	5.2
Pine Crest CDP	1,546	1,439	879	560	107	15	1.04	5.1

TABLE 6.8– NUMBER OF HOUSING UNITS, BY TENURE AND VACANCY STATUS AND BY NUMBER OF PERSONS PER ROOM, AND MEAN NUMBER OF ROOMS PER HOUSING UNIT, INCORPORATED AND CENSUS DESIGNATED PLACES, 1990 (Continued)

| Place | Total | Number of housing units | | | | Occupied with 1.01 or more persons per room | | Mean number of rooms per housing unit |
		Total occupied	Owner-occupied	Renter-occupied	Vacant	Number	Percent	
Piperton	245	234	207	27	11	8	3.42	6.4
Pitman Center	291	206	155	51	85	3	1.46	5.1
Pleasant Hill	228	202	125	77	26	1	0.50	5.0
Portland	2,101	1,949	1,383	566	152	67	3.44	5.3
Powell CDP	3,023	2,919	2,237	682	104	30	1.03	6.0
Powell's Crossroads	395	381	344	37	14	9	2.36	5.5
Pulaski	3,545	3,302	1,821	1,481	243	86	2.60	5.2
Puryear	268	247	203	44	21	3	1.21	5.4
Ramer	142	128	110	18	14	3	2.34	5.7
Red Bank	6,262	5,595	3,052	2,543	667	86	1.54	5.0
Red Boiling Springs	420	371	259	112	49	10	2.70	5.2
Ridgely	723	710	415	295	13	13	1.83	5.2
Ridgeside	162	159	152	7	3	0	0.00	8.4
Ridgetop	389	375	337	38	14	6	1.60	6.1
Ripley	2,490	2,288	1,178	1,110	202	118	5.16	5.0
Rives	141	126	106	20	15	8	6.35	5.2
Roan Mountain CDP	508	477	375	102	31	16	3.35	5.2
Rockford	256	247	179	68	9	2	0.81	5.8
Rockwood	2,326	2,174	1,389	785	152	55	2.53	5.2
Rogersville	1,995	1,854	1,089	765	141	34	1.83	5.1
Rossville	111	105	76	29	6	8	7.62	5.6
Rural Hill CDP	474	451	426	25	23	1	0.22	6.5
Rutherford	590	554	431	123	36	12	2.17	5.4
Rutledge	378	342	217	125	36	4	1.17	5.1
St. Joseph	331	306	238	68	25	6	1.96	5.5

TABLE 6.8-- NUMBER OF HOUSING UNITS, BY TENURE AND VACANCY STATUS AND BY NUMBER OF PERSONS PER ROOM, AND MEAN NUMBER OF ROOMS PER HOUSING UNIT, INCORPORATED AND CENSUS DESIGNATED PLACES, 1990 (Continued)

Place	Total	Total occupied	Owner-occupied	Renter-occupied	Vacant	Occupied with 1.01 or more persons per room		Mean number of rooms per housing unit
						Number	Percent	
Salitllo	209	161	136	25	48	6	3.73	4.9
Samburg	181	149	92	57	32	11	7.38	4.5
Sardis	144	133	110	23	11	2	1.50	5.6
Saulsbury	54	44	37	7	10	0	0.00	5.5
Savannah	2,796	2,601	1,669	932	195	58	2.23	5.3
Scotts Hill	284	257	215	42	27	2	0.78	5.4
Selmer	1,780	1,629	1,052	577	151	23	1.41	5.2
Sevierville	3,321	2,980	1,663	1,317	341	76	2.55	5.0
Sewanee CDP	548	513	317	196	35	2	0.39	6.2
Seymour CDP	2,662	2,544	2,158	386	118	31	1.22	6.0
Sharon	493	458	341	117	35	7	1.53	5.4
Shelbyville	6,163	5,684	3,413	2,271	479	167	2.94	5.1
Signal Mountain	2,718	2,593	2,134	459	125	7	0.27	7.3
Silerton	37	31	28	3	6	0	0.00	5.8
Slayden	49	44	38	6	5	5	11.36	4.9
Smithville	1,693	1,588	971	617	105	32	2.02	5.2
Smyrna	5,312	4,836	2,701	2,135	476	132	2.73	5.3
Sneedville	551	513	326	187	38	13	2.53	5.1
Soddy-Daisy	3,356	3,193	2,486	707	163	83	2.60	5.3
Somerville	911	865	467	398	46	47	5.43	5.0
South Carthage	376	343	231	112	33	7	2.04	5.3
South Cleveland CDP	2,036	1,918	1,488	430	118	42	2.19	5.4
South Fulton	1,182	1,121	809	312	61	15	1.34	5.4
South Pittsburg	1,444	1,314	816	498	130	28	2.13	5.3
Sparta	2,034	1,898	1,232	666	136	52	2.74	5.4

Number of housing units

TABLE 6.8– NUMBER OF HOUSING UNITS, BY TENURE AND VACANCY STATUS AND BY NUMBER OF PERSONS PER ROOM, AND MEAN NUMBER OF ROOMS PER HOUSING UNIT, INCORPORATED AND CENSUS DESIGNATED PLACES, 1990 (Continued)

| Place | Total | Number of housing units | | | | Occupied with 1.01 or more persons per room | | Mean number of rooms per housing unit |
		Total occupied	Owner-occupied	Renter-occupied	Vacant	Number	Percent	
Spencer	466	429	344	85	37	11	2.56	5.3
Spring City	967	867	608	259	100	11	1.27	5.5
Springfield	4,530	4,243	2,412	1,831	287	160	3.77	5.2
Spring Hill	580	515	383	132	65	19	3.69	5.5
Spurgeon CDP	1,266	1,217	893	324	49	18	1.48	5.6
Stanton	210	188	95	93	22	12	6.38	5.2
Stantonville	131	112	85	27	19	3	2.68	5.1
Surgoinsville	625	578	457	121	47	14	2.42	5.4
Sweetwater	2,168	2,017	1,431	586	151	36	1.78	5.4
Tazewell	919	861	544	317	58	12	1.39	5.3
Tellico Plains	328	276	210	66	52	4	1.45	5.1
Tennessee Ridge	499	470	402	68	29	4	0.85	5.7
Tiptonville	844	807	459	348	37	29	3.59	5.2
Toone	102	97	72	25	5	3	3.09	5.5
Townsend	199	150	123	27	49	2	1.33	5.3
Tracy City	667	619	510	109	48	12	1.94	5.5
Trenton	2,150	1,954	1,119	835	196	38	1.94	5.2
Trezevant	396	375	320	55	21	5	1.33	5.4
Trimble	300	280	212	68	20	4	1.43	5.3
Troy	454	436	313	123	18	13	2.98	5.1
Tullahoma	7,119	6,607	4,289	2,318	512	112	1.70	5.7
Tusculum	526	500	393	107	26	3	0.60	5.8
Union City	4,609	4,305	2,452	1,853	304	98	2.28	5.3
Vanleer	153	139	112	27	14	6	4.32	5.3
Viola	55	48	35	13	7	0	0.00	5.9

TABLE 6.8— NUMBER OF HOUSING UNITS, BY TENURE AND VACANCY STATUS AND BY NUMBER OF PERSONS PER ROOM, AND MEAN NUMBER OF ROOMS PER HOUSING UNIT, INCORPORATED AND CENSUS DESIGNATED PLACES, 1990 (Continued)

Place	Total	Number of housing units				Occupied with 1.01 or more persons per room		Mean number of rooms per housing unit
		Total occupied	Owner-occupied	Renter-occupied	Vacant	Number	Percent	
Vonore	272	248	194	54	24	7	2.82	5.6
Walden	598	567	485	82	31	4	0.71	7.1
Walnut Hill CDP	1,291	1,242	1,053	189	49	14	1.13	6.1
Walterhill CDP	378	346	308	38	32	12	3.47	5.7
Wartburg	375	342	178	164	33	4	1.17	5.2
Wartrace	227	202	156	46	25	5	2.48	5.9
Watauga	161	148	125	23	13	2	1.35	5.3
Watertown	566	510	399	111	56	7	1.37	5.6
Waverly	1,787	1,641	1,081	560	146	26	1.58	5.6
Waynesboro	775	723	559	164	52	5	0.69	5.7
Westmoreland	709	668	442	226	41	21	3.14	5.1
White Bluff	851	763	540	223	88	14	1.83	5.2
White House	1,122	1,031	806	225	91	20	1.94	5.6
White Pine	768	723	506	217	45	15	2.07	5.2
Whiteville	444	413	311	102	31	20	4.84	5.5
Whitwell	689	636	496	140	53	19	2.99	5.1
Wildwood Lake CDP	1,033	989	798	191	44	12	1.21	5.5
Williston	151	141	117	24	10	9	6.38	5.3
Winchester	2,625	2,466	1,653	813	159	61	2.47	5.5
Winfield	226	206	155	51	20	5	2.43	5.3
Woodbury	1,034	946	587	359	88	18	1.90	5.1
Woodland Mills	161	155	127	28	6	1	0.65	5.8
Yorkville	137	134	105	29	3	3	2.24	5.8

Note: CDP indicates a Census Designated Place.

Source: U.S. Department of Commerce, Bureau of the Census, 1990 Census of Population and Housing, *Summary Population and Housing Characteristics, Tennessee.*

TABLE 6.9-- HOUSING UNITS, BY TYPE, PERSONS IN HOUSEHOLDS, AND MEDIAN VALUE AND RENT OF SPECIFIED OCCUPIED HOUSING UNITS, INCORPORATED AND CENSUS DESIGNATED PLACES, 1990

Place	Persons in households	Persons per household	Type of structure[1] Single-family	Multifamily 2 to 9 units	Multifamily 10 or more units	Mobile home or trailer and other	Median value of owner-occupied units[2]	Median rent of renter-occupied units[3]
Adams	552	2.59	179	0	0	57	37,900	193
Adamsville	1,604	2.27	615	101	5	43	39,600	188
Alamo	2,283	2.30	851	105	22	71	39,400	167
Alcoa	6,400	2.38	2,474	229	145	44	46,500	228
Alexandria	730	2.27	284	42	0	26	40,400	145
Algood	2,234	2.38	722	191	35	68	42,800	183
Allardt	609	2.50	223	2	0	33	42,700	181
Altamont	668	2.88	177	1	0	78	23,600	114
Ardmore	796	2.38	287	24	3	41	52,700	203
Arlington	1,052	2.96	359	2	0	11	53,900	203
Ashland City	2,487	2.46	701	154	101	138	52,800	270
Athens	11,545	2.38	3,666	1,143	143	232	45,000	193
Atoka	659	2.83	230	3	0	26	61,400	221
Atwood	1,066	2.53	377	13	0	62	36,200	215
Auburntown	240	2.38	99	2	0	10	34,400	192
Baileyton	309	2.41	109	0	0	34	34,400	188
Baneberry	218	2.42	103	6	0	0	90,400	433
Banner Hill CDP	1,717	2.49	598	15	0	111	34,600	168
Bartlett	26,637	3.15	8,487	243	45	32	91,200	469
Baxter	1,274	2.42	418	55	23	83	39,900	160
Beersheba Springs	596	2.58	226	2	0	62	26,900	150
Belinda City CDP	2,098	3.12	656	46	2	3	70,200	462
Bell Buckle	326	2.47	122	7	0	13	49,600	170
Belle Meade	2,839	2.58	1,054	23	62	10	383,700	650
Bells	1,519	2.44	534	15	12	115	39,800	173
Benton	965	2.68	274	31	1	91	36,700	143
Berry Hill	759	1.89	239	49	186	1	66,600	308

TABLE 6.9– HOUSING UNITS, BY TYPE, PERSONS IN HOUSEHOLDS, AND MEDIAN VALUE AND RENT OF SPECIFIED OCCUPIED HOUSING UNITS, INCORPORATED AND CENSUS DESIGNATED PLACES, 1990 (Continued)

Place	Persons in households	Persons per household	Single-family	Multifamily 2 to 9 units	Multifamily 10 or more units	Mobile home or trailer and other	Median value of owner-occupied units [2]	Median rent of renter-occupied units [3]
Bethel Springs	755	2.42	299	3	0	46	32,000	161
Big Sandy	505	2.05	213	12	0	64	32,000	149
Blaine	1,326	2.82	347	20	0	138	46,500	189
Bloomingdale CDP	10,953	2.59	3,378	224	20	825	45,400	231
Blountville CDP	2,296	2.61	755	44	0	120	57,400	259
Bluff City	1,390	2.56	408	24	0	177	42,700	209
Bolivar	5,331	2.67	1,537	263	98	200	43,300	182
Braden	354	2.58	126	0	1	23	42,800	147
Bradford	1,154	2.44	437	27	0	39	33,500	173
Brentwood	16,306	3.09	5,355	101	16	42	179,400	717
Brighton	717	2.61	255	19	0	27	50,700	190
Bristol	22,862	2.35	7,149	1,544	846	864	49,500	234
Brownsville	9,881	2.67	2,980	647	108	113	41,500	192
Bruceton	1,498	2.34	592	54	3	50	33,500	180
Bulls Gap	659	2.43	227	19	23	43	38,600	173
Burlison	394	2.45	158	0	0	13	48,000	254
Burns	1,127	2.76	329	23	12	76	57,600	319
Byrdstown	949	2.43	284	76	28	41	34,700	100[4]
Calhoun	552	2.71	194	1	0	24	38,400	185
Camden	3,428	2.24	1,242	163	69	193	40,400	170
Carthage	2,241	2.26	691	237	39	113	44,900	172
Caryville	1,740	2.57	546	51	0	135	40,400	188
Cedar Hill	347	2.75	100	7	0	26	33,800	138
Celina	1,422	2.22	468	82	38	97	41,800	149
Centertown	332	3.05	104	1	0	15	41,400	194
Centerville	3,415	2.31	1,178	94	161	171	47,300	166

TABLE 6.9.– HOUSING UNITS, BY TYPE, PERSONS IN HOUSEHOLDS, AND MEDIAN VALUE AND RENT OF SPECIFIED OCCUPIED HOUSING UNITS, INCORPORATED AND CENSUS DESIGNATED PLACES, 1990 (Continued)

Place	Persons in households	Persons per household	Single-family	2 to 9 units	10 or more units	Mobile home or trailer and other	Median value of owner-occupied units [2]	Median rent of renter-occupied units [3]
				Type of structure [1] — Multifamily				
Central CDP	2,635	2.50	745	89	0	296	49,100	215
Chapel Hill	833	2.56	302	9	0	35	48,400	255
Charleston	653	2.59	226	5	0	34	45,000	171
Charlotte	854	2.41	281	43	1	49	48,400	232
Chattanooga	147,497	2.37	41,880	15,920	9,968	1,833	54,100	271
Church Hill	4,712	2.49	1,416	235	149	204	53,500	261
Clarksburg	300	2.34	106	3	0	31	38,000	131
Clarksville	68,596	2.70	18,548	4,674	2,150	2,270	59,000	302
Cleveland	28,968	2.41	8,357	3,472	837	384	60,900	247
Clifton	600	2.50	230	1	0	53	30,800	131
Clinton	8,894	2.34	2,564	564	648	230	55,700	258
Coalmont	813	2.87	228	3	0	62	30,500	188
Collegedale	4,113	2.71	779	396	9	457	71,700	269
Collierville	14,313	3.23	4,161	157	219	76	104,500	366
Collinwood	1,014	2.50	349	22	0	69	31,200	129
Colonial Heights CDP	6,711	2.64	2,205	232	66	110	74,000	275
Columbia	27,954	2.48	8,354	2,111	686	991	61,500	303
Cookeville	19,117	2.23	5,466	2,337	911	570	62,000	246
Copperhill	362	2.08	164	32	0	9	29,200	178
Cornersville	664	2.33	265	13	0	29	38,500	219
Cottage Grove	85	2.36	38	0	0	4	23,300	125
Covington	7,245	2.65	2,067	661	96	96	52,100	191
Cowan	1,738	2.57	565	95	5	63	31,700	137
Crab Orchard	876	2.67	269	65	0	86	24,600	152
Cross Plains	1,025	2.89	243	12	0	127	63,400	241
Crossville	6,662	2.35	1,947	664	172	271	42,100	208
Crump	2,028	2.59	647	10	0	280	36,200	174

TABLE 6.9-- HOUSING UNITS, BY TYPE, PERSONS IN HOUSEHOLDS, AND MEDIAN VALUE AND RENT OF SPECIFIED OCCUPIED HOUSING UNITS, INCORPORATED AND CENSUS DESIGNATED PLACES, 1990 (Continued)

Place	Persons in households	Persons per household	Single-family	2 to 9 units	10 or more units	Mobile home or trailer and other	Median value of owner-occupied units [2]	Median rent of renter-occupied units [3]
				Type of structure [1]				
				Multifamily				
Cumberland City	319	2.44	114	21	4	18	32,900	100 [a]
Cumberland Gap	210	2.31	73	19	0	12	38,800	242
Dandridge	1,294	2.32	463	82	13	67	49,200	188
Dayton	5,235	2.46	1,597	531	49	129	49,400	191
Decatur	1,256	2.49	348	91	16	95	46,000	162
Decaturville	857	2.53	301	37	1	46	34,200	163
Dechard	2,193	2.59	751	128	11	23	39,000	216
Dickson	8,479	2.41	2,469	816	342	191	57,600	262
Dover	1,246	2.21	468	57	50	32	51,600	130
Dowelltown	308	2.18	127	14	0	10	29,300	117
Doyle	338	2.43	114	0	0	35	24,300	141
Dresden	2,392	2.32	805	219	3	75	40,200	177
Ducktown	421	2.08	162	21	13	18	30,600	171
Dunlap	3,646	2.57	1,067	120	36	278	38,300	180
Dyer	2,204	2.39	874	92	0	16	34,500	176
Dyersburg	15,814	2.36	4,790	1,589	420	242	44,700	217
Eagleton Village CDP	5,169	2.38	1,865	215	62	139	46,600	246
Eagleville	462	2.54	176	7	0	11	55,900	241
East Brainerd CDP	11,410	3.10	3,623	95	1	91	91,300	348
East Cleveland CDP	1,249	2.63	361	54	12	93	27,700	186
East Ridge	20,958	2.30	6,554	1,775	1,208	94	55,200	339
Eastview	563	2.31	227	1	1	38	41,900	175
Elizabethton	11,362	2.30	3,746	881	308	256	43,300	174
Elkton	448	2.72	143	2	0	39	42,200	188
Englewood	1,611	2.41	542	72	8	97	32,500	166
Enville	211	2.24	98	0	0	10	22,800	117
Erin	1,423	2.32	461	91	44	72	32,100	128

TABLE 6.9— HOUSING UNITS, BY TYPE, PERSONS IN HOUSEHOLDS, AND MEDIAN VALUE AND RENT OF SPECIFIED OCCUPIED HOUSING UNITS, INCORPORATED AND CENSUS DESIGNATED PLACES, 1990 (Continued)

| Place | Persons in households | Persons per household | Type of structure [1] | | | | Median value of owner-occupied units [2] | Median rent of renter-occupied units [3] |
| | | | Single-family | Multifamily | | Mobile home or trailer and other | | |
				2 to 9 units	10 or more units			
Erwin	4,920	2.29	1,748	289	106	116	47,900	183
Estill Springs	1,408	2.46	466	25	1	113	52,600	260
Ethridge	565	2.58	195	4	0	37	35,800	178
Etowah	3,651	2.30	1,341	298	16	82	37,400	188
Fairfield Glade CDP	2,209	2.04	1,304	63	19	180	95,200	422
Fairmount CDP	1,578	2.92	529	56	0	20	82,800	333
Fairview	4,210	2.98	1,236	43	30	170	64,000	258
Fall Branch CDP	1,203	2.51	387	15	0	107	50,600	190
Farragut	12,688	2.98	4,199	80	1	176	127,900	458
Fayetteville	6,747	2.24	2,231	769	197	80	44,600	172
Finger	279	2.58	105	0	0	15	31,900	142
Forest Hills	4,231	2.73	1,577	17	1	2	231,400	588
Franklin	19,693	2.52	4,828	1,893	1,567	460	95,900	413
Friendship	459	2.32	177	13	0	20	30,000	140
Friendsville	792	2.63	292	1	0	44	46,900	253
Gadsden	561	2.89	199	3	0	12	33,800	175
Gainesboro	989	2.15	359	89	13	34	40,300	106
Gallatin	18,242	2.60	5,248	1,282	504	601	61,900	306
Gallaway	632	3.19	105	76	3	27	43,900	152
Garland	194	2.55	73	0	0	6	52,500	325
Gates	608	2.76	206	10	3	22	32,700	207
Gatlinburg	3,357	2.26	1,970	316	496	141	88,700	307
Germantown	32,893	3.07	10,266	598	237	30	145,100	530
Gibson	281	2.53	97	5	0	11	38,600	170
Gilt Edge	447	2.68	145	0	0	35	56,300	192
Gleason	1,402	2.55	491	45	0	47	31,500	144

TABLE 6.9— HOUSING UNITS, BY TYPE, PERSONS IN HOUSEHOLDS, AND MEDIAN VALUE AND RENT OF SPECIFIED OCCUPIED HOUSING UNITS, INCORPORATED AND CENSUS DESIGNATED PLACES, 1990 (Continued)

Place	Persons in households	Persons per household	Type of structure [1]				Median value of owner-occupied units [2]	Median rent of renter-occupied units [3]
			Single-family	Multifamily		Mobile home or trailer and other		
				2 to 9 units	10 or more units			
Goodlettsville	11,135	2.53	3,174	560	848	179	82,800	404
Gordonsville	891	2.57	303	13	1	55	52,100	198
Grand Junction	365	2.28	159	10	0	15	42,900	138
Gray CDP	1,071	2.48	285	41	3	115	61,000	230
Graysville	1,301	2.69	333	5	0	194	36,900	220
Greenback	611	2.65	215	0	0	35	51,800	192
Greenbrier	2,873	2.73	896	76	66	73	57,800	318
Greeneville	12,850	2.30	4,419	1,064	333	242	47,700	203
Greenfield	2,098	2.35	833	81	6	29	32,600	155
Green Hill CDP	6,763	3.04	2,260	70	10	29	92,000	481
Gruetli-Laager	1,810	2.81	497	8	0	175	30,700	164
Guys	497	2.72	142	2	0	50	36,500	138
Halls CDP	6,450	2.61	2,247	79	118	95	74,400	205
Halls	2,431	2.49	856	133	4	60	36,500	174
Harriman	6,940	2.37	2,310	539	213	172	36,300	168
Harrison CDP	7,191	2.78	2,194	265	162	88	71,700	303
Harrogate-Shawnee CDP	2,490	2.62	811	74	1	149	49,900	248
Hartsville	2,063	2.35	660	138	88	78	38,300	188
Henderson	3,732	2.49	1,266	214	67	53	39,900	162
Hendersonville	31,728	2.77	9,372	1,459	1,401	240	86,300	399
Henning	802	2.77	215	49	2	50	35,700	109
Henry	317	2.71	94	0	0	38	30,300	173
Hickory Valley	159	2.41	60	3	0	6	40,000	113
Hohenwald	3,611	2.35	1,226	202	8	249	36,100	164
Hollow Rock	902	2.53	286	6	0	105	30,200	159
Hopewell CDP	2,565	2.60	713	271	0	32	59,900	282
Hornbeak	445	2.65	157	0	1	27	34,300	145

TABLE 6.9— HOUSING UNITS, BY TYPE, PERSONS IN HOUSEHOLDS, AND MEDIAN VALUE AND RENT OF SPECIFIED OCCUPIED HOUSING UNITS, INCORPORATED AND CENSUS DESIGNATED PLACES, 1990 (Continued)

Place	Persons in households	Persons per household	Single-family	Multifamily 2 to 9 units	Multifamily 10 or more units	Mobile home or trailer and other	Median value of owner-occupied units [2]	Median rent of renter-occupied units [3]
Homsby	313	2.61	111	0	0	17	28,900	138
Humboldt	9,464	2.50	3,081	469	111	339	38,900	181
Hunter CDP	1,250	2.40	395	37	1	114	44,800	219
Huntingdon	3,980	2.39	1,457	211	7	115	40,400	179
Huntland	885	2.56	325	7	0	35	37,300	186
Huntsville	546	2.54	153	51	0	36	38,600	154
Iron City	402	2.68	142	0	0	19	20,700	115
Jacksboro	1,537	2.54	448	80	49	73	54,700	224
Jackson	46,631	2.43	13,893	5,025	1,389	432	50,600	240
Jamestown	1,752	2.23	563	200	19	122	31,400	134
Jasper	2,751	2.49	924	104	56	115	50,000	220
Jefferson City	4,208	2.23	1,209	445	204	148	43,300	200
Jellico	2,447	2.37	659	106	141	198	35,500	131
Johnson City	45,325	2.30	13,072	4,498	2,439	1,232	60,000	245
Jonesborough	2,914	2.46	923	179	91	69	55,500	226
Karns CDP	1,458	2.56	511	23	0	49	70,100	351
Kenton	1,366	2.41	456	107	4	39	35,400	147
Kimball	1,243	2.64	315	10	4	178	53,400	270
Kingsport	35,682	2.28	11,517	2,569	2,109	547	55,400	231
Kingston	4,479	2.31	1,570	220	165	116	49,600	249
Kingston Springs	1,480	2.97	412	3	0	104	94,100	317
Knoxville	154,089	2.20	44,335	13,982	16,734	1,402	49,800	261
Lafayette	3,567	2.25	1,260	252	52	131	38,400	182
LaFollette	7,095	2.42	2,162	542	167	245	33,000	180[a]
LaGrange	167	2.65	71	6	0	1	81,300	100[a]
Lake City	2,045	2.39	552	223	32	105	36,600	171
Lakeland	1,199	2.64	333	1	0	141	164,000	267

TABLE 6.9— HOUSING UNITS, BY TYPE, PERSONS IN HOUSEHOLDS, AND MEDIAN VALUE AND RENT OF SPECIFIED OCCUPIED HOUSING UNITS, INCORPORATED AND CENSUS DESIGNATED PLACES, 1990 (Continued)

| Place | Persons in households | Persons per household | Type of structure[1] | | | | Median value of owner-occupied units[2] | Median rent of renter-occupied units[3] |
| | | | Single-family | Multifamily | | Mobile home or trailer and other | | |
				2 to 9 units	10 or more units			
Lakesite	732	2.88	246	31	18	7	79,000	315
Lakewood	2,009	2.51	652	63	57	81	64,500	313
LaVergne	7,475	2.90	1,982	107	57	664	65,200	312
Lawrenceburg	10,249	2.32	3,500	875	128	208	45,600	184
Lebanon	14,713	2.49	4,444	1,533	391	224	67,300	301
Lenoir City	6,147	2.39	1,877	323	182	352	39,200	177
Lewisburg	9,621	2.40	3,016	688	351	220	47,200	229
Lexington	5,598	2.32	1,802	438	21	351	44,500	173
Liberty	391	2.61	128	11	0	21	31,800	157
Linden	1,018	2.30	355	56	6	87	38,000	188
Livingston	3,608	2.32	1,138	236	82	223	40,600	150
Lobelville	830	2.39	274	37	4	72	36,200	113
Lookout Mountain	1,901	2.46	744	50	20	4	198,300	393
Loretto	1,515	2.56	548	33	0	39	40,900	182
Loudon	4,026	2.35	1,462	194	62	114	41,700	180
Luttrell	812	2.92	217	5	0	81	34,200	161
Lynchburg	4,714	2.72	1,549	43	1	319	50,400	214
Lynnville	344	2.42	138	2	0	14	41,300	144
McEwen	1,442	2.40	474	50	6	102	39,700	167
McKenzie	4,892	2.45	1,644	345	1	168	37,100	175
McLemoresville	280	2.31	122	1	0	17	29,600	155
McMinnville	10,833	2.29	3,497	1,166	338	122	41,100	203
Madisonville	2,953	2.35	990	159	25	170	41,400	197
Manchester	7,449	2.44	2,414	412	224	280	51,200	250
Martin	6,530	2.22	1,889	720	344	151	46,500	200
Maryville	18,140	2.35	5,896	1,418	723	243	64,900	230

TABLE 6.9-- HOUSING UNITS, BY TYPE, PERSONS IN HOUSEHOLDS, AND MEDIAN VALUE AND RENT OF SPECIFIED OCCUPIED HOUSING UNITS, INCORPORATED AND CENSUS DESIGNATED PLACES, 1990 (Continued)

Place	Persons in households	Persons per household	Type of structure[1] Single-family	Multifamily 2 to 9 units	Multifamily 10 or more units	Mobile home or trailer and other	Median value of owner-occupied units[2]	Median rent of renter-occupied units[3]
Mascot CDP	2,138	2.61	629	16	0	232	40,400	209
Mason	337	2.67	116	0	0	19	33,800	100[4]
Maury City	782	2.66	272	3	0	36	31,200	146
Maynardville	1,217	2.43	262	125	38	119	50,900	195
Medina	658	2.14	293	12	0	27	37,100	201
Medon	137	2.40	49	0	0	10	38,800	140
Memphis	594,322	2.59	157,760	48,962	37,138	4,713	55,700	282
Michie	677	2.51	225	9	0	60	38,100	163
Middleton	536	2.36	212	5	16	14	43,200	189
Middle Valley CDP	12,255	2.98	3,883	187	0	227	68,300	348
Midway CDP	2,953	2.59	836	98	49	209	54,700	214
Milan	7,319	2.37	2,543	623	34	100	43,700	204
Milledgeville	279	2.20	117	3	0	24	32,000	150
Millersville	2,575	2.66	536	54	3	451	62,900	357
Millington	12,225	2.93	2,667	1,001	286	486	64,700	307
Minor Hill	372	2.40	163	2	0	14	34,500	200
Mitchellville	193	2.61	64	5	0	12	37,000	269
Monteagle	985	2.41	327	53	2	62	42,100	192
Monterey	2,446	2.42	749	184	9	171	36,000	181
Morrison	564	2.52	193	36	1	21	38,900	192
Morristown	20,660	2.37	6,134	1,981	614	519	43,500	206
Moscow	384	2.36	125	43	0	16	40,000	155
Mosheim	1,451	2.57	462	22	23	79	43,000	204
Mountain City	2,141	2.24	692	198	67	93	47,600	127
Mount Carmel	4,082	2.61	1,432	49	0	149	53,800	224
Mount Juliet	5,389	2.94	1,542	30	2	352	104,700	364
Mount Pleasant	4,222	2.48	1,382	311	70	116	45,600	207

TABLE 6.9-- HOUSING UNITS, BY TYPE, PERSONS IN HOUSEHOLDS, AND MEDIAN VALUE AND RENT OF SPECIFIED OCCUPIED HOUSING UNITS, INCORPORATED AND CENSUS DESIGNATED PLACES, 1990 (Continued)

Place	Persons in households	Persons per household	Single-family	Type of structure[1] Multifamily 2 to 9 units	Type of structure[1] Multifamily 10 or more units	Mobile home or trailer and other	Median value of owner-occupied units[2]	Median rent of renter-occupied units[3]
Munford	2,326	2.73	719	76	41	76	61,600	224
Murfreesboro	40,685	2.38	10,038	4,505	3,448	717	78,200	326
Nashville-Davidson	467,419	2.35	121,860	40,035	51,992	5,641	74,400	358
Newbern	2,515	2.49	769	240	9	40	43,100	173
New Hope	854	2.75	235	1	0	111	47,000	197
New Johnsonville	1,643	2.78	549	14	18	99	44,700	276
New Market	1,086	2.78	362	3	0	47	49,700	189
Newport	6,972	2.35	2,084	543	172	372	41,200	146
New Tazewell	1,730	2.38	484	154	22	125	45,400	147
Niota	745	2.37	254	39	3	48	33,900	210
Nolensville CDP	1,570	3.04	488	4	0	45	99,000	425
Normandy	118	2.81	36	0	0	9	31,700	313
Norris	1,303	2.24	523	59	36	4	59,300	246
Oakdale	268	2.76	93	9	1	8	17,100	159
Oak Grove CDP	3,375	2.50	920	283	69	184	60,800	289
Oak Hill	4,301	2.49	1,691	89	0	8	166,100	488
Oakland	392	3.02	121	0	0	13	48,400	238
Oak Ridge	27,066	2.30	8,967	2,078	1,587	62	64,100	307
Obion	1,241	2.47	430	52	7	47	30,800	135
Oliver Springs	3,433	2.62	1,145	120	26	94	46,100	213
Oneida	3,447	2.42	1,020	269	44	173	41,900	158
Ooltewah CDP	4,755	2.75	1,280	61	2	504	69,300	247
Orlinda	469	2.55	185	0	0	15	46,400	225
Orme	150	3.13	33	0	0	19	20,000	200
Palmer	769	2.71	228	2	0	68	21,700	167
Paris	9,127	2.17	3,263	799	135	341	40,400	167
Parker's Crossroads	159	2.48	43	0	1	25	53,000	163

TABLE 6.9– HOUSING UNITS, BY TYPE, PERSONS IN HOUSEHOLDS, AND MEDIAN VALUE AND RENT OF SPECIFIED OCCUPIED HOUSING UNITS, INCORPORATED AND CENSUS DESIGNATED PLACES, 1990 (Continued)

Place	Persons in households	Persons per household	Single-family	Type of structure[1] Multifamily 2 to 9 units	10 or more units	Mobile home or trailer and other	Median value of owner-occupied units[2]	Median rent of renter-occupied units[3]
Parrotsville	121	2.88	35	2	0	7	36,700	163
Parsons	1,915	2.29	714	67	1	146	36,300	158
Pegram	1,328	2.74	457	18	0	60	76,400	299
Petersburg	514	2.41	191	21	0	25	26,800	170
Philadelphia	463	2.50	165	3	0	28	35,800	200
Pigeon Forge	2,914	2.44	956	133	47	235	66,600	308
Pikeville	1,706	2.37	536	97	66	103	39,400	144
Pine Crest CDP	3,318	2.31	833	321	141	251	54,500	278
Piperton	612	2.62	232	2	0	11	99,500	113
Pittman Center	475	2.31	231	20	12	28	80,000	281
Pleasant Hill	391	1.94	145	68	1	14	48,300	205
Portland	5,165	2.65	1,588	241	53	219	49,600	275
Powell CDP	7,533	2.58	2,185	126	220	492	74,900	210
Powell's Crossroads	1,098	2.88	363	2	0	30	43,000	204
Pulaski	7,582	2.30	2,200	906	185	254	46,600	196
Puryear	573	2.32	226	12	0	30	35,800	160
Ramer	337	2.63	118	0	0	24	34,400	146
Red Bank	12,322	2.20	3,612	1,402	1,156	92	54,400	289
Red Boiling Springs	905	2.44	330	32	9	49	29,600	143
Ridgely	1,775	2.50	477	146	5	95	35,000	126
Ridgeside	400	2.52	158	3	0	1	127,100	342
Ridgetop	1,086	2.90	359	14	0	16	74,200	335
Ripley	5,875	2.57	1,613	697	54	126	42,200	185
Rives	344	2.73	109	0	0	32	22,800	196
Roan Mountain CDP	1,220	2.56	316	30	2	160	41,800	159
Rockford	646	2.62	236	3	0	17	67,300	100[4]

TABLE 6.9-- HOUSING UNITS, BY TYPE, PERSONS IN HOUSEHOLDS, AND MEDIAN VALUE AND RENT OF SPECIFIED OCCUPIED HOUSING UNITS, INCORPORATED AND CENSUS DESIGNATED PLACES, 1990 (Continued)

Place	Persons in households	Persons per household	Type of structure[1]				Median value of owner-occupied units[2]	Median rent of renter-occupied units[3]
			Single-family	Multifamily		Mobile home or trailer and other		
				2 to 9 units	10 or more units			
Rockwood	5,153	2.37	1,693	196	196	241	33,700	142
Rogersville	3,972	2.14	1,354	401	134	106	45,100	195
Rossville	291	2.77	97	1	0	13	66,300	100[4]
Rural Hill CDP	1,329	2.95	451	4	0	19	108,900	340
Rutherford	1,303	2.35	501	54	0	35	33,100	155
Rutledge	757	2.21	237	70	17	54	40,000	144
St. Joseph	789	2.58	277	7	0	47	35,300	143
Saltillo	383	2.38	150	0	0	59	23,300	105
Samburg	374	2.51	125	14	0	42	25,000	158
Sardis	305	2.29	129	0	0	15	31,400	125
Saulsbury	106	2.41	47	0	0	7	23,200	150
Savannah	6,332	2.43	2,259	300	83	154	39,900	165
Scotts Hill	594	2.31	232	4	0	48	34,000	146
Selmer	3,737	2.29	1,341	193	62	184	38,700	160
Sevierville	6,978	2.34	1,964	756	217	384	62,400	253
Sewanee CDP	1,173	2.29	460	67	2	19	71,900	333
Seymour CDP	6,949	2.73	2,240	150	9	263	65,200	270
Sharon	1,042	2.28	399	71	0	23	35,000	187
Shelbyville	13,702	2.41	4,434	868	278	583	46,400	228
Signal Mountain	6,921	2.67	2,337	163	197	21	120,600	537
Silerton	59	1.90	28	0	0	9	26,000	175
Slayden	111	2.52	40	0	0	9	29,200	117
Smithville	3,685	2.32	1,266	265	76	86	44,000	192
Smyrna	13,442	2.78	3,176	1,293	440	403	71,600	359
Sneedville	1,278	2.49	354	113	11	73	35,800	100[4]
Soddy-Daisy	8,240	2.58	2,425	216	4	711	48,500	254
Somerville	1,987	2.30	603	146	125	37	49,600	119

TABLE 6.9— HOUSING UNITS, BY TYPE, PERSONS IN HOUSEHOLDS, AND MEDIAN VALUE AND RENT OF SPECIFIED OCCUPIED HOUSING UNITS, INCORPORATED AND CENSUS DESIGNATED PLACES, 1990 (Continued)

| Place | Persons in households | Persons per household | Type of structure[1] | | | | Median value of owner-occupied units [2] | Median rent of renter-occupied units [3] |
| | | | Single-family | Multifamily | | Mobile home or trailer and other | | |
				2 to 9 units	10 or more units			
South Carthage	851	2.48	273	67	8	28	46,200	164
South Cleveland CDP	5,372	2.80	1,619	82	99	236	46,300	256
South Fulton	2,678	2.39	983	128	14	57	36,800	187
South Pitsburg	3,129	2.38	992	230	95	127	43,800	161
Sparta	4,499	2.37	1,571	324	79	60	39,400	180
Spencer	1,125	2.62	372	21	0	73	32,700	123
Spring City	2,068	2.39	777	81	15	94	41,400	212
Springfield	10,846	2.56	3,210	804	248	268	53,300	215
Spring Hill	1,410	2.74	472	46	20	42	60,600	282
Spurgeon CDP	3,149	2.59	911	169	56	130	58,500	267
Stanton	487	2.59	132	42	16	20	40,000	100[4]
Stantonville	264	2.36	104	1	0	26	36,000	114
Surgoinsville	1,499	2.59	509	15	14	87	45,400	161
Sweetwater	4,928	2.44	1,689	265	44	170	40,300	178
Tazewell	2,065	2.40	676	106	58	79	41,700	181
Tellico Plains	657	2.38	231	25	1	71	32,700	154
Tennessee Ridge	1,258	2.68	432	7	0	60	38,600	192
Tiptonville	1,960	2.43	675	117	12	40	35,600	114
Toone	261	2.69	81	2	0	19	31,300	195
Townsend	329	2.19	156	2	0	41	79,800	221
Tracy City	1,556	2.51	527	22	3	115	32,300	162
Trenton	4,535	2.32	1,501	468	122	59	40,200	156
Trezevant	874	2.33	353	1	0	42	28,700	169
Trimble	694	2.48	233	16	0	51	33,400	173
Troy	1,047	2.40	352	45	15	42	36,500	199
Tullahoma	16,563	2.51	5,184	1,166	290	479	55,800	230
Tusculum	1,215	2.43	419	21	16	70	58,600	227

TABLE 6.9.– HOUSING UNITS, BY TYPE, PERSONS IN HOUSEHOLDS, AND MEDIAN VALUE AND RENT OF SPECIFIED OCCUPIED HOUSING UNITS, INCORPORATED AND CENSUS DESIGNATED PLACES, 1990 (Continued)

Place	Persons in households	Persons per household	Single-family	Multifamily 2 to 9 units	Multifamily 10 or more units	Mobile home or trailer and other	Median value of owner-occupied units [2]	Median rent of renter-occupied units [3]
Union City	10,275	2.39	3,101	1,177	144	187	48,800	216
Vanleer	355	2.55	118	9	0	26	40,400	185
Viola	123	2.56	45	2	0	8	37,500	167
Vonore	605	2.44	214	2	0	56	41,800	197
Walden	1,523	2.69	556	27	0	15	136,500	327
Walnut Hill CDP	3,332	2.68	1,047	54	1	189	63,900	236
Walterhill CDP	1,043	3.01	324	5	0	49	71,600	308
Wartburg	793	2.32	225	106	14	30	46,900	145
Wartrace	494	2.45	182	12	1	32	40,100	200
Watauga	389	2.63	99	0	0	62	44,700	219
Watertown	1,250	2.45	471	39	0	56	38,100	237
Waverly	3,887	2.37	1,356	269	49	113	45,800	193
Waynesboro	1,651	2.28	635	51	0	89	35,600	180
Westmoreland	1,726	2.58	512	79	14	104	37,900	188
White Bluff	1,988	2.61	602	125	4	120	49,800	241
White House	2,987	2.90	952	126	3	41	61,900	301
White Pine	1,771	2.45	532	83	15	138	41,600	174
Whiteville	1,050	2.54	357	34	4	49	36,000	181
Whitwell	1,602	2.52	538	20	20	111	34,900	179
Wildwood Lake CDP	2,680	2.71	761	58	0	214	49,500	245
Williston	427	3.03	128	1	0	22	42,500	217
Winchester	6,024	2.44	2,004	451	49	121	46,000	200
Winfield	564	2.74	154	2	0	70	36,000	163

TABLE 6.9-- HOUSING UNITS, BY TYPE, PERSONS IN HOUSEHOLDS, AND MEDIAN VALUE AND RENT OF SPECIFIED OCCUPIED HOUSING UNITS, INCORPORATED AND CENSUS DESIGNATED PLACES, 1990 (Continued)

Place	Persons in households	Persons per household	Type of structure[1]				Median value of owner-occupied units [2]	Median rent of renter-occupied units [3]
			Single-family	Multifamily		Mobile home or trailer and other		
				2 to 9 units	10 or more units			
Woodbury	2,188	2.31	753	160	80	41	39,300	176
Woodland Mills	398	2.57	158	3	0	0	53,800	175
Yorkville	347	2.59	122	1	0	14	36,500	158

1. Includes vacant-for-sale and vacant-for-rent housing units.
2. Value data are limited to owner-occupied one-family houses on less than ten acres, without a commercial establishment or medical office on the property. Mobile homes, boats, trailers, and owner-occupied noncondominium units in multifamily buildings are excluded.
3. Contract rent data are tabulated for specified renter-occupied housing units paying cash rent, and exclude one-family houses on ten acres or more.
a. The median value falls within the lower interval of an open-ended distribution. The median is shown as the upper value of the category.
Source: U.S. Department of Commerce, Bureau of the Census, 1990 Census of Population and Housing, Summary Population and Housing Characteristics, Tennessee.

TABLE 6.10--NUMBER OF NEW PRIVATELY OWNED HOUSING UNITS AUTHORIZED BY BUILDING PERMITS, SELECTED CITIES, TENNESSEE, 1968–1993

Year	Chattanooga	Clarksville	Jackson	Johnson City	Kingsport	Knoxville	Memphis[1]	Nashville-Davidson County[2]	Oak Ridge
1993	517	1,373	164	495	259	762	7,391	2,311	140
1992	452	1,019	135	297	252	487	6,331	1,914	126
1991	380	899	154	294	152	346	5,100	1,479	81
1990	305	623	114	214	154	452	5,806	1,597	135
1989	527	921	111	241	149	635	8,142	1,863	147
1988	750	886	101	255	166	528	7,670	3,772	156
1987	1,228	971	263	192	136	945	7,669	3,507	111
1986	1,327	917	412	253	172	418	8,388	8,127	40
1985	1,910	769	351	170	110	510	10,001	10,095	177
1984	581	717	285	139	592	179	8,812	12,334	70
1983	995	914	351	222	191	484	932	6,698	169
1982	423	741	109	294	198	1,048	432	2,284	178
1981	297	157	214	97	98	646	564	1,333	136
1980	1,064	553	344	210	393	1,149	1,324	1,892	116
1979	632	494	416	219	250	1,024	1,367	3,253	122
1978	434ᵃ	565	497	245	316	1,957	1,565	3,532	137
1977	893	641	315	295	82	929	2,381	4,928	244
1976	1,140	876	128	101	94	928	577	3,385	158
1975	628	417	127	118	72	373	1,000	1,900	132
1974	711	400ᵃ	266	285	159	509	869	4,425	120
1973	1,878	1,211	246	247	840	2,796	6,609	6,001	331
1972	940	1,042	257	307	260	2,730	9,159	8,165	88
1971	878	483	632	186	163	2,313	6,826	6,819	110
1970	916	208	522	124ᵃ	178ᵃ	993	4,260	3,655	92
1969	355	127	294	304	99	1,071	3,641	4,826	206
1968	749	268	277	281	266	2,120	4,047	6,023	156

1. Beginning in 1984 data are no longer available separately for Memphis city. Number of permits shown is for the entire Memphis MSA; therefore, data are not comparable to earlier years.

2. Permit system covers entire unincorporated area of the county and Nashville city.

a. Data shown are for 11 months.

Source: U.S. Department of Commerce, Bureau of the Census, *Current Construction Reports, Housing Units Authorized by Building Permits: Annual 1993*, and earlier editions.

TABLE 6.11--VALUATION OF CONSTRUCTION AUTHORIZED BY PERMIT, BY TYPE OF CONSTRUCTION, SOUTHEASTERN STATES, 1992 [In millions of dollars]

State	Total [1]	Residential	Nonresidential Total [2]	Nonresidential Industrial	Nonresidential Office	Nonresidential Stores
TENNESSEE	3,916	2,020	835	106	150	205
Alabama	1,965	865	522	117	120	157
Arkansas	1,051	504	303	64	36	128
Florida	13,615	8,563	2,124	144	287	790
Georgia	5,854	3,559	1,117	227	121	439
Kentucky	1,858	1,017	361	78	55	116
Louisiana	1,366	701	304	31	39	103
Mississippi	692	348	160	19	16	79
North Carolina	6,317	3,849	1,091	180	182	274
South Carolina	2,724	1,469	569	51	101	199
Virginia	5,453	3,130	855	76	258	280
West Virginia	371	147	93	6	9	42

1. Includes residential and nonresidential additions and alterations, residential nonhousekeeping buildings, and residential garages and carports, not shown separately.
2. Includes other types of construction not shown separately.
Source: U.S. Department of Commerce, Bureau of the Census, *Statistical Abstract of the United States, 1993.*

TABLE 6.12--EXISTING HOME SALES, SOUTHEASTERN STATES, 1985–1992 [In thousands]

State	1992	1991	1990	1989	1988	1987	1986	1985
TENNESSEE	102.2	92.0	92.7	95.2	93.9	111.2	112.0	89.3
Alabama	72.5	64.0	61.1	59.4	61.5	59.7	60.8	54.8
Arkansas	47.8	43.4	44.8	47.5	47.5	48.2	52.8	49.9
Florida	179.2	176.0	183.3	177.6	179.2	184.2	169.4	142.7
Georgia	n.a.	70.7	73.2	73.6	78.2	89.0	75.1	58.7
Kentucky	78.7	67.8	66.4	62.2	60.9	64.1	58.6	51.8
Louisiana	47.0	47.1	41.6	40.8	39.8	40.4	34.0	36.4
Mississippi	39.2	35.2	34.7	36.5	36.6	34.2	34.2	34.7
North Carolina	160.2	139.9	135.9	127.5	134.7	140.6	139.2	107.9
South Carolina	58.9	53.9	57.8	52.2	55.0	60.9	58.0	48.4
Virginia	101.3	90.3	96.9	116.0	130.7	113.0	130.4	116.0
West Virginia	46.8	43.3	42.0	36.8	36.4	36.6	39.7	31.1

n.a. not available.
Source: National Association of Realtors, *Existing Home Sales*, monthly, as printed in the U.S. Department of

TABLE 6.13--HOUSING PRICE INDEX AND MEDIAN AND AVERAGE SALES PRICES OF NEW
ONE-FAMILY HOMES IN THE SOUTH, 1963-1993

Year	Median sales price	Average sales price	Housing price index (1987 = 100)
1993	115,000	133,600	114.3
1992	105,500	126,900	108.5
1991	100,000	123,000	107.4
1990	99,000	123,500	105.4
1989	96,400	123,100	105.2
1988	92,000	114,800	102.3
1987	88,000	106,600	100.0
1986	80,200	95,300	96.6
1985	75,000	88,900	93.8
1984	72,000	86,000	91.9
1983	70,900	83,000	89.0
1982	66,100	78,300	86.6
1981	64,400	75,600	83.9
1980	59,600	69,100	77.2
1979	57,300	63,800	69.2
1978	50,300	55,600	60.1
1977	44,100	48,100	54.0
1976	40,500	43,800	n.a.
1975	37,300	39,600	n.a.
1974	34,500	36,800	n.a.
1973	30,900	33,200	n.a.
1972	25,800	28,500	n.a.
1971	22,500	25,900	n.a.
1970	20,300	24,000	n.a.
1969	22,800	25,300	n.a.
1968	21,500	23,600	n.a.
1967	19,400	21,100	n.a.
1966	18,200	20,200	n.a.
1965	17,500	18,900	n.a.
1964	16,700	18,100	n.a.
1963	16,100	16,800	n.a.

Note: Median and average sales prices are collected from a sample of all new one-family house sales and include
the value of land. The price index presented here is intended to reflect the changing cost of a typical house sold
in the base weighting period of 1982 and is calculated from a sample of houses with similar characteristics with
respect to lot size, square footage, presence of a garage, and seven other characteristics.

n.a. not available.

Source: U.S. Department of Commerce and U.S. Department of Housing and Urban Development, *Current
Construction Reports, New One-Family Houses Sold*, March 1994; and U.S. Department of Commerce, Bureau
of Industrial Economics, Construction and Building Products Division, *Construction Review*, Vol. 29, No. 4.

TABLE 6.14—NUMBER AND AVERAGE SALES PRICE OF NEW MOBILE HOMES PLACED FOR RESIDENTIAL USE, SOUTHEASTERN STATES, 1992 AND 1993
[Number in thousands]

State	1993						1992					
	Total[1]		Single-wide		Double-wide		Total[1]		Single-wide		Double-wide	
	Number	Price	Number	Price	Number	Price	Number	Price	Number	Price	Number	Price
TENNESSEE	12.0	$24,900	7.9	$19,500	4.0	$34,400	10.8	$22,700	7.7	$18,200	3.1	$33,100
Alabama	11.1	25,200	7.4	19,900	3.6	34,900	9.7	23,300	6.7	18,700	3.0	33,100
Arkansas	5.1	26,000	3.6	21,300	1.5	37,000	3.5	24,600	2.2	19,600	1.3	32,700
Florida	17.7	31,200	5.6	17,700	11.6	36,700	19.9	27,300	8.7	16,800	11.0	33,900
Georgia	12.9	26,200	6.3	18,700	6.4	33,000	10.6	24,100	4.6	17,300	5.8	28,700
Kentucky	7.8	25,800	5.2	19,700	2.6	37,400	8.0	22,300	5.8	18,100	2.3	32,900
Louisiana	4.7	25,200	4.0	22,500	0.7	40,400	3.2	23,300	2.7	21,100	0.5	35,600
Mississippi	6.0	23,700	4.5	19,400	1.5	36,200	4.9	22,000	3.7	19,300	1.2	30,200
North Carolina	24.3	27,600	14.3	20,200	9.8	38,100	20.5	26,200	12.0	19,600	8.3	35,100
South Carolina	13.8	27,900	7.1	20,600	6.5	35,500	11.4	25,000	6.5	18,600	4.8	33,400
Virginia	6.1	28,900	3.5	19,900	2.6	40,400	5.5	27,900	3.3	19,900	2.2	39,200
West Virginia	4.6	27,300	2.9	21,200	1.7	37,400	3.8	26,100	2.2	19,300	1.5	35,700

Note: Detail may not add to total due to rounding.
1. Includes mobile homes with more than two sections.
Source: U.S. Department of Commerce, Bureau of the Census, *Construction Reports, Housing Starts, May 1994.*

The historical order of appearance of the economic censuses is an indicator of increasing diversity in the American economy. The first population census was conducted in 1790, and the first official measures of the economy appeared with the *Census of Manufacturing* in 1810, no doubt as a result of the belief that an independent nation must develop its own manufactures. The *Census of Agriculture* did not appear until 1840. For nearly a century, these two sources were the only measures of the U.S. economy. The first *Census of Business*, covering only retail and wholesale concerns, was not taken until 1929. Then, in 1933, a few service activities were added. As trade and services have come to account for an increasing share of the economy, the data collected have been more detailed, and in 1972 the *Census of Business* was replaced by three separate reports: *The Census of Retail Trade, The Census of Wholesale Trade*, and the *Census of Selected Service Industries*. The reports on *Minority-Owned Business Enterprises* and *Women-Owned Businesses* are other recent additions to the business censuses. Also, data on business starts and business failures, collected and published by Dun and Bradstreet Corporation, are included in this chapter.

Zip code area data are available from the Censuses of Retail Trade and Selected Service Industries for 1982 and 1987. These data are not published in the print medium, but can be obtained on compact disc read-only memory (CD-ROM) or from a local State Data Center (SDC). A list of SDC affiliates is detailed in the front of this *Abstract*.

The *Census of Retail Trade* includes all establishments primarily engaged in selling for personal or household consumption, including liquor stores operated by governments and post exchanges and other military retail operations of the federal government. Data by type of retail establishment are available by county, place and Zip code area where detail does not disclose the operation of an individual business. The *Census of Wholesale Trade* covers establishments primarily engaged in selling goods to dealers and distributors for resale or to purchasers, for business and farm uses. Since wholesale establishments are fewer in number, data are not broken down by category; yet data are more frequently suppressed to avoid disclosure. The *Census of Service Industries* covers a wide variety of establishments providing selected personal and business services.

The 1987 Standard Industrial Classification (SIC) was used to categorize data in this edition of the *Abstract*. Figure 7.2 is the only exception because it provides a comparison of 1987 data with 1982 data. Classifications in the 1982 Census were based on 1972 SIC. Also, 1982 data were revised to show the number of establishments in business during 1982. This revision provides a comparable count of firms for 1982 and 1987. In censuses prior to 1987, the count of establishments had been restricted to those in business at the end of the year.

TABLE OF CONTENTS

TABLE 7.1– MONTHLY RETAIL SALES, TENNESSEE, 1978–1992 [In millions of dollars]

Year	January	February	March	April	May	June	July	August	September	October	November	December	Annual
1992	2,654	2,757	2,945	3,011	3,177	3,110	3,230	3,263	3,158	3,395	3,428	4,012	38,140
1991ʳ	2,304	2,369	2,772	2,723	3,020	2,853	2,883	3,017	2,696	2,892	2,936	3,358	33,823
1990ʳ	2,374	2,347	2,691	2,597	2,824	2,756	2,752	2,924	2,648	2,740	2,825	3,169	32,647
1989ʳ	2,132	2,087	2,511	2,488	2,651	2,567	2,590	2,783	2,557	2,532	2,655	3,076	30,629
1988ʳ	1,839	2,000	2,317	2,320	2,404	2,384	2,389	2,547	2,307	2,409	2,474	2,988	28,378
1987ʳ	1,749	1,788	2,097	2,230	2,349	2,294	2,313	2,416	2,173	2,257	2,233	2,679	26,578
1986	1,693	1,556	1,925	1,983	2,106	1,992	2,061	2,040	1,982	2,056	1,982	2,495	23,871
1985	1,478	1,426	1,735	1,773	1,853	1,800	1,869	1,938	1,841	1,925	1,920	2,343	21,901
1984	1,427	1,390	1,642	1,612	1,691	1,707	1,647	1,690	1,646	1,730	1,794	2,079	20,055
1983	1,207	1,181	1,458	1,440	1,462	1,539	1,590	1,564	1,550	1,586	1,602	1,918	18,097
1982	1,134	1,096	1,289	1,316	1,354	1,354	1,404	1,380	1,327	1,376	1,406	1,716	16,152
1981	1,201	1,150	1,368	1,383	1,390	1,396	1,393	1,455	1,368	1,396	1,374	1,736	16,610
1980	1,091	1,083	1,223	1,206	1,281	1,266	1,289	1,314	1,284	1,362	1,382	1,688	15,469
1979	966	953	1,266	1,221	1,252	1,247	1,218	1,295	1,215	1,219	1,300	1,533	14,685
1978	813	869	1,098	1,124	1,129	1,190	1,151	1,180	1,144	1,159	1,172	1,426	13,455

Note: Not adjusted for seasonal variations.
r revised.

Source: U.S. Department of Commerce, Bureau of the Census, *Current Business Reports, Combined Annual and Revised Monthly Retail Trade, January 1983 through December 1992*; and *Current Business Reports, Revised Monthly Retail Sales and Inventories: January 1982 through December 1991*, and earlier editions.

TABLE 7.2-- RETAIL TRADE DATA, BY TYPE OF ESTABLISHMENT, TENNESSEE, 1987
[Dollar amounts in thousands]

Type of establishment	Number of establishments	Sales	Annual payroll	Number of paid employees [1]
TOTAL	29,373	$28,532,933	$3,198,060	338,168
Building materials and garden supply stores	1,537	1,652,247	181,963	12,878
General merchandise stores	953	3,805,353	392,120	42,089
Food stores	4,214	5,654,155	515,427	58,735
Automotive dealers	2,435	7,140,596	581,616	29,169
Gasoline service stations	2,491	2,206,641	136,210	15,532
Apparel and accessory stores	2,943	1,333,823	161,806	19,755
Furniture and home furnishings stores	2,244	1,347,652	176,463	13,517
Eating and drinking places	6,209	2,595,902	667,377	108,720
Drug and proprietary stores	1,228	1,019,097	126,883	11,176
Miscellaneous retail stores	5,119	1,777,467	258,195	26,597

Note: Includes only establishments with payroll.
1. Survey taken during week of March 12.
Source: U.S. Department of Commerce, Bureau of the Census, *1987 Census of Retail Trade, Geographic Area Series, Tennessee.*

FIGURE 7.1
Retail Sales and Percentage Change, by Type of Business, Establishments with Payroll, Tennessee, 1982 and 1987

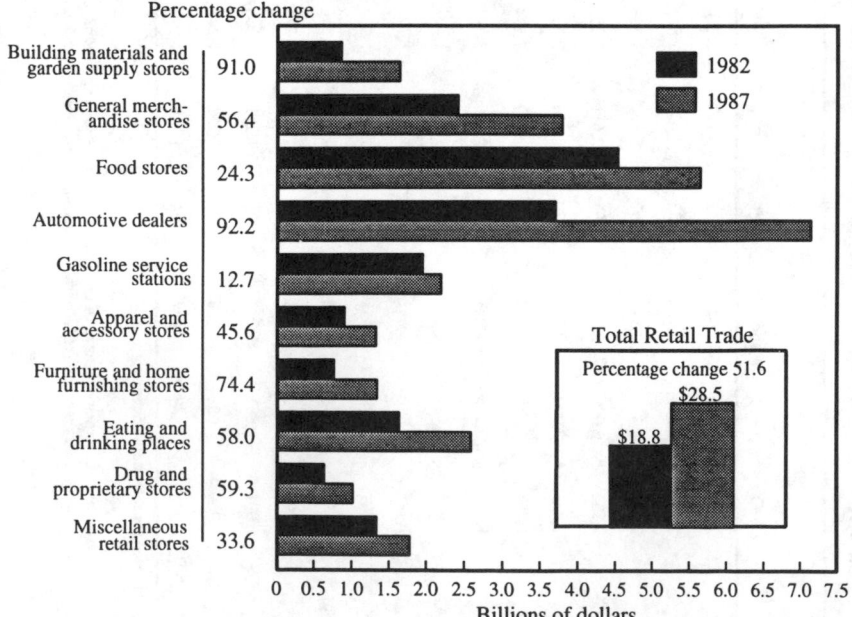

Note: Comparative statistics based on 1972 SIC. Includes only establishments with payroll.
Source: U.S. Department of Commerce, Bureau of the Census, 1987 *Census of Retail Trade, Tennessee.*

TABLE 7.3.-- WHOLESALE TRADE DATA, BY TYPE OF OPERATION, TENNESSEE, 1987 [Dollar amounts in thousands]

Kind of business	Number of establishments	Sales	Annual payroll	Number of paid employees [1]	Operating expenses	End-of-1987 inventories	End-of-1986 inventories
Total	8,782	$48,278,891	$2,518,097	115,927	$5,171,868	$3,428,029	$3,092,312
Merchant wholesalers	7,237	25,707,687	1,880,233	93,186	3,836,643	2,946,289	2,632,295
Wholesale distributors and jobbers	6,954	22,336,474	1,798,208	89,470	3,610,357	2,490,759	2,241,193
Importers	155	1,657,285	58,419	2,428	143,066	253,082	204,321
Exporters	42	674,422	9,359	393	20,778	30,113	25,973
Terminal grain elevators	5	(D)	(D)	(D)	(D)	(D)	(D)
Country grain elevators	42	(D)	(D)	(D)	(D)	(D)	(D)
Assemblers of farm products, except country grain elevators	39	787,903	7,381	459	45,695	159,852	147,060
Manufacturers' sales branches and sales offices	742	17,514,804	532,576	17,310	1,122,854	458,874	441,642
Sales branches with stock	463	7,016,520	334,543	12,005	663,388	458,874	441,642
Sales offices without stock	279	10,498,284	198,033	5,305	459,466	0	0
Agents, brokers, and commission merchants	803	5,056,400	105,288	5,431	212,371	22,866	18,375
Auction companies	55	687,302	6,136	1,015	14,140	1,751	1,206
Brokers	209	2,174,114	33,333	1,567	66,404	1,648	1,711
Commission merchants	115	467,378	14,074	851	29,788	5,766	6,147
Import agents	9	171,877	3,967	107	12,594	6,272	2,886
Export agents	4	17,912	105	27	719	0	0
Manufacturers' agents	411	1,537,817	47,673	1,864	88,726	7,429	6,425

(D) Withheld to avoid disclosing operations of individual companies.
1. Survey taken during week of March 12.
Source: U.S. Department of Commerce, Bureau of the Census, *1987 Census of Wholesale Trade, Geographic Area Series, Tennessee.*

TABLE 7.4-- SERVICE INDUSTRY ESTABLISHMENTS, RECEIPTS, PAYROLL AND EMPLOYMENT, BY
TYPE OF ESTABLISHMENT, TENNESSEE, 1987 [Dollar amounts in thousands]

| Kind of business | Number of establishments | | | | | |
	Total	Individual proprietor- ships	Partner- ships	Receipts	Annual payroll	Number of paid employees [1]
TOTAL	27,829	11,761	2,838	$12,010,161	$4,486,948	282,908
Hotels, motels, and other lodging places	993	310	213	814,385	210,756	24,580
Personal services	3,500	1,928	366	646,984	226,989	23,420
Business services	4,046	1,110	263	2,009,604	811,020	74,268
Automotive repair, services, and parking	2,718	1,292	268	892,497	188,564	13,088
Miscellaneous repair services	1,176	606	97	299,711	87,235	5,444
Amusement and recreation services	1,905	590	244	675,592	168,298	15,293
Health services	7,399	3,410	433	3,797,943	1,648,366	75,344
Legal services	2,018	1,134	564	605,799	192,545	8,523
Selected educational services	160	37	9	50,311	19,106	1,250
Social services	769	342	46	106,577	42,028	5,476
Engineering, accounting, research, management, and related services	2,878	970	311	2,081,243	882,352	35,506
Other services	267	32	24	29,515	9,689	716

Note: Includes only those establishments with payroll that were subject to Federal Income Tax.

1. Survey taken during week of March 12.

Source: U.S. Department of Commerce, Bureau of the Census, *1987 Census of Service Industries, Geographic Area Series, Tennessee.*

TABLE 7.5-- NUMBER AND LIABILITIES OF BUSINESS FAILURES, TENNESSEE, 1955-1993, SELECTED YEARS [Liabilities in thousands of dollars]

Year	Number of failures [1]	Current liabilities [2]
1993[p]	1,209	109,930
1992	1,660	304,050
1991	1,995	446,794
1990	1,475	861,177
1989	1,164	362,486
1988	1,169	415,668
1987	1,134	324,557
1986	1,180	321,114
1985	1,217	442,025
1984	1,326	1,044,724
1983	989	252,874
1982	814	226,795
1981	603	129,000
1980	449	115,000
1979	234	47,123
1978	155	28,369
1977	150	65,936
1976	214	52,281
1975	190	81,625
1974	147	25,025
1973	118	13,499
1972	130	13,990
1971	119	18,283
1970	170	48,090
1969	123	23,024
1968	115	9,486
1967	145	13,513
1966	134	13,802
1965	188	19,938
1960	172	10,850
1955	129	8,717

Note: Data are for commercial and industrial failures only through 1983, excluding failures of banks, railroads, real estate, insurance, holding and financial companies, steamship lines, travel agencies, etc. Beginning in 1984, data are based on expanded coverage and new methodology and are, therefore, not comparable with earlier years.

p preliminary.

1. Includes concerns discontinuing following assignment, voluntary or involuntary petition in bankruptcy, attachment, execution, foreclosure, etc.; voluntary withdrawals from business with known loss to creditors; also enterprises involved in court action, such as receivership and reorganization or arrangement which may or may not lead to discontinuance; and businesses making voluntary compromise with creditors out of court.

2. Liabilities exclude long-term publicly held obligations; offsetting assets are not taken into account.

Source: Printed by permission from The Dun and Bradstreet Corporation, *Business Failure Record*, corresponding years, and direct correspondence.

TABLE 7.6-- RETAIL TRADE DATA, BY TYPE OF ESTABLISHMENT, METROPOLITAN STATISTICAL
AREAS, 1987 [Dollar amounts in thousands]

MSA and type of establishment	Number of establish- ments	Sales	Annual payroll	Number of paid employees [1]
CHATTANOOGA				
Total retail trade	2,702	$2,661,888	$307,524	31,288
Building materials and garden supply stores	139	150,264	16,852	1,003
General merchandise stores	80	327,912	37,861	3,902
Food stores	287	561,625	47,887	5,120
Automotive dealers	195	592,607	52,617	2,444
Gasoline service stations	271	234,569	14,011	1,436
Apparel and accessory stores	287	135,747	16,384	1,956
Furniture and home furnishings stores	216	134,611	17,874	1,444
Eating and drinking places	614	245,332	61,919	10,185
Drug and proprietary stores	102	78,169	10,894	988
Miscellaneous retail stores	511	201,052	31,225	2,810
CLARKSVILLE-HOPKINSVILLE				
Total retail trade	970	881,628	103,284	11,032
Building materials and garden supply stores	51	63,387	7,066	474
General merchandise stores	28	119,819	14,058	1,661
Food stores	110	144,510	14,346	1,539
Automotive dealers	76	265,583	22,191	1,223
Gasoline service stations	69	55,364	3,405	439
Apparel and accessory stores	103	36,114	4,378	563
Furniture and home furnishings stores	74	40,281	5,284	416
Eating and drinking places	232	82,148	22,139	3,647
Drug and proprietary stores	38	24,123	3,316	262
Miscellaneous retail stores	189	50,299	7,101	808
JACKSON				
Total retail trade	584	589,142	64,282	6,882
Building materials and garden supply stores	32	50,296	4,864	287
General merchandise stores	20	112,907	11,654	1,307
Food stores	74	110,358	9,306	1,127
Automotive dealers	51	112,945	9,157	465
Gasoline service stations	56	49,698	3,235	384
Apparel and accessory stores	62	29,161	4,066	518
Furniture and home furnishings stores	49	26,071	3,757	319
Eating and drinking places	107	42,457	10,520	1,696
Drug and proprietary stores	20	16,262	1,895	170
Miscellaneous retail stores	113	38,987	5,828	609
JOHNSON CITY-KINGSPORT-BRISTOL				
Total retail trade	2,459	2,256,191	247,716	27,664
Building materials and garden supply stores	133	160,844	14,250	1,079
General merchandise stores	81	336,470	36,854	4,007
Food stores	327	474,047	40,077	4,643
Automotive dealers	219	554,181	43,061	2,580
Gasoline service stations	203	141,729	8,156	997
Apparel and accessory stores	235	91,453	10,606	1,340
Furniture and home furnishings stores	207	95,279	11,989	1,086
Eating and drinking places	515	203,678	53,567	8,856
Drug and proprietary stores	123	85,259	11,970	993
Miscellaneous retail stores	416	113,251	17,186	2,083

TABLE 7.6-- RETAIL TRADE DATA, BY TYPE OF ESTABLISHMENT, METROPOLITAN STATISTICAL
AREAS, 1987 [Dollar amounts in thousands] (Continued)

MSA and type of establishment	Number of establish-ments	Sales	Annual payroll	Number of paid employees [1]
KNOXVILLE				
Total retail trade	4,296	4,216,793	482,421	50,694
Building materials and				
garden supply stores	216	239,570	27,217	1,803
General merchandise stores	104	525,797	56,071	5,571
Food stores	599	794,861	75,253	9,032
Automotive dealers	307	1,041,630	83,372	4,096
Gasoline service stations	345	366,895	22,106	2,587
Apparel and accessory stores	446	218,162	23,834	2,877
Furniture and home				
furnishings stores	334	203,944	25,087	2,074
Eating and drinking places	948	441,247	115,862	17,252
Drug and proprietary stores	167	132,863	17,125	1,443
Miscellaneous retail stores	830	251,824	36,494	3,959
MEMPHIS				
Total retail trade	5,404	6,280,063	712,253	72,495
Building materials and				
garden supply stores	215	261,736	32,806	2,422
General merchandise stores	181	861,738	87,331	9,368
Food stores	765	1,124,401	104,811	12,407
Automotive dealers	427	1,655,584	143,791	6,593
Gasoline service stations	434	527,821	32,797	3,477
Apparel and accessory stores	623	337,987	44,068	5,075
Furniture and home				
furnishings stores	405	320,462	42,336	2,903
Eating and drinking places	1,159	531,050	138,673	22,043
Drug and proprietary stores	160	245,823	25,805	2,291
Miscellaneous retail stores	1,035	413,461	59,835	5,916
NASHVILLE-DAVIDSON				
Total retail trade	5,840	6,893,335	808,691	83,116
Building materials and				
garden supply stores	274	376,687	40,479	2,894
General merchandise stores	139	952,190	96,468	9,483
Food stores	740	1,228,077	124,842	12,661
Automotive dealers	440	1,736,361	142,687	6,634
Gasoline service stations	445	527,317	34,400	3,846
Apparel and accessory stores	628	321,611	39,913	4,778
Furniture and home				
furnishings stores	481	363,496	48,080	3,312
Eating and drinking places	1,371	717,042	186,516	30,233
Drug and proprietary stores	240	207,070	26,464	2,403
Miscellaneous retail stores	1,082	463,484	68,842	6,872

Note: Includes only establishments with payroll.

1. Survey taken during week March 12.

Source: U.S. Department of Commerce, Bureau of the Census, *1987 Census of Retail Trade, Geographic Area Series, Tennessee.*

TABLE 7.7.– WHOLESALE TRADE DATA, BY TYPE OF BUSINESS ESTABLISHMENT, METROPOLITAN STATISTICAL AREAS, 1987 [Dollar amounts in thousands]

Metropolitan Statistical Area	Total				Merchant wholesalers			
	Number of establishments	Sales	Annual payroll	Number of paid employees [1]	Number of establishments	Sales	Annual payroll	Number of paid employees [1]
Chattanooga	944	$4,213,833	$248,854	11,937	790	$2,182,896	$198,229	9,926
Clarksville-Hopkinsville	195	468,871	29,384	1,824	176	405,360	26,617	1,548
Jackson	167	453,130	34,171	1,922	155	419,715	31,630	1,832
Johnson City-Kingsport-Bristol	605	3,622,213	191,030	9,230	528	1,396,322	105,618	6,524
Knoxville	1,178	4,637,599	352,233	15,264	975	(D)	(D)	(D)
Memphis	2,241	22,205,695	848,663	35,802	1,706	10,603,471	593,006	26,885
Nashville	2,101	10,742,878	679,133	29,652	1,662	6,098,910	541,037	24,707

(D) Withheld to avoid disclosing operations of individual companies.

1. Survey taken during week of March 12.

Source: U.S. Department of Commerce, Bureau of the Census, *1987 Census of Wholesale Trade, Geographic Area Series, Tennessee.*

TABLE 7.8-- SERVICE INDUSTRIES DATA, BY TYPE OF ESTABLISHMENT, METROPOLITAN
STATISTICAL AREAS, 1987 [Dollar amounts in thousands]

Metropolitan Statistical Area	Number of establish-ments	Receipts	Annual payroll	Number of paid employees [1]
CHATTANOOGA				
TOTAL	2,565	$1,120,612	$419,745	26,871
Hotels, motels, and other lodging places	74	63,852	16,831	2,171
Personal services	335	66,158	24,258	2,318
Business services	409	180,421	75,299	8,064
Automotive repair, services, and parking	268	86,313	19,690	1,274
Miscellaneous repair services	98	30,222	9,242	585
Amusement and recreation services, including motion pictures	135	46,803	11,720	1,027
Health services	711	446,780	183,063	7,770
Legal services	168	73,826	26,949	1,008
Selected educational services	15	5,504	1,994	137
Social services	61	15,872	4,780	603
Engineering, accounting, research, management, and related services	260	101,308	44,872	1,812
Other services	31	3,553	1,047	102
CLARKSVILLE-HOPKINSVILLE				
TOTAL	700	155,200	54,207	4,361
Hotels, motels, and other lodging places	29	10,765	2,449	433
Personal services	126	14,930	5,262	629
Business services	77	18,997	7,099	715
Automotive repair, services, and parking	92	18,080	4,137	352
Miscellaneous repair services	30	4,275	1,243	93
Amusement and recreation services, including motion pictures	40	6,283	1,326	184
Health services	176	55,012	23,443	1,209
Legal services	48	11,196	2,792	185
Selected educational services	3	2,186	766	39
Social services	23	4,055	1,614	232
Engineering, accounting, research, management, and related services	50	9,243	4,031	281
Other services	6	178	45	9
JACKSON				
TOTAL	542	208,938	96,318	5,101
Hotels, motels, and other lodging places	24	9,465	2,094	284
Personal services	68	12,355	4,201	489
Business services	76	26,502	12,381	1,200
Automotive repair, services, and parking	59	(D)	(D)	(D)
Miscellaneous repair services	26	6,115	2,347	141
Amusement and recreation services, including motion pictures	38	(D)	(D)	(D)
Health services	133	113,622	60,299	2,037
Legal services	43	10,114	4,156	166
Selected educational services	3	(D)	(D)	(D)
Social services	18	1,437	607	84
Engineering, accounting, research, management, and related services	53	8,903	4,734	215
Other services	1	(D)	(D)	(D)
JOHNSONCITY-KINGSPORT-BRISTOL				
TOTAL	2,184	681,869	261,573	16,841
Hotels, motels, and other lodging places	67	45,825	11,394	1,359
Personal services	345	50,648	18,529	1,934
Business services	230	89,718	37,246	3,277
Automotive repair, services, and parking	212	50,372	11,235	889
Miscellaneous repair services	91	14,879	4,353	336
Amusement and recreation services, including motion pictures	151	25,699	5,650	749
Health services	628	320,144	140,826	6,460
Legal services	195	40,922	13,686	680

TABLE 7.8-- SERVICE INDUSTRIES DATA, BY TYPE OF ESTABLISHMENT, METROPOLITAN
STATISTICAL AREAS, 1987 [Dollar amounts in thousands] (Continued)

Metropolitan Statistical Area	Number of establish- ments	Receipts	Annual payroll	Number of paid employees [1]
Selected educational services	3	(D)	(D)	(D)
Social services	59	7,389	3,245	393
Engineering, accounting, research, management, and related services	187	35,463	15,187	742
Other services	16	(D)	(D)	(D)
KNOXVILLE				
TOTAL	4,209	2,136,442	746,209	41,410
Hotels, motels, and other lodging places	262	175,287	40,383	4,174
Personal services	488	83,613	28,053	3,046
Business services	583	235,662	97,294	7,722
Automotive repair, services, and parking	370	116,546	25,106	1,712
Miscellaneous repair services	172	37,017	12,148	798
Amusement and recreation services, including motion pictures	285	99,112	24,500	2,569
Health services	1,122	531,064	239,914	9,822
Legal services	250	90,262	29,148	1,262
Selected educational services	30	5,418	1,947	131
Social services	92	14,875	6,063	761
Engineering, accounting, research, management, and related services	507	743,244	240,283	9,298
Other services	48	4,342	1,371	115
MEMPHIS				
TOTAL	5,810	2,672,602	1,031,415	66,574
Hotels, motels, and other lodging places	149	171,018	46,930	5,008
Personal services	705	148,886	56,656	5,799
Business services	1,021	592,517	254,026	23,730
Automotive repair, services, and parking	613	292,724	59,012	3,887
Miscellaneous repair services	288	88,246	27,497	1,568
Amusement and recreation services, including motion pictures	264	139,417	31,223	3,051
Health services	1,484	729,973	343,502	12,917
Legal services	445	149,400	49,470	2,059
Selected educational services	35	8,265	3,593	237
Social services	146	17,884	7,814	1,070
Engineering, accounting, research, management, and related services	613	328,638	150,396	7,149
Other services	47	5,634	1,296	99
NASHVILLE-DAVIDSON				
TOTAL	7,107	3,505,767	1,275,052	81,033
Hotels, motels, and other lodging places	195	295,748	81,097	9,596
Personal services	727	149,421	55,771	5,368
Business services	1,228	687,468	256,486	22,958
Automotive repair, services, and parking	611	236,861	52,382	3,404
Miscellaneous repair services	286	87,912	22,925	1,350
Amusement and recreation services, including motion pictures	630	325,655	86,647	6,234
Health services	1,686	994,862	429,681	18,877
Legal services	489	183,153	56,018	2,377
Selected educational services	49	17,232	6,902	406
Social services	233	38,261	16,117	2,014
Engineering, accounting, research, management, and related services	881	476,312	206,318	8,198
Other services	92	12,882	4,708	251

Note: Includes only those establishments with payroll that were subject to Federal Income Tax.
(D) Withheld to avoid disclosing operations of individual companies.
1. Survey taken during week March 12.
Source: U.S. Department of Commerce, Bureau of the Census, *1987 Census of Service Industries, Geographic Area Series, Tennessee.*

TABLE 7.9-- WHOLESALE TRADE EMPLOYEES AND PAYROLL, AND NUMBER OF
ESTABLISHMENTS BY EMPLOYMENT-SIZE CLASS, COUNTIES, 1991

County	Number of employees [1]	Annual payroll ($1,000)	Total	Employment-size class				
				1 to 4	5 to 9	10 to 19	20 to 49	50 or more
Anderson	344	$9,259	66	38	20	5	3	0
Bedford	341	6,413	34	16	11	2	4	1
Benton	211	4,107	24	10	6	6	1	1
Bledsoe	(a)	(D)	4	2	1	1	0	0
Blount	1,075	23,237	98	51	17	16	10	4
Bradley	1,994	43,233	115	60	31	9	11	4
Campbell	290	5,265	29	11	8	5	5	0
Cannon	(b)	(D)	6	5	0	1	0	0
Carroll	249	3,567	32	16	9	5	2	0
Carter	210	3,493	31	17	8	4	1	1
Cheatham	99	2,496	12	5	3	2	2	0
Chester	84	1,176	12	7	2	1	2	0
Claiborne	224	1,630	21	9	5	2	4	1
Clay	(b)	(D)	5	4	0	0	1	0
Cocke	132	1,657	28	18	6	3	1	0
Coffee	444	8,531	59	31	14	9	5	0
Crockett	169	3,056	16	10	3	1	1	1
Cumberland	291	6,696	35	20	4	8	3	0
Davidson	26,027	756,108	1,520	602	332	268	204	114
Decatur	63	986	9	5	1	3	0	0
DeKalb	77	1,632	12	8	1	2	1	0
Dickson	375	8,030	29	11	5	6	7	0
Dyer	595	10,989	58	22	12	18	5	1
Fayette	120	2,561	14	7	2	3	2	0
Fentress	59	752	9	6	0	3	0	0
Franklin	250	4,161	27	12	6	7	2	0
Gibson	543	10,767	68	38	18	8	2	2
Giles	277	5,572	35	16	10	6	3	0
Grainger	107	1,939	13	8	2	2	1	0
Greene	672	8,184	71	35	16	13	5	2
Grundy	57	891	9	4	3	2	0	0
Hamblen	1,081	19,402	82	37	22	15	3	5
Hamilton	10,501	262,083	820	355	190	148	90	37
Hancock	(b)	(D)	5	4	1	0	0	0
Hardeman	191	2,655	22	12	3	5	2	0
Hardin	154	3,254	22	10	8	1	3	0
Hawkins	97	1,728	19	12	5	1	1	0
Haywood	129	2,371	19	8	6	4	1	0
Henderson	221	2,934	22	7	8	4	3	0
Henry	610	11,648	42	17	11	7	5	2
Hickman	53	1,046	13	9	3	1	0	0
Houston	(b)	(D)	9	9	0	0	0	0
Humphreys	158	2,481	19	8	3	6	2	0
Jackson	(b)	(D)	6	4	1	0	1	0
Jefferson	198	3,813	37	23	6	7	1	0
Johnson	(b)	(D)	9	4	0	3	2	0
Knox	13,450	343,184	1,001	411	231	183	127	49
Lake	52	679	11	4	7	0	0	0
Lauderdale	227	5,210	32	17	5	7	3	0
Lawrence	370	6,866	48	24	15	5	4	0

TABLE 7.9-- WHOLESALE TRADE EMPLOYEES AND PAYROLL, AND NUMBER OF
ESTABLISHMENTS BY EMPLOYMENT-SIZE CLASS, COUNTIES, 1991 (Continued)

County	Number of employees [1]	Annual payroll ($1,000)	Total	Employment-size class				
				1 to 4	5 to 9	10 to 19	20 to 49	50 or more
Lewis	95	1,633	9	4	3	0	2	0
Lincoln	344	5,024	35	13	10	8	3	1
Loudon	251	3,998	31	15	6	8	2	0
McMinn	495	7,869	51	21	11	13	6	0
McNairy	666	10,191	31	13	8	7	1	2
Macon	54	588	12	7	3	2	0	0
Madison	2,351	49,781	179	58	40	46	26	9
Marion	124	2,201	19	11	2	5	1	0
Marshall	149	3,324	17	11	2	1	2	1
Maury	853	18,063	78	27	23	17	9	2
Meigs	(a)	(D)	1	1	0	0	0	0
Monroe	281	5,358	29	12	8	4	5	0
Montgomery	757	14,506	95	52	25	8	9	1
Moore	(a)	(D)	3	2	1	0	0	0
Morgan	(b)	(D)	7	3	3	1	0	0
Obion	613	12,360	60	27	19	6	4	4
Overton	106	1,227	16	9	3	3	1	0
Perry	(c)	(D)	5	2	1	0	1	1
Pickett	(c)	(D)	6	3	1	0	1	1
Polk	130	3,530	14	4	5	4	1	0
Putnam	1,159	23,582	120	60	25	17	15	3
Rhea	75	888	16	11	3	2	0	0
Roane	290	5,708	33	17	8	4	3	1
Robertson	516	8,035	49	21	13	6	7	2
Rutherford	3,434	76,806	150	56	33	31	19	11
Scott	104	1,452	16	10	1	4	1	0
Sequatchie	(b)	(D)	7	5	1	1	0	0
Sevier	241	5,437	43	26	11	4	2	0
Shelby	36,582	1,035,899	2,132	837	495	373	279	148
Smith	(c)	(D)	18	10	4	3	1	0
Stewart	(a)	(D)	1	1	0	0	0	0
Sullivan	4,116	133,815	253	98	71	46	29	9
Sumner	976	23,825	124	72	30	12	7	3
Tipton	179	3,053	28	19	3	4	2	0
Trousdale	75	557	14	9	2	3	0	0
Unicoi	(b)	(D)	7	3	4	0	0	0
Union	44	784	7	2	4	1	0	0
Van Buren	(b)	(D)	2	1	0	0	1	0
Warren	392	6,992	48	22	10	12	4	0
Washington	2,796	60,266	197	81	50	35	20	11
Wayne	64	860	9	5	1	1	2	0
Weakley	450	9,512	49	24	13	8	2	2
White	247	3,551	30	17	3	7	2	1
Williamson	1,542	51,052	198	119	37	27	10	5
Wilson	780	15,653	82	50	17	6	7	2

(D) Withheld to avoid disclosing operations of individual companies.

1. Number of employees for week including March 12.

a. 0–19 employees.

b. 20–99 employees.

c. 100–249 employees.

Source: U.S. Department of Commerce, Bureau of the Census, *County Business Patterns*, 1991.

TABLE 7.10--WHOLESALE TRADE DATA, TENNESSEE, COUNTIES AND MUNICIPALITIES WITH POPULATION OF 2,500 OR MORE, 1987 [Dollar amounts in thousands]

| County and municipality | Total | Number of establishments | | Sales | Annual payroll | Number of paid employees [1] |
		Merchant whole-salers	Other operating types			
Anderson	56	47	9	$133,172	$15,666	723
Clinton	11	11	0	(D)	(D)	(D)
Oak Ridge (part)	31	26	5	29,316	2,632	155
Oliver Springs (part)	1	1	0	(D)	(D)	(D)
Bedford	39	36	3	(D)	(D)	(D)
Shelbyville	30	28	2	81,214	5,135	278
Benton	18	17	1	18,248	1,475	104
Camden	15	14	1	(D)	(D)	(D)
Bledsoe	2	2	0	(D)	(D)	(D)
Blount	85	74	11	350,836	23,479	1,258
Alcoa	20	17	3	55,669	3,345	245
Maryville	37	33	4	182,884	11,564	599
Bradley	97	90	7	582,046	20,865	1,234
Cleveland	82	76	6	570,179	20,251	1,184
Campbell	27	27	0	(D)	(D)	(D)
Jellico	3	3	0	(D)	(D)	(D)
LaFollette	11	11	0	31,592	2,484	130
Cannon	4	4	0	(D)	(D)	(D)
Carroll	34	31	3	(D)	(D)	(D)
Huntingdon	14	13	1	38,096	1,336	98
McKenzie (part)	11	9	2	6,553	712	52
Carter	23	23	0	(D)	(D)	(D)
Elizabethton	17	17	0	20,055	2,031	135
Johnson City (part)	0	0	0	0	0	0
Cheatham	7	7	0	(D)	(D)	(D)
Chester	14	14	0	19,769	1,062	73
Henderson	12	12	0	(D)	(D)	(D)
Claiborne	19	15	4	(D)	(D)	(D)
Clay	4	4	0	(D)	(D)	(D)
Cocke	26	21	5	52,613	1,558	146
Newport	17	15	2	25,652	1,138	89
Coffee	55	52	3	(D)	(D)	(D)
Manchester	16	15	1	37,169	1,583	135
Tullahoma (part)	23	22	1	46,960	4,266	218
Crockett	16	15	1	(D)	(D)	(D)
Alamo	3	3	0	(D)	(D)	(D)
Cumberland	33	32	1	(D)	(D)	(D)
Crossville	22	22	0	(D)	(D)	(D)
Davidson	1,506	1,179	327	8,818,393	575,227	24,329
Belle Meade	6	3	3	(D)	(D)	(D)
Forest Hills	5	2	3	9,386	476	11
Goodlettsville (part)	38	31	7	(D)	(D)	(D)
Nashville-Davidson	1,454	1,141	313	8,124,514	552,492	23,360
Oak Hill	3	2	1	(D)	(D)	(D)
Decatur	10	8	2	(D)	(D)	(D)
DeKalb	11	11	0	9,144	930	75
Smithville	8	8	0	(D)	(D)	(D)
Dickson	34	30	4	(D)	(D)	(D)
Dickson	24	22	2	(D)	(D)	(D)
Dyer	68	61	7	176,343	8,920	573
Dyersburg	51	46	5	143,842	7,898	510

TABLE 7.10--WHOLESALE TRADE DATA, TENNESSEE, COUNTIES AND MUNICIPALITIES WITH
POPULATION OF 2,500 OR MORE, 1987 [Dollar amounts in thousands] (Continued)

County and municipality	Number of establishments			Sales	Annual payroll	Number of paid employees [1]
	Total	Merchant whole-salers	Other operating types			
Newbern	6	5	1	14,673	694	43
Fayette	16	16	0	41,868	3,231	204
Fentress	6	6	0	6,286	421	33
Franklin	24	22	2	45,563	3,139	217
Tullahoma (part)	0	0	0	0	0	0
Winchester	7	7	0	(D)	(D)	(D)
Gibson	67	63	4	140,669	7,608	467
Humboldt	14	14	0	16,890	1,073	74
Milan	19	17	2	45,337	2,212	124
Trenton	21	20	1	63,699	2,811	189
Giles	38	35	3	60,272	4,338	283
Pulaski	23	21	2	48,912	3,478	210
Grainger	10	10	0	11,520	1,139	68
Greene	67	49	18	170,180	8,532	718
Greeneville	51	35	16	155,906	6,614	542
Grundy	9	9	0	6,510	683	53
Hamblen	86	75	11	275,508	19,542	1,135
Morristown	70	63	7	(D)	(D)	(D)
Hamilton	816	670	146	3,957,120	226,165	10,530
Chattanooga	717	594	123	(D)	(D)	(D)
Collegedale	2	1	1	(D)	(D)	(D)
East Ridge	26	23	3	34,829	1,862	152
Red Bank	15	14	1	13,429	2,229	101
Signal Mountain	9	5	4	8,495	512	40
Soddy-Daisy	7	6	1	5,977	546	35
Hancock	5	5	0	2,635	184	24
Hardeman	23	21	2	31,596	2,134	195
Bolivar	10	9	1	17,739	986	94
Hardin	21	20	1	44,236	2,348	135
Savannah	13	13	0	(D)	(D)	(D)
Hawkins	20	18	2	(D)	(D)	(D)
Church Hill	1	0	1	(D)	(D)	(D)
Kingsport (part)	0	0	0	0	0	0
Mount Carmel	1	1	0	(D)	(D)	(D)
Rogersville	11	10	1	(D)	(D)	(D)
Haywood	20	16	4	26,259	1,583	139
Brownsville	17	14	3	(D)	(D)	(D)
Henderson	22	21	1	59,037	3,137	252
Lexington	14	14	0	(D)	(D)	(D)
Henry	50	45	5	99,594	8,036	547
McKenzie (part)	0	0	0	0	0	0
Paris	34	30	4	80,592	6,283	403
Hickman	10	9	1	6,693	467	40
Centerville	7	6	1	(D)	(D)	(D)
Houston	9	8	1	3,628	281	27
Humphreys	16	15	1	37,991	1,687	101
Waverly	11	11	0	(D)	(D)	(D)
Jackson	9	7	2	(D)	(D)	(D)
Jefferson	24	21	3	22,729	2,289	169
Jefferson City	6	6	0	4,584	439	36
Johnson	11	11	0	9,586	749	65

TABLE 7.10--WHOLESALE TRADE DATA, TENNESSEE, COUNTIES AND MUNICIPALITIES WITH POPULATION OF 2,500 OR MORE, 1987 [Dollar amounts in thousands] (Continued)

County and municipality	Number of establishments			Sales	Annual payroll	Number of paid employees [1]
	Total	Merchant whole-salers	Other operating types			
Knox	956	780	176	4,066,833	305,605	12,780
Farragut	1	1	0	(D)	(D)	(D)
Knoxville	753	627	126	3,128,958	203,653	9,568
Lake	14	12	2	42,499	2,029	211
Lauderdale	30	30	0	50,191	3,027	212
Ripley	13	13	0	28,762	1,524	108
Lawrence	40	35	5	74,573	3,887	271
Lawrenceburg	31	27	4	64,607	3,415	222
Lewis	9	9	0	19,496	1,277	109
Hohenwald	9	9	0	19,496	1,277	109
Lincoln	43	39	4	72,192	4,813	383
Fayetteville	31	27	4	59,042	3,717	319
Loudon	26	23	3	48,697	3,436	228
Lenoir City	11	9	2	27,671	1,485	112
Loudon	6	5	1	14,448	1,342	69
McMinn	51	50	1	91,859	6,790	453
Athens	31	31	0	(D)	(D)	(D)
Etowah	2	2	0	(D)	(D)	(D)
McNairy	27	25	2	87,452	11,440	540
Selmer	14	12	2	63,637	10,037	468
Macon	12	12	0	15,134	631	66
Lafayette	9	9	0	14,439	578	61
Madison	167	155	12	453,130	34,171	1,922
Jackson	149	138	11	420,418	30,821	1,680
Marion	19	18	1	28,378	2,093	132
Jasper	5	4	1	14,415	982	56
South Pittsburg	4	4	0	9,555	538	43
Marshall	14	13	1	18,072	1,922	121
Lewisburg	10	10	0	(D)	(D)	(D)
Maury	83	78	5	135,677	10,496	636
Columbia	66	63	3	100,392	8,819	514
Mount Pleasant	7	6	1	14,614	876	42
Meigs	0	0	0	0	0	0
Monroe	36	31	5	102,805	4,253	321
Madisonville	10	10	0	7,179	1,159	96
Sweetwater	13	10	3	20,362	1,532	104
Montgomery	90	85	5	169,871	11,798	726
Clarksville	81	76	5	151,707	9,940	660
Moore	2	2	0	(D)	(D)	(D)
Morgan	10	10	0	9,965	616	43
Oliver Springs (part)	0	0	0	0	0	0
Obion	64	58	6	161,251	8,324	553
South Fulton	9	7	2	8,124	506	37
Union City	35	31	4	124,922	6,126	389
Overton	18	18	0	23,904	1,053	80
Livingston	11	11	0	18,999	586	45
Perry	5	5	0	11,606	1,532	97
Pickett	5	5	0	3,873	348	32
Polk	12	12	0	40,537	2,207	98

TABLE 7.10--WHOLESALE TRADE DATA, TENNESSEE, COUNTIES AND MUNICIPALITIES WITH POPULATION OF 2,500 OR MORE, 1987 [Dollar amounts in thousands] (Continued)

County and municipality	Number of establishments					
	Total	Merchant whole-salers	Other operating types	Sales	Annual payroll	Number of paid employees[1]
Putnam	101	94	7	206,970	15,492	1,033
Cookeville	96	89	7	(D)	(D)	(D)
Monterey	0	0	0	0	0	0
Rhea	11	10	1	14,310	568	54
Dayton	8	7	1	(D)	(D)	(D)
Roane	29	26	3	98,349	6,507	392
Harriman	11	11	0	(D)	(D)	(D)
Kingston	4	4	0	(D)	(D)	(D)
Oak Ridge (part)	0	0	0	0	0	0
Oliver Springs (part)	0	0	0	0	0	0
Rockwood	10	8	2	53,543	3,929	227
Robertson	46	37	9	105,086	6,157	471
Greenbrier	2	2	0	(D)	(D)	(D)
Springfield	31	25	6	78,334	4,781	346
Rutherford	146	132	14	432,465	40,024	1,956
LaVergne	23	21	2	210,649	19,793	783
Murfreesboro	95	85	10	173,395	15,716	866
Smyrna	17	16	1	36,906	4,135	254
Scott	15	13	2	21,007	1,229	115
Oneida	10	8	2	19,795	1,080	96
Sequatchie	5	5	0	8,671	343	26
Dunlap	5	5	0	8,671	343	26
Sevier	42	38	4	44,355	3,595	225
Gatlinburg	3	3	0	(D)	(D)	(D)
Sevierville	17	16	1	28,968	2,346	130
Shelby	2,081	1,562	519	21,108,532	803,832	33,584
Bartlett	30	21	9	102,332	4,600	189
Collierville	16	13	3	68,599	3,475	244
Germantown	87	43	44	1,352,674	29,003	928
Memphis	1,840	1,400	440	18,447,612	721,381	30,227
Millington	5	5	0	2,692	445	24
Smith	19	16	3	33,430	1,504	199
Carthage	11	10	1	14,150	491	68
Stewart	4	3	1	(D)	(D)	(D)
Sullivan	253	212	41	(D)	(D)	(D)
Bristol	82	64	18	267,868	56,704	2,070
Kingsport (part)	114	94	20	2,028,762	47,210	1,709
Sumner	123	94	29	219,076	14,779	834
Gallatin	32	28	4	(D)	(D)	(D)
Goodlettsville (part)	1	1	0	(D)	(D)	(D)
Hendersonville	62	38	24	74,844	5,757	299
Portland	14	14	0	18,046	2,085	138
Tipton	26	24	2	60,475	2,433	204
Covington	21	19	2	(D)	(D)	(D)
Trousdale	12	10	2	21,904	559	93
Hartsville	11	9	2	(D)	(D)	(D)
Unicoi	5	5	0	(D)	(D)	(D)
Erwin	3	3	0	(D)	(D)	(D)
Union	5	5	0	8,154	460	41
Van Buren	5	5	0	(D)	(D)	(D)
Warren	49	44	5	84,731	6,453	449

TABLE 7.10--WHOLESALE TRADE DATA, TENNESSEE, COUNTIES AND MUNICIPALITIES WITH
POPULATION OF 2,500 OR MORE, 1987 [Dollar amounts in thousands] (Continued)

County and municipality	Number of establishments			Sales	Annual payroll	Number of paid employees [1]
	Total	Merchant whole- salers	Other operating types			
McMinnville	28	26	2	43,382	3,726	199
Washington	177	157	20	597,450	43,430	2,783
Johnson City (part)	142	126	16	501,252	35,699	2,122
Jonesborough	4	4	0	(D)	(D)	(D)
Wayne	11	11	0	12,804	695	70
Weakley	50	49	1	88,395	6,454	372
McKenzie (part)	0	0	0	0	0	0
Martin	17	17	0	(D)	(D)	(D)
White	28	25	3	55,731	2,905	251
Sparta	16	14	2	38,823	2,264	174
Williamson	168	119	49	839,611	24,371	1,076
Brentwood	77	47	30	(D)	(D)	(D)
Fairview	3	3	0	(D)	(D)	(D)
Franklin	67	54	13	151,858	8,390	441
Wilson	71	64	7	235,192	11,821	631
Lebanon	39	36	3	115,481	8,222	433
Mt. Juliet	15	14	1	22,276	2,220	119
TENNESSEE	8,782	7,237	1,545	48,278,891	2,518,097	115,927

(D) Withheld to avoid disclosing operations of individual companies.

1. Survey taken during week of March 12.

Source: U.S. Department of Commerce, Bureau of the Census, *1987 Census of Wholesale Trade, Geographic Area Series, Tennessee.*

TABLE 7.11--RETAIL SALES OF ESTABLISHMENTS, BY TYPE OF ESTABLISHMENT, COUNTIES, 1992
[In thousands of dollars]

County	Total	Building material dealers, etc.	General merchandise stores	Food stores	Autos, boats and aircraft
Anderson	530,964	25,347	93,862	125,375	124,297
Bedford	164,956	8,175	21,383	50,003	23,132
Benton	85,044	3,448	15,011	23,066	7,777
Bledsoe	21,033	(D)	3,075	10,030	1,885
Blount	720,071	47,846	97,368	145,857	224,732
Bradley	514,181	48,065	67,108	133,502	99,952
Campbell	167,547	11,971	29,282	40,518	15,650
Cannon	26,707	(D)	2,077	11,949	3,587
Carroll	128,303	7,561	16,778	41,195	29,385
Carter	215,929	16,783	35,232	64,229	33,964
Cheatham	90,794	4,990	12,355	40,630	3,430
Chester	63,050	6,547	1,519	15,456	21,021
Claiborne	97,172	5,501	13,906	32,873	7,658
Clay	(D)	2,518	1,159	8,967	1,164
Cocke	167,042	6,626	34,844	51,067	15,000
Coffee	361,701	36,364	70,372	78,589	65,033
Crockett	39,336	2,039	1,665	16,014	5,526
Cumberland	255,820	28,945	38,691	63,787	35,396
Davidson	5,843,998	279,751	859,785	792,312	1,006,956
Decatur	53,875	3,108	4,795	14,365	8,899
DeKalb	57,839	2,811	3,682	21,304	9,200
Dickson	252,076	15,402	46,140	68,072	35,924
Dyer	259,817	16,890	49,475	64,274	50,285
Fayette	59,960	4,914	5,062	22,192	6,157
Fentress	60,572	6,131	11,584	20,974	5,138
Franklin	146,932	8,943	22,088	48,090	23,954
Gibson	245,188	11,922	40,457	65,957	55,673
Giles	142,060	7,228	16,867	38,615	22,390
Grainger	41,607	701	356	17,648	6,776
Greene	311,966	33,881	55,495	86,215	44,977
Grundy	35,180	5,251	2,157	14,084	3,474
Hamblen	480,546	27,930	74,881	91,348	95,706
Hamilton	2,627,161	158,209	403,125	460,419	390,438
Hancock	13,387	822	(D)	5,797	936
Hardeman	106,025	18,468	16,193	32,303	14,114
Hardin	132,197	7,238	24,065	33,771	28,200
Hawkins	151,931	13,263	13,370	60,957	17,381
Haywood	93,269	5,347	14,118	23,031	16,875
Henderson	126,352	7,822	21,580	40,770	20,363
Henry	199,348	36,772	28,322	38,078	36,286
Hickman	(D)	4,568	2,213	21,201	3,173
Houston	20,988	(D)	(D)	10,887	1,481
Humphreys	76,627	5,170	13,904	23,196	6,581
Jackson	(D)	1,411	1,286	10,770	1,272
Jefferson	151,247	4,579	19,010	53,438	19,803
Johnson	47,248	5,534	3,623	19,063	3,748
Knox	3,540,530	262,064	499,182	538,173	530,358
Lake	23,061	5,524	1,104	8,353	842
Lauderdale	89,639	6,698	16,635	32,311	7,088
Lawrence	204,475	12,847	29,873	60,023	38,726

TABLE 7.11--RETAIL SALES OF ESTABLISHMENTS, BY TYPE OF ESTABLISHMENT, COUNTIES, 1992
[In thousands of dollars] (Continued)

Gasoline service stations	Apparel, accessory stores	Furniture equipment stores	Eating, drinking places	Miscellaneous retail stores	County
23,157	14,594	8,765	52,965	62,602	Anderson
7,607	1,949	5,803	15,232	31,672	Bedford
18,503	1,335	775	6,175	8,954	Benton
(D)	(D)	(D)	1,155	2,654	Bledsoe
40,135	8,495	23,760	55,446	76,431	Blount
19,707	22,663	18,084	49,778	55,320	Bradley
23,452	4,948	4,483	18,093	19,150	Campbell
1,908	(D)	1,153	2,204	2,955	Cannon
4,346	3,784	3,856	8,423	12,974	Carroll
11,843	3,607	5,572	19,863	24,836	Carter
16,106	363	456	4,789	7,675	Cheatham
2,615	1,377	2,445	5,395	6,675	Chester
5,350	933	1,898	11,764	17,288	Claiborne
1,684	(D)	197	3,024	6,886	Clay
18,745	2,511	4,091	20,124	14,034	Cocke
20,568	8,723	8,924	35,211	37,915	Coffee
2,514	874	1,554	1,439	7,712	Crockett
13,389	22,140	6,845	25,652	20,975	Cumberland
549,603	304,199	288,004	683,490	1,079,898	Davidson
6,348	1,311	502	3,953	10,593	Decatur
5,885	814	1,777	4,583	7,782	DeKalb
29,824	8,485	8,124	22,621	17,484	Dickson
8,972	8,763	11,340	22,168	27,649	Dyer
8,459	514	520	2,934	9,208	Fayette
5,345	946	375	4,145	5,933	Fentress
6,114	1,944	4,758	12,535	18,506	Franklin
11,734	6,990	6,550	20,703	25,202	Gibson
19,599	4,198	5,683	13,377	14,102	Giles
3,975	189	470	3,525	7,966	Grainger
19,541	3,449	7,243	27,539	33,626	Greene
2,537	21	441	2,739	4,476	Grundy
79,528	10,811	5,936	42,223	52,183	Hamblen
178,798	167,095	114,948	293,052	461,077	Hamilton
(D)	(D)	(D)	1,084	3,392	Hancock
7,352	1,033	1,657	7,115	7,790	Hardeman
7,418	2,331	3,825	11,331	14,017	Hardin
9,418	2,442	2,917	17,592	14,590	Hawkins
11,144	1,862	3,792	11,597	5,502	Haywood
6,334	2,002	5,226	9,313	12,941	Henderson
8,557	4,572	6,304	17,260	23,197	Henry
6,539	(D)	733	3,387	6,070	Hickman
693	(D)	490	1,365	3,392	Houston
8,436	656	1,198	7,789	9,697	Humphreys
1,184	(D)	291	1,550	3,047	Jackson
17,359	1,141	2,558	16,307	17,051	Jefferson
4,145	252	1,077	3,207	6,599	Johnson
469,798	177,416	169,485	352,978	541,076	Knox
1,972	(D)	190	2,598	2,479	Lake
6,907	1,665	1,479	5,239	11,618	Lauderdale
7,841	5,703	14,440	16,566	18,456	Lawrence

TABLE 7.11--RETAIL SALES OF ESTABLISHMENTS, BY TYPE OF ESTABLISHMENT, COUNTIES, 1992
[In thousands of dollars] (Continued)

County	Total	Building material dealers, etc.	General merchandise stores	Food stores	Autos, boats and aircraft
Lewis	(D)	2,440	9,489	12,636	2,514
Lincoln	144,491	6,543	22,831	38,652	28,600
Loudon	168,782	15,647	21,598	45,063	28,550
McMinn	281,712	36,777	46,300	71,030	41,001
McNairy	78,841	4,164	12,503	24,014	8,117
Macon	70,595	8,873	11,949	19,787	5,196
Madison	736,661	50,569	140,832	147,028	106,663
Marion	158,636	5,818	30,531	45,141	14,992
Marshall	131,316	8,247	16,570	40,008	25,323
Maury	393,483	30,395	60,593	96,990	63,686
Meigs	21,904	1,551	1,117	12,413	938
Monroe	144,059	10,645	22,103	48,453	15,105
Montgomery	674,426	63,196	114,254	138,559	113,787
Moore	11,457	(D)	228	3,368	(D)
Morgan	31,719	1,359	1,464	13,849	5,266
Obion	196,033	13,090	29,678	44,127	38,218
Overton	66,783	5,475	3,971	26,210	11,740
Perry	17,722	1,301	1,129	8,285	1,155
Pickett	14,061	1,112	(D)	4,283	2,010
Polk	(D)	1,126	2,694	17,349	2,603
Putnam	421,674	41,269	66,998	89,070	69,677
Rhea	104,319	6,458	15,555	36,809	14,977
Roane	215,737	12,531	29,938	61,521	41,809
Robertson	232,910	12,279	29,020	56,941	43,199
Rutherford	805,550	59,931	105,591	190,331	152,034
Scott	75,743	8,175	15,651	21,970	6,184
Sequatchie	39,696	5,255	1,888	13,407	6,901
Sevier	724,717	31,956	64,550	122,788	24,372
Shelby	6,778,127	323,955	1,110,338	988,338	1,258,949
Smith	72,385	5,907	10,094	23,500	8,817
Stewart	(D)	718	1,177	12,226	5,214
Sullivan	1,214,889	62,620	269,076	198,606	244,434
Sumner	472,968	34,088	61,366	143,279	75,855
Tipton	157,411	10,538	21,127	50,444	34,092
Trousdale	19,787	(D)	789	9,873	1,722
Unicoi	57,488	3,140	1,199	23,734	9,698
Union	(D)	3,317	2,027	10,703	2,903
Van Buren	7,295	(D)	(D)	4,797	261
Warren	210,700	28,377	34,470	54,653	24,463
Washington	757,970	68,684	128,025	152,883	125,474
Wayne	42,951	4,583	2,685	18,445	2,618
Weakley	140,088	9,045	23,386	36,706	19,173
White	94,654	9,385	14,585	29,505	19,861
Williamson	661,247	36,029	118,854	153,761	121,006
Wilson	351,640	24,339	37,695	79,023	66,304

TABLE 7.11--RETAIL SALES OF ESTABLISHMENTS, BY TYPE OF ESTABLISHMENT, COUNTIES, 1992
[In thousands of dollars] (Continued)

Gasoline service stations	Apparel, accessory stores	Furniture equipment stores	Eating, drinking places	Miscellaneous retail stores	County
17,668	(D)	922	3,561	5,278	Lewis
15,257	2,458	3,781	12,630	13,738	Lincoln
24,519	595	2,187	18,237	12,387	Loudon
13,919	4,049	7,332	26,985	34,320	McMinn
9,383	2,277	2,014	5,754	10,615	McNairy
7,189	419	5,528	4,743	6,912	Macon
58,062	38,840	30,803	78,470	85,394	Madison
19,173	4,964	5,915	16,974	15,127	Marion
15,411	1,053	4,032	9,597	11,075	Marshall
17,078	19,859	9,798	40,095	54,989	Maury
(D)	(D)	(D)	1,737	2,865	Meigs
6,757	2,627	4,056	19,534	14,777	Monroe
21,514	42,743	27,281	83,916	69,175	Montgomery
(D)	(D)	(D)	809	6,546	Moore
2,629	563	312	2,648	3,627	Morgan
6,959	13,024	8,678	15,323	26,936	Obion
4,041	724	1,464	5,477	7,683	Overton
3,167	94	257	552	1,781	Perry
1,731	(D)	(D)	1,442	3,116	Pickett
1,059	(D)	264	3,953	3,336	Polk
30,590	23,011	17,122	45,478	38,460	Putnam
7,923	2,534	1,218	10,549	8,295	Rhea
11,813	5,048	6,359	21,601	25,116	Roane
35,608	4,004	6,081	19,331	26,447	Robertson
49,089	38,065	26,694	99,367	84,449	Rutherford
4,213	930	2,053	7,826	8,741	Scott
5,032	363	337	2,520	3,992	Sequatchie
25,699	128,343	28,217	138,839	159,953	Sevier
641,608	377,406	294,318	695,520	1,087,696	Shelby
2,627	419	7,812	4,025	9,185	Smith
1,183	(D)	858	2,110	3,118	Stewart
67,734	48,243	41,194	117,246	165,735	Sullivan
28,474	6,249	10,235	47,628	65,794	Sumner
7,953	3,980	2,361	10,612	16,304	Tipton
1,611	(D)	329	847	3,960	Trousdale
2,192	1,546	1,608	6,894	7,478	Unicoi
942	(D)	655	772	3,044	Union
(D)	(D)	(D)	211	1,210	Van Buren
13,535	10,448	5,014	19,354	20,387	Warren
31,502	27,472	23,088	90,745	110,097	Washington
3,549	493	1,819	4,245	4,516	Wayne
10,567	3,633	3,275	15,605	18,698	Weakley
2,231	1,218	1,539	8,274	8,055	White
40,556	35,931	17,033	56,067	82,008	Williamson
40,863	11,802	6,965	36,254	48,393	Wilson

(D) Withheld to avoid disclosing operations of individual companies; may also represent no sales.
Source: Tennessee Department of Revenue, direct correspondence.

TABLE 7-12--RETAIL TRADE EMPLOYEES AND PAYROLL, AND NUMBER OF ESTABLISHMENTS BY EMPLOYMENT-SIZE CLASS, COUNTIES, 1991

County	Number of employees [1]	Annual payroll ($1,000)	Total	1 to 4	5 to 9	10 to 19	20 to 49	50 or more
						Employment-size class		
Anderson	4,982	$57,946	428	225	86	55	39	23
Bedford	1,665	16,985	190	94	49	31	11	5
Benton	697	6,097	96	56	23	11	4	2
Bledsoe	170	1,370	34	24	5	3	2	0
Blount	6,276	81,855	492	225	121	69	51	26
Bradley	5,081	56,184	455	231	95	58	53	18
Campbell	1,877	18,144	199	101	46	28	17	7
Cannon	240	2,664	42	28	6	6	2	0
Carroll	1,211	11,050	179	108	34	21	14	2
Carter	2,031	18,480	214	119	44	24	22	5
Cheatham	667	6,480	77	43	17	8	7	2
Chester	393	4,837	73	52	11	4	5	1
Claiborne	1,213	9,727	124	78	24	8	8	6
Clay	148	1,108	36	25	7	4	0	0
Cocke	1,546	14,995	148	78	29	19	16	6
Coffee	3,816	36,592	334	164	84	35	38	13
Crockett	450	3,613	70	40	14	13	3	0
Cumberland	2,425	29,651	239	137	40	30	24	8
Davidson	65,203	841,469	4,107	1,662	1,022	653	508	262
Decatur	476	5,012	75	43	15	13	3	1
DeKalb	461	4,670	82	50	18	10	4	0
Dickson	2,185	24,162	210	96	51	35	23	5
Dyer	2,659	27,108	271	135	71	33	23	9
Fayette	480	5,565	83	47	22	11	3	0
Fentress	606	6,110	78	46	19	5	7	1
Franklin	1,512	17,642	170	90	34	33	8	5
Gibson	2,364	23,433	312	181	62	41	23	5
Giles	1,253	13,584	158	84	39	20	11	4
Grainger	301	2,982	53	34	8	7	4	0
Greene	3,215	30,634	306	157	71	36	33	9
Grundy	531	4,863	71	42	15	7	5	2
Hamblen	4,168	43,444	370	168	109	40	34	19
Hamilton	28,481	343,463	2,163	943	540	335	227	118
Hancock	101	750	23	17	3	2	1	0
Hardeman	1,010	11,067	139	89	25	15	6	4
Hardin	1,390	13,791	167	96	40	19	8	4
Hawkins	1,614	15,913	162	93	24	24	13	8
Haywood	979	9,434	108	66	18	12	8	4
Henderson	1,202	11,194	147	84	34	11	15	3
Henry	1,959	19,446	214	89	72	32	16	5
Hickman	392	3,206	74	54	9	7	4	0
Houston	183	1,785	35	24	8	2	1	0
Humphreys	748	7,687	92	49	24	10	8	1
Jackson	232	1,980	50	38	6	3	3	0
Jefferson	1,388	13,976	142	76	35	11	14	6
Johnson	301	3,253	59	36	18	3	2	0
Knox	38,012	445,891	2,638	1,104	693	388	294	159
Lake	232	1,999	35	19	10	3	3	0
Lauderdale	867	7,661	134	82	23	20	8	1
Lawrence	1,800	20,105	218	130	41	29	13	5

TABLE 7-12--RETAIL TRADE EMPLOYEES AND PAYROLL, AND NUMBER OF ESTABLISHMENTS BY
EMPLOYMENT-SIZE CLASS, COUNTIES, 1991 (Continued)

County	Number of employees [1]	Annual payroll ($1,000)	Employment-size class					
			Total	1 to 4	5 to 9	10 to 19	20 to 49	50 or more
Lewis	389	3,211	53	35	7	8	1	2
Lincoln	1,450	13,871	170	92	45	15	14	4
Loudon	1,400	14,243	142	82	25	18	10	7
McMinn	3,127	28,659	281	160	47	32	29	13
McNairy	642	6,102	111	78	17	9	6	1
Macon	577	6,052	86	58	16	5	5	2
Madison	8,153	81,441	633	274	155	101	70	33
Marion	1,418	13,589	138	73	34	13	12	6
Marshall	1,096	11,952	129	77	29	11	7	5
Maury	4,117	48,657	398	191	109	55	30	13
Meigs	202	1,780	30	19	7	2	1	1
Monroe	1,650	16,138	188	104	44	19	15	6
Montgomery	7,242	83,432	630	277	189	80	53	31
Moore	58	441	16	10	3	3	0	0
Morgan	225	2,107	38	26	6	2	4	0
Obion	2,160	23,450	243	120	60	35	23	5
Overton	528	4,669	66	34	19	6	6	1
Perry	148	1,107	31	21	5	4	1	0
Pickett	73	593	19	14	3	2	0	0
Polk	293	2,494	52	33	12	3	4	0
Putnam	4,536	47,649	416	218	86	51	47	14
Rhea	1,088	10,378	119	65	29	11	11	3
Roane	2,133	22,118	224	108	59	31	19	7
Robertson	2,005	21,072	161	84	32	18	16	11
Rutherford	9,238	101,994	624	268	160	87	78	31
Scott	778	6,848	89	55	15	11	4	4
Sequatchie	315	3,159	45	26	8	8	2	1
Sevier	6,335	78,247	708	376	170	87	54	21
Shelby	75,493	959,741	4,903	1,927	1,241	848	574	313
Smith	608	7,116	87	55	13	12	5	2
Stewart	227	2,337	42	23	11	5	3	0
Sullivan	12,347	136,164	899	395	209	135	106	54
Sumner	5,142	53,364	488	249	111	59	54	15
Tipton	1,477	15,711	185	110	33	26	13	3
Trousdale	215	2,199	42	31	6	3	2	0
Unicoi	560	5,280	76	38	19	14	5	0
Union	157	1,854	46	34	9	2	1	0
Van Buren	17	174	6	5	1	0	0	0
Warren	2,190	22,256	213	113	47	29	17	7
Washington	8,257	87,975	626	283	144	89	70	40
Wayne	388	3,390	64	39	12	9	4	0
Weakley	1,519	13,265	181	102	31	32	13	3
White	826	8,262	92	52	17	11	11	1
Williamson	8,129	139,474	538	289	104	58	60	27
Wilson	3,885	60,692	315	162	61	43	35	14

1. Number of employees for week including March 12.
Source: U.S. Department of Commerce, Bureau of the Census, *County Business Patterns*, 1991.

TABLE 7.13--SERVICES EMPLOYEES AND PAYROLL, AND NUMBER OF ESTABLISHMENTS BY
EMPLOYMENT-SIZE CLASS, COUNTIES, 1991

County	Number of employees [1]	Annual payroll ($1,000)	Total	1 to 4	5 to 9	10 to 19	20 to 49	50 or more
Anderson	13,721	$438,115	649	382	124	70	37	36
Bedford	1,587	20,420	187	124	39	11	7	6
Benton	621	7,710	85	59	17	3	3	3
Bledsoe	330	3,870	32	24	5	1	0	2
Blount	5,815	101,481	609	378	121	70	26	14
Bradley	8,479	138,510	577	309	131	67	32	38
Campbell	1,089	15,484	150	102	27	13	5	3
Cannon	302	4,357	38	27	6	3	0	2
Carroll	1,455	17,813	172	132	26	3	5	6
Carter	2,253	31,363	276	188	54	18	10	6
Cheatham	392	4,957	78	62	8	6	0	2
Chester	403	6,734	37	24	8	3	0	2
Claiborne	863	14,132	101	63	22	7	6	3
Clay	323	3,923	28	16	5	5	0	2
Cocke	1,017	15,488	138	90	34	5	6	3
Coffee	7,300	223,120	354	224	62	37	21	10
Crockett	397	4,359	63	47	13	1	0	2
Cumberland	2,452	34,587	233	168	33	15	8	9
Davidson	123,628	2,647,010	6,679	3,782	1,278	747	511	361
Decatur	444	7,147	60	41	9	5	3	2
DeKalb	1,256	17,348	85	62	15	4	0	4
Dickson	1,979	33,387	178	115	35	13	8	7
Dyer	2,129	34,701	259	169	47	27	10	6
Fayette	568	7,348	79	57	12	5	2	3
Fentress	619	9,417	61	45	10	3	0	3
Franklin	2,416	36,467	197	136	35	13	5	8
Gibson	2,226	26,437	327	238	52	20	8	9
Giles	1,213	19,005	150	97	31	10	6	6
Grainger	295	2,479	52	42	6	1	2	1
Greene	3,678	54,278	377	253	64	34	13	13
Grundy	240	2,415	50	41	6	2	0	1
Hamblen	3,833	57,736	390	230	82	44	23	11
Hamilton	44,181	831,303	2,993	1,624	627	378	226	138
Hancock	121	1,689	17	13	0	2	2	0
Hardeman	1,851	24,828	122	84	20	9	3	6
Hardin	609	6,503	113	82	20	6	3	2
Hawkins	1,019	12,715	166	115	33	12	2	4
Haywood	629	8,983	106	72	20	8	4	2
Henderson	730	8,840	102	73	14	7	4	4
Henry	1,324	19,874	209	133	46	17	9	4
Hickman	453	5,435	64	47	11	3	1	2
Houston	335	4,194	29	19	5	2	1	2
Humphreys	501	7,203	78	52	14	7	4	1
Jackson	355	4,498	45	30	7	4	2	2
Jefferson	1,788	20,451	167	117	34	9	3	4
Johnson	357	4,407	61	51	3	3	2	2
Knox	50,880	1,045,701	3,642	2,037	715	472	279	139
Lake	206	1,947	37	27	7	2	0	1
Lauderdale	632	7,657	96	72	15	4	3	2
Lawrence	1,352	18,969	187	125	42	13	2	5

TABLE 7.13--SERVICES EMPLOYEES AND PAYROLL, AND NUMBER OF ESTABLISHMENTS BY
EMPLOYMENT-SIZE CLASS, COUNTIES, 1991 (Continued)

County	Number of employees [1]	Annual payroll ($1,000)	Employment-size class					
			Total	1 to 4	5 to 9	10 to 19	20 to 49	50 or more
Lewis	512	6,775	55	42	5	3	1	4
Lincoln	1,028	14,387	163	115	33	6	5	4
Loudon	1,708	20,838	182	123	26	16	11	6
McMinn	2,097	28,567	279	187	60	15	8	9
McNairy	2,603	46,715	113	80	19	7	2	5
Macon	453	5,280	61	43	11	4	1	2
Madison	12,484	253,293	773	408	147	112	72	34
Marion	796	10,963	96	65	19	7	2	3
Marshall	1,051	13,577	131	83	31	10	2	5
Maury	4,743	84,732	450	268	96	42	26	18
Meigs	133	1,334	24	18	5	0	0	1
Monroe	1,238	15,561	147	107	19	9	4	8
Montgomery	4,104	56,573	576	357	129	52	29	9
Moore	47	389	15	14	0	1	0	0
Morgan	324	3,912	33	22	4	3	3	1
Obion	1,843	28,302	219	147	45	17	5	5
Overton	504	7,699	70	56	8	3	1	2
Perry	276	4,955	30	22	6	0	0	2
Pickett	118	1,174	14	9	2	0	3	0
Polk	449	5,390	86	68	12	4	0	2
Putnam	3,906	59,343	433	266	93	39	20	15
Rhea	927	11,202	111	70	32	4	2	3
Roane	1,836	25,828	240	169	41	15	8	7
Robertson	2,173	20,395	197	135	35	15	6	6
Rutherford	9,839	183,173	743	442	144	81	48	28
Scott	1,011	13,632	75	49	14	5	3	4
Sequatchie	327	4,928	42	30	6	3	0	3
Sevier	6,629	89,655	620	383	97	75	46	19
Shelby	122,534	2,416,707	7,032	3,789	1,354	924	582	383
Smith	607	8,171	73	53	13	3	1	3
Stewart	137	1,520	22	15	6	0	0	1
Sullivan	15,386	309,845	1,182	690	205	172	84	31
Sumner	6,779	106,918	697	443	136	70	28	20
Tipton	1,319	16,352	178	121	38	9	7	3
Trousdale	264	3,596	31	23	5	0	1	2
Unicoi	671	10,050	85	54	21	8	0	2
Union	136	1,231	26	18	7	0	0	1
Van Buren	18	447	8	7	1	0	0	0
Warren	1,620	25,531	211	143	33	19	13	3
Washington	12,145	220,809	830	491	164	98	45	32
Wayne	377	4,428	53	38	9	4	1	1
Weakley	2,612	34,020	188	121	36	17	9	5
White	491	6,211	92	71	15	4	0	2
Williamson	10,435	210,022	881	519	166	101	58	37
Wilson	4,042	68,236	445	277	85	45	26	12

1. Number of employees for week including March 12.

Source: U.S. Department of Commerce, Bureau of the Census, *County Business Patterns*, 1991.

TABLE 7.14--SERVICE INDUSTRIES DATA, COUNTIES AND MUNICIPALITIES WITH POPULATION
OF 2,500 OR MORE, 1987 [Dollar amounts in thousands]

County and municipality	Number of establish-ments	Receipts	Annual payroll	Number of paid employees [1]
Anderson	447	$683,054	$200,812	8,439
Clinton	50	14,837	3,721	383
Oak Ridge (part)	324	(D)	(D)	(D)
Oliver Springs (part)	16	(D)	(D)	(D)
Bedford	134	34,491	12,224	1,093
Shelbyville	119	32,183	11,442	1,006
Benton	61	19,096	5,910	514
Camden	45	14,219	5,124	419
Bledsoe	29	7,324	2,349	180
Blount	442	132,163	48,403	3,139
Alcoa	61	22,076	6,103	583
Maryville	274	77,107	30,816	1,794
Bradley	388	179,674	64,743	5,329
Cleveland	342	141,576	50,288	3,720
Campbell	108	21,327	6,353	679
Jellico	15	2,162	807	60
LaFollette	66	13,398	3,947	459
Cannon	27	8,934	3,307	239
Carroll	107	17,289	5,681	508
Huntingdon	42	8,128	2,881	282
McKenzie (part)	35	(D)	(D)	(D)
Carter	157	41,363	15,030	1,055
Elizabethton	132	37,678	13,237	967
Johnson City (part)	0	0	0	0
Cheatham	41	4,136	967	95
Chester	22	3,067	953	123
Henderson	19	2,898	903	105
Claiborne	65	15,226	4,134	465
Clay	26	12,190	4,816	317
Cocke	90	20,144	6,104	594
Newport	69	16,948	4,863	462
Coffee	257	387,307	219,824	8,153
Manchester	82	(D)	(D)	(D)
Tullahoma (part)	146	(D)	(D)	(D)
Crockett	35	5,942	2,387	197
Alamo	19	4,373	1,978	158
Cumberland	145	29,898	10,546	898
Crossville	125	25,123	9,099	728
Davidson	4,843	2,786,669	1,006,911	63,282
Belle Meade	72	66,424	32,565	506
Forest Hills	11	903	421	17
Goodlettsville (part)	116	39,747	17,261	1,570
Nashville-Davidson	4,633	2,678,407	956,334	61,156
Oak Hill	11	1,188	330	33
Decatur	39	9,324	2,966	316
DeKalb	54	19,919	6,743	391
Smithville	42	17,429	5,920	316
Dickson	130	31,142	12,296	975
Dickson	87	24,377	10,554	819
Dyer	181	37,279	11,385	829
Dyersburg	162	34,801	10,589	746
Newbern	8	838	242	22

TABLE 7.14--SERVICE INDUSTRIES DATA, COUNTIES AND MUNICIPALITIES WITH POPULATION OF 2,500 OR MORE, 1987 [Dollar amounts in thousands] (Continued)

County and municipality	Number of establish- ments	Receipts	Annual payroll	Number of paid employees [1]
Fayette	44	6,790	2,207	212
Fentress	52	16,240	5,970	466
Franklin	122	18,451	6,148	439
Tullahoma (part)	1	(D)	(D)	(D)
Winchester	82	12,925	4,150	332
Gibson	212	46,748	15,142	1,383
Humboldt	62	13,593	4,282	392
Milan	59	12,836	4,849	377
Trenton	51	15,826	4,889	497
Giles	100	35,083	12,629	910
Pulaski	76	29,259	10,406	654
Grainger	27	4,798	1,443	177
Greene	249	58,027	20,158	1,517
Greeneville	214	49,482	17,150	1,238
Grundy	26	5,544	1,545	229
Hamblen	275	82,751	28,013	1,869
Morristown	254	80,058	27,100	1,780
Hamilton	2,147	1,005,624	377,696	23,946
Chattanooga	1,710	878,848	335,856	20,854
Collegedale	15	8,075	2,940	230
East Ridge	157	59,759	18,949	1,401
Red Bank	95	24,522	8,805	557
Signal Mountain	42	4,536	1,728	103
Soddy-Daisy	23	1,626	401	42
Hancock	13	2,024	653	89
Hardeman	66	14,635	4,169	416
Bolivar	41	8,401	2,932	287
Hardin	78	13,924	4,018	352
Savannah	66	12,259	3,542	310
Hawkins	95	17,248	5,507	494
Church Hill	21	4,961	1,582	148
Kingsport (part)	5	364	159	20
Mount Carmel	3	159	38	9
Rogersville	44	6,362	1,746	154
Haywood	65	15,969	4,971	361
Brownsville	60	15,003	4,786	336
Henderson	76	9,142	2,860	262
Lexington	56	7,790	2,528	223
Henry	148	37,759	10,757	705
McKenzie (part)	0	0	0	0
Paris	122	32,189	9,312	589
Hickman	46	6,906	2,057	212
Centerville	30	5,755	1,784	181
Houston	16	6,308	2,362	172
Humphreys	61	15,955	4,673	373
Waverly	43	13,240	4,056	297
Jackson	30	7,702	2,501	227
Jefferson	88	15,116	4,455	430
Jefferson City	43	8,096	2,645	280
Johnson	35	7,242	2,278	196
Knox	2,715	1,111,249	441,485	25,018
Farragut	1	(D)	(D)	(D)
Knoxville	2,142	838,374	325,327	19,451

TABLE 7.14--SERVICE INDUSTRIES DATA, COUNTIES AND MUNICIPALITIES WITH POPULATION
OF 2,500 OR MORE, 1987 [Dollar amounts in thousands] (Continued)

County and municipality	Number of establishments	Receipts	Annual payroll	Number of paid employees [1]
Lake	24	3,489	1,244	178
Lauderdale	67	11,422	3,655	374
Ripley	52	8,623	2,847	279
Lawrence	133	29,742	9,257	777
Lawrenceburg	102	17,860	4,827	419
Lewis	32	8,891	3,421	299
Hohenwald	26	8,034	2,901	279
Lincoln	122	18,717	5,495	563
Fayetteville	94	16,489	4,755	495
Loudon	106	22,054	7,510	703
Lenoir City	43	7,582	2,545	235
Loudon	38	11,447	3,982	386
McMinn	172	60,639	19,332	1,597
Athens	124	49,826	15,725	1,293
Etowah	30	6,024	2,474	200
McNairy	70	29,121	13,440	953
Selmer	42	6,425	1,770	144
Macon	47	8,016	2,352	234
Lafayette	38	5,328	1,534	120
Madison	542	208,938	96,318	5,101
Jackson	517	205,860	95,525	5,026
Marion	70	22,278	7,906	625
Jasper	24	3,144	1,248	79
South Pittsburg	27	10,453	3,845	324
Marshall	88	25,384	8,745	972
Lewisburg	71	23,467	8,265	919
Maury	310	96,157	32,253	2,276
Columbia	262	89,549	30,151	2,083
Mount Pleasant	25	4,239	1,260	129
Meigs	13	2,197	897	82
Monroe	83	18,901	5,957	524
Madisonville	19	2,617	761	67
Sweetwater	42	9,059	3,111	266
Montgomery	418	93,041	30,720	2,501
Clarksville	386	87,021	28,620	2,300
Moore	3	(D)	(D)	(D)
Morgan	17	3,536	1,269	146
Oliver Springs (part)	0	0	0	0
Obion	161	41,320	12,799	901
South Fulton	23	2,082	494	58
Union City	108	36,644	11,504	764
Overton	49	16,053	4,849	378
Livingston	43	15,121	4,673	358
Perry	22	8,537	2,880	244
Pickett	12	2,267	677	88
Polk	44	7,423	2,279	201
Putnam	320	91,189	36,137	2,968
Cookeville	293	83,401	33,480	2,702
Monterey	8	2,129	852	94
Rhea	73	10,060	3,097	235
Dayton	45	5,539	1,656	134

TABLE 7.14--SERVICE INDUSTRIES DATA, COUNTIES AND MUNICIPALITIES WITH POPULATION OF 2,500 OR MORE, 1987 [Dollar amounts in thousands] (Continued)

County and municipality	Number of establish-ments	Receipts	Annual payroll	Number of paid employees [1]
Roane	167	32,086	10,412	791
Harriman	65	13,604	4,914	415
Kingston	35	6,622	1,888	133
Oak Ridge (part)	3	(D)	(D)	(D)
Oliver Springs (part)	1	(D)	(D)	(D)
Rockwood	37	6,695	2,126	128
Robertson	128	22,605	7,250	664
Greenbrier	8	1,165	445	35
Springfield	92	17,552	5,776	510
Rutherford	538	180,466	67,559	4,350
LaVergne	32	20,559	10,545	365
Murfreesboro	403	136,073	48,741	3,319
Smyrna	77	21,120	7,581	583
Scott	44	8,265	2,919	229
Oneida	33	4,704	1,872	127
Sequatchie	32	8,745	3,214	249
Dunlap	22	7,149	2,860	218
Sevier	470	185,749	48,405	4,061
Gatlinburg	142	67,871	17,234	1,756
Sevierville	129	20,160	6,683	558
Shelby	5,289	2,517,776	984,817	63,148
Bartlett	125	29,591	11,419	881
Collierville	71	12,258	4,070	368
Germantown	295	114,481	55,130	2,139
Memphis	4,475	2,255,617	877,757	56,983
Millington	54	11,638	4,211	340
Smith	55	14,266	4,469	375
Carthage	42	9,119	2,875	269
Stewart	14	1,706	453	42
Sullivan	893	346,288	135,537	7,374
Bristol	245	93,987	39,361	1,859
Kingsport (part)	516	203,813	81,265	4,412
Sumner	521	163,826	61,262	4,305
Gallatin	153	44,389	16,934	1,306
Goodlettsville (part)	3	311	104	10
Hendersonville	282	108,033	40,897	2,691
Portland	27	3,975	1,491	99
Tipton	103	15,365	4,137	361
Covington	65	11,082	3,001	249
Trousdale	23	5,637	2,025	155
Hartsville	19	5,203	1,915	142
Unicoi	60	10,927	4,308	326
Erwin	50	(D)	(D)	(D)
Union	20	4,313	1,206	146
Van Buren	3	(D)	(D)	(D)
Warren	151	40,473	13,142	996
McMinnville	127	38,474	12,557	914
Washington	588	173,566	67,289	5,117
Johnson City (part)	480	157,832	61,691	4,551
Jonesborough	30	5,915	2,290	199
Wayne	30	7,415	2,685	208
Weakley	111	33,003	11,936	1,114
McKenzie (part)	1	(D)	(D)	(D)

TABLE 7.14--SERVICE INDUSTRIES DATA, COUNTIES AND MUNICIPALITIES WITH POPULATION
OF 2,500 OR MORE, 1987 [Dollar amounts in thousands] (Continued)

County and municipality	Number of establish-ments	Receipts	Annual payroll	Number of paid employees[1]
Martin	51	24,223	9,527	884
White	71	12,367	3,740	323
Sparta	59	10,954	3,475	305
Williamson	601	213,404	85,546	4,756
Brentwood	284	120,278	52,669	2,598
Fairview	10	975	233	23
Franklin	255	76,712	27,667	1,973
Wilson	305	103,519	33,261	2,606
Lebanon	214	88,689	27,861	2,238
Mt. Juliet	49	7,374	2,172	171

Note: Includes only those establishments with payroll that were subject to Federal Income Tax.

(D) Withheld to avoid disclosing operations of individual companies.

1. Survey taken during week of March 12.

Source: U.S. Department of Commerce, Bureau of the Census, *1987 Census of Service Industries, Geographic Area Series, Tennessee.*

TABLE 7.15--RETAIL TRADE STATISTICS, SOUTHEASTERN STATES, 1987 [Dollar amounts in thousands]

State	Number of establishments			Sales	Annual payroll	Number of paid employees[1]
	Total	Individual proprietor-ships	Partner-ships			
TENNESSEE	29,373	10,123	2,761	$28,532,933	$3,198,060	338,168
Alabama	24,092	7,936	1,558	21,260,901	2,357,486	249,847
Arkansas	15,096	5,692	1,111	11,631,735	1,245,802	138,671
Florida	83,808	13,814	2,964	87,925,609	10,297,035	1,022,862
Georgia	39,782	10,836	2,169	39,994,882	4,791,594	486,992
Kentucky	21,731	6,663	1,798	18,939,911	2,132,223	243,641
Louisiana	24,262	6,459	1,048	21,627,111	2,569,763	277,708
Mississippi	15,729	6,062	1,312	11,357,667	1,264,565	140,361
North Carolina	42,991	11,846	2,676	39,051,791	4,422,835	464,862
South Carolina	21,859	6,300	1,245	18,949,588	2,177,453	237,122
Virginia	34,916	7,704	1,643	38,960,210	4,556,660	453,325
West Virginia	10,737	3,405	595	9,029,979	994,297	109,220

Note: Includes only establishments with payroll.

1. Survey taken during week of March 12.

Source: U.S. Department of Commerce, Bureau of the Census, *1987 Census of Retail Trade, Geographic Area Series,* individual states.

TABLE 7.16--WHOLESALE TRADE DATA, SOUTHEASTERN STATES, 1987 [Dollar amounts in thousands]

State	Number of establish-ments	Sales	Annual payroll	Number of paid employees [1]	Operating expenses
TENNESSEE	8,782	$48,278,891	$2,518,097	115,927	$5,171,868
Alabama	6,671	24,343,595	1,548,477	77,559	3,196,662
Arkansas	4,024	12,780,741	705,452	38,940	1,495,469
Florida	25,636	97,360,044	5,554,657	261,765	11,638,571
Georgia	13,678	86,853,971	4,116,577	178,235	8,529,135
Kentucky	5,650	24,461,486	1,240,003	63,606	2,538,774
Louisiana	7,643	31,477,276	1,652,536	80,533	3,459,995
Mississippi	3,850	12,249,754	733,066	39,936	1,563,650
North Carolina	12,109	57,027,579	3,064,076	140,158	6,051,686
South Carolina	5,271	17,084,415	1,064,842	54,551	2,221,689
Virginia	8,446	44,758,793	2,625,045	115,126	5,409,943
West Virginia	2,444	5,935,356	476,934	24,217	963,763

1. Survey taken during week of March 12.
Source: U.S. Department of Commerce, Bureau of the Census, *1987 Census of Wholesale Trade, Geographic Area Series*, individual states.

TABLE 7.17--SERVICE INDUSTRIES DATA, SOUTHEASTERN STATES, 1987 [Dollar amounts in thousands]

State	Number of establish-ments	Receipts	Annual payroll	Number of paid employees [1]
TENNESSEE	27,829	$12,010,161	$4,486,948	282,908
Alabama	20,474	8,397,181	3,066,890	189,566
Arkansas	12,437	3,703,250	1,365,908	93,960
Florida	98,713	45,530,941	16,909,560	974,746
Georgia	39,189	18,645,815	6,908,896	414,969
Kentucky	18,415	6,325,252	2,315,487	166,228
Louisiana	25,513	10,243,284	3,788,155	240,551
Mississippi	11,663	3,331,645	1,208,449	84,293
North Carolina	36,016	12,829,836	4,928,270	331,402
South Carolina	18,810	6,354,990	2,396,984	169,535
Virginia	38,337	20,414,594	8,128,443	438,728
West Virginia	8,909	2,917,003	1,030,947	67,281

Note: Includes only those establishments with payroll that were subject to Federal Income Tax.
1. Survey taken during week of March 12.
Source: U.S. Department of Commerce, Bureau of the Census, *1987 Census of Service Industries, Geographic Area Series*, individual states.

TABLE 7.18--NUMBER OF BUSINESS STARTS, BY INDUSTRY SECTOR, SOUTHEASTERN STATES, 1987

State	Total[1]		Agriculture, forestry and fishing	Mining	Construction	Manufacturing	Transportation and public utilities	Wholesale and retail trade	Finance, insurance and real estate	Services
	Firms	Employees								
TENNESSEE	3,852	21,784	47	9	495	326	122	1,716	232	802
Alabama	3,015	16,019	59	8	369	220	79	1,367	119	644
Arkansas	1,732	9,829	40	18	195	149	79	850	61	318
Florida	15,088	80,027	210	12	2,353	1,113	555	6,338	1,133	3,236
Georgia	6,972	36,341	96	8	881	556	233	2,737	433	1,591
Kentucky	2,876	14,212	49	92	345	202	108	1,270	130	603
Louisiana	3,490	19,687	44	85	380	187	127	1,580	219	833
Mississippi	1,743	8,625	50	15	160	127	64	876	84	345
North Carolina	5,072	26,881	69	2	733	509	126	2,235	292	962
South Carolina	2,843	18,335	44	5	335	212	96	1,290	197	567
Virginia	5,519	26,763	100	43	1,136	305	166	1,788	393	1,277
West Virginia	1,197	5,015	15	91	160	37	33	519	53	262

1. Total includes categories not shown separately.

Source: Printed by permission from The Dun and Bradstreet Corporation, *Business Starts Record, 1986/1987.*

TABLE 7.19--FAILURE RATES PER 10,000 BUSINESSES, SOUTHEASTERN STATES AND
UNITED STATES, 1940-1993, SELECTED YEARS

State	1993 p	1992	1991	1990	1989	1985	1980	1970	1960	1950	1940
TENNESSEE	88	120	145	111	95	149	101	41	40	15	36
Alabama	80	86	100	67	53	97	45	21	24	17	31
Arkansas	23	65	64	38	44	130	39	19	28	13	43
Florida	121	130	135	100	89	113	25	38	94	31	58
Georgia	121	130	203	119	109	87	46	34	46	22	70
Kentucky	81	105	122	108	71	142	25	25	22	11	29
Louisiana	57	74	96	103	132	163	32	32	44	18	14
Mississippi	46	70	74	64	80	112	39	18	25	17	36
North Carolina	62	78	72	56	44	65	34	15	25	18	45
South Carolina	42	52	66	46	22	45	n.a.	9	60	5	31
Virginia	87	117	133	94	70	106	52	29	31	21	63
West Virginia	64	85	85	52	37	130	25	33	35	20	26
UNITED STATES	96	110	107	76	65	115	42	44	57	34	63

Note: Businesses are those listed by The Dun and Bradstreet Corporation. Data are for commercial and industrial
failures only through 1983, excluding failures of banks, railroads, real estate, insurance, holding and financial
companies, steamship lines, travel agencies, etc. Beginning in 1984 data are based on expanded coverage and
new methodology and are, therefore, not comparable with earlier years.

p preliminary.

n.a. not available.

Source: Printed by permission from Dun and Bradstreet Corporation, direct correspondence; and *The Business
Failure Record, 1991/1992*, and earlier editions.

The communications media covered in this section include newspapers, telephones, radio and television stations, and the cable television industry.

The Federal Communications Commission's (FCC) annual *Statistics of Communications Common Carriers* was the source for statistics on the telephone industry until 1982. Reports submitted by the American Telephone and Telegraph Company and other independent companies were compiled in this publication. However, due to recent industry changes, these data are no longer published. The Tennessee Telephone Association currently provides information on telephone companies serving each county in Tennessee. Sometimes as many as five companies serve one county. The *Census of Housing* also provides data on telephone availability in occupied housing units. Data from the 1990 Census provide information on this industry.

Earlier data for the cable television industry were also from the FCC's *Annual Report*. The current source for statistics on cable television is *Television and Cable Factbook*, published by Warren Publishing, Inc. The previous publisher of this report was *Television Digest, Inc*.

Comprehensive data for Tennessee newspapers are detailed in the *Tennessee Newspaper Directory*, a semi-annual publication of the Tennessee Press Association. Included are data on paid circulation and publication of both daily and nondaily newspapers in Tennessee. Figure 8.1, also from the *Tennessee Newspaper Directory*, shows the location of newspaper publishers across the state.

Data on FM and AM radio stations for each Tennessee town and city are given in Table 8.7. These data are available in the yearbook issue of *Broadcasting Cablecasting*. Television data in Table 8.6 are also from this source.

TABLE OF CONTENTS

TABLE 8.1-- NUMBER AND PAID CIRCULATION OF NEWSPAPERS PUBLISHED, TENNESSEE, 1955-1990

Year	Total[1]	Number of newspapers published					Net paid circulation (1,000)		
		Daily morning	Daily evening	Sunday edition	Weekly	Others[2]	Daily morning[3]	Daily evening	Sunday edition[4]
1990	143	12	17	20	96	17	679.1	361.2	1,162.9
1989[a]	n.a.	28[a]	(a)	16	n.a.	n.a.	965.0[a]	(a)	1,073.0
1988	135	10	18	16	92	14	650.2	382.7	1,112.3
1987	132	10	18	15	90	13	603.2	387.7	1,109.7
1986	135	9	18	16	93	13	594.4	400.6	1,099.5
1985	135	8	18	15	93	14	550.6	434.8	1,080.4
1984	143	8	19	16	96	17	585.2	448.3	1,083.4
1983	139	7	19	15	93	17	494.7	448.9	1,046.2
1982	153	7	22	16	104	18	494.0	564.9	1,061.9
1981	153	7	22	16	105	17	492.7	558.6[b]	1,044.6
1980	154	7	22	16	106	17	500.4	578.4	1,038.7
1979	154	7	22	16	105	18	515.5	588.5	1,062.3
1978	163	7	25	14	118	13	454.6	594.1	968.0
1977	160	7	25	14	116	12	450.7	611.8	950.1
1976	158	6	25	14	115	12	448.5	609.2	948.2
1975	158	6	25	14	116	11	473.3	627.8	972.5
1974	160	6	25	14	118	11	496.5	625.2	952.3
1973	160	6	24	14	120	10	493.8	626.5	939.8
1972	164	6	23	14	122	13	494.9	604.5	881.8
1971	159	6	24	13	122	7	492.7	607.9	900.5
1970	159	6	23	13	123	7	492.0	638.0	901.3
1969	162	6	23	13	126	7	500.1	622.9	896.4
1968	160	6	23	13	123	8	498.0	601.7	874.4
1967	162	6	23	12	125	8	497.9	573.8	832.5
1966	162	6	21	10	127	8	486.8	568.3	819.3
1965	161	6	21	10	128	6	489.2	559.8	800.3
1964	159	6	21	10	126	6	481.6	557.5	788.7
1963	160	6	22	10	126	6	478.6	551.6	771.0
1962	158	6	22	9	124	6	487.0	562.5	765.3
1961	156	6	21	7	122	7	475.9	558.2	763.4
1960	156	6	21	10	123	6	462.8	546.5	753.5
1959	156	6	21	10	121	8	456.7	527.4	731.2
1958	156	6	21	10	120	9	462.7	535.0	706.1
1957	160	6	21	9	124	9	471.2	523.4	810.9
1956	158	7	21	12	121	9	469.7	517.2	807.8
1955	159	7	21	13	123	8	468.4	509.4	796.6

Note: Data beginning in 1979 were compiled by the Center for Business and Economic Research from data for individual newspaper publishers listed in the sources cited.

n.a. not available.

1. The difference between "total" column and the sum of "daily," "weekly," and "others" columns represents the number of all-day daily newspapers.

2. Newspapers published more than once per week; computed by the Center for Business and Economic Research.

3. Beginning in 1988 includes circulation of all-day daily newspapers.

4. Where source did not give separate figure for Sunday edition, daily circulation was counted.

a. Source for 1989 data differs from that for other years. Daily figures were not broken down by time of edition.

b. Excludes Union City data which were not available, separately.

Source: Tennessee Press Service, Inc., *Tennessee Newspaper Directory, 1991*, and earlier editions; Editor & Publisher Co., New York, NY, *Editor & Publisher International Year Book*, annual, as printed in U.S. Statistical Abstract, 1991 (1989 data); and IMS Press, *IMS/Ayer Directory of Publications, 1955-1978*, used by special permission.

TABLE 8.2-- TENNESSEE TELEPHONE COMPANIES, COUNTY SERVICE AREAS, 1987

County	Telephone company	Location of telephone company offices
Anderson	South Central Bell Telephone Company	Nashville
	Highland Telephone Cooperative, Inc.	Sunbright
	ALLTEL Tennessee, Inc.	Powell
Bedford	South Central Bell Telephone Company	Nashville
	Ben Lomand Rural Telephone Cooperative, Inc.	McMinnville
	United Telephone Company, Inc.	Chapel Hill
Benton	South Central Bell Telephone Company	Nashville
Bledsoe	Bledsoe Telephone Cooperative	Pikeville
Blount	South Central Bell Telephone Company	Nashville
Bradley	South Central Bell Telephone Company	Nashville
	Ooltewah-Collegedale Telephone Company, Inc.	Chickamauga, Ga.
Campbell	South Central Bell Telephone Company	Nashville
Cannon	DeKalb Telephone Cooperative	Alexandria
Carroll	South Central Bell Telephone Company	Nashville
	Peoples Telephone Company, Inc.	Erin
	Tennessee Telephone Company	Knoxville
	West Tennessee Telephone Company	Bradford
Carter	United Inter-Mountain Telephone Company	Bristol
Cheatham	South Central Bell Telephone Company	Nashville
Chester	South Central Bell Telephone Company	Nashville
	Adamsville Telephone Company, Inc.	Adamsville
Claiborne	South Central Bell Telephone Company	Nashville
	Claiborne Telephone Company, Inc.	New Tazewell
Clay	Twin Lakes Telephone Cooperative Corporation	Gainesboro
Cocke	South Central Bell Telephone Company	Nashville
Coffee	South Central Bell Telephone Company	Nashville
	Ben Lomand Rural Telephone Cooperative, Inc.	McMinnville
Crockett	South Central Bell Telephone Company	Nashville
	Crockett Telephone Company	Friendship
Cumberland	General Telephone Company of the Southeast	Cookeville
Davidson	South Central Bell Telephone Company	Nashville
	Tennessee Telephone Company	Knoxville
	United Telephone Company, Inc.	Chapel Hill
Decatur	Tennessee Telephone Company	Knoxville
DeKalb	DeKalb Telephone Cooperative	Alexandria
	Twin Lakes Telephone Cooperative Corporation	Gainesboro
Dickson	South Central Bell Telephone Company	Nashville
Dyer	South Central Bell Telephone Company	Nashville
	Yorkville Telephone Cooperative, Inc.	Yorkville
Fayette	South Central Bell Telephone Company	Nashville
	Millington Telephone Company, Inc.	Millington
Fentress	Twin Lakes Telephone Cooperative Corporation	Gainesboro
Franklin	South Central Bell Telephone Company	Nashville
	United Telephone Company, Inc.	Chapel Hill
Gibson	South Central Bell Telephone Company	Nashville
	West Tennessee Telephone Company	Bradford

TABLE 8.2-- TENNESSEE TELEPHONE COMPANIES, COUNTY SERVICE AREAS, 1987 (Continued)

County	Telephone company	Location of telephone company offices
Giles	Yorkville Telephone Cooperative, Inc.	Yorkville
	South Central Bell Telephone Company	Nashville
	Ardmore Telephone Company, Inc.	Ardmore
	Tennessee Telephone Company	Knoxville
Grainger	South Central Bell Telephone Company	Nashville
	ALLTEL Tennessee, Inc.	Powell
Greene	United Inter-Mountain Telephone Company	Bristol
Grundy	Ben Lomand Rural Telephone Cooperative, Inc.	McMinnville
Hamblen	South Central Bell Telephone Company	Nashville
Hamilton	South Central Bell Telephone Company	Nashville
	Ooltewah-Collegedale Telephone Company, Inc.	Chickamauga, Ga.
Hancock	South Central Bell Telephone Company	Nashville
	United Inter-Mountain Telephone Company	Bristol
Hardeman	South Central Bell Telephone Company	Nashville
Hardin	South Central Bell Telephone Company	Nashville
	Adamsville Telephone Company, Inc.	Adamsville
	Tennessee Telephone Company	Knoxville
Hawkins	South Central Bell Telephone Company	Nashville
	United Inter-Mountain Telephone Company	Bristol
Haywood	South Central Bell Telephone Company	Nashville
	Millington Telephone Company, Inc.	Millington
Henderson	South Central Bell Telephone Company	Nashville
	Tennessee Telephone Company	Knoxville
Henry	South Central Bell Telephone Company	Nashville
	Peoples Telephone Company, Inc.	Erin
	West Kentucky Rural Telephone Cooperative Corporation, Inc.	Mayfield, Ky.
Hickman	South Central Bell Telephone Company	Nashville
Houston	South Central Bell Telephone Company	Nashville
	Peoples Telephone Company, Inc.	Erin
Humphreys	South Central Bell Telephone Company	Nashville
	Humphreys County Telephone Company	New Johnsonville
Jackson	Twin Lakes Telephone Cooperative Corporation	Gainesboro
Jefferson	South Central Bell Telephone Company	Nashville
Johnson	United Inter-Mountain Telephone Company	Bristol
Knox	South Central Bell Telephone Company	Nashville
	ALLTEL Tennessee, Inc.	Powell
	Tennessee Telephone Company	Knoxville
Lake	South Central Bell Telephone Company	Nashville
Lauderdale	South Central Bell Telephone Company	Nashville
Lawrence	South Central Bell Telephone Company	Nashville
	Loretto Telephone Company, Inc.	Loretto
Lewis	South Central Bell Telephone Company	Nashville
Lincoln	South Central Bell Telephone Company	Nashville
	Ardmore Telephone Company, Inc.	Ardmore
Loudon	South Central Bell Telephone Company	Nashville

TABLE 8.2-- TENNESSEE TELEPHONE COMPANIES, COUNTY SERVICE AREAS, 1987 (Continued)

County	Telephone company	Location of telephone company offices
McMinn	South Central Bell Telephone Company	Nashville
	Englewood Telephone Company, Inc.	Englewood
	Tellico Telephone Company, Inc.	Tellico Plains
McNairy	South Central Bell Telephone Company	Nashville
	Adamsville Telephone Company, Inc.	Adamsville
Macon	North Central Telephone Cooperative, Inc.	Lafayette
Madison	South Central Bell Telephone Company	Nashville
Marion	South Central Bell Telephone Company	Nashville
	Ben Lomand Rural Telephone Cooperative, Inc.	McMinnville
	Bledsoe Telephone Cooperative	Pikeville
Marshall	South Central Bell Telephone Company	Nashville
	Tennessee Telephone Company	Knoxville
	United Telephone Company, Inc.	Chapel Hill
Maury	South Central Bell Telephone Company	Nashville
Meigs	South Central Bell Telephone Company	Nashville
Monroe	South Central Bell Telephone Company	Nashville
	Englewood Telephone Company, Inc.	Englewood
	Tellico Telephone Company, Inc.	Tellico Plains
Montgomery	South Central Bell Telephone Company	Nashville
Moore	South Central Bell Telephone Company	Nashville
Morgan	Highland Telephone Cooperative, Inc.	Sunbright
Obion	South Central Bell Telephone Company	Nashville
	Yorkville Telephone Cooperative, Inc.	Yorkville
Overton	Twin Lakes Telephone Cooperative Corporation	Gainesboro
Perry	Tennessee Telephone Company	Knoxville
Pickett	Twin Lakes Telephone Cooperative Corporation	Gainesboro
Polk	South Central Bell Telephone Company	Nashville
Putnam	General Telephone Company of the Southeast	Cookeville
	Twin Lakes Telephone Cooperative Corporation	Gainesboro
Rhea	South Central Bell Telephone Company	Nashville
Roane	South Central Bell Telephone Company	Nashville
Robertson	South Central Bell Telephone Company	Nashville
Rutherford	South Central Bell Telephone Company	Nashville
	Ben Lomand Rural Telephone Cooperative, Inc.	McMinnville
Scott	South Central Bell Telephone Company	Nashville
	Highland Telephone Cooperative, Inc.	Sunbright
Sequatchie	South Central Bell Telephone Company	Nashville
	Bledsoe Telephone Cooperative	Pikeville
Sevier	South Central Bell Telephone Company	Nashville
Shelby	South Central Bell Telephone Company	Nashville
	Millington Telephone Company, Inc.	Millington
Smith	South Central Bell Telephone Company	Nashville
	DeKalb Telephone Cooperative	Alexandria
	North Central Telephone Cooperative, Inc.	Lafayette
	Twin Lakes Telephone Cooperative Corporation	Gainesboro

TABLE 8.2-- TENNESSEE TELEPHONE COMPANIES, COUNTY SERVICE AREAS, 1987 (Continued)

County	Telephone company	Location of telephone company offices
Stewart	South Central Bell Telephone Company	Nashville
Sullivan	United Inter-Mountain Telephone Company	Bristol
Sumner	South Central Bell Telephone Company	Nashville
	North Central Telephone Cooperative, Inc.	Lafayette
Tipton	South Central Bell Telephone Company	Nashville
	Millington Telephone Company, Inc.	Millington
Trousdale	South Central Bell Telephone Company	Nashville
	North Central Telephone Cooperative, Inc.	Lafayette
Unicoi	United Inter-Mountain Telephone Company	Bristol
Union	South Central Bell Telephone Company	Nashville
	Claiborne Telephone Company, Inc.	New Tazewell
	ALLTEL Tennessee, Inc.	Powell
Van Buren	Ben Lomand Rural Telephone Cooperative, Inc.	McMinnville
	Bledsoe Telephone Cooperative	Pikeville
Warren	Ben Lomand Rural Telephone Cooperative, Inc.	McMinnville
	General Telephone Company of the Southeast	Cookeville
Washington	United Inter-Mountain Telephone Company	Bristol
Wayne	Tennessee Telephone Company	Knoxville
Weakley	South Central Bell Telephone Company	Nashville
	General Telephone Company of the Southeast	Cookeville
White	Ben Lomand Rural Telephone Cooperative, Inc.	McMinnville
	General Telephone Company of the Southeast	Cookeville
Williamson	South Central Bell Telephone Company	Nashville
	United Telephone Company, Inc.	Chapel Hill
Wilson	South Central Bell Telephone Company	Nashville
	Tennessee Telephone Company	Knoxville

Source: Tennessee Telephone Association, *1986–87 Membership Directory.*

FIGURE 8.1
Percentage of Occupied Housing Units Lacking Telephone, Tennessee Counties, 1990
(Tennessee percentage = 7.14)

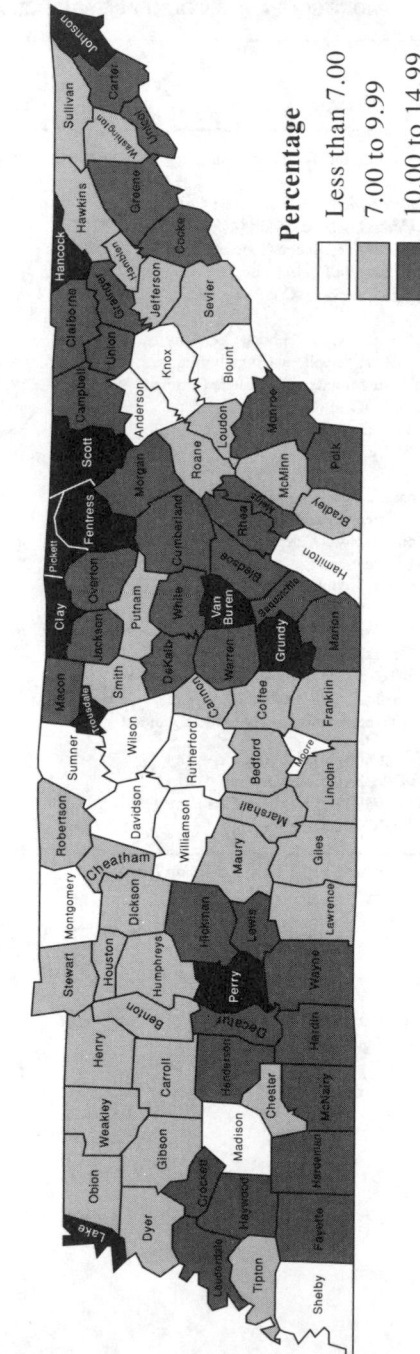

Percentage

Less than 7.00
7.00 to 9.99
10.00 to 14.99
15.00 or more

Source: U.S. Department of Commerce, Bureau of the Census, *1990 Census of Population and Housing, Summary Tape File 3A, Tennessee.*

TABLE 8.3-- TELEPHONE AVAILABILITY IN OCCUPIED HOUSING UNITS, COUNTIES, 1990

County	Occupied housing units	Units lacking telephone	Percent lacking telephone
Anderson	27,384	1,690	6.17
Bedford	11,608	1,033	8.90
Benton	5,784	493	8.52
Bledsoe	3,261	401	12.30
Blount	33,624	2,112	6.28
Bradley	27,604	2,072	7.51
Campbell	13,150	1,591	12.10
Cannon	3,980	346	8.69
Carroll	10,727	973	9.07
Carter	20,189	2,203	10.91
Cheatham	9,515	863	9.07
Chester	4,558	419	9.19
Claibome	9,629	1,109	11.52
Clay	2,855	550	19.26
Cocke	11,191	1,616	14.44
Coffee	15,500	1,364	8.80
Crockett	5,183	548	10.57
Cumberland	13,426	1,357	10.11
Davidson	207,530	9,362	4.51
Decatur	4,216	495	11.74
DeKalb	5,696	794	13.94
Dickson	13,019	940	7.22
Dyer	13,617	1,279	9.39
Fayette	8,453	973	11.51
Fentress	5,511	846	15.35
Franklin	12,660	1,170	9.24
Gibson	18,361	1,341	7.30
Giles	9,832	846	8.60
Grainger	6,394	938	14.67
Greene	21,482	2,298	10.70
Grundy	4,784	731	15.28
Hamblen	19,429	1,896	9.76
Hamilton	111,799	5,881	5.26
Hancock	2,484	486	19.57
Hardeman	8,276	900	10.87
Hardin	8,726	1,032	11.83
Hawkins	17,167	1,541	8.98
Haywood	7,014	730	10.41
Henderson	8,527	936	10.98
Henry	11,362	1,047	9.21
Hickman	5,976	663	11.09
Houston	2,683	261	9.73
Humphreys	6,063	453	7.47
Jackson	3,642	471	12.93
Jefferson	12,329	1,072	8.69
Johnson	5,406	878	16.24
Knox	133,639	6,485	4.85
Lake	2,418	396	16.38
Lauderdale	8,423	1,048	12.44
Lawrence	13,338	1,148	8.61

TABLE 8.3-- TELEPHONE AVAILABILITY IN OCCUPIED HOUSING UNITS, COUNTIES, 1990 (Continued)

County	Occupied housing units	Units lacking telephone	Percentage lacking telephone
Lewis	3,533	503	14.24
Lincoln	10,881	866	7.96
Loudon	12,155	1,011	8.32
McMinn	16,351	1,431	8.75
McNairy	8,834	901	10.20
Macon	6,159	884	14.35
Madison	29,609	1,618	5.46
Marion	9,215	1,023	11.10
Marshall	8,268	788	9.53
Maury	20,608	1,540	7.47
Meigs	2,996	402	13.42
Monroe	11,363	1,497	13.17
Montgomery	34,345	1,700	4.95
Moore	1,734	100	5.77
Morgan	5,841	811	13.88
Obion	12,412	1,194	9.62
Overton	6,734	740	10.99
Perry	2,512	382	15.21
Pickett	1,786	307	17.19
Polk	5,092	732	14.38
Putnam	19,753	1,509	7.64
Rhea	9,185	949	10.33
Roane	18,453	1,324	7.17
Robertson	14,801	1,180	7.97
Rutherford	42,118	2,191	5.20
Scott	6,534	1,046	16.01
Sequatchie	3,287	461	14.02
Sevier	19,520	1,491	7.64
Shelby	303,571	14,138	4.66
Smith	5,358	512	9.56
Stewart	3,678	300	8.16
Sullivan	56,729	4,252	7.50
Sumner	36,850	2,058	5.58
Tipton	13,033	1,218	9.35
Trousdale	2,261	345	15.26
Unicoi	6,621	740	11.18
Union	4,932	674	13.67
Van Buren	1,799	295	16.40
Warren	12,681	1,490	11.75
Washington	35,823	3,214	8.97
Wayne	5,174	720	13.92
Weakley	11,992	946	7.89
White	7,722	843	10.92
Williamson	27,928	681	2.44
Wilson	24,070	1,247	5.18
TENNESSEE	1,853,725	132,331	7.14

Source: U.S. Department of Commerce, Bureau of the Census, *1990 Census of Population and Housing, Summary Tape File 3A, Tennessee.*

TABLE 8.4-- PAID CIRCULATION OF NON-DAILY NEWSPAPERS, COUNTIES, 1990

County	City	Newspaper	Paid circulation
Anderson	Clinton	Clinton Courier-News	7,293
Anderson	Lake City	The Town Crier	1,292
Anderson	Lake City	Clinch Valley Chronicle	3,873
Benton	Camden	The Camden Chronicle	4,620
Bledsoe	Pikeville	The Bledsonian-Banner	2,682
Campbell	Jellico	The Advance-Sentinel	567
Campbell	LaFollette	The LaFollette Press	7,435
Cannon	Woodbury	Cannon Courier	3,586
Carroll	Huntingdon	Carroll County News	5,420
Carroll	Huntingdon	The Carroll Leader	4,579
Carroll	McKenzie	The McKenzie Banner	4,894
Cheatham	Ashland City	Ashland City Times	4,416
Chester	Henderson	Chester County Independent	3,801
Claiborne	Tazewell	The Claiborne Progress	6,736
Clay	Celina	Citizen-Statesman	2,176
Cocke	Newport	The Newport Plain Talk	9,403
Coffee	Manchester	Manchester Times	6,073
Coffee	Tullahoma	The Tullahoma News	7,786
Crockett	Alamo	The Crockett Times	3,886
Cumberland	Crossville	Crossville Chronicle	5,437
Cumberland	Crossville	Cumberland Times	2,500
Davidson	Nashville	Nashville Record	1,267
Davidson	Nashville	Nashville Business Journal	8,312
Davidson	Nashville	Westview	3,219
Decatur	Parsons	The News Leader	3,862
DeKalb	Smithville	Smithville Review	4,152
Dickson	Dickson	The Dickson Herald	7,023
Dyer	Newbern	Dyer County Tennessean	2,083
Fayette	Somerville	Fayette County Review	2,183
Fayette	Somerville	The Fayette Falcon	2,991
Fentress	Jamestown	Fentress Courier	4,770
Franklin	Winchester	The Herald-Chronicle	8,379
Gibson	Dyer	The Tri-City Reporter	3,396
Gibson	Humboldt	The Courier-Chronicle	4,136
Gibson	Milan	The Milan Mirror-Exchange	5,550
Gibson	Trenton	The Herald Gazette	4,375
Giles	Ardmore	Your Community Shopper	3,680
Giles	Pulaski	The Giles Free Press	6,546
Giles	Pulaski	The Pulaski Citizen	6,628
Grainger	Rutledge	Grainger County News	2,829
Grundy	Tracy City	Grundy County Herald	4,317
Hamilton	Chattanooga	Hamilton County Herald	203
Hardeman	Bolivar	The Bolivar Bulletin-Times	4,390
Hardin	Savannah	The Courier	8,695
Hawkins	Rogersville	Rogersville Review	7,279
Haywood	Brownsville	The States-Graphic	4,319
Henderson	Lexington	The Lexington Progress	7,684
Hickman	Centerville	Hickman County Times	6,038
Humphreys	Waverly	The News-Democrat	3,612
Jackson	Gainesboro	Jackson County Sentinel	3,000
Jefferson	Jefferson City	Standard-Banner	5,612
Johnson	Mountain City	The Tomahawk	5,664
Knox	Knoxville	West Side Story	3,900
Lake	Tiptonville	The Lake County Banner	3,045
Lauderdale	Halls	The Halls Graphic	1,205
Lauderdale	Ripley	The Lauderdale Voice	3,397
Lauderdale	Ripley	The Lauderdale County Enterprise	4,459
Lawrence	Lawrenceburg	The Democrat-Union	7,301
Lewis	Hohenwald	Lewis County Herald	3,066

TABLE 8.4-- PAID CIRCULATION OF NON-DAILY NEWSPAPERS, COUNTIES, 1990 (Continued)

County	City	Newspaper	Paid circulation
Lincoln	Fayetteville	Elk Valley Times	7,270
Loudon	Lenoir City	The News-Herald	5,954
Macon	Lafayette	Macon County Times	6,140
Marion	Jasper	The Jasper Journal	3,927
Marion	South Pittsburg	South Pittsburg Hustler	3,697
Marshall	Lewisburg	Lewisburg Tribune	6,441
Marshall	Lewisburg	Marshall Gazette	6,300
Maury	Mt. Pleasant	The Record	774
McMinn	Etowah	The Etowah Enterprise	1,411
McNairy	Selmer	Independent-Appeal	6,777
Monroe	Madisonville	The Democrat/Laker	3,150
Monroe	Sweetwater	Monroe County Advocate	3,438
Moore	Lynchburg	The Moore County News	1,524
Morgan	Wartburg	The Morgan County News	4,322
Overton	Livingston	Overton County News	3,577
Overton	Livingston	Livingston Enterprise	5,036
Perry	Linden	Buffalo River Review	2,618
Pickett	Byrdstown	Pickett County Press	1,507
Polk	Benton	The Polk County News/Citizen Advance	2,931
Rhea	Dayton	The Herald-News	4,660
Roane	Harriman	The Harriman Record	735
Roane	Kingston	The Roane County News	7,786
Roane	Rockwood	The Rockwood Times	758
Robertson	Springfield	Robertson County Times	9,207
Rutherford	Smyrna	The Rutherford Courier	3,722
Scott	Oneida	Independent Herald	3,929
Scott	Oneida	Scott County News	6,800
Sequatchie	Dunlap	The Dunlap Tribune	2,423
Sevier	Pigeon Forge	Weekly Star	2,193
Shelby	Bartlett	Bartlett Express	4,431
Shelby	Collierville	Collierville Independent	4,158
Shelby	Germantown	Germantown News	6,023
Shelby	Memphis	Memphis Business Journal	10,989
Shelby	Millington	The Millington Star	2,525
Smith	Carthage	Carthage Courier	4,766
Stewart	Dover	The Stewart-Houston Times	5,397
Sullivan	Blountville	Sullivan County News	3,085
Sumner	Gallatin	The News-Examiner	9,545
Sumner	Portland	The Portland Leader	2,401
Sumner	Westmoreland	Westmoreland World	823
Tipton	Covington	The Covington Leader	7,027
Trousdale	Hartsville	The Hartsville Vidette	1,933
Unicoi	Erwin	The Erwin Record	4,843
Warren	McMinnville	Southern Standard	8,214
Washington	Jonesborough	Herald and Tribune	3,950
Wayne	Waynesboro	The Wayne County News	6,465
Weakley	Dresden	Dresden Enterprise	5,476
Weakley	Martin	Weakley County Press	5,576
White	Sparta	The Expositor	4,166
Williamson	Fairview	The Fairview Observer	1,257
Williamson	Franklin	The Williamson Leader	6,800
Williamson	Franklin	The Review-Appeal	9,339
Wilson	Lebanon	The Wilson World	4,260
Wilson	Mt. Juliet	Mt. Juliet News	3,619

Note: Paid circulation is that reported to the U.S. Postal Service in 1990 annual statement or the Publisher's Statement for Audit Bureau of Circulation (ABC) members, as of September 30, 1990.

Source: Tennessee Press Service, Inc., *Tennessee Newspaper Directory, 1991.*

FIGURE 8.2

Newspapers Published in Tennessee, by Frequency of Publication, by County, 1994

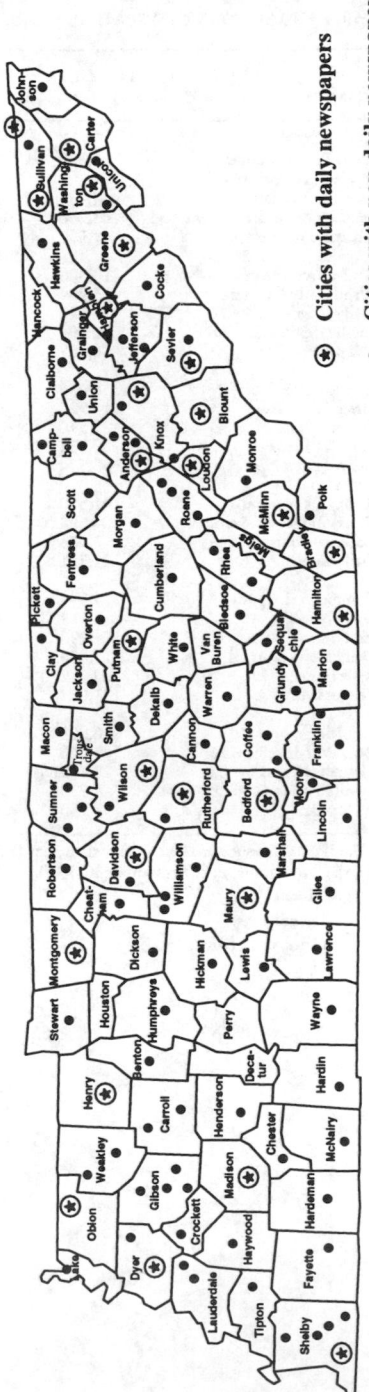

(✪) Cities with daily newspapers

• Cities with non-daily newspapers

Note: Where more than one newspaper is published, both are represented by one symbol. The following cities have both daily and non-daily newspaper:Cleveland, Clarksville, Cookeville, Chattanooga, Knoxville, Lenoir City, Lebanon, Memphis and Nashville. See Tables 8.4 and 8.5 for circulation detail.

Source: News Media Directories, *Tennessee News Media Directory, 1995.* Used by special permission.

TABLE 8.5-- PAID CIRCULATION OF DAILY AND SUNDAY NEWSPAPERS, CITIES, 1990

City	County	Newspaper name	Paid daily circulation	Sunday circulation
Athens	McMinn	The Daily Post-Athenian	10,322	0
Bristol	Sullivan	Bristol Herald Courier/		
		Virginia-Tennessean	44,437	45,998
Chattanooga	Hamilton	Chattanooga News-Free Press	63,206	107,373
		The Chattanooga Times	47,156	0
Clarksville	Montgomery	The Leaf-Chronicle	18,300	21,282
Cleveland	Bradley	Cleveland Daily Banner	16,904	18,321
Columbia	Maury	The Daily Herald	12,873	14,355
Cookeville	Putnam	Cookeville Herald-Citizen	10,204	11,590
Dyersburg	Dyer	State Gazette	8,485	0
Elizabethton	Carter	Elizabethton Star	8,460	8,460[a]
Greeneville	Greene	The Greeneville Sun	14,925	0
Jackson	Madison	The Jackson Sun	37,570	39,924
Johnson City	Washington	Johnson City Press	30,334	32,686
Kingsport	Sullivan	Kingsport Times-News[1]	46,574	47,992
Knoxville	Knox	The Knoxville Journal	41,370	0
		The Knoxville News-Sentinel	104,628	171,888
Lebanon	Wilson	The Lebanon Democrat	8,933	0
Maryville	Blount	The Daily Times	21,781	0
Memphis	Shelby	The Commercial Appeal	214,544	291,084
		The Daily News	2,513	0
Morristown	Hamblen	Citizen Tribune	21,293	24,011
Murfreesboro	Rutherford	The Daily News Journal	15,854	17,600
Nashville	Davidson	Nashville Banner	63,232	0
		The Tennessean	131,027	270,291
Oak Ridge	Anderson	The Oak Ridger	10,528	11,721
Paris	Henry	The Paris Post-Intelligencer	8,045	0
Sevierville	Sevier	The Mountain Press	8,863	0
Shelbyville	Bedford	Shelbyville Times-Gazette	8,230	0
Union City	Obion	Union City Daily Messenger	8,280	0

Note: Paid circulation is that reported to the U.S. Postal Service in 1990 annual statement or the Publisher's
Statement for Audit Bureau of Circulation (ABC) members, as of September 30, 1990.
1. These papers have both morning and evening editions.
a. Separate circulation not listed for daily and Sunday editions.
Source: Tennessee Press Service, Inc., *Tennessee Newspaper Directory, 1991.*

TABLE 8.6-- SELECTED DATA ON TELEVISION STATIONS, CITIES, 1990

City	Channel	Call letters	Air date	Major network affiliation
Chattanooga	12	WDEF-TV	1954	CBS
	61	WDSI-TV	1972	Ind.; Fox
	3	WRCB-TV (Stereo)	1956	NBC
	45	WTCI[1]	1970	PBS
	9	WTVC	1958	ABC
Cleveland	53	WFLI-TV	1987	Ind.
Cookeville	22	WCTE[1]	1978	PBS
	28	WMTT	(a)	n.a.
Crossville	20	WINT-TV	1983	Ind.
Greeneville	39	WEMT (Stereo)	1985	Ind.; Fox
Hendersonville	50	WPGD	(a)	n.a.
Jackson	7	WBBJ-TV	1955	ABC
	16	WJWT	1985	Ind.; Fox
Jellico	54	WPMC	(a)	n.a.
Johnson City	11	WJHL-TV	1953	CBS
Kingsport	19	WKPT-TV (Stereo)	1969	ABC
Knoxville	6	WATE-TV (Stereo)	1953	ABC
	10	WBIR-TV	1956	NBC
	43	WKCH-TV	1983	Ind.; Fox
	8	WKXT-TV (Stereo)	1988	CBS
	15	(b)	(a)	n.a.
Lebanon	66	WJFB	1989	Ind.
Lexington	11	WLJT-TV[1]	1968	PBS
Memphis	13	WHBQ-TV	1953	ABC
	10	WKNO-TV[1]	1956	PBS
	30	WLMT	1983	Ind.; Fox
	5	WMC-TV (Stereo)	1948	NBC
	24	WPTY-TV	1978	Ind.
	3	WREG-TV	1956	CBS
Murfreesboro	39	WHTN	1983	Ind.
Nashville	8	WDCN[1] (Stereo)	1962	PBS
	2	WKRN-TV	1953	ABC
	58	WNAB	(a)	n.a.
	42	WSDA[1]	(a)	n.a.
	4	WSMV (Stereo)	1950	NBC
	5	WTVF (Stereo)	1954	CBS
	30	WXMT	1984	Ind.
	17	WZTV	1976	Ind.; Fox
Sneedville	2	WSJK-TV[1]	1967	PBS
Union City	41	WYDL	(a)	n.a.

ABC - American Broadcasting Company   Ind. - Independent
CBS - Columbia Broadcasting System   PBS - Public Broadcasting System
NBC - National Broadcasting Company
n.a. not available.
1. Non-commercial.
a. Not on air, target date unknown.
b. New station; call letters not available.
Source: Broadcasting Publications, Inc., *Broadcasting Yearbook 1990*. Used by special permission.

TABLE 8.7-- SELECTED DATA ON AM AND FM RADIO STATIONS, MUNICIPALITIES, 1990

Municipality	AM stations			FM stations		
	Call letters	Frequency (khz)	Air date	Call letters	Frequency (mhz)	Air date
Adamsville	WEAB	960	1978			
Alamo	WCTA	810	1983	WNBE	93.1	(a)
Alcoa	WMDR	1470	1957	WYLV[1]	89.1	(a)
Algood	WWRT	1590	1981			
Ardmore	WSLV	1110	1968			
Ashland City	WAJN	790	1982			
Athens	WLAR	1450	1946	WJSQ	101.7	1979
	WYXI	1390	1966			
Benton	WBIN	1540	1977			
Berry Hill	WVOL	1470	1951			
Blountville	WJTZ	640	(a)			
Bolivar	WBOL	1560	1962	WMOD	96.7	1975
Brentwood	WYOR	560	1985			
Bristol	WBCV	1550	1962	WHCB[1]	91.5	1984
	WOPI	1490	1929	WXBQ	96.9	1945
Brownsville	WBHT	1520	1963	WTBG	95.3	1965
Camden	WFWL	1220	1956	WRJB	98.3	1976
Carthage	WRKM	1350	1959	WUCZ	102.3	1975
Centerville	WHLP	1570	1955	WHLP	96.7	1974
Chattanooga	WTYR	1550	1970	WDEF	92.3	1964
	WDEF	1370	1941	WDOD	96.5	1960
	WDOD	1310	1925	WDYN[1]	89.7	1968
	WDXB	1490	1948	WSKZ	106.5	1960
	WGOW	1150	1936	WMBW[1]	88.9	1969
	WMOC	1450	1961	WFXS	102.3	1977
	WNOO	1260	1951	WUTC[1]	88.1	1980
Church Hill	WMCH	1260	1954			
Clarksville	WCTZ	1550	1980	WAPX[1]	91.7	1984
	WDXN	540	1954			
	WJZM	1400	1941			
Cleveland	WBAC	1340	1945	WALV	95.3	1980
	WCLE	1570	1957	WUSY	100.7	1961
Clinton	WYSH	1380	1960	WYFC	95.3	1966
Collegedale				WSMC[1]	90.5	1961
Collierville	WCRV	640	1966			
Colonial Heights	WPRQ	870	1984			
Columbia	WKRM	1340	1946	WKOM	101.7	1967
	WMCP	1280	1956			
Cookeville	WHUB	1400	1940	WHUB	98.3	1964
	WPTN	780	1962	WGSQ	94.3	1963
				WTTU[1]	88.5	1972
Copperhill	WLSB	1400	1958			
Covington	WKBL	1250	1954	WKBL	93.5	1965
Cowan	WZYX	1440	1957			
Crossville	WAEW	1330	1952	WXVL	99.3	1967
	WCSV	1490	1968			
Dayton	WDNT	1280	1957	WTCX	104.9	1976
	WREA	1520	1979			
Dickson	WDKN	1260	1955	WQZQ	102.5	1964
Dunlap	WSDQ	1190	1980			
Dyersburg	WDSG	1450	1946	WASL	100.1	1968
	WTRO	1330	1957			
Elizabethton	WBEJ	1240	1946	WUSJ	99.3	1968
	WIDD	1520	1964			
Englewood	WENR	1090	1967			
Erwin	WEMB	1420	1956	WXIS	103.9	1968
Etowah	WCPH	1220	1955	WDRZ	103.1	1977
Fairview	WPFD	850	1982			
Farragut	WTNN	670	1988			
Fayetteville	WEKR	1240	1948	WYTM	105.5	1970

TABLE 8.7-- SELECTED DATA ON AM AND FM RADIO STATIONS, MUNICIPALITIES, 1990 (Continued)

Municipality	AM stations			FM stations		
	Call letters	Frequency (khz)	Air date	Call letters	Frequency (mhz)	Air date
Franklin	WAKM	950	1953	WRLT	100.1	1961
	WIZO	1380	1969			
Gallatin	WAMG	1130	1966	WGFX	104.5	1960
	WHIN	1010	1948	WVCP[1]	88.5	1979
Gatlinburg				WSEV	105.5	1983
Graysville				WAYB	95.7	(a)
Greeneville	WGRV	1340	1946	WIKQ	94.9	1956
	WSMG	1450	1961			
Harriman	WKCE	1230	1983	WWBR	92.7	1981
	WWBR	1600	1947			
Harrogate	WSVQ	740	1980	WLMU[1]	91.3	n.a.
Hartsville	WJKM	1090	1966			
Henderson	WHHM	1580	1967	WFHC[1]	91.5	1967
				WFKX	95.9	1984
Hendersonville	WMII	1330	(a)	WQQK	92.1	1970
Hohenwald	WMLR	1230	1970			
Humboldt	WHMT	1190	1972	WLSZ	105.3	1989
	WIRJ	740	1949	WZDQ	102.3	1964
Huntingdon	WFOT	1530	1975	WHZZ	100.9	1979
				WBVD	93.7	(a)
Jackson	WDXI	1310	1948	WMXX	103.1	1979
	WJAK	1460	1954	WTNV	104.1	1947
	WTJS	1390	1931	(b)	90.1	(a)
Jamestown	WCLC	1260	1957	WCLC	103.1	1985
	WDEB	1500	1968	WDEB	103.9	1972
Jasper	WAPO	820	1987			
Jefferson City	WJFC	1480	1961	WNOX	99.3	1976
Jellico	WJJT	1540	1972			
Johnson City	WETB	790	1947	WETS[1]	89.5	1974
	WJCW	910	1938	WQUT	101.5	1948
Jonesborough	WKTP	1590	1958			
Karns				WCKS	93.1	(a)
Kingsport	WGOC	640	1967	WCSK[1]	90.3	1984
	WKIN	1320	1951	WZXY	104.9	1970
	WKPT	1400	1940	WTFM	98.5	1948
Kingston	WBBX	1410	1978			
Knoxville	WEMG	1430	1960	WEZK	97.5	1967
	WHJM	1180	1988	WHGG[1]	88.3	(a)
	WIMZ	1240	1941	WIMZ	103.5	1949
	WITA	1490	1960	WIVK	107.7	1965
	WIVK	990	1953	WKCS[1]	91.1	1952
	WKGN	1340	1947	WOKI	100.3	1974
	WKNL	760	(a)	WUOT[1]	91.9	1949
	WKXV	900	1953	WUTK[1]	90.3	1982
	WMRE	1580	1961			
	WRJZ	620	1927			
	WUTK	850	1989			
Lafayette	WEEN	1460	1958			
LaFollette	WLAF	1450	1953	WQLA	104.9	1982
	WWGR	960	1983			
Lawrenceburg	WCMG	910	1982	WDXE	95.9	1964
	WDXE	1370	1951			
	WWLX	590	1987			
Lebanon	WCOR	900	1949	WFMQ[1]	91.5	1966
	WQDQ	1200	1979	WYHY	107.5	1962
Lenoir City	WBLC	1360	1965	WLIL	93.5	1967
	WLIL	730	1950			
Lewisburg	WAXO	1220	1980	WJJM	94.3	1969
	WJJM	1490	1947			
Lexington	WDXL	1490	1954	WZLT	99.3	1964

TABLE 8.7-- SELECTED DATA ON AM AND FM RADIO STATIONS, MUNICIPALITIES, 1990 (Continued)

Municipality	AM stations			FM stations		
	Call letters	Frequency (khz)	Air date	Call letters	Frequency (mhz)	Air date
Livingston	WLIV	920	1956	WXKG	95.9	1966
Lobelville				WIST	94.3	1974
Lookout Mountain	WFLI	1070	1961			
Loudon	WLOD	1140	1983	WLOD	99.1	1989
Lynchburg	WTNX	1290	1981			
McKenzie	WHDM	1440	1954	WWYN	106.9	1963
McKinnon				WTWL	101.5	(a)
McMinnville	WAKI	1230	1947	WTRZ	103.9	1964
	WBMC	960	1955			
Madison	WRLT	1430	1958			
Madisonville	WRKQ	1250	1967			
Manchester	WMSR	1320	1957	WMSR	99.7	1962
Martin	WCMT	1410	1957	WCMT	101.7	1968
				WUTM[1]	90.3	1971
Maryville	WCGM	1120	1989	WYNQ	95.7	(a)
	WGAP	1400	1947			
Memphis	KWAM	990	1946	KMPZ	98.1	1960
	WDIA	1070	1947	KRNB	101.1	1965
	WGSF	1210	1986	WHRK	97.1	1961
	WHBQ	560	1925	WEVL[1]	89.9	1976
	WLOK	1340	1956	WGKX	105.9	1968
	WMC	790	1923	WKNO[1]	91.1	1972
	WMQM	1480	1964	WLYX[1]	89.3	1972
	WNWZ	1430	1955	WMC	99.7	1947
	WODZ	680	1925	WEZI	94.3	1977
	WPLX	1170	1987	WQOX[1]	88.5	1974
	WREC	600	1922	WEGR	102.7	1967
	WXSS	1030	(a)	WRVR	104.5	1968
				WSMS[1]	91.7	1975
Milan	WKBJ	1600	1955	WYNU	92.3	1964
	WWHY	1360	1983			
Millington	WMPS	1380	1962			
Minor Hill				WLLX	92.1	1983
Monterey				WRJT	107.1	1986
Morristown	WCRK	1150	1947	WAZI	95.9	1964
	WMTN	1300	1957			
Mountain City	WMCT	1390	1967			
Mt. Carmel	WRVX	1200	(a)			
Mt. Pleasant	WXRQ	1460	1981			
Murfreesboro	WGNS	1450	1947	WMOT[1]	89.5	1969
	WMTS	810	1953	WRMX	96.3	1963
Nashville	WAMB	1160	1971	WFSK[1]	88.1	1973
	WENO	760	1988	WKDF	103.3	1967
	WKDA	1240	1948	WLAC	105.9	1953
	WLAC	1510	1926	WNAZ[1]	89.1	1967
	WMDB	880	1983	WPLN[1]	90.3	1962
	WNAH	1360	1949	WRVU[1]	91.1	1971
	WNQM	1300	1948	WSIX	97.9	1948
	WSIX	980	1927	WSM	95.5	1962
	WSM	650	1925	WZEZ	92.9	1976
	WWGM	1560	1967			
Newport	WLIK	1270	1954			
	WNPC	1060	1978			
Oak Ridge	WATO	1290	1948	WKNF	94.3	1967
	WORI	1550	1973			
Olive Hill				WDNX[1]	89.1	1975
Oliver Springs				WXVO	98.7	1989
Oneida	WOCV	1310	1959	WBNT	105.5	1965
Paris	WMUF	1000	1980	WAKQ	105.5	1967
	WTPR	710	1947			

TABLE 8.7-- SELECTED DATA ON AM AND FM RADIO STATIONS, MUNICIPALITIES, 1990 (Continued)

Municipality	AM stations			FM stations		
	Call letters	Frequency (khz)	Air date	Call letters	Frequency (mhz)	Air date
Parsons	WKJY	1550	1970			
Pikeville	WUAT	1110	1972	WIKU[1]	91.3	(a)
Portland	WQKR	1270	1980			
Powell	WQBB	1040	1984			
Pulaski	WKSR	1420	1947	WINJ	98.3	1970
Red Bank				WJTT	94.3	1972
Ripley	WTRB	1570	1954			
Rockwood	WOFE	580	1957			
Rogersville	WRGS	1370	1954			
St. Joseph	WJOR	1040	1986			
Savannah	WORM	1010	1956	WKWX	93.5	1980
				WORM	101.7	1966
Selmer	WDTM	1150	1967	WXOQ	105.5	1986
				WSIB	93.9	(a)
Sevierville	WSEV	930	1955	WMYU	102.1	1961
Sewanee				WUTS[1]	91.5	1972
Seymour				WMEY	96.3	(a)
Shelbyville	WHAL	1400	1946	WYCQ	102.9	1962
	WLIJ	1580	1959			
Signal Mountain				WAWL[1]	91.5	1980
Smithville	WJLE	1480	1964	WJLE	101.7	1970
Smyrna	WSVT	710	1981			
Soddy-Daisy	WSDT	1240	1970			
Somerville	WSTN	1410	1982			
South Pittsburg	WEPG	910	1954	(b)	97.3	(a)
Sparta	WSMT	1050	1953	WSMT	105.5	1964
	WTZX	860	1971			
Spencer				(b)	98.7	(a)
Spring City	WXQK	970	1979	WAYA	93.9	(a)
Springfield	WDBL	1590	1950	WDBL	94.3	1964
	WSGI	1100	1982			
Static	WSBI	1210	1986			
Summertown				WUTZ[1]	88.3	1979
Surgoinsville				WOTH	104.3	(a)
Sweetwater	WDEH	800	1955	WDEH	98.3	1967
Tazewell	WNTT	1250	1960	WFSM	94.1	(a)
Thompson Station	WQDQ	1100	1983			
Trenton	WTNE	1500	1966	WLOT	97.7	1980
Tullahoma	WDFZ	740	1947	WKQD	93.3	1962
Union City	WENK	1240	1946	WKWT	104.9	1974
Wartburg	WECO	940	1970	WECO	101.3	(a)
Waverly	WPHC	1060	1963	WVRY	104.9	1972
Waynesboro	WTNR	930	1970			
White Bluff	WJKZ	1030	1982			
Winchester	WCDT	1340	1948			
Woodbury	WBRY	1540	1963			

Note: Stations are listed in the municipality in which they are located.

1. Non-commercial.

a. Air date unavailable.

b. New station; no call letters available yet.

Source: Broadcasting Publications, Inc., *Broadcasting Yearbook, 1990*. Used by special permission.

TABLE 8.8-- TELEPHONE AVAILABILITY IN OCCUPIED HOUSING UNITS, SOUTHEASTERN STATES
AND UNITED STATES, 1990

State	Occupied housing units	Units lacking telephone	Percent lacking telephone
TENNESSEE	1,853,725	132,331	7.1
Alabama	1,506,790	131,554	8.7
Arkansas	891,179	97,536	10.9
Florida	5,134,869	270,242	5.3
Georgia	2,366,615	195,689	8.3
Kentucky	1,379,782	140,881	10.2
Louisiana	1,499,269	124,455	8.3
Mississippi	911,374	115,130	12.6
North Carolina	2,517,026	178,690	7.1
South Carolina	1,258,044	114,695	9.1
Virginia	2,291,830	123,638	5.4
West Virginia	688,557	70,754	10.3
UNITED STATES	91,947,410	4,817,457	5.2

Source: U.S. Department of Commerce, Bureau of the Census, 1990 *Census of Population and Housing, Summary Tape File 3A.*

TABLE 8.9-- NUMBER AND CIRCULATION OF DAILY AND SUNDAY NEWSPAPERS,
SOUTHEASTERN STATES, 1990

| State | Daily | | | Sunday | |
| | Number | Circulation[1] | | Number | Net paid circu- lation (1,000) |
		Net paid (1,000)	Per capita[2]		
TENNESSEE	28	969.5	0.20	16	1,082.6
Alabama	27	766.5	0.19	21	766.9
Arkansas	32	566.0	0.24	17	675.2
Florida	43	3,175.0	0.25	36	3,920.0
Georgia	36	1,211.4	0.19	18	1,311.6
Kentucky	23	662.4	0.18	12	673.7
Louisiana	28	780.4	0.18	21	892.1
Mississippi	22	403.2	0.16	14	379.5
North Carolina	53	1,453.4	0.22	35	1,452.7
South Carolina	17	675.5	0.19	13	727.5
Virginia	34	2,525.4	0.41	15	990.3
West Virginia	23	436.0	0.24	11	412.0

1. Circulation figures based on the principal community served by a newspaper which is not necessarily the same
location as the publisher's office.
2. Per capita based on total resident population estimated as of April 1.

Source: Editor & Publisher Co., New York, NY, *Editor and Publisher International Year Book*, annual, (copyright) as printed in U.S. Department of Commerce, Bureau of the Census, *Statistical Abstract of the United
States, 1992.*

TABLE 8.10—SELECTED STATISTICS ON THE CABLE TELEVISION INDUSTRY, SOUTHEASTERN STATES, 1980–1990, SELECTED YEARS

State	1990			1989			1988			1980		
	No. of cable systems	No. of communities	No. of subscribers	No. of cable systems	No. of communities	No. of subscribers	No. of cable systems	No. of communities	No. of subscribers	No. of cable systems	No. of communities	No. of subscribers
TENNESSEE	177	472	968,660	166	473	930,766	155	400	890,359	57	111	250,489
Alabama	216	485	771,633	195	522	741,076	180	462	684,736	53	128	330,840
Arkansas	283	502	455,588	252	469	437,992	233	408	421,366	76	128	209,609
Florida	288	816	3,160,758	264	800	3,025,060	248	680	2,929,931	91	342	876,132
Georgia	257	677	1,248,716	244	666	1,190,992	209	573	1,101,908	67	175	387,961
Kentucky	295	966	783,196	273	977	784,818	255	841	752,453	97	239	234,212
Louisiana	206	407	868,851	168	376	835,967	161	333	788,114	38	97	294,539
Mississippi	180	348	438,831	154	307	426,874	142	268	450,526	41	107	241,471
North Carolina	215	704	1,343,992	191	703	1,258,595	189	597	1,142,073	54	135	339,051
South Carolina	143	334	623,798	126	344	537,847	111	266	558,880	33	104	176,649
Virginia	159	477	1,317,816	159	446	1,252,292	153	376	1,166,743	48	144	320,801
West Virginia	226	899	469,410	216	927	463,961	213	833	446,725	73	278	191,136

Note: Number of subscribers refers to number of basic subscribers.

Source: Warren Publishing, Inc., 2115 Ward Court, N.W., Washington, D.C. 20037, (202)872-9200, *Television and Cable Fact Book, 1991* (by special permission), and earlier editions; and U.S. Federal Communications Commission, *47th Annual Report, Fiscal Year 1981*.

Tennessee is fortunate to have not only a well-developed system of highways and railroads connecting its metropolitan areas and traversing the state, but also an extensive water transport system. Figure 9.1 shows the location of Tennessee's interstate highways, while Figure 9.2 provides the network of railway routes, including the latest changes in lines. Data on the location and facilities of Tennessee's riverports and airports are provided in Table 9.13 and Table 9.8, respectively.

Comprehensive statistics on public roads are provided by the U.S. Department of Transportation, Federal Highway Administration, Highway Statistics Division. That agency's annual publication, *Highway Statistics*, includes data on mileage, construction, maintenance, motor vehicle registrations, and tax collections for each state. The Federal Aviation Administration issues a variety of publications which have provided data for this chapter, including the *FAA Statistical Handbook of Aviation, Census of U.S. Civil Aircraft*, and *Airport Activity Statistics of Certificated Route Air Carriers*. Reports on Tennessee airports and roads are also issued by the State Department of Transportation.

The U.S. Department of Commerce, Bureau of the Census, publishes its *Census of Transportation* every five years. Data from the Truck Inventory and Use Survey from the 1987 Census describe the size and type of trucks registered in Tennessee and truck use by industry. The number of trucks and truck miles is reported for each of the southeastern states. Table 9.25, also from this survey, presents information on the transportation of hazardous materials. Transportation questions were also included in the 1980 and 1990 Censuses of Population. These data tell us how Tennesseans travel to work.

County-specific data detail motor vehicle registrations and highway systems throughout the state. These data are collected by the Motor Vehicle Division of the Department of Revenue and the Tennessee Department of Transportation. The Tennessee Valley Authority's Economic Development and Analysis Branch provides information on waterfront development. River freight traffic on the Tennessee River is reported by type of commodity shipped by TVA and the U.S. Department of the Army, Corps of Engineers. TVA's Navigation Development Branch issues information on the location and shipping characteristics of Tennessee's public river terminals.

Another important component of the transportation industry in Tennessee is the liquid petroleum pipelines. These are regulated as common carriers. However, the petroleum pipeline is featured with the natural gas pipeline in Figure 10.2. Readers should consult the Energy chapter for information on the transportation of petroleum.

TABLE OF CONTENTS

TABLE OF CONTENTS
(Continued)

FIGURE 9.1
Principal Highways in Tennessee

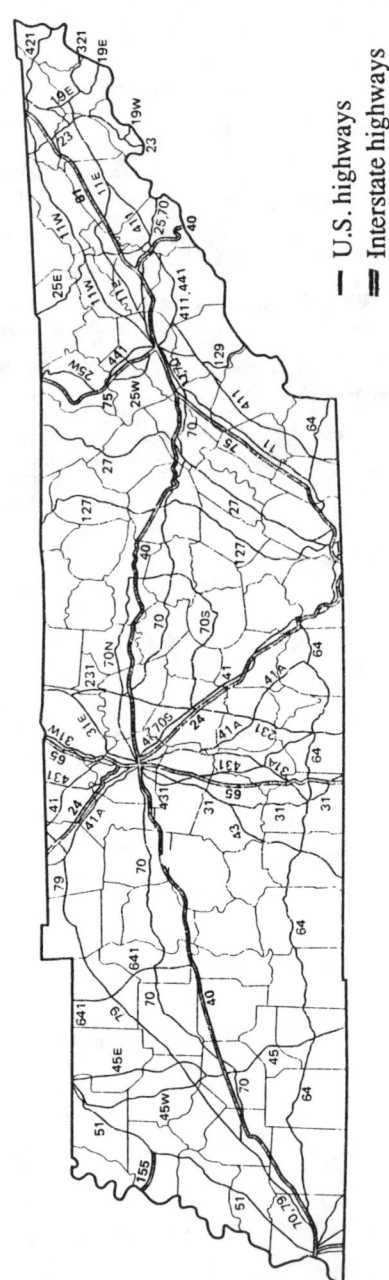

— U.S. highways
═ Interstate highways

Source: Official Tourist Development Map of Tennessee.

TABLE 9.1-- EXPENDITURES FOR CONSTRUCTION AND MAINTENANCE OF STATE-ADMINISTERED
HIGHWAYS, TENNESSEE AND UNITED STATES, 1925-1992, SELECTED YEARS
[In thousands of dollars]

	Construction[1]		Maintenance[2]	
Year	Tennessee	United States[3]	Tennessee	United States[3]
1992	613,159	27,143,028	192,392	8,746,808
1991	518,735	25,716,047	192,580	8,209,125
1990	552,827	24,813,063	204,532	8,266,037
1989	446,303	22,985,539	176,942	7,761,022
1988	487,011	22,397,781	169,839	7,480,811
1987	355,074	21,221,467	154,738	7,179,665
1986	319,414	20,426,870	131,783	6,646,641
1985	332,400	18,882,214	136,447	6,385,453
1984	295,641	15,757,546	109,025	5,824,109
1983	337,126	13,713,084	79,878	5,487,063
1982	241,139	12,398,955	90,688	5,266,909
1981	282,881	12,430,807	76,477	4,866,185
1980	341,813	14,013,201	60,503	4,566,982
1979	310,544	11,798,070	48,204	4,352,592
1978	232,310	10,015,634	50,585	4,037,821
1977	200,799	8,882,863	42,241	3,465,798
1976	234,081	9,676,656	35,764	3,116,821
1975	258,952	10,168,550	34,532	2,946,178
1974	192,254	9,390,755	36,788	2,656,449
1973	163,971	8,981,484	31,966	2,458,251
1972	183,169	9,383,859	26,284	2,236,190
1971	162,960	9,416,682	25,372	2,086,947
1970	155,363	8,866,017	26,432	1,928,819
1969	149,341	7,876,135	22,473	1,723,160
1968	132,908	7,866,362	18,522	1,593,652
1967	129,301	7,339,818	18,157	1,513,502
1966	146,985	7,056,353	18,055	1,402,296
1965	143,548	6,458,214	15,017	1,309,786
1964	146,360	6,362,372	14,787	1,054,199
1963	135,023	5,649,619	14,045	992,117
1962	119,892	5,608,404	13,583	1,093,279
1961	103,164	5,105,084	10,998	1,019,839
1960	93,739	4,669,349	10,144	985,648
1955	29,373	3,102,994	8,184	675,629
1950	24,675	1,533,859	9,114	501,487
1945	5,910	210,467	2,491	289,368
1940	5,712	563,074	2,442	218,776
1935	6,243	438,306	2,070	187,122
1930	29,915	728,887	5,060	193,928
1925	9,243	403,843	1,560	119,304

1. Includes acquisition of right-of-way, engineering, construction of roads and major structures, and installation of
   traffic service facilities.

2. Includes physical maintenance and traffic services.

3. U.S. data through 1958 are for 48 states; after 1958 data include Alaska and Hawaii.

Source: U.S. Department of Transportation, Federal Highway Administration, Highway Statistics Division,
   Highway Statistics, 1992, and earlier editions; *Summary to 1955*.

TABLE 9.2-- MEANS OF TRANSPORTATION AND TRAVEL TIME TO WORK, WORKERS 16 YEARS
AND OVER, TENNESSEE, 1980 AND 1990 [In thousands of persons]

	1990		1980	
	Number	Percent	Number	Percent
MEANS OF TRANSPORTAION TO WORK				
Workers 16 years and older	2,239.3	100.0	1,891.7	100.0
Private vehicle	2,087.2	93.2	1,727.8	91.3
Drive alone	1,763.0	78.7	1,289.5	68.2
Carpool	324.2	14.5	438.3	23.2
Public transportation	29.6	1.3	46.6	2.5
Bicycle	1.8	0.1	2.1	0.1
Motorcycle	1.9	0.1	3.8	0.2
Walked only	50.8	2.3	66.6	3.5
Other means	15.8	0.7	12.5	0.7
Worked at home	52.2	2.3	32.2	1.7
TRAVEL TIME TO WORK				
Workers 16 years and older	2,187.1	100.0	1,863.1	100.0
Less than 10 minutes	329.9	15.1	297.9	16.0
10 to 19 minutes	762.7	34.9	646.5	34.7
20 to 29 minutes	480.3	22.0	398.7	21.4
30 to 44 minutes	397.0	18.2	340.4	18.3
45 or more minutes	217.2	9.9	179.5	9.6
Mean (in minutes)	21.5		21.2	

Note: Data may not add to total due to independent rounding.

Source: U.S. Department of Commerce, Bureau of the Census, *Census of Population and Housing, 1990:
Summary Tape File 3A, Tennessee*; and 1980 Census of Population, *General Social and Economic
Characteristics, Tennessee.*

TABLE 9.3-- MOTOR VEHICLE REGISTRATIONS, BY TYPE OF VEHICLE, TENNESSEE, 1925-1992,
SELECTED YEARS

Year	Total	Automobiles	Buses	Trucks
1992	4,645,083	3,726,216	15,001	903,866
1991	4,541,676	3,642,146	14,467	885,063
1990	4,444,108	3,552,828	13,867	877,413
1989	4,315,702	3,451,763	13,191	850,748
1988	4,225,490	3,373,276	12,814	839,400
1987	4,026,565	3,194,605	12,078	819,882
1986	3,932,220	3,097,473	12,499	822,248
1985	3,753,926	2,944,971	12,049	796,906
1984	3,568,661	2,822,315	11,555	734,791
1983	3,537,012	2,904,367	11,228	621,417
1982	3,381,216	2,765,974	11,624	603,618
1981	3,533,299	2,870,407	10,475	652,147
1980	3,271,345	2,564,551	10,374	696,420
1979	2,995,305	2,337,221	9,424	648,660
1978	2,911,222	2,351,910	9,175	550,137
1977	2,996,157	2,307,783	8,774	679,600
1976	2,804,840	2,153,922	8,705	642,213
1975	2,725,569	2,092,996	8,303	624,270
1974	2,568,381	1,987,890	7,906	572,585
1973	2,466,821	1,938,735	7,796	520,290
1972	2,293,635	1,819,121	7,608	466,906
1971	2,135,635	1,703,756	7,527	424,352
1970	2,049,992	1,638,268	7,432	404,292
1969	1,971,160	1,583,187	7,185	380,788
1968	1,906,774	1,543,887	6,498	356,389
1967	1,869,918	1,523,452	6,268	340,198
1966	1,757,575	1,426,481	5,415	325,679
1965	1,654,682	1,353,463	5,340	295,879
1964	1,573,437	1,288,397	5,301	279,739
1963	1,500,566	1,231,600	5,115	263,851
1962	1,429,055	1,175,489	4,793	248,773
1961	1,362,868	1,118,664	6,295	237,909
1960	1,307,010	1,070,432	5,537	231,041
1959	1,264,255	1,032,023	5,519	226,713
1958	1,203,405	980,438	5,739	217,228
1957	1,160,042	941,346	5,801	212,895
1956	1,131,437	914,470	5,666	211,301
1955	1,168,295	925,292	4,578	238,425
1950	858,111	672,966	4,092	181,053
1945	466,677	378,121	4,174	84,382
1940	461,183	380,210	2,154	78,819
1935	359,618	310,520	1,312	47,786
1930	373,534	330,978	1,179	41,377
1925	246,511	221,707	720	24,084

Note: The automobile classification includes taxicabs.

Source: U.S. Department of Transportation, Federal Highway Administration, Highway Statistics Division,
Highway Statistics, 1992, and earlier editions; *Summary to 1955*.

TABLE 9.4-- LOCATION AND NUMBER OF MOTOR FREIGHT TERMINALS, TENNESSEE, 1992

City	County	Number of terminals
Athens	McMinn	1
Blountville	Sullivan	1
Carthage	Smith	1
Centerville	Hickman	1
Chattanooga	Hamilton	26
Cleveland	Bradley	3
Columbia	Maury	2
Cookeville	Putnam	8
Cowan	Franklin	1
Dayton	Rhea	1
Decherd	Franklin	1
Dresden	Weakley	2
Dyersburg	Dyer	5
Fayetteville	Lincoln	1
Gallatin	Sumner	2
Greeneville	Greene	2
Jackson	Madison	10
Johnson City	Washington-Carter	5
Kingsport	Hawkins-Sullivan	10
Knoxville	Knox	18
La Grange	Fayette	1
Lawrenceburg	Lawrence	2
Lebanon	Wilson	1
Lewisburg	Marshall	1
Lexington	Henderson	1
McMinnville	Warren	3
Maryville	Blount	1
Memphis	Shelby	47
Milan	Gibson	1
Morristown	Hamblen	6
Murfreesboro	Rutherford	3
Nashville	Davidson	37
Oak Ridge	Anderson-Roane	1
Paris	Henry	2
Portland	Sumner	2
Pulaski	Giles	1
Savannah	Hardin	1
Shelbyville	Bedford	2
Sparta	White	2
Springfield	Robertson	1
Tullahoma	Franklin-Coffee	2
Union City	Obion	2
Winchester	Franklin	1

Source: International Thomson Transport Press, *American Motor Carrier Directory*, Spring 1992. Copyright
material presented here with permission of the publisher.

TABLE 9.5-- MOTOR FUEL CONSUMPTION, BY TYPE, TENNESSEE, 1976–1988 [In thousands of gallons]

Year	Total	Gasoline[1]	Highway gasohol	Highway diesel	Highway LPG[2]
1988	3,220,571	2,058,956	580,277	578,470	2,868
1987	3,053,936	2,236,792	524,300	555,974	3,737
1986	3,002,210	2,257,066	214,700	527,361	3,083
1985	2,896,757	2,169,930	209,372	513,329	4,125
1984	2,857,614	2,237,227	109,762	503,273	7,350
1983	2,798,191	2,331,654	n.a.	458,245	8,292
1982	2,767,843	2,355,395	n.a.	404,754	7,694
1981	2,804,155	2,388,466	n.a.	410,866	4,823
1980	2,811,901	2,417,938	n.a.	391,393	2,570
1979	2,922,305	2,527,837	n.a.	392,749	1,719
1978	3,045,694	2,664,296	n.a.	379,463	1,934
1977	2,899,101	2,554,607	n.a.	342,756	1,738
1976	2,784,787	2,479,795	n.a.	303,405	1,587

Note: Totals may not equal sum of components due to independent rounding.

n.a. not available.

1. Includes aviation gasoline and losses.

2. Includes butane, propane, ethane-propane mixtures, etc.

Source: Tennessee Department of Economic and Community Development, Energy Division, *Tennessee Energy Statistical Annual, 1988*; and *Tennessee Energy Statistics Quarterly*, Fourth Quarter 1985.

TABLE 9.6-- SIZE AND WEIGHT LIMITATIONS FOR TRUCKS, TENNESSEE, 1989

Maximum overall height: 8 feet[1]

Maximum overall length, single truck: 13 feet 6 inches

Maximum overall length tractor and semi-trailer combination:[2]

    Straight truck and semi-trailer or combination: 65 feet
    Combination transporting poles or logs (in single length pieces): 75 feet
    Twin trailer combination: There is no maximum overall length.

Maximum length of semi-trailers used in twin trailer combination:
    Neither trailer shall exceed twenty-eight feet six inches.

Maximum gross weight:
    Two axle single truck: 40,000 pounds
    Three axle single truck: 54,000 pounds
    Four axle single truck: 74,000 pounds
    Three axle tractor and semi-trailer combination: 60,000 pounds
    Four axle tractor and semi-trailer combination: 74,000 pounds
    Five axle tractor and semi-trailer combination or five axle tractor,
    Semi-trailers and converter gear (twin trailers): 80,000 pounds

Maximum gross axle weight:
    Steering axle for single truck: 20,000 pounds
    Steering axle for tractor: 20,000 pounds
    Single axle for single truck, tractor, semi-trailer or converter gear:
       20,000 pounds
    Tandem axle for single truck, tractor or semi-trailer: 34,000 pounds

Note: Data are meant to give basic information pertaining to the trucking rules in Tennessee. They are not meant to provide all the requirements. For further information, contact Tennessee Department of Revenue, Motor Vehicle Enforcement.

1. 102 inches authorized on Interstate system and other designated routes.

2. When a motor vehicle consists of a truck-tractor and semi-trailer or trailer combination, the towed vehicle shall not exceed forty-eight feet in length from the point of attachment to the tractor except that this length may be increased to fifty-two feet when the load on such vehicle consists of livestock or automobiles and/or motor vehicles.

Source: Tennessee Department of Revenue, Motor Vehicle Division, *Proportional Registration Manual, 1988.*

TABLE 9.7-- TRUCKS COMPARATIVE USE SUMMARY, TENNESSEE, 1967–1987, CENSUS YEARS

| | Percent of trucks registered in Tennessee | | | | |
	1987	1982	1977	1972	1967 [a]
Major use					
Agriculture	8.6	10.5	18.0	24.8	39.0
Forestry and lumbering	0.3	0.6	0.3	(b)	(b)
Mining and quarrying	0.1	0.1	0.4	(b)	(b)
Construction	7.3	7.2	4.8	7.0	8.6
Manufacturing	1.1	1.9	1.7	2.7	3.3
Wholesale, retail trade	4.7	5.5	8.1	9.7	9.2
For-hire, transportation	2.1	2.4	2.3	3.3	2.4
Utilities and service	5.0	5.0	4.0	6.2	5.8
Personal transportation	69.6	66.5	58.2	44.4	27.1
Other	1.1	0.3	2.1	1.8	4.6
Body type					
Pickup, panel, or mini-van[1]	90.7	87.4	87.8	74.5	74.0
Platform and cattle rack	3.1	5.1	4.9	12.1	13.8
Van[1]	2.5	3.5	3.9	6.7	5.4
Public utility	0.2	0.1	0.2	0.9	1.2
Other	3.5	3.9	3.2	5.8	5.6
Vehicle size					
Light (10,000 lbs. or less)	92.9	91.2	89.9	82.0	77.1
Medium (10,001--19,500 lbs.)	1.9	3.3	4.6	8.5	14.8
Light-heavy (19,501--26,000 lbs.)	1.5	1.7	2.0	2.1	2.6
Heavy-heavy (26,001 lbs. or more)	3.7	3.9	3.5	7.4	5.5
Year model					
1 to 2 years old	18.3	10.1	8.2	16.9	12.6
3 to 4 years old	15.4	15.9	17.9	19.6	20.1
Over 4 years old	66.3	74.0	73.9	63.6	67.3
Annual miles					
Less than 5,000	23.6	24.3	26.2	23.0	(c)
5,000 to 9,999	20.3	30.0	35.2	29.8	(c)
10,000 to 19,999	37.9	34.5	35.2	33.8	31.0
20,000 to 29,999	10.2	6.2	8.4	7.7	7.6
30,000 miles or more	7.9	5.0	4.7	5.8	5.8

Note: Detail may not add to total due to independent rounding.

1. Vans similar to panel trucks are included in pickup, panel category.

a. May not be comparable to later years due to revisions in categorization.

b. Less than 0.05 percent.

c. For 1967 survey, data were presented for "less than 6,000 miles" (39.4 percent) and "6,000 to 9,999 miles" (16.2 percent).

Source: U.S. Department of Commerce, Bureau of the Census, *1987 Census of Transportation, Truck Inventory and Use Survey, Tennessee*; and earlier editions.

TABLE 9.8-- SELECTED AIRPORT STATISTICS, TENNESSEE, 1989

City	County	Airport name	Class[1]	Runway length (in feet)
Arlington	Shelby	Municipal	General Utility	3,800
Athens	McMinn	McMinn County	General Utility	4,700
Bolivar	Hardeman	Bolivar-Hardeman County	General Utility	4,000
Bristol	Sullivan	Tri-City Airport	Air Carrier	8,000
Camden	Benton	Benton County	Basic Utility II	3,500
Centerville	Hickman	Municipal	General Utility	4,000
Chattanooga	Hamilton	Dallas Bay Sky Park	Basic Utility	3,100
Chattanooga	Hamilton	Lovell Field	Air Carrier	7,400
Clarksville	Montgomery	Outlaw Field	Basic Transport	6,000
Cleveland	Bradley	Hardwick Field	Basic Utility I	3,300
Clifton	Wayne	Hassell Field	General Utility	4,600
Collegedale	Hamilton	Municipal	Basic Utility I	4,700
Columbia-Mt. Pleasant	Maury	Maury County	Basic Transport	5,000
Cookeville	Putnam	Putnam County	General Utility	3,800
Copper Hill	Polk	Martin Campbell	Basic Utility	3,500
Covington	Tipton	Municipal	General Utility	4,000
Crossville	Cumberland	Memorial	Basic Transport	5,400
Dayton	Rhea	Mark Anton	General Utility	4,500
Dickson	Dickson	Municipal	General Utility	4,000
Dyersburg	Dyer	Municipal	Basic Transport	5,000
Elizabethton	Carter	Municipal	Basic Utility II	4,000
Fayetteville	Lincoln	Municipal	Basic Transport	4,900
Gainesboro	Jackson	Jackson County	Basic Utility II	3,500
Gallatin	Sumner	Municipal	Basic Transport	5,000
Greeneville	Greene	Municipal	Basic Transport	6,300
Halls	Lauderdale	Arnold Field	General Utility	4,700
Hohenwald	Lewis	John A. Baker Field	General Utility	4,000
Humboldt	Gibson	Municipal	General Utility	4,000
Huntingdon-McKenzie	Carroll	Carroll County	Basic Transport	5,000
Jacksboro	Campbell	Campbell County	Basic Utility	3,500
Jackson	Madison	McKellar Field	General Transport	6,000
Jamestown	Fentress	Municipal	Basic Utility II	3,500
Jasper	Marion	Marion County	Basic Utility II	3,500
Johnson City	Carter	Johnson City (STOL)	Basic Utility I	3,000
Knoxville	Knox	Downtown Island	Basic Utility II	3,500
Knoxville	Blount	McGhee Tyson	Air Carrier	9,000
Lafayette	Macon	Municipal	General Utility	4,000
Lawrenceburg	Lawrence	Municipal	Basic Transport	5,000
Lebanon	Wilson	Municipal	Basic Utility II	4,000
Lewisburg	Marshall	Ellington Airport	Basic Transport	5,000
Lexington	Henderson	Franklin-Wilkins	General Utility	4,500
Linden	Perry	Perry County	Basic Utility II	3,600
Livingston	Overton	Municipal	General Utility	4,000
McKinnon	Houston	Houston County	Basic Utility I	3,000
McMinnville	Warren	Warren County Memorial	Basic Tranport	5,000
Madisonville	Monroe	Monroe County	Basic Utility II	3,500
Memphis	Shelby	General de Witt Spain	General Utility	3,800
Memphis	Shelby	International	Air Carrier	9,300
Milan-Trenton	Gibson	Gibson County	Basic Transport	4,800
Millington	Shelby	Charles W. Baker	Basic Utility II	3,500
Morristown	Hamblen	Moore-Murrell	General Transport	5,700
Mountain City	Johnson	Johnson County	General Utility	4,500

TABLE 9.8-- SELECTED AIRPORT STATISTICS, TENNESSEE, 1989 (Continued)

City	County	Airport name	Class[1]	Runway length (in feet)
Murfreesboro	Rutherford	Municipal	General Utility	3,900
Nashville	Davidson	Cornelia Fort	Basic Utility	2,800
Nashville	Davidson	John C. Tune	Basic Transport	5,000
Nashville	Davidson	Municipal	Air Carrier	8,500
Oneida	Scott	Scott Municipal	Basic Transport	5,500
Paris	Henry	Henry County	Basic Transport	5,000
Parsons	Decatur	Scott Field	General Utility	4,000
Portland	Sumner	Municipal	General Utility	4,000
Powell	Knox	Powell (STOL)	Basic Utility I	2,600
Pulaski	Giles	Abernathy Field	Basic Transport	5,000
Reelfoot Lake	Obion	Reelfoot Lake Airpark	Basic Utility II	3,500
Rockwood	Roane	Municipal	Basic Transport	5,000
Rogersville	Hawkins	Hawkins County	Basic Utility II	3,500
Savannah	Hardin	Savannah	Basic Transport	5,000
Selmer	McNairy	Robert Sibley Airport	General Utility	4,300
Sevierville	Sevier	Gatlinburg-Pigeon Forge	General Transport	5,500
Sewanee	Franklin	University of the South-Franklin County	Basic Utility I	3,300
Shelbyville	Bedford	Bomar	Basic Transport	5,000
Smithville	DeKalb	Municipal	Basic Utility II	4,100
Smyrna	Rutherford	Symrna	General Transport	8,000
Somerville	Fayette	Fayette County	Basic Utility II	3,500
Sparta	White	Sparta-White County	Basic Transport	5,000
Springfield	Robertson	Springfield-Robertson County	Basic Utility II	3,700
Tazewell	Claiborne	Tazewell Claiborne County	Basic Utility I	3,000
Tullahoma	Coffee	Soesbe-Martin	Basic Transport	5,000
Union City	Obion	Everett-Stewart Field	Basic Transport	5,000
Waverly	Humphreys	Humphreys County	General Utility	4,000
Winchester	Franklin	Municipal	General Utility	5,000

Note: Only airports with paved runways are listed. Military airports have been excluded.

1. Basic Utility I: Airport accommodating about 75 percent of propeller airplanes under 12,500 pounds.
   Basic Utility II: Airport accommodating about 95 percent of propeller airplanes under 12,500 pounds.
   General Utility: Accommodates all propeller airplanes under 12,500 pounds.
   Basic Transport: Accommodates turbojets up to 60,000 pounds.
   General Transport: Accommodates airplanes up to 175,000 pounds.
   Air Carrier: Airport serving regularly scheduled commercial airlines.

Source: Tennessee Department of Transportation, *Tennessee Airport Directory, 1982*, and direct correspondence; and Tennessee Department of Economic and Community Development, Industrial Development Division, *Transportation in Tennessee, 1979*.

TABLE 9.9-- STATUS OF THE AIRPORT IMPROVEMENT PROGRAM, BY TYPE OF AIRPORT, TENNESSEE, 1971-1989

| Year | Air carriers | | General aviation | |
	Total federal funds ($1,000)	Total projects	Total federal funds ($1,000)	Total projects
1989	36,744	12	2,815	6
1988	37,910	12	3,310	9
1986	15,322	13	1,809	6
1985	14,236	10	1,718	5
1984	11,470	16	2,627	8
1983	12,377	16	1,827	9
1982	6,948	6	1,275	5
1981	74,305	86	8,337	35
1980	65,733	80	7,912	32
1979	60,401	72	6,833	28
1978	56,271	66	6,197	23
1977	46,699	58	5,739	20
1976	32,802	46	4,469	16
1975	26,685	42	2,974	10
1974	25,908	38	2,505	9
1973	1,580	8	17,124	30
1972	10,751	19	581	5
1971	4,026	8	502	4

Note: Beginning in 1982, air carriers refer to primary, commercial, and reliever airports. This reclassification of data resulted from the Airport and Airway Improvement Act of 1982.

Source: U.S. Department of Transportation, Federal Aviation Administration, *FAA Statistical Handbook of Aviation, Calendar Year 1989*, and earlier editions.

TABLE 9.10--NUMBER OF AIRPORTS, BY LENGTH OF LONGEST RUNWAY, TENNESSEE, AS OF DECEMBER 31, 1989

Length of runway	Number
Total	208
Less than 3,000 feet	120
3,000–3,999	31
4,000–4,999	27
5,000–5,999	19
6,000–6,999	3
7,000–7,999	2
8,000–8,999	3
9,000–9,999	2
10,000 and over	1

Note: Includes seaplane bases, heliports, and military fields having joint civil-military use.

Source: U.S. Department of Transportation, Federal Aviation Administration, *FAA Statistical Handbook of Aviation, 1989.*

TABLE 9.11--AIRCRAFT DEPARTURES AND REVENUE TRAFFIC AT ON-LINE AIRPORTS, SELECTED TENNESSEE COMMUNITIES, DECEMBER 31, 1989

	TENNESSEE	Chattanooga	Johnson City-Kingsport-Bristol	Knoxville	Memphis	Nashville
Aircraft departures						
performed	178,741	5,158	3,760	10,732	97,431	61,657
Scheduled	178,645	5,158	3,757	10,719	97,375	61,633
Nonscheduled	96	0	3	13	56	24
Passenger enplanements	8,620,578	253,807	148,694	481,896	3,989,814	3,746,367
Revenue Tons						
Enplaned[1]	628,256.62	875.04	897.60	6,941.42	604,337.00	15,203.46
Freight	601,703.12	568.95	214.22	5,353.76	588,577.07	6,987.02
U.S. mail	26,553.50	306.09	683.38	1,587.66	15,759.93	8,216.44

1. Includes express and foreign mail not shown separately.

Source: U.S. Department of Transportation, Federal Aviation Administration, *Airport Activity Statistics of Certificated Route Air Carriers, 12 Months Ending December 31, 1989.*

TABLE 9.12--AIRCRAFT DEPARTURES AND PASSENGER ENPLANEMENTS AT ON-LINE AIRPORTS, TENNESSEE AND SELECTED COMMUNITIES, 1965-1989, SELECTED YEARS

Year	TENNESSEE	Chattanooga	Johnson City-Kingsport-Bristol	Knoxville	Memphis	Nashville
1989						
Departures	178,741	5,158	3,760	10,732	97,431	61,657
Enplanements	8,620,578	253,807	148,694	481,896	3,989,814	3,746,367
1988						
Departures	182,902	5,297	4,048	11,178	103,759	58,617
Enplanements	8,729,764	259,032	162,356	531,790	4,532,572	3,244,014
1987						
Departures	183,922	5,313	3,290	11,545	107,295	56,471
Enplanements	8,947,174	276,100	140,131	520,482	5,023,047	2,987,233
1986						
Departures	171,551	5,483	3,869	11,043	104,695	46,461
Enplanements	7,215,559	250,389	144,941	477,252	4,177,169	2,165,808
1985						
Departures	126,632	4,556	4,679	9,132	77,942	30,313
Enplanements	5,663,875	216,862	157,005	425,203	3,469,318	1,395,487
1984						
Departures	105,715	4,493	4,932	10,161	57,528	28,801
Enplanements	4,265,622	207,552	150,213	408,244	2,283,425	1,216,188
1983						
Departures	99,619	4,812	5,023	9,386	56,248	24,150
Enplanements	4,232,731	219,190	150,907	394,620	2,359,442	1,108,572
1982						
Departures	96,162	4,941	5,712	9,651	51,153	24,735
Enplanements	4,019,261	180,715	156,308	413,512	2,189,650	1,079,076
1981						
Departures	96,738	4,765	6,817	8,301	50,377	25,943
Enplanements	3,732,147	212,086	173,326	364,338	1,945,933	1,033,206
1980						
Departures	108,233	5,571	7,983	9,195	55,840	28,315
Enplanements	4,174,472	252,245	211,280	430,153	2,148,730	1,122,084
1979						
Departures	123,231	6,620	8,658	11,049	64,275	30,094
Enplanements	4,829,801	291,335	236,473	487,724	2,576,902	1,223,219
1978						
Departures	127,836	9,137	9,567	12,145	62,406	31,390
Enplanements	4,534,079	307,600	228,945	476,799	2,344,531	1,156,836
1977						
Departures	120,790	9,589	9,177	13,387	57,003	29,195
Enplanements	4,014,837	281,791	206,952	443,202	2,072,202	987,193
1976						
Departures	118,835	10,105	9,172	13,716	54,696	28,271
Enplanements	3,801,264	259,578	191,304	406,522	2,015,073	904,325
1975						
Departures	115,732	9,557	9,696	13,580	51,867	27,909
Enplanements	3,519,249	237,266	185,695	375,442	1,857,207	840,438
1965						
Departures	85,383	10,119	10,095	14,888	28,898	16,815
Enplanements	1,622,057	121,562	112,616	225,972	761,919	386,184

Source: U.S. Department of Transportation, Federal Aviation Administration, *Airport Activity Statistics of Certificated Route Air Carriers, 12 Months Ended December 31, 1989*, and earlier editions.

TABLE 9.13--PUBLIC RIVER TERMINALS, LOCATION AND FACILITIES, TENNESSEE RIVER AND ITS TRIBUTARIES, TENNESSEE, 1991

River	County	River mile	Facility name	Handling equipment[1]	Storage facility[2]	Transport access	
						Rail	Major highway[3]
TENNESSEE RIVER							
Tennessee	Humphreys	100.3R	Herbert Sangravel Co., Inc.	A,C,D,E	III	CSX	U.S. 70
	Humphreys	100.3R	Merchants Grain, Inc.	A,C	IV	CSX	U.S. 70
	Perry	135.5	Tinker Sand & Gravel, Inc.	A,C,D,E	III	None	TN. 100
	Marion	421.6R	Jasper Bulk Terminals, Inc.	None	None	None	I-24
	Marion	424.0L	Port of Nickajack	F	III	None	I-24
	Marion	430.3L	Serodino, Inc.	F	III,VI	None	I-24
	Hamilton	456.1R	Mid-South Terminals, Inc.	F	III,IV	Norfolk Southern	I-24
	Hamilton	462.0L	Combustion Engineering Co.	F	III	CSX	I-124
	Hamilton	463.1R	Southern Electric Fleeting Co.	F	III	None	I-124
	Hamilton	463.6R	Concrete Service Co.	F	III	Norfolk Southern	I-124
	Hamilton	463.8R	JIT Terminals, Inc.	B,F	II,VI,VIb (humidity controlled)	Norfolk Southern	I-124
	Loudon	600.2R	Fort Loudon Terminal	D,E	II,III	Norfolk Southern	U.S. 11
	Knox	652.2R	Burkhart Enterprises	D,E,F	III	Norfolk Southern	I-40,I-75
TENNESSEE RIVER TRIBUTARIES							
Little Tennessee	Monroe	18.9L	Burkhart Enterprises	F	III	CSX	U.S. 411
Emory	Monroe	11.0L	Harbert International	F	II,III,V	Norfolk Southern	I-40
Hiwassee	Monroe	18.2R	Hiwassee River Terminal	F	III,IV	Norfolk Southern	U.S. 11

1. Codes: Type of Handling Equipment
A. Conveyor system
B. Pipeline
C. Hopper facilities
D. Clamshell bucket
E. Fixed crane or derrick
F. Mobile crane or derrick
G. Floating crane/derrick
H. Hoists (fixed or mobile)

2. Codes: Type of Storage Facilities
I. Covered shed
II. Enclosed shed (warehouse)
III. Open storage area
IV. Grain elevators
V. Bins
VI. Liquid storage tanks
VI.a. Petroleum
VI.b. Other

3. Highway is within 10-mile radius.

Source: Tennessee Valley Authority, Navigation Development, direct correspondence.

TABLE 9.14--PRIVATE INVESTMENT IN WATERFRONT PLANTS AND TERMINALS ON THE
TENNESSEE RIVER, 1933–1992 [In thousands of dollars]

Year	Investment in new and expanded plants	Cumulative investment in new and expanded plants	Cumulative percent of total
1992	58,250	7,881,129	100.0
1991	602,733	7,822,879	99.3
1990	709,400	7,220,146	91.6
1989[r]	752,900	6,510,746	82.6
1988	465,500	5,757,846	73.1
1987	204,400	5,292,346	67.2
1986	146,350	5,087,946	64.6
1985	150,000	4,941,596	62.7
1984	211,065	4,791,596	60.8
1983	147,775	4,580,531	58.1
1982	40,000	4,432,756	56.2
1981	317,872	4,392,756	55.7
1980	316,886	4,074,884	51.7
1979	156,243	3,757,998	47.7
1978	97,523	3,601,755	45.7
1977	437,248	3,504,232	44.5
1976	71,632	3,066,984	38.9
1975	300,488	2,995,352	38.0
1974	162,273	2,694,864	34.2
1973	365,915	2,532,591	32.1
1972	46,195	2,166,676	27.5
1971	27,895	2,120,481	26.9
1970	78,943	2,092,586	26.6
1969	133,050	2,013,643	25.6
1968	311,251	1,880,593	23.9
1967	95,876	1,569,342	19.9
1966	180,755	1,473,466	18.7
1965	214,620	1,292,711	16.4
1964	62,157	1,078,091	13.7
1963	83,529	1,015,934	12.9
1962	110,050	932,405	11.8
1961	67,961	822,355	10.4
1960	27,937	754,394	9.6
1959	57,471	726,457	9.2
1958	21,788	668,986	8.5
1957	159,449	647,198	8.2
1956	169,703	487,749	6.2
1955	56,633	318,046	4.0
1954	94,985	261,413	3.3
1953	37,792	166,428	2.1
1952	44,805	128,636	1.6
1951	24,491	83,831	1.1
1950	3,506	59,340	0.8
1949	10,012	55,834	0.7
1948	32,767	45,822	0.6
1947	1,768	13,055	0.2
1946	729	11,287	0.1
1933–1945	10,558	10,558	0.1

r revised.

Source: Tennessee Valley Authority, Economic Development and Analysis Branch, "Industrial Development Along the Tennessee River 1992."

TABLE 9.15--NET TONS OF RIVER FREIGHT TRAFFIC, BY COMMODITY, MAINSTREAM OF TENNESSEE RIVER, 1935-1992, SELECTED YEARS [In thousands of tons]

Year	Total	Chemicals	Coal and coke	Forest products	Grains and products	Iron and steel	Petroleum products	Stone, sand, and gravel[1]	All other
1992	46,167.0	2,318.0	21,683.0	730.0	4,181.0	1,344.0	2,471.0	11,380.0	2,060.0
1991	42,164.0	2,459.0	21,076.0	643.0	3,689.0	1,389.0	2,344.0	8,520.0	2,044.0
1990	44,636.0	2,150.0	22,271.0	611.0	4,097.0	1,500.0	2,580.0	9,014.0	2,413.0
1989	43,452.6	2,088.1	21,792.1	551.0	3,535.4	1,349.0	2,508.0	9,700.5	1,928.6
1988	47,289.0	3,363.0	24,194.0	560.0	4,044.0	1,664.0	2,756.0	8,670.0	2,038.0
1987	41,788.9	2,233.4	20,694.2	593.9	3,970.9	1,285.1	2,385.1	8,190.0	2,436.1
1986	39,998.9	2,215.0	21,884.4	519.4	4,340.8	1,187.5	2,079.7	5,248.9	2,519.0
1985	36,683.3	2,313.4	19,144.2	547.7	3,911.8	1,114.8	1,788.8	5,591.1	2,271.6
1984	33,182.0	2,440.0	16,275.9	548.2	4,604.8	1,334.3	1,677.3	4,214.4	2,087.1
1983	27,988.0	1,800.0	13,450.0	627.0	3,776.0	916.0	2,259.0	3,547.0	1,613.0
1982	25,513.0	1,752.0	14,081.0	583.0	3,285.0	690.0	1,598.0	2,051.0	1,473.0
1981	26,006.0	2,095.0	13,197.0	697.0	2,915.0	1,073.0	1,503.0	2,534.0	1,992.0
1980	29,397.0	2,488.0	15,651.0	591.0	2,895.0	937.0	1,918.0	3,158.0	1,759.0
1979	31,398.0	2,765.2	15,029.1	476.5	2,453.9	1,156.5	2,414.8	5,608.9	1,493.1
1978	31,634.5	2,829.8	13,412.4	449.5	2,506.5	1,270.9	3,303.1	6,099.4	1,683.0
1977	26,583.2	2,730.8	10,114.7	361.2	2,255.5	1,086.5	3,544.8	4,901.2	1,688.5
1976	26,254.2	2,619.8	9,354.3	320.5	1,921.7	1,132.2	3,472.2	5,839.1	1,590.4
1975	28,316.5	2,142.5	12,110.9	302.7	1,885.8	835.6	2,820.6	6,824.2	1,394.3
1974	27,123.6	2,513.3	9,329.1	336.5	1,963.3	1,193.2	2,140.9	8,146.5	1,500.8
1973	29,346.6	2,395.4	11,689.6	375.8	1,990.9	1,099.0	2,425.1	7,816.9	1,554.0
1972	28,529.7	2,204.0	12,021.7	372.8	1,918.9	1,079.3	3,185.5	6,352.1	1,395.4
1971	27,685.2	1,836.6	10,802.9	342.9	2,927.1	1,080.5	3,328.6	5,994.1	1,372.4
1970	25,489.2	1,609.8	9,714.1	328.2	2,939.0	868.6	2,927.8	5,506.7	1,595.1
1969	24,530.3	1,651.0	9,593.9	341.3	2,565.8	962.2	2,739.7	5,386.6	1,289.6
1968	23,018.3	1,280.6	8,827.5	297.7	1,815.4	810.3	2,651.8	5,929.6	1,405.4
1967	21,511.7	1,019.9	8,123.8	252.2	2,065.8	462.9	1,983.5	6,356.2	1,247.5
1966	19,709.1	581.4	7,892.6	245.4	2,200.1	515.8	1,082.8	6,292.8	898.2
1965	17,395.9	401.6	6,640.8	212.8	1,724.3	438.6	1,097.7	6,014.9	865.2
1964	15,373.9	352.6	6,328.3	202.3	1,784.2	375.8	875.9	4,723.1	731.8
1963	14,432.7	286.9	5,917.3	195.5	2,203.4	340.6	846.7	3,943.6	698.7
1962	13,115.4	311.7	4,655.1	168.3	2,908.3	259.7	790.4	3,531.3	490.5
1961	11,614.7	305.1	4,664.0	161.7	2,099.2	250.3	604.4	3,155.9	374.0
1960	12,440.7	345.8	5,177.4	183.1	2,261.4	306.5	794.2	3,000.5	371.7
1959	12,036.9	245.0	5,206.3	168.5	1,901.1	353.7	717.8	3,089.5	354.9
1958	12,040.8	246.3	5,052.8	176.0	1,773.0	286.3	787.4	2,879.2	839.8
1957	12,742.2	171.3	6,725.6	149.4	1,079.4	325.8	731.7	2,799.3	759.6
1956	12,299.4	86.8	7,473.8	109.2	649.8	293.0	826.3	2,162.3	698.2
1955	9,975.0	111.2	5,661.9	112.0	736.1	258.2	914.8	1,881.7	299.1
1950	3,051.2	(a)	207.2	29.3	160.7	117.5	754.3	1,657.1	125.0
1945	2,163.4	0.0	505.3	62.9	122.9	17.5	215.6	1,198.3	40.9
1940	2,206.9	0.0	(a)	141.9	43.1	20.6	102.9	1,842.1	56.3
1935	1,899.3	0.0	(a)	111.0	(a)	34.9	0.0	1,598.7	154.7

1. Includes waterway improvement material.

a. Included in all other category.

Source: Tennessee Valley Authority and U.S. Department of the Army, Corps of Engineers, direct correspondence.

TRANSPORTATION

TABLE 9.16–TON-MILES OF RIVER FREIGHT TRAFFIC, BY COMMODITY, MAINSTREAM OF
TENNESSEE RIVER, 1935–1992, SELECTED YEARS [In millions of ton miles]

Year	Total	Chemicals	Coal and coke	Forest products	Grains and products	Iron and steel	Petroleum products	Stone, sand, and gravel [1]	All other
1992	6,964.8	405.4	3,380.1	86.1	1,491.1	221.3	442.7	479.0	459.1
1991	6,408.6	409.0	3,106.4	80.5	1,325.6	226.8	339.9	450.2	470.2
1990	6,597.2	367.8	2,934.9	70.8	1,499.0	252.5	397.6	503.1	571.5
1989	6,598.2	328.1	3,343.8	63.7	1,246.1	241.3	417.6	461.3	496.4
1988	7,355.2	560.2	3,297.8	76.7	1,437.5	314.8	521.2	595.1	552.0
1984	6,127.0	400.0	2,913.2	72.8	1,726.2	214.1	253.0	142.4	405.3
1983	5,405.2	302.7	2,742.9	71.6	1,341.3	161.1	372.7	116.9	295.9
1982	5,101.9	329.5	2,947.6	76.2	1,045.6	148.0	265.2	82.7	207.1
1981	4,842.3	395.0	2,523.0	85.9	969.3	216.2	280.3	101.6	271.0
1980	5,330.0	502.6	2,967.1	60.9	932.9	169.3	313.0	102.8	281.3
1979	5,061.9	529.2	2,501.7	53.7	818.8	201.9	584.0	142.8	229.8
1978	4,416.6	583.4	1,535.0	50.4	904.8	221.5	712.0	149.0	260.6
1977	3,747.6	581.7	1,073.7	40.0	805.0	191.7	695.7	126.8	233.0
1976	3,663.7	522.2	1,099.2	33.0	728.6	214.6	705.5	159.2	201.6
1975	3,915.8	434.4	1,590.9	30.8	730.2	152.6	601.0	181.4	194.4
1974	3,578.8	437.9	1,259.1	36.5	769.9	202.8	497.0	205.2	170.4
1973	3,954.3	454.8	1,576.7	40.9	772.6	193.1	438.5	268.4	209.3
1972	3,755.9	412.7	1,404.0	36.9	739.7	175.2	540.1	234.6	212.8
1971	3,960.5	317.2	1,247.5	32.4	1,144.6	196.6	545.1	230.3	246.8
1970	3,667.7	256.2	1,173.6	33.2	1,145.2	144.3	447.3	208.8	259.2
1969	3,341.9	288.8	1,038.9	36.6	999.0	128.9	403.5	203.6	242.7
1968	2,757.8	242.7	848.8	35.5	706.7	138.9	374.9	186.6	223.7
1967	2,598.8	191.0	840.2	31.2	798.7	72.8	222.6	218.1	224.2
1966	2,556.4	142.6	874.0	28.9	855.0	77.4	203.0	206.5	169.1
1965	2,190.1	91.3	664.5	23.9	672.5	74.8	295.0	204.4	163.7
1964	2,053.9	71.0	604.8	22.6	699.2	71.2	280.7	153.5	150.8
1963	2,218.1	58.1	534.5	22.4	880.5	57.6	398.1	133.5	133.5
1962	2,268.8	66.4	423.7	19.0	1,171.9	43.8	347.7	85.2	111.2
1961	1,875.8	61.3	538.5	19.3	814.4	38.0	240.3	98.3	65.7
1960	2,312.7	62.7	712.2	25.3	923.9	73.7	359.8	76.9	78.2
1959	2,164.0	37.7	745.3	25.8	793.6	86.7	334.2	67.4	73.4
1958	2,103.3	48.0	712.0	28.2	744.9	85.2	343.0	80.8	61.1
1957	2,112.8	37.8	1,056.8	24.4	461.2	90.8	312.6	76.0	53.2
1956	2,003.4	22.9	1,130.3	17.4	273.0	83.5	342.1	55.1	79.3
1955	1,631.3	23.0	702.3	16.9	292.6	70.2	400.5	44.3	81.5
1950	589.4	(a)	54.2	4.6	57.1	42.5	359.8	49.0	22.2
1945	258.5	0.0	148.5	9.4	46.9	4.4	24.8	20.1	4.4
1940	97.4	0.0	(a)	21.4	17.9	4.9	33.5	15.3	4.4
1935	69.4	0.0	(a)	15.9	(a)	1.8	0.0	43.5	8.2

Note: The U.S. Army Corps of Engineers did not provide ton-mile data for the years 1985–1987.

1. Includes waterway improvement material.

a. Included in all other category.

Source: U.S. Department of the Army, Corps of Engineers and Tennessee Valley Authority, direct correspondence.

TABLE 9.17--MOTOR VEHICLE REGISTRATIONS, BY TYPE OF VEHICLE, TENNESSEE AND COUNTIES, 1990

County	Total	Auto-mobiles	Motor-cycles	Buses	Taxis	Trucks	Semi-trailers	Mobile homes
Anderson	84,131	79,079	1,530	12	14	2,609	885	2
Bedford	31,638	28,355	574	0	6	1,881	822	0
Benton	16,558	14,950	354	0	4	905	345	0
Bledsoe	8,536	7,748	105	0	0	538	145	0
Blount	96,454	89,537	2,096	1	22	3,966	831	1
Bradley	76,538	69,777	1,932	7	8	3,022	1,790	2
Campbell	32,071	29,220	523	0	5	1,407	916	0
Cannon	9,653	8,982	122	0	0	428	121	0
Carroll	25,442	23,752	380	0	3	979	328	0
Carter	47,772	44,516	1,123	0	16	1,617	500	0
Cheatham	22,497	20,541	458	1	1	1,077	419	0
Chester	10,961	10,029	113	0	1	537	280	1
Claiborne	26,902	24,358	507	0	0	1,327	710	0
Clay	7,940	7,336	136	0	0	308	160	0
Cocke	29,420	27,455	448	2	1	1,159	355	0
Coffee	41,651	38,324	788	2	7	1,999	531	0
Crockett	12,036	10,803	175	0	0	714	344	0
Cumberland	34,923	31,535	606	2	4	2,094	681	1
Davidson	537,746	408,489	6,755	214	311	25,850	96,117	10
Decatur	12,210	11,053	177	0	0	687	293	0
DeKalb	15,022	13,900	233	0	0	696	193	0
Dickson	33,952	31,058	575	0	6	1,846	467	0
Dyer	33,920	30,666	745	0	8	1,894	603	4
Fayette	22,838	21,328	290	0	0	836	384	0
Fentress	13,431	12,202	156	0	0	766	307	0
Franklin	32,011	29,043	573	0	1	1,374	1,020	0
Gibson	39,614	36,526	620	0	6	1,724	737	1
Giles	25,354	23,244	385	1	8	1,260	456	0
Grainger	15,084	13,928	256	0	0	693	207	0
Greene	48,028	44,100	821	6	5	2,029	1,067	0
Grundy	12,370	11,387	127	0	1	548	307	0
Hamblen	61,086	55,810	1,363	3	11	2,430	1,469	0
Hamilton	307,462	245,937	4,643	26	102	14,267	42,487	0
Hancock	4,901	4,596	41	0	0	226	38	0
Hardeman	19,834	18,579	217	0	0	761	277	0
Hardin	21,809	20,063	252	0	0	1,004	488	2
Hawkins	37,482	35,412	701	0	1	1,145	223	0
Haywood	14,170	13,051	180	0	0	728	211	0
Henderson	19,617	17,692	258	4	1	970	692	0
Henry	27,532	24,956	400	5	4	1,567	600	0
Hickman	14,967	13,818	279	0	1	715	154	0
Houston	6,537	6,155	90	0	1	203	88	0
Humphreys	16,416	14,934	266	0	1	804	409	2
Jackson	7,956	7,413	124	0	0	354	65	0
Jefferson	26,319	24,030	338	6	1	1,179	765	0
Johnson	13,941	13,072	305	0	0	449	115	0
Knox	305,989	276,102	4,725	30	86	18,030	7,007	9
Lake	4,872	4,525	27	0	0	228	92	0
Lauderdale	20,624	18,940	236	0	1	925	522	0
Lawrence	30,921	28,823	358	3	3	1,210	522	2
Lewis	8,584	7,693	153	0	1	473	264	0
Lincoln	25,755	23,469	316	0	2	1,442	525	1

TABLE 9.17--MOTOR VEHICLE REGISTRATIONS, BY TYPE OF VEHICLE, TENNESSEE AND
COUNTIES, 1990 (Continued)

County	Total	Auto-mobiles	Motor-cycles	Buses	Taxis	Trucks	Semi-trailers	Mobile homes
Loudon	35,057	32,695	571	0	3	1,429	359	0
McMinn	40,980	37,819	750	0	9	1,762	640	0
McNairy	24,255	22,409	327	3	0	1,113	401	2
Macon	13,788	12,752	187	0	0	621	227	1
Madison	72,823	65,795	1,120	4	27	4,640	1,233	4
Marion	25,141	23,269	395	4	1	1,093	379	0
Marshall	20,383	17,609	312	0	2	892	1,568	0
Maury	58,859	53,240	1,232	6	12	3,326	1,043	0
Meigs	7,864	7,300	129	0	0	353	82	0
Monroe	30,904	28,597	568	4	0	1,330	405	0
Montgomery	99,670	92,802	2,657	0	31	3,539	638	3
Moore	6,179	5,437	136	0	0	462	144	0
Morgan	13,721	12,736	188	0	0	687	110	0
Obion	28,238	25,572	451	0	1	1,552	662	0
Overton	13,694	12,625	119	1	5	684	259	1
Perry	6,844	6,255	127	0	0	343	119	0
Pickett	5,001	4,565	73	0	0	261	101	1
Polk	14,599	13,625	295	0	0	499	180	0
Putnam	52,187	46,828	1,001	11	5	2,988	1,350	4
Rhea	31,403	29,273	636	0	1	1,198	295	0
Roane	41,975	39,350	758	6	9	1,349	503	0
Robertson	36,587	33,671	619	6	7	1,885	399	0
Rutherford	106,157	96,899	2,747	11	36	4,679	1,785	0
Scott	18,496	16,848	218	0	0	1,009	421	0
Sequatchie	12,134	11,186	198	0	0	606	144	0
Sevier	53,146	49,423	1,091	8	8	2,411	205	0
Shelby	686,092	600,302	7,096	50	340	25,940	52,364	0
Smith	13,798	12,607	228	0	1	762	200	0
Stewart	10,782	10,003	234	0	0	458	87	0
Sullivan	156,568	140,227	3,618	7	76	6,991	5,649	0
Sumner	91,226	83,594	1,956	41	21	4,202	1,412	0
Tipton	31,820	29,588	410	0	3	1,529	288	2
Trousdale	6,565	6,044	116	0	0	320	84	1
Unicoi	17,589	16,463	389	0	0	636	101	0
Union	20,323	18,857	358	16	0	966	126	0
Van Buren	4,040	3,763	82	0	0	156	39	0
Warren	34,178	30,379	609	0	5	2,333	852	0
Washington	94,719	84,560	2,021	0	22	4,732	3,384	0
Wayne	13,584	12,541	169	0	0	648	226	0
Weakley	26,552	24,450	413	0	1	1,165	523	0
White	20,680	18,659	301	0	4	1,004	712	0
Williamson	82,132	76,009	1,291	31	3	3,807	991	0
Wilson	66,436	60,411	1,245	6	12	3,740	1,022	0
TENNESSEE	5,072,084	4,319,644	80,299	598	1,362	251,230	418,891	60

Note: With the exception of automobiles, all registrations are renewable by March 1. Automobile registrations
include all renewals from March 1, 1989, through February 28, 1990. Tennessee total includes registrations not
assigned to a particular county.

Source: Tennessee Department of Revenue, Motor Vehicle Division, direct correspondence.

TABLE 9.18--ROAD MILEAGE, BY TYPE, TENNESSEE AND COUNTIES, AS OF DECEMBER 31, 1991
[In miles]

County	Total	Inter-state system	State highway system	Local county roads	Local city streets	State park roads
Anderson	833.43	12.12	127.11	423.99	263.02	5.58
Bedford	918.43	0.46	159.12	662.26	96.59	0.00
Benton	726.63	8.77	91.84	572.55	40.98	12.49
Bledsoe	507.96	0.00	62.96	409.12	22.72	13.16
Blount	1,209.17	0.00	162.41	807.57	216.08	0.00
Bradley	1,027.11	19.35	113.73	688.06	204.75	1.22
Campbell	807.84	31.64	84.00	573.97	117.38	0.85
Cannon	462.44	0.00	79.89	366.32	16.23	0.00
Carroll	1,037.24	0.66	223.98	675.05	122.84	14.71
Carter	760.55	0.00	120.61	503.58	132.29	4.07
Cheatham	623.29	11.44	96.77	457.50	51.00	2.78
Chester	544.63	0.00	91.81	412.72	33.48	6.62
Claiborne	815.30	0.00	99.44	664.40	49.92	0.00
Clay	406.65	0.00	68.96	325.27	12.42	0.00
Cocke	839.74	21.95	120.09	449.68	51.97	0.00
Coffee	951.23	30.12	111.04	620.51	181.72	3.42
Crockett	539.44	0.00	101.32	395.91	42.21	0.00
Cumberland	956.75	36.05	151.30	676.56	87.13	5.71
Davidson	2,683.82	88.65	270.16	64.68	2,254.81	5.52
Decatur	623.00	5.67	102.83	476.32	38.18	0.00
DeKalb	598.97	0.00	100.96	435.95	53.08	8.98
Dickson	1,058.91	17.86	154.74	734.17	140.46	11.48
Dyer	884.40	15.93	157.25	590.80	120.42	0.00
Fayette	935.18	16.09	187.87	684.59	46.63	0.00
Fentress	572.54	0.00	115.24	427.76	26.67	2.87
Franklin	882.66	0.00	154.99	595.65	128.08	3.94
Gibson	1,265.36	0.00	227.09	857.31	180.96	0.00
Giles	1,105.92	22.40	151.71	855.70	76.11	0.00
Grainger	632.83	0.00	94.21	522.63	15.99	0.00
Greene	1,527.14	32.16	191.14	1,157.79	144.04	2.01
Grundy	445.60	7.31	93.33	245.55	96.44	2.97
Hamblen	631.52	9.92	81.70	397.38	138.77	2.93
Hamilton	2,246.98	32.45	233.41	542.87	1,427.02	11.23
Hancock	411.67	0.00	64.39	337.25	10.03	0.00
Hardeman	892.43	0.00	149.96	660.46	72.57	9.44
Hardin	926.29	0.00	164.93	670.39	71.22	5.26
Hawkins	1,047.41	0.00	162.38	754.25	130.78	0.00
Haywood	738.04	23.89	139.91	519.66	54.58	0.00
Henderson	949.07	24.64	160.83	661.26	47.31	55.03
Henry	1,065.71	0.00	176.27	804.54	79.13	5.77
Hickman	986.89	14.45	137.50	801.58	33.36	0.00
Houston	361.86	0.00	63.06	267.30	31.50	0.00
Humphreys	794.69	14.12	78.49	624.21	77.87	0.00
Jackson	599.91	0.00	126.28	455.58	18.05	0.00
Jefferson	856.40	27.69	121.56	626.02	81.13	0.00
Johnson	448.96	0.00	95.54	326.10	20.14	0.00
Knox	2,706.88	59.82	226.10	1,492.32	928.64	0.00
Lake	279.40	0.00	58.05	193.56	22.79	5.00
Lauderdale	724.89	0.00	133.35	508.35	77.80	5.39
Lawrence	1,272.92	0.00	149.78	980.54	136.34	6.26

TABLE 9.18--ROAD MILEAGE, BY TYPE, TENNESSEE AND COUNTIES, AS OF DECEMBER 31, 1991
[In miles] (Continued)

County	Total	Inter-state system	State highway system	Local county roads	Local city streets	State park roads
Lewis	433.32	0.00	69.78	306.06	31.63	0.00
Lincoln	1,018.33	0.00	181.47	786.52	50.34	0.00
Loudon	651.08	23.97	81.02	451.32	90.82	0.00
McMinn	1,115.16	24.99	136.57	787.29	166.31	0.00
McNairy	996.10	0.00	164.64	714.39	111.86	5.21
Macon	697.36	0.00	98.03	553.78	45.55	0.00
Madison	1,145.08	27.94	163.18	742.29	208.78	2.89
Marion	585.62	32.13	155.43	285.35	112.71	0.00
Marshall	743.60	12.77	143.31	500.26	82.22	5.04
Maury	1,209.80	17.68	209.69	784.62	188.26	0.00
Meigs	422.54	0.00	74.69	330.44	12.38	0.00
Monroe	1,116.00	6.51	158.75	765.92	112.77	1.22
Montgomery	1,149.10	17.20	166.67	701.72	262.89	0.62
Moore	281.52	0.00	42.06	235.79	3.67	0.00
Morgan	573.90	0.00	108.66	447.64	15.77	1.83
Obion	1,015.27	0.00	187.99	703.26	124.02	0.00
Overton	776.13	0.00	142.26	590.59	32.31	10.97
Perry	500.76	0.00	97.42	378.61	23.24	1.49
Pickett	272.14	0.00	45.49	196.49	12.28	17.88
Polk	708.59	0.00	108.23	382.60	22.65	1.89
Putnam	1,017.75	37.06	140.60	627.98	210.64	0.76
Rhea	597.79	0.00	91.52	434.57	71.70	0.00
Roane	929.81	22.98	128.13	592.93	185.77	0.00
Robertson	1,037.24	28.23	151.68	724.70	132.63	0.00
Rutherford	1,458.23	33.29	201.32	877.66	344.81	1.15
Scott	541.88	0.00	70.13	429.77	41.98	0.00
Sequatchie	321.11	0.00	59.54	215.61	45.96	0.00
Sevier	1,208.16	4.76	155.30	869.01	145.77	0.00
Shelby	3,503.25	62.18	277.66	680.67	2,451.15	31.59
Smith	589.28	17.17	105.09	432.93	34.09	0.00
Stewart	642.35	0.00	100.16	387.05	31.25	0.00
Sullivan	1,548.75	31.94	183.57	948.20	378.46	6.58
Sumner	1,430.24	5.93	220.01	789.93	412.36	2.01
Tipton	846.47	0.00	125.12	627.18	94.17	0.00
Trousdale	224.80	0.00	43.37	161.09	20.34	0.00
Unicoi	310.41	0.00	67.22	198.16	31.11	0.00
Union	479.49	0.00	71.83	376.63	27.45	3.58
Van Buren	295.17	0.00	75.48	178.47	18.32	22.90
Warren	901.15	0.00	161.94	644.62	88.40	6.19
Washington	1,193.54	17.91	138.10	723.40	314.13	0.00
Wayne	942.45	0.00	145.76	715.99	51.25	0.00
Weakley	1,177.23	0.00	199.59	863.70	113.73	0.21
White	750.13	0.00	101.95	600.10	48.08	0.00
Williamson	1,167.84	24.48	182.84	766.48	194.04	0.00
Wilson	1,200.07	27.35	165.82	828.64	143.69	34.57
TENNESSEE	84,852.07	1,062.08	12,490.46	54,297.95	15,865.37	373.27

Note: Federal reservation roads are not listed separately but are included in the total.

Source: Tennessee Department of Transportation, Office of Research and Planning, Research and Statistics Division, direct correspondence.

TABLE 9.19--MILEAGE OF EXISTING PUBLIC ROADS AND STREETS, BY FUNCTIONAL CLASSIFICATION, SOUTHEASTERN STATES AND UNITED STATES, 1992

State	Total	Rural					Urban				
		Total	Inter-state	Other arterial	Collector	Local	Total	Inter-state	Other arterial[1]	Collector	Local
TENNESSEE	85,144	68,830	733	5,152	16,142	46,803	16,314	329	2,883	2,425	10,677
Alabama	92,201	72,835	602	5,761	18,187	48,285	19,366	298	2,953	2,128	13,987
Arkansas	77,162	69,471	419	5,118	19,069	44,865	7,691	123	1,720	982	4,866
Florida	110,640	62,003	1,057	6,017	9,825	45,104	48,637	417	4,715	4,854	38,651
Georgia	110,790	84,643	809	8,276	20,963	54,595	26,147	434	4,755	2,106	18,852
Kentucky	71,765	61,757	546	3,355	16,625	41,231	10,008	217	1,744	998	7,049
Louisiana	58,629	46,310	648	2,658	11,551	31,453	12,319	221	2,248	1,213	8,637
Mississippi	72,795	64,907	557	5,672	14,538	44,140	7,888	128	1,334	973	5,453
North Carolina	95,582	74,131	636	5,146	16,206	52,143	21,451	334	3,953	1,683	15,481
South Carolina	64,129	53,612	668	5,091	11,950	35,903	10,517	142	1,759	1,461	7,155
Virginia	68,429	52,848	788	5,066	12,613	34,381	15,581	318	2,829	1,395	11,039
West Virginia	34,919	31,829	458	2,207	8,526	20,638	3,090	92	622	403	1,973
UNITED STATES	3,901,715	3,116,555	33,027	232,435	718,881	2,132,212	785,160	12,466	140,998	82,657	549,039

Note: Data are mileages of routes that were serving traffic as of December 31.

1. Includes other freeways and expressways.

Source: U.S. Department of Transportation, Federal Highway Administration, Highway Statistics Division, *Highway Statistics, 1992.*

TABLE 9.20--MOTOR VEHICLE REGISTRATIONS, BY OWNERSHIP AND BY TYPE OF VEHICLE,
SOUTHEASTERN STATES, 1992

| | Total | | Ownership | | | | |
| | | Percent | Private | | | Type of vehicle | |
State	Registra-tions	change 1991–92	and commercial	Publicly owned	Automobiles	Buses	Trucks
TENNESSEE	4,645,083	2.3	4,567,986	77,097	3,726,216	15,001	903,866
Alabama	3,304,064	-5.2	3,259,463	44,601	2,196,269	8,270	1,099,525
Arkansas	1,501,480	1.5	1,477,666	23,814	974,023	5,585	521,872
Florida	10,232,336	2.5	9,988,576	243,760	8,131,392	38,135	2,062,809
Georgia	5,899,437	3.2	5,811,957	87,480	4,121,018	15,399	1,763,020
Kentucky	2,983,220	1.4	2,901,585	81,635	1,938,605	10,325	1,034,290
Louisiana	3,093,511	1.6	3,044,787	48,724	2,005,710	19,681	1,068,120
Mississippi	1,953,973	3.5	1,922,731	31,242	1,496,099	8,911	448,963
North Carolina	5,306,911	1.7	5,197,293	109,618	3,778,448	33,592	1,494,871
South Carolina	2,600,929	5.2	2,560,674	40,255	1,948,340	14,360	638,229
Virginia	5,238,706	4.3	5,161,910	76,796	3,960,758	16,315	1,261,633
West Virginia	1,272,907	0.0	1,217,027	55,880	778,169	3,628	491,110

Source: U.S. Department of Transportation, Federal Highway Administration, Highway Statistics Division,
Highway Statistics, 1992.

TABLE 9.21--NUMBER OF TRUCKS AND TRUCK-MILES, SOUTHEASTERN STATES, 1987

| | All trucks | | | Trucks and truck miles, excluding pickups, panels, utilities, and station wagons | | |
State	Number of trucks (1,000)	Truck-miles (1,000,000)	Average miles per truck (1,000)	Trucks (1,000)	Truck-miles (1,000,000)	Average miles per truck (1,000)
TENNESSEE	1,017.0	12,749.5	12.5	94.7	2,593.2	27.4
Alabama	893.7	11,045.2	12.4	99.9	2,814.4	28.2
Arkansas	520.7	5,817.6	11.2	8.8	494.3	56.2
Florida	1,924.0	24,498.1	12.7	156.8	3,922.3	25.0
Georgia	1,210.1	15,619.8	12.9	142.5	3,417.3	24.0
Kentucky	808.1	8,700.5	10.8	102.7	1,502.7	14.6
Louisiana	926.8	11,337.8	12.2	84.2	1,740.8	20.7
Mississippi	500.6	5,963.2	11.9	30.3	1,040.9	34.4
North Carolina	1,371.2	15,941.0	11.6	173.3	3,796.9	21.9
South Carolina	597.5	7,070.1	11.8	62.0	1,158.2	18.7
Virginia	1,139.1	12,887.8	11.3	127.3	2,273.7	17.9
West Virginia	422.8	4,056.4	9.6	37.1	546.4	14.7

Source: U.S. Department of Commerce, Bureau of the Census, *1987 Census of Transportation, Truck Inventory
and Use Survey*, individual states.

TABLE 9.22--MOTOR TRUCK REGISTRATIONS, SOUTHEASTERN STATES, 1970-1992, SELECTED YEARS

State	Total regis- tered	Private and commer- cial	Fed- eral	State, county, and muni- cipal	Total regis- tered	Private and commer- cial	Fed- eral	State, county, and muni- cipal
	1992				1991			
TENNESSEE	903,866	857,442	7,601	38,823	885,063	840,618	7,254	37,191
Alabama	1,099,525	1,075,273	3,986	20,266	978,402	954,462	3,804	20,136
Arkansas	521,872	511,569	2,230	8,073	516,531	506,370	2,128	8,033
Florida	2,062,809	1,938,379	12,141	112,289	2,032,321	1,910,644	11,589	110,088
Georgia	1,763,020	1,709,154	5,916	47,950	1,708,001	1,655,908	5,648	46,445
Kentucky	1,034,290	984,040	3,541	46,709	1,010,517	962,250	3,380	44,887
Louisiana	1,068,120	1,049,903	3,914	14,303	1,024,145	1,006,282	3,735	14,128
Mississippi	448,963	432,953	2,816	13,194	435,740	420,189	2,688	12,863
North Carolina	1,494,871	1,438,599	4,293	51,979	1,468,522	1,414,033	4,098	50,391
South Carolina	638,229	616,760	3,898	17,571	587,755	566,809	3,720	17,226
Virginia	1,261,633	1,230,396	7,024	24,213	1,180,242	1,148,914	6,704	24,624
West Virginia	491,110	456,031	1,589	33,490	491,110	455,421	1,516	34,173
	1980				1970			
TENNESSEE	696,420	666,054	6,697	23,669	404,292	385,045	4,592	14,655
Alabama	823,846	801,957	3,283	18,606	399,028	382,743	2,418	13,867
Arkansas	531,726	522,374	1,687	7,665	310,754	304,352	1,213	5,189
Florida	1,387,642	1,294,734	7,661	85,247	556,210	518,897	5,060	32,253
Georgia	873,420	836,610	3,847	32,963	510,886	493,432	2,604	14,850
Kentucky	777,278	753,117	2,448	21,713	380,867	367,978	1,559	11,330
Louisiana	791,628	776,511	2,931	12,186	365,228	352,455	1,825	10,948
Mississippi	349,075	339,199	2,337	7,539	290,301	279,571	1,838	8,892
North Carolina	1,109,666	1,048,977	3,221	57,468	578,302	533,156	2,146	43,000
South Carolina	451,888	436,593	2,272	13,023	250,518	238,363	1,512	10,643
Virginia	541,128	517,411	4,583	19,134	359,090	340,257	2,998	15,835
West Virginia	387,313	362,798	1,296	23,219	173,437	166,325	910	6,202

Source: U.S. Department of Transportation, Federal Highway Administration, Highway Statistics Division, *Highway Statistics, 1992*, and earlier editions.

TABLE 9.23--MOTOR FUEL CONSUMPTION AND TAXES, SOUTHEASTERN STATES, 1992

State	Gross gallons reported[1] (1,000)	Net total gallons taxed (1,000)	Gasoline tax rate[2] (¢ per gallon)	Diesel tax rate[2] (¢ per gallon)	Gross receipts from motor fuel taxes ($1,000)
TENNESSEE	3,162,803	3,052,880	20.0	17.0	618,352
Alabama	2,779,400	2,750,294	13.0[a]	14.0[a]	434,919
Arkansas	1,691,951	1,649,230	18.7[b]	18.7[b]	302,332
Florida	7,163,851	7,155,485	11.6[c]	18.7[c]	1,058,752
Georgia	4,505,454	4,498,659	7.5	7.5	338,873
Kentucky	2,438,541	2,433,479	15.4[d]	12.4[d]	370,239
Louisiana	2,301,690	2,290,554	20.0	20.0	480,657
Mississippi	1,682,640	1,654,829	18.2[e]	18.2[e]	296,921
North Carolina	4,039,158	3,969,965	22.3[f]	22.3[f]	871,504
South Carolina	2,292,435	2,265,847	16.0	16.0	335,244
Virginia	3,686,471	3,619,466	17.7[g]	16.2[g]	637,487
West Virginia	1,056,509	1,050,835	20.35[h]	20.35[h]	219,552

Note: Tax rates are as of January 1.

1. Export sales and other amounts not consumed as motor fuel in state have been excluded wherever possible.

2. Only taxes that are levied as a dollar amount per volume of motor fuel are included. Taxes that apply to all petroleum products without distinguishing motor fuel are omitted. Local option taxes are included only when they have been adopted uniformly statewide.

a. Includes a 2 cents per gallon inspection fee.

b. Includes a 0.2 cent per gallon Environmental Assurance Fee.

c. Tax rates are variable, adjusted annually. For gasoline, in addition to the rate shown, there is a state-imposed State Comprehensive Enhanced Transportation System (SCETS) tax that varies by county from 0–4.2 cents per gallon. All but 2 counties levy the maximum rate.

d. Tax rates are variable, adjusted quarterly. A 2% surtax is imposed on gasoline and 4.7% on special fuels for any vehicle with 3 or more axles. There is an additional 2 cents per gallon surtax on vehicles with a combined license weight over 59,999 pounds. Includes a 0.4 cent per gallon Petroleum Environmental Assurance Fee.

e. Includes a 0.2 cent per gallon fee dedicated to the Groundwater Protection Trust Fund.

f. Rates are variable, adjusted semiannually.

g. Through 6/30/92, rates shown include 0.2 cent per gallon for the Virginia Underground Petroleum Storage Tank Fund. Motor carrier road tractors, tractor trucks and straight trucks with more than 2 axles pay an additional 3.5 cents per gallon.

h. Rates are variable. Adjusted annually.

Source: U.S. Department of Transportation, Federal Highway Administration, Highway Statistics Division, *Highway Statistics, 1992.*

TABLE 9.24--STATE MOTOR FUEL TAX RATE AND REVENUE, SOUTHEASTERN STATES, 1970-1992, SELECTED YEARS

State	1992		1991		1990		1980		1970	
	Gasoline tax rate per gallon (¢)	Gross tax collections ($1,000)	Gasoline tax rate per gallon (¢)	Gross tax collections ($1,000)	Gasoline tax rate per gallon (¢)	Gross tax collections ($1,000)	Gasoline tax rate per gallon (¢)	Gross tax collections[1] ($1,000)	Gasoline tax rate per gallon (¢)	Gross tax collections[1] ($1,000)
TENNESSEE	20.0	626,455	20.0	605,600	20.0	632,071	7.0	198,506	7.0	136,877
Alabama	13.0	437,554	13.0	345,688	13.0	355,178	11.0	189,504	7.0	118,032
Arkansas	18.7	302,332	18.7	219,698	13.7	214,689	9.5	135,031	7.5	77,191
Florida	11.6	1,060,993	11.2	986,293	9.7	716,078	8.0	417,685	7.0	236,148
Georgia	7.5	342,827	7.5	329,638	10.9	333,006	7.0	253,457	6.5	164,573
Kentucky	15.4	370,239	15.4	350,422 [a]	15.0	357,595	9.0	192,146	7.0	110,325
Louisiana	20.0	483,591	20.0	464,270	15.4	480,890	8.0	185,278	8.0	124,172
Mississippi	18.2	296,921	18.2	278,821	18.0	282,439	9.0	126,351	8.0	90,195
North Carolina	22.3	871,504	22.6	855,384	21.7	849,637	9.0	293,202	9.0	227,255
South Carolina	16.0	337,131	16.0	349,504	16.0	358,214	11.0	179,043	7.0	92,387
Virginia	17.7	638,829	17.7	634,957	17.7	616,806	11.0	289,784	7.0	158,234
West Virginia	20.35	219,552	20.35	212,152	20.35	152,830	10.0	100,034	8.5	59,425

Note: Data are on a calendar year basis. Tax rates are as of December 31. See footnotes, Table 9.21 for more detail regarding tax rates.

a. Federal Highway Administration estimate.

1. Includes revenues from state taxes on motor vehicle fuels and for most states, only the portion of the tax on special fuels that is applicable to gallonage used on highways. Includes in some states receipts in the form of tax credits for refund claims accepted by distributors acting as agents of the state and refund credits to users who are licensed as distributors.

Source: U.S. Department of Transportation, Federal Highway Administration, Highway Statistics Division, *Highway Statistics, 1992,* and earlier editions.

TABLE 9.25--TRUCK MILES FOR TRANSPORTATION OF HAZARDOUS MATERIALS, BY STATE OF TRUCK REGISTRATION, SOUTHEASTERN STATES, 1987
[In millions of truck miles]

State	Flammable liquids	Combustible liquids	Corrosive liquids	Poison B solids	Poison B liquids	Flammable solids	Oxidizers	Flammable gas	Nonflammable gas	Poison A	Corrosive solids
TENNESSEE	402.8	301.7	291.8	207.6	209.0	209.0	208.6	204.8	204.8	207.6	198.0
Alabama	342.0	290.6	240.0	211.6	203.7	203.7	215.9	201.2	197.5	81.8	84.7
Arkansas	17.8	0.3	15.0	(a)	0.1	(a)	(a)	(a)	(a)	(a)	(a)
Florida	193.7	92.8	51.1	11.4	11.4	11.4	11.4	11.4	11.4	5.4	5.4
Georgia	233.2	141.8	120.3	27.5	27.5	23.3	23.3	23.3	23.3	6.6	6.6
Kentucky	120.7	71.7	53.9	3.5	(b)	(b)	(b)	0.2	0.2	0.2	0.2
Louisiana	178.1	97.5	52.4	5.6	5.6	5.6	5.6	5.6	5.6	5.6	5.6
Mississippi	46.5	26.5	11.8	8.5	5.9	2.2	2.2	2.2	2.2	(a)	(a)
North Carolina	453.4	389.9	358.2	237.7	219.5	219.5	233.0	219.5	219.5	205.3	205.3
South Carolina	87.0	41.2	27.4	3.8	3.8	2.7	2.7	2.7	2.7	2.7	2.7
Virginia	152.5	70.9	41.4	29.2	29.2	29.2	29.2	3.8	3.8	2.8	2.8
West Virginia	26.1	10.9	8.4	0.6	1.1	0.6	1.4	1.1	1.1	0.6	0.6

Note: Multiple responses were possible, and not all responses are included.

a. Less than 50,000 truck miles.

b. Withheld because estimate did not meet publication standards on the basis of either the response rate, associated standard error, or a consistency review.

Source: U.S. Department of Commerce, Bureau of the Census, 1987 Census of Transportation, Truck Inventory and Use Survey, individual states.

TABLE 9.26–ESTIMATED ACTIVE PILOTS AND FLIGHT INSTRUCTORS, BY SEX, SOUTHEASTERN
STATES, DECEMBER 31, 1989

State	Pilots						Flight instructor[2]
	Total	Students	Private	Commercial	Airline transport	Miscellaneous[1]	
				Total			
TENNESSEE	12,242	2,564	4,694	2,240	2,482	262	1,220
Alabama	9,394	1,808	3,699	2,275	748	864	883
Arkansas	5,962	1,183	2,681	1,551	475	72	506
Florida	47,220	9,061	17,960	11,015	8,335	849	4,192
Georgia	18,607	3,458	6,461	3,719	4,617	352	1,448
Kentucky	5,775	1,206	2,496	995	939	139	522
Louisiana	8,136	1,612	3,110	2,182	929	303	741
Mississippi	4,628	992	1,797	1,360	380	99	397
North Carolina	15,415	3,358	6,180	2,993	2,486	398	1,205
South Carolina	6,969	1,614	2,836	1,609	786	124	574
Virginia	15,525	3,037	5,468	3,878	2,681	461	1,413
West Virginia	2,502	575	1,205	474	181	67	214
				Female			
TENNESSEE	662	279	229	77	64	13	55
Alabama	400	177	150	25	7	41	19
Arkansas	277	121	127	24	3	2	17
Florida	2,854	1,202	1,090	367	148	47	223
Georgia	820	363	313	81	48	15	47
Kentucky	263	111	93	30	28	1	22
Louisiana	338	158	126	40	10	4	26
Mississippi	233	116	80	22	10	5	13
North Carolina	808	365	291	87	46	19	61
South Carolina	340	178	109	29	16	8	17
Virginia	939	410	349	109	46	25	79
West Virginia	123	55	48	13	3	4	6

1. Includes helicopter, glider, and lighter-than-air.

2. Not included in total.

Source: U. S. Department of Transportation, Federal Aviation Administration, *FAA Statistical Handbook of Aviation, 1989.*

TABLE 9.27--NUMBER OF ACTIVE CIVILIAN PILOTS AND ACTIVE CIVIL GENERAL AVIATION AIRCRAFT, SOUTHEASTERN STATES, 1989

			General aviation aircraft							
			Fixed wing aircraft							
	Total		Piston		Turboprop		Turbojet			
	active		Single-	Multi-	Single-	Multi-	Single-	Multi-	Roto-	
State	civilian pilots	Total	engine	engine	engine	engine	engine	engine	craft	Other
TENNESSEE	12,242	4,214	3,129	535	37	165	2	67	120	159
Alabama	9,394	4,062	3,157	459	0	140	3	67	153	83
Arkansas	5,962	3,085	2,445	375	24	88	1	41	76	35
Florida	47,220	16,817	11,448	3,309	8	410	13	355	799	475
Georgia	18,607	6,083	4,681	723	7	179	0	136	176	181
Kentucky	5,775	2,070	1,556	219	0	47	0	39	78	131
Louisiana	8,136	3,785	2,797	341	3	86	3	31	479	45
Mississippi	4,628	2,332	1,881	244	16	61	2	24	49	55
North Carolina	15,415	6,078	4,631	688	8	256	1	149	140	205
South Carolina	6,969	2,387	1,778	280	2	81	1	28	115	102
Virginia	15,525	4,102	3,157	369	2	124	6	92	140	212
West Virginia	2,502	1,266	994	141	0	37	1	8	48	37

Source: U.S. Department of Transportation, Federal Aviation Administration, Office of Management Systems, *Census of U.S. Civil Aircraft, Calendar Year 1989.*

TABLE 9.28--RAILROAD MILEAGE OPERATED, SOUTHEASTERN STATES AND UNITED STATES, 1979-1988, SELECTED YEARS

State	1988	1987	1986	1985	1981	1980	1979
TENNESSEE	2,475	2,234	2,537	2,597	3,035	3,136	3,136
Alabama	3,448	3,600	3,650	3,832	4,322	4,455	4,497
Arkansas	2,491	2,539	2,594	2,712	2,720	2,763	2,749
Florida	2,678	2,976	3,085	3,230	3,421	3,681	3,698
Georgia	4,792	4,954	5,031	5,119	4,747	5,468	5,471
Kentucky	2,518	2,521	2,846	3,175	3,569	3,515	3,572
Louisiana	3,237	2,691	2,785	3,050	3,310	3,373	3,452
Mississippi	666	1,496	1,510	1,744	2,823	3,063	3,161
North Carolina	2,986	3,090	3,217	3,334	2,845	3,577	3,640
South Carolina	2,391	2,490	2,533	2,579	2,558	2,736	2,772
Virginia	3,345	3,430	3,729	3,766	3,451	3,503	3,511
West Virginia	3,013	3,149	3,156	3,209	3,534	3,565	3,513
UNITED STATES	139,856	146,584	154,657	159,360	173,809	183,077	188,304

Note: Beginning in 1981, the miles of line shown represents mileage operated by Class I roads only. Prior to 1981, the miles shown represents mileage operated by Class I and Class II roads. Miles operated jointly by two or more · railroads and two or more parallel tracks are not duplicated in this listing. Mileage of yard tracks and sidings are also excluded from these totals.

Source: Association of American Railroads, *Railroad Facts, 1989 Edition*, and earlier editions.

FIGURE 9.2
Principal Railroads in Tennessee as of March, 1988

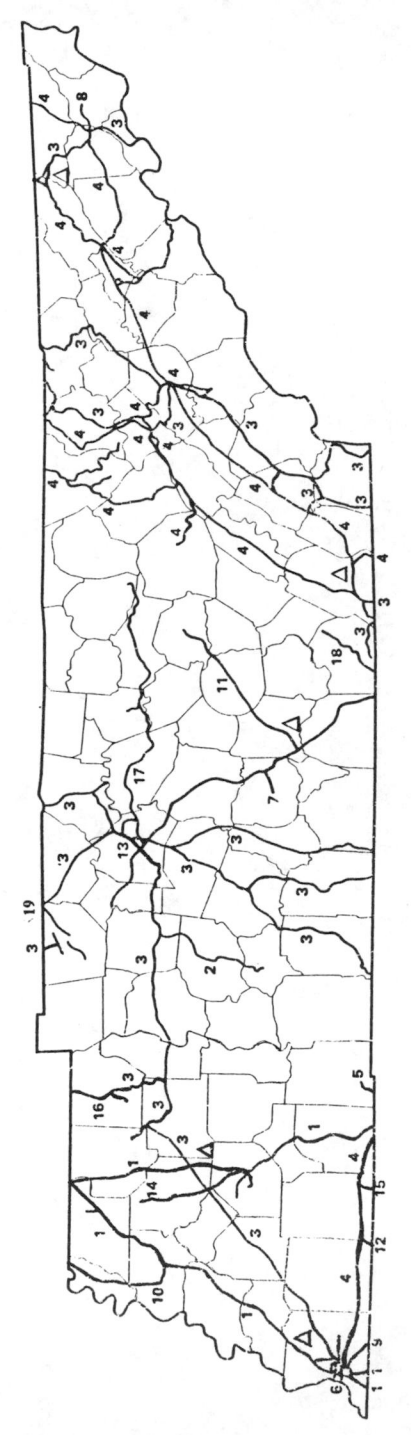

1   Illinois Central R.R.
2   South Central Tennessee R.R.
3   CSX T R.R.
4   Norfolk Southern R.R.
5   Corinth and Counce R.R.
6   Union Pacific R.R.
7   Walking Horse and Eastern R.R.

8   East Tennessee Railway
9   Burlington Northern R.R.
10   Tennken R.R.
11   Caney Fork and Western R.R.
12   Natchez Trace R.R.
13   Nashville and Ashland City R.R.
14   West Tennessee R.R.

15   South Rail Corporation
16   KWT R.R.
17   Nashville and Eastern R.R.
18   Sequatchie Valley R.R.
19   Corman R.R.

△   U.S. Government

Source: Prepared from data supplied by the Tennessee Department of Transportation, Office of Public Transportation.

375

The U.S. Department of Energy was created in October 1977 to centralize the responsibilities of the Federal Power Commission, the U.S. Bureau of Mines, the Federal Energy Administration, and the U.S. Energy Research Administration. Data from publications of the U.S. Department of Energy, Energy Information Administration (EIA), provide information on energy consumption by type of fuel and consuming sector. At the present time, data on traditional energy sources are abundant. Not only are statistics on the many phases of production and utilization available, but in addition, a historical time series has been constructed in order to provide a reference for current and future changes in the energy picture. Publications of EIA include the *State Energy Data Report*, the *Electric Power Annual*, the *Petroleum Supply Annual*, the *Natural Gas Annual*, and *Coal Production*. Another EIA publication, *Cost and Quality of Fuels for Electric Utility Plants*, provides important comparative data for the industry. While the utilization of fuel minerals is presented as "energy" data, information on mineral production and reserves is included in Chapter 5 on Mining. In addition to reports published by the U.S. Department of Energy, the American Gas Association provides a comprehensive collection of data on sales, customers, consumption and prices of gas at state, national and international levels. These data are published in a yearbook titled *Gas Facts*.

Data on the electric utility industry, previously reported by the Federal Power Commission, are now reported in the *Electric Power Annual*. New information features data on the origin, destination, cost and quality of coal received by electric utilities for the southeastern states, as seen in Table 10.16. The average retail prices of electricity by consumer sector, also reported in the *Electric Power Annual*, are included in Table 10.19.

For the TVA region and its local power distributors, a major source of data is *Electricity Sales Statistics*, published monthly. An important component of the energy picture is the climate of the area. TVA issues degree-day heating and cooling requirements for weather stations across Tennessee. These data are also published in *Electricity Sales Statistics* and reprinted with other climatic data in Chapter 12.

The production capability and generation of nuclear power plants in each of the southeastern states is reported in the EIA's *Electric Power Annual*. The *State Energy Data Book* also reports on nuclear energy consumption. The status of Tennessee nuclear power facilities is reported in Table 10.10 from a statement issued by TVA, August 1991. Because other newer energy sources–such as solar and geothermal–are not in wide use and the technology is still largely experimental on any scale appropriate to public use, consistent and accessible statistics are not available.

TABLE OF CONTENTS

TABLE OF CONTENTS
(Continued)

FIGURE 10.1
Tennessee Energy Consumption by Sector and Fuel Type, 1991

CONSUMPTION BY SECTOR

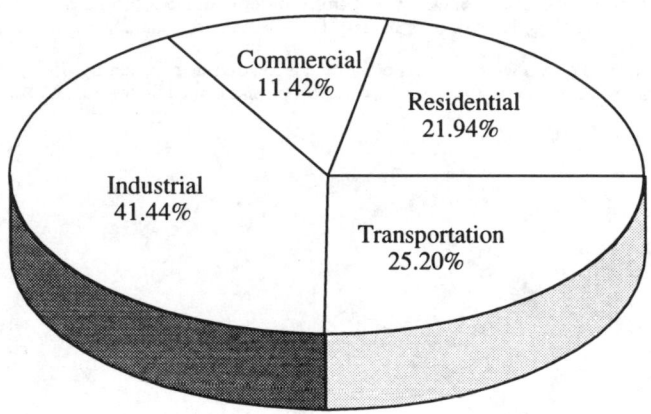

CONSUMPTION BY TYPE

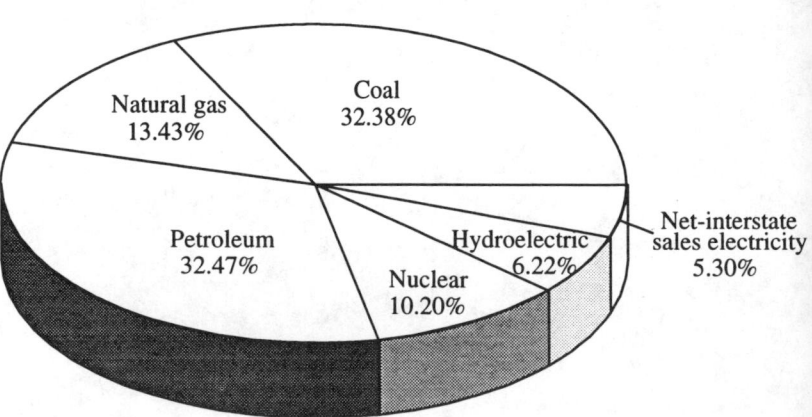

Source: U.S. Department of Energy, Energy Information Administration, Office of Energy Markets and End Use,
  State Energy Data Report, 1991.

TABLE 10.1--CONSUMPTION OF ENERGY, BY TYPE, TENNESSEE, 1960–1991 [In trillions of BTU]

Year	Total [r]	Coal	Natural gas [1]	Petroleum [r]	Nuclear	Hydro-electric [2]	Net interstate sales of electricity [3]
1991	1,748.5	565.5	234.6	567.1	178.1	108.7	92.5
1990	1,752.9	600.3	227.5	586.9	149.5	98.6	90.0
1989	1,757.2	564.4	228.6	594.1	167.3	122.5	80.5
1988	1,714.8	610.6	220.9	581.1	42.3	47.0	212.3
1987	1,687.0	598.6	207.0	599.1	-1.2	77.6	206.6
1986	1,643.4	607.4	194.0	582.8	-1.1	54.6	205.6
1985	1,643.4	599.7	196.7	552.8	104.6	67.6	120.9
1984	1,673.6	555.3	211.3	540.7	135.6	105.1	124.4
1983	1,601.5	547.1	199.1	493.3	153.2	104.7	104.1
1982	1,557.3	470.7	212.1	502.6	111.9	102.1	157.8
1981	1,653.9	565.9	227.1	518.1	51.9	61.8	229.1
1980	1,692.4	576.9	233.3	530.4	5.7	91.0	255.0
1979	1,753.8	542.3	233.9	593.5	0.0	127.4	256.7
1978	1,717.5	564.7	189.2	630.6	0.0	91.0	242.1
1977	1,735.8	553.7	208.4	600.6	0.0	108.5	264.6
1976	1,676.3	561.5	218.5	565.7	0.0	98.3	232.3
1975	1,573.9	471.9	224.1	503.8	0.0	122.9	251.3
1974	1,538.0	470.3	265.4	483.2	0.0	122.9	196.2
1973	1,572.0	532.9	300.1	498.3	0.0	119.0	121.7
1972	1,430.3	444.3	283.4	455.9	0.0	115.5	131.2
1971	1,328.1	370.0	270.8	413.2	0.0	98.7	175.4
1970	1,330.7	403.7	261.8	407.4	0.0	84.7	173.2
1969	1,304.9	436.7	257.5	400.7	0.0	78.1	131.8
1968	1,250.0	439.3	243.4	377.8	0.0	80.3	109.2
1967	1,204.6	352.0	242.0	348.4	0.0	100.4	161.9
1966	1,196.6	363.7	236.8	339.6	0.0	79.5	177.1
1965	1,101.1	338.8	211.1	301.6	0.0	91.5	158.1
1964	1,053.8	336.1	191.2	284.6	0.0	95.2	146.8
1963	1,026.1	386.3	179.2	273.2	0.0	80.9	106.5
1962	973.4	347.2	174.0	254.9	0.0	101.7	95.6
1961	936.1	354.2	166.7	237.0	0.0	93.2	85.0
1960	919.6	374.4	151.7	228.8	0.0	93.4	71.4

Note: Some changes in methodology were made and, where necessary, revisions were applied to the entire historical series. Totals may not equal sum of components due to independent rounding. Excludes small quantities of other energy sources for which consistent historical data are not available.

r revised.

1. Includes supplemental gaseous fuels.
2. Includes industrial and utility production, and net imports of electricity.
3. Net interstate sales of electricity is the difference between the amounts of energy in the electricity sold within a state (including associated losses) and the energy input at the electric utilities within the state. The net interstate sales, therefore, include associated electrical system energy losses. A positive number indicates that more electricity (including associated losses) came into the state than went out of the state during the year.

Source: U.S. Department of Energy, Energy Information Administration, Office of Energy Markets and End Use, *State Energy Data Report, 1991*, and earlier editions.

TABLE 10.2–TOTAL ENERGY CONSUMPTION, BY SECTOR, TENNESSEE, 1960–1991 [In trillions of BTU]

Year	Residential	Commercial	Industrial	Transportation
1991	383.2	199.5	723.8	440.1
1990	371.8	198.4	720.2	462.5
1989	378.6	197.0	708.8	472.8
1988	373.1	179.0	701.6	461.0
1987	362.5	172.2	671.2	481.1
1986	341.7	167.3	670.0	464.4
1985	344.2	182.3	685.4	431.5
1984	356.4	183.4	702.9	430.9
1983	342.8	256.1	607.5	395.1
1982	339.8	236.1	583.1	398.3
1981	338.7	234.2	672.4	408.7
1980	364.9	225.1	693.6	408.9
1979	352.9	218.9	731.7	450.3
1978	367.1	206.3	700.9	443.2
1977	375.3	173.5	768.6	418.4
1976	343.0	146.7	780.4	406.1
1975	335.4	144.3	704.0	390.2
1974	298.8	153.4	704.8	380.9
1973	308.5	156.0	719.3	388.2
1972	300.6	149.5	624.6	355.6
1971	286.4	142.1	574.2	325.4
1970	282.9	134.6	604.9	308.4
1969	269.1	129.2	610.6	296.1
1968	246.8	119.2	606.5	277.5
1967	219.9	108.3	618.6	257.8
1966	214.8	102.0	630.8	249.0
1965	195.0	94.3	581.0	230.9
1964	185.8	89.7	556.4	221.9
1963	182.8	86.4	541.0	215.9
1962	169.3	94.0	508.3	201.9
1961	155.3	84.6	506.6	189.7
1960	155.1	77.2	513.3	174.0

Note: Some changes in methodology were made and, where necessary, revisions were applied to the entire historical series.

Source: U.S. Department of Energy, Energy Information Administration, Office of Energy Markets and End Use, *State Energy Data Report, 1991*, and earlier editions.

TABLE 10.3--CONSUMPTION OF COAL, BY SECTOR, TENNESSEE, 1960-1991

Year	Residential		Commercial		Industrial	
	Trillion BTU	Thousand short tons	Trillion BTU	Thousand short tons	Trillion BTU	Thousand short tons
1991	1.6	63	2.7	109	93.5	3,720
1990	1.9	78	3.5	140	96.8	3,846
1989	1.9	78	3.5	142	100.3	4,058
1988	1.6	66	3.0	123	99.8	4,020
1987	0.8	34	1.5	64	100.4	4,034
1986	0.7	28	1.2	51	104.2	4,205
1985	1.4	59	2.7	110	102.2	4,145
1984	2.6	108	4.9	200	96.7	3,941
1983	4.1	168	7.7	312	95.5	3,936
1982	1.5	62	2.7	114	75.9	3,122
1981	1.2	50	2.2	92	86.4	3,573
1980	2.0	82	3.6	152	67.2	2,774
1979	1.5	66	2.8	122	74.4	3,092
1978	1.8	75	3.2	139	71.8	3,018
1977	2.0	83	3.6	154	66.6	2,821
1976	2.1	86	3.8	159	54.1	2,270
1975	2.7	114	5.0	211	49.9	2,134
1974	2.8	120	5.1	222	56.6	2,450
1973	3.2	134	5.8	248	59.5	2,551
1972	3.6	152	6.6	280	53.2	2,286
1971	4.8	204	8.9	377	45.7	1,947
1970	4.5	191	8.4	352	58.0	2,452
1969	5.4	225	10.1	416	66.8	2,747
1968	4.5	184	8.3	339	82.7	3,365
1967	4.5	183	8.3	338	76.9	3,127
1966	5.2	214	9.7	395	79.4	3,203
1965	5.7	233	10.6	430	71.4	2,862
1964	5.7	230	10.4	423	63.8	2,550
1963	7.1	288	13.1	531	64.6	2,575
1962	7.6	308	14.0	568	59.3	2,355
1961	7.1	288	13.1	530	63.5	2,522
1960	8.3	336	15.3	618	58.1	2,307

Note: Some changes in methodology were made and, where necessary, revisions were applied to the entire historical series.

Source: U.S. Department of Energy, Energy Information Administration, Office of Energy Markets and End Use, *State Energy Data Report, 1991*, and earlier editions.

FIGURE 10.2
Natural Gas and Petroleum Products Pipelines, Tennessee, 1987

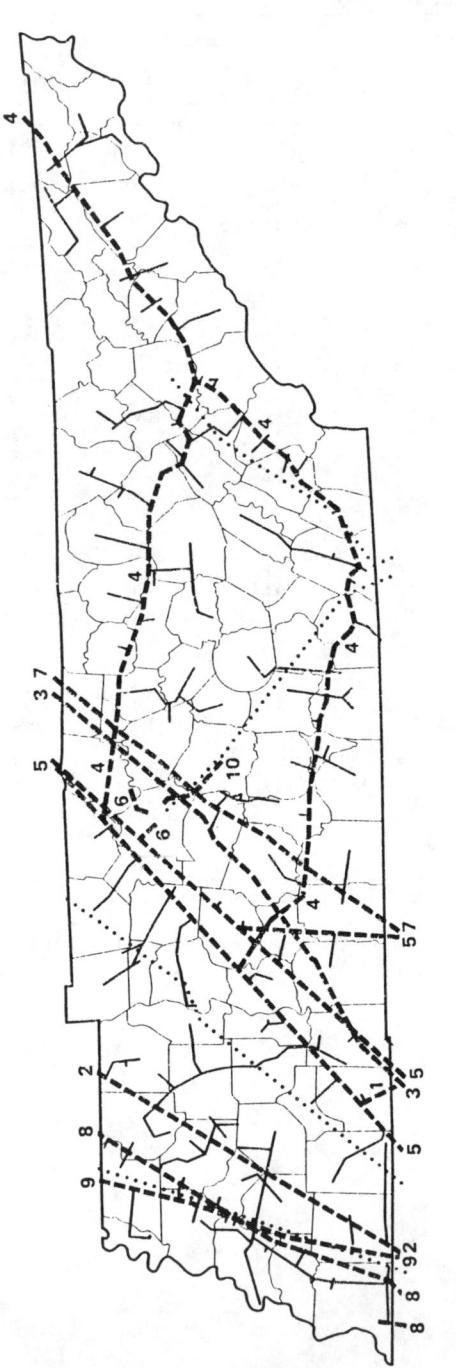

- - - Interstate Natural Gas Pipelines
——— Intrastate Natural Gas Pipelines
• • • • Petroleum Products Pipelines

1   Alabama-Tennessee Natural Gas Company
2   Michigan-Wisconsin Pipe Line Company
3   Columbia Gulf Transmission Company
4   East Tennessee Natural Gas Company
5   Tennessee Gas Pipeline Company

6   Tennessee Natural Gas Lines, Incorporated
7   Texas Eastern Transmission Corporation
8   Texas Gas Transmission Corporation
9   Trunkline Gas Company
10 Tennessee Gas Pipe Line Company

Note: The four large metropolitan areas contain several satellite communities which are served by natural gas lines, but are not detailed here.
Source: Tennessee Public Service Commission, direct correspondence.

TABLE 10.4-- CONSUMPTION OF NATURAL GAS,[1] BY SECTOR, TENNESSEE, 1960-1991

	Residential		Commercial		Industrial		Transportation	
Year	Trillion BTU	Billion cubic feet	Trillion BTU	Billion cubic feet	Trillion BTU	Billion cubic feet	Trillion BTU	Billion cubic feet
1991	51.0	49	47.5	46	119.7	116	16.3	16
1990	48.0	46	45.1	44	113.6	110	20.3	20
1989	50.8	49	49.0	48	110.4	107	18.4	18
1988	49.1	48	47.3	46	106.6	103	17.6	17
1987	44.9	43	45.6	44	100.8	98	15.8	15
1986	41.5	40	44.0	43	94.5	92	14.0	14
1985	40.8	39	44.9	43	100.6	97	10.5	10
1984	45.1	44	47.7	47	105.5	103	13.0	13
1983	41.5	41	43.9	43	102.4	100	11.1	11
1982	43.0	42	39.6	39	112.5	110	17.0	17
1981	42.5	42	43.4	43	123.1	121	17.8	18
1980	45.6	45	44.7	44	125.1	123	16.8	16
1979	46.6	45	44.1	43	122.3	118	20.8	20
1978	40.9	40	31.8	31	101.7	99	14.8	14
1977	44.9	44	36.2	35	113.0	110	14.3	14
1976	45.0	44	39.4	38	118.4	115	15.5	15
1975	45.4	44	43.8	42	115.1	112	19.7	19
1974	44.5	44	45.5	45	150.9	148	24.5	24
1973	46.9	46	46.9	46	164.5	161	29.0	28
1972	54.9	54	46.6	46	139.1	136	25.9	25
1971	48.0	47	45.0	44	132.1	129	27.2	27
1970	47.6	47	43.7	43	125.9	123	27.0	26
1969	47.2	45	42.7	41	122.8	118	25.9	25
1968	45.5	44	39.8	38	112.4	108	23.3	22
1967	43.4	42	35.8	34	113.5	109	23.2	22
1966	42.7	41	32.8	31	114.6	109	23.0	22
1965	38.9	37	29.6	28	101.9	97	23.7	23
1964	38.4	37	29.7	28	95.6	91	19.9	19
1963	42.8	41	28.6	27	83.7	79	19.3	18
1962	36.8	36	39.3	38	73.1	71	16.7	16
1961	35.1	34	34.2	33	74.4	72	16.0	15
1960	35.1	34	25.1	24	78.6	76	5.5	5

Note: Some changes in methodology were made and, where necessary, revisions were applied to the entire historical series.

1. Includes supplemental gaseous fuels.

Source: U.S. Department of Energy, Energy Information Administration, Office of Energy Markets and End Use, *State Energy Data Report, 1991*, and earlier editions.

TABLE 10.5--CONSUMPTION OF PETROLEUM, BY SECTOR, TENNESSEE, 1960–1991

Year	Residential Trillion BTU	Residential Thousand barrels	Commercial Trillion BTU	Commercial Thousand barrels	Industrial Trillion BTU[r]	Industrial Thousand barrels[r]	Transportation Trillion BTU[r]	Transportation Thousand barrels[r]
1991	10.1	2,472	7.2	1,409	124.4	21,345	423.8	78,318
1990	9.4	2,277	7.8	1,502	126.1	21,545	442.2	81,648
1989	12.2	2,840	9.1	1,737	116.2	19,920	454.5	83,990
1988	11.3	2,604	12.1	2,247	112.1	19,391	443.5	82,030
1987	9.0	2,084	10.8	1,976	112.7	19,436	465.3	86,178
1986	8.0	1,920	12.6	2,283	110.5	19,021	450.4	83,401
1985	10.0	2,205	22.1	3,901	98.4	16,740	420.9	78,073
1984	10.8	2,323	17.9	3,214	92.8	15,850	417.9	77,469
1983	10.3	2,282	17.0	3,060	80.3	13,597	383.9	71,285
1982	9.3	2,030	11.2	2,031	99.2	16,888	381.3	70,899
1981	10.6	2,139	10.5	1,901	104.2	17,838	390.9	72,557
1980	10.4	2,358	10.2	1,897	115.3	19,853	392.1	72,828
1979	12.4	2,728	9.6	1,795	138.0	23,516	429.4	79,525
1978	18.9	4,148	11.0	2,101	142.1	23,792	428.4	79,572
1977	19.9	4,372	11.1	2,119	143.7	23,953	404.1	75,139
1976	21.2	4,663	11.7	2,222	127.8	21,431	390.5	72,639
1975	19.1	4,320	8.9	1,757	97.6	16,405	370.5	68,953
1974	19.3	4,244	8.6	1,674	97.1	16,368	358.4	66,353
1973	22.2	4,843	9.4	1,841	105.8	17,701	359.2	66,893
1972	20.1	4,425	8.5	1,666	96.6	16,218	329.7	61,427
1971	21.4	4,551	8.2	1,607	85.3	14,352	298.1	55,637
1970	21.2	4,512	8.3	1,622	96.6	16,360	281.2	52,469
1969	20.5	4,366	8.1	1,574	102.0	17,308	270.0	50,437
1968	19.7	4,063	8.1	1,559	95.9	16,267	254.0	47,466
1967	17.9	3,699	7.5	1,429	88.5	15,011	234.4	43,913
1966	13.3	2,780	6.1	1,171	94.3	15,887	225.7	42,273
1965	10.1	2,117	4.7	899	79.9	13,521	206.9	38,819
1964	8.5	1,811	4.3	822	70.1	11,955	201.6	37,799
1963	10.1	2,121	4.5	861	62.3	10,585	196.1	36,769
1962	9.1	1,889	4.3	821	56.5	9,483	184.9	34,732
1961	8.2	1,707	4.0	764	51.3	8,644	173.3	32,583
1960	8.4	1,740	3.6	682	49.2	8,346	167.6	31,527

Note: Some changes in methodology were made and, where necessary, revisions were applied to the entire historical series.

r revised.

Source: U.S. Department of Energy, Energy Information Administration, Office of Energy Markets and End Use, *State Energy Data Report, 1991*, and earlier editions.

TABLE 10.6--NET ELECTRIC ENERGY GENERATION BY ENERGY SOURCE, TENNESSEE, 1980–1991, SELECTED YEARS [In gigawatthours]

Type of generation	1991	1990	1989	1988	1987	1986	1985	1984	1983	1982	1980
Total	73,932	73,903	73,959	59,858	58,312	56,455	66,581	68,764	69,441	59,505	60,211
Coal	46,671	50,187	46,324	51,122	50,730	51,108	50,242	45,963	45,279	39,479	50,617
Petroleum	160	134	178	187	124	126	128	118	153	153	198
Gas	17	41	1	16	(a)	(a)	(a)	(a)	7	(a)	114
Nuclear	16,587	14,003	15,603	3,940	-108	-105	9,672	12,501	14,051	10,104	519
Hydroelectric	10,497	9,537	11,853	4,591	7,566	5,326	6,539	10,181	9,952	9,769	8,764

Note: Negative generation denotes that electric power consumed for plant use exceeds gross generation. Totals may not equal sum of components because of independent rounding.

a. Less than 0.5 gigawatthours.

Source: U.S. Department of Energy, Energy Information Administration, Office of Coal, Nuclear, Electric, and Alternate Fuels, *Electric Power Annual, 1991,* and earlier editions.

TABLE 10.7–FUEL CONSUMPTION FOR ELECTRIC ENERGY, TENNESSEE, 1976–1991

Year	Coal (1,000 short tons)	Petroleum (1,000 barrels)	Gas (million cubic feet)
1991	19,216	272	211
1990	20,814	232	565
1989	19,283	356	18
1988	21,010	365	225
1987	20,697	222	0
1986	21,051	232	0
1985	20,853	237	0
1984	19,106	207	0
1983	18,672	291	107
1982	16,532	287	0
1981	20,497	322	316
1980	21,679	406	1,105
1979	20,173	700	0
1978	21,621	5,177	0
1977	21,694	3,739	0
1976	22,362	2,486	176

Source: U.S. Department of Energy, Energy Information Administration, Office of Coal, Nuclear, Electric, and Alternate Fuels, *Electric Power Annual, 1991*, and earlier editions.

TABLE 10.8–AVERAGE FUEL COSTS AT ELECTRIC UTILITIES, TENNESSEE, 1977–1991

Year	Coal ¢ per mil. BTU	Coal $ per ton	Petroleum ¢ per mil. BTU	Petroleum $ per barrel
1991	125.2	30.48	498.3	29.05
1990	134.2	32.12	560.8	32.70
1989	134.3	31.94	394.7	22.92
1988	133.5	32.17	350.9	20.39
1987	136.7	32.74	392.8	22.82
1986	141.9	33.79	336.8	19.57
1985	153.6	36.34	585.1	33.95
1984	162.2	38.30	611.3	35.58
1983	172.0	40.51	650.2	37.80
1982	174.5	41.22	810.2	47.15
1981	173.5	40.29	823.7	47.86
1980	155.7	36.21	639.0	37.28
1979	136.0	31.25	452.8	26.39
1978	119.6	26.99	264.8	15.47
1977	103.1	22.88	264.1	15.51

Note: Data are for plants with a capacity of 25 megawatts or greater prior to 1979. Beginning in 1979, data are for plants with a capacity of 50 megawatts or greater.

Source: U.S. Department of Energy, Energy Information Administration, Office of Coal, Nuclear, Electric, and Alternative Fuels, *Electric Power Annual, 1991*, and earlier editions.

TABLE 10.9--TOTAL ELECTRICITY SALES TO FINAL CUSTOMERS, AND RELATED STATISTICS, TVA AND LOCAL DISTRIBUTORS, 1980-1991, SELECTED FISCAL YEARS

Item	1991	1990	1989	1988	1987	1986	1985	1984	1983	1982	1980
Customers served--June (1,000)											
Total	3,404	3,353	3,302	3,231	3,165	3,086	3,005	2,946	2,887	2,842	2,757
Residential	2,920	2,877	2,902	2,846	2,796	2,733	2,665	2,614	2,565	2,531	2,455
Commercial and industrial	472	464	391	377	360	346	332	325	317	308	299
Other	12	12	9	9	8	8	7	7	4	4	3
Electricity sales (1,000,000 kwh)											
Total	92,188	89,830	88,217	85,817	83,042	78,466	76,697	76,982	69,971	71,863	71,331
Residential	41,382	40,289	40,219	39,655	38,968	36,439	35,958	37,369	33,497	34,989	34,977
Commercial and industrial	49,652	48,410	46,885	45,054	42,991	40,943	39,658	38,513	35,331	35,734	35,275
Street and outdoor lighting	1,154	1,130	1,113	1,108	1,083	1,084	1,081	1,100	1,143	1,140	1,079
Revenue from electricity sales ($1,000,000)											
Total	5,166.0	5,038.5	4,941.6	4,858.0	4,605.9	4,080.1	3,812.1	3,761.4	3,385.0	3,351.7	2,368.7
Residential	2,359.1	2,301.8	2,239.6	2,280.2	2,132.3	1,831.2	1,725.2	1,764.2	1,568.3	1,581.5	1,121.1
Commercial and industrial	2,714.5	2,647.3	2,561.7	2,493.4	2,330.0	2,113.5	1,960.5	1,874.8	1,706.2	1,665.7	1,167.5
Street and outdoor lighting	92.4	89.3	86.3	84.4	80.2	77.4	73.9	72.1	64.6	61.4	47.6
Other	0.0	0.0	54.0	(a)	63.4	58.0	52.5	50.3	45.9	43.1	32.5

Note: Totals may not equal sum of components due to independent rounding.

a. Less than 0.05.

Source: Tennessee Valley Authority, Division of Power Utilization, *Electricity Sales Statistics*, Monthly Report 677, July 1991, and earlier editions.

FIGURE 10.3
TVA Generating Plants in Tennessee

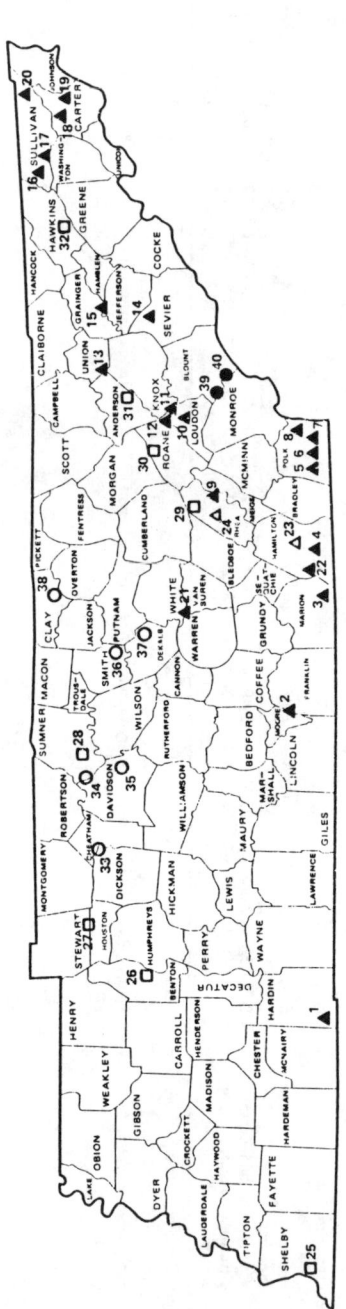

Please see legend on facing page

Legend for Figure 10.3

▲		TVA HYDRO PLANTS	Kw Capacity
	1.	Pickwick Landing	224,080
	2.	Tims Ford	45,000
	3.	Nickajack	103,950
	4.	Chickamauga	120,000
	5.	Ocoee 1	18,000
	6.	Ocoee 2	21,000
	7.	Ocoee 3	28,800
	8.	Appalachia	82,800
	9.	Watts Bar	166,500
	10.	Tellico	(a)
	11.	Fort Loudon	139,140
	12.	Melton Hill	72,000
	13.	Norris	100,800
	14.	Douglas	120,600
	15.	Cherokee	135,180
	16.	Ft. Patrick Henry	36,000
	17.	Boone	76,400
	18.	Wilbur	10,700
	19.	Watauga	57,600
	20.	South Holston	38,500
	21.	Great Falls	31,860
	22.	Raccoon Mtn. Pumped Storage Station	1,530,000

△		TVA NUCLEAR	Kw Capacity
	23.	Sequoyah Nuclear	2,441,160
	24.	Watts Bar Nuclear (under construction)	2,539,800

□		TVA COAL-FIRED, STEAM ELECTRIC	
	25.	Thomas H. Allen	990,000
	26.	Johnsonville	1,485,200
	27.	Cumberland	2,600,000
	28.	Gallatin	1,255,200
	29.	Watts Bar ("mothballed" in 1983)	240,000
	30.	Kingston	1,700,000
	31.	Bull Run	950,000
	32.	John Sevier	800,000

○		CORPS ENGINEER DAMS	
	33.	Cheatham	36,000
	34.	Old Hickory	100,000
	35.	J. Percy Priest	28,000
	36.	Cordell Hull	100,000
	37.	Center Hill	135,000
	38.	Dale Hollow	54,000

●		ALCOA DAMS	
	39.	Chilhowee	50,000
	40.	Calderwood	121,500

Note: In addition, combustion turbine peaking units have been installed at Allen (620,800 Kw), Johnsonville (1,088,000 Kw), and Gallatin (325,200 Kw).
a. Tellico Dam does not have generating capacity. Water from the Tellico Reservoir is used to increase flow through Fort Loudon generators via a canal linking the two reservoirs, resulting in an average annual energy increase of 200 million Kwh.
Source: Tennessee Valley Authority, Information Office, direct correspondence.

TABLE 10.10--STATUS OF TENNESSEE VALLEY AUTHORITY'S NUCLEAR PLANTS, AS OF
AUGUST 12, 1991

Unit	Status
Bellefonte Unit One	Construction deferred, scheduled for operation in 1997
Bellefonte Unit Two	Construction deferred, scheduled for operation in 1999
Browns Ferry Unit One	Undergoing repair
Browns Ferry Unit Two	Full power operations began August 14
Browns Ferry Unit Three	Likely to be next operational unit, scheduled for operation in 1993
Sequoyah Unit One	Restarted November 1988
Sequoyah Unit Two	Restarted May 1988
Watts Bar Unit One	Construction work on hold for quality review
Watts Bar Unit Two	Construction deferred, scheduled for operation in 1997

Note: Scheduled operation dates are subject to change; a forecast was made for budget planning purposes.
Source: Tennessee Valley Authority, Information statement of August 12, 1991.

TABLE 10.11--TVA AVERAGE ANNUAL ELECTRICAL USE, BILLS, AND RATES FOR RETAIL
COMMERCIAL AND INDUSTRIAL CONSUMERS, DISTRIBUTORS SERVING
TENNESSEE, CALENDAR YEAR 1990

	Demand under 50 kw			Demand 50 kw and over	
Distributor	Average annual kwh use [1]	Average annual bill	Average rate (¢/kwh)	Total consumption (1,000 kwh)	Average rate (¢/kwh)
Cities					
Alcoa	16,003	1,090.44	6.81	102,979	5.54
Athens	20,068	1,298.42	6.47	296,683	4.99
Bolivar	16,296	1,062.60	6.52	69,333	5.40
Bristol	18,725	1,169.02	6.24	284,046	5.31
Brownsville	21,481	1,314.98	6.12	103,564	5.17
Chattanooga	28,600	1,846.59	6.46	2,679,474	5.04
Clarksville	28,124	1,761.34	6.26	235,955	5.48
Cleveland	27,405	1,723.16	6.29	402,710	5.08
Clinton	20,906	1,355.71	6.48	171,393	5.55
Columbia	25,472	1,572.55	6.17	182,221	5.27
Cookeville	22,093	1,431.20	6.48	236,136	5.36
Covington	21,284	1,373.89	6.45	125,501	5.37
Dayton	15,202	999.94	6.58	79,792	5.22
Dickson	17,867	1,191.06	6.67	143,918	5.66
Dyersburg	24,325	1,620.47	6.66	351,225	4.74
Elizabethton	17,970	1,156.75	6.44	148,219	5.38
Erwin	19,005	1,196.35	6.30	92,718	4.98
Etowah	18,941	1,220.10	6.44	66,787	4.95
Fayetteville	16,368	1,120.73	6.85	116,354	5.56
Gallatin	26,531	1,587.79	5.98	237,883	4.98
Greeneville	15,454	994.50	6.44	390,220	5.27
Harriman	18,695	1,315.84	7.04	123,920	5.39
Humboldt	21,190	1,249.56	5.90	120,943	4.85
Jackson	28,527	1,757.94	6.16	640,591	5.04
Jellico	17,212	1,149.09	6.68	13,904	6.65
Johnson City	23,032	1,394.22	6.05	518,473	5.07
Knoxville	27,545	1,773.37	6.44	1,896,220	5.12
LaFollette	14,824	989.64	6.68	114,753	6.02
Lawrenceburg	17,408	1,111.19	6.38	162,146	5.33
Lebanon	26,198	1,637.51	6.25	153,842	5.26
Lenoir City	19,358	1,303.16	6.73	283,131	5.64
Lewisburg	27,228	1,762.01	6.47	166,539	5.42
Lexington	12,757	865.86	6.79	121,284	5.78
Loudon	19,094	1,298.05	6.80	111,055	5.30
McMinnville	19,506	1,256.41	6.44	106,676	5.47
Maryville	25,570	1,590.61	6.22	176,136	5.18
Memphis	30,806	2,080.74	6.75	5,715,269	5.12
Milan	16,122	1,001.30	6.21	87,036	5.24
Morristown	29,311	1,858.17	6.34	365,918	5.41
Mount Pleasant	21,913	1,433.35	6.54	33,851	5.25
Murfreesboro	31,632	1,914.02	6.05	382,296	5.10
Nashville	33,878	2,214.22	6.54	4,920,502	5.08
Newbern	20,289	1,268.84	6.25	45,120	5.69
Newport	15,755	1,083.67	6.88	159,706	5.38
Oak Ridge	29,737	1,818.04	6.11	174,867	5.30
Paris	14,467	915.11	6.33	135,643	5.32
Pulaski	16,982	1,101.48	6.49	164,727	5.00

TABLE 10.11--TVA AVERAGE ANNUAL ELECTRICAL USE, BILLS, AND RATES FOR RETAIL
COMMERCIAL AND INDUSTRIAL CONSUMERS, DISTRIBUTORS SERVING
TENNESSEE, CALENDAR YEAR 1990 (Continued)

	Demand under 50 kw			Demand 50 kw and over	
Distributor	Average annual kwh use [1]	Average annual bill	Average rate (¢/kwh)	Total consumption (1,000 kwh)	Average rate (¢/kwh)
Ripley	21,294	1,308.66	6.15	147,400	5.06
Rockwood	18,004	1,205.59	6.70	65,302	5.50
Sevierville	21,123	1,423.92	6.74	287,697	5.68
Shelbyville	28,673	1,788.08	6.24	170,481	5.27
Smithville	23,197	1,468.64	6.33	39,331	5.35
Somerville	24,824	1,576.01	6.35	8,940	6.15
Sparta	23,862	1,563.89	6.55	41,212	5.46
Springfield	31,952	2,123.66	6.65	81,161	5.99
Sweetwater	16,674	1,040.88	6.24	68,450	5.80
Trenton	22,603	1,456.14	6.44	39,847	5.19
Tullahoma	24,500	1,540.20	6.29	107,659	5.34
Union City	27,071	1,597.25	5.90	247,316	4.27
Winchester	23,964	1,563.41	6.52	38,891	5.52
Counties					
Benton County	14,202	951.19	6.70	69,739	5.62
Carroll County	14,722	997.95	6.78	123,730	5.35
Weakley County	16,225	1,040.43	6.41	149,662	5.55
Cooperatives					
Appalachian	13,453	969.20	7.20	192,962	5.73
Caney Fork	11,833	757.97	6.41	110,528	5.87
Chickasaw	11,584	779.24	6.73	79,612	5.47
Cumberland	13,333	911.91	6.84	250,550	5.84
Duck River	14,699	1,046.77	7.12	210,201	6.26
Forked Deer	6,506	523.22	8.04	52,785	5.49
Fort Loudoun	14,789	1,057.06	7.15	47,695	6.12
Gibson County	13,148	871.67	6.63	142,489	5.60
Holston	11,934	831.05	6.96	228,705	4.99
Meriwether Lewis	15,338	1,064.37	6.94	342,219	5.18
Middle Tennessee	16,481	1,075.28	6.52	736,422	4.98
Mountain	14,449	1,000.50	6.92	76,608	6.46
Pickwick	13,082	897.28	6.86	93,328	5.93
Plateau	15,636	1,167.10	7.46	72,776	6.53
Powell Valley, VA.	11,279	912.70	8.09	72,223	6.92
Sequachee Valley	17,994	1,218.94	6.77	195,196	5.67
Southwest Tennessee	12,719	916.28	7.20	150,785	5.81
Tennessee Valley	14,632	1,035.66	7.08	58,717	6.60
Tippah, MS.	12,500	833.41	6.67	94,321	5.76
Tri-County	11,474	819.88	7.15	261,819	5.76
Tri-State, GA.	16,072	1,220.89	7.60	29,352	6.70
Upper Cumberland	12,816	914.87	7.14	208,347	5.72
Volunteer	15,297	1,086.06	7.10	290,714	5.85

1. Annual kwh per consumer; this is derived by dividing total consumption during the year by the average number of consumers.

Source: Tennessee Valley Authority, Division of Power Utilization, *Electricity Sales Statistics, Calendar Year 1990*.

TABLE 10.12--ELECTRICITY SALES STATISTICS, DISTRIBUTORS SERVING TENNESSEE USING TVA POWER, CALENDAR YEAR 1990

	All service classes		Residential service		
Distributor	Total sales (1,000 kwh)	Average rate (¢/kwh)	Kwh per consumer	Average annual bill	Average rate (¢/kwh)
Cities					
Alcoa	376,355	5.74	14,518	812.77	5.60
Athens	469,062	5.29	14,005	773.10	5.52
Bolivar	211,352	5.69	13,733	762.79	5.55
Bristol	706,407	5.45	15,138	812.47	5.37
Brownsville	171,008	5.33	13,239	706.68	5.34
Chattanooga	5,050,007	5.42	15,176	863.33	5.69
Clarksville	714,976	5.64	14,757	814.06	5.52
Cleveland	783,084	5.38	15,353	847.89	5.52
Clinton	525,280	5.72	14,557	820.33	5.64
Columbia	477,869	5.49	14,496	790.79	5.46
Cookeville	406,482	5.57	13,144	738.29	5.62
Covington	176,038	5.53	12,505	705.58	5.64
Dayton	173,454	5.56	12,429	692.84	5.57
Dickson	478,130	5.79	14,863	845.16	5.69
Dyersburg	509,738	5.17	12,523	730.10	5.83
Elizabethton	448,782	5.60	13,604	751.70	5.53
Erwin	189,711	5.32	12,142	664.17	5.47
Etowah	129,925	5.35	13,317	737.13	5.54
Fayetteville	319,901	5.87	13,604	790.31	5.81
Gallatin	392,097	5.17	16,002	842.80	5.27
Greeneville	789,267	5.48	13,948	757.92	5.43
Harriman	261,001	5.84	13,241	799.49	6.04
Humboldt	185,736	5.02	12,935	659.75	5.10
Jackson	1,031,569	5.32	12,698	696.13	5.48
Jellico	64,844	6.15	11,145	649.75	5.83
Johnson City	1,340,019	5.31	15,068	795.75	5.28
Knoxville	4,344,749	5.54	15,053	855.04	5.68
LaFollette	318,596	5.89	12,331	694.71	5.63
Lawrenceburg	391,346	5.47	13,857	743.73	5.37
Lebanon	287,076	5.50	14,957	825.43	5.52
Lenoir City	889,130	5.84	17,765	1,022.34	5.75
Lewisburg	243,745	5.59	13,503	769.12	5.70
Lexington	335,019	5.87	12,297	692.25	5.63
Loudon	189,518	5.64	13,703	809.66	5.91
McMinnville	200,730	5.61	12,898	703.60	5.46
Maryville	405,997	5.47	13,100	715.28	5.46
Memphis	11,106,179	5.55	14,087	817.67	5.80
Milan	198,885	5.40	15,259	811.88	5.32
Morristown	545,252	5.56	12,531	705.10	5.63
Mount Pleasant	83,290	5.63	13,503	769.65	5.70
Murfreesboro	730,455	5.33	13,950	752.67	5.40
Nashville	9,635,519	5.52	15,150	876.74	5.79
Newbern	66,208	5.69	13,503	737.25	5.46
Newport	363,419	5.74	12,558	724.05	5.77
Oak Ridge	382,402	5.52	13,133	717.72	5.47
Paris	369,584	5.49	13,782	735.00	5.33
Pulaski	333,028	5.34	13,802	752.11	5.45

TABLE 10.12--ELECTRICITY SALES STATISTICS, DISTRIBUTORS SERVING TENNESSEE USING TVA POWER, CALENDAR YEAR 1990 (Continued)

	All service classes		Residential service		
Distributor	Total sales (1,000 kwh)	Average rate (¢/kwh)	Kwh per consumer	Average annual bill	Average rate (¢/kwh)
Ripley	232,902	5.27	12,634	675.79	5.35
Rockwood	231,928	5.79	14,695	838.20	5.70
Sevierville	699,562	5.96	13,677	796.31	5.82
Shelbyville	277,824	5.46	12,679	701.70	5.53
Smithville	72,034	5.52	12,018	649.91	5.41
Somerville	31,288	5.96	13,975	785.30	5.62
Sparta	80,637	5.74	11,969	685.24	5.73
Springfield	168,555	6.09	13,343	790.41	5.92
Sweetwater	158,003	5.68	13,499	719.23	5.33
Trenton	81,139	5.56	13,821	776.65	5.62
Tullahoma	245,502	5.58	14,626	807.58	5.52
Union City	329,165	4.58	11,879	624.37	5.26
Winchester	106,696	5.76	14,770	838.89	5.68
Counties					
Benton County	184,037	5.81	12,686	716.46	5.65
Carroll County	327,456	5.70	14,354	816.23	5.69
Weakley County	435,330	5.61	15,627	850.82	5.44
Cooperatives					
Appalachian	596,676	5.97	13,855	818.04	5.90
Caney Fork	412,020	5.58	13,606	717.28	5.27
Chickasaw	227,447	5.59	16,125	879.76	5.46
Cumberland	1,138,726	5.85	16,792	951.75	5.67
Duck River	893,962	6.20	15,267	913.78	5.99
Forked Deer	169,289	5.92	14,844	873.80	5.89
Fort Loudoun	292,700	6.20	13,402	810.59	6.05
Gibson County	582,053	5.77	14,929	838.86	5.62
Holston	508,144	5.49	13,286	757.37	5.70
Meriwether Lewis	679,194	5.60	12,123	706.76	5.83
Middle Tennessee	2,167,248	5.41	17,387	957.32	5.51
Mountain	328,725	6.16	9,668	563.12	5.82
Pickwick	314,295	5.90	13,776	772.00	5.60
Plateau	210,771	6.67	9,907	643.05	6.49
Powell Valley, VA.	318,654	6.83	11,236	743.78	6.62
Sequachee Valley	539,567	5.91	13,294	770.49	5.80
Southwest Tennessee	675,111	6.02	15,773	927.46	5.88
Tennessee Valley	259,786	6.29	12,800	758.84	5.93
Tippah, MS.	241,122	5.78	13,172	728.30	5.53
Tri-County	745,429	5.98	12,290	715.95	5.83
Tri-State, GA.	153,397	6.79	10,796	708.84	6.57
Upper Cumberland	645,609	6.00	13,220	782.40	5.92
Volunteer	1,243,184	6.08	13,156	780.23	5.93

Source: Tennessee Valley Authority, Division of Power Utilization, *Electricity Sales Statistics, Calendar Year 1990.*

TABLE 10.13--ENERGY CONSUMPTION, BY SOURCE, SOUTHEASTERN STATES, 1980 AND 1988 [In trillions of BTU]

State	Total 1988	Total 1980	Coal 1988	Coal 1980	Natural gas[1] 1988	Natural gas[1] 1980	Petroleum 1988	Petroleum 1980	Nuclear 1988	Nuclear 1980	Hydroelectric[2] 1988	Hydroelectric[2] 1980
TENNESSEE	1,714.2	1,692.8	610.6	576.9	220.9	233.3	581.1	530.9	42.3	5.7	47.0	91.0
Percent	100.0	100.0	35.6	34.1	12.9	13.8	33.9	31.4	2.5	0.3	2.7	5.4
Alabama	1,614.1	1,516.2	652.7	661.0	243.2	278.4	578.6	457.7	139.5	256.3	55.1	97.7
Percent	100.0	100.0	40.4	43.6	15.1	18.4	35.8	30.2	8.6	16.9	3.4	6.4
Arkansas	790.3	821.7	218.8	36.6	218.8	274.0	309.1	312.0	95.6	85.4	28.5	17.6
Percent	100.0	100.0	27.7	4.5	27.7	33.3	39.1	38.0	12.1	10.4	3.6	2.1
Florida	2,928.8	2,444.1	611.5	225.5	305.8	329.6	1,559.2	1,661.6	281.4	182.6	2.1	2.2
Percent	100.0	100.0	20.9	9.2	10.4	13.5	53.2	68.0	9.6	7.5	0.1	0.1
Georgia	2,038.1	1,638.4	699.0	521.5	331.1	325.3	831.0	706.4	162.8	92.0	21.1	45.9
Percent	100.0	100.0	34.3	31.8	16.2	19.9	40.8	43.1	8.0	5.6	1.0	2.8
Kentucky	1,400.8	1,384.0	821.8	641.7	190.9	204.1	522.2	517.3	0.0	0.0	24.8	30.5
Percent	100.0	100.0	58.7	46.4	13.6	14.7	37.3	37.4	0.0	0.0	1.8	2.2
Louisiana	3,449.8	3,594.3	212.1	2.5	1,506.4	1,862.2	1,530.6	1,604.4	148.1	0.0	0.0	0.0
Percent	100.0	100.0	6.1	0.1	43.7	51.8	44.4	44.6	4.3	0.0	0.0	0.0
Mississippi	938.1	794.8	129.6	75.0	216.4	270.9	444.4	379.3	102.9	0.0	0.0	0.0
Percent	100.0	100.0	13.8	9.4	23.1	34.1	47.4	47.7	11.0	0.0	0.0	0.0
North Carolina	1,946.5	1,603.7	515.4	624.7	156.6	155.2	774.1	667.7	313.1	63.0	29.6	57.0
Percent	100.0	100.0	26.5	39.0	8.0	9.7	39.8	41.6	16.1	3.9	1.5	2.9 r
South Carolina	1,143.2	977.2	301.8	245.8	115.3	146.9	375.8	366.5	437.7	189.8	7.0	31.4
Percent	100.0	100.0	26.4	25.2	10.1	15.0	32.9	37.5	38.3	19.4	0.6	2.7 r
Virginia	1,840.1	1,499.7	342.9	231.8	170.2	161.0	792.4	778.1	226.0	125.1	-2.0	9.3
Percent	100.0	100.0	18.6	15.5	9.2	10.7	43.1	51.9	12.3	8.3	-0.1	0.5
West Virginia	777.7	872.3	915.4	857.8	131.8	147.6	267.6	311.5	0.0	0.0	10.1	11.6
Percent	100.0	100.0	117.7	98.3	16.9	16.9	34.4	35.7	0.0	0.0	1.3	1.5 r

Note: Total includes net interstate sales of electricity not shown separately. A negative figure for net interstate sales of electricity will account for the sum of individual percentages being greater than 100 percent, while a positive figure will result in a sum less than 100 percent. Percentages were computed by the Center for Business and Economic Research. r revised.

1. Includes supplemental gaseous fuels.

2. May include small quantities of electricity generated at industrial hydropower sites.

Source: U.S. Department of Energy, Energy Information Administration, Office of Energy Markets and End Use, *State Energy Data Report, 1960 through 1988.*

TABLE 10.14--NET ELECTRIC ENERGY GENERATION, BY ENERGY SOURCE, SOUTHEASTERN
STATES, 1989 [In gigawatthours]

State	Total	Coal	Petroleum	Gas	Nuclear	Hydro-electric
TENNESSEE	73,959	46,324	178	1	15,603	11,853
Alabama	77,600	52,612	128	183	11,524	13,153
Arkansas	33,400	18,604	144	2,723	8,844	3,084
Florida	124,254	59,418	26,280	17,407	20,916	234
Georgia	92,448	63,405	158	50	24,961	3,874
Kentucky	70,760	66,214	112	29	(X)	4,404
Louisiana	54,292	18,081	298	23,522	12,391	(X)
Mississippi	21,055	8,724	738	3,767	7,826	(X)
North Carolina	87,103	50,524	256	115	29,212	6,996
South Carolina	66,984	23,800	134	255	40,780	2,016
Virginia	43,360	24,059	4,237	399	14,264	401
West Virginia	82,860	82,105	264	16	(X)	476

Note: Negative generation denotes that electric power consumed for plant use exceeds gross generation. Totals may
not equal sum of components because of independent rounding.

(X) Not applicable.

Source: U.S. Department of Energy, Energy Information Administration, Office of Coal, Nuclear, Electric, and
Alternate Fuels, *Electric Power Annual, 1989.*

TABLE 10.15--FUEL CONSUMPTION FOR ELECTRIC ENERGY, SOUTHEASTERN STATES AND
UNITED STATES, 1989

State	Coal (1,000 short tons)	Petroleum (1,000 barrels)	Gas (million cubic feet)
TENNESSEE	19,283	356	18
Alabama	21,884	216	1,760
Arkansas	11,278	278	29,462
Florida	24,292	42,966	186,814
Georgia	25,839	346	684
Kentucky	29,109	230	328
Louisiana	11,770	521	244,984
Mississippi	3,566	1,363	44,927
North Carolina	19,516	557	1,673
South Carolina	9,472	285	2,705
Virginia	9,573	6,786	3,796
West Virginia	32,391	402	124
UNITED STATES	766,888	267,451	2,787,012

Source: U.S. Department of Energy, Energy Information Administration, Office of Coal, Nuclear, Electric, and
Alternate Fuels, *Electric Power Annual, 1989.*

TABLE 10.16--ORIGIN AND DESTINATION OF COAL RECEIVED BY ELECTRIC UTILITY PLANTS, SOUTHEASTERN STATES, 1989

Destination Origin	Quantity (1,000 short tons)	Average quality			Average delivered cost	
		BTU (per pound)	Sulfur (percent by weight)	Ash (percent by weight)	(¢ per million BTU)	($ per short ton)
TENNESSEE	18,300	11,895	1.99	9.56	134.3	31.94
Illinois	1,495	11,719	1.99	7.79	111.8	26.21
Indiana	6	11,601	1.60	7.60	129.1	29.95
Kentucky	13,638	11,735	2.08	9.73	140.5	32.97
TENNESSEE	1,866	12,481	1.40	10.15	115.9	28.93
Virginia	1,276	12,951	1.87	9.01	123.8	32.06
West Virginia	18	12,421	2.60	11.40	139.5	34.65
Alabama	21,311	12,023	1.64	11.87	186.5	44.84
Alabama	14,725	12,152	1.34	12.38	201.9	49.06
Illinois	874	11,590	2.27	8.08	109.8	25.45
Indiana	374	11,609	3.42	7.94	105.9	24.58
Kentucky	2,125	11,785	2.78	10.94	123.3	29.06
Ohio	2,352	11,562	2.30	11.62	206.3	47.71
TENNESSEE	745	12,321	0.77	11.95	126.2	31.10
West Virginia	117	11,971	0.79	10.90	159.2	38.11
Arkansas	11,502	8,720	0.34	5.26	163.1	28.45
Wyoming	11,502	8,720	0.34	5.26	163.1	28.45
Florida	23,375	12,383	1.75	8.58	178.7	44.26
Alabama	13	11,802	3.01	13.94	114.3	26.98
Illinois	4,107	11,672	2.78	8.80	198.6	46.36
Indiana	508	11,357	3.40	9.55	130.2	29.58
Kentucky	14,980	12,592	1.61	8.31	172.0	43.31
TENNESSEE	90	12,733	1.02	6.79	216.1	55.03
Virginia	838	12,498	0.72	8.96	232.8	58.18
West Virginia	1,999	12,615	1.21	10.40	181.8	45.86
Imported	841	12,043	0.73	7.21	171.8	41.38
Georgia	25,434	12,100	1.68	10.13	174.9	42.33
Alabama	246	12,131	2.00	12.11	153.3	37.20
Illinois	5,188	11,366	2.61	9.07	182.0	41.37
Kentucky	13,963	12,196	1.56	10.62	165.6	40.38
Montana	54	9,348	0.32	4.13	181.1	33.86
TENNESSEE	1,140	12,854	1.07	8.04	198.0	50.90
Virginia	3,277	12,836	1.40	10.00	171.6	44.06
West Virginia	1,355	12,054	0.65	11.71	242.9	58.55
Wyoming	188	8,736	0.38	5.64	137.3	23.98
Imported	23	13,189	0.71	8.47	172.5	45.52
Kentucky	30,733	11,493	2.74	12.47	113.7	26.13
Illinois	9	11,200	1.93	8.60	115.7	25.92
Indiana	2,107	11,210	2.50	8.82	104.7	23.47
Kentucky	25,475	11,433	2.96	12.92	114.1	26.10
Ohio	124	11,280	2.51	12.01	129.4	29.20
Pennsylvania	19	12,322	2.51	13.24	128.1	31.57
TENNESSEE	541	12,433	2.60	11.56	105.2	26.15
West Virginia	2,435	12,191	0.81	11.24	117.5	28.65
Wyoming	22	8,397	0.31	5.40	124.2	20.86
Louisiana	11,594	8,187	0.48	7.27	162.7	26.64
Louisiana	2,981	6,858	0.54	12.18	127.4	17.48
West Virginia	195	13,003	0.66	6.71	201.7	52.46
Wyoming	8,418	8,546	0.45	5.54	171.4	29.29
Mississippi	3,455	12,654	1.56	7.77	167.1	42.29
Illinois	1,116	12,600	2.51	8.22	146.7	36.97
Kentucky	2,311	12,686	1.10	7.54	177.2	44.95
West Virginia	27	12,132	1.57	9.16	143.4	34.79
North Carolina	18,413	12,531	0.92	9.93	177.0	44.35
Kentucky	9,169	12,553	0.94	8.81	180.5	45.31
TENNESSEE	166	12,511	1.35	9.60	186.8	46.74

TABLE 10.16--ORIGIN AND DESTINATION OF COAL RECEIVED BY ELECTRIC UTILITY PLANTS, SOUTHEASTERN STATES, 1989 (Continued)

Destination Origin	Quantity (1,000 short tons)	Average quality			Average delivered cost	
		BTU (per pound)	Sulfur (percent by weight)	Ash (percent by weight)	(¢ per million BTU)	($ per short ton)
Virginia	4,283	12,700	1.02	10.66	171.7	43.61
West Virginia	4,795	12,337	0.77	11.42	174.7	43.10
South Carolina	9,805	12,618	1.12	9.16	170.7	43.08
Kentucky	8,596	12,564	1.09	9.16	172.7	43.39
TENNESSEE	135	12,530	1.40	9.09	156.8	39.29
Virginia	1,047	13,074	1.30	9.09	156.8	41.00
West Virginia	27	12,482	1.26	11.58	171.7	42.87
Virginia	9,739	12,693	0.94	9.44	154.8	39.29
Kentucky	3,553	12,670	1.02	8.55	156.2	39.58
Virginia	3,601	12,729	0.90	10.44	156.8	39.92
West Virginia	2,585	12,675	0.87	9.27	150.0	38.03
West Virginia	31,143	12,395	1.85	11.71	142.5	35.33
Kentucky	1,109	12,143	1.06	10.20	165.5	40.20
Maryland	925	12,140	1.71	15.13	116.6	28.32
Ohio	935	12,203	4.04	10.94	102.3	24.97
Pennsylvania	308	12,885	1.60	8.19	119.8	30.87
West Virginia	27,866	12,415	1.82	11.72	144.1	35.77

Source: U. S. Department of Energy, Energy Information Administration, *Cost and Quality of Fuels for Electric Utility Plants 1989*.

TABLE 10.17--FUEL COSTS AT ELECTRIC UTILITIES, SOUTHEASTERN STATES AND UNITED STATES, 1989

State	Coal		Petroleum		Gas	
	¢ per million BTU	Dollars per ton	¢ per million BTU	Dollars per barrel	¢ per million BTU	Dollars per million cubic feet
TENNESSEE	31.94	134.3	22.92	394.7	(X)	(X)
Alabama	44.84	186.5	23.87	414.3	2.27	220.5
Arkansas	28.45	163.1	22.44	370.6	1.69	165.4
Florida	44.26	178.7	17.19	271.1	2.49	246.2
Georgia	42.96	177.5	24.95	426.7	3.23	315.6
Kentucky	26.13	113.7	27.71	475.2	2.73	267.3
Louisiana	26.64	162.7	23.86	379.4	1.78	170.2
Mississippi	42.29	167.1	16.91	267.6	1.88	183.4
North Carolina	44.35	177.0	23.17	398.9	(X)	(X)
South Carolina	43.08	170.7	24.71	426.3	2.27	222.1
Virginia	39.29	154.8	17.48	284.4	2.58	247.9
West Virginia	35.33	142.5	26.33	450.5	4.59	458.8
UNITED STATES	30.15	144.6	18.17	289.3	2.42	235.5

Note: Data are for plants with a capacity of 50 megawatts or greater.
(X) Not applicable.
Source: U.S. Department of Energy, Energy Information Administration, Office of Coal, Nuclear, Electric, and Alternate Fuels, *Electric Power Annual, 1989*.

TABLE 10.18--SALES OF ELECTRIC ENERGY TO ULTIMATE CUSTOMERS, BY CLASS OF SERVICE,
1989, AND TOTAL SALES, 1980-1989, SELECTED YEARS, SOUTHEASTERN STATES
[In gigawatthours]

State	Class of service , 1989[P]				
	Total	Residential	Commercial	Industrial	Other[1]
TENNESSEE	75,113	28,355	11,297	34,520	940
Alabama	58,187	19,842	10,517	27,232	596
Arkansas	26,085	9,957	5,982	9,562	584
Florida	138,474	68,184	48,943	17,040	4,307
Georgia	77,060	28,349	21,431	26,388	891
Kentucky	58,487	16,922	8,952	30,173	2,440
Louisiana	61,842	20,515	13,437	24,762	3,128
Mississippi	29,574	11,516	6,495	10,958	605
North Carolina	88,209	32,784	22,506	31,152	1,768
South Carolina	53,857	17,464	11,343	24,301	749
Virginia	73,461	29,223	19,920	16,395	7,922
West Virginia	22,847	7,634	4,926	10,195	93

	Total sales						
	1989[P]	1988	1987	1986	1985	1984	1980
TENNESSEE	75,113	72,872	69,730	68,893	68,457	71,751	73,391
Alabama	58,187	56,638	54,703	52,844	49,662	49,649	50,367
Arkansas	26,085	25,273	24,196	22,194	23,064	24,584	26,499
Florida	138,474	130,241	122,468	116,443	108,665	101,458	90,766
Georgia	77,060	74,346	71,680	66,056	59,972	57,042	51,209
Kentucky	58,487	54,078	50,787	50,493	39,325	41,352	49,787
Louisiana	61,842	60,011	59,156	57,499	58,809	59,639	52,877
Mississippi	29,574	28,080	27,186	27,385	25,725	25,166	23,258
North Carolina	88,209	85,540	82,967	74,216	70,959	70,535	58,737
South Carolina	53,857	52,809	51,967	49,198	42,507	41,769	37,264
Virginia	73,461	70,115	66,847	62,823	58,513	55,586	48,369
West Virginia	22,847	22,388	21,075	20,600	21,844	22,022	20,831

Note: Totals may not equal sum of components because of independent rounding.

p preliminary.

1. Includes public street and highway lighting, other sales to public authorities, sales to railroads and railways, and interdepartmental sales.

Source: U.S. Department of Energy, Energy Information Administration, Office of Coal, Nuclear, Electric, and Alternate Fuels, *Electric Power Annual, 1989*, and earlier editions.

TABLE 10.19--AVERAGE REVENUE PER KILOWATT-HOUR, BY SECTOR, SOUTHEASTERN STATES, 1988 AND 1989 [In cents]

State	Total			Residential			Commercial			Industrial			Other[1]		
	1989 P	1988	Percent change	1989 P	1988	Percent change	1989 P	1988	Percent change	1989 P	1988	Percent change	1989 P	1988	Percent change
TENNESSEE	5.4	5.5	-2.2	5.7	5.7	-0.2	6.1	6.1	0.5	5.0	5.2	-3.3	6.8	7.0	-2.6
Alabama	5.6	5.5	1.3	6.6	6.5	1.5	6.8	6.6	2.4	4.3	4.4	-2.7	5.6	5.6	0.0
Arkansas	6.4	6.4	0.6	7.8	7.6	2.5	6.7	6.5	2.9	4.9	4.8	1.4	6.7	6.7	-0.4
Florida	7.0	7.1	-0.8	7.7	7.8	-1.5	6.6	6.7	-2.1	5.1	5.1	0.0	6.7	6.8	-0.9
Georgia	6.4	6.2	2.7	7.2	7.0	2.6	7.3	7.1	2.5	4.7	4.7	0.6	7.8	7.3	6.4
Kentucky	4.8	5.1	-6.6	5.6	5.7	-1.1	5.3	5.4	-1.1	4.3	4.8	-9.9	4.6	4.7	-2.5
Louisiana	6.0	5.8	3.4	7.3	7.1	2.4	7.0	6.8	3.1	4.3	4.2	2.9	6.1	6.2	-2.1
Mississippi	6.2	6.2	0.3	6.8	6.5	4.0	7.2	7.1	1.1	4.8	5.1	-5.1	7.7	8.8	-12.4
North Carolina	6.2	6.1	1.0	7.7	7.5	3.1	6.3	6.2	1.6	4.7	4.6	1.3	6.4	6.4	-0.5
South Carolina	5.6	5.6	0.0	7.2	7.1	1.0	6.2	6.2	0.0	4.3	4.2	1.4	5.8	5.5	5.5
Virginia	5.9	5.7	4.1	6.9	6.6	4.9	6.0	5.7	5.1	4.2	4.1	2.9	5.2	5.5	-5.5
West Virginia	4.8	4.8	0.0	5.9	5.9	-0.5	5.4	5.4	-0.7	3.6	3.6	-0.3	8.3	8.2	1.3
UNITED STATES	6.5	6.4	2.4	7.6	7.5	1.6	7.2	7.0	2.3	4.7	4.7	0.0	6.2	6.2	0.0

Note: Percent change computed by the Center for Business and Economic Research.

p preliminary.

1. Includes public street and highway lighting, other sales to public authorities, sales to railroads and railways, and interdepartmental sales.

Source: U.S. Department of Energy, Energy Information Administration, Office of Coal, Nuclear, Electric, and Alternate Fuels, *Electric Power Annual, 1989.*

TABLE 10.20--NATURAL GAS DELIVERED TO CONSUMERS, BY CLASS OF SERVICE, 1989, AND TOTAL, 1980-1989, SELECTED YEARS, SOUTHEASTERN STATES [In millions of cubic feet]

State	Total	Class of service, 1989			
		Residential	Commercial	Industrial	Electric utilities
TENNESSEE	203,588	49,136	47,573	106,860	18
Alabama	225,124	47,932	26,438	149,047	1,707
Arkansas	228,392	42,312	27,284	129,333	29,462
Florida	310,493	13,089	35,105	75,485	186,814
Georgia	309,970	103,657	53,114	152,516	684
Kentucky	165,562	65,086	36,145	64,003	328
Louisiana	1,209,158	57,705	26,617	897,754	227,082
Mississippi	188,597	26,312	17,568	99,790	44,927
North Carolina	156,105	38,658	33,145	82,629	1,673
South Carolina	114,237	20,472	16,525	74,534	2,705
Virginia	167,450	61,712	44,181	57,761	3,796
West Virginia	110,452	37,128	23,257	49,943	124

State	Total delivered to consumers						
	1989	1988	1987	1986	1985	1984	1980
TENNESSEE	203,588	197,095	185,200	174,333	179,942	193,489	213,169
Alabama	225,124	217,586	189,112	187,654	202,901	213,516	242,793
Arkansas	228,392	197,208	151,856	184,148	174,991	193,694	260,319
Florida	310,493	282,792	288,317	278,439	278,666	291,128	304,638
Georgia	309,970	316,108	297,249	273,799	276,446	301,331	307,827
Kentucky	165,562	160,332	147,258	140,704	149,102	162,985	180,368
Louisiana	1,209,158	1,116,676	1,147,961	1,149,230	1,086,006	1,241,850	1,523,691
Mississippi	188,597	171,186	168,075	179,610	195,058	228,840	219,828
North Carolina	156,105	146,790	143,500	130,787	129,081	138,228	147,448
South Carolina	114,237	109,817	103,273	96,175	95,225	105,842	139,214
Virginia	167,450	154,756	151,880	135,725	134,589	136,757	149,980
West Virginia	110,452	100,595	94,065	89,533	92,218	101,023	127,343

Source: U.S. Department of Energy, Energy Information Administration, *Natural Gas Annual, 1989*, and earlier editions.

TABLE 10.21–NUMBER OF NATURAL GAS CONSUMERS, BY CLASS OF SERVICE, SOUTHEASTERN
STATES, 1980–1989, SELECTED YEARS [In thousands]

State	1989 Resi-dential	Commer-cial	Indus-trial	1988 Resi-dential	Commer-cial	Indus-trial	1987 Resi-dential	Commer-cial	Indus-trial
TENNESSEE	599	84	3	566	81	2	535	77	2
Alabama	681	57	2	668	55	2	662	54	2
Arkansas	491	62	1	485	62	1	481	60	1
Florida	453	44	(a)	447	43	1	445	42	1
Georgia	1,309	107	3	1,275	102	3	1,237	99	3
Kentucky	614	65	1	606	64	1	596	63	1
Louisiana	937	64	2	947	66	2	952	67	2
Mississippi	376	44	1	372	44	1	370	43	1
North Carolina	493	64	3	473	61	3	436	56	3
South Carolina	328	39	1	314	37	1	302	35	1
Virginia	602	61	1	574	55	1	550	54	1
West Virginia	349	34	(a)	350	33	(a)	351	31	(a)

State	1986 Resi-dential	Commer-cial	Indus-trial	1985 Resi-dential	Commer-cial	Indus-trial	1980 Resi-dential	Commer-cial	Indus-trial
TENNESSEE	507	73	2	494	71	2	457	63	2
Alabama	656	53	2	640	53	2	634	49	2
Arkansas	475	60	1	470	60	2	456	58	2
Florida	442	41	(a)	439	40	1	416	34	1
Georgia	1,190	94	3	1,138	91	3	993	79	2
Kentucky	592	62	1	588	60	1	587	57	1
Louisiana	963	70	1	975	70	2	970	69	2
Mississippi	367	44	1	367	43	1	353	44	1
North Carolina	426	54	2	407	51	3	373	46	2
South Carolina	298	34	1	293	33	1	263	27	1
Virginia	536	48	(a)	525	46	1	534	46	1
West Virginia	352	31	(a)	355	31	(a)	367	33	(a)

a. Less than 500 industrial consumers.

Source: U. S. Department of Energy, Energy Information Administration, *Natural Gas Annual, 1989*, and earlier
editions.

TABLE 10.22--AVERAGE CONSUMPTION AND ANNUAL COST OF NATURAL GAS PER CONSUMER,
BY CLASS OF SERVICE, 1989, AND AVERAGE RESIDENTIAL CONSUMPTION,
1980-1989, SELECTED YEARS, SOUTHEASTERN STATES AND UNITED STATES
[Consumption in thousands of cubic feet]

| | 1989 | | | | |
| | Residential | | Commercial | | |
State	Consumption	Cost	Consumption	Cost	Industrial consumption
TENNESSEE	82	$397	566	$2,539	41,824
Alabama	70	441	466	2,408	62,625
Arkansas	86	418	441	1,932	91,596
Florida	29	233	801	3,884	164,097
Georgia	79	494	498	2,720	49,534
Kentucky	106	496	556	2,417	44,354
Louisiana	62	368	415	2,182	586,767
Mississippi	70	357	397	1,880	77,839
North Carolina	78	514	521	2,680	24,439
South Carolina	63	421	425	2,402	57,027
Virginia	103	675	724	3,567	64,537
West Virginia	106	609	686	3,601	235,578
UNITED STATES	97	547	647	3,068	30,810

| | Average annual residential consumption per customer | | | | | | |
	1989	1988	1987	1986	1985	1984	1980
TENNESSEE	82	84	81	79	80	92	98
Alabama	70	73	74	68	68	78	83
Arkansas	86	88	83	81	86	99	103
Florida	29	33	33	31	31	34	36
Georgia	79	85	81	75	74	87	91
Kentucky	106	106	99	100	102	114	126
Louisiana	62	63	64	60	62	71	75
Mississippi	70	72	72	69	70	79	83
North Carolina	78	81	82	74	70	83	91
South Carolina	63	66	67	59	56	66	72
Virginia	103	102	101	96	93	100	103
West Virginia	106	108	102	103	104	111	132
UNITED STATES	97	96	90	92	96	100	108

Source: U. S. Department of Energy, Energy Information Administration, *Natural Gas Annual, 1989*, and earlier editions.

TABLE 10.23--AVERAGE PRICE OF NATURAL GAS DELIVERED TO CONSUMERS, BY CLASS OF
SERVICE, 1989, AND TOTAL, 1980-1989, SELECTED YEARS, SOUTHEASTERN STATES
AND UNITED STATES [In dollars per thousand cubic feet]

| State | Class of service, 1989 | | | | |
	Total	Residential	Commercial	Industrial	Electric utilities
TENNESSEE	4.13	4.83	4.49	3.37	2.83
Alabama	4.60	6.27	5.17	3.02	2.27
Arkansas	3.63	4.85	4.38	3.09	1.69
Florida	3.15	8.06	4.85	3.13	2.49
Georgia	5.38	6.24	5.46	3.73	3.23
Kentucky	4.42	4.68	4.35	3.69	2.73
Louisiana	2.34	5.97	5.26	1.97	1.78
Mississippi	3.09	5.10	4.73	2.54	1.88
North Carolina	4.87	6.55	5.14	3.64	3.57
South Carolina	4.47	6.73	5.65	3.46	2.27
Virginia	5.48	6.59	4.93	3.91	2.57
West Virginia	5.02	5.73	5.25	2.92	4.59
UNITED STATES	4.22	5.64	4.74	2.97	2.43

| State | Average prices to all consumers | | | | | | |
	1989	1988	1987	1986	1985	1984	1980
TENNESSEE	4.13	3.97	3.91	4.33	4.60	4.50	2.73
Alabama	4.60	4.53	4.74	4.57	4.86	4.95	2.97
Arkansas	3.63	3.67	3.44	3.59	3.88	3.99	2.27
Florida	3.15	2.92	3.34	2.86	3.91	3.96	2.28
Georgia	5.38	5.24	5.17	5.07	5.38	5.36	3.16
Kentucky	4.42	4.20	4.23	4.53	4.91	4.86	2.87
Louisiana	2.34	2.29	2.15	2.19	3.19	3.40	1.65
Mississippi	3.09	3.40	3.49	3.43	3.86	3.96	2.62
North Carolina	4.87	4.67	4.88	4.93	5.46	5.78	3.59
South Carolina	4.47	4.49 r	4.79	4.53	5.20	5.45	3.17
Virginia	5.48	4.82	4.94	5.25	5.88	6.00	3.67
West Virginia	5.02	5.11	5.53	5.35	5.61	5.50	3.28
UNITED STATES	4.22	4.09	4.05	4.13	4.72	4.85	2.91

r revised.

Source: U. S. Department of Energy, Energy Information Administration, *Natural Gas Annual, 1989*, and earlier
editions.

TABLE 10.24--NUMBER AND CAPACITY OF OPERABLE PETROLEUM REFINERIES, SOUTHEASTERN
STATES AND UNITED STATES, AS OF JANUARY 1, 1991

	Number of operable refineries			Crude capacity (in barrels per calendar day)		
State	Total	Operating	Idle[1]	Total	Operating	Idle[1]
TENNESSEE	1	1	0	60,000	60,000	0
Alabama	3	2	1	140,100	113,500	26,600
Arkansas	3	3	0	59,700	53,900	5,800
Georgia	2	1	1	33,540	5,540	28,000
Kentucky	2	2	0	218,900	218,900	0
Louisiana	22	19	3	2,627,207	2,286,707	340,500
Mississippi	6	5	1	368,400	362,400	6,000
North Carolina	1	1	0	3,000	3,000	0
Virginia	2	2	0	56,700	56,700	0
West Virginia	1	1	0	12,500	12,500	0
UNITED STATES	202	184	18	15,675,627	14,958,777	716,850

1. Refineries where distillation units are completely idle but not permanently shut down on January 1.

Source: U.S. Department of Energy, Energy Information Administration, Office of Oil and Gas, *Petroleum Supply Annual, 1990, Volume 1.*

TABLE 10.25--NUCLEAR POWER PLANTS: NUMBER OF UNITS AND NET SUMMER CAPABILITY,
1988, AND NET GENERATION, 1989, SOUTHEASTERN STATES AND UNITED STATES

	1988 Number of units	1988 Net summer capability		1989 Net generation	
State		Nuclear (million kw)	Percent of total	Nuclear (million kwh)	Percent of total
TENNESSEE	2	2.3	13.5	20,916	16.8
Alabama	5	4.8	25.7	34,954	14.4
Arkansas	2	1.7	17.7	11,524	14.9
Florida	5	3.7	11.4	29,212	33.5
Georgia	3	2.6	13.4	0	0.0
Kentucky	0	0.0	0.0	24,961	27.0
Louisiana	2	2.0	11.9	7,826	37.2
Mississippi	1	1.1	16.4	0	0.0
North Carolina	5	4.7	23.5	0	0.0
South Carolina	7	6.3	42.8	14,264	32.9
Virginia	4	3.4	26.5	0	0.0
West Virginia	0	0.0	0.0	2,719	7.6
UNITED STATES	108	94.7	14.0	529,355	19.1

Source: U.S. Department of Commerce, Bureau of the Census, *Statistical Abstract of the United States, 1991*, and earlier editions.

A principal source of data on agriculture is the *Census of Agriculture*, conducted by the U.S. Department of Commerce, Bureau of the Census, in five-year intervals beginning in 1840. The four-year intervals seen in the 1978 and 1982 agricultural censuses were used to put this census on the same schedule as the other economic censuses conducted by the Bureau. Data from the 1992 Census are presented in this edition of the *Abstract* for Tennessee and its counties. As reports for most states have not been published, comparative tables on Tennessee and the other southeastern states report 1987 data.

Although states and counties are the primary geographic units for printed data, the *Census of Agriculture* CD-ROM (compact disc read-only memory) provides data for Zip Code areas beginning in 1987.

Another comprehensive set of agricultural data, published annually, is the United States Department of Agriculture (USDA) Statistical Reporting Service's *Agricultural Statistics*, which provides estimates on crop production, livestock inventory, farm income, prices received, and taxes on farm real estate. Tennessee Agricultural Statistics Service, in cooperation with the USDA, publishes a similar annual state report, *Tennessee Agricultural Statistics, Annual Bulletin*, and a monthly bulletin, *Farm Facts*. These publications also provide indexes of prices received by farmers and prices paid by farmers for major production items. Price indexes for Tennessee and the U.S. are reported in Tables 11.11 and 11.25, respectively.

Farm income is reported by the USDA, Economic Research Service (ERS), in an annual bulletin titled *Economic Indicators of the Farm Sector,* which provides information on cash receipts by commodity, as shown in Table 11.5. This source also provides data on the various farm programs by state. Time-series data on farm debt outstanding for southeastern states and current information on primary agricultural crops for states are also detailed in this report.

Another source of farm income data is the U.S. Department of Commerce, Bureau of Economic Analysis (BEA). These estimates are produced annually for states and counties and distributed by the Center for Business and Economic Research and other members of the BEA User Group. These data are also distributed on CD-ROM. Rural farm populations, detailed in Table 11.17 and 11.18, are from the Census Bureau's decennial *Census of Population*.

Forestry data are gathered and published by the USDA, Forest Service, on a 10-year cycle. Data for this edition of the *Abstract* are for 1989 and were collected by the Southern Forest Experiment Station, New Orleans. Both state and county tables on forestry are published together at the end of this chapter beginning with Table 11.29.

TABLE OF CONTENTS

TABLE OF CONTENTS
(Continued)

411

TABLE 11.1-- NUMBER OF FARMS AND SUMMARY FARM STATISTICS, TENNESSEE, 1930–1992, SELECTED YEARS

Year	Number of farms	Total land in farms (1,000 acres)	Average size of farm (acres)	Average dollar value of land and buildings Per farm	Per acre
1992	75,076	11,169	149	186,171	1,245
1987	79,711	11,731	147	146,126	1,001
1982	90,565	12,475	138	139,141	1,014
1978[r]	86,910[a]	12,681	146	125,238	856
1974	93,659[a]	13,103	140	65,308	467
1969	121,406	15,057	124	33,176	268
1964	133,446	15,266	114	20,509	179
1959	157,688	16,081	102	13,288	130
1954	203,149	17,654	87	8,049	93
1950	231,631	18,534	80	6,182	77
1945	234,431	17,789	76	3,715	49
1940	247,617	18,493	75	2,683	36
1935	273,783	19,086	70	2,030	29
1930	245,657	18,003	73	3,025	41

Note: Beginning with the 1974 Census, a farm is defined as any place having annual sales of agricultural products of $1,000 or more. Earlier data include places of 10 or more acres that had annual sales of agricultural products of $50 or more and places of less than 10 acres that had annual sales of $250 or more.

r revised so as to be comparable with later years. Beginning in 1982, the area sample survey was discontinued; thus data represent only farms on the mail list. The adjustment to the 1978 data was made by subtracting the area sample results from the 1978 totals.

a. Number of farms adjusted to 1969 definition:

    1974 = 103,219

    1978 = 117,233

Source: U.S. Department of Commerce, Bureau of the Census, *1992 Census of Agriculture, Tennessee*, and earlier editions.

TABLE 11.2-- FARM LAND USE PATTERN, TENNESSEE, 1945–1992, CENSUS YEARS [In acres]

Land use	1992	1987	1982	1978 [r]	1974
Total land in use for farms	11,169,086	11,731,386	12,474,931	12,680,809	13,103,224
Cropland total	7,086,879	7,185,903	7,602,106	7,786,086	7,756,516
Harvested	3,817,720	3,854,302	4,548,895	4,409,331	3,746,117
Pastured	2,597,907	2,472,453	2,608,138	2,886,362	3,500,924
Other	671,252	859,148	445,073	490,393	509,475
Woodland including woodland pastures	2,771,296	2,957,874	3,248,631	3,362,986	3,410,625
All other land[1]	1,310,911	1,587,609	1,624,194	1,531,737	1,936,083
Irrigated land	36,974	37,776	17,745	13,163	9,860

Land use	1969	1964	1959	1950	1945
Total land in use for farms	15,056,907	15,266,213	16,081,285	18,534,380	17,788,997
Cropland total	8,403,509	7,855,209	8,499,211	9,920,008	9,273,021
Harvested	3,472,039	3,617,961	4,116,418	5,575,106	5,843,567
Pastured	3,780,947	3,059,139	3,216,771	2,855,786	2,259,571
Other	1,150,523	1,178,109	1,166,022	1,489,116	1,169,883
Woodland including woodland pastures	4,375,196	4,859,186	5,201,315	5,868,607	5,053,051
All other land[1]	2,278,202	2,551,818	2,380,759	2,745,765	3,462,925
Irrigated land	12,158	10,737	10,979	1,012	393

Note: Total land area in Tennessee is 26,728,000 acres.

r revised data, comparable to later years. See Table 11.1 for details.

1. Includes pastureland other than cropland and woodland pasture, rangeland, and land in house lots, ponds, roads, wasteland, etc.

Source: U.S. Department of Commerce, Bureau of the Census, *1992 Census of Agriculture, Tennessee*, and earlier editions.

TABLE 11.3-- GROSS AND NET INCOME FROM FARMING, TENNESSEE, 1950–1992, SELECTED YEARS [In millions of dollars]

Year	Agricultural cash receipts	Government payments	Non-cash income[1]	Other farm income[2]	Net inventory adjustment[3]	Gross farm income[4]	Production expenses[4]	Net farm income
1992	2,103.5	115.9	182.0	143.4	61.3	2,606.0	1,997.7	608.3
1991r	1,936.4	70.3	177.4	150.3	58.9	2,393.4	1,970.5	422.9
1990f	2,056.9	91.0	195.1	156.9	-45.0	2,454.9	1,996.5	458.3
1989f	1,945.7	141.0	206.0	179.5	17.2	2,489.4	1,992.2	497.2
1988f	1,925.3	140.4	209.2	176.6	49.4	2,501.0	2,046.6	454.4
1987	1,947.7	156.7	196.2	155.9	-54.7	2,401.8	1,999.5	402.4
1986	1,826.3	98.4	196.0	113.4	-146.6	2,087.6	1,915.1	172.5
1985	1,987.1	61.7	313.5	96.6	-42.0	2,416.9	2,041.0	375.9
1984	2,118.1	76.6	509.2	85.4	89.6	2,878.8	2,261.6	617.2
1983	1,803.4	65.8	489.6	78.2	-122.8	2,314.2	2,178.5	135.7
1982	1,949.2	28.1	509.5	57.6	98.2	2,642.6	2,176.1	466.5
1981	1,933.0	20.7	501.9	58.9	124.0	2,638.5	2,124.8	513.7
1980	1,849.5	18.7	439.5	68.0	-101.8	2,273.9	1,977.1	296.8
1979	1,776.5	8.4	375.0	30.6	-19.2	2,171.3	1,769.3	402.0
1978	1,578.6	15.5	276.2	31.7	-29.5	1,872.5	1,532.9	339.5
1977	1,391.7	12.4	266.3	17.1	-53.3	1,634.2	1,363.5	270.4
1976	1,289.3	11.4	229.2	15.7	57.9	1,603.5	1,261.8	341.7
1975	1,116.3	16.6	171.1	15.8	-4.6	1,315.2	1,131.8	183.4
1970	702.5	71.0	114.4	9.8	8.6	906.3	676.6	229.8
1965	603.3	36.7	112.9	6.4	-4.0	755.3	514.3	240.9
1960	503.3	14.9	102.5	3.8	-0.3	624.2	406.0	218.2
1955	440.4	5.6	121.0	1.2	46.0	614.2	325.0	289.3
1950	431.3	6.7	130.4	0.2	5.2	573.8	271.4	302.4

r revised.

1. Includes the rental value of housing provided by farm dwellings and the value of farm products consumed directly in farm dwellings.

2. Includes cash income from machine hire, custom work, other farm business-related income, forest product sales and custom feeding fees.

3. The estimated physical change in livestock and crops owned by farmers, valued at average prices prevailing during the year.

4. Includes operator dwellings. New data sources and methods are used in deriving the gross imputed rental income and expenses related to farm dwellings.

Source: U.S. Department of Agriculture and Tennessee Department of Agriculture, Tennessee Agricultural Statistics Service, *Tennessee Agriculture, 1994*, and earlier editions (formerly titled *Tennessee Agricultural Statistics*); and *Agricultural Trends in Tennessee*.

TABLE 11.4-- FARM BALANCE SHEET, TENNESSEE, 1988–1992

Item	1992	1991	1990	1989	1988
	Millions of dollars				
TOTAL FARM ASSETS	15,648.4	14,695.9	14,830.5	14,946.5	14,359.0
Real estate	10,728.6	9,940.4	10,074.6	10,274.8	9,978.2
Livestock and poultry	1,297.5	1,265.6	1,319.4	1,267.4	1,219.9
Machinery and motor vehicles	1,977.5	1,965.9	1,969.3	1,979.9	1,866.0
Crops[1]	304.7	338.2	350.0	378.8	293.4
Purchased inputs	43.1	31.3	34.0	28.6	33.0
Financial	1,277.0	1,154.5	1,083.3	1,017.0	968.5
TOTAL FARM DEBT	1,976.8	1,987.8	1,993.3	1,966.6	2,016.0
Real estate[2]	1,056.4	1,036.2	1,056.2	1,068.9	1,095.7
Nonreal estate[3]	920.4	951.5	937.1	897.7	920.3
EQUITY	13,671.5	12,708.1	12,837.2	12,979.9	12,343.0
	Percent				
RATIOS					
Debt to equity	14.5	15.6	15.5	15.2	16.3
Debt to assets	12.6	13.5	13.4	13.2	14.0

Note: Includes farm households. Data are for farms with sales of $1,000 or more annually.

1. All crops held on farms including value above loan rates for crops held under CCC.

2. Includes CCC storage and drying facilities loans.

3. Includes debt owed to both institutional and noninstitutional lenders.

Source: U.S. Department of Agriculture and Tennessee Department of Agriculture, Tennessee Agricultural
Statistics Service, *Tennessee Agriculture, 1994* (previously titled *Tennessee Agricultural Statistics*).

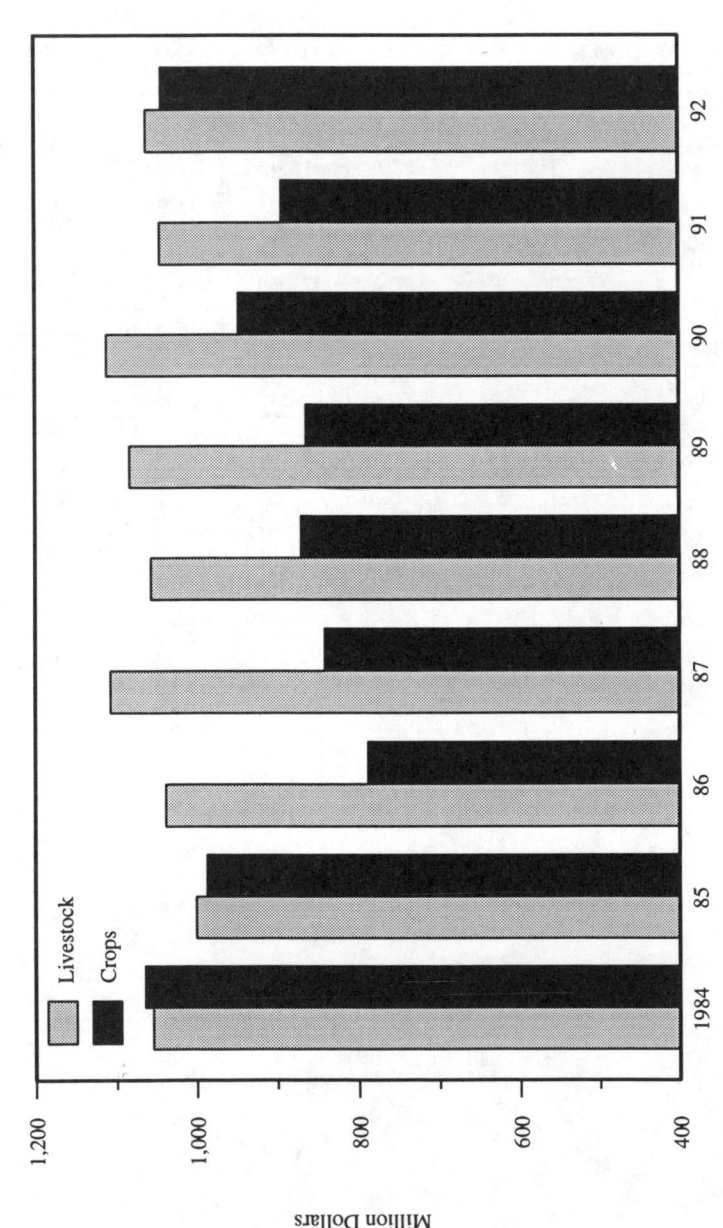

FIGURE 11.1

Cash Receipts: Livestock and Crops, Tennessee, 1984–1992

Source: U.S. Department of Agriculture, Economic Research Service, *Economic Indicators of the Farm Sector, State Financial Summary, 1992,* and earlier editions.

TABLE 11.5-- CASH RECEIPTS, BY COMMODITY, TENNESSEE, 1989–1992 [In thousands of dollars]

Commodity	1992		1991 [r]		1990 [r]		1989 [r]	
	Value	Percent of total	Value	Percent of total	Value	Percent of total	Value	Percent of total
All commodities	2,103,471	100.0	1,936,439	100.0	2,056,909	100.0	1,945,650	100.0
Livestock products	1,061,246	50.5	1,043,782	53.9	1,110,587	54.0	1,082,435	55.6
Meat animals	579,972	27.6	598,953	30.9	635,830	30.9	611,362	31.4
Cattle, calves	478,167	22.7	484,791	25.0	497,213	24.2	451,524	23.2
Hogs	101,609	4.8	113,768	5.9	138,247	6.7	159,393	8.2
Dairy products	287,980	13.7	260,985	13.5	302,606	14.7	285,316	14.7
Milk, retail	n.a.	n.a.	n.a.	n.a.	1,256	0.1	1,726	0.1
Milk, wholesale	287,980	13.7	260,985	13.5	301,350	14.7	283,590	14.6
Poultry and eggs	169,198	8.0	159,782	8.3	147,641	7.2	167,599	8.6
Eggs, chicken	15,895	0.8	18,763	1.0	16,204	0.8	21,557	1.1
Miscellaneous livestock	24,096	1.1	24,062	1.2	24,510	1.2	18,158	0.9
Crops	1,042,225	49.5	892,657	46.1	946,322	46.0	863,215	44.4
Wheat	39,399	1.9	21,533	1.1	48,749	2.4	67,648	3.5
Feed crops	113,120	5.4	89,032	4.6	99,433	4.8	100,614	5.2
Corn	79,857	3.8	57,313	3.0	66,831	3.2	70,530	3.6
Hay	23,739	1.1	23,010	1.2	25,775	1.3	26,243	1.3
Sorghum, grain	9,524	0.5	8,709	0.4	6,827	0.3	3,841	0.2
Cotton	246,996	11.7	173,251	8.9	196,810	9.6	168,046	8.6
Cotton lint	219,439	10.4	156,085	8.1	176,152	8.6	151,433	7.8
Cottonseed	27,557	1.3	17,166	0.9	20,658	1.0	16,613	0.9
Tobacco	246,389	11.7	209,638	10.8	186,379	9.1	147,509	7.6
Soybean	179,967	8.6	184,681	9.5	192,142	9.3	176,007	9.0
Vegetables	47,224	2.2	48,160	2.5	47,990	2.3	34,414	1.8
Snap beans	6,813	0.3	1,992	0.1	2,047	0.1	2,184	0.1
Tomatoes	15,120	0.7	17,766	0.9	20,640	1.0	12,600	0.6
Other vegetables	25,291	1.2	28,402	1.5	25,303	1.2	19,630	1.0
Fruits and nuts	10,563	0.5	10,594	0.5	9,276	0.5	8,953	0.5
Apples	2,184	0.1	2,001	0.1	1,523	0.1	1,480	0.1
Other fruits and nuts	8,379	0.4	8,593	0.4	7,753	0.4	7,473	0.4
All other crops	158,350	7.5	155,177	8.0	165,543	8.0	160,024	8.2
Greenhouse nursery	130,682	6.2	128,646	6.6	135,540	6.6	128,944	6.6
Other crops	27,668	1.3	26,531	1.4	30,003	1.5	31,080	1.6

Note: "Other" and "miscellaneous" categories include commodities which are not enumerated separately for the state, as well as items protected for reasons of confidentiality. Percentages were computed by the Center for Business and Economic Research.

r revised.

n.a. not available.

Source: U.S. Department of Agriculture, Economic Research Service, *Economic Indicators of the Farm Sector, State Financial Summary, 1992.*

TABLE 11.6-- PRODUCTION OF SELECTED CROPS, TENNESSEE, 1950–1993, SELECTED YEARS

Commodity	1993	1992	1991	1990	1989	1980	1970	1960	1950
Hay (all types)									
Production (1,000 tons)	3,478	3,465	3,263	3,255	3,499	1,764	1,718	1,717	1,965
Average yield per acre (tons)	2.05	2.17	1.98	2.17	2.06	1.49	1.55	1.29	1.25
Soybeans (for beans)									
Production (1,000 bu.)	30,690	33,250	31,500	33,750	29,760	45,900	26,450	8,865	3,822
Average yield per acre (bu.)	31.0	35.0	30.0	27.0	24.0	18.0	23.0	22.5	21.0
Corn (for grain)									
Production (1,000 bu.)	46,200	79,360	43,860	43,860	56,710	29,440	25,605	52,806	66,170
Average yield per acre (bu.)	84.0	124.0	86.0	86.0	107.0	46.0	45.0	39.0	32.5
Cotton									
Lint-production[1] (1,000 bales)	545	834	701	495	476	200	392	583	409
Seed-production (1,000 tons)	216	332	277	192	176	82	160	238	165
Average yield per acre, lint (lbs.)	425	651	552	461	497	349	483	545	310
Wheat									
Production (1,000 bu.)	13,940	13,440	7,680	17,640	18,900	18,620	6,545	3,288	3,050
Average yield per acre (bu.)	41.0	48.0	24.0	36.0	42.0	38.0	35.0	24.0	12.5
Tobacco (all types)									
Production (1,000 lbs.)	139,423	146,556	121,524	112,218	79,820	111,931	114,269	115,336	132,385
Average yield per acre (lbs.)	1,993	2,030	1,969	2,094	1,754	1,728	2,123	1,561	1,284
Snap beans									
Production (tons)	6,600	7,100	8,300	8,900	9,100	12,710	26,850	20,400	13,700
Average yield per acre (tons)	1.70	1.78	1.66	1.78	1.75	1.05	2.20	2.20	1.91
Sorghum (for silage)									
Production (1,000 tons)	36	72	91	42	66	132	88	180	n.a.
Average yield per acre (tons)	9	18	13	14	11	11	11	9	n.a.
Sorghum (for grain)									
Production (1,000 bu.)	3,120	5,600	4,225	4,235	2,025	1,750	1,224	1,088	n.a.
Average yield per acre (bu.)	80	80	65	77	75	50	51	34	n.a.
Tomatoes									
Production (1,000 cwt.)	704	720	846	860	504	407	242	230	441
Average yield per acre (cwt.)	160	160	180	200	140	110	115	85	76

n.a. not available.

1. Bales of 500 pounds gross weight through 1963. Beginning with 1964, production is given in 480 pound net weight bales.

Source: U.S. Department of Agriculture and Tennessee Department of Agriculture, Tennessee Agricultural Statistics Service, *Tennessee Agriculture, 1994,* and earlier editions (formerly titled *Tennessee Agricultural Statistics*); and *Agricultural Trends in Tennessee.*

TABLE 11.7-- NUMBER AND VALUE OF LIVESTOCK ON FARMS, TENNESSEE, JANUARY 1, 1930–1994, SELECTED YEARS [In thousands]

Year	Cattle		Milk cows, number [1]	Hogs[2]		Sheep and lambs	
	Number	Value		Number	Value	Number	Value
1994	2,440	$1,342,000	175	470	$34,310	12	$1,104
1993	2,300	1,253,500	190	600	38,400	16	1,360
1992	2,290	1,213,700	195	670	44,890	13	1,131
1991	2,250	1,260,000	195	620	53,320	14	1,232
1990	2,300	1,207,500	195	700	56,350	12	1,128
1989	2,300	1,184,500	198	1,000	66,500	10	785
1988	2,300	1,069,500	198	820	65,190	12	876
1987	2,400	804,000	198	770	70,070	13	988
1986	2,500	800,000	205	950	65,550	10	670
1985	2,535	823,875	210	1,100	78,100	9	572
1984	2,750	866,250	214	950	50,825	6	348
1983	2,675	949,625	217	750	64,875	8	508
1982	2,500	862,500	215	900	59,850	10	560
1981	2,350	951,750	215	1,140	77,520	11	583
1980	2,300	1,081,000	214	920	67,620	12	504
1975	3,300	445,500	217	1,395	30,690	21	599
1970	2,308	369,280	296	922	20,007	50	975
1965	2,240	215,040	437	1,453	23,539	95	1,216
1960	1,858	219,244	532	970	24,929	245	3,944
1955	1,771	116,886	695	1,371	30,573	286	4,376
1950	1,490	150,490	668	1,316	17,371	251	4,317
1945	1,483	73,112	666	1,450	8,410	333	3,330
1940	1,211	39,236	564	1,002	5,592	402	2,653
1935	1,233	19,632	594	982	9,525	411	1,877
1930	992	44,045	468	1,035	8,901	368	3,533

1. In years prior to 1970 the definition is "cows and heifers 2 years and older kept for milk." Beginning in 1970 the definition is "milk cows that have calved."

2. Data are as of December 1 of the previous year.

Source: U.S. Department of Agriculture and Tennessee Department of Agriculture, Tennessee Agricultural Statistics Service, *Tennessee Agriculture, 1994*, and earlier editions (formerly titled *Agricultural Statistics*); and *Agricultural Trends in Tennessee*.

TABLE 11.8-- MANUFACTURED DAIRY PRODUCTS, TENNESSEE, 1970–1993, SELECTED YEARS

	(1,000 pounds)			
Year	Creamery butter	American cheese made from whole milk	Cottage cheese curd	Cottage cheese creamed
1993	(D)	(D)	5,348	5,988
1992	(D)	(D)	5,585	6,435
1991	(D)	(D)	5,262	6,151
1990	(D)	9,950	6,289	6,668
1989	(D)	6,018	6,139	7,865
1988	(D)	(D)	7,592	8,967
1987	(D)	(D)	7,128	8,284
1986	(D)	(D)	(D)	(D)
1985	(D)	(D)	7,099	9,625
1984	(D)	10,613	6,970	9,297
1983	28,463	21,696	6,768	9,173
1982	27,329	19,274	5,981	8,896
1981	26,785	20,834	3,961	6,034
1980	23,285	21,826	4,439	6,357
1979	21,697	20,279	4,846	7,292
1978	20,675	18,892	4,898	6,961
1977	21,263	20,509	4,458	6,831
1976	18,277	20,536	4,787	7,002
1975	19,121	21,389	4,994	7,726
1974	16,839	27,051	5,257	7,555
1970	12,762	36,253	7,971	11,523

	(1,000 gallons)					
Year	Total ice cream	Sherbet (milk)	Ice milk	Ice cream mix	Ice milk mix	Milk sherbet mix
1993	17,137	786	5,640	8,908	2,689	589
1992	17,651	647	5,618	9,172	2,503	522
1991	17,006	811	4,007	9,244	2,769	553
1990	15,291	894	5,405	8,408	3,499	558
1989	18,611	867	5,587	9,856	4,238	619
1988	18,800	923	5,562	10,155	2,970	625
1987	21,267	1,005	6,794	11,049	2,900	662
1986	21,075	909	6,023	10,468	2,710	640
1985	19,119	918	6,636	9,702	2,769	590
1984	19,135	933	5,536	9,823	2,397	601
1983	18,633	916	5,413	9,507	2,379	588
1982	19,053	899	4,912	9,577	2,293	587
1981	18,095	1,031	5,164	9,236	2,501	670
1980	18,751	1,141	5,772	9,592	3,000	746
1979	18,371	1,114	6,446	9,360	3,183	741
1978	19,417	1,247	7,496	9,614	3,676	815
1977	18,008	1,454	7,665	9,562	4,053	858
1976	17,441	1,115	7,823	8,860	4,044	720
1975	18,465	1,261	8,892	9,353	4,532	813
1974	16,713	1,324	8,849	10,580	5,008	854
1970	15,827	1,465	9,829	9,539	6,320	908

(D) Withheld to avoid disclosing individual operations.

Source: U.S. Department of Agriculture and Tennessee Department of Agriculture, Tennessee, Agricultural Statistics Service, *Tennessee Agriculture, 1994* (previously titled *Tennessee Agricultural Statistics*).

TABLE 11.9-- EGG PRODUCTION, PRICE, AND VALUE OF PRODUCTION, TENNESSEE, 1960-1993

Year	Average number of layers during year (1,000 birds)	Eggs per layer (number)	Eggs produced (millions)	Price per dozen [1] (¢)	Value of production [2] ($1,000)
1993	1,091	236	258	50.0	10,750
1992	1,168	241	282	55.0	12,925
1991	1,112	250	279	80.7	18,763
1990	1,217	227	277	70.2	16,204
1989	1,612	241	389	66.5	21,557
1988	2,120	251	532	46.0	20,393
1987	2,684	250	670	46.0	25,683
1986	2,637	251	663	61.1	33,758
1985	2,948	256	756	56.7	35,721
1984	2,901	256	744	71.0	44,020
1983	3,232	254	822	59.6	40,826
1982	3,649	242	884	63.3	46,631
1981	3,747	246	922	67.0	51,479
1980	3,961	243	962	56.5	45,294
1979	4,050	247	999	58.6	48,785
1978	4,016	243	974	53.4	43,343
1977	4,178	238	993	57.8	47,829
1976	4,136	235	974	59.0	47,889
1975	4,238	235	1,002	55.2	46,092
1974	4,295	237	1,028	58.2	49,858
1973	4,697	231	1,088	56.4	51,136
1972	4,832	230	1,113	37.0	34,318
1971	4,725	213	1,010	37.0	31,142
1970	5,228	203	1,064	43.0	38,127
1969	4,673	207	965	42.4	34,097
1968	5,013	205	1,029	36.6	31,385
1967	5,289	199	1,052	32.9	28,843
1966	4,900	198	972	39.9	32,319
1965	4,982	193	963	36.7	29,451
1964	5,058	194	979	36.3	29,614
1963	4,853	190	922	37.6	28,889
1962	4,916	189	927	36.1	27,888
1961	4,871	187	909	37.6	28,482
1960	5,228	183	957	38.0	30,305

Note: Annual estimates cover the period December 1 previous year through November 30 current year.

1. Average of all eggs sold by producers, including hatching eggs.

2. Includes home consumption by producers.

Source: U.S. Department of Agriculture and Tennessee Department of Agriculture, Tennessee Agricultural Statistics Service, *Tennessee Agriculture, 1994* (previously titled *Tennessee Agricultural Statistics*).

TABLE 11.10--FARM PRODUCTION EXPENSES, TENNESSEE, 1988–1992 [In millions of dollars]

Item	1992	1991 [r]	1990 [r]	1989 [r]	1988 [r]
Total	1,997.7	1970.5	1,996.5	1,992.2	2,046.6
Feed	177.6	153.0	180.8	217.7	227.8
Livestock	95.6	89.0	78.2	66.6	127.3
Seed	66.3	69.0	62.2	61.7	58.0
Fertilizer and lime	124.3	126.1	126.1	131.3	139.8
Pesticides	76.6	75.7	65.2	61.8	51.9
Fuel and oil	71.8	72.8	74.9	62.2	62.3
Electricity	23.5	25.0	25.1	25.8	23.3
Repair and maintenance	147.4	175.4	173.6	175.2	168.8
Other operations[1]	242.0	239.5	224.2	221.0	243.7
Interest					
Real estate	85.7	91.4	102.4	107.4	110.6
Nonreal estate	80.1	82.3	88.7	92.9	93.3
Labor expenses[2]	151.8	148.4	153.8	131.5	120.7
Net rent to landlords	115.3	95.6	103.8	91.7	96.3
Capital consumption[3]	469.3	462.1	470.2	482.2	461.6
Property taxes	70.5	65.4	67.4	63.1	61.3

Note: Includes operator households.

r revised.

1. Includes machine hire and custom work expenses; marketing, storage, and transportation expenses; and miscellaneous expenses.

2. Includes contract labor expenses, hired labor wages, perquisites, and Social Security payments.

3. Includes depreciation and accidental damage.

Source: U.S. Department of Agriculture and Tennessee Department of Agriculture, Tennessee Agricultural Statistics Service, *Tennessee Agriculture, 1994* (previously titled *Tennessee Agricultural Statistics*).

TABLE 11.11–INDEX NUMBERS OF PRICES RECEIVED BY FARMERS, TENNESSEE, MONTHLY, 1980–1993, SELECTED YEARS [1977 = 100]

Year	Jan.	Feb.	March	April	May	June	July	August	Sept.	Oct.	Nov.	Dec.	Average
						All farm products							
1993	140	144	145	143	143	144	147	146	143	139	141	142	143
1992	138	144	139	137	141	141	142	143	139	137	136	139	140
1991ʳ	140	145	143	142	145	143	146	146	143	139	137	135	142
1990	146	148	144	147	151	148	151	150	146	144	141	144	147
1989	144	143	144	138	137	140	139	141	138	140	142	143	141
1988	129	131	133	132	136	135	138	141	139	139	138	141	136
1985	128	128	128	129	126	125	121	119	118	118	118	117	123
1980	133	135	129	123	122	125	130	135	137	138	141	139	132
						All crops							
1993	107	117	115	114	110	110	116	114	112	111	114	118	113
1992	111	118	111	111	113	114	110	108	105	105	105	106	110
1991ʳ	107	116	112	113	111	111	109	111	110	109	108	107	110
1990	112	115	107	114	115	114	114	113	112	114	109	110	112
1989	120	119	121	118	118	116	114	110	105	108	109	109	114
1988	101	101	104	107	112	120	126	122	121	117	117	119	114
1985	124	111	112	112	111	111	108	104	101	100	97	99	108
1980	110	110	107	105	105	106	112	117	123	124	131	127	115
						All livestock							
1993	170	168	171	170	173	175	175	174	172	165	165	164	170
1992	162	169	164	161	166	165	171	175	170	166	165	169	167
1991ʳ	167	172	171	168	177	172	179	178	173	167	164	160	171
1990	177	178	178	178	184	180	185	184	177	174	171	175	178
1989	166	165	165	157	155	163	162	170	168	170	172	173	166
1988	154	158	160	155	157	147	148	158	156	160	156	161	156
1985	145	144	143	143	140	139	132	133	133	134	137	134	138
1980	153	157	149	139	139	142	146	151	151	151	150	149	148

r revised.

Source: U.S. Department of Agriculture and Tennessee Department of Agriculture, Tennessee Agricultural Statistics Service, *Tennessee Agriculture, 1994* (previously titled *Tennessee Agricultural Statistics*).

TABLE 11.12--AVERAGE PRICES RECEIVED BY FARMERS FOR SELECTED CROPS, LIVESTOCK, AND POULTRY PRODUCTS, BY TYPE OF PRODUCT, TENNESSEE, 1960–1993, SELECTED YEARS

Commodity	1993	1992	1991	1990	1989	1980	1970	1960
Crops								
Cotton								
Lint (¢ per lb.)	58.7 [p]	53.1	53.9	65.8	63.0	78.4	22.1	31.4
Seed ($ per ton)	95.5 [p]	86.0	62.5	112.0	102.0	128.0	53.8	41.7
Tobacco ($ per lb.)	1.86	1.85	1.83	1.78	1.73	1.61	0.70	0.61
Corn ($ per bushel)	2.55 [p]	2.10	2.50	2.43	2.50	3.50	1.55	1.12
Hay ($ per ton)	50.50	52.00	51.00	49.00	48.50	46.00	29.00	25.60
Soybeans ($ per bushel)	6.60 [p]	5.61	5.73	5.95	5.99	7.88	2.79	2.04
Wheat ($ per bushel)	2.80 [p]	3.40	2.85	3.03	3.65	3.80	1.34	1.77
Sorghum ($ per bushel)	2.38 [p]	1.99	2.35	2.26	2.32	2.97	1.20	1.00
Snap beans ($ per ton)	233.00	227.00	240.00	230.00	240.00	211.00	113.80	122.00
Tomatoes ($ per cwt.)	27.00	21.00	21.00	24.00	25.00	21.20	10.40	6.89
Apples (¢ per lb.)	17.30	17.60	15.40	17.90	14.80	16.40	5.66	4.29
Peaches (¢ per lb.)	38.00	35.40	30.00	37.00	36.90	17.80	6.77	4.89
Livestock								
Beef cattle ($ per cwt.)	64.70	63.80	65.40	65.50	61.70	52.00	24.30	17.70
Calves ($ per cwt.)	85.00	80.90	93.30	88.10	85.00	70.40	35.00	22.60
Milk ($ per cwt.)	13.60	14.00	12.70	14.70	13.80	13.30	5.69	4.23
Hogs ($ per cwt.)	43.50	39.30	46.80	50.40	39.90	38.20	22.50	15.20
Sheep ($ per cwt.)	28.50	26.00	20.20	23.00	24.60	19.50	7.70	5.10
Lambs ($ per cwt.)	61.40	59.70	53.90	55.90	64.00	62.10	26.00	18.90
Wool (¢ per lb.)	38.00	40.00	39.00	37.00	80.00	73.00	43.00	50.00
Poultry								
Eggs (¢ per doz.)	50.00	55.00	54.70	52.00	51.70	56.50	43.00	38.00
Commercial broilers (¢ per lb.)	33.00	30.00	29.50	30.00	34.00	25.00	14.10	16.10

Note: Prices are season or marketing year averages. See original source for specific time periods for each commodity.

p preliminary.

Source: U.S. Department of Agriculture and Tennessee Department of Agriculture, Tennessee Agricultural Statistics Service, *Tennessee Agriculture, 1994*, and earlier editions (formerly titled *Tennessee Agricultural Statistics*); and *Agricultural Trends in Tennessee.*

TABLE 11.13--SELECTED FARM STATISTICS, COUNTIES, 1992

County	Number of farms	Average size (acres)	Average dollar value of land and buildings per farm	Value of farm products sold Amount ($1,000)	Value of farm products sold Average per farm ($)	Operators with major occupation farming
Anderson	441	95	198,332	5,646	12,804	120
Bedford	1,259	170	176,926	59,101	46,943	562
Benton	355	177	149,064	4,328	12,193	110
Bledsoe	502	185	163,324	11,567	23,042	229
Blount	1,012	95	227,358	17,385	17,179	362
Bradley	704	130	233,914	42,519	60,397	301
Campbell	425	71	114,827	3,860	9,082	144
Cannon	712	136	118,771	13,617	19,125	272
Carroll	783	211	147,098	21,617	27,608	304
Carter	662	55	105,477	6,999	10,572	203
Cheatham	512	114	153,544	6,766	13,216	204
Chester	347	206	133,857	7,025	20,244	142
Claiborne	1,565	91	130,201	23,913	15,280	656
Clay	507	139	109,996	6,321	12,468	181
Cocke	995	84	113,533	14,822	14,897	405
Coffee	838	158	184,171	29,288	34,950	359
Crockett	425	341	358,929	36,875	86,764	247
Cumberland	639	152	196,503	16,144	25,264	241
Davidson	440	108	346,853	5,968	13,563	145
Decatur	443	196	113,877	5,759	13,000	151
DeKalb	775	124	127,149	18,488	23,856	290
Dickson	1,012	143	160,725	11,454	11,318	368
Dyer	510	453	449,501	48,880	95,844	291
Fayette	671	385	357,037	50,051	74,592	297
Fentress	453	156	147,637	18,824	41,555	186
Franklin	1,022	133	190,470	41,613	40,717	436
Gibson	898	303	280,966	62,444	69,537	482
Giles	1,426	180	168,801	30,033	21,061	548
Grainger	1,242	84	98,323	15,541	12,513	521
Greene	3,380	70	110,912	52,665	15,581	1,353
Grundy	353	121	152,598	23,270	65,921	178
Hamblen	769	74	159,455	13,990	18,192	284
Hamilton	559	112	204,939	11,329	20,266	185
Hancock	736	109	80,328	8,376	11,380	357
Hardeman	457	350	269,809	15,532	33,988	183
Hardin	517	213	151,408	8,400	16,248	225
Hawkins	1,933	80	109,419	19,026	9,843	672
Haywood	432	519	473,458	50,314	116,468	269
Henderson	767	191	159,942	20,405	26,604	281
Henry	779	246	204,085	31,210	40,064	340
Hickman	642	203	192,271	8,720	13,582	262
Houston	241	184	142,270	3,396	14,089	90
Humphreys	505	236	302,475	9,014	17,849	193
Jackson	667	131	90,611	5,709	8,559	269
Jefferson	1,234	80	170,283	18,569	15,048	438
Johnson	828	66	99,128	8,059	9,733	298
Knox	1,157	81	254,326	13,871	11,989	417
Lake	85	1,075	1,217,662	23,925	281,473	60
Lauderdale	472	387	420,562	37,123	78,650	249
Lawrence	1,424	138	170,198	25,731	18,070	480

425

TABLE 11.13--SELECTED FARM STATISTICS, COUNTIES, 1992 (Continued)

County	Number of farms	Average size (acres)	Average dollar value of land and buildings per farm	Value of farm products sold Amount ($1,000)	Value of farm products sold Average per farm ($)	Operators with major occupation farming
Lewis	195	190	164,796	2,448	12,553	72
Lincoln	1,578	174	165,498	38,686	24,516	629
Loudon	715	103	243,652	38,546	53,910	256
McMinn	970	127	177,402	32,929	33,947	370
McNairy	605	201	157,306	13,133	21,707	227
Macon	1,359	102	93,736	17,261	12,701	482
Madison	505	280	311,830	27,166	53,794	231
Marion	278	183	223,671	8,858	31,864	106
Marshall	960	169	201,614	23,074	24,035	380
Maury	1,506	163	217,564	25,872	17,179	599
Meigs	319	176	164,306	5,039	15,797	117
Monroe	881	114	184,144	23,517	26,693	310
Montgomery	941	186	222,646	30,503	32,416	438
Moore	359	134	122,998	7,725	21,517	126
Morgan	300	144	124,855	5,213	17,378	98
Obion	697	369	347,805	51,849	74,388	362
Overton	818	129	110,963	10,591	12,947	313
Perry	219	242	150,694	3,573	16,316	96
Pickett	395	95	96,570	4,955	12,544	140
Polk	251	125	214,379	19,037	75,844	111
Putnam	1,081	108	153,251	13,305	12,308	389
Rhea	346	152	155,430	7,908	22,855	136
Roane	510	103	140,310	4,825	9,462	189
Robertson	1,447	161	207,212	57,025	39,409	700
Rutherford	1,417	141	229,100	21,170	14,940	508
Scott	235	139	169,804	5,120	21,787	64
Sequatchie	164	151	166,212	3,094	18,865	67
Sevier	863	86	261,624	9,554	11,071	331
Shelby	609	238	493,974	28,305	46,477	213
Smith	1,115	135	120,360	14,799	13,272	432
Stewart	342	157	183,484	5,226	15,280	118
Sullivan	1,331	70	198,654	22,318	16,768	511
Sumner	1,669	106	200,346	30,562	18,312	629
Tipton	588	312	343,309	39,904	67,864	270
Trousdale	389	142	168,770	7,632	19,620	191
Unicoi	237	48	128,881	1,555	6,561	86
Union	541	91	155,583	5,395	9,973	235
Van Buren	210	157	127,979	4,062	19,344	83
Warren	1,313	126	147,767	56,453	42,996	597
Washington	1,856	63	170,502	44,778	24,126	737
Wayne	617	203	129,722	6,423	10,411	208
Weakley	857	238	178,894	46,265	53,985	374
White	1,043	119	130,386	17,833	17,098	384
Williamson	1,296	158	358,284	25,474	19,656	475
Wilson	1,637	131	200,250	19,062	11,645	648

Source: U.S. Department of Commerce, Bureau of the Census, *1992 Census of Agriculture, Tennessee.*

TABLE 11.14--FARM OPERATOR CHARACTERISTICS, COUNTIES, 1987

		All farms		Type of organization[2] (%)		
County	Number	Percent full owners	Percent with nonfarm principal occupation[1]	Individual or family	Partner- ship	Corpo- ration
Anderson	463	70.2	72.1	93.3	5.8	0.9
Bedford	1,244	74.9	57.3	91.6	6.8	1.4
Benton	392	71.7	68.1	93.4	5.6	1.0
Bledsoe	482	72.0	54.4	93.4	5.8	0.4
Blount	1,185	66.9	64.4	91.4	7.6	0.6
Bradley	738	73.0	64.0	90.7	8.1	0.9
Campbell	470	78.7	68.1	92.6	7.0	0.0
Cannon	694	75.2	65.9	92.1	7.5	0.1
Carroll	848	70.5	59.1	89.4	9.4	0.5
Carter	686	70.6	73.5	93.3	6.4	0.1
Cheatham	567	68.1	67.0	87.8	9.9	1.9
Chester	387	64.1	59.2	90.2	9.0	0.8
Claiborne	1,528	75.0	58.8	88.8	10.7	0.2
Clay	528	77.5	60.8	89.0	10.2	0.4
Cocke	1,081	73.5	60.5	90.1	9.7	0.1
Coffee	887	72.6	58.7	91.5	7.6	0.6
Crockett	506	45.7	44.9	88.7	10.7	0.6
Cumberland	622	73.2	63.7	93.6	5.9	0.3
Davidson	561	73.1	71.5	87.0	10.0	2.3
Decatur	474	71.7	62.7	91.4	8.4	0.0
DeKalb	823	77.2	63.7	92.1	7.2	0.6
Dickson	1,068	75.2	65.0	90.5	9.2	0.0
Dyer	603	47.9	34.8	85.9	13.1	0.8
Fayette	765	60.5	54.9	89.4	9.2	0.9
Fentress	454	73.8	59.9	93.0	5.5	1.3
Franklin	1,126	69.4	56.3	88.7	9.6	1.2
Gibson	1,057	60.2	46.5	90.5	9.0	0.1
Giles	1,551	76.9	64.0	91.0	8.4	0.5
Grainger	1,219	76.2	60.2	90.6	8.9	0.2
Greene	3,580	73.7	59.2	89.2	10.3	0.3
Grundy	333	77.5	56.2	91.6	7.2	0.9
Hamblen	843	75.8	67.0	91.1	8.2	0.1
Hamilton	587	73.8	71.9	92.3	6.0	1.5
Hancock	760	72.9	50.4	91.4	8.6	0.0
Hardeman	488	62.1	57.0	90.0	8.2	1.6
Hardin	570	64.9	54.7	90.4	8.8	0.9
Hawkins	1,985	77.2	65.3	90.9	8.2	0.1
Haywood	527	46.7	40.0	84.8	13.1	1.5
Henderson	849	69.0	63.3	87.8	11.4	0.6
Henry	805	66.6	52.3	88.2	10.8	0.7
Hickman	650	76.0	63.4	92.6	6.6	0.3
Houston	245	74.3	64.1	92.7	7.3	0.0
Humphreys	506	68.8	63.2	91.3	7.5	1.0
Jackson	732	74.3	63.4	90.8	8.9	0.0
Jefferson	1,326	74.7	62.9	90.6	8.5	0.5
Johnson	888	79.5	63.1	90.8	9.0	0.2
Knox	1,253	72.9	68.4	93.0	5.9	0.6
Lake	85	17.6	21.2	76.5	11.8	11.8
Lauderdale	572	51.7	49.3	86.5	11.2	1.7
Lawrence	1,428	76.2	66.7	91.9	7.3	0.5

TABLE 11.14--FARM OPERATOR CHARACTERISTICS, COUNTIES, 1987 (Continued)

County		All farms		Type of organization[2] (%)		
	Number	Percent full owners	Percent with nonfarm principal occupation[1]	Individual or family	Partner-ship	Corpo-ration
Lewis	223	75.8	68.2	95.1	4.5	0.0
Lincoln	1,628	74.0	61.3	88.9	10.7	0.2
Loudon	760	74.2	67.5	90.5	8.0	0.8
McMinn	1,076	73.8	63.4	91.7	7.7	0.4
McNairy	715	67.8	61.1	92.9	7.1	0.0
Macon	1,242	76.4	65.9	89.0	10.3	0.2
Madison	614	64.8	53.1	90.6	7.3	1.0
Marion	310	67.7	68.4	91.3	8.7	0.0
Marshall	1,013	77.4	60.9	90.7	8.4	0.1
Maury	1,575	72.6	60.8	91.0	8.2	0.3
Meigs	322	73.6	65.8	90.4	9.0	0.6
Monroe	930	72.7	64.5	92.8	6.3	0.5
Montgomery	998	70.2	57.1	83.6	15.7	0.4
Moore	427	77.8	74.2	92.0	6.6	0.9
Morgan	304	66.8	74.0	93.8	5.9	0.0
Obion	761	55.8	48.5	82.1	15.5	1.7
Overton	842	77.6	62.7	91.4	6.7	1.4
Perry	220	63.6	61.8	89.5	10.0	0.0
Pickett	369	72.4	66.9	96.2	3.5	0.0
Polk	260	78.5	64.2	94.6	5.0	0.4
Putnam	1,072	75.0	62.6	93.5	6.0	0.2
Rhea	374	67.6	62.0	91.4	7.2	1.1
Roane	542	73.4	66.6	93.7	5.7	0.6
Robertson	1,543	70.1	53.0	86.2	12.6	0.6
Rutherford	1,562	73.6	67.8	93.0	6.4	0.3
Scott	239	65.3	72.4	92.1	5.4	2.5
Sequatchie	156	71.8	68.6	91.7	7.7	0.6
Sevier	953	70.4	64.5	93.3	5.4	0.8
Shelby	733	58.7	62.9	85.4	8.5	4.1
Smith	1,123	72.8	60.8	87.1	12.3	0.4
Stewart	371	67.7	67.4	93.3	6.5	0.0
Sullivan	1,432	72.4	65.4	91.5	7.5	0.4
Sumner	1,864	76.1	65.2	88.6	10.5	0.6
Tipton	650	54.6	51.8	85.8	11.8	2.0
Trousdale	439	66.3	53.1	85.0	14.6	0.0
Unicoi	266	77.1	65.4	93.6	4.9	0.8
Union	612	77.5	61.3	95.1	4.6	0.2
Van Buren	217	79.3	60.4	87.6	12.4	0.0
Warren	1,238	70.6	57.6	88.4	9.5	1.9
Washington	1,909	72.3	62.8	91.0	8.3	0.2
Wayne	698	79.9	69.9	89.8	9.0	0.4
Weakley	926	61.7	54.4	89.7	9.5	0.5
White	1,006	76.1	64.1	91.2	7.8	0.6
Williamson	1,421	73.9	67.6	87.9	9.7	1.7
Wilson	1,755	77.1	60.5	91.6	7.4	0.7

Note: Percentages were computed by the Center for Business and Economic Research.

1. Farms whose operators spent 50 percent or more of their time at nonfarm occupations. Does not apply to corporate farms.

2. Percentages representing cooperative, estate or trust, and institutional farms are not shown.

Source: U.S. Department of Commerce, Bureau of the Census, *1987 Census of Agriculture, Tennessee.*

FIGURE 11.2

Cash Receipts from Farm Marketings, Tennessee Counties, 1992

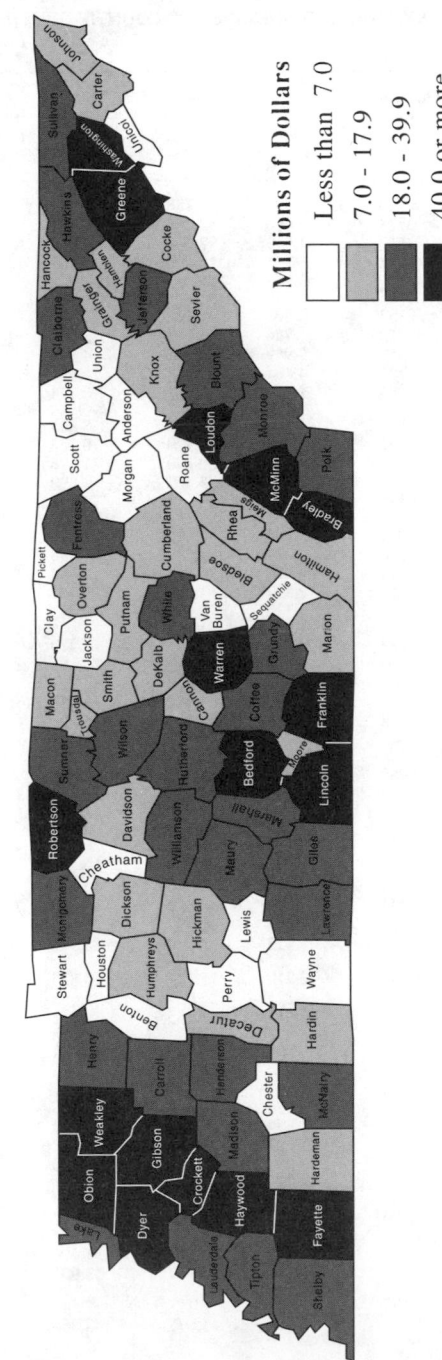

Millions of Dollars

Less than 7.0

7.0 - 17.9

18.0 - 39.9

40.0 or more

Source: U.S. Department of Commerce, Bureau of Economic Analysis, Regional Economic Measurement Division, *Regional Economic Information System 1969–1992* CD-ROM.

TABLE 11.15--FARM INCOME, BY SOURCE, TENNESSEE AND COUNTIES, 1992 [In thousands of dollars]

County	Receipts from marketing	Govern-ment pay-ments	Other income [1]	Total income	Expenses	Inventory change	Net income
Anderson	6,344	(L)	1,396	7,788	7,733	55	110
Bedford	52,029	773	5,066	57,868	48,611	608	9,865
Benton	4,567	617	1,919	7,103	7,190	237	150
Bledsoe	14,005	547	5,344	19,896	15,562	418	4,752
Blount	18,479	86	3,466	22,031	22,232	577	376
Bradley	41,848	152	3,308	45,308	33,026	113	12,395
Campbell	5,003	(L)	784	5,805	5,591	197	411
Cannon	12,932	350	1,989	15,271	14,842	496	925
Carroll	20,043	2,701	4,484	27,228	24,937	2,826	5,117
Carter	7,698	85	1,219	9,002	8,674	313	641
Cheatham	6,745	115	2,213	9,073	8,824	394	643
Chester	6,767	1,351	1,811	9,929	10,363	579	145
Claiborne	26,451	89	3,310	29,850	21,678	1,402	9,574
Clay	6,575	122	1,865	8,562	6,890	371	2,043
Cocke	16,750	231	3,674	20,655	15,584	703	5,774
Coffee	27,497	1,025	5,803	34,325	28,559	1,077	6,843
Crockett	41,087	9,330	4,223	54,640	47,695	7,057	14,002
Cumberland	13,340	754	2,674	16,768	14,053	166	2,881
Davidson	10,383	253	2,857	13,493	13,401	85	177
Decatur	7,128	409	1,132	8,669	9,213	171	-373
DeKalb	16,396	399	2,979	19,774	16,270	377	3,881
Dickson	11,262	200	3,885	15,347	15,192	465	620
Dyer	44,201	4,703	3,073	51,977	42,659	4,804	14,122
Fayette	54,064	7,152	4,206	65,422	63,461	3,537	5,498
Fentress	19,142	328	1,756	21,226	15,291	235	6,170
Franklin	42,393	1,175	4,011	47,579	40,286	1,325	8,618
Gibson	61,965	7,960	6,584	76,509	64,592	8,333	20,250
Giles	32,582	858	7,195	40,635	35,950	775	5,460
Grainger	17,914	102	2,806	20,822	14,936	930	6,816
Greene	60,303	497	10,089	70,889	59,074	2,558	14,373
Grundy	27,134	492	1,446	29,072	19,471	135	9,736
Hamblen	12,444	115	1,975	14,534	13,313	511	1,732
Hamilton	15,508	343	2,169	18,020	15,050	89	3,059
Hancock	8,907	78	1,594	10,579	8,355	605	2,829
Hardeman	14,869	3,168	3,712	21,749	18,943	1,557	4,363
Hardin	11,280	1,603	2,218	15,101	14,825	728	1,004
Hawkins	21,220	193	4,221	25,634	25,630	1,265	1,269
Haywood	51,578	11,166	4,511	67,255	54,076	9,100	22,279
Henderson	21,080	2,212	3,042	26,334	23,518	878	3,694
Henry	27,912	1,821	5,509	35,242	28,568	2,392	9,066
Hickman	8,967	228	1,977	11,172	11,797	291	-334
Houston	3,744	76	824	4,644	4,296	130	478
Humphreys	7,477	219	1,854	9,550	9,880	505	175
Jackson	6,261	98	2,502	8,861	8,408	348	801
Jefferson	22,850	117	3,297	26,264	22,950	785	4,099
Johnson	8,932	(L)	1,445	10,418	9,422	547	1,543
Knox	13,878	96	3,658	17,632	20,407	271	-2,504
Lake	25,583	1,563	1,281	28,427	20,996	2,775	10,206
Lauderdale	39,230	8,162	2,600	49,992	37,476	5,957	18,473
Lawrence	30,966	1,811	4,140	36,917	33,901	1,463	4,479
Lewis	2,062	134	581	2,777	2,943	58	-108
Lincoln	39,515	1,592	4,568	45,675	43,984	1,559	3,250

TABLE 11.15--FARM INCOME, BY SOURCE, TENNESSEE AND COUNTIES, 1992 [In thousands of dollars] (Continued)

County	Receipts from marketing	Government payments	Other income [1]	Total income	Expenses	Inventory change	Net income
Loudon	43,416	139	2,954	46,509	41,848	403	5,064
McMinn	40,036	345	4,438	44,819	37,052	478	8,245
McNairy	27,189	2,131	3,159	32,479	21,146	958	12,291
Macon	14,892	236	3,785	18,913	13,761	1,297	6,449
Madison	23,225	6,742	3,354	33,321	28,000	4,111	9,432
Marion	7,392	92	1,142	8,626	7,434	233	1,425
Marshall	25,406	193	4,097	29,696	26,435	420	3,681
Maury	29,686	501	7,580	37,767	33,809	1,242	5,200
Meigs	7,249	119	1,194	8,562	8,086	149	625
Monroe	21,857	255	4,558	26,670	24,175	617	3,112
Montgomery	30,536	1,015	6,457	38,008	29,833	2,373	10,548
Moore	6,967	(L)	1,737	8,724	8,934	114	-96
Morgan	4,356	111	610	5,077	5,068	90	99
Obion	55,960	4,247	4,829	65,036	52,783	5,925	18,178
Overton	13,682	301	2,275	16,258	12,647	379	3,990
Perry	3,060	302	1,578	4,940	3,797	218	1,361
Pickett	5,630	92	787	6,509	4,915	314	1,908
Polk	18,660	162	1,433	20,255	13,614	143	6,784
Putnam	12,612	346	5,671	18,629	16,401	426	2,654
Rhea	14,077	788	1,198	16,063	10,466	98	5,695
Roane	5,461	65	2,082	7,608	7,548	93	153
Robertson	62,720	1,428	7,560	71,708	60,736	3,930	14,902
Rutherford	24,851	822	6,137	31,810	32,663	657	-196
Scott	6,183	(L)	668	6,882	6,752	52	182
Sequatchie	3,636	148	547	4,331	3,371	107	1,067
Sevier	10,049	75	2,313	12,437	12,813	452	76
Shelby	31,696	3,587	3,840	39,123	35,816	2,252	5,559
Smith	15,867	140	2,232	18,239	16,798	830	2,271
Stewart	4,270	78	721	5,069	4,648	445	866
Sullivan	20,398	(L)	4,398	24,825	22,647	693	2,871
Sumner	37,975	519	10,456	48,950	40,359	1,695	10,286
Tipton	34,864	6,182	6,861	47,907	39,432	5,427	13,902
Trousdale	9,896	(L)	1,018	10,953	8,118	562	3,397
Unicoi	1,611	(L)	434	2,049	2,187	148	(L)
Union	5,640	(L)	1,487	7,173	5,429	324	2,068
Van Buren	3,618	69	1,277	4,964	4,029	(L)	944
Warren	73,600	972	6,085	80,657	74,049	510	7,118
Washington	45,006	190	6,711	51,907	43,952	1,417	9,372
Wayne	6,916	399	2,173	9,488	9,658	182	(L)
Weakley	44,496	4,299	4,409	53,204	40,737	3,916	16,383
White	19,094	316	2,391	21,801	21,675	443	569
Williamson	31,614	401	8,244	40,259	40,750	762	271
Wilson	22,408	132	4,822	27,362	27,680	529	211
TENNESSEE	2,055,047	115,866	313,947	2,484,860	2,142,629	118,556	460,787

1. Includes imputed income such as gross rental value of dwellings and value of home consumption and other farm related income components such as machine hire and custom work income, rental income, and income from forest products (1978 to present).

(L) Less than $50,000. Estimates are included in totals.

Source: U.S. Department of Commerce, Bureau of Economic Analysis, Regional Economic Measurement Division, *Regional Economic Information System 1969–1992 CD-ROM*.

TABLE 11.16--CASH RECEIPTS FROM FARM MARKETINGS, TENNESSEE AND COUNTIES, 1992
[In thousands of dollars]

County	Cash receipts	Percent of total	County	Cash receipts	Percent of total
Anderson			Cocke		
Marketing total	6,344	100.0	Marketing total	16,750	100.0
Livestock	3,392	53.5	Livestock	8,871	53.0
Crops	2,952	46.5	Crops	7,879	47.0
Bedford			Coffee		
Marketing total	52,029	100.0	Marketing total	27,497	100.0
Livestock	47,290	90.9	Livestock	17,231	62.7
Crops	4,739	9.1	Crops	10,266	37.3
Benton			Crockett		
Marketing total	4,567	100.0	Marketing total	41,087	100.0
Livestock	3,113	68.2	Livestock	2,236	5.4
Crops	1,454	31.8	Crops	38,851	94.6
Bledsoe			Cumberland		
Marketing total	14,005	100.0	Marketing total	13,340	100.0
Livestock	9,021	64.4	Livestock	8,741	65.5
Crops	4,984	35.6	Crops	4,599	34.5
Blount			Davidson		
Marketing total	18,479	100.0	Marketing total	10,383	100.0
Livestock	12,169	65.9	Livestock	4,394	42.3
Crops	6,310	34.1	Crops	5,989	57.7
Bradley			Decatur		
Marketing total	41,848	100.0	Marketing total	7,128	100.0
Livestock	40,817	97.5	Livestock	6,164	86.5
Crops	1,031	2.5	Crops	964	13.5
Campbell			DeKalb		
Marketing total	5,003	100.0	Marketing total	16,396	100.0
Livestock	3,189	63.7	Livestock	5,488	33.5
Crops	1,814	36.3	Crops	10,908	66.5
Cannon			Dickson		
Marketing total	12,932	100.0	Marketing total	11,262	100.0
Livestock	9,429	72.9	Livestock	6,888	61.2
Crops	3,503	27.1	Crops	4,374	38.8
Carroll			Dyer		
Marketing total	20,043	100.0	Marketing total	44,201	100.0
Livestock	6,935	34.6	Livestock	3,745	8.5
Crops	13,108	65.4	Crops	40,456	91.5
Carter			Fayette		
Marketing total	7,698	100.0	Marketing total	54,064	100.0
Livestock	4,643	60.3	Livestock	30,663	56.7
Crops	3,055	39.7	Crops	23,401	43.3
Cheatham			Fentress		
Marketing total	6,745	100.0	Marketing total	19,142	100.0
Livestock	2,241	33.2	Livestock	15,912	83.1
Crops	4,504	66.8	Crops	3,230	16.9
Chester			Franklin		
Marketing total	6,767	100.0	Marketing total	42,393	100.0
Livestock	3,191	47.2	Livestock	26,771	63.1
Crops	3,576	52.8	Crops	15,622	36.9
Claiborne			Gibson		
Marketing total	26,451	100.0	Marketing total	61,965	100.0
Livestock	12,991	49.1	Livestock	12,512	20.2
Crops	13,460	50.9	Crops	49,453	79.8
Clay			Giles		
Marketing total	6,575	100.0	Marketing total	32,582	100.0
Livestock	2,995	45.6	Livestock	28,644	87.9
Crops	3,580	54.4	Crops	3,938	12.1

TABLE 11.16--CASH RECEIPTS FROM FARM MARKETINGS, TENNESSEE AND COUNTIES, 1992
[In thousands of dollars] (Continued)

County	Cash receipts	Percent of total	County	Cash receipts	Percent of total
Grainger			Humphreys		
Marketing total	17,914	100.0	Marketing total	7,477	100.0
Livestock	8,224	45.9	Livestock	5,139	68.7
Crops	9,690	54.1	Crops	2,338	31.3
Greene			Jackson		
Marketing total	60,303	100.0	Marketing total	6,261	100.0
Livestock	34,925	57.9	Livestock	2,982	47.6
Crops	25,378	42.1	Crops	3,279	52.4
Grundy			Jefferson		
Marketing total	27,134	100.0	Marketing total	22,850	100.0
Livestock	21,597	79.6	Livestock	15,165	66.4
Crops	5,537	20.4	Crops	7,685	33.6
Hamblen			Johnson		
Marketing total	12,444	100.0	Marketing total	8,932	100.0
Livestock	7,305	58.7	Livestock	3,686	41.3
Crops	5,139	41.3	Crops	5,246	58.7
Hamilton			Knox		
Marketing total	15,508	100.0	Marketing total	13,878	100.0
Livestock	11,958	77.1	Livestock	8,206	59.1
Crops	3,550	22.9	Crops	5,672	40.9
Hancock			Lake		
Marketing total	8,907	100.0	Marketing total	25,583	100.0
Livestock	3,305	37.1	Livestock	0	0.0
Crops	5,602	62.9	Crops	25,583	100.0
Hardeman			Lauderdale		
Marketing total	14,869	100.0	Marketing total	39,230	100.0
Livestock	6,227	41.9	Livestock	3,891	9.9
Crops	8,642	58.1	Crops	35,339	90.1
Hardin			Lawrence		
Marketing total	11,280	100.0	Marketing total	30,966	100.0
Livestock	5,664	50.2	Livestock	22,123	71.4
Crops	5,616	49.8	Crops	8,843	28.6
Hawkins			Lewis		
Marketing total	21,220	100.0	Marketing total	2,062	100.0
Livestock	8,780	41.4	Livestock	1,765	85.6
Crops	12,440	58.6	Crops	297	14.4
Haywood			Lincoln		
Marketing total	51,578	100.0	Marketing total	39,515	100.0
Livestock	3,846	7.5	Livestock	27,788	70.3
Crops	47,732	92.5	Crops	11,727	29.7
Henderson			Loudon		
Marketing total	21,080	100.0	Marketing total	43,416	100.0
Livestock	16,552	78.5	Livestock	12,944	29.8
Crops	4,528	21.5	Crops	30,472	70.2
Henry			McMinn		
Marketing total	27,912	100.0	Marketing total	40,036	100.0
Livestock	12,651	45.3	Livestock	36,451	91.0
Crops	15,261	54.7	Crops	3,585	9.0
Hickman			McNairy		
Marketing total	8,967	100.0	Marketing total	27,189	100.0
Livestock	7,216	80.5	Livestock	19,698	72.4
Crops	1,751	19.5	Crops	7,491	27.6
Houston			Macon		
Marketing total	3,744	100.0	Marketing total	14,892	100.0
Livestock	2,916	77.9	Livestock	4,562	30.6
Crops	828	22.1	Crops	10,330	69.4

TABLE 11.16--CASH RECEIPTS FROM FARM MARKETINGS, TENNESSEE AND COUNTIES, 1992
[In thousands of dollars] (Continued)

County	Cash receipts	Percent of total	County	Cash receipts	Percent of total
Madison			Putnam		
Marketing total	23,225	100.0	Marketing total	12,612	100.0
Livestock	3,339	14.4	Livestock	8,260	65.5
Crops	19,886	85.6	Crops	4,352	34.5
Marion			Rhea		
Marketing total	7,392	100.0	Marketing total	14,077	100.0
Livestock	5,537	74.9	Livestock	5,812	41.3
Crops	1,855	25.1	Crops	8,265	58.7
Marshall			Roane		
Marketing total	25,406	100.0	Marketing total	5,461	100.0
Livestock	23,222	91.4	Livestock	4,303	78.8
Crops	2,184	8.6	Crops	1,158	21.2
Maury			Robertson		
Marketing total	29,686	100.0	Marketing total	62,720	100.0
Livestock	21,617	72.8	Livestock	23,199	37.0
Crops	8,069	27.2	Crops	39,521	63.0
Meigs			Rutherford		
Marketing total	7,249	100.0	Marketing total	24,851	100.0
Livestock	5,060	69.8	Livestock	21,058	84.7
Crops	2,189	30.2	Crops	3,793	15.3
Monroe			Scott		
Marketing total	21,857	100.0	Marketing total	6,183	100.0
Livestock	17,248	78.9	Livestock	3,833	62.0
Crops	4,609	21.1	Crops	2,350	38.0
Montgomery			Sequatchie		
Marketing total	30,536	100.0	Marketing total	3,636	100.0
Livestock	9,731	31.9	Livestock	2,921	80.3
Crops	20,805	68.1	Crops	715	19.7
Moore			Sevier		
Marketing total	6,967	100.0	Marketing total	10,049	100.0
Livestock	6,239	89.6	Livestock	6,773	67.4
Crops	728	10.4	Crops	3,276	32.6
Morgan			Shelby		
Marketing total	4,356	100.0	Marketing total	31,696	100.0
Livestock	3,762	86.4	Livestock	6,258	19.7
Crops	594	13.6	Crops	25,438	80.3
Obion			Smith		
Marketing total	55,960	100.0	Marketing total	15,867	100.0
Livestock	13,904	24.8	Livestock	8,208	51.7
Crops	42,056	75.2	Crops	7,659	48.3
Overton			Stewart		
Marketing total	13,682	100.0	Marketing total	4,270	100.0
Livestock	10,226	74.7	Livestock	1,285	30.1
Crops	3,456	25.3	Crops	2,985	69.9
Perry			Sullivan		
Marketing total	3,060	100.0	Marketing total	20,398	100.0
Livestock	2,318	75.8	Livestock	12,489	61.2
Crops	742	24.2	Crops	7,909	38.8
Pickett			Sumner		
Marketing total	5,630	100.0	Marketing total	37,975	100.0
Livestock	3,014	53.5	Livestock	21,452	56.5
Crops	2,616	46.5	Crops	16,523	43.5
Polk			Tipton		
Marketing total	18,660	100.0	Marketing total	34,864	100.0
Livestock	17,864	95.7	Livestock	2,791	8.0
Crops	796	4.3	Crops	32,073	92.0

TABLE 11.16--CASH RECEIPTS FROM FARM MARKETINGS, TENNESSEE AND COUNTIES, 1992
[In thousands of dollars] (Continued)

County	Cash receipts	Percent of total	County	Cash receipts	Percent of total
Trousdale			Wayne		
Marketing total	9,896	100.0	Marketing total	6,916	100.0
Livestock	3,502	35.4	Livestock	5,915	85.5
Crops	6,394	64.6	Crops	1,001	14.5
Unicoi			Weakley		
Marketing total	1,611	100.0	Marketing total	44,496	100.0
Livestock	262	16.3	Livestock	19,924	44.8
Crops	1,349	83.7	Crops	24,572	55.2
Union			White		
Marketing total	5,640	100.0	Marketing total	19,094	100.0
Livestock	2,438	43.2	Livestock	15,938	83.5
Crops	3,202	56.8	Crops	3,156	16.5
Van Buren			Williamson		
Marketing total	3,618	100.0	Marketing total	31,614	100.0
Livestock	3,091	85.4	Livestock	20,467	64.7
Crops	527	14.6	Crops	11,147	35.3
Warren			Wilson		
Marketing total	73,600	100.0	Marketing total	22,408	100.0
Livestock	19,879	27.0	Livestock	18,715	83.5
Crops	53,721	73.0	Crops	3,693	16.5
Washington			TENNESSEE		
Marketing total	45,006	100.0	Marketing total	2,055,047	100.0
Livestock	24,150	53.7	Livestock	1,061,246	51.6
Crops	20,856	46.3	Crops	993,801	48.4

Source: U.S. Department of Commerce, Bureau of Economic Analysis, Regional Economic Measurement Division, *Regional Economic Information System 1969–1992 CD-ROM*.

TABLE 11.17--RURAL FARM POPULATION, TENNESSEE AND COUNTIES, 1980 AND 1990

	Farm population[1]			Farm population[1]	
County	1990	1980	County	1990	1980
Anderson	391	717	Lewis	193	532
Bedford	1,892	2,591	Lincoln	2,455	4,086
Benton	627	867	Loudon	887	1,396
Bledsoe	709	938	McMinn	960	1,449
Blount	1,544	1,961	McNairy	847	1,527
Bradley	849	1,356	Macon	2,211	3,019
Campbell	758	950	Madison	863	1,856
Cannon	873	1,760	Marion	280	791
Carroll	1,388	2,280	Marshall	1,283	2,451
Carter	594	957	Maury	2,198	3,402
Cheatham	598	1,169	Meigs	429	434
Chester	577	861	Monroe	1,019	1,677
Claiborne	2,192	3,261	Montgomery	1,439	2,720
Clay	972	1,611	Moore	557	818
Cocke	1,431	2,622	Morgan	319	577
Coffee	1,423	2,194	Obion	1,390	3,117
Crockett	1,501	2,174	Overton	1,090	1,839
Cumberland	791	917	Perry	215	664
Davidson	81	411	Pickett	502	576
Decatur	488	1,105	Polk	529	475
DeKalb	1,109	1,459	Putnam	1,275	1,878
Dickson	1,868	2,253	Rhea	291	546
Dyer	1,028	1,917	Roane	687	855
Fayette	1,276	2,119	Robertson	2,915	4,849
Fentress	781	906	Rutherford	2,198	3,276
Franklin	1,658	2,518	Scott	135	407
Gibson	2,685	4,133	Sequatchie	203	282
Giles	2,111	3,258	Sevier	800	1,859
Grainger	1,591	2,277	Shelby	747	1,042
Greene	4,362	6,780	Smith	1,656	3,067
Grundy	590	939	Stewart	723	1,029
Hamblen	1,209	1,897	Sullivan	1,478	2,118
Hamilton	569	762	Sumner	2,608	4,063
Hancock	1,134	1,670	Tipton	1,143	1,983
Hardeman	663	1,029	Trousdale	752	1,021
Hardin	490	1,127	Unicoi	520	519
Hawkins	2,700	3,343	Union	763	1,011
Haywood	888	1,506	Van Buren	221	355
Henderson	1,448	2,151	Warren	1,774	2,995
Henry	1,810	2,636	Washington	2,641	3,744
Hickman	1,378	1,531	Wayne	542	1,566
Houston	224	408	Weakley	2,024	3,370
Humphreys	826	985	White	1,194	2,314
Jackson	965	1,433	Williamson	1,463	3,362
Jefferson	1,812	2,359	Wilson	2,447	3,042
Johnson	1,748	1,740	TENNESSEE		175,673
Knox	1,233	1,466			
Lake	201	374			
Lauderdale	845	1,907			
Lawrence	1,933	4,129			

Note: For total county population see Table 1.8. For county, urban and rural population see Table 1.14.

1. The farm population includes all persons living in rural areas on places of 1 or more acres from which at least $1,000 worth of agricultural products were sold during 1989.

Source: U.S. Department of Commerce, Bureau of the Census, *1990 Census of Population, Social and Economic Characteristics, Tennessee*; and earlier editions.

TABLE 11.18--RURAL FARM POPULATION AND PERCENT OF TOTAL POPULATION, SOUTHEASTERN STATES, 1950-1990, DECENNIAL CENSUS YEARS

State	1990 Number (1,000)	1990 %	1980 Number (1,000)	1980 %	1980[a] Number (1,000)	1980[a] %	1970 Number (1,000)	1970 %	1960 Number (1,000)	1960 %	1950 Number (1,000)	1950 %
TENNESSEE	112	2.3	176	3.8	263	5.7	317	8.1	587	16.5	1,016	30.9
Alabama	59	1.5	88	2.3	139	3.6	160	4.6	403	12.3	960	31.4
Arkansas	64	2.7	108	4.7	142	6.2	174	9.0	332	18.6	802	42.0
Florida	47	0.4	59	0.6	85	0.9	72	1.1	105	2.1	233	8.4
Georgia	80	1.2	121	2.2	164	3.0	172	3.7	407	10.3	962	27.9
Kentucky	174	4.7	245	6.7	326	8.9	382	11.9	548	18.0	974	33.1
Louisiana	40	1.0	59	1.4	85	2.0	114	3.1	233	7.2	567	21.1
Mississippi	56	2.2	85	3.4	131	5.2	210	9.5	543	24.9	1,097	50.4
North Carolina	117	1.8	188	3.2	269	4.6	375	7.4	808	17.7	1,377	33.9
South Carolina	49	1.4	54	1.7	84	2.7	112	4.3	351	14.7	701	33.1
Virginia	81	1.3	113	2.1	166	3.1	193	4.1	397	10.0	723	22.1
West Virginia	24	1.3	29	1.5	51	2.6	57	3.3	121	6.5	411	20.5

Note: Percentages computed by the Center for Business and Economic Research.

a. This set of population figures for 1980 is based on the previous farm definition which allowed a place that had as little as $50 of agricultural sales per year to qualify as a farm. For the 1980 Census, the annual dollar value of agricultural sales required for a place to be considered a farm was raised to $1,000. This definitional change is reflected in the 1980 farm population figures shown in the first column.

Source: U.S. Department of Commerce, Bureau of the Census, *1990 Census of Population, General Social and Economic Characteristics*, individual states; *Rural Population by Farm-Nonfarm Residence for Counties in the United States: 1970*; and *Characteristics of the Population*, for 1950 and 1960.

TABLE 11.19--SELECTED FARM STATISTICS, SOUTHEASTERN STATES, 1987

State	Farm acreage	Number of farms	Average size of farm (acres)	Average value of land and buildings Per farm	Per acre	Market value of products sold Total (1,000)	Per farm
TENNESSEE	11,731,386	79,711	147	$146,126	$1,001	$1,617,636	$20,294
Alabama	9,145,753	43,318	211	168,161	800	1,908,303	44,053
Arkansas	14,355,611	48,242	298	225,604	761	3,320,258	68,825
Florida	11,194,090	36,556	306	543,830	1,790	4,351,383	119,033
Georgia	10,744,718	43,552	247	226,217	920	2,814,592	64,626
Kentucky	14,012,700	92,453	152	135,696	896	2,075,571	22,450
Louisiana	8,007,173	27,350	293	268,630	940	1,340,162	49,000
Mississippi	10,746,190	34,074	315	215,209	697	1,862,903	54,672
North Carolina	9,447,705	59,284	159	199,781	1,263	3,541,419	59,737
South Carolina	4,758,631	20,517	232	201,169	871	878,683	42,827
Virginia	8,676,336	44,799	194	232,374	1,198	1,588,770	35,464
West Virginia	3,372,955	17,237	196	130,802	682	270,639	15,701

Source: U.S. Department of Commerce, Bureau of the Census, *1987 Census of Agriculture*, individual states.

TABLE 11.20–NUMBER AND PERCENT OF FARMS, BY ECONOMIC CLASS, SOUTHEASTERN STATES, 1987

State	Total	Economic class (based on farm product sales)							
		$500,000 or more	$250,000– 499,999	$100,000– 249,999	$40,000– 99,999	$20,000– 39,999	$10,000– 19,999	$5,000– 9,999	Less than $5,000
TENNESSEE									
Number	79,711	296	780	2,388	3,815	5,005	9,472	14,398	43,557
Percent	100.0	0.4	1.0	3.0	4.8	6.3	11.9	18.1	54.6
Alabama									
Number	43,318	540	1,253	2,693	2,657	2,615	4,218	6,534	22,808
Percent	100.0	1.2	2.9	6.2	6.1	6.0	9.7	15.1	52.7
Arkansas									
Number	48,242	903	2,511	5,686	4,199	3,139	4,964	7,101	19,739
Percent	100.0	1.9	5.2	11.8	8.7	6.5	10.3	14.7	40.9
Florida									
Number	36,556	1,455	1,139	2,202	3,151	3,044	3,676	4,470	17,419
Percent	100.0	4.0	3.1	6.0	8.6	8.3	10.1	12.2	47.7
Georgia									
Number	43,552	935	2,025	3,936	3,821	3,227	4,167	5,805	19,636
Percent	100.0	2.1	4.6	9.0	8.8	7.4	9.6	13.3	45.1
Kentucky									
Number	92,453	249	631	2,667	6,615	9,413	14,457	17,620	40,801
Percent	100.0	0.3	0.7	2.9	7.2	10.2	15.6	19.1	44.1
Louisiana									
Number	27,350	386	927	2,396	2,636	1,812	2,441	3,448	13,304
Percent	100.0	1.4	3.4	8.8	9.6	6.6	8.9	12.6	48.6
Mississippi									
Number	34,074	694	1,318	2,405	2,178	2,066	3,307	5,012	17,094
Percent	100.0	2.0	3.9	7.1	6.4	6.1	9.7	14.7	50.2
North Carolina									
Number	59,284	1,084	2,177	4,857	5,726	5,213	6,664	8,344	25,219
Percent	100.0	1.8	3.7	8.2	9.7	8.8	11.2	14.1	42.5

TABLE 11.20--NUMBER AND PERCENT OF FARMS, BY ECONOMIC CLASS, SOUTHEASTERN STATES, 1987 (Continued)

State	Total	Economic class (based on farm product sales)							
		$500,000 or more	$250,000– 499,999	$100,000– 249,999	$40,000– 99,999	$20,000– 39,999	$10,000– 19,999	$5,000– 9,999	Less than $5,000
South Carolina									
Number	20,517	313	478	1,114	1,343	1,395	2,039	2,900	10,935
Percent	100.0	1.5	2.3	5.4	6.5	6.8	9.9	14.1	53.3
Virginia									
Number	44,799	467	966	2,144	2,963	3,567	5,495	7,580	21,617
Percent	100.0	1.0	2.2	4.8	6.6	8.0	12.3	16.9	48.3
West Virginia									
Number	17,237	72	115	299	553	699	1,512	2,547	11,440
Percent	100.0	0.4	0.7	1.7	3.2	4.1	8.8	14.8	66.4

Note: Farms include institutional farms, experiment and research farms, and Indian reservations. Percentages computed by Center for Business and Economic Research.

Source: U.S. Department of Commerce, Bureau of the Census, *1987 Census of Agriculture*, individual states.

TABLE 11.21--FARM REAL ESTATE: VALUE OF LAND AND BUILDINGS, SOUTHEASTERN STATES
AND UNITED STATES, 1980-1992, SELECTED YEARS

State	Average value of land and buildings per acre ($)					Value of land and buildings (mil $)				
	1992	1991	1990	1989	1980	1992	1991	1990	1989	1980
TENNESSEE	985	988	996	1,002	976	12,219	12,251	12,350	12,625	13,274
Alabama	832	791	839	822	780	8,153	7,752	8,474	8,713	9,516
Arkansas	724	770	750	778	918	11,219	11,935	11,625	12,215	15,147
Florida	2,062	2,133	2,085	1,887	1,381	21,648	22,397	22,727	21,134	18,505
Georgia	902	995	1,012	998	896	10,917	12,040	12,650	12,575	13,440
Kentucky	993	962	981	911	976	13,998	13,564	13,832	12,936	14,250
Louisiana	905	905	915	954	1,256	7,961	7,964	8,144	8,681	12,686
Mississippi	738	754	728	713	819	9,441	9,651	9,464	9,483	11,957
North Carolina	1,264	1,243	1,263	1,317	1,219	12,136	11,933	12,251	13,170	14,262
South Carolina	931	948	909	939	900	4,747	4,835	4,727	4,977	5,760
Virginia	1,363	1,295	1,516	1,333	1,028	11,998	11,396	13,492	11,997	10,074
West Virginia	719	625	613	702	669	2,659	2,313	2,268	2,599	2,810
UNITED STATES	685	681	668	661	737	670,798	667,504	658,187	653,511	763,285

Source: U.S. Department of Commerce, Bureau of the Census, *Statistical Abstract of the United States, 1993*, and
earlier editions.

TABLE 11.22--TAXES ON FARM REAL ESTATE, SOUTHEASTERN STATES, 1985–1988, SELECTED YEARS

State	Amount levied on farm real estate ($1,000,000)				Taxes per acre ($)				Taxes per $100 of full value ($)			
	1988	1987	1986	1985	1988	1987	1986	1985	1988	1987	1986	1985
TENNESSEE	47.1	46.1	48.8	46.4	4.06	3.97	3.92	3.73	0.41	0.42	0.40	0.38
Alabama	11.0	10.5	12.4	12.4	1.23	1.16	1.14	1.14	0.15	0.15	0.15	0.15
Arkansas	40.0	39.5	38.1	37.0	2.83	2.79	2.69	2.61	0.37	0.39	0.38	0.31
Florida	107.2	101.9	93.0	85.3	10.04	9.34	7.60	6.97	0.56	0.58	0.53	0.46
Georgia	52.6	48.7	67.5	63.7	4.93	4.57	4.71	4.44	0.54	0.51	0.57	0.51
Kentucky	32.7	33.6	30.0	30.0	2.36	2.41	2.16	2.16	0.26	0.27	0.25	0.24
Louisiana	19.2	19.0	19.8	19.8	2.47	2.39	2.21	2.21	0.26	0.26	0.22	0.18
Mississippi	19.8	19.4	29.3	28.1	1.93	1.85	2.23	2.14	0.28	0.27	0.30	0.26
North Carolina	51.7	50.0	53.7	51.6	5.62	5.33	5.14	4.94	0.44	0.42	0.45	0.40
South Carolina	14.4	13.1	14.1	14.1	3.06	2.79	2.56	2.56	0.35	0.35	0.29	0.28
Virginia	50.2	44.5	41.5	41.5	5.83	5.16	4.57	4.57	0.49	0.45	0.40	0.42
West Virginia	3.4	3.3	3.4	3.4	1.01	0.99	0.94	0.94	0.15	0.16	0.18	0.17

Source: U.S. Department of Agriculture, Statistical Reporting Service, *Agricultural Statistics, 1990*, and earlier editions.

TABLE 11.23--TYPE OF FARM OWNERSHIP, SOUTHEASTERN STATES, 1987

State	Farm acreage	Number of farms	Family farms		Partnership farms		Corporate farms	
			Number	%	Number	%	Number	%
TENNESSEE	11,731,386	79,711	71,976	90.3	6,947	8.7	496	0.6
Alabama	9,145,753	43,318	39,553	91.3	3,014	7.0	570	1.3
Arkansas	14,355,611	48,242	42,885	88.9	3,626	7.5	1,542	3.2
Florida	11,194,090	36,556	28,943	79.2	3,289	9.0	3,961	10.8
Georgia	10,744,718	43,552	38,806	89.1	3,382	7.8	1,106	2.5
Kentucky	14,012,700	92,453	78,463	84.9	12,717	13.8	817	0.9
Louisiana	8,007,173	27,350	24,322	88.9	1,926	7.0	905	3.3
Mississippi	10,746,190	34,074	30,326	89.0	2,770	8.1	823	2.4
North Carolina	9,447,705	59,284	52,398	88.4	5,238	8.8	1,355	2.3
South Carolina	4,758,631	20,517	18,337	89.4	1,583	7.7	488	2.4
Virginia	8,676,336	44,799	39,344	87.8	4,004	8.9	1,173	2.6
West Virginia	3,372,955	17,237	15,988	92.8	971	5.6	197	1.1

Note: Percentages computed by Center for Business and Economic Research. Percentages will not add to 100 because cooperative, estate, and institutional farms are not shown separately.

Source: U.S. Department of Commerce, Bureau of the Census, *1987 Census of Agriculture*, individual states.

TABLE 11.24--FARM DEBT OUTSTANDING (INCLUDING OPERATOR HOUSEHOLDS), SOUTHEASTERN STATES, 1980-1992, SELECTED YEARS
[In millions of dollars]

State	1992 Real estate	1992 Nonreal estate	1991 Real estate	1991 Nonreal estate	1990ʳ Real estate	1990ʳ Nonreal estate	1985 Real estate	1985 Nonreal estate	1980 Real estate	1980 Nonreal estate
TENNESSEE	1,056	920	1,036	952	1,056	937	1,509	1,085	1,583	1,493
Alabama	694	772	703	698	681	690	1,312	849	1,241	1,129
Arkansas	1,766	1,340	1,697	1,407	1,643	1,372	2,062	1,581	1,967	1,642
Florida	2,613	1,009	2,585	960	2,662	968	2,893	1,039	2,334	1,294
Georgia	1,638	1,141	1,590	1,162	1,581	1,159	2,225	1,829	2,273	2,253
Kentucky	1,686	990	1,692	1,041	1,579	980	2,180	1,467	2,151	1,627
Louisiana	723	980	750	956	752	953	1,520	1,287	1,565	1,170
Mississippi	1,185	1,227	1,241	1,218	1,216	1,221	2,022	1,866	1,841	1,742
North Carolina	1,387	1,236	1,522	1,176	1,433	1,133	2,165	1,296	1,885	1,818
South Carolina	495	381	519	386	531	402	918	601	820	707
Virginia	1,224	685	1,195	726	1,161	743	1,247	980	1,149	852
West Virginia	290	113	277	117	274	121	258	90	235	125

Note: Data are for farms with annual sales of $1,000 or more. Real estate debt includes CCC storage and drying facilities loans. Nonreal estate debt includes that owed to both institutional and noninstitutional lenders. Data are as of December 31.

r revised.

Source: U.S. Department of Agriculture, Economic Research Service, *Economic Indicators of the Farm Sector, State Financial Summary, 1992*, and earlier editions.

TABLE 11.25-INDEXES OF PRICES RECEIVED AND PAID BY FARMERS, UNITED STATES, 1973–1992

Year	Prices received			Prices paid								Ratio[4]	Parity ratio[5] (1910–14=100)
	All farm products	All crops	Livestock and products	Total[1]	Total[2]	Production items							
						Feed	Seed	Fuels and energy	Interest	Taxes	Wage rates[3]		
1992[p]	139	121	157	191	174	123	162	199	167	171	210	73	48
1991	145[r]	129[r]	161[r]	189	174[r]	123	163	203	172	160	201	77	51
1990	149	127	170	184	171	128	165	204	177[r]	158[r]	193[r]	81	54
1989	147	134	160	178	165[r]	136[r]	165	180[r]	176[r]	151[r]	185[r]	83	55
1988	138	126	150	170	157	128	150	167[r]	182[r]	147[r]	171[r]	81	54
1987	127[r]	106	146	162[r]	148[r]	103	148	161	189[r]	144[r]	166[r]	78	52
1986	123	107	138	159	144	108	148	162	211[r]	134	159[r]	77	51
1985	128	120	136	162	151	116	152	201	228	133	154	79	52
1984	142	138[r]	146	164[r]	155	135	151	201	248[r]	133[r]	151	87	58[r]
1983	135	128	141	161	152	134	141	202	250	129	148	84	56
1982	133	121	145	159	153	122	141	210	242[r]	124	144	84	55[r]
1981	139	134	143	150	148	134	138	213	211[r]	123	138[r]	93	60[r]
1980	134	125	144	138	138	123	118	188	174	115	127	97	65
1979	132	116	147	123	125	110	110	137	143	107	117	107	71
1978	115	105	124	108	108	98	105	105	117	100	107	106	70
1976	102	102	101	95	97	103	92	93	88	94	93	107	71
1975	101	105	98	89	91	100	94	88	77	87	85	113	76
1974	105	117	94	81	83	104	82	79	65	81	79	130	86
1973	98	91	104	71	73	86	64	57	55	77	69	138	91

Note: Base year is 1977=100 for prices received, prices paid, and ratio unless otherwise specified.

p preliminary.

r revised.

1. Includes production items. interest, taxes, wage rates, and a family living component. The family living component is the Consumer Price Index for all urban consumers from the Bureau of Labor Statistics.

2. Includes items not shown separately.

3. Straight average of seasonally adjusted indexes.

4. Ratio of index of prices received by farmers for all farm products to index of prices paid for commodities, services, interest, taxes, and wage rates. Computed by the Center for Business and Economic Research.

5. Ratio of prices received by farmers to prices paid.

Source: U.S. Department of Commerce, Bureau of the Census, *Statistical Abstract of the United States, 1993*, and earlier editions.

TABLE 11.26--FARM MARKETINGS, 1987-1991, AND PRINCIPAL COMMODITIES RANKING, SOUTHEASTERN STATES AND UNITED STATES, 1991
[In millions of dollars]

State	Farm marketings								Principal commodities in order of marketing receipts, 1991
	1991			Rank in United States	1990 r	1989	1988	1987	
	Total	Crops	Live-stock and prod-ucts						
TENNESSEE	1,978	933	1,045	30	2,061	1,946	1,933	1,984	Cattle, dairy products, tobacco, cotton
Alabama	2,978	759	2,219	23	2,826	2,671	2,422	2,154	Broilers, cattle, greenhouse, peanuts
Arkansas	4,311	1,631	2,680	12	4,256	4,157	3,831	3,195	Broilers, cattle, soybeans, rice
Florida	6,141	4,969	1,172	8	5,744	6,238	5,820	5,454	Oranges, greenhouse, tomatoes, sugar
Georgia	3,978	1,825	2,153	13	3,866	3,908	3,570	3,124	Broilers, peanuts, eggs, cattle
Kentucky	3,179	1,475	1,704	21	3,103	2,928	2,510	2,448	Tobacco, cattle, horses, dairy products
Louisiana	1,793	1,172	621	32	1,929	1,712	1,876	1,476	Cotton, cattle, sugar, soybeans
Mississippi	2,422	1,147	1,275	28	2,433	2,276	2,305	1,987	Cotton, broilers, cattle, soybeans
North Carolina	4,924	2,316	2,608	10	4,926	4,592	4,038	3,768	Tobacco, broilers, hogs, turkeys
South Carolina	1,225	677	549	36	1,169	1,236	1,106	929	Tobacco, cattle, broilers, greenhouse
Virginia	2,095	732	1,363	29	2,122	2,039	1,914	1,759	Cattle, broilers, dairy products, tobacco
West Virginia	330	77	253	46	339	310	286	234	Cattle, broilers, dairy products, turkeys
UNITED STATES	167,292	80,547	86,745	(X)	169,920	161,027	150,192	139,468	Cattle, dairy products, corn, hogs

Note: Cattle include calves.
(X) Not applicable.
r revised.
Source: U.S. Department of Commerce, Bureau of the Census, *Statistical Abstract of the United States, 1993*, and earlier editions.

TABLE 11.27.-CASH RECEIPTS, BY COMMODITY, SOUTHEASTERN STATES, 1992 [In thousands of dollars]

State	Total	Total livestock	Percent of total	Livestock Meat animals	Dairy products	Poultry and eggs	Other livestock
TENNESSEE	2,103,471	1,061,246	50.5	579,972	287,980	169,198	24,086
Alabama	2,830,062	2,062,559	72.9	556,658	72,500	1,368,509	64,892
Arkansas	4,602,230	2,701,729	58.7	514,997	106,057	2,000,405	80,270
Florida	6,144,508	1,159,595	18.9	356,337	401,700	259,678	141,880
Georgia	4,073,125	2,309,283	56.7	459,881	229,860	1,578,285	41,257
Kentucky	3,221,305	1,641,069	50.9	839,842	284,960	78,570	437,697
Louisiana	1,846,181	587,253	31.8	173,422	135,360	210,542	67,929
Mississippi	2,601,966	1,355,116	52.1	255,649	106,500	765,236	227,731
North Carolina	5,181,017	2,794,849	53.9	918,212	215,350	1,608,773	52,514
South Carolina	1,176,746	545,246	46.3	188,491	58,099	286,879	11,777
Virginia	2,134,353	1,352,915	63.4	431,222	291,888	555,479	74,326
West Virginia	342,548	267,072	78.0	123,007	36,448	101,205	6,412

State	Total crop	Percent of total	Food grains	Feed crops	Crops Cotton	Tobacco	Oil crops	Vege- tables	Fruits and nuts	Other crops
TENNESSEE	1,042,225	49.5	39,399	113,120	246,996	246,389	180,184	47,224	10,563	158,350
Alabama	767,503	27.1	12,691	48,232	172,137	1,282	222,923	82,449	16,508	211,281
Arkansas	1,900,501	41.3	659,830	113,962	520,422		543,104	21,729	8,666	32,788
Florida	4,984,913	81.1	2,376	22,719	21,837	31,729	64,843	1,658,050	1,607,117	1,576,242
Georgia	1,763,842	43.3	47,814	152,043	212,632	170,101	649,831	245,303	89,978	196,140
Kentucky	1,580,236	49.1	65,840	300,061	0	877,357	221,305	30,278	10,605	74,790
Louisiana	1,258,928	68.2	206,400	92,785	429,039	0	192,048	76,911	15,370	246,375
Mississippi	1,246,850	47.9	148,008	62,165	667,831	0	293,436	41,999	6,820	26,591
North Carolina	2,386,168	46.1	83,295	211,153	143,928	1,049,524	327,778	201,642	46,597	322,251
South Carolina	631,500	53.7	41,880	58,072	74,433	190,448	88,001	52,678	28,047	96,941
Virginia	781,438	36.6	45,340	99,583	7,624	189,907	163,008	113,799	48,853	113,324
West Virginia	75,476	22.0	972	16,553	0	5,851	12	5,800	27,205	19,083

Note: Percentages were computed by the Center for Business and Economic Research.

Source: U.S. Department of Agriculture, Economic Research Service, *Economic Indicators of the Farm Sector, State Financial Summary, 1992.*

TABLE 11.28--GOVERNMENT PAYMENTS FOR FARM PROGRAMS, SOUTHEASTERN STATES, 1992 [In thousands of dollars]

State	Total	Feed grain	Wheat	Rice	Cotton	Wool Act	Conservation[1]	Miscellaneous[2]
TENNESSEE	115,866	12,221	6,728	92	28,911	92	27,603	40,219
Alabama	119,132	4,086	4,165	0	28,731	101	29,144	52,905
Arkansas	410,026	6,969	25,758	198,861	45,173	303	17,658	115,304
Florida	53,085	2,327	560	273	2,457	15	14,569	32,884
Georgia	182,300	14,791	13,197	0	25,525	41	32,954	95,792
Kentucky	72,125	28,989	6,209	0	0	192	29,615	7,120
Louisiana	270,835	4,070	4,339	78,784	60,908	27	10,389	112,318
Mississippi	279,904	3,568	6,649	40,763	103,746	9	39,696	85,473
North Carolina	74,805	21,048	5,400	0	9,964	85	10,809	27,499
South Carolina	72,588	10,892	6,792	0	11,717	5	13,859	29,323
Virginia	29,072	9,525	2,971	0	224	755	7,331	8,266
West Virginia	6,862	1,254	75	0	0	408	2,100	3,025

Note: Includes both cash payments and payment-in-kind (PIK).

1. Includes amount paid under agriculture and conservation programs (Conservation Reserve, Agriculture Conservation, Emergency Conservation, and Great Plains Program.)
2. Programs included are Rural Clean Water, Animal Waste Management, Forest Incentive, Water Bank, Dairy Indemnity, Dairy Termination, Extended Warehouse Storage, Extended Farm Storage, Colorado River Salinity, Livestock Emergency Assistance, Market Gains, Naval Stores Conservation, Milk Marketing Fee, Interest Penalty Payments, Disaster, Loan Deficiency, and Interest on CCC-6S.

Source: U.S. Department of Agriculture, Economic Research Service, *Economic Indicators of the Farm Sector, State Financial Summary, 1992.*

TABLE 11.29--AREA OF TIMBERLAND, BY OWNERSHIP AND STOCKING CLASSES OF GROWING-STOCK TREES, TENNESSEE, 1989 [In thousands of acres]

Ownership class	All classes	Stocking class (percent)				
		> 130	100–130	60–100	16.7–60	< 16.7
All ownerships	13,265.2	133.7	2,470.9	8,518.4	2,076.9	65.3
National forest	556.0	15.7	198.5	315.2	26.6	0.0
Other public	952.9	0.0	217.6	561.9	161.6	11.8
Forest industry	1,121.5	45.4	288.9	674.4	107.2	5.7
Forest industry leased	22.4	0.0	0.0	16.7	5.7	0.0
Other private	10,612.5	72.7	1,765.9	6,950.3	1,775.8	47.8

Source: U.S. Department of Agriculture, Forest Service, Southern Forest Experiment Station, New Orleans, direct correspondence.

TABLE 11.30--VOLUME OF GROWING STOCK AND SAWTIMBER ON COMMERCIAL FOREST LAND, TENNESSEE, 1989

Ownership class	Growing stock (million cu. ft.)			Sawtimber (million board ft.)		
	All species	Softwood	Hardwood	All species	Softwood	Hardwood
All ownerships	16,682.7	2,895.3	13,787.4	53,613.6	9,615.4	43,998.2
National forest	1,005.0	303.0	702.1	3,611.9	1,302.1	2,309.8
Other public	1,391.2	302.2	1,089.0	4,999.4	1,245.1	3,754.3
Forest industry	1,223.6	302.6	921.0	3,466.9	750.0	2,716.9
Farm	4,724.9	573.6	4,151.3	15,172.3	1,698.7	13,473.6
Miscellaneous private	8,337.9	1,414.0	6,924.0	26,363.1	4,619.4	21,743.7

Source: U.S. Department of Agriculture, Forest Service, Southern Forest Experiment Station, New Orleans, direct correspondence.

TABLE 11.31--AVERAGE ANNUAL GROWTH AND REMOVAL OF GROWING STOCK ON TIMBERLAND, BY OWNERSHIP CLASS, AND BY TYPE OF WOOD, TENNESSEE, 1980–1989 [In millions of cubic feet]

Ownership class	Net annual growth			Annual removals		
	All species	Softwood	Hardwood	All species	Softwood	Hardwood
All ownerships[1]	637.4	99.8	537.6	219.4	52.2	167.2
National forest	24.4	5.7	18.8	14.3	5.4	8.9
Other public	36.4	4.9	31.6	4.5	0.7	3.8
Forest industry	52.5	20.8	31.6	28.9	7.9	20.9
Farmer	192.8	19.4	173.4	65.8	11.9	53.9
Miscellaneous private	331.3	49.1	282.2	106.0	26.3	79.6

1. Totals may not add due to independent rounding.

Source: U.S. Department of Agriculture, Forest Service, Southern Forest Experiment Station, New Orleans, direct correspondence.

TABLE 11.32.–CHANGES IN TIMBERLAND, TENNESSEE, 1980–1989 [In thousands of acres]

Resource region	Total area[1]	Timberland	Net change	Additions from:			Diversions to:		
				Total	Agri-culture	Other[2]	Total	Agri-culture	Other[2]
All regions	26,339.1	13,265.1	305.8	824.6	574.8	249.8	518.8	283.3	235.5
West	6,007.0	1,963.0	-189.9	30.8	21.6	9.2	220.7	189.2	31.5
West Central	3,287.6	2,333.7	148.1	155.2	105.8	49.4	7.1	5.8	1.2
Central	6,163.2	2,461.3	298.9	344.7	268.1	76.6	45.8	16.7	29.1
Plateau	4,394.9	3,064.8	86.8	150.9	90.5	60.4	64.1	19.8	44.3
East	6,486.4	3,442.3	-38.1	143.0	88.8	54.2	181.1	51.7	129.4

Note: Totals may not equal sum of components due to rounding.

1. U.S. Bureau of the Census, *Land and Water Area of the United States.*

2. Includes urban, industrial, highway, noncommercial forest, water, rights-of-way, and other land uses.

Source: U.S. Department of Agriculture, Forest Service, Southern Forest Experiment Station, New Orleans, direct correspondence.

TABLE 11.33--AREA OF COMMERCIAL FOREST LAND, BY FOREST TYPE, AND BY RESOURCE
REGION, TENNESSEE, 1989 [In thousands of acres]

| Forest type | State | Resource region | | | | |
		West	West Central	Central	Plateau	East
All types	13,265.2	1,963.0	2,333.7	2,461.4	3,064.8	3,442.4
White pine-hemlock	64.0	0.0	0.0	4.9	22.4	36.7
Loblolly-shortleaf pine	1,115.3	167.9	126.8	10.2	321.1	489.3
Oak-pine	1,126.5	95.6	76.9	11.4	362.6	580.0
Red cedar	683.5	64.0	23.2	456.1	34.3	105.9
Oak-hickory	9,476.5	1,102.1	2,030.9	1,940.5	2,301.9	2,101.2
Oak-gum-cypress	639.3	490.4	75.9	38.3	16.8	17.9
Elm-ash-cottonwood	43.0	43.0	0.0	0.0	0.0	0.0
Maple-beech-birch	111.4	0.0	0.0	0.0	0.0	111.4
Not typed	5.7	0.0	0.0	0.0	5.7	0.0

Source: U.S. Department of Agriculture, Forest Service, Southern Forest Experiment Station, New Orleans, direct
correspondence.

TABLE 11.34--SELECTED DATA ON THE LUMBER AND WOOD PRODUCTS INDUSTRY, TENNESSEE,
1987 [Dollar amounts in millions]

| Sector of industry | Number of establishments | | All employees | | Production workers | | Value added by manu- facture | Value of ship- ments | New capital expen- ditures |
	Total	With 20 or more employees	Number (1,000)	Payroll	Number (1,000)	Wages			
Total lumber and wood products industry	831	193	17.9	$259.3	15.0	$191.3	$612.1	$1,333.0	$40.6
Logging	126	2	0.6	6.6	0.5	5.1	56.0	83.8	(D)
Sawmills and planing mills	345	80	9.0	133.3	7.8	102.8	289.7	632.3	26.9
Millwork, plywood, and structural members	153	46	3.3	48.9	2.7	34.2	113.4	242.4	4.5
Wood containers	87	20	1.4	17.3	1.2	12.6	31.5	69.7	(D)
Wood buildings and mobile homes	32	20	1.9	32.0	1.4	20.7	66.7	187.9	4.2
Miscellaneous wood products	88	25	1.8	21.2	1.6	15.8	54.8	117.0	(D)

Note: Includes industry groups and industries with 500 employees or more.

(D) Withheld to avoid disclosing operations of individual companies.

Source: U.S. Department of Commerce, Bureau of the Census, *1987 Census of Manufactures, Geographic Area
Series, Tennessee.*

TABLE 11.35--TOTAL LAND AREA AND FOREST LAND, BY TYPE, TENNESSEE AND COUNTIES, 1989
[Area in thousands of acres]

| County | All land [1] | Forest land | | Reserved timberland | Nonforest land |
		Total	Timberland [2]		
Anderson	216.8	124.0	124.0	0.0	92.8
Bedford	304.1	74.6	74.6	0.0	229.5
Benton	279.1	172.7	172.7	0.0	106.4
Bledsoe	260.7	186.3	186.3	0.0	74.4
Blount	357.2	165.5	69.9	95.6	191.7
Bradley	209.5	92.5	92.5	0.0	117.0
Campbell	306.6	250.3	250.2	0.1	56.2
Cannon	170.0	88.5	88.5	0.0	81.5
Carroll	383.7	169.1	169.1	0.0	214.7
Carter	218.0	161.3	155.5	5.8	56.6
Cheatham	194.3	118.2	118.2	0.0	76.1
Chester	184.7	99.4	99.4	0.0	85.3
Claiborne	276.8	167.5	167.5	0.0	109.2
Clay	145.3	105.1	105.1	0.0	40.2
Cocke	276.5	182.0	163.4	18.6	94.5
Coffee	274.2	114.4	114.2	0.2	159.8
Crockett	170.2	15.1	15.1	0.0	155.1
Cumberland	436.7	320.3	320.3	0.0	116.3
Davidson	320.5	108.7	108.1	0.6	211.8
Decatur	220.8	134.8	134.8	0.0	86.0
DeKalb	186.0	114.2	114.2	0.0	71.8
Dickson	314.0	174.3	174.3	0.0	139.7
Dyer	332.6	40.4	40.4	0.0	292.2
Fayette	451.5	152.0	152.0	0.0	299.5
Fentress	318.7	244.1	244.1	0.1	74.6
Franklin	347.5	183.4	183.0	0.4	164.1
Gibson	385.6	36.4	36.4	0.0	349.2
Giles	390.7	171.8	171.8	0.0	218.9
Grainger	174.7	102.6	102.6	0.0	72.1
Greene	395.8	179.9	171.8	8.1	215.9
Grundy	231.2	174.5	165.9	8.6	56.7
Hamblen	100.1	32.8	32.8	0.0	67.3
Hamilton	345.0	210.7	210.7	0.0	134.3
Hancock	143.0	92.9	92.9	0.0	50.1
Hardeman	429.0	247.1	247.1	0.0	181.9
Hardin	380.9	219.9	219.9	0.0	161.0
Hawkins	310.7	177.3	177.3	0.0	133.4
Haywood	341.6	71.2	71.2	0.0	270.4
Henderson	332.8	158.4	158.4	0.0	174.4
Henry	358.3	176.1	176.1	0.0	182.2
Hickman	391.8	297.2	297.2	0.0	94.6
Houston	132.4	94.2	94.2	0.0	38.3
Humphreys	356.2	241.2	241.2	0.0	115.0
Jackson	197.0	135.9	135.9	0.0	61.1
Jefferson	169.9	62.2	62.2	0.0	107.7
Johnson	190.2	144.4	144.4	0.0	45.8
Knox	323.8	127.5	127.0	0.5	196.2
Lake	107.8	18.0	18.0	0.0	89.8
Lauderdale	303.7	90.0	88.8	1.2	213.6
Lawrence	395.4	199.8	199.8	0.0	195.5

TABLE 11.35--TOTAL LAND AREA AND FOREST LAND, BY TYPE, TENNESSEE AND COUNTIES, 1989
[Area in thousands of acres] (Continued)

County	All land [1]	Forest land			Nonforest land
		Total	Timberland [2]	Reserved timberland	
Lewis	180.8	158.0	158.0	0.0	22.9
Lincoln	365.3	136.7	136.7	0.0	228.6
Loudon	150.5	62.3	62.3	0.0	88.1
McMinn	274.5	136.5	136.5	0.0	138.0
McNairy	359.4	224.4	224.4	0.0	135.0
Macon	196.6	77.0	77.0	0.0	119.6
Madison	357.2	140.7	140.7	0.0	216.6
Marion	328.0	251.7	251.7	0.0	76.2
Marshall	241.0	89.6	89.6	0.0	151.3
Maury	394.4	133.0	133.0	0.0	261.4
Meigs	121.1	82.9	82.9	0.0	38.2
Monroe	414.9	301.5	279.0	22.5	113.3
Montgomery	344.7	136.9	136.9	0.1	207.8
Moore	82.4	36.6	36.6	0.0	45.8
Morgan	334.5	287.8	276.2	11.6	46.7
Obion	352.2	67.6	67.6	0.0	284.6
Overton	277.2	170.4	170.4	0.0	106.8
Perry	271.1	223.6	223.6	0.0	47.5
Pickett	102.0	68.4	68.4	0.0	33.6
Polk	280.0	224.7	214.1	10.5	55.3
Putnam	255.5	152.5	152.3	0.1	103.0
Rhea	197.7	126.5	126.4	0.2	71.2
Roane	228.3	153.1	153.1	0.0	75.2
Robertson	304.6	53.0	53.0	0.0	251.5
Rutherford	387.5	155.7	155.7	0.0	231.8
Scott	338.0	300.3	300.3	0.0	37.7
Sequatchie	169.9	137.3	137.3	0.0	32.6
Sevier	377.8	254.5	127.5	127.1	123.3
Shelby	493.8	111.6	111.6	0.0	382.2
Smith	200.2	81.0	81.0	0.0	119.1
Stewart	316.1	219.7	219.7	0.0	96.5
Sullivan	265.8	123.6	123.6	0.0	142.1
Sumner	338.6	88.2	88.2	0.0	250.4
Tipton	290.7	50.9	50.9	0.0	239.8
Trousdale	73.1	30.0	30.0	0.0	43.2
Unicoi	119.3	99.3	89.4	9.9	20.0
Union	139.7	102.5	102.5	0.0	37.2
Van Buren	174.4	145.0	135.4	9.6	29.4
Warren	275.6	93.6	93.6	0.0	182.0
Washington	208.8	54.8	50.3	4.5	154.0
Wayne	470.7	372.6	372.6	0.0	98.1
Weakley	372.1	96.1	95.9	0.2	276.0
White	238.7	129.4	129.4	0.0	109.3
Williamson	373.6	142.0	142.0	0.0	231.6
Wilson	365.1	98.1	97.0	1.1	267.0
TENNESSEE	26,447.0	13,602.5	13,265.2	337.3	12,844.5

Source: U.S. Department of Agriculture, Forest Service, Southern Forest Experiment Station: New Orleans, direct correspondence.

Tennessee offers great variety in climate and topography. Elevations range from more than 6,600 feet at the eastern boundary to approximately 200 feet at the Mississippi River. There are nearly 60 national and state parks and recreations areas in Tennessee, as shown in Figure 12.2.

Data on travel-generated employment and revenue for Tennessee and its counties are published annually by the Tennessee Department of Tourist Development. The report, *The Economic Impact of Travel on Tennessee Counties*, results from an annual study conducted by the U.S. Travel Data Center.

Acreage which is owned by various federal agencies but located in Tennessee and other southeastern states is shown in Table 12.16. Additional information on selected federally owned Tennessee lands is given in other tables throughout the chapter. The Army Corps of Engineers maintains the Cumberland River areas in Tennessee, while TVA maintains all Tennessee River areas except for National Wildlife Refuge areas (managed by the U.S. Fish and Wildlife Service). The U.S. Department of the Interior, National Park Service, maintains the Great Smoky Mountains National Park as well as a variety of other areas, as listed in Table 12.9. The Cherokee National Forest is managed by the U.S. Department of Agriculture, National Forest Service. In regard to state-owned properties, the Tennessee Department of Conservation has primary responsibility for these parks and recreation areas. Records of visitations and use, collected and maintained by each of these agencies, are presented in several tables throughout this chapter.

The U.S. Department of Commerce, National Oceanic and Atmospheric Administration, through the Environmental Data Service, National Climate Center, publishes data on weather and climate. The monthly data in Table 12.1 are published for seven metropolitan areas in Tennessee in *Climatological Data Annual Summary, Tennessee*. "Normal" values of temperature and precipitation shown in this table are based on records for the 30 years between 1951 and 1980. Actual minimum and maximum weekday temperatures and normal and actual cooling degree days and heating degree days are reported for more than 70 Tennessee locations in *Electricity Sales Statistics*, issued by the Tennessee Valley Authority.

Summary information about land and water areas of counties is presented in Table 12.8. These data are collected and published by the U.S. Department of Commerce, Bureau of the Census. Latest measurements were made in 1990.

Other tables in this chapter provide information for each of the southeastern states on environmental concerns such as hazardous waste sites, water usage and air quality.

TABLE OF CONTENTS

FIGURE 12.1
Physiographic Map of Tennessee

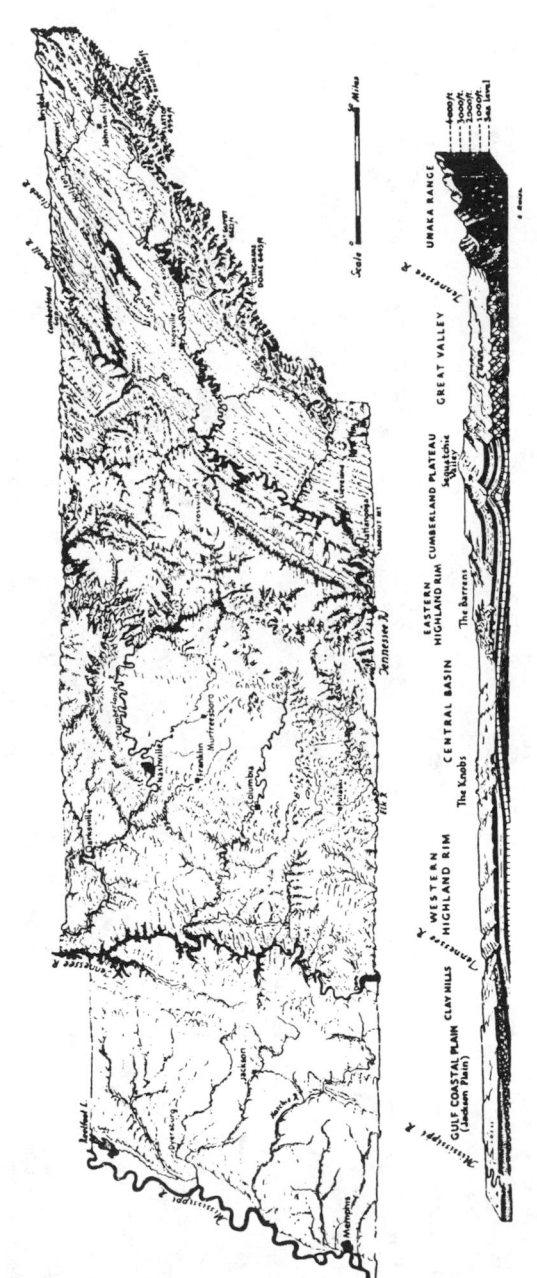

Source: Tennessee Department of Finance and Administration, *Tennessee, Its Resources and Economy*, Volume II.

TABLE 12.1-- CLIMATOLOGICAL DATA, SELECTED METROPOLITAN STATIONS, 1989 AND 30-YEAR NORMALS [Temperatures in degrees Fahrenheit]

Weather station	Jan.	Feb.	Mar.	Apr.	May	June	July	Aug.	Sept.	Oct.	Nov.	Dec.	Annual
BRISTOL - Elevation 1,525 feet, Latitude 36°29'N, Longitude 82°24'W													
1989 average temperature	42.3	39.5	51.2	54.7	59.8	71.9	75.1	73.3	67.8	56.6	45.6	28.1	55.5
Normal average temperature	35.0	37.9	46.3	56.1	64.4	71.5	74.9	74.3	68.8	57.1	46.2	38.2	55.9
1989 precipitation (inches)	3.69	4.07	3.76	2.97	4.10	6.97	3.81	3.41	6.95	1.77	3.18	3.16	47.84
Normal precipitation	3.56	3.43	4.29	3.46	3.61	3.46	4.19	3.23	3.00	2.50	2.98	3.53	41.24
1989 cooling degree days[1]	0	0	5	24	42	218	322	268	144	11	0	0	1,034
CHATTANOOGA - Elevation 692 feet, Latitude 35°02'N, Longitude 85°12'W													
1989 average temperature	45.3	43.2	54.5	59.6	65.4	74.8	78.9	78.4	71.7	60.9	50.7	35.0	59.9
Normal average temperature	38.7	41.9	49.8	60.1	67.8	75.1	78.7	78.1	72.3	60.0	48.9	41.5	59.4
1989 precipitation (inches)	5.30	7.16	5.86	3.99	4.56	9.19	9.93	3.46	11.22	1.77	5.45	3.71	71.60
Normal precipitation	5.20	4.69	6.31	4.57	4.00	3.32	4.55	3.41	4.30	2.92	4.19	5.14	52.60
1989 cooling degree days[1]	0	2	16	68	109	300	437	424	236	43	0	0	1,635
CLARKSVILLE[2] - Elevation 382 feet, Latitude 36°33'N, Longitude 87°22'W													
1989 average temperature	42.7	35.6	50.0	57.8	64.8	73.6	78.2	77.4	69.5	59.2	48.6	27.7	57.1
Normal average temperature	35.7	39.0	47.9	59.0	66.9	74.8	78.7	77.4	71.0	58.9	47.8	39.5	58.1
1989 precipitation (inches)	6.69	10.80	7.52	3.31	3.76	6.20	4.10	3.13	4.30	2.80	3.04	2.45	58.10
Normal precipitation	4.52	4.26	5.92	4.46	4.14	3.74	3.81	3.79	3.31	2.83	4.22	4.64	49.64
1989 cooling degree days[1]	0	0	10	67	112	267	416	393	186	25	4	0	1,480
JACKSON[2] - Elevation 400 feet, Latitude 35°37'N, Longitude 88°50'W													
1989 average temperature	44.4	37	51.3	59.2	65.9	74.6	78.3	78.0	69.7	61.1	49.6	30.3	58.3
Normal average temperature	37.0	40.6	49.1	60.3	68.3	75.8	79.2	77.9	71.8	60.2	49.1	41.0	59.2
1989 precipitation (inches)	8.78	9.31	6.78	2.68	3.20	6.74	5.72	1.50	7.19	1.48	3.64	2.21	59.23
Normal precipitation	4.74	4.46	5.24	5.39	4.94	3.84	4.06	2.88	3.69	2.47	4.22	4.50	50.43
1989 cooling degree days[1]	0	0	16	85	117	297	420	410	198	44	1	0	1,588
KNOXVILLE - Elevation 949 feet, Latitude 35°48'N, Longitude 84°00'W													
1989 average temperature	42.8	41.3	53.5	57.8	62.4	73.3	77.5	76.8	70.9	59.4	48.1	32.2	58.0
Normal average temperature	38.2	41.5	49.7	59.6	67.4	74.3	77.6	77.0	71.5	59.5	48.8	41.1	58.9
1989 precipitation (inches)	4.96	6.26	3.82	3.50	5.31	8.21	2.68	3.16	9.19	1.47	4.92	2.74	56.22
Normal precipitation	4.65	4.18	5.49	3.87	3.71	3.95	4.33	3.02	2.99	2.73	3.78	4.59	47.29
1989 cooling degree days[1]	0	2	10	47	76	257	395	374	219	35	0	0	1,415

TABLE 12.1-- CLIMATOLOGICAL DATA, SELECTED METROPOLITAN STATIONS, 1989 AND 30-YEAR NORMALS [Temperatures in degrees Fahrenheit] (Continued)

Weather station	Jan.	Feb.	Mar.	Apr.	May	June	July	Aug.	Sept.	Oct.	Nov.	Dec.	Annual
MEMPHIS - Elevation 265 feet, Latitude 35°03'N, Longitude 90°00'W													
1989 average temperature	47.3	40.0	53.8	62.6	69.5	77.6	80.7	81.2	72.4	64.2	54.2	33.6	61.4
Normal average temperature	39.6	43.6	51.7	62.6	71.0	78.7	82.1	80.6	74.2	62.9	51.3	43.3	61.8
1989 precipitation (inches)	7.91	10.51	5.50	2.13	2.36	7.20	7.55	1.43	6.08	2.37	3.65	2.20	58.89
Normal precipitation	4.61	4.33	5.44	5.77	5.06	3.58	4.03	3.74	3.62	2.37	4.17	4.85	51.57
1989 cooling degree days[1]	0	2	27	109	186	386	496	510	254	84	20	0	2,074
NASHVILLE - Elevation 580 feet, Latitude 36°07'N, Longitude 86°41'W													
1989 average temperature	44.9	39.0	52.6	59.3	65.7	74.7	79.1	78.0	70.5	61.0	51.4	29.5	58.8
Normal average temperature	37.1	40.4	49.0	59.7	68.1	75.8	79.4	78.4	72.3	60.2	48.6	40.9	59.2
1989 precipitation (inches)	4.52	9.36	5.31	2.68	4.61	7.87	3.18	3.67	6.30	3.62	3.94	1.97	57.03
Normal precipitation	4.49	4.03	5.58	4.47	4.56	3.70	3.82	3.40	3.71	2.58	3.52	4.63	48.49
1989 cooling degree days[1]	0	0	21	93	120	298	446	408	208	39	8	0	1,641

Note: Normals are computed over the thirty-year period from 1951 to 1980. They are updated after every tenth year.

1. One cooling degree day is accumulated for each degree that the daily mean temperature exceeds 65°F.

2. Normals computed by the Center for Business and Economic Research.

Source: U.S. Department of Commerce, National Oceanic and Atmospheric Administration, Environmental Data Service, National Climatic Data Center, Asheville, North Carolina, *Climatological Data Annual Summary, Tennessee,* 1989; and *Comparative Climatic Data for the United States,* 1984.

457

TABLE 12.2-- MAXIMUM RECORDED TEMPERATURE AND COOLING DEGREE DAYS, SELECTED TENNESSEE LOCATIONS, 1989 COOLING YEAR
[Degree day base = 65°F]

Weather station and county	Maximum weekday temperature recorded	Cooling degree days[1]			Weather station and county[3]	Maximum weekday temperature recorded	Actual degree days[2]
		Normal	Actual[2]	Actual as percent of normal			
Allardt, Fentress	88	905	817	90	Ames Plantation, Fayette	96	1,515
Bolivar Water Works, Hardeman	95	1,587	1,549	98	Athens, McMinn	92	1,200
Bristol, Sullivan	91	1,066	1,034	97	Carthage, Smith	94	1,496
Brownsville, Haywood	95	1,873	1,650	88	Centerville Water Plant, Hickman	96	1,279
Chattanooga, Hamilton	94	1,578	1,635	104	Cleveland, Bradley	92	1,272
Clarksville Sewage Plant, Montgomery	95	1,514	1,480	98	Cookeville, Putnam	91[a]	1,064
Columbia, Maury	94	1,497	1,217	81	Crossville, Cumberland	91	875
Covington, Tipton	95	1,733	1,609	93	Dayton, Rhea	90	1,175
Crossville, Cumberland	89	798	617	77	Dickson, Dickson	94	1,364
Dyersburg, Dyer	98	1,840	1,837	100	Dover, Stewart	94	1,307
Franklin Sewage Plant, Williamson	93	1,466	1,199	82	Dresden, Weakley	93	n.a.
Greeneville, Greene	92	1,167	1,063	91	Elizabethton, Carter	90	727
Jackson Exp. Station, Madison	95	1,625	1,588	98	Erwin, Unicoi	89	859
Jackson, Madison	96	1,802	1,729	96	Fayetteville, Lincoln	93	1,265
Kingsport, Hawkins-Sullivan	92	1,164	1,199	103	Huntingdon Water Plant, Carroll	96	1,499
Knoxville, Knox	94	1,449	1,415	98	Kingston Springs, Cheatham	94	1,286
Lenoir City, Loudon	94	1,306	1,377	105	LaFayette, Macon	96	1,487

TABLE 12.2-- MAXIMUM RECORDED TEMPERATURE AND COOLING DEGREE DAYS, SELECTED TENNESSEE LOCATIONS, 1989 COOLING YEAR
[Degree day base = 65°F] (Continued)

Weather station and county	Maximum weekday temperature recorded	Cooling degree days[1]			Weather station and county[3]	Maximum weekday temperature recorded	Actual degree days[2]
		Normal	Actual[2]	Actual as percent of normal			
Lewisburg Exp. Station, Marshall	96	1,383	1,132	82	Lawrenceburg Filtration Plant, Lawrence	93	1,189
McMinnville, Warren	96	1,689	1,354	80	Lebanon, Wilson	95	1,397
Martin, Weakley	92	1,375	1,313	95	Lexington, Henderson	97	1,600
Memphis, Shelby	98	2,067	2,074	100	Livingston, Overton	92	1,289
Milan, Gibson	98	1,580	1,533	97	Morristown Radio, WCRK, Overton	91	1,106
Monteagle, Grundy-Marion	89	1,087	987	91	Moscow, Fayette	94	1,742
Murfreesboro, Rutherford	93	1,573	1,332	85	Mountain City, Johnson	88	538
Nashville, Davidson	96	1,661	1,641	99	Mount Pleasant, Maury	94	1,423
Newbern, Dyer	96	1,653	1,522	92	Neapolis Exp. Station, Maury	96	1,321
Newport, Cocke	93	1,293	1,206	93	Norris, Anderson	91	950
Oak Ridge, Anderson-Roane	94	1,294	1,346	104	Oneida, Scott	89[a]	840
Paris, Henry	92	1,422	1,291	91	Pikeville, Bledsoe	93	1,251
Rogersville, Hawkins	90	1,054	969	92	Portland Sewage Plant, Sumner	95[a]	1,423
Samburg Wildlife Refuge, Obion	97	1,667	1,366	82	Pulaski Water Plant, Giles	95	1,619
Savannah, Hardin	97	1,734	1,534	88	Ripley, Lauderdale	96	1,638
Shelbyville, Bedford	94	1,472	1,427	97	Rockwood, Roane	96	1,080
Springfield Exp. Station, Robertson	95	1,380	1,193	86	Selmer, McNairy	95	1,513

TABLE 12.2-- MAXIMUM RECORDED TEMPERATURE AND COOLING DEGREE DAYS, SELECTED TENNESSEE LOCATIONS, 1989 COOLING YEAR
[Degree day base = 65°F] (Continued)

Weather station and county	Maximum weekday temperature recorded	Cooling degree days[1]		
		Normal	Actual[2]	Actual as percent of normal
Union City, Obion	94	1,426	1,360	95
Waynesboro, Wayne	93	1,265	1,127	89

Weather station and county[3]	Maximum weekday temperature recorded	Actual degree days[2]
Sevierville, Sevier	91	n.a.
Smithville, DeKalb	92	1,048
Sparta, White	93	1,241
Tazewell, Claiborne	92	936
Tullahoma, Coffee-Franklin	94	1,373
Waverly, Humphreys	97	1,313
Winchester, Franklin	94	1,410
Woodbury, Cannon	95	1,275

1. A degree day measures the amount by which the mean daily temperature at a location exceeds or falls below a base temperature (usually 65°F). Degree days for a cooling season are the sum of every day's variation from 65°F. TVA's cooling year is from July 1 to June 30.
2. Where temperatures for one or more days are not reported, they are estimated.
3. Data on normal degree days are not available for these stations.
Source: Tennessee Valley Authority, Division of Power Utilization, *Electricity Sales Statistics*, Report No. 662.

TABLE 12.3-- MINIMUM RECORDED TEMPERATURE AND HEATING DEGREE DAYS, SELECTED TENNESSEE LOCATIONS, 1989 HEATING YEAR
[Degree day base = 65°F]

Weather station and county	Minimum weekday temperature recorded	Heating degree days[1]			Weather station and county[3]	Minimum weekday temperature recorded	Actual degree days[2]
		Normal	Actual[2]	Actual as percent of normal			
Allardt, Fentress	4	4,491	4,308	96	Ames Plantation, Fayette	13	3,664
Bolivar Water Works, Hardeman	15	3,608	3,437	95	Athens, McMinn	10	3,945
Bristol, Sullivan	12	4,356	4,192	96	Centerville Water Plant, Hickman	8	3,812
Brownsville, Haywood	15	3,356	3,615	108	Cheatham, Cheatham	n.a.	n.a.
Chattanooga, Hamilton	15	3,583	3,260	91	Cookeville, Putnam	8	4,353
Clarksville Sewage Plant, Montgomery	8	4,014	3,998	100	Crossville, Cumberland	5	4,373
Columbia, Maury	12	3,761	4,044	108	Dayton, Rhea	11	3,661
Covington, Tipton	14	3,707	3,726	101	Dresden, Weakley	10	n.a.
Crossville, Cumberland	2	4,896	4,929	101	Elizabethton, Carter	n.a.	n.a.
Dickson, Dickson	10	3,759	3,835	102	Erwin, Unicoi	6	4,439
Dover, Stewart	9	4,115	4,170	101	Fayetteville, Lincoln	9	3,941
Dyersburg, Dyer	13	3,559	3,324	93	Huntingdon Water Plant, Carroll	12	3,919
Franklin Sewage Plant, Williamson	11	3,664	4,174	114	Jefferson City, Jefferson	11	4,108
Gatinburg, Sevier	8	4,263	4,411	103	Kingston Springs, Cheatham	8	n.a.
Greeneville, Greene	9	4,063	4,333	107	LaFayette, Macon	8	3,727
Jackson Exp. Sta., Madison	14	3,707	3,655	99	Lawrenceburg Filtration Plant, Lawrence	12	3,729
Jackson, Madison	15	3,540	3,374	95	Lebanon, Wilson	9	4,145

TABLE 12.3-- MINIMUM RECORDED TEMPERATURE AND HEATING DEGREE DAYS, SELECTED TENNESSEE LOCATIONS, 1989 HEATING YEAR
[Degree day base = 65°F] (Continued)

Weather station and county	Minimum weekday temperature recorded	Heating degree days[1] Normal	Actual[2]	Actual as percent of normal
Kingsport, Hawkins-Sullivan	13	3,920	3,795	97
Knoxville, Knox	14	3,658	3,664	100
Lenoir City, Loudon	14	4,023	3,765	94
Lewisburg Experimental Sta., Marshall	10	4,056	4,160	103
McMinnville, Warren	11	3,663	3,522	96
Martin, Weakley	8	3,781	4,342	115
Memphis, Shelby	17	3,207	2,968	93
Monteagle, Grundy-Marion	7	4,030	4,176	104
Murfreesboro, Rutherford	11	3,734	4,040	108
Nashville, Davidson	12	3,756	3,516	94
Newbern, Dyer	13	3,837	3,896	102
Newport, Cocke	12	4,081	3,790	93
Oak Ridge, Anderson-Roane	12	4,006	3,907	98
Paris, Henry	7	4,077	4,253	104
Rogersville, Hawkins	9	4,220	4,195	99
Samburg Wildlife Refuge, Obion	10	3,953	4,126	104
Savannah, Hardin	12	3,326	3,135	94

Weather station and county[3]	Minimum weekday temperature recorded	Actual degree days[2]
Linden, Perry	10	4,125
Livingston Radio, WLIV, Hamblen	n.a.	n.a.
Morristown Radio, WCRK, Overton	11	3,926
Mt. Pleasant, Maury	11	3,902
Mountain City, Johnson	3	5,207
Neapolis Experimental Station, Maury	10	4,000
Norris, Anderson	8	4,421
Pikeville, Bledsoe	10	3,648
Portland Sewage Plant, Sumner	10	n.a.
Pulaski Water Plant, Giles	13	3,100
Rockwood, Roane	11	4,240
Selmer, McNairy	13	3,541
Sevierville, Sevier	13	3,674
Smithville, DeKalb	10	4,379
Sparta, White	10	3,634
Tazewell, Claiborne	8	4,819
Waverly, Humphreys	7	4,056

TABLE 12.3-- MINIMUM RECORDED TEMPERATURE AND HEATING DEGREE DAYS, SELECTED TENNESSEE LOCATIONS, 1989 HEATING YEAR

[Degree day base = 65°F] (Continued)

Weather station and county	Minimum weekday temperature recorded	Heating degree days[1]			Weather station and county[3]	Minimum weekday temperature recorded	Actual degree days[2]
		Normal	Actual[2]	Actual as percent of normal			
Shelbyville, Bedford	11	3,610	3,469	96	Winchester, Franklin	12	3,284
Springfield Exp. Station, Robertson	8	4,305	4,420	103	Woodbury, Cannon	9	3,743
Tullahoma, Coffee-Franklin	11	3,618	n.a.	n.a.			
Union City, Obion	12	4,224	4,234	100			
Waynesboro, Wayne	11	4,170	4,094	98			

n.a. not available.

a. Indicates Saturday or Sunday temperature was lower.

1. A degree day measures the amount by which the mean daily temperature at a location exceeds or falls below a base temperature (usually 65°F). Degree days for a heating season are the sum of every day's variation from 65°F. TVA's heating year is from July 1 to June 30.

2. Where temperatures for one or more days are not reported, they are estimated.

3. Data on normal degree days are not available for these stations.

Source: Tennessee Valley Authority, Division of Power Utilization, *Electricity Sales Statistics*, Report No. 656.

TABLE 12.4-- MINIMUM TEMPERATURES AND HEATING DEGREE DAYS, TVA REGION,[1] HEATING
YEARS 1972–1989

Heating year	Minimum weekday temperatures			Heating degree days[2]				
	Dec.	Jan.	Feb.	Dec.	Jan.	Feb.	Total season	Percent of normal
1989	23 [a]	25	15	683	601	663	3,311	93
1988	23	7	16 [a]	607	918	708	3,550	99
1987	24	13	19	736	825	569	3,278	92
1986	11	6	15	899	817	520	3,157	88
1985	12	-10	14	463	1,050	727	3,399	95
1984	2 [a]	6 [a]	10	909	953	614	3,977	111
1983	20	18	21	533	805	616	3,416	96
1982	17 [a]	-1 [a]	16 [a]	813	919	649	3,717	104
1981	16	8	5	730	902	603	3,644	102
1980	17	18	15 [a]	715	753	823	3,719	104
1979	22 [a]	9	10 [a]	664	1,023	794	3,642	102
1978	12	9	11	774	1,105	901	4,129	115
1977	9	-3	13	852	1,180	671	4,197	117
1976	11	7	17	728	899	440	3,292	92
1975	19	15	16	709	669	569	3,514	98
1974	17	26	14	734	538	618	2,943	82
1973	14	13	19	673	852	726	3,635	102
1972	31	15	19	476	686	689	3,099	87
Normal	17	12	17	724	826	651	3,569	100

1. TVA Region is city temperatures weighted by size of heating loads.
2. A degree day measures the amount by which the mean daily temperature at a location exceeds or falls below a base temperature (usually 65°F). Degree days for a heating season are the sum of every day's variation from 65°F. TVA's heating year is from July 1 to June 30.
a. Indicates Saturday or Sunday temperature was lower.
Source: Tennessee Valley Authority, Division of Power Utilization, *Electricity Sales Statistics*, Report No. 656.

TABLE 12.5-- TRAVEL-GENERATED EMPLOYMENT, BY CATEGORY, TENNESSEE, 1991 AND 1992

	1992 ᵖ		1991	
	Employment (1,000)	Percent of total	Employment (1,000)	Percent of total
TOTAL	128.8	100.0	125.7	100.0
Public transportation	30.3	23.5	30.5	24.3
Auto transportation	4.0	3.1	3.9	3.1
Lodging	21.8	16.9	21.9	17.4
Food service	47.1	36.6	44.7	35.6
Entertainment and recreation	14.1	10.9	13.8	11.0
General retail trade	9.2	7.1	8.5	6.8
Planning	2.3	1.8	2.4	1.9

Note: Detail may not add to total due to independent rounding.

p preliminary.

Source: U.S. Travel Data Center, *The Economic Impact of Travel on Tennessee Counties, 1992,* a study prepared for the Tennessee Department of Tourist Development; and earlier editions.

TABLE 12.6-- ESTIMATES OF TRAVEL ECONOMIC IMPACT, TENNESSEE, 1988–1992

	1992 ᵖ	1991	1990	1989	1988
Travel expenditures ($1,000,000)	6,365.7	6,010.2	5,779.2	5,530.1	4,980.1
Travel-generated payroll ($1,000,000)	2,126.5	2,020.9	1,963.0	1,746.2	1,566.4
Travel-generated employment (1,000)	128.8	125.7	125.8	124.2	114.5
Travel-generated state tax revenue ($1,000,000)	325.5	306.2	295.9	285.7	265.4
Travel-generated local tax revenue ($1,000,000)	160.0	150.6	144.9	134.4	116.2
Out-of-state visitor expenditures (billions of dollars)	5.3	4.8	4.8	4.5	3.5
Out-of-state travelers (1,000,000)	30.9	35.8	26.5	28.7ʳ	22.7ʳ

Note: Detail may not add to total due to independent rounding.

p preliminary.

r revised.

Source: U.S. Travel Data Center, *The Economic Impact of Travel on Tennessee Counties, 1992,* a study prepared for the Tennessee Department of Tourist Development; and earlier editions.

TABLE 12.7 -- TRAVEL EXPENDITURES AND TRAVEL-GENERATED STATE AND LOCAL TAX RECEIPTS AND EMPLOYMENT, TENNESSEE AND COUNTIES, 1991 AND 1992 [Expenditures and receipts in millions of dollars; employment in thousands]

County	1992 P				1991			
	Total travel expenditures	State tax receipts	Local tax receipts	Travel-generated employment	Total travel expenditures	State tax receipts	Local tax receipts	Travel-generated employment
Anderson	47.90	2.97	0.97	0.76	48.49	2.97	0.96	0.80
Bedford	11.97	0.72	0.45	0.18	12.63	0.76	0.45	0.20
Benton	10.46	0.65	0.99	0.12	10.15	0.63	0.93	0.11
Bledsoe	1.86	0.10	0.28	0.02	1.79	0.09	0.27	0.02
Blount	107.01	6.28	3.39	1.80	100.74	5.84	3.19	1.74
Bradley	51.41	3.10	1.03	0.83	50.02	2.98	1.02	0.85
Campbell	29.20	1.66	1.23	0.47	28.42	1.65	1.19	0.48
Cannon	1.91	0.12	0.12	0.02	1.79	0.11	0.11	0.02
Carroll	9.24	0.58	0.32	0.11	9.15	0.57	0.31	0.11
Carter	13.18	0.80	0.81	0.16	12.85	0.79	0.77	0.16
Cheatham	7.94	0.44	0.26	0.12	6.07	0.34	0.22	0.09
Chester	3.96	0.27	0.11	0.04	3.48	0.24	0.11	0.03
Claiborne	9.80	0.55	0.63	0.16	9.67	0.54	0.60	0.17
Clay	5.94	0.32	0.36	0.11	6.06	0.33	0.35	0.12
Cocke	22.01	1.26	0.86	0.41	21.03	1.22	0.81	0.40
Coffee	32.55	1.95	0.78	0.57	32.23	1.94	0.76	0.58
Crockett	2.91	0.16	0.13	0.04	3.32	0.22	0.13	0.04
Cumberland	39.81	2.26	1.58	0.77	38.12	2.18	1.50	0.76
Davidson	1,869.05	89.56	38.49	42.20	1,776.72	84.69	36.05	41.13
Decatur	5.87	0.37	0.88	0.06	6.26	0.39	0.84	0.07
DeKalb	10.73	0.60	1.41	0.15	10.57	0.60	1.34	0.14
Dickson	23.87	1.44	0.53	0.39	21.23	1.29	0.48	0.36
Dyer	17.85	1.12	0.39	0.28	15.93	1.03	0.35	0.25
Fayette	3.81	0.24	0.16	0.04	3.72	0.24	0.15	0.04
Fentress	6.26	0.35	0.33	0.08	5.13	0.29	0.32	0.07
Franklin	10.21	0.63	0.44	0.14	10.23	0.63	0.42	0.14
Gibson	18.20	1.18	0.50	0.20	18.45	1.20	0.48	0.20
Giles	12.36	0.76	0.44	0.16	11.94	0.76	0.42	0.16

TABLE 12.7.-- TRAVEL EXPENDITURES AND TRAVEL-GENERATED STATE AND LOCAL TAX RECEIPTS AND EMPLOYMENT, TENNESSEE AND COUNTIES, 1991 AND 1992 [Expenditures and receipts in millions of dollars; employment in thousands] (Continued)

County	1992 [P]				1991			
	Total travel expenditures	State tax receipts	Local tax receipts	Travel-generated employment	Total travel expenditures	State tax receipts	Local tax receipts	Travel-generated employment
Grainger	7.46	0.42	1.44	0.07	6.90	0.39	1.35	0.06
Greene	27.84	1.71	0.71	0.40	26.22	1.62	0.68	0.39
Grundy	4.00	0.25	0.60	0.03	3.91	0.25	0.57	0.03
Hamblen	40.93	2.52	0.84	0.60	37.63	2.30	0.77	0.56
Hamilton	374.20	21.30	7.27	6.53	340.45	19.28	6.57	6.02
Hancock	0.61	0.04	0.11	0.00	0.64	0.04	0.11	0.00
Hardeman	8.40	0.53	0.48	0.09	8.32	0.53	0.46	0.09
Hardin	16.54	0.98	1.16	0.23	14.47	0.87	1.08	0.20
Hawkins	11.69	0.69	0.67	0.14	11.21	0.66	0.64	0.14
Haywood	8.00	0.52	0.31	0.10	7.55	0.50	0.29	0.10
Henderson	10.60	0.65	0.33	0.14	10.40	0.64	0.33	0.15
Henry	30.10	1.70	3.36	0.40	25.55	1.46	3.09	0.33
Hickman	3.39	0.19	0.30	0.04	3.56	0.20	0.28	0.04
Houston	2.17	0.12	0.25	0.02	1.86	0.10	0.23	0.02
Humphreys	15.01	0.77	0.89	0.24	14.76	0.74	0.84	0.25
Jackson	1.55	0.09	0.14	0.02	1.40	0.08	0.13	0.02
Jefferson	19.77	1.21	1.38	0.28	18.09	1.11	1.29	0.25
Johnson	5.26	0.30	0.37	0.08	5.17	0.29	0.35	0.08
Knox	380.30	20.55	7.78	7.39	381.11	20.26	7.70	7.61
Lake	4.46	0.25	0.38	0.08	3.85	0.21	0.35	0.07
Lauderdale	6.77	0.39	0.54	0.08	6.99	0.41	0.51	0.08
Lawrence	16.23	1.02	0.40	0.20	15.08	0.95	0.38	0.20
Lewis	2.83	0.16	0.13	0.04	2.74	0.15	0.12	0.04
Lincoln	9.87	0.62	0.29	0.13	10.49	0.66	0.29	0.14
Loudon	16.22	0.98	0.39	0.25	15.94	0.97	0.38	0.25
McMinn	19.65	1.16	0.45	0.28	18.62	1.10	0.41	0.27
McNairy	5.99	0.35	0.28	0.07	6.07	0.36	0.27	0.07

TABLE 12.7-- TRAVEL EXPENDITURES AND TRAVEL-GENERATED STATE AND LOCAL TAX RECEIPTS AND EMPLOYMENT, TENNESSEE AND COUNTIES, 1991 AND 1992 [Expenditures and receipts in millions of dollars; employment in thousands] (Continued)

County	1992 [P]				1991			
	Total travel expenditures	State tax receipts	Local tax receipts	Travel-generated employment	Total travel expenditures	State tax receipts	Local tax receipts	Travel-generated employment
Macon	2.91	0.17	0.16	0.04	2.91	0.17	0.16	0.04
Madison	83.20	4.94	1.66	1.49	80.40	4.78	1.61	1.50
Marion	13.37	0.77	0.45	0.22	12.75	0.73	0.42	0.21
Marshall	13.50	0.85	0.32	0.20	12.16	0.75	0.30	0.19
Maury	35.22	2.11	0.72	0.49	34.26	2.06	0.70	0.49
Meigs	3.41	0.18	0.46	0.04	2.75	0.15	0.43	0.03
Monroe	20.11	1.13	1.23	0.32	19.27	1.09	1.16	0.31
Montgomery	64.19	4.11	1.11	0.97	62.15	3.94	1.08	0.99
Moore	1.07	0.06	0.04	0.01	0.90	0.05	0.04	0.01
Morgan	2.32	0.15	0.25	0.02	2.32	0.15	0.24	0.02
Obion	20.95	1.24	0.62	0.32	19.39	1.17	0.57	0.29
Overton	4.17	0.26	0.21	0.05	4.00	0.25	0.20	0.05
Perry	3.82	0.21	0.85	0.03	3.57	0.20	0.80	0.03
Pickett	2.57	0.14	0.44	0.03	2.51	0.14	0.41	0.03
Polk	4.40	0.24	0.27	0.07	4.33	0.24	0.26	0.07
Putnam	40.28	2.42	0.87	0.68	39.34	2.41	0.83	0.67
Rhea	14.79	0.86	0.98	0.22	12.31	0.72	0.89	0.18
Roane	26.48	1.59	1.29	0.38	26.05	1.56	1.24	0.38
Robertson	16.70	1.11	0.40	0.21	15.56	1.05	0.37	0.20
Rutherford	80.29	4.96	1.61	1.21	83.33	4.75	1.70	1.46
Scott	4.70	0.27	0.31	0.06	5.15	0.30	0.29	0.06
Sequatchie	3.62	0.20	0.21	0.04	3.06	0.19	0.20	0.04
Sevier	539.09	28.58	15.06	12.25	482.01	25.59	13.59	11.38
Shelby	1,496.92	63.40	29.59	34.33	1,394.37	58.68	28.01	33.83
Smith	4.69	0.29	0.19	0.05	4.63	0.29	0.18	0.05
Stewart	3.71	0.21	0.49	0.04	3.37	0.19	0.46	0.04
Sullivan	123.87	7.10	2.90	2.12	119.52	6.84	2.71	2.05
Sumner	36.68	2.30	0.76	0.51	32.52	2.07	0.66	0.42

TABLE 12.7-- TRAVEL EXPENDITURES AND TRAVEL-GENERATED STATE AND LOCAL TAX RECEIPTS AND EMPLOYMENT, TENNESSEE AND COUNTIES, 1991 AND 1992 [Expenditures and receipts in millions of dollars; employment in thousands] (Continued)

County	1992 P				1991			
	Total travel expenditures	State tax receipts	Local tax receipts	Travel-generated employment	Total travel expenditures	State tax receipts	Local tax receipts	Travel-generated employment
Tipton	10.17	0.66	0.33	0.12	9.61	0.62	0.32	0.12
Trousdale	1.74	0.10	0.05	0.02	1.83	0.12	0.05	0.02
Unicoi	4.22	0.24	0.32	0.06	5.72	0.33	0.31	0.08
Union	3.46	0.20	0.44	0.04	3.70	0.21	0.43	0.05
Van Buren	5.77	0.30	0.52	0.11	4.64	0.25	0.48	0.09
Warren	13.68	0.82	0.46	0.18	14.56	0.88	0.45	0.19
Washington	91.27	5.40	1.97	1.49	88.30	5.20	1.96	1.53
Wayne	4.45	0.25	0.28	0.06	4.17	0.24	0.26	0.05
Weakley	10.04	0.59	0.32	0.14	9.77	0.60	0.30	0.13
White	9.50	0.59	0.37	0.08	8.13	0.52	0.33	0.07
Williamson	73.61	4.54	1.40	1.17	68.99	4.27	1.32	1.12
Wilson	33.64	2.01	0.99	0.58	30.76	1.86	0.91	0.54
TENNESSEE	6,365.74	325.47	160.00	128.75	6,010.22	306.22	150.63	125.70

Note: Estimates represent expenditures by U.S. residents traveling away from home overnight, or on day trips to places 100 miles or more away from home.

p preliminary.

Source: U.S. Travel Data Center, *The Economic Impact of Travel on Tennessee Counties, 1992*, a study prepared for the Tennessee Department of Tourist Development.

TABLE 12.8-- LAND AND INLAND WATER AREA, TENNESSEE AND COUNTIES [In square miles]

County	Total area	Land area	Inland water area
Anderson	344.83	337.52	7.31
Bedford	474.89	473.72	1.17
Benton	436.23	394.81	41.42
Bledsoe	406.73	406.33	0.40
Blount	566.66	558.57	8.08
Bradley	331.52	328.76	2.77
Campbell	498.27	480.08	18.19
Cannon	265.73	265.67	0.06
Carroll	599.89	599.06	0.84
Carter	347.64	341.06	6.57
Cheatham	307.16	302.69	4.48
Chester	288.76	288.54	0.22
Claiborne	441.56	434.29	7.27
Clay	259.26	236.12	23.15
Cocke	443.17	434.42	8.75
Coffee	434.49	428.91	5.59
Crockett	265.49	265.29	0.21
Cumberland	684.97	681.63	3.34
Davidson	526.16	502.26	23.90
Decatur	344.93	333.92	11.02
DeKalb	329.00	304.59	24.41
Dickson	491.34	489.92	1.42
Dyer	526.52	510.59	15.93
Fayette	706.27	704.55	1.73
Fentress	499.00	498.66	0.34
Franklin	574.37	553.13	21.24
Gibson	603.64	602.72	0.92
Giles	611.22	610.97	0.25
Grainger	302.46	280.35	22.10
Greene	624.27	621.84	2.42
Grundy	361.16	360.59	0.58
Hamblen	175.78	161.04	14.74
Hamilton	575.76	542.50	33.27
Hancock	223.51	222.30	1.21
Hardeman	670.44	667.58	2.86
Hardin	596.36	577.91	18.45
Hawkins	499.66	486.69	12.98
Haywood	534.19	533.25	0.95
Henderson	525.95	520.06	5.89
Henry	593.49	561.75	31.74
Hickman	612.75	612.70	0.05
Houston	206.94	200.22	6.71
Humphreys	556.75	532.24	24.50
Jackson	319.57	308.90	10.67
Jefferson	314.34	273.83	40.51
Johnson	302.76	298.49	4.26
Knox	525.81	508.49	17.32
Lake	193.81	163.43	30.38
Lauderdale	507.17	470.48	36.69
Lawrence	617.96	617.22	0.74

TABLE 12.8-- LAND AND INLAND WATER AREA, TENNESSEE AND COUNTIES [In square miles]
(Continued)

County	Total area	Land area	Inland water area
Lewis	282.50	282.12	0.38
Lincoln	570.68	570.29	0.39
Loudon	247.04	228.62	18.43
McMinn	432.24	430.30	1.94
McNairy	560.87	560.08	0.79
Macon	307.20	307.15	0.06
Madison	558.68	557.12	1.56
Marion	513.80	499.84	13.96
Marshall	376.13	375.39	0.75
Maury	615.57	612.92	2.65
Meigs	216.79	194.87	21.92
Monroe	652.88	635.25	17.64
Montgomery	543.87	539.16	4.71
Moore	130.38	129.17	1.20
Morgan	522.41	522.07	0.34
Obion	555.38	544.95	10.43
Overton	434.83	433.36	1.47
Perry	422.93	414.92	8.00
Pickett	174.58	162.92	11.66
Polk	442.39	435.11	7.28
Putnam	402.44	400.97	1.47
Rhea	336.40	315.95	20.45
Roane	394.99	360.99	34.00
Robertson	476.72	476.51	0.20
Rutherford	624.00	618.97	5.02
Scott	533.25	532.12	1.13
Sequatchie	266.04	265.86	0.18
Sevier	597.77	592.33	5.44
Shelby	783.69	754.87	28.82
Smith	325.38	314.44	10.94
Stewart	493.22	457.70	35.52
Sullivan	429.71	413.05	16.66
Sumner	543.16	529.35	13.81
Tipton	474.76	459.39	15.36
Trousdale	116.65	114.25	2.40
Unicoi	186.49	186.14	0.35
Union	247.14	223.57	23.57
Van Buren	274.61	273.47	1.14
Warren	434.11	432.70	1.41
Washington	329.71	326.22	3.49
Wayne	735.66	734.02	1.63
Weakley	581.85	580.28	1.57
White	379.54	376.74	2.80
Williamson	583.67	582.73	0.94
Wilson	583.27	570.64	12.63
TENNESSEE	42,146.00	41,219.51	926.49

Source: U.S. Department of Commerce, Bureau of the Census, *Census of Population and Housing, 1990:
Summary Tape File 1A, Tennessee.*

TABLE 12.9-- NATIONAL PARKS, ACREAGE, AND RECREATIONAL VISITS, TENNESSEE, 1989–1993
[Visits in thousands]

Name of park	Acreage[1]	Recreational visits				
		1993	1992	1991	1990	1989
Andrew Johnson National Historic Site[8,9]	16.0	41.7	64.5	82.1	71.0	71.4
Big South Fork National River [2]	120,000.0	737.9	752.2	860.0	794.5	730.2
Chickamauga and Chattanooga National Military Park [3]	8,095.0	1,015.9	995.6	1,002.3	955.1	851.5
Cumberland Gap National Historic Park [4,5]	20,273.0	976.0	962.4	951.7	897.8	887.6
Fort Donelson National Battlefield [6]	536.0	207.5	218.9	206.5	285.7	277.7
Great Smoky Mountains National Park[7]	241,206.0	9,283.8	8,931.7	8,654.5	8,151.8	8,333.6
Obed Wild and Scenic River [5,6,8,9]	5,101.0	226.1	186.3	86.4	104.9	21.3
Shiloh National Military Park[9]	3,753.0	341.2	408.0	401.0	337.2	338.9
Stones River National Battlefield [9]	330.0	283.3	243.8	222.6	192.4	189.9

Note: Data for Appalachian National Scenic Trail are not reported.

n.a. not available.

1. Includes only that part of park located in Tennessee.
2. A part is located in Kentucky.
3. A part is located in Georgia.
4. Parts are located in Kentucky and Virginia.
5. 1990 visits may not be comparable with earlier years.
6. 1991 visits may not be comparable with earlier years.
7. A part is located in North Carolina.
8. 1992 visits are not comparable with earlier years.
9. 1993 visits are not comparable with earlier years.

Source: U.S. Department of the Interior, National Park Service, *National Park Service Statistical Abstract 1993*, and earlier editions; and direct correspondence.

TABLE 12.10--SELECTED STATISTICS ON THE GREAT SMOKY MOUNTAINS NATIONAL PARK, NORTH CAROLINA-TENNESSEE, 1960–1990, SELECTED YEARS

Visitor activity	1990	1989	1988	1987
Total number of visitors[1]	8,152,000	8,338,000	8,786,100	10,210,000
Campground campers in tents	182,927	170,866	200,518	206,530
Campground campers in trailers or recreational vehicles	166,774	176,792	187,092	183,141
Campers in organized groups	25,771	22,754	21,477	19,156
Backcountry campers	77,061	69,228	72,152	76,714
Picnickers	400,375	449,518	622,171	708,717
Hikers using park trails	324,625	305,281	277,389	317,915
Horseback riders	77,919	71,753	72,339	59,546
Bicycle riders (Cades Cove Loop)	40,254	40,891	43,020	48,521
	1986	1980	1970	1960
Total number of visitors[1]	9,836,000	8,441,000	6,778,500	4,528,500
Campground campers in tents	179,204	198,189	274,300	336,900
Campground campers in trailers or recreational vehicles	177,336	207,223	314,400	23,600
Campers in organized groups	17,343	26,793	n.a.	n.a.
Backcountry campers	68,375	81,500	88,600	19,100
Picnickers	546,728	470,161	627,400	558,800
Hikers using park trails	276,466	328,951	304,800	203,800
Horseback riders	49,957	60,468	43,700	24,000
Bicycle riders (Cades Cove Loop)	49,664	16,942	n.a.	n.a.

Note: Starting on January 1, 1988, the method for computing recreational visits was modified; therefore, figures for years after 1987 are not comparable to earlier years.
n.a. not available.
1. Includes categories not shown separately.
Source: U.S. Department of the Interior, National Park Service, direct correspondence.

TABLE 12.11--NUMBER OF VISITORS TO THE GREAT SMOKY MOUNTAINS NATIONAL PARK,
NORTH CAROLINA-TENNESSEE, MONTHLY, 1970–1990, SELECTED YEARS
[In thousands]

Month	1990	1989	1988[a]	1987	1986	1985	1984	1980	1975	1970
TOTAL	8,152	8,338	8,786	10,210	9,836	9,319	8,508	8,441	8,542	6,779
January	189	214	169	260	207	174	158	208	173	104
February	235	200	176	228	200	198	231	192	191	126
March	373	341	309	415	457	422	301	260	353	228
April	597	507	504	570	649	599	546	553	491	325
May	626	812	664	869	825	632	638	716	771	544
June	1,062	1,195	1,246	1,317	1,284	1,216	1,141	1,106	1,222	1,017
July	1,395	1,340	1,670	1,628	1,762	1,611	1,445	1,439	1,492	1,335
August	1,158	1,231	1,471	1,513	1,400	1,391	1,282	1,410	1,612	1,325
September	914	809	987	990	920	996	926	803	714	601
October	888	1,077	969	1,577	1,285	1,340	1,134	1,076	983	807
November	468	422	390	587	560	503	430	448	356	208
December	247	190	232	277	286	237	279	231	183	160

a. New method of computing visitation; figures are not comparable to earlier years. In general, the change in
computations had a greater impact on the winter months (October through April).

Source: U.S. Department of the Interior, National Park Service, January news releases, and direct correspondence.

TABLE 12.12--NUMBER OF VISITORS TO THE CHEROKEE NATIONAL FOREST, BY TYPE OF
ACTIVITY, FISCAL YEAR 1993 [In thousands]

Activity	Visitors	Activity	Visitors
Automobile travel	1,776	Picnicking	798
Bicycling	71	Recreation summer homes	50
Boating and sailing	251	Resorts	165
Camping	2,124	Sports and games	110
Fishing	552	Swimming related activities	785
Hiking and walking	450	Viewing scenery	670
Horseback riding	102	White-water activities	485
Hunting	726	Winter sports	42
Off-road vehicle travel	352	Other	393
		TOTAL	9,985

Note: Cherokee National Forest has 628,265 total acres; within this, there are 29 campgrounds, 29 picnic grounds,
9 swimming beaches, 13 boat launching sites.

Source: U.S. Department of Agriculture, Forest Service, Cleveland, Tennessee, direct correspondence.

TABLE 12.13--STATE PARKS AND RECREATION AREAS: LOCATION, ACREAGE, AND NUMBER OF
VISITS, TENNESSEE, FISCAL YEAR 1991

Name of park	County	Size (acres)	Number of visits
Big Cypress Tree	Weakley	330	12,459
Big Hill Pond	McNairy	4,218	96,434
Big Ridge	Union	3,642	283,954
Bledsoe Creek Camping Park	Sumner	164	106,383
Booker T. Washington	Hamilton	353	365,549
Burgess Falls	Putnam-White	155	143,921
Cedars of Lebanon	Wilson	832	509,366
Chickasaw	Chester-Hardeman	1,280	652,182
Cove Lake	Campbell	673	584,804
Cumberland Mountain	Cumberland	1,562	947,694
Cumberland Trail	Campbell	90	21,500
David Crockett Birth Place	Greene	67	336,704
David Crockett State Park	Lawrence	1,071	746,794
Dunbar Cave/Port Royal	Montgomery-Robertson	136	148,644
Edgar Evins	DeKalb	6,279	278,840
Fall Creek Falls	Bledsoe-Van Buren	16,092	761,533
Fort Loudoun	Monroe	407	180,824
Fort Pillow	Lauderdale	1,629	81,213
Frozen Head	Morgan	11,651	162,562
Harrison Bay	Hamilton	1,199	633,242
Henry Horton	Marshall	1,141	1,131,978
Hiwassee/Ocoee Rivers	Polk	181	511,182
Indian Mountain	Campbell	213	241,837
Long Hunter	Davidson-Rutherford-Wilson	2,315	439,630
Meeman-Shelby Forest	Shelby	12,467	2,160,348
Montgomery Bell	Dickson	3,751	1,344,386
Mousetail Landing	Perry	1,219	249,341
Natchez Trace	Benton-Carroll-Henderson	11,100	1,139,763
Nathan Bedford Forrest	Benton-Humphreys	2,587	463,298
Norris Dam	Anderson-Campbell	4,038	717,841
Old Stone Fort	Coffee	796	279,085
Panther Creek	Hamblen	1,965	668,566
Paris Landing	Henry	773	1,389,033
Pickett	Pickett	865	343,416
Pickwick Landing	Hardin	1,392	1,673,743
Pinson Mounds	Madison	1,086	144,345
Radnor Lake	Davidson	957	648,872
Red Clay	Bradley	258	242,280
Reelfoot Lake	Lake-Obion	338	516,906
Roan Mountain	Carter	1,998	626,046
Rock Island	Warren-White	870	342,262
South Cumberland[1]	Franklin-Grundy-Marion	11,510	878,715
Standing Stone	Overton	1,055	362,299
Sycamore Shoals	Carter	49	209,270
Tims Ford	Franklin	413	272,817
T. O. Fuller	Shelby	384	337,659
Warriors' Path	Sullivan	870	2,274,055

1. The South Cumberland Park is made up of seven smaller parks or areas.

Source: Tennessee Department of Conservation, Division of State Parks, direct correspondence.

FIGURE 12.2
National and State Parks, Tennessee

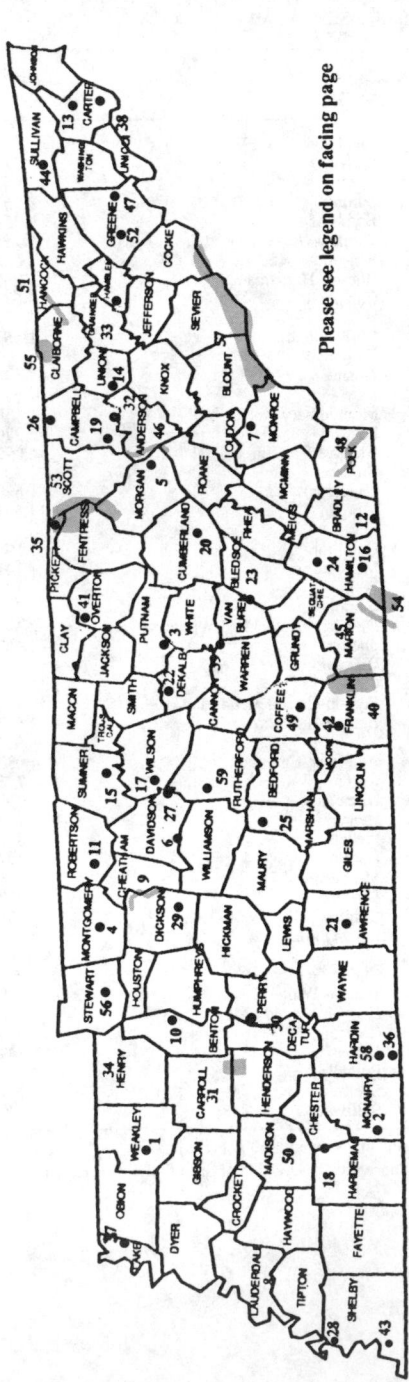

Please see legend on facing page

Legend for Figure 12.2

State Natural Areas

1 Big Cypress Tree
2 Big Hill Pond
3 Burgess Falls
4 Dunbar Cave
5 Frozen Head
6 Radnor Lake

State Historical Areas

7 Fort Loudoun
8 Fort Pillow
9 Harpeth River
10 Nathan Bedford Forrest
11 Port Royal
12 Red Clay
13 Sycamore Shoals

State Parks and Recreation Areas

14 Big Ridge
15 Bledsoe Creek
16 Booker T. Washington
17 Cedars of Lebanon
18 Chickasaw
19 Cove Lake
20 Cumberland Mountain

State Parks and Recreation Areas (Cont.)

21 David Crockett
22 Edgar Evins
23 Fall Creek Falls
24 Harrison Bay
25 Henry Horton
26 Indian Mountain
27 Long Hunter
28 Meeman-Shelby Forest
29 Montgomery Bell
30 Mousetail Landing
31 Natchez Trace
32 Norris Dam
33 Panther Creek
34 Paris Landing
35 Pickett
36 Pickwick Landing
37 Reelfoot Lake
38 Roan Mountain
39 Rock Island
40 South Cumberland[1]
41 Standing Stone
42 Tims Ford
43 T.O. Fuller
44 Warrior's Path

Other State Areas

45 Cumberland State Scenic Trail I
46 Cumberland State Scenic Trail II
47 Davy Crockett Birthplace
48 Hiawassee State Scenic River
49 Old Stone Fort State Archaeological Area
50 Pinson Mounds State Archaeological Area
51 Trail of the Lonesome Pine

National Parks

52 Andrew Johnson
53 Big South Fork
54 Chickamauga
55 Cumberland Gap
56 Fort Donnelson
57 Great Smoky Mountains
58 Shiloh
59 Stones River

〜 Trail or River

▨ Location of largest parks

Note: Does not include national forests.
1. South Cumberland is comprised of seven separate parks and state areas.

Source: Tennessee Department of Tourist Development and Tennessee Department of Conservation, direct correspondence.

TABLE 12.14--EXTREME AND MEAN ELEVATIONS, SOUTHEASTERN STATES AND UNITED STATES
[Elevations in feet]

	Highest point		Lowest Point		Approximate mean elevation
State	Name	Elevation	Name	Elevation	
TENNESSEE	Clingmans Dome	6,643	Mississippi River	178	900
Alabama	Cheaha Mountain	2,405	Gulf of Mexico	Sea level	500
Arkansas	Magazine Mountain	2,753	Oachita River	55	650
Florida	Sec. 30, T6N, R20W, Walton County[1]	345	Atlantic Ocean	Sea level	100
Georgia	Brasstown Bald	4,784	Atlantic Ocean	Sea level	600
Kentucky	Black Mountain	4,139	Mississippi River	257	750
Louisiana	Driskill Mountain	535	New Orleans	-8	100
Mississippi	Woodall Mountain	806	Gulf of Mexico	Sea level	300
North Carolina	Mount Mitchell	6,684	Atlantic Ocean	Sea level	700
South Carolina	Sassafras Mountain	3,560	Atlantic Ocean	Sea level	350
Virginia	Mount Rogers	5,729	Atlantic Ocean	Sea level	950
West Virginia	Spruce Knob	4,861	Potomac River	240	1,500
UNITED STATES	Mt. McKinley (Alaska)	20,320	Death Valley (CA)	-282	2,500

1. Sec. denotes section; T, township; R, range; N, north; W, west.
Source: U.S. Department of Commerce, Bureau of the Census, *Statistical Abstract of the United States, 1993.*

TABLE 12.15--STATE PARKS AND RECREATION AREAS: ACREAGE, VISITORS AND REVENUE, SOUTHEASTERN STATES AND UNITED STATES, 1987–1991

	Acreage, 1991 (1,000)	Visitors[1] (1,000)					Revenue, 1991	
State		1991	1990	1989	1988	1987	Total ($1,000)	Percent of operating budget
TENNESSEE	133	26,974	26,093	26,060	24,774	24,343	19,737	53.9
Alabama	50	6,084	5,800	5,775	7,009	6,099	22,505	80.7
Arkansas	47	6,949	6,765	6,660	6,363	7,148	11,227	59.5
Florida	444	13,087	14,124	15,147	14,344	14,290	16,248	41.3
Georgia	57	16,262	14,924	14,351	13,717	13,310	14,811	39.7
Kentucky	42	27,272	26,704	26,192	25,182	24,210	37,668	69.1
Louisiana	39	1,107	1,090	1,028	1,086	740	1,860	30.5
Mississippi	23	3,912	3,703	4,385	4,474	4,434	4,796	44.3
North Carolina	134	9,463	8,549	7,938	8,033	7,152	1,700	16.0
South Carolina	80	7,970	7,236	8,392	8,000	7,803	10,587	61.4
Virginia	59	3,862	3,688	3,873	3,899	3,635	2,686	28.5
West Virginia	202	8,278	8,470	8,767	9,129	9,129	12,973	58.6
UNITED STATES	11,148	736,897	722,819	726,842	710,342	694,432	454,248	41.5

1. Includes overnight visitors.
Source: U.S. Department of Commerce, Bureau of the Census, *Statistical Abstract of the United States, 1993,* and earlier editions.

TABLE 12.16--FEDERALLY OWNED LAND, BY AGENCY, SOUTHEASTERN STATES, AS OF SEPTEMBER 30, 1989 [In acres]

State	Total federally owned land[1] Acres	Percent of total state land area	Forest Service	National Park Service	Fish and Wildlife Service
TENNESSEE	1,322,215.2	5.0	62,541.6	265,951.0	40,533.1
Alabama	549,857.6	1.7	62,164.1	6,348.4	13,544.5
Arkansas	3,421,060.9	10.3	2,496,952.4	97,706.2	220,858.5
Florida	3,355,543.5	9.7	110,008.9	2,172,338.1	204,650.8
Georgia	2,292,378.5	6.2	867,370.7	34,270.5	464,682.5
Kentucky	1,391,208.2	5.5	667,461.0	62,440.4	2,153.8
Louisiana	6,537,587.7	23.4	6,002,965.3	9,115.8	328,219.6
Mississippi	1,670,523.7	5.6	1,104,364.4	102,068.5	130,723.7
North Carolina	1,140,931.3	3.7	122,560.4	357,762.9	276,699.4
South Carolina	433,771.4	2.3	60,538.3	21,021.8	146,188.2
Virginia	1,918,344.3	7.6	1,043,522.6	354,368.6	103,182.1
West Virginia	2,099,135.6	13.6	1,884,948.2	29,108.0	455.3

	Military services	Veterans Administration	Corps of Engineers	Tennessee Valley Authority	Department of Energy
TENNESSEE	115,236.8	922.4	272,324.8	559,902.3	3,646.9
Alabama	171,813.2	674.0	69,654.9	221,711.6	0.0
Arkansas	94,350.0	295.1	508,412.3	0.0	1.0
Florida	674,047.6	534.2	19,483.3	0.0	0.0
Georgia	548,042.0	378.4	362,741.9	9,507.9	0.0
Kentucky	160,605.6	264.1	335,251.7	161,383.2	0.0
Louisiana	119,344.9	80.6	69,293.8	0.0	0.0
Mississippi	18,760.7	290.7	255,277.5	10,570.8	0.0
North Carolina	307,920.3	325.8	44,083.7	21,845.6	0.0
South Carolina	107,482.8	145.7	96,851.5	0.0	0.0
Virginia	277,734.3	1,273.5	109,964.3	1,624.5	11.0
West Virginia	49.8	424.2	84,134.7	0.0	0.0

Note: Percentages computed by the Center for Business and Economic Research using total land area from the *Census of Population and Housing, 1990: Summary Tape File 1A.*

1. Total includes categories not detailed separately.

Source: General Services Administration, Public Buildings Service, direct correspondence.

TABLE 12.17--NATIONAL FOREST LAND, SOUTHEASTERN STATES AND UNITED STATES, AS OF
        SEPTEMBER 30, 1991 [In thousands of acres]

State	Total[1]	National forest system[2]	Other lands within boundaries
TENNESSEE	1,212	628	585
Alabama	1,280	658	622
Arkansas	3,490	2,509	981
Florida	1,246	1,128	118
Georgia	1,846	859	987
Kentucky	2,102	670	1,431
Louisiana	1,022	601	422
Mississippi	2,310	1,150	1,160
North Carolina	3,165	1,232	1,934
South Carolina	1,376	607	768
Virginia	3,223	1,645	1,578
West Virginia	1,863	1,025	838
UNITED STATES	231,443	191,324	40,119

1. Comprises all publicly and privately owned land within authorized boundaries of national forests, purchase
   units, national grasslands, land utilization projects, research and experimental areas, and other areas.
2. Federally owned land within the "Gross area within unit boundaries."
Source: U.S. Department of Commerce, Bureau of the Census, *Statistical Abstract of the United States, 1993.*

TABLE 12.18--NUMBER OF HAZARDOUS WASTE SITES ON THE NATIONAL PRIORITY LIST,
        SOUTHEASTERN STATES AND UNITED STATES, 1986–1992

State	1992	1991	1990	1989	1988	1987	1986
TENNESSEE	14	14	14	14	17	10	8
Alabama	12	12	12	12	12	10	10
Arkansas	12	10	10	11	10	10	8
Florida	55	52	51	51	51	39	39
Georgia	13	13	13	13	7	7	5
Kentucky	19	19	17	17	10	10	10
Louisiana	12	11	11	11	11	8	7
Mississippi	2	2	2	3	3	2	2
North Carolina	23	22	22	22	21	11	8
South Carolina	24	23	23	23	21	15	12
Virginia	22	20	20	20	22	19	13
West Virginia	5	5	5	5	6	6	6
UNITED STATES	1,224	1,201	1,197	1,209	1,167	933	879

Source: U.S. Department of Commerce, Bureau of the Census, *Statistical Abstract of the United States, 1993*, and
        earlier editions.

TABLE 12.19--WATER WITHDRAWN, BY SOURCE AND BY USE, SOUTHEASTERN STATES AND UNITED STATES, 1990 [In millions of gallons per day, except as noted]

State	Total	Per capita, fresh (gallons per day)	Water withdrawn							Consumptive use, fresh water[3]
			Source		Use					
			Ground water	Surface water	Irrigation	Public supply[1]	Industrial[2]	Thermo-electric		
TENNESSEE	9,190	1,880	503	8,690	38	754	972	7,320		252
Alabama	8,090	2,000	403	7,680	94	735	804	6,310		454
Arkansas	7,840	3,330	4,710	3,130	5,250	360	179	1,640		4,140
Florida	17,900	582	4,660	13,200	3,730	2,229	774	11,000		3,130
Georgia	5,350	816	996	4,360	441	1,063	702	3,060		822
Kentucky	4,320	1,170	247	4,070	12	483	331	3,440		309
Louisiana	9,350	2,200	1,340	8,010	708	669	2,467	4,950		1,590
Mississippi	3,640	1,290	2,670	963	1,880	353	272	702		1,800
North Carolina	8,940	1,350	435	8,510	114	908	492	7,210		390
South Carolina	6,000	1,720	282	5,720	55	455	644	4,820		293
Virginia	6,860	762	443	6,420	36	822	652	5,290		224
West Virginia	4,580	2,560	728	3,860	0	209	659	3,710		509
UNITED STATES	404,796	1,340	80,440	323,960	136,860	41,481	27,486	192,427		93,799

Note: Total includes "Use" categories not shown separately.
1. Includes domestic withdrawals for normal household purposes.
2. Includes water used in mining.
3. Water that has been evaporated, transpired, or incorporated into products, plant or animal tissue and therefore is not available for immediate reuse.

Source: U.S. Department of Commerce, Bureau of the Census, *Statistical Abstract of the United States, 1993*.

TABLE 12.20--METROPOLITAN AREAS FAILING TO MEET NATIONAL AMBIENT AIR QUALITY
STANDARDS FOR OZONE: NUMBER OF DAYS EXCEEDING STANDARDS,
SOUTHEASTERN STATES, 1989–1991

Metropolitan area	1991	Average, 1989–1991
Atlanta, GA	4.0	3.8
Baton Rouge, LA	2.0	4.1
Birmingham, AL	0	1.4
Charleston, WV	1.0	0.3
Charlotte-Gastonia-Rock Hill, NC-SC[1]	1.0	1.1
Cherokee Co, SC[2]	0	0
Cincinnati-Hamilton, OH-KY-IN[3]	3.0	2.3
Edmonson County, KY[2]	0	0
Evansville, IN-KY	0	0.4
Greenbrier County, WV[2]	1.1	0.4
Greensboro-Winston-Salem-High Point, NC	0	0.3
Huntington-Ashland, WV-KY-OH	3.1	1.9
Knoxville, TN	0	0.3
Lake Charles, LA	1.0	1.7
Lexington-Fayette, KY	0	0.3
Louisville, KY-IN	3.4	2.2
Memphis, TN-AR-MS	0	0.3
Miami-Fort Lauderdale, FL[3]	0	0.3
Nashville, TN	1.1	3.0
Norfolk-Virginia Beach-Newport News, VA	1.0	0
Owensboro, KY	0	1.0
Paducah, KY[2]	0	0
Parkersburg-Marietta, WV-OH	1.0	1.0
Raleigh-Durham, NC	0	1.0
Richmond-Petersburg, VA	0	0.3
Smyth County, VA[2]	n.a.	n.a.
Tampa-St. Petersburg-Clearwater, FL	0	0.5
Washington, DC-MD-VA	6.1	2.4

n.a. not available.

1. Excludes York County, South Carolina.

2. Not a metropolitan area.

3. Consolidated Metropolitan Statistical Area.

Source: U.S. Department of Commerce, Bureau of the Census, *Statistical Abstract of the United States, 1993*.

State-chartered Tennessee banks come under the jurisdiction of the State Department of Financial Institutions, whereas national banks in Tennessee are organized under federal law and fall under the jurisdiction of the U.S. Comptroller of the Currency. The Federal Reserve System, including all national banks and those state banks which join voluntarily, was established in 1913 in order to provide some control over bank lending practices across the country. Summary data of U.S. banks are published quarterly in the *Federal Reserve Bulletin*. Some state-level data for Tennessee are available in monthly releases from the Atlanta and St. Louis Federal Reserve District Banks.

The Federal Deposit Insurance Corporation (FDIC) was established in 1933 to insure accounts in its member banks. Nearly all banks belong to the FDIC, and it is a primary source of statistical data on commercial banks. Their semi-annual *Data Book, Operating Banks and Branches* provides deposit information for states, their Metropolitan Statistical Areas, and for counties. The *Annual Report* includes information on bank failures and data on banks receiving FDIC disbursements. A third FDIC publication, *Statistics on Banking*, provides balance sheet and income statement data at the state level. Sheshunoff and Company, Inc. also provides these data at the state level, but its most valuable contribution to banking statistics is the information it provides on individual banks. Performance statistics on banks in Tennessee are taken from *Sheshunoff Banks of Tennessee* and published here by special permission.

For savings and loan institutions, annual statistics of members in the Federal Savings and Loan Insurance Corporation (FSLIC) are reported in *Savings and Home Financing Sourcebook*, published by the Federal Home Loan Bank Board. The name of this supervisory agency was changed to the Office of Thrift Supervision in July 1989. Data on credit unions are available from the Credit Union National Association (CUNA), Inc., established in 1970. The *Credit Union Report*, a statistical supplement formerly included in the *Credit Union National Association Yearbook,* is the source of credit union data for the southeastern states. Additional data on Tennessee credit unions are provided by the Tennessee Department of Financial Institutions in its annual report.

The *Annual Report of the Commissioner of Commerce and Insurance* gives complete data about insurance written in the state of Tennessee by both in-state and out-of-state companies. Premiums and losses are reported for mutual fire insurance companies; stock fire and casualty insurance companies; title insurance companies; and non-profit hospital and medical associations. Information on life insurance companies features amount of insurance in force by type. Because insurance is regulated by the individual states, the federal government does not collect detailed statistics on insurance; however, the American Council of Life Insurance (New York) publishes *Life Insurance Fact Book*, and the Insurance Information Institute publishes *Insurance Facts*. Both are comprehensive statistical booklets on the industry.

TABLE OF CONTENTS

TABLE OF CONTENTS
(Continued)

TABLE 13.1-- NUMBER OF BANKING OFFICES, FDIC-INSURED COMMERCIAL BANKS AND TRUST
COMPANIES, BY TYPE OF CHARTER, TENNESSEE, 1940–1993, SELECTED YEARS

| | | | State charter | |
| | | | --- | --- |
Year	Total	National charter	Federal Reserve member	Federal Reserve nonmember
1993	1,619	835	22	762
1992	1,564	658	130	776
1991	1,511	635	139	737
1990	1,497	587	134	776
1989	1,451	529	134	788
1988	1,420	529	98	793
1987	1,370	538	83	749
1986	1,348	546	69	733
1985	1,334	533	66	735
1984	1,317	525	63	729
1983	1,341	478	65	798
1982	1,335	423	72	840
1981	1,407	481	62	864
1980	1,382	479	62	841
1979	1,342	480	60	802
1978	1,301	483	59	759
1977	1,256	474	64	718
1976	1,160	427	66	667
1975	1,114	443	65	606
1974	1,056	427	58	571
1973	974	402	53	519
1972	904	389	55	460
1971	834	371	51	412
1970	791	353	46	392
1969	749	338	44	367
1968	715	324	41	350
1967	698	322	39	337
1966	671	309	36	326
1965	622	281	33	308
1964	585	257	31	297
1963	560	239	31	290
1962	544	224	31	289
1961	526	217	26	283
1960	507	205	25	277
1955	430	153	23	254
1950	387	123	22	242
1945	348	98	21	229
1940	339	89	16	234

Note: Data are as of December 31.

Source: Federal Deposit Insurance Corporation, *Statistics on Banking, 1993,* and earlier editions; and *Annual
Report, 1990,* and earlier editions.

TABLE 13.2-- STATEMENT OF CONDITION OF FDIC-INSURED COMMERCIAL BANKS, TENNESSEE, AS OF DECEMBER 31, 1991–1993 [In millions of dollars]

Account	1993	1992	1991
TOTAL ASSETS	57,016	52,852	49,092
Cash and due from depository institutions	3,465	3,795	4,028
Securities	16,342	15,702	13,562
Federal funds sold	1,529	2,560	1,758
Loans and leases, net	32,763	28,110	27,033
Allowance for losses	-674	-669	-617
Unearned income	-208	-202	-225
Total loans and leases	33,644	28,981	27,875
Real estate	17,665	13,954	12,771
Depository institutions	93	135	169
Agricultural production	327	294	303
Commercial and industrial	7,319	6,542	6,562
Loans to individuals	6,638	6,421	6,269
Other loans	1,358	1,433	1,589
Lease financing	244	203	212
Other assets	2,917	2,634	2,710
Trading accounts	456	468	269
Bank premises	888	806	773
Other real estate, owned	185	227	339
Intangible assets	196	104	114
All other assets	1,192	1,029	1,215
TOTAL LIABILITIES AND EQUITY CAPITAL	57,016	52,852	49,092
Total liabilities	52,276	48,837	45,538
Total deposits	46,595	44,105	41,339
Federal funds purchased	3,602	3,367	2,653
Demand notes	143	40	58
Other borrowed money	990	465	277
Mortgage indebtedness	27	32	35
Subordinated notes and debentures	76	101	104
Other liabilities	843	728	1,072
Total equity capital	4,740	4,016	3,554
Number of banks	250	251	250

Note: Detail may not add to total due to independent rounding.

Source: Federal Deposit Insurance Corporation, *Statistics on Banking, 1993,* and earlier editions.

TABLE 13.3-- INCOME STATEMENT OF COMMERCIAL BANKS, TENNESSEE, 1991–1993
[In millions of dollars]

Income and expenses	1993	1992	1991
TOTAL OPERATING INCOME	4,523	4,393	4,678
Total interest and fee income	3,651	3,669	4,038
Interest and fees on loans	2,557	2,500	2,845
Income from lease financing receivables	15	16	21
Interest on balances with banks	19	28	66
Income on securities	981	1,025	951
Assets in trading accounts	58	23	25
Income on federal funds sold	21	78	130
Total non-interest income	872	724	640
Fiduciary activities	78	71	67
Service charges on deposit accounts	295	268	251
Foreign transaction income	2	2	2
Trading account gains and fees	121	108	98
Other non-interest income	376	275	221
TOTAL OPERATING EXPENSES	3,434	3,414	3,896
Total interest expense	1,438	1,621	2,218
Interest on deposits	1,294	1,494	2,045
Expense of federal funds purchased	101	100	140
Interest on other borrowings	32	15	19
Mortgages indebtedness	3	3	3
Interest on subordinated notes and debentures	8	9	10
Total non-interest expense	1,996	1,793	1,678
Salaries and employee benefits	895	806	768
Expenses of premises and fixed assets	245	226	221
Other non-interest expense	855	761	689
Provision for loan and lease losses and allocated transfer risk	96	254	329
Pre-tax net opperating income	993	725	453
Securities gains (losses), gross	17	32	34
Income taxes	331	236	126
Income before extraordinary items	679	521	360
Extraordinary items, net of tax	11	3	1
NET INCOME	690	525	361
Full-time equivalent employees (units)	27,274	25,643	25,088
Number of banks (units)	250	251	250

Note: Detail may not add to total due to independent rounding.

Source: Federal Deposit Insurance Corporation, *Statistics on Banking, 1993*, and earlier editions.

FIGURE 13.1
Deposits of Insured Commercial Banks in Tennessee
Annual Percent Change, 1970–1993

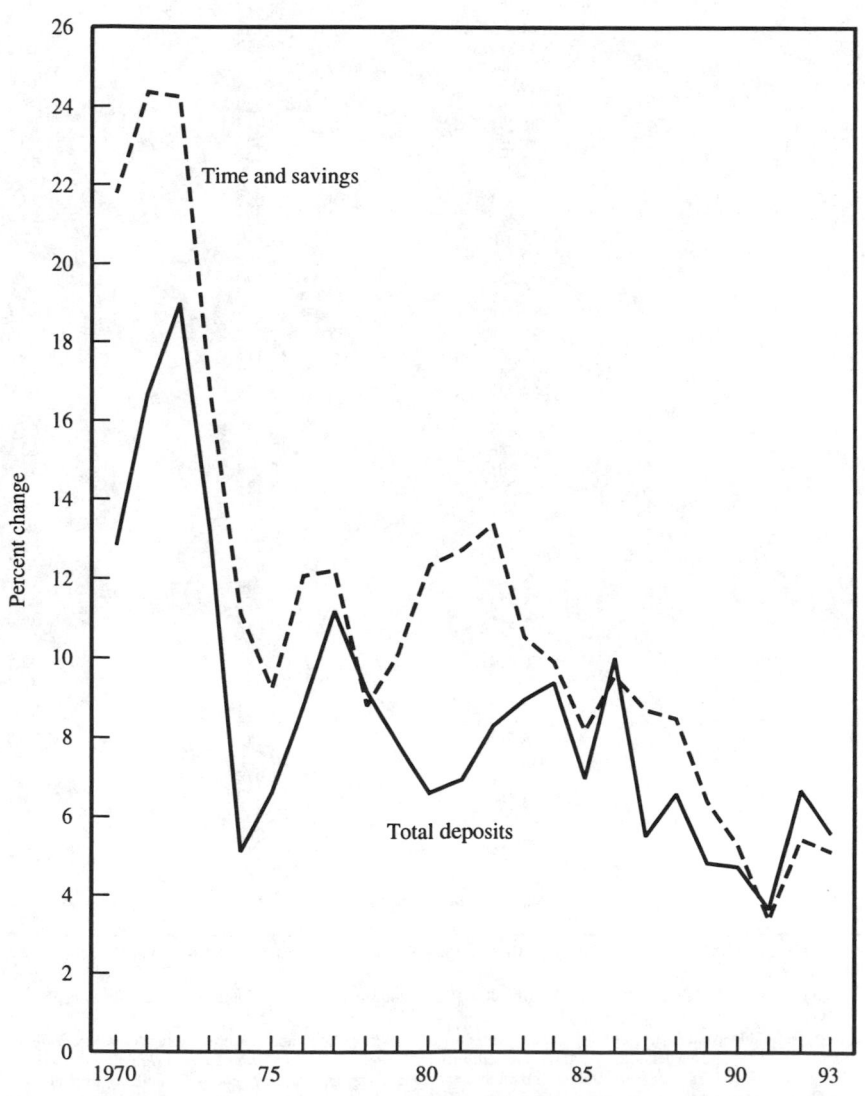

Source: Federal Deposit Insurance Corporation, *Statistics on Banking*, 1993; *Bank Operating Statistics*, 1984, and earlier editions; and U.S. Department of Commerce, Bureau of the Census, *Statistical Abstract of the United States*, 1987.

TABLE 13.4-- DEPOSITS OF INSURED COMMERCIAL BANKS, BY TYPE OF DEPOSIT, TENNESSEE, AS OF DECEMBER 31, 1950–1993, SELECTED YEARS [In millions of dollars]

| Year | Total deposits [1] | Time and savings[2] | |
		Amount	Percent
1993	46,595	38,318	82.2
1992	44,105	36,439	82.6
1991	41,339	34,550	83.6
1990	39,871	33,416	83.8
1989	38,060	31,729	83.4
1988	36,297	29,817	82.1
1987	34,054	27,486	80.7
1986	32,271	25,285	78.4
1985	29,334	23,081	78.7
1984	27,422	21,334	77.8
1983	25,070	19,412	77.4
1982	23,012	17,562	76.3
1981	21,251	15,490	72.9
1980	19,875	13,741	69.1
1979	18,645	12,232	65.6
1978	17,288	11,111	64.3
1977	15,840	10,213	64.5
1976	14,249	9,103	63.9
1975	13,098	8,124	62.0
1974	12,288	7,438	60.5
1973	11,691	6,696	57.3
1972	10,329	5,735	55.5
1971	8,682	4,616	53.2
1970	7,442	3,712	49.9
1969	6,593	3,047	46.2
1968	6,209	2,744	44.2
1967	5,839	2,576	44.1
1966	5,365	2,299	42.9
1965	5,050	2,159	42.8
1964	4,717	1,951	41.4
1963	4,183	1,671	39.9
1962	3,806	1,424	37.4
1961	3,617	1,175	32.5
1960	3,314	1,075	32.4
1959	3,212	1,009	31.4
1958	3,044	967	31.8
1957	2,789	838	30.0
1956	2,729	747	27.4
1955	2,632	695	26.4
1950	2,056	459	22.3

1. For 1978 through 1982, deposits in foreign offices were included only in total deposits, as data on the actual breakdown were not available.

2. Beginning in 1986, refers to all interest-bearing deposits, including those held in interest-bearing checking accounts.

Source: Federal Deposit Insurance Corporation, *Statistics on Banking, 1993*, and earlier editions; *Bank Operating Statistics, 1983*, and earlier editions; *Assets and Liabilities, Commercial and Mutual Savings Banks, December 31, 1977*, and earlier editions; and direct correspondence; U.S. Department of Commerce, Bureau of the Census, *Statistical Abstract of the United States, 1987*.

TABLE 13.5-- SELECTED BALANCE SHEET ITEMS OF INSURED SAVINGS INSTITUTIONS,
TENNESSEE, AS OF DECEMBER 31, 1950–1989, SELECTED YEARS
[Dollar amounts in millions]

Year	Number of institutions	Total assets	Mortgage loans	Total deposits
1989	58	$11,600	$6,637	$9,911
1988	60	12,147	7,014	9,860
1987	63	11,515	6,422	9,240
1986	64	10,624	6,197	8,942
1985	62	9,819	6,207	8,570
1984	66	9,628	5,932	8,562
1983	70	7,814	5,276	6,949
1982	81	7,933	5,907	6,826
1981	92	7,684	6,244	6,473
1980	99	7,425	6,097	6,270
1979	98	6,904	5,858	5,728
1978	97	6,417	5,485	5,321
1977	96	5,529	4,699	4,711
1976	76	4,669	3,924	4,036
1975	78	4,031	3,386	3,458
1974	76	3,461	2,963	2,944
1973	72	3,152	2,715	2,696
1972	71	2,817	2,383	2,436
1971	71	2,358	1,969	2,061
1970	70	1,996	1,674	1,727
1969	70	1,808	1,563	1,568
1968	70	1,690	1,443	1,488
1967	68	1,538	1,301	1,362
1966	66	1,375	1,182	1,219
1965	65	1,285	1,103	1,126
1964	65	1,172	1,005	1,031
1963	64	1,080	918	944
1962	63	953	805	840
1961	59	854	718	764
1960	56	744	629	665
1959	52	644	544	570
1958	49	564	471	505
1957	46	492	411	443
1955	44	395	340	349
1950	39	158	132	137

Source: Federal Home Loan Bank Board, *Savings and Home Financing Source Book, 1989,* and earlier editions.

TABLE 13.6-- SELECTED DATA ON STATE–CHARTERED CREDIT UNIONS, TENNESSEE, 1980–1990, SELECTED YEARS

	1990	1989	1988	1987	1986	1985	1984	1983	1980
Number of credit unions	221	229	241	248	263	280	303	313	365
Average credit union membership	2,978	3,048	2,755	2,588	2,353	2,078	1,820	1,680	1,353
Total number of members	658,246	698,496	664,059	641,979	618,913	581,793	551,497	526,072	494,007
Per member share average	$1,186	$1,372	$1,520	$1,428	$1,507	$1,018	$918	$958	$964
Total number of borrowers	n.a.	n.a.	n.a.	264,267	277,716	254,797	244,497	227,232	245,573
Total number of non-borrowers	n.a.	n.a.	n.a.	377,712	341,197	326,996	307,000	298,840	248,434
Total percent borrowing	n.a.	n.a.	n.a.	41.2	44.9	43.8	44.3	43.2	49.7
Total number of loans	n.a.	n.a.	365,724	n.a.	n.a.	n.a.	n.a.	n.a.	n.a.
Average loan per borrower	n.a.	n.a.	$4,054	$4,977	$4,080	$3,936	$2,861	$3,162	$2,421

n.a. not available.
Source: Tennessee Department of Financial Institutions, direct correspondence, and *1988 Fifteenth Annual Report*, and earlier editions.

TABLE 13.7-- CONSOLIDATED STATEMENT OF CONDITION OF STATE-CHARTERED CREDIT
UNIONS, TENNESSEE, AS OF DECEMBER 31, 1991 [In thousands of dollars]

Assets		Liabilities	
Cash	48,651	Current liabilities	24,091
		Promissory notes	90
Loans	1,445,316	Reverse repurchase agreements	0
Unsecured loans	302,747	Other notes and interest payable	11,947
New auto loans	351,011	Accounts payable and other liabilities	12,054
Used auto loans	141,457		
First mortgage real estate	361,682	Shares and deposits	2,165,363
Other real estate	199,767	Share certificates	526,954
All other loans to members	102,139	Share drafts	141,942
Other loans	402	Regular shares	885,436
Allowance for loan losses	-13,889	Money Market shares	306,374
		IRA/Keogh and retirement accounts	304,258
		Non-member deposits	399
Investments	885,492		
U.S. Government and agency securities	291,875		
GSPS, NIFCUS	3,672	TOTAL LIABILITIES	2,232,270
Mutual fund shares	12,573		
Corporate central credit union deposits	352,015	Reserves	144,813
Commercial bank deposits	112,580	Regular reserve	110,336
S & L and mutual savings bank deposits	78,590	Other reserves	34,477
NCUA share insurance capital deposit	8,291		
Credit union deposits	751	Undivided earnings	63,093
Loans to credit unions	0		
Other investments	25,145		
		TOTAL LIABILITIES	
		AND RESERVES	2,440,176
Allowances for investment losses	-285		
Land and buildings	28,209		
Other real estate owned	2,478		
Other fixed assets	10,082		
Other assets	20,233		
TOTAL ASSETS	2,440,176		

Note: Detail may not add to total due to independent rounding.
Source: Tennessee Department of Financial Institutions, *1991 Eighteenth Annual Report*, and earlier editions.

TABLE 13.8-- OPERATIONS OF COUNTY MUTUAL FIRE INSURANCE COMPANIES, TENNESSEE, 1930–1992, SELECTED YEARS [In thousands of dollars]

Year	Net risks in force at end of year	New membership fees and assessments	Net losses paid	Net losses paid as percent of membership fees and assessments
1992	693,280	4,336	2,118	48.8
1991	627,491	4,182	2,590	61.9
1990	624,022	3,888	1,929	49.6
1989	692,294	3,942	1,960	49.7
1988	677,804	3,811	2,125	55.8
1987	647,484	3,777	1,928	51.0
1986	669,221	3,678	1,977	53.8
1985	556,097	3,380	1,763	52.2
1984	497,438	3,001	1,916	63.8
1983	497,623	2,965	1,520	51.3
1982	501,184	3,015	1,409	46.7
1981	482,171	2,874	1,785	62.1
1980	500,043	2,492	1,596	64.0
1979	445,629	2,336	1,315	56.3
1978	429,662	2,215	1,048	47.3
1977	398,271	1,906	1,316	69.0
1976	364,401	1,655	926	56.0
1975	353,693	1,408	968	68.8
1974	334,434	1,511	1,135	75.1
1973	334,797	1,876	847	45.1
1972	558,201	1,719	931	54.2
1971	401,022	1,652	972	58.8
1970	378,275	1,418	908	64.0
1960	223,096	853	523	61.3
1950	101,862	416	159	38.2
1940	41,649	171	105	61.4
1930	47,959	266	230	86.5

Note: Percentages computed by the Center for Business and Economic Research.

Source: Tennessee Department of Commerce and Insurance, *Annual Report of the Commissioner of Commerce and Insurance, December 31, 1992,* and earlier editions.

TABLE 13.9-- OPERATIONS OF STOCK FIRE AND CASUALTY INSURANCE COMPANIES, TENNESSEE, 1972–1992 [In thousands of dollars]

Year	Premiums earned	Losses incurred	Losses incurred as percent of premiums earned
1992	336,680	181,787	54.0
1991	157,879	102,302	64.8
1990	97,617	65,543	67.1
1989	76,324	55,546	72.8
1988	69,834	47,537	68.1
1987	90,233	104,441	115.7
1986	109,779	91,341	83.2
1985	209,816	184,459	87.9
1984	74,247	63,231	85.2
1983	68,803	49,763	72.3
1982	52,524	40,204	76.5
1981	61,825	42,392	68.6
1980	62,436	40,787	65.3
1979	74,858	50,064	66.9
1978	61,231	34,597	56.5
1977	30,461	15,491	50.9
1976	28,808	17,643	61.2
1975	33,532	20,906	62.3
1974	39,921	26,098	65.4
1973	50,415	29,760	59.0
1972	49,688	24,413	49.1

Note: Refers to companies domiciled in Tennessee.

Source: Tennessee Department of Commerce and Insurance, *Annual Report of the Commissioner of Commerce and Insurance, December 31, 1992,* and earlier editions.

TABLE 13.10--NUMBER OF LICENSED INSURANCE COMPANIES, BY TYPE AND BY STATE OF
DOMICILE, TENNESSEE, DECEMBER 31, 1987–1992

Type of company	Total						Tennessee					
	1992	1991	1990	1989	1988	1987	1992	1991	1990	1989	1988	1987
ife companies	735	741	736	736	739	717	23	24	26	27	27	26
Fraternal orders or associations	14	14	14	14	15	15	1	1	1	1	1	1
Nonprofit hospital and medical associations	5	5	5	4	4	4	5	5	5	4	4	4
Health maintenance organizations	10	10	10	11	12	14	8	10	10	11	12	14
Stock fire and casualty companies	665	637	597	577	566	553	16	17	16	15	14	17
Captive companies	14	15	16	14	13	12	14	15	16	14	13	12
Mutual fire and casualty companies	77	76	78	79	81	80	3	4	4	4	4	5
Reciprocal or inter-insurers	14	15	14	13	14	15	1	1	1	0	0	0
Lloyds, New York	1	1	1	1	1	1	0	0	0	0	0	0
Title companies	25	25	27	28	27	27	3	3	3	3	3	3
County mutual fire companies	19	19	19	19	19	19	19	19	19	19	19	19

Source: Tennessee Department of Commerce and Insurance, *Annual Report of the Commissioner of Commerce and Insurance, December 31, 1992,* and earlier editions.

TABLE 13.11--NUMBER, ASSETS, LIABILITIES, AND SURPLUS OF INSURANCE COMPANIES, BY
TYPE AND BY STATE OF DOMICILE, TENNESSEE, DECEMBER 31, 1992
[In thousands of dollars]

Type of company	Admitted assets [1]	Liabilities	Surplus
Life insurance	1,544,663,897	1,445,278,695	99,385,199
Tennessee	28,551,058	25,748,811	2,802,247
Out-of-state	1,516,112,839	1,419,529,884	96,582,952
Fraternal orders or associations	32,423,651	29,694,037	2,729,611
Tennessee	67,727	53,664	14,062
Out-of-state	32,355,924	29,640,373	2,715,549
Nonprofit hospital and medical associations, Tennessee	777,427	456,280	321,147
Health maintenance organizations,	849,422	564,099	n.a.
Tennessee	81,578	55,162	n.a.
Out-of-state	767,844	508,937	n.a.
Stock fire and casualty	431,445,303	324,586,793	106,858,417
Tennessee	483,448	340,959	142,478
Out-of-state	430,961,855	324,245,834	106,715,939
Mutual fire and casualty	114,453,366	76,663,752	37,789,621
Tennessee	960,324	435,524	524,800
Out-of-state	113,493,042	76,228,228	37,264,821
Mutual Risk Retention, Tennessee	76,383	56,224	20,139
Reciprocal or inter-insurers	20,860,979	14,243,107	6,617,872
Tennessee	5,494	2,218	3,276
Out-of-state	20,855,485	14,240,889	6,614,596
Captive companies, Tennessee	558,112	290,163	267,946
Title companies	2,650,519	1,677,006	973,503
Tennessee	17,986	7,199	10,785
Out-of-state	2,632,533	1,669,807	962,718
County mutual fire companies, Tennessee	21,134	69	21,063
Surplus lines companies	13,761,178	8,068,426	5,692,758

Note: Detail may not add to total due to independent rounding.

n.a. not available.

1. Includes capital or guaranty fund for life insurance companies.

Source: Tennessee Department of Commerce and Insurance, *Annual Report of the Commissioner of Commerce and Insurance, December 31, 1992.*

TABLE 13.12--PREMIUMS EARNED AND LOSSES INCURRED BY INSURANCE COMPANIES, BY TYPE AND BY STATE OF DOMICILE, TENNESSEE, 1992 [In thousands of dollars]

Type of company	Premiums earned	Losses incurred	Losses incurred as percent of premiums earned
Stock fire and casualty	126,279,288	97,163,034	76.9
Tennessee	336,680	181,787	54.0
Out-of-state	125,942,608	96,981,247	77.0
Mutual fire and casualty	46,916,846	33,787,099	72.0
Tennessee	210,404	125,747	59.7
Out-of-state	46,706,442	33,661,352	72.0
Mutual risk retention, Tennessee	19,736	13,816	70.0
Reciprocal or inter-insurers	10,103,977	7,671,513	75.9
Tennessee	548	392	71.5
Out-of-state	10,103,429	7,671,121	75.9
Captive companies, Tennessee	51,536	189	0.3
County mutual fire companies, Tennessee[1]	5,602	2,118	37.8
Fraternal orders or associations[2]	7,509,628	5,578,803	74.3
Tennessee	19,787	14,294	72.2
Out-of-state	7,489,841	5,564,509	74.3
Title insurance	3,518,771	311,827	8.9
Tennessee	7,291	666	9.1
Out-of-state	3,511,480	311,161	8.9
Nonprofit hospital and medical associations	1,408,519	1,314,448	93.3

Note: Percentages computed by Center for Business and Economic Research when not given in source.

1. Refers to total income and net losses paid.

2. Refers to total income and total paid to policyholders.

Source: Tennessee Department of Commerce and Insurance, *Annual Report of the Commissioner of Commerce and Insurance, December 31, 1992.*

TABLE 13.13--LIFE INSURANCE IN FORCE, BY TYPE, TENNESSEE, 1955–1989 [In millions of dollars]

Year	Total	Ordinary	Group	Industrial	Credit
1989	166,478	92,792	66,273	792	6,621
1988	154,096	84,709	62,201	807	6,379
1987	143,106	76,098	60,398	826	5,784
1986	130,746	67,708	56,618	878	5,542
1985	116,766	60,249	50,353	903	5,261
1984	105,333	53,780	46,180	953	4,420
1983	96,501	47,571	43,739	1,039	4,152
1982	86,316	41,154	40,132	1,105	3,925
1981	77,230	36,064	36,047	1,180	3,939
1980	66,672	32,109	29,011	1,281	4,271
1979	61,051	29,323	25,327	1,383	5,018
1978	54,767	26,438	22,289	1,438	4,602
1977	49,206	23,159	20,791	1,599	3,657
1976	43,512	20,696	18,083	1,597	3,136
1975	39,334	18,679	16,172	1,628	2,855
1974	35,128	16,936	13,808	1,626	2,758
1973	32,348	15,389	12,841	1,625	2,493
1972	29,203	13,663	11,351	1,558	2,631
1971	26,291	12,440	10,140	1,513	2,198
1970	24,077	11,428	9,186	1,533	1,930
1969	21,828	10,611	7,832	1,477	1,908
1968	20,242	9,813	7,221	1,466	1,742
1967	18,265	8,956	6,472	1,436	1,401
1966	16,510	8,070	5,729	1,414	1,297
1965	14,909	7,289	5,020	1,378	1,222
1964	12,762	6,496	3,910	1,332	1,024
1963	11,583	5,838	3,587	1,306	852
1962	10,779	5,329	3,408	1,283	759
1961	9,896	4,890	3,094	1,224	688
1960	9,179	4,527	2,784	1,200	668
1959	8,367	4,145	2,471	1,165	586
1958	7,580	3,716	2,202	1,150	512
1957	7,121	3,387	2,041	1,171	522
1956	6,422	3,064	1,784	1,137	437
1955	5,821	2,762	1,563	1,115	381

Note: Life insurance in force is the sum of the face amounts, plus dividend additions, of life insurance policies outstanding at a given time. Additional amounts payable under accidental death or other special provisions are not included.

Beginning in 1973, credit is limited to life insurance on loans of ten years' duration or less. Ordinary and group include credit life insurance on loans of more than ten years' duration.

Source: American Council of Life Insurance, Washington, D.C., *1990 Life Insurance Fact Book,* and earlier editions.

TABLE 13.14--LIFE INSURANCE AND ANNUITY BENEFIT PAYMENTS, TENNESSEE, 1960–1989, SELECTED YEARS [In thousands of dollars]

Benefits	1989	1988	1987	1986	1980	1970	1960
TOTAL	1,456,400	1,436,300	1,347,600	1,229,700	612,800	235,100	104,200
Death payments	438,100	395,500	381,200	369,600	230,700	116,300	51,200
Matured endowments	12,700	12,500	11,200	12,100	11,600	12,100	6,700
Disability payments	11,700	10,100	8,300	10,100	11,600	4,400	2,400
Annuity payments	479,700	535,800	497,600	371,200	118,400	20,100	5,500
Surrender values	275,900	250,900	241,100	261,600	118,400	37,600	20,500
Policy and contract dividends	238,300	231,500	208,200	205,100	122,100	44,600	17,900

Source: American Council of Life Insurance, Washington, D.C., *1990 Life Insurance Fact Book,* and earlier editions.

TABLE 13.15--OPERATIONS OF NONPROFIT HOSPITAL AND MEDICAL ASSOCIATIONS, TENNESSEE, 1950–1992, SELECTED YEARS [In thousands of dollars]

Year	Premiums earned	Claims incurred	Claims incurred as percent of premiums earned
1992	1,408,519	1,314,448	93.3
1991	1,322,894	1,231,605	93.1
1990	1,143,984	1,071,647	93.7
1989	926,158	874,065	94.4
1988	796,505	759,603	95.4
1987	740,230	744,202	100.5
1986	663,053	706,206	106.5
1985	646,410	590,890	91.4
1984	644,872	599,077	92.9
1983	348,428	321,096	92.2
1982	348,890	319,331	91.5
1981	344,671	324,071	94.0
1980	347,495	336,416	96.8
1979	321,424	298,104	92.7
1978	314,692	287,815	91.5
1977	279,190	253,904	90.9
1975	210,596	198,279	94.2
1970	98,245	90,377	92.0
1965	55,028	48,660	88.4
1960	31,525	28,090	89.1
1955	14,674	11,596	79.0
1950	4,349	3,273	75.3

Note: Percentages computed by the Center for Business and Economic Research.

Source: Tennessee Department of Commerce and Insurance, *Annual Report of the Commissioner of Commerce and Insurance, December 31, 1992,* and earlier editions.

TABLE 13.16--NUMBER OF BANKS AND AMOUNT OF DEPOSITS IN INSURED COMMERCIAL BANKS, BY TYPE OF DEPOSIT, METROPOLITAN STATISTICAL AREAS, AS OF JUNE 30, 1989
[Deposits in thousands of dollars]

Metropolitan Statistical Area	Banks	Banking offices	Deposits		
			Total	IPC	Other
Chattanooga	21	113	2,855,678	2,553,093	302,585
Clarksville-Hopkinsville	7	38	831,332	769,479	61,853
Jackson	5	27	684,374	647,821	36,553
Johnson City-Kingsport-Bristol	20	122	2,545,138	2,402,162	142,976
Knoxville	24	161	4,081,170	3,827,793	253,377
Memphis	36	215	7,240,938	6,532,640	708,298
Nashville-Davidson	31	258	9,073,888	8,472,209	601,679

Source: Federal Deposit Insurance Corporation, *Data Book, Operating Banks and Branches, June 30, 1989.*

TABLE 13.17--SELECTED OPERATING STATISTICS AND ASSET SIZE RANKINGS, BY BANK, CITIES, DECEMBER 31, 1989

City	Name of bank	Rank	Total assets ($1,000)	Total loans to deposits[1]
Adamsville	Bank of Adamsville	214	25,968	64.7
Adamsville	Farmers and Merchants Bank	237	19,828	64.2
Alamo	Bank of Alamo	164	39,527	55.4
Alcoa	American Fidelity Bank	203	28,243	76.0
Alexandria	DeKalb County Bank and Trust Company	109	68,579	70.6
Athens	Citizens National Bank of Athens	97	77,158	62.0
Athens	City and County Bank of McMinn County	163	39,930	62.6
Athens	First National Bank and Trust Co. Athens	62	113,602	65.7
Atwood	Citizens Bank and Trust Company	266	8,304	55.0
Barretville	Barretville Bank and Trust Company	32	186,025	61.8
Bartlett	Bank of Bartlett	56	121,275	72.9
Bartlett	Shelby Bank	213	26,153	84.0
Belfast	Bank of Belfast	264	10,480	56.6
Bells	Bank of Crockett	170	36,424	51.4
Bells	Bells Banking Company	224	24,579	75.3
Benton	Benton Banking Company	208	27,467	81.5
Benton	Peoples Bank of Polk County	249	17,622	77.6
Blountville	Tri-City Bank and Trust Company	28	194,883	70.0
Bolivar	Bank of Bolivar	180	34,484	59.5
Bolivar	Hardeman County Bank	114	66,385	81.7
Bradford	Bank of Bradford	205	27,777	38.2
Brentwood	Brentwood National Bank	133	51,772	82.2
Brighton	Brighton Bank	247	17,763	73.6
Brownsville	Brownsville Bank	76	94,203	81.1
Brownsville	First State Bank	95	77,559	57.4
Byrdstown	Peoples Bank and Trust Co. Pickett County	211	26,420	85.4
Byrdstown	Pickett County Bank and Trust Company	200	28,501	33.5
Camden	Bank of Camden	99	75,668	55.2
Carthage	Citizens Bank	38	164,881	65.6
Centerville	First National Bank of Centerville	103	70,803	58.0
Centerville	Sovran Bank Hickman County	162	40,418	64.6
Chapel Hill	First State Bank	250	17,187	29.5
Chattanooga	American National Bank and Trust Company	9	1,190,561	90.2
Chattanooga	First American National Bank	21	263,003	79.1
Chattanooga	Pioneer Bank	18	380,502	53.8
Chattanooga	Sovran Bank Chattanooga	19	326,670	82.7
Chattanooga	Volunteer Bank and Trust Company	159	41,556	73.9
Clarksville	First American Bank	22	261,836	97.2
Clarksville	Heritage Bank	261	12,252	80.2
Cleveland	Bank of Cleveland	144	46,642	78.8
Cleveland	Cleveland Bank and Trust Company	33	185,324	70.5
Cleveland	First Citizens Bank	69	105,453	79.2
Cleveland	Merchants Bank	59	117,782	76.4
Clifton	Peoples Bank	217	25,481	66.7
Clinton	Anderson County Bank	222	24,980	68.8
Collierville	Citizens Bank	238	19,506	63.4
Columbia	First Bank of Maury County	252	16,414	38.9
Columbia	First Farmers and Merchants National Bank	20	271,172	77.9
Columbia	Middle Tennessee Bank	36	168,092	54.8
Cookeville	Bank of Putnam County	82	87,581	68.8

TABLE 13.17--SELECTED OPERATING STATISTICS AND ASSET SIZE RANKINGS, BY BANK, CITIES,
DECEMBER 31, 1989 (Continued)

Total capital as a percent of total assets	Income before extraordinary items ($1,000)	Return on average assets	Return on average equity	Yield on average earning assets	Rate on funds [2]	City
9.88	329	1.31	13.95	11.13	5.78	Adamsville
8.46	112	0.57	7.42	10.66	6.31	Adamsville
12.10	407	1.08	9.67	11.04	6.34	Alamo
8.00	218	0.81	10.82	11.68	6.12	Alcoa
7.84	801	1.22	16.98	11.31	6.58	Alexandria
11.25	1,165	1.58	14.79	10.68	5.83	Athens
9.82	469	1.20	13.82	10.71	5.70	Athens
7.99	1,460	1.29	17.43	10.91	5.91	Athens
8.23	11	0.14	1.51	11.05	7.40	Atwood
18.67	3,270	1.80	10.22	10.30	5.04	Barretville
7.56	473	0.41	6.12	12.12	6.80	Bartlett
13.67	228	1.11	7.40	12.01	6.89	Bartlett
9.08	-38	-0.39	-4.89	11.28	6.33	Belfast
9.16	410	1.17	14.03	11.26	6.57	Bells
8.61	220	0.98	12.17	11.10	6.60	Bells
8.34	323	1.23	15.53	11.60	5.36	Benton
9.68	158	0.91	10.39	11.74	7.05	Benton
8.78	1,410	0.76	9.02	10.25	5.90	Blountville
7.66	248	0.75	10.89	11.19	6.21	Bolivar
8.34	484	0.74	10.39	11.00	6.56	Bolivar
9.66	288	1.07	11.45	9.99	6.30	Bradford
20.32	279	0.61	2.79	10.61	6.01	Brentwood
8.26	208	1.23	16.54	11.42	6.99	Brighton
10.92	1,038	1.13	10.77	10.82	6.78	Brownsville
11.10	771	1.03	9.91	10.46	6.32	Brownsville
9.17	310	1.23	15.54	12.26	7.20	Byrdstown
8.49	-30	-0.10	-0.87	10.47	6.96	Byrdstown
10.90	715	0.97	9.30	10.62	6.23	Camden
14.51	3,436	2.23	15.75	11.13	6.28	Carthage
11.11	841	1.22	11.50	11.63	6.31	Centerville
13.04	344	0.89	6.88	10.88	6.36	Centerville
12.33	217	1.27	10.95	10.12	5.58	Chapel Hill
8.67	12,330	1.06	14.40	10.71	6.32	Chattanooga
6.87	2,200	0.92	14.78	11.09	6.48	Chattanooga
10.88	477	1.67	18.77	11.46	5.72	Chattanooga
8.02	-321	-1.11	-16.94	10.09	6.60	Chattanooga
7.96	-40	-0.09	-1.29	10.61	6.96	Chattanooga
7.12	1,759	0.68	9.40	11.88	6.60	Clarksville
35.04	-257	-3.22	-6.34	5.53	2.18	Clarksville
9.06	517	1.21	14.80	11.39	6.66	Cleveland
9.55	1,703	0.97	10.59	10.99	6.32	Cleveland
8.81	1,351	1.32	17.60	11.95	6.49	Cleveland
9.59	-726	-0.62	-6.88	11.30	6.29	Cleveland
5.46	132	0.51	13.24	11.40	6.90	Clifton
3.19	-1,669	-5.59	-96.75	9.84	7.21	Clinton
8.18	144	0.80	10.35	11.55	6.71	Collierville
3.21	-332	-1.94	-89.88	10.20	7.16	Columbia
10.17	-30	-0.10	-0.87	10.47	6.96	Columbia
9.60	1,650	1.00	11.14	10.56	6.18	Columbia
9.11	841	1.00	11.88	10.66	5.92	Cookeville

TABLE 13.17--SELECTED OPERATING STATISTICS AND ASSET SIZE RANKINGS, BY BANK, CITIES, DECEMBER 31, 1989 (Continued)

City	Name of bank	Rank	Total assets ($1,000)	Total loans to deposits [1]
Cookeville	Citizens Bank	42	145,674	57.0
Cookeville	First American Bank	30	187,191	68.5
Cookeville	Peoples Bank and Trust Company Cumberlands	212	26,410	76.7
Copperhill	First National Bank of Polk County	118	62,290	84.1
Cordova	Cordova Bank and Trust Company	254	15,197	62.8
Cornersville	Farmers Bank	228	22,580	71.8
Covington	First State Bank of Covington	89	82,166	78.4
Covington	Tipton County Bank	39	160,397	61.7
Covington	Union Savings Bank	130	54,501	60.9
Crossville	Cumberland County Bank	134	51,630	61.0
Crossville	First National Bank of Crossville	51	131,499	51.7
Cumberland City	Cumberland City Bank	233	20,734	56.6
Dayton	Rhea County National Bank	179	34,584	72.4
Decatur	Meigs County Bank	153	43,153	70.6
Decaturville	Decatur County Bank	168	36,687	39.2
Dickson	Bank of Dickson	98	76,816	55.1
Dover	Farmers and Merchants Bank	225	24,427	76.5
Dresden	Weakley County Bank	199	28,543	68.2
Ducktown	Home Banking Tennessee	142	47,892	77.4
Dunlap	Citizens Bank Dunlap/Pikeville	204	27,853	76.1
Dunlap	Sequatchie County Bank	191	31,314	60.4
Dyer	Bank of Dyer	253	16,297	67.9
Dyer	Farmers and Merchants Bank	197	29,009	71.9
Dyersburg	First Citizens National Bank	26	220,978	72.3
East Ridge	Bank of East Ridge	235	20,486	68.5
Elizabethton	Carter County Bank	63	112,758	52.0
Elizabethton	Citizens Bank	54	123,750	102.0
Erin	Erin Bank and Trust Company	184	34,224	44.1
Erwin	Erwin National Bank	149	44,278	61.1
Etowah	Southern United Bank McMinn County	229	22,286	36.9
Fayetteville	Lincoln County Bank	111	67,492	82.4
Fayetteville	Peoples Bank of Elk Valley	210	27,189	70.2
Finger	Home Banking Company	258	13,446	49.7
Frankewing	Bank of Frankewing	231	21,615	77.4
Franklin	First Citizens Bank	192	30,836	78.8
Franklin	Franklin National Bank	265	8,835	36.8
Friendship	Bank of Friendship	240	18,969	35.6
Gainesboro	Citizens Bank	232	21,576	53.2
Gainesboro	Jackson County Bank	145	45,183	52.9
Gates	Gates Banking and Trust Company	234	20,508	56.0
Gatlinburg	First National Bank of Gatlinburg	55	123,276	81.0
Gatlinburg	Tennessee State Bank	77	94,090	79.3
Germantown	Community Bank of Germantown	25	239,507	77.2
Gleason	Bank of Gleason	161	41,278	63.1
Goodlettsville	Bank of Goodlettsville	50	135,596	72.5
Greeneville	Andrew Johnson Bank	169	36,667	71.1
Greeneville	Greene County Bank	27	209,623	67.9
Greeneville	Sovran Bank - Grennville	49	137,699	66.1
Greenfield	Greenfield Banking Company	181	34,310	47.3
Halls	Bank of Halls	189	31,800	50.1

TABLE 13.17--SELECTED OPERATING STATISTICS AND ASSET SIZE RANKINGS, BY BANK, CITIES, DECEMBER 31, 1989 (Continued)

Total capital as a percent of total assets	Income before extraordinary items ($1,000)	Return on average assets	Return on average equity	Yield on average earning assets	Rate on funds [2]	City
9.39	2,206	1.54	24.56	10.76	6.66	Cookeville
6.71	1,801	1.04	16.56	10.86	6.65	Cookeville
21.84	133	0.72	2.60	11.07	5.46	Cookeville
8.55	733	1.24	16.71	11.60	7.34	Copperhill
37.19	-58	-0.68	-1.64	6.02	2.39	Cordova
10.01	416	2.12	23.54	12.55	6.50	Cornersville
8.75	905	1.16	14.74	11.10	6.28	Covington
8.31	1,085	0.71	9.31	10.52	6.67	Covington
7.78	556	1.14	15.85	10.45	6.07	Covington
7.31	424	0.84	12.53	10.05	5.83	Crossville
7.78	1,370	1.07	14.58	10.11	6.29	Crossville
8.80	125	0.60	5.86	6.32	4.02	Cumberland City
8.15	378	1.14	15.92	12.26	6.65	Dayton
7.53	336	0.84	11.57	11.96	6.60	Decatur
10.83	172	0.47	4.73	10.26	6.11	Decaturville
10.01	914	1.23	13.56	10.74	6.02	Dickson
10.02	60	0.28	4.51	11.80	7.17	Dover
6.45	-321	-1.11	-16.94	10.09	6.60	Dresden
8.18	253	0.53	7.42	11.50	6.73	Ducktown
7.68	321	1.19	16.33	12.27	6.76	Dunlap
14.05	366	1.19	8.83	10.33	5.98	Dunlap
5.53	-326	-2.04	-28.97	10.58	6.46	Dyer
8.97	341	1.27	16.73	11.41	6.33	Dyer
7.24	1,309	0.61	9.22	11.00	6.54	Dyersburg
10.09	158	0.83	8.91	10.91	6.31	East Ridge
6.95	1,048	0.96	14.43	11.07	6.48	Elizabethton
9.81	1,762	1.45	15.18	12.29	6.47	Elizabethton
14.13	487	1.48	10.68	10.59	5.40	Erin
7.69	206	0.50	6.68	10.62	6.22	Erwin
8.05	169	0.76	10.33	10.19	5.77	Etowah
8.80	1,116	1.72	20.17	12.73	6.09	Fayetteville
4.32	-1,160	-3.88	-89.49	11.69	6.95	Fayetteville
8.50	138	1.05	13.40	10.63	6.44	Finger
11.97	409	1.91	17.39	12.11	6.54	Frankewing
12.68	71	0.26	1.97	10.92	7.08	Franklin
66.93	-419	-5.77	-7.63	0.63	0.14	Franklin
10.22	165	0.90	9.07	10.51	6.50	Friendship
11.54	181	0.85	8.05	10.95	6.52	Gainesboro
10.09	407	0.92	10.38	10.65	6.30	Gainesboro
8.50	128	0.66	8.06	10.96	6.60	Gates
7.64	281	0.24	3.65	2.96	1.86	Gatlinburg
7.57	1,064	1.18	16.71	11.62	6.83	Gatlinburg
9.48	1,691	0.75	9.03	11.57	6.77	Germantown
11.18	549	1.40	13.26	10.83	6.45	Gleason
8.48	1,113	0.86	10.96	11.34	6.61	Goodlettsville
8.03	361	1.06	14.29	10.67	6.34	Greeneville
11.71	3,015	1.51	13.20	10.42	5.95	Greeneville
10.22	1,932	1.49	15.93	11.11	6.10	Greeneville
10.15	360	1.11	11.59	10.31	6.56	Greenfield
9.51	290	0.94	10.14	10.40	6.49	Halls

TABLE 13.17--SELECTED OPERATING STATISTICS AND ASSET SIZE RANKINGS, BY BANK, CITIES, DECEMBER 31, 1989 (Continued)

City	Name of bank	Rank	Total assets ($1,000)	Total loans to deposits [1]
Halls	Lauderdale County Bank	257	14,697	67.2
Harriman	Bank of Roane County	53	130,396	57.4
Harrogate	Commercial Bank Claiborne County	101	73,189	67.9
Hartsville	Bank of Hartsville	158	41,915	71.3
Hartsville	Citizens Bank	206	27,587	71.0
Henderson	Chester County Bank	236	19,900	86.3
Henderson	First State Bank	83	86,689	32.4
Hohenwald	First Citizens Bank Hohenwald	155	42,726	54.8
Hohenwald	Lewis County Bank	220	25,202	88.2
Hornbeak	Reelfoot Bank	110	67,831	67.8
Humboldt	Merchants State Bank	65	110,658	57.5
Huntingdon	Bank of Huntingdon	75	94,234	52.2
Huntland	Bank of Huntland	256	14,875	84.0
Jacksboro	First State Bank	178	35,236	55.9
Jackson	First American National Bank	15	454,748	66.8
Jackson	First National Bank Jackson	128	56,165	87.7
Jackson	Jackson National Bank	24	242,433	81.7
Jamestown	Fentress County Bank	198	28,913	62.6
Jamestown	Union Bank	127	56,325	58.7
Jasper	Marion Trust and Banking Company	138	49,160	84.8
Jefferson City	First Peoples Bank	165	39,206	62.5
Jellico	Union Bank	186	33,515	28.6
Johnson City	Hamilton Bank of Upper East Tennessee	23	251,784	80.0
Johnson City	Sovran Bank Tri-Cities	84	85,404	68.7
Kenton	First State Bank	117	64,550	69.6
Kingsport	Bank of Tennessee	52	131,014	77.2
Kingsport	Executive Park National Bank	171	36,392	56.4
Kingsport	First American National Bank	11	596,869	87.1
Kingston Springs	Cheatham State Bank	140	48,689	74.2
Knoxville	Bank of East Tennessee	35	168,187	86.5
Knoxville	First American Bank	8	1,431,157	83.6
Knoxville	First National Bank Knoxville	173	36,123	81.1
Knoxville	NBC Knoxville Bank	73	98,605	56.6
Knoxville	Third National Bank in Knoxville	16	407,977	82.9
Knoxville	Valley Fidelity Bank and Trust Company	13	495,669	68.7
Lafayette	Citizens Bank	71	103,387	60.9
Lafayette	Macon Bank and Trust Company	91	80,509	55.7
LaFollette	First National Bank of LaFollette	112	67,342	53.4
LaFollette	Peoples National Bank LaFollette	102	71,476	47.2
Lake City	Third National Bank in Anderson County	45	140,828	63.6
Lawrenceburg	Community Bank and Trust Company	219	25,223	50.0
Lawrenceburg	First National Bank of Lawrenceburg	68	108,113	41.6
Lebanon	Lebanon Bank	41	147,407	59.8
Lebanon	Peoples Bank	104	70,482	73.8
Lebanon	Wilson Bank and Trust Company	94	78,638	72.2
Lenoir City	First National Bank of Loudon County	48	138,821	66.9
Lenoir City	Third National Bank	93	78,710	73.6
Lewisburg	Peoples and Union Bank	92	79,941	65.1
Lexington	Central State Bank	78	94,019	41.5
Lexington	First Bank	100	73,863	70.4

TABLE 13.17--SELECTED OPERATING STATISTICS AND ASSET SIZE RANKINGS, BY BANK, CITIES,
DECEMBER 31, 1989 (Continued)

Total capital as a percent of total assets	Income before extra-ordinary items ($1,000)	Return on average assets	Return on average equity	Yield on average earning assets	Rate on funds [2]	City
9.74	7	0.05	0.56	11.27	6.38	Halls
7.91	2,676	2.11	27.03	10.76	6.27	Harriman
6.45	471	0.69	9.56	10.80	6.48	Harrogate
8.77	317	0.78	8.79	10.83	6.20	Hartsville
9.90	362	1.34	14.89	11.57	5.96	Hartsville
11.04	164	0.82	8.16	11.78	6.59	Henderson
12.82	1,092	1.29	10.35	10.03	6.24	Henderson
7.72	416	0.96	12.10	10.54	6.42	Hohenwald
8.92	324	1.36	17.21	11.59	7.39	Hohenwald
8.88	383	0.77	9.44	14.81	8.97	Hornbeak
8.99	1,852	1.70	20.37	10.63	6.58	Humboldt
8.32	969	1.05	13.34	10.29	6.26	Huntingdon
7.80	379	2.54	36.86	11.44	5.91	Huntland
9.03	459	1.36	15.52	10.10	6.01	Jacksboro
7.10	291	1.03	13.30	11.18	6.59	Jackson
5.48	-824	-1.49	-23.72	10.98	9.75	Jackson
8.77	1,761	0.73	8.88	10.74	6.46	Jackson
9.60	477	1.67	18.77	11.46	5.72	Jamestown
14.91	995	1.81	12.85	11.17	5.87	Jamestown
9.33	1,029	2.15	25.75	12.11	6.16	Jasper
7.74	-916	-2.16	-32.36	10.49	5.73	Jefferson City
13.21	396	1.22	9.48	10.18	5.54	Jellico
8.94	2,633	1.07	13.37	11.65	5.74	Johnson City
7.74	640	0.80	10.64	10.89	6.26	Johnson City
6.78	460	0.83	13.70	10.94	6.73	Kenton
7.64	1,079	0.87	12.05	11.04	6.93	Kingsport
8.76	11	0.03	0.36	10.54	7.23	Kingsport
6.78	366	1.19	8.83	10.33	5.98	Kingsport
7.51	467	1.03	16.08	12.36	6.88	Kingston Springs
6.65	200	0.12	1.51	11.31	6.47	Knoxville
7.17	12,229	0.86	13.53	10.55	6.18	Knoxville
20.55	-847	-3.30	-12.11	10.35	5.58	Knoxville
6.94	764	0.92	15.70	11.10	8.01	Knoxville
9.40	809	2.70	90.90	11.35	4.61	Knoxville
10.39	187	0.64	10.67	11.44	6.89	Knoxville
8.55	1,059	1.06	13.33	10.62	6.54	Lafayette
9.13	522	0.66	7.69	10.53	6.41	Lafayette
11.15	804	1.22	11.54	10.52	5.84	LaFollette
12.12	1,008	1.39	12.29	10.29	5.69	LaFollette
7.50	1,418	1.02	13.76	11.02	5.94	Lake City
10.55	140	0.59	5.69	10.85	6.29	Lawrenceburg
9.89	1,309	1.21	13.13	10.24	5.90	Lawrenceburg
9.09	329	0.22	2.62	11.22	6.47	Lebanon
9.21	-145	-0.20	-2.56	12.24	6.36	Lebanon
8.97	957	1.43	16.17	12.19	7.39	Lebanon
9.98	1,431	1.06	11.40	10.69	6.55	Lenoir City
9.41	754	0.94	11.36	11.16	6.52	Lenoir City
12.48	1,126	1.44	13.48	10.19	5.86	Lewisburg
11.18	18	0.02	0.18	10.84	6.50	Lexington
7.80	653	0.91	11.73	11.29	6.24	Lexington

TABLE 13.17--SELECTED OPERATING STATISTICS AND ASSET SIZE RANKINGS, BY BANK, CITIES,
            DECEMBER 31, 1989 (Continued)

City	Name of bank	Rank	Total assets ($1,000)	Total loans to deposits [1]
Lexington	Henderson County Bank	248	17,699	86.5
Liberty	Liberty State Bank	193	30,098	66.2
Linden	First State Bank	185	33,537	53.1
Livingston	First National Bank Cumberlands	120	61,037	79.8
Livingston	Union Bank and Trust Company	196	29,585	70.4
Lobelville	Bank of Perry County	221	25,027	71.2
Loudon	First Heritage National Bank	121	60,962	72.9
Lynchburg	Farmers Bank	136	51,045	25.0
McKenzie	McKenzie Banking Company	139	49,157	46.7
McLemoresville	Carroll Bank and Trust Company	125	58,121	72.1
McMinnville	City Bank and Trust Company	34	179,252	60.3
McMinnville	First National Bank of McMinnville	47	139,074	51.4
Madison	First Cumberland Bank	150	43,948	71.1
Madisonville	Bank of Madisonville	81	89,777	61.2
Manchester	Coffee County Bank	239	19,307	81.9
Manchester	First National Bank of Manchester	126	57,756	55.4
Manchester	Peoples Bank and Trust Company	175	35,879	56.7
Martin	City State Bank	129	55,915	62.0
Martin	Martin Bank	147	44,397	49.2
Maryville	Citizens Bank of Blount County	58	119,905	73.5
Mason	Bank of Mason	268	5,773	47.1
Maury City	Planters Bank	263	11,263	56.4
Maynardville	First State Bank	227	23,115	43.3
Medina	Medina Banking Company	230	21,814	47.3
Memphis	Boatmen's Bank of Tennessee	12	550,559	92.0
Memphis	First American Bank	10	680,731	53.5
Memphis	First Tennessee Bank	1	6,142,997	77.4
Memphis	National Bank of Commerce	7	1,632,720	67.5
Memphis	Sovran Bank	17	385,078	94.3
Memphis	Tri-State Bank of Memphis	123	59,300	45.8
Memphis	Union Planters National Bank	5	2,584,207	82.4
Memphis	United American Bank	31	187,106	74.9
Middleton	Bank of Middleton	226	23,461	70.8
Milan	Milan Banking Company	113	66,629	66.2
Millington	Tennessee Bank and Trust Company	223	24,583	75.9
Morristown	Third National Bank Hamblen County	57	120,948	72.8
Morristown	United Southern Bank	176	35,286	69.5
Moscow	Moscow Savings Bank	244	18,448	76.5
Mt. Juliet	First Bank and Trust Company	177	35,240	79.4
Mountain City	Farmers State Bank	122	60,087	56.2
Mountain City	Johnson County Bank	218	25,349	54.8
Munford	Munford Union Bank	183	34,258	66.2
Murfreesboro	First American Bank	60	117,735	47.7
Murfreesboro	First City Bank	46	139,175	59.2
Murfreesboro	Mid-South Bank and Trust Company	14	488,099	79.8
Nashville	Bank Nashville	148	44,298	129.0
Nashville	Citizens Savings Bank and Trust Company	167	38,432	65.0
Nashville	Dominion Bank of Middle Tennessee	6	1,649,345	83.3
Nashville	First American National Bank	3	3,047,923	91.4
Nashville	First American Trust Company	267	5,858	(a)

TABLE 13.17--SELECTED OPERATING STATISTICS AND ASSET SIZE RANKINGS, BY BANK, CITIES, DECEMBER 31, 1989 (Continued)

Total capital as a percent of total assets	Income before extra- ordinary items ($1,000)	Return on average assets	Return on average equity	Yield on average earning assets	Rate on funds [2]	City
13.15	19	0.14	0.96	11.03	6.88	Lexington
7.12	187	0.64	10.67	11.44	6.89	Liberty
11.27	380	1.12	11.60	10.28	5.99	Linden
7.57	580	1.02	14.36	10.94	6.41	Livingston
6.72	809	2.70	90.90	11.35	4.61	Livingston
9.77	302	1.29	14.06	10.94	6.71	Lobelville
6.78	445	0.82	11.97	11.48	6.67	Loudon
11.74	391	0.80	6.93	9.71	6.48	Lynchburg
8.96	557	1.19	12.16	10.94	6.32	McKenzie
8.27	546	0.98	13.08	11.70	6.82	McLemoresville
9.95	2,434	1.40	15.33	10.82	6.30	McMinnville
13.70	2,200	1.64	12.54	10.63	5.73	McMinnville
9.75	-753	-2.00	-18.03	11.53	7.03	Madison
9.24	752	0.86	10.01	10.60	6.34	Madisonville
13.75	351	1.91	14.04	11.87	5.29	Manchester
8.97	709	1.26	15.32	10.84	6.09	Manchester
8.48	340	0.98	12.29	10.79	5.70	Manchester
8.80	446	0.82	10.05	10.98	6.87	Martin
10.27	586	1.32	13.66	9.49	5.81	Martin
8.19	1,384	1.20	16.42	10.47	6.42	Maryville
11.54	19	0.36	3.03	10.58	5.93	Mason
11.56	173	1.72	15.04	10.66	5.03	Maury City
8.61	106	0.46	6.13	10.42	6.11	Maynardville
10.37	132	0.63	6.41	10.62	6.19	Medina
7.85	71	0.26	1.97	10.92	7.08	Memphis
6.68	-4,015	-0.62	-10.00	10.16	6.55	Memphis
8.32	27,112	0.45	7.84	11.20	6.62	Memphis
7.31	20,941	1.36	19.38	11.18	6.64	Memphis
8.17	341	1.27	16.73	11.41	6.33	Memphis
11.04	678	1.15	11.67	10.10	5.23	Memphis
6.75	-25,296	-0.91	-16.26	10.98	7.27	Memphis
7.15	580	0.33	4.62	10.97	5.67	Memphis
9.22	204	0.89	10.80	10.78	6.34	Middleton
8.28	480	0.71	9.12	10.17	6.80	Milan
12.28	102	0.45	4.41	12.02	6.74	Millington
9.19	1,253	1.06	13.39	10.68	5.71	Morristown
8.14	550	1.62	22.78	10.83	6.01	Morristown
10.49	207	1.19	12.30	11.90	6.65	Moscow
20.38	-66	-0.29	-1.07	11.00	4.97	Mt. Juliet
12.17	856	1.47	13.66	11.73	6.10	Mountain City
9.11	142	0.56	6.76	11.16	6.57	Mountain City
10.37	389	1.19	12.24	11.50	6.42	Munford
6.86	467	0.41	6.13	10.94	6.79	Murfreesboro
8.57	316	0.26	4.47	10.76	7.04	Murfreesboro
8.55	373	1.28	15.91	11.85	6.87	Murfreesboro
61.22	-559	-1.70	-2.64	2.00	0.19	Nashville
6.31	58	0.17	4.31	10.66	4.94	Nashville
7.64	3,063	0.19	2.76	11.53	6.54	Nashville
6.57	-20,590	-0.65	-11.50	10.69	7.01	Nashville
57.26	1,014	19.36	31.59	8.27	0.00	Nashville

509

TABLE 13.17--SELECTED OPERATING STATISTICS AND ASSET SIZE RANKINGS, BY BANK, CITIES, DECEMBER 31, 1989 (Continued)

City	Name of bank	Rank	Total assets ($1,000)	Total loans to deposits [1]
Nashville	First Union National Bank Tennessee	182	34,279	207.9
Nashville	Nashville Bank of Commerce	64	111,881	54.4
Nashville	Southtrust Bank Middle Tennessee	146	44,829	81.4
Nashville	Sovran Bank Central South	2	3,986,337	86.7
Nashville	Third National Bank in Nashville	4	2,618,347	96.9
New Tazewell	Citizens Bank	115	66,127	55.1
Newbern	Security Bank	131	54,090	37.3
Newport	Merchants and Planters Bank	43	141,749	47.9
Newport	National Bank of Newport	108	69,418	59.1
Niota	Bank of Niota	251	16,436	63.4
Oakland	Oakland Deposit Bank	243	18,709	74.0
Obion	Commercial Bank	215	25,882	42.5
Oneida	First National Bank of Oneida	90	81,489	75.3
Oneida	First Trust and Savings Bank	132	53,710	67.3
Paris	Commercial Bank and Trust Company	44	141,427	67.8
Paris	Security Bank and Trust Company	107	69,973	85.1
Parsons	Citizens State Bank	246	17,893	64.7
Parsons	Farmers Bank	202	28,363	72.7
Pikeville	First National Bank of Pikeville	172	36,280	62.8
Portland	Farmers Bank	88	82,464	67.1
Portland	Volunteer State Bank	86	83,924	70.7
Pulaski	First National Bank of Pulaski	40	149,997	68.5
Pulaski	Union Bank	70	103,975	53.8
Ripley	Bank of Ripley	87	83,665	58.6
Ripley	Farmers Union Bank	119	61,123	75.0
Rogersville	Citizens Union Bank	29	189,800	59.4
Rutledge	Citizens Bank & Trust Co. Grainger County	106	70,053	53.8
Sardis	Peoples Bank	242	18,713	31.4
Savannah	Citizens Bank	141	48,161	54.1
Savannah	Hardin County Bank	105	70,152	70.9
Selmer	First National Bank	174	35,904	83.6
Selmer	Selmer Bank and Trust Company	116	65,011	56.1
Sevierville	Citizens National Bank	96	77,479	83.4
Sevierville	Sevier County Bank	67	109,152	53.6
Sevierville	Third National Bank in Sevier County	61	115,960	60.7
Sharon	Bank of Sharon	137	49,507	53.6
Shelbyville	First Community Bank Bedford County	209	27,390	69.0
Shelbyville	First National Bank of Shelbyville	37	165,445	67.4
Smithville	Citizens Bank	72	100,545	64.3
Sneedville	Citizens Bank	241	18,914	76.2
Somerville	First State Bank of Fayette County	201	28,391	64.3
Somerville	Somerville Bank and Trust Company	85	84,992	73.5
South Pittsburg	Citizens State Bank	194	29,985	84.3
Spencer	Citizens Bank	260	12,955	73.5
Spring City	First Bank of Rhea County	154	42,777	81.3
Sweetwater	Sweetwater Valley Bank	74	97,303	58.5
Tazewell	First Claiborne Bank	80	91,233	58.7
Tiptonville	First State Bank and Trust Company	216	25,528	70.0
Toone	Merchants and Planters Bank	166	38,685	70.0
Trenton	Bank of Commerce	190	31,571	53.6

TABLE 13.17--SELECTED OPERATING STATISTICS AND ASSET SIZE RANKINGS, BY BANK, CITIES, DECEMBER 31, 1989 (Continued)

Total capital as a percent of total assets	Income before extra-ordinary items ($1,000)	Return on average assets	Return on average equity	Yield on average earning assets	Rate on funds [2]	City
12.99	-1,597	-4.67	-40.95	13.01	8.77	Nashville
7.08	1,101	1.17	19.21	12.47	7.82	Nashville
16.63	-19	-0.06	-0.27	10.93	6.74	Nashville
8.39	41,414	1.10	15.27	10.80	6.49	Nashville
9.91	22,828	0.86	11.96	10.94	6.54	Nashville
9.93	529	0.82	8.62	10.65	5.84	New Tazewell
7.52	338	0.64	8.41	10.25	6.72	Newbern
7.08	1,425	1.02	14.44	10.37	6.46	Newport
8.81	544	0.82	10.23	10.40	5.71	Newport
8.75	88	0.55	6.67	10.31	5.60	Niota
8.25	140	0.80	11.00	12.14	6.79	Oakland
9.80	298	1.16	11.86	10.47	6.43	Obion
8.78	882	1.08	13.17	10.78	6.54	Oneida
9.56	393	0.72	8.49	10.71	6.33	Oneida
7.50	2,119	1.55	22.57	11.23	6.28	Paris
7.96	789	1.17	16.85	11.62	7.18	Paris
5.43	-162	-0.90	-17.74	10.95	6.31	Parsons
9.26	271	1.00	11.84	11.29	6.16	Parsons
10.02	506	1.42	16.36	11.24	6.43	Pikeville
10.06	1,300	1.66	16.91	11.64	5.96	Portland
7.66	-215	-0.27	-3.41	11.56	6.14	Portland
11.65	2,095	1.44	13.74	11.53	6.15	Pulaski
10.60	1,283	1.34	13.53	10.88	5.93	Pulaski
11.73	703	0.87	8.05	11.24	6.41	Ripley
8.48	584	1.01	11.64	10.57	6.63	Ripley
10.02	2,301	1.23	12.90	10.79	6.22	Rogersville
11.40	1,232	1.83	16.83	11.15	5.43	Rutledge
8.23	68	0.41	5.22	9.24	6.58	Sardis
8.74	668	1.40	17.79	10.67	5.93	Savannah
8.13	648	0.97	13.00	11.17	6.38	Savannah
10.32	423	1.23	12.28	11.29	6.23	Selmer
11.08	698	1.10	10.19	10.08	6.05	Selmer
7.90	1,003	1.39	19.34	11.31	5.96	Sevierville
8.25	529	0.49	5.92	10.35	6.27	Sevierville
9.51	1,615	1.38	16.14	10.71	5.85	Sevierville
11.05	843	1.79	17.54	11.68	6.70	Sharon
14.50	181	0.84	5.51	11.84	6.26	Shelbyville
7.75	1,579	1.02	14.63	11.52	6.57	Shelbyville
6.55	1,056	0.91	14.64	10.67	6.75	Smithville
9.86	228	1.29	13.79	10.83	5.73	Sneedville
10.58	166	0.60	6.98	10.29	7.18	Somerville
14.52	1,347	1.73	12.29	11.57	6.25	Somerville
8.75	373	1.28	15.91	11.85	6.87	South Pittsburg
10.12	142	1.12	11.34	11.34	5.94	Spencer
10.10	844	2.07	23.43	12.23	6.06	Spring City
9.51	1,071	1.18	12.90	11.09	5.97	Sweetwater
10.03	317	0.36	3.77	10.86	6.67	Tazewell
12.27	270	1.05	9.19	11.45	5.69	Tiptonville
7.83	439	1.21	17.30	12.09	6.88	Toone
8.83	255	0.86	10.06	10.14	6.23	Trenton

TABLE 13.17--SELECTED OPERATING STATISTICS AND ASSET SIZE RANKINGS, BY BANK, CITIES, DECEMBER 31, 1989 (Continued)

City	Name of bank	Rank	Total assets ($1,000)	Total loans to deposits [1]
Trenton	Bank of Trenton and Trust Company	188	33,024	46.6
Trenton	Citizens State Bank	207	27,551	80.1
Trezevant	Farmers and Merchants Bank	259	13,314	60.7
Troy	Bank of Troy	187	33,068	62.4
Tullahoma	American City Bank Tullahoma	157	42,344	80.1
Tullahoma	First National Bank of Tullahoma	143	47,316	68.5
Tullahoma	Traders National Bank of Tullahoma	160	41,512	83.2
Union City	First Volunteer Bank	255	15,178	75.2
Union City	Sovran Bank	66	109,557	80.2
Vanleer	Peoples Bank	124	59,015	72.7
Wartburg	Citizens Bank and Trust Company	135	51,375	61.2
Waynesboro	Bank of Waynesboro	152	43,206	54.9
Waynesboro	Wayne County Bank	151	43,369	80.0
White Bluff	Farmers and Merchants Bank	245	18,384	56.0
Whiteville	Whiteville Bank	195	29,608	69.3
Winchester	Franklin County Bank	156	42,404	64.0
Woodbury	Bank of Commerce	79	91,896	38.0
Woodland Mills	Farmers Bank	262	11,638	41.2

TABLE 13.17--SELECTED OPERATING STATISTICS AND ASSET SIZE RANKINGS, BY BANK, CITIES, DECEMBER 31, 1989 (Continued)

Total capital as a percent of total assets	Income before extra-ordinary items ($1,000)	Return on average assets	Return on average equity	Yield on average earning assets	Rate on funds [2]	City
8.28	262	0.80	10.21	10.46	6.42	Trenton
10.04	237	0.88	9.81	10.63	5.96	Trenton
7.68	85	0.64	9.56	11.81	7.03	Trezevant
6.34	-365	-1.13	-24.07	11.03	7.09	Troy
7.73	381	0.94	12.72	11.01	6.24	Tullahoma
7.53	348	0.72	10.92	10.32	5.85	Tullahoma
7.86	901	2.26	32.25	11.20	5.11	Tullahoma
10.38	161	1.14	13.17	12.25	6.38	Union City
10.64	1,579	1.50	15.29	11.43	6.41	Union City
9.01	762	1.31	14.56	11.27	6.11	Vanleer
9.16	63	0.13	1.57	0.99	0.54	Wartburg
12.59	322	0.76	6.52	11.05	6.18	Waynesboro
13.28	740	1.75	14.85	12.45	6.56	Waynesboro
9.63	216	1.29	15.95	11.23	6.44	White Bluff
9.10	291	1.03	13.30	11.18	6.59	Whiteville
9.19	476	1.15	13.80	11.11	6.00	Winchester
7.75	452	0.50	6.23	10.11	6.71	Woodbury
11.40	81	0.68	6.72	9.71	6.29	Woodland Mills

Note: 1989 averages are calculated using each quarter during the year plus year-end 1988. Certain adjustments are made for banks chartered during the year to reflect the number of quarters available. For more information on income statement items, see the original source.

a. Number is too large to be relevant or is otherwise not meaningful.

1. Total loans to deposits less public funds.

2. Rate on funds = Total interest expense - Interest on mortgage indebtedness and obligations under capitalized leases/average earning assets.

Source: Sheshunoff Information Services, Inc., *Sheshunoff Banks of Tennessee, 1990.* Used by special permission.

TABLE 13.18--NUMBER OF BANKS AND AMOUNT OF DEPOSITS IN INSURED COMMERCIAL BANKS,
BY TYPE OF DEPOSIT, TENNESSEE AND COUNTIES, AS OF JUNE 30, 1992 [Deposits in thousands of dollars]

	Number		Deposits		
County	Banks [1]	Banking offices	Total	IPC	Other
Anderson	6	18	480,678	461,149	19,529
Bedford	4	10	280,115	265,081	15,034
Benton	4	6	167,508	158,779	8,729
Bledsoe	2	2	52,006	48,769	3,237
Blount	6	26	676,612	624,751	51,861
Bradley	6	23	676,962	630,731	46,231
Campbell	6	13	314,185	298,909	15,276
Cannon	3	5	96,374	92,856	3,518
Carroll	6	15	244,137	230,437	13,700
Carter	2	12	243,649	225,168	18,481
Cheatham	4	8	139,101	135,057	4,044
Chester	2	7	119,102	112,083	7,019
Claiborne	3	10	206,603	195,882	10,721
Clay	2	3	52,349	50,208	2,141
Cocke	2	9	173,458	160,654	12,804
Coffee	7	14	274,611	247,124	27,487
Crockett	8	11	164,980	153,032	11,948
Cumberland	4	11	240,976	229,279	11,697
Davidson	17	150	7,024,304	6,547,403	476,901
Decatur	4	7	89,937	83,552	6,385
DeKalb	4	8	161,561	146,521	15,040
Dickson	5	13	274,090	258,138	15,952
Dyer	5	15	357,073	334,149	22,924
Fayette	5	8	161,088	148,721	12,367
Fentress	2	4	88,391	80,477	7,914
Franklin	5	11	206,535	191,019	15,516
Gibson	12	27	611,496	576,327	35,169
Giles	4	10	294,602	277,701	16,901
Grainger	1	4	77,792	73,833	3,959
Greene	5	20	523,942	507,128	16,814
Grundy	2	5	56,518	53,120	3,398
Hamblen	4	15	343,178	329,908	13,270
Hamilton	11	98	3,015,939	2,807,872	208,067
Hancock	2	2	25,424	23,390	2,034
Hardeman	5	9	217,386	198,719	18,667
Hardin	4	11	199,107	186,991	12,116
Hawkins	5	14	297,759	269,354	28,405
Haywood	3	8	213,019	198,999	14,020
Henderson	4	14	217,397	200,778	16,618
Henry	4	14	277,112	249,946	27,166
Hickman	2	3	113,664	106,956	6,708
Houston	2	2	35,827	32,554	3,273
Humphreys	2	5	117,330	108,434	8,896
Jackson	2	4	73,438	68,894	4,544
Jefferson	4	12	226,126	214,970	11,156
Johnson	2	4	95,026	88,377	6,649
Knox	10	81	2,610,854	2,406,586	204,268
Lake	2	5	38,558	33,965	4,593
Lauderdale	7	13	233,512	207,439	26,073
Lawrence	5	13	353,174	342,218	10,956

TABLE 13.18--NUMBER OF BANKS AND AMOUNT OF DEPOSITS IN INSURED COMMERCIAL BANKS, BY TYPE OF DEPOSIT, TENNESSEE AND COUNTIES, AS OF JUNE 30, 1992 [Deposits in thousands of dollars] (Continued)

County	Number Banks [1]	Banking offices	Deposits Total	IPC	Other
Lewis	2	4	77,308	69,862	7,446
Lincoln	5	14	234,734	219,085	15,649
Loudon	6	14	330,131	295,403	34,728
McMinn	6	16	299,320	283,301	16,019
McNairy	7	13	204,663	195,068	9,595
Macon	3	8	188,823	179,202	9,621
Madison	6	32	703,154	695,860	7,294
Marion	4	9	186,758	173,604	13,154
Marshall	7	13	282,817	262,325	20,492
Maury	6	23	660,859	614,647	46,212
Meigs	1	3	41,938	38,686	3,252
Monroe	3	14	207,330	196,207	11,123
Montgomery	6	23	597,365	532,222	65,143
Moore	1	1	64,405	62,173	2,232
Morgan	1	3	55,905	52,877	3,028
Obion	8	20	416,073	380,656	35,417
Overton	3	5	116,232	113,764	2,468
Perry	2	3	62,893	56,960	5,933
Pickett	2	2	54,958	52,003	2,955
Polk	4	9	171,251	160,780	10,471
Putnam	7	23	622,599	596,087	26,512
Rhea	4	7	187,822	177,678	10,144
Roane	3	10	248,622	228,319	20,303
Robertson	7	15	330,317	317,762	12,555
Rutherford	8	33	782,652	702,606	80,046
Scott	2	7	131,358	124,220	7,138
Sequatchie	2	4	51,923	48,397	3,526
Sevier	5	25	649,922	578,622	71,300
Shelby	24	196	7,469,676	6,683,158	786,518
Smith	3	7	202,783	193,368	9,415
Stewart	3	5	90,479	87,178	3,301
Sullivan	8	35	1,180,424	1,109,032	71,392
Sumner	14	41	780,962	762,050	18,912
Tipton	6	14	280,503	261,898	18,605
Trousdale	2	2	64,432	60,305	4,127
Unicoi	3	5	114,069	107,327	6,742
Union	3	6	65,293	61,675	3,618
Van Buren	1	1	15,441	13,245	2,196
Warren	4	15	358,254	334,467	23,787
Washington	8	31	872,635	848,973	23,662
Wayne	3	8	134,987	127,847	7,140
Weakley	9	17	323,909	307,873	16,036
White	4	6	236,683	228,204	8,479
Williamson	11	34	1,009,087	975,146	33,941
Wilson	9	23	591,126	560,920	30,206
TENNESSEE	247	1,611	44,987,440	41,805,430	3,182,009

1. Total number of banks for each county includes each bank operating at least one office in the county, irrespective of the location of its main office. State bank totals are based on the location of each bank's main office.

Source: Federal Deposit Insurance Corporation, *Data Book, Operating Banks and Branches, June 30, 1992.*

TABLE 13.19--SELECTED BALANCE SHEET STATISTICS OF INSURED COMMERCIAL BANKS,
SOUTHEASTERN STATES AND UNITED STATES, AS OF DECEMBER 31, 1990
[In millions of dollars]

		Assets			Deposits	
		Gross loans				
State	Total	Total	Commercial and industrial	Real estate	Total	Interest-bearing
TENNESSEE	47,405	28,550	7,020	12,197	39,871	33,416
Alabama	38,903	23,922	6,260	10,302	31,881	26,615
Arkansas	21,502	11,222	2,293	5,531	19,053	16,339
Florida	137,237	89,620	14,320	52,114	116,977	97,112
Georgia	70,296	44,214	11,775	17,891	53,226	41,397
Kentucky	41,426	24,962	6,181	10,818	33,488	27,749
Louisiana	37,341	19,748	5,084	8,617	32,584	26,511
Mississippi	21,416	11,710	2,551	5,015	18,502	15,726
North Carolina	80,246	51,083	15,280	22,913	58,361	47,619
South Carolina	25,219	16,879	3,558	8,224	18,511	15,259
Virginia	69,600	44,999	10,826	20,257	54,672	45,589
West Virginia	17,446	9,598	1,705	4,968	14,826	12,974
UNITED STATES	3,388,926	2,123,083	615,311	829,446	2,650,035	2,161,492

Note: Totals include items not shown separately.
Source: Federal Deposit Insurance Corporation, *Statistics on Banking, 1990.*

TABLE 13.20--NUMBER AND ASSETS OF INSURED COMMERCIAL BANKS, BY ASSET SIZE, SOUTHEASTERN STATES, AS OF DECEMBER 31, 1990 [Assets in millions of dollars]

State	All banks	Less than $25 million	$25 to $100 million	$100 to $1 billion	More than $1 billion
TENNESSEE					
Banks	253	43	148	54	8
Assets	47,405	816	7,886	10,597	28,107
Alabama					
Banks	221	49	125	42	5
Assets	38,903	814	6,320	8,092	23,677
Arkansas					
Banks	256	49	154	53	0
Assets	21,502	812	8,187	12,504	0
Florida					
Banks	430	84	200	127	19
Assets	137,237	1,352	9,694	37,435	88,757
Georgia					
Banks	409	87	243	71	8
Assets	70,296	1,420	12,025	15,049	41,802
Kentucky					
Banks	332	53	195	80	4
Assets	41,426	852	10,539	15,767	14,269
Louisiana					
Banks	231	28	145	53	5
Assets	37,341	490	7,832	11,777	17,241
Mississippi					
Banks	123	19	69	30	5
Assets	21,416	312	3,884	5,608	11,612
North Carolina					
Banks	78	11	35	23	9
Assets	80,246	203	1,928	4,930	73,185
South Carolina					
Banks	85	17	51	12	5
Assets	25,219	282	2,769	3,851	18,318
Virginia					
Banks	178	27	97	46	8
Assets	69,600	481	5,667	10,343	53,109
West Virginia					
Banks	180	29	106	44	1
Assets	17,446	521	5,968	9,884	1,074

Note: Detail may not add to total due to independent rounding.
Source: Federal Deposit Insurance Corporation, *Statistics on Banking, 1990.*

TABLE 13.21.–SELECTED BALANCE SHEET AND INCOME STATEMENT ITEMS OF INSURED COMMERCIAL BANKS, SOUTHEASTERN STATES, DECEMBER 31, 1990 [In percent unless otherwise noted]

State	Number of banks	Total assets ($1,000,000)	Income before extraordinary items ($1,000)	Net interest income to average earning assets	Net income to average assets	Net income to average equity	Total non-current loans to total loans [1]	Equity capital to total assets
TENNESSEE	253	47,405	181,424	4.60	0.92	10.48	1.58	8.52
Alabama	221	38,903	378,612	4.56	0.96	10.36	1.35	9.38
Arkansas	256	21,502	207,406	4.36	1.05	11.70	1.60	9.03
Florida	430	137,237	351,505	4.66	0.27	4.50	1.98	8.73
Georgia	409	70,296	596,227	4.99	0.81	8.36	1.51	9.78
Kentucky	332	41,426	307,716	4.46	1.00	11.10	1.56	8.75
Louisiana	231	37,341	72,298	4.36	0.55	8.09	3.59	7.38
Mississippi	123	21,416	153,551	4.35	0.94	10.04	1.71	8.89
North Carolina	78	80,246	681,192	4.62	0.59	5.92	1.25	10.28
South Carolina	85	25,219	204,375	4.73	0.86	8.55	0.98	10.43
Virginia	178	69,600	302,655	4.71	0.78	7.81	1.68	9.26
West Virginia	180	17,446	176,594	4.61	0.98	10.40	1.80	9.08

Note: Ratios correspond to adjusted mean values.
1. Includes lease receivables.
Source: Federal Deposit Insurance Corporation, *Statistics on Banking, 1990.*

TABLE 13.22.--NUMBER OF FAILED BANKS, BY TYPE OF LIQUIDATION, SOUTHEASTERN STATES AND UNITED STATES, 1986–1989

State	1989				1988				1987				1986			
	Total	Purchase and assumptions	Pay-offs	Insured deposit trans-fers	Total	Purchase and assumptions	Pay-offs	Insured deposit trans-fers	Total	Purchase and assumptions	Pay-offs	Insured deposit trans-fers	Total	Purchase and assumptions	Pay-offs	Insured deposit trans-fers
TENNESSEE	0	0	0	0	0	0	0	0	0	0	0	0	2	1	0	1
Alabama	0	0	0	0	0	0	0	0	2	2	0	0	1	1	0	0
Arkansas	0	0	0	0	0	0	0	0	0	0	0	0	0	0	0	0
Florida	5	4	1	0	3	2	0	1	3	2	0	1	3	2	1	0
Kentucky	0	0	0	0	0	0	0	0	1	1	0	0	2	1	0	1
Louisiana	21	19	1	1	11	10	0	1	14[a]	14[a]	0	0	8	8	0	0
Mississippi	0	0	0	0	0	0	0	0	0	0	0	0	0	0	0	0
Virginia	1	1	0	0	0	0	0	0	0	0	0	0	0	0	0	0
West Virginia	1	1	0	0	0	0	0	0	0	0	0	0	0	0	0	0
UNITED STATES	206	174	9	23	200	164	6	30	184	133	11	40	138	98	21	19

Note: The U.S. figures include Puerto Rico.

a. Includes one failure handled as a bridge bank.

Source: Federal Deposit Insurance Corporation, *1989 Annual Report*, and earlier editions.

TABLE 13.23.–CREDIT UNION MEMBERSHIP AND LOANS OUTSTANDING, SOUTHEASTERN STATES, 1980–1990, SELECTED YEARS
[Loans in thousands of dollars]

State	1990		1988		1987		1980	
	Members	Loans	Members	Loans	Members	Loans	Members	Loans
TENNESSEE	1,203,003	2,731,144	1,166,895	2,591,556	1,125,035	2,340,534	829,780	989,561
Alabama	1,056,736	2,286,222	1,017,867	2,080,069	974,441	1,866,245	665,008	721,265
Arkansas	190,506	357,344	176,854	305,394	167,836	262,483	139,890	115,439
Florida	2,632,831	5,965,105	2,453,011	5,415,680	2,373,607	4,829,587	1,773,488	1,923,023
Georgia	1,212,603	2,479,702	1,151,646	2,259,472	1,091,907	3,308,954	880,791	949,478
Kentucky	519,484	994,575	509,055	939,623	512,478	836,790	373,077	330,570
Louisiana	750,258	1,510,395	708,610	1,358,465	678,391	1,235,509	589,682	600,302
Mississippi	336,289	588,043	319,309	538,143	312,839	472,639	286,343	246,770
North Carolina	1,243,634	3,687,736	1,107,688	3,144,261	1,041,839	2,581,752	752,589	875,689
South Carolina	730,111	1,641,188	685,998	1,466,486	625,857	1,265,718	443,583	438,129
Virginia	2,853,069	7,043,863	2,574,546	5,777,825	1,720,127	5,166,621	1,690,349	1,844,777
West Virginia	250,575	509,649	247,376	463,050	240,342	401,487	182,606	197,883

Note: Refers to both state and federally chartered credit unions. All data is stated as preliminary when released.

Source: Credit Union National Association, Inc., direct correspondence; *Credit Union Report, 1990*, and earlier editions.

TABLE 13.24—SELECTED FINANCIAL DATA FOR FSLIC-INSURED THRIFT INSTITUTIONS, SOUTHEASTERN STATES AND UNITED STATES, AS OF DECEMBER 31, 1989 [In millions of dollars]

State	Number of institutions	Total assets	Mortgage loans	Mortgage-backed securities	Cash and investments	Total deposits	FHLB advances and other borrowed money	Regulatory capital	Net deposit gain[1]
TENNESSEE	58	11,600	6,637	1,455	1,623	9,911	783	716	111
Alabama	36	9,276	4,723	2,162	897	7,273	1,618	213	-648
Arkansas	34	5,359	2,712	746	815	5,476	1,221	-1,427	-79
Florida	140	79,126	41,383	12,818	10,685	61,482	14,299	2,066	-483
Georgia	69	18,765	10,442	3,211	1,870	14,319	3,369	773	84
Kentucky	62	7,787	4,806	1,063	1,162	6,788	414	521	86
Louisiana	86	13,190	7,960	1,137	1,765	11,996	1,420	-368	138
Mississippi	39	4,379	2,190	697	638	3,891	578	-174	-50
North Carolina	129	21,180	14,013	1,948	2,166	17,887	1,778	1,236	499
South Carolina	47	11,547	7,552	835	1,050	9,377	1,415	517	345
Virginia	62	29,510	18,523	3,928	2,614	21,915	5,877	1,288	625
West Virginia	16	2,167	1,233	228	327	1,767	220	143	36
UNITED STATES[2]	2,878	1,249,025	708,929	170,532	166,023	945,656	255,981	23,583	-16,158

Note: Data are preliminary.

1. New deposits received less deposits withdrawn plus interest credited.

2. Includes Guam and other territories.

Source: Federal Home Loan Bank Board, *Savings and Home Financing Source Book, 1989.*

TABLE 13.25--SELECTED OPERATING STATISTICS FOR INSURED SAVINGS ASSOCIATIONS,
SOUTHEASTERN STATES AND UNITED STATES, 1988 AND 1989

	1989				1988			
State	Return on assets [1]	Cost of funds [2]	Cost of deposits [3]	Mortgage portfolio yield [4]	Return on assets [1]	Cost of funds [2]	Cost of deposits [3]	Mortgage portfolio yield [4]
TENNESSEE	-0.14	7.95	7.72	10.11	0.16	7.23	6.95	9.74
Alabama	-1.04	8.3	7.97	10.57	-0.31	7.64	7.31	10.29
Arkansas	-7.37	8.1	7.83	9.16	-7.26	7.49	7.22	8.51
Florida	-1.11	8.26	7.91	10.05	-0.57	7.46	7.18	9.46
Georgia	-0.7	7.92	7.61	10.36	0.20	7.44	7.23	10.06
Kentucky	0.62	7.59	7.52	9.85	0.52	7.01	6.98	9.54
Louisiana	-3.07	8.07	7.77	9.62	-1.00	7.32	7.19	9.23
Mississippi	-4.09	7.91	7.54	9.77	-1.71	7.19	6.98	9.28
North Carolina	-0.2	7.98	7.84	10.3	0.43	7.16	7.05	9.88
South Carolina	-0.01	8.02	7.68	9.91	0.38	7.11	6.90	9.79
Virginia	0.03	8.47	8.14	10.74	0.01	7.75	7.52	10.13
West Virginia	0.48	7.04	6.99	9.89	0.45	6.32	6.27	9.06
UNITED STATES	-1.47	8.26	7.91	10.32	-0.97	7.49	7.20	9.62

1. Net income after taxes divided by average assets.
2. Interest and dividends paid on deposits, FHL Bank advances, and other borrowings divided by average deposits and borrowings balance.
3. Interest and dividends paid on deposits divided by average deposit balance.
4. Interest and discounts earned on mortgage loans divided by average mortgage balance (net of loans in process).
Source: Federal Home Loan Bank Board, *Savings and Home Financing Source Book, 1989.*

TABLE 13.26--NUMBER OF LIFE INSURANCE COMPANIES, SOUTHEASTERN STATES, 1960–1989,
SELECTED YEARS

State	1989	1988	1987	1986	1985	1984	1980	1975	1970	1960
TENNESSEE	27	26	24	25	24	24	24	22	21	26
Alabama	30	30	31	31	32	34	34	39	54	42
Arkansas	33	33	25	25	23	23	23	29	29	35
Florida	47	41	44	44	41	44	38	38	28	26
Georgia	32	32	30	30	31	32	27	26	30	30
Kentucky	15	15	16	16	15	15	14	14	19	11
Louisiana	107	115	114	115	114	108	99	93	103	127
Mississippi	30	29	30	28	28	32	25	16	16	19
North Carolina	23	24	23	24	25	24	21	21	22	26
South Carolina	23	21	21	22	24	23	29	30	35	54
Virginia	16	17	17	16	15	12	15	16	16	20
West Virginia	2	2	2	2	2	2	2	3	4	4

Note: Data as of midyear.
Source: American Council of Life Insurance, Washington, D.C., *1990 Life Insurance Fact Book,* and earlier editions.

TABLE 13.27--LIFE INSURANCE IN FORCE, BY TYPE, SOUTHEASTERN STATES AND UNITED STATES, 1989 [In thousands of policies and millions of dollars]

	Total		Ordinary		Group	
State	Number	Amount	Number	Amount	Certifi-cates	Amount
TENNESSEE	9,999	166,478	3,119	92,792	3,167	66,273
Alabama	12,285	142,114	3,075	79,333	2,533	55,444
Arkansas	2,866	55,015	1,026	34,229	1,089	18,750
Florida	17,885	379,604	6,750	237,203	5,075	126,820
Georgia	12,881	246,364	4,599	145,686	3,612	90,442
Kentucky	6,237	101,804	2,404	58,615	1,708	38,493
Louisiana	8,078	135,901	2,433	86,518	1,983	43,769
Mississippi	4,394	70,340	1,186	41,499	1,192	24,714
North Carolina	12,535	222,454	4,871	132,024	3,314	81,661
South Carolina	8,139	112,460	2,924	68,029	1,919	38,732
Virginia	13,083	239,212	3,695	126,459	4,542	101,180
West Virginia	3,105	46,200	1,028	23,391	994	19,997
UNITED STATES	393,951	8,694,015	143,565	4,939,964	141,556	3,469,498

	Industrial		Credit[1]	
	Number	Amount	Number	Amount
TENNESSEE	1,700	792	2,013	6,621
Alabama	5,064	2,064	1,613	5,273
Arkansas	237	126	514	1,910
Florida	2,095	1,456	3,965	14,125
Georgia	2,139	1,277	2,531	8,959
Kentucky	935	567	1,190	4,129
Louisiana	2,440	1,501	1,222	4,113
Mississippi	807	465	1,209	3,662
North Carolina	1,984	975	2,366	7,794
South Carolina	1,476	885	1,820	4,814
Virginia	1,574	938	3,272	10,635
West Virginia	337	225	746	2,587
UNITED STATES	36,614	24,446	72,216	260,107

1. Includes group credit certificates. "Credit" is limited to life insurance on loans of 10 years' duration or less. "Ordinary" and "Group" include credit insurance on loans of more than 10 years.

Source: American Council of Life Insurance, Washington, D.C., *1990 Life Insurance Fact Book.*

TABLE 13.28.--DIRECT WRITTEN PREMIUMS, SELECTED INSURANCE LINES, SOUTHEASTERN STATES AND UNITED STATES, 1988 [In thousands of dollars]

State	Automobile		Homeowners	Farmowners	Commercial multiperil	Workers' compensation	Medical malpractice	Fire	Burglary and theft	Earthquake	Accident and health
	Liability	Physical damage									
TENNESSEE	790,507	683,729	326,963	33,735	280,838	487,402	82,691	82,866	1,742	3,532	53,937
Alabama	532,927	515,750	292,585	25,297	233,984	344,252	77,764	71,420	1,292	316	57,815
Arkansas	406,160	276,591	162,776	6,449	120,476	221,951	26,777	51,925	630	1,016	22,011
Florida	3,337,676	1,660,634	879,613	6,323	1,015,434	1,272,512	143,993	134,388	5,092	1,581	165,035
Georgia	1,479,979	952,009	433,420	27,378	392,197	769,979	169,766	94,678	2,944	737	72,763
Kentucky	577,331	418,868	195,902	46,189	181,547	317,399	69,854	50,834	1,018	2,607	31,481
Louisiana	843,793	422,699	348,911	1,829	222,903	465,889	55,602	91,958	1,357	442	44,450
Mississippi	359,437	299,366	193,969	998	105,064	209,964	26,369	71,026	1,186	743	34,447
North Carolina	1,263,886	756,254	386,513	19,404	313,596	453,879	79,486	91,170	2,272	753	53,105
South Carolina	712,915	437,154	223,913	1,852	168,212	337,868	10,236	63,177	869	2,455	28,241
Virginia	1,343,000	754,797	335,117	14,175	376,238	539,201	112,351	72,640	2,686	629	57,869
West Virginia	311,803	226,363	103,184	3,790	81,091	2,634	38,779	29,741	443	102	13,092
UNITED STATES	53,758,394	33,976,532	17,430,617	965,412	19,125,092	28,538,403	5,011,782	3,448,300	114,479	364,159	3,436,153

Note: Direct written premiums are the amounts actually paid by policy holders. These do not reflect the additional exchanges of premiums among insurance companies which contract, through a process known as reinsurance, to absorb specified portions of each other's losses.

Source: Insurance Information Institute, *1990 Property/Casualty Insurance Facts.* Data used by special permission.

Official returns from the national elections are collected by the clerk of the U.S. House of Representatives, and state election statistics are collected by the office of the Tennessee Secretary of State. National data are published biennially in *Statistics of Presidential and Congressional Elections.* These data are also included in the *U.S. Statistical Abstract* and the *Tennessee Blue Book* (last published in 1990). The Bureau of the Census publishes information about the voting age population in each decennial Census of Population. Estimates of these populations between decennial censuses are provided in *Current Population Reports*, Series P-25 and P-20. Several tables, beginning with 14.10, include the most current information on voter registration, participation, and voting age population.

The organization of governments below the state level is covered in the Bureau of the Census publication, *Governmental Organization*, from the *Census of Governments.* In addition to the 94 county governments (Nashville-Davidson metropolitan government is classified as municipal), data from the 1987 Census cover 334 municipal governments, 14 school districts, and 462 special districts, including airport authorities, housing authorities, and sanitation districts. Information on the number of state and local elected officials is also taken from this Census. The *Census of Governments*, like the economic censuses, is conducted every five years. Since results of the 1992 Census are not yet available, the latest Census published is 1987.

In addition to government units, Tennessee has a number of regional planning areas. Local officials and citizens who wish to receive planning assistance or discuss regional planning coordination will find the names and locations of each of these regional planning agencies in Table 14.2. For information on the counties served by each district office, see the map in Figure 14.1.

In the first judicial restructuring act of this century, Public Chapter 931 established 31 districts in which judges and chancellors serve the same geographical area. The plan allots one judge or chancellor per 42,333 persons per district. Figure 14.2 outlines the geographic boundaries of Tennessee's Judicial Districts.

United States congressional and state legislative districts are redrawn following each decennial census. Figure 14.3 shows the results of redistricting following the 1990 census for U.S. congressional districts in Tennessee. Voting in the 1992 elections was in accordance with these new district boundaries.

TABLE OF CONTENTS

TABLE 14.1-- NUMBER OF COUNTY AND MUNICIPAL GOVERNMENTS, BY POPULATION SIZE,
TENNESSEE, 1972–1987, CENSUS YEARS

| Population size | Number of county governments | | | | Distribution of 1986 county population (1,000) | Percent of total Tennessee county population |
	1987	1982	1977	1972		
Total	94	94	94	94	4,305	100.0
500,000 or more	1	1	(a)	(a)	810	18.8
250,000 to 499,999[a]	2	2	3	3	614	14.3
100,000 to 249,999	2	1	1	1	249	5.8
50,000 to 99,999	14	13	9	8	985	22.9
25,000 to 49,999	27	28	30	25	943	21.9
10,000 to 24,999	34	34	33	38	604	14.0
Less than 10,000	14	15	18	19	101	2.3

| Population size | Number of municipalities | | | | Distribution of 1986 municipal population (1,000) | Percent of total Tennessee municipal population |
	1987	1982	1977	1972		
Total	334	335	326	316	2,840	100.0
300,000 or more	2	2	2	2	1,126	39.6
200,000 to 299,999	0	0	0	0	0	0.0
100,000 to 199,999	2	2	2	2	335	11.8
50,000 to 99,999	2	1	1	0	114	4.0
25,000 to 49,999	8	8	7	6	258	9.1
10,000 to 24,999	25	24	22	20	387	13.6
5,000 to 9,999	34	33	32	28	245	8.6
2,500 to 4,999	46	45	44	41	166	5.8
1,000 to 2,499	88	87	70	68	141	5.0
Less than 1,000	127	133	146	149	68	2.4

Note: The Metropolitan Government of Nashville and Davidson County is classified as a municipality in the Census of Governments. Percentages computed by the Center for Business and Economic Research.

a. Data for 1972 and 1977 are for populations of 250,000 or greater.

Source: U.S. Department of Commerce, Bureau of the Census, *1987 Census of Governments, Volume I, Governmental Organization*, and earlier editions.

FIGURE 14.1
Tennessee Development Districts

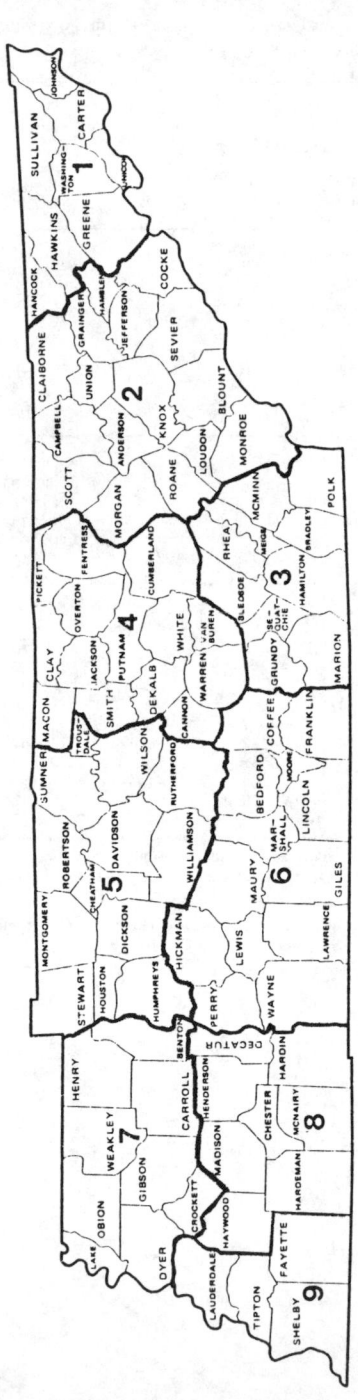

1 First Tennessee-Virginia
2 East Tennessee
3 Southeast Tennessee
4 Upper Cumberland
5 Greater Nashville Regional Council
6 South Central Tennessee
7 Northwest Tennessee
8 Southwest Tennessee
9 Memphis Delta

Source: Tennessee State Planning Office.

TABLE 14.2-- TENNESSEE DEVELOPMENT DISTRICTS

East Tennessee Development District
5616 Kingston Pike
P. O. Box 19806
Knoxville, Tennessee 37939-2806

First Tennessee-Virginia Development District
Suite 800
207 North Boone Street
Johnson City, Tennessee 37601

Memphis Delta Development District
157 Poplar Avenue, B-150
Memphis, Tennessee 38103

Greater Nashville Regional Council
Seventh Floor, Stahlman Building
Box 233, 211 Union Street
Nashville, Tennessee 37201

Northwest Tennessee Development District
124 Weldon Street
P. O. Box 63
Martin, Tennessee 38237

South Central Tennessee Development
  District
P. O. Box 1346
Columbia, Tennessee 38402-1346

Southeast Tennessee Development
  District
216 W. 8th Street, Suite 300
Chattanooga, Tennessee 37402

Southwest Tennessee Development District
27 Conrad Drive, Suite 150
Jackson, Tennessee 38305

Upper Cumberland Development District
1225 South Willow Avenue
Cookeville, Tennessee 38506-4194

Source: Tennessee State Planning Office, direct correspondence.

TABLE 14.3-- GUBERNATORIAL ELECTION RETURNS, PRIMARY AND GENERAL, TENNESSEE, 1970–1990, ELECTION YEARS

| | | Primary | |
| | Democratic | | Republican | |
Name	Popular vote	Name	Popular vote
		1990	
McWherter	454,464	Henry	92,100
Write-ins	90	Moffett	26,363
		Patty	10,097
		Turner	16,293
		Watson	8,893
		Williams	18,153
		Write-ins	102
		1986	
Eskind	225,551	Dunn	222,458
Fulton	190,016	Patty	7,660
McWherter	314,449	Vick	5,954
Others[1]	10,425	Write-ins	69
		1982	
Henry	19,453	Alexander	259,497
Kindall	7,792	Write-ins	9
Love	10,600		
McCall	2,577		
McKnight	10,761		
Nyabongo	5,885		
O'Brien	254,500		
Thomas	6,052		
Tyree	318,205		
Write-ins	5		
		1978	
Butcher	320,329	Alexander	230,922
Clement	228,577	Harper	2,527
Fulton	122,101	Patty	1,132
Others[2]	51,888	Sterling	34,037
		Write-ins	2
		1974	
Blanton	148,062	Alexander	120,773
Butcher	132,173	Oldham	35,683
Crockett	86,852	Waldron	1,674
Haney	84,155	Winston	90,980
Snodgrass	40,211	Write-ins	2
Wiseman	89,061		
Others[3]	70,806		
		1970[a]	
Anderson	29,175	Dunn	81,475
Emerson	12,608	Jarman	70,420
Hooker	261,580	Jenkins	50,910
Newton	3,490	Patty	1,647
Snodgrass	193,199	Robertson	40,547
Taylor	90,009		
Write-ins	48		

TABLE 14.3-- GUBERNATORIAL ELECTION RETURNS, PRIMARY AND GENERAL, TENNESSEE, 1970–1990, ELECTION YEARS (Continued)

	General				
	Democratic		Republican		Independent
Name	Popular vote	Name	Popular vote	Name	Popular vote
		1990			
Ned McWherter	479,990	Dwight Henry	288,904	Curtis Jacox	10,980
				David Shepard	9,094
				Write-ins	100
		1986			
Ned McWherter	656,602	Winfield Dunn	553,449	Write-ins	288
		1982			
Randy Tyree	500,937	Lamar Alexander	737,963	Write-ins	27
		1978			
Jake Butcher	523,495	Lamar Alexander	661,959	Jessie D. McDonald	1,988
				Claude E. Montgomery	921
				William B. Thompson	1,230
				Write-ins	102
		1974			
Ray Blanton	576,833	Lamar Alexander	455,467	Jack Comer	2,431
				Hubert D. Patty	845
				James E. Reesor	1,986
				Alfred W. Taylor	2,338
				Arnold J. Zandi	784
				Write-ins	30
		1970[a]			
John J. Hooker, Jr.	509,521	Winfield Dunn	575,777	Write-ins	4

1. Joseph L. Crichton, 6,582 votes; Bill Jacox, 3,817 votes; and Write-ins, 26 votes.

2. William Jackson, 1,365 votes; Willie Jacox, 2,010 votes; Ben Miller, 1,317 votes; Roger Murray, 40,871 votes; and Shelley Stiles, 6,325 votes.

3. Ross Bass, 36,091 votes; Washington Butler, 14,801 votes; Johnnie David Elkins, 1,694 votes; David Pack, 13,625 votes; James Powers, 13,464 votes; Charles G. Vick, 1,121 votes; and Write-ins, 10 votes.

a. American Party candidate, Douglas L. Heinsohn, received 1,000 votes in the Primary and 22,945 votes in the general election.

Source: Office of the Secretary of State (Nashville), Certificate of Election Returns for the August 1990, Primary Election, and the November 1990, General Election, State of Tennessee; and corresponding dates for earlier years.

TABLE 14.4-- COMPOSITION OF THE STATE LEGISLATURE, BY POLITICAL AFFILIATION, TENNESSEE, 1940–1992, ELECTION YEARS

Year	Senate		House	
	Democrat	Republican	Democrat	Republican
1992	19	14	64	35
1990	20	13	57	42
1988	22	11	59	40
1986	23	10	61	38
1984[a]	23	10	62	37
1982[a]	22	11	60	38
1980[b,c]	20	12	57	39
1978[d]	20	12	60	38
1976[d]	23	9	66	32
1974[a,e]	20	12	63	35
1972[e]	19	13	51	48
1970[e]	19	13	55	44
1968[a]	20	13	49	49
1966[a]	25	8	59	39
1964	25	8	75	24
1962	27	6	78	21
1960	27	6	80	19
1958	28	5	82	17
1956	27	6	78	21
1954	28	5	80	19
1952	28	5	81	18
1950	28	5	80	19
1948	29	4	80	19
1946	28	5	84	15
1944	28	5	75	24
1942	30	3	78	21
1940	29	4	84	15

a. One Independent candidate was also elected to the House of Representatives.

b. Two Independent candidates were also elected to the House of Representatives.

c. One Independent candidate was also elected to the Senate.

d. One Independent candidate was also elected to the House and Senate.

e. One American party candidate was also elected to the Senate.

Source: Office of the Secretary of State, direct correspondence; and *Tennessee Blue Book*, 1942–1982.

TABLE 14.5-- ELECTION RETURNS FOR UNITED STATES SENATOR, PRIMARY AND GENERAL
ELECTIONS, TENNESSEE, 1972–1990, ELECTION YEARS

	Democratic popular vote			Republican popular vote	
Candidate	Primary	General election	Candidate	Primary	General election
			1990[a]		
Albert Gore	479,961	529,914	William Hawkins	54,317	233,324
Write-ins	54		Brown	53,873	
			Hales	31,515	
			Write-ins	70	
			1988[b]		
Jim Sasser	332,560	1,020,061	Bill Andersen	115,341	541,033
Write-ins	14		Alice Algood	34,413	
			Hubert Patty	8,358	
			Write-ins	11	
			1984[c]		
Albert Gore	345,527	1,000,607	Victor Ashe	145,744	557,016
Write-ins	113		Jack McNeil	17,970	
			Hubert Patty	4,777	
			Write-ins	49	
			1982		
Jim Sasser	511,059	780,113	Robin Beard	205,271	479,642
Charles G. Vick	63,488		William B. Thompson, Jr.	19,277	
			1978		
Jane Eskind	196,156	466,228	Howard H. Baker	205,680	642,644
Jim Boyd	48,458		James D. Boles	8,899	
Walter Bradley	22,130		Harvey Howard	21,154	
Bill Bruce	170,795		Hubert D. Patty	3,941	
James Foster	10,671		Dayton Seiler	3,381	
Douglas Heinsohn	17,787		Francis Tapp	2,994	
J. D. Lee	89,939				
Virginia Nyabongo	7,682				
Charles G. Vick	4,414				
Write-ins	134				
			1976		
Jim Sasser	244,930	751,180	William Brock	173,743	673,231
David Bolin	44,056		Write-ins	1,266	
Edward Brown	4,695				
William T. Hardison	4,461				
John J. Hooker, Jr.	171,716				
Lester Kefauver	29,864				
Harry Sadler	54,125				

a. Independent candidates Bill Jacox and Charles Vick received 11,172 and 7,995 votes, respectively; there were
109 Write-in votes.

b. Independent candidate, Muhaymin, received 6,042 votes; there were 45 Write-in votes.

c. Independent candidate, McAteer, received 87,234 votes, Muhaymin received 3,179.

Source: Office of the Secretary of State, Certificate of Election Returns for August 1990, Primary Election, and
November 1990, General Election, State of Tennessee; and corresponding sources for earlier elections.

FIGURE 14.2
Judicial Districts for Tennessee

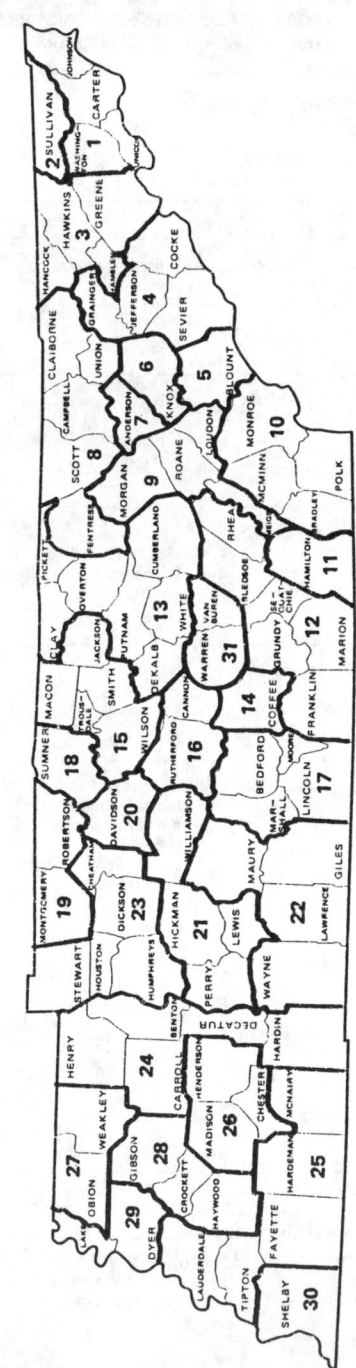

Note: For detail see Public Chapter 931, 93rd General Assembly. See also Table 14.6.
Source: Tennessee Supreme Court, direct correspondence.

TABLE 14.6-- TRIAL COURT CHANCELLORS AND JUDGES, AND POPULATION SERVED, TENNESSEE
JUDICIAL DISTRICTS, 1992–1993

District	Counties	Population 1992	Chancery Court Judges	Population served per Chancellor[1]	Circuit Court Judges[2]	Criminal Court Judges	Population served per Judge[1]
1	Carter	52,029	1	178,963	2	2	44,741
	Johnson	15,209					
	Unicoi	16,791					
	Washington	94,934					
2	Sullivan	146,676	1	146,676	2	1	48,892
3	Greene	57,243	1	161,580	3	1	40,395
	Hamblen	51,657					
	Hancock	6,725					
	Hawkins	45,955					
4	Cocke	29,490	1 [a]	227,099	3	0	45,565
	Grainger	17,766					
	Jefferson	34,770					
	Sevier	54,670					
5	Blount	90,403	(a)	227,099	2	0	45,202
6	Knox	347,583	3	115,861	4	3	49,655
7	Anderson	70,525	1	70,525	1	0	70,525
8	Campbell	35,656	1	110,546	1	1	55,273
	Claiborne	27,079					
	Fentress	14,916					
	Scott	18,836					
	Union	14,059					
9	Loudon	33,242	1	107,462	1	1	53,731
	Meigs	8,412					
	Morgan	17,714					
	Roane	48,094					
10	Bradley	75,934	1	164,765	3	1	41,191
	McMinn	43,552					
	Monroe	31,376					
	Polk	13,903					
11	Hamilton	288,637	2	144,319	4	3	41,234
12	Bledsoe	9,779	1 [b]	193,428	3	0	39,436
	Franklin	35,301					
	Grundy	13,475					
	Marion	25,297					
	Rhea	25,270					
	Sequatchie	9,186					
13	Clay	7,226	1	154,621	2	1	51,540
	Cumberland	36,743					
	DeKalb	14,637					
	Overton	17,809					
	Pickett	4,554					
	Putnam	53,162					
	White	20,490					
14	Coffee	41,641	(b)	193,428	2	0	20,821
15	Jackson	9,107	1	116,966	1	1	58,483
	Macon	16,343					
	Smith	14,407					
	Trousdale	5,949					
	Wilson	71,160					
16	Cannon	10,756	1	139,487	3	0	46,496
	Rutherford	128,731					

TABLE 14.6-- TRIAL COURT CHANCELLORS AND JUDGES, AND POPULATION SERVED, TENNESSEE
JUDICIAL DISTRICTS, 1992–1993 (Continued)

District	Counties	Population 1992	Chancery Court Judges	Population served per Chancellor [1]	Circuit Court Judges [2]	Criminal Court Judges	Population served per Judge [1]
17	Bedford	31,738	1	88,069	2	0	44,035
	Lincoln	28,451					
	Marshall	22,974					
	Moore	4,906					
18	Sumner	107,937	1	107,937	1	1	53,969
19	Montgomery	109,992	1 [c]	163,881	3	0	51,246
	Robertson	43,745					
20	Davidson	517,798	3	172,599	6	4	51,780
21	Hickman	17,579	0	(X)	3	0	40,955
	Lewis	9,820					
	Perry	6,825					
	Williamson	88,640					
22	Giles	26,667	0	(X)	3	0	46,016
	Lawrence	36,436					
	Maury	59,740					
	Wayne	15,204					
23	Cheatham	28,795	(c)	(X)	3	0	32,830
	Dickson	36,509					
	Houston	7,177					
	Humphreys	15,864					
	Stewart	10,144					
24	Benton	15,073	1	104,938	2	0	52,469
	Carroll	27,641					
	Decatur	10,393					
	Hardin	23,508					
	Henry	28,323					
25	Fayette	25,995	2	67,594	2	0	67,594
	Hardeman	23,770					
	Lauderdale	23,639					
	McNairy	22,563					
	Tipton	39,221					
26	Chester	12,961	1	115,327	2	0	57,664
	Henderson	22,136					
	Madison	80,230					
27	Obion	31,558	1	63,489	1	0	63,489
	Weakley	31,931					
28	Crockett	13,286	1	79,152	1	0	79,152
	Gibson	46,392					
	Haywood	19,474					
29	Dyer	34,847	1	42,151	1	0	42,151
	Lake	7,304					
30	Shelby	844,847	3	281,616	9	10	44,466
31	Van Buren	4,891	(b)	(X)	1	0	38,370
	Warren	33,479					

(X) not applicable.

1. Computed by the Center for Business and Economic Research.

2. Circuit Court Judges may hear both civil and criminal cases.

a. Blount is served by the Chancellor of the 4th District.

b. Coffee (District 14) and Warren (District 31) are served by the 12th District Chancellor.

c. Stewart (District 23) is served by the 19th District Chancellor.

Source: Tennessee Supreme Court, direct correspondence, and U.S. Department of Commerce, Bureau of the Census, direct correspondence.

TABLE 14.7-- RETURNS FROM THE GENERAL ELECTION FOR THE UNITED STATES HOUSE OF
REPRESENTATIVES, CONGRESSIONAL DISTRICTS AND COUNTIES, NOVEMBER 1992

County and district	Democratic candidate	Republican candidate	Independent candidates		
FIRST DISTRICT	**Christian**	**Quillen**	**(a)**		
Total	47,809	114,797			
Carter	3,125	10,603			
Cocke	1,245	6,008			
Greene	4,895	11,538			
Hancock	376	1,201			
Hawkins	5,189	8,022			
Jefferson	2,140	6,669			
Johnson	1,005	3,423			
Knox	336	593			
Sevier	4,042	12,977			
Sullivan	16,404	30,718			
Unicoi	1,186	4,148			
Washington	7,866	18,897			
SECOND DISTRICT	**Goodale**	**Duncan**	**Krieg**		
Total					
Blount	7,059	26,320	720		
Bradley	3,154	8,301	473		
Knox	33,126	87,033	2,421		
Loudon	2,903	8,596	0		
McMinn	3,359	10,964	396		
Monroe	3,286	7,163	124		
THIRD DISTRICT	**Lloyd**	**Wamp**	**Hagan**	**Martin**	**Melcher**
Total	105,693	102,763	4,433	1,593	2,048
Anderson	15,802	9,520	568	169	123
Bledsoe	1,753	2,112	92	26	24
Bradley	6,072	9,415	321	130	148
Grundy	2,735	1,003	66	20	28
Hamilton	52,649	60,755	2,607	908	1,476
Marion	5,883	4,156	137	71	76
Meigs	1,570	1,540	49	19	10
Morgan	3,063	1,968	60	28	23
Polk	2,730	2,145	99	44	24
Roane	10,776	8,036	353	138	84
Sequatchie	1,797	1,583	49	18	22
Van Buren	863	530	32	22	10
FOURTH DISTRICT	**Cooper**	**Johnson**	**Fox**	**Parks**	
Total	98,984	50,340	3,970	1,210	
Bedford	7,319	1,876	192	44	
Campbell	5,535	2,009	166	65	
Claiborne	4,409	1,916	128	77	
Coffee	8,556	3,556	347	102	
Cumberland	6,982	4,439	266	94	
Fentress	2,782	926	58	34	
Franklin	7,666	2,746	270	70	
Giles	5,646	1,582	203	49	
Grainger	2,178	1,615	97	25	
Hamblen	7,184	8,387	396	83	
Hardin	2,504	2,533	318	49	
Knox	1,948	1,761	287	30	
Lawrence	6,911	2,514	171	59	
Lincoln	5,385	2,387	196	59	
Moore	1,170	358	44	23	
Pickett	808	582	19	4	
Rhea	3,810	3,490	121	62	
Scott	2,839	1,361	76	33	
Union	2,165	1,150	90	30	
Warren	7,029	2,055	249	86	

TABLE 14.7-- RETURNS FROM THE GENERAL ELECTION FOR THE UNITED STATES HOUSE OF
REPRESENTATIVES, CONGRESSIONAL DISTRICTS AND COUNTIES, NOVEMBER 1992
(Continued)

County and district	Democratic candidate	Republican candidate	Independent candidates			
FOURTH DISTRICT (Con't)	**Cooper**	**Johnson**	**Fox**	**Parks**		
Wayne	1,622	1,748	61	36		
White	4,536	1,349	215	96		
FIFTH DISTRICT	**Clement**	**Stone**	**Edmondson**	**Haury**	**Tomeo**	**Wyatt**
Total	125,233	49,417	6,724	1,685	1,002	3,507
Davidson	116,731	46,863	6,368	1,661	980	3,335
Robertson	8,502	2,554	356	24	22	172
SIXTH DISTRICT	**Gordon**	**Blackburn**	**Benson**			
Total	120,177	86,289	5,952			
Cannon	2,817	1,078	75			
Clay	1,874	643	39			
Davidson	906	1,347	49			
DeKalb	4,052	1,572	123			
Jackson	3,055	629	65			
Macon	2,940	1,781	57			
Marshall	4,907	2,492	133			
Overton	4,358	1,275	81			
Putnam	11,210	7,648	548			
Rutherford	26,551	17,267	1,384			
Smith	4,349	1,628	95			
Sumner	21,600	15,110	1,152			
Trousdale	1,734	517	43			
Williamson	15,273	22,280	1,130			
Wilson	14,551	11,022	978			
SEVENTH DISTRICT	**Davis**	**Sundquist**	**Boyette**	**Osburn**	**Tapp**	
Total	72,062	125,101	2,290	1,831	1,573	
Cheatham	5,225	3,109	78	69	51	
Chester	1,661	2,954	25	29	9	
Decatur	2,227	1,774	24	13	11	
Dickson	6,108	4,924	79	98	52	
Fayette	3,254	4,352	64	88	71	
Hardeman	2,641	3,331	147	28	24	
Henderson	2,340	4,771	32	47	21	
Hickman	3,004	2,747	42	46	19	
Lewis	1,881	1,211	9	19	14	
Maury	9,065	7,431	185	128	67	
McNairy	3,259	4,630	268	42	26	
Montgomery	10,702	16,571	377	338	432	
Perry	1,513	850	16	15	12	
Robertson	1,231	1,173	33	20	39	
Shelby	17,951	65,273	911	851	725	
EIGHTH DISTRICT	**Tanner**	**(a)**	**Barnes**	**McKissack**	**Vinson**	**Ward**
Total	136,852		9,605	4,600	5,435	6,930
Benton	4,009		272	92	86	181
Carroll	6,673		202	155	146	127
Crockett	3,689		238	95	101	140
Dyer	9,300		601	170	275	538
Gibson	11,141		302	118	127	151
Haywood	4,337		334	102	73	159
Henry	7,443		332	98	140	157
Houston	1,448		89	49	78	59
Humphreys	3,392		245	228	115	257
Lake	1,528		37	4	26	11
Lauderdale	5,819		320	107	175	203
Madison	22,756		1,736	941	819	1,265
Obion	8,964		196	184	120	125
Shelby	25,696		3,248	1,520	2,121	2,525

TABLE 14.7-- RETURNS FROM THE GENERAL ELECTION FOR THE UNITED STATES HOUSE OF REPRESENTATIVES, CONGRESSIONAL DISTRICTS AND COUNTIES, NOVEMBER 1992 (Continued)

County and district	Democratic candidate	Republican candidate	Independent candidates			
EIGHTH DISTRICT (Con't)	**Tanner**	**(a)**	**Barnes**	**McKissack**	**Vinson**	**Ward**
Stewart	2,270		106	62	93	98
Tipton	9,453		873	293	463	647
Weakley	8,934		474	382	477	287
NINTH DISTRICT	**Ford**	**Black**	**Liptock**	**Rolen**	**Vandergriff**	
Total (Shelby)	123,276	60,606	14,075	2,517	12,265	

a. No candidates for designated party.

Source: State of Tennessee, Office of the Secretary of State (Nashville), Certificate of Election Returns for the November 1992, General Election.

FIGURE 14.3

United States Congressional Districts in Tennessee

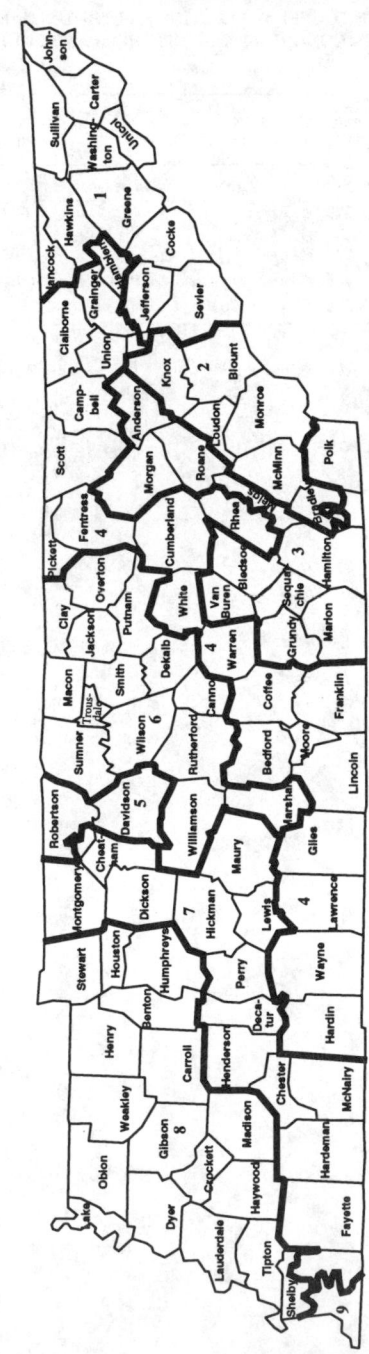

Note: Congressional Districts as of May 1992 per House Bill 2085; Senate Bill 2127.
Source: State of Tennessee, Office of Legislative Services of the Tennessee General Assembly.

TABLE 14.8-- RETURNS FROM THE GENERAL ELECTION FOR THE UNITED STATES SENATE, TOP
TWO CANDIDATES, TENNESSEE AND COUNTIES, 1988 AND 1990

County	1990		1988	
	Democratic candidate Gore	Republican candidate Hawkins	Democratic candidate Sasser	Republican candidate Andersen
Anderson	9,542	4,018	14,997	8,459
Bedford	2,259	621	6,275	2,182
Benton	1,735	441	4,042	998
Bledsoe	1,229	734	1,824	1,353
Blount	7,563	4,803	15,039	13,016
Bradley	4,942	3,533	11,834	10,578
Campbell	3,527	1,253	5,852	2,919
Cannon	992	316	2,445	728
Carroll	3,306	998	6,188	2,759
Carter	3,431	2,042	8,484	6,751
Cheatham	1,818	672	4,890	1,870
Chester	1,468	758	2,659	1,612
Claiborne	2,486	938	4,568	2,273
Clay	711	219	1,522	673
Cocke	1,996	914	3,523	3,119
Coffee	3,994	2,013	8,955	4,069
Crockett	1,361	535	2,866	1,093
Cumberland	3,680	2,513	6,074	4,872
Davidson	54,267	19,008	126,569	55,900
Decatur	1,200	509	2,885	1,086
DeKalb	1,342	421	3,279	1,019
Dickson	3,740	1,127	7,312	2,621
Dyer	3,536	1,374	6,992	3,015
Fayette	2,378	1,137	4,727	2,109
Fentress	1,446	519	2,871	1,295
Franklin	3,971	1,210	7,549	2,721
Gibson	6,972	1,671	11,403	3,350
Giles	2,558	608	5,060	1,787
Grainger	936	625	2,126	1,727
Greene	3,511	2,283	8,895	6,982
Grundy	1,251	344	2,957	672
Hamblen	4,792	2,842	8,280	6,125
Hamilton	28,928	20,671	60,154	49,296
Hancock	651	260	987	760
Hardeman	3,873	1,034	4,828	1,624
Hardin	3,343	1,374	4,234	2,196
Hawkins	4,943	2,239	8,184	5,589
Haywood	1,685	568	4,150	1,462
Henderson	1,857	1,141	4,309	2,915
Henry	2,756	868	7,104	2,044
Hickman	1,741	421	3,564	1,079
Houston	1,017	185	1,840	436
Humphreys	1,605	393	4,067	1,000
Jackson	1,243	231	2,485	506
Jefferson	2,454	1,504	5,060	4,251
Johnson	1,027	561	2,459	2,118
Knox	37,254	18,675	66,540	45,081
Lake	486	113	1,187	268
Lauderdale	1,748	593	5,164	1,555
Lawrence	5,198	1,862	6,778	3,612
Lewis	1,704	404	2,007	643
Lincoln	2,743	807	5,327	1,765
Loudon	2,479	1,655	5,886	4,087

TABLE 14.8-- RETURNS FROM THE GENERAL ELECTION FOR THE UNITED STATES SENATE, TOP TWO CANDIDATES, TENNESSEE AND COUNTIES, 1988 AND 1990 (Continued)

| County | 1990 | | 1988 | |
	Democratic candidate Gore	Republican candidate Hawkins	Democratic candidate Sasser	Republican candidate Andersen
McMinn	1,030	3,065	7,262	5,875
McNairy	12,516	1,654	5,205	2,419
Macon	3,743	392	2,721	1,370
Madison	1,629	4,120	18,824	9,130
Marion	5,289	1,399	6,079	2,646
Marshall	5,442	623	4,073	1,416
Maury	3,622	2,332	9,431	4,457
Meigs	900	556	1,412	991
Monroe	2,715	1,922	5,337	4,713
Montgomery	11,567	2,864	13,959	6,617
Moore	465	156	1,039	370
Morgan	1,457	457	2,983	1,297
Obion	3,210	858	7,105	1,836
Overton	1,761	317	3,304	834
Perry	762	194	1,602	391
Pickett	506	262	818	703
Polk	1,485	615	2,738	1,528
Putnam	6,663	2,032	10,719	4,304
Rhea	3,124	1,954	3,951	3,434
Roane	7,583	3,069	10,583	6,152
Robertson	3,602	883	8,374	2,645
Rutherford	10,184	3,860	21,070	10,687
Scott	1,021	465	2,385	1,379
Sequatchie	996	538	1,786	876
Sevier	3,278	2,158	6,657	7,642
Shelby	98,841	49,860	204,815	88,768
Smith	1,996	341	3,455	914
Stewart	1,247	337	2,454	707
Sullivan	14,871	7,398	29,928	19,046
Sumner	10,376	3,539	19,851	9,903
Tipton	2,375	1,465	6,853	3,104
Trousdale	1,867	216	1,643	337
Unicoi	1,395	567	2,933	2,241
Union	1,054	629	1,993	1,321
Van Buren	728	124	1,195	289
Warren	5,837	1,117	6,417	2,293
Washington	10,730	3,973	17,527	10,512
Wayne	896	632	2,329	1,932
Weakley	4,290	1,072	7,239	2,559
White	1,818	459	3,967	1,305
Williamson	8,664	5,189	14,764	13,294
Wilson	11,704	3,103	14,025	6,776
TENNESSEE	529,914	233,324	1,020,061	541,033

Source: State of Tennessee, Office of the Secretary of State (Nashville), Certificate of Election Returns for the November 1988, and the November 1990 General Election.

TABLE 14.9-- POPULAR VOTE FOR UNITED STATES PRESIDENT, TOP THREE CANDIDATES,
TENNESSEE AND COUNTIES, 1988 AND 1992

County	1992			1988		
	William Clinton	George Bush	Ross Perot	Michael Dukakis	George Bush	Ron Paul
Anderson	13,482	11,838	3,149	9,589	15,056	35
Bedford	5,978	3,836	1,541	4,046	4,856	9
Benton	3,896	1,625	559	2,826	2,167	1
Bledsoe	1,884	1,776	352	1,274	1,858	5
Blount	14,655	18,415	4,468	9,602	20,027	38
Bradley	9,889	16,528	3,212	6,122	15,829	16
Campbell	6,756	4,897	1,240	4,188	5,197	5
Cannon	2,593	1,229	495	1,726	1,604	4
Carroll	5,741	4,842	1,139	4,151	5,635	3
Carter	6,502	10,712	1,898	4,634	12,036	18
Cheatham	4,817	3,496	1,433	3,067	4,132	15
Chester	2,317	2,834	439	1,757	2,781	2
Claiborne	4,509	4,065	860	2,977	4,071	6
Clay	1,922	1,072	223	1,183	1,291	0
Cocke	3,495	5,298	1,124	2,115	5,430	9
Coffee	8,534	6,047	2,420	5,686	7,837	29
Crockett	2,657	2,180	507	1,742	2,214	0
Cumberland	6,393	7,116	2,200	3,964	7,557	22
Davidson	106,355	76,567	20,184	89,270	98,599	299
Decatur	2,633	1,667	351	1,880	2,286	7
DeKalb	4,382	1,714	608	2,452	2,098	6
Dickson	7,863	4,450	1,730	5,129	5,343	13
Dyer	5,845	5,668	1,241	3,690	6,508	5
Fayette	4,211	3,713	657	3,292	3,573	11
Fentress	2,730	2,391	606	1,856	3,103	2
Franklin	7,773	4,507	1,837	5,442	5,381	16
Gibson	9,555	7,161	1,536	7,542	8,415	16
Giles	5,601	2,827	1,309	3,918	3,518	10
Grainger	2,242	2,772	513	1,423	2,734	5
Greene	7,857	9,912	2,930	5,077	11,947	44
Grundy	2,997	1,004	366	2,415	1,429	0
Hamblen	7,114	8,898	1,760	5,061	10,418	27
Hamilton	46,770	53,476	14,400	40,990	68,111	157
Hancock	1,000	1,274	151	737	1,303	8
Hardeman	4,832	3,122	594	3,526	3,547	13
Hardin	3,922	3,875	734	2,808	4,252	5
Hawkins	6,623	7,758	1,847	5,212	9,356	24
Haywood	3,511	2,518	331	2,923	2,687	3
Henderson	3,502	4,719	785	2,296	5,418	21
Henry	6,797	3,661	1,588	5,138	4,784	3
Hickman	4,093	1,820	795	2,643	2,246	14
Houston	2,012	648	280	1,467	882	4
Humphreys	3,875	1,641	609	3,037	2,132	1
Jackson	3,208	708	332	1,962	1,168	5
Jefferson	4,740	6,184	1,385	3,168	6,832	13
Johnson	1,781	3,170	574	1,329	3,715	3
Knox	59,702	66,607	15,669	41,829	73,092	190
Lake	1,449	680	151	935	806	1
Lauderdale	4,452	2,928	561	3,296	3,308	4
Lawrence	6,816	5,608	1,403	4,903	6,273	0

TABLE 14.9-- POPULAR VOTE FOR UNITED STATES PRESIDENT, TOP THREE CANDIDATES,
TENNESSEE AND COUNTIES, 1988 AND 1992 (Continued)

	1992			1988		
County	William Clinton	George Bush	Ross Perot	Michael Dukakis	George Bush	Ron Paul
Lewis	2,491	1,218	434	1,419	1,324	8
Lincoln	5,063	3,814	1,371	3,672	4,288	21
Loudon	5,414	6,444	1,602	3,480	7,122	14
McMinn	6,682	7,453	1,812	4,568	8,462	19
McNairy	4,691	4,093	774	3,510	4,625	10
Macon	2,961	2,299	443	1,538	2,962	5
Madison	13,629	14,869	2,634	11,001	16,952	3
Marion	5,589	3,262	1,186	4,175	4,407	6
Marshall	4,491	2,516	1,050	2,795	2,975	2
Maury	9,997	7,440	2,821	6,280	8,397	11
Meigs	1,673	1,355	453	1,048	1,507	2
Monroe	5,384	6,025	936	4,000	6,355	9
Montgomery	14,507	13,011	3,753	9,145	12,599	24
Moore	1,151	661	327	731	786	3
Morgan	3,190	2,306	658	1,941	2,576	2
Obion	6,497	4,812	1,494	4,785	6,037	8
Overton	4,489	1,657	468	2,511	1,873	1
Perry	1,889	708	317	1,208	854	3
Pickett	1,144	1,094	121	634	1,118	0
Polk	2,583	1,584	419	2,073	2,297	3
Putnam	10,858	7,998	2,473	6,606	9,547	24
Rhea	4,289	4,860	1,163	2,595	5,144	6
Roane	9,812	8,719	2,396	6,535	10,881	6
Robertson	8,498	5,271	1,978	5,884	5,714	12
Rutherford	21,084	18,877	7,005	12,245	20,397	34
Scott	2,730	3,011	643	1,611	2,562	3
Sequatchie	1,754	1,381	405	1,196	1,659	2
Sevier	6,719	11,714	2,760	3,643	11,920	13
Shelby	191,322	153,310	20,223	149,759	157,457	375
Smith	5,061	1,482	486	2,522	2,138	2
Stewart	2,779	1,046	487	1,979	1,302	2
Sullivan	20,935	28,801	6,730	17,396	32,996	33
Sumner	19,387	17,401	5,177	11,702	19,523	41
Tipton	5,652	6,757	1,279	3,824	6,052	6
Trousdale	1,846	565	243	1,193	969	1
Unicoi	2,375	3,344	709	1,794	3,664	5
Union	2,478	2,274	580	1,431	2,110	3
Van Buren	1,329	555	191	796	780	0
Warren	7,189	3,704	1,415	4,646	4,529	5
Washington	13,071	18,206	4,002	10,087	19,615	63
Wayne	1,868	2,955	424	1,516	3,405	3
Weakley	5,691	4,800	1,355	4,239	5,701	15
White	4,102	2,118	821	2,562	2,646	10
Williamson	13,053	22,015	5,026	7,864	20,847	52
Wilson	13,861	12,061	3,848	8,360	13,317	24
TENNESSEE	933,521	841,300	199,968	679,794	947,233	2,041

Source: State of Tennessee, Office of the Secretary of State (Nashville), Certificate of Election Returns for the
November 1992, General Election, State of Tennessee, and corresponding source for 1988 election year.

TABLE 14.10--VOTING AGE POPULATION, 1990, AND NUMBER OF REGISTERED VOTERS AND VOTES, TENNESSEE AND COUNTIES, 1992

| County | Population aged 18 and over in 1990 | Registered voters as percent of voting age population, 1990 | | Registered voters as of 12/1/92 | Voters 1992[a] | |
		Number	Percent		Number	Percent
Anderson	51,916	33,083	63.7	36,402	28,611	78.6
Bedford	22,696	14,784	65.1	15,324	11,421	74.5
Benton	11,184	9,602	85.9	9,290	6,114	65.8
Bledsoe	7,301	6,751	92.5	6,357	4,018	63.2
Blount	66,307	44,086	66.5	51,642	37,651	72.9
Bradley	55,464	34,000	61.3	39,687	29,696	74.8
Campbell	26,076	18,952	72.7	19,817	12,931	65.3
Cannon	7,830	6,014	76.8	5,783	4,331	74.9
Carroll	20,983	16,629	79.2	16,080	11,799	73.4
Carter	40,116	24,710	61.6	25,473	19,190	75.3
Cheatham	19,534	10,764	55.1	12,470	9,788	78.5
Chester	9,805	7,844	80.0	7,806	5,596	71.7
Claiborne	19,469	15,373	79.0	14,861	9,485	63.8
Clay	5,564	5,437	97.7	4,954	3,226	65.1
Cocke	22,157	15,832	71.5	15,879	10,000	63.0
Coffee	29,960	20,624	68.8	22,084	17,044	77.2
Crockett	10,121	8,233	81.3	8,230	5,357	65.1
Cumberland	26,615	17,718	66.6	21,120	15,792	74.8
Davidson	394,243	261,863	66.4	278,359	203,807	73.2
Decatur	8,080	7,190	89.0	6,737	4,661	69.2
DeKalb	10,898	10,190	93.5	9,730	6,722	69.1
Dickson	25,485	17,834	70.0	18,754	14,093	75.1
Dyer	25,947	20,426	78.7	19,550	12,787	65.4
Fayette	17,918	13,308	74.3	12,780	8,609	67.4
Fentress	10,840	9,722	89.7	9,160	5,759	62.9
Franklin	26,195	18,370	70.1	19,373	14,176	73.2
Gibson	35,264	22,945	65.1	24,231	18,332	75.7
Giles	19,312	14,217	73.6	15,161	9,781	64.5
Grainger	12,924	8,915	69.0	8,767	5,553	63.3
Greene	43,056	28,626	66.5	27,845	20,875	75.0
Grundy	9,644	5,064	52.5	6,187	4,386	70.9
Hamblen	38,398	24,807	64.6	26,190	17,854	68.2
Hamilton	216,526	143,966	66.5	162,534	115,085	70.8
Hancock	5,038	4,653	92.4	5,007	2,449	48.9
Hardeman	16,756	12,917	77.1	13,281	8,627	65.0
Hardin	16,981	12,110	71.3	12,206	8,592	70.4
Hawkins	33,971	22,373	65.9	22,954	16,285	70.9
Haywood	13,799	10,073	73.0	10,019	6,376	63.6
Henderson	16,392	13,376	81.6	13,473	9,024	67.0
Henry	21,517	14,935	69.4	15,352	12,095	78.8
Hickman	12,735	9,687	76.1	9,626	6,727	69.9
Houston	5,327	4,197	78.8	3,892	2,951	75.8
Humphreys	11,824	8,722	73.8	9,454	6,135	64.9
Jackson	7,183	6,692	93.2	6,422	4,258	66.3
Jefferson	25,778	14,923	57.9	15,592	12,362	79.3
Johnson	10,575	7,927	75.0	7,633	5,563	72.9
Knox	260,637	157,948	60.6	187,762	142,476	75.9
Lake	5,564	3,670	66.0	3,517	2,306	65.6
Lauderdale	17,088	13,872	81.2	13,308	7,958	59.8
Lawrence	26,088	18,895	72.4	18,367	13,864	75.5
Lewis	6,768	5,858	86.6	5,986	4,152	69.4
Lincoln	21,177	13,504	63.8	13,554	10,302	76.0
Loudon	23,923	18,881	78.9	18,787	13,510	71.9

TABLE 14.10--VOTING AGE POPULATION, 1990, AND NUMBER OF REGISTERED VOTERS AND
VOTES, TENNESSEE AND COUNTIES, 1992 (Continued)

| County | Population aged 18 and over in 1990 | Registered voters as percent of voting age population, 1990 | | Registered voters as of 12/1/92 | Voters 1992[a] | |
		Number	Percent		Number	Percent
McMinn	32,009	20,972	65.5	21,787	15,990	73.4
McNairy	16,919	12,723	75.2	12,879	9,595	74.5
Macon	11,882	8,530	71.8	9,363	5,726	61.2
Madison	57,657	39,888	69.2	43,129	31,196	72.3
Marion	18,333	19,944	(b)	20,116	10,068	50.0
Marshall	16,085	10,699	66.5	10,643	8,098	76.1
Maury	40,534	24,642	60.8	27,635	20,459	74.0
Meigs	6,036	6,425	(b)	5,788	3,484	60.2
Monroe	22,810	18,845	82.6	19,044	12,411	65.2
Montgomery	73,865	30,629	41.5	39,461	31,341	79.4
Moore	3,518	2,825	80.3	2,934	2,145	73.1
Morgan	12,838	8,632	67.2	8,872	6,184	69.7
Obion	23,880	16,276	68.2	17,098	12,864	75.2
Overton	13,394	10,048	75.0	9,551	6,651	69.6
Perry	4,952	4,236	85.5	4,175	2,919	69.9
Pickett	3,431	3,864	(b)	3,688	2,368	64.2
Polk	10,349	8,596	83.1	8,300	4,610	55.5
Putnam	40,128	24,063	60.0	27,279	21,482	78.7
Rhea	18,186	13,502	74.2	14,827	10,348	69.8
Roane	36,120	35,113	97.2	36,240	20,999	57.9
Robertson	30,109	18,412	61.2	20,436	15,779	77.2
Rutherford	86,797	49,777	57.3	62,389	47,140	75.6
Scott	12,977	11,264	86.8	10,852	6,418	59.1
Sequatchie	6,577	5,548	84.4	5,068	3,559	70.2
Sevier	38,834	25,747	66.3	28,772	21,266	73.9
Shelby	600,023	423,080	70.5	498,719	366,110	73.4
Smith	10,604	9,497	89.6	9,797	7,044	71.9
Stewart	7,373	5,917	80.3	5,764	4,323	75.0
Sullivan	111,342	73,059	65.6	72,494	56,980	78.6
Sumner	74,833	46,980	62.8	52,600	42,132	80.1
Tipton	26,081	17,440	66.9	19,403	13,717	70.7
Trousdale	4,499	3,930	87.4	3,915	2,664	68.0
Unicoi	12,952	9,428	72.8	8,973	6,447	71.8
Union	10,025	7,883	78.6	9,025	5,354	59.3
Van Buren	3,573	3,738	(b)	3,420	2,080	60.8
Warren	24,698	16,199	65.6	17,616	12,355	70.1
Washington	72,230	39,593	54.8	45,354	35,483	78.2
Wayne	10,359	8,856	85.5	8,147	5,266	64.6
Weakley	24,935	15,720	63.0	16,215	11,869	73.2
White	15,286	11,520	75.4	11,229	7,074	63.0
Williamson	57,463	42,275	73.6	51,756	40,195	77.7
Wilson	49,136	32,161	65.5	36,887	29,903	81.1
TENNESSEE	3,660,581	2,491,568	68.1	2,726,449	1,982,638	72.7

Note: Percentages were computed by the Center for Business and Economic Research.
a. Total who voted for President in Tennessee General Election, November 1992.
b. Percent is greater than 100.
Source: Office of the Secretary of State, Registered Voters and Certificate of Election Returns, November 1992,
General Election, State of Tennessee; and U.S. Department of Commerce, Bureau of the Census, *1990 Census of
Population, General Population Characteristics, Tennessee.*

TABLE 14.11--ESTIMATES OF THE PERCENT OF THE VOTING AGE POPULATION VOTING FOR
PRESIDENTIAL ELECTORS, 1960-1992, AND VOTING FOR U.S. REPRESENTATIVES,
1960-1992, SOUTHEASTERN STATES AND UNITED STATES, SELECTED ELECTION
YEARS

State	Percent voting for presidential electors[1]								
	1992	1988	1984	1980	1976	1972	1968	1964	1960
TENNESSEE	52.4	44.7	49.1	48.7	48.7	43.5	53.7	51.7	49.8
Alabama	55.2	46.0	49.9	48.7	46.3	43.3	52.7	35.9	30.8
Arkansas	53.8	47.3	51.8	51.5	51.1	48.1	53.3	50.6	40.8
Florida	50.2	44.7	48.3	48.7	49.2	48.6	53.0	51.2	48.6
Georgia	46.9	39.4	42.0	41.3	42.0	37.3	43.4	43.3	29.2
Kentucky	53.7	48.1	50.8	49.9	48.0	48.0	51.2	53.3	57.6
Louisiana	59.8	52.3	54.5	53.0	48.7	44.0	54.8	47.3	44.6
Mississippi	52.8	50.5	52.2	51.8	48.0	44.2	53.2	33.9	25.3
North Carolina	50.1	43.7	47.4	43.4	43.0	42.8	54.3	52.3	52.9
South Carolina	45.0	39.0	40.7	40.4	40.3	38.2	46.7	39.4	30.4
Virginia	52.8	48.0	50.7	47.5	47.0	44.7	50.1	41.1	32.8
West Virginia	50.6	46.7	51.7	52.7	57.2	62.5	71.1	75.5	78.0
UNITED STATES	55.2	50.1	53.1	52.6	53.5	55.2	60.7	61.8	63.1

	Percent voting for U.S. representatives[1]												
	1992	1990	1988	1986	1984	1982	1980	1976	1972	1968	1964	1960
TENNESSEE	45.5	19.5	38.5	31.0	37.7	34.5	39.3	41.2	39.9	43.6	46.8	30.5
Alabama	52.1	34.0	39.3	37.9	39.7	34.0	36.8	38.5	41.8	45.7	32.2	23.7
Arkansas[2]	50.1	38.3	34.6	38.5	27.1	45.5	12.4	22.4	13.8	26.1	11.7	36.0
Florida[2]	47.2	23.4	31.6	23.4	28.2	27.2	40.9	32.5	36.4	42.9	39.1	39.3
Georgia	44.2	29.1	36.4	24.0	36.0	22.4	35.0	35.8	28.3	33.1	31.7	22.9
Kentucky	48.6	27.9	40.2	23.2	44.1	26.4	40.7	40.6	44.4	41.9	48.6	46.8
Louisiana[3]	22.5	3.5	6.6	12.4	20.5	16.9	26.3	38.7	28.4	31.4	31.7	28.7
Mississippi	51.5	20.1	49.8	28.7	48.2	36.2	45.8	39.7	40.2	36.5	29.9	21.9
North Carolina	48.7	39.7	40.7	33.2	47.1	29.9	40.6	40.2	38.1	47.9	47.9	50.4
South Carolina	41.8	25.9	39.2	29.2	39.0	28.5	37.5	39.3	35.8	44.0	32.9	25.8
Virginia	48.8	24.4	41.4	23.7	43.4	32.8	39.5	40.5	39.0	46.7	36.6	27.2
West Virginia	40.8	27.8	40.7	28.0	49.4	38.4	49.0	51.3	59.1	67.1	73.4	76.3
UNITED STATES	50.8	33.1	44.7	33.4	47.7	38.0	47.4	48.9	50.7	55.2	57.8	58.7

r revised.

1. Votes cast as a percent of the population of voting age.
2. State law does not require tabulation of votes for unopposed candidates.
3. Since 1978, Congressional seats in Louisiana have been determined by open primaries. Run-off elections are
held only when no single candidate receives a majority of the votes.

Source: U.S. Department of Commerce, Bureau of the Census, *Statistical Abstract of the United States, 1993*, and
earlier editions; and U.S. Department of Commerce, Bureau of the Census, Current Population Reports, Series
P25-1117, *Projections of the Voting-Age Population, for States: November 1994.*

TABLE 14.12–POPULAR VOTE FOR PRESIDENTIAL ELECTORS, BY MAJOR POLITICAL PARTY, SOUTHEASTERN STATES, 1980–1992, ELECTION YEARS
[In thousands of votes]

State	1992				1988ʳ			1984			1980		
	Total[1]	Democratic	Republican	Independent	Total[1]	Democratic	Republican	Total[1]	Democratic	Republican	Total[1]	Democratic	Republican
TENNESSEE	1,983	934	841	200	1,636	680	947	1,712	712	990	1,618	783	788
Alabama	1,688	690	804	183	1,378	550	816	1,442	552	873	1,342	637	654
Arkansas	951	506	337	99	828	349	467	884	339	535	838	398	403
Florida	5,314	2,073	2,173	1,053	4,302	1,657	2,619	4,180	1,449	2,730	3,687	1,419	2,047
Georgia	2,321	1,009	995	310	1,810	715	1,081	1,776	707	1,069	1,597	891	654
Kentucky	1,493	665	617	204	1,323	580	734	1,369	540	822	1,295	616	635
Louisiana	1,790	816	733	211	1,628	717	884	1,707	652	1,037	1,549	708	793
Mississippi	982	400	488	86	932	364	558	941	352	582	893	429	441
North Carolina	2,612	1,114	1,135	358	2,134	890	1,237	2,175	824	1,346	1,856	876	915
South Carolina	1,203	480	578	139	986	371	606	969	344	616	894	430	442
Virginia	2,559	1,039	1,151	349	2,192	860	1,309	2,147	796	1,337	1,866	752	990
West Virginia	684	331	242	109	653	341	310	736	328	405	738	367	334

r revised.

1. Includes candidates other than official Democratic and Republican nominees.

Source: U.S. Department of Commerce, Bureau of the Census, *Statistical Abstract of the United States, 1993*, and earlier editions; original source for data is Elections Research Center, *America Votes*, biennial, used by special permission; and Congressional Quarterly, Inc., Washington, D.C., *Congressional Quarterly Weekly Report*, Vol. 46, No. 46, Nov. 12, 1988, used by special permission.

TABLE 14.13.--POPULATION OF VOTING AGE, SOUTHEASTERN STATES AND UNITED STATES, NOVEMBER 1, 1964-1994, SELECTED ELECTION YEARS

[In thousands of voters]

State	1994[a]	1992[r]	1990	1988[r]	1986[r]	1984[r]	1982	1980	1976	1972	1968	1964
TENNESSEE	3,913	3,796	3,685	3,609	3,532	3,464	3,408	3,293	3,033	2,763	2,325	2,212
Alabama	3,138	3,080	2,995	2,950	2,912	2,867	2,827	2,732	2,554	2,325	1,993	1,919
Arkansas	1,817	1,774	1,737	1,717	1,706	1,690	1,667	1,615	1,502	1,354	1,143	1,108
Florida	10,856	10,422	10,180	9,651	9,158	8,656	8,138	7,387	6,408	5,313	4,124	3,623
Georgia	5,159	5,006	4,791	4,631	4,450	4,243	4,038	3,817	3,494	3,153	2,851	2,634
Kentucky	2,857	2,798	2,740	2,710	2,688	2,672	2,656	2,578	2,434	2,223	2,063	1,964
Louisiana	3,100	3,045	2,988	3,006	3,069	3,072	3,063	2,875	2,623	2,389	2,002	1,894
Mississippi	1,905	1,873	1,832	1,816	1,805	1,787	1,771	1,706	1,603	1,462	1,229	1,207
North Carolina	5,364	5,190	5,061	4,903	4,749	4,598	4,421	4,224	3,907	3,548	2,921	2,723
South Carolina	2,740	2,669	2,587	2,505	2,437	2,368	2,305	2,180	1,993	1,762	1,427	1,333
Virginia	4,967	4,855	4,716	4,572	4,394	4,234	4,077	3,872	3,613	3,257	2,717	2,539
West Virginia	1,389	1,376	1,349	1,358	1,381	1,402	1,422	1,390	1,314	1,219	1,061	1,049
UNITED STATES	193,650	189,524	185,812	181,956	177,922	173,995	169,936	162,791	152,308	140,777	120,285	114,085

Note: Data include Armed Forces stationed in each state. Data through 1970 are for population 21 years old and over, except in Georgia and Kentucky, where it is 18 years. Beginning in 1972, data are for population 18 years old and over. Estimates for 1990, 1992, and 1994 consistent with the 1990 Census of Population. Estimates for 1984-1988 consistent with the 1980 Census of Population.

r revised.

a. Projected for November 1.

Source: U.S. Department of Commerce, Bureau of the Census, *Current Population Reports, Series P25-1117, Projections of the Voting-Age Population, for States: November 1994,* and earlier editions.

TABLE 14.14--REPORTED VOTING AND REGISTRATION, BY RACE AND BY SEX, SOUTHEASTERN
STATES AND UNITED STATES, NOVEMBER 1992

State	All persons 18 years and over (1,000)	Reported registered (percent)	Reported voted (percent)
Tennessee	3,714	65.0	55.6
Male	1,689	64.8	57.2
Female	2,024	65.1	54.3
White	3,132	63.4	54.8
Black	529	77.4	62.9
Alabama	3,007	77.1	63.6
Male	1,415	77.3	62.7
Female	1,592	76.8	64.4
White	2,210	79.3	65.9
Black	775	71.8	58.1
Arkansas	1,745	66.5	58.0
Male	820	65.7	57.6
Female	924	67.3	58.4
White	1,434	67.8	60.7
Black	291	62.4	46.4
Florida	10,342	62.7	55.8
Male	4,858	60.2	53.7
Female	5,484	64.9	57.7
White	8,742	64.5	57.9
Black	1,410	54.7	46.3
Hispanic origin	1,349	35.0	30.5
Georgia	4,723	62.0	54.1
Male	2,270	59.9	51.9
Female	2,453	63.9	56.2
White	3,136	67.3	58.7
Black	1,505	53.9	47.1
Kentucky	2,724	64.9	57.6
Male	1,319	66.1	59.0
Female	1,405	63.8	56.3
White	2,496	65.5	58.2
Black	217	61.4	53.0
Louisiana	2,972	77.0	68.6
Male	1,394	77.3	67.9
Female	1,579	76.8	69.3
White	2,198	76.2	68.3
Black	721	82.3	71.5
Mississippi	1,839	79.3	66.7
Male	856	78.8	66.8
Female	983	79.7	66.6
White	1,230	80.2	69.4
Black	602	78.5	61.9
North Carolina	4,976	68.7	60.0
Male	2,358	67.6	59.4
Female	2,619	69.7	60.6
White	3,797	70.8	62.4
Black	1,107	64.0	54.1
South Carolina	2,580	67.0	58.0
Male	1,188	66.4	56.7
Female	1,392	67.6	59.1
White	1,842	69.2	61.6
Black	693	62.0	48.8

TABLE 14.14--REPORTED VOTING AND REGISTRATION, BY RACE AND BY SEX, SOUTHEASTERN STATES AND UNITED STATES, NOVEMBER 1992 (Continued)

State	All persons 18 years and over (1,000)	Reported registered (percent)	Reported voted (percent)
Virginia	4,585	65.4	61.2
Male	2,143	65.8	62.0
Female	2,442	65.1	60.4
White	3,628	67.2	63.4
Black	799	64.5	59.0
West Virginia	1,367	64.9	57.3
Male	652	64.1	57.0
Female	715	65.7	57.6
White	1,317	65.0	57.6
United States	185,684	68.2	61.3
Male	88,557	66.9	60.2
Female	97,126	69.3	62.3
White	157,837	70.1	63.6
Black	21,039	63.9	54.0
Hispanic origin	14,688	35.0	28.9

Note: Data are percentages of total voting age population by race and by sex. Data from household surveys have the limitation of generally overestimating voter turnout. For example, data from the November 1992 CPS indicate that 113.9 million persons reported voting in the November 1992 election--9.5 million more than the 104.4 million preliminary count from the Committee for the Study of the American Electorate.

Source: U.S. Department of Commerce, Bureau of the Census, *Current Population Reports*, Series P-20, No. 466.

TABLE 14.15--POPULATION, BY VOTING AGE, SOUTHEASTERN STATES, JULY 1, 1993 [In thousands]

State	Total, 18 and over	Age			
		18–24	25–44	45–64	65 and over
TENNESSEE					
Number	3,830	530	1,604	1,045	651
Percent of total	100.0	13.8	41.9	27.3	17.0
Alabama					
Number	3,111	454	1,277	835	545
Percent of total	81.2	11.9	33.3	21.8	14.2
Arkansas					
Number	1,790	247	695	486	362
Percent of total	46.7	6.4	18.1	12.7	9.5
Florida					
Number	10,509	1,160	4,037	2,773	2,539
Percent of total	274.4	30.3	105.4	72.4	66.3
Georgia					
Number	5,077	738	2,316	1,328	695
Percent of total	132.6	19.3	60.5	34.7	18.1
Kentucky					
Number	2,818	404	1,177	755	482
Percent of total	73.6	10.5	30.7	19.7	12.6
Louisiana					
Number	3,052	457	1,331	777	487
Percent of total	79.7	11.9	34.8	20.3	12.7
Mississippi					
Number	1,885	305	763	488	329
Percent of total	49.2	8.0	19.9	12.7	8.6
North Carolina					
Number	5,241	755	2,224	1,397	865
Percent of total	136.8	19.7	58.1	36.5	22.6
South Carolina					
Number	2,690	406	1,151	707	426
Percent of total	70.2	10.6	30.1	18.5	11.1
Virginia					
Number	4,904	682	2,214	1,296	712
Percent of total	128.0	17.8	57.8	33.8	18.6
West Virginia					
Number	1,387	195	532	382	278
Percent of total	36.2	5.1	13.9	10.0	7.3

Note: Detail may not add to total due to independent rounding.
Source: U.S. Department of Commerce, Bureau of the Census, *Census and You*, April 1994.

TABLE 14.16--NUMBER OF LOCAL GOVERNMENT UNITS, BY TYPE, SOUTHEASTERN STATES, 1987

State	Total	County	Municipal	School district	Special district
TENNESSEE	904	94	334	14	462
Alabama	1,053	67	436	129	421
Arkansas	1,396	75	483	333	505
Florida	965	66	390	95	414
Georgia	1,286	158	532	186	410
Kentucky	1,303	119	437	178	569
Louisiana	452	61	301	66	24
Mississippi	853	82	293	171	307
North Carolina	916	100	495	0	321
South Carolina	707	46	269	92	300
Virginia	430	95	229	0	106
West Virginia	630	55	230	55	290

Source: U.S. Department of Commerce, Bureau of the Census, *1987 Census of Governments, Volume I, Number 1, Government Organization.*

TABLE 14.17--NUMBER OF STATE AND LOCAL ELECTED OFFICIALS, SOUTHEASTERN STATES, 1987

State	Elected officials			Number of local governments	Elected officials per local government
	Total	State	Local		
TENNESSEE	6,841	322	6,519	905	7.2
Alabama	4,315	423	3,892	1,054	3.7
Arkansas	8,331	310	8,021	1,397	5.7
Florida	5,256	817	4,439	966	4.6
Georgia	6,556	447	6,109	1,287	4.7
Kentucky	7,388	560	6,828	1,304	5.2
Louisiana	4,966	586	4,380	453	9.7
Mississippi	4,944	294	4,650	854	5.4
North Carolina	5,531	549	4,982	917	5.4
South Carolina	3,692	195	3,497	708	4.9
Virginia	3,112	143	2,969	431	6.9
West Virginia	2,838	205	2,633	631	4.2
United States	497,155	18,134	479,021	83,235	5.8

Source: United States Department of Commerce, Bureau of the Census, *1987 Census of Governments, Volume 1, Number 2, Government Organization, Popularly Elected Officials.*

Because governments have traditionally been required to maintain records in order to answer to constituents or serve the needs of higher levels of government, revenues and expenditures are among the best documented fields. One principal source of data concerning state and local government finances is the Bureau of the Census, which publishes the annual reports, *State Government Finances, City Government Finances,* and *County Government Finances.* In addition, the multiple volume, *Census of Governments,* is issued quinquennially. The geographic distribution of federal funds is reported in an annual report, *Federal Expenditures by State.* Another report that provides data at the county level is *Consolidated Federal Funds Report,* Volume I.

For those who need a variety of statistics on state finance, including relative tax burdens, *Facts and Figures on Government Finance* is a convenient compendium of state-level governmental data published biennially by the Tax Foundation, Inc. Data relating to federal tax collections by source are available in the *Statistics of Income Bulletin* and the *Annual Report of the Commissioner of Internal Revenue,* Department of the Treasury.

A comprehensive collection of data on Tennessee local and county government finances is published by the Tennessee Association of Business (formerly the Tennessee Manufacturers and Taxpayers Association) in a report titled *Annual Survey of State and Local Government in Tennessee.* Much of the data used to report sales and use tax collections, property taxes, valuations and tax rates in the *Annual Survey* are provided by the Tennessee State Board of Equalization and the Office of the Comptroller of the Treasury, State of Tennessee. The State Board of Equalization publishes the annual *Tax Aggregate Report,* and the Comptroller's Office provides fiscal year data in a report titled *County and Municipal Finances.* The *Tennessee Budget,* available from the Department of Finance and Administration, and the *Monthly Statement of Revenue Collections* published by the Department of Revenue are other sources of Tennessee financial information. Data from each of these state agencies will be more comprehensive and more current than data published in multi-state reports. For example, state sales and use tax collections are detailed in the *1994/95 Abstract* for each county for fiscal year 1994.

Tennessee Rankings, Chapter 20 of the *Abstract,* provides interesting comparative statistics on per capita measures of state tax collections in Figure 20.1 and its corresponding table. However, data users should exercise caution when making comparisons among governments in *Rankings* and throughout the *Abstract.* Programs may be administered by different levels of governments in different states, and sources of funding and program content may vary greatly. Rigorous use of the data may require that the user make specific inquiries of the governments concerned.

TABLE OF CONTENTS

TABLE OF CONTENTS
(Continued)

FIGURE 15.1
General Revenues and Expenditures of Tennessee Government,
by Source and Percent Distribution, 1992

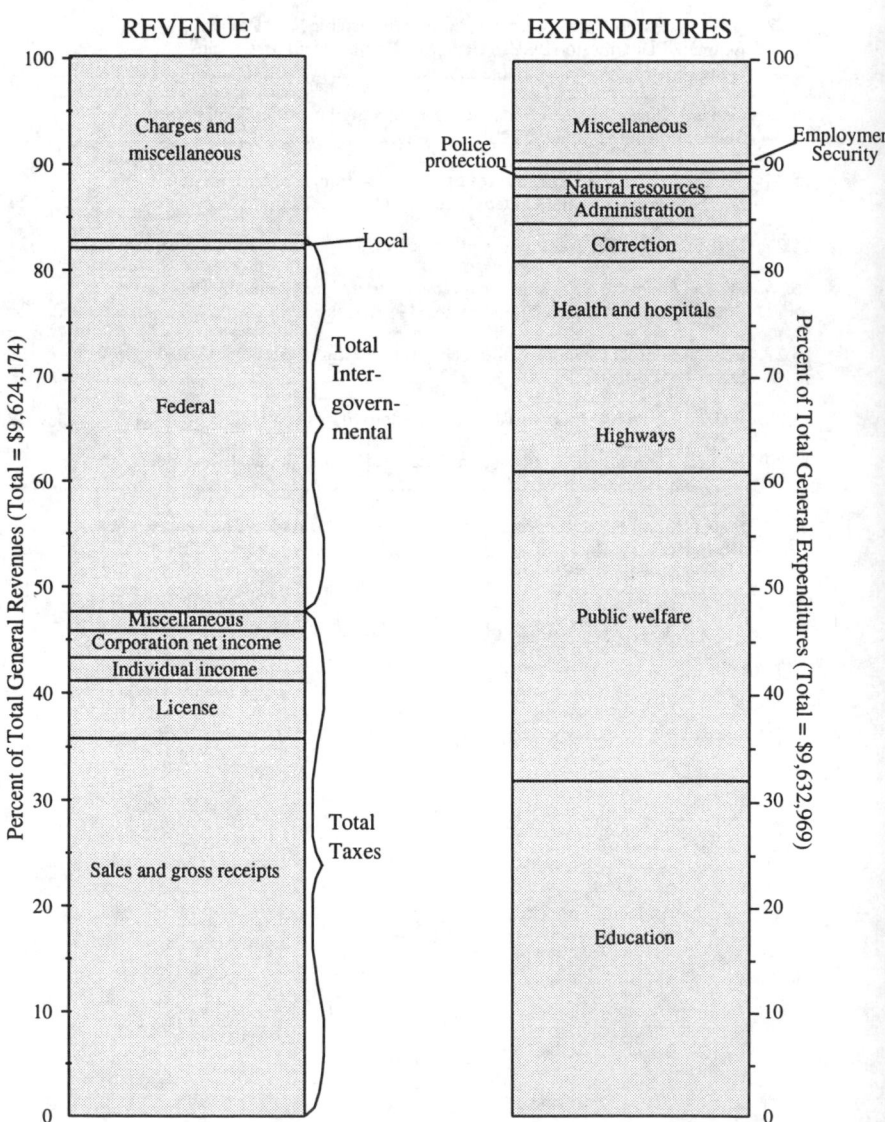

Note: See Tables 15.3 and 15.6 for data.
Source: U.S. Department of Commerce, Bureau of the Census, *State Government Finances: 1992.*

TABLE 15.1-- STATE GOVERNMENT REVENUE AND EXPENDITURE, TENNESSEE, 1950–1992,
SELECTED YEARS [In thousands of dollars]

	Revenue[1]		
Year	Total	Tax [2]	Expenditure[3]
1992	11,126,342	4,525,662	10,405,568
1991	9,544,386	4,310,573	9,237,787
1990	9,109,677	4,245,024	8,402,652
1989	8,325,303	4,066,459	7,741,816
1988	7,798,219	3,855,027	7,082,137
1987	7,382,678	3,603,331	6,641,241
1986	6,812,908	3,271,963	6,080,204
1985	6,142,245	2,998,373	5,439,026
1984	5,334,595	2,511,631	4,829,728
1983	4,783,433	2,246,288	4,578,341
1982	4,521,319	2,146,242	4,298,381
1981	4,271,237	1,958,427	4,230,952
1980	4,028,047	1,886,992	3,873,736
1979	3,614,601	1,843,906	3,361,000
1978	3,275,928	1,703,951	3,091,556
1977	2,933,213	1,529,531	2,854,020
1976	2,643,189	1,273,215	2,807,698
1975	2,234,018	1,152,054	2,417,217
1974	2,036,318	1,092,405	1,910,117
1973	1,882,304	1,002,356	1,675,600
1972	1,636,377	887,450	1,522,748
1971	1,422,737	735,440	1,457,612
1970	1,272,728	686,936	1,271,209
1969	1,127,971	645,758	1,113,043
1968	1,034,971	577,320	993,351
1967	962,743	514,422	956,603
1966	858,856	480,949	841,020
1965	751,947	432,844	702,747
1964	706,179	408,244	658,856
1963	618,321	352,098	591,100
1962	557,035	329,078	559,975
1961	535,316	311,352	522,299
1960	517,311	304,590	494,351
1955	314,935	204,761	320,469
1950	238,860	149,782	247,803

1. Revenue is all money received from external sources, net of refunds and correcting transactions, other than from issue of debt, liquidation of investments, and agency and private trust transactions. State university student fees are included in revenue.

2. Tax revenue is all money received from taxes imposed, including interest, penalties, and money shared or redistributed to local governments, but excluding protested amounts, refunds, and local government revenues collected by the state as agent.

3. Expenditure is all money paid out, net of recoveries and correcting transactions, other than for retirement of debt, investment in securities, extension of credit, or agency transactions. Expenditure includes only external transactions. All state university general spending is included in expenditure.

Source: U.S. Department of Commerce, Bureau of the Census, *State Government Finances: 1992*, and earlier editions.

TABLE 15.2-- PER CAPITA GENERAL REVENUE AND EXPENDITURES OF THE STATE
GOVERNMENT, BY TYPE, TENNESSEE, 1960–1992, SELECTED YEARS [In dollars]

Revenue, by source	1992	1991	1990	1989	1980	1970	1960
Total general revenue	1,915.64	1,692.88	1,637.86	1,509.56	778.01	301.24	133.39
Taxes, total [1]	900.81	870.30	870.42	823.17	411.02	175.05	85.39
General sales	500.56	477.14	480.60	452.81	213.95	61.45	29.41
Motor fuel sales	130.69	128.26	129.20	108.27	49.40	33.29	21.38
Motor vehicle licenses [2]	36.98	35.07	35.31	34.77	20.28	14.81	7.10
Individual income	18.58	19.59	21.11	19.32	6.71	3.09	1.46
Corporation net income [2]	58.77	69.76	68.08	75.21	43.18	15.20	6.00
Total aid received from other governments [2]	682.15	559.75	516.73	461.27	270.38	95.21	41.62
Federal	673.74	551.42	508.20	454.73	263.09	91.29	39.34
Local	8.41	8.33	8.53	6.54	7.29	3.92	2.28
Charges and miscellaneous	332.67	262.84	250.71	225.12	96.61	30.97	6.39

Expenditures, by function	1992	1991	1990	1989	1980	1970	1960
Total general expenditures	1,917.39	1,735.52	1,615.55	1,471.24	771.81	308.64	128.85
Education	617.16	620.67	578.33	555.32	308.45	133.65	41.82
Highways	225.81	214.14	210.98	190.25	132.76	67.96	45.67
Public welfare	560.64	399.26	343.38	286.59	124.24	39.09	16.54
Health and hospitals [2]	146.47	142.03	132.46	122.35	62.96	21.33	8.47
Correction	75.64	79.50	75.72	69.36	21.43	5.35	1.34
Natural resources [2]	30.82	22.41	22.51	19.96	15.66	9.17	3.30
Employment security administration [2]	13.78	12.47	11.95	11.50	9.20	2.86	n.a.
Governmental administration [2]	48.50	48.22	48.69	40.80	17.48	6.21	1.78
Miscellaneous [3]	198.58	196.82	191.54	175.10	79.63	23.02	9.93

Note: Detail may not add to total due to independent rounding.

n.a. not available.

1. Includes amounts for categories not shown separately.

2. Calculated by the Center for Business and Economic Research when not given in the source. Per capita amounts
are based on population estimates as of July 1, for intercensal years and are computed on the basis of amounts
rounded to the nearest thousand.

3. Calculated by the Center for Business and Economic Research as the residual of total general expenditures and
the sum of all other per capita expenditure classifications.

Source: U.S. Department of Commerce, Bureau of the Census, *State Government Finances: 1992*, and earlier
editions.

TABLE 15.3– GENERAL REVENUE OF THE STATE GOVERNMENT, BY SOURCE, TENNESSEE, 1970-1992, SELECTED YEARS [Amounts in thousands of dollars]

Source of revenue	1992		1991		1990		1980		1970	
	Amount	%	Amount	%	Amount	%	Amount	%	Amount	%
Total general revenue[1]	9,624,174	100.0	8,384,829	100.0	7,987,822	100.0	3,571,842	100.0	1,182,101	100.0
Taxes, total	4,525,662	47.0	4,310,573	51.4	4,245,024	53.1	1,886,992	52.8	686,936	58.1
Sales and gross receipts	3,515,642	36.5	3,299,700	39.4	3,268,457	40.9	1,415,967	39.6	473,806	40.1
General	2,514,798	26.1	2,363,252	28.2	2,343,908	29.3	982,251	27.5	241,151	20.4
Selective[2]	1,000,844	10.4	936,448	11.2	924,549	11.6	433,716	12.1	232,655	19.7
License	500,876	5.2	454,329	5.4	429,511	5.4	181,522	5.1	116,417	9.8
Motor vehicle and operator[3]	185,810	1.9	173,685	2.1	172,224	2.2	102,651	2.9	62,631	5.3
Other[3]	315,066	3.3	280,644	3.3	257,287	3.2	78,871	2.2	53,786	4.6
Individual income	93,360	1.0	97,033	1.2	102,954	1.3	30,800	0.9	12,113	1.0
Corporation net income[4]	295,266	3.1	345,542	4.1	332,036	4.2	198,222	5.5	59,633	5.0
Miscellaneous[4]	120,518	1.3	113,969	1.4	112,066	1.4	60,481	1.7	24,967	2.1
Intergovernmental revenue	3,427,157	35.6	2,772,431	33.1	2,520,103	31.5	1,241,306	34.8	373,623	31.6
Federal	3,384,884	35.2	2,731,190	32.6	2,478,513	31.0	1,207,833	33.8	358,231	30.3
Local	42,273	0.4	41,241	0.5	41,590	0.5	33,473	0.9	15,392	1.3
Charges and miscellaneous	1,671,355	17.4	1,301,825	15.5	1,222,695	15.3	443,544	12.4	121,542	10.3

Note: For each source item, the percentage relates to total general revenue, not to category totals. Percentages were computed by the Center for Business and Economic Research.
1. General revenue is all state revenue except insurance trust revenue.
2. Includes motor fuels, alcoholic beverages, tobacco products, insurance, public utilities, amusements, and parimutuels.
3. Includes corporations in general, public utilities, alcoholic beverage, amusements, occupations and businesses not elsewhere classified, and hunting and fishing.
4. Includes property (back taxes only), death and gift, document and stock transfer, and severance.
Source: U.S. Department of Commerce, Bureau of the Census, *State Government Finances: 1992*, and earlier editions.

GOVERNMENT FINANCES

TABLE 15.4-- INTERGOVERNMENTAL REVENUE FROM LOCAL GOVERNMENTS TO THE STATE
GOVERNMENT, BY FUNCTION, TENNESSEE, 1955–1992 [In thousands of dollars]

Year	Total	Education	Highways	Public welfare	Health and hospitals	Other
1992	42,273	10,869	16,494	224	5,062	9,624
1991	41,241	9,828	12,373	78	4,778	14,184
1990	41,590	9,971	13,028	206	7,129	11,256
1989	32,294	9,432	5,297	207	7,185	10,173
1988	16,344	6,909	0	854	7,597	984
1987	31,161	5,966	10,758	895	10,678	2,864
1986	40,730	5,391	18,426	911	12,872	3,130
1985	36,428	6,500	13,074	1,349	11,955	3,550
1984	31,713	4,498	11,820	1,250	12,042	2,103
1983	29,484	4,686	10,366	1,264	11,022	2,146
1982	34,101	3,560	16,005	766	10,847	2,923
1981	32,332	6,239	7,363	5,265	11,976	1,489
1980	33,473	6,224	10,436	5,539	9,784	1,490
1979	25,103	4,353	6,376	4,816	8,096	1,462
1978	23,004	4,095	6,676	3,183	7,804	1,246
1977	16,325	3,309	3,900	1,417	6,640	1,059
1976	14,816	2,296	4,167	508	6,472	1,373
1975	17,384	2,670	5,943	547	7,310	914
1974	24,068	2,806	9,453	477	10,232	1,100
1973	29,859	1,955	5,216	9,333	12,416	939
1972	22,635	1,147	4,460	7,067	9,286	675
1971	20,117	1,329	3,774	6,888	7,706	420
1970	15,392	1,570	2,099	5,885	5,380	458
1969	12,086	1,159	981	5,103	4,397	446
1968	15,784	1,010	5,854	4,608	3,814	498
1967	21,702	1,703	11,387	4,008	3,166	1,438
1966	9,780	1,109	1,338	3,290	3,121	922
1965	7,362	313	459	2,668	3,580	342
1964	7,307	638	265	2,383	3,558	463
1963	6,168	149	125	2,256	3,232	406
1962	6,401	235	0	2,412	3,267	487
1961	8,609	230	2,276	2,401	3,118	584
1960	8,129	312	1,756	2,564	2,902	595
1959	6,376	0	122	2,277	3,184	793
1958	5,686	0	146	2,154	2,633	753
1957	5,203	0	314	2,168	2,347	374
1956	5,232	0	593	2,439	1,640	560
1955	4,687	0	125	2,207	1,535	820

Source: U.S. Department of Commerce, Bureau of the Census, *State Government Finances: 1992*, and earlier
editions.

TABLE 15.5.– INTERGOVERNMENTAL REVENUE FROM THE FEDERAL GOVERNMENT TO THE STATE GOVERNMENT, BY FUNCTION, TENNESSEE, 1950–1992, SELECTED YEARS [In thousands of dollars]

Year	Total	Education	Highways	Public welfare	Health and hospitals	Employment security adminis- tration	Natural resources	Other[1]
1992	3,384,884	473,522	307,093	2,022,888	121,582	67,581	34,782	357,436
1991	2,731,190	459,571	257,418	1,488,292	117,849	60,915	11,677	335,468
1990	2,478,513	416,059	290,164	1,273,431	98,625	57,037	13,388	329,809
1989	2,246,378	391,817	262,618	1,076,646	90,392	56,982	9,891	358,032
1988	2,075,922	372,980	231,425	1,031,458	81,867	50,168	25,496	282,528
1987	1,852,262	323,953	277,766	835,821	82,331	45,318	24,203	262,870
1986	1,812,191	328,882	341,393	729,678	83,435	48,097	20,692	260,014
1985	1,611,640	311,171	282,280	599,975	90,955	48,093	24,302	254,864
1984	1,462,876	285,676	263,483	553,208	71,534	46,498	24,036	218,441
1983	1,287,327	274,438	182,782	495,982	59,761	51,181	20,040	203,143
1982	1,230,529	263,578	194,847	463,593	52,056	47,697	20,632	188,126
1981	1,322,402	292,940	256,755	454,090	49,511	46,664	20,155	202,287
1980	1,207,833	266,546	230,308	404,750	43,929	43,441	21,430	197,429
1979	1,004,156	221,430	170,027	342,945	38,261	40,139	18,835	172,519
1978	909,753	196,660	155,146	307,416	37,645	39,413	17,192	156,281
1977	817,356	177,321	155,885	280,990	30,819	33,691	19,179	119,471
1976	769,930	178,392	165,940	245,829	25,718	27,830	16,181	110,040
1975	635,458	159,406	125,903	193,007	19,904	23,157	15,056	99,025
1974	523,553	129,768	80,444	174,467	16,347	18,182	13,814	90,531
1973	524,875	132,135	87,020	188,681	13,467	16,199	11,907	75,466
1972	452,402	116,498	110,163	161,729	13,868	15,126	9,887	25,131
1971	434,029	117,981	114,243	145,128	14,936	13,041	10,971	17,729
1970	358,231	98,709	101,691	111,351	13,592	11,436	8,146	13,306
1965	209,587	20,733	110,379	54,463	6,893	6,195	4,734	6,190
1960	140,319	11,398	66,825	43,115	6,811	4,401	3,703	4,066
1955	63,737[a]	4,956	11,801	35,497	3,353	3,286	2,556	2,288
1950	58,495	12,251	8,488	28,162	0	3,063	0	6,531

1. Before 1982 "Other" category may include general revenue sharing.
a. Total includes defense revenue.
Source: U.S. Department of Commerce, Bureau of the Census, *State Government Finances: 1992*, and earlier editions.

TABLE 15.6-- GENERAL EXPENDITURES OF THE STATE GOVERNMENT, BY FUNCTION,
TENNESSEE, 1970–1992, SELECTED YEARS [Amounts in thousands of dollars]

Function	1992		1991		1990	
	Amount	%	Amount	%	Amount	%
Total general expenditure	9,632,969	100.0	8,596,037	100.0	7,879,053	100.0
Education	3,100,593	32.2	3,074,195	35.8	2,820,523	35.8
Highways	1,134,464	11.8	1,060,615	12.3	1,028,958	13.1
Public welfare	2,816,658	29.2	1,977,532	23.0	1,674,661	21.3
Health and hospitals	735,876	7.6	703,490	8.2	645,994	8.2
Police protection	65,338	0.7	62,139	0.7	60,309	0.8
Correction	380,028	3.9	393,752	4.6	369,268	4.7
Natural resources	154,836	1.6	110,973	1.3	109,782	1.4
Employment security administration	69,206	0.7	61,779	0.7	58,257	0.7
Governmental administration	243,659	2.5	238,818	2.8	237,448	3.0
Miscellaneous[1]	932,311	9.7	912,744	10.6	873,853	11.1

Function	1989		1980		1970	
	Amount	%	Amount	%	Amount	%
Total general expenditure	7,267,950	100.0	3,543,378	100.0	1,211,150	100.0
Education	2,743,279	37.7	1,416,092	40.0	524,467	43.3
Highways	939,827	12.9	609,508	17.2	266,680	22.0
Public welfare	1,415,771	19.5	570,382	16.1	153,411	12.7
Health and hospitals	604,437	8.3	289,093	8.2	83,699	6.9
Police protection	63,116	0.9	23,629	0.7	8,301	0.7
Correction	342,642	4.7	98,408	2.8	20,999	1.7
Natural resources	98,610	1.4	71,906	2.0	35,982	3.0
Employment security administration	56,829	0.8	42,241	1.2	11,213	0.9
Governmental administration	201,553	2.8	94,923	2.7	31,380	2.6
Miscellaneous[1]	801,886	11.0	327,196	9.2	75,018	6.2

Note: Percentages computed by the Center for Business and Economic Research.

1. Calculated by the Center for Business and Economic Research as the residual of total general expenditure and the sum of all other general expenditure classifications.

Source: U.S. Department of Commerce, Bureau of the Census, *State Government Finances: 1992*, and earlier editions.

TABLE 15.7-- OPERATING REVENUE, BY SOURCE, COUNTY GOVERNMENTS, FISCAL YEAR 1992
[In dollars]

County	Total	Federal government	State government	Total [1]	Property taxes	Local sales taxes
				Local sources		
Anderson	52,436,109	4,085,732	13,195,251	35,155,126	17,314,744	8,945,021
Bedford	25,016,959	1,694,387	10,038,849	13,283,723	7,707,118	2,898,176
Benton	12,453,253	1,004,710	5,844,409	5,604,134	2,119,033	1,744,451
Bledsoe	7,889,460	911,585	4,194,900	2,782,975	1,615,415	496,127
Blount	64,089,425	2,748,049	16,522,235	44,819,141	19,338,931	14,390,346
Bradley	54,414,775	2,434,139	14,531,312	37,449,324	16,603,800	10,885,376
Campbell	28,978,674	3,406,878	12,418,161	13,153,635	6,286,090	3,599,416
Cannon	8,160,700	747,802	3,957,983	3,454,915	1,783,588	537,291
Carroll	12,850,298	300,131	3,042,812	9,507,355	4,738,550	2,555,534
Carter	31,102,016	3,387,935	11,364,070	16,350,011	7,624,911	4,710,222
Cheatham	23,331,682	1,720,152	8,937,712	12,673,818	6,423,470	1,864,631
Chester	9,951,455	1,146,886	4,905,980	3,898,589	1,628,858	988,696
Claiborne	21,652,409	3,293,284	8,611,892	9,747,233	5,119,337	1,992,894
Clay	7,081,281	923,174	3,743,555	2,414,552	1,246,913	260,976
Cocke	22,479,249	3,348,181	8,059,463	11,071,605	4,686,156	3,885,987
Coffee	28,593,933	1,666,809	7,626,416	19,300,708	8,101,354	7,588,070
Crockett	9,702,699	712,230	3,777,336	5,213,133	2,406,761	859,001
Cumberland	29,459,877	2,585,678	10,155,536	16,718,663	7,124,384	5,704,414
Davidson	821,050,000	49,617,000	154,756,000	616,677,000	269,084,000	145,263,000
Decatur	8,163,254	774,803	4,315,573	3,072,878	1,328,686	825,691
DeKalb	10,390,717	1,339,572	4,947,897	4,103,248	2,370,945	843,395
Dickson	33,622,269	2,024,165	11,810,478	19,787,626	8,406,087	4,861,817
Dyer	25,629,476	1,718,653	7,319,142	16,591,681	5,027,295	6,617,909
Fayette	22,023,772	3,996,966	8,311,552	9,715,254	5,496,990	1,314,704
Fentress	11,455,944	1,549,422	5,477,908	4,428,614	1,850,008	887,940
Franklin	23,762,783	2,102,688	10,593,581	11,066,514	5,328,191	3,218,737
Gibson	17,502,417	191,486	2,746,663	14,564,268	6,292,201	5,167,016
Giles	22,336,095	1,690,361	8,389,342	12,256,392	6,420,035	1,964,363
Grainger	11,864,375	1,285,760	6,171,691	4,406,924	2,596,176	688,168
Greene	39,741,175	3,195,851	12,406,508	24,138,816	9,777,260	7,674,080
Grundy	11,678,208	1,700,301	5,760,234	4,217,673	2,270,849	678,573
Hamblen	39,726,165	3,556,163	14,204,115	21,965,887	11,304,098	5,975,871
Hamilton	195,250,945	4,678,586	41,617,691	148,954,668	74,311,147	30,963,148
Hancock	7,805,094	1,514,171	3,485,194	2,805,729	597,972	215,814
Hardeman	19,595,204	2,635,371	9,924,254	7,035,579	3,065,721	1,918,358
Hardin	19,595,434	2,690,622	7,641,254	9,263,558	4,318,289	1,928,015
Hawkins	32,592,932	2,858,255	11,806,726	17,927,951	9,700,614	4,148,887
Haywood	19,102,859	3,072,503	7,662,391	8,367,965	3,622,029	1,207,404
Henderson	15,054,124	1,227,062	6,985,459	6,841,603	2,525,061	2,498,775
Henry	21,342,446	1,171,653	7,775,846	12,394,947	5,992,624	3,901,927
Hickman	14,271,539	1,287,270	6,270,173	6,714,096	3,740,081	973,217
Houston	6,221,474	540,783	3,242,467	2,438,224	1,254,323	514,466
Humphreys	14,590,019	1,201,662	6,131,989	7,256,368	3,947,536	1,781,297
Jackson	8,452,772	968,518	3,711,523	3,772,731	1,829,406	482,023
Jefferson	24,192,542	2,309,913	9,258,330	12,624,299	6,381,782	3,030,551
Johnson	12,813,828	2,105,195	5,222,876	5,485,757	2,938,941	720,487
Knox	311,946,749	13,961,075	89,843,892	208,141,782	90,113,870	75,226,829
Lake	6,666,598	804,122	3,471,837	2,390,639	1,125,019	469,861
Lauderdale	18,036,203	2,483,754	8,826,478	6,725,971	2,842,482	1,762,824
Lawrence	29,198,565	2,838,078	11,323,230	15,037,257	6,730,338	4,288,382

TABLE 15.7-- OPERATING REVENUE, BY SOURCE, COUNTY GOVERNMENTS, FISCAL YEAR 1992
[In dollars] (Continued)

County	Total	Federal government	State government	Total [1]	Property taxes	Local sales taxes
				Local sources		
Lewis	7,763,087	1,013,634	3,863,064	2,886,389	1,193,954	799,043
Lincoln	20,079,370	1,545,780	8,916,329	9,617,261	5,018,085	2,045,222
Loudon	22,380,437	1,570,368	7,753,015	13,057,054	8,370,573	2,300,932
McMinn	30,455,892	1,631,284	10,084,805	18,739,803	11,280,461	3,064,432
McNairy	17,448,632	1,683,798	7,836,049	7,928,785	3,772,054	1,804,198
Macon	12,001,933	837,687	5,277,669	5,886,577	3,226,210	1,396,857
Madison	79,012,815	5,291,361	23,619,482	50,101,972	17,674,097	21,165,884
Marion	20,543,603	2,643,229	8,584,653	9,315,721	3,617,872	3,083,848
Marshall	19,444,756	997,635	7,647,231	10,799,890	5,199,460	2,702,144
Maury	51,533,702	3,029,342	17,715,381	30,788,979	12,370,954	9,653,604
Meigs	7,770,267	1,086,956	3,986,090	2,697,221	1,339,935	381,288
Monroe	22,119,316	2,321,480	8,733,466	11,064,370	4,795,456	3,396,302
Montgomery	92,605,637	8,946,317	28,026,600	55,632,720	20,764,839	16,470,424
Moore	5,423,825	473,980	2,624,882	2,324,963	1,539,912	280,968
Morgan	15,490,027	1,744,729	6,889,475	6,855,823	4,888,277	594,530
Obion	24,941,000	1,657,439	8,098,765	15,184,796	6,613,962	4,177,232
Overton	13,953,107	1,655,668	6,187,058	6,110,381	2,835,894	1,050,985
Perry	6,902,402	687,275	3,541,982	2,673,145	1,548,619	368,736
Pickett	4,780,541	689,736	2,528,128	1,562,677	607,707	187,583
Polk	13,552,812	2,439,091	5,642,072	5,471,649	3,251,418	783,137
Putnam	41,844,410	2,461,254	14,640,251	24,742,905	7,865,233	9,439,689
Rhea	18,384,999	1,681,445	6,976,640	9,726,914	4,794,432	2,371,443
Roane	35,164,239	2,408,724	10,895,576	21,859,939	9,617,806	7,335,456
Robertson	35,597,796	2,385,911	13,503,008	19,708,877	10,127,597	4,328,713
Rutherford	108,091,079	3,029,535	29,413,564	75,647,980	37,833,491	19,423,459
Scott	15,985,990	2,552,883	6,587,540	6,845,567	3,813,205	1,613,619
Sequatchie	9,037,582	1,099,644	4,296,236	3,641,702	1,605,179	839,231
Sevier	57,226,088	3,239,590	15,010,017	38,976,481	10,777,810	21,525,473
Shelby	637,953,807	10,269,001	119,165,931	508,518,875	218,828,291	160,109,241
Smith	11,658,093	811,968	4,980,299	5,865,826	2,497,064	1,324,365
Stewart	8,816,925	1,304,365	5,022,197	2,490,363	1,054,713	646,085
Sullivan	139,682,322	8,086,728	26,504,440	105,091,154	57,730,540	28,335,500
Sumner	97,049,818	3,670,914	30,862,751	62,516,153	29,543,558	10,696,830
Tipton	30,750,726	2,556,128	11,565,876	16,628,722	8,819,483	3,222,639
Trousdale	5,740,941	270,211	3,030,051	2,440,679	1,552,311	438,747
Unicoi	12,808,177	1,250,958	5,555,837	6,001,382	3,149,552	1,215,758
Union	9,238,310	1,161,073	4,941,610	3,135,627	1,675,171	606,974
Van Buren	4,928,699	664,632	2,453,611	1,810,456	986,751	264,787
Warren	29,934,426	2,751,303	11,213,785	15,969,338	6,020,357	4,110,118
Washington	56,311,246	2,270,394	13,855,994	40,184,858	17,845,703	16,648,584
Wayne	12,593,929	1,497,504	6,442,933	4,653,492	2,300,687	763,028
Weakley	21,932,612	1,538,927	9,391,897	11,001,788	4,752,988	3,116,888
White	16,038,503	1,343,111	6,831,107	7,864,285	3,301,039	1,877,175
Williamson	89,745,123	2,039,087	20,103,828	67,602,208	38,994,860	14,778,493
Wilson	52,975,261	1,599,337	16,171,766	35,204,158	21,100,663	4,870,665
TENNESSEE	4,373,014,493	263,100,942	1,229,313,107	2,880,600,444	1,310,957,692	791,530,467

Note: Detail may not add to total due to independent rounding.

1. Includes items not shown separately.

2. Data are for Metropolitan Nashville-Davidson County.

Source: State of Tennessee, Report of the Comptroller of the Treasury, Division of Local Finance, *County and Municipal Finances for Fiscal Year Ended June 30, 1992.*

TABLE 15.8-- PER CAPITA MAJOR OPERATING REVENUE SOURCES AND PERCENT OF OPERATING
REVENUES FROM FEDERAL, STATE, AND LOCAL SOURCES, TENNESSEE AND
COUNTIES, YEAR ENDING JUNE 30, 1992

County	Per capita major revenue sources[1]				Percent of total operating revenue by source		
	Property tax	Local sales tax	Federal government	State government	Federal	State	Local
Anderson	254	131	60	193	7.8	25.2	67.0
Bedford	253	95	56	330	6.8	40.1	53.1
Benton	146	120	69	402	8.1	46.9	45.0
Bledsoe	167	51	94	434	11.6	53.2	35.3
Blount	225	167	32	192	4.3	25.8	69.9
Bradley	225	148	33	197	4.5	26.7	68.8
Campbell	179	103	97	354	11.8	42.9	45.4
Cannon	170	51	71	378	9.2	48.5	42.3
Carroll	172	93	11	111	2.3	23.7	74.0
Carter	148	91	66	221	10.9	36.5	52.6
Cheatham	237	69	63	329	7.4	38.3	54.3
Chester	127	77	89	383	11.5	49.3	39.2
Claibome	196	76	126	329	15.2	39.8	45.0
Clay	172	36	128	517	13.0	52.9	34.1
Cocke	161	133	115	277	14.9	35.9	49.3
Coffee	201	188	41	189	5.8	26.7	67.5
Crockett	180	64	53	282	7.3	38.9	53.7
Cumberland	205	164	74	292	8.8	34.5	56.8
Davidson[2]	527	284	97	303	6.0	18.8	75.1
Decatur	127	79	74	412	9.5	52.9	37.6
DeKalb	165	59	93	345	12.9	47.6	39.5
Dickson	240	139	58	337	6.0	35.1	58.9
Dyer	144	190	49	210	6.7	28.6	64.7
Fayette	215	51	156	325	18.1	37.7	44.1
Fentress	126	61	106	373	13.5	47.8	38.7
Franklin	153	93	61	305	8.8	44.6	46.6
Gibson	136	112	4	59	1.1	15.7	83.2
Giles	249	76	66	326	7.6	37.6	54.9
Grainger	152	40	75	361	10.8	52.0	37.1
Greene	175	137	57	222	8.0	31.2	60.7
Grundy	170	51	127	431	14.6	49.3	36.1
Hamblen	224	118	70	281	9.0	35.8	55.3
Hamilton	260	108	16	146	2.4	21.3	76.3
Hancock	89	32	225	517	19.4	44.7	35.9
Hardeman	131	82	113	425	13.4	50.6	35.9
Hardin	191	85	119	338	13.7	39.0	47.3
Hawkins	218	93	64	265	8.8	36.2	55.0
Haywood	186	62	158	394	16.1	40.1	43.8
Henderson	116	114	56	320	8.2	46.4	45.4
Henry	215	140	42	279	5.5	36.4	58.1
Hickman	223	58	77	374	9.0	43.9	47.0
Houston	179	73	77	462	8.7	52.1	39.2
Humphreys	250	113	76	388	8.2	42.0	49.7
Jackson	197	52	104	399	11.5	43.9	44.6
Jefferson	193	92	70	280	9.5	38.3	52.2
Johnson	213	52	153	379	16.4	40.8	42.8
Knox	268	224	42	268	4.5	28.8	66.7
Lake	158	66	113	487	12.1	52.1	35.9
Lauderdale	121	75	106	376	13.8	48.9	37.3
Lawrence	191	121	80	321	9.7	38.8	51.5
Lewis	129	86	110	418	13.1	49.8	37.2
Lincoln	178	73	55	317	7.7	44.4	47.9

567

TABLE 15.8-- PER CAPITA MAJOR OPERATING REVENUE SOURCES AND PERCENT OF OPERATING
REVENUES FROM FEDERAL, STATE, AND LOCAL SOURCES, , TENNESSEE AND
COUNTIES, YEAR ENDING JUNE 30, 1992 (Continued)

| County | Per capita major revenue sources[1] | | | | Percentage of total operating revenue by source | | |
	Property tax	Local sales tax	Federal government	State government	Federal	State	Local
Loudon	268	74	50	248	7.0	34.6	58.3
McMinn	266	72	38	238	5.4	33.1	61.5
McNairy	168	80	75	349	9.7	44.9	45.4
Macon	203	88	53	332	7.0	44.0	49.0
Madison	227	271	68	303	6.7	29.9	63.4
Marion	146	124	106	345	12.9	41.8	45.3
Marshall	241	125	46	355	5.1	39.3	55.5
Maury	226	176	55	323	5.9	34.4	59.7
Meigs	167	47	135	496	14.0	51.3	34.7
Monroe	157	111	76	286	10.5	39.5	50.0
Montgomery	207	164	89	279	9.7	30.3	60.1
Moore	326	60	100	556	8.7	48.4	42.9
Morgan	283	34	101	398	11.3	44.5	44.3
Obion	209	132	52	255	6.6	32.5	60.9
Overton	161	60	94	351	11.9	44.3	43.8
Perry	234	56	104	536	10.0	51.3	38.7
Pickett	134	41	152	556	14.4	52.9	32.7
Polk	238	57	179	414	18.0	41.6	40.4
Putnam	153	184	48	285	5.9	35.0	59.1
Rhea	197	97	69	287	9.1	37.9	52.9
Roane	204	155	51	231	6.8	31.0	62.2
Robertson	244	104	58	325	6.7	37.9	55.4
Rutherford	319	164	26	248	2.8	27.2	70.0
Scott	208	88	139	359	16.0	41.2	42.8
Sequatchie	181	95	124	485	12.2	47.5	40.3
Sevier	211	422	63	294	5.7	26.2	68.1
Shelby	265	194	12	144	1.6	18.7	79.7
Smith	177	94	57	352	7.0	42.7	50.3
Stewart	111	68	138	530	14.8	57.0	28.2
Sullivan	402	197	56	185	5.8	19.0	75.2
Sumner	286	104	36	299	3.8	31.8	64.4
Tipton	235	86	68	308	8.3	37.6	54.1
Trousdale	262	74	46	512	4.7	52.8	42.5
Unicoi	190	73	76	336	9.8	43.4	46.9
Union	122	44	85	361	12.6	53.5	33.9
Van Buren	204	55	137	506	13.5	49.8	36.7
Warren	182	125	83	340	9.2	37.5	53.3
Washington	193	180	25	150	4.0	24.6	71.4
Wayne	165	55	107	462	11.9	51.2	37.0
Weakley	149	97	48	294	7.0	42.8	50.2
White	164	93	67	340	8.4	42.6	49.0
Williamson	481	182	25	248	2.3	22.4	75.3
Wilson	312	72	24	239	3.0	30.5	66.5
TENNESSEE	269	162	54	252	6.0	28.1	65.9

Note: Figures computed by the Center for Business and Economic Research. Sum of percentages may not equal
    100 due to independent rounding.

1. Population figures used are from 1990 Census of Population and Housing.

2. Data are for Metropolitan Nashville-Davidson County.

Source: State of Tennessee, Report of the Comptroller of the Treasury, Division of Local Finance, *County and
    Municipal Finances For Fiscal Year Ended June 30, 1992.*

TABLE 15.9-- OPERATING EXPENDITURES, BY FUNCTION, COUNTY GOVERNMENTS, FISCAL YEAR 1992 [In dollars]

County	Total [1]	General purpose	Schools	Highways and streets	Debt service	
					Principal	Interest
Anderson	41,533,213	11,809,809	24,012,879	2,031,502	1,984,346	1,694,677
Bedford	23,178,630	4,343,158	15,299,166	1,905,790	1,003,761	626,755
Benton	12,152,596	2,522,176	7,349,568	1,734,910	294,623	251,319
Bledsoe	7,624,671	1,633,779	4,081,786	1,459,164	303,208	146,734
Blount	53,130,442	14,491,327	29,597,973	3,066,923	3,762,433	2,211,786
Bradley	45,336,562	11,561,805	25,440,827	3,404,436	3,080,667	1,848,827
Campbell	27,552,258	3,776,857	19,892,682	1,725,956	1,370,000	786,763
Cannon	8,274,224	2,030,474	4,818,651	1,118,201	233,490	73,408
Carroll	7,070,794	3,255,399	1,682,392	1,997,362	117,166	18,475
Carter	27,502,842	5,648,611	18,422,472	1,951,729	987,520	492,510
Cheatham	22,736,324	4,773,554	13,200,065	1,849,969	1,423,212	1,489,524
Chester	9,427,405	2,283,032	5,286,816	1,315,407	355,602	186,548
Claiborne	20,870,570	3,241,751	14,057,630	1,277,570	1,762,123	531,496
Clay	7,235,066	1,415,572	4,275,081	1,280,156	198,451	65,806
Cocke	19,636,481	3,712,578	12,699,745	1,796,200	1,158,581	269,377
Coffee	20,675,589	6,005,727	11,677,268	1,755,629	865,368	371,597
Crockett	9,381,200	2,112,993	4,484,826	1,780,667	503,739	498,975
Cumberland	26,158,224	5,501,737	16,169,747	1,834,953	1,780,056	871,731
Davidson[2]	691,994,000	295,138,000	303,473,000	30,376,000	26,635,000	36,372,000
Decatur	7,617,302	1,610,554	4,726,640	978,579	164,807	136,722
DeKalb	10,303,384	2,122,178	6,448,128	1,285,129	309,101	138,848
Dickson	31,645,321	7,948,310	18,879,255	2,544,550	1,248,330	1,024,876
Dyer	19,025,384	3,748,508	11,108,447	2,947,438	329,072	891,919
Fayette	21,140,142	4,011,011	12,836,990	3,056,832	731,462	503,847
Fentress	12,130,132	2,410,917	7,685,163	1,499,605	416,807	117,640
Franklin	24,050,087	4,589,137	15,800,792	2,154,896	946,264	558,998
Gibson	9,312,075	4,596,268	1,689	3,401,764	1,037,717	274,637
Giles	20,845,650	2,742,562	13,219,172	2,610,477	1,299,831	973,608
Grainger	11,308,367	1,695,234	7,563,977	1,304,860	512,350	231,946
Greene	31,790,342	8,452,818	18,583,766	3,026,291	1,165,000	562,467
Grundy	11,287,427	1,980,339	7,706,398	1,090,581	331,314	178,795
Hamblen	40,003,789	6,073,638	29,295,307	1,488,411	1,776,267	1,370,166
Hamilton	156,514,414	59,073,904	76,880,262	6,535,611	8,155,000	5,869,637
Hancock	7,532,326	1,997,772	4,235,728	1,054,013	200,258	44,555
Hardeman	18,921,533	3,140,067	13,232,096	2,088,146	168,411	292,813
Hardin	18,336,514	2,887,494	11,069,909	2,393,978	1,250,000	735,133
Hawkins	29,867,607	5,460,017	19,196,472	2,323,161	1,725,864	1,162,093
Haywood	18,185,436	3,496,839	12,080,619	2,024,583	369,531	213,864
Henderson	14,307,526	2,561,965	8,208,778	1,911,925	1,142,914	481,944
Henry	17,202,603	3,231,266	10,019,663	2,752,535	878,850	320,289
Hickman	13,285,789	2,054,872	8,027,012	1,740,147	871,000	592,758
Houston	5,892,243	1,105,024	3,314,109	1,192,145	196,315	84,650
Humphreys	13,484,251	2,314,302	8,592,471	1,696,758	442,900	437,820
Jackson	7,621,529	1,427,703	4,416,419	1,379,156	193,323	204,928
Jefferson	22,402,181	3,261,945	14,988,237	2,045,943	1,305,352	800,704
Johnson	11,656,878	2,785,645	7,183,830	1,194,048	300,002	193,353
Knox	298,706,963	83,767,150	185,841,555	8,127,991	11,919,686	9,050,581
Lake	6,255,139	1,559,521	3,307,770	1,034,840	182,984	170,024
Lauderdale	16,647,079	1,708,906	11,962,903	2,273,739	330,000	371,531
Lawrence	27,957,746	5,316,971	17,758,988	3,011,083	987,553	883,151

569

TABLE 15.9-- OPERATING EXPENDITURES, BY FUNCTION, COUNTY GOVERNMENTS, FISCAL YEAR 1992 [In dollars] (Continued)

County	Total[1]	General purpose	Schools	Highways and streets	Debt service Principal	Debt service Interest
Lewis	7,275,775	1,501,123	4,144,306	1,205,602	323,813	100,931
Lincoln	18,466,980	2,816,322	11,006,926	2,289,927	1,042,600	1,311,205
Loudon	21,190,816	4,777,745	12,237,041	1,385,528	1,478,100	1,312,402
McMinn	27,240,989	4,859,510	16,010,668	2,753,802	2,265,821	1,351,188
McNairy	17,845,815	1,998,858	12,181,932	2,141,743	831,864	691,418
Macon	11,093,345	2,221,124	6,653,926	1,397,281	228,333	592,681
Madison	74,946,422	14,499,188	49,165,386	4,055,097	5,234,044	1,992,707
Marion	18,718,654	3,462,521	12,525,516	1,981,233	455,000	294,384
Marshall	18,949,451	2,750,533	12,641,375	1,634,075	1,324,346	599,122
Maury	48,382,079	9,957,971	31,376,846	2,647,065	2,867,942	1,532,255
Meigs	7,589,923	1,626,937	4,452,010	1,018,866	214,147	277,963
Monroe	19,379,010	3,747,578	12,809,993	2,128,748	517,975	174,716
Montgomery	89,784,002	20,036,880	50,696,960	3,935,303	9,523,823	5,591,036
Moore	5,491,258	1,294,212	2,830,648	1,250,102	77,641	38,655
Morgan	14,844,753	2,234,259	8,689,327	1,554,631	1,346,000	1,020,536
Obion	20,829,760	2,768,755	12,762,525	3,201,575	1,412,890	684,015
Overton	14,655,540	2,473,804	9,014,278	1,377,215	1,187,329	602,914
Perry	6,595,327	1,179,410	3,214,539	1,502,754	345,326	353,298
Pickett	4,839,262	1,233,796	2,422,448	1,013,630	22,787	146,601
Polk	13,567,073	3,147,668	7,176,535	2,389,138	420,000	433,732
Putnam	35,873,291	9,211,509	23,015,605	2,428,234	1,060,000	157,943
Rhea	16,846,921	2,927,840	10,677,972	1,346,956	1,331,488	562,665
Roane	28,754,660	5,670,181	19,448,296	1,860,916	1,352,954	422,313
Robertson	34,517,670	6,191,109	21,768,127	2,425,076	1,983,247	2,150,111
Rutherford	92,313,834	19,826,237	57,232,050	4,356,539	5,900,713	4,998,295
Scott	14,560,139	3,427,861	8,483,205	1,526,256	652,848	469,969
Sequatchie	8,902,685	1,850,501	5,359,678	1,300,135	211,188	181,183
Sevier	46,147,689	9,934,677	28,461,183	3,149,700	2,584,353	2,017,776
Shelby	410,525,610	221,062,274	120,028,784	18,454,073	25,270,863	25,709,616
Smith	12,064,536	2,981,605	6,888,704	1,463,847	420,557	309,823
Stewart	8,308,444	1,253,149	5,222,847	1,398,010	309,562	124,876
Sullivan	99,329,369	27,465,979	59,097,575	6,030,068	5,530,000	1,205,747
Sumner	90,561,441	18,452,278	58,064,216	3,489,783	7,030,000	3,525,164
Tipton	27,631,442	3,433,747	17,353,433	3,450,878	1,236,258	2,157,126
Trousdale	5,375,765	1,215,614	2,777,369	1,082,430	147,843	152,509
Unicoi	12,278,561	2,636,380	7,491,182	1,312,425	382,051	456,523
Union	9,330,994	1,849,876	5,826,500	1,307,371	285,000	62,247
Van Buren	4,661,298	1,096,795	2,113,912	1,291,162	48,005	111,424
Warren	27,284,453	5,495,454	17,069,463	2,013,802	1,133,833	1,571,901
Washington	40,554,257	10,428,302	24,462,679	3,477,735	1,455,000	730,541
Wayne	12,538,731	2,228,292	7,735,255	1,880,843	367,774	326,567
Weakley	20,074,639	2,308,996	14,321,466	2,528,294	633,727	282,156
White	15,646,061	3,138,112	9,380,942	1,727,831	1,027,105	372,071
Williamson	70,128,369	12,950,078	40,013,492	4,775,678	5,778,106	6,611,015
Wilson	45,762,939	8,689,113	27,190,650	3,103,208	3,239,677	3,540,291

1. Includes detail not shown separately.

2. Data are for Metropolitan Nashville-Davidson County.

Source: State of Tennessee, Report of the Comptroller of the Treasury, Division of Local Finance, *County and Municipal Finances for Fiscal Year Ended June 30, 1992.*

TABLE 15.10--LOCAL SALES TAX RATES, COUNTIES AND SELECTED MUNICIPALITIES, AS OF
JULY 1994

County Municipality	Tax rate (%)	Effective date	County Municipality	Tax rate (%)	Effective date
Anderson	2.25	5/87	Lauderdale	2.00	7/76
Clinton	2.75	7/87	Lawrence	2.25	12/83
Lake City	2.75	9/87	Lewis	2.00	7/79
Bedford	1.75	7/74	Lincoln	2.50	5/92
Benton	2.25	1/79	Loudon	1.50	10/71
Bledsoe	2.25	11/77	Lenoir City	2.00	6/88
Blount	2.25	10/80	McMinn	2.00	5/78
Bradley	2.25	1/83	McNairy	2.25	9/79
Campbell	2.25	7/84	Macon	2.25	7/84
Lake City	2.75	9/87	Madison	2.75	7/89
Cannon	1.75	1/76	Marion	2.25	6/77
Carroll	2.25	1/81	Marshall	2.25	11/78
Huntingdon	2.75	1/91	Maury	2.25	12/83
Carter	2.25	3/83	Meigs	2.00	7/78
Cheatham	2.25	7/76	Monroe	2.25	10/80
Chester	2.25	10/82	Montgomery	2.50	1/89
Claiborne	2.25	9/83	Moore	2.50	10/86
Clay	1.00	2/69	Morgan	2.00	7/80
Cocke	2.75	3/88	Wartburg	2.75	1/89
Coffee	2.00	8/81	Obion	2.25	11/83
Crockett	2.25	3/81	Overton	1.75	9/73
Cumberland	2.25	6/79	Perry	2.00	7/86
Davidson	2.25	10/80	Pickett	1.50	8/75
Decatur	1.50	7/73	Polk	2.25	7/84
DeKalb	1.50	1/70	Putnam	2.25	7/80
Dickson	2.25	7/81	Rhea	2.25	1/83
Dyer	2.75	1/91	Roane	2.50	1/89
Fayette	2.25	1/82	Oak Ridge	2.75	1/87
Fentress	2.50	10/92	Robertson	2.25	1/83
Franklin	2.25	12/86	Rutherford	2.25	10/83
Gibson	2.25	9/83	Scott	2.25	7/83
Humboldt	2.75	11/91	Sequatchie	2.25	1/77
Giles	1.50	1/75	Sevier	2.50	10/91
Grainger	2.75	7/94	Shelby	2.25	1/84
Greene	2.50	11/87	Smith	2.00	1/77
Grundy	2.25	9/77	Stewart	2.25	7/77
Hamblen	2.50	10/86	Sullivan	2.25	4/83
Hamilton	1.75	10/72	Kingsport	2.50	7/92
Hancock	2.00	1/83	Sumner	2.25	12/83
Hardeman	2.00	5/78	Tipton	2.25	5/78
Hardin	1.50	11/73	Trousdale	2.25	10/76
Hawkins	2.75	10/88	Unicoi	2.25	6/83
Haywood	2.00	1/94	Union	2.25	10/88
Henderson	2.25	1/77	Van Buren	2.75	9/89
Henry	2.25	10/83	Warren	2.00	7/85
Hickman	2.25	10/81	Washington	2.50	7/94
Houston	2.75	10/86	Wayne	1.75	1/75
Humphreys	2.25	8/83	Weakley	2.25	5/83
Jackson	2.00	10/77	White	2.25	1/85
Jefferson	2.25	11/81	Williamson	2.25	4/91
Johnson	1.50	3/69	Wilson	2.25	11/93
Knox	2.25	1/89	Mount Juliet	2.25	10/83
Lake	2.25	12/80			

Note: Municipalities with the same rate as the county are not shown. The state rate is 6% beginning April 1992.

Source: Tennessee Department of Revenue, direct correspondence.

TABLE 15.11--STATE SALES AND USE TAX COMPARISON, COUNTIES, FISCAL YEAR 1994

County	Total collections	Percent of state total	Percent change 1993-1994	Per capita collections [1]
Anderson	$44,263,680	1.46	8.95	$628
Bedford	12,508,847	0.41	6.96	394
Benton	5,771,208	0.19	15.46	383
Bledsoe	1,426,627	0.05	9.63	146
Blount	54,359,501	1.79	11.30	601
Bradley	38,215,506	1.26	10.76	503
Campbell	11,499,029	0.38	8.67	322
Cannon	2,068,050	0.07	3.10	192
Carroll	8,007,367	0.26	1.67	290
Carter	15,583,317	0.51	11.06	300
Cheatham	6,115,013	0.20	12.68	212
Chester	4,331,789	0.14	15.74	334
Claiborne	6,124,835	0.20	7.79	226
Clay	1,661,826	0.05	2.55	230
Cocke	9,875,807	0.33	7.25	335
Coffee	29,594,787	0.98	6.94	711
Crockett	2,737,692	0.09	9.88	206
Cumberland	18,543,120	0.61	12.07	505
Davidson	499,567,932	16.49	12.88	965
Decatur	3,975,478	0.13	9.71	383
DeKalb	4,546,142	0.15	7.95	311
Dickson	18,610,033	0.61	13.20	510
Dyer	19,005,107	0.63	8.12	545
Fayette	4,063,170	0.13	10.95	156
Fentress	4,061,510	0.13	5.28	272
Franklin	11,021,130	0.36	13.68	312
Gibson	18,167,367	0.60	6.91	392
Giles	10,224,284	0.34	8.92	383
Grainger	2,213,381	0.07	1.51	125
Greene	22,482,596	0.74	11.40	393
Grundy	2,083,580	0.07	7.89	155
Hamblen	33,998,165	1.12	13.21	658
Hamilton	198,455,750	6.55	9.47	688
Hancock	714,132	0.02	12.77	106
Hardeman	6,479,746	0.21	5.77	273
Hardin	10,000,025	0.33	7.02	425
Hawkins	11,296,686	0.37	5.86	246
Haywood	6,298,831	0.21	2.57	323
Henderson	8,926,919	0.29	10.90	403
Henry	14,240,629	0.47	10.27	503
Hickman	3,354,360	0.11	9.04	191
Houston	1,358,988	0.04	11.57	189
Humphreys	5,642,455	0.19	4.12	356
Jackson	1,423,964	0.05	4.55	156
Jefferson	9,964,354	0.33	9.18	287
Johnson	3,465,215	0.11	8.49	228
Knox	262,397,145	8.66	10.80	755
Lake	1,272,006	0.04	4.14	174
Lauderdale	6,391,802	0.21	7.17	270
Lawrence	15,219,359	0.50	11.79	418

TABLE 15.11--STATE SALES AND USE TAX COMPARISON, COUNTIES, FISCAL YEAR 1994 (Continued)

County	Total collections	Percent of state total	Percent change 1993–1994	Per capita collections [1]
Lewis	2,607,189	0.09	4.23	265
Lincoln	9,784,344	0.32	9.07	344
Loudon	13,201,517	0.44	10.68	397
McMinn	20,697,086	0.68	9.05	475
McNairy	5,552,307	0.18	2.93	246
Macon	4,715,668	0.16	6.09	289
Madison	58,752,975	1.94	11.06	732
Marion	10,372,236	0.34	8.52	410
Marshall	9,117,511	0.30	4.02	397
Maury	33,514,698	1.11	15.04	561
Meigs	2,417,376	0.08	10.96	287
Monroe	11,264,457	0.37	11.23	359
Montgomery	50,689,813	1.67	12.34	461
Moore	626,216	0.02	5.41	128
Morgan	2,116,081	0.07	7.61	119
Obion	14,353,806	0.47	7.44	455
Overton	4,278,237	0.14	5.22	240
Perry	1,201,777	0.04	4.39	176
Pickett	859,737	0.03	3.62	189
Polk	2,310,091	0.08	9.28	166
Putnam	34,044,917	1.12	15.77	640
Rhea	7,594,476	0.25	10.12	301
Roane	24,921,969	0.82	9.89	518
Robertson	15,222,761	0.50	9.17	348
Rutherford	72,201,863	2.38	11.45	561
Scott	5,403,395	0.18	11.35	287
Sequatchie	2,687,287	0.09	8.76	293
Sevier	56,707,634	1.87	8.77	1037
Shelby	522,587,424	17.25	11.20	619
Smith	5,129,890	0.17	6.85	356
Stewart	2,334,833	0.08	8.16	230
Sullivan	89,502,922	2.95	4.01	610
Sumner	36,529,211	1.21	13.31	338
Tipton	11,086,593	0.37	10.35	283
Trousdale	1,234,783	0.04	8.37	208
Unicoi	3,860,291	0.13	-1.14	230
Union	1,876,184	0.06	9.32	133
Van Buren	529,751	0.02	5.71	108
Warren	15,009,584	0.50	9.53	448
Washington	55,990,227	1.85	9.57	590
Wayne	3,042,880	0.10	7.06	200
Weakley	10,265,218	0.34	6.69	321
White	7,514,744	0.25	12.60	367
Williamson	61,813,324	2.04	18.41	697
Wilson	25,852,053	0.85	13.32	363

Note: Percent change was computed by the Center for Business and Economic Research.

1. Per capita figures were computed by the Center for Business and Economic Research using population as of July 1, 1992.

Source: Tennessee Department of Revenue, *Monthly Statement of Revenue Collections*, June 1994.

TABLE 15.12–ESTIMATED CURRENT PROPERTY VALUE, ASSESSED VALUE, BY CLASSIFICATION, AND PROPERTY TAXES LEVIED, COUNTIES, 1992 [In thousands of dollars]

County	County taxes levied	Estimated current property value	Assessed value					
					Real property		Personal property[2]	Public utilities[3]
			Total	Total[1]	Residential and farm	Industrial and commercial		
Anderson	17,315	2,203,732	657,477	565,388	347,379	218,009	60,402	31,686
Bedford	7,707	805,534	231,935	189,768	148,890	40,878	17,573	24,595
Benton	2,119	300,552	76,193	66,070	54,342	11,729	3,968	6,155
Bledsoe	1,615	227,251	58,722	49,686	43,752	5,934	1,151	7,885
Blount	19,339	3,161,715	929,009	715,555	477,834	237,721	161,787	51,667
Bradley	16,604	2,336,459	617,761	509,865	316,999	192,866	73,954	33,942
Campbell	6,286	806,352	190,793	162,803	117,575	45,227	12,051	15,940
Cannon	1,784	215,328	60,957	52,008	44,236	7,772	1,521	7,429
Carroll	4,739	550,781	155,818	127,795	100,244	27,551	15,931	12,092
Carter	7,625	926,981	263,933	232,389	172,172	60,218	18,802	12,741
Cheatham	6,423	702,790	193,552	169,909	146,507	23,402	8,502	15,141
Chester	1,629	256,097	72,839	62,114	50,847	11,268	2,354	8,370
Claiborne	5,119	593,733	170,332	145,430	113,142	32,289	7,226	17,676
Clay	1,247	146,681	35,837	30,441	24,513	5,927	1,834	3,562
Cocke	4,686	579,147	146,719	119,924	84,555	35,369	14,392	12,403
Coffee	8,101	1,103,910	326,506	273,847	180,790	93,057	32,038	20,621
Crockett	2,407	374,050	105,417	90,153	73,396	16,757	6,109	9,155
Cumberland	7,124	1,447,089	389,781	341,010	274,883	66,128	21,833	26,938
Davidson	269,084	23,710,813	6,020,172	5,194,649	2,275,507	2,919,142	466,910	358,613
Decatur	1,329	238,712	68,272	57,918	45,148	12,770	4,577	5,778
DeKalb	2,371	456,810	98,585	81,128	63,685	17,443	7,847	9,610
Dickson	8,406	1,012,197	291,166	247,644	182,217	65,426	24,130	19,392
Dyer	5,027	964,787	285,797	235,894	159,853	76,041	24,616	25,287
Fayette	5,497	695,351	197,735	154,072	129,317	24,755	19,001	24,662
Fentress	1,850	289,932	79,101	66,902	53,531	13,372	3,636	8,562
Franklin	5,328	936,594	248,144	216,499	177,420	39,079	12,957	18,689
Gibson	6,292	1,039,069	271,500	222,091	164,114	57,977	25,769	23,639

TABLE 15.12–ESTIMATED CURRENT PROPERTY VALUE, ASSESSED VALUE, BY CLASSIFICATION, AND PROPERTY TAXES LEVIED, COUNTIES, 1992 [In thousands of dollars] (Continued)

County	County taxes levied	Estimated current property value	Assessed value					
				Real property			Personal property[2]	Public utilities[3]
			Total	Total[1]	Residential and farm	Industrial and commercial		
Giles	6,420	722,800	148,548	119,175	86,235	32,940	17,266	12,107
Grainger	2,596	325,672	79,240	68,290	60,723	7,566	2,189	8,761
Greene	9,777	1,409,984	409,395	344,218	240,467	103,751	41,134	24,043
Grundy	2,271	225,461	65,587	52,813	45,183	7,630	1,022	11,753
Hamblen	11,304	1,561,179	434,458	342,227	204,079	138,148	63,922	28,310
Hamilton	74,311	11,118,471	3,293,013	2,824,877	1,557,387	1,267,490	265,206	202,931
Hancock	598	124,602	35,460	30,091	25,565	4,526	751	4,618
Hardeman	3,066	510,689	143,761	118,315	97,736	20,579	10,722	14,725
Hardin	4,318	780,616	176,540	130,040	102,496	27,544	29,796	16,704
Hawkins	9,701	1,141,717	334,360	249,747	191,138	58,609	44,024	40,589
Haywood	3,622	580,547	171,687	129,260	97,154	32,106	19,683	22,744
Henderson	2,525	482,949	110,173	93,310	70,693	22,618	10,184	6,679
Henry	5,993	680,634	190,200	155,853	116,603	39,250	18,697	15,650
Hickman	3,740	501,410	102,045	85,016	73,041	11,975	5,061	11,968
Houston	1,254	130,653	37,089	31,703	26,097	5,606	1,546	3,840
Humphreys	3,948	586,177	138,755	92,857	63,082	29,774	33,520	12,378
Jackson	1,829	202,794	47,118	37,328	31,920	5,409	2,205	7,584
Jefferson	6,382	904,739	261,653	216,060	162,757	53,303	19,834	25,759
Johnson	2,939	267,869	76,750	63,458	52,460	10,999	3,745	9,547
Knox	90,114	11,180,499	2,933,905	2,569,443	1,524,999	1,044,444	213,364	151,098
Lake	1,125	133,418	37,706	32,480	25,838	6,642	1,289	3,937
Lauderdale	2,842	502,380	126,588	97,362	72,770	24,592	15,634	13,591
Lawrence	6,730	843,147	243,210	202,369	146,803	55,565	25,606	15,236
Lewis	1,194	216,420	63,508	49,922	39,131	10,791	5,224	8,362
Lincoln	5,018	717,019	201,037	175,782	136,856	38,926	16,036	9,219
Loudon	8,371	1,128,650	316,626	250,860	173,791	77,069	47,189	18,577

575

TABLE 15.12—ESTIMATED CURRENT PROPERTY VALUE, ASSESSED VALUE, BY CLASSIFICATION, AND PROPERTY TAXES LEVIED, COUNTIES, 1992 [In thousands of dollars] (Continued)

County	County taxes levied	Estimated current property value	Assessed value					
			Total	Real property			Personal property [2]	Public utilities [3]
				Total [1]	Residential and farm	Industrial and commercial		
McMinn	11,280	1,614,901	485,044	292,513	179,737	112,776	167,334	25,197
McNairy	3,772	505,016	133,987	103,264	81,589	21,675	10,655	20,068
Macon	3,226	382,497	94,792	74,021	62,069	11,951	5,104	15,667
Madison	17,674	2,588,145	633,964	510,198	303,036	207,162	86,683	37,083
Marion	3,618	596,698	175,896	143,890	104,668	39,221	10,700	21,306
Marshall	5,199	735,548	217,736	160,195	113,395	46,801	36,957	20,584
Maury	12,371	2,108,400	400,555	332,007	223,488	108,519	41,529	27,020
Meigs	1,340	209,711	59,229	48,514	42,753	5,761	3,038	7,678
Monroe	4,795	902,647	268,832	195,950	134,721	61,229	48,370	24,512
Montgomery	20,765	2,600,242	773,950	668,736	423,914	244,822	63,346	41,869
Moore	1,540	197,798	51,805	43,053	25,330	17,724	6,430	2,322
Morgan	4,888	283,082	82,289	60,926	54,153	6,773	2,706	18,657
Obion	6,614	770,650	226,624	183,752	133,208	50,544	16,290	26,582
Overton	2,836	345,529	99,668	83,405	67,563	15,842	3,752	12,512
Perry	1,549	182,466	57,081	38,751	32,131	6,620	2,155	16,175
Pickett	608	94,030	26,860	22,301	18,925	3,377	1,014	3,545
Polk	3,251	295,484	84,231	64,260	55,281	8,979	5,576	14,395
Putnam	7,865	1,489,990	444,797	374,253	246,308	127,945	33,500	37,043
Rhea	4,794	625,820	136,565	115,561	85,001	30,560	8,965	12,038
Roane	9,618	1,150,573	293,585	248,825	198,587	50,239	22,620	22,140
Robertson	10,128	1,213,061	346,918	295,751	226,875	68,876	23,382	27,784
Rutherford	37,833	4,261,113	1,182,605	963,731	585,958	377,773	147,616	71,258
Scott	3,813	353,471	104,948	75,726	58,897	16,830	8,955	20,267
Sequatchie	1,605	267,289	66,544	53,640	39,320	14,320	8,260	4,643
Sevier	10,778	2,889,094	885,337	828,889	436,270	392,620	38,694	17,754
Shelby	218,828	29,432,831	8,560,308	7,179,598	4,055,208	3,124,390	790,853	589,857
Smith	2,497	498,189	86,309	69,372	49,632	19,740	9,307	7,631

TABLE 15.12--ESTIMATED CURRENT PROPERTY VALUE, ASSESSED VALUE, BY CLASSIFICATION, AND PROPERTY TAXES LEVIED, COUNTIES, 1992 [In thousands of dollars] (Continued)

County	County taxes levied	Estimated current property value	Assessed value					
			Total	Real property			Personal property[2]	Public utilities[3]
				Total[1]	Residential and farm	Industrial and commercial		
Stewart	1,055	244,997	68,072	58,184	51,255	6,929	2,941	6,948
Sullivan	57,731	5,545,520	1,381,818	981,347	604,718	376,629	318,824	81,647
Sumner	29,544	3,380,468	960,846	844,282	633,875	210,407	66,173	50,390
Tipton	8,819	939,830	265,597	221,471	181,509	39,962	17,940	26,186
Trousdale	1,552	136,555	41,790	31,922	23,914	8,008	1,811	8,057
Unicoi	3,150	373,039	106,282	85,058	65,350	19,708	12,499	8,725
Union	1,675	271,894	70,387	62,334	51,933	10,401	3,592	4,460
Van Buren	987	106,650	29,342	26,291	23,212	3,079	323	2,727
Warren	6,020	991,069	293,360	237,850	158,455	79,395	37,599	17,911
Washington	17,846	2,858,235	671,895	584,126	358,792	225,334	50,293	37,475
Wayne	2,301	305,886	89,626	70,311	59,584	10,727	3,262	16,054
Weakley	4,753	739,978	215,893	177,205	126,175	51,030	21,726	16,962
White	3,301	482,944	138,344	114,276	89,216	25,060	12,299	11,769
Williamson	38,995	4,878,489	1,411,828	1,224,701	919,430	305,271	60,437	126,690
Wilson	21,101	2,555,745	523,879	467,370	371,450	95,920	22,858	33,651

1. Includes categories not shown separately.
2. Includes utilities assessed by the Public Service Commission as well as those locally assessed.
3. Includes utilities assessed by the Public Service Commission as well as those locally assessed.

Source: Tennessee State Board of Equalization, *1992 Tax Aggregate Report*; and State of Tennessee, Report of the Comptroller of the Treasury, Division of Local Finance, *County and Municipal Finances for Fiscal Year Ended June 30, 1992.*

TABLE 15.13--ACTUAL AND EFFECTIVE PROPERTY TAX RATES, APPRAISAL RATIO, AND YEAR OF LATEST APPRAISAL, COUNTIES, 1992

County	Actual tax rate [1]	Appraisal ratio (%) [2]	Year of appraisal	Equalized tax rate [3]	Effective tax rate by class of property [4]				Weighted average effective rate [5]
					Commercial and industrial real (40%)	Residential and farm real (25%)	Commercial and industrial personal (30%)	Public utilities (55%)	
Anderson	$2.98	100.00	1992	$2.98	$1.19	$0.75	$0.89	$1.64	$0.89
Bedford	3.36	100.00	1991	3.36	1.34	0.84	1.01	1.85	0.97
Benton	3.30	91.04	1983	3.00	1.20	0.75	0.90	1.65	0.84
Bledsoe	2.89	91.66	1984	2.65	1.06	0.66	0.79	1.46	0.75
Blount	2.37	100.00	1991	2.37	0.95	0.59	0.71	1.30	0.70
Bradley	3.06	88.32	1986	2.70	1.08	0.68	0.81	1.49	0.81
Campbell	3.59	81.79	1983	2.94	1.17	0.73	0.88	1.61	0.85
Cannon	2.96	100.00	1991	2.96	1.18	0.74	0.89	1.63	0.84
Carroll	1.55	100.00	1991	1.55	0.62	0.39	0.47	0.85	0.44
Carter	3.18	100.00	1991	3.18	1.27	0.80	0.95	1.75	0.91
Cheatham	3.41	100.00	1991	3.41	1.36	0.85	1.02	1.88	0.94
Chester	2.04	100.00	1992	2.04	0.82	0.51	0.61	1.12	0.58
Claiborne	3.14	100.00	1992	3.14	1.26	0.79	0.94	1.73	0.90
Clay	3.53	85.56	1984	3.02	1.21	0.76	0.91	1.66	0.86
Cocke	3.15	86.80	1984	2.73	1.09	0.68	0.82	1.50	0.80
Coffee	2.99	100.00	1991	2.99	1.20	0.75	0.90	1.64	0.88
Crockett	2.34	100.00	1992	2.34	0.94	0.59	0.70	1.29	0.66
Cumberland	1.93	96.00	1990	1.85	0.74	0.46	0.56	1.02	0.52
Davidson	3.64	77.67	1984	2.83	1.13	0.71	0.85	1.55	0.92
Decatur	1.99	100.00	1992	1.99	0.80	0.50	0.60	1.09	0.57
DeKalb	2.43	74.71	1983	1.82	0.73	0.45	0.54	1.00	0.52
Dickson	2.89	100.00	1991	2.89	1.16	0.72	0.87	1.59	0.83
Dyer	1.85	100.00	1992	1.85	0.74	0.46	0.56	1.02	0.55
Fayette	2.82	100.00	1991	2.82	1.13	0.71	0.85	1.55	0.80
Fentress	3.00	95.00	1985	2.85	1.14	0.71	0.86	1.57	0.82
Franklin	2.47	94.82	1990	2.34	0.94	0.59	0.70	1.29	0.65
Gibson	1.07	90.00	1983	0.96	0.39	0.24	0.29	0.53	0.28
Giles	4.51	70.53	1983	3.18	1.27	0.80	0.95	1.75	0.93

TABLE 15.13–ACTUAL AND EFFECTIVE PROPERTY TAX RATES, APPRAISAL RATIO, AND YEAR OF LATEST APPRAISAL, COUNTIES, 1992 (Continued)

| County | Actual tax rate [1] | Appraisal ratio (%) [2] | Year of appraisal | Equalized tax rate [3] | Effective tax rate by class of property [4] | | | | Weighted average effective rate [5] |
					Commercial and industrial real (40 %)	Residential and farm real (25 %)	Commercial and industrial personal (30%)	Public utilities (55 %)	
Grainger	3.29	88.26	1984	2.90	1.16	0.73	0.87	1.60	0.80
Greene	2.62	100.00	1992	2.62	1.05	0.66	0.79	1.44	0.76
Grundy	3.41	100.00	1992	3.41	1.36	0.85	1.02	1.88	0.99
Hamblen	2.88	91.81	1986	2.64	1.06	0.66	0.79	1.45	0.80
Hamilton	2.93	95.93	1989	2.81	1.12	0.70	0.84	1.55	0.87
Hancock	1.82	100.00	1992	1.82	0.73	0.46	0.55	1.00	0.52
Hardeman	2.28	100.00	1992	2.28	0.91	0.57	0.68	1.25	0.64
Hardin	2.54	78.29	1986	1.99	0.80	0.50	0.60	1.09	0.57
Hawkins	3.20	100.00	1992	3.20	1.28	0.80	0.96	1.76	0.94
Haywood	2.30	100.00	1991	2.30	0.92	0.58	0.69	1.27	0.68
Henderson	2.33	79.92	1983	1.86	0.74	0.47	0.56	1.02	0.53
Henry	3.04	96.90	1985	2.95	1.18	0.74	0.88	1.62	0.85
Hickman	3.81	72.00	1986	2.74	1.10	0.69	0.82	1.51	0.78
Houston	3.29	100.00	1992	3.29	1.32	0.82	0.99	1.81	0.93
Humphreys	2.84	79.24	1984	2.25	0.90	0.56	0.68	1.24	0.67
Jackson	3.93	80.15	1984	3.15	1.26	0.76	0.94	1.73	0.91
Jefferson	2.40	100.00	1992	2.40	0.96	0.60	0.72	1.32	0.69
Johnson	3.85	100.00	1988	3.85	1.54	0.96	1.16	2.12	1.10
Knox	3.25	86.21	1983	2.80	1.12	0.70	0.84	1.54	0.85
Lake	3.00	100.00	1992	3.00	1.20	0.75	0.90	1.65	0.85
Lauderdale	2.33	86.59	1986	2.02	0.81	0.50	0.61	1.11	0.59
Lawrence	2.78	100.00	1992	2.78	1.11	0.70	0.83	1.53	0.80
Lewis	2.09	100.00	1992	2.09	0.84	0.52	0.63	1.15	0.61
Lincoln	2.56	100.00	1991	2.56	1.02	0.64	0.77	1.41	0.72
Loudon	2.80	96.06	1983	2.69	1.08	0.67	0.81	1.48	0.79
McMinn	2.53	100.00	1992	2.53	1.01	0.63	0.76	1.39	0.76
McNairy	2.85	90.80	1985	2.59	1.04	0.65	0.78	1.42	0.76

TABLE 15.13--ACTUAL AND EFFECTIVE PROPERTY TAX RATES, APPRAISAL RATIO, AND YEAR OF LATEST APPRAISAL, COUNTIES, 1992 (Continued)

| County | Actual tax rate[1] | Appraisal ratio (%)[2] | Year of appraisal | Equalized tax rate[3] | Effective tax rate by class of property[4] | | | | Weighted average effective rate[5] |
					Commercial and industrial real (40%)	Residential and farm real (25%)	Commercial and industrial personal (30%)	Public utilities (55%)	
Macon	3.38	84.66	1986	2.86	1.14	0.72	0.86	1.57	0.84
Madison	3.55	81.01	1981	2.88	1.15	0.72	0.86	1.58	0.87
Marion	2.14	100.00	1992	2.14	0.86	0.54	0.64	1.18	0.63
Marshall	2.71	100.00	1991	2.71	1.08	0.68	0.81	1.49	0.80
Maury	3.44	64.00	1985	2.20	0.88	0.55	0.66	1.21	0.65
Meigs	2.32	100.00	1991	2.32	0.93	0.58	0.70	1.28	0.66
Monroe	2.00	100.00	1991	2.00	0.80	0.50	0.60	1.10	0.60
Montgomery	2.73	100.00	1991	2.73	1.09	0.68	0.82	1.50	0.81
Moore	3.05	85.00	1984	2.59	1.04	0.65	0.78	1.43	0.80
Morgan	6.05	100.00	1991	6.05	2.42	1.51	1.82	3.33	1.76
Obion	3.31	100.00	1991	3.31	1.32	0.83	0.99	1.82	0.97
Overton	2.79	100.00	1992	2.79	1.12	0.70	0.84	1.53	0.80
Perry	3.27	100.00	1991	3.27	1.31	0.82	0.98	1.80	1.02
Pickett	3.44	100.00	1992	3.44	1.38	0.86	1.03	1.89	0.98
Polk	3.69	100.00	1992	3.69	1.48	0.92	1.11	2.03	1.05
Putnam	2.00	100.00	1992	2.00	0.80	0.50	0.60	1.10	0.60
Rhea	3.48	75.66	1984	2.63	1.05	0.66	0.79	1.45	0.76
Roane	3.51	90.62	1986	3.18	1.27	0.80	0.95	1.75	0.90
Robertson	3.29	100.00	1991	3.29	1.32	0.82	0.99	1.81	0.94
Rutherford	3.39	92.06	1986	3.12	1.25	0.78	0.94	1.72	0.94
Scott	3.93	100.00	1992	3.93	1.57	0.98	1.18	2.16	1.17
Sequatchie	2.62	86.02	1984	2.25	0.90	0.56	0.68	1.24	0.65
Sevier	1.26	100.00	1992	1.26	0.50	0.32	0.38	0.69	0.39
Shelby	3.16	95.57	1991	3.02	1.21	0.76	0.91	1.66	0.92
Smith	2.93	58.87	1984	1.72	0.69	0.43	0.52	0.95	0.51
Stewart	1.55	100.00	1992	1.55	0.62	0.39	0.47	0.85	0.43
Sullivan	4.24	82.75	1983	3.51	1.40	0.88	1.05	1.93	1.06
Sumner	3.15	100.00	1992	3.15	1.26	0.79	0.95	1.73	0.90

TABLE 15.13--ACTUAL AND EFFECTIVE PROPERTY TAX RATES, APPRAISAL RATIO, AND YEAR OF LATEST APPRAISAL, COUNTIES, 1992 (Continued)

County	Actual tax rate [1]	Appraisal ratio (%) [2]	Year of appraisal	Equalized tax rate [3]	Effective tax rate by class of property [4]				Weighted average effective rate [5]
					Commercial and industrial real (40 %)	Residential and farm real (25 %)	Commercial and industrial personal (30%)	Public utilities (55 %)	
Tipton	3.57	100.00	1992	3.57	1.43	0.89	1.07	1.96	1.01
Trousdale	4.10	100.00	1992	4.10	1.64	1.03	1.23	2.26	1.25
Unicoi	3.29	100.00	1991	3.29	1.32	0.82	0.99	1.81	0.94
Union	2.50	93.68	1990	2.34	0.94	0.59	0.70	1.29	0.65
Van Buren	3.48	100.00	1991	3.48	1.39	0.87	1.04	1.91	0.96
Warren	2.11	100.00	1992	2.11	0.84	0.53	0.63	1.16	0.62
Washington	3.01	78.26	1983	2.36	0.94	0.59	0.71	1.30	0.71
Wayne	2.57	100.00	1992	2.57	1.03	0.64	0.77	1.41	0.75
Weakley	2.54	100.00	1991	2.54	1.02	0.64	0.76	1.40	0.74
White	2.48	100.00	1992	2.48	0.99	0.62	0.74	1.36	0.71
Williamson	2.91	100.00	1992	2.91	1.16	0.73	0.87	1.60	0.84
Wilson	3.78	72.86	1986	2.75	1.17	0.73	0.87	1.60	0.82

1. Does not include special school district rates or differing county rates charged in municipalities by some counties.
2. Based on sales ratio studies and certified by the Tennessee State Board of Equalization.
3. Computed by the Center for Business and Economic Research. Equalized rate = actual rate x appraisal ratio.
4. Effective tax rate is the percentage that tax liability is of the market value. Effective rate = equalized rate x assessment ratio.
5. Weighted average effective rate is the ratio of the total assessed value to the total estimated current property value multiplied by the appropriate tax rate.

Source: State of Tennessee, State Board of Equalization, *1992 Tax Aggregate Report of Tennessee.*

GOVERNMENT FINANCES

FIGURE 15.2
Equalized Property Tax Rate, Tennessee Counties, 1992
(Tennessee Mean Rate = $2.72)

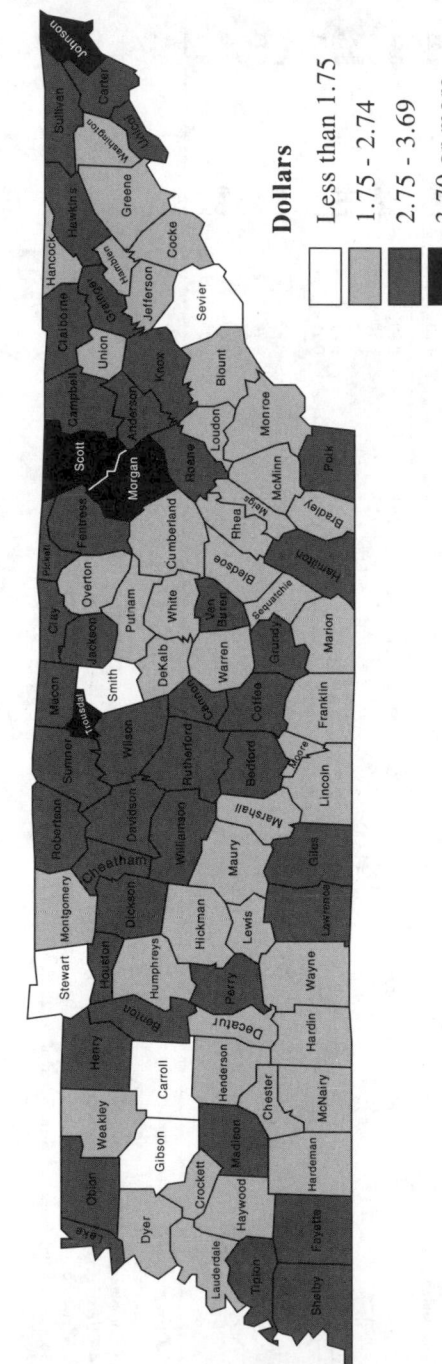

Dollars

Less than 1.75
1.75 - 2.74
2.75 - 3.69
3.70 or more

Source: State of Tennessee, State Board of Equalization, *1992 Tax Aggregate Report of Tennessee.*

TABLE 15.14--FEDERAL GOVERNMENT DIRECT EXPENDITURES OR OBLIGATIONS, COUNTIES, FISCAL YEAR 1993 [In thousands of dollars]

County	Total	Grant awards	Total salaries and wages	Total direct payments for individuals	Total procurement contract awards	Other federal expenditures or obligations
Anderson	2,669,320	40,877	81,503	207,939	2,338,857	144
Bedford	93,249	18,692	4,242	68,535	816	964
Benton	57,522	6,429	2,079	47,342	981	691
Bledsoe	30,423	7,833	712	21,087	251	539
Blount	281,839	30,924	13,426	227,607	9,544	338
Bradley	202,639	32,981	11,679	153,786	3,772	420
Campbell	170,297	32,674	4,769	113,929	18,828	97
Cannon	35,027	5,456	1,463	27,515	241	352
Carroll	197,303	19,967	4,752	84,748	84,409	3,427
Carter	149,597	26,807	5,957	115,542	1,038	252
Cheatham	57,712	7,650	3,461	45,825	540	237
Chester	43,048	11,823	1,959	27,621	185	1,459
Claiborne	101,755	26,525	3,613	67,706	3,756	156
Clay	27,982	9,161	1,897	15,528	1,224	172
Cocke	108,997	34,061	3,205	70,636	705	390
Coffee	422,771	42,407	19,731	115,422	243,576	1,636
Crockett	60,132	11,719	2,246	34,289	2,408	9,469
Cumberland	129,006	18,896	4,002	104,516	749	843
Davidson	2,059,443	347,656	362,319	1,249,213	92,272	7,983
Decatur	37,039	7,101	1,676	27,420	287	555
DeKalb	52,214	10,195	2,150	38,211	1,062	595
Dickson	104,760	13,695	4,339	85,637	754	335
Dyer	130,211	27,938	5,102	91,014	1,338	4,819
Fayette	84,263	27,885	2,573	45,237	692	7,875
Fentress	61,411	16,346	1,929	42,346	314	476
Franklin	121,782	16,671	6,848	90,931	5,353	1,978
Gibson	199,022	38,812	11,746	136,372	2,185	9,906
Giles	95,573	16,323	3,813	73,469	781	1,188
Grainger	61,966	18,293	2,889	39,879	762	142
Greene	206,361	31,905	7,888	130,314	35,420	833
Grundy	48,037	10,836	1,400	34,672	292	838
Hamblen	166,009	33,287	7,400	118,524	6,586	211
Hamilton	1,782,828	174,724	383,001	784,434	438,118	2,549
Hancock	27,989	10,915	540	16,382	93	59
Hardeman	106,309	26,345	3,126	64,414	8,626	3,798
Hardin	85,823	19,702	5,058	58,661	521	1,881
Hawkins	202,404	29,468	14,045	99,892	58,680	319
Haywood	97,094	38,669	2,415	44,316	501	11,194
Henderson	73,727	14,551	2,728	53,278	440	2,729
Henry	119,670	16,986	6,176	93,007	1,226	2,275
Hickman	52,640	8,604	3,016	39,839	809	373
Houston	27,195	5,724	969	20,192	213	97
Humphreys	72,302	8,311	18,534	43,622	1,527	309
Jackson	31,238	8,626	1,151	20,976	337	147
Jefferson	111,764	17,154	5,669	87,883	842	215
Johnson	58,024	13,952	1,834	41,718	364	156
Knox	1,434,707	226,126	214,248	863,156	128,785	2,392
Lake	37,601	7,504	2,291	25,748	223	1,835
Lauderdale	103,915	27,363	3,097	63,275	1,006	9,174
Lawrence	121,398	23,252	4,970	90,019	1,164	1,994

TABLE 15.14--FEDERAL GOVERNMENT DIRECT EXPENDITURES OR OBLIGATIONS, COUNTIES, FISCAL YEAR 1993 [In thousands of dollars] (Continued)

County	Total	Grant awards	Total salaries and wages	Total direct payments for individuals	Total procurement contract awards	Other federal expenditures or obligations
Lewis	30,089	5,882	1,184	22,716	130	174
Lincoln	99,464	19,980	3,043	73,097	1,435	1,910
Loudon	112,742	16,806	6,652	88,198	834	251
McMinn	134,799	22,185	7,052	104,093	1,011	459
McNairy	114,009	43,977	3,702	63,305	565	2,459
Macon	49,085	13,240	1,820	33,350	339	337
Madison	288,113	51,355	28,674	195,806	5,222	7,056
Marion	86,927	16,887	4,027	65,090	737	186
Marshall	68,658	12,503	3,212	55,328	-2,711	324
Maury	188,873	28,753	11,198	135,833	12,142	947
Meigs	28,828	6,346	1,521	20,592	196	172
Monroe	107,799	20,503	5,772	73,736	7,405	384
Montgomery	302,283	53,460	11,294	226,656	9,229	1,645
Moore	10,095	2,366	315	7,319	56	39
Morgan	54,668	11,761	5,422	35,791	1,332	362
Obion	113,441	19,744	4,429	82,937	739	5,591
Overton	62,532	16,206	2,408	43,160	370	388
Perry	26,516	5,279	955	19,783	139	359
Pickett	16,457	4,770	471	11,018	74	123
Polk	57,388	11,298	3,891	41,237	698	264
Putnam	193,897	41,197	10,910	137,968	3,269	553
Rhea	194,675	15,754	84,860	69,321	24,059	682
Roane	197,665	28,820	26,662	138,453	3,118	612
Robertson	107,879	16,479	4,246	84,296	763	2,095
Rutherford	348,583	53,316	79,485	208,431	5,844	1,508
Scott	81,373	21,295	3,265	52,794	3,818	201
Sequatchie	26,012	6,652	1,075	16,916	1,164	205
Sevier	155,029	20,643	11,330	114,443	8,359	254
Shelby	3,880,040	631,472	800,907	1,975,490	460,280	11,890
Smith	52,943	7,9	7,999	34,970	1,918	538
Stewart	61,416	5,742	23,162	32,066	313	134
Sullivan	572,693	66,681	25,191	380,591	99,778	453
Sumner	263,181	35,257	23,082	198,329	5,618	896
Tipton	125,709	26,393	4,363	87,514	725	6,714
Trousdale	18,908	3,030	2,680	13,015	126	57
Unicoi	161,341	15,217	3,230	48,780	94,052	61
Union	32,961	8,368	1,025	23,279	223	67
Van Buren	11,967	3,223	286	8,099	46	313
Warren	116,426	19,581	5,299	85,892	891	4,763
Washington	394,473	46,711	72,260	255,821	18,841	841
Wayne	43,148	9,807	1,675	30,894	269	503
Weakley	121,223	28,948	7,791	77,873	1,281	5,331
White	77,426	22,045	2,564	51,850	549	419
Williamson	161,297	20,664	12,514	123,433	3,695	992
Wilson	161,778	20,418	6,698	131,966	2,271	427

Note: Detail may not add to total because of independent rounding. Undistributed federal obligations of $1,116,112,000 are not shown.

Source: U.S. Department of Commerce, Bureau of the Census, *Consolidated Federal Funds Report, Volume I: County Areas, Fiscal Year 1993.*

TABLE 15.15--OPERATING REVENUE, BY SOURCE, MUNICIPALITIES, FISCAL YEAR 1992 [In dollars]

Municipality	Total	Local sources Total	Property taxes	County government Total	Local sales tax	State government	Federal government
Adams	94,166	30,686	15,237	9,995	9,995	53,485	0
Adamsville	878,874	542,290	208,180	165,356	165,356	171,228	0
Alamo	1,893,396	400,833	185,077	419,983	120,488	929,943	142,637
Alcoa	14,691,329	7,441,235	3,582,251	4,143,952	3,187,225	2,726,480	379,662
Alexandria	189,902	94,920	74,958	23,060	23,060	71,922	0
Algood	649,805	383,794	154,967	98,453	98,453	167,558	0
Allardt	62,713	6,429	0	6,296	6,296	49,988	0
Altamont	191,525	20,311	0	16,016	16,016	155,198	0
Ardmore	337,559	173,240	29,832	99,347	74,955	64,972	0
Arlington	597,501	376,239	195,919	76,410	76,410	144,852	0
Ashland City	1,042,074	370,357	215,604	461,265	461,265	210,452	0
Athens	13,474,819	4,493,672	2,063,296	3,688,234	1,849,997	4,326,543	966,370
Atoka	209,882	82,371	5,357	74,013	71,513	53,498	0
Atwood	122,808	9,815	0	31,732	31,732	81,261	0
Auburntown	59,658	35,884	0	5,420	5,420	18,354	0
Baileyton	110,929	30,563	0	54,407	54,407	25,959	0
Baneberry	75,236	43,909	35,997	11,236	11,236	20,091	0
Bartlett	11,611,180	7,983,884	4,794,047	1,400,910	1,400,910	2,226,386	0
Baxter	319,471	184,369	94,624	31,547	31,547	103,555	0
Beersheba Springs	220,648	174,080	0	4,679	4,679	41,889	0
Bell Buckle	56,958	19,255	6,911	3,832	3,832	33,871	0
Belle Meade	3,292,139	1,589,197	1,099,876	0	0	1,702,942	0
Bells	1,018,235	461,924	279,355	249,025	51,477	192,292	114,994
Benton	241,966	91,178	29,852	72,114	72,114	78,674	0
Berry Hill	1,399,377	478,343	0	817,184	817,184	103,850	0
Bethel Springs	134,978	60,176	19,965	19,571	19,571	55,231	0
Big Sandy	229,001	149,799	19,202	30,684	30,684	48,518	0
Blaine	270,749	38,969	0	38,379	38,379	193,401	0
Bluff City	415,259	199,945	94,949	92,407	92,407	122,907	0
Bolivar	2,824,605	1,613,639	280,238	728,428	527,762	482,538	0
Braden	121,265	13,439	0	3,525	3,525	104,301	0
Bradford	261,415	127,609	49,274	41,078	41,078	92,728	0
Brentwood	11,390,607	7,516,852	3,908,076	1,841,716	1,811,866	1,912,420	119,619
Brighton	189,310	62,247	13,840	69,954	67,454	57,109	0
Bristol	28,749,675	9,531,668	6,121,512	10,079,902	2,770,248	7,737,055	1,401,050
Brownsville	3,965,831	2,507,685	973,066	643,861	518,573	814,285	0
Bruceton	433,570	256,257	133,413	55,607	55,607	121,706	0
Bulls Gap	178,675	99,021	50,545	27,183	27,183	52,471	0
Burlison	35,804	4,174	0	4,081	4,081	27,549	0
Burns	271,989	142,358	32,561	22,164	22,164	107,467	0
Byrdstown	198,250	76,463	62,074	46,676	46,676	75,111	0
Calhoun	274,988	43,801	23,572	14,855	14,855	95,456	120,876
Camden	1,595,454	696,750	138,079	604,794	604,794	293,910	0
Carthage	1,138,209	687,185	349,935	218,240	218,240	232,784	0
Caryville	477,753	163,053	0	158,766	158,766	155,934	0
Cedar Hill	43,787	9,028	5,316	5,763	5,763	28,996	0
Celina	443,452	250,295	117,765	64,705	64,705	128,452	0
Centertown	27,055	1,873	0	0	0	25,182	0
Centerville	1,333,380	597,929	244,674	397,578	348,522	284,539	53,334
Chapel Hill	245,058	154,482	111,446	19,475	19,475	71,101	0
Charleston	280,052	152,860	32,054	65,485	55,485	61,707	0
Charlotte	209,651	74,146	12,192	57,547	57,547	77,958	0
Chattanooga	200,380,831	97,994,586	53,838,816	44,181,390	25,178,146	50,992,208	7,212,647
Church Hill	1,027,970	365,277	173,376	223,085	223,085	439,608	0
Clarksburg	45,063	7,192	0	13,672	13,672	24,199	0

TABLE 15.15--OPERATING REVENUE, BY SOURCE, MUNICIPALITIES, FISCAL YEAR 1992 [In dollars]
(Continued)

| Municipality | Total | Local sources | | County government | | State government | Federal government |
		Total	Property taxes	Total	Local sales tax		
Clarksville	23,146,000	12,803,500	6,371,100	3,322,100	3,322,100	7,020,400	0
Cleveland	29,276,351	9,959,071	5,336,367	9,155,945	3,675,671	8,740,796	1,420,539
Clifton	355,851	178,031	46,013	0	0	177,820	0
Clinton	8,649,833	2,686,866	820,979	2,781,139	1,319,412	2,156,859	1,024,969
Coalmont	233,317	13,502	0	9,427	9,427	210,388	0
Collegedale	1,842,766	1,071,585	622,530	193,834	193,834	577,347	0
Collierville	7,813,741	5,088,344	2,824,528	1,493,541	1,493,541	1,231,856	0
Collinwood	271,266	191,087	128,662	0	0	80,179	0
Columbia	11,776,022	5,871,508	3,164,251	3,516,439	3,516,439	2,388,075	0
Cookeville	9,785,778	4,920,139	2,051,547	3,052,035	3,052,035	1,813,604	0
Copperhill	246,842	145,445	47,810	68,661	68,661	32,736	0
Cornersville	145,399	77,966	56,307	11,311	11,311	56,122	0
Cottage Grove	19,363	7,279	1,549	6,139	6,139	5,945	0
Covington	7,693,868	1,486,235	0	3,539,131	2,756,042	2,668,502	0
Cowan	364,363	272,422	71,028	30,209	30,209	61,732	0
Crab Orchard	158,487	41,410	0	50,451	50,451	66,626	0
Cross Plains	202,160	71,926	0	52,171	51,371	78,063	0
Crossville	4,589,704	1,913,857	707,536	2,058,846	2,058,846	617,001	0
Cumberland City	112,908	73,654	18,360	13,853	13,853	25,401	0
Cumberland Gap	358,310	256,670	2,601	42,450	42,450	59,190	0
Dandridge	547,828	241,578	173,546	163,211	163,211	143,039	0
Dayton	4,504,329	1,111,868	237,556	1,137,693	793,921	2,104,232	150,536
Decatur	454,237	205,461	75,533	95,806	95,806	152,970	0
Decaturville	307,430	113,577	76,296	43,793	43,793	105,404	44,656
Decherd	889,258	471,392	251,308	258,358	258,358	159,508	0
Dickson	6,556,850	4,469,033	1,414,665	1,308,960	1,308,960	778,857	0
Dover	565,945	318,482	103,944	144,277	144,277	103,186	0
Dowelltown	32,548	8,395	0	893	893	23,260	0
Doyle	52,278	18,255	0	8,045	8,045	25,978	0
Dresden	1,175,256	702,801	368,040	231,868	231,868	240,587	0
Ducktown	706,173	49,454	27,143	69,770	69,770	586,949	0
Dunlap	922,107	422,146	195,303	137,224	137,224	362,737	0
Dyer	623,294	275,363	142,514	170,639	170,639	177,292	0
Dyersburg	21,154,811	8,735,001	3,509,493	4,508,746	3,863,947	7,093,359	817,705
Eagleville	162,532	59,522	41,299	62,164	53,164	40,846	0
East Ridge	6,082,815	2,906,011	1,518,482	1,357,640	1,357,640	1,819,164	0
Eastview	93,888	32,661	0	19,192	19,192	42,035	0
Elizabethton	12,853,944	5,261,055	2,780,314	3,744,430	1,702,241	3,100,710	747,749
Elkton	171,531	110,774	5,508	9,318	9,318	51,439	0
Englewood	411,111	231,250	125,821	42,845	40,391	137,016	0
Erin	528,789	228,114	104,383	165,327	165,327	135,348	0
Erwin	1,854,128	1,066,844	620,150	378,875	378,875	408,409	0
Estill Springs	337,515	184,432	76,749	28,824	28,824	124,259	0
Ethridge	145,344	46,788	0	54,012	54,012	44,544	0
Etowah	2,861,680	1,206,444	451,425	614,893	244,531	865,243	175,100
Fairview	1,107,913	583,336	257,486	176,757	176,757	347,820	0
Farragut	2,951,061	702,985	0	1,130,270	1,130,270	1,117,806	0
Fayetteville	6,876,284	3,302,332	1,362,253	1,396,340	530,797	1,918,665	258,947
Finger	43,542	14,749	0	5,341	5,341	23,452	0
Forest Hills	815,190	170,415	0	172,366	172,366	472,409	0
Franklin	13,383,701	7,276,926	3,400,226	4,352,111	4,309,194	1,754,664	0
Friendship	141,504	87,207	48,985	16,626	9,126	37,671	0
Friendsville	102,795	27,971	0	11,706	11,706	63,118	0

TABLE 15.15--OPERATING REVENUE, BY SOURCE, MUNICIPALITIES, FISCAL YEAR 1992 [In dollars]
(Continued)

| Municipality | Total | Local sources | | County government | | State government | Federal government |
		Total	Property taxes	Total	Local sales tax		
Gadsden	96,090	40,606	0	8,102	7,102	47,382	0
Gainesboro	588,802	334,630	79,186	175,316	175,316	78,856	0
Gallatin	8,644,780	5,163,845	2,534,629	2,012,660	2,012,660	1,468,275	0
Gallaway	205,033	119,497	0	26,021	0	59,515	0
Garland	35,400	12,153	2,011	8,690	6,190	14,557	0
Gates	128,911	72,303	37,033	8,652	8,652	47,956	0
Gatlinburg	15,767,853	10,916,023	599,479	2,998,969	2,839,282	1,852,861	0
Germantown	15,522,577	10,014,482	6,527,206	2,536,878	2,536,878	2,971,217	0
Gibson	133,222	90,876	14,931	9,360	9,360	32,986	0
Gilt Edge	64,285	25,524	0	4,408	1,908	34,353	0
Gleason	387,760	223,195	81,014	50,215	50,215	114,350	0
Goodlettsville	5,962,480	1,749,809	370,040	3,224,312	3,224,312	988,359	0
Gordonsville	285,461	171,143	117,758	45,684	45,684	68,634	0
Grand Junction	196,072	119,860	37,779	47,108	47,108	29,104	0
Graysville	184,984	55,303	21,571	11,622	11,622	118,059	0
Greenback	125,204	55,262	0	12,365	12,365	57,577	0
Greenbrier	647,337	327,186	212,846	79,074	79,074	241,077	0
Greeneville	19,848,451	8,191,292	4,638,358	5,632,391	3,182,669	5,079,752	945,016
Greenfield	677,695	399,826	144,143	111,441	111,441	166,428	0
Gruetli-Laager	268,137	76,557	0	55,856	55,856	135,724	0
Guys	121,270	71,100	0	10,049	10,049	40,121	0
Halls	948,595	657,546	247,680	98,025	98,025	193,024	0
Harriman	8,823,394	2,023,448	894,647	2,667,463	706,543	3,606,228	526,255
Hartsville	1,189,982	701,513	227,517	173,210	173,210	315,259	0
Henderson	1,563,044	952,146	334,407	181,571	101,185	429,327	0
Hendersonville	10,028,102	5,503,357	2,389,782	1,949,874	1,949,874	2,574,871	0
Henning	218,156	115,446	28,267	26,798	20,798	75,912	0
Henry	142,095	106,730	17,090	11,674	11,674	23,691	0
Hickory Valley	40,554	12,069	1,842	16,281	16,281	12,204	0
Hohenwald	1,648,081	939,751	290,679	395,349	308,530	312,981	0
Hollow Rock	201,636	109,728	14,298	21,209	21,209	70,699	0
Hornbeak	233,401	174,422	9,709	23,917	23,917	35,062	0
Hornsby	59,183	29,047	6,069	6,593	6,593	23,543	0
Humboldt	11,288,944	4,020,575	1,520,446	1,480,396	766,703	4,350,663	1,437,310
Huntingdon	1,991,214	745,000	298,703	882,411	662,064	363,803	0
Huntland	357,997	237,813	64,764	47,854	34,931	72,330	0
Huntsville	144,545	62,146	13,336	27,562	27,562	54,837	0
Iron City	58,545	18,563	2,604	9,562	9,562	30,420	0
Jacksboro	384,323	80,894	0	80,752	80,752	222,677	0
Jackson	35,710,757	24,213,587	11,423,383	5,525,552	5,262,202	5,143,645	827,973
Jamestown	619,105	314,399	134,419	158,279	158,279	146,427	0
Jasper	766,527	332,846	92,369	207,899	207,899	225,782	0
Jefferson City	1,923,756	817,984	427,004	656,471	656,471	449,301	0
Jellico	910,697	591,876	88,877	127,246	127,246	191,575	0
Johnson City	53,688,210	23,545,151	12,394,059	14,856,676	7,205,268	13,120,087	2,166,296
Jonesborough	1,502,676	776,148	414,335	344,058	324,058	382,470	0
Kenton	358,274	168,067	101,288	80,554	80,554	109,653	0
Kimball	742,083	259,643	25,773	388,974	388,974	93,466	0
Kingsport	55,745,162	20,177,099	14,489,084	20,504,861	9,132,574	13,127,396	1,935,806
Kingston	1,915,214	1,174,535	554,344	351,893	351,893	388,786	0
Kingston Springs	384,296	192,508	98,179	73,530	73,530	118,258	0
Knoxville	107,003,466	72,409,611	46,271,528	15,344,765	15,344,765	15,096,688	4,152,402
Lafayette	1,560,966	744,485	286,264	515,380	515,380	289,678	11,423
LaFollette	3,286,435	1,382,632	512,421	1,143,479	1,143,479	760,324	0

TABLE 15.15--OPERATING REVENUE, BY SOURCE, MUNICIPALITIES, FISCAL YEAR 1992 [In dollars]
    (Continued)

| Municipality | Total | Local sources | | County government | | State government | Federal government |
		Total	Property taxes	Total	Local sales tax		
LaGrange	108,389	92,965	15,995	2,236	2,236	13,188	0
Lake City	954,273	439,974	119,413	313,514	313,514	200,785	0
Lakeland	714,571	239,084	0	380,204	380,204	95,283	0
Lakesite	118,257	51,133	38,516	3,714	3,714	63,410	0
Lakewood	410,386	150,674	0	57,631	0	202,081	0
LaVergne	3,447,798	2,046,314	1,010,968	830,107	830,107	571,377	0
Lawrenceburg	6,557,807	4,254,216	1,198,687	1,592,899	1,542,134	668,223	42,469
Lebanon	7,552,940	3,740,512	900,931	1,749,418	1,749,418	2,063,010	0
Lenoir City	8,828,986	2,829,188	641,280	2,900,693	1,109,018	2,909,113	189,992
Lewisburg	6,296,539	5,041,683	2,183,645	475,677	475,677	779,179	0
Lexington	6,076,324	2,162,580	564,347	908,326	183,267	3,005,418	0
Liberty	74,422	26,275	3,457	11,863	11,863	36,284	0
Linden	403,468	185,071	61,635	119,355	119,355	99,042	0
Livingston	1,237,037	834,067	512,515	250,939	250,939	152,031	0
Lobelville	240,759	132,688	70,538	33,696	33,696	74,375	0
Lookout Mountain	2,060,813	1,069,216	798,483	24,703	24,703	966,894	0
Loretto	354,663	93,298	28,558	126,682	125,682	134,683	0
Loudon	2,553,256	1,961,154	760,075	232,234	232,234	359,868	0
Lynnville	64,406	32,562	10,768	4,597	4,597	27,247	0
McEwen	349,941	167,249	57,217	66,345	66,345	116,347	0
McKenzie	2,077,583	1,173,951	321,831	515,168	515,168	388,464	0
McLemoresville	60,787	31,231	13,424	6,601	6,601	22,955	0
McMinnville	5,808,625	4,349,196	1,841,605	352,930	352,930	1,106,499	0
Madisonville	1,385,928	538,702	126,079	560,663	560,663	286,563	0
Manchester	8,260,379	3,294,195	1,404,781	2,317,208	1,024,278	2,271,054	377,922
Martin	5,451,492	3,903,511	671,843	903,083	903,083	636,093	8,805
Maryville	24,000,887	9,011,939	5,553,908	7,569,336	3,245,023	6,822,549	597,063
Mason	304,928	192,951	31,240	38,384	35,884	73,593	0
Maury City	247,398	138,447	40,467	29,656	22,156	79,295	0
Maynardville	269,537	48,518	0	122,940	122,940	98,079	0
Medina	264,185	117,127	56,852	0	0	147,058	0
Medon	71,221	58,515	0	1,951	1,951	10,755	0
Memphis	749,848,344	274,008,689	133,824,462	197,172,915	62,682,797	189,308,037	89,358,703
Michie	95,440	28,273	0	15,235	15,235	51,932	0
Middleton	315,979	151,756	37,075	105,550	105,550	58,673	0
Milan	3,150,591	1,802,970	408,160	742,204	742,204	605,417	0
Milledgeville	72,356	11,710	0	12,914	12,914	47,732	0
Millersville	425,343	153,044	70,120	70,625	70,625	201,674	0
Millington	5,188,005	2,265,787	623,426	1,520,106	1,507,120	1,402,112	0
Minor Hill	195,017	154,747	0	10,445	10,445	29,825	0
Mitchellville	25,854	8,760	4,872	820	820	16,274	0
Monteagle	436,700	198,320	0	138,373	138,373	100,007	0
Monterey	615,312	277,801	140,297	142,577	142,577	194,934	0
Morrison	63,078	19,050	5,344	0	0	44,028	0
Morristown	12,712,553	6,216,070	3,345,629	4,659,647	4,193,417	1,789,093	47,743
Moscow	245,666	161,886	24,807	45,806	39,596	37,974	0
Mosheim	283,662	93,977	0	69,165	69,165	120,520	0
Mount Carmel	811,310	243,827	0	232,935	232,935	334,548	0
Mount Juliet	2,220,630	1,026,243	0	627,716	627,716	566,671	0
Mount Pleasant	1,452,812	834,287	279,107	241,551	238,451	336,179	40,795
Mountain City	1,118,844	438,454	265,061	233,575	233,575	446,815	0
Munford	603,279	282,037	89,350	110,867	110,867	210,375	0
Murfreesboro	45,147,860	20,291,523	11,470,848	12,972,598	6,108,384	10,034,760	1,848,979
New Hope	89,477	22,156	10,020	3,266	3,266	64,055	0

TABLE 15.15--OPERATING REVENUE, BY SOURCE, MUNICIPALITIES, FISCAL YEAR 1992 [In dollars]
(Continued)

		Local sources		County government			
Municipality	Total	Total	Property taxes	Total	Local sales tax	State government	Federal government
New Johnsonville	566,431	320,394	86,812	115,191	115,191	130,846	0
New Market	215,175	58,559	0	61,496	41,198	95,120	0
New Tazewell	1,151,572	138,082	0	476,243	476,243	537,247	0
Newbern	1,078,536	713,108	251,019	141,867	125,547	223,561	0
Newport	6,707,762	2,381,394	1,191,460	2,045,969	1,483,452	1,998,438	281,961
Niota	187,700	99,007	48,623	21,566	21,566	67,127	0
Normandy	16,679	6,849	1,471	321	321	9,509	0
Norris	603,867	465,784	262,540	26,517	26,517	111,566	0
Oak Hill	853,674	263,816	0	70,996	0	518,862	0
Oak Ridge	34,643,554	11,537,458	5,419,908	11,021,554	5,471,204	10,997,310	1,087,232
Oakdale	481,375	41,355	23,659	3,018	3,018	437,002	0
Obion	263,433	166,629	81,188	25,492	25,492	71,312	0
Oliver Springs	1,022,148	507,399	285,103	234,512	234,512	280,237	0
Oneida	1,411,328	537,414	305,262	572,295	572,295	301,619	0
Orlinda	117,835	54,709	0	29,084	28,284	34,042	0
Orme	59,658	1,238	0	323	323	58,097	0
Palmer	97,006	30,152	0	8,719	8,719	58,135	0
Paris	4,451,763	2,132,588	725,907	1,549,431	1,549,431	769,744	0
Parker's Crossroads	105,442	56,073	0	33,988	33,988	15,381	0
Parrottsville	52,384	40,759	0	0	0	11,625	0
Parsons	772,777	333,026	188,621	254,273	254,273	185,478	0
Pegram	217,080	71,516	0	36,446	36,446	109,118	0
Petersburg	142,243	91,053	21,506	34,903	34,903	16,287	0
Philadelphia	52,725	8,998	0	3,942	3,942	39,785	0
Pigeon Forge	16,126,328	8,281,662	340,283	4,422,929	4,422,929	3,421,737	0
Pikeville	440,693	221,778	81,518	76,145	76,145	142,770	0
Piperton	95,857	13,389	0	35,599	35,599	46,869	0
Pittman Center	149,725	81,211	34,344	31,269	31,269	37,245	0
Pleasant Hill	79,155	17,438	0	13,581	13,581	48,136	0
Portland	2,269,589	1,166,749	562,918	421,900	421,900	680,940	0
Powell's Crossroads	118,325	28,284	0	9,996	9,996	80,045	0
Pulaski	3,096,063	1,933,137	524,614	509,339	490,855	653,587	0
Puryear	370,155	166,277	22,687	22,370	22,370	181,508	0
Red Bank	2,659,975	1,110,171	561,685	634,559	634,559	915,245	0
Red Boiling Springs	324,197	166,765	68,305	74,469	74,469	82,963	0
Ridgely	479,146	306,315	103,797	35,881	35,881	136,950	0
Ridgeside	173,161	123,215	105,563	3,763	3,763	46,183	0
Ridgetop	243,215	117,378	66,566	27,393	27,393	98,444	0
Ripley	2,813,474	1,839,914	718,439	406,350	406,350	567,210	0
Rives	150,809	118,628	12,769	1,099	1,099	31,082	0
Rockford	161,233	11,931	0	59,068	59,068	90,234	0
Rockwood	2,567,659	1,128,920	426,401	824,186	824,186	506,981	107,572
Rogersville	3,601,727	1,007,669	550,044	1,310,771	852,029	1,090,009	193,278
Rossville	261,279	220,403	134,718	18,067	18,067	22,809	0
Rutherford	390,385	227,977	86,005	59,932	59,932	102,476	0
Rutledge	227,722	60,354	0	75,498	75,498	91,870	0
St. Joseph	222,506	130,433	7,454	31,362	31,362	60,711	0
Saltillo	274,370	30,768	0	6,713	6,713	236,889	0
Samburg	112,984	63,109	0	21,447	21,447	28,428	0
Sardis	44,863	11,887	6,666	8,873	7,373	24,103	0
Saulsbury	27,110	9,886	0	7,508	7,508	9,716	0
Savannah	2,465,522	1,425,941	395,206	514,327	439,338	525,254	0
Scotts Hill	179,802	65,454	17,021	67,426	65,715	46,922	0
Selmer	1,545,850	689,592	291,547	517,445	517,445	338,813	0

TABLE 15.15--OPERATING REVENUE, BY SOURCE, MUNICIPALITIES, FISCAL YEAR 1992 [In dollars]
          (Continued)

| | | | | County government | | | |
| | | Local sources | | | | | |
Municipality	Total	Total	Property taxes	Total	Local sales tax	State government	Federal government
Sevierville	6,166,618	2,484,127	651,437	2,764,955	2,764,955	917,536	0
Sharon	428,102	290,812	107,659	46,721	46,721	90,569	0
Shelbyville	6,739,414	4,987,308	2,369,321	715,920	715,920	1,036,186	0
Signal Mountain	3,018,817	1,982,198	1,418,481	163,487	163,487	873,132	0
Silerton	5,332	703	0	184	184	4,445	0
Slayden	11,225	195	0	5,574	5,574	5,456	0
Smithville	1,288,701	739,044	279,753	188,440	188,440	361,217	0
Smyrna	7,371,064	4,715,820	744,318	1,681,500	1,681,500	973,744	0
Sneedville	290,695	69,321	0	159,000	159,000	62,374	0
Soddy-Daisy	1,962,032	871,170	282,323	403,574	403,574	687,288	0
Somerville	1,212,806	697,371	95,898	324,058	324,058	191,377	0
South Carthage	399,387	285,107	73,922	49,135	49,135	65,145	0
South Fulton	835,184	533,542	157,362	88,352	88,352	213,290	0
South Pittsburg	1,552,459	882,892	186,398	292,568	292,568	376,999	0
Sparta	2,803,145	1,648,995	659,249	731,602	731,602	422,548	0
Spencer	233,167	98,611	0	40,348	40,348	94,208	0
Spring City	1,132,810	343,064	170,355	141,533	141,533	648,213	0
Spring Hill	875,071	537,321	60,575	63,799	63,799	273,951	0
Springfield	5,731,008	3,989,123	1,488,039	829,889	829,889	911,996	0
Stanton	166,211	22,788	18,484	4,218	4,218	139,205	0
Stantonville	34,305	9,416	0	2,586	2,586	22,303	0
Sunbright	83,163	673	0	39,923	39,923	42,567	0
Surgoinsville	366,777	202,438	52,574	50,207	50,207	114,132	0
Sweetwater	5,542,935	1,518,778	499,558	1,720,337	1,020,609	1,893,828	409,992
Tazewell	530,585	191,420	0	180,142	180,142	159,023	0
Tellico Plains	514,182	353,188	59,510	87,080	87,080	73,914	0
Tennessee Ridge	236,684	77,047	51,028	62,874	61,374	96,763	0
Thompson Station	99,450	33,548	16,150	15,494	15,494	50,408	0
Tiptonville	610,444	380,163	128,425	55,605	55,605	174,676	0
Toone	64,977	29,734	2,339	12,582	7,182	22,661	0
Townsend	198,493	57,075	0	115,610	106,571	25,808	0
Tracy City	389,807	164,373	70,024	104,708	104,708	120,726	0
Trenton	3,291,678	2,106,812	487,452	452,819	452,819	732,047	0
Trezevant	192,106	98,956	27,741	29,596	29,596	63,554	0
Trimble	147,389	67,092	42,184	12,162	12,162	68,135	0
Troy	336,269	179,394	111,022	61,488	61,488	95,387	0
Tullahoma	20,833,677	7,645,208	4,332,709	3,327,610	3,327,610	9,860,859	0
Tusculum	247,033	84,700	0	17,557	17,557	144,776	0
Union City	12,243,625	4,302,714	2,006,621	3,633,156	2,217,956	3,740,188	567,567
Vanleer	55,774	20,464	2,386	5,350	5,350	29,960	0
Viola	10,342	820	0	0	0	9,522	0
Vonore	209,918	126,856	0	24,518	24,518	58,544	0
Walden	451,013	244,650	198,740	18,316	18,316	188,047	0
Wartburg	446,225	95,507	0	283,215	283,215	67,503	0
Wartrace	140,935	96,974	33,457	6,669	6,669	37,292	0
Watauga	92,136	16,206	4,975	48,377	48,377	27,553	0
Watertown	224,325	110,505	77,270	18,052	18,052	95,768	0
Waverly	1,931,254	966,868	350,493	613,701	490,314	345,739	4,946
Waynesboro	629,824	479,747	253,556	83,189	83,189	66,888	0
Westmoreland	504,503	270,973	119,926	101,393	101,393	132,137	0
White Bluff	484,442	239,482	117,893	91,082	91,082	153,878	0
White House	1,576,961	1,058,364	683,325	277,931	268,034	240,666	0
White Pine	617,948	328,644	127,790	155,185	155,185	134,119	0

TABLE 15.15--OPERATING REVENUE, BY SOURCE, MUNICIPALITIES, FISCAL YEAR 1992 [In dollars] (Continued)

		Local sources		County government			
					Local		
			Property		sales	State	Federal
Municipality	Total	Total	taxes	Total	tax	government	government
Whiteville	325,152	189,659	57,637	34,388	34,388	101,105	0
Whitwell	305,809	121,611	12,436	0	0	184,198	0
Williston	53,154	15,153	0	4,895	4,895	33,106	0
Winchester	2,654,960	1,619,134	990,017	508,808	504,808	527,018	0
Winfield	729,627	633,382	0	53,524	53,524	42,721	0
Woodbury	723,908	439,339	268,025	101,248	101,248	183,321	0
Woodland Mills	57,428	23,032	0	4,204	4,204	30,192	0
Yorkville	80,397	52,673	0	3,404	3,404	24,320	0

Note: Detail may not add to total due to independent rounding. Nashville (unified city and county government) data are presented in Table 15.7.

Source: State of Tennessee, Report of the Comptroller of the Treasury, Division of Local Finance, *County and Municipal Finances for Fiscal Year Ended June 30, 1992.*

TABLE 15.16--OPERATING EXPENDITURES, BY FUNCTION, MUNICIPALITIES, FISCAL YEAR 1992
[In dollars]

| Municipality | Total [1] | General purpose | Schools | Highways and streets | Debt service | |
					Principal	Interest
Adams	70,677	57,934	0	12,743	0	0
Adamsville	959,667	752,416	0	109,757	43,295	54,199
Alamo	1,813,707	396,334	1,208,825	124,854	34,525	49,169
Alcoa	15,552,897	6,937,847	6,236,024	605,426	1,012,555	761,045
Alexandria	198,613	137,544	0	43,021	17,099	949
Algood	519,300	365,628	0	102,812	25,000	25,860
Allardt	76,738	34,761	0	41,977	0	0
Altamont	199,728	162,104	0	28,143	5,508	3,973
Ardmore	347,190	276,395	0	44,331	24,980	1,484
Arlington	609,627	459,590	0	41,500	78,041	30,496
Ashland City	942,316	620,877	0	321,439	0	0
Athens	13,847,711	4,831,461	7,209,114	1,055,950	350,000	401,186
Atoka	347,687	327,649	0	20,038	0	0
Atwood	92,532	54,825	0	30,249	7,458	0
Auburntown	54,801	43,284	0	5,842	3,423	2,252
Baileyton	61,872	57,116	0	4,756	0	0
Baneberry	54,664	43,976	0	0	9,000	1,688
Bartlett	13,691,158	10,201,689	0	1,555,139	989,231	945,099
Baxter	360,616	237,389	0	59,942	40,567	22,718
Beersheba Springs	197,508	192,968	0	4,540	0	0
Bell Buckle	78,158	64,577	0	13,581	0	0
Belle Meade	2,643,132	1,448,013	0	827,327	250,000	117,792
Bells	1,315,547	333,818	761,023	91,744	35,621	93,341
Benton	301,492	207,539	0	66,272	20,358	7,323
Berry Hill	973,971	957,145	0	16,826	0	0
Bethel Springs	150,034	83,513	0	61,521	1,983	3,017
Big Sandy	187,884	172,004	0	15,880	0	0
Blaine	260,964	236,269	0	24,695	0	0
Bluff City	372,450	218,984	0	44,279	40,750	68,437
Bolivar	2,560,328	2,164,173	0	332,030	48,328	15,797
Braden	101,838	98,747	0	3,091	0	0
Bradford	236,754	183,054	0	36,328	10,000	7,372
Brentwood	8,366,172	4,943,385	0	2,118,509	558,500	745,778
Brighton	372,737	127,349	0	233,469	6,427	5,492
Bristol	36,322,695	8,611,869	20,070,405	2,262,423	2,736,000	2,641,998
Brownsville	3,561,128	2,064,993	0	1,232,624	157,707	105,804
Bruceton	383,183	328,795	0	54,388	0	0
Bulls Gap	169,669	132,689	0	23,091	11,066	2,823
Burlison	28,581	16,862	0	11,719	0	0
Burns	204,908	156,025	0	36,353	9,422	3,108
Byrdstown	177,364	153,189	0	0	15,000	9,175
Calhoun	284,728	235,043	0	49,253	432	0
Camden	1,343,704	995,152	0	348,552	0	0
Carthage	840,310	607,308	0	222,678	9,031	1,293
Caryville	654,924	478,315	0	73,000	74,562	29,047
Cedar Hill	23,689	16,643	0	1,100	3,628	2,318
Celina	467,990	326,326	0	62,453	46,463	32,748
Centertown	9,701	4,823	0	4,878	0	0
Centerville	1,211,199	1,012,686	0	77,162	85,674	35,677
Chapel Hill	416,305	209,570	0	206,735	0	0
Charleston	274,393	214,345	0	36,710	20,924	2,414
Charlotte	227,964	165,934	0	18,788	37,527	5,715
Chattanooga	187,120,490	96,789,993	79,042,473	4,757,961	4,339,929	2,190,134
Church Hill	905,803	660,692	0	245,111	0	0
Clarksburg	17,461	10,844	0	6,617	0	0
Clarksville	25,388,000	19,764,700	0	3,154,400	1,492,000	976,900
Cleveland	27,432,294	10,083,513	14,545,182	1,466,822	788,478	548,299

TABLE 15.16--OPERATING EXPENDITURES, BY FUNCTION, MUNICIPALITIES, FISCAL YEAR 1992
[In dollars] (Continued)

Municipality	Total [1]	General purpose	Schools	Highways and streets	Debt service Principal	Interest
Clifton	358,585	295,923	0	35,211	23,734	3,717
Clinton	9,324,356	4,279,787	3,779,514	357,012	445,000	463,043
Coalmont	248,534	236,781	0	11,753	0	0
Collegedale	1,457,903	1,163,888	0	64,817	132,344	96,854
Collierville	7,649,063	5,997,350	0	852,324	393,735	405,654
Collinwood	213,072	183,117	0	29,955	0	0
Columbia	11,336,807	9,290,894	0	1,761,468	105,000	179,445
Cookeville	11,327,591	7,603,044	0	1,627,705	1,614,000	482,842
Copperhill	274,517	191,407	0	83,110	0	0
Cornersville	179,972	117,985	0	53,841	6,192	1,954
Cottage Grove	8,604	6,843	0	1,761	0	0
Covington	7,124,052	3,259,830	2,931,160	506,766	351,427	74,869
Cowan	420,758	268,001	0	105,186	41,219	6,352
Crab Orchard	233,040	187,788	0	38,372	6,028	852
Cross Plains	213,064	152,038	0	21,539	24,309	15,178
Crossville	3,712,702	2,833,775	0	606,498	172,246	100,183
Cumberland City	96,008	91,934	0	4,074	0	0
Cumberland Gap	293,794	249,098	0	44,696	0	0
Dandridge	444,879	345,975	0	98,904	0	0
Dayton	3,816,307	1,711,406	1,452,840	329,603	296,966	25,492
Decatur	324,359	215,296	528	108,535	0	0
Decaturville	323,556	276,987	0	46,569	0	0
Decherd	1,063,069	754,588	0	283,558	9,095	15,828
Dickson	5,561,755	4,354,207	0	1,207,548	0	0
Dover	481,176	406,233	0	30,099	33,726	11,118
Dowelltown	28,155	20,012	0	8,143	0	0
Doyle	28,722	22,611	0	6,111	0	0
Dresden	1,667,980	1,459,023	0	159,452	39,805	9,700
Ducktown	221,867	188,900	0	32,967	0	0
Dunlap	1,017,266	816,375	0	183,459	8,992	8,440
Dyer	591,617	452,241	0	109,802	28,726	848
Dyersburg	19,666,753	7,509,404	11,009,749	324,114	310,471	513,015
Eagleville	145,032	131,739	0	13,293	0	0
East Ridge	7,188,622	5,452,491	0	1,149,543	303,909	282,679
Eastview	84,373	69,707	0	14,666	0	0
Elizabethton	15,136,959	5,206,917	8,257,159	945,209	631,830	95,844
Elkton	150,325	126,686	0	23,639	0	0
Englewood	366,585	312,693	0	53,892	0	0
Erin	492,418	361,534	0	108,750	15,200	6,934
Erwin	1,652,977	1,063,327	0	437,430	95,000	57,220
Estill Springs	261,925	171,552	0	90,373	0	0
Ethridge	127,731	82,670	0	45,061	0	0
Etowah	2,645,131	1,228,715	1,063,678	352,738	0	0
Fairview	1,001,660	836,317	0	165,343	0	0
Farragut	2,208,475	1,253,581	0	566,933	226,025	161,936
Fayetteville	6,270,924	2,469,937	2,875,831	635,577	102,991	186,588
Finger	26,378	22,773	0	3,605	0	0
Forest Hills	490,270	269,907	0	220,363	0	0
Franklin	10,530,740	8,607,168	0	756,705	520,000	646,867
Friendship	140,384	99,744	0	40,640	0	0
Friendsville	112,382	78,932	0	33,450	0	0
Gadsden	87,882	62,392	0	25,490	0	0
Gainesboro	492,130	434,245	0	57,885	0	0
Gallatin	7,991,194	6,070,154	0	1,002,118	630,000	288,922
Gallaway	189,341	173,986	0	14,897	458	0
Garland	40,977	27,797	0	13,180	0	0

TABLE 15.16--OPERATING EXPENDITURES, BY FUNCTION, MUNICIPALITIES, FISCAL YEAR 1992
[In dollars] (Continued)

Municipality	Total [1]	General purpose	Schools	Highways and streets	Debt service Principal	Debt service Interest
Gates	116,337	83,977	0	32,360	0	0
Gatlinburg	15,389,506	12,005,349	203,932	57,879	1,074,887	2,047,459
Germantown	13,350,867	10,171,318	0	433,481	1,720,000	1,026,068
Gibson	139,014	117,266	0	19,590	0	2,158
Gilt Edge	29,656	25,218	0	4,438	0	0
Gleason	396,776	258,671	0	138,105	0	0
Goodlettsville	4,798,650	4,163,041	0	635,609	0	0
Gordonsville	345,721	286,295	0	59,426	0	0
Grand Junction	175,887	143,403	0	32,484	0	0
Graysville	154,242	136,398	0	17,844	0	0
Greenback	114,944	109,366	0	5,578	0	0
Greenbrier	614,367	452,500	0	161,867	0	0
Greeneville	19,120,302	6,484,905	10,921,895	1,028,713	572,964	111,825
Greenfield	718,384	637,014	0	67,630	5,695	8,045
Gruetli-Laager	248,552	206,338	0	42,214	0	0
Guys	94,388	27,473	0	66,915	0	0
Halls	876,666	730,648	0	57,741	66,667	21,610
Harriman	9,287,709	2,327,067	6,378,013	207,327	287,199	88,103
Hartsville	1,080,964	936,385	0	90,807	53,772	0
Henderson	1,355,801	1,104,407	0	207,509	25,580	18,305
Hendersonville	1,678,690	47,793	0	526,657	358,069	746,171
Henning	234,137	158,172	0	75,965	0	0
Henry	136,500	105,479	0	4,178	15,000	11,843
Hickory Valley	26,031	23,137	0	2,894	0	0
Hohenwald	1,540,341	1,241,786	0	258,766	32,616	7,173
Hollow Rock	215,652	179,238	0	36,414	0	0
Hornbeak	233,399	215,421	0	13,728	4,000	250
Hornsby	55,675	46,786	0	8,889	0	0
Humboldt	17,310,501	4,505,418	8,455,497	400,666	3,562,416	386,504
Huntingdon	2,158,683	1,396,632	0	376,310	222,563	163,178
Huntland	340,092	279,160	0	60,932	0	0
Huntsville	145,196	111,771	0	25,102	5,323	3,000
Iron City	32,710	24,898	0	7,812	0	0
Jacksboro	414,700	341,971	0	60,898	9,410	2,421
Jackson	32,380,366	27,147,228	0	1,755,566	2,035,000	1,442,572
Jamestown	550,420	411,294	0	133,826	2,000	3,300
Jasper	876,550	764,556	0	111,994	0	0
Jefferson City	2,011,804	1,449,068	0	505,381	42,889	14,466
Jellico	965,404	753,668	0	155,617	2,000	54,119
Johnson City	56,204,825	25,772,173	22,595,220	3,799,840	1,947,897	2,089,695
Jonesborough	1,557,521	1,275,705	0	113,028	93,200	75,588
Kenton	372,626	284,757	0	87,869	0	0
Kimball	735,885	704,660	0	31,225	0	0
Kingsport	62,201,267	22,559,510	29,783,238	1,001,145	6,394,373	2,463,001
Kingston	1,634,203	1,401,757	0	199,623	23,500	9,323
Kingston Springs	368,168	151,842	0	184,006	21,000	11,320
Knoxville	118,233,421	83,797,659	0	4,276,031	21,076,680	9,083,051
Lafayette	1,413,846	1,137,166	0	276,680	0	0
LaFollette	3,340,358	2,612,326	0	489,820	160,672	77,540
LaGrange	106,031	94,147	0	11,884	0	0
Lake City	969,871	773,407	0	177,063	16,783	2,618
Lakeland	508,609	430,915	0	77,694	0	0
Lakesite	101,693	86,507	0	15,186	0	0
Lakewood	407,963	378,871	0	29,092	0	0
LaVergne	3,069,392	2,358,074	0	693,914	3,957	13,447
Lawrenceburg	6,103,682	5,085,944	0	996,513	17,000	4,225
Lebanon	7,784,212	6,708,569	0	1,056,082	11,552	8,009

TABLE 15.16--OPERATING EXPENDITURES, BY FUNCTION, MUNICIPALITIES, FISCAL YEAR 1992
[In dollars] (Continued)

Municipality	Total [1]	General purpose	Schools	Highways and streets	Debt service Principal	Debt service Interest
Lenoir City	8,518,830	2,096,435	5,267,365	527,001	275,000	353,029
Lewisburg	5,398,140	4,258,311	0	779,629	290,890	69,310
Lexington	6,064,672	2,440,490	2,416,887	812,324	170,000	224,971
Liberty	67,231	34,118	0	33,113	0	0
Linden	347,694	306,379	0	36,411	3,220	1,684
Livingston	1,396,620	1,013,334	0	244,069	75,796	63,421
Lobelville	160,857	135,384	0	25,473	0	0
Lookout Mountain	2,191,394	1,491,176	160,551	114,350	260,000	165,317
Loretto	406,316	353,091	0	53,225	0	0
Loudon	2,909,918	2,256,884	0	461,559	82,000	109,475
Lynnville	52,114	44,074	0	8,040	0	0
McEwen	313,907	240,563	0	0	72,993	351
McKenzie	2,453,677	1,952,487	0	357,195	102,100	41,895
McLemoresville	65,852	34,034	0	31,818	0	0
McMinnville	6,404,207	4,873,848	0	882,456	333,000	314,903
Madisonville	1,263,675	1,111,105	0	116,717	24,000	11,853
Manchester	8,072,863	3,064,254	4,251,516	460,965	183,549	112,579
Martin	3,886,156	3,228,382	0	657,774	0	0
Maryville	24,082,550	7,172,753	13,920,862	523,407	1,684,191	781,337
Mason	288,924	257,861	0	31,063	0	0
Maury City	195,247	174,983	0	20,264	0	0
Maynardville	218,435	188,766	0	29,669	0	0
Medina	344,863	274,071	0	68,372	2,000	420
Medon	50,477	44,622	0	5,855	0	0
Memphis	772,709,317	319,872,187	388,826,899	8,156,339	34,603,934	21,249,958
Michie	80,431	75,964	0	0	3,599	868
Middleton	275,293	232,574	0	35,094	3,000	4,625
Milan	3,859,194	2,865,891	62,132	604,553	198,333	128,285
Milledgeville	99,393	92,315	0	7,078	0	0
Millersville	477,073	314,937	0	57,076	77,879	27,181
Millington	3,799,407	2,681,502	0	1,087,566	25,000	5,339
Minor Hill	232,887	199,136	0	33,751	0	0
Mitchellville	24,519	22,084	0	2,435	0	0
Monteagle	462,622	397,965	0	64,657	0	0
Monterey	610,523	402,980	0	154,019	50,000	3,524
Morrison	25,854	23,264	0	2,590	0	0
Morristown	12,527,095	10,635,064	0	1,311,338	500,000	80,693
Moscow	204,531	188,569	0	15,962	0	0
Mosheim	188,075	120,968	0	67,107	0	0
Mount Carmel	881,062	663,437	0	163,631	46,477	7,517
Mount Juliet	2,516,129	1,791,337	0	165,151	233,834	325,807
Mount Pleasant	1,417,648	1,152,294	0	189,057	32,917	43,380
Mountain City	1,136,132	1,033,408	0	102,724	0	0
Munford	578,295	450,113	0	128,182	0	0
Murfreesboro	43,187,038	17,174,128	17,538,231	2,312,862	2,955,000	3,206,817
New Hope	131,203	97,338	0	30,184	1,788	1,893
New Johnsonville	701,971	645,205	0	18,884	14,721	23,161
New Market	126,137	116,567	0	9,570	0	0
New Tazewell	1,041,767	837,497	0	204,270	0	0
Newbern	1,210,950	893,154	0	260,118	30,632	27,046
Newport	6,327,310	2,960,216	2,528,050	725,559	83,454	30,031
Niota	219,192	117,278	0	101,914	0	0
Normandy	8,075	4,688	0	3,387	0	0
Norris	546,984	514,070	0	8,295	21,422	3,197
Oak Hill	813,979	564,101	0	249,878	0	0
Oak Ridge	38,026,617	11,116,035	23,797,208	829,688	983,521	1,300,165
Oakdale	487,526	475,774	0	11,752	0	0

TABLE 15.16--OPERATING EXPENDITURES, BY FUNCTION, MUNICIPALITIES, FISCAL YEAR 1992
[In dollars] (Continued)

Municipality	Total [1]	General purpose	Schools	Highways and streets	Debt service Principal	Debt service Interest
Obion	246,589	195,030	0	51,559	0	0
Oliver Springs	930,016	578,947	0	328,594	9,000	13,475
Oneida	1,531,477	758,392	0	549,660	185,000	38,425
Orlinda	113,314	89,047	0	24,267	0	0
Orme	10,935	7,774	0	3,161	0	0
Palmer	112,849	74,302	0	38,547	0	0
Paris	6,360,157	3,293,489	0	855,631	2,027,339	183,698
Parker's Crossroads	109,631	92,442	0	17,189	0	0
Parrottsville	26,855	21,232	0	5,623	0	0
Parsons	895,453	604,226	0	134,228	146,739	10,260
Pegram	190,400	111,420	0	78,980	0	0
Petersburg	146,504	118,360	0	28,144	0	0
Philadelphia	39,909	29,029	0	5,942	3,333	1,605
Pigeon Forge	13,755,707	12,557,254	0	1,124,137	60,555	13,761
Pikeville	454,683	382,980	0	58,715	6,232	6,756
Piperton	62,535	58,660	0	3,875	0	0
Pittman Center	253,641	139,449	0	88,395	20,000	5,797
Pleasant Hill	57,778	19,607	0	29,853	7,027	1,291
Portland	1,850,592	1,494,855	0	257,481	0	98,256
Powell's Crossroads	105,232	62,441	0	42,791	0	0
Pulaski	3,713,598	3,032,047	0	681,551	0	0
Puryear	306,034	258,401	0	47,633	0	0
Red Bank	3,265,982	2,934,467	0	331,515	0	0
Red Boiling Springs	288,802	251,356	0	37,446	0	0
Ridgely	446,277	331,002	0	115,275	0	0
Ridgeside	167,261	71,663	0	36,771	35,568	23,259
Ridgetop	223,355	146,675	0	65,219	6,820	4,641
Ripley	2,731,816	2,378,427	0	241,656	97,212	14,521
Rives	151,230	132,683	0	18,547	0	0
Rockford	149,240	111,942	0	37,298	0	0
Rockwood	2,558,305	1,960,337	0	539,605	12,000	46,363
Rogersville	3,892,227	1,712,762	1,505,152	431,387	121,422	121,504
Rossville	271,547	256,492	0	15,055	0	0
Rutherford	370,000	307,134	0	62,866	0	0
Rutledge	175,022	109,380	0	65,642	0	0
St. Joseph	271,530	243,281	0	28,249	0	0
Saltillo	339,393	259,550	0	71,026	6,260	2,557
Samburg	94,512	91,780	0	2,732	0	0
Sardis	48,783	28,342	0	20,441	0	0
Saulsbury	18,284	13,931	0	4,353	0	0
Savannah	3,483,518	3,025,924	0	422,319	9,000	26,275
Scotts Hill	171,784	132,860	0	38,924	0	0
Selmer	1,418,540	976,012	0	389,196	36,111	17,221
Sevierville	5,164,367	3,693,435	0	1,005,989	262,568	202,375
Sharon	409,106	368,500	0	40,606	0	0
Shelbyville	4,197,207	3,952,343	0	228,574	0	16,290
Signal Mountain	3,074,072	2,439,697	0	476,612	101,442	56,321
Silerton	9,725	5,720	0	4,005	0	0
Slayden	6,262	5,303	0	959	0	0
Smithville	1,104,209	920,440	0	183,769	0	0
Smyrna	5,762,130	4,682,071	0	791,967	151,933	136,159
Sneedville	278,568	153,431	0	96,485	28,652	0
Soddy-Daisy	2,576,268	2,107,793	0	286,562	150,140	31,773
Somerville	1,151,187	1,066,708	0	84,479	0	0
South Carthage	410,553	374,299	0	31,409	3,000	1,845
South Fulton	705,286	588,705	0	116,581	0	0
South Pittsburg	1,483,306	1,009,478	0	293,011	105,000	75,817

TABLE 15.16--OPERATING EXPENDITURES, BY FUNCTION, MUNICIPALITIES, FISCAL YEAR 1992
[In dollars] (Continued)

Municipality	Total [1]	General purpose	Schools	Highways and streets	Debt service	
					Principal	Interest
Sparta	2,963,833	2,448,908	0	80,752	197,840	236,333
Spencer	229,704	148,299	0	65,369	15,000	1,036
Spring City	1,074,409	1,040,124	0	34,285	0	0
Spring Hill	694,949	581,133	0	113,816	0	0
Springfield	5,279,548	3,797,109	0	688,269	600,431	193,739
Stanton	81,282	56,395	0	20,471	1,483	2,933
Stantonville	37,024	21,328	0	6,017	3,679	6,000
Sunbright	38,833	38,714	0	119	0	0
Surgoinsville	282,307	251,077	0	31,230	0	0
Sweetwater	5,546,468	1,798,419	3,160,750	495,464	70,000	21,835
Tazewell	569,332	459,693	0	109,639	0	0
Tellico Plains	401,551	356,434	0	45,117	0	0
Tennessee Ridge	234,851	205,674	0	4,920	24,257	0
Thompson Station	32,800	17,500	0	15,300	0	0
Tiptonville	593,113	389,272	0	191,273	12,015	553
Toone	47,881	43,973	0	3,908	0	0
Townsend	195,843	184,204	0	11,639	0	0
Tracy City	440,677	357,628	0	51,138	26,661	5,250
Trenton	2,807,218	2,197,502	0	320,652	188,232	100,832
Trezevant	210,315	183,698	0	26,617	0	0
Trimble	152,465	128,823	0	23,642	0	0
Troy	234,808	231,919	0	2,889	0	0
Tullahoma	19,808,199	5,157,704	11,306,781	775,274	1,168,730	1,399,710
Tusculum	262,705	183,829	0	78,876	0	0
Union City	11,660,625	4,405,001	6,432,587	823,037	0	0
Vanleer	81,223	44,888	0	13,843	22,492	0
Viola	20,975	3,199	0	17,776	0	0
Vonore	207,664	178,487	0	29,177	0	0
Walden	354,229	279,663	0	72,166	2,400	0
Wartburg	432,191	163,336	0	238,270	28,785	1,800
Wartrace	231,554	219,519	0	12,035	0	0
Watauga	89,585	81,508	0	8,077	0	0
Watertown	215,787	164,980	0	50,807	0	0
Waverly	2,077,358	1,063,749	0	746,825	266,784	0
Waynesboro	712,222	538,285	0	173,937	0	0
Westmoreland	494,632	450,794	0	43,838	0	0
White Bluff	417,355	320,702	0	96,653	0	0
White House	1,475,570	1,033,237	0	94,793	342,502	5,038
White Pine	607,046	512,211	0	94,835	0	0
Whiteville	309,754	210,081	0	90,422	8,334	917
Whitwell	311,721	266,097	0	33,621	12,003	0
Williston	48,173	40,511	1,632	6,030	0	0
Winchester	1,967,619	1,526,297	0	439,127	2,080	115
Winfield	1,063,298	906,558	0	60,046	65,192	31,502
Woodbury	649,291	532,632	0	84,555	27,957	4,147
Woodland Mills	43,800	35,529	0	8,271	0	0
Yorkville	74,339	65,851	0	7,695	152	641

Note: Detail may not add to total due to independent rounding. Nashville (unified city and county government) data are presented in Table 15.9.

1. Includes detail not shown separately.

Source: State of Tennessee, Report of the Comptroller of the Treasury, Division of Local Finance, *County and Municipal Finances for Fiscal Year Ended June 30, 1992.*

TABLE 15.17–ESTIMATED CURRENT PROPERTY VALUE, ASSESSED VALUE, BY CLASSIFICATION, AND PROPERTY TAXES LEVIED, MUNICIPALITIES, 1992

[In thousands of dollars]

| Municipality | City property taxes levied[1] | Estimated current property value | Assessed value | | | | | | County |
| | | | Total | Real property | | | Personal property[3] | Public utilities[4] | |
				Total[2]	Residential and farm	Industrial and commercial			
Adams	15	10,026	3,027	2,028	1,837	191	9	980	Robertson
Adamsville	208	65,000	19,375	13,732	5,599	8,134	66	1,699	McNairy
Alamo	185	51,965	15,849	12,528	7,290	5,239	345	912	Crockett
Alcoa	3,582	684,145	227,185	121,804	31,140	90,664	85,934	12,652	Blount
Alexandria	75	21,795	5,883	3,092	2,084	1,008	21	2,548	DeKalb
Algood	155	54,569	16,660	14,141	8,568	5,372	104	1,364	Putnam
Ardmore	30	28,494	6,241	5,326	2,728	2,599	10	318	Giles
Arlington	196	71,108	21,196	10,738	6,404	4,334	8,754	1,705	Shelby
Ashland City	216	96,324	31,095	22,123	9,969	12,153	5,209	2,916	Cheatham
Athens	2,063	419,273	134,219	96,897	41,130	55,767	1,969	7,255	McMinn
Atoka	5	15,093	4,194	3,488	2,896	584	55	375	Tipton
Barlett	4,794	1,090,972	292,295	265,980	206,047	59,933	14,467	11,848	Shelby
Baxter	95	20,816	6,271	5,221	3,720	1,500	65	890	Putnam
Bell Buckle	7	5,823	1,578	1,413	1,280	133	0	164	Bedford
Belle Meade	1,100	348,602	69,412	68,227	65,215	3,012	251	934	Davidson
Bells	279	51,574	16,997	13,811	5,110	8,701	174	951	Crockett
Benton	30	16,431	5,340	3,647	2,453	1,193	22	1,333	Polk
Bethel Springs	20	11,517	3,091	2,336	2,025	311	17	735	McNairy
Big Sandy	19	7,329	2,008	1,576	1,218	358	13	397	Benton
Bluff City	95	25,587	6,292	5,281	3,824	1,457	23	865	Sullivan
Bolivar	280	113,278	33,687	27,105	17,417	9,688	213	1,738	Hardeman
Bradford	49	19,537	5,246	4,195	3,150	1,045	48	885	Gibson
Brentwood	3,908	1,733,271	523,223	427,082	305,637	121,445	2,529	75,334	Williamson
Brighton	14	16,183	4,469	3,798	3,280	518	0	511	Tipton
Bristol	6,122	752,011	195,129	160,128	87,261	72,867	1,387	16,981	Sullivan
Brownsville	973	263,020	81,657	59,739	30,809	28,930	341	3,902	Haywood
Bruceton	133	42,762	13,199	8,428	4,628	3,800	3,412	994	Carroll

TABLE 15.17--ESTIMATED CURRENT PROPERTY VALUE, ASSESSED VALUE, BY CLASSIFICATION, AND PROPERTY TAXES LEVIED, MUNICIPALITIES, 1992
[In thousands of dollars] (Continued)

Municipality	City property taxes levied [1]	Estimated current property value	Assessed value					Public utilities [4]	County
			Total	Real property			Personal property [3]		
				Total [2]	Residential and farm	Industrial and commercial			
Bulls Gap	51	16,092	5,135	3,303	2,305	998	20	1,567	Hawkins
Burns	33	23,955	6,438	6,122	5,198	924	50	179	Dickson
Byrdstown	62	17,915	5,998	4,469	2,146	2,322	60	1,049	Pickett
Calhoun	24	11,432	3,372	2,670	1,899	771	1	605	McMinn
Camden	138	77,764	22,166	18,863	9,884	8,979	229	1,725	Benton
Carthage	350	94,055	17,956	14,165	5,984	8,181	115	996	Smith
Cedar Hill	5	4,069	1,213	907	750	156	2	300	Robertson
Celina	118	31,523	8,476	6,848	3,575	3,272	30	646	Clay
Centerville	245	113,400	25,033	19,575	11,937	7,638	175	2,181	Hickman
Chapel Hill	111	22,410	6,687	5,253	4,204	1,048	7	1,228	Marshall
Charleston	32	16,402	4,702	3,108	2,077	1,032	10	1,396	Bradley
Charlotte	12	21,937	6,310	5,395	4,152	1,242	265	553	Dickson
Chattanooga	53,839	6,497,469	2,068,383	1,695,858	639,423	1,056,435	233,094	139,431	Hamilton
Church Hill	173	120,599	34,799	29,518	22,431	7,087	118	3,320	Hawkins
Clarksville	6,371	1,848,716	559,464	504,675	287,963	216,382	3,174	19,773	Montgomery
Cleveland	5,336	1,248,688	355,413	275,005	113,875	161,071	8,224	15,221	Bradley
Clifton	46	10,596	3,225	2,493	1,755	739	11	583	Wayne
Clinton	821	351,931	111,003	84,477	38,021	46,456	8,021	3,786	Anderson
Collegedale	623	171,336	52,284	38,670	17,435	21,235	11,123	2,491	Hamilton
Collierville	2,825	709,555	194,181	169,398	120,975	48,423	19,833	4,950	Shelby
Collinwood	129	21,491	7,002	5,322	2,833	2,489	383	1,099	Wayne
Columbia	3,164	1,053,694	210,809	181,782	96,123	85,659	4,798	10,029	Maury
Cookeville	2,052	778,442	248,703	203,142	93,148	109,994	1,901	16,106	Putnam
Copperhill	48	11,883	4,232	2,555	1,267	1,289	46	1,468	Polk
Comersville	56	15,344	4,486	3,554	2,886	669	13	784	Marshall
Cottage Grove	2	1,541	552	254	209	46	0	296	Henry

TABLE 15.17—ESTIMATED CURRENT PROPERTY VALUE, ASSESSED VALUE, BY CLASSIFICATION, AND PROPERTY TAXES LEVIED, MUNICIPALITIES, 1992
[In thousands of dollars] (Continued)

Municipality	City property taxes levied [1]	Estimated current property value	Assessed value						County
			Total	Real property			Personal property [3]	Public utilities [4]	
				Total [2]	Residential and farm	Industrial and commercial			
Covington	0	223,646	70,891	50,689	23,762	26,927	188	5,446	Tipton
Cowan	71	23,732	6,317	5,500	4,464	1,037	50	547	Franklin
Crossville	708	314,889	100,150	76,775	29,700	47,074	1,586	8,245	Cumberland
Cumberland City	18	6,171	1,950	1,400	1,088	312	11	530	Stewart
Cumberland Gap	3	5,248	1,681	1,566	733	833	0	115	Claiborne
Dandridge	174	50,856	16,282	12,880	6,671	6,208	972	1,916	Jefferson
Dayton	238	196,505	47,637	37,746	16,234	21,512	288	2,286	Rhea
Decatur	76	33,120	11,532	7,331	4,228	3,103	111	3,678	Meigs
Decaturville	76	17,431	5,616	4,960	2,373	2,586	86	490	Decatur
Decherd	251	54,353	16,379	13,836	6,800	7,036	103	1,297	Franklin
Dickson	1,415	414,161	130,860	103,143	48,437	54,706	1,337	6,321	Dickson
Dover	104	47,426	14,654	10,972	6,616	4,356	2,035	1,459	Stewart
Dresden	368	92,139	29,452	20,666	9,247	11,419	1,648	2,110	Weakley
Ducktown	27	10,823	3,676	3,303	1,028	2,276	10	161	Polk
Dunlap	195	84,683	22,566	18,457	10,456	8,001	264	1,988	Sequatchie
Dyer	143	40,975	10,770	9,134	6,430	2,704	37	709	Gibson
Dyersburg	3,509	470,496	147,790	120,573	57,541	63,032	261	6,204	Dyer
Eagleville	41	13,625	3,781	3,103	2,113	990	8	455	Rutherford
East Ridge	1,518	613,588	179,079	169,888	93,013	76,875	5,391	3,799	Hamilton
Elizabethton	2,780	286,646	89,755	77,054	39,088	37,966	419	4,935	Carter
Elkton	6	10,673	2,270	2,059	1,259	800	10	133	Giles
Englewood	126	22,258	6,308	5,436	4,359	1,078	43	663	McMinn
Erin	104	29,342	9,768	7,637	3,230	4,406	168	1,127	Houston
Erwin	620	145,396	44,093	32,722	19,089	13,611	657	3,295	Unicoi
Estill Springs	77	40,124	10,790	9,361	7,408	1,953	170	966	Franklin
Etowah	451	71,773	21,629	19,108	11,640	7,468	27	1,654	McMinn
Fairview	257	93,057	26,366	23,688	18,322	5,366	114	1,703	Williamson

TABLE 15.17--ESTIMATED CURRENT PROPERTY VALUE, ASSESSED VALUE, BY CLASSIFICATION, AND PROPERTY TAXES LEVIED, MUNICIPALITIES, 1992
[In thousands of dollars] (Continued)

Municipality	City property taxes levied [1]	Estimated current property value	Assessed value Total	Real property Total [2]	Real property Residential and farm	Real property Industrial and commercial	Personal property [3]	Public utilities [4]	County
Fayetteville	1,362	235,629	75,270	57,804	24,903	32,901	694	3,314	Lincoln
Franklin	3,400	1,155,759	364,348	314,338	151,527	162,217	2,140	16,813	Williamson
Friendship	49	7,606	2,349	1,664	1,295	369	106	517	Crockett
Gainesboro	79	30,602	8,528	5,873	2,289	3,584	2	1,668	Jackson
Gallatin	2,535	630,248	193,578	155,729	82,279	73,450	1,328	6,387	Sumner
Gates	37	8,704	2,191	1,803	1,292	511	71	281	Lauderdale
Gatlinburg	599	762,571	252,710	242,261	83,680	157,828	2,719	3,029	Sevier
Germantown	6,527	1,967,759	505,800	486,314	410,099	76,215	9,468	10,018	Shelby
Gibson	15	5,686	1,601	1,040	935	106	0	545	Gibson
Gleason	81	20,116	5,789	5,030	3,712	1,318	14	452	Weakley
Goodlettsville (pt.)	370	128,603	34,700	33,317	27,989	5,328	92	1,008	Sumner
Goodlettsville (pt.)	-	483,882	131,274	116,201	32,951	83,250	10,216	4,857	Davidson
Gordonsville	118	68,069	13,024	8,202	3,185	4,728	5	874	Smith
Grand Junction	38	15,385	4,864	2,716	1,462	1,254	82	676	Hardeman
Graysville	22	14,530	2,934	2,714	2,434	280	8	175	Rhea
Greenbrier	213	62,531	18,114	15,025	11,773	3,252	218	2,246	Robertson
Greeneville	4,638	528,558	170,918	130,944	52,752	78,192	8,984	8,788	Greene
Greenfield	144	43,118	12,681	10,322	7,015	3,306	373	854	Weakley
Halls	248	63,224	16,925	8,436	4,855	3,581	311	1,568	Lauderdale
Harriman	895	139,616	39,820	31,839	16,811	15,027	2,334	3,574	Roane
Hartsville	228	53,739	17,518	14,102	6,289	7,813	929	1,654	Trousdale
Henderson	334	86,550	26,626	22,725	13,978	8,747	211	2,933	Chester
Hendersonville	2,390	1,278,987	365,551	337,110	237,718	99,392	2,717	10,615	Sumner
Henning	28	9,969	2,768	2,256	1,225	1,030	3	437	Lauderdale
Henry	17	10,900	3,332	1,641	680	961	6	147	Henry
Hickory Valley	2	2,447	686	660	482	178	5	10	Hardeman
Hohenwald	291	83,195	25,462	18,531	11,213	7,318	310	2,051	Lewis

TABLE 15.17—ESTIMATED CURRENT PROPERTY VALUE, ASSESSED VALUE, BY CLASSIFICATION, AND PROPERTY TAXES LEVIED, MUNICIPALITIES, 1992
[In thousands of dollars] (Continued)

| Municipality | City property taxes levied [1] | Estimated current property value | Assessed value | | | | Personal property [3] | Public utilities [4] | County |
| | | | Total | Real property | | | | | |
				Total [2]	Residential and farm	Industrial and commercial			
Hollow Rock	14	11,548	3,167	2,861	2,389	472	20	256	Carroll
Hombeak	10	6,627	2,019	1,505	1,218	287	9	447	Obion
Hornsby	6	5,565	1,592	1,150	891	260	4	90	Hardeman
Humboldt	1,520	209,952	58,209	42,809	23,395	19,415	338	3,311	Gibson
Huntingdon	299	102,640	31,380	24,998	14,215	10,783	334	1,971	Carroll
Huntland	65	18,619	5,143	4,437	3,169	1,268	31	357	Franklin
Huntsville	13	17,227	5,475	3,901	2,250	1,650	39	803	Scott
Iron City	3	3,920	1,026	971	888	83	24	31	Lawrence
Jackson	11,423	1,684,792	437,360	337,281	145,148	192,133	5,926	21,597	Madison
Jamestown	134	46,941	15,545	12,299	3,486	8,813	91	1,500	Fentress
Jasper	92	74,700	23,405	19,336	10,497	8,819	252	2,090	Marion
Jefferson City	427	116,877	38,474	31,512	13,518	17,986	1,763	3,732	Jefferson
Jellico	89	45,948	12,118	9,882	5,140	4,742	153	1,714	Campbell
Johnson City (pt.)	12,394	54,798	17,489	9,871	3,328	6,543	0	282	Carter
Johnson City (pt.)	-	3,221	797	728	429	299	34	7	Sullivan
Johnson City (pt.)	-	1,703,534	424,747	362,064	170,666	191,399	6,217	23,329	Washington
Jonesborough	414	84,967	20,124	17,757	10,910	6,847	120	1,702	Washington
Kenton (pt.)	101	14,455	4,448	3,064	1,605	1,459	5	150	Obion
Kenton (pt.)	-	10,063	2,590	2,230	1,831	399	20	314	Gibson
Kimball	26	42,037	13,927	12,262	4,724	7,520	92	966	Marion
Kingsport (pt.)	14,489	2,365,785	626,123	387,921	153,931	233,990	2,251	26,462	Sullivan
Kingsport (pt.)	-	87,417	22,053	20,542	11,614	8,927	326	860	Hawkins
Kingston	554	114,136	30,050	27,056	19,270	7,756	216	2,070	Roane
Kingston Springs	98	50,541	13,871	12,609	10,286	2,323	48	742	Cheatham
Knoxville	46,272	5,119,374	1,467,294	1,238,073	495,018	743,055	132,547	96,675	Knox
Lafayette	286	105,637	28,526	20,676	11,266	9,410	224	3,579	Macon

TABLE 15.17–ESTIMATED CURRENT PROPERTY VALUE, ASSESSED VALUE, BY CLASSIFICATION, AND PROPERTY TAXES LEVIED, MUNICIPALITIES, 1992
[In thousands of dollars] (Continued)

Municipality	City property taxes levied [1]	Estimated current property value	Assessed value Total	Real property Total [2]	Real property Residential and farm	Real property Industrial and commercial	Personal property [3]	Public utilities [4]	County
LaFollette	512	173,309	46,092	40,053	17,453	22,600	557	3,239	Campbell
LaGrange	16	6,355	1,730	1,324	1,247	77	0	403	Fayette
Lake City	119	37,223	12,375	10,347	4,046	6,301	483	1,181	Anderson
Lakesite	39	28,050	6,965	6,896	6,351	545	11	58	Hamilton
LaVergne	1,011	587,438	173,837	104,648	37,374	67,274	2,121	7,285	Rutherford
Lawrenceburg	1,199	347,884	110,228	83,151	36,177	46,974	8,784	3,532	Lawrence
Lebanon	901	654,805	152,576	127,600	56,959	70,642	2,824	5,854	Wilson
Lenoir City	641	151,532	47,591	37,616	15,462	22,154	292	3,484	Loudon
Lewisburg	2,184	394,526	122,710	82,479	39,841	42,638	896	4,364	Marshall
Lexington	564	184,056	46,742	35,061	16,284	18,778	1,865	1,913	Henderson
Liberty	3	6,686	1,557	1,104	893	211	5	402	DeKalb
Linden	62	27,383	9,233	6,427	2,626	3,801	30	1,449	Perry
Livingston	513	89,356	29,354	22,901	10,814	12,053	294	3,862	Overton
Lobelville	71	30,020	12,482	4,086	2,768	1,318	16	8,177	Perry
Lookout Mountain	798	170,162	41,772	40,592	39,658	934	55	1,125	Hamilton
Loretto	29	31,969	9,370	8,117	5,905	2,212	36	1,027	Lawrence
Loudon	760	239,696	77,004	54,089	14,158	39,931	366	2,395	Loudon
Lynnville	11	5,713	1,170	917	805	112	2	246	Giles
McEwen	57	23,910	5,546	4,579	3,570	1,009	20	778	Humphreys
McKenzie (pt.)	322	3,405	1,041	664	335	329	0	22	Weakley
McKenzie (pt.)	-	87,759	26,464	22,575	13,608	8,967	620	1,727	Carroll
McKenzie (pt.)	-	14,357	4,322	1,820	698	1,122	3	17	Henry
McLemoresville	13	4,621	1,287	1,194	926	268	0	85	Carroll
McMinnville	1,842	342,855	112,403	94,547	38,545	56,002	1,114	7,290	Warren
Madisonville	126	88,164	27,825	23,404	12,844	10,560	190	3,150	Monroe
Manchester	1,405	217,076	69,415	56,948	26,293	30,629	519	4,668	Coffee
Martin	672	189,942	60,201	48,497	22,886	25,611	446	3,403	Weakley

TABLE 15.17—ESTIMATED CURRENT PROPERTY VALUE, ASSESSED VALUE, BY CLASSIFICATION, AND PROPERTY TAXES LEVIED, MUNICIPALITIES, 1992

[In thousands of dollars] (Continued)

Municipality	City property taxes levied [1]	Estimated current property value	Assessed value						County
			Total	Real property			Personal property [3]	Public utilities [4]	
				Total [2]	Residential and farm	Industrial and commercial			
Maryville	5,554	833,538	255,905	194,805	101,610	93,194	1,193	6,784	Blount
Mason	31	16,226	5,899	5,217	1,021	4,197	15	442	Tipton
Maury City	40	10,820	3,166	2,646	2,055	591	100	405	Crockett
Medina	57	9,998	2,683	2,104	1,600	505	10	452	Gibson
Memphis	133,824	19,767,664	5,905,760	4,789,857	2,390,138	2,399,719	602,565	513,338	Shelby
Middleton	37	19,133	5,967	3,439	2,129	1,310	21	916	Hardeman
Milan	408	160,780	43,973	36,754	21,018	15,736	279	2,481	Gibson
Millersville	70	33,279	9,282	8,422	6,718	1,705	101	479	Sumner
Millington	623	204,250	61,566	50,929	27,884	23,044	4,189	6,448	Shelby
Mitchellville	5	2,530	730	534	506	28	0	196	Sumner
Monterey	140	40,582	12,508	9,990	6,608	3,382	82	1,807	Putnam
Morrison	5	27,684	8,252	3,000	1,930	1,069	10	161	Warren
Morristown	3,346	835,516	250,367	185,508	71,428	114,079	5,215	14,488	Hamblen
Moscow	25	9,690	3,131	2,258	1,326	932	6	812	Fayette
Mount Pleasant	279	114,773	21,298	18,533	12,675	5,858	200	846	Maury
Mountain City	265	54,635	18,018	14,461	7,162	7,299	166	2,852	Johnson
Munford	89	55,531	16,084	14,152	10,546	3,606	9	1,393	Tipton
Murfreesboro	11,471	1,760,068	515,194	437,031	200,927	236,104	9,476	22,456	Rutherford
Nashville	269,084	16,968,943	4,431,595	3,761,409	1,420,827	2,340,582	374,529	295,657	Davidson
New Hope	10	14,343	3,856	3,286	3,222	64	4	566	Marion
New Johnsonville	87	40,413	9,592	7,569	5,690	1,878	188	1,729	Humphreys
Newbern	251	65,775	20,676	17,596	8,520	9,076	33	1,117	Dyer
Newport	1,191	155,845	43,874	36,430	15,801	20,628	504	3,421	Cocke
Niota	49	18,547	5,671	4,495	2,547	1,948	7	453	McMinn
Normandy	1	2,106	579	478	444	33	0	102	Bedford
Norris	263	42,128	11,642	10,259	8,883	1,375	366	963	Anderson
Oak Ridge (pt.)	5,420	1,101,160	342,834	299,090	151,982	147,108	8,585	13,793	Anderson

TABLE 15.17—ESTIMATED CURRENT PROPERTY VALUE, ASSESSED VALUE, BY CLASSIFICATION, AND PROPERTY TAXES LEVIED, MUNICIPALITIES, 1992
[In thousands of dollars] (Continued)

Municipality	City property taxes levied [1]	Estimated current property value	Assessed value Total	Real property Total [2]	Residential and farm	Industrial and commercial	Personal property [3]	Public utilities [4]	County
Oak Ridge (pt.)	-	119,089	33,082	27,093	22,657	4,435	6	1,717	Roane
Oakdale	24	3,995	1,495	433	412	21	0	1,062	Morgan
Oakland	n.a.	12,157	3,772	2,268	1,270	998	8	293	Fayette
Obion	81	18,652	5,633	3,993	3,051	942	23	1,022	Obion
Oliver Springs (pt.)	285	627	201	187	88	99	1	13	Morgan
Oliver Springs (pt.)	-	55,931	16,293	14,835	9,778	5,057	348	699	Anderson
Oliver Springs (pt.)	-	13,818	4,358	3,039	2,308	731	32	1,218	Roane
Oneida	305	91,102	29,156	22,201	11,093	11,108	1,282	3,403	Scott
Paris	726	229,342	69,830	56,431	27,619	28,812	867	4,216	Henry
Parsons	189	56,335	18,150	14,351	6,865	7,487	615	1,716	Decatur
Petersburg (pt.)	22	5,949	1,681	1,523	1,099	425	1	25	Lincoln
Petersburg (pt.)	-	2,866	996	506	449	57	0	473	Marshall
Pigeon Forge	340	545,214	197,053	185,762	29,285	156,095	6,046	915	Sevier
Pikeville	82	37,163	11,755	8,674	3,905	4,769	496	2,584	Bledsoe
Pitman Center	34	35,062	9,703	9,534	7,241	2,261	5	162	Sevier
Portland	563	186,460	60,231	38,866	20,724	18,141	246	9,073	Sumner
Pulaski	525	190,406	41,804	36,548	18,769	17,780	198	1,829	Giles
Puryear	23	11,184	3,226	2,560	1,949	610	15	609	Henry
Red Bank	562	334,770	98,084	86,410	52,768	33,642	3,318	8,355	Hamilton
Red Boiling Springs	68	20,454	5,460	4,025	2,485	1,540	11	833	Macon
Ridgely	104	21,619	6,597	5,691	3,484	2,208	4	591	Lake
Ridgeside	106	20,620	4,986	4,922	4,901	21	4	60	Hamilton
Ridgetop (pt.)	67	28,474	7,529	7,272	6,435	837	10	201	Robertson
Ridgetop (pt.)	-	813	174	124	122	2	0	50	Davidson
Ripley	718	139,236	38,554	30,472	13,749	16,723	454	2,529	Lauderdale
Rives	13	3,669	1,065	727	673	53	0	332	Obion

TABLE 15.17–ESTIMATED CURRENT PROPERTY VALUE, ASSESSED VALUE, BY CLASSIFICATION, AND PROPERTY TAXES LEVIED, MUNICIPALITIES, 1992
[In thousands of dollars] (Continued)

Municipality	City property taxes levied [1]	Estimated current property value	Assessed value						County
			Total	Real property			Personal property [3]	Public utilities [4]	
				Total [2]	Residential and farm	Industrial and commercial			
Rockwood	426	109,901	30,929	22,314	11,988	10,325	275	3,107	Roane
Rogersville	550	115,519	37,260	28,161	14,339	13,822	401	4,502	Hawkins
Rossville	135	42,657	14,563	8,021	960	7,061	1	700	Fayette
Rutherford	86	22,657	5,999	4,603	3,615	988	71	802	Gibson
St. Joseph	7	14,031	3,987	3,369	2,717	652	0	395	Lawrence
Sardis	7	4,966	1,153	947	808	138	5	194	Henderson
Savannah	395	171,916	42,160	36,507	19,388	17,101	123	3,103	Hardin
Scotts Hill (pt.)	17	4,594	1,284	1,225	943	281	1	56	Decatur
Scotts Hill (pt.)	-	10,047	2,503	2,068	1,292	776	19	340	Henderson
Selmer	292	104,486	30,277	21,208	10,915	10,293	225	3,326	McNairy
Sevierville	651	359,456	115,864	97,377	41,363	55,861	1,143	5,581	Sevier
Sharon	108	23,769	7,348	5,136	3,164	1,973	649	955	Weakley
Shelbyville	2,369	376,426	116,630	89,052	50,883	38,169	1,024	10,801	Bedford
Signal Mountain	1,418	370,555	94,356	90,652	80,999	9,654	434	3,270	Hamilton
Smithville	280	138,309	33,295	23,517	11,096	12,421	716	2,787	DeKalb
Smyrna	744	514,715	148,765	115,267	57,829	57,438	1,119	11,845	Rutherford
Soddy Daisy	282	199,464	55,545	49,417	34,827	14,589	1,757	4,371	Hamilton
Somerville	96	53,728	17,746	13,811	6,810	7,002	88	2,838	Fayette
South Carthage	74	33,890	6,638	5,257	2,644	2,584	73	1,113	Smith
South Fulton	157	46,343	13,447	11,696	7,781	3,915	100	514	Obion
South Pittsburg	186	84,371	27,680	19,763	8,116	11,647	44	2,550	Marion
Sparta	659	131,694	42,572	32,544	14,338	18,188	302	3,222	White
Spring City	170	50,832	11,838	9,922	6,152	3,770	15	1,580	Rhea
Spring Hill (pt.)	61	15,863	4,012	3,997	3,884	114	0	4	Williamson
Spring Hill (pt.)	-	51,818	10,452	8,279	4,907	3,372	274	1,668	Maury
Springfield	1,488	337,591	105,620	88,239	43,497	44,742	998	4,772	Robertson
Stanton	18	7,007	2,134	1,604	1,142	463	8	430	Haywood

TABLE 15.17—ESTIMATED CURRENT PROPERTY VALUE, ASSESSED VALUE, BY CLASSIFICATION, AND PROPERTY TAXES LEVIED, MUNICIPALITIES, 1992
[In thousands of dollars] (Continued)

Municipality	City property taxes levied[1]	Estimated current property value	Assessed value						County
			Total	Real property			Personal property[3]	Public utilities[4]	
				Total[2]	Residential and farm	Industrial and commercial			
Sweetwater	500	145,331	45,956	38,927	18,652	20,276	621	2,640	Monroe
Tellico Plains	60	20,864	7,357	5,054	2,472	2,582	29	2,085	Monroe
Tennessee Ridge	51	19,657	5,411	4,636	4,376	260	1	742	Houston
Thompson Station	16	29,208	7,609	7,093	6,784	280	8	477	Williamson
Tiptonville	128	28,774	9,128	7,591	4,475	3,116	24	1,387	Lake
Toone	2	3,575	998	826	670	156	0	81	Hardeman
Tracy City	70	25,904	8,117	6,224	4,396	1,828	28	1,702	Grundy
Trenton	487	105,807	30,929	23,137	10,938	12,198	2,065	2,936	Gibson
Trezevant	28	14,214	3,995	3,216	2,682	534	252	451	Carroll
Trimble (pt.)	42	10,223	2,911	2,413	1,982	431	0	356	Dyer
Trimble (pt.)	-	88	27	9	9	0	0	18	Obion
Troy	111	20,636	6,373	4,799	3,093	1,706	107	833	Obion
Tullahoma (pt.)	4,333	468,862	143,171	121,744	66,213	55,531	1,347	4,648	Coffee
Tullahoma (pt.)	-	31,344	8,648	7,432	6,004	1,429	66	258	Franklin
Union City	2,007	271,336	85,527	74,399	36,909	37,490	1,178	5,233	Obion
Vanleer	2	6,389	1,890	1,491	1,272	219	9	385	Dickson
Walden	n.a.	96,572	23,624	23,092	22,523	569	113	419	Hamilton
Wartrace	33	9,131	2,818	2,184	1,603	581	0	633	Bedford
Watauga	5	6,469	1,815	1,340	1,085	155	2	113	Carter
Watertown	77	23,904	5,143	4,657	3,166	1,491	24	395	Wilson
Waverly	350	105,547	26,002	20,819	12,313	8,507	420	2,909	Humphreys
Waynesboro	254	46,146	15,056	10,817	5,462	5,355	196	2,153	Wayne
Westmoreland	120	30,004	9,210	7,702	4,725	2,978	20	951	Sumner
White Bluff	118	44,234	13,330	11,348	7,557	3,791	177	1,477	Dickson
White House (pt.)	683	100,440	31,664	23,370	10,662	12,707	661	1,073	Robertson
White House (pt.)	-	42,460	12,698	10,544	7,872	2,672	7	1,931	Sumner
White Pine	128	39,917	12,525	10,433	5,651	4,782	296	1,576	Jefferson

TABLE 15.17—ESTIMATED CURRENT PROPERTY VALUE, ASSESSED VALUE, BY CLASSIFICATION, AND PROPERTY TAXES LEVIED, MUNICIPALITIES, 1992
[In thousands of dollars] (Continued)

Municipality	City property taxes levied [1]	Estimated current property value	Assessed value						County
			Total	Real property			Personal property [3]	Public utilities [4]	
				Total [2]	Residential and farm	Industrial and commercial			
Whiteville	58	17,903	5,342	4,334	3,127	1,207	20	710	Hardeman
Whitwell	12	24,325	7,398	6,205	4,078	2,075	27	1,022	Marion
Winchester	990	195,823	56,951	46,407	25,700	20,707	398	2,660	Franklin
Woodbury	268	52,084	16,815	13,768	7,004	6,764	79	2,000	Cannon

Note: Data for Special School Districts are not shown. Detail may not add to total due to independent rounding.

n.a. not available.

1. For municipalities located in more than one county, the property taxes shown for the first part of the municipality are actually taxes levied for the entire municipality (all parts combined).

2. Includes categories not shown separately.

3. Includes industrial and commercial, residential, farm, and intangible personal property.

4. Includes utilities assessed by the Public Service Commission as well as those locally assessed.

Source: Tennessee State Board of Equalization, *1992 Tax Aggregate Report*; and State of Tennessee, Report of the Comptroller of the Treasury, Division of Local Finance, *County and Municipal Finances for Fiscal Year Ended June 30, 1992.*

TABLE 15.18--ACTUAL AND EFFECTIVE PROPERTY TAX RATES AND APPRAISAL RATIO, MUNICIPALITIES, 1993

Municipality	Actual tax rates			Appraisal ratio (%)	Equalized tax rate [1]	Effective tax rate by class of property				Weighted average effective rate [2]	County
	City tax rate	County tax rate in city	Total tax rate			Commercial and industrial real (40 %)	Residential and farm real (25 %)	Commercial and industrial personal (30 %)	Public utilities (55 %)		
Adams	0.51	3.29	3.80	0.95	3.61	1.25	0.78	1.14	1.72	1.09	Robertson
Adamsville	0.82	2.85	3.67	0.90	3.30	1.02	0.64	1.10	1.41	1.09	McNairy
Alamo	1.26	2.34	3.60	1.00	3.60	0.94	0.58	1.08	1.29	1.10	Crockett
Alcoa	2.15	2.27	4.42	1.00	4.42	0.91	0.57	1.33	1.25	1.45	Blount
Alexandria	0.90	1.80	2.70	1.00	2.70	0.72	0.45	0.81	0.99	0.94	DeKalb
Algood	1.07	2.54	3.61	1.00	3.61	1.02	0.64	1.08	1.40	1.09	Putnam
Ardmore (pt.)	0.39	3.31	3.70	1.00	3.70	1.32	0.83	1.11	1.82	1.15	Giles
Ardmore (pt.)	0.38	2.59	2.97	1.00	2.97	1.04	0.65	0.89	1.42	0.77	Lincoln
Arlington	1.20	3.16	4.36	1.00	4.36	1.26	0.79	1.31	1.74	1.34	Shelby
Ashland City	0.70	3.56	4.26	0.95	4.05	1.35	0.85	1.28	1.86	1.32	Cheatham
Athens	1.68	2.53	4.21	1.00	4.21	1.01	0.63	1.26	1.39	1.35	McMinn
Atoka	0.10	3.57	3.67	1.00	3.67	1.43	0.89	1.10	1.96	1.01	Tipton
Baneberry	1.20	2.50	3.70	1.00	3.70	1.00	0.62	1.11	1.38	0.97	Jefferson
Bartlett	1.49	3.16	4.65	1.00	4.65	1.26	0.79	1.40	1.74	1.31	Shelby
Baxter	2.00	2.54	4.54	1.00	4.54	1.02	0.64	1.36	1.40	1.36	Putnam
Bell Buckle	0.45	3.47	3.92	1.00	3.92	1.39	0.87	1.18	1.91	1.06	Bedford
Belle Meade	0.73	3.50	4.23	1.00	4.23	1.40	0.88	1.27	1.93	1.08	Davidson
Bells	1.63	2.34	3.97	1.00	3.97	0.94	0.58	1.19	1.29	1.31	Crockett
Benton	0.75	3.59	4.34	1.00	4.34	1.44	0.90	1.30	1.97	1.42	Polk
Bethel Springs	0.75	2.85	3.60	0.90	3.24	1.02	0.64	1.08	1.41	0.96	McNairy
Big Sandy	1.00	3.04	4.04	1.00	4.04	1.22	0.76	1.21	1.67	1.23	Benton
Bluff City	1.50	2.92	4.42	1.00	4.42	1.17	0.73	1.33	1.61	1.30	Sullivan
Bolivar	1.15	2.28	3.43	1.00	3.43	0.91	0.57	1.03	1.25	1.02	Hardeman
Bradford	0.87	2.63	3.50	1.00	3.50	1.05	0.66	1.05	1.45	1.06	Gibson
Brentwood	0.89	2.92	3.81	1.00	3.81	1.17	0.73	1.14	1.61	1.15	Williamson

TABLE 15.18—ACTUAL AND EFFECTIVE PROPERTY TAX RATES AND APPRAISAL RATIO, MUNICIPALITIES, 1993 (Continued)

| Municipality | Actual tax rates | | | Appraisal ratio (%) | Equalized tax rate[1] | Effective tax rate by class of property | | | | | County |
	City tax rate	County tax rate in city	Total tax rate			Commercial and industrial real (40 %)	Residential and farm real (25 %)	Commercial and industrial personal (30 %)	Public utilities (55 %)	Weighted average effective rate[2]	
Brighton	0.33	3.57	3.90	1.00	3.90	1.43	0.89	1.17	1.96	1.08	Tipton
Bristol	2.71	2.92	5.63	1.00	5.63	1.17	0.73	1.69	1.61	1.75	Sullivan
Brownsville	1.40	2.50	3.90	0.97	3.78	0.97	0.60	1.17	1.33	1.18	Haywood
Bruceton	1.11	3.34	4.45	0.91	4.05	1.22	0.76	1.33	1.67	1.27	Carroll
Bulls Gap	1.06	3.20	4.26	1.00	4.26	1.28	0.80	1.28	1.76	1.37	Hawkins
Burns	0.50	2.90	3.40	0.98	3.32	1.13	0.70	1.02	1.55	0.91	Dickson
Byrdstown	1.05	3.44	4.49	1.00	4.49	1.38	0.86	1.35	1.89	1.50	Pickett
Calhoun	0.70	2.53	3.23	1.00	3.23	1.01	0.63	0.97	1.39	0.96	McMinn
Camden	0.60	3.04	3.64	1.00	3.64	1.22	0.76	1.09	1.67	1.14	Benton
Carthage	1.95	2.93	4.88	0.60	2.91	0.70	0.44	1.46	0.96	0.95	Smith
Cedar Hill	0.50	3.29	3.79	0.95	3.60	1.25	0.78	1.14	1.72	1.09	Robertson
Celina	1.44	3.53	4.97	0.88	4.39	1.24	0.78	1.49	1.71	1.38	Clay
Centerville	0.95	3.81	4.76	0.74	3.50	1.12	0.70	1.43	1.54	1.08	Hickman
Chapel Hill	1.75	2.90	4.65	0.99	4.62	1.15	0.72	1.40	1.58	1.38	Marshall
Charleston	0.75	3.06	3.81	0.83	3.15	1.01	0.63	1.14	1.39	1.01	Bradley
Charlotte	0.25	2.90	3.15	0.98	3.07	1.13	0.70	0.95	1.55	0.89	Dickson
Chattanooga	2.62	2.81	5.43	1.00	5.43	1.12	0.70	1.63	1.55	1.79	Hamilton
Church Hill	0.64	3.20	3.84	1.00	3.84	1.28	0.80	1.15	1.76	1.11	Hawkins
Clarksville	1.19	2.73	3.92	0.95	3.74	1.04	0.65	1.18	1.43	1.13	Montgomery
Cleveland	1.52	2.70	4.22	0.83	3.49	0.89	0.56	1.27	1.23	1.12	Bradley
Clifton	1.60	2.57	4.17	1.00	4.17	1.03	0.64	1.25	1.41	1.30	Wayne
Clinton	0.85	2.97	3.82	1.00	3.82	1.19	0.74	1.15	1.63	1.20	Anderson
Collegedale	1.17	2.81	3.98	1.00	3.98	1.12	0.70	1.19	1.55	1.25	Hamilton
Collierville	1.59	3.16	4.75	1.00	4.75	1.26	0.79	1.43	1.74	1.35	Shelby
Collinwood	1.88	2.57	4.45	1.00	4.45	1.03	0.64	1.33	1.41	1.44	Wayne

TABLE 15.18--ACTUAL AND EFFECTIVE PROPERTY TAX RATES AND APPRAISAL RATIO, MUNICIPALITIES, 1993 (Continued)

| Municipality | Actual tax rates | | | Appraisal ratio (%) | Equalized tax rate[1] | Effective tax rate by class of property | | | | Weighted average effective rate[2] | County |
	City tax rate	County tax rate in city	Total tax rate[1]			Commercial and industrial real (40%)	Residential and farm real (25%)	Commercial and industrial personal (30%)	Public utilities (55%)		
Columbia	1.35	3.79	5.14	0.62	3.17	0.93	0.58	1.54	1.28	0.99	Maury
Cookeville	1.00	2.54	3.54	1.00	3.54	1.02	0.64	1.06	1.40	1.13	Putnam
Copperhill	1.19	3.59	4.78	1.00	4.78	1.44	0.90	1.43	1.97	1.70	Polk
Cornersville	1.19	2.90	4.09	0.99	4.06	1.15	0.72	1.23	1.58	1.21	Marshall
Cottage Grove	0.30	3.08	3.38	0.93	3.13	1.14	0.71	1.01	1.57	1.15	Henry
Covington	1.59	3.57	5.16	1.00	5.16	1.43	0.89	1.55	1.96	1.63	Tipton
Cowan	2.00	2.40	4.39	0.98	4.31	0.94	0.58	1.32	1.29	1.21	Franklin
Crossville	0.77	1.87	2.64	1.00	2.64	0.75	0.47	0.79	1.03	0.87	Cumberland
Cumberland City	1.00	1.55	2.55	1.00	2.55	0.62	0.39	0.76	0.85	0.80	Stewart
Cumberland Gap	0.16	3.22	3.38	1.00	3.38	1.29	0.81	1.01	1.77	1.09	Claiborne
Dandridge	0.89	2.50	3.39	1.00	3.39	1.00	0.62	1.02	1.38	1.09	Jefferson
Dayton	0.60	2.74	3.34	1.00	3.34	1.10	0.69	1.00	1.51	1.05	Rhea
Decatur	0.65	2.32	2.97	1.00	2.97	0.93	0.58	0.89	1.28	1.03	Meigs
Decaturville	1.30	1.99	3.29	1.00	3.29	0.80	0.50	0.99	1.09	1.08	Decatur
Dechard	1.60	2.40	4.00	0.98	3.92	0.94	0.58	1.20	1.29	1.25	Franklin
Dickson	1.10	2.90	4.00	0.98	3.90	1.13	0.70	1.20	1.55	1.24	Dickson
Dover	0.73	1.55	2.28	1.00	2.28	0.62	0.39	0.68	0.85	0.71	Stewart
Dresden	1.32	2.54	3.86	0.98	3.78	0.99	0.62	1.16	1.36	1.21	Weakley
Ducktown	0.80	3.59	4.39	1.00	4.39	1.44	0.90	1.32	1.97	1.48	Polk
Dunlap	0.84	2.36	3.20	1.00	3.20	0.94	0.59	0.96	1.30	0.99	Sequatchie
Dyer	1.12	2.31	3.43	1.00	3.43	0.92	0.58	1.03	1.27	1.01	Gibson
Dyersburg	1.65	1.85	3.50	1.00	3.50	0.74	0.46	1.05	1.02	1.09	Dyer
Eagleville	1.10	3.39	4.49	0.91	4.10	1.24	0.77	1.35	1.70	1.24	Rutherford
East Ridge	1.00	2.81	3.81	1.00	3.81	1.12	0.70	1.14	1.55	1.16	Hamilton
Elizabethton	3.22	3.18	6.40	1.00	6.40	1.27	0.80	1.92	1.75	2.01	Carter

TABLE 15.18–ACTUAL AND EFFECTIVE PROPERTY TAX RATES AND APPRAISAL RATIO, MUNICIPALITIES, 1993 (Continued)

Municipality	City tax rate	County tax rate in city	Total tax rate	Appraisal ratio (%)	Equalized tax rate [1]	Commercial and industrial real (40%)	Residential and farm real (25%)	Commercial and industrial personal (30%)	Public utilities (55%)	Weighted average effective rate [2]	County
Elkton	0.13	3.31	3.44	1.00	3.44	1.32	0.83	1.03	1.82	1.02	Giles
Englewood	2.00	2.53	4.53	1.00	4.53	1.01	0.63	1.36	1.39	1.29	McMinn
Erin	1.25	3.29	4.54	1.00	4.54	1.32	0.82	1.36	1.81	1.52	Houston
Erwin	1.40	3.29	4.69	0.88	4.15	1.16	0.73	1.41	1.60	1.26	Unicoi
Estill Springs	0.75	2.40	3.15	0.98	3.08	0.94	0.58	0.94	1.29	0.88	Franklin
Etowah	2.02	2.53	4.55	1.00	4.55	1.01	0.63	1.37	1.39	1.37	McMinn
Fairview	1.00	2.92	3.92	1.00	3.92	1.17	0.73	1.18	1.61	1.12	Williamson
Fayetteville	1.83	2.59	4.42	1.00	4.42	1.04	0.65	1.33	1.42	1.41	Lincoln
Franklin	0.94	3.63	4.57	1.00	4.57	1.45	0.91	1.37	2.00	1.44	Williamson
Friendship	2.05	2.34	4.39	1.00	4.39	0.94	0.58	1.32	1.29	1.33	Crockett
Gainesboro	0.84	3.17	4.01	1.00	4.01	1.27	0.79	1.20	1.74	1.41	Jackson
Gallatin	1.45	3.15	4.60	1.00	4.60	1.26	0.79	1.38	1.73	1.41	Sumner
Gates	1.80	2.68	4.48	0.78	3.47	0.83	0.52	1.34	1.14	1.00	Lauderdale
Gatlinburg	0.24	1.26	1.50	1.00	1.50	0.50	0.32	0.45	0.69	0.50	Sevier
Germantown	1.72	3.16	4.88	1.00	4.88	1.26	0.79	1.46	1.74	1.31	Shelby
Gibson	0.95	2.31	3.26	1.00	3.26	0.92	0.58	0.98	1.27	0.98	Gibson
Gleason	1.43	2.54	3.97	0.98	3.89	0.99	0.62	1.19	1.36	1.12	Weakley
Goodlettsville (pt.)	0.17	3.50	3.67	1.00	3.67	1.40	0.88	1.10	1.93	1.25	Davidson
Goodlettsville (pt.)	0.22	3.15	3.37	1.00	3.37	1.26	0.79	1.01	1.73	0.91	Sumner
Gordonsville	0.91	2.93	3.84	0.60	2.29	0.70	0.44	1.15	0.96	0.74	Smith
Grand Junction	0.74	2.28	3.02	1.00	3.02	0.91	0.57	0.91	1.25	0.96	Hardeman
Graysville	0.62	2.74	3.36	1.00	3.36	1.10	0.69	1.01	1.51	0.90	Rhea
Greenbrier	1.20	3.29	4.49	0.95	4.26	1.25	0.78	1.35	1.72	1.23	Robertson
Greeneville	2.96	2.20	5.16	1.00	5.16	0.88	0.55	1.55	1.21	1.67	Greene
Greenfield	1.17	2.54	3.71	0.98	3.64	0.99	0.62	1.11	1.36	1.07	Weakley
Halls	1.41	2.68	4.09	0.78	3.17	0.83	0.52	1.23	1.14	1.03	Lauderdale
Harriman	2.87	3.04	5.92	0.83	4.88	1.00	0.63	1.77	1.38	1.55	Roane

TABLE 15.18--ACTUAL AND EFFECTIVE PROPERTY TAX RATES AND APPRAISAL RATIO, MUNICIPALITIES, 1993 (Continued)

| Municipality | Actual tax rates | | | Appraisal ratio (%) | Equalized tax rate[1] | Effective tax rate by class of property | | | | Weighted average effective rate[2] | County |
	City tax rate	County tax rate in city	Total tax rate			Commercial and industrial real (40%)	Residential and farm real (25%)	Commercial and industrial personal (30%)	Public utilities (55%)		
Hartsville	1.35	4.05	5.40	1.00	5.40	1.62	1.01	1.62	2.23	1.76	Trousdale
Henderson	1.36	2.48	3.84	1.00	3.84	0.99	0.62	1.15	1.36	1.19	Chester
Hendersonville	0.79	3.15	3.94	1.00	3.94	1.26	0.79	1.18	1.73	1.12	Sumner
Henning	1.80	2.68	4.48	0.78	3.47	0.83	0.52	1.34	1.14	1.12	Lauderdale
Henry	0.57	3.08	3.65	0.93	3.39	1.14	0.71	1.10	1.57	1.07	Henry
Hickory Valley	0.25	2.28	2.53	1.00	2.53	0.91	0.57	0.76	1.25	0.71	Hardeman
Hohenwald	1.50	2.09	3.59	1.00	3.59	0.84	0.52	1.08	1.15	1.10	Lewis
Hollow Rock	0.70	3.34	4.04	0.91	3.68	1.22	0.76	1.21	1.67	1.01	Carroll
Hombeak	0.48	3.31	3.79	0.95	3.60	1.26	0.79	1.14	1.73	1.10	Obion
Hornsby	0.39	2.28	2.67	1.00	2.67	0.91	0.57	0.80	1.25	0.76	Hardeman
Humboldt (pt.)	3.70	0.94	4.64	1.00	4.64	0.38	0.23	1.39	0.52	1.44	Gibson
Humboldt (pt.)	3.70	3.50	7.20	0.80	5.76	1.12	0.70	2.16	1.54	1.54	Madison
Huntingdon	0.95	3.44	4.39	0.91	4.00	1.25	0.78	1.32	1.72	1.22	Carroll
Huntland	1.23	2.40	3.63	0.98	3.55	0.94	0.58	1.09	1.29	1.04	Franklin
Huntsville	0.36	3.72	4.08	1.00	4.08	1.49	0.93	1.22	2.05	1.34	Scott
Iron City	0.28	2.78	3.06	1.00	3.06	1.11	0.70	0.92	1.53	0.80	Lawrence
Jackson	2.75	3.50	6.25	0.80	5.00	1.12	0.70	1.88	1.54	1.60	Madison
Jamestown	0.95	3.00	3.95	0.94	3.70	1.12	0.70	1.19	1.54	1.29	Fentress
Jasper	0.43	2.14	2.57	1.00	2.57	0.86	0.54	0.77	1.18	0.80	Marion
Jefferson City	1.17	2.50	3.67	1.00	3.67	1.00	0.62	1.10	1.38	1.20	Jefferson
Jellico	0.67	2.96	3.63	1.00	3.63	1.18	0.74	1.09	1.63	1.18	Campbell
Johnson City (pt.)	2.61	3.18	5.79	0.98	5.68	1.24	0.78	1.74	1.71	1.81	Carter
Johnson City (pt.)	2.61	2.92	5.53	1.00	5.53	1.17	0.73	1.66	1.61	1.58	Sullivan
Johnson City (pt.)	2.61	2.41	5.02	1.00	5.02	0.96	0.60	1.51	1.33	1.57	Washington
Jonesborough	1.70	2.41	4.11	1.00	4.11	0.96	0.60	1.23	1.33	1.23	Washington
Kenton (pt.)	1.36	2.38	3.74	1.00	3.74	0.95	0.60	1.12	1.31	1.08	Gibson

TABLE 15.18--ACTUAL AND EFFECTIVE PROPERTY TAX RATES AND APPRAISAL RATIO, MUNICIPALITIES, 1993 (Continued)

| Municipality | Actual tax rates | | | Appraisal ratio (%) | Equalized tax rate [1] | Effective tax rate by class of property | | | | Weighted average effective rate [2] | County |
	City tax rate	County tax rate in city	Total tax rate			Commercial and industrial real (40 %)	Residential and farm real (25 %)	Commercial and industrial personal (30 %)	Public utilities (55 %)		
Kenton (pt.)	1.30	3.38	4.68	0.95	4.45	1.28	0.80	1.40	1.76	1.37	Obion
Kimball	0.19	2.14	2.33	1.00	2.33	0.86	0.54	0.70	1.18	0.77	Marion
Kingsport (pt.)	2.06	3.20	5.26	1.00	5.26	1.28	0.80	1.58	1.76	1.60	Hawkins
Kingsport (pt.)	2.06	2.92	4.98	1.00	4.98	1.17	0.73	1.49	1.61	1.56	Sullivan
Kingston	2.00	3.83	5.83	0.83	4.81	1.26	0.79	1.75	1.73	1.39	Roane
Kingston Springs	0.70	3.56	4.26	0.95	4.05	1.35	0.85	1.28	1.86	1.11	Cheatham
Knoxville	2.73	2.91	5.64	0.99	5.60	1.15	0.72	1.69	1.58	1.84	Knox
Lafayette	1.00	3.29	4.29	0.83	3.57	1.10	0.69	1.29	1.51	1.14	Macon
LaFollette	1.07	2.96	4.03	1.00	4.03	1.18	0.74	1.21	1.63	1.32	Campbell
LaGrange	0.74	2.92	3.66	0.84	3.07	0.98	0.61	1.10	1.35	0.83	Fayette
Lake City (pt.)	1.15	2.98	4.13	1.00	4.13	1.19	0.75	1.24	1.64	1.38	Anderson
Lake City (pt.)	1.15	2.96	4.11	1.00	4.11	1.18	0.74	1.23	1.63	1.26	Campbell
Lakesite	0.56	2.81	3.38	1.00	3.38	1.12	0.70	1.01	1.55	0.87	Hamilton
Lavergne	0.57	3.39	3.96	0.91	3.62	1.24	0.77	1.19	1.70	1.16	Rutherford
Lawrenceburg	1.17	2.78	3.95	1.00	3.95	1.11	0.70	1.18	1.53	1.25	Lawrence
Lebanon	0.60	3.20	3.80	1.00	3.80	1.28	0.80	1.14	1.76	1.21	Wilson
Lenoir City	1.23	2.29	3.52	1.00	3.52	0.92	0.57	1.06	1.26	1.14	Loudon
Lewisburg	1.79	2.90	4.69	0.99	4.66	1.15	0.72	1.41	1.58	1.46	Marshall
Lexington	0.99	1.91	2.90	1.00	2.90	0.76	0.48	0.87	1.05	0.91	Henderson
Liberty	0.19	1.80	1.99	1.00	1.99	0.72	0.45	0.60	0.99	0.61	DeKalb
Linden	0.72	3.27	3.99	0.99	3.95	1.29	0.81	1.20	1.78	1.31	Perry
Livingston	1.79	2.79	4.58	1.00	4.58	1.12	0.70	1.37	1.53	1.51	Overton
Lobelville	0.95	3.27	4.22	0.99	4.18	1.29	0.81	1.27	1.78	1.77	Perry
Lookout Mountain	1.68	2.81	4.50	1.00	4.50	1.12	0.70	1.35	1.55	1.15	Hamilton
Loretto	0.31	2.78	3.09	1.00	3.09	1.11	0.70	0.93	1.53	0.92	Lawrence

TABLE 15.18--ACTUAL AND EFFECTIVE PROPERTY TAX RATES AND APPRAISAL RATIO, MUNICIPALITIES, 1993 (Continued)

| Municipality | Actual tax rates | | | Appraisal ratio (%) | Equalized tax rate [1] | Effective tax rate by class of property | | | | Weighted average effective rate [2] | County |
	City tax rate	County tax rate in city	Total tax rate			Commercial and industrial real (40 %)	Residential and farm real (25 %)	Commercial and industrial personal (30 %)	Public utilities (55 %)		
Loudon	1.00	2.51	3.51	1.00	3.51	1.00	0.63	1.05	1.38	1.16	Loudon
Lynnville	0.70	3.31	4.01	1.00	4.01	1.32	0.83	1.20	1.82	1.16	Giles
McEwen	0.81	2.23	3.04	1.00	3.04	0.89	0.56	0.91	1.23	0.90	Humphreys
McKenzie (pt.)	1.04	3.33	4.37	0.91	3.98	1.21	0.76	1.31	1.67	1.20	Carroll
McKenzie (pt.)	1.10	3.08	4.18	0.93	3.87	1.14	0.71	1.25	1.57	1.21	Henry
McKenzie (pt.)	1.04	2.54	3.58	0.98	3.51	0.99	0.62	1.07	1.36	1.09	Weakley
McLemoresville	1.05	3.42	4.47	0.91	4.07	1.24	0.78	1.34	1.71	1.12	Carroll
McMinnville	1.86	2.24	4.10	1.00	4.10	0.90	0.56	1.23	1.23	1.34	Warren
Madisonville	0.54	2.00	2.54	0.97	2.47	0.78	0.49	0.76	1.07	0.78	Monroe
Manchester	2.85	2.65	5.50	0.91	4.99	0.96	0.60	1.65	1.32	1.60	Coffee
Martin	1.16	2.54	3.70	0.98	3.63	0.99	0.62	1.11	1.36	1.15	Weakley
Maryville	2.25	2.27	4.52	1.00	4.52	0.91	0.57	1.36	1.25	1.37	Blount
Mason	0.50	3.57	4.07	1.00	4.07	1.43	0.89	1.22	1.96	1.48	Tipton
Maury City	1.25	2.34	3.59	1.00	3.59	0.94	0.58	1.08	1.29	1.05	Crockett
Medina	1.90	2.31	4.21	1.00	4.21	0.92	0.58	1.26	1.27	1.25	Gibson
Memphis	3.18	3.16	6.34	1.00	6.34	1.26	0.79	1.90	1.74	1.96	Shelby
Middleton	0.65	2.28	2.93	1.00	2.93	0.91	0.57	0.88	1.25	0.91	Hardeman
Milan	0.82	2.49	3.31	1.00	3.31	1.00	0.62	0.99	1.37	1.03	Gibson
Millersville (pt.)	0.80	3.29	4.09	0.95	3.88	1.25	0.78	1.23	1.72	1.24	Robertson
Millersville (pt.)	0.80	3.15	3.95	1.00	3.95	1.26	0.79	1.19	1.73	1.09	Sumner
Millington	1.10	3.16	4.26	1.00	4.26	1.26	0.79	1.28	1.74	1.36	Shelby
Mitchellville	0.89	3.15	4.04	1.00	4.04	1.26	0.79	1.21	1.73	1.18	Sumner
Monterey	1.40	2.54	3.94	1.00	3.94	1.02	0.64	1.18	1.40	1.21	Putnam
Morrison	0.17	2.24	2.41	1.00	2.41	0.90	0.56	0.72	1.23	0.72	Warren
Morristown	1.41	2.81	4.22	0.90	3.80	1.01	0.63	1.27	1.39	1.24	Hamblen

TABLE 15.18.--ACTUAL AND EFFECTIVE PROPERTY TAX RATES AND APPRAISAL RATIO, MUNICIPALITIES, 1993 (Continued)

| Municipality | Actual tax rates | | | | | Effective tax rate by class of property | | | | | County |
	City tax rate	County tax rate in city	Total tax rate	Appraisal ratio (%)	Equalized tax rate[1]	Commercial and industrial real (40%)	Residential and farm real (25%)	Commercial and industrial personal (30%)	Public utilities (55%)	Weighted average effective rate[2]	
Moscow	0.85	2.92	3.77	0.84	3.17	0.98	0.61	1.13	1.35	1.02	Fayette
Mount Pleasant	1.60	3.79	5.39	0.62	3.32	0.93	0.58	1.62	1.28	0.97	Maury
Mountain City	1.46	3.85	5.31	1.00	5.31	1.54	0.96	1.59	2.12	1.73	Johnson
Munford	0.58	3.57	4.15	1.00	4.15	1.43	0.89	1.24	1.96	1.19	Tipton
Murfreesboro	2.29	3.39	5.68	0.91	5.19	1.24	0.77	1.70	1.70	1.64	Rutherford
Nashville	0.00	4.50	4.50	1.00	4.50	1.80	1.13	1.35	2.48	1.47	Davidson
New Hope	0.25	2.14	2.39	1.00	2.39	0.86	0.54	0.72	1.18	0.64	Marion
New Johnsonville	0.82	2.23	3.05	1.00	3.05	0.89	0.56	0.91	1.23	0.90	Humphreys
Newbern	1.10	1.85	2.95	1.00	2.95	0.74	0.46	0.89	1.02	0.92	Dyer
Newport	2.58	3.15	5.73	0.85	4.86	1.07	0.67	1.72	1.47	1.58	Cocke
Niota	0.96	2.53	3.49	1.00	3.49	1.01	0.63	1.05	1.39	1.07	McMinn
Normandy	0.27	3.47	3.74	1.00	3.74	1.39	0.87	1.12	1.91	1.03	Bedford
Norris	2.70	2.98	5.68	1.00	5.68	1.19	0.75	1.70	1.64	1.57	Anderson
Oak Ridge (pt.)	1.73	2.72	4.45	1.00	4.45	1.09	0.68	1.33	1.50	1.39	Anderson
Oak Ridge (pt.)	1.73	3.04	4.78	1.00	4.78	1.22	0.76	1.43	1.67	1.33	Roane
Oakdale	2.00	6.04	8.04	1.00	8.04	2.42	1.51	2.41	3.32	2.87	Morgan
Oakland	0.38	2.92	3.30	0.84	2.77	0.98	0.61	0.99	1.35	0.88	Fayette
Obion	1.33	3.31	4.64	0.95	4.41	1.26	0.79	1.39	1.73	1.33	Obion
Oliver Springs (pt.)	1.35	2.98	4.33	1.00	4.33	1.19	0.75	1.30	1.64	1.27	Anderson
Oliver Springs (pt.)	1.35	6.04	7.39	1.00	7.39	2.42	1.51	2.22	3.32	2.38	Morgan
Oliver Springs (pt.)	1.35	3.83	5.18	1.00	5.18	1.53	0.95	1.55	2.10	1.68	Roane
Oneida	1.40	3.72	5.12	1.00	5.12	1.49	0.93	1.54	2.05	1.62	Scott
Paris	1.12	3.34	4.46	0.93	4.13	1.24	0.77	1.34	1.70	1.30	Henry
Parsons	1.10	1.99	3.09	1.00	3.09	0.80	0.50	0.93	1.09	1.00	Decatur
Petersburg (pt.)	0.98	2.59	3.57	1.00	3.57	1.04	0.65	1.07	1.42	1.01	Lincoln

TABLE 15.18--ACTUAL AND EFFECTIVE PROPERTY TAX RATES AND APPRAISAL RATIO, MUNICIPALITIES, 1993 (Continued)

| Municipality | Actual tax rates | | | Appraisal ratio (%) | Equalized tax rate [1] | Effective tax rate by class of property | | | | Weighted average effective rate [2] | County |
	City tax rate	County tax rate in city	Total tax rate			Commercial and industrial real (40%)	Residential and farm real (25%)	Commercial and industrial personal (30%)	Public utilities (55%)		
Petersburg (pt.)	0.98	2.90	3.88	0.99	3.86	1.15	0.72	1.17	1.58	1.34	Marshall
Pigeon Forge	0.17	1.26	1.43	1.00	1.43	0.50	0.32	0.43	0.69	0.52	Sevier
Pikeville	0.64	2.55	3.19	1.00	3.19	1.02	0.64	0.96	1.40	1.10	Bledsoe
Pitman Center	0.32	1.26	1.58	1.00	1.58	0.50	0.32	0.47	0.69	0.44	Sevier
Portland	1.18	3.15	4.33	1.00	4.33	1.26	0.79	1.30	1.73	1.40	Sumner
Pulaski	0.85	3.31	4.16	1.00	4.16	1.32	0.83	1.25	1.82	1.31	Giles
Puryear	0.67	3.08	3.75	0.93	3.48	1.14	0.71	1.13	1.57	1.03	Henry
Red Bank	1.03	2.81	3.84	1.00	3.84	1.12	0.70	1.15	1.55	1.18	Hamilton
Red Boiling Springs	1.43	3.29	4.72	0.83	3.93	1.10	0.69	1.42	1.51	1.24	Macon
Ridgely	1.72	3.00	4.72	1.00	4.72	1.20	0.75	1.42	1.65	1.44	Lake
Ridgeside	2.13	2.18	4.31	1.00	4.31	0.87	0.55	1.29	1.20	1.09	Hamilton
Ridgetop (pt.)	0.66	3.50	4.16	1.00	4.16	1.40	0.88	1.25	1.93	1.13	Davidson
Ridgetop (pt.)	0.84	3.29	4.13	0.95	3.92	1.25	0.78	1.24	1.72	1.04	Robertson
Ripley	2.00	2.68	4.68	0.78	3.63	0.83	0.52	1.40	1.14	1.17	Lauderdale
Rives	2.00	3.31	5.31	0.95	5.04	1.26	0.79	1.59	1.73	1.45	Obion
Rockwood	1.30	3.83	5.13	0.83	4.23	1.26	0.79	1.54	1.73	1.32	Roane
Rogersville	1.67	3.20	4.87	1.00	4.87	1.28	0.80	1.46	1.76	1.58	Hawkins
Rossville	0.98	2.92	3.90	0.84	3.27	0.98	0.61	1.17	1.35	1.09	Fayette
Rutherford	1.33	0.94	2.27	1.00	2.27	0.38	0.23	0.68	0.52	0.68	Gibson
St. Joseph	0.20	2.78	2.98	1.00	2.98	1.11	0.70	0.89	1.53	0.85	Lawrence
Sardis	0.51	1.91	2.42	1.00	2.42	0.76	0.48	0.73	1.05	0.71	Henderson
Savannah	0.92	2.54	3.46	0.78	2.71	0.79	0.50	1.04	1.09	0.85	Hardin
Scotts Hill (pt.)	0.38	1.99	2.37	1.00	2.37	0.80	0.50	0.71	1.09	0.67	Decatur
Scotts Hill (pt.)	0.42	1.91	2.33	1.00	2.33	0.76	0.48	0.70	1.05	0.72	Henderson
Selmer	0.95	2.85	3.80	0.90	3.42	1.02	0.64	1.14	1.41	1.07	McNairy

TABLE 15.18–ACTUAL AND EFFECTIVE PROPERTY TAX RATES AND APPRAISAL RATIO, MUNICIPALITIES, 1993 (Continued)

Municipality	Actual tax rates			Appraisal ratio (%)	Equalized tax rate [1]	Effective tax rate by class of property				Weighted average effective rate [2]	County
	City tax rate	County tax rate in city	Total tax rate			Commercial and industrial real (40 %)	Residential and farm real (25 %)	Commercial and industrial personal (30 %)	Public utilities (55 %)		
Sevierville	0.56	1.26	1.82	1.00	1.82	0.50	0.32	0.55	0.69	0.59	Sevier
Sharon	1.57	2.54	4.11	0.98	4.03	0.99	0.62	1.23	1.36	1.26	Weakley
Shelbyville	2.30	3.47	5.77	1.00	5.77	1.39	0.87	1.73	1.91	1.79	Bedford
Signal Mountain	1.58	2.81	4.39	1.00	4.39	1.12	0.70	1.32	1.55	1.17	Hamilton
Smithville	0.85	1.80	2.65	1.00	2.65	0.72	0.45	0.79	0.99	0.83	DeKalb
Smyrna	0.55	3.39	3.94	0.91	3.60	1.24	0.77	1.18	1.70	1.12	Rutherford
Soddy Daisy	0.68	2.81	3.49	1.00	3.49	1.12	0.70	1.05	1.55	1.02	Hamilton
Somerville	0.51	2.92	3.43	0.84	2.88	0.98	0.61	1.03	1.35	0.94	Fayette
South Carthage	1.10	2.93	4.03	0.60	2.41	0.70	0.44	1.21	0.96	0.79	Smith
South Fulton	1.14	3.31	4.45	0.95	4.23	1.26	0.79	1.33	1.73	1.23	Obion
South Pittsburg	0.70	2.35	3.05	1.00	3.05	0.94	0.59	0.91	1.29	1.01	Marion
Sparta	1.72	2.48	4.20	1.00	4.20	0.99	0.62	1.26	1.36	1.36	White
Spring City	1.35	2.74	4.09	1.00	4.09	1.10	0.69	1.23	1.51	1.27	Rhea
Spring Hill (pt.)	0.75	3.79	4.54	0.62	2.80	0.93	0.58	1.36	1.28	0.87	Maury
Spring Hill (pt.)	0.47	3.09	3.56	1.00	3.56	1.24	0.77	1.07	1.70	0.90	Williamson
Springfield	1.42	3.29	4.71	0.95	4.47	1.25	0.78	1.41	1.72	1.40	Robertson
Stanton	0.93	2.50	3.43	0.97	3.33	0.97	0.60	1.03	1.33	1.01	Haywood
Surgoinsville	0.72	3.20	3.92	1.00	3.92	1.28	0.80	1.18	1.76	1.12	Hawkins
Sweetwater	1.10	2.00	3.10	0.97	3.01	0.78	0.49	0.93	1.07	0.96	Monroe
Tellico Plains	0.84	2.00	2.84	0.97	2.75	0.78	0.49	0.85	1.07	0.98	Monroe
Tennessee Ridge	0.96	3.29	4.25	1.00	4.25	1.32	0.82	1.27	1.81	1.18	Houston
Thompson Station	0.00	3.09	3.09	1.00	3.09	1.24	0.77	0.93	1.70	0.80	Williamson
Tiptonville	1.70	3.00	4.70	1.00	4.70	1.20	0.75	1.41	1.65	1.52	Lake
Toone	0.21	2.28	2.49	1.00	2.49	0.91	0.57	0.75	1.25	0.70	Hardeman
Tracy City	0.61	3.41	4.02	1.00	4.02	1.36	0.85	1.21	1.88	1.25	Grundy
Trenton	1.85	2.38	4.23	1.00	4.23	0.95	0.60	1.27	1.31	1.37	Gibson
Trezevant	0.90	3.42	4.32	0.91	3.94	1.24	0.78	1.30	1.71	1.11	Carroll

TABLE 15.18–ACTUAL AND EFFECTIVE PROPERTY TAX RATES AND APPRAISAL RATIO, MUNICIPALITIES, 1993 (Continued)

| Municipality | Actual tax rates | | | Appraisal ratio (%) | Equalized tax rate [1] | Effective tax rate by class of property | | | | | County |
	City tax rate	County tax rate in city	Total tax rate			Commercial and industrial real (40%)	Residential and farm real (25%)	Commercial and industrial personal (30%)	Public utilities (55%)	Weighted average effective rate [2]	
Trimble (pt.)	1.63	1.85	3.48	1.00	3.48	0.74	0.46	1.04	1.02	0.99	Dyer
Trimble (pt.)	1.63	3.31	4.94	0.95	4.69	1.26	0.79	1.48	1.73	1.45	Obion
Troy	1.70	3.31	5.01	0.95	4.76	1.26	0.79	1.50	1.73	1.49	Obion
Tullahoma (pt.)	2.80	2.65	5.45	0.91	4.95	0.96	0.60	1.63	1.32	1.51	Coffee
Tullahoma (pt.)	2.80	2.07	4.87	0.91	4.42	0.75	0.47	1.46	1.03	1.22	Franklin
Union City	2.40	2.40	4.80	0.95	4.56	0.91	0.57	1.44	1.25	1.43	Obion
Vanleer	0.12	2.90	3.02	0.98	2.95	1.13	0.70	0.91	1.55	0.87	Dickson
Vonore	0.50	2.00	2.50	0.97	2.42	0.78	0.49	0.75	1.07	0.78	Monroe
Walden	0.90	2.81	3.71	1.00	3.71	1.12	0.70	1.11	1.55	0.95	Hamilton
Wartrace	1.20	3.47	4.67	1.00	4.67	1.39	0.87	1.40	1.91	1.44	Bedford
Watauga	0.30	3.18	3.48	0.98	3.41	1.24	0.78	1.04	1.71	0.96	Carter
Watertown	1.14	3.06	4.20	1.00	4.20	1.22	0.77	1.26	1.68	1.27	Wilson
Waverly	1.08	2.23	3.31	1.00	3.31	0.89	0.56	0.99	1.23	1.03	Humphreys
Waynesboro	1.60	2.57	4.17	1.00	4.17	1.03	0.64	1.25	1.41	1.33	Wayne
Westmoreland	1.65	3.15	4.80	1.00	4.80	1.26	0.79	1.44	1.73	1.47	Sumner
White Bluff	0.92	2.90	3.82	0.98	3.73	1.13	0.70	1.15	1.55	1.13	Dickson
White House (pt.)	1.62	3.29	4.91	0.95	4.66	1.25	0.78	1.47	1.72	1.47	Robertson
White House (pt.)	1.62	3.15	4.77	1.00	4.77	1.26	0.79	1.43	1.73	1.41	Sumner
White Pine	1.04	2.50	3.54	1.00	3.54	1.00	0.62	1.06	1.38	1.11	Jefferson
Whiteville	1.20	2.28	3.48	1.00	3.48	0.91	0.57	1.04	1.25	1.05	Hardeman
Whitwell	0.20	2.14	2.34	1.00	2.34	0.86	0.54	0.70	1.18	0.71	Marion
Winchester	1.57	2.07	3.64	0.98	3.57	0.81	0.50	1.09	1.11	1.10	Franklin
Woodbury	1.70	2.79	4.49	1.00	4.49	1.12	0.70	1.35	1.53	1.43	Cannon

1. Equal to total tax rate (excluding Special School District rate) multiplied by the appraisal ratio; computed by the Center for Business and Economic Research; see Table 15.13 for additional footnotes.

2. The average tax burden for all property is calculated by dividing the estimated current value of the property into the total assessed value and multiplying by the total tax rate.

Source: State of Tennessee, State Board of Equalization, *1993 Tax Aggregate Report of Tennessee.*

TABLE 15.19--GENERAL REVENUE OF STATE GOVERNMENTS, BY SOURCE, SOUTHEASTERN
STATES AND UNITED STATES, 1992 [In thousands of dollars]

| State | Total | Intergovernmental revenue | | Taxes | Current charges | Miscel- laneous |
		Federal	Local			
TENNESSEE	9,624,174	3,384,884	42,273	4,525,662	939,489	731,866
Alabama	8,910,315	2,707,431	29,749	4,217,916	1,347,766	607,453
Arkansas	5,190,388	1,629,989	5,973	2,748,292	552,610	253,524
Florida	23,651,927	5,406,514	304,938	14,411,775	1,281,046	2,247,654
Georgia	12,377,277	3,723,847	46,829	7,266,981	947,088	392,532
Kentucky	9,221,972	2,593,515	15,771	5,080,971	846,268	685,447
Louisiana	10,361,962	3,676,223	19,032	4,250,245	1,093,446	1,323,016
Mississippi	5,289,771	2,011,434	65,847	2,494,392	494,515	223,583
North Carolina	14,980,885	3,695,376	322,220	9,009,742	1,194,139	759,408
South Carolina	7,861,740	2,347,127	96,714	3,935,500	1,044,255	438,144
Virginia	13,086,581	2,563,170	162,730	7,025,345	2,010,012	1,325,324
West Virginia	4,558,622	1,475,928	14,159	2,351,858	415,006	301,671
UNITED STATES	605,333,551	159,041,447	10,860,625	327,821,571	52,941,024	54,668,884

Source: U.S. Department of Commerce, Bureau of the Census, *State Government Finances: 1992.*

TABLE 15.20--PER CAPITA GENERAL REVENUE OF STATE GOVERNMENTS, BY SOURCE,
SOUTHEASTERN STATES AND UNITED STATES, 1992 [In dollars]

| State | Total | Intergovernmental revenue | | Taxes | Current charges [1] | Miscel- laneous [1] |
		Federal	Local			
TENNESSEE	1,915.64	673.74	8.41	900.81	187.00	145.67
Alabama	2,154.33	654.60	7.19	1,019.81	325.86	146.87
Arkansas	2,163.56	679.45	2.49	1,145.60	230.35	105.68
Florida	1,753.55	400.84	22.61	1,068.49	94.98	166.64
Georgia	1,833.40	551.60	6.94	1,076.43	140.29	58.14
Kentucky	2,455.92	690.68	4.20	1,353.12	225.37	182.54
Louisiana	2,417.07	857.53	4.44	991.43	255.06	308.61
Mississippi	2,023.63	769.49	25.19	954.24	189.18	85.53
North Carolina	2,189.23	540.20	47.09	1,316.64	174.51	110.98
South Carolina	2,182.00	651.44	26.84	1,092.28	289.83	121.61
Virginia	2,052.15	401.94	25.52	1,101.67	315.20	207.83
West Virginia	2,515.80	814.53	7.81	1,297.93	229.03	166.49
UNITED STATES	2,378.59	624.93	42.68	1,288.14	208.03	214.82

Note: Population estimates are as of July 1.

1. Computed by Center for Business and Economic Research. Per capita amounts are computed on the basis of
figures rounded to nearest thousand.

Source: U.S. Department of Commerce, Bureau of the Census, *State Government Finances: 1992.*

TABLE 15.21--STATE TAX REVENUE, BY SOURCE, SOUTHEASTERN STATES, FISCAL YEAR 1992 [In thousands of dollars]

State	Total	General sales and gross receipts	Selective sales and gross receipts [1]	Total license	Individual income	Corporation net income	Property	Severance	Death and gift	Other taxes [2]
TENNESSEE	4,525,662	2,514,798	1,000,844	500,876	93,360	295,266	0	1,199	42,414	76,905
Alabama	4,217,916	1,115,516	1,103,368	395,202	1,233,824	164,779	98,027	61,864	30,279	15,057
Arkansas	2,748,292	1,032,536	485,252	195,634	850,111	125,525	11,089	14,996	8,587	24,562
Florida	14,411,775	8,325,978	2,958,850	997,465	0	695,114	490,073	67,000	281,368	595,927
Georgia	7,266,981	2,687,346	815,737	211,443	3,081,708	375,286	27,758	0	37,584	30,119
Kentucky	5,080,971	1,366,872	861,114	281,006	1,678,526	271,027	338,548	203,329	77,355	3,194
Louisiana	4,250,245	1,268,695	892,957	412,425	867,478	232,061	42,584	487,887	46,158	0
Mississippi	2,494,392	1,182,356	494,777	155,912	439,577	146,308	22,617	41,994	10,851	0
North Carolina	9,009,742	2,171,041	1,801,940	601,150	3,583,018	643,865	112,183	1,621	94,924	0
South Carolina	3,935,500	1,452,014	599,816	279,459	1,410,893	141,895	12,585	0	26,145	12,693
Virginia	7,025,345	1,570,789	1,286,863	390,242	3,321,243	273,258	15,351	1,426	48,791	117,382
West Virginia	2,351,858	796,889	425,259	141,056	612,619	182,081	2,053	180,833	7,410	3,658

Note: Total does not include unemployment insurance tax collections.

1. Includes collections of motor fuels, alcoholic beverages, tobacco products, insurance, public utilities, parimutuels, and amusements.

2. Includes document and stock transfer taxes.

Source: U.S. Department of Commerce, Bureau of the Census, *State Government Finances: 1992.*

TABLE 15.22—GROSS ASSESSED VALUE OF LOCALLY ASSESSED TAXABLE REAL PROPERTY, ESTIMATED DISTRIBUTION BY USE CATEGORY, SOUTHEASTERN STATES AND UNITED STATES, 1986 [In millions of dollars]

State	Total	Residential (nonfarm)			Acreage	Vacant platted lots	Commercial and industrial		
		Total	Single-family	Multi-family			Total	Commercial	Industrial
TENNESSEE[1]	24,345	12,284	11,562	722	2,961	935	8,104	6,825	1,280
Alabama[2]	8,874	5,084	4,603	481	1,535	324	1,915	1,635	280
Arkansas	8,871	5,014	4,699	315	1,752	348	1,745	1,329	416
Florida	344,042	227,631	203,481	24,150	16,035	29,217	70,151	59,775	10,377
Georgia[3]	50,768	31,481	28,086	3,395	6,209	1,837	11,189	9,210	1,979
Kentucky[1]	54,240	32,616	30,098	2,519	9,575	842	10,900	8,586	2,314
Louisiana[4]	8,852	5,424	4,858	567	805	377	2,242	2,001	241
Mississippi	4,807	2,824	2,544	280	866	189	920	764	156
North Carolina[3,5]	121,397	75,767	69,902	5,865	16,645	4,050	24,327	18,137	6,190
South Carolina[1,2]	3,174	1,819	1,607	212	241	213	881	519	362
Virginia[3]	166,460	110,689	100,852	9,837	15,475	7,186	32,536	27,088	5,448
West Virginia[2]	8,697	5,369	5,025	344	562	294	1,802	1,169	632
UNITED STATES	4,104,549	2,511,599	2,180,289	331,310	309,308	189,224	997,462	710,546	286,916

Note: These data are estimates subject to sampling variation. Valuation date was January 1, 1986, unless otherwise stated.

1. Estimates for "Single-family" residential may include all or some parcels in "Multifamily" use.

2. Alabama valuation date was October 1, 1985; South Carolina, December 31, 1985; and West Virginia, July 1, 1985.

3. Estimates for "Vacant platted lots" may include "Acreage" parcels, and vice versa.

4. Louisiana manufacturing plant value was inconsistently allocated between realty and personalty components in reported data. As a result, the total realty value amount shown may be overstated or understated to the extent influenced by inconsistent reporting.

5. North Carolina assessed values reported as gross are actually net values for those counties which did not report the amounts of their partial exemptions.

Source: U.S. Department of Commerce, Bureau of the Census, *1987 Census of Governments, Volume 2, Taxable Property Values*.

TABLE 15.23—GENERAL EXPENDITURES OF STATE GOVERNMENTS, BY FUNCTION, SOUTHEASTERN STATES AND UNITED STATES, 1992 [In thousands of dollars]

State	Total[1]	Education	Highways	Public welfare	Health and hospitals	Natural resources	Governmental administration	Interest on general debt
TENNESSEE	9,632,969	3,100,593	1,134,464	2,816,658	735,876	154,836	243,659	202,680
Alabama	8,788,293	3,570,524	694,874	1,853,436	1,174,934	151,432	274,088	280,179
Arkansas	5,061,654	2,122,905	576,635	1,176,619	359,846	117,150	129,695	130,387
Florida	24,851,056	8,814,361	2,175,460	5,333,949	1,924,004	840,390	1,065,427	740,022
Georgia	12,781,046	5,184,261	875,483	3,313,204	1,025,265	244,118	236,694	280,715
Kentucky	9,235,218	3,572,415	933,960	2,382,835	493,807	236,480	343,955	434,180
Louisiana	10,682,706	3,687,009	879,977	2,544,821	1,072,239	237,919	293,438	733,312
Mississippi	5,216,887	1,993,166	538,749	1,210,496	395,752	125,371	130,576	115,741
North Carolina	14,671,144	6,312,907	1,448,093	2,948,994	1,153,674	279,626	451,702	273,409
South Carolina	7,968,594	3,070,613	530,144	1,617,805	967,257	133,692	216,422	241,042
Virginia	12,694,076	4,930,767	1,521,447	2,094,146	1,424,235	163,418	544,265	478,499
West Virginia	4,395,674	1,753,193	510,002	1,094,068	197,092	103,038	170,728	172,304
UNITED STATES	611,921,919	211,569,798	48,746,992	156,363,573	48,123,553	10,520,664	21,140,110	24,621,601

1. Includes items not shown separately.

Source: U.S. Department of Commerce, Bureau of the Census, *State Government Finances: 1992.*

623

TABLE 15.24--PER CAPITA GENERAL EXPENDITURES OF STATE GOVERNMENTS, BY FUNCTION, SOUTHEASTERN STATES AND UNITED STATES, 1992
[In dollars]

State	Total[1]	Education	Highways	Public welfare	Health and hospitals	Natural resources[2]	Governmental administration[2]	Interest on general debt
TENNESSEE	1,917.39	617.16	225.81	560.64	146.47	30.82	48.50	40.34
Alabama	2,124.83	863.28	168.01	448.12	284.08	36.61	66.27	67.74
Arkansas	2,109.90	884.91	240.36	490.46	149.99	48.83	54.06	54.35
Florida	1,842.46	653.50	161.29	395.46	142.65	62.31	78.99	54.87
Georgia	1,893.21	767.92	129.68	490.77	151.87	36.16	35.06	41.58
Kentucky	2,459.45	951.38	248.72	634.58	131.51	62.98	91.60	115.63
Louisiana	2,491.88	860.04	205.27	593.61	250.11	55.50	68.45	171.05
Mississippi	1,995.75	762.50	206.10	463.08	151.39	47.96	49.95	44.28
North Carolina	2,143.96	922.53	211.62	430.95	168.59	40.86	66.01	39.95
South Carolina	2,211.66	852.24	147.14	449.02	268.46	37.11	60.07	66.90
Virginia	1,990.60	773.21	238.58	328.39	223.34	25.63	85.35	75.04
West Virginia	2,425.87	967.55	281.46	603.79	108.77	56.86	94.22	95.09
UNITED STATES	2,404.47	831.34	191.55	614.41	189.10	41.34	83.07	96.75

Note: Per capita amounts are based on population estimates as of July 1.

1. Includes items not shown separately.

2. Computed by Center for Business and Economic Research. Per capita amounts are computed on the basis of figures rounded to nearest thousand.

Source: U.S. Department of Commerce, Bureau of the Census, *State Government Finances: 1992.*

TABLE 15.25–DISTRIBUTION OF FEDERAL FUNDS AND RANK BY STATE, SOUTHEASTERN STATES, 1993

| State | Per capita federal funds ($) | | Federal funds received ($1,000,000) | | | | | |
	Amount	Rank	Total	Grants to state and local governments	Salaries and wages	Direct payments to individuals	Procurement	Other
TENNESSEE	4,663.16	28	23,778	3,925	2,600	12,544	4,285	425
Alabama	5,058.43	14	21,180	3,081	3,085	11,135	3,333	545
Arkansas	4,473.33	32	10,843	1,855	969	6,848	533	637
Florida	5,009.33	16	68,523	7,579	7,351	43,391	8,982	1,220
Georgia	4,357.30	35	30,139	4,408	5,832	14,505	4,670	725
Kentucky	4,433.19	33	16,797	3,041	2,535	9,376	1,461	384
Louisiana	4,684.60	25	20,204	4,817	2,099	9,965	2,601	722
Mississippi	4,948.98	17	13,080	2,285	1,469	6,825	2,014	488
North Carolina	3,917.95	46	27,210	4,498	4,727	15,350	1,868	767
South Carolina	4,492.73	31	16,367	2,521	2,537	8,275	2,734	299
Virginia	6,824.10	3	44,295	2,945	12,346	16,086	11,432	1,487
West Virginia	4,905.62	18	8,928	1,884	756	5,663	463	163

Note: Detail may not add to total due to independent rounding.

Source: U.S. Department of Commerce, Bureau of the Census, *Federal Expenditures by State for Fiscal Year 1993.*

TABLE 15.26—FEDERAL GRANTS TO STATE AND LOCAL GOVERNMENTS, PER CAPITA, BY PROGRAM, SOUTHEASTERN STATES AND UNITED STATES, 1993

[In dollars]

State	Total	Dept. of Agriculture child nutrition programs	Dept. of Education compensatory education for disadvantaged	EPA construction of wastewater treatment works	Medical assistance (Medicaid)	Social services block grant	Family support payments (AFDC)
TENNESSEE	769.72	25.71	26.23	5.82	364.50	8.30	40.52
Alabama	735.90	32.56	32.82	5.38	287.54	10.80	26.48
Arkansas	765.23	35.29	32.51	6.63	322.75	10.66	23.59
Florida	554.04	24.81	21.62	5.61	208.89	11.47	42.99
Georgia	637.32	28.90	26.93	3.52	254.77	10.48	50.62
Kentucky	802.46	29.95	30.77	8.73	342.47	11.01	51.65
Louisiana	1,121.55	43.71	35.91	5.31	656.62	9.38	38.69
Mississippi	864.40	51.43	46.96	6.12	353.01	10.91	31.75
North Carolina	647.62	26.33	23.07	6.13	277.34	10.34	47.48
South Carolina	692.10	31.44	26.92	4.06	332.15	6.74	29.45
Virginia	453.73	14.96	18.79	5.40	141.97	10.47	26.34
West Virginia	1,035.05	28.26	29.97	8.60	504.02	11.59	61.50
UNITED STATES	745.65	24.22	25.14	8.12	289.45	10.59	59.75

TABLE 15.26—FEDERAL GRANTS TO STATE AND LOCAL GOVERNMENTS, PER CAPITA, BY PROGRAM, SOUTHEASTERN STATES AND UNITED STATES, 1993
[In dollars] (Continued)

State	Department of Housing and Urban Development		Department of Labor		Department of Transportation		
	Community development	Housing assistance	Job Training Partnership Act	State employment services	Highway trust fund	Federal Transit Administration	Other
TENNESSEE	9.80	37.91	13.98	8.60	47.94	5.88	115.54
Alabama	11.92	36.91	17.87	9.57	73.40	3.85	186.80
Arkansas	8.63	38.18	14.27	11.71	84.07	3.64	173.32
Florida	9.22	29.60	8.40	8.71	46.06	9.11	127.56
Georgia	9.39	36.38	9.03	8.69	59.21	8.42	130.97
Kentucky	12.78	49.71	16.43	8.46	56.78	4.69	179.02
Louisiana	14.37	37.28	14.41	8.22	68.05	6.74	182.88
Mississippi	12.06	40.68	15.32	9.45	71.91	3.30	211.53
North Carolina	7.68	34.06	12.06	8.71	61.23	3.45	129.73
South Carolina	8.88	32.21	12.41	9.22	58.61	2.56	158.91
Virginia	7.79	37.20	8.63	8.22	34.78	4.31	141.37
West Virginia	9.88	44.14	16.75	10.28	77.68	3.25	209.48
UNITED STATES	12.22	47.59	12.57	13.13	61.70	13.43	167.75

Note: Detail may not add to total due to independent rounding.

Source: U.S. Department of Commerce, Bureau of the Census, *Federal Expenditures by State for Fiscal Year 1993*.

TABLE 15.27--FEDERAL INTERNAL REVENUE COLLECTIONS, SOUTHEASTERN STATES AND
UNITED STATES, 1949-1991, SELECTED FISCAL YEARS [In millions of dollars]

State	1991 Total	1991 Income and employment taxes	1989 Total	1989 Income and employment taxes	1979 Total	1979 Income and employment taxes
TENNESSEE	16,703.2	16,258.3	23,040.9	22,459.6	5,669.7	5,447.1
Alabama	10,241.1	10,029.9	7,838.2	7,667.2	4,130.5	3,948.6
Arkansas	7,118.3	6,874.7	5,754.1	5,575.8	2,018.9	1,939.4
Florida	42,777.7	41,339.1	42,437.4	41,254.0	13,328.6	12,482.9
Georgia	24,832.8	23,461.4	22,764.1	21,683.4	7,314.7	6,735.2
Kentucky	10,195.4	9,409.0	8,850.9	8,299.3	5,272.0	3,928.0
Louisiana	11,217.3	10,598.0	7,662.9	7,319.0	5,486.7	5,334.5
Mississippi	4,745.8	4,595.0	3,430.9	3,326.5	1,755.6	1,702.8
North Carolina	20,385.9	20,015.4	19,198.6	18,668.6	8,936.4	7,427.8
South Carolina	8,793.3	8,621.5	7,768.0	7,593.1	3,030.6	2,959.5
Virginia	23,454.8	22,496.8	18,138.9	17,671.8	7,626.9	6,761.7
West Virginia	3,679.4	3,523.2	3,254.2	3,122.2	1,770.7	1,708.7
UNITED STATES	1,086,851.4	1,044,926.7	1,013,322.1	978,371.7	453,859.1	432,697.8

State	1969 Total	1969 Income and employment taxes	1959 Total	1959 Income and employment taxes	1949 Total	1949 Income and employment taxes
TENNESSEE	1,868.1	1,788.4	644.7	605.4	333.2	295.7
Alabama	1,332.6	1,222.5	534.7	512.6	259.5	236.2
Arkansas	651.8	609.5	197.5	188.6	115.9	105.6
Florida	3,625.6	3,381.7	1,147.3	1,039.3	342.6	286.6
Georgia	2,614.8	2,428.8	888.9	778.7	403.5	322.9
Kentucky	2,541.0	1,314.1	1,541.0	547.3	812.3	282.1
Louisiana	1,639.9	1,542.3	689.2	610.7	357.4	291.8
Mississippi	619.6	574.0	193.1	176.7	100.7	91.6
North Carolina	4,065.6	2,801.4	1,983.7	875.0	1,166.7	423.7
South Carolina	963.1	931.4	287.6	272.6	205.0	191.5
Virginia	2,829.1	2,250.5	1,231.5	843.3	770.3	393.4
West Virginia	630.1	595.6	308.0	287.4	242.7	219.8
UNITED STATES	187,919.3	168,846.7	78,652.1	66,642.2	40,351.4	31,983.3

Note: Collections in various states do not necessarily indicate the actual Federal tax burden on the residents of each state.

Source: Tax Foundation, Inc., *Facts and Figures on Government Finance, 1993.*

TABLE 15.28--FEDERAL INDIVIDUAL INCOME TAX, SOUTHEASTERN STATES AND UNITED STATES, 1991 [Money amounts in thousands of dollars, except as indicated]

State	Number of returns	Adjusted gross income	Salaries and wages	Tax liability	
				Total	Average ($)
TENNESSEE	2,207,814	57,975,796	46,091,675	7,784,122	4,423
Alabama	1,747,049	45,108,672	35,612,143	5,682,313	4,217
Arkansas	984,063	22,981,206	17,465,272	2,790,806	3,676
Florida	6,249,819	177,888,512	120,692,234	25,503,780	5,105
Georgia	2,946,924	84,162,097	67,591,430	10,932,796	4,632
Kentucky	1,538,049	39,331,477	30,448,156	4,932,573	4,002
Louisiana	1,723,112	43,422,532	34,093,712	5,743,196	4,418
Mississippi	1,035,518	22,782,594	18,088,245	2,644,862	3,534
North Carolina	3,093,762	82,314,527	64,598,223	10,191,496	4,072
South Carolina	1,567,377	39,604,857	31,460,452	4,703,324	3,821
Virginia	2,907,900	93,151,332	74,094,085	12,516,503	5,064
West Virginia	699,738	17,540,137	13,401,581	2,165,505	3,878
United States	115,766,796	3,453,028,487	2,659,733,424	473,533,243	5,005

Source: U.S. Department of the Treasury, Internal Revenue Service, *Statistics of Income Bulletin, Fall 1993*.

TABLE 15.29--FEDERAL TAX BURDEN, SOUTHEASTERN STATES AND UNITED STATES, FISCAL YEARS 1987 AND 1992

State	Amount ($1,000,000)		Percent of total burden		Per capita ($)	
	1992	1987	1992	1987	1992	1987[a]
TENNESSEE	17,449	13,141	1.65	1.60	3,473	2,725
Alabama	13,138	10,227	1.24	1.25	3,177	2,515
Arkansas	7,243	5,558	0.68	0.68	3,019	2,355
Florida	55,364	39,348	5.23	4.81	4,105	3,269
Georgia	24,590	17,869	2.32	2.18	3,642	2,893
Kentucky	11,771	9,241	1.11	1.13	3,135	2,466
Louisiana	13,407	12,418	1.27	1.52	3,127	2,770
Mississippi	6,700	5,375	0.63	0.66	2,563	2,031
North Carolina	23,664	17,476	2.23	2.13	3,458	2,732
South Carolina	11,319	8,259	1.07	1.01	3,142	2,406
Virginia	26,931	20,065	2.54	2.45	4,223	3,435
West Virginia	5,231	4,542	0.49	0.55	2,887	2,356
UNITED STATES	1,059,276	818,856	100.00	100.00	4,153	3,365

Note: The burden by state is estimated on the basis of a special formula designed by the Tax Foundation, Inc. Data on federal tax collections by state do not accurately reflect the distribution of the burden.
a. Based on estimates of resident population as of July 1, 1987.
Source: Tax Foundation, Inc., *Facts and Figures on Government Finance, 1993*; and earlier editions.

TABLE 15.30--STATE GENERAL FUND RESOURCES, EXPENDITURES, AND BALANCE,
SOUTHEASTERN STATES, 1991–1993 [In millions of dollars]

State	Resources[1,2]			Expenditures[2]			Balance[3]		
	1993	1992	1991	1993	1992	1991	1993	1992	1991
TENNESSEE	4,568	4,017	3,870	4,528	3,916	3,863	40	101	7
Alabama	3,449	3,405	3,387	3,445	3,400	3,386	4	5	1
Arkansas	2,055	1,935	1,879	2,055	1,935	1,879	0	0	0
Florida	11,901	11,169	11,085	11,901	11,047	10,943	0	123	142
Georgia	8,152	7,421	7,408	8,134	7,403	7,373	18	18	35
Kentucky	4,658	4,595	4,358	4,625	4,546	4,188	34	49	170
Louisiana	4,318	4,426	4,938	4,411	4,426	4,520	93	0	418
Mississippi	2,000	1,945	1,949	1,993	1,925	1,945	7	20	4
North Carolina	8,255	7,818	7,430	8,210	7,652	7,430	45	165	0
South Carolina	3,770	3,404	3,524	3,729	3,396	3,462	41	8	62
Virginia	6,429	6,271	6,331	6,374	6,203	6,331	55	68	0
West Virginia	2,119	2,016	1,977	2,116	1,959	1,888	3	57	89

Note: 1993 data are estimated. General funds exclude special funds earmarked for particular purposes, such as
highway trust funds and federal funds; they support most on-going broad-based state services, and are available
for appropriation to support any governmental activity.
1. Includes funds budgeted, adjustments, and balances from previous year.
2. May or may not include budget stabilization fund transfers, depending on state accounting practices.
3. Resources less expenditures.
Source: U.S. Department of Commerce, Bureau of the Census, *Statistical Abstract of the United States, 1993* from
National Association of State Budget Officers, Washington, DC, National Governors' Association and NASBO,
Fiscal Survey of States, semi-annual (copyright), used by special permission.

Many of the tables in Chapter 16 are from the Tennessee Department of Education's *Annual Statistical Report*, which provides detailed data for counties, school districts, special education, and vocational-technical education. Public library data are available from *Tennessee Public Library Statistics*, a report of the Tennessee State Library and Archives. The Tennessee Higher Education Commission publishes data on public and private institutions of higher education in its annual *Statistical Abstract of Tennessee Higher Education*. Additional information on private institutions of higher education can be obtained from the Tennessee Council of Private Colleges. Because of its interests in the number of persons entering the labor force and the educational level of the work force, Tennessee Department of Employment Security collects and publishes information on graduating high school students each year. In addition to reporting the number of graduates by county, this report gives the number and percentage of seniors continuing their education beyond high school.

The Tennessee Education Association (TEA) publishes an annual series of research bulletins which provide details on economic status, taxing effort and ability, revenue sources, salaries, and employment in education for county, state, and local areas. The National Education Association (NEA) publication, *Estimates of School Statistics*, is a detailed comparison of the 50 states and is the source for many of the southeastern comparisons. The U.S. Department of Education, National Center for Education Statistics, collects data such as enrollments, degrees conferred, current revenues and current expenditures on educational institutions.

The Bureau of the Census, in its decennial censuses, provides data on the educational attainment of the population. The first data were percentages of the illiterate population and number of children attending school. Beginning in 1950, data became available concerning school attendance and number of years of school completed, by sex and race. Tables 16.16 and 16.17 contain information on the educational level of the population in 1990. These "attainment" data are not exactly comparable to the "education" levels reported in earlier censuses. Beginning in 1990, educational attainment refers to highest grade "completed" rather than "attended." The 1990 Census also provides information on educational degrees earned. Other data from the 1980 and 1990 Censuses detail school enrollment for persons 3 years and older by level and public or private school status.

TABLE OF CONTENTS

TABLE OF CONTENTS
(Continued)

TABLE 16.1– NET ENROLLMENT, AVERAGE DAILY MEMBERSHIP, AND AVERAGE DAILY ATTENDANCE IN PUBLIC SCHOOLS, TENNESSEE, 1950–1993, SELECTED SCHOLASTIC YEARS

Year	Net enrollment[1]					Average daily membership	Average daily attendance
	Total	Kindergarten	Elementary (grades 1–8)	Secondary (grades 9–12)	Special education[2]		
1993	906,975	69,680	567,201	249,570	20,524	841,098	786,146
1992	893,272	68,392	560,180	243,741	20,959	827,525	774,596
1991	880,246	68,100	553,241	240,515	18,390	817,793	767,738
1990	858,991	65,934	535,395	239,516	18,146	812,020	761,766
1989	860,004	66,510	530,861	244,946	17,687	816,507	764,354
1988	860,101	66,429	524,432	250,110	19,130	816,678	766,651
1987	855,157	66,060	518,069	251,440	19,588	813,576	766,521
1986	846,823	62,079	517,685	247,284	19,775	808,303	762,225
1985	849,047	63,571	524,175	243,224	18,077	811,232	769,862
1984	854,318	61,568	533,431	242,289	17,030	816,666	774,346
1983	860,708	61,083	539,171	245,465	14,989	821,719	778,321
1982	874,589	57,576	547,925	253,075	16,013	831,854	785,336
1981	889,847	58,647	553,514	260,744	16,942	846,922	797,237
1980	898,997	58,815	561,173	263,785	15,224	857,373	806,696
1979	911,347	59,069	570,384	268,076	13,818	865,509	808,512
1978	918,552	59,642	579,383	265,995	13,532	873,317	819,028
1977	925,184	62,905	581,974	263,407	16,898	877,030	821,698
1976	918,684	59,482	584,922	261,327	12,953	876,322	826,335
1975	913,103	53,245	587,208	256,853	15,797	871,681	823,394
1970	916,862	(X)	645,315	256,661	14,886	880,172	836,010
1965	893,908	(X)	647,175	235,833	10,900	859,198	821,192
1960	810,300	(X)	628,562	181,738	(a)	775,516	735,660
1955	740,933	(X)	590,408	150,525	(a)	n.a.	663,738
1950	659,785	(X)	539,445	120,340	(a)	n.a.	583,126

(X) Not applicable.

n.a. not available.

1. Represents the total number of original entries in public schools; pupils enrolled who change school districts during the school year are counted more than once.

2. Only that portion of students receiving special education who are in the comprehensive development classrooms; the remainder of special education students are included in the regular graded classifications. Prior to 1962, all types of special education were included in the regular graded classifications. Prior to 1976, includes ungraded or unclassified enrollment.

a. Included in regular graded classifications.

Source: Tennessee Department of Education, *Annual Statistical Report, 1993*; and earlier editions.

TABLE 16.2-- NUMBER OF PUPILS IN PROGRAMS OTHER THAN KINDERGARTEN THROUGH
TWELFTH GRADES RUN BY LOCAL BOARDS OF EDUCATION, TENNESSEE,
SCHOLASTIC YEARS 1972-1993

Year	Total	Headstart	Summer school	Adult education	Other
1993	254,103	1,008	44,810	48,394	159,891
1992	123,271	1,160	36,320	49,662	36,129
1991	133,584	846	39,202	44,406	49,130
1990	133,716	675	41,935	38,507	52,599
1989	104,113	445	27,393	32,333	43,942
1988	104,616	404	26,882	29,855	47,475
1987	97,778	448	20,617	24,549	52,164
1986	93,459	1,031	17,946	25,972	48,510
1985	84,730	802	15,485	23,956	44,487
1984	84,363	682	16,629	25,553	41,499
1983	54,664	894	16,737	25,729	11,304
1982	n.a.	n.a.	n.a.	n.a.	n.a.
1981	82,541	1,845	17,605	26,999	36,092
1980	86,870	2,017	24,501	26,277	34,075
1979	77,372	1,842	20,449	21,964	33,117
1978	96,959	6,497	20,812	64,229	5,421
1977	116,492	1,693	27,427	73,358	14,014
1976	100,261	1,945	23,772	56,719	17,825
1975	92,150	6,837	21,683	55,785	7,845
1974	84,850	2,985	24,529	48,125	9,211
1973	102,291	6,052	27,872	56,143	12,224
1972	101,322	7,421	36,113	41,426	16,362

n.a. not available.
Source: Tennessee Department of Education, *Annual Statistical Report, 1993*, and earlier editions.

TABLE 16.3-- SCHOOL ENROLLMENT, BY TYPE OF SCHOOL, URBAN AND RURAL AREAS,
TENNESSEE, 1980 AND 1990

	Total		Urban		Rural	
	1990	1980	1990	1980	1990	1980
Persons 3 years old and over enrolled in school	1,171,640	1,217,290	739,543	765,575	432,097	451,715
Preprimary[1]	70,274	107,995	47,420	69,981	22,854	38,014
Public	44,693	72,939	28,204	42,576	16,489	30,363
Percent public	63.6	67.5	59.5	60.8	72.1	79.9
Elementary and High School	821,881	892,793	358,645	518,015	343,417	374,778
Public	762,103	822,793	316,775	460,670	329,269	362,123
Percent public	92.7	92.2	88.3	88.9	95.9	96.6
College	279,485	216,502	213,659	177,579	65,826	38,923
Public	216,855	172,171	162,650	139,547	54,205	32,624
Percent public	77.6	79.5	76.1	78.6	82.3	83.8

Note: Percentages were computed by the Center for Business and Economic Research.

1. Includes Kindergarten.

Source: U.S. Department of Commerce, Bureau of the Census, *Census of Population, General Social and Economic Characteristics, Tennessee, 1980 and 1990.*

TABLE 16.4-- TOTAL AND AVERAGE ANNUAL EXPENDITURES IN PUBLIC SCHOOL SYSTEMS, TENNESSEE, 1930-1993, SELECTED FISCAL YEARS

Year	Total expenditures ($1,000)	Current expenditures ($1,000)		Number of pupils in ADA [2]	Average expenditures per pupil in ADA [2] ($)		
		Total [1]	Operating		Total	Current Total [1]	Operating
1993	3,733,577	3,170,255	3,107,339	786,146	4,749.22	4,032.65	3,952.62
1992	3,112,634	2,890,606	2,673,481	774,596	4,018.40	3,731.76	3,451.45
1991	3,000,507	2,827,839	2,578,741	767,738	3,908.24	3,683.34	3,358.88
1990	2,841,756	2,680,081	2,443,076	761,766	3,730.48	3,518.25	3,207.12
1989	2,658,587	2,525,618	2,297,957	764,354	3,478.21	3,304.25	3,006.40
1988	2,489,574	2,370,392	2,130,743	766,651	3,247.34	3,091.88	2,779.29
1987	2,312,393	2,198,866	1,963,035	766,521	3,016.74	2,868.63	2,560.97
1986	2,140,542	2,035,219	1,762,328	762,225	2,808.28	2,670.10	2,312.08
1985	1,958,473	1,855,909	1,625,030	769,862	2,543.93	2,410.70	2,110.81
1984	1,747,960	1,657,646	1,451,590	774,346	2,257.34	2,140.70	1,874.60
1983	1,658,544	1,602,577	1,399,623	778,321	2,130.92	2,059.01	1,798.26
1982	1,530,144	1,522,227	1,319,432	785,336	1,948.39	1,938.31	1,680.09
1981	1,539,979	1,462,835	1,275,764	797,237	1,931.65	1,834.89	1,600.23
1980	1,391,576	1,322,072	1,176,179	806,696	1,725.03	1,638.87	1,458.02
1979	1,247,582	1,194,166	1,056,241	808,512	1,543.06	1,476.99	1,307.50
1978	1,133,315	1,094,249	960,126	819,028	1,383.73	1,336.03	1,172.27
1977	1,018,612	993,196	875,767	821,698	1,239.64	1,208.71	1,065.80
1976	959,114	877,524	783,168	826,335	1,160.68	1,061.95	947.76
1975	878,926	789,868	727,404	823,394	1,067.44	959.28	883.42
1974	735,743	671,882	611,881	817,902	899.55	821.47	748.11
1973	660,292	616,726	555,301	832,087	793.54	741.18	667.36
1972	642,122	578,766	516,091	846,190	758.84	683.97	609.90
1971	598,667	519,937	472,882	849,882	704.41	611.78	556.41
1970	509,164	472,440	427,920	836,010	609.04	565.11	511.86
1969	470,809	421,460	376,960	835,076	563.79	504.70	451.41
1968	430,620	382,884	342,084	830,568	518.46	460.99	411.87
1967	395,855	337,531	312,581	828,091	478.03	407.60	377.47
1965	275,555	249,733	231,633	821,192	335.55	304.11	282.07
1960	205,446	n.a.	159,885	735,660	279.27	n.a.	217.34
1955	130,794	n.a.	103,965	663,738	196.06	n.a.	156.64
1950	109,680	n.a.	78,715	583,126	188.09	n.a.	134.99
1945	36,574	n.a.	34,773	498,305	73.40	n.a.	69.78
1940	29,035	n.a.	23,371	536,717	54.10	n.a.	43.54
1935	20,257	n.a.	17,189	521,079	38.88	n.a.	32.99
1930	23,837	n.a.	20,614	481,962	49.46	n.a.	42.77

Note: Averages computed by the Center for Business and Economic Research when not available in the source.
n.a. not available.

1. Beginning in 1965 the Department of Education calculated a second series of current expenditures including administration of State Department of Education, retirement of teachers, and value of commodities distributed by the U.S. Department of Agriculture.
2. Average daily attendance in regular classes and special education classes.
Source: Tennessee Department of Education, *Annual Statistical Report, 1993*, and earlier editions.

EDUCATION

TABLE 16.5-- NUMBER OF TEACHERS EMPLOYED IN PUBLIC SCHOOL SYSTEMS, BY LEVEL OF
TRAINING, TENNESSEE, SCHOLASTIC YEARS, 1950-1993, SELECTED YEARS

Year	Total	Ph.D. degree	Ed.S. degree	Master's degree [1]	Bachelor's degree	3 years college	2 years college	1 year college or less
1993	53,883	659	1,298	26,674	24,527	10	15	700
1992	50,732	641	1,228	25,480	22,664	14	11	694
1991	50,217	616	1,164	24,880	22,804	14	18	721
1990	50,009	601	1,136	24,370	23,150	21	16	715
1989	48,863	581	1,087	23,268	23,169	28	18	712
1988	49,920	538	1,002	22,920	23,375	38	13	34
1987	48,965	508	949	21,926	25,428	27	16	111
1986	48,645	470	926	21,653	25,430	39	20	107
1985	47,487	439	874	20,911	25,118	55	22	68
1984	47,022	401	846	20,283	25,318	65	34	75
1983	46,691	378	799	19,780	25,545	69	40	80
1982	47,494	365	751	19,465	26,661	118	57	77
1981	49,021	340	709	19,329	28,311	165	81	86
1980	49,133	289	619	18,560	29,298	217	112	38
1979	48,479	253	534	17,613	29,599	288	117	75
1978	48,302	217	466	16,897	30,142	364	155	61
1977	47,569	186	386	15,918	30,289	472	216	102
1976	46,483	144	267	14,626	30,450	603	295	98
1975	45,942	97	186	13,361	31,008	795	405	90
1974	44,161	77	116	11,969	30,296	1,064	534	105
1973	43,124	67	93	11,007	29,771	1,285	728	173
1972	41,942	62	(X)	10,030	29,219	1,552	975	104
1971	41,531	36	(X)	9,084	29,115	1,957	1,163	176
1970	40,458	29	(X)	8,502	28,385	2,023	1,331	188
1969	39,164	28	(X)	7,860	27,278	2,253	1,485	260
1968	38,016	29	(X)	7,612	26,204	2,230	1,698	243
1967	36,111	33	(X)	7,341	24,624	2,185	1,708	220
1966	35,123	28	(X)	7,015	23,363	2,666	1,877	174
1965	34,231	27	(X)	6,954	22,632	2,387	2,028	203
1964	33,393	27	(X)	6,636	21,744	2,501	2,239	246
1963	32,402	26	(X)	6,306	20,744	2,567	2,483	276
1962	31,635	21	(X)	6,036	19,903	2,590	2,724	361
1961	30,907	25	(X)	5,808	19,028	2,642	2,967	437
1960	29,936	34	(X)	5,358	18,076	2,685	3,162	621
1959	29,092	29	(X)	5,034	17,265	2,607	3,412	745
1958	28,252	23	(X)	4,788	16,172	2,724	3,593	952
1957	27,899	17	(X)	4,551	15,412	2,764	3,933	1,222
1956	27,088	20	(X)	4,112	14,689	2,775	4,265	1,227
1955	26,363	16	(X)	3,726	14,019	2,730	4,582	1,290
1950	23,067	5	(X)	1,787	9,886	2,394	5,795	3,200

(X) Not applicable.

1. Includes master's degree plus 45 hours.

Source: Tennessee Department of Education, *Annual Statistical Report, 1993*, and earlier editions.

TABLE 16.6-- NUMBER OF TEACHERS EMPLOYED IN PUBLIC SCHOOL SYSTEMS, BY SEX,
TENNESSEE, 1930–1993, SELECTED SCHOLASTIC YEARS

Year	Total	Male	Female
1993	53,883	12,561	41,322
1992	50,732	11,992	38,740
1991	50,217	12,017	38,200
1990	50,009	12,268	37,741
1989	48,863	12,122	36,741
1988	49,920	12,252	37,668
1987	48,965	12,318	36,647
1986	48,645	12,320	36,325
1985	47,487	12,463	35,024
1984	47,022	12,370	34,652
1983	46,691	12,406	34,285
1982	47,494	12,647	34,847
1981	49,021	13,242	35,779
1980	49,133	13,277	35,856
1979	48,479	13,179	35,300
1978	48,302	13,304	34,998
1977	47,569	13,196	34,373
1976	46,483	12,679	33,804
1975	45,942	12,269	33,673
1974	44,161	11,898	32,263
1973	43,124	11,815	31,309
1972	41,942	11,157	30,785
1971	41,531	10,890	30,641
1970	40,458	10,452	30,006
1969	39,164	9,885	29,279
1968	38,016	9,414	28,602
1967	36,111	8,843	27,268
1966	35,123	8,763	26,360
1965	34,231	8,591	25,640
1964	33,393	8,307	25,086
1963	32,402	7,967	24,435
1962	31,635	7,751	23,884
1961	30,907	7,415	23,492
1960	29,936	7,118	22,818
1959	29,092	6,725	22,367
1958	28,252	6,353	21,899
1957	27,899	6,121	21,778
1956	27,088	5,947	21,141
1955	26,363	5,719	20,644
1954	25,251	5,410	19,841
1953	24,532	5,349	19,183
1952	24,106	5,234	18,872
1951	23,897	5,252	18,645
1950	23,067	4,734	18,333
1945	20,562	2,916	17,646
1940	20,664	5,353	15,311
1935	19,592	4,869	14,723
1930	19,058	4,050	15,008

Source: Tennessee Department of Education, *Annual Statistical Report, 1993*, and earlier editions.

TABLE 16.7-- AVERAGE ANNUAL SALARIES IN PUBLIC SCHOOL SYSTEMS, TENNESSEE, 1956–1993,
        SCHOLASTIC YEARS

Year	Average, all salaries
1993	$30,062.77
1992	29,726.06
1991	29,370.73
1990	27,949.00
1989	26,512.00
1988	24,535.86
1987	23,323.46
1986	21,874.02
1985	20,812.05
1984	18,243.65
1983	17,697.58
1982	16,581.52
1981	15,395.82
1980	14,072.70
1979	13,158.45
1978	12,272.02
1977	11,338.44
1976	10,326.93
1975	9,949.37
1974	9,028.70
1973	8,470.07
1972	8,153.89
1971	7,694.73
1970	7,187.29
1969	6,621.43
1968	6,145.71
1967	5,755.06
1966	5,216.57
1965	4,941.49
1964	4,769.39
1963	4,329.10
1962	4,151.47
1961	4,136.85
1960	3,818.85
1959	3,538.32
1958	3,427.45
1957	3,174.33
1956	3,051.50

Note: After 1980, refers to instructional personnel, which includes teachers, principals, supervisors, guidance
    counselors, attendance teachers, librarians and psychological personnel.

Source: Tennessee Department of Education, *Annual Statistical Report, 1993*, and earlier editions.

TABLE 16.8-- SELECTED PUBLIC LIBRARY STATISTICS, METROPOLITAN AND CITY LIBRARIES
AND REGIONAL LIBRARY CENTERS, FISCAL YEAR 1990

Location and name of library or regional library center	Total personnel	Bookstock Local	Regional	Total circulation	Total expenditures
Metropolitan and independent city libraries	816	3,522,245	0	7,397,513	27,300,529
Chattanooga, Chattanooga-Hamilton County Bicentennial Library	93	395,307	0	790,676	$3,071,191
East Ridge	3	18,573	0	18,949	452,845
Kingsport, Kingsport Public Library	14	122,876	0	234,736	457,733
Knoxville, Knox County Public Library	131	656,857	0	1,637,705	3,968,832
Memphis, Memphis Public Library and Information Center	353	1,500,000	0	2,587,331	11,410,752
Nashville, Public Library of Nashville and Davidson County	203	702,595	0	1,820,188	7,258,790
Oak Ridge, Oak Ridge Public Library	17	106,037	0	274,928	598,136
Signal Mountain	2	20,000	0	33,000	82,250
Regional centers[1]	573	2,065,939	2,394,508	9,396,839	15,446,783
Athens, Fort Loudoun Regional Library System	68	161,419	268,503	1,132,813	1,703,214
Clarksville, Warioto Regional Library System	51	182,801	139,546	826,486	1,306,209
Clinton, Clinch-Powell Regional Library System	22	24,913	201,650	376,680	713,790
Columbia, Blue Grass Regional Library System	69	207,667	151,512	1,117,787	1,693,702
Cookeville, Upper Cumberland Regional Library System	37	138,272	96,920	595,376	872,297
Halls, Forked Deer Regional Library System	25	103,189	263,749	421,180	707,223
Jackson, Shiloh Regional Library System	41	201,600	223,871	524,087	1,328,940
Johnson City, Watauga Regional Library System	83	285,193	185,723	1,104,835	2,244,253
Martin, Reelfoot Regional Library System	39	197,612	134,828	815,745	1,083,520
Morristown, Nolichucky Regional Library System	36	138,942	173,136	694,095	1,162,333
Murfreesboro, Highland Rim Regional Library System	71	328,731	439,089	1,237,139	1,796,812
Sparta, Caney Fork Regional Library System	31	95,600	115,981	550,616	834,490

1. Statistics include local libraries in each region.
Source: Tennessee State Library and Archives, *Tennessee Public Library Statistics, July 1, 1989-June 30, 1990.*

FIGURE 16.1
Public Higher Educational Institutions in Tennessee

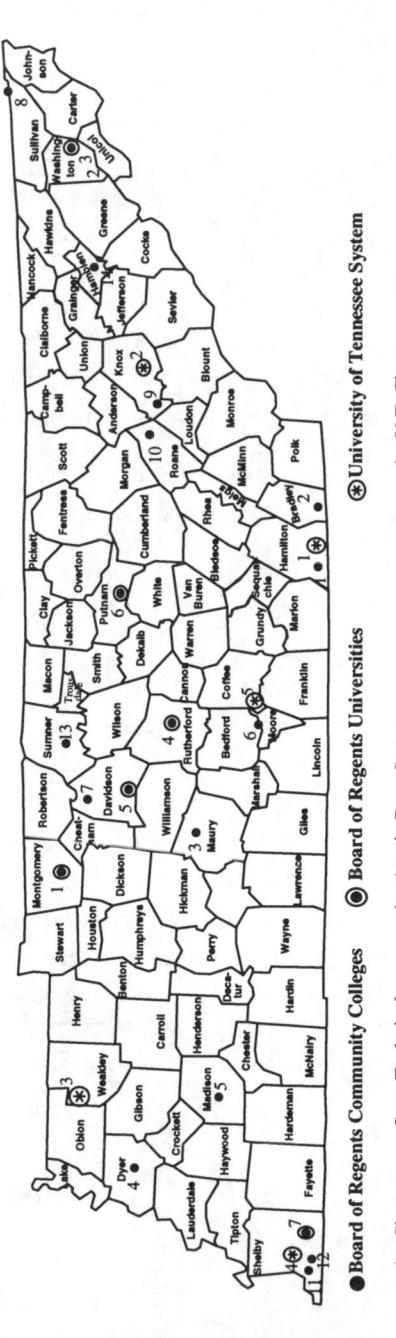

● **Board of Regents Community Colleges**

1 Chattanooga State Technical
2 Cleveland State
3 Columbia State
4 Dyersburg State
5 Jackson State
6 Motlow State
7 Nashville State Technical
8 Northeast State Technica
9 Pellissippi State Technical
10 Roane State
11 Shelby State
12 State Technical, Memphis
13 Volunteer State
14 Walters State

● **Board of Regents Universities**

1 Austin Peay State
2 East Tennessee State
3 East Tennessee State University, Medical
4 Middle Tennessee State
5 Tennessee State
6 Tennessee Technological
7 University of Memphis

✳ **University of Tennessee System**

1 U.T. Chattanooga
2 U.T. Knoxville
3 U.T. Martin
4 U.T. Center for Health Sciences
5 U.T. Space Institute

Source: Tennessee Higher Education Commission, *Statistical Abstract of Tennessee Higher Education, 1991-92.*

TABLE 16.9-- FALL ENROLLMENT IN STATE INSTITUTIONS OF HIGHER EDUCATION, TENNESSEE,
1989-1991

Institution	1991 Headcount enrollment	1991 Full-time equated enrollment[1]	1990 Headcount enrollment	1990 Full-time equated enrollment[1]	1989 Headcount enrollment	1989 Full-time equated enrollment[1]
Board of Regents' Universities	71,011	56,862	69,021	55,195	67,877	54,264
Austin Peay State	7,670	5,440	6,347	4,629	6,292	4,630
East Tennessee State	11,711	9,547	11,358	9,218	11,185	9,066
Memphis State	20,454	15,421	20,688	15,610	20,613	15,532
Middle Tennessee State	15,673	13,346	14,865	12,751	14,136	12,151
Tennessee State	7,405	5,802	7,393	5,690	7,362	5,805
Tennessee Technological	7,863	7,071	8,134	7,297	8,063	7,080
East Tennessee State-Medical	235	235	236	(X)	226	(X)
The University of Tennessee System	41,492	34,935	40,928	32,352	39,911	31,619
U.T. Chattanooga	7,888	6,216	7,725	6,000	7,564	5,850
U.T. Knoxville	25,817	21,609	25,579	21,094	25,187	20,885
U.T. Martin	5,479	5,210	5,363	5,055	5,088	4,744
U.T. Center for Health Sciences, Memphis	1,859	1,716	1,785	(X)	1,747	(X)
U.T. Space Institute	449	184	476	203	325	140
Two-Year Institutions	71,315	43,739	64,467	38,641	58,761	34,566
Chattanooga State	8,395	5,107	7,793	4,660	7,412	4,243
Cleveland State	3,306	2,137	3,315	2,052	3,098	1,860
Columbia State	3,527	2,177	3,402	2,045	3,053	1,821
Dyersburg State	2,112	1,357	1,993	1,230	1,851	1,114
Jackson State	3,332	2,159	3,252	2,035	3,010	1,850
Motlow State	3,033	2,013	2,782	1,794	2,544	1,574
Nashville State Tech	6,130	2,743	5,974	2,632	5,586	2,436
Northeast State	3,133	2,058	2,787	1,804	2,228	1,399
Pellissippi	7,236	4,818	5,983	4,022	4,702	3,145
Roane State	5,269	3,589	4,928	3,376	4,319	3,044
Shelby State	6,069	4,068	4,763	2,946	4,216	2,845
State Tech Memphis	10,010	5,110	8,768	4,526	8,852	4,353
Volunteer State	4,721	3,046	4,160	2,585	3,670	2,246
Walters State	5,042	3,357	4,567	2,934	4,220	2,636

(X) Not applicable.

1. Full-time equated enrollment is the total number of degree credits taken by undergraduate students divided by 15; for graduate/professional, divided by 12. Enrollments in medical schools are not included before 1991.

Source: Tennessee Higher Education Commission, *Statistical Abstract of Tennessee Higher Education, 1991–92.*

TABLE 16.10–NUMBER OF DEGREES CONFERRED BY STATE INSTITUTIONS OF HIGHER
EDUCATION, BY TYPE OF DEGREE, TENNESSEE, SCHOLASTIC YEAR 1991

Institution and location	Bachelor's degrees	Master's degrees	Ed.S. or education specialist degrees	Professional degrees	Doctoral degrees
U.T. Chattanooga	926	243	0	0	0
U.T. Knoxville	3,168	1,103	11	158	214
U.T. Martin	649	73	0	0	0
U.T. Memphis	149	32	0	279	12
Austin Peay State University, Clarksville	568	111	0	0	0
East Tennessee State University, Johnson City	1,204	318	1	56	11
Middle Tennessee State University, Murfreesboro	1,703	291	20	0	16
Tennessee State University, Nashville	517	181	8	0	27
Tennessee Technological University, Cookeville	1,029	185	35	0	4
University of Memphis	1,859	802	7	131	81

Note: Excludes duplicates for double majors.
Source: Tennessee Higher Education Commission, *Statistical Abstract of Tennessee Higher Education, 1991–92.*

FIGURE 16.2
State Area Vocational Technical Schools

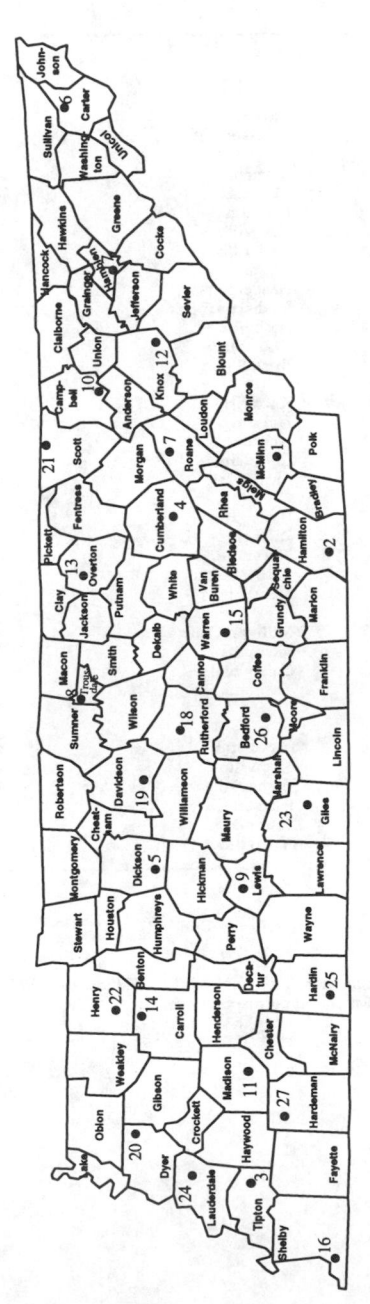

● **Vocational-Technical Schools**

1	Athens	8	Hartsville	15	McMinnville
2	Chattanooga	9	Hohenwald	16	Memphis
3	Covington	10	Jacksboro	17	Morristown
4	Crossville	11	Jackson	18	Murfreesboro
5	Dickson	12	Knoxville	19	Nashville
6	Elizabethton	13	Livingston	20	Newbern
7	Harriman	14	McKenzie	21	Oneida

22	Paris
23	Pulaski
24	Ripley
25	Savannah
26	Shelbyville
27	Whiteville

Source: Tennessee Higher Education Commission, *Statistical Abstract of Tennessee Higher Education, 1991-92.*

TABLE 16.11--PRIVATE INSTITUTIONS OF HIGHER EDUCATION, TENNESSEE, 1992

Institution	Location	Controlling body
Aquinas Junior College[1]	Nashville	Roman Catholic
Belmont College	Nashville	Southern Baptist
Bethel College	McKenzie	Cumberland Presbyterian
Bryan (Wm. Jennings) College	Dayton	Independent
Carson-Newman College	Jefferson City	Southern Baptist
Christian Brothers University	Memphis	Roman Catholic
Crichton College	Memphis	Independent
Cumberland University	Lebanon	Independent
David Lipscomb University	Nashville	Church of Christ
Fisk University	Nashville	Independent
Freed-Hardeman University	Henderson	Church of Christ
Hiwassee College[1]	Madisonville	United Methodist
John A. Gupton College[2]	Nashville	Independent
Johnson Bible College	Knoxville	Christian
King College	Bristol	Presbyterian
Knoxville College	Knoxville	Presbyterian
Lambuth College	Jackson	United Methodist
Lane College	Jackson	United Methodist
Lee College	Cleveland	Church of God
LeMoyne-Owen College	Memphis	United Church of Christ
Lincoln Memorial University	Harrogate	Independent
Martin College[1]	Pulaski	United Methodist
Maryville College	Maryville	Presbyterian
Meharry Medical College	Nashville	Independent
Memphis College of Arts	Memphis	Independent
Milligan College	Milligan College	Christian
Rhodes College[3]	Memphis	Presbyterian
Southern College[4]	Collegedale	Seventh Day Adventist
Southern College of Optometry[2]	Memphis	Independent
Tennessee Wesleyan College	Athens	United Methodist
Tomlinson College	Cleveland	Church of God
Trevecca Nazarene College	Nashville	Church of the Nazarene
Tusculum College	Greeneville	Presbyterian
Union University	Jackson	Southern Baptist
University of the South	Sewanee	Episcopal
Vanderbilt University	Nashville	Independent

1. Junior college.

2. Private professional schools.

3. Formerly Southwestern at Memphis.

4. Formerly Southern Missionary College.

Source: Tennessee Higher Education Commission, *Statistical Abstract of Tennessee Higher Education, 1991–92*; and Tennessee Council of Private Colleges, direct correspondence.

TABLE 16.12--FALL ENROLLMENT IN PRIVATE INSTITUTIONS OF HIGHER EDUCATION, TENNESSEE, 1988–1991

Institution	Headcount				Full-time equivalent[1]			
	1991	1990	1989	1988	1991	1990	1989	1988
TOTAL	45,233	44,454	44,045	43,219	40,621	40,126	39,487	39,276
Aquinas	400	399	440	443	282	279	324	284
Belmont	2,821	2,812	2,706	2,580	2,279	2,175	2,167	2,104
Bethel	581	613	674	596	457	462	531	486
Bryan	568	502	551	517	483	479	485	460
Carson-Newman	2,118	2,110	2,016	1,974	1,991	1,956	1,939	1,870
Christian Brothers	1,730	1,765	1,774	1,798	1,391	1,349	1,409	1,542
Crichton[2]	322	n.a.	n.a.	n.a.	256	n.a.	n.a.	n.a.
Cumberland	775	691	632	645	585	542	473	415
David Lipscomb	2,244	2,399	2,542	2,330	2,062	2,479	2,303	2,208
Fisk	838	912	891	774	868	962	936	786
Freed-Hardeman	1,247	1,194	1,174	1,169	1,241	1,176	1,181	1,154
Hiwassee	494	522	542	584	438	464	529	503
John A. Gupton	49	44	50	55	41	41	48	56
Johnson Bible	474	458	434	430	455	433	405	419
King	543	535	595	589	526	502	565	632
Knoxville[3]	1,177	1,266	1,225	1,310	1,105	1,242	1,134	1,199
Lambuth	1,040	819	804	767	859	702	728	687
Lane	562	530	526	541	542	498	500	514
Lee	1,827	1,740	1,645	1,535	1,751	1,679	1,612	1,483
LeMoyne-Owen	973	1,067	1,103	1,130	868	1,009	963	1,020
Lincoln Memorial	1,859	1,819	1,780	1,582	1,360	1,387	1,357	1,315
Martin	395	390	376	330	406	334	342	319
Maryville	827	841	856	787	698	713	729	648
Meharry Medical	791	790	751	683	791	790	751	683
Memphis College of Arts	263	272	257	254	236	247	232	225
Milligan	764	811	760	658	720	771	741	636
Morristown[3]	(X)	(X)	(X)	(X)	(X)	(X)	(X)	(X)
Rhodes	1,429	1,407	1,386	1,346	1,345	1,314	1,288	1,293
Southern	1,532	1,534	1,526	1,443	1,340	1,360	1,320	1,208
Southern College of Optometry	382	345	364	382	394	373	384	407
Tennessee Wesleyan	631	605	601	600	525	519	518	510
Tomlinson	207	243	228	248	220	252	246	255
Trevecca Nazarene	1,534	1,795	1,761	1,977	1,152	1,232	1,257	1,378
Tusculum	812	718	659	953	745	651	594	1,252
Union	2,262	2,106	2,211	2,017	1,886	1,748	1,787	1,636
University of the South	1,181	1,164	1,146	1,171	1,170	1,233	1,121	1,160
Vanderbilt	9,581	9,236	9,059	9,021	9,153	8,773	8,589	8,529

Note: Scarritt College excluded as it does not report to the Higher Education Commission.

n.a. not available.

(X) not applicable.

1. Represents the total number of degree credits taken by undergraduates divided by 15; for graduates the total is divided by 12.

2. Crichton College became a member of the Tennessee Independent Colleges and Universities in 1991.

3. Morristown College merged with Knoxville College in 1988.

Source: Tennessee Higher Education Commission, *Statistical Abstract of Tennessee Higher Education, 1991–92.*

EDUCATION

TABLE 16.13-SCHOOL ENROLLMENT BY TYPE OF SCHOOL, TENNESSEE AND COUNTIES, 1990

County	Preprimary School		Elementary/High School		College		Not enrolled in school
	Public	Private	Public	Private	Public	Private	
Anderson	877	258	10,875	323	2,749	336	50,416
Bedford	267	53	5,365	139	782	60	22,526
Benton	112	30	2,331	91	262	62	11,188
Bledsoe	90	6	1,570	39	204	79	7,320
Blount	694	289	13,624	296	2,998	1,028	63,875
Bradley	534	430	11,693	555	2,788	1,848	53,060
Campbell	354	19	6,057	104	708	257	26,227
Cannon	67	11	1,767	44	302	32	7,818
Carroll	243	40	4,553	80	733	336	20,595
Carter	506	177	7,554	105	1,741	809	38,884
Cheatham	149	90	4,731	339	560	252	19,704
Chester	56	21	1,894	102	305	1,049	8,874
Claiborne	250	22	4,609	209	491	597	19,008
Clay	87	2	1,226	2	193	52	5,468
Cocke	201	48	4,853	54	655	81	22,390
Coffee	367	145	6,834	251	1,395	128	29,560
Crockett	166	24	2,136	38	254	15	10,313
Cumberland	338	82	5,469	169	935	134	26,281
Davidson	3,791	3,730	62,830	12,652	20,092	18,325	367,616
Decatur	71	6	1,647	41	202	39	8,114
De Kalb	153	12	2,376	79	340	28	10,854
Dickson	395	126	6,246	123	733	169	25,718
Dyer	378	91	6,003	69	1,269	151	25,560
Fayette	162	111	4,462	777	652	180	18,163
Fentress	245	3	2,541	28	459	43	10,828
Franklin	248	164	5,740	273	1,023	1,174	24,836
Gibson	576	66	7,367	193	1,272	278	34,913
Giles	288	79	4,295	130	599	374	19,037
Grainger	132	24	2,880	28	379	22	13,059
Greene	489	159	8,440	303	1,590	383	42,636
Grundy	151	9	2,454	126	347	28	9,816
Hamblen	342	198	7,952	275	1,752	381	37,678
Hamilton	2,529	2,118	39,792	6,762	14,555	4,225	204,312
Hancock	99	0	1,165	5	110	17	5,117
Hardeman	143	54	4,435	95	728	123	16,828
Hardin	162	36	3,746	83	507	65	17,151
Hawkins	431	64	7,121	278	1,222	115	33,773
Haywood	218	27	4,054	41	505	74	13,738
Henderson	175	16	3,745	70	613	83	16,453
Henry	306	60	4,336	156	678	115	21,363
Hickman	70	35	2,644	97	411	76	12,777
Houston	69	7	1,209	26	108	25	5,352
Humphreys	122	59	2,846	80	371	72	11,613
Jackson	86	0	1,534	15	287	27	7,025
Jefferson	162	33	4,885	80	972	1,603	24,329
Johnson	118	12	2,204	56	249	37	10,694
Knox	3,193	2,139	46,610	3,255	28,712	2,997	235,993
Lake	98	11	1,186	22	218	10	5,359
Lauderdale	219	56	4,390	11	590	38	17,179
Lawrence	442	78	5,716	365	900	164	26,106
Lewis	145	39	1,616	94	205	14	6,810
Lincoln	236	78	4,682	74	864	104	20,971

TABLE 16.13–SCHOOL ENROLLMENT BY TYPE OF SCHOOL, TENNESSEE AND COUNTIES, 1990 (Continued)

County	Preprimary School		Elementary/High School		College		Not enrolled in school
	Public	Private	Public	Private	Public	Private	
Loudon	176	94	4,813	221	836	121	23,877
McMinn	320	60	6,873	103	1,025	435	32,013
McNairy	182	51	3,795	110	476	53	16,921
Macon	176	18	2,757	9	240	46	11,996
Madison	912	394	12,757	1,168	2,513	2,325	54,648
Marion	193	58	4,534	105	668	55	18,265
Marshall	156	28	3,790	52	647	52	16,032
Maury	671	237	9,066	549	1,809	251	39,991
Meigs	20	24	1,464	37	212	17	5,975
Monroe	169	35	5,541	64	744	481	22,359
Montgomery	1,134	612	16,085	508	7,176	735	68,789
Moore	20	24	867	11	224	6	3,392
Morgan	221	10	3,124	121	639	155	12,383
Obion	353	112	5,640	26	962	58	23,453
Overton	177	45	2,937	92	390	29	13,408
Perry	52	0	1,063	49	145	13	5,019
Pickett	38	0	767	10	99	4	3,497
Polk	76	32	2,350	53	320	35	10,254
Putnam	572	288	7,465	71	6,253	172	34,821
Rhea	135	11	4,333	154	492	532	17,817
Roane	438	126	7,560	356	2,148	192	34,677
Robertson	430	206	7,138	406	978	133	30,171
Rutherford	1,556	705	20,033	838	10,953	662	78,401
Scott	143	24	3,833	38	578	89	12,888
Sequatchie	58	24	1,541	61	168	52	6,586
Sevier	413	145	8,386	292	1,175	229	38,616
Shelby	7,808	6,664	131,150	17,515	45,353	11,851	565,664
Smith	142	9	2,409	9	362	59	10,612
Stewart	62	2	1,544	5	236	31	7,340
Sullivan	1,208	934	21,546	1,131	5,047	1,106	107,794
Sumner	1,308	649	18,159	1,247	3,276	712	73,681
Tipton	365	188	7,534	189	1,021	152	26,208
Trousdale	60	2	983	27	131	36	4,483
Unicoi	64	6	2,728	6	529	41	12,661
Union	106	15	2,494	25	270	88	10,057
Van Buren	20	7	855	24	88	12	3,643
Warren	283	70	5,345	218	871	120	24,847
Washington	666	476	13,424	361	7,785	511	65,942
Wayne	96	9	2,391	18	244	41	10,569
Weakley	267	69	4,728	36	3,657	166	21,890
White	155	48	3,247	67	407	50	15,408
Williamson	877	1,189	13,390	2,558	2,168	1,199	56,353
Wilson	613	434	11,374	1,136	1,971	809	48,425
TENNESSEE	44,693	25,581	762,103	59,778	216,855	62,630	3,507,104

Source: U.S. Department of Commerce, Bureau of the Census, *Census of Population and Housing, 1990: Summary Tape File 3A, Tennessee.*

FIGURE 16.3
Expenditures per Pupil in Average Daily Attendance in Tennessee County School Districts, Scholastic Year 1992
(Tennessee average = $3,732)

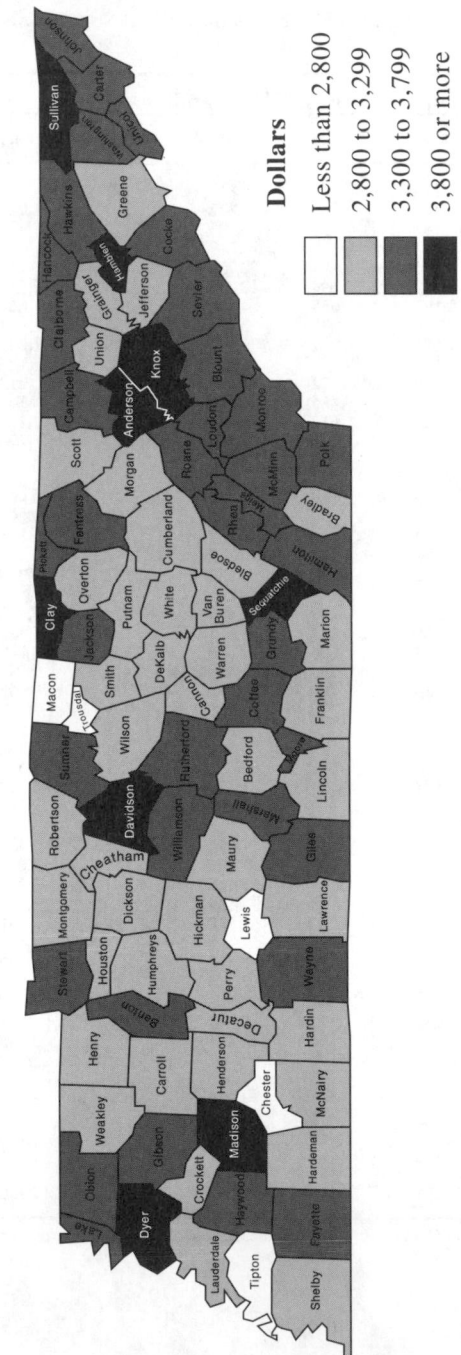

Dollars

- Less than 2,800
- 2,800 to 3,299
- 3,300 to 3,799
- 3,800 or more

Note: For city school district per capita expenditures, see Table 16.14.

*Per pupil expenditures for the highest school district (or special school district) within the county were used for Carroll and Gibson counties. They include special school systems.

Source: Tennessee Department of Education, Annual Statistical Report, 1992.

TABLE 16.14--SELECTED PUBLIC SCHOOL STATISTICS, COUNTY AND CITY SCHOOL DISTRICTS,
SCHOLASTIC YEAR 1992

County and local district	Net enrollment[1]	Average daily attendance	Number of teachers employed	Number of public schools	Total current expenditures ($1,000)	Expenditure per pupil in ADA[2] ($)
Anderson	7,159	6,116	442	16	25,164	4,115
Clinton	1,251	1,062	76	3	3,984	3,751
Oak Ridge	4,827	4,370	354	8	24,200	5,538
Bedford	5,865	5,282	321	9	16,323	3,090
Benton	2,640	2,339	157	6	7,914	3,383
Bledsoe	1,723	1,411	85	4	4,333	3,071
Blount	10,641	8,974	535	16	31,474	3,507
Alcoa	1,515	1,422	106	3	6,930	4,874
Maryville	3,728	3,465	234	5	14,404	4,157
Bradley	9,698	8,176	519	16	26,587	3,252
Cleveland	4,628	4,010	284	8	15,332	3,823
Campbell	6,761	5,770	424	17	20,580	3,567
Cannon	1,987	1,701	115	7	5,070	2,981
Carroll	0	0	16	2	1,578	0
Hollow Rock-Bruceton[3]	852	747	49	2	2,175	2,912
Huntingdon[3]	1,446	1,365	89	3	4,312	3,159
McKenzie[3]	1,506	1,337	82	3	3,652	2,731
South Carroll[3]	422	372	24	1	1,045	2,809
West Carroll[3]	1,207	1,019	65	3	3,157	3,098
Carter	6,815	5,638	405	16	20,137	3,572
Elizabethton	2,633	2,179	160	5	9,346	4,289
Cheatham	5,948	5,088	281	10	14,431	2,836
Chester	2,398	2,130	123	6	5,743	2,696
Claiborne	5,158	4,226	318	11	14,502	3,432
Clay	1,379	1,230	105	5	4,756	3,867
Cocke	4,838	4,010	271	12	13,527	3,373
Newport	854	740	48	1	2,515	3,398
Coffee	3,964	3,412	234	9	12,444	3,647
Manchester	1,307	1,058	79	3	4,443	4,199
Tullahoma	3,582	3,031	219	7	12,523	4,132
Crockett	1,716	1,464	100	6	4,716	3,221
Alamo	594	540	31	1	1,315	2,436
Bells	366	313	19	1	811	2,591
Cumberland	6,072	5,409	326	9	17,269	3,193
Davidson-Nashville (Metro)	71,351	62,224	4,179	120	289,125	4,647
Decatur	1,871	1,698	115	5	5,326	3,137
DeKalb	2,839	2,406	146	4	6,849	2,846
Dickson	7,269	6,604	388	11	20,544	3,111
Dyer	3,667	3,097	198	8	12,227	3,948
Dyersburg	3,504	3,052	206	4	12,223	4,005
Fayette	4,671	3,908	274	8	13,557	3,469
Fentress	2,471	2,131	165	8	8,070	3,787
Franklin	6,483	5,497	363	15	16,922	3,078
Gibson	0	0	0	0	0	0
Humboldt	2,498	2,193	145	5	7,110	3,242
Milan[3]	2,155	1,902	130	4	6,349	3,338
Trenton[3]	1,323	1,221	88	3	4,219	3,455
Bradford[3]	673	592	38	1	1,748	2,953
Gibson[3]	2,218	2,020	121	6	6,565	3,250
Giles	4,871	4,216	275	8	14,286	3,389
Grainger	3,187	2,791	178	6	8,257	2,958
Greene	6,740	6,116	396	15	19,642	3,212

TABLE 16.14--SELECTED PUBLIC SCHOOL STATISTICS, COUNTY AND CITY SCHOOL DISTRICTS,
SCHOLASTIC YEAR 1992 (Continued)

County and local district	Net enrollment[1]	Average daily attendance	Number of teachers employed	Number of public schools	Total current expenditures ($1,000)	Expenditure per pupil in ADA[2] ($)
Greeneville	2,799	2,403	214	7	12,499	5,202
Grundy	2,712	2,278	178	7	8,008	3,515
Hamblen	9,586	8,039	583	19	31,654	3,938
Hamilton	26,155	21,821	1,296	41	76,643	3,512
Chattanooga	20,931	18,594	1,370	39	86,958	4,677
Hancock	1,301	1,145	101	6	4,067	3,552
Hardeman	5,346	4,659	313	9	14,120	3,031
Hardin	4,160	3,679	253	10	12,046	3,274
Hawkins	7,150	6,022	405	16	20,668	3,432
Rogersville	575	539	36	1	1,805	3,348
Haywood	4,372	3,909	258	6	12,983	3,321
Henderson	3,313	3,071	189	9	8,793	2,863
Lexington	874	771	46	1	2,444	3,170
Henry	3,768	3,285	214	7	10,784	3,283
Paris[3]	1,316	1,161	77	3	4,372	3,765
Hickman	3,145	2,729	168	4	8,439	3,092
Houston	1,429	1,213	72	3	3,582	2,953
Humphreys	3,109	2,724	174	6	8,835	3,243
Jackson	1,582	1,349	106	4	4,493	3,330
Jefferson	5,702	5,039	316	10	16,292	3,233
Johnson	2,535	2,103	157	8	7,333	3,487
Knox	54,504	46,716	3,383	86	182,356	3,904
Lake	1,246	1,044	80	3	3,631	3,478
Lauderdale	5,052	4,750	278	6	13,357	2,812
Lawrence	6,683	5,931	377	14	18,824	3,174
Lewis	1,939	1,704	106	3	4,482	2,630
Lincoln	4,405	3,906	245	9	11,928	3,054
Fayetteville	1,063	897	60	2	2,980	3,323
Loudon	4,087	3,662	255	10	13,575	3,707
Lenoir City	2,048	1,709	102	3	5,446	3,187
McMinn	5,940	5,208	337	9	17,512	3,363
Athens	2,044	1,724	114	5	6,902	4,004
Etowah	445	347	24	1	1,252	3,608
McNairy	4,375	3,807	242	8	11,686	3,069
Macon	3,128	2,781	164	6	7,418	2,667
Madison	15,345	12,827	868	27	53,410	4,164
Marion	4,996	4,173	261	10	13,570	3,252
Richard City[3]	289	245	15	1	616	2,515
Marshall	4,367	4,039	246	6	13,424	3,324
Maury	11,329	10,119	650	15	33,345	3,295
Meigs	1,688	1,409	93	6	4,732	3,358
Monroe	5,014	4,207	257	12	13,892	3,302
Sweetwater	1,220	1,037	62	3	3,229	3,114
Montgomery-Clarksville	19,927	16,506	990	23	54,448	3,299
Moore	967	870	56	2	3,027	3,479
Morgan	3,554	3,088	201	7	9,458	3,063
Obion	4,464	3,735	256	8	13,698	3,668
Union City	1,862	1,734	126	5	7,112	4,102
Overton	3,163	2,765	192	7	9,034	3,267
Perry	1,212	1,075	76	3	3,393	3,157

TABLE 16.14--SELECTED PUBLIC SCHOOL STATISTICS, COUNTY AND CITY SCHOOL DISTRICTS,
SCHOLASTIC YEAR 1992 (Continued)

County and local district	Net enrollment [1]	Average daily attendance	Number of teachers employed	Number of public schools	Total current expenditures ($1,000)	Expenditure per pupil in ADA [2] ($)
Pickett	829	758	60	2	2,571	3,392
Polk	2,439	2,098	146	6	7,416	3,535
Putnam	9,193	8,238	503	14	24,392	2,961
Rhea	4,123	3,456	220	6	11,420	3,305
Dayton	762	618	34	1	1,670	2,702
Roane	6,338	5,384	358	13	20,122	3,737
Harriman	1,947	1,613	122	5	6,532	4,049
Robertson	8,983	7,702	478	16	23,841	3,095
Rutherford	20,258	17,350	1,078	25	61,384	3,538
Murfreesboro	4,779	4,416	300	8	17,129	3,879
Scott	3,168	2,837	184	7	9,068	3,196
Oneida[3]	1,169	1,065	73	2	3,695	3,469
Sequatchie	1,699	1,450	114	4	5,624	3,879
Sevier	9,723	8,731	556	18	30,582	3,503
Shelby	45,423	37,411	2,052	39	122,560	3,276
Memphis	110,766	96,259	6,270	162	420,228	4,366
Smith	2,907	2,560	158	9	7,430	2,902
Stewart	1,741	1,509	96	3	5,425	3,595
Sullivan	14,974	13,063	946	31	59,091	4,524
Bristol	3,938	3,457	269	8	18,146	5,249
Kingsport	6,276	5,618	418	9	30,515	5,432
Sumner	20,568	18,796	1,093	34	62,244	3,312
Tipton	8,357	7,031	376	6	19,221	2,734
Covington	1,234	1,024	59	1	3,284	3,208
Trousdale	1,177	1,065	65	2	2,957	2,776
Unicoi	2,797	2,409	164	6	8,054	3,343
Union	2,507	2,229	138	5	6,290	2,822
Van Buren	807	722	48	2	2,228	3,086
Warren	6,421	5,637	390	10	17,563	3,116
Washington	8,516	7,719	493	14	25,890	3,354
Johnson City	6,123	5,495	385	10	24,391	4,439
Wayne	2,986	2,417	172	8	7,979	3,301
Weakley	5,266	4,755	306	12	14,583	3,067
White	3,606	3,263	213	8	10,066	3,085
Williamson	12,554	11,516	729	20	43,527	3,780
Franklin[3]	3,783	3,447	247	6	13,755	3,990
Wilson	11,171	9,613	519	15	27,444	2,855
Lebanon[3]	2,477	2,243	157	4	8,022	3,576
TENNESSEE	893,272	774,596	50,732	1,532	2,890,606	3,732

1. Net enrollment consists of ungraded or unclassified, special education, and grades K-12.
2. Average daily attendance.
3. Special school district.
Source: Tennessee Department of Education, *Annual Statistical Report, 1992.*

TABLE 16.15--HIGH SCHOOL GRADUATES, TENNESSEE AND COUNTIES, 1992

County	Number of schools	Number of graduates	Number continuing education	Percent of graduates continuing education
Anderson[1]	3	565	426	75.4
Bedford	4	367	201	54.8
Benton	2	170	103	60.6
Bledsoe	1	80	38	47.5
Blount	4	984	615	62.5
Bradley	3	782	407	52.0
Campbell	3	361	148	41.0
Cannon[a]	1	90	n.a.	n.a.
Carroll	5	343	210	61.2
Carter	5	582	330	56.7
Cheatham	3	327	114	34.9
Chester	1	121	93	76.9
Claibome	3	261	154	59.0
Clay[a]	2	83	10	12.0
Cocke[1]	2	230	140	60.9
Coffee	2	453	309	68.2
Crockett	1	130	53	40.8
Cumberland	1	348	140	40.2
Davidson[1]	31	3,819	3,123	81.8
Decatur[2]	2	170	60	35.3
DeKalb	1	156	76	48.7
Dickson	1	465	154	33.1
Dyer	2	345	213	61.7
Fayette	3	287	169	58.9
Fentress[3,a]	2	173	28	16.2
Franklin	3	425	319	75.1
Gibson	5	522	289	55.4
Giles	3	254	119	46.9
Grainger	2	190	70	36.8
Greene	5	594	315	53.0
Grundy	1	158	55	34.8
Hamblen	2	600	420	70.0
Hamilton	21	2,954	2,243	75.9
Hancock	1	67	40	59.7
Hardeman	2	268	129	48.1
Hardin	1	247	162	65.6
Hawkins	2	462	266	57.6
Haywood	1	216	135	62.5
Henderson[2]	2	292	175	59.9
Henry	1	264	196	74.2
Hickman	1	188	84	44.7
Houston	1	94	54	57.4
Humphreys	2	194	82	42.3
Jackson	1	84	26	31.0
Jefferson	1	347	205	59.1
Johnson	1	139	53	38.1
Knox	19	3,088	2,097	67.9
Lake	1	64	38	59.4
Lauderdale	2	241	104	43.2
Lawrence	3	408	286	70.1
Lewis	1	111	64	57.7
Lincoln	1	301	196	65.1
Loudon	3	400	167	41.8
McMinn	3	494	309	62.6
McNairy	2	281	100	35.6

TABLE 16.15--HIGH SCHOOL GRADUATES, TENNESSEE AND COUNTIES, 1992 (Continued)

County	Number of schools	Number of graduates	Number continuing education	Percent of graduates continuing education
Macon	2	160	76	47.5
Madison	6	735	474	64.5
Marion	3	262	108	41.2
Marshall	3	269	123	45.7
Maury	7	599	390	65.1
Meigs	1	89	62	69.7
Monroe	4	317	133	42.0
Montgomery	6	996	454	45.6
Moore	1	62	61	98.4
Morgan	4	248	157	63.3
Obion	3	387	275	71.1
Overton	1	188	80	42.6
Perry	1	58	34	58.6
Pickett	1	47	40	85.1
Polk	2	147	55	37.4
Putnam	3	490	320	65.3
Rhea	1	227	129	56.8
Roane	5	525	273	52.0
Robertson	4	422	220	52.1
Rutherford	8	1,332	678	50.9
Scott[a]	2	252	103	40.9
Sequatchie	1	79	58	73.4
Sevier	4	584	429	73.5
Shelby[1]	56	7,463	6,083	81.5
Smith	2	137	71	51.8
Stewart	1	112	55	49.1
Sullivan[a]	7	1,698	922	54.3
Sumner	7	1,286	842	65.5
Tipton	2	418	151	36.1
Trousdale	1	48	35	72.9
Unicoi	1	190	100	52.6
Union	1	128	49	38.3
Van Buren	1	42	15	35.7
Warren	1	364	200	54.9
Washington	4	838	557	66.5
Wayne	3	150	79	52.7
Weakley	6	301	194	64.5
White	1	230	120	52.2
Williamson	6	1,040	863	83.0
Wilson[1]	5	382	183	47.9
Special schools	4	201	27	13.4
TENNESSEE[1,a]	362	48,964	31,370	64.1

n.a. not available.

a. One or more schools reported the number of graduates only.

1. Less than 100.0 percent response.

2. Scotts Hill High School has students from both Decatur and Henderson County. The school's figures are included in both counties' tabulations but added only once to the state total.

3. Includes Alvin C. York Agricultural Institute, which is also listed as a state special school.

Source: Tennessee Department of Employment Security, Research and Statistics Division, *Tennessee's High School Graduates, 1992.*

TABLE 16.16–EDUCATIONAL ATTAINMENT OF PERSONS 25 YEARS AND OLDER, COUNTIES, 1990

County	Less than 9th grade		High school graduate or higher		Bachelor' degree or higher	
	Number	Percent	Number	Percent	Number	Percent
Anderson	6,643	14.4	33,439	72.4	8,583	18.6
Bedford	4,401	22.2	11,401	57.6	2,083	10.5
Benton	2,251	22.6	5,598	56.3	737	7.4
Bledsoe	1,782	27.9	3,324	52.1	347	5.4
Blount	8,878	15.3	39,695	68.5	8,290	14.3
Bradley	8,893	19.0	30,160	64.4	5,586	11.9
Campbell	7,199	31.9	10,713	47.5	1,483	6.6
Cannon	1,761	25.7	3,734	54.6	473	6.9
Carroll	4,514	24.5	10,200	55.3	1,340	7.3
Carter	7,687	22.3	19,803	57.5	3,722	10.8
Cheatham	2,364	13.8	11,140	65.0	1,800	10.5
Chester	1,872	24.1	4,231	54.6	677	8.7
Claibome	5,533	33.4	8,415	50.8	1,329	8.0
Clay	1,734	35.6	2,366	48.5	380	7.8
Cocke	5,900	30.8	9,671	50.4	1,057	5.5
Coffee	4,741	18.0	17,144	65.1	4,040	15.3
Crockett	1,907	21.2	5,152	57.2	576	6.4
Cumberland	5,444	23.1	14,112	59.8	2,402	10.2
Davidson	28,202	8.4	254,732	75.9	81,852	24.4
Decatur	1,917	26.8	3,788	52.9	345	4.8
DeKalb	2,828	29.6	4,809	50.3	803	8.4
Dickson	4,115	18.6	13,631	61.5	2,037	9.2
Dyer	5,636	25.0	12,456	55.3	2,116	9.4
Fayette	3,549	22.7	8,673	55.5	1,244	8.0
Fentress	3,498	37.4	4,196	44.9	620	6.6
Franklin	4,214	18.8	14,253	63.5	2,934	13.1
Gibson	6,459	20.7	17,926	57.5	2,496	8.0
Giles	3,246	19.4	10,076	60.1	1,494	8.9
Grainger	3,886	34.9	5,153	46.3	532	4.8
Greene	8,984	23.9	21,851	58.1	3,857	10.3
Grundy	3,006	36.2	3,715	44.7	451	5.4
Hamblen	6,856	20.6	20,474	61.6	3,727	11.2
Hamilton	21,076	11.2	136,069	72.5	36,958	19.7
Hancock	1,823	41.5	1,860	42.4	223	5.1
Hardeman	3,192	21.9	7,723	53.0	1,105	7.6
Hardin	3,578	24.0	8,168	54.8	904	6.1
Hawkins	7,054	23.9	17,136	58.0	2,481	8.4
Haywood	3,001	24.9	6,379	53.0	1,046	8.7
Henderson	3,592	24.9	7,960	55.2	984	6.8
Henry	3,989	20.7	11,560	60.0	1,642	8.5
Hickman	2,639	23.5	6,239	55.6	807	7.2
Houston	1,255	26.6	2,491	52.8	298	6.3
Humphreys	1,812	17.4	6,625	63.5	956	9.2
Jackson	2,458	38.8	2,860	45.2	432	6.8
Jefferson	4,858	22.6	13,002	60.5	2,524	11.7
Johnson	2,951	31.6	4,402	47.2	465	5.0
Knox	23,831	10.9	162,819	74.6	52,211	23.9
Lake	1,406	29.9	2,329	49.6	237	5.0
Lauderdale	3,745	25.4	7,684	52.1	883	6.0
Lawrence	6,379	28.3	12,096	53.7	1,499	6.7

TABLE 16.16–EDUCATIONAL ATTAINMENT OF PERSONS 25 YEARS AND OLDER, COUNTIES, 1990
(Continued)

County	Less than 9th grade		High school graduate or higher		Bachelor' degree or higher	
	Number	Percent	Number	Percent	Number	Percent
Lewis	1,634	27.7	3,041	51.5	296	5.0
Lincoln	3,595	19.3	10,682	57.5	1,696	9.1
Loudon	4,028	19.1	13,418	63.8	2,014	9.6
Macon	3,506	34.1	5,054	49.2	565	5.5
Madison	6,679	13.6	33,453	68.3	8,113	16.6
Marion	3,995	25.0	8,299	51.9	1,031	6.4
Marshall	2,633	18.7	8,453	60.0	1,085	7.7
Maury	5,820	16.4	23,173	65.2	4,294	12.1
McMinn	6,687	24.0	15,900	57.1	2,920	10.5
McNairy	3,404	22.5	8,668	57.4	785	5.2
Meigs	1,405	27.1	2,733	52.7	342	6.6
Monroe	6,252	32.0	9,744	49.9	1,489	7.6
Montgomery	5,521	9.5	45,232	77.9	9,565	16.5
Moore	538	17.4	2,061	66.7	363	11.7
Morgan	2,654	23.9	6,281	56.7	409	3.7
Obion	3,801	18.2	12,808	61.3	1,780	8.5
Overton	4,249	36.4	5,149	44.1	804	6.9
Perry	1,167	26.3	2,336	52.7	308	6.9
Pickett	1,161	38.0	1,400	45.8	277	9.1
Polk	2,670	29.7	4,604	51.3	522	5.8
Putnam	6,860	21.8	19,887	63.2	5,300	16.8
Rhea	3,660	23.5	8,728	56.0	1,330	8.5
Roane	5,689	17.8	21,291	66.7	4,222	13.2
Robertson	3,681	13.9	17,381	65.5	2,559	9.6
Rutherford	7,786	11.1	51,787	73.9	13,092	18.7
Scott	3,411	30.7	5,685	51.2	736	6.6
Sequatchie	1,603	28.3	2,910	51.4	431	7.6
Sevier	6,944	20.4	21,472	63.0	3,682	10.8
Shelby	45,674	9.0	381,850	75.1	105,711	20.8
Smith	2,584	27.6	5,074	54.2	569	6.1
Stewart	1,596	24.4	3,855	58.9	505	7.7
Sullivan	16,688	17.1	65,156	66.8	15,209	15.6
Sumner	8,712	13.3	46,258	70.6	9,446	14.4
Tipton	4,138	18.4	13,882	61.8	1,505	6.7
Trousdale	1,264	32.0	1,888	47.7	277	7.0
Unicoi	2,612	22.8	6,847	59.6	1,087	9.5
Union	2,889	33.7	3,911	45.6	382	4.5
Van Buren	994	32.1	1,488	48.0	128	4.1
Warren	4,636	21.5	12,290	57.0	1,748	8.1
Washington	9,142	15.1	41,438	68.4	11,422	18.9
Wayne	2,766	30.8	4,586	51.0	448	5.0
Weakley	4,172	21.2	11,194	56.9	2,025	10.3
White	4,021	29.8	7,180	53.2	1,025	7.6
Williamson	4,223	8.2	42,275	81.8	17,685	34.2
Wilson	5,246	12.1	30,917	71.4	6,741	15.6

Source: U.S. Department of Commerce, Bureau of the Census, *1990 Census of Population and Housing, Summary Tape File 3A, Tennessee.*

TABLE 16.17–EDUCATIONAL ATTAINMENT OF PERSONS 25 YEARS AND OLDER BY RACE,
SOUTHEASTERN STATES AND UNITED STATES, 1990

State	Percent of total		Percent of white		Percent of black	
	High school graduate or higher	Bachelor's degree or higher	High school graduate or higher	Bachelor's degree or higher	High school graduate or higher	Bachelor's degree or higher
TENNESSEE	67.1	16.0	68.2	16.7	59.4	10.2
Alabama	66.9	15.7	70.3	17.3	54.6	9.3
Arkansas	66.3	13.3	68.6	14.1	51.5	8.4
Florida	74.4	18.3	77.0	19.3	56.4	9.8
Georgia	70.9	19.3	74.9	21.8	58.6	11.0
Kentucky	64.6	13.6	64.7	13.9	61.7	7.7
Louisiana	68.3	16.1	74.2	18.7	53.1	9.1
Mississippi	64.3	14.7	71.7	17.2	47.3	8.8
North Carolina	70.0	17.4	73.1	19.3	58.1	9.5
South Carolina	68.3	16.6	73.6	19.8	53.3	7.6
Virginia	75.2	24.5	78.3	27.0	60.3	11.1
West Virginia	66.0	12.3	66.0	12.2	64.7	10.9
UNITED STATES	75.2	20.3	77.9	21.5	63.1	11.4

Source: U.S. Department of Commerce, Bureau of the Census, *1990 Census of Population and Housing,
Education in the United States.*

TABLE 16.18--ESTIMATED PUBLIC SCHOOL FALL ENROLLMENT, AVERAGE DAILY MEMBERSHIP
AND ATTENDANCE, DAILY ATTENDANCE AS A PERCENT OF FALL ENROLLMENT,
AND NUMBER OF PUBLIC HIGH SCHOOL GRADUATES, SOUTHEASTERN STATES
AND UNITED STATES, SCHOLASTIC YEAR 1991

| | Fall enrollment | | | Average daily membership | Average daily attendance | | Number of public high school graduates |
State	Total	Elementary	Secondary		Number	Percent of fall enrollment	
TENNESSEE	833,590	600,185	233,405	816,918	766,337	91.9	43,160
Alabama	726,158	409,571	316,587	718,859	681,865	93.9	37,071
Arkansas[1]	436,460	245,652	190,808	429,586	409,535	93.8	28,189
Florida[1]	1,861,592	1,099,976	761,616	1,834,198	1,778,494	95.5	89,276
Georgia	1,151,687	849,082	302,605	1,147,308	1,057,025	91.8	60,426
Kentucky	630,091	439,698	190,393	599,658	569,200	90.3	36,200
Louisiana[1]	779,161	580,275	198,886	762,056	715,168	91.8	38,803
Mississippi	500,122	316,032	184,090	497,614	474,109	94.8	24,237
North Carolina	1,082,558	779,591	302,967	1,070,850	1,010,040	93.3	62,005
South Carolina	622,618	452,968	169,650	600,862	582,351	93.5	33,000
Virginia	998,463	645,368	353,095	990,176	932,143	93.4	58,955
West Virginia	323,021	191,555	131,466	n.a.	297,309	92.0	21,256
UNITED STATES	41,047,643	26,910,963	14,136,680	n.a.	38,099,634	92.8	2,285,030

Note: With some exceptions, enrollment data are based on organizational level; i.e., kindergarten and grades 1–6 as
elementary; and junior and senior high school, grades 7–12, as secondary.
n.a. not available.
1. NEA Research estimates based on regression equations. Used where state did not submit data.
Source: National Education Association, *Estimates of School Statistics, 1990–91.* Used by special permission.

TABLE 16.19--HIGH SCHOOL DROPOUT RATES, 1990, HIGH SCHOOL GRADUATES, 1994, AND
         COLLEGE ENTRANCE EXAM SCORES, 1992 AND 1993, SOUTHEASTERN STATES AND
         UNITED STATES

| State | High school dropout rate 1990[a] | High school graduates 1994 | College entrance exams | |
			Test taken[1]	Score
TENNESSEE	13.4	46,361	A.C.T.	20.2
Alabama	12.6	42,120	A.C.T.	19.8
Arkansas	11.4	26,385	A.C.T.	20.0
Florida	14.3	102,274	S.A.T.	882
Georgia	14.1	63,852	S.A.T.	844
Kentucky	13.3	39,144	A.C.T.	20.0
Louisiana	12.5	41,321	A.C.T.	19.4
Mississippi	11.8	26,843	A.C.T.	18.8
North Carolina	12.5	60,733	S.A.T.	859
South Carolina	11.7	35,222	S.A.T.	838
Virginia	10.0	62,175	S.A.T.	894
West Virginia	10.9	20,802	A.C.T.	19.8
UNITED STATES	11.2	2,490,832	A.C.T./S.A.T.	20.6/902

1. A.C.T. results are for 1992. The A.C.T. is scored on a scale from 1 to 36. S.A.T. results are for 1993. The
   S.A.T. is scored on a scale from 400 to 1,600.

a. Dropout rates are from the 1990 Census of Population. The figures represent the percentage of 16- to 19-year
   olds who are not high school graduates and who are not enrolled in school.

Source: The Chronicle of Higher Education, *Almanac*, August 25, 1993; and U.S. Department of Commerce,
   Bureau of the Census, 1990 Census of Population and Housing, *Social and Economic Characteristics*.

TABLE 16.20-ESTIMATED TOTAL CURRENT EXPENDITURES AND AVERAGE EXPENDITURE PER PUPIL IN PUBLIC SCHOOLS, SOUTHEASTERN STATES AND UNITED STATES, SCHOLASTIC YEARS 1990 AND 1991

State	Total current expenditures[1] (1,000)		Average expenditure per pupil in ADA	
	1991	1990[r]	1991	1990[r]
TENNESSEE	2,840,884	$2,680,081	3,707	$3,518
Alabama	2,487,250	2,266,432	3,648	3,314
Arkansas[2]	1,400,083	1,340,814	3,419	3,272
Florida[2]	8,897,191	8,287,905	5,003	5,051
Georgia[2]	5,128,711	4,691,939	4,852	4,468
Kentucky	2,498,946	2,161,238	4,390	3,793
Louisiana	2,890,000	2,730,000	4,041	3,836
Mississippi	1,575,000	1,484,904	3,322	3,119
North Carolina[2]	4,681,787	4,394,800	4,635	4,373
South Carolina	2,238,000	2,122,998	3,843	3,731
Virginia	4,972,901	4,736,096	5,335	5,149
West Virginia	1,395,847	1,361,802	4,695	4,510
UNITED STATES	198,435,420	185,400,429	5,208	4,952

1. Refers to expenditures for public elementary and secondary day schools. Excludes current expenditures for other programs, capital outlay, and interest on school debt.
2. NEA Research estimates based on regression equations. Used where state did not submit data.
Source: National Education Association, *Estimates of School Statistics, 1990–91*. Used by special permission.

TABLE 16.21–ESTIMATED AVERAGE ANNUAL SALARIES OF TOTAL INSTRUCTIONAL STAFF AND OF CLASSROOM TEACHERS, SOUTHEASTERN STATES AND UNITED STATES, SCHOLASTIC YEARS 1990 AND 1991 [In dollars except percentages]

| State | 1991 | | | | | 1990[r] | | | |
| | Average salary of instructional staff | Average salary of classroom teachers | | | | Average salary of instructional staff | Average salary of classroom teachers | | |
		All teachers	Percent change 1990–91	Elementary school	Secondary school		All teachers	Elementary school	Secondary school
TENNESSEE	29,371	28,248	4.4	27,772	29,398	27,949	27,052	26,700	28,345
Alabama	28,800	27,300	7.9	27,300	27,300	26,700	25,300	25,300	25,300
Arkansas[1]	23,345	23,040	3.1	21,919	23,211	22,693	22,352	21,393	22,603
Florida[1]	31,940	30,387	5.5	30,348	30,072	30,275	28,803	28,766	28,504
Georgia	33,522	28,855	3.0	28,855	28,855	31,685	28,006	28,006	28,006
Kentucky	30,395	29,089	10.6	28,362	30,620	27,482	26,292	25,643	27,685
Louisiana	27,040	26,240	8.0	26,240	26,240	25,036	24,300	23,921	25,078
Mississippi	25,256	24,443	0.3	24,057	25,020	25,146	24,364	23,944	24,991
North Carolina	30,196	29,082	4.3	29,233	28,984	28,952	27,883	28,028	27,789
South Carolina	29,430	28,174	3.5	27,556	29,379	28,453	27,217	26,615	28,376
Virginia	33,151	32,382	4.6	31,287	33,911	31,693	30,958	29,913	32,420
West Virginia	26,967	25,958	13.6	25,574	26,439	23,842	22,842	22,467	23,350
UNITED STATES	34,456	33,015	5.4	32,448	33,701	32,723	31,331	30,769	32,017

r revised.

1. NEA Research estimates based on regression equation. Used where state did not submit data.

Source: National Education Association, *Estimates of School Statistics, 1990–91*. Used by special permission.

TABLE 16.22–STATE AND LOCAL GOVERNMENT FULL-TIME EQUIVALENT EMPLOYMENT AND PAYROLL IN EDUCATION, SOUTHEASTERN STATES, OCTOBER 1991

State	Number of employees				October payroll ($1,000)			
	Total	Elementary and secondary schools	Institutions of higher education	Other education[1]	Total	Elementary and secondary schools	Institutions of higher education	Other education[1]
TENNESSEE	117,800	86,613	29,256	1,931	235,643	168,133	63,421	4,090
Alabama	114,394	80,436	29,885	4,073	220,856	142,895	68,418	9,544
Arkansas	68,343	52,634	13,085	2,624	124,750	91,610	28,047	5,093
Florida	297,648	237,152	57,833	2,663	624,271	481,749	136,711	5,811
Georgia	181,122	144,363	32,067	4,692	356,482	269,685	75,617	11,180
Kentucky	110,877	79,796	26,810	4,271	231,364	155,644	65,982	9,738
Louisiana	124,444	94,287	26,683	3,474	239,009	171,859	59,572	7,577
Mississippi	81,068	60,947	18,267	1,854	133,150	91,688	37,823	3,640
North Carolina	188,626	134,690	50,908	3,028	420,190	288,559	124,303	7,327
South Carolina	103,670	72,370	28,317	2,983	201,410	138,804	56,144	6,461
Virginia	178,838	134,580	41,165	3,093	390,418	286,081	96,309	8,029
West Virginia	53,146	40,370	11,241	1,535	109,971	81,005	25,939	3,027

Note: Detail may not add to total due to independent rounding.
1. State government only.
Source: U.S. Department of Commerce, Bureau of the Census, *Public Employment in 1991*.

TABLE 16.23–ESTIMATED PUBLIC SCHOOL REVENUE AND PERCENT DISTRIBUTION, BY SOURCE, SOUTHEASTERN STATES AND UNITED STATES, SCHOLASTIC YEAR 1991

State	Total receipts[1] ($1,000)	Total revenue receipts ($1,000)	Percent of revenue receipts by source		
			Federal	State	Local and other
TENNESSEE	3,086,355	2,946,355	9.4	48.0	42.6
Alabama	2,643,019	2,533,236	12.6	68.1	19.3
Arkansas[2]	1,567,803	1,530,849	9.5	58.7	31.8
Florida[2]	11,102,217	10,298,447	5.8	53.6	40.6
Georgia[2]	5,338,072	5,328,036	6.4	61.2	32.4
Kentucky	2,969,376	2,736,376	8.4	70.4	21.2
Louisiana[2]	3,317,904	3,268,002	9.5	52.6	37.9
Mississippi	1,789,540	1,744,540	15.5	54.9	29.6
North Carolina[2]	5,381,220	5,255,990	6.1	66.4	27.5
South Carolina	2,816,800	2,713,900	8.0	51.7	40.3
Virginia	5,272,191	5,201,662	4.6	34.6	60.8
West Virginia	1,454,982	1,453,918	7.8	65.4	26.8
UNITED STATES	227,247,145	217,980,540	6.2	49.3	44.5

Note: Data are preliminary estimates.

1. Includes non-revenue receipts.

2. NEA Research estimates based on regression equations. Used where state did not submit data.

Source: National Education Association, *Estimates of School Statistics, 1990–91*. Used by special permission.

TABLE 16.24--NUMBER OF AND ENROLLMENT IN INSTITUTIONS OF HIGHER EDUCATION AND PERCENT MINORITY ENROLLMENT, FALL 1991, SOUTHEASTERN STATES

	Public						Private					
	4-year			2-year			4-year			2-year		
		Enrollment			Enrollment			Enrollment			Enrollment	
State	Number	Total	Percent minority	Number	Total	Percent minority	Number	Total	Percent minority	Number	Total	Percent minority
TENNESSEE	10	112,789	15.9	14	73,652	17.5	42	46,848	18.1	15	4,753	19.6
Alabama	18	127,754	19.6	37	74,557	21.0	18	18,788	45.5	13	3,232	38.6
Arkansas	10	63,464	16.1	10	18,688	14.8	10	10,070	15.7	5	2,118	36.2
Florida	9	183,117	24.6	29	323,225	25.9	50	98,099	27.1	16	7,340	38.2
Georgia	20	151,218	19.7	46	67,706	25.4	30	49,783	39.0	15	8,316	29.2
Kentucky	8	109,780	7.9	14	45,993	8.0	26	26,941	6.0	16	5,244	16.2
Louisiana	14	143,219	28.3	6	25,603	30.9	12	26,624	32.0	4	1,992	42.7
Mississippi	9	60,187	31.5	20	51,199	26.2	12	10,996	33.9	5	2,968	47.2
North Carolina	16	152,320	21.7	58	153,153	21.4	37	62,053	21.4	11	4,442	25.5
South Carolina	12	85,518	17.9	21	51,494	26.1	22	25,268	25.1	6	2,627	44.6
Virginia	15	163,232	20.7	24	134,875	18.7	33	54,270	22.7	11	3,948	41.5
West Virginia	13	70,937	5.2	3	7,278	3.8	9	7,815	6.2	3	2,572	6.1

Source: The Chronicle of Higher Education, *Almanac*, August 25, 1993.

TABLE 16.25--GRADUATE ENROLLMENT IN THE SCIENCE, ENGINEERING, AND HEALTH FIELDS IN ALL INSTITUTIONS OF HIGHER EDUCATION, BY SELECTED FIELDS, SOUTHEASTERN STATES, 1991

State	Total science, engineering and health fields	Science fields								
		Total	Physical	Earth, atmospheric and oceanic	Mathematical	Computer	Agricultural	Biological	Psychological	Social
TENNESSEE	6,891	4,428	431	136	322	311	76	963	1,118	1,071
Alabama	6,486	3,606	414	66	262	538	287	841	513	685
Arkansas	2,313	1,225	114	17	70	54	160	260	289	261
Florida	14,600	8,579	831	602	561	1,112	382	1,142	1,664	2,285
Georgia	8,701	5,160	583	125	342	475	209	1,039	885	1,502
Kentucky	4,119	2,692	273	66	282	113	132	573	500	753
Louisiana	5,921	3,699	364	231	278	544	165	762	548	807
Mississippi	2,847	2,071	263	57	99	261	259	343	292	497
North Carolina	10,282	6,809	762	444	551	422	368	1,958	738	1,566
South Carolina	3,993	2,356	329	162	203	269	137	593	193	470
Virginia	11,588	7,292	620	379	488	1,294	266	1,090	1,136	2,019
West Virginia	2,363	1,331	94	115	141	83	89	220	252	337

TABLE 16.25--GRADUATE ENROLLMENT IN THE SCIENCE, ENGINEERING, AND HEALTH FIELDS IN ALL INSTITUTIONS OF HIGHER EDUCATION, BY SELECTED FIELDS, SOUTHEASTERN STATES, 1991 (Continued)

| State | Health fields | Total | | Engineering fields | | | | | | |
			Chemical	Civil	Electrical	Industrial	Mechanical	Metallurgical/materials	All other engineering
TENNESSEE	661	1,730	109	299	356	251	210	72	433
Alabama	1,072	1,808	115	132	546	263	403	190	159
Arkansas	418	669	32	34	135	391	24	0	53
Florida	2,147	3,874	90	564	1,262	381	443	137	997
Georgia	891	2,650	153	429	728	570	329	129	312
Kentucky	545	882	74	120	283	168	141	34	62
Louisiana	965	1,257	124	146	225	93	124	0	545
Mississippi	328	448	52	53	161	38	71	0	73
North Carolina	1,645	1,828	107	271	581	108	309	207	245
South Carolina	505	1,132	33	288	174	65	126	39	407
Virginia	1,340	2,956	132	343	668	587	427	118	681
West Virginia	520	512	59	77	70	131	108	0	67

Note: The data published here represent estimates based on a survey sent to all institutions in the United States with departments or programs offering courses of study at the postbaccalaureate level in any science and engineering field.

Source: National Science Foundation, *Academic Science and Engineering: Graduate Enrollment and Support,* Fall 1991, NSF 93-309.

TABLE 16.26–FINANCES OF PUBLIC INSTITUTIONS OF HIGHER EDUCATION, SOUTHEASTERN STATES AND UNITED STATES, 1991

State	FTE enrollment [1] (1,000)	Appropriations for current operations [2]		Net tuition revenues [3]	
		Total (mil. $)	Per FTE student ($)	Total (mil. $)	Per FTE student ($)
TENNESSEE	144.5	562.8	3,896	218.5	1,512
Alabama	170.5	557.1	3,268	289.2	1,697
Arkansas	64.9	229.6	3,537	109.5	1,687
Florida	334.4	1,685.4	5,040	346.2	1,035
Georgia	183.7	807.4	4,395	238.4	1,298
Kentucky	114.8	429.2	3,739	148.7	1,295
Louisiana	125.7	381.8	3,037	231.6	1,842
Mississippi	95.5	288.7	3,023	146.4	1,533
North Carolina	224.5	1,153.8	5,139	223.2	995
South Carolina	105.6	455.1	4,311	239.6	2,270
Virginia	215.4	812.9	3,774	417.8	1,940
West Virginia	60.6	167.2	2,758	97.2	1,603
UNITED STATES	8,119.2	35,083.1	4,321	12,415.4	1,529

1. Full-time equivalent. Credit and non-credit program enrollment including summer session. Excludes medical enrollments.

2. State and local appropriations. Includes aid to students attending in-state public institutions. Excludes sums for research, agriculture stations and cooperative extension, and hospitals and medical schools.

3. Excludes appropriated aid to students attending in-state public institutions.

Source: U.S. Department of Commerce, Bureau of the Census, *Statistical Abstract of the United States, 1993*; original source for data is Research Associates of Washington, Washington, D.C., *State Profiles: Financing Public Higher Education*, annual, used by special permission..

TABLE 16.27--HIGHER EDUCATION FINANCING, SOUTHEASTERN STATES, FISCAL YEARS 1991-93 [In thousands of dollars, unless otherwise noted]

| State | Average tuition and fees FY 1992 (dollars) | | | Expenditures FY 1991 | | State appropriations, FY 93 | State spending on student aid, FY 93 | Research | |
| | Public | | Private | | | | | | |
	4-year	2-year	4-year	Public institutions	Private institutions			Spending by universities FY 91	Federal funds for college- and university-based, FY 91
TENNESSEE	1,586	849	7,493	1,585,614	1,097,066	747,525	24,471	240,054	148,877
Alabama	1,699	1,046	6,355	2,054,798	244,425	824,000	14,183	244,901	155,818
Arkansas	1,540	714	5,046	797,291	114,655	411,827	7,304	55,081	25,785
Florida	1,484	905	8,556	2,896,046	1,274,196	1,415,262	76,339	438,054	217,377
Georgia	1,763	934	8,159	1,929,993	1,227,745	951,726	25,990	484,019	194,164
Kentucky	1,574	817	5,658	1,400,529	282,937	621,794	27,783	97,989	46,190
Louisiana	1,794	852	10,367	1,439,415	572,049	620,791	7,666	239,533	101,680
Mississippi	2,125	817	5,597	978,366	101,330	437,215	1,351	96,471	42,970
North Carolina	1,224	504	8,502	2,581,156	1,704,643	1,541,926	70,406	501,841	340,513
South Carolina	2,471	920	7,353	1,475,074	319,782	633,379	18,315	151,204	54,996
Virginia	3,026	1,060	8,288	2,812,109	671,912	934,776	26,879	337,874	181,418
West Virginia	1,625	1,031	9,022	548,802	108,334	284,606	14,894	50,772	33,711

Source: The Chronicle of Higher Education, *Almanac*, August 25, 1993.

TABLE 16.28-NUMBER AND AVERAGE PAY OF FACULTY MEMBERS OF INSTITUTIONS OF HIGHER EDUCATION, SOUTHEASTERN STATES AND UNITED STATES, FISCAL YEAR 1991

State	Number of faculty members	Average pay of full-time faculty members		Private 4-year
		Public		
		4-year	2-year	4-year
TENNESSEE	7,270	$41,089	$30,509	$35,883
Alabama	5,942	38,481	33,240	30,947
Arkansas	2,957	34,960	26,811	31,410
Florida	13,038	43,855	32,294	35,881
Georgia	7,648	39,909	31,709	36,501
Kentucky	5,249	38,818	28,463	30,086
Louisiana	6,006	36,705	29,878	41,362
Mississippi	3,920	33,717	28,195	34,888
North Carolina	9,675	43,035	26,141	35,798
South Carolina	5,520	40,541	27,649	31,510
Virginia	9,974	47,650	35,361	36,269
West Virginia	2,552	35,610	27,610	28,904
UNITED STATES	379,373	44,497	37,064	42,183

Source: The Chronicle of Higher Education, *Almanac*, August 25, 1993.

The main agency for health data is the National Center for Health Statistics (NCHS) in the Centers for Disease Control (CDC). NCHS is responsible for the collection, analysis, and dissemination of statistics on the nature and extent of the health, illness, and disability of the population; the impact of illness and disability on the economy; the effects of environmental, social, and other health hazards; the use of health care services; health resources; family formation, growth, and dissolution; and vital events. The CDC also provides data on morbidity, infectious diseases, and occupational diseases and injuries.

The U.S. Health Care Financing Administration is also a major source of administrative data on Medicare and Medicaid programs. Other national data sources providing comparative data for states include the American Medical Association; the American Dental Association; the American Hospital Association, publisher of *Hospital Statistics* (copyright); and the Health Insurance Association of America, which publishes the *Source Book of Health Insurance*. The *Statistical Abstract of the United States* is an intermediary source for much of the state and national data used in this chapter.

In Tennessee, the Department of Health, Division of Information Resources, provides state and county data on births, deaths, marriage, and divorce, as well as details of morbidity, health care, and medical personnel and facilities. Publications include the *Annual Bulletin of Vital Statistics*; *Teenage Childbearing; Induced Abortions Reported in Tennessee*; *Vital Signs*, and *Tennessee's Health, A Picture of the Present*.

A new publication of the Department of Health, *The Messenger*, specifically addresses the present need for information and services for victims of AIDS (Acquired Immune Deficiency Syndrome) and HIV positive patients. Table 17.14 provides information on this disease.

The State Licensing Board for the Healing Arts and the State Board of Dentistry, also in the Department of Health, publish annual directories of doctors of medicine, osteopathy and dentistry. These reports provide a good picture of health care resources and vital statistics in Tennessee and its counties; but the most comprehensive source of data for local areas is *Tennessee's Heath*.

In most cases, the tables of this chapter contain "resident data." These include all births or deaths of residents of the specific area, regardless of the place of occurrence. "Recorded data," data by place of occurrence, are for a specific area, regardless of the place of residence of the individual. Recorded data are used for marriage and divorce information.

TABLE OF CONTENTS

TABLE OF CONTENTS
(Continued)

FIGURE 17.1
Live Birth and Death Rates per 1,000 Population, Tennessee, 1940–1992

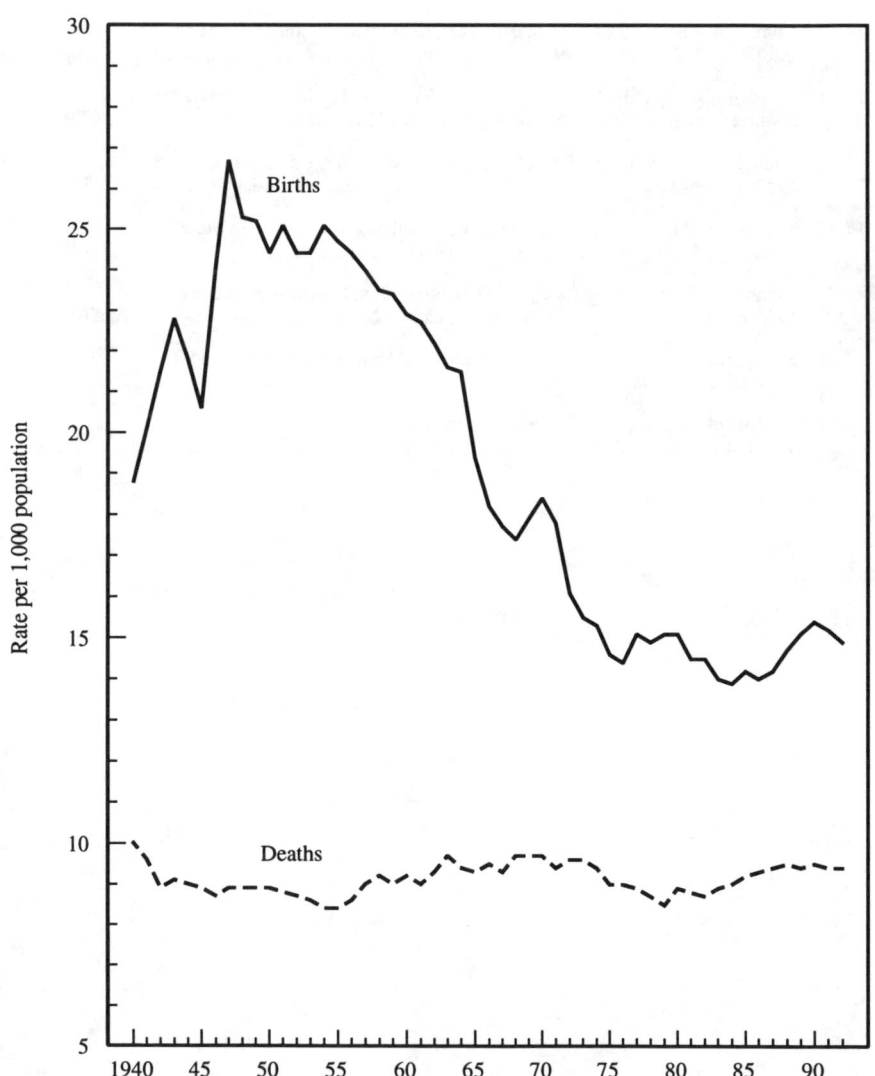

Source: Tennessee Department of Health, Division of Information Resources, *Annual Bulletin of Vital Statistics,* *1991,* and earlier editions; *Tennessee Vital Statistics Summary. Resident Data, 1992 and earlier editions.*

TABLE 17.1--NUMBER OF LIVE BIRTHS, NUMBER OF DEATHS, AND BIRTH AND DEATH RATES,
BY RACE, TENNESSEE, 1935-1992, SELECTED YEARS

Year	Number of live births			Total live birth rate	Number of deaths			Total death rate
	Total	White	Nonwhite		Total	White	Nonwhite	
1992	73,560	55,214	18,335	14.9	46,412	38,605	7,802	9.4
1991	74,392	55,869	18,513	15.2	46,158	38,443	7,709	9.4
1990	74,870	55,919 ʳ	18,941 ʳ	15.4	46,204	38,348	7,856	9.5
1989	73,137	54,504	18,620	15.1	45,362	37,575	7,782	9.4
1988	70,685	53,053	17,625	14.7	45,728	38,157	7,567	9.5
1987	67,942	51,410	16,528	14.2	44,884	37,307	7,572	9.4
1986	66,246	50,445	15,798	14.0	44,237	36,674	7,561	9.3
1985	66,730	50,989	15,735	14.2	43,176	35,729	7,444	9.2
1984	64,937	49,951	14,979	13.9	42,221	35,031	7,183	9.0
1983	65,465	50,469	14,989	14.0	41,604	34,438	7,161	8.9
1982	67,078	51,748	15,327	14.5	40,260	33,238	7,021	8.7
1981	67,050	51,429	15,614	14.5	40,480	33,533	6,941	8.8
1980	69,102	52,967	16,129	15.1	40,713	33,416	7,291	8.9
1979	68,326	52,303	16,021	15.1	38,712	31,837	6,875	8.5
1978	66,466	51,183	15,275	14.9	38,654	31,964	6,690	8.7
1977	66,632	52,110	14,521	15.1	39,080	32,110	6,970	8.9
1976	62,514	48,750	13,760	14.4	38,933	32,086	6,847	9.0
1975	62,265	48,453	13,808	14.6	38,522	31,504	7,013	9.0
1974	64,154	50,201	13,952	15.3	39,376	32,214	7,158	9.4
1973	64,303	50,113	14,187	15.5	39,724	32,319	7,394	9.6
1972	65,802	51,609	14,191	16.1	39,345	32,039	7,306	9.6
1971	71,202	56,075	15,125	17.8	37,783	30,671	7,112	9.4
1970	72,273	56,777	15,493	18.4	38,079	30,878	7,200	9.7
1969	69,921	55,133	14,788	17.9	37,832	30,441	7,391	9.7
1968	67,029	52,779	14,249	17.4	37,373	29,827	7,545	9.7
1967	67,740	52,991	14,749	17.7	35,736	28,843	6,893	9.3
1966	68,871	53,769	15,102	18.2	36,108	28,873	7,235	9.5
1965	72,990	56,380	16,610	19.4	35,049	28,116	6,933	9.3
1964	80,100	62,526	17,572	21.5	34,815	27,597	7,218	9.4
1963	79,715	62,145	17,570	21.6	35,633	28,223	7,410	9.7
1962	80,893	62,945	17,948	22.2	34,025	26,852	7,173	9.3
1961	82,067	63,830	18,236	22.7	32,625	25,744	6,880	9.0
1960	81,892	63,551	18,341	22.9	32,892	25,849	7,043	9.2
1959	82,956	64,555	18,401	23.4	31,813	24,990	6,823	9.0
1958	82,679	64,963	17,716	23.5	32,305	25,256	7,049	9.2
1957	83,923	65,469	18,454	24.0	31,329	24,328	7,001	9.0
1956	84,527	66,026	18,499	24.4	29,698	23,232	6,465	8.6
1955	84,713	66,661	18,048	24.7	28,886	22,463	6,422	8.4
1954	85,401	67,492	17,907	25.1	28,517	22,222	6,295	8.4
1953	82,585	65,402	17,183	24.4	29,106	22,362	6,744	8.6
1952	81,750	65,334	16,406	24.4	29,124	22,380	6,744	8.7
1951	83,521	67,007	16,501	25.1	29,281	22,425	6,856	8.8
1950	80,559	64,541	16,016	24.4	29,197	22,395	6,802	8.9
1949	82,307	67,047	15,258	25.2	29,012	22,248	6,764	8.9
1948	81,490	67,006	14,480	25.3	28,597	21,990	6,607	8.9
1947	85,284	71,845	13,437	26.7	28,456	21,891	6,563	8.9
1946	75,839	64,234	11,588	24.1	27,356	20,920	6,432	8.7
1945	64,101	53,473	10,622	20.6	27,680	21,052	6,624	8.9
1944	67,100	56,357	10,731	21.8	27,652	21,036	6,610	9.0
1943	69,205	58,391	10,808	22.8	27,782	20,752	7,030	9.1
1942	64,557	54,319	10,224	21.5	26,787	19,896	6,886	8.9
1941	59,415	50,127	9,284	20.1	28,373	20,959	7,406	9.6
1940	54,958	46,445	8,510	18.8	29,231	21,488	7,733	10.0
1935	52,827	44,511	8,302	19.0	29,425	21,632	7,785	10.6

Note: All data are by place of residence. Rates are per 1,000 population. For years where total does not equal the
sum of the components, the total includes births and deaths with race unknown. Beginning in 1991, race is race
of mother not race of child.

ʳ revised.

Source: Tennessee Department of Health, Bureau of Information Resources, *Annual Bulletin of Vital Statistics*,
1991, and earlier editions; and *Tennessee Vital Statistics Summary, Resident Data, 1992*, and earlier editions.

TABLE 17.2--NUMBER OF DEATHS, BY SELECTED MAJOR CAUSE, TENNESSEE, 1960–1991

Year	All causes [1]	Diseases of heart	Athero-sclerosis	Malignant neoplasms	Pneumonia and influenza	Conditions origi-nating in perinatal period
1991	46,158	15,358	357	10,611	1,695	355
1990	46,204	15,415	405	10,504	1,696	367
1989	45,362	15,364	419	10,181	1,509	399
1988	45,728	16,010	416	9,894	1,621	364
1987	44,884	15,779	347	10,004	1,361	405
1986	44,237	15,722	411	9,549	1,471	338
1985	43,176	15,740	429	9,220	1,437	367
1984	42,221	15,361	475	9,127	1,133	366
1983	41,604	15,206	495	8,768	1,117	395
1982	40,260	14,843	552	8,660	973	376
1981	40,480	14,894	620	8,355	1,174	445
1980	40,713	14,872	570	8,304	1,037	454
1979	38,712	14,115	642	7,792	908	464
1978	38,654	14,176	615	7,492	1,159	460
1977	39,080	14,497	582	7,507	1,070	481
1976	38,938	14,580	570	7,198	1,240	522
1975	38,522	14,303	622	6,869	1,101	526
1974	39,376	14,738	669	6,718	1,024	619
1973	39,724	15,011	641	6,501	1,197	726
1972	39,345	14,946	617	6,266	1,264	754
1971	37,783	14,528	558	6,070	1,193	847
1970	38,079	14,312	538	5,984	1,351	889
1969	37,832	14,345	634	5,737	1,402	881
1968	37,373	14,182	633	5,713	1,377	859
1967	35,736	13,173	709	5,465	1,247	913
1966	36,108	13,518	761	5,202	1,435	965
1965	35,049	12,763	744	5,108	1,356	1,094
1964	34,815	12,558	690	4,888	1,523	1,209
1963	35,633	12,561	668	5,134	1,880	1,192
1962	34,025	11,996	756	4,650	1,443	1,269
1961	32,625	11,119	701	4,634	1,326	1,256
1960	32,892	11,284	666	4,381	1,449	1,293

TABLE 17.2--NUMBER OF DEATHS, BY SELECTED MAJOR CAUSE, TENNESSEE, 1960-1991 (Continued)

Congenital anomalies	Diabetes Mellitus	Accidents (including motor vehicle)	Motor vehicle accidents	Suicide	Homicide and legal inter-vention	Year
233	936	2,135	1,167	681	584	1991
253	914	2,264	1,210	654	564	1990
231	915	2,277	1,138	671	462	1989
223	725	2,435	1,288	662	509	1988
230	701	2,334	1,298	623	495	1987
247	672	2,435	1,289	642	517	1986
244	597	2,185	1,135	598	431	1985
267	627	2,144	1,154	658	414	1984
275	646	2,173	1,076	604	440	1983
271	557	2,093	1,091	589	482	1982
262	609	2,205	1,132	577	510	1981
317	514	2,453	1,178	566	551	1980
280	552	2,350	1,268	607	474	1979
278	525	2,460	1,294	548	456	1978
281	565	2,440	1,245	588	477	1977
228	548	2,262	1,160	559	492	1976
298	612	2,310	1,142	567	568	1975
304	629	2,510	1,290	544	569	1974
325	610	2,698	1,442	490	550	1973
384	651	2,602	1,401	469	549	1972
339	675	2,467	1,337	490	486	1971
381	619	2,582	1,406	497	441	1970
339	607	2,531	1,358	461	423	1969
376	571	2,502	1,252	413	412	1968
372	498	2,466	1,286	404	379	1967
391	492	2,468	1,250	385	333	1966
387	461	2,247	1,143	379	316	1965
447	448	2,162	1,061	395	307	1964
422	428	2,100	977	359	266	1963
405	455	1,967	901	401	264	1962
420	419	1,825	795	346	263	1961
434	420	1,969	859	333	268	1960

Note: Data are by place of residence at time of death. Cause titles are shown according to the *Ninth Revision International Classification of Disease, 1975*, adopted for use January 1, 1979. Where necessary, regrouping of causes for 1960-1978 has been done to make numbers for these years correspond as nearly as possible with those for 1979-1991.

1. Includes categories not detailed separately.

Source: Tennessee Department of Health, Bureau of Information Resources, *Annual Bulletin of Vital Statistics, 1991*; and unpublished data.

TABLE 17.3--DEATH RATES PER 100,000 POPULATION, BY MAJOR CAUSE, TENNESSEE, 1960-1991

Year	Diseases of the heart	Malignant neoplasms	Cerebrovascular disease	Accidents and adverse effects	Chronic obstructive pulmonary disease and allied conditions	Pneumonia and influenza	Suicide	Homicide and legal intervention	Diabetes mellitus
1991	312.9	216.2	71.0	43.5	38.5	34.5	13.9	11.9	19.1
1990	316.1	215.4	74.3	46.4	38.5	34.8	13.4	11.6	18.7
1989	317.2	210.2	74.3	47.0	36.8	31.2	13.9	9.5	18.9
1988	332.9	205.7	78.2	50.6	36.4	33.7	13.8	10.6	15.1
1987	330.4	209.5	79.4	48.9	33.7	28.5	13.0	10.4	14.7
1986	331.5	201.4	76.5	51.3	35.4	31.0	13.5	10.9	14.2
1985	334.3	195.8	76.5	46.4	33.7	28.5	12.7	9.2	12.7
1984	327.9	194.8	83.3	45.8	31.1	31.0	14.0	8.8	13.4
1983	326.2	188.1	88.8	46.6	27.7	24.0	13.0	9.4	13.9
1982	320.0	186.7	85.5	45.1	27.3	21.0	12.7	10.4	12.0
1981	322.8	181.1	88.6	47.8	28.1	25.4	12.5	11.1	13.2
1980	323.9	180.9	93.9	53.4	26.9	22.6	12.3	12.0	11.2
1979	311.4	171.9	92.9	51.8	23.2	20.0	13.4	10.5	12.2
1978	317.7	167.9	96.0	55.1	25.7	26.0	12.3	10.2	11.8
1977	329.3	170.5	103.6	55.4	23.7	24.3	13.4	10.8	12.8
1976	336.8	166.3	112.3	52.3	23.0	28.6	12.9	11.4	12.7
1975	335.7	161.2	115.0	54.2	21.9	25.8	13.3	13.3	14.4
1974	350.8	159.9	123.9	59.7	22.4	24.4	12.9	13.5	15.0
1973	362.7	157.1	129.0	65.2	21.8	28.9	11.8	13.3	14.7
1972	365.6	153.3	127.6	63.7	20.5	30.9	11.5	13.4	15.9
1971	362.3	151.4	124.6	61.5	17.0	29.8	12.2	12.1	16.8
1970	364.5	152.4	128.8	65.8	18.3	34.4	12.7	11.2	15.8
1969	368.1	147.2	130.8	64.9	17.9	36.0	11.8	10.9	15.6
1968	367.3	148.0	133.3	64.8	16.8	35.7	10.7	10.7	14.8
1967	344.3	142.9	131.2	64.5	16.5	32.6	10.6	9.9	13.0
1966	356.7	137.3	132.6	65.1	16.5	37.9	10.2	8.8	13.0
1965	340.0	136.1	131.4	59.9	17.2	36.1	10.1	8.4	12.3
1964	337.7	131.4	131.2	58.1	13.5	41.0	10.6	8.3	12.0
1963	341.1	139.4	136.0	57.0	14.4	51.0	9.7	7.2	11.6
1962	328.9	127.5	135.0	53.9	13.1	39.6	11.0	7.2	12.5
1961	307.9	128.3	130.2	50.5	11.4	36.7	9.6	7.3	11.6
1960	315.5	122.5	130.9	55.1	11.3	40.5	9.3	7.5	11.7

Note: Cause titles are shown according to the *Ninth Revision International Classification of Disease, 1975*, adopted for use on January 1, 1979. Where necessary, regrouping of causes for 1960-1978 has been done to make numbers for these years correspond as closely as possible with those for 1979-1991. Rates are based on number of deaths by place of residence at time of death.

Source: Tennessee Department of Health, Bureau of Information Resources, *Annual Bulletin of Vital Statistics, 1991*; and unpublished data.

TABLE 17.4-- NUMBER OF INFANT AND NEONATAL DEATHS AND RATES PER 1,000 LIVE BIRTHS, BY RACE, RESIDENT DATA, TENNESSEE, 1960-1991, SELECTED YEARS

| | Infant deaths[1] | | | | | | Neonatal deaths[2] | | | | | |
| | Total | | White | | All other races | | Total | | White | | All other races | |
Year	Number	Rate	Number	Rate	Number	Rate	Number	Rate	Number	Rate	Number	Rate
1991	738	9.9	405	7.2	333	18.0	459	6.2	250	4.5	209	11.3
1990	770	10.3	449	8.0	321	16.9	490	6.5	282	5.0	208	11.0
1989	789	10.8	459	8.4	330	17.7	500	6.8	279	5.1	221	11.9
1988	762	10.8	438	8.3	324	18.4	458	6.5	258	4.9	200	11.3
1987	792	11.7	473	9.2	319	19.3	515	7.6	302	5.9	213	12.9
1986	726	11.0	437	8.7	289	18.3	456	6.9	281	5.6	175	11.1
1985	757	11.3	451	8.8	306	19.4	501	7.5	277	5.4	224	14.2
1984	768	11.8	491	9.8	277	18.5	516	7.9	319	6.4	197	13.2
1983	833	12.7	537	10.6	296	19.7	545	8.3	352	7.0	193	12.9
1982	804	12.0	519	10.0	285	18.6	532	7.9	339	6.6	193	12.6
1981	846a	12.6	522	10.1	321	20.6	593a	8.8	356	6.9	235	15.1
1980	929	13.4	625	11.8	304	18.8	626	9.1	424	8.0	202	12.5
1979	925	13.5	600	11.5	325	20.3	620	9.1	397	7.6	223	13.9
1978	981	14.8	664	13.0	317	20.8	691	10.4	461	9.0	230	15.1
1977	1,022	15.3	691	13.3	331	22.8	719	10.8	487	9.3	232	16.0
1976	1,007	16.1	674	13.8	333	24.2	724	11.6	491	10.1	233	16.9
1975	1,004	16.1	672	13.9	332	24.0	729	11.7	485	10.0	244	17.7
1974	1,110	17.3	756	15.1	354	25.4	828	12.9	570	11.4	258	18.5
1973	1,303a	20.3	898	17.9	404	28.5	956a	14.9	670	13.4	285	20.1
1972	1,384	21.0	925	17.9	459	32.3	1,021	15.5	687	13.3	334	23.5
1971	1,469	20.6	1,054	18.8	415	27.4	1,092	15.3	791	14.1	301	19.9
1970	1,540	21.3	1,061	18.7	479	30.9	1,173	16.2	839	14.8	334	21.6
1969	1,529	21.9	1,031	18.7	498	33.7	1,126	16.1	770	14.0	356	24.1
1968	1,549a	23.1	1,039	19.7	509	35.7	1,117	16.7	787	14.9	330	23.2
1967	1,649	24.3	1,107	20.9	542	36.7	1,176	17.4	825	15.6	351	23.8
1966	1,790	26.0	1,186	22.1	604	40.0	1,243	18.0	854	15.9	389	25.8
1965	2,024	27.7	1,327	23.5	697	42.0	1,409	19.3	970	17.2	439	26.4
1964	2,255	28.2	1,547	24.7	708	40.3	1,569	19.6	1,098	17.6	471	26.8
1960	2,399	29.3	1,610	25.3	789	43.0	1,651	20.2	1,180	18.6	471	25.7

1. A death of a live-born infant under one year of age.
2. A death of a live-born infant under 28 days of age.
a. Includes deaths with race not stated.
Source: Tennessee Department of Health, Bureau of Information Resources, *Annual Bulletin of Vital Statistics*, 1991; and unpublished data.

TABLE 17.5--NUMBER OF INFANT DEATHS AND RATES PER 1,000 LIVE BIRTHS, BY CAUSE AND BY
RACE, RESIDENT DATA, TENNESSEE, 1991

Cause of death	Total		White		Nonwhite	
	Number	Rate	Number	Rate	Number	Rate
Total [1]	738	9.9	405	7.2	333	18.0
Sudden infant death syndrome	125	1.7	71	1.3	54	2.9
Congenital anomalies	143	1.9	101	1.8	42	2.3
Immaturity	85	1.1	34	0.6	51	2.8
Respiratory distress syndrome	41	0.6	28	0.5	13	0.7
Infections specific to the perinatal period	33	0.4	15	0.3	18	1.0
Complications of placenta, cord and membranes	15	0.2	7	0.1	8	0.4
Accidents and adverse effects	21	0.3	17	0.3	4	0.2
Maternal complications of pregnancy	32	0.4	21	0.4	11	0.6
Intrauterine hypoxia and birth asphyxia	14	0.2	9	0.2	5	0.3
Homicide	11	0.1	6	0.1	5	0.3

1. Total includes subcategories not listed separately.

Source: Tennessee Department of Health, Bureau of Information Resources, *Tennessee Vital Statistics, 1991*; and unpublished data.

TABLE 17.6--ILLEGITIMATE BIRTHS AS A PERCENT OF LIVE BIRTHS, BY RACE, TENNESSEE, 1950–1991

Year	Total	White	Nonwhite
1991	32.2	19.4	71.0
1990	30.2	17.5	67.8
1989	29.1	16.1	67.0
1988	27.6	14.7	66.3
1987	26.3	13.8	65.3
1986	25.3	13.0	64.6
1985	24.3	12.2	63.3
1984	22.9	11.2	62.0
1983	22.0	10.5	60.9
1982	20.9	9.7	58.7
1981	20.4	9.2	57.0
1980	19.8	8.8	56.2
1979	19.1	8.1	55.1
1978	18.2	7.4	54.1
1977	16.6	6.7	52.2
1976	16.5	6.1	53.3
1975	15.8	5.9	50.6
1974	14.9	5.4	49.3
1973	14.9	5.3	49.0
1972	14.4	5.2	47.9
1971	12.9	4.5	43.9
1970	12.5	4.6	41.5
1969	11.8	4.5	39.3
1968	11.8	4.4	39.1
1967	11.8	4.1	39.6
1966	11.3	4.0	37.2
1965	11.2	3.8	36.4
1964	9.9	3.2	33.9
1963	9.7	3.1	32.8
1962	9.5	3.1	32.1
1961	9.3	3.0	31.3
1960	8.7	2.7	29.4
1959	8.4	2.8	27.8
1958	8.0	2.7	27.3
1957	7.8	2.6	26.2
1956	7.6	2.5	25.7
1955	7.3	2.4	25.5
1954	7.0	2.4	24.6
1953	6.7	2.2	24.0
1952	6.0	2.2	21.1
1951	6.1	2.7	19.7
1950	5.8	2.1	20.6

Source: Tennessee Department of Health, Bureau of Information Resources, *Annual Bulletin of Vital Statistics, 1991*; and unpublished data.

TABLE 17.7--TEENAGE PREGNANCIES, LIVE BIRTHS, AND PERCENT OF LIVE BIRTHS THAT WERE ILLEGITIMATE, BY AGE GROUP AND BY RACE OF MOTHER, TENNESSEE, 1974-1989

	Females 10–14 years of age								
			Live births						
	Teenage pregnancies, all races[1]		All races			White		Other races	
					Percent illegit-imate				
Year	Number	Rate	Number	Rate		Number	Rate	Number	Rate
1989	517	3.1	310	1.9	91.9	98	0.8	211	5.7
1988	491	2.9	316	1.9	93.0	87	0.7	229	6.2
1987	521	3.1	279	1.7	92.8	100	0.8	179	4.9
1986	580	3.4	293	1.7	91.8	99	0.7	194	5.3
1985	555	3.2	294	1.7	89.5	99	0.7	195	5.3
1984	497	2.9	252	1.5	90.9	80	0.6	172	5.0
1983	506	2.9	272	1.6	91.5	104	0.8	168	4.8
1982	494	2.8	292	1.6	85.3	113	0.8	179	5.1
1981	495	2.8	299	1.7	87.0	105	0.7	194	5.4
1980	527	2.9	291	1.6	85.2	118	0.8	173	4.7
1979	574	3.4	334	2.0	80.2	148	1.1	186	5.9
1978	565	3.2	359	2.0	81.3	159	1.1	200	6.0
1977	595	3.3	380	2.1	81.8	168	1.2	212	6.2
1976	616	3.4	384	2.1	77.1	150	1.0	234	6.7
1975	596	3.1	425	2.2	80.0	164	1.1	261	6.8
1974	606	3.1	455	2.4	75.2	175	1.1	280	7.1

	Females 15–19 years of age								
			Live births						
	Teenage pregnancies, all races[1]		All races			White		Other races	
					Percent illegit-imate				
Year	Number	Rate	Number	Rate		Number	Rate	Number	Rate
1989	17,331	95.6	12,479	68.8	57.9	8,237	57.4	4,240	112.4
1988	17,235	93.6	11,832	64.3	57.4	7,772	53.3	4,060	106.3
1987	16,313	87.3	11,145	59.6	55.9	7,309	49.3	3,836	99.1
1986	16,110	84.9	10,972	57.8	52.2	7,326	48.7	3,646	93.0
1985	16,052	83.3	11,120	57.7	51.4	7,521	49.2	3,599	90.6
1984	15,927	80.1	11,016	55.9	48.7	7,562	47.8	3,454	89.1
1983	16,685	82.7	11,557	57.7	47.4	7,907	49.3	3,650	91.5
1982	17,511	85.5	12,221	59.7	44.7	8,434	51.4	3,787	93.1
1981	18,012	86.7	12,716	61.2	43.9	8,713	52.5	4,003	95.5
1980	19,276	91.5	13,468	63.9	42.5	9,206	54.9	4,262	98.8
1979	19,816	100.4	13,841	70.2	41.1	9,386	58.6	4,455	119.7
1978	18,759	94.5	13,830	69.7	40.3	9,376	58.3	4,453	118.1
1977	18,706	94.0	14,176	71.2	37.9	9,809	60.9	4,347	114.0
1976	18,964	95.8	14,243	71.9	37.0	9,660	60.5	4,583	120.0
1975	18,371	91.7	14,950	74.6	33.8	10,252	64.4	4,698	113.9
1974	18,538	93.6	15,943	80.5	32.1	10,858	68.8	5,085	126.0

Note: Rate is per 1,000 female population in specified race and age group.

1. Live births plus fetal deaths plus abortions.

Source: Tennessee Department of Health, Division of Information Resources, *Teenage Childbearing, Resident Data, Tennessee, 1950–1982*, April 1984; and unpublished data.

TABLE 17.8-- NUMBER AND PERCENT DISTRIBUTION OF WOMEN RECEIVING ABORTIONS, BY SELECTED CHARACTERISTICS, TENNESSEE, 1980-1989, SELECTED YEARS

Characteristics	1989 Number	1989 %	1988 Number	1988 %	1987 Number	1987 %	1986 Number	1986 %	1985 Number	1985 %	1980 Number	1980 %
Total	21,050	100.0	21,589	100.0	21,621	100.0	21,938	100.0	21,069	100.0	23,274	100.0
Age												
19 years or less	5,873	27.9	6,148	28.5	6,232	28.8	6,210	28.3	6,056	28.7	7,400	31.8
20-24 years	6,819	32.4	6,990	32.4	7,097	32.8	7,342	33.5	7,208	34.2	8,101	34.8
25 years and over	8,337	39.6	8,432	39.1	8,286	38.3	8,373	38.2	7,794	37.0	7,741	33.3
Race												
White	13,837	65.7	14,492	67.1	14,754	68.2	15,039	68.6	14,721	69.9	17,199	73.9
All other races	7,166	34.0	7,035	32.6	6,826	31.6	6,878	31.4	6,305	29.9	5,950	25.6
Marital status												
Unmarried	16,389	77.9	16,303	75.5	16,496	76.3	16,936	77.2	16,146	76.6	17,131	73.6
Married[1]	4,449	21.1	4,654	21.6	4,817	22.3	4,850	22.1	4,835	22.9	5,982	25.7
Number of living children												
None	10,956	52.0	11,560	53.5	11,846	54.8	12,198	55.6	12,117	57.5	13,619	58.5
One	5,475	26.0	5,460	25.3	5,277	24.4	5,235	23.9	4,788	22.7	4,841	20.8
Two	3,214	15.3	3,168	14.7	3,089	14.3	3,079	14.0	2,884	13.7	3,034	13.0
Three	959	4.6	974	4.5	961	4.4	976	4.4	861	4.1	1,072	4.6
Four	286	1.4	271	1.3	287	1.3	283	1.3	270	1.3	337	1.4
Five or more	125	0.6	137	0.6	140	0.6	152	0.7	133	0.6	225	1.0
Number of previous abortions												
None	14,058	66.8	14,763	68.4	14,799	68.4	15,138	69.0	14,522	68.9	17,190	73.9
One	4,917	23.4	4,875	22.6	4,904	22.7	4,887	22.3	4,788	22.7	4,718	20.3
Two	1,438	6.8	1,363	6.3	1,287	6.0	1,295	5.9	1,229	5.8	890	3.8
Three	369	1.8	383	1.8	398	1.8	401	1.8	340	1.6	164	0.7
Four	133	0.6	94	0.4	121	0.6	125	0.6	110	0.5	45	0.2
Five or more	79	0.4	77	0.4	79	0.4	64	0.3	60	0.3	10	(a)

Note: Percentages do not add to 100 as total includes observations with "chracteristics not stated."
1. Married includes separated.
a. Percent less than 0.05.
Source: Tennessee Department of Health, Center for Health Statistics, *Induced Abortions Reported in Tennessee, 1989.*

TABLE 17.9-- REPORTED CASES OF SELECTED COMMUNICABLE DISEASES, TENNESSEE, 1960–1989, SELECTED YEARS

Year	Encephalitis (all types)	Hepatitis (all types)	Measles	Meningococcal infections	Pertussis (whooping cough)	Salmonellosis[1]	Primary and secondary syphilis	Gonorrhea
1989	6	842	157	158	111	580	1,161	14,424
1988	14	830	0	29	35	530	968	19,497
1987	14	636	0	35	23	507	721	19,886
1986	13	793	55	45	18	474	624	26,891
1985	8	818	0	44	27	486	631	29,658
1984	22	901	2	52	7	450	543	30,748
1983	23	1,004	0	58	8	521	588	30,949
1982	33	1,012	6	79	26	455	656	32,663
1981	89	1,029	2	71	16	598	686	31,817
1980	35	1,023	170	61	37	546	926	29,932
1979	38	1,149	69	54	31	508	686	31,059
1978	34	1,249	952	58	60	513	387	31,201
1977	55	1,582	769	47	56	588	253	35,195
1976	78	1,663	187	64	33	363	289	35,362
1975	181	1,631	165	62	78	525	416	33,124
1974	98	1,976	54	51	80	485	450	30,188
1973	42	1,886	164	40	55	686	453	26,688
1972	41	1,548	195	35	128	527	509	26,891
1971	59	1,531	1,028	85	192	429	355	20,783
1970	64	1,344	608	75	161	880	179	16,366
1969	53	1,097	21	75	110	277	289	14,432
1968	48	1,058	64	72	180	313	310	12,456
1967	84	860	2,058	78	479	436	298	12,163
1966	58	1,015	12,955	100	313	229	305	11,105
1965	28	805	8,994	75	286	191	497	9,905
1964	47	910	25,309	71	578	220	480	9,369
1963	26	1,459	7,880	79	865	148	396	8,210
1960	36	2,100	19,202	66	1,111	97	448	9,881

1. Excluding typhoid fever.

Source: Tennessee Department of Health, Division of Communicable Diseases, unpublished data; and Division of Information Resources, unpublished data..

TABLE 17.10--SELECTED DATA ON SHORT-TERM NON-FEDERAL HOSPITALS, BY TYPE OF OWNERSHIP, TENNESSEE, 1986–1992

| Year and type of ownership | Number of hospitals | Staffed beds | | Average daily census | Average length of stay (days) | Staffed percent occupancy | Full-time equivalent employees per 100 staffed beds |
		Number	Per 1,000 popu- lation				
1992							
Total	135	21,643	4.4	13,005	6.3	60.2	n.a.
1991							
Total	137	22,220	4.5	13,350	6.3	60.0	n.a.
1990							
Total	138	22,418	4.6	13,809	6.4	61.8	n.a.
1989							
Total	138	22,262	4.4	13,714	6.3	62.0	350.2
State/local							
government	28	4,343	0.9	2,684	5.6	62.1	382.3
Nonprofit	59	12,685	2.5	8,634	6.8	68.3	383.3
Profit	51	5,234	1.0	2,396	5.5	46.6	243.2
1988							
Total	139	22,088	4.5	13,357	6.2	60.7	337.9
State/local							
government	32	4,479	0.9	2,840	5.7	65.0	363.3
Nonprofit	54	12,422	2.5	8,450	6.9	67.5	370.4
Profit	53	5,187	1.0	2,066	4.9	40.3	238.2
1987							
Total	143	22,851	4.7	12,656	5.9	55.2	315.0
State/local							
government	31	4,653	0.9	2,383	4.8	51.0	329.5
Nonprofit	53	12,544	2.6	8,371	6.7	66.3	355.7
Profit	59	5,654	1.2	1,902	4.7	33.8	212.8
1986							
Total	145	23,001	4.8	13,428	5.9	57.3	334.1
State/local							
government	33	4,607	1.0	2,439	4.6	50.9	320.2
Nonprofit	52	12,466	2.6	8,552	6.5	67.1	348.2
Profit	60	5,928	1.2	2,437	5.8	41.3	203.5

Note: Computed variables such as average length of stay were based on only those facilities which reported sufficient data necessary for the calculations. In addition, not every hospital reported every variable.

n.a. not available.

Source: Tennessee Department of Health, Bureau of Information Resources, *Tennessee's Health, Picture of the Present Part 2, 1992* and earlier editions; and unpublished data.

TABLE 17.11--NUMBER OF HOSPITALS, BY OWNERSHIP AND BY TYPE, TENNESSEE, 1983–1989,
         SELECTED YEARS

| | | Ownership of hospital | | | |
| | | Government | | Private | |
Year and type of hospital	Total	Federal	State and local	Nonprofit	Proprietary
1989 Total	162	6	35	63	58
Short-term	144	5	29	59	51
General	139	5	29	56	49
Specialty	5	0	0	3	2
Long-term	18	1	6	4	7
Psychiatric	17	1	5	4	7
Geriatric	1	0	1	0	0
1988 Total	162	6	38	58	60
Short-term	144	5	32	54	53
General	143	5	32	54	52
Specialty	1	0	0	0	1
Long-term	18	1	6	4	7
Psychiatric	17	1	5	4	7
Geriatric	1	0	1	0	0
1987 Total	168	6	37	58	67
Short-term	150	5	31	54	60
General	149	5	31	54	59
Specialty	1	0	0	0	1
Long-term	18	1	6	4	7
Psychiatric	17	1	5	4	7
Geriatric	1	0	1	0	0
1985 Total	173	6	39	64	64
Short-term	156	5	33	59	59
General	149	5	33	54	57
Specialty	7	0	0	5	2
Long-term	17	1	6	5	5
Psychiatric	15	1	5	4	5
Geriatric	2	0	1	1	0
1984 Total	172	6	41	61	64
Short-term	157	5	35	57	60
General	150	5	35	53	57
Specialty	7	0	0	4	3
Long-term	15	1	6	4	4
Psychiatric	13	1	5	3	4
Geriatric	2	0	1	1	0
1983 Total	171	5	44	57	65
Short-term	155	4	38	53	60
General	149	4	38	49	58
Specialty	6	0	0	4	2
Long-term	16	1	6	4	5
Psychiatric	14	1	5	3	5
Geriatric	2	0	1	1	0

Source: Tennessee Department of Health, Division of Information Resources, unpublished data.

TABLE 17.12--NUMBER OF NURSING HOMES AND SELECTED UTILIZATION DATA, TENNESSEE, 1970–1992

Year	Nursing homes	Staffed beds	Admissions[1]	Patient days[2]	Staffed percent occupancy
1992	313	35,900	34,809	n.a.	95.2
1991	304	35,116	33,326	n.a.	94.2
1990	302	34,886	31,075	n.a.	94.1
1989	293	33,831	26,561	11,541,017	94.6
1988	291	32,738	27,111	11,097,964	94.5
1987	284	31,993	25,625	10,685,768	94.4
1986	278	30,200	23,638	10,103,795	93.7
1985	268	29,128	21,834	9,702,449	94.7
1984	261	27,756	21,539	9,503,802	95.5
1983	258	27,169	20,155	9,116,368	94.2
1982	251	26,208	18,664	8,696,774	92.9
1981	242	24,984	17,961	8,210,423	93.4
1980	235	22,990	15,989	7,484,862	95.4
1979	218	20,557	14,715	6,778,172	94.7
1978	209	18,369	13,326	6,196,139	96.0
1977	205	17,320	12,636	5,618,718	94.1
1976	200	15,700	12,090	5,226,232	95.1
1975	199	14,410	12,510	4,766,637	94.6
1974	203	13,109	11,375	4,243,999	94.0
1973	198	11,924	12,681	3,934,953	92.0
1972	200	11,977	14,023	3,693,078	88.1
1971	207	11,792	14,348	3,445,248	82.1
1970	208	11,475	14,281	3,186,815	80.4

n.a. not available.

1. Beginning in 1990, admissions refer to total patients.

2. 1970–1978 data are inpatient days. After 1978 data are patient days of care.

Source: Tennessee Department of Health, Bureau of Information Resources, *Tennessee's Health, Picture of the Present, Part 2, 1992*, and earlier editions; and *Annual Report of Hospitals, Nursing Homes, and Homes for the Aged in Tennessee, 1980*, and earlier editions; and unpublished data.

FIGURE 17.2

Birth Rates per 1,000 Population by County of Residence, Tennessee, 1992
(Tennessee average birth rate = 14.9)

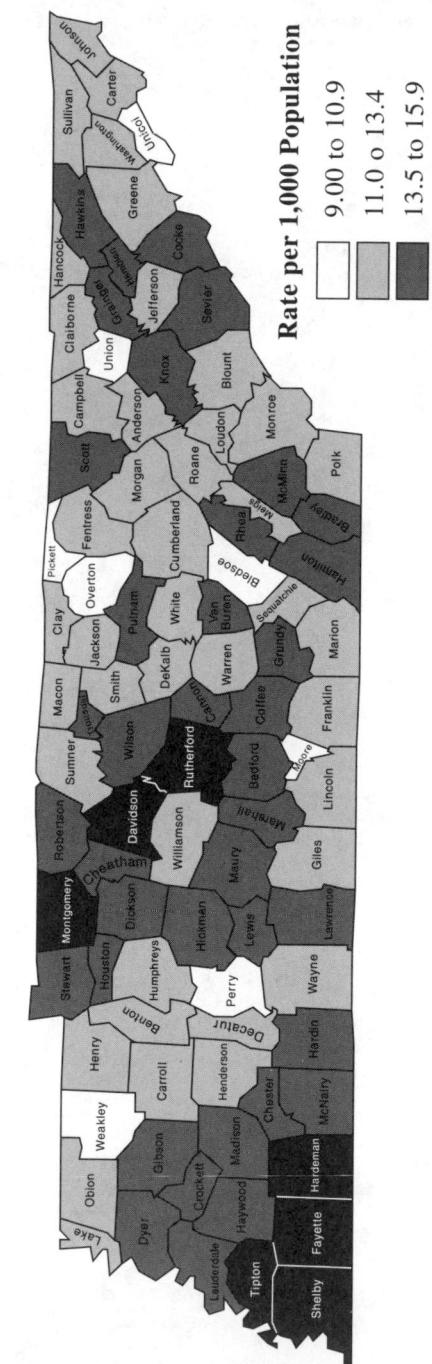

Rate per 1,000 Population

☐	9.00 to 10.9
▨	11.0 o 13.4
▨	13.5 to 15.9
■	16.0 or more

Source: Tennessee Department of Health, Division of Information Resources, Tennessee Vital Statistics Summary, Residence Data, 1992.

TABLE 17.13–LIVE BIRTHS AND DEATHS, BY RACE, TENNESSEE AND COUNTY OF RESIDENCE, 1992

	Live births						Deaths					
	Total[1]		White		Nonwhite		Total[2]		White		Nonwhite	
County	Number	Rate	Number	Rate	Number	Rate	Number	Rate	Number	Rate	Number	Rate
Anderson	916	13.4	851	13.2	63	17.0	660	9.7	634	9.8	26	7.0
Bedford	424	13.7	371	13.4	53	15.8	343	11.1	296	10.7	47	14.0
Benton	173	11.9	165	11.7	8	18.8	186	12.8	183	13.0	3	7.0
Bledsoe	90	9.2	89	9.6	1	2.2	96	9.8	92	9.9	4	8.7
Blount	1,158	13.2	1,099	13.1	59	16.4	798	9.1	765	9.1	33	9.2
Bradley	1,066	14.2	1,003	14.1	63	17.0	605	8.1	573	8.0	32	8.7
Campbell	462	13.2	462	13.3	0	0.0	400	11.4	398	11.5	2	5.4
Cannon	162	15.4	159	15.4	3	12.8	109	10.3	106	10.3	3	12.8
Carroll	333	12.2	288	11.9	45	14.1	361	13.2	322	13.3	39	12.3
Carter	577	11.2	563	11.1	14	17.8	544	10.5	535	10.5	9	11.5
Cheatham	406	14.2	400	14.3	6	8.7	189	6.6	187	6.7	2	2.9
Chester	183	14.2	154	13.5	29	19.7	111	8.6	104	9.1	7	4.7
Claiborne	355	13.4	349	13.4	4	9.0	264	10.0	259	10.0	5	11.3
Clay	88	12.3	88	12.5	0	0.0	102	14.3	97	13.8	5	37.9
Cocke	411	14.1	404	14.2	7	9.3	317	10.9	308	10.8	9	11.9
Coffee	590	14.5	553	14.2	37	19.0	406	9.9	395	10.2	11	5.6
Crockett	192	14.7	147	13.5	45	20.7	175	13.4	160	14.7	15	6.9
Cumberland	462	12.8	462	12.9	0	0.0	358	9.9	358	10.0	0	0.0
Davidson	8,439	16.3	5,714	14.9	2,724	20.4	4,629	9.0	3,446	9.0	1,183	8.9
Decatur	134	12.9	130	13.1	4	8.6	143	13.8	137	13.8	6	12.9
DeKalb	167	11.5	165	11.6	2	7.2	166	11.4	160	11.2	6	21.5
Dickson	527	14.5	484	14.1	43	21.0	362	9.9	343	10.0	19	9.3
Dyer	514	14.7	416	13.6	98	22.4	363	10.4	315	10.3	48	11.0
Fayette	409	16.0	209	14.3	200	18.2	228	8.9	132	9.0	96	8.8
Fentress	189	12.9	189	13.0	0	(a)	143	9.8	143	9.8	0	(a)
Franklin	412	11.7	391	11.9	21	9.3	332	9.4	313	9.5	19	8.4
Gibson	629	13.8	456	12.4	173	19.2	592	13.0	498	13.6	94	10.4
Giles	347	13.4	299	13.3	48	13.6	318	12.2	271	12.1	47	13.3
Grainger	234	13.6	234	13.8	0	0.0	161	9.4	158	9.3	3	19.0
Greene	638	11.4	626	11.5	12	8.5	630	11.2	615	11.3	14	10.0

TABLE 17.13–LIVE BIRTHS AND DEATHS, BY RACE, TENNESSEE AND COUNTY OF RESIDENCE, 1992 (Continued)

County	Live births						Deaths					
	Total[1]		White		Nonwhite		Total[2]		White		Nonwhite	
	Number	Rate	Number	Rate	Number	Rate	Number	Rate	Number	Rate	Number	Rate
Grundy	187	14.1	185	14.0	2	(a)	154	11.6	154	11.7	0	(a)
Hamblen	716	14.1	676	14.1	40	15.2	533	10.5	511	10.6	22	8.4
Hamilton	4,021	14.1	2,835	12.5	1,186	20.4	2,774	9.8	2,162	9.6	612	10.5
Hancock	81	12.1	81	12.4	0	0.0	66	9.9	66	10.1	0	0.0
Hardeman	416	17.9	197	13.6	219	24.7	236	10.1	152	10.5	84	9.5
Hardin	309	13.6	285	13.2	24	21.4	274	12.0	264	12.2	10	8.9
Hawkins	618	13.8	598	13.7	20	22.2	474	10.6	464	10.6	10	11.1
Haywood	291	15.1	111	11.6	180	18.7	230	12.0	127	13.2	103	10.7
Henderson	262	12.0	236	11.8	26	14.1	239	10.9	215	10.7	24	13.0
Henry	339	12.3	293	11.8	45	15.7	392	14.2	353	14.2	39	13.6
Hickman	236	13.8	225	13.9	11	11.5	185	10.8	182	11.3	3	3.1
Houston	102	14.5	94	13.9	8	27.1	86	12.2	81	12.0	5	16.9
Humphreys	182	11.6	165	10.9	17	27.0	175	11.1	168	11.1	7	11.1
Jackson	105	11.3	105	11.4	0	(a)	116	12.5	115	12.5	1	(a)
Jefferson	419	12.6	409	12.7	10	9.2	324	9.7	314	9.7	10	9.2
Johnson	184	13.4	184	13.5	0	(a)	131	9.6	129	9.5	2	(a)
Knox	4,664	13.8	4,037	13.3	627	17.8	3,057	9.0	2,749	9.1	308	8.8
Lake	89	12.5	72	13.6	17	9.5	78	11.0	65	12.2	13	7.3
Lauderdale	356	15.3	222	14.0	134	18.1	296	12.7	207	13.0	89	12.0
Lawrence	519	14.6	512	14.6	7	10.8	395	11.1	386	11.0	9	13.8
Lewis	125	13.7	125	13.9	0	0.0	81	8.9	77	8.6	4	25.2
Lincoln	375	13.1	339	13.0	36	14.2	318	11.1	286	11.0	32	12.6
Loudon	381	12.0	370	11.8	11	20.6	319	10.0	319	10.2	0	0.0
McMinn	592	13.9	538	13.4	54	23.3	405	9.5	382	9.5	23	9.9
McNairy	342	15.3	315	15.1	27	18.0	279	12.5	260	12.4	19	12.7
Macon	215	13.5	215	13.5	0	0.0	164	10.3	164	10.3	0	0.0
Madison	1,251	15.9	708	13.2	543	21.7	821	10.4	573	10.7	248	9.9
Marion	322	12.9	312	13.1	10	9.2	223	8.9	207	8.7	16	14.7
Marshall	326	14.8	310	15.5	16	8.0	239	10.8	221	11.0	18	9.0
Maury	789	14.2	658	14.1	131	14.5	541	9.7	432	9.3	109	12.1

TABLE 17.13--LIVE BIRTHS AND DEATHS, BY RACE, TENNESSEE AND COUNTY OF RESIDENCE, 1992 (Continued)

| | Live births | | | | | | Deaths | | | | | |
| | Total[1] | | White | | Nonwhite | | Total[2] | | White | | Nonwhite | |
County	Number	Rate	Number	Rate	Number	Rate	Number	Rate	Number	Rate	Number	Rate
Meigs	92	11.3	91	11.4	1	6.8	90	11.1	88	11.0	2	13.7
Monroe	406	13.1	387	12.9	19	19.2	320	10.4	301	10.1	19	19.2
Montgomery	2,343	22.5	1,737	21.3	606	26.7	622	6.0	482	5.9	140	6.2
Moore	52	10.9	50	10.9	2	11.4	46	9.7	40	8.7	6	34.1
Morgan	197	11.3	197	11.5	0	0.0	163	9.3	162	9.5	1	2.7
Obion	419	13.3	347	12.4	72	20.9	381	12.1	352	12.5	29	8.4
Overton	167	9.5	167	9.5	0	(a)	184	10.4	184	10.5	0	(a)
Perry	71	10.6	67	10.2	4	28.6	97	14.5	95	14.5	2	14.3
Pickett	43	9.4	43	9.4	0	(a)	41	9.0	41	9.0	0	(a)
Polk	160	11.7	159	11.7	1	(a)	155	11.4	153	11.3	2	(a)
Putnam	735	14.1	723	14.3	12	7.6	524	10.0	519	10.2	5	3.2
Rhea	332	13.6	323	13.7	9	11.5	245	10.1	238	10.1	7	8.9
Roane	560	12.0	540	12.0	20	11.1	506	10.8	488	10.8	18	10.0
Robertson	608	14.3	525	13.8	83	18.2	409	9.6	352	9.3	57	12.5
Rutherford	2,038	16.0	1,786	15.7	252	18.4	803	6.3	693	6.1	110	8.0
Scott	264	14.5	264	14.6	0	0.0	167	9.2	167	9.2	0	0.0
Sequatchie	111	12.4	111	12.5	0	(a)	92	10.3	92	10.3	0	(a)
Sevier	747	14.0	741	14.1	6	8.9	453	8.5	453	8.6	0	0.0
Shelby	15,607	18.7	6,159	13.5	9,445	24.9	7,260	8.7	3,864	8.5	3,394	9.0
Smith	172	12.1	170	12.4	2	4.0	154	10.8	147	10.7	7	13.8
Stewart	133	13.7	131	13.8	2	10.3	105	10.9	104	11.0	1	5.2
Sullivan	1,805	12.6	1,763	12.6	42	11.7	1,350	9.4	1,310	9.4	40	11.2
Sumner	1,454	13.4	1,364	13.4	90	14.1	776	7.2	718	7.0	58	9.1
Tipton	640	16.5	436	14.8	204	22.3	344	8.9	253	8.6	91	9.9
Trousdale	91	15.3	76	15.0	15	17.2	68	11.4	58	11.4	10	11.5
Unicoi	174	10.5	174	10.6	0	(a)	196	11.9	196	11.9	0	(a)
Union	150	10.6	150	10.7	0	(a)	120	8.5	119	8.5	1	(a)
Van Buren	70	14.5	70	14.6	0	(a)	39	8.1	39	8.1	0	(a)
Warren	437	13.2	417	13.2	20	13.2	348	10.5	335	10.6	13	8.6
Washington	1,104	11.9	1,049	11.8	54	13.5	868	9.4	823	9.3	44	11.0

TABLE 17.13--LIVE BIRTHS AND DEATHS, BY RACE, TENNESSEE AND COUNTY OF RESIDENCE, 1992 (Continued)

	Live births						Deaths					
	Total[1]		White		Nonwhite		Total[2]		White		Nonwhite	
County	Number	Rate	Number	Rate	Number	Rate	Number	Rate	Number	Rate	Number	Rate
Wayne	184	13.2	183	13.3	1	5.9	133	9.5	132	9.6	1	5.9
Weakley	329	10.3	305	10.5	24	8.9	355	11.1	339	11.6	16	6.0
White	246	12.2	241	12.2	5	11.7	248	12.3	234	11.8	14	32.7
Williamson	1,140	13.1	1,039	12.8	101	16.5	477	5.5	432	5.3	45	7.4
Wilson	978	13.9	897	13.7	80	15.8	577	8.2	514	7.9	62	12.2
TENNESSEE	73,560	14.9	55,214	13.5	18,335	21.7	46,412	9.4	38,605	9.4	7,802	9.2

Note: Data are by place of residence. Rates are per 1,000 population. Beginning in 1991, race is race of mother not race of child.
1. Includes births with race unknown for Anderson, Claiborne, Davidson, Henry, Shelby, Washington and Wilson counties.
2. Includes deaths with race unknown for Greene, Shelby, Washington and Wilson counties.
a. Rate not calculated when population is less than 100.
Source: Tennessee Department of Health, Bureau of Information Resources, *Tennessee Vital Statistics Summary, Resident Data, 1992.*

TABLE 17.14– CUMULATIVE AIDS CASES REPORTED SINCE 1982, TENNESSEE AND SELECTED
COUNTIES, FEBRUARY 29, 1990–1994

County	2/94	2/93	2/92	2/91	2/90	County	2/94	2/93	2/92	2/91	2/90
Anderson	19	12	11	9	6	Lincoln	11	8	8	8	7
Bedford	8	(a)	(a)	(a)	(a)	Loudon	11	6	6	5	(a)
Blount	24	17	13	10	7	McMinn	15	9	5	(a)	(a)
Bradley	33	25	17	11	5	McNairy	5	(a)	(a)	(a)	(a)
Campbell	8	7	7	(a)	(a)	Madison	38	27	18	13	9
Cannon	5	5	(a)	(a)	(a)	Maury	13	10	7	5	(a)
Carter	8	6	(a)	(a)	(a)	Montgomery	37	24	21	16	12
Cheatham	14	12	11	10	9	Morgan	6	(a)	(a)	(a)	(a)
Cocke	5	(a)	(a)	(a)	(a)	Obion	10	8	6	(a)	(a)
Coffee	13	11	9	6	(a)	Putnam	17	9	7	6	(a)
Crockett	7	5	(a)	(a)	(a)	Rhea	5	(a)	(a)	(a)	(a)
Cumberland	12	11	8	6	(a)	Roane	7	5	(a)	(a)	(a)
Davidson	889	602	456	351	248	Robertson	18	10	8	7	5
Decatur	5	(a)	(a)	(a)	(a)	Rutherford	48	33	24	17	15
Dickson	9	8	7	6	(a)	Sequatchie	6	5	5	(a)	(a)
Dyer	7	5	(a)	(a)	(a)	Sevier	19	16	14	10	9
Fayette	11	5	(a)	(a)	(a)	Shelby	1,105	723	517	392	287
Fentress	6	(a)	(a)	(a)	(a)	Sullivan	56	34	28	20	16
Franklin	13	10	8	7	7	Sumner	32	22	17	14	11
Gibson	11	7	7	6	6	Tipton	17	6	(a)	(a)	(a)
Giles	9	9	7	(a)	(a)	Unicoi	6	(a)	(a)	(a)	(a)
Grainger	5	5	5	(a)	(a)	Warren	11	(a)	(a)	(a)	(a)
Greene	20	12	8	7	6	Washington	55	38	34	23	20
Hamblen	18	13	9	5	5	Weakley	9	9	8	6	6
Hamilton	254	172	132	99	66	White	9	7	(a)	(a)	(a)
Hardeman	6	5	(a)	(a)	(a)	Williamson	24	17	13	8	7
Hawkins	9	6	6	6	(a)	Wilson	16	10	7	6	(a)
Haywood	8	6	5	(a)	(a)						
Henry	9	8	6	5	(a)						
Humphries	5	(a)	(a)	(a)	(a)	TENNESSEE	3,755	2,521	1,909	1,457	1,061
Jefferson	17	14	12	5	(a)						
Johnson	8	(a)	(a)	(a)	(a)						
Knox	228	139	115	90	71						
Lauderdale	9	6	(a)	(a)	(a)						
Lawrence	9	7	6	6	(a)						

Note: Any county reporting five or more resident cases is indicated. No individual county information will be
released for counties reporting 0–4 cases. Data are reported as of the last day of the month.

a. County reported less than five resident cases.

Source: Tennessee Department of Health, AIDS Program, Bureau of Health Services, *The Messenger*, various
issues.

TABLE 17.15--NUMBER OF MARRIAGES AND DIVORCES, TENNESSEE AND COUNTY OF
OCCURRENCE, 1991

County	Marriages	Divorces	County	Marriages	Divorces
Anderson	800	406	Lewis	133	101
Bedford	353	288	Lincoln	885	224
Benton	197	143	Loudon	386	196
Bledsoe	109	56	McMinn	547	294
Blount	979	610	McNairy	431	165
Bradley	1,022	574	Macon	203	133
Campbell	870	245	Madison	877	496
Cannon	202	80	Marion	449	218
Carroll	315	191	Marshall	254	164
Carter	632	398	Maury	559	351
Cheatham	227	251	Meigs	123	49
Chester	178	127	Monroe	399	207
Claiborne	475	118	Montgomery	1,593	993
Clay	127	46	Moore	83	35
Cocke	505	180	Morgan	237	88
Coffee	501	274	Obion	351	238
Crockett	151	63	Overton	180	94
Cumberland	469	305	Perry	73	46
Davidson	5,970	3,206	Pickett	80	17
Decatur	131	58	Polk	315	54
DeKalb	194	89	Putnam	568	378
Dickson	459	314	Rhea	316	195
Dyer483	266	Roane	514		
Fayette	245	288	Robertson	1,347	282
Fentress	245	161	Rutherford	1,182	941
Franklin	465	226	Scott	268	128
Gibson	541	368	Sequatchie	158	57
Giles	482	173	Sevier	8,977	414
Grainger	187	120	Shelby	8,277	3,806
Greene	711	474	Smith	195	103
Grundy	165	110	Stewart	120	50
Hamblen	702	450	Sullivan	1,562	716
Hamilton	3,413	1,949	Sumner	1,023	784
Hancock	95	14	Tipton	560	779
Hardeman	326	172	Trousdale	163	48
Hardin	412	172	Unicoi	259	120
Hawkins	463	372	Union	220	98
Haywood	229	126	Van Buren	62	22
Henderson	281	217	Warren	398	276
Henry	339	202	Washington	1,000	657
Hickman	161	96	Wayne	126	86
Houston	83	49	Weakley	334	236
Humphreys	179	75	White	258	133
Jackson	110	43	Williamson	559	456
Jefferson	357	168	Wilson	660	440
Johnson	280	105			
Knox	3,474	2,492	TENNESSEE	67,501	33,156
Lake93	50				
Lauderdale	298	219			
Lawrence	445	275			

Source: Tennessee Department of Health, Bureau of Information Resources, *Tennessee Vital Statistics, 1991.*

TABLE 17.16--ILLEGITIMATE LIVE BIRTHS, BY RACE, TENNESSEE AND COUNTY OF RESIDENCE OF
MOTHER, 1991

County	Total		White		Nonwhite	
	Number	Percent of live births	Number	Percent of live births	Number	Percent of live births
Anderson	230	24.4	183	21.1	47	62.7
Bedford	130	30.6	95	25.4	35	68.6
Benton	36	17.6	26	13.6	10	76.9
Bledsoe	19	17.6	19	17.8	0	0.0
Blount	232	20.5	208	19.2	24	54.5
Bradley	254	23.8	212	21.1	42	68.9
Campbell	140	28.5	140	28.6	0	0.0
Cannon	29	20.6	24	17.8	5	(a)
Carroll	107	29.1	76	23.5	31	68.9
Carter	152	24.8	144	24.0	8	72.7
Cheatham	95	21.7	90	21.1	5	50.0
Chester	28	15.9	14	9.0	14	66.7
Claiborne	62	16.9	62	17.0	0	0.0
Clay	11	16.9	10	15.6	1	(a)
Cocke	137	34.6	126	33.2	11	68.8
Coffee	159	26.4	142	25.0	17	48.6
Crockett	41	21.5	23	14.2	18	62.1
Cumberland	102	22.9	102	23.0	0	0.0
Davidson	3,278	37.9	1,285	22.1	1,993	70.6
Decatur	35	25.9	26	21.3	9	69.2
DeKalb	38	19.7	37	19.3	1	(a)
Dickson	140	24.6	103	20.4	37	57.8
Dyer	181	32.7	98	21.9	82	78.1
Fayette	210	49.6	36	20.2	174	71.0
Fentress	46	20.6	46	20.6	0	0.0
Franklin	90	21.6	70	18.0	20	74.1
Gibson	228	37.4	72	18.3	156	72.6
Giles	96	26.4	54	17.6	42	75.0
Grainger	27	13.0	27	13.0	0	0.0
Greene	174	25.4	160	24.2	14	63.6
Grundy	57	26.6	57	26.6	0	0.0
Hamblen	214	29.2	180	26.3	34	69.4
Hamilton	1,569	37.3	629	21.2	939	75.9
Hancock	15	20.3	15	20.3	0	0.0
Hardeman	188	46.8	36	19.5	152	70.0
Hardin	78	23.8	63	20.3	15	88.2
Hawkins	112	18.5	109	18.4	3	27.3
Haywood	165	50.6	23	20.0	142	67.3
Henderson	60	20.3	46	17.4	14	45.2
Henry	86	25.9	59	20.2	27	67.5
Hickman	57	25.2	44	21.4	13	65.0
Houston	24	23.5	19	20.7	5	50.0
Humphreys	42	19.5	31	16.0	11	52.4
Jackson	14	18.2	14	18.2	0	0.0
Jefferson	61	15.7	57	14.9	4	(a)
Johnson	50	28.7	50	28.7	0	0.0
Knox	1,191	25.8	776	19.6	415	62.8
Lake	37	45.1	19	31.1	18	85.7
Lauderdale	140	34.6	36	14.1	104	69.3
Lawrence	77	14.2	72	13.5	5	(a)

TABLE 17.16--ILLEGITIMATE LIVE BIRTHS, BY RACE, TENNESSEE AND COUNTY OF RESIDENCE OF MOTHER, 1991 (Continued)

County	Total		White		Nonwhite	
	Number	Percent of live births	Number	Percent of live births	Number	Percent of live births
Lewis	22	16.5	22	16.5	0	0.0
Lincoln	74	20.9	47	14.9	27	71.1
Loudon	88	22.1	86	21.7	2	(a)
McMinn	144	22.9	114	19.6	30	65.6
McNairy	68	21.9	53	18.5	15	60.0
Macon	42	19.4	42	19.4	0	0.0
Madison	560	41.9	121	15.9	438	75.9
Marion	91	27.8	83	26.3	8	72.7
Marshall	87	27.3	63	22.0	24	72.7
Maury	291	33.4	165	23.8	126	71.2
Meigs	20	22.2	20	22.2	0	0.0
Monroe	93	21.2	86	20.3	7	46.7
Montgomery	418	23.7	240	17.7	178	43.7
Moore	7	14.6	6	12.8	1	(a)
Morgan	63	25.9	62	25.6	1	(a)
Obion	115	28.9	64	19.2	51	78.5
Overton	38	16.8	38	17.0	0	0.0
Perry	10	15.6	8	12.9	2	(a)
Pickett	8	17.0	8	17.0	0	0.0
Polk	28	16.9	28	16.9	0	0.0
Putnam	130	18.6	120	17.7	10	47.6
Rhea	109	31.5	102	30.4	7	63.6
Roane	140	25.4	128	24.1	12	60.0
Robertson	176	25.8	100	17.1	76	78.4
Rutherford	473	23.6	335	18.9	138	58.5
Scott	75	24.9	74	24.7	1	(a)
Sequatchie	27	21.1	27	21.1	0	0.0
Sevier	156	22.7	150	22.1	6	(a)
Shelby	7,668	48.6	878	13.5	6,789	73.2
Smith	26	15.2	23	13.8	3	(a)
Stewart	18	15.9	17	15.3	1	(a)
Sullivan	353	20.1	337	19.4	16	59.3
Sumner	369	24.6	289	20.8	80	73.4
Tipton	240	36.1	77	17.8	163	70.3
Trousdale	15	20.5	13	20.3	2	(a)
Unicoi	32	16.8	32	16.9	0	0.0
Union	22	13.3	22	13.3	0	0.0
Van Buren	11	26.2	11	26.2	0	0.0
Warren	106	22.9	96	21.3	10	76.9
Washington	270	23.3	228	20.8	42	63.6
Wayne	32	16.5	31	16.1	1	(a)
Weakley	73	19.9	50	15.1	23	63.9
White	54	19.4	51	18.7	3	(a)
Williamson	176	15.8	98	9.9	78	63.4
Wilson	217	21.2	144	15.7	73	67.0
TENNESSEE	23,979	32.2	10,834	19.4	13,141	71.0

a. Percent not calculated when number of births is less than 10.

Source: Tennessee Department of Health, Bureau of Information Resources, *Tennessee Vital Statistics, 1991.*

TABLE 17.17--SELECTED STATISTICS ON MEDICAL RESOURCES, TENNESSEE AND COUNTIES, 1992

County	Number of hospitals	Number of staffed beds	Number of medical doctors (M.D.)	Number of dentists	Number of registeredf nurses
Anderson	1	273	169	57	484
Bedford	1	75	19	13	95
Benton	1	93	10	4	47
Bledsoe	1	32	4	2	29
Blount	1	203	127	47	488
Bradley	2	260	103	35	415
Campbell	2	121	25	7	103
Cannon	1	55	8	3	31
Carroll	2	109	13	10	84
Carter	1	100	35	15	140
Cheatham	1	29	5	5	46
Chester	0	0	4	3	12
Claibome	1	72	17	5	98
Clay	1	28	5	2	19
Cocke	1	55	18	7	91
Coffee	3	217	57	28	253
Crockett	0	0	5	3	16
Cumberland	1	184	45	11	149
Davidson	11	3,655	2,373	407	7,184
Decatur	1	40	6	2	46
DeKalb	1	53	14	5	34
Dickson	1	147	31	14	127
Dyer	1	125	48	15	148
Fayette	1	38	8	6	48
Fentress	1	71	9	3	38
Franklin	1	99	42	12	149
Gibson	3	216	34	20	153
Giles	1	95	22	7	95
Grainger	0	0	3	2	14
Greene	2	280	69	21	268
Grundy	0	0	4	2	16
Hamblen	2	302	64	30	267
Hamilton	7	1,443	802	195	3,197
Hancock	0	0	3	0	21
Hardeman	1	47	19	8	101
Hardin	1	58	13	6	71
Hawkins	1	55	19	10	91
Haywood	1	52	10	6	47
Henderson	1	35	8	6	53
Henry	1	83	30	14	91
Hickman	1	28	5	4	33
Houston	1	37	4	3	23
Humphreys	1	52	10	4	39
Jackson	1	41	14	3	23
Jefferson	1	91	15	12	86
Johnson	1	65	12	3	26
Knox	7	2,087	1,105	239	3,952
Lake	0	0	3	1	23
Lauderdale	1	70	11	6	52
Lawrence	1	83	26	11	114
Lewis	1	42	6	3	27
Lincoln	1	52	23	11	94
Loudon	1	30	18	15	69

TABLE 17.17--SELECTED STATISTICS ON MEDICAL RESOURCES, TENNESSEE AND COUNTIES, 1992
(Continued)

County	Number of hospitals	Number of staffed beds	Number of medical doctors (M.D.)	Number of dentists	Number of registeredf onurses
McMinn	2	169	49	18	153
McNairy	1	86	14	5	58
Macon	1	43	7	3	32
Madison	2	736	237	52	965
Marion	2	102	16	7	54
Marshall	1	119	19	6	70
Maury	1	275	97	27	375
Meigs	0	0	2	1	5
Monroe	1	59	18	8	80
Montgomery	1	188	111	31	383
Moore	0	0	0	1	8
Morgan	0	0	6	3	25
Obion	1	133	28	14	122
Overton	1	91	12	3	52
Perry	1	53	3	1	30
Pickett	0	0	2	2	6
Polk	1	40	8	6	43
Putnam	1	184	78	25	230
Rhea	1	36	10	6	58
Roane	2	168	43	19	171
Robertson	1	115	30	12	182
Rutherford	1	217	149	58	679
Scott	1	76	16	5	62
Sequatchie	0	0	2	2	25
Sevier	1	58	31	19	152
Shelby	11	4,570	2,436	629	7,736
Smith	2	82	14	3	46
Stewart	0	0	1	2	16
Sullivan	3	966	449	95	1,424
Sumner	3	245	104	47	424
Tipton	1	100	23	13	86
Trousdale	1	34	3	3	11
Unicoi	1	48	12	6	60
Union	0	0	2	3	20
Van Buren	0	0	1	1	4
Warren	1	114	35	12	126
Washington	3	573	391	56	1,131
Wayne	1	70	4	3	31
Weakley	1	100	28	12	111
White	1	60	16	6	42
Williamson	1	130	86	47	453
Wilson	1	125	70	19	316
TENNESSEE	135	21,643	10,217	2,654	35,479

Source: Tennessee Department of Health, Bureau of Information Resources, *Tennessee's Health, Picture of the Present Part 2, 1992*.

TABLE 17.18--LIVE BIRTHS AND DEATHS, BY RESIDENCE, CITIES WITH 1980 POPULATION OF 10,000 OR MORE, 1991

City	Live births		Deaths	
	Number	Rate[1]	Number	Rate[1]
Athens	195	16.2	143	11.8
Bartlett	320	11.8	110	4.1
Bristol	283	12.1	300	12.8
Chattanooga	2,640	17.3	1,896	12.5
Clarksville	1,418	18.4	462	6.0
Cleveland	498	16.2	426	13.9
Columbia	498	17.3	298	10.3
Cookeville	309	14.1	207	9.4
Dyersburg	331	20.2	213	13.0
East Ridge	173	8.2	193	9.2
Elizabethton	177	14.8	201	16.8
Franklin	441	21.2	195	9.4
Gallatin	344	17.9	222	11.5
Germantown	247	7.4	119	3.6
Greeneville	184	13.5	215	15.7
Hendersonville	454	13.8	187	5.7
Humboldt	163	17.0	150	15.6
Jackson	895	18.2	632	12.8
Johnson City	611	12.2	497	9.9
Kingsport	513	13.1	517	13.2
Knoxville	2,614	15.8	1,965	11.8
Lawrenceburg	161	15.4	127	12.1
Lebanon	293	18.7	217	13.9
McMinnville	185	16.4	164	14.6
Maryville	328	16.9	223	11.5
Memphis	12,549	20.2	6,552	10.5
Millington	431	24.1	86	4.8
Morristown	396	18.5	328	15.3
Murfreesboro	736	15.8	364	7.8
Nashville	8,645	16.8	4,677	9.1
Oak Ridge	291	10.6	238	8.7
Paris	111	12.0	159	17.1
Red Bank	40	3.3	86	7.0
Shelbyville	220	15.5	197	13.9
Springfield	235	20.8	179	15.8
Tullahoma	245	14.5	183	10.9
Union City	140	13.3	134	12.8

1. Rates are per 1,000 population and are based on population estimates from the Census Bureau.

Source: Tennessee Department of Health, Bureau of Information Resources, *Tennessee Vital Statistics, 1991.*

TABLE 17.19--NUMBER OF DEATHS AND RATE PER 1,000 POPULATION, SOUTHEASTERN STATES AND UNITED STATES, 1950–1991, SELECTED YEARS [Number in thousands]

State	1991P Number	1991P Rate	1990 Number	1990 Rate	1989 Number	1989 Rate	1988 Number	1988 Rate	1987 Number	1987 Rate
TENNESSEE	45	9.2	46	9.5	45	9.4	46	9.4	45	9.3
Alabama	38	9.3	39	9.7	39	9.7	39	9.5	38	9.2
Arkansas	24	10.2	25	10.5	25	10.5	25	10.4	24	10.2
Florida	135	10.2	134	10.4	133	10.5	131	10.6	127	10.6
Georgia	53	8.0	52	8.0	52	8.2	52	8.1	50	8.1
Kentucky	35	9.5	35	9.5	35	9.6	36	9.6	35	9.3
Louisiana	38	9.0	38	8.9	38	8.9	38	8.5	36	8.2
Mississippi	26	9.9	25	9.8	25	9.9	25	9.5	25	9.4
North Carolina	59	8.7	57	8.6	57	8.8	58	8.9	55	8.6
South Carolina	30	8.4	30	8.5	30	8.6	29	8.5	28	8.3
Virginia	49	7.8	48	7.8	47	7.7	48	7.9	47	7.9
West Virginia	20	11.0	19	10.8	20	10.8	20	10.6	20	10.4
UNITED STATES	2,165	8.6	2,148	8.6	2,150	8.7	2,168	8.8	2,123	8.7

State	1985 Number	1985 Rate	1980 Number	1980 Rate	1970 Number	1970 Rate	1960 Number	1960 Rate	1950 Number	1950 Rate
TENNESSEE	43	9.1	41	8.9	38	9.7	33	9.2	29	8.9
Alabama	38	9.3	36	9.1	34	9.8	30	9.3	27	8.8
Arkansas	24	10.2	23	9.9	21	10.7	18	10.0	15	8.1
Florida	121	10.7	105	10.7	75	11.0	48	9.7	27	9.6
Georgia	49	8.1	44	8.1	42	9.1	35	9.0	30	8.8
Kentucky	35	9.4	34	9.2	33	10.3	30	9.9	28	9.5
Louisiana	37	8.3	36	8.5	33	9.2	30	9.1	24	8.8
Mississippi	25	9.4	24	9.4	23	10.5	22	10.0	21	9.5
North Carolina	53	8.5	48	8.2	45	8.8	38	8.4	31	7.7
South Carolina	27	8.1	25	8.1	23	8.8	21	8.7	18	8.5
Virginia	45	7.9	43	8.0	39	8.4	34	8.7	30	9.0
West Virginia	19	10.0	19	9.9	20	11.5	18	9.7	17	8.7
UNITED STATES	2,086	8.7	1,990	8.8	1,921	9.5	1,712	9.5	1,452	9.6

Note: Data by place of residence. Rates are based on total population residing in area. Beginning in 1970, data exclude nonresidents of the U.S.

p preliminary.

Source: U.S. Department of Commerce, Bureau of the Census, *Statistical Abstract of the United States, 1993*, and earlier editions.

TABLE 17.20--DEATH RATES, BY CAUSE, SOUTHEASTERN STATES AND UNITED STATES, 1990

State	All causes [1]	Diseases of heart	Cancer	Cerebro-vascular diseases	Accidents and adverse effects	Chronic obstructive pulmonary [2] diseases	Pneumonia and influenza	Diabetes Mellitus	Suicide	Chronic liver disease and cirrhosis	Athero-sclerosis
TENNESSEE	949.6	317.8	215.1	73.6	47.6	38.2	34.8	18.7	13.4	10.5	8.3
Alabama	974.6	319.1	214.3	71.7	57.5	37.5	30.3	21.5	12.7	10.7	7.0
Arkansas	1,048.7	339.9	242.6	88.3	50.4	42.2	38.5	22.0	12.5	8.7	6.9
Florida	1,038.7	354.3	261.7	65.7	40.0	43.9	27.0	22.9	16.1	13.1	8.7
Georgia	799.8	252.2	170.3	59.0	44.4	29.5	27.7	15.5	13.6	8.7	6.6
Kentucky	951.8	322.4	228.6	65.9	45.9	42.2	36.7	21.7	14.9	8.6	6.2
Louisiana	890.3	294.4	206.0	56.8	45.7	29.0	24.0	28.8	13.2	8.6	7.6
Mississippi	976.5	358.3	206.9	70.6	58.0	34.2	33.8	17.1	11.2	8.2	5.5
North Carolina	864.7	280.1	199.6	67.3	44.0	30.9	29.3	19.8	14.0	10.9	5.0
South Carolina	852.2	267.7	194.8	69.5	47.8	29.9	23.4	20.8	12.4	10.3	4.7
Virginia	776.0	248.9	187.9	56.9	35.5	29.2	27.9	14.4	12.9	8.0	5.8
West Virginia	1,080.9	395.8	245.8	65.9	47.1	50.9	39.7	27.2	12.2	10.0	8.6
UNITED STATES	863.8	289.5	203.2	57.9	37.0	34.9	32.0	19.2	12.4	10.4	7.3

Note: Deaths per 100,000 resident population estimated as of April 1.
1. Includes other causes not shown separately.
2. Includes allied conditions.
Source: U.S. Department of Commerce, Bureau of the Census, *Statistical Abstract of the United States, 1993.*

TABLE 17.21--LEGAL ABORTIONS, SOUTHEASTERN STATES AND UNITED STATES, 1980–1988, SELECTED YEARS

State	Number (1,000)			Rate[1]			Ratio[2]		
	1988	1985	1980	1988	1985	1980	1988	1985	1980
TENNESSEE	22.1	22.4	25.6	18.9	19.1	23.6	292	315	352
Alabama	18.2	19.4	20.8	18.7	20.2	23.1	284	333	331
Arkansas	6.3	5.4	6.2	11.6	10.1	12.3	182	159	173
Florida	82.9	76.7	73.6	31.5	31.8	35.5	437	465	547
Georgia	36.7	38.3	37.9	23.5	26.1	28.4	333	397	395
Kentucky	11.5	9.8	12.8	13.0	11.0	15.1	215	189	215
Louisiana	17.3	19.2	17.7	16.3	17.4	17.6	243	240	218
Mississippi	5.1	5.9	6.1	8.4	9.7	10.6	123	142	132
North Carolina	39.7	34.2	31.9	25.4	22.6	22.8	392	379	377
South Carolina	14.2	11.2	13.7	16.7	13.7	18.2	259	228	274
Virginia	35.4	34.2	31.8	23.7	24.0	24.2	385	412	417
West Virginia	3.3	4.6	3.0	7.5	10.1	6.9	141	185	104
UNITED STATES	1,590.8	1,588.6	1,553.9	27.3	28.0	29.3	404	422	428

1. Rate per 1,000 women, 15–44 years old.
2. Abortions per 1,000 live births.
Source: U.S. Department of Commerce, Bureau of the Census, *Statistical Abstract of the United States, 1993*; original source is S.K. Henshaw and J. Van Vort, eds., *Abortion Factbook, 1992 Edition: Readings, Trends, and State and Local Data to 1988*, The Alan Gutmacher Institute, New York, NY, 1992 (copyright). Used by special permission.

TABLE 17.22--NUMBER OF LIVE BIRTHS AND RATE PER 1,000 POPULATION, SOUTHEASTERN STATES AND UNITED STATES, 1950–1991, SELECTED YEARS [Number in thousands]

State	1991[P] Number	Rate	1990 Number	Rate	1988 Number	Rate	1987 Number	Rate	1986 Number	Rate
TENNESSEE	73	14.5	75	15.4	71	14.4	68	14.0	66	13.8
Alabama	61	14.6	63	15.7	61	14.8	60	14.6	59	14.7
Arkansas	35	14.2	36	15.5	35	14.6	35	14.5	34	14.5
Florida	194	14.6	199	15.4	184	14.9	175	14.6	168	14.3
Georgia	110	16.6	113	17.4	106	16.7	103	16.5	98	16.1
Kentucky	55	14.7	54	14.8	51	13.7	51	13.8	52	13.9
Louisiana	75	17.2	72	17.1	74	16.8	74	16.6	78	17.3
Mississippi	44	16.6	44	16.9	42	16.1	41	15.7	42	16.0
North Carolina	102	15.2	105	15.8	98	15.0	94	14.6	90	14.3
South Carolina	58	16.0	59	16.8	55	15.9	53	15.4	52	15.3
Virginia	97	15.4	99	16.1	93	15.5	90	15.3	87	15.0
West Virginia	22	12.2	23	12.6	22	11.6	22	11.8	23	12.1
UNITED STATES [1]	4,111	16.2	4,158	16.7	3,910	15.9	3,809	15.7	3,757	15.6

State	1985 Number	Rate	1980 Number	Rate	1970 Number	Rate	1960 Number	Rate	1950 Number	Rate
TENNESSEE	67	14.0	69	15.1	72	18.4	82	23.0	84	25.6
Alabama	60	14.9	64	16.3	67	19.4	81	24.7	86	28.1
Arkansas	35	14.9	37	16.3	35	18.5	41	22.7	52	27.1
Florida	164	14.4	132	13.5	115	16.9	116	23.3	66	23.9
Georgia	96	16.1	92	16.9	97	21.1	100	25.3	97	28.0
Kentucky	53	14.2	60	16.3	60	18.7	72	23.8	79	26.9
Louisiana	81	18.2	82	19.5	74	20.4	90	27.7	80	29.7
Mississippi	43	16.6	48	19.0	49	22.1	59	27.2	66	30.4
North Carolina	89	14.3	84	14.4	98	19.3	110	24.1	111	27.3
South Carolina	52	15.6	52	16.6	52	20.1	60	25.1	64	30.2
Virginia	86	15.1	78	14.7	86	18.6	96	24.1	84	25.4
West Virginia	24	12.5	29	15.1	31	17.8	39	21.2	53	26.6
UNITED STATES [1]	3,761	15.8	3,612	15.9	3,731	18.4	4,258	23.7	3,632	24.1

Note: Data are by place of residence. Rates are based on total population residing in area. Beginning in 1970, births to nonresidents of the U.S. are excluded.

p preliminary.

1. Beginning in 1960, includes Alaska and Hawaii.

Source: U.S. Department of Commerce, Bureau of the Census, *Statistical Abstract of the United States, 1993,* and earlier editions.

TABLE 17.23--LOW BIRTH WEIGHT AND BIRTHS TO TEENAGE MOTHERS AND TO UNMARRIED WOMEN, SOUTHEASTERN STATES AND UNITED STATES, 1980 AND 1990

State	Percent of births with low birth weight[1]		Births to teenage mothers (percent of total)		Births to unmarried women (percent of total)	
	1990	1980	1990	1980	1990	1980
TENNESSEE	8.2	8.0	17.6	19.9	30.2	19.9
Alabama	8.4	7.9	18.2	20.6	30.1	22.2
Arkansas	8.2	7.6	19.7	21.6	29.4	20.5
Florida	7.4	7.6	13.9	18.2	31.7	23.0
Georgia	8.7	8.6	16.7	20.7	32.8	23.2
Kentucky	7.1	6.8	17.5	21.1	23.6	15.1
Louisiana	9.2	8.6	17.6	20.1	36.8	23.4
Mississippi	9.6	8.7	21.3	23.2	40.5	28.0
North Carolina	8.0	7.9	16.2	19.2	29.4	19.0
South Carolina	8.7	8.6	17.1	19.8	32.7	23.0
Virginia	7.2	7.5	11.7	15.5	26.0	19.2
West Virginia	7.1	6.7	17.8	20.1	25.4	13.1
UNITED STATES	7.0	6.8	12.8	15.6	28.0	18.4

1. Less than 2,500 grams (5 pounds, 8 ounces).
Source: U.S. Department of Commerce, Bureau of the Census, *Statistical Abstract of the United States, 1993*, and earlier editions.

TABLE 17.24--INFANT MORTALITY RATES, BY RACE, SOUTHEASTERN STATES AND UNITED STATES, 1980 AND 1990 [Deaths per 1,000 live births, by place of residence]

State	Total[1]		White		Black	
	1990	1980	1990	1980	1990	1980
TENNESSEE	10.3	13.5	8.0	11.9	17.5	19.3
Alabama	10.8	15.1	8.3	11.6	15.9	21.6
Arkansas	9.2	12.7	8.0	10.3	13.6	20.0
Florida	9.6	14.6	7.6	11.8	16.2	22.8
Georgia	12.4	14.5	9.1	10.8	18.0	21.0
Kentucky	8.5	12.9	8.0	12.0	13.6	22.0
Louisiana	11.1	14.3	7.3	10.5	16.5	20.6
Mississippi	12.1	17.0	8.5	11.1	16.1	23.7
North Carolina	10.6	14.5	8.3	12.1	16.0	20.0
South Carolina	11.7	15.6	8.3	10.8	17.1	22.9
Virginia	10.2	13.6	7.5	11.9	18.8	19.8
West Virginia	9.9	11.8	9.6	11.4	16.6	21.5
UNITED STATES	9.2	12.6	7.7	11.0	17.0	21.4

1. Includes other races not shown separately.
Source: U.S. Department of Commerce, Bureau of the Census, *Statistical Abstract of the United States, 1993*, and earlier editions.

TABLE 17.25--NUMBER OF MARRIAGES, AND RATE PER 1,000 POPULATION, SOUTHEASTERN STATES AND UNITED STATES, 1950-1991, SELECTED YEARS [Number in thousands]

State	1991[p] Number	Rate	1990 Number	Rate	1989[p] Number	Rate	1988[p] Number	Rate	1987[p] Number	Rate
TENNESSEE	68.8	13.7	66.6	13.4	65.0	13.2	69.4	14.2	57.5	11.8
Alabama	42.7	10.3	43.3	10.5	41.8	10.2	44.5	10.9	44.0	10.8
Arkansas	38.1	15.7[a]	35.7	14.8	34.6	14.4	34.8	14.5	32.2	13.5
Florida	136.9	10.3	142.3	10.9	138.4	10.9	137.1	11.1	138.2	11.5
Georgia	70.5	10.6	64.4	9.8	63.1	9.8	73.3	11.6	65.3	10.5
Kentucky	47.3[a]	12.7[a]	51.3	13.8	50.2	13.5	49.9	13.4	47.6	12.8
Louisiana	36.8	8.5[a]	41.2	9.4	39.0	8.9	33.9	7.7	36.8	8.2
Mississippi	23.4	8.9	24.3	9.3	24.3	9.3	24.8	9.5	23.9	9.1
North Carolina	49.0	7.3	52.1	7.8	50.6	7.7	51.7	8.0	50.5	7.9
South Carolina	53.3	14.8	55.8	15.7	54.3	15.5	54.3	15.7	53.5	15.6
Virginia	68.8	11.0	71.3	11.5	68.9	11.3	69.0	11.5	67.1	11.4
West Virginia	12.6	6.9	13.2	7.2	13.4	7.2	14.4	7.7	13.5	7.1
UNITED STATES	2,371.0	9.4	2,448.0[b]	9.8[b]	2,404.0	9.7	2,389.0	9.7	2,421.0	9.9

State	1985 Number	Rate	1980 Number	Rate	1970 Number	Rate	1960 Number	Rate	1950 Number	Rate
TENNESSEE	55.0	11.5	59.2	12.9	45.4	11.6	30.7	8.6	21.7	6.6
Alabama	46.1	11.5	49.0	12.6	47.0	13.6	31.9	9.8	22.8	7.5
Arkansas	31.7	13.4	26.5	11.6	23.3	12.1	18.3	10.3	51.6	27.0
Florida	125.5	11.0	108.3	11.1	69.2	10.2	39.3	7.9	27.6	10.0
Georgia	72.3	12.1	70.6	12.9	63.9	13.9	49.4	12.5	44.1	12.8
Kentucky	46.0	12.3	32.7[a]	8.9[a]	36.3	11.3	26.5	8.7	33.0	11.2
Louisiana	39.4	8.8	43.5	10.3	35.4	9.7	23.5	7.2	26.9	10.0
Mississippi	24.8	9.5	27.9	11.1	26.3	11.9	21.2	9.7	56.7	26.0
North Carolina	50.5	8.1	46.7	7.9	48.3	9.5	31.7	6.9	29.8	7.3
South Carolina	52.8	15.8	53.9	17.3	57.9	22.3	39.0	16.4	46.2	21.8
Virginia	66.5	11.7	60.2	11.3	52.0	11.2	37.5	9.5	36.7	11.1
West Virginia	14.6	7.5	17.4	8.9	15.9	9.1	13.6	7.3	17.2	8.6
UNITED STATES	2,412.6	10.1	2,390.3	10.6	2,158.8	10.6	1,523.4	8.5	1,667.2	11.1

Note: Data are by place of occurrence. Rates are based on total population residing in area.

p preliminary.

a. Incomplete.

b. Estimate for U.S. is based on monthly reports adjusted for observed differences from final monthly figures. State figures are not adjusted in this manner.

Source: U.S. Department of Commerce, Bureau of the Census, *Statistical Abstract of the United States, 1993,* and earlier editions.

TABLE 17.26--NUMBER OF DIVORCES, AND RATE PER 1,000 POPULATION, SOUTHEASTERN STATES
AND UNITED STATES, 1950-1991, SELECTED YEARS [Number in thousands]

State	1991[p] Number	Rate	1990 Number	Rate	1989[p] Number	Rate	1988[p] Number	Rate	1987[p] Number	Rate
TENNESSEE	32.5	6.5	32.3	6.5	32.3	6.5	32.0	6.5	31.0	6.4
Alabama	27.1	6.5	25.3	6.1	24.9	6.1	23.4	5.7	24.7	6.0
Arkansas	18.9[a]	7.8	16.8	6.9	16.4	6.8	16.7	7.0	16.2	6.8
Florida	82.7	6.2	81.7	6.3	80.0	6.3	78.0	6.3	79.7	6.6
Georgia	42.0	6.3	35.7	5.5	30.0	4.7	35.7	5.6	33.5	5.4
Kentucky	22.3[a]	6.0	21.8	5.8	20.6	5.5	20.5	5.5	19.9	5.3
Louisiana	n.a.	n.a.	n.a.	n.a.	n.a.	n.a.	n.a.	n.a.	n.a.	n.a.
Mississippi	12.9	4.9	14.4	5.5	12.8	4.9	12.2	4.7	12.4	4.7
North Carolina	33.8	5.0	34.0	5.1	32.4	4.9	32.4	5.0	31.6	4.9
South Carolina	14.7	4.1	16.1	4.5	14.9	4.2	14.6	4.2	14.0	4.1
Virginia	28.2	4.5	27.3	4.4	25.8	4.2	26.1	4.3	25.6	4.3
West Virginia	10.1	5.6	9.7	5.3	9.4	5.1	9.1	4.9	9.1	4.8
UNITED STATES[1]	1,187.0	4.7	1,175.0	4.7	1,163.0	4.7	1,183.0	4.8	1,157.0	4.8

State	1985 Number	Rate	1980 Number	Rate	1970 Number	Rate	1960 Number	Rate	1950 Number	Rate
TENNESSEE	29.9	6.3	30.2	6.6	16.6	4.2	9.0	2.5	7.8	2.4
Alabama	25.0	6.2	26.7	6.9	15.1	4.4	17.3	5.3	8.7	2.9
Arkansas	16.5	7.0	15.9[a]	6.9[a]	9.3[a]	4.8[a]	5.4[a]	(b)	8.8	4.6
Florida	77.5	6.8	71.6	7.3	37.2	5.5	19.6	3.9	18.0	6.5
Georgia	33.4	5.6	34.7	6.4	18.6	4.1	8.9	2.3	9.5	2.8
Kentucky	18.3	4.9	16.7[a]	4.6[a]	10.7	3.3	7.5[a]	(b)	8.1	2.8
Louisiana	17.6[a]	n.a.	18.1[a]	4.3[a]	5.1[a]	(b)	4.1[a]	(b)	5.4	2.0
Mississippi	13.0	5.0	13.8	5.5	8.2	3.7	5.2	2.4	6.1	2.8
North Carolina	30.2	4.8	28.1	4.8	13.7	2.7	6.0	1.3	6.4	1.6
South Carolina	13.5	4.0	13.6	4.4	5.8	2.3	3.0	1.3	2.3	1.1
Virginia	24.1	4.2	23.6	4.4	11.9	2.6	7.4	1.9	5.9	1.8
West Virginia	9.9	5.1	10.3	5.3	5.6	3.2	3.6	1.9	4.2	2.1
UNITED STATES[1]	1,190.0	5.0	1,189.0	5.2	708.0	3.5	393.0	2.2	385.0	2.6

Note: Data are by place of occurrence and include reported annulments. Rates are based on total population
   residing in area.
n.a. not available.
p preliminary.
1. Estimated.
a. Incomplete.
b. Does not meet publication standards because reporting was less than 90 percent complete.
Source: U.S. Department of Commerce, Bureau of the Census, *Statistical Abstract of the United States, 1993*, and
   earlier editions.

TABLE 17.27--NUMBER OF PHYSICIANS, SOUTHEASTERN STATES AND UNITED STATES, 1980-1990, SELECTED YEARS

State	1990 Number	1990 Rate	1988 Number	1988 Rate	1986	1985	1983	1980
TENNESSEE	9,619	196	9,022	187	8,673	8,492	7,851	7,169
Alabama	6,464	158	6,137	151	5,903	5,769	5,336	4,856
Arkansas	3,595	150	3,414	144	3,342	3,274	3,059	2,772
Florida	26,123	208	24,235	203	23,083	22,295	19,899	17,479
Georgia	11,144	175	10,294	167	9,863	9,614	8,732	7,728
Kentucky	6,202	168	5,953	161	5,754	5,640	5,364	4,820
Louisiana	8,173	188	8,126	184	7,999	7,936	7,392	6,501
Mississippi	3,455	133	3,257	125	3,176	3,081	2,933	2,664
North Carolina	12,262	190	11,276	179	10,755	10,489	9,708	8,874
South Carolina	5,441	161	5,246	156	5,052	4,912	4,490	4,129
Virginia	12,615	213	11,701	204	11,331	11,075	10,110	9,154
West Virginia	3,086	166	3,120	164	3,117	3,122	2,940	2,610
UNITED STATES	532,638	213	506,474	210	491,503	483,905	455,192	413,692

Note: "Physicians" refers to all active, non-federal physicians. Rates are per 100,000 civilian population and are based on U.S. Bureau of the Census estimates as of July 1.

Source: American Medical Association, Chicago, IL, *Physician Characteristics and Distribution in the U.S.*, annual (copyright) as printed in U.S. Department of Commerce, Bureau of the Census, *Statistical Abstract of the United States*, 1993, 113th edition, page 119; and earlier editions.

TABLE 17.28--NUMBER OF DENTISTS, SOUTHEASTERN STATES AND UNITED STATES, 1979-1992, SELECTED YEARS

State	1992 Number	1992 Rate	1990	1989	1987	1982	1979
TENNESSEE	2,767	55	2,660	2,630	2,491	2,226	2,034
Alabama	1,776	43	1,700	1,680	1,615	1,489	1,314
Arkansas	989	41	970	960	911	838	714
Florida	7,079	53	6,230	6,160	5,960	4,878	4,323
Georgia	3,165	47	2,950	2,920	2,864	2,388	2,167
Kentucky	2,113	57	2,020	2,000	1,944	1,741	1,490
Louisiana	2,005	47	2,050	2,030	1,953	1,808	1,586
Mississippi	1,019	39	990	980	962	872	763
North Carolina	2,895	43	2,730	2,700	2,674	2,451	2,175
South Carolina	1,521	43	1,410	1,400	1,412	1,242	1,130
Virginia	3,502	57	3,210	3,180	3,264	2,876	2,599
West Virginia	867	48	850	840	784	797	703
UNITED STATES	155,058	61	145,500	144,000	n.a.	126,985	117,223

Note: "Dentists" refers to all professionally active dentists. Active occupation categories include the following: clinical practitioners, dental school faculty or staff, armed forces dentists, government-employed dentists, health/dental organization staff members, interns/residents, and other students. Rates are per 100,000 civilian population and are based on U.S. Bureau of the Census estimates as of July 1.

Source: U.S. Department of Commerce, Bureau of the Census, *Statistical Abstract of the United States, 1993*; and American Dental Association, *Distribution of Dentists in the United States by Region and State*, 1979, 1982 and 1987.

Information on payments to individuals for reasons of public assistance, unemployment, or retirement benefits is the subject of this chapter. These payments are considered transfer payments–income payments which are not a compensation for current work effort. Program payments are frequently from a combination of federal, state, and local sources, and total payments distributed to local areas are reported in two sources. The Tennessee Department of Human Services provides data on levels of funding for various programs in its *Annual Report*. Comparisons of assistance funds to Tennessee counties for Aid to Families with Dependent Children, medical assistance and food stamps, previously found in the *Annual Report*, were provided from departmental records in Tables 18.6, 18.7 and 18.8.

The second and most comprehensive source of local information on transfer payments is compiled by the Bureau of Economic Analysis (BEA), U.S. Department of Commerce, as part of personal income estimates. Estimates of transfer payments to residents of metropolitan statistical areas and counties are available for dissemination to members of BEA's Regional Economics Information System. While total transfer payments are reported as part of personal income in Chapter 2 tables, details of transfer payments by type of program are included in this chapter with other statistics on public assistance and social insurance programs. Complete details are reported in Table 18.1 for the state, and major categories are shown in Table 18.4 for each county. However, the same level of detail is available for counties and may be requested from the Center for Business and Economic Research. Revisions for earlier years are also available upon request.

The effects of changes in the level of transfer payments may be estimated by consideration of two additional measures shown in Table 18.5. These are per capita transfer payments and transfers as a percentage of total personal income. Transfer payments to residents in local areas are often substantial. In some counties transfer payments represent more than 25 percent of personal income. Similarly, data from the 1990 decennial Census of Population reports on the incidence of poverty in counties and municipalities. These data are presented in Chapter 2. For state- and United States-level information on public assistance or social insurance programs, a number of federal publications are available to the public. The Social Security Administration, in its monthly *Social Security Bulletin*, gives information on Supplemental Security Income, Aid to Families with Dependent Children, and Social Security payments. Year-end data are published in the *Annual Statistical Supplement*. Table 18.12 provides data on the Food and Nutrition Service Programs for Tennessee and other southeastern states. These data are published in *Agricultural Statistics* by the U.S. Department of Agriculture, Statistical Reporting Service.

TABLE OF CONTENTS

TABLE 18.1.—TRANSFER PAYMENTS BY MAJOR SOURCE, TENNESSEE, 1987–1992 [In thousands of dollars]

Source	1992	1991	1990	1989	1988	1987
TOTAL TRANSFER PAYMENTS	15,650,453	14,038,025	12,407,350	11,173,121	10,738,119	10,010,037
Government payments to individuals	14,918,849	13,355,786	11,813,820	10,592,041	10,158,788	9,437,674
Retirement and disability insurance benefit	7,407,227	6,916,553	6,385,039	5,925,054	5,576,624	5,216,467
Old-age, survivors and disability insurance	5,589,654	5,198,512	4,788,194	4,433,794	4,129,294	3,874,914
Railroad retirement and disability	150,275	146,355	141,673	137,514	133,295	128,202
Federal civilian employee retirement	520,492	511,491	477,692	444,599	421,115	385,441
Military retirement	503,323	470,584	434,584	402,890	378,089	353,899
State and local government employee retirement	530,043	481,726	439,355	403,909	415,715	377,004
Workers' compensation (Federal and State)	60,324	56,481	52,175	49,087	44,650	43,221
Other government disability insurance and retirement[1]	53,116	51,404	51,366	53,261	54,466	53,786
Medical[2]	4,859,464	4,181,466	3,469,009	2,954,772	3,012,582	2,777,625
Income maintenance benefit	1,560,003	1,295,767	1,121,161	966,427	867,206	772,164
Supplemental security income (SSI)	528,117	435,858	384,507	351,095	327,335	307,024
Aid to families with dependent children (AFDC)	221,615	211,339	182,831	151,228	133,445	121,665
Food stamps	574,304	485,882	389,943	325,925	298,134	279,296
Other income maintenance[3]	235,967	162,688	163,880	138,179	108,292	64,179
Unemployment insurance benefit	495,575	388,828	290,031	221,146	211,460	197,212
State unemployment insurance compensation	457,834	363,710	273,929	202,951	192,317	180,398
Unemployment compensation for Federal civilian employees (UCFE)	17,883	14,361	8,186	11,413	11,245	7,092
Unemployment compensation for railroad employees	1,409	1,531	1,270	1,507	1,571	2,844
Unemployment compensation for veterans (UCX)	13,822	3,815	2,844	2,175	2,405	2,324
Other unemployment compensation[4]	4,627	5,411	3,802	3,100	3,922	4,554
Veterans' benefit	435,850	421,191	405,895	390,395	385,061	376,789
Veterans' pensions and compensation	390,350	375,150	366,490	350,860	341,736	331,759
Educational assistance to veterans, dependents, and survivors[5]	11,525	9,997	8,394	11,568	12,431	14,246
Veterans' life insurance benefit	32,664	35,571	30,521	27,500	30,488	30,061
Other assistance to veterans[6]	1,311	473	490	467	406	723
Federal educational and training assistance (excluding veterans)[7]	143,030	136,338	130,567	128,427	102,607	91,992
Other payments to individuals[8]	17,700	15,643	12,118	5,820	3,248	5,425
Payments to nonprofit institutions	420,758	388,266	297,331	290,372	296,983	289,845
Federal government	105,792	91,876	82,897	80,296	80,838	74,254
State and local government[9]	201,099	182,870	96,286	88,049	96,670	90,118
Business	113,867	113,520	118,148	122,027	119,475	125,473
Business payments to individuals[10]	310,846	293,973	296,199	290,708	282,348	282,518

Notes on following page.

TABLE 18.1.–TRANSFER PAYMENTS BY MAJOR SOURCE, TENNESSEE, 1987–1992 [In thousands of dollars] (Continued)

1. Includes temporary disability payments and Black Lung payments.

2. Consists of Medicare payments, medical vendor payments, and CHAMPUS payments.

3. Includes general, emergency, refugee, and energy assistance, foster home care payments, and earned income tax credits.

4. Consists of trade readjustment allowance payments, Redwood Park benefit payments, public service employment benefit payments, and transitional benefit payments.

5. Includes Veterans' Readjustment benefit payments and Educational Assistance to spouses/children of disabled/deceased veterans.

6. Includes payments to paraplegics, payments for autos and conveyances for disabled veterans, veterans' aid & veterans' bonuses.

7. Includes federal fellowship payments (National Science Foundation, fellowships and traineeships, subsistence payments to State Maritime Academy cadets, and other federal fellowships), interest subsidy on higher education loans, Basic Educational Opportunity Grants, and Job Corps payments.

8. Includes Bureau of Indian Affairs payments, education exchange payments, compensation of survivors of public safety officers, compensation of victims of crime, and other special payments to individuals.

9. Consists of state and local government payments for foster home care supervised by private agencies, state and local government educational assistance payments to nonprofit institutions, and other state and local government payments to nonprofit institutions.

10. Includes personal injury payments to individuals other than employees, and other business transfer payments.

Source: U.S. Department of Commerce, Bureau of Economic Analysis, Regional Economic Measurement Division, *Regional Economic Information System 1969–1992 CD-ROM.*

TABLE 18.2--EXPENDITURES FOR HUMAN SERVICES PROGRAMS, TENNESSEE, FISCAL YEARS 1989 AND 1990

	Amount		Percent change 1989-90
Program	1989–90	1988–89	
Total expenditures	527,272,998	$476,979,078	10.5
Rehabilitation services	34,110,455	32,846,926	3.8
Case services	25,385,229	24,188,933	4.9
Workshops for the blind	511,298	487,700	4.8
Facility operation	7,723,916	7,670,284	0.7
Hearing impaired contracts	490,012	500,009	-2.0
Family assistance[1]	178,315,605	157,342,807	13.3
Aid to dependent children grants	160,626,375	141,176,352	13.8
Child support	17,046,876	16,103,455	5.9
Contracted services	6,721,722	6,595,010	1.9
Family and incentive payments	10,325,154	9,508,445	8.6
Refugee assistance grants	102,073	63,000	62.0
Social services	117,720,625	96,501,830	22.0
Vendor day care	3,574,700	3,431,358	4.2
Board and care (includes foster care)	42,432,656	28,426,865	49.3
Work incentive program	232,548	157,423	47.7
Day care	229,857	78,772	191.8
Other	2,691	78,651	-96.6
Social services contracts	48,192,700	42,100,531	14.5
Refugee resettlement contracts	821,700	484,617	69.6
Low income energy assistance contracts	16,542,521	14,714,493	12.4
Weatherization assistance contracts	5,923,800	7,186,543	-17.6
Administration	197,126,313	190,287,515	3.6
General	67,303,933	67,080,921	0.3
Direct services	36,820,961	33,562,633	9.7
Purchased services	3,040,600	2,811,258	8.2
Family assistance	62,371,760	58,160,840	7.2
Disability determination	16,476,917	15,881,654	3.7
Child support	2,395,979	2,056,936	16.5
Rehabilitation services	8,716,163	10,733,273	-18.8

Note: The following amounts in Certified Public Expenditures were not included in the figures above:

	1989-1990	1988-1989
Child support	$1,569,631	$1,439,518
Social services contracts	6,327,600	6,711,576

1. 1989–90 data includes Individual and Family Grant of $540,281.
Source: Tennessee Department of Human Services, direct correspondence.

TABLE 18.3--CONTRIBUTIONS, BENEFIT PAYMENTS, AND FUND ASSETS UNDER UNEMPLOYMENT
INSURANCE PROGRAM, TENNESSEE, 1955-1990, SELECTED YEARS
[In thousands of dollars]

Year	Contributions	Benefit payments	Payments as percent of contributions [1]	Assets [2]		
				Total	Trust fund account in United States Treasury [1]	Other [1]
1990	276,231	256,182	92.7	657,476	663,188	-5,712
1989	268,771	198,528	73.9	637,427	642,767	-5,340
1988	258,031	183,399	71.1	567,185	569,816	-2,631
1987	243,069	167,358	68.9	492,553	495,636	-3,083
1986	233,053	177,255	76.1	416,842	421,401	-4,559
1985	272,008	182,067	66.9	361,044	365,438	-4,394
1984	344,617	149,488	43.4	271,103	271,957	-854
1983	276,646	309,237	111.8	37,771	40,847	-3,076
1982	181,031	275,098	152.0	69,571	76,461	-6,890
1981	143,308	228,197	159.2	156,905	159,876	-2,971
1980	157,304	182,349	115.9	249,065	249,115	-50
1979	161,735	112,949	69.8	254,841	254,406	435
1978	130,972	100,838	77.0	192,145	190,950	1,195
1977	93,209	115,617	124.0	156,446	155,950	497
1976	79,996	135,503	169.4	180,676	179,273	1,402
1975	80,367	160,492	199.7	247,423	245,783	1,640
1974	80,939	48,002	59.3	316,101	315,705	396
1973	69,117	38,101	55.1	267,079	266,710	369
1972	52,346	45,721	87.3	224,145	223,993	152
1971	45,807	57,714	126.0	207,006	206,662	344
1970	45,766	40,490	88.5	208,013	207,383	630
1969	45,056	27,148	60.3	193,481	193,539	-58
1968	48,439	30,753	63.5	167,465	166,999	466
1967	50,524	23,853	47.2	149,884	149,745	139
1966	46,604	18,922	40.6	123,060	122,855	205
1965	42,663	23,112	54.2	94,316	94,014	302
1964	39,295	29,123	74.1	76,897	74,711	2,186
1963	35,936	31,187	86.8	65,001	64,356	645
1962	33,079	32,610	98.6	62,136	61,629	507
1961	30,619	42,987	140.4	63,461	62,970	491
1960	30,120	34,508	114.6	72,886	72,127	759
1955	21,528	29,009	134.8	92,855	91,879	976

Note: Prior to 1984, the data were obtained from *State Government Finances*. Beginning in 1984, the source
becomes the Tennessee Department of Employment Security. As a result, the data may not be directly
comparable.

1. Computed by the Center for Business and Economic Research when not given in the source.

2. Beginning in 1984 assets are as of end of calendar year. Assets were counted at end of fiscal year for all previous
years.

Source: Tennessee Department of Employment Security, "Statement of Revenues, Expenditures, and Changes in
Fund Balance, 1990," and earlier editions; U.S. Department of Commerce, Bureau of the Census, *State
Government Finances in 1984*, and earlier editions; and Tennessee Department of Employment Security, *30th
Annual Report, 1966.*

TABLE 18.4—TRANSFER PAYMENTS, BY TYPE, COUNTIES, 1992 [In thousands of dollars]

Type of payments	Anderson	Bedford	Benton	Bledsoe	Blount	Bradley	Campbell	Cannon
Total transfer payments	242,819	86,306	52,475	27,930	260,790	181,944	156,360	32,601
Retirement and disability insurance benefit	139,487	44,040	27,510	11,473	147,535	96,378	72,370	15,836
Medical[1]	58,304	22,278	15,321	8,723	61,816	41,132	43,765	10,512
Income maintenance benefit	21,867	7,970	4,272	4,243	20,861	18,143	23,150	2,732
Unemployment insurance benefit	6,490	4,134	1,528	831	8,716	7,342	6,297	1,007
Veterans' benefit	5,588	2,906	1,535	1,103	7,329	4,881	5,086	835
Federal educational and training assistance[2]	579	285	104	71	1,252	2,675	352	77
Payments to nonprofit institutions	5,896	2,640	1,240	836	7,469	6,407	3,002	901
Business payments to individuals[3]	4,355	1,949	916	617	5,518	4,733	2,219	666

Type of payments	Carroll	Carter	Cheatham	Chester	Claiborne	Clay	Cocke	Coffee
Total transfer payments	102,204	153,815	58,733	34,955	91,499	21,398	107,167	132,013
Retirement and disability insurance benefit	51,615	77,871	30,673	16,809	43,975	8,459	41,586	71,488
Medical[1]	30,863	36,800	14,267	8,858	22,798	6,613	35,559	34,673
Income maintenance benefit	8,547	17,205	5,208	4,005	14,478	3,411	15,989	11,282
Unemployment insurance benefit	3,563	5,834	2,372	1,020	1,551	924	5,799	3,866
Veterans' benefit	2,767	7,428	1,728	1,193	3,174	840	3,566	3,847
Federal educational and training assistance[2]	666	803	202	1,114	1,528	53	211	681
Payments to nonprofit institutions	2,351	4,428	2,409	1,100	2,246	617	2,506	3,473
Business payments to individuals[3]	1,739	3,272	1,779	813	1,660	456	1,852	2,566

Type of payments	Crockett	Cumberland	Davidson	Decatur	DeKalb	Dickson	Dyer	Fayette
Total transfer payments	45,511	116,755	1,617,927	32,727	46,745	100,756	118,001	88,949
Retirement and disability insurance benefit	20,310	66,168	728,531	16,682	21,914	51,193	53,928	27,635
Medical[1]	15,707	26,286	564,845	7,849	13,797	26,615	38,474	40,692
Income maintenance benefit	4,918	10,590	142,030	3,195	5,471	9,708	12,418	12,286
Unemployment insurance benefit	1,355	4,249	47,287	1,803	1,927	4,090	4,080	2,578
Veterans' benefit	1,111	3,717	36,999	1,397	1,329	3,346	3,110	1,652
Federal educational and training assistance[2]	96	297	19,450	76	104	310	651	185
Payments to nonprofit institutions	1,133	3,063	44,276	893	1,239	3,090	3,002	2,204
Business payments to individuals[3]	837	2,264	32,708	659	915	2,282	2,219	1,630

TABLE 18.4--TRANSFER PAYMENTS, BY TYPE, COUNTIES, 1992 [In thousands of dollars] (Continued)

	Fentress	Franklin	Gibson	Giles	Grainger	Greene	Grundy	Hamblen
Total transfer payments	56,931	106,541	168,948	87,092	52,111	165,891	51,219	156,749
Retirement and disability insurance benefit[1]	22,523	56,587	81,688	39,592	24,783	84,548	21,849	76,622
Medical[1]	19,028	29,042	54,754	30,435	13,744	37,987	16,539	42,398
Income maintenance benefit	8,675	8,742	14,799	7,635	7,602	19,141	7,589	17,605
Unemployment insurance benefit	1,970	2,889	5,975	2,821	1,862	9,365	1,736	6,685
Veterans' benefit	2,399	3,410	4,014	1,993	1,384	5,337	1,385	4,312
Federal educational and training assistance[2]	105	517	545	657	123	984	96	1,463
Payments to nonprofit institutions	1,255	3,010	3,943	2,225	1,469	4,796	1,140	4,311
Business payments to individuals[3]	926	2,225	2,913	1,646	1,086	3,544	841	3,183

	Hamilton	Hancock	Hardeman	Hardin	Hawkins	Haywood	Henderson	Henry
Total transfer payments	966,700	26,803	95,556	74,042	132,178	75,836	64,854	101,853
Retirement and disability insurance benefit[1]	461,734	8,303	34,861	35,034	68,864	24,250	33,398	55,574
Medical[1]	320,800	10,293	39,696	18,609	31,568	33,237	15,590	27,572
Income maintenance benefit	79,317	5,895	13,275	10,401	16,588	11,022	6,905	8,193
Unemployment insurance benefit	23,470	434	2,024	3,693	4,037	2,832	3,355	2,728
Veterans' benefit	25,119	803	1,913	2,624	3,978	1,399	1,949	3,297
Federal educational and training assistance[2]	12,420	(a)	218	212	324	139	159	251
Payments to nonprofit institutions	24,654	576	2,007	1,950	3,835	1,664	1,879	2,383
Business payments to individuals[3]	18,214	427	1,483	1,442	2,833	1,228	1,390	1,761

	Hickman	Houston	Humphreys	Jackson	Jefferson	Johnson	Knox	Lake
Total transfer payments	49,400	26,372	52,497	27,922	103,307	55,242	1,043,313	28,547
Retirement and disability insurance benefit[1]	25,536	13,272	25,835	12,000	52,577	22,820	527,379	10,812
Medical[1]	12,606	7,464	15,784	7,859	26,408	17,674	306,979	11,683
Income maintenance benefit	4,688	2,195	4,052	4,040	9,992	7,524	90,086	3,803
Unemployment insurance benefit	2,375	1,350	2,772	1,450	4,277	2,975	26,273	591
Veterans' benefit	1,482	962	1,528	1,082	3,331	2,028	27,403	531
Federal educational and training assistance[2]	122	52	113	67	1,668	99	13,653	52
Payments to nonprofit institutions	1,457	605	1,356	800	2,841	1,177	28,985	604
Business payments to individuals[3]	1,076	448	1,003	592	2,101	870	21,413	447

TABLE 18.4--TRANSFER PAYMENTS, BY TYPE, COUNTIES, 1992 [In thousands of dollars] (Continued)

	Lauderdale	Lawrence	Lewis	Lincoln	Loudon	McMinn	McNairy	Macon
Total transfer payments	92,749	110,204	29,344	85,651	99,466	128,937	78,706	43,692
Retirement and disability insurance benefit[1]	34,628	56,564	14,079	46,579	56,137	65,284	38,391	20,126
Medical[1]	37,467	27,109	8,126	22,067	24,232	33,379	21,510	12,130
Income maintenance benefit[1]	12,033	10,017	3,461	7,482	7,712	13,215	10,174	5,061
Unemployment insurance benefit	2,997	7,622	1,255	2,582	3,350	5,536	2,219	2,213
Veterans' benefit	1,860	3,222	905	2,394	2,975	4,325	2,821	1,327
Federal educational and training assistance[2]	189	257	117	206	231	717	163	115
Payments to nonprofit institutions	2,011	3,043	788	2,441	2,715	3,646	1,928	1,373
Business payments to individuals[3]	1,485	2,250	582	1,804	2,007	2,692	1,424	1,014

	Madison	Marion	Marshall	Maury	Meigs	Monroe	Montgomery	Moore
Total transfer payments	256,623	86,211	64,401	174,546	26,742	96,048	277,350	10,077
Retirement and disability insurance benefit[1]	117,155	39,672	32,237	84,984	13,960	47,274	161,323	5,812
Medical[1]	83,114	27,039	20,458	51,080	5,449	23,276	49,706	1,847
Income maintenance benefit[1]	26,376	10,093	4,962	16,888	3,136	12,489	21,477	793
Unemployment insurance benefit	7,332	3,027	1,633	7,643	1,731	4,632	9,817	504
Veterans' benefit	6,086	2,374	1,630	4,660	1,156	2,903	17,852	366
Federal educational and training assistance[2]	4,488	181	156	835	60	776	2,734	(a)
Payments to nonprofit institutions	6,722	2,151	1,870	4,755	703	2,642	8,082	407
Business payments to individuals[3]	4,967	1,589	1,382	3,513	519	1,952	5,971	299

	Morgan	Obion	Overton	Perry	Pickett	Polk	Putnam	Rhea
Total transfer payments	61,388	98,706	56,180	22,610	13,968	48,144	152,841	85,558
Retirement and disability insurance benefit[1]	30,349	50,299	25,857	10,802	6,098	26,454	79,802	37,146
Medical[1]	16,811	27,612	15,033	7,449	3,923	11,909	36,958	26,639
Income maintenance benefit[1]	7,696	9,431	7,475	1,895	2,084	4,409	13,008	11,082
Unemployment insurance benefit	1,834	3,627	2,659	683	401	1,712	6,122	3,326
Veterans' benefit	1,904	2,695	2,278	712	733	1,471	4,888	2,971
Federal educational and training assistance[2]	125	230	186	(a)	(a)	99	4,142	665
Payments to nonprofit institutions	1,500	2,706	1,513	573	391	1,176	4,455	2,097
Business payments to individuals[3]	1,110	2,000	1,119	424	290	868	3,291	1,549

TABLE 18.4—TRANSFER PAYMENTS, BY TYPE, COUNTIES, 1992 [In thousands of dollars] (Continued)

	Roane	Robert-son	Ruther-ford	Scott	Sequat-chie	Sevier	Shelby	Smith
Total transfer payments	165,249	111,359	258,098	79,090	28,919	142,775	3,040,025	43,491
Retirement and disability insurance benefit[1]	87,354	55,022	143,145	31,679	13,457	76,351	1,170,104	19,758
Medical[1]	43,554	32,825	49,798	25,442	8,270	30,791	1,244,998	13,791
Income maintenance benefit	15,739	8,928	18,660	13,588	3,678	13,235	340,665	4,174
Unemployment insurance benefit	5,104	4,894	11,808	3,116	1,198	9,174	61,458	2,090
Veterans' benefit	5,119	2,914	9,057	2,281	894	4,819	61,913	1,425
Federal educational and training assistance[2]	1,193	306	6,722	211	65	379	35,221	102
Payments to nonprofit institutions	4,039	3,638	10,620	1,559	763	4,514	70,682	1,210
Business payments to individuals[3]	2,986	2,689	7,846	1,152	564	3,334	52,198	894

	Stewart	Sulli-van	Sumner	Trousdale	Unicoi	Union	Van Buren
Total transfer payments	35,327	440,149	245,498	17,071	60,801	38,247	11,191
Retirement and disability insurance benefit[1]	20,599	255,858	130,934	7,774	34,199	16,784	4,859
Medical[1]	6,940	99,898	58,065	4,991	13,792	11,163	2,869
Income maintenance benefit	3,043	37,693	19,641	1,894	5,174	5,642	1,518
Unemployment insurance benefit	1,294	8,657	13,099	839	2,693	1,072	655
Veterans' benefit	1,920	13,610	6,492	571	2,304	1,342	514
Federal educational and training assistance[2]	70	2,501	1,065	92	118	101	(a)
Payments to nonprofit institutions	822	12,334	9,098	511	1,417	1,206	418
Business payments to individuals[3]	607	9,112	6,722	378	1,048	890	307

	Warren	Wash-ington	Wayne	Weakley	White	William-son	Wilson
Total transfer payments	100,077	298,556	39,957	89,987	62,370	164,986	169,820
Retirement and disability insurance benefit[1]	47,501	156,674	19,693	45,060	31,638	94,008	85,081
Medical[1]	28,780	75,759	9,522	24,563	15,247	38,861	46,640
Income maintenance benefit	10,856	24,661	4,928	6,773	6,384	8,793	12,954
Unemployment insurance benefit	4,343	7,715	2,062	2,849	3,497	5,868	7,526
Veterans' benefit	3,223	13,243	1,528	2,570	2,379	3,945	6,083
Federal educational and training assistance[2]	305	6,414	100	3,317	145	607	926
Payments to nonprofit institutions	2,851	7,923	1,194	2,730	1,732	7,234	5,968
Business payments to individuals[3]	2,106	5,854	883	2,018	1,280	5,344	4,407

Notes on following page.

TABLE 18.4–TRANSFER PAYMENTS, BY TYPE, COUNTIES, 1992 [In thousands of dollars] (Continued)

Note: Includes items not detailed separately.

1. Consists of Medicare payments, medical vendor payments, and CHAMPUS payments.

2. Includes federal fellowship payments (National Science Foundation, fellowships and traineeships, subsistence payments to State Maritime Academy cadets, and other federal fellowships), interest subsidy on higher education loans, Basic Educational Opportunity Grants, and Job Corps payments.   Excludes veterans.

3. Includes personal injury payments to individuals other than employees, and other business transfer payments.

a. Less than $50,000.   Estimates are included in totals.

Source: U.S. Department of Commerce, Bureau of Economic Analysis, Regional Economic Measurement Division, *Regional Economic Information System 1969–1992 CD-ROM.*

TABLE 18.5--TOTAL AND PER CAPITA TRANSFER PAYMENTS, AND TRANSFER PAYMENTS AS PERCENT OF PERSONAL INCOME, TENNESSEE AND COUNTIES, 1992

County	Total ($1,000)	Per capita ($)	Percent of personal income	County	Total ($1,000)	Per capita ($)	Percent of personal income
Anderson	242,819	3,444	18.5	Lewis	29,344	2,994	23.7
Bedford	86,306	2,723	17.4	Lincoln	85,651	3,005	20.1
Benton	52,475	3,475	25.0	Loudon	99,466	2,996	19.2
Bledsoe	27,930	2,850	24.6	McMinn	128,937	2,957	20.6
Blount	260,790	2,885	16.9	McNairy	78,706	3,483	24.9
Bradley	181,944	2,397	14.2	Macon	43,692	2,680	19.6
Campbell	156,360	4,380	37.0	Madison	256,623	3,200	18.4
Cannon	32,601	3,019	20.3	Marion	86,211	3,408	24.6
Carroll	102,204	3,703	25.3	Marshall	64,401	2,800	16.2
Carter	153,815	2,958	22.4	Maury	174,546	2,924	17.7
Cheatham	58,733	2,039	13.8	Meigs	26,742	3,184	25.2
Chester	34,955	2,689	23.1	Monroe	96,048	3,059	24.3
Claiborne	91,499	3,376	26.9	Montgomery	277,350	2,521	17.0
Clay	21,398	2,972	22.8	Moore	10,077	2,057	15.0
Cocke	107,167	3,633	27.1	Morgan	61,388	3,468	29.7
Coffee	132,013	3,173	18.2	Obion	98,706	3,124	18.5
Crockett	45,511	3,422	21.2	Overton	56,180	3,156	26.5
Cumberland	116,755	3,181	24.0	Perry	22,610	3,325	26.3
Davidson	1,617,927	3,125	14.0	Pickett	13,968	3,037	23.6
Decatur	32,727	3,147	24.7	Polk	48,144	3,464	26.3
DeKalb	46,745	3,202	20.8	Putnam	152,841	2,873	18.0
Dickson	100,756	2,760	17.7	Rhea	85,558	3,382	26.0
Dyer	118,001	3,391	20.8	Roane	165,249	3,436	21.5
Fayette	88,949	3,421	24.0	Robertson	111,359	2,548	16.2
Fentress	56,931	3,821	30.9	Rutherford	258,098	2,005	11.2
Franklin	106,541	3,018	20.7	Scott	79,090	4,207	35.3
Gibson	168,948	3,641	22.8	Sequatchie	28,919	3,143	23.8
Giles	87,092	3,262	20.4	Sevier	142,775	2,610	16.6
Grainger	52,111	2,928	24.6	Shelby	3,040,025	3,599	17.6
Greene	165,891	2,900	20.9	Smith	43,491	3,020	19.8
Grundy	51,219	3,794	32.8	Stewart	35,327	3,498	27.8
Hamblen	156,749	3,032	19.0	Sullivan	440,149	3,000	16.9
Hamilton	966,700	3,350	16.9	Sumner	245,498	2,275	12.8
Hancock	26,803	4,000	39.3	Tipton	126,984	3,239	21.5
Hardeman	95,556	4,015	30.7	Trousdale	17,071	2,893	23.0
Hardin	74,042	3,151	24.4	Unicoi	60,801	3,619	24.5
Hawkins	132,178	2,873	19.5	Union	38,247	2,713	23.5
Haywood	75,836	3,889	25.8	Van Buren	11,191	2,284	22.5
Henderson	64,854	2,935	21.1	Warren	100,077	2,987	20.6
Henry	101,853	3,599	23.6	Washington	298,556	3,146	18.3
Hickman	49,400	2,807	22.1	Wayne	39,957	2,629	22.0
Houston	26,372	3,663	31.6	Weakley	89,987	2,821	19.1
Humphreys	52,497	3,302	23.6	White	62,370	3,042	23.0
Jackson	27,922	3,068	24.0	Williamson	164,986	1,862	7.1
Jefferson	103,307	2,969	21.1	Wilson	169,820	2,385	13.1
Johnson	55,242	3,634	36.4				
Knox	1,043,313	3,001	15.3	TENNESSEE	15,650,453	3,114	17.6
Lake	28,547	3,911	32.8				
Lauderdale	92,749	3,930	28.8				
Lawrence	110,204	3,028	19.9				

Note: The per capita amounts are based on population as of July 1.

Source: U.S. Department of Commerce, Bureau of Economic Analysis, Regional Economic Measurement Division, *Regional Economic Information System 1969–1992 CD-ROM.*

FIGURE 18.1

Transfer Payments as Percent of Personal Income, Tennessee Counties, 1992

(Tennessee = 17.6)

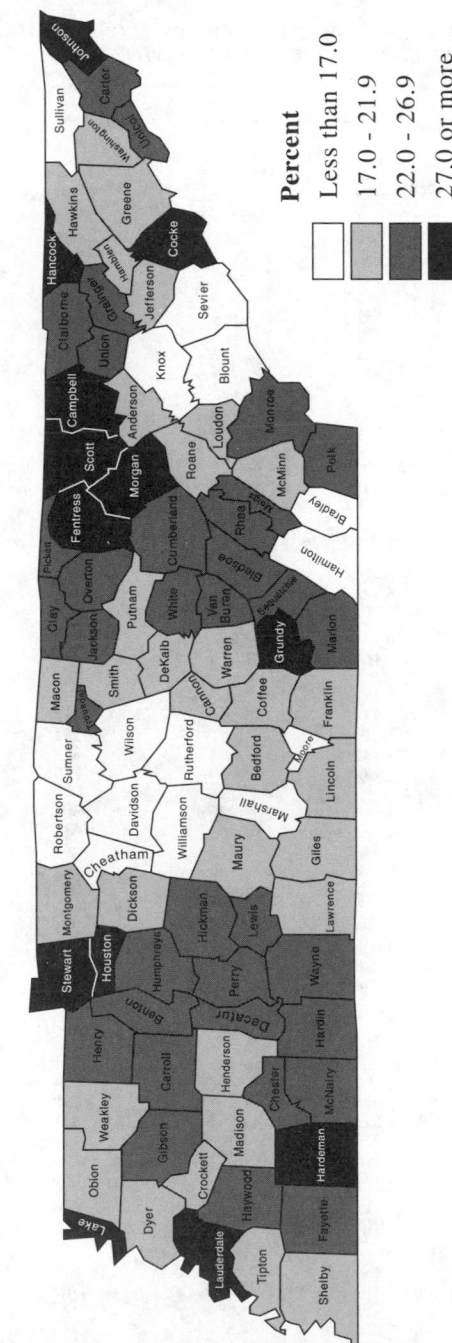

Percent

Less than 17.0
17.0 - 21.9
22.0 - 26.9
27.0 or more

Source: U.S. Department of Commerce, Bureau of Economic Analysis, Regional Economic Measurement Division, Regional Economic Information System 1969–1992 CD-ROM.

TABLE 18.6--AID TO FAMILIES WITH DEPENDENT CHILDREN, CASES AND GRANT PAYMENTS,
TENNESSEE AND COUNTIES, FISCAL YEARS 1990 AND 1991

| | | 1991 | | | 1990 | |
County	Families	Children	Grant payments ($)	Families	Children	Grant payments ($)
Anderson	1,027	1,780	2,277,245	964	1,709	2,007,793
Bedford	359	633	783,534	282	519	597,849
Benton	148	251	320,960	131	238	278,159
Bledsoe	163	263	346,663	145	233	292,542
Blount	978	1,581	2,140,384	852	1,370	1,747,872
Bradley	664	1,131	1,552,041	516	900	1,132,951
Campbell	1,017	1,748	2,188,214	927	1,620	1,876,426
Cannon	90	162	196,135	85	142	169,003
Carroll	316	558	731,128	295	513	653,890
Carter	647	1,086	1,437,320	596	995	1,264,864
Cheatham	231	395	516,291	175	304	371,996
Chester	154	281	355,684	141	251	303,700
Claiborne	505	868	1,077,380	458	778	920,184
Clay	97	164	210,661	85	146	172,145
Cocke	670	1,078	1,425,764	643	1,043	1,279,171
Coffee	523	891	1,232,407	426	730	921,026
Crockett	176	326	417,575	158	284	348,930
Cumberland	331	556	722,182	312	548	656,295
Davidson	10,531	20,134	24,117,977	9,106	17,436	19,842,204
Decatur	100	163	223,515	81	139	167,807
DeKalb	205	357	482,866	181	327	395,604
Dickson	528	941	1,230,390	413	725	918,774
Dyer	614	1,070	1,354,781	572	993	1,191,396
Fayette	667	1,385	1,537,358	632	1,328	1,369,357
Fentress	282	482	629,910	256	441	536,091
Franklin	379	644	807,926	307	514	613,336
Gibson	708	1,297	1,617,567	635	1,185	1,371,924
Giles	370	649	840,419	347	604	722,743
Grainger	248	412	549,856	214	355	427,842
Greene	738	1,205	1,596,677	573	958	1,162,563
Grundy	350	604	767,983	284	505	589,191
Hamblen	947	1,606	2,085,250	809	1,413	1,708,845
Hamilton	5,014	9,280	11,429,343	4,375	8,137	9,443,489
Hancock	224	376	479,286	217	370	437,722
Hardeman	690	1,310	1,562,712	654	1,231	1,378,329
Hardin	363	639	788,839	326	573	674,365
Hawkins	658	1,104	1,459,761	551	949	1,166,636
Haywood	642	1,197	1,464,908	614	1,134	1,310,565
Henderson	214	358	460,597	190	328	382,790
Henry	300	513	654,671	261	450	550,258
Hickman	194	323	408,861	158	268	326,410
Houston	93	141	194,123	86	136	172,963
Humphreys	168	283	374,178	133	236	295,491
Jackson	89	152	200,493	87	138	170,178
Jefferson	434	691	931,313	372	585	732,639
Johnson	266	449	580,121	254	435	539,174
Knox	5,173	9,103	11,406,599	4,742	8,339	9,897,899
Lake	178	298	389,896	157	265	326,738
Lauderdale	684	1,283	1,592,952	593	1,114	1,289,346
Lawrence	392	674	883,170	319	543	663,114

TABLE 18.6--AID TO FAMILIES WITH DEPENDENT CHILDREN, CASES AND GRANT PAYMENTS,
TENNESSEE AND COUNTIES, FISCAL YEARS 1990 AND 1991 (Continued)

		1991			1990	
County	Families	Children	Grant payments ($)	Families	Children	Grant payments ($)
Lewis	142	243	321,245	118	193	243,469
Lincoln	294	510	654,215	236	406	488,608
Loudon	306	507	657,610	289	479	574,018
McMinn	596	997	1,301,474	493	816	1,002,706
McNairy	383	641	818,439	336	560	683,855
Macon	152	274	361,223	132	244	292,833
Madison	1,659	3,193	3,814,068	1,525	2,891	3,268,269
Marion	505	854	1,105,730	458	763	941,802
Marshall	200	340	445,662	193	324	387,328
Maury	810	1,396	1,809,660	707	1,227	1,464,145
Meigs	141	258	338,976	108	190	235,635
Monroe	495	855	1,136,360	399	685	838,239
Montgomery	1,039	1,905	2,451,068	817	1,493	1,830,448
Moore	27	34	52,156	23	31	40,379
Morgan	295	510	651,370	279	470	556,025
Obion	411	721	940,685	332	617	725,862
Overton	197	332	442,408	171	276	349,120
Perry	46	76	101,868	38	61	77,745
Pickett	59	107	143,926	46	81	102,745
Polk	112	183	245,948	116	188	233,146
Putnam	394	665	881,568	326	554	689,948
Rhea	544	963	1,242,264	496	864	1,063,939
Roane	644	1,059	1,396,076	572	940	1,156,830
Robertson	404	745	941,171	369	649	791,559
Rutherford	977	1,790	2,341,383	818	1,496	1,807,734
Scott	506	913	1,121,068	471	864	999,902
Sequatchie	161	260	338,901	138	232	280,362
Sevier	518	861	1,109,212	417	687	826,412
Shelby	24,031	50,284	57,869,787	22,037	46,363	50,089,072
Smith	141	242	317,506	126	221	267,994
Stewart	64	110	145,128	63	106	130,204
Sullivan	1,495	2,483	3,417,972	1,336	2,255	2,894,785
Sumner	715	1,272	1,757,956	535	966	1,220,676
Tipton	931	1,982	2,231,578	876	1,833	1,943,794
Trousdale	65	117	149,603	51	90	106,185
Unicoi	168	259	365,064	152	223	297,162
Union	251	427	563,822	215	359	450,221
Van Buren	53	92	120,571	49	82	100,777
Warren	356	643	840,699	306	549	677,973
Washington	1,121	1,908	2,499,027	1,020	1,735	2,133,432
Wayne	136	227	289,243	116	198	226,709
Weakley	270	460	615,943	231	396	491,016
White	184	321	433,736	140	233	296,990
Williamson	511	917	1,183,963	440	793	936,564
Wilson	581	1,025	1,316,925	462	807	970,541
TENNESSEE	83,627	156,828	192,320,123	74,263	139,958	160,957,737

Note: Number of families and children are monthly averages.

Source: Tennessee Department of Human Services, direct correspondence.

PUBLIC ASSISTANCE AND SOCIAL INSURANCE

TABLE 18.7--MEDICAL ASSISTANCE CASELOAD, TENNESSEE AND COUNTIES, FISCAL YEAR 1991
[Average caseload]

| County | Medically needy | Categorically needy | | | | AFDC Medicaid only |
		Aged	Blind	Disabled	Women and children	
Anderson	361	359	9	107	811	97
Bedford	96	257	0	24	288	31
Benton	76	217	0	25	209	16
Bledsoe	82	55	0	8	133	14
Blount	345	544	1	95	940	81
Bradley	383	509	0	94	904	58
Campbell	415	282	0	84	677	61
Cannon	56	83	0	12	114	6
Carroll	125	376	2	59	318	51
Carter	232	522	0	84	544	49
Cheatham	111	106	0	23	282	17
Chester	70	120	0	29	170	17
Claibome	182	182	0	58	472	41
Clay	61	54	0	10	112	5
Cocke	281	247	0	64	478	64
Coffee	278	280	0	75	534	47
Crockett	76	248	2	26	184	22
Cumberland	186	301	0	61	514	36
Davidson	1,341	2,726	1	870	3,993	684
Decatur	76	167	5	22	155	11
DeKalb	101	115	0	16	194	17
Dickson	249	242	0	43	391	39
Dyer	149	343	0	67	381	64
Fayette	126	177	1	29	274	69
Fentress	178	130	0	74	309	28
Franklin	192	240	0	40	324	27
Gibson	232	589	1	147	533	80
Giles	130	227	2	29	243	42
Grainger	133	134	0	32	259	15
Greene	370	518	0	473	667	47
Grundy	166	144	0	39	253	25
Hamblen	322	352	0	81	526	59
Hamilton	1,176	1,713	0	283	2,741	371
Hancock	78	59	0	11	138	13
Hardeman	184	184	0	115	313	53
Hardin	227	228	4	48	426	30
Hawkins	258	258	0	72	495	43
Haywood	158	179	0	39	293	80
Henderson	128	224	1	46	314	23
Henry	167	294	0	52	365	42
Hickman	81	178	0	26	221	13
Houston	58	120	0	10	84	6
Humphreys	84	130	0	19	204	14
Jackson	64	106	0	17	148	10
Jefferson	247	285	0	62	382	36
Johnson	146	148	0	39	212	25
Knox	1,253	1,913	0	468	2,921	398
Lake	56	123	0	23	107	19
Lauderdale	133	264	0	39	237	56
Lawrence	199	304	0	40	481	41

TABLE 18.7--MEDICAL ASSISTANCE CASELOAD, TENNESSEE AND COUNTIES, FISCAL YEAR 1991
[Average caseload] (Continued)

| County | Medically needy | Categorically needy | | | | |
		Aged	Blind	Disabled	Women and children	AFDC Medicaid only
Lewis	60	98	1	16	149	15
Lincoln	67	304	0	32	249	23
Loudon	147	190	0	121	293	21
McMinn	249	388	0	47	464	44
McNairy	139	251	4	42	301	35
Macon	84	107	0	19	191	14
Madison	368	637	5	106	757	194
Marion	224	199	0	22	393	36
Marshall	90	132	0	32	190	17
Maury	316	465	0	74	663	61
Meigs	52	80	0	14	104	9
Monroe	278	273	0	90	591	42
Montgomery	512	382	0	101	981	78
Moore	18	10	0	1	38	2
Morgan	192	91	13	35	291	33
Obion	121	338	1	51	362	46
Overton	90	181	0	33	253	16
Perry	50	91	0	13	71	2
Pickett	21	56	1	7	67	5
Polk	84	116	0	11	140	7
Putnam	213	400	1	71	593	30
Rhea	194	241	0	42	296	45
Roane	300	470	0	82	497	46
Robertson	159	295	0	33	449	61
Rutherford	278	501	4	112	1,000	97
Scott	271	181	1	64	445	21
Sequatchie	66	92	0	15	126	11
Sevier	293	295	0	39	735	51
Shelby	1,659	3,542	2	900	5,390	1,762
Smith	73	127	1	19	128	13
Stewart	41	84	0	12	101	7
Sullivan	592	977	1	190	1,489	102
Sumner	356	521	1	88	960	56
Tipton	156	220	1	33	389	75
Trousdale	45	67	0	10	84	3
Unicoi	66	194	0	33	172	16
Union	101	98	0	20	215	11
Van Buren	42	26	0	10	80	6
Warren	260	254	0	44	472	28
Washington	402	591	10	111	979	75
Wayne	107	140	4	20	321	16
Weakley	88	407	0	39	336	36
White	99	177	0	47	305	26
Williamson	184	322	1	34	446	54
Wilson	269	314	0	57	618	40
TENNESSEE	21,349	32,478	80	7,301	49,440	6,576

Note: These data do not include SSI or AFDC recipients who also hold Medicaid cards.

Source: Research and Statistics, Tennessee Department of Human Services, direct correspondence.

TABLE 18.8--VALUE OF FOOD STAMP COUPONS AND NUMBER OF HOUSEHOLDS PARTICIPATING,
TENNESSEE AND COUNTIES, FISCAL YEARS 1990 AND 1991

| | 1991 | | 1990 | |
County	Number of households [1]	Value of coupons	Number of households [1]	Value of coupons
Anderson	3,141	6,003,828	2,800	$5,030,824
Bedford	1,081	1,974,106	885	1,463,965
Benton	673	1,175,980	574	857,842
Bledsoe	658	1,201,476	565	943,652
Blount	3,106	5,322,602	2,791	4,472,393
Bradley	2,558	4,470,127	2,030	3,205,273
Campbell	3,217	6,131,387	2,884	5,066,016
Cannon	386	691,187	334	523,468
Carroll	1,371	1,955,886	1,244	1,572,647
Carter	2,507	4,364,477	2,256	3,674,080
Cheatham	717	1,573,420	518	1,064,254
Chester	726	1,124,765	669	924,660
Claiborne	1,709	3,108,300	1,505	2,572,705
Clay	454	657,335	417	566,984
Cocke	2,227	3,750,477	2,035	3,203,291
Coffee	1,695	3,113,542	1,428	2,352,463
Crockett	638	962,089	534	704,307
Cumberland	1,475	2,619,794	1,294	2,147,509
Davidson	22,201	43,417,928	18,934	36,500,655
Decatur	574	777,939	488	561,477
DeKalb	707	1,254,966	638	1,024,008
Dickson	1,372	2,827,718	1,098	2,067,990
Dyer	2,106	3,121,419	1,864	2,478,003
Fayette	1,782	3,336,133	1,630	2,900,072
Fentress	1,292	2,358,056	1,150	1,979,872
Franklin	1,229	2,139,274	1,062	1,674,034
Gibson	2,396	3,870,524	2,157	3,172,020
Giles	1,221	2,058,245	1,116	1,761,854
Grainger	936	1,760,735	793	1,319,418
Greene	2,610	4,568,595	2,197	3,475,123
Grundy	1,142	2,259,079	978	1,785,625
Hamblen	2,358	4,386,238	1,990	3,426,031
Hamilton	13,329	21,400,646	11,765	18,378,528
Hancock	670	1,282,029	628	1,161,787
Hardeman	1,979	3,458,153	1,837	2,975,247
Hardin	1,768	2,797,844	1,610	2,326,523
Hawkins	2,305	4,230,411	2,069	3,550,263
Haywood	1,954	3,130,387	1,829	2,707,404
Henderson	1,159	1,669,722	1,031	1,321,566
Henry	1,334	2,081,151	1,190	1,646,493
Hickman	705	1,231,241	569	879,593
Houston	313	544,671	286	458,775
Humphreys	533	942,102	430	662,957
Jackson	483	831,638	415	650,355
Jefferson	1,544	2,654,504	1,308	2,003,679
Johnson	1,126	1,795,960	1,052	1,593,699
Knox	13,313	24,402,633	11,744	20,474,906
Lake	659	990,837	581	775,791
Lauderdale	1,880	3,250,240	1,621	2,530,459
Lawrence	1,573	2,600,055	1,388	2,093,380

TABLE 18.8--VALUE OF FOOD STAMP COUPONS AND NUMBER OF HOUSEHOLDS PARTICIPATING, TENNESSEE AND COUNTIES, FISCAL YEARS 1990 AND 1991 (Continued)

	1991		1990	
	Number of	Value	Number of	Value
	households [1]	of	households [1]	of
County		coupons		coupons
Lewis	593	989,946	496	733,838
Lincoln	990	1,598,082	786	1,145,349
Loudon	1,197	2,030,056	1,059	1,655,130
McMinn	1,876	3,497,983	1,558	2,613,227
McNairy	1,487	2,328,239	1,344	1,897,846
Macon	616	1,142,882	526	885,395
Madison	3,896	6,855,389	3,607	5,850,518
Marion	1,583	3,032,073	1,336	2,404,067
Marshall	764	1,282,159	642	990,732
Maury	2,467	4,358,389	2,038	3,249,651
Meigs	468	949,607	388	735,071
Monroe	1,842	3,486,408	1,529	2,645,461
Montgomery	3,271	6,388,906	2,640	4,631,437
Moore	125	201,899	97	134,222
Morgan	1,191	2,259,215	1,057	1,855,375
Obion	1,547	2,398,154	1,334	1,887,593
Overton	947	1,586,357	819	1,241,273
Perry	311	511,642	272	391,257
Pickett	219	382,718	196	314,681
Polk	622	1,106,670	562	894,825
Putnam	1,552	2,714,168	1,254	1,947,895
Rhea	1,708	3,154,908	1,506	2,587,553
Roane	2,283	3,929,054	2,064	3,296,995
Robertson	1,235	2,209,692	1,023	1,587,993
Rutherford	2,505	4,959,408	2,063	3,745,334
Scott	1,903	3,515,238	1,722	2,922,338
Sequatchie	568	997,005	499	807,297
Sevier	1,932	3,561,907	1,670	2,804,367
Shelby	48,703	102,448,346	43,940	89,927,866
Smith	508	921,916	418	697,358
Stewart	356	625,447	315	472,836
Sullivan	5,540	9,958,646	5,073	8,487,591
Sumner	2,563	5,031,721	1,952	3,435,328
Tipton	2,416	4,708,418	2,194	3,984,410
Trousdale	248	475,873	194	340,668
Unicoi	903	1,397,829	806	1,142,725
Union	732	1,453,571	597	1,112,408
Van Buren	223	410,612	198	338,694
Warren	1,345	2,430,059	1,150	1,950,245
Washington	3,506	6,416,553	3,110	5,259,055
Wayne	713	1,179,422	635	971,235
Weakley	1,153	1,684,166	1,034	1,333,618
White	787	1,341,919	619	948,011
Williamson	1,270	2,400,390	1,045	1,849,848
Wilson	1,769	3,442,334	1,377	2,468,901
TENNESSEE	229,321	425,387,227	200,953	351,241,437

1. Monthly average number of participating households.

Source: Tennessee Department of Human Services, Research and Statistics Division, direct correspondence.

TABLE 18.9--MEDICARE AND MEDICAID BENEFITS, SOUTHEASTERN STATES, 1991

| State | Medicare[1] | | Medicaid[2] | |
	Benefits paid ($1,000,000)	Persons enrolled (1,000)	Benefits paid ($1,000,000)	Recipients[3] (1,000)
TENNESSEE	2,405	706	1,485	697
Alabama	2,124	593	805	403
Arkansas	1,257	397	688	285
Florida	8,443	2,402	2,944	1,249
Georgia	2,588	750	1,799	746
Kentucky	1,801	543	1,200	525
Louisiana	2,283	541	1,723	641
Mississippi	1,154	371	755	470
North Carolina	2,607	917	1,788	667
South Carolina	1,212	454	910	375
Virginia	2,341	741	1,218	442
West Virginia	949	312	542	284

Note: Preliminary data.

1. Payments are for calendar year and represent total disbursements from federal hospital and supplementary medical insurance trust funds. Estimates of distribution by state based on interim reimbursements. Enrollment is as of July 1.

2. For fiscal year ending September 30.

3. Persons receiving Medicaid at any time during year.

Source: U.S. Department of Commerce, Bureau of the Census, *Statistical Abstract of the United States, 1993.*

TABLE 18.10--EXPENDITURES OF STATE HEALTH AGENCIES AND LOCAL HEALTH DEPARTMENTS, BY PROGRAM AREA, SOUTHEASTERN STATES, 1988

State	Total public health expenditures	Direct state health agency expenditures	Intergovernmental transfers [1]	Additional expenditures of local health departments
TENNESSEE	220,633	158,877	19,720	42,036
Alabama	135,021	82,463	8,101	44,456
Arkansas	67,265	678,265	(a)	(a)
Florida	366,796	150,395	216,402	(a)
Georgia	239,924	148,552	50,293	41,078
Kentucky	154,857	76,179	34,053	44,625
Louisiana	116,726	116,042	685	(a)
Mississippi	105,899	75,856	30,043	(a)
North Carolina	286,642	128,125	50,747	107,770
South Carolina	181,959	105,038	76,891	(a)
Virginia	206,196	96,111	110,084	(a)
West Virginia	172,664	153,192	6,528	12,944

1. Transfers from state health agencies to local health departments.
a. No data or data unobtainable.
Source: Health Insurance Association of America, *Source Book of Health Insurance Data, 1990*, used by special permission.

TABLE 18.11--AID TO FAMILIES WITH DEPENDENT CHILDREN, NUMBER OF RECIPIENTS AND AMOUNT OF PAYMENTS, SOUTHEASTERN STATES AND UNITED STATES, 1991

State	Recipients [1] (1,000)	Amount of payments	
		Total ($1,000,000)	Monthly average per family ($)
TENNESSEE	266	200	187
Alabama	142	73	125
Arkansas	76	60	191
Florida	546	560	267
Georgia	383	392	267
Kentucky	230	208	217
Louisiana	276	189	170
Mississippi	178	88	122
North Carolina	308	312	238
South Carolina	137	111	203
Virginia	185	208	270
West Virginia	119	116	252
UNITED STATES	13,285	20,843	394

Note: Recipients are as of December.

1. Includes the children and one or both parents, or one caretaker relative other than a parent, in families where the needs of such adults were considered in determining the amount of assistance.
Source: U.S. Department of Commerce, Bureau of the Census, *Statistical Abstract of the United States, 1993*.

TABLE 18.12--CASH PAYMENTS MADE UNDER FOOD AND NUTRITION SERVICE PROGRAMS, SOUTHEASTERN STATES, FISCAL YEAR 1989
[In thousands of dollars]

State	Total	Child Nutrition Program					Special Supplemental Food (WIC)[1]	Commodity Distribution[1]	Food Stamp[1]	TEFAP[2]
		Child Care Food	Summer Food	Special Milk	National School Lunch	Breakfast				
TENNESSEE	467,128	8,474	1,562	36	65,667	16,252	30,298	26,150	312,362	6,328
Alabama	429,971	11,680	3,625	33	74,428	12,918	26,678	18,716	276,056	5,838
Arkansas	218,155	5,609	600	26	39,364	7,535	19,375	11,470	130,440	3,737
Florida	745,075	22,266	11,536	110	141,256	26,426	50,996	29,057	455,257	8,171
Georgia	523,363	16,198	4,203	53	99,281	18,808	47,766	29,688	301,773	5,594
Kentucky	433,473	6,433	1,217	274	58,186	14,491	29,118	18,788	299,965	5,000
Louisiana	707,040	14,547	3,885	80	100,109	17,600	42,604	38,061	484,489	5,665
Mississippi	471,200	15,919	4,418	17	72,178	15,841	26,672	13,980	318,740	3,435
North Carolina	424,490	13,331	2,981	`118	84,732	19,860	42,282	28,431	227,688	5,067
South Carolina	291,425	6,603	3,930	22	56,659	10,362	29,406	15,325	167,229	1,889
Virginia	340,049	9,274	1,486	256	56,387	8,465	29,160	21,210	206,418	7,394
West Virginia	232,231	3,244	464	29	28,027	9,111	12,956	6,824	169,187	2,388

Note: Data are preliminary.

1. The amounts shown for WIC, Commodity Distribution, Food Stamp, and TEFAP programs are the values of the food benefits provided.
2. Temporary Emergency Food Assistance Program.
Source: U.S. Department of Agriculture, Statistical Reporting Service, *Agricultural Statistics, 1990.*

TABLE 18.13– SOCIAL SECURITY BENEFICIARIES AND BENEFIT PAYMENTS, SOUTHEASTERN STATES AND UNITED STATES, 1991

State	Number of beneficiaries (1,000)				Benefit payments ($1,000,000)				Average monthly payments ($)		
	Total	Retired workers [1,2]	Survivors	Disabled workers [2]	Total	Retired workers [1,2]	Survivors [3]	Disabled workers [2]	Retired workers [4]	Disabled workers	Widows and widowers [5]
TENNESSEE	846	557	165	123	5,189	3,343	1,143	703	588	577	524
Alabama	722	460	155	107	4,357	2,706	1,046	605	581	582	512
Arkansas	473	311	91	72	2,791	1,784	604	403	565	576	502
Florida	2,728	2,092	403	234	18,170	13,532	3,143	1,495	628	620	602
Georgia	905	583	181	141	5,550	3,519	1,215	816	587	582	519
Kentucky	658	407	139	113	3,963	2,365	951	647	579	605	520
Louisiana	663	397	157	108	3,989	2,304	1,085	600	584	617	535
Mississippi	459	282	96	81	2,577	1,559	588	430	546	560	471
North Carolina	1,111	758	201	152	6,858	4,599	1,361	898	588	573	512
South Carolina	558	371	104	84	3,415	2,245	678	492	588	583	506
Virginia	857	593	159	105	5,387	3,607	1,149	631	595	596	542
West Virginia	373	230	82	61	2,409	1,422	616	371	622	654	554
UNITED STATES	39,621	28,241	7,028	4,352	264,049	183,287	53,806	26,956	n.a.	n.a.	n.a.

Note: A person eligible to receive more than one type of benefit is generally classified or counted only once as a retired worker beneficiary.

n.a. not available.

1. Includes special benefits for persons aged 72 and over not insured under regular or transitional provisions of Social Security Act.

2. Includes benefits payable to dependents.

3. Includes lump-sum payments to survivors of deceased workers.

4. Excludes persons with special benefits.

5. Nondisabled only.

Source: U.S. Department of Commerce, Bureau of the Census, *Statistical Abstract of the United States, 1993.*

TABLE 18.14--SUPPLEMENTAL SECURITY INCOME FOR THE AGED, BLIND, AND DISABLED, SOUTHEASTERN STATES, 1989

| | State-administered supplementation | | Federally administered supplementation[1] | | | | | | | |
| | | | | | Aged | | Blind | | Disabled | |
	Total recipients	Total payments ($1,000)	Total recipients	Total payments ($1,000)	Recipients	Average monthly payment ($)	Recipients	Average monthly payment ($)	Recipients	Average monthly payment ($)
TENNESSEE	0	0	135,683	350,389	42,480	267.27	1,953	248.21	91,250	261.86
Alabama	11,601	8,210	130,894	325,492	51,001	264.74	1,698	255.28	78,195	260.74
Arkansas	0	0	74,489	171,428	28,488	270.16	1,265	253.56	44,736	260.46
Florida	11,322	12,528	210,866	588,631	80,887	278.58	3,166	258.67	126,813	273.28
Georgia	0	0	156,938	386,857	52,229	276.88	2,680	253.19	102,029	268.43
Kentucky	6,474	10,574	109,840	303,357	29,962	261.29	1,964	232.86	77,914	253.29
Louisiana	0	0	130,020	350,043	41,634	265.39	2,257	249.03	86,129	254.61
Mississippi	0	0	112,511	280,048	43,079	260.37	1,667	243.31	67,765	253.63
North Carolina	15,334	58,811	144,663	362,876	49,219	265.89	2,624	253.36	92,820	256.01
South Carolina	3,312	7,840	88,701	218,985	29,596	269.83	1,790	249.84	57,315	263.30
Virginia	5,849	15,287	91,990	235,110	29,354	272.64	1,487	255.26	61,149	263.57
West Virginia	0	0	45,656	133,972	9,285	269.67	669	252.09	35,702	250.71

Note: Number of recipients and average monthly payments are for the month of December.

1. Includes federal SSI payments and federally administered state supplementation.

Source: U.S. Department of Health and Human Services, Social Security Administration, Social Security Bulletin, Annual Statistical Supplement, 1990.

TABLE 18.15--INSURANCE SUMMARY FOR COVERED EMPLOYMENT, SOUTHEASTERN STATES, 1991

State	Insured unemployment		Average weekly unemployment benefits ($)	Beneficiaries, first payments (1,000)	Benefits paid ($1,000,000)
	Number (1,000)	Percent [1]			
TENNESSEE	63.0	3.0	118	221	333
Alabama	41.7	2.7	119	171	221
Arkansas	31.7	3.6	140	103	176
Florida	120.8	2.3	158	353	823
Georgia	66.3	2.3	149	278	469
Kentucky	40.6	3.0	145	145	273
Louisiana	35.2	2.3	111	102	163
Mississippi	28.2	3.2	116	85	127
North Carolina	80.3	2.7	157	332	510
South Carolina	41.0	2.8	141	148	235
Virginia	45.3	1.7	157	169	313
West Virginia	22.9	3.9	160	66	153

1. Insured unemployment as a percent of average covered employment in preceding year.
Source: U.S. Department of Commerce, Bureau of the Census, *Statistical Abstract of the United States, 1993*.

TABLE 18.16--WORKERS' COMPENSATION PAYMENTS, SOUTHEASTERN STATES, 1980–1990, SELECTED YEARS [In millions of dollars]

State	1990	1989	1988	1987	1986	1985	1980
TENNESSEE	463	390	341	289	234	204	129
Alabama	444	380	311	274	244	203	112
Arkansas	229	196	177	160	143	129	83
Florida	1,976	1,732	1,422	1,178	979	815	362
Georgia	735	661	581	510	427	360	185
Kentucky	383	326	293	274	245	225	161
Louisiana	575	586	565	544	485	466	301
Mississippi	198	171	155	137	122	98	60
North Carolina	480	386	328	272	245	236	131
South Carolina	277	240	208	186	162	152	79
Virginia	507	465	409	354	313	276	182
West Virginia	389	375	363	355	322	285	176

Source: U.S. Department of Commerce, Bureau of the Census, *Statistical Abstract of the United States, 1993*.

Law enforcement statistics are generally either records of police agencies or prison data. Records of prosecutions and court actions do not lend themselves to statistical presentation because of the complexity of reporting litigation. The U.S. Department of Justice, Federal Bureau of Investigation, reports the most common local crimes in its *Crime in the United States, Uniform Crime Reports.* It is important to remember that crime statistics included here represent only those crimes reported to police and represent fewer than the number actually committed; that reporting procedures vary from place to place or over time; that differences exist among governmental units in the scope of responsibilities and administration; and finally, that many factors influence the frequency of crimes and the level of enforcement needed. Therefore, data users are advised to exercise caution in making comparisons in the area of law enforcement statistics.

The *Sourcebook of Criminal Justice Statistics,* published by the U.S. Department of Justice, Bureau of Justice Statistics (BJS), provides prisoner detail and governmental expenditures data for criminal justice. In addition to the Bureau of Justice, departments of state government publish prisoner and expenditure data in their annual reports. The most current data on Tennessee state and local expenditures for law enforcement can be found in Chapter 15, Government Finance. Prisoner and prison statistics are published by the Department of Corrections. When published reports are not available in time to be included in the *Abstract,* the Department of Corrections has graciously provided these data from their files. Information on the number of deaths from homicide is supplied by Tennessee Department of Health.

Traffic accidents and deaths are reported in the Tennessee Department of Safety's *Tennessee Motor Vehicle Traffic Accident Facts.* Note that a change in reporting laws and procedures occurred in 1971; therefore, data reported prior to this date are not comparable to data reported later. However, two years of comparable data have been given here in order to provide a bridge for the data user.

New to this edition of the *Abstract,* a table on lawyers licensed in Tennessee and each of the southeastern states shows a doubling of this profession between 1970 and the mid-1980s. However, the number of licensed attorneys has begun to level off in recent years.

A map featuring judicial districts in Tennessee might also be of interest to data users interested in law enforcement. A corresponding table details the number of chancellors and criminal and civil court judges serving each district. This information is included in Chapter 14.

TABLE OF CONTENTS

TABLE OF CONTENTS
(Continued)

FIGURE 19.1

Crime Rates per 100,000 Population by Type of Crime, Tennessee, 1982–1992

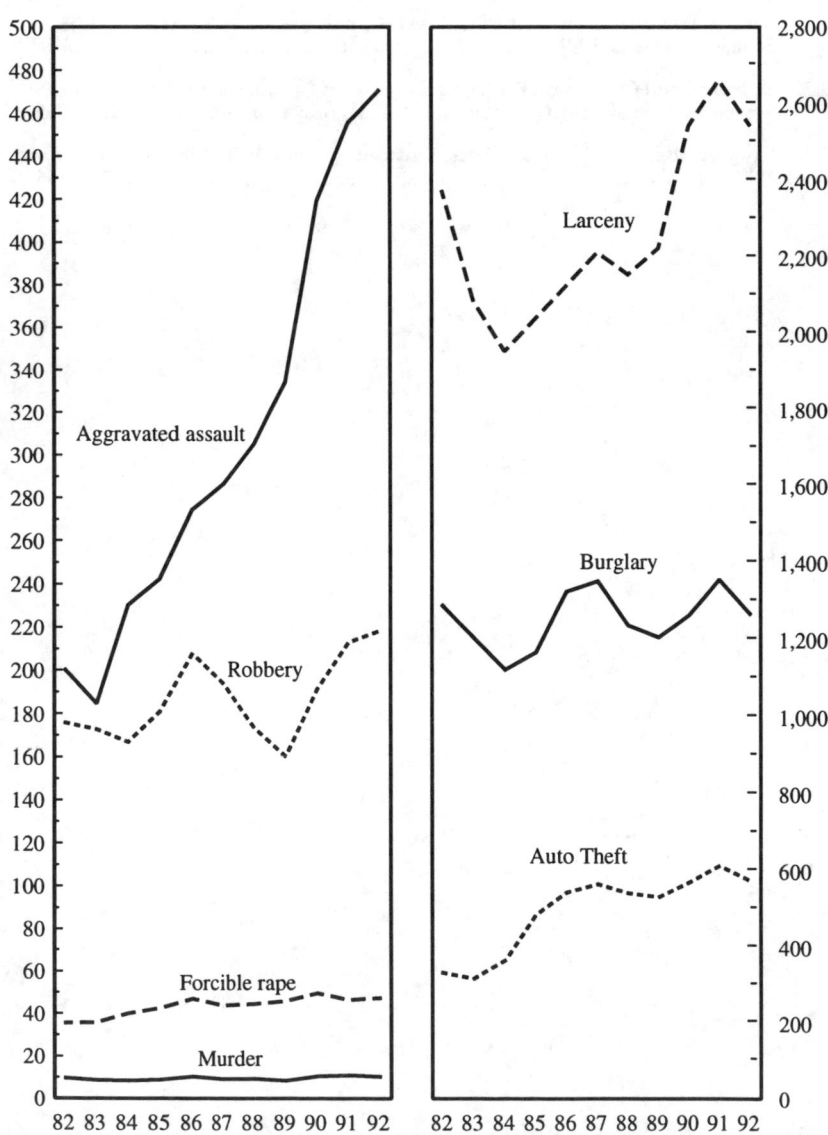

Note: Rates are known offenses based on Bureau of the Census population estimates as of July 1 except in decennial census years, when it is April 1.

Source: U.S. Department of Justice F.B.I., *Crime in the United States, Uniform Crime Reports*, 1992, and earlier editions.

TABLE 19.1-- CRIME RATES PER 100,000 POPULATION, BY TYPE OF CRIME, TENNESSEE, 1957–1992

Year	Total offenses	Murder[1]	Forcible rape	Robbery	Aggra- vated assault	Burglary	Larceny $50 and over[2]	Auto theft
1992	5,135.8	10.4	47.3	218.2	470.3	1,267.2	2,546.5	575.9
1991	5,366.7	11.0	46.4	212.9	455.6	1,365.0	2,662.1	613.6
1990	5,051.0	10.5	49.5	191.2	419.2	1,264.0	2,545.1	571.5
1989	4,513.6	8.4	46.0	160.4	334.1	1,206.9	2,224.9	532.9
1988	4,469.4	9.4	44.7	173.6	305.1	1,237.9	2,156.0	542.8
1987	4,665.6	9.1	43.9	193.8	286.6	1,351.8	2,213.4	566.9
1986	4,534.2	10.4	47.0	207.7	274.5	1,325.2	2,125.8	543.6
1985	4,166.7	9.0	42.6	180.9	242.0	1,166.8	2,040.3	485.2
1984	3,889.6	8.4	40.0	166.8	230.3	1,123.6	1,954.1	366.4
1983	4,011.7	8.8	35.9	172.8	184.6	1,205.9	2,087.2	316.5
1982	4,413.6	9.7	35.5	175.7	200.2	1,288.6	2,371.9	332.0
1981	4,311.4	9.7	37.6	171.7	193.5	1,384.2	2,180.6	334.1
1980	4,497.9	10.8	37.4	180.6	229.4	1,501.5	2,175.2	363.1
1979	4,013.4	9.8	34.5	166.1	203.6	1,294.7	1,937.2	367.4
1978	3,690.4	9.4	30.6	152.4	190.2	1,213.6	1,766.1	328.1
1977	3,739.7	10.1	29.7	145.8	203.9	1,259.7	1,776.5	314.0
1976	4,258.4	11.0	25.4	147.5	209.4	1,320.5	2,218.6	325.9
1975	4,270.5	11.4	26.1	166.8	192.6	1,379.3	2,129.5	364.7
1974	3,659.1	13.4	25.7	157.2	190.4	1,350.1	1,575.6	346.7
1973	3,060.1	13.2	26.9	130.5	187.5	1,009.8	1,362.2	330.1
1972	2,101.5	11.3	19.9	101.1	186.7	894.3	587.4	300.9
1971	2,060.3	12.4	18.1	86.5	196.8	901.4	541.7	303.5
1970	1,888.3	8.8	15.5	82.0	168.6	806.7	517.4	289.3
1969	1,665.5	9.6	12.7	75.2	134.3	715.0	437.2	281.6
1968	1,598.0	8.7	11.6	71.2	129.0	719.7	390.3	267.4
1967	1,531.3	8.9	12.5	56.5	130.5	711.8	368.0	243.1
1966	1,275.6	7.8	10.8	34.4	105.2	602.5	321.7	193.1
1965	1,082.9	8.0	11.1	28.6	91.1	523.0	254.5	166.7
1964	1,103.8	5.9	8.8	30.2	73.6	561.4	248.0	175.8
1963	1,014.0	6.5	6.7	28.4	60.7	515.9	230.2	165.7
1962	919.2	6.1	6.6	34.8	56.1	461.6	195.9	158.1
1961	875.5	8.0	6.7	30.4	63.0	462.0	166.1	139.2
1960	847.2	8.5	5.2	27.8	50.4	469.4	153.5	132.2
1959	821.5	7.0	6.6	26.9	56.2	437.8	151.4	135.7
1958	791.7	8.4	7.4	26.2	59.2	416.5	142.1	131.9
1957	745.0	9.2	n.a.	27.1	70.5	360.5	139.2	138.6

Note: Rates represent offenses known per 100,000 population, based on the Bureau of the Census provisional population estimate as of July 1, except in decennial census years, when it is April 1.

n.a. not available.

1. Murder includes nonnegligent manslaughter.

2. Beginning in 1973, includes all larceny-theft not using force or fraud.

Source: U.S. Department of Justice, Federal Bureau of Investigation, *Crime in the United States, Uniform Crime Reports, 1992*, and earlier editions (prior to 1961 titled *Uniform Crime Reports for the United States*).

TABLE 19.2-- NUMBER OF CRIMINAL OFFENSES, BY TYPE OF CRIME, TENNESSEE, 1957–1992

Year	Total offenses	Murder[1]	Forcible rape	Robbery	Aggra- vated assault	Burglary	Larceny $50 and over[2]	Auto theft
1992	258,021	520	2,377	10,964	23,626	63,665	127,934	28,935
1991	265,811	547	2,299	10,543	22,566	67,608	131,855	30,393
1990	246,346	511	2,415	9,325	20,447	61,646	124,127	27,875
1989	222,972	417	2,270	7,926	16,505	59,621	109,908	26,325
1988	219,852	461	2,201	8,537	15,006	60,894	106,052	26,701
1987	226,516	444	2,133	9,409	13,914	65,632	107,459	27,525
1986	217,780	501	2,256	9,978	13,184	63,649	102,103	26,109
1985	198,419	429	2,027	8,614	11,522	55,563	97,159	23,105
1984	183,472	394	1,887	7,867	10,862	53,002	92,176	17,284
1983	187,946	410	1,682	8,094	8,650	56,498	97,785	14,827
1982	205,278	452	1,651	8,173	9,310	59,934	110,316	15,442
1981	198,756	448	1,735	7,916	8,920	63,811	100,526	15,400
1980	204,456	489	1,700	8,208	10,427	68,251	98,876	16,505
1979	175,786	430	1,511	7,277	8,917	56,710	84,850	16,091
1978	160,792	411	1,335	6,639	8,286	52,876	76,948	14,297
1977	160,768	434	1,276	6,266	8,767	54,154	76,371	13,500
1976	179,448	462	1,072	6,215	8,825	55,647	93,493	13,734
1975	178,850	477	1,095	6,987	8,068	57,766	89,184	15,273
1974	151,085	555	1,062	6,490	7,862	55,745	65,055	14,316
1973	126,259	544	1,108	5,383	7,736	41,663	56,206	13,619
1972	84,713	455	802	4,076	7,525	36,049	23,678	12,128
1971	82,207	496	721	3,452	7,851	35,964	21,612	12,111
1970	74,101	346	607	3,218	6,616	31,656	20,305	11,353
1969	66,371	382	505	2,996	5,352	28,492	17,421	11,223
1968	63,535	345	460	2,830	5,131	28,616	15,520	10,633
1967	59,605	347	486	2,199	5,079	27,703	14,323	9,468
1966	49,529	304	421	1,337	4,083	23,394	12,492	7,498
1965	41,635	307	425	1,100	3,501	20,107	9,787	6,408
1964	41,920	225	336	1,148	2,796	21,321	9,418	6,676
1963	37,458	239	247	1,048	2,243	19,056	8,503	6,122
1962	33,404	220	241	1,266	2,040	16,772	7,119	5,746
1961	31,648	290	242	1,100	2,278	16,702	6,005	5,031
1960	30,220	304	187	993	1,799	16,744	5,477	4,716
1959	29,014	247	232	950	1,984	15,461	5,347	4,793
1958	27,468	293	258	908	2,054	14,448	4,930	4,577
1957	25,651	316	n.a.	932	2,427	12,411	4,794	4,771

n.a. not available.

1. Murder includes nonnegligent manslaughter.

2. Beginning in 1973, includes all larceny-theft not using force or fraud.

Source: U.S. Department of Justice, Federal Bureau of Investigation, *Crime in the United States, Uniform Crime Reports, 1992*, and earlier editions (prior to 1961 titled *Uniform Crime Reports for the United States*).

TABLE 19.3--POPULATION AND PER CAPITA EXPENDITURES OF ADULT CORRECTIONAL
INSTITUTIONS, TENNESSEE, FISCAL YEAR 1993

Institution	Population[1]	Average daily count	Designated capacity	Average daily cost per resident
Brushy Mountain State Penitentiary	490	456	495	$63.57
Carter County Work Camp	209	192	210	44.01
Chattanooga Community Service Center	121	115	120	47.87
DeBerry Special Needs Facility	538	399	612	160.25
Fort Pillow Prison and Farm	655	641	700	47.56
Knoxville Community Service Center	147	130	150	54.28
Lake County Regional Correctional Facility	731	701	715	40.94
Mark H. Luttrell Reception Center	424	380	411	58.96
Middle Tennessee Reception Center	606	575	594	50.07
Morgan County Regional Correctional Facility	808	796	791	40.25
Nashville Community Service Center	327	310	325	42.59
Northeast Correctional Center	972	944	960	41.04
Northwest Correctional Center	947	828	960	44.06
Riverbend Maximum Security Institution	571	571	574	66.45
South Central Correctional Center	966	930	960	36.46
Southeastern Tennessee State Regional Correctional Facility	808	792	782	42.57
Tennessee Prison For Women	354	339	341	67.48
Turney Center Industrial Prison	790	691	728	54.49
Wayne County Work Camp	144	119	150	58.52
West Tennessee High Security Facility	607	601	606	51.38

1. As of June 30, 1993.
Source: Tennessee Department of Correction, direct correspondence.

TABLE 19.4-- SENTENCED PRISONERS RECEIVED FROM COURT DURING YEAR AND PRESENT AT
END OF YEAR IN STATE PRISONS, TENNESSEE AND UNITED STATES, 1940–1991,
SELECTED YEARS

| Year | Received from court[1] | | | Present at end of year | | |
	Tennessee	United States	Tennessee as percent of U.S.	Tennessee	United States	Tennessee as percent of U.S.
1991	4,026	317,237	1.27	11,474	789,347	1.45
1990	3,144 e	323,069	0.97	10,388	738,894	1.41
1989	2,924 e	316,215	0.92	10,630	680,809	1.56
1988	1,492	261,242	0.57	7,732	603,732	1.28
1987	1,920	241,887	0.79	7,624	556,748	1.37
1986	3,011	219,382	1.37	7,591	522,245	1.45
1985	n.a.	n.a.	n.a.	7,127	480,568	1.48
1984	3,991	180,418	2.21	7,302	443,838	1.65
1983	3,632	187,408	1.94	8,201	419,346	1.96
1982	3,238	177,109	1.83	7,869	395,516	1.99
1981	3,814	160,272	2.38	7,897	353,167	2.24
1980	2,947	142,122	2.07	7,022	315,974	2.22
1979	2,809	131,047	2.14	6,629	301,470	2.20
1978	2,415	126,121	1.91	5,835	293,546	1.99
1977	2,608	128,050	2.04	5,480	278,141	1.97
1976	2,482	121,997	2.03	4,817	262,833	1.83
1975	2,353	122,715	1.92	4,371	233,900	1.87
1974	1,895	103,754	1.83	3,771	218,205	1.73
1973	1,861	127,686	1.46	3,454	204,349	1.69
1972	1,797	119,316	1.51	3,329	196,183	1.70
1971	1,741	n.a.	n.a.	3,454	198,061	1.74
1970	1,611	67,304	2.39	3,268	176,391	1.85
1969	1,474	63,688	2.31	3,148	176,384	1.78
1968	1,379	60,938	2.26	2,999	167,211	1.79
1967	1,313	66,403	1.98	2,980	175,317	1.70
1966	1,214	66,349	1.83	2,968	180,409	1.65
1965	1,403	74,724	1.88	3,213	189,855	1.69
1964	1,300	75,096	1.73	3,187	192,627	1.65
1963	1,275	74,944	1.70	3,246	194,155	1.67
1962	1,221	75,568	1.62	3,167	194,886	1.63
1961	1,288	79,996	1.61	3,144	196,453	1.60
1960	1,294	74,852	1.73	3,134	189,735	1.65
1959	1,283	73,394	1.75	2,914	185,613	1.57
1958	1,073	74,922	1.43	2,712	184,094	1.47
1957	956	67,252	1.42	2,657	174,994	1.52
1956	931	64,534	1.44	2,713	169,431	1.60
1955	984	63,128	1.56	2,723	165,692	1.64
1950	1,026	55,236	1.86	2,780	148,989	1.87
1945	624	39,041	1.60	2,232	115,011	1.94
1940	1,278	57,995	2.20	3,233	154,446	2.09

Note: Percentages computed by the Center for Business and Economic Research. The United States numbers
include federal institutions.

e estimate.

n.a. not available.

1. New court commitments. Includes all inmates admitted with new sentences and probation violators entering
prison for the first time on the probated offenses. Does not include inmates readmitted for any sentences with
prison time already served or parole violators with new sentences.

Source: U.S. Department of Justice, Bureau of Justice Statistics, *Sourcebook of Criminal Justice Statistics, 1992*,
and earlier editions; and *National Prisoner Statistics, Prisoners in State and Federal Institutions on
December 31, 1980*, and earlier editions.

TABLE 19.5-- MOTOR VEHICLE TRAFFIC ACCIDENTS AND DEATHS ON TENNESSEE HIGHWAYS, 1955–1992

	Accidents					
Year	Total	Fatal	Injury	Property damage only	Number of deaths	Number of injuries
1992	142,386	1,027	47,039	94,320	1,153	73,481
1991	136,820	1,002	45,362	90,456	1,113	71,181
1990	140,260	1,045	46,411	92,804	1,177	72,536
1989	149,314	977	47,222	101,115	1,088	73,571
1988	156,310	1,116	48,014	107,180	1,266	73,969
1987	153,859	1,101	47,386	105,372	1,247	69,995
1986	167,584	1,102	45,990	120,492	1,230	67,741
1985	164,317	997	42,760	120,560	1,101	62,092
1984	156,957	1,006	39,868	116,083	1,111	57,380
1983	149,706	927	37,521	111,258	1,046	54,229
1982	135,491	961	34,134	100,396	1,074	49,266
1981	137,098	978	34,884	101,236	1,119	50,338
1980	137,829	1,014	34,989	101,826	1,161	50,712
1979	149,942	1,070	35,944	112,928	1,268	51,955
1978	144,572	1,109	35,091	108,372	1,252	51,199
1977	133,723	1,072	32,828	99,823	1,218	47,940
1976	126,947	1,009	31,191	94,747	1,146	45,789
1975	121,046	1,002	29,535	90,509	1,162	43,194
1974	111,981	1,081	26,354	84,546	1,274	38,439
1973	140,020	1,256	31,322	108,328	1,444	42,800
(1972)[a]	(23,578)	(1,205)	(7,840)	(14,533)	(1,414)	(12,100)
1972[a]	133,626	1,205	30,487	101,934	1,431	38,315
(1971)[a]	(21,750)	(1,146)	(7,324)	(13,280)	(1,373)	(11,513)
1971[a]	107,154	1,158	26,690	79,306	1,373	36,754
1970	15,661	1,153	5,826	8,682	1,390	9,655
1969	16,877	1,126	6,161	9,590	1,371	9,551
1968	17,925	1,045	6,249	10,631	1,201	9,809
1967	18,720	1,043	6,509	11,160	1,258	10,639
1966	63,802	1,064	n.a.	n.a.	1,272	27,475
1965	49,595	925	17,259	31,411	1,077	27,787
1964	48,688	904	17,853	29,931	1,060	26,047
1963	49,255	779	17,305	31,171	941	25,405
1962	44,810	688	16,366	27,756	811	24,238
1961	50,508	628	16,153	33,727	742	23,725
1960	68,209	663	14,916	52,630	787	22,079
1959	51,344	674	11,706	38,964	771	17,706
1958	43,208	606	9,789	32,813	719	15,360
1957	39,414	600	8,886	29,928	699	13,741
1956	35,468	670	7,732	27,066	765	12,029
1955	29,758	708	6,558	22,492	906	10,135

n.a. not available.

a. Data prior to 1971 are not comparable to data reported after this date due to changes in reporting laws and procedures. Comparable data based on earlier reporting procedures are given in parentheses for 1971 and 1972.

Source: Tennessee Department of Safety, Planning and Research Section, *Tennessee Motor Vehicle Traffic Accident Facts, 1988–1992*, and earlier editions.

TABLE 19.6-- ALCOHOL TEST RESULTS OF DRIVERS IN FATAL TRAFFIC CRASHES, BY AGE, TENNESSEE, 1992

Age of driver	Total [1]	Number tested	Percent of total	Negative blood alcohol content	Percent of tested	Positive blood alcohol content	Percent of tested	Blood alcohol content >=0.10	Percent of tested
TOTAL	1,522	955	63	542	57	413	43	341	36
15 or younger	18	6	33	3	50	3	50	1	17
16–17	82	48	59	40	83	8	17	2	4
18–20	137	93	68	53	57	40	43	36	39
21–24	188	134	71	64	48	70	52	53	40
25–34	385	266	69	117	44	149	56	125	47
35–44	251	158	63	85	54	73	46	62	39
45–54	169	105	62	63	60	42	40	36	34
55–64	114	66	58	46	70	20	30	18	27
65 or older	167	79	47	71	90	8	10	8	10
Age unknown	11	0	(X)	0	(X)	0	(X)	0	(X)

(X) Not applicable.

1. Total number of drivers involved in fatal traffic crashes.

Source: Tennessee Department of Safety, Planning and Research Section, *Tennessee Motor Vehicle Traffic Accident Facts, 1988–1992.*

TABLE 19.7-- NUMBER OF DEATHS FROM HOMICIDE AND LEGAL INTERVENTION, BY RACE AND BY SEX, RESIDENT DATA, TENNESSEE, 1971–1991

| | | | White | | | | All other races | | | |
| | All races | | Male | | Female | | Male | | Female | |
Year	Number[1]	Rate	Number	Rate	Number	Rate	Number	Rate	Number	Rate
1991	584	11.9	188	9.5	72	3.4	264	67.7	60	13.4
1990	564	11.6	175	8.9	65	3.1	261	67.5	63	14.2
1989	462	9.5	177	9.1	56	2.7	183	48.0	45	10.3
1988	509	10.6	155	8.0	85	4.1	216	57.4	53	12.3
1987	495	10.4	181	9.4	49	2.4	204	54.9	61	14.4
1986	517	10.9	192	10.0	56	2.7	223	60.8	46	11.0
1985	431	9.2	174	9.1	59	2.9	157	43.4	41	9.9
1984	414	8.8	181	9.5	55	2.7	157	43.6	21	5.1
1983	440	9.4	168	8.9	54	2.7	179	49.9	39	9.6
1982	482	10.4	194	10.3	57	2.9	189	52.9	42	10.3
1981	510	11.1	223	11.9	60	3.0	181	50.9	46	11.4
1980	551	12.0	234	12.6	66	3.3	207	58.5	44	11.0
1979	474	10.5	187	10.0	57	2.9	190	60.7	40	11.1
1978	456	10.2	193	10.5	48	2.5	181	58.3	34	9.5
1977	477	10.8	195	10.8	49	2.5	185	59.8	48	13.5
1976	492	11.4	209	11.7	56	3.0	186	60.4	41	11.6
1975	568	13.3	244	13.9	58	3.1	213	69.5	53	15.1
1974	569	13.5	232	13.5	58	3.2	232	76.0	47	13.5
1973	550	13.3	214	12.6	48	2.7	224	74.1	64	18.6
1972	549	13.4	219	13.1	59	3.3	222	73.5	49	14.3
1971	486	12.1	220	13.4	49	2.8	185	62.0	32	9.5

Note: Rate is per 100,000 population. Rates for 1981–1988 are revised in accordance with revised intercensal population estimates.

1. May include one or more deaths with race and/or sex not stated.

Source: Tennessee Department of Health, Division of Information Resources, *Tennessee Vital Statistics, 1991.*

TABLE 19.8-- NUMBER OF CRIMES AND CRIME RATES PER 100,000 POPULATION, BY TYPE OF CRIME, METROPOLITAN STATISTICAL AREAS, 1992

Metropolitan Statistical Area	Total offenses	Murder[1]	Forcible rape	Robbery	Aggravated assault	Burglary	Larceny-theft	Auto theft
Chattanooga								
Number	23,164	36	189	796	2,570	5,153	11,970	2,450
Rate	5,610.6	8.7	45.8	192.8	622.5	1,248.1	2,899.3	593.4
Clarksville								
Number	8,167	11	67	128	1,877	1,792	4,005	287
Rate	4,700.1	6.3	38.6	73.7	1,080.2	1,031.3	2,304.9	165.2
Jackson								
Number	6,937	14	60	235	833	1,610	3,888	297
Rate	8,636.0	17.4	74.7	292.6	1,037.0	2,004.3	4,840.2	369.7
Johnson City-Kingsport-Bristol								
Number	13,897	15	114	135	896	3,490	8,468	779
Rate	3,095.7	3.3	25.4	30.1	199.6	777.4	1,886.3	173.5
Knoxville								
Number	n.a.	n.a.	n.a.	n.a.	n.a.	n.a.	n.a.	n.a.
Rate	n.a.	n.a.	n.a.	n.a.	n.a.	n.a.	n.a.	n.a.
Memphis								
Number	74,052	201	858	5,591	4,365	19,775	29,108	14,154
Rate	7,145.7	19.4	82.8	539.5	421.2	1,908.2	2,808.8	1,365.8
Nashville-Davidson								
Number	69,771	114	753	2,903	6,794	14,792	38,305	6,110
Rate	6,875.2	11.2	74.2	286.1	669.5	1,457.6	3,774.6	602.1

Note: Where reporting area is less than 100% of the Metropolitan Statistical Area, data are estimated to include that portion not reporting. Where reporting area is less than 75%, data are not reported. See Figure 0.1 for area of each Metropolitan Statistical Area.

n.a. not available.

1. Includes nonnegligent manslaughter.

Source: U.S. Department of Justice, Federal Bureau of Investigation, *Crime in the United States, Uniform Crime Reports, 1992.*

TABLE 19.9--NUMBER OF OFFENSES KNOWN TO POLICE, BY TYPE OF CRIME, CITIES AND TOWNS WITH POPULATION OF 10,000 OR MORE, 1992

City	Total	Murder[1]	Forcible rape	Robbery	Aggra-vated assault	Burglary	Larceny $50 and over[2]	Auto theft
Athens	708	1	1	6	72	137	446	45
Bartlett	874	0	2	5	85	182	600	0
Brentwood	380	0	3	2	7	102	255	11
Bristol	975	1	13	5	67	178	677	34
Brownsville	680	2	11	16	142	159	323	27
Chattanooga	15,452	31	146	734	2,011	3,077	7,617	1,836
Clarksville	5,028	7	46	72	1,366	995	2,363	179
Cleveland	1,768	2	7	22	211	347	1,033	146
Collierville	482	0	2	4	12	84	348	32
Columbia	2,097	0	8	57	162	481	1,307	82
Cookeville	835	2	1	4	37	149	599	43
Dyersburg	1,507	2	8	26	113	268	1,048	42
East Ridge	1,264	0	2	15	134	236	759	118
Franklin	1,420	0	16	23	107	213	985	76
Gallatin	1,053	2	15	11	154	174	658	39
Germantown	705	1	0	10	5	45	613	31
Goodlettsville	1,303	0	1	29	22	123	1,056	72
Greeneville	779	0	1	5	7	280	411	75
Hendersonville	1,094	0	17	3	137	263	663	11
Jackson	6,039	12	50	230	757	1,302	3,437	251
Johnson City	2,752	1	21	29	74	573	1,880	174
Kingsport	2,894	1	16	34	239	474	1,980	150
Knoxville	15,231	35	116	792	2,164	3,340	6,903	1,881
Lawrenceburg	564	0	3	2	79	122	335	23
McMinnville	719	0	2	8	67	155	434	53
Maryville	668	0	19	8	27	120	436	58
Memphis	61,935	176	688	5,341	3,559	16,284	22,673	13,214
Morristown	1,380	1	8	7	38	180	1,018	128
Murfreesboro	3,701	3	21	62	333	622	2,480	180
Nashville	49,864	90	498	2,668	5,126	10,238	26,106	5,138
Oak Ridge	1,682	0	7	34	61	257	1,249	74
Red Bank	650	1	6	10	81	148	356	48
Shelbyville	667	0	5	13	63	192	353	41
Smyrna	731	2	15	8	36	233	403	34
Springfield	1,013	4	11	16	184	92	678	28
Tullahoma	920	0	1	7	18	237	607	50
Union City	921	1	8	10	97	199	585	21

1. Murder includes nonnegligent manslaughter.
2. Includes all larceny-theft not using force or fraud.

Source: U.S. Department of Justice, Federal Bureau of Investigation, *Crime in the United States, Uniform Crime Reports, 1992.*

TABLE 19.10—NUMBER OF TOTAL OFFENSES AND MURDERS KNOWN TO POLICE, SELECTED CITIES, 1980-1992, SELECTED YEARS

Year	Chattanooga	Clarksville	Jackson	Johnson City	Kingsport	Knoxville	Memphis	Nashville	Oak Ridge
1992									
Total	15,452	5,028	6,039	2,752	2,894	15,231	61,935	49,864	1,682
Murder	31	7	12	1	1	35	176	90	0
1991									
Total	19,610	5,774	6,055	3,254	2,905	15,529	63,137	43,958	1,505
Murder	49	11	10	0	2	35	169	88	1
1990									
Total	19,481	4,989	5,275	3,171	2,757	13,113	60,255	39,360	1,370
Murder	32	5	4	4	1	25	195	67	0
1988									
Total	15,092	3,048	4,569	2,371	2,379	11,059	61,159	37,185	1,368
Murder	22	4	7	1	2	21	174	79	3
1987									
Total	14,589	2,854	4,826	2,322	2,352	11,728	63,824	43,001	1,270
Murder	26	3	3	3	5	20	143	99	1
1986									
Total	13,283	2,825	4,462	2,496	2,117	11,872	64,856	38,240	1,278
Murder	25	6	6	3	0	29	161	93	0
1985									
Total	13,461	2,630	4,310	2,308	2,160	10,838	59,965	31,863	1,163
Murder	26	4	5	2	3	16	122	81	0
1984									
Total	13,212	2,623	4,088	2,128	2,026	9,796	52,792	31,125	1,259
Murder	22	4	10	0	1	20	113	72	1
1983									
Total	13,051	2,546	3,828	2,319	1,923	9,994	55,222	31,213	1,543
Murder	22	3	9	1	2	19	127	81	0
1980									
Total	16,019	2,585	4,660	2,563	2,385	12,423	50,921	34,886	1,731
Murder	26	5	2	2	1	21	152	87	4

Note: Murder includes nonnegligent manslaughter.

n.a. not available.

Source: U.S. Department of Justice, Federal Bureau of Investigation, *Crime in the United States, Uniform Crime Reports, 1992,* and earlier editions.

TABLE 19.11–NUMBER OF FULL-TIME POLICE AND CIVILIAN LAW ENFORCEMENT PERSONNEL, SELECTED CITIES, 1980-1992, SELECTED YEARS

City	Total						Police officers						Civilians[1]					
	1992	1991	1990	1988	1985	1980	1992	1991	1990	1988	1985	1980	1992	1991	1990	1988	1985	1980
Chattanooga	508	504	507	500	481	482	368	374	363	363	364	387	140	130	144	137	117	95
Clarksville	157	157	150	138	n.a.	n.a.	137	138	131	117	n.a.	n.a.	20	19	19	21	n.a	n.a.
Jackson	201	199	193	175	167	153	150	152	143	128	130	124	51	47	50	47	37	29
Johnson City	151	132	146	130	120	127	126	111	123	104	96	105	25	21	23	26	24	22
Kingsport	130	126	127	110	89	87	91	89	90	76	71	72	39	37	37	34	18	15
Knoxville	n.a.	351	355	343	389	431	n.a.	293	296	289	288	325	n.a.	58	59	54	101	106
Memphis	1,710	1,805	1,798	1,696	1,563	1,661	1,371	1,390	1,379	1,269	1,154	1,210	339	415	419	427	409	451
Nashville	1,393	1,303	1,294	1,410	1,238	1,157	1,043	990	994	1,100	984	1,006	350	313	300	310	254	151
Oak Ridge	55	56	52	56	54	51	46	47	43	44	44	42	9	9	9	12	10	9

Note: Data are as of October 31.
n.a. not available.
1. Employees of police departments who are not sworn personnel.
Source: U.S. Department of Justice, Federal Bureau of Investigation, *Crime in the United States, Uniform Crime Reports, 1992*, and earlier editions.

TABLE 19.12--NUMBER OF ADULT COMMITMENTS TO INCARCERATION (PRISON AND JAIL), TENNESSEE AND COUNTY OF COMMITMENT, FISCAL YEARS 1991-1993

| County | Commitments | | | County | Commitments | | |
	1993	1992	1991		1993	1992	1991
Anderson	84	76	54	Lewis	21	19	11
Bedford	76	72	74	Lincoln	48	42	41
Benton	21	21	30	Loudon	21	19	16
Bledsoe	5	10	8	McMinn	51	39	30
Blount	109	64	74	McNairy	18	11	26
Bradley	118	89	166	Macon	13	17	5
Campbell	37	26	19	Madison	151	128	186
Cannon	8	15	11	Marion	29	30	18
Carroll	48	35	37	Marshall	71	59	65
Carter	53	44	36	Maury	77	70	67
Cheatham	34	39	43	Meigs	10	7	7
Chester	11	15	15	Monroe	46	43	39
Claiborne	11	13	9	Montgomery	79	67	73
Clay	5	16	3	Moore	4	1	1
Cocke	76	59	46	Morgan	15	8	10
Coffee	93	59	68	Obion	50	50	36
Crockett	27	28	23	Overton	16	9	15
Cumberland	28	29	29	Perry	3	1	6
Davidson	1,237	1,074	1,024	Pickett	1	2	2
Decatur	17	9	15	Polk	16	15	19
DeKalb	17	20	17	Putnam	59	46	38
Dickson	42	28	27	Rhea	27	16	21
Dyer	84	81	90	Roane	22	19	22
Fayette	78	75	63	Robertson	35	43	34
Fentress	10	18	14	Rutherford	267	207	168
Franklin	36	26	33	Scott	20	9	8
Gibson	142	68	104	Sequatchie	6	4	7
Giles	33	35	26	Sevier	68	67	55
Grainger	13	18	10	Shelby	3,690	3,576	3,408
Greene	121	110	82	Smith	17	6	12
Grundy	15	10	8	Stewart	7	5	3
Hamblen	154	125	122	Sullivan	253	230	260
Hamilton	519	591	630	Sumner	149	108	133
Hancock	19	9	13	Tipton	39	38	36
Hardeman	59	39	42	Trousdale	14	12	4
Hardin	59	39	30	Unicoi	15	18	24
Hawkins	76	61	52	Union	8	7	6
Haywood	37	30	47	Van Buren	4	4	6
Henderson	18	28	27	Warren	36	24	39
Henry	40	37	35	Washington	127	103	93
Hickman	20	24	14	Wayne	10	6	5
Houston	12	5	5	Weakley	52	36	33
Humphreys	18	17	21	White	12	16	29
Jackson	8	11	5	Williamson	121	134	109
Jefferson	43	32	29	Wilson	76	66	43
Johnson	21	12	10				
Knox	475	342	347	TENNESSEE	10,287	9,213	9,199
Lake	18	11	10				
Lauderdale	90	50	33				
Lawrence	38	31	30				

Note: State total includes data for incarcerations where county is unknown.

Source: Tennessee Department of Correction, direct correspondence.

TABLE 19.13–COMMITMENTS TO TENNESSEE DEPARTMENT OF YOUTH DEVELOPMENT CUSTODY, PROBATION REGIONS, SELECTED FISCAL YEARS 1985–1993

Probation region	1993	1992	1991	1990	1989	1988	1985
TOTAL	1,541	1,610	1,613	1,492	1,286	1,363	1,548
East Tennessee	225	249	235	219	179	178	206
First Tennessee-Virginia	132	160	139	112	115	138	131
Greater Nashville Regional Council	275	294	290	277	130	204	188
Memphis Delta	96	149	265	209	180	144	395
Northwest Tennessee	154	131	112	103	90	81	72
South Central Tennessee	215	154	133	123	114	120	98
Southeast Tennessee	194	239	208	234	235	228	227
Southwest Tennessee	149	136	143	142	104	117	79
Upper Cumberland	101	98	88	73	139	153	152

Source: Tennessee Department of Youth Development, direct correspondence.

TABLE 19.14--CRIME RATES PER 100,000 POPULATION, BY TYPE OF CRIME, SOUTHEASTERN STATES, 1992

State	Total offenses	Murder[1]	Forcible rape	Robbery	Aggra-vated assault	Burglary	Larceny-theft	Auto theft
TENNESSEE	5,135.8	10.4	47.3	218.2	470.3	1,267.2	2,546.5	575.9
Alabama	5,268.1	11.0	41.2	164.9	654.6	1,186.0	2,848.2	362.3
Arkansas	4,761.7	10.8	41.3	125.5	399.0	1,092.7	2,763.2	329.3
Florida	8,358.2	9.0	54.2	366.9	777.2	1,888.8	4,434.3	828.0
Georgia	6,405.4	11.0	45.3	249.8	427.1	1,442.8	3,653.1	576.4
Kentucky	3,323.5	5.8	32.2	87.2	410.4	729.1	1,842.5	216.5
Louisiana	6,546.5	17.4	42.3	271.4	653.4	1,366.3	3,567.5	628.1
Mississippi	4,282.5	12.2	44.6	124.5	230.4	1,282.8	2,251.4	336.5
North Carolina	5,802.2	10.6	35.9	186.8	447.7	1,653.0	3,181.6	286.6
South Carolina	5,893.1	10.4	57.5	170.6	706.0	1,378.5	3,224.7	345.4
Virginia	4,298.5	8.8	31.5	137.8	196.8	709.1	2,909.0	305.6
West Virginia	2,609.7	6.3	21.7	43.5	140.0	622.9	1,611.5	163.8

Note: Rates represent offenses known per 100,000 population, based on the Bureau of the Census provisional population estimate as of July 1.

1. Murder includes nonnegligent manslaughter.

Source: U.S. Department of Justice, Federal Bureau of Investigation, *Crime in the United States, Uniform Crime Reports, 1992.*

TABLE 19.15--PRISON POPULATION IN STATE INSTITUTIONS, SOUTHEASTERN STATES, AS OF DECEMBER 31, 1950–1991, SELECTED YEARS

State	1991	1990[r]	1989	1988	1987	1985	1984	1983	1980	1975	1970	1960	1950
TENNESSEE[1]	11,474	10,388	10,630	7,720	7,624	7,127	7,302	8,201	7,022	4,561	3,268	3,134	2,780
Alabama[1]	16,760	15,665	13,907	12,610	12,827	11,015	10,482	9,856	6,543	4,420	3,790	5,369	4,454
Arkansas[1]	7,766	7,322	6,649	5,519	5,441	4,611	4,454	4,244	2,911	2,162	n.a.	2,016	1,541
Florida[2]	46,533	44,387	39,999	34,732	32,445	28,600	27,106	26,334	20,735	15,315	9,187	7,084	3,973
Georgia[2]	23,644	22,411	20,885	18,787	18,575	16,014	15,731	15,358	12,178	10,102	5,113	6,985	4,545
Kentucky	9,799	9,023	8,289	7,119	6,436	5,801	5,502	4,752	3,588	3,393	2,849	3,603	3,259
Louisiana	20,003	18,599	17,257	16,242	15,375	13,890	13,919	12,812	8,889	4,835	4,196	3,749	2,674
Mississippi	8,904	8,375	7,911	7,384	6,880	6,392	6,115	5,586	3,902	2,422	1,730	1,975	2,158
North Carolina[2]	18,903	18,411	17,454	17,078	17,218	17,344	16,371	15,395	15,513	11,449	5,969	5,977	5,004
South Carolina	18,269	17,319	15,720	13,888	12,664	10,510	10,011	9,576	7,862	5,600	2,726	2,080	1,513
Virginia[3]	19,829	17,593	16,477	14,184	13,321	12,073	10,667	10,093	8,920	5,497	4,648	5,775	4,439
West Virginia	1,502	1,565	1,536	1,455	1,461	1,725	1,599	1,624	1,257	1,176	938	2,407	2,904

r revised.

n.a. not available.

1. Excludes state prisoners held in local jails because of overcrowding.

2. Numbers are custodial, not jurisdictional counts.

3. Year-end 1983 data are for January 1, 1984; 1984 data are for December 28, 1984; and 1985 data are for January 3, 1986.

Source: U.S. Department of Commerce, Bureau of the Census, Statistical Abstract of the United States, 1993, and earlier editions; and U.S. Department of Justice, Bureau of Justice Statistics, National Prisoner Statistics, Prisoners in State and Federal Institutions on December 31, 1982, and earlier editions.

TABLE 19.16--ADULTS UNDER CORRECTIONAL SUPERVISION, SOUTHEASTERN STATES AND UNITED STATES, 1990 [In thousands, except rate]

State	Total	Rate[1]	Prison[2]	Parole[3]	Probation[4]
TENNESSEE	63.8	174.2	8.5	11.3	32.7
Alabama	55.4	185.7	15.4	6.0	27.7
Arkansas	28.9	166.8	6.6	4.0	16.0
Florida	288.6	286.6	44.0	2.1	210.8
Georgia	201.0	423.0	22.3	22.6	134.8
Kentucky	24.7	90.4	8.3	3.2	7.5
Louisiana	66.6	222.4	14.1	8.9	30.2
Mississippi	23.3	127.7	7.6	3.5	8.2
North Carolina	114.6	228.3	18.6	9.9	77.8
South Carolina	57.0	222.2	15.6	3.5	32.3
Virginia	55.4	118.3	14.6	9.0	21.3
West Virginia	9.4	69.9	1.6	1.0	5.1
UNITED STATES	4,349.8	235.0	745.2	531.4	2,670.2

Note: Excludes juveniles, persons incarcerated in mental health institutions in lieu of prison, persons held by the armed services, persons held on Indian reservations, parolees under county jurisdiction, parolees whose sentences were for 1 year or less, and court probationers (those not placed under the supervisory authority of a probation agency). Total includes persons in jail not shown separately.

1. Rate per 10,000 persons 18 years old and over.

2. Includes all inmates of Federal and State institutions.

3. Includes all adults under State parole supervision, whether released from prison via parole board decision or mandatory release, who were sentenced to more than 1 year in prison.

4. Includes all adults who, as part of a State, or local court order, have been placed under the supervisory authority of a probation agency.

Source: U.S. Department of Commerce, Bureau of the Census, *Statistical Abstract of the United States, 1993.*

TABLE 19.17--PRISONERS EXECUTED UNDER CIVIL AUTHORITY, SOUTHEASTERN STATES AND UNITED STATES, 1940–1991

State	1991	1990	1980 to 1989	1970 to 1979	1960 to 1969	1950 to 1959	1940 to 1949
TENNESSEE	0	0	0	0	1	8	37
Alabama	0	1	7	0	5	20	50
Arkansas	0	2	0	0	9	18	38
Florida	2	4	20	1	12	49	65
Georgia	1	0	14	0	14	85	130
Kentucky	0	0	0	0	1	16	34
Louisiana	1	1	18	0	1	27	47
Mississippi	0	0	4	0	10	36	60
North Carolina	1	0	3	0	1	19	112
South Carolina	1	1	2	0	8	26	61
Virginia	2	3	7	0	6	23	35
West Virginia	0	0	0	0	0	9	11
UNITED STATES	14	23	117	3	191	717	1,284

Source: U.S. Department of Commerce, Bureau of the Census, *Statistical Abstract of the United States, 1993.*

TABLE 19.18--DEATHS FROM MOTOR VEHICLE ACCIDENTS, SOUTHEASTERN STATES AND UNITED STATES, 1970-1991, SELECTED YEARS

State	1991 Number	Mileage rate[1]	1990	1989	1988	1986	1985	1980	1975	1972[a]	1970
TENNESSEE	1,112	2.4	1,172	1,081	1,404	1,372	1,219	1,280	1,280	1,526	1,525
Alabama	1,108	2.0	1,095	1,025	1,158	1,180	1,005	1,054	1,087	1,356	1,297
Arkansas	608	2.9	604	648	667	624	580	607	577	750	595
Florida	2,519	2.3	2,951	3,016	3,247	2,925	2,968	2,967	2,067	2,570	2,181
Georgia	1,393	1.9	1,563	1,632	1,756	1,604	1,462	1,558	1,420	1,940	1,825
Kentucky	828	2.5	850	782	843	829	749	865	885	1,114	1,081
Louisiana	824	2.2	912	857	946	987	1,011	1,261	993	1,136	1,194
Mississippi	701	2.9	751	728	791	785	691	796	629	976	947
North Carolina	1,365	2.2	1,383	1,464	1,669	1,727	1,553	1,588	1,560	2,026	1,801
South Carolina	890	2.6	983	996	1,012	1,077	943	895	837	1,148	1,070
Virginia	937	1.6	1,073	999	1,093	1,141	1,021	1,111	1,069	1,256	1,251
West Virginia	414	2.7	481	468	491	470	461	583	499	578	561
UNITED STATES	43,500	2.0	46,300	47,100	49,391	48,140	45,901	53,476	46,032	56,528	54,845

1. Deaths per 100 million vehicle miles.
a. Represents peak year for deaths from motor vehicle accidents.
Source: National Safety Council, Itasca, IL, *Accident Facts 1991* (copyright); 1985, National Center for Health Statistics; as printed in U.S. Department of Commerce, Bureau of the Census, *Statistical Abstract of the United States, 1993*, and earlier editions.

TABLE 19.19--SELECTED DATA ON FULL-TIME STATE POLICE AND HIGHWAY PATROL EMPLOYEES, SOUTHEASTERN STATES, 1992

State	Total	Police officers	Civilians	Miles of state-controlled highway per police officer[1]	State motor vehicle registrations per police officer[2]
TENNESSEE	1,566	757	809	19.2	6,136.2
Alabama	1,256	608	648	18.1	5,434.3
Arkansas	687	491	196	33.0	3,058.0
Florida	2,078	1,583	495	7.5	6,463.9
Georgia	1,775	757	1,018	23.6	7,793.2
Kentucky	1,605	918	687	30.0	3,249.7
Louisiana	1,033	683	350	24.4	4,529.3
Mississippi	831	493	338	21.2	3,963.4
North Carolina	1,598	1,259	339	61.9	4,215.2
South Carolina	1,208	994	214	41.9	2,616.6
Virginia	2,279	1,667	612	33.9	3,142.6
West Virginia	798	526	272	60.6	2,420.0

Note: Data as of October 31.
1. Miles of state-controlled highway taken from U.S. Department of Transportation publication, *Highway Statistics, 1992.* Includes urban and rural mileage.
2. State motor vehicle registration data, which include automobile, bus, and truck registrations, taken from U.S. Department of Transportation publication, *Highway Statistics, 1992.*
Source: U.S. Department of Justice, Federal Bureau of Investigation, *Crime in the United States, Uniform Crime Reports, 1992.*

TABLE 19.20--STATE AND LOCAL GOVERNMENT PER CAPITA EXPENDITURES FOR CRIMINAL JUSTICE SYSTEM, BY TYPE OF ACTIVITY, SOUTHEASTERN STATES, FISCAL YEAR 1990 [In dollars]

State	Total justice system	Police protection	Judicial and legal services			Corrections	Other justice activities
			Courts only	Prosecution and legal services	Public defense		
TENNESSEE	193.63	77.90	20.71	8.33	3.33	82.94	0.41
Alabama	159.12	76.78	21.85	8.70	2.05	48.73	1.01
Arkansas	115.29	55.44	13.25	6.46	0.88	38.35	0.91
Florida	288.13	121.69	30.58	16.04	6.87	108.17	4.77
Georgia	238.81	90.28	29.62	10.10	1.92	105.28	1.62
Kentucky	152.13	62.73	19.98	10.42	2.00	55.80	1.19
Louisiana	196.28	90.29	24.74	11.75	0.11	68.66	0.73
Mississippi	122.56	59.26	15.16	6.91	1.02	40.03	0.19
North Carolina	186.16	86.59	17.69	7.01	3.30	69.38	2.20
South Carolina	188.62	82.83	17.23	5.99	1.07	80.04	1.47
Virginia	234.97	101.20	27.54	9.47	3.86	90.26	2.64
West Virginia	97.30	45.60	19.01	5.80	3.59	23.05	0.25

Source: U.S. Department of Justice, Bureau of Justice Statistics, *Sourcebook of Criminal Justice Statistics, 1992.*

TABLE 19.21–LAWYERS LICENSED IN THE UNITED STATES, SOUTHEASTERN STATES, 1970, 1980, 1985 AND 1988

State	1988 Total	1988 Private practice	1988 Population per lawyer [1]	1985	1980	1970
TENNESSEE	9,515	6,771	514	8,782	7,802	4,770
Alabama	7,261	5,276	565	6,679	5,466	3,291
Arkansas	3,939	2,746	608	3,741	3,188	1,969
Florida	33,259	24,634	371	30,444	23,521	10,917
Georgia	15,314	11,528	414	13,652	11,087	5,517
Kentucky	7,517	5,447	496	7,017	6,200	3,625
Louisiana	11,515	9,244	383	10,569	8,752	5,089
Mississippi	4,384	3,316	598	4,270	3,850	2,517
North Carolina	10,238	7,324	634	9,265	7,459	4,367
South Carolina	5,482	4,177	633	5,021	4,195	2,236
Virginia	14,916	9,846	403	13,390	10,895	6,401
West Virginia	3,016	2,238	622	2,835	2,566	1,719

Note: Data are weighted to account for nonreporters and duplicate listings.

1. Based on Bureau of the Census estimated resident population, including Armed Forces stationed in area as of July 1, 1988.

Source: U.S. Department of Commerce, Bureau of the Census, *Statistical Abstract of the United States, 1993* and earlier editions; and American Bar Foundation, Chicago, IL., *The 1971 Lawyer Statistical Report, 1971* (copyright); 1980, *The Lawyer Statistical Report: A Statistical Profile of the U.S. Legal Profession in the 1980's*, 1985 (copyright) and 1988, *Supplement to The Lawyer Statistical Report: The U.S. Legal Profession in 1988*, 1991 (copyright) by special permission.

Tennessee Rankings presents comparative socioeconomic data for Tennessee and other southeastern states in key interest areas. This section is a particularly useful feature for speech writers, planners and others who need readily accessible comparative information on Tennessee. *Tennessee Rankings* changes substantially from one edition to the next in accordance with current interests and the availability of new data.

The first five tables are from primary data areas: population, income and employment. Ranking of states and metropolitan areas according to these topics provides a current assessment of growth and general well-being. Population rankings are published by the U.S. Department of Commerce, Bureau of the Census. Income items include measures of per capita disposable personal income for states as well as per capita personal income for metropolitan areas. These are estimated and published by the Bureau of Economic Analysis (BEA), also in the U.S. Department of Commerce. Employment data are collected and published by the U.S. Department of Labor, Bureau of Labor Statistics. Rankings include percentage change in total nonagricultural jobs and manufacturing jobs and an analysis of part-time employment by reason for part-time status.

Interest in foreign trade led to the inclusion of Census Bureau data on exports and BEA data on foreign investment and employment in Tennessee and other southeastern states by non-bank U.S. affiliates of foreign companies.

Many of the other tables in this chapter were published previously in the *Statistical Abstract of the United States*. Although this source is noted on the tables, information on the original publishing agency is often important.

Research and development is the subject of Tables 20.10 and 20.16. The first features data on patents issued by type for each of the southeastern states. The original source of this information is the U.S. Patent and Trademark Office. Table 20.16 provides R&D data collected and published by the National Science Foundation.

Comparisons of energy prices by type were taken from a report issued by the U.S. Energy Information Administration, and the Census Bureau is responsible for collection of the revenue and expenditure data of state governments. Comparative data on public aid recipients are from the U.S. Social Security Administration *Bulletin* and the *Quarterly Public Assistance Statistics* published by the U.S. Family Support Administration. State legislative arts appropriations data are from the National Assembly of Arts Agencies.

TABLE OF CONTENTS

TABLE 20.1.– RESIDENT POPULATION, BY AGE, SOUTHEASTERN STATES AND UNITED STATES, 1992 [In thousands]

State	Total	Under 5 years	5 to 17 years	18 to 24 years	25 to 34 years	35 to 44 years	45 to 54 years	55 to 64 years	65 to 74 years	75 to 84 years	85 years and over	16 years and over	65 years+ Percent	65 years+ Rank
TENNESSEE	5,024	353	893	529	807	787	574	440	367	211	63	3,915	12.7	24
Alabama	4,136	298	778	449	639	621	449	363	307	178	52	3,181	13.0	23
Arkansas	2,399	171	458	244	349	344	262	213	198	123	37	1,841	14.9	6
Florida	13,488	943	2,163	1,173	2,081	1,946	1,415	1,282	1,414	838	232	10,690	18.4	1
Georgia	6,751	530	1,270	732	1,184	1,089	749	514	399	220	62	5,138	10.1	47
Kentucky	3,755	258	706	402	596	580	415	322	270	157	50	2,901	12.7	25
Louisiana	4,287	340	898	462	691	646	435	335	281	154	45	3,180	11.2	39
Mississippi	2,614	203	545	302	388	372	265	214	182	110	34	1,951	12.5	29
North Carolina	6,843	491	1,171	767	1,140	1,070	764	594	501	268	76	5,359	12.4	30
South Carolina	3,603	273	672	409	589	557	390	296	255	128	34	2,760	11.6	37
Virginia	6,377	468	1,094	688	1,136	1,050	735	509	415	217	64	4,974	10.9	43
West Virginia	1,812	108	330	191	250	284	204	171	158	91	27	1,429	15.2	5
UNITED STATES	255,082	19,512	46,655	25,919	42,463	39,904	27,418	20,927	18,461	10,565	3,259	195,672	12.7	(X)

Note: Population includes Armed Forces residing in each state. Detail may not add to total because of independent rounding.
(X) not applicable.
Source: U.S. Department of Commerce, Bureau of the Census, *Statistical Abstract of the United States, 1993.*

TABLE 20.2– PER CAPITA PERSONAL INCOME, METROPOLITAN AREAS, SOUTHEASTERN STATES, 1989–1992

Metropolitan area	Dollars				Percentage change		Percentage of U.S.				Rank 1992
	1992	1991	1990	1989	1991 to 1992	1990 to 1992	1992	1991	1990	1989	
Albany, GA	15,461	15,063	14,190	13,325	2.6	9.0	76.9	78.6	76.0	75.3	275
Alexandria, LA	15,186	14,420	13,969	13,055	5.3	8.7	75.5	75.2	74.8	73.8	277
Anniston, AL	15,158	14,452	13,570	12,888	4.9	11.7	75.4	75.4	72.7	72.9	279
Asheville, NC	18,283	17,187	16,622	15,276	6.4	10.0	90.9	89.7	89.0	86.4	146
Athens, GA	16,316	15,576	15,063	14,217	4.8	8.3	81.2	81.3	80.7	80.4	241
Atlanta, GA	21,849	20,806	20,439	19,477	5.0	6.9	108.7	108.6	109.5	110.1	38
Augusta-Aiken, GA-SC	17,414	16,865	16,528	15,264	3.3	5.4	86.6	88.0	88.5	86.3	184
Baton Rouge, LA	17,831	16,733	15,938	14,756	6.6	11.9	88.7	87.3	85.4	83.4	165
Biloxi-Gulfport-Pascagoula, MS	14,744	13,965	13,301	12,535	5.6	10.8	73.3	72.9	71.3	70.9	283
Birmingham, AL	19,428	18,303	17,594	16,468	6.1	10.4	96.6	95.5	94.3	93.1	94
Charleston-North Charleston, SC	16,239	15,703	15,406	12,952	3.4	5.4	80.8	81.9	82.5	73.2	248
Charleston, WV	19,119	18,009	17,214	15,908	6.2	11.1	95.1	94.0	92.2	89.9	107
Charlotte-Gastonia-Rock Hill, NC-SC	19,884	18,876	18,592	17,178	5.3	6.9	98.9	98.5	99.6	97.1	87
Charlottesville, VA	20,796	19,906	19,248	18,374	4.5	8.0	103.4	103.9	103.1	103.9	58
CHATTANOOGA, TN-GA	17,895	16,906	16,572	15,664	5.8	8.0	89.0	88.2	88.8	88.5	163
CLARKSVILLE-HOPKINSVILLE, TN-KY	14,295	13,066	12,091	12,096	9.4	18.2	71.1	68.2	64.8	68.4	288
Columbia, SC	18,472	17,699	17,339	16,206	4.4	6.5	91.9	92.4	92.9	91.6	134
Columbus, GA-AL	16,115	15,624	14,594	13,667	3.1	10.4	80.2	81.5	78.2	77.3	254
Danville, VA	15,705	14,775	14,461	13,756	6.3	8.6	78.1	77.1	77.5	77.8	271
Daytona Beach, FL	16,348	15,805	15,650	15,278	3.4	4.5	81.3	82.5	83.8	86.4	240
Decatur, AL	17,100	16,267	15,419	14,424	5.1	10.9	85.1	84.9	82.6	81.5	204
Dothan, AL	16,359	15,372	14,624	13,915	6.4	11.9	81.4	80.2	78.3	78.7	239
Fayetteville, NC	16,050	13,725	12,928	12,382	16.9	24.1	79.8	71.6	69.3	70.0	259
Fayetteville-Springdale-Rogers, AR	17,339	16,101	15,500	14,856	7.7	11.9	86.2	84.0	83.0	84.0	190
Florence, AL	15,949	15,099	14,543	13,142	5.6	9.7	79.3	78.8	77.9	74.3	262
Florence, SC	16,192	15,352	14,786	13,281	5.5	9.5	80.5	80.1	79.2	75.1	251
Fort Lauderdale, FL (PMSA)	23,107	22,393	22,276	21,535	3.2	3.7	114.9	116.9	119.3	121.7	27
Fort Myers-Cape Coral, FL	20,312	19,603	19,396	18,906	3.6	4.7	101.0	102.3	103.9	106.9	72
Fort Pierce-Port St. Lucie, FL	21,233	20,649	20,361	19,504	2.8	4.3	105.6	107.8	109.1	110.3	49
Fort Smith, AR-OK	15,806	14,533	14,023	13,413	8.8	12.7	78.6	75.8	75.1	75.8	267
Fort Walton Beach, FL	17,656	16,987	16,139	15,310	3.9	9.4	87.8	88.6	86.5	86.5	171
Gadsden, AL	15,500	14,320	13,889	13,234	8.2	11.6	77.1	74.7	74.4	74.8	274

TABLE 20.2-- PER CAPITA PERSONAL INCOME, METROPOLITAN AREAS, SOUTHEASTERN STATES, 1989-1992 (Continued)

Metropolitan area	Dollars				Percentage change		Percentage of U.S.				Rank 1992
	1992	1991	1990	1989	1991 to 1992	1990 to 1992	1992	1991	1990	1989	
Gainesville, FL	17,468	16,692	16,078	15,136	4.6	8.6	86.9	87.1	86.1	85.6	180
Goldsboro, NC	14,325	13,571	13,146	12,322	5.6	9.0	71.3	70.8	70.4	69.7	286
Greensboro-Winston-Salem-High Point, NC	19,940	18,865	18,467	17,464	5.7	8.0	99.2	98.4	98.9	98.7	86
Greenville, NC	16,809	15,854	15,417	14,230	6.0	9.0	83.6	82.7	82.6	80.4	222
Greenville-Spartanburg-Anderson, SC	16,945	16,216	15,836	14,989	4.5	7.0	84.3	84.6	84.8	84.7	214
Hickory-Morganton, NC	17,233	16,148	15,904	14,988	6.7	8.4	85.7	84.3	85.2	84.7	194
Houma, LA	13,389	13,094	12,445	11,399	2.3	7.6	66.6	68.3	66.7	64.4	290
Huntington-Ashland, WV-KY-OH	15,711	14,631	13,981	13,018	7.4	12.4	78.1	76.4	74.9	73.6	270
Huntsville, AL	20,082	18,955	18,206	17,099	5.9	10.3	99.9	98.9	97.5	96.7	78
Jackson, MS	16,945	16,089	15,354	14,698	5.3	10.4	84.3	84.0	82.3	83.1	214
JACKSON, TN	17,340	16,032	15,418	14,108	8.2	12.5	86.2	83.7	82.6	79.8	189
Jacksonville, FL	19,146	18,409	18,010	17,119	4.0	6.3	95.2	96.1	96.5	96.8	104
Jacksonville, NC	12,782	10,638	10,201	10,517	20.2	25.3	63.6	55.5	54.6	59.5	295
JOHNSON CITY-KINGSPORT-BRISTOL, TN-VA	16,232	15,313	14,699	13,575	6.0	10.4	80.7	79.9	78.7	76.7	250
KNOXVILLE, TN	18,364	17,272	16,498	15,616	6.3	11.3	91.3	90.1	88.4	88.3	142
Lafayette, LA	14,954	14,300	13,630	12,378	4.6	9.7	74.4	74.6	73.0	70.0	281
Lake Charles, LA	16,137	15,438	14,322	13,172	4.5	12.7	80.3	80.6	76.7	74.5	253
Lakeland-Winter Haven, FL	16,268	15,676	15,292	15,025	3.8	6.4	80.9	81.8	81.9	84.9	245
Lexington, KY	18,893	18,008	17,351	16,073	4.9	8.9	94.0	94.0	93.0	90.9	118
Little Rock-North Little Rock, AR	18,650	17,367	16,481	15,638	7.4	13.2	92.8	90.6	88.3	88.4	127
Louisville, KY-IN	20,211	18,959	18,197	17,097	6.6	11.1	100.5	98.9	97.5	96.6	75
Lynchburg, VA	17,276	16,625	16,341	15,617	3.9	5.7	85.9	86.8	87.5	88.3	192
Macon, GA	17,528	16,800	16,187	15,416	4.3	8.3	87.2	87.7	86.7	87.1	177
Melbourne-Titusville-Palm Bay, FL	18,715	18,019	17,621	17,105	3.9	6.2	93.1	94.0	94.4	96.7	124
MEMPHIS, TN-AR-MS	19,517	18,405	17,821	16,913	6.0	9.5	97.1	96.0	95.5	95.6	91
Miami, FL (PMSA)	17,124	17,807	17,629	17,090	-3.8	-2.9	85.2	92.9	94.4	96.6	201
Mobile, AL	15,806	15,054	14,135	13,271	5.0	11.8	78.6	78.6	75.7	75.0	267
Monroe, LA	15,181	14,368	13,655	12,874	5.7	11.2	75.5	75.0	73.2	72.8	278
Montgomery, AL	17,931	17,126	16,465	15,548	4.7	8.9	89.2	89.4	88.2	87.9	162
Myrtle Beach, SC	16,040	15,524	15,182	13,544	3.3	5.7	79.8	81.0	81.3	76.6	260
Naples, FL	27,232	27,327	27,300	26,254	-0.3	-0.2	135.4	142.6	146.2	148.4	9

TABLE 20.2-- PER CAPITA PERSONAL INCOME, METROPOLITAN AREAS, SOUTHEASTERN STATES, 1989–1992 (Continued)

Metropolitan area	Dollars				Percentage change		Percentage of U.S.				Rank 1992
	1992	1991	1990	1989	1991 to 1992	1990 to 1992	1992	1991	1990	1989	
NASHVILLE, TN	20,569	19,144	18,333	17,509	7.4	12.2	102.3	99.9	98.2	99.0	64
New Orleans, LA	18,087	17,227	16,382	15,302	5.0	10.4	90.0	89.9	87.8	86.5	156
Norfolk-Virginia Beach-Newport News, VA-NC	18,077	17,412	16,735	16,090	3.8	8.0	89.9	90.9	89.7	91.0	157
Ocala, FL	15,375	14,799	14,500	14,034	3.9	6.0	76.5	77.2	77.7	79.3	276
Orlando, FL	18,596	17,734	17,465	16,916	4.9	6.5	92.5	92.5	93.6	95.6	130
Owensboro, KY	16,736	15,908	15,103	14,309	5.2	10.8	83.2	83.0	80.9	80.9	226
Panama City, FL	16,445	15,787	14,988	13,961	4.2	9.7	81.8	82.4	80.3	78.9	234
Parkersburg-Marietta, WV-OH	16,736	15,761	15,044	14,099	6.2	11.2	83.2	82.2	80.6	79.7	226
Pensacola, FL	16,287	15,481	14,972	14,073	5.2	8.8	81.0	80.8	80.2	79.6	243
Pine Bluff, AR	14,386	13,476	13,136	12,515	6.8	9.5	71.6	70.3	70.4	70.7	285
Punta Gorda, FL	17,761	17,251	17,265	16,913	3.0	2.9	88.3	90.0	92.5	95.6	167
Raleigh-Durham-Chapel Hill, NC	21,086	19,986	19,420	18,152	5.5	8.6	104.9	104.3	104.0	102.6	52
Richmond-Petersburg, VA	22,303	21,517	21,314	20,372	3.7	4.6	110.9	112.3	114.2	115.2	34
Roanoke, VA	20,661	19,400	19,117	18,010	6.5	8.1	102.8	101.2	102.4	101.8	61
Rocky Mount, NC	16,262	15,734	15,100	14,207	3.4	7.7	80.9	82.1	80.9	80.3	246
Sarasota-Bradenton, FL	24,804	23,726	23,233	22,565	4.5	6.8	123.4	123.8	124.5	127.6	17
Savannah, GA	18,222	17,372	16,992	16,030	4.9	7.2	90.6	90.7	91.0	90.6	147
Shreveport-Bossier City, LA	17,061	16,002	14,975	14,014	6.6	13.9	84.9	83.5	80.2	79.2	206
Sumter, SC	13,171	12,523	12,081	11,251	5.2	9.0	65.5	65.3	64.7	63.6	292
Tallahassee, FL	17,103	16,365	15,824	14,840	4.5	8.1	85.1	85.0	84.8	83.9	203
Tampa-St. Petersburg-Clearwater, FL	19,400	18,405	17,964	17,489	5.4	8.0	96.5	96.0	96.2	98.9	96
Tuscaloosa, AL	16,092	15,145	14,666	13,492	6.3	9.7	80.0	79.0	78.6	76.3	256
Washington, DC-MD-VA-WV (PMSA)	26,817	25,801	25,129	24,173	3.9	6.7	133.4	134.6	134.6	136.6	11
West Palm Beach-Boca Raton, FL	30,901	30,347	29,103	26,737	1.8	6.2	153.7	158.4	155.9	151.1	2
Wheeling, WV-OH	16,964	16,191	15,272	14,269	4.8	11.1	84.4	84.5	81.8	80.7	213
Wilmington, NC	16,997	16,353	15,603	14,411	3.9	8.9	84.5	85.3	83.6	81.5	211
UNITED STATES	20,105	19,163	18,667	17,690	4.9	7.7	(X)	(X)	(X)	(X)	(X)

Note: Rank is out of 299 metropolitan areas. Includes Metropolitan Statistical Areas and Primary Metropolitan Statistical Areas.

Source: U.S. Department of Commerce, Bureau of Economic Analysis, Regional Economic Measurement Division, *Regional Economic Information System 1969–1992* CD-ROM.

TABLE 20.3– PER CAPITA DISPOSABLE PERSONAL INCOME, SOUTHEASTERN STATES AND UNITED STATES, 1988–1993 [In dollars]

State	Amount	1993 Percent of U.S. average	Rank	1992[r]	1991[r]	1990	1989	1988
TENNESSEE	16,486	91	33	15,812	14,864	14,315	13,544	12,827
Alabama	15,264	84	40	14,754	13,846	13,227	12,374	11,662
Arkansas	14,239	79	48	13,905	12,879	12,236	11,662	10,976
Florida	18,272	101	18	17,414	17,049	16,535	15,826	14,591
Georgia	16,815	93	29	16,235	15,464	14,891	14,126	13,572
Kentucky	14,777	82	45	14,378	13,498	12,901	12,024	11,229
Louisiana	14,843	82	44	14,208	13,438	12,728	11,948	11,389
Mississippi	13,380	74	50	12,852	12,100	11,491	10,839	10,259
North Carolina	16,307	90	34	15,591	14,726	14,243	13,269	12,629
South Carolina	14,943	82	43	14,423	13,730	13,327	12,174	11,733
Virginia	18,694	103	13	18,137	17,406	16,886	16,040	15,077
West Virginia	14,544	80	47	14,029	13,142	12,479	11,566	11,030
SOUTHEAST	16,459	91	(X)	15,825	15,092	14,532	13,702	12,896
UNITED STATES	18,124	100	(X)	17,593	16,729	16,173	15,291	14,457

(X) not applicable.
r revised.
Source: U.S. Department of Commerce, Bureau of Economic Analysis, *Survey of Current Business*, August 1994, Volume 74, Number 8.

TABLE 20.4– NONFARM AND MANUFACTURING PAYROLL EMPLOYEES, SOUTHEASTERN STATES, 1990–1993 [In thousands of persons]

State	Total nonfarm employees				1992–1993		Manufacturing employees				1992–1993	
	1993	1992	1991	1990	Percent change	Rank	1993	1992	1991	1990	Percent change	Rank
TENNESSEE	2,327.5	2,245.0	2,183.6	2,193.2	3.67	17	528.3	514.5	502.7	520.3	2.68	12
Alabama	1,712.2	1,674.5	1,642.0	1,635.7	2.25	21	383.3	380.7	379.3	384.5	0.68	19
Arkansas	989.5	963.1	936.4	923.5	2.74	33	243.2	237.0	233.7	232.8	2.62	25
Florida	5,567.4	5,358.7	5,294.3	5,387.4	3.89	4	484.2	482.9	492.8	522.1	0.27	14
Georgia	3,106.1	2,987.2	2,937.5	2,991.8	3.98	11	554.6	545.2	541.0	561.1	1.72	11
Kentucky	1,534.0	1,508.5	1,474.7	1,470.5	1.69	26	292.4	286.9	281.4	287.5	1.92	23
Louisiana	1,643.1	1,626.9	1,613.0	1,589.9	1.00	23	185.6	185.0	186.4	184.4	0.32	29
Mississippi	998.1	960.3	937.5	936.6	3.94	32	254.5	251.9	246.9	246.5	1.03	24
North Carolina	3,244.6	3,125.5	3,072.2	3,117.7	3.81	10	845.9	834.4	826.1	861.5	1.38	8
South Carolina	1,569.6	1,527.7	1,513.4	1,545.0	2.74	25	373.6	371.0	369.2	383.3	0.70	20
Virginia	2,919.5	2,848.4	2,828.9	2,896.3	2.50	12	404.7	407.4	412.0	426.4	-0.66	18
West Virginia	651.7	640.0	629.1	630.1	1.83	37	82.9	82.2	83.2	87.5	0.85	39

Source: U.S. Department of Labor, Bureau of Labor Statistics, *Employment and Earnings*, May 1994, and earlier editions.

TABLE 20.5– CIVILIAN EMPLOYED PERSONS BY FULL OR PART-TIME STATUS, AND BY REASON FOR PART-TIME STATUS, SOUTHEASTERN STATES, 1990 ANNUAL AVERAGES (Numbers in thousands)

State	Total employment	Full-time	Part-time Total		Part-time Economic reasons			Part-time Voluntary reasons	
			Number	Percent of total	Number	%	Percent of total Rank	Number	Percent of total
TENNESSEE	2,272	1,941	331	14.57	53	2.33	38	278	12.24
Alabama	1,764	1,513	251	14.23	56	3.17	18	195	11.05
Arkansas	1,056	887	169	16.00	35	3.31	16	134	12.69
Florida	5,987	5,043	944	15.77	166	2.77	27	778	12.99
Georgia	3,041	2,627	414	13.61	57	1.87	44	358	11.77
Kentucky	1,664	1,375	289	17.37	55	3.31	17	234	14.06
Louisiana	1,758	1,472	285	16.21	65	3.70	12	220	12.51
Mississippi	1,095	935	160	14.61	41	3.74	11	119	10.87
North Carolina	3,262	2,788	474	14.53	70	2.15	41	404	12.39
South Carolina	1,643	1,399	243	14.79	50	3.04	22	193	11.75
Virginia	3,060	2,605	454	14.84	68	2.22	39	387	12.65
West Virginia	708	588	120	16.95	37	5.23	2	83	11.72

Note: Persons employed on a part-time basis for economic reasons are those working fewer than 35 hours per week whose employers are experiencing slack work, material shortages, or repairs to plant and equipment or persons who are unable to find a full-time job.

Source: U.S. Department of Labor, Bureau of Labor Statistics, *Geographic Profile of Employment and Unemployment, 1990.*

TABLE 20.6-- GROSS PROPERTY, PLANT AND EQUIPMENT OF NONBANK U.S. AFFILIATES OF FOREIGN COMPANIES, SOUTHEASTERN STATES AND UNITED STATES, 1987–1990[1] [In millions of dollars]

State	1990 Total	1990 Commercial property	1989 Total	1989 Commercial property	1988 Total	1988 Commercial property	1987 Total	1987 Commercial property
TENNESSEE	10,124	1,681	8,940	1,486	7,292	1,135	5,604	780
Alabama	7,346	480	5,973	609	4,852	466	4,011	163
Arkansas	2,478	480	2,312	485	1,707	375	1,289	252
Florida	17,677	8,527	14,902	7,317	11,905	6,190	9,574	5,105
Georgia	16,506	5,485	13,895	4,806	10,856	3,678	9,059	3,092
Kentucky	9,011	835	6,799	601	5,581	655	4,557	641
Louisiana	17,221	1,492	15,994	1,216	15,898	1,323	14,292	1,320
Mississippi	2,912	236	2,686	224	2,579	193	2,425	191
North Carolina	15,160	2,000	13,619	1,702	11,792	1,584	9,727	1,509
South Carolina	10,153	1,400	8,664	1,516	7,289	1,002	6,182	732
Virginia	10,618	3,052	9,155	2,583	7,982	2,040	6,808	2,029
West Virginia	8,023	185	5,532	271	5,020	191	5,060	78
UNITED STATES[1]	572,342	146,611	489,461	124,839	418,069	104,048	353,278	89,919

Note: A U.S. affiliate is a U.S. business enterprise in which there is foreign direct investment–that is, in which a single foreign person owns or controls, directly or indirectly, 10 percent or more of the voting securities of an incorporated U.S. business enterprise or an equivalent interest in an unincorporated U.S. business enterprise. An affiliate is called a U.S. affiliate to denote that it is located in the United States.

1. More recent data are provided for the nation only (in millions of dollars):

   1992 gross property, plant and equipment 660,817 and commercial property 168, 277
   1991 gross property, plant and equipment 640,140 and commercial property 165,759.

Source: U.S. Department of Commerce, Bureau of Economic Analysis, *Survey of Current Business*, Volume 74, Number 7, July 1994.

TABLE 20.7-- TOTAL AND MANUFACTURING EMPLOYMENT OF NONBANK U.S. AFFILIATES OF
FOREIGN COMPANIES, SOUTHEASTERN STATES AND UNITED STATES, 1987–1992
[In thousands of employees]

State	Total employment					
	1992	1991	1990	1989	1988	1987
TENNESSEE	121.7	120.4	115.8	114.1	98.2	82.2
Alabama	60.7	65.0	55.0	64.7	42.0	35.4
Arkansas	30.8	30.4	29.7	32.2	25.7	21.3
Florida	194.9	211.2	200.1	178.3	154.1	124.0
Georgia	154.3	162.6	159.8	157.2	143.7	122.4
Kentucky	69.4	71.3	63.4	56.0	47.7	38.5
Louisiana	62.1	62.2	61.2	65.2	56.2	51.3
Mississippi	23.8	23.6	22.8	24.1	20.2	17.5
North Carolina	191.3	181.0	180.8	176.7	157.4	134.1
South Carolina	111.1	110.1	102.4	101.4	85.1	75.7
Virginia	119.9	119.1	112.2	106.2	92.7	79.7
West Virginia	34.1	34.7	35.2	29.4	26.6	25.4
UNITED STATES	4,705.5	4,871.9	4,705.3	4,511.5	3,844.2	3,224.3

	Manufacturing employment					
TENNESSEE	75.0	71.3	68.5	68.3	62.0	51.9
Alabama	38.1	36.9	34.8	27.0	25.0	21.7
Arkansas	18.7	18.5	18.7	18.3	15.2	11.2
Florida	45.0	48.7	47.4	44.8	33.7	30.6
Georgia	70.9	74.4	71.6	68.4	62.2	55.8
Kentucky	445.9	47.4	41.1	37.4	27.1	21.1
Louisiana	24.3	23.1	20.9	20.4	16.8	15.8
Mississippi	13.5	14.3	14.8	15.2	13.6	11.2
North Carolina	116.8	108.6	107.3	101.1	93.4	74.8
South Carolina	65.7	63.7	63.4	52.3	47.4	37.7
Virginia	50.2	48.4	49.3	45.1	39.6	30.5
West Virginia	19.5	18.1	17.9	17.6	14.7	14.5
UNITED STATES	2,014.5	2,053.1	2,005.4	1,885.4	1,611.9	1,315.4

Note: For definition of a U.S. affiliate, see Table 20.6.

Source: U.S. Department of Commerce, Bureau of Economic Analysis, *Survey of Current Business*, Volume 74,
Number 7, July 1994.

TABLE 20.8-- EMPLOYMENT OF NONBANK U.S. AFFILIATES OF FOREIGN COMPANIES, BY COUNTRY OF ULTIMATE BENEFICIAL OWNER, SOUTHEASTERN STATES AND UNITED STATES, 1992 [In thousands of employees]

State	All countries	Canada	Europe						Latin America and other Western Hemisphere	Africa	Middle East	Asia and Pacific			
			Total	France	Federal Republic of Germany	Netherlands	Switzerland	United Kingdom				Total	Australia	Japan	United States
TENNESSEE	121.7	16.9	76.3	9.6	7.3	6.2	6.9	30.7	1.6	0.2	0.3	26.1	4.7	20.3	0.5
Alabama	60.7	7.6	38.6	12.8	4.0	1.6	4.2	8.8	G	0.5	0.4	10.8	1.9	7.8	G
Arkansas	30.8	5.8	15.7	2.7	0.9	1.8	1.7	4.4	F	0.5	(a)	6.7	1.4	4.9	G
Florida	194.9	20.4	125.1	18.0	18.1	9.6	8.3	42.7	13.5	0.2	1.9	30.6	4.8	22.1	3.2
Georgia	154.3	21.2	95.6	12.7	13.1	10.4	10.1	34.5	G	2.3	2.8	28.7	5.3	21.0	G
Kentucky	69.4	10.7	33.9	4.7	7.9	2.4	1.8	12.8	1.1	0.2	0.9	21.7	1.2	19.1	0.9
Louisiana	62.1	10.0	36.8	3.6	7.0	7.3	2.6	11.6	8.5	0.1	0.7	5.2	1.0	2.3	0.9
Mississippi	23.8	4.3	13.8	2.2	2.3	0.7	2.7	3.8	1.7	0.3	(a)	3.2	1.0	2.0	0.4
North Carolina	191.3	29.0	140.1	14.0	29.5	6.7	12.6	43.0	1.5	0.2	0.7	16.1	1.6	13.3	3.7
South Carolina	111.1	8.4	84.6	15.0	17.4	18.3	5.1	14.0	G	0.3	0.7	13.0	0.6	11.7	G
Virginia	119.9	15.3	79.8	8.5	15.1	4.9	5.7	23.3	H	(a)	0.9	16.5	0.6	15.0	H
West Virginia	34.1	7.1	23.9	2.1	7.1	2.8	3.2	7.0	1.0	(a)	(a)	1.9	(a)	1.9	0.0
UNITED STATES	4,705.5	587.9	2,888.8	358.7	519.5	306.1	295.1	961.4	132.0	15.7	31.0	956.0	137.8	728.2	94.1

Note: For definition of a U.S. affiliate, see Table 20.6. An "ultimate beneficial owner" (UBO) is that person, proceeding up a U.S. affiliate's ownership chain, beginning with and including the foreign parent, that is not owned more than 50 percent by another person. The foreign parent is the first foreign person in the affiliate's ownership chain. Unlike the foreign parent, the UBO of an affiliate may be located in the United States. The UBO of each U.S. affiliate is identified to ascertain the person that ultimately owns or controls and that, therefore, ultimately derives the benefits from owning or controlling the U.S. affiliate. Size ranges are given where employment is suppressed: F–500 to 999; G–1,000 to 2,499; H–2,500 to 4,999.

a. Less than 50 employees.

Source: U.S. Department of Commerce, Bureau of Economic Analysis, *Survey of Current Business*, Volume 74, Number 7, July 1994.

TABLE 20.9– AVERAGE ANNUAL PAY, SOUTHEASTERN STATES AND UNITED STATES, 1989–1991

| State | Average annual pay | | | | Percent change | |
| | 1991ᴾ | | 1990ʳ | 1989 | | |
	Amount	Rank			1990–1991	1989–1990
TENNESSEE	21,541	29	20,611	19,712	4.5	4.6
Alabama	21,287	33	20,468	19,593	4.0	4.5
Arkansas	19,008	46	18,204	17,418	4.4	4.5
Florida	21,991	27	21,030	20,072	4.6	4.8
Georgia	23,164	20	22,115	21,072	4.7	4.9
Kentucky	20,730	39	19,947	19,001	3.9	5.0
Louisiana	21,501	30	20,646	19,750	4.1	4.5
Mississippi	18,411	48	17,718	17,047	3.9	3.9
North Carolina	21,087	34	20,220	19,321	4.3	4.7
South Carolina	20,439	41	19,668	18,797	3.9	4.6
Virginia	23,804	16	22,750	21,882	4.6	4.0
West Virginia	21,356	31	20,715	19,788	3.1	4.7
UNITED STATES	24,575	(X)	23,602	22,563	4.1	4.6

Note: For workers covered by state unemployment insurance laws and for federal civilian workers covered by unemployment compensation for federal employees, approximately 90 percent of total civilian employment. Excludes most agricultural workers on small farms, all Armed Forces, elected officials in most states, railroad employees, most domestic workers, employees of certain nonprofit organizations and most self-employed individuals. Pay includes bonuses, cash value of meals and lodging, and tips and other gratuities.

(X) Not applicable.

p preliminary.

r revised.

Source: U.S. Department of Commerce, Bureau of the Census, *Statistical Abstract of the United States, 1993*, and earlier editions.

TABLE 20.10--U.S. PATENTS, BY TYPE, SOUTHEASTERN STATES AND UNITED STATES, 1991

State	Total Number	Rank	Inventions	Designs	Botanical plants	Reissues
TENNESSEE	590	25	515	68	5	2
Alabama	370	32	319	50	1	0
Arkansas	149	41	113	36	0	0
Florida	1,950	10	1,688	247	10	5
Georgia	757	22	641	109	5	2
Kentucky	371	31	321	49	0	1
Louisiana	503	27	469	33	0	1
Mississippi	124	42	98	25	0	1
North Carolina	980	16	882	95	2	1
South Carolina	450	28	409	37	1	3
Virginia	938	18	827	108	0	3
West Virginia	170	40	162	7	0	1
UNITED STATES[1]	57,656	(X)	51,176	6,072	237	171

Note: Includes only U.S. patents granted to residents of the United States and territories.

1. Includes patents not distributed by state.

(X) Not applicable.

Source: U.S. Department of Commerce, Bureau of the Census, *Statistical Abstract of the United States, 1993.*

TABLE 20.11–ENERGY PRICES, BY TYPE, SOUTHEASTERN STATES AND UNITED STATES, 1989 [In dollars per million Btu]

State	All energy		Petroleum		Motor gasoline		Natural gas		Coal		Electricity	
	Price	Rank	Price	Rank	Price	Rank	Price	Rank	Price	Rank	Price	Rank
TENNESSEE	8.03	21	7.27	13	8.25	22	3.87	34	1.36	35	15.91	41
Alabama	7.04	40	6.43	38	7.96	35	3.92	33	1.83	7	16.43	36
Arkansas	7.56	33	6.74	29	7.69	44	3.39	43	1.64	20	19.04	18
Florida	9.83	6	6.04	46	7.68	45	3.02	45	1.79	9	20.45	16
Georgia	8.15	19	6.41	39	7.12	50	4.76	12	1.75	15	18.70	21
Kentucky	7.47	34	7.07	16	8.08	31	4.07	27	1.22	44	14.17	44
Louisiana	5.18	50	5.26	49	7.90	37	2.13	49	1.62	24	17.64	26
Mississippi	7.13	39	5.84	47	8.07	32	2.89	46	1.67	18	18.25	24
North Carolina	9.31	9	7.27	12	8.10	30	4.56	17	1.77	11	18.33	23
South Carolina	8.52	14	7.05	17	7.84	38	4.22	21	1.71	17	16.53	35
Virginia	8.39	16	6.97	20	8.55	13	4.95	11	1.57	26	17.26	30
West Virginia	6.13	47	6.97	21	8.52	14	4.07	26	1.43	33	14.04	45
UNITED STATES	7.72	(X)	6.48	(X)	8.01	(X)	3.85	(X)	1.48	(X)	18.98	(X)

Note: Rank is among the fifty states.
(X) Not applicable.
Source: Energy Information Administration, *State Energy Price and Expenditure Report, 1989.*

771

TABLE 20.12–STATE LEGISLATIVE ARTS APPROPRIATIONS, SOUTHEASTERN STATES, 1980–1992, SELECTED FISCAL YEARS [In thousands of dollars]

State	Total	1992 Per capita[1] Amount ($)	Rank	1991	1990	1989	1985	1980
TENNESSEE	1,422	3.53	5	4,299	3,783	3,506	719	517
Alabama	2,079	1.99	18	1,579	1,949	1,476	1,000	525
Arkansas	1,032	2.32	8	973	1,016	1,021	796	846
Florida	16,180	0.83	43	23,386	23,635	24,179	9,045	2,378
Georgia	3,059	2.21	11	3,338	3,413	3,248	1,720	1,102
Kentucky	3,348	1.12	36	3,202	2,387	2,368	1,536	857
Louisiana	859	4.99	3	936	909	996	1,133	857
Mississippi	489	5.35	2	514	497	496	436	307
North Carolina	4,729	1.45	25	5,428 [a]	4,978	4,996	2,921	1,379
South Carolina	3,525	1.02	40	3,633	3,534	3,159	1,858	941
Virginia	1,500	4.25	4	4,016	5,392	3,771	1,748	1,230
West Virginia	1,727	1.05	39	2,384 [b]	1,675 [b]	1,133 [b]	1,849	1,563

1. Based on enumerated resident population as of July 1, 1992.

a. Includes $522,000 one-time appropriation.

b. Excludes administrative expenses.

Source: U.S. Department of Commerce, Bureau of the Census, *Statistical Abstract of the United States, 1993*, and earlier editions.

TABLE 20.13–STATE GOVERNMENT PER CAPITA GENERAL EXPENDITURES, BY TYPE OF EXPENDITURE, SOUTHEASTERN STATES AND UNITED STATES, 1992

State	Total general expenditures ($1,000)	Per capita general expenditures ($)											
		Total[1]		Education		Public welfare		Hospitals		Highways		Police	
		Amount	Rank	Amount	Rank	Amount	Rank	Amount	Rank	Amount	Rank	Amount	Rank
TENNESSEE	9,632,969	1917.4	45	617.2	47	225.8	24	560.6	19	83.0	29	13.0	46
Alabama	8,788,293	2124.8	37	863.3	23	168.0	43	448.1	35	188.8	2	18.8	31
Arkansas	5,061,654	2109.9	38	884.9	21	240.4	19	490.5	26	75.2	34	16.1	36
Florida	24,851,056	1842.5	48	653.5	44	161.3	44	395.5	45	37.6	47	16.7	34
Georgia	12,781,046	1893.2	46	767.9	37	129.7	50	490.8	25	78.7	31	15.0	39
Kentucky	9,235,218	2459.5	20	951.4	13	248.7	17	634.6	13	77.4	33	28.1	12
Louisiana	10,682,706	2491.9	19	860.0	24	205.3	32	593.6	15	170.2	4	27.9	14
Mississippi	5,216,887	1995.8	43	762.5	40	206.1	31	463.1	31	92.5	24	14.1	40
North Carolina	14,671,144	2144.0	36	922.5	18	211.6	29	431.0	38	93.5	23	21.8	24
South Carolina	7,968,594	2211.7	29	852.2	25	147.1	46	449.0	34	156.7	7	22.7	20
Virginia	12,694,076	1990.6	44	773.2	35	238.6	20	328.4	50	150.5	8	40.6	4
West Virginia	4,395,674	2425.9	22	967.6	12	281.5	10	603.8	14	49.3	42	13.2	45
UNITED STATES	611,921,919	2404.5	(X)	831.3	(X)	191.6	(X)	614.4	(X)	102.7	(X)	21.6	(X)

1. Includes categories not shown separately.

(X) Not applicable.

Source: U.S. Department of Commerce, Bureau of the Census, *State Government Finances: 1992.*

TABLE 20.14–STATE GOVERNMENT PER CAPITA TAX COLLECTIONS, BY TYPE OF TAX, SOUTHEASTERN STATES, 1991

State	Total tax collections ($1,000)	Per capita tax collections ($)											
		Total[1]		General sales		Personal income		Motor fuel		Motor vehicle license		Death and gift	
		Amount	Rank	Amount	Rank	Amount	Rank	Amount	Rank	Amount	Rank	Amount	Rank
TENNESSEE	4,310,573	870.30	48	477.14	10	19.59	43	128.26	3	30.76	39	8.89	30
Alabama	3,942,565	964.19	44	256.67	41	287.17	35	71.03	41	34.49	35	4.47	42
Arkansas	2,366,105	997.51	42	369.69	26	334.69	32	94.83	25	31.28	38	3.60	45
Florida	13,764,055	1,036.68	39	612.99	5	(X)	(X)	61.89	46	40.15	25	22.18	9
Georgia	7,154,525	1,080.25	35	401.15	21	445.07	16	68.12	44	11.89	50	6.23	34
Kentucky	5,043,183	1,358.25	13	350.03	32	456.06	14	94.36	27	38.00	29	18.51	12
Louisiana	4,309,467	1,013.52	40	307.64	39	188.99	38	104.37	15	18.41	49	9.92	26
Mississippi	2,460,836	949.40	46	432.16	16	185.03	39	117.71	7	24.79	45	2.99	46
North Carolina	7,850,043	1,165.21	26	250.83	42	524.64	10	122.52	4	31.81	37	12.54	19
South Carolina	3,933,214	1,104.84	31	403.78	19	389.51	24	95.54	24	20.35	47	10.13	25
Virginia	6,852,365	1,090.10	33	247.99	44	514.80	11	98.25	20	39.12	26	7.46	32
West Virginia	2,328,132	1,292.69	17	453.84	12	320.01	34	114.37	9	46.46	16	4.20	44

Note: Rank is among 50 states and is based on unrounded figures.

(X) Not applicable.

1. Includes categories not shown separately.

Source: U.S. Department of Commerce, Bureau of the Census, *State Government Tax Collections in 1991*.

FIGURE 20.1
State Tax Collections Per Capita by Selected Categories
Southeastern States, 1991

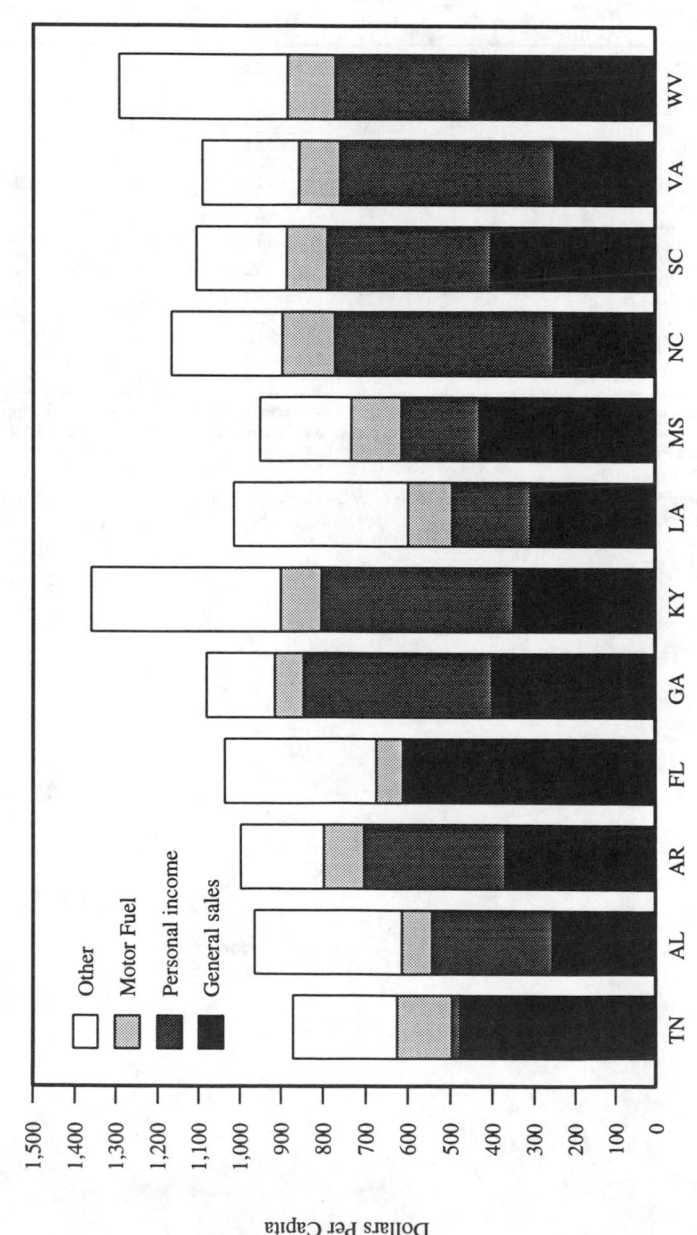

Source: U.S. Department of Commerce, Bureau of the Census, *State Government Tax Collections in 1991.*

TABLE 20.15--PUBLIC AID RECIPIENTS AS PERCENT OF POPULATION, SOUTHEASTERN STATES
AND UNITED STATES, 1980, 1990 AND 1991

State	1991 Percent	1991 Rank	1990 Percent	1990 Rank	1980 Percent	1980 Rank
TENNESSEE	7.9	8	7.2	9	6.4	19
Alabama	6.6	17	6.5	14	8.1	7
Arkansas	6.4	20	6.3	17	7.2	12
Florida	5.3	33	4.6	35	4.4	35
Georgia	7.9	8	7.1	10	6.9	16
Kentucky	9.1	4	7.9	6	7.2	12
Louisiana	9.7	3	9.8	2	8.3	5
Mississippi	11.4	1	11.4	1	11.4	1
North Carolina	6.5	19	5.7	23	5.8	27
South Carolina	6.3	23	5.8	20	7.6	8
Virginia	4.3	42	3.9	42	4.6	32
West Virginia	8.9	5	8.8	4	6.0	24
UNITED STATES	7.0	(X)	6.5	(X)	6.5	(X)

Note: Total recipients as of June of Aid to Families with Dependent Children and of Federal Supplemental Security
Income as percent of resident population. Based on resident population as of July 1 for 1980 and 1991; April 1
for 1990.

(X) Not applicable.

Source: U.S. Department of Commerce, Bureau of the Census, *Statistical Abstract of the United States, 1993*, and
earlier editions.

TABLE 20.16—RESEARCH AND DEVELOPMENT EXPENDITURES AT DOCTORATE-GRANTING INSTITUTIONS, BY SOURCE OF FUNDS, SOUTHEASTERN STATES, FISCAL YEAR 1991 [In thousands of dollars]

State	Total		Industry		Federal government		State and local government		Universities and colleges		Other sources	
	Amount	Rank	Amount	Rank	Amount	Rank	Amount	Rank	Amount	Rank	Amount	Rank
TENNESSEE	240,054	25	12,351	28	146,573	21	32,927	18	34,772	29	13,431	24
Alabama	244,901	24	20,348	16	125,184	25	26,256	22	52,460	22	20,653	17
Arkansas	55,081	42	4,514	42	20,178	45	13,958	30	12,945	39	3,486	39
Florida	438,054	12	35,690	12	220,683	13	36,736	15	116,339	9	28,606	12
Georgia	484,019	11	39,882	10	238,032	12	43,222	13	149,775	6	13,108	26
Kentucky	97,989	35	10,569	30	38,386	39	6,122	39	38,008	28	4,904	35
Louisiana	239,533	26	15,539	26	98,834	28	62,167	7	48,024	25	14,969	23
Mississippi	96,471	36	8,879	32	49,424	34	20,886	24	11,662	43	5,620	34
North Carolina	501,841	10	55,079	6	303,921	9	71,990	5	51,758	24	19,093	19
South Carolina	151,204	31	15,903	25	54,045	32	16,858	27	54,011	20	10,387	31
Virginia	337,874	16	31,347	13	178,896	17	52,727	10	52,191	23	22,713	16
West Virginia	50,772	43	11,170	29	20,479	44	1,564	49	13,191	38	4,368	37

Note: Rank is among the fifty states and the District of Columbia.

Source: National Science Foundation, *Selected Data on Academic Science and Engineering R&D Expenditures: Fiscal Year 1991*.

TABLE 20.17–VALUE OF EXPORTS, SOUTHEASTERN STATES, 1991 AND 1992 [Dollar amounts in millions]

State	1992			1991		
	Value	Percent of U.S.	Rank	Value	Percent of U.S.	Rank
TENNESSEE	5,156	1.4	21	4,344	1.2	21
Alabama	3,629	1.0	26	3,325	0.9	26
Arkansas	1,324	0.3	37	1,147	0.3	37
Florida	14,431	3.8	9	13,257	3.8	9
Georgia	7,652	2.0	15	6,815	1.9	15
Kentucky	3,648	1.0	27	3,217	0.9	27
Louisiana	16,151	4.3	6	15,456	4.4	6
Mississippi	1,963	0.5	34	1,738	0.5	34
North Carolina	10,374	2.7	14	8,540	2.4	14
South Carolina	4,222	1.1	23	3,741	1.1	23
Virginia	9,784	2.6	11	10,004	2.8	11
West Virginia	1,746	0.5	35	1,656	0.5	35

Note: Exports are on a f.a.s. value basis.
Source: U.S. Department of Commerce, Bureau of the Census, *Statistical Abstract of the United States, 1993.*

TABLE 20.18.–TENNESSEE: SIGNIFICANT RANKINGS AMONG 50 STATES

Item	Rank	Tennessee	U.S.
Total population, 1992 (1,000)	17th	5,024	255,082
Land area, 1990 (square miles)	34th	41,220	3,536,342
Population per square mile, 1992	19th	121.9	72.1
Percent change in population, 1980–1990	24th	6.2 %	9.8 %
Median age, 1990 (years)	13th	33.6	32.9
Population 65 years old and over, 1992	24th	12.7 %	12.7 %
Black population, 1990	10th	16.0 %	12.1 %
Hispanic population, 1990	44th	0.7%	9.0 %
Metropolitan population, 1990	31st	65.5%	79.4 %
Persons living in different state in 1985 (5 yrs. +) 1990	25th	11.0%	9.4 %
Birth rate,[1] 1990	32nd	15.4	16.7
Infant mortality rate,[2] 1990	10th	10.3	9.2
Marriage rate,[1] 1991 (preliminary)	5th	13.7	9.4
Divorce rate,[1] 1991 (preliminary)	5th	6.5	4.7
Abortions per 1,000 live births, 1988	26th	292	404
Physicians per 100,000 population, 1990	21st	196	216
Community hospital beds per 100,000 population, 1991	8th	474	366
Total housing units, 1990 (1,000)	18th	2,026	102,264
Built between 1980 and 1990	15th	31.1 %	25.9 %
Prior to 1940	37th	16.7%	26.1 %
Percent condominium	30th	2.19%	4.74%
Median value of specified owner-occupied units, 1990	37th	$58,400	$79,100
Median gross rent of specified renter-occupied units, 1990	38th	$273	$374
Violent crime rate,[3] 1991	15th	726	758
Adults under correctional supervision, rate,[4] 1990	31st	174.2	235.0
Public elementary and secondary schools, 1992			
Expenditures per capita	50th	$611	$957
Current expenditures per pupil	47th	$3,736	$5,466
Public school teachers' salaries, 1992	36th	$28,600	$34,100
Percent high school graduates (25 years old +), 1990	45th	67.1 %	75.2 %
Percent Bachelor's degree or higher (25 years old +), 1990	43rd	16.0 %	20.3 %
Enrollment, higher education, 1990 (1,000)	21st	238	14,359
Percent change in nonagricultural employment, 1980–1992	16th	27.8 %	19.9 %
Unemployment rate, 1992	33rd	6.4 %	7.4 %
Manufacturing employment, 1992			
Number (1,000)	13th	513	18,190
Percent of total employed	7th	23.0 %	16.8 %
Average annual pay, 1991	29th	$21,541	$24,575
Median household money income, 1989	39th	$24,807	$30,056

TABLE 20.18–TENNESSEE: SIGNIFICANT RANKINGS AMONG 50 STATES (Continued)

Item	Rank	Tennessee	U.S.
Median family income, 1989	38th	$29,546	$35,225
Per capita money income, 1989	36th	$12,255	$14,420
Percent of households with income $75,000 or more, 1989	45th	5.6 %	9.5 %
Percent of population receiving food stamps, 1989	7th	10.0 %	7.6 %
Percent below poverty level, 1989			
Persons	12th	15.7 %	13.1 %
Children under 18 years	12th	20.7 %	17.9 %
Families	9th	12.4 %	10.0 %
Female householder families	16th	45.2 %	42.3 %
State and local governments, 1991			
Direct general expenditures per capita	47th	$1,735	$2,199
General revenues per capita	46th	$1,693	$2,188
Debt outstanding per capita	45th	$563	$1,370
Federal funds per capita, 1992	23rd	$4,485	$4,631
Percent of population casting votes for			
U.S. President, 1992	39th	52.4 %	55.2 %
Automobile registration per 1,000 population, 1991	2nd	735	567
Means of transportation to work, 1990			
Percent of workers commuting in carpools	20th	14.5 %	2.0 %
Percent drove alone	7th	78.7 %	73.2 %
Percent using public transportation	33rd	1.3 %	5.3 %
Vehicle traffic fatalities per 100,000 population, 1991	11th	22.5	17.3
Energy consumption per capita, 1990 (mil. Btu)	17th	359.4	326.2
Temperature, average annual (°F)	14th	58.5	53.2
Precipitation, average annual (inches)	5th	51.7	28.8
Number of hazardous waste sites, 1992	25th	14	1,224
Domestic travel expenditures, 1990 (millions)	15th	$5,780	$290,446
Percent change in average value per farm acre, 1985–1990	17th	11.4 %	-2.8 %
Percent change in land in farms, 1982–1987	32nd	-6.0	-2.3
Farm debt/asset ratio, 1991	37th	11.1	14.6
Percent change in housing starts, 1991–1992	25th	19.1 %	18.3 %
Manufacturing value added, 1991 (billions)	15th	$32.5	$1,313.8
Percent change in retail sales per household, 1990–1991	15th	1.7 %	-0.2 %

1. Per 1,000 resident population.   2. Deaths of infants under 1 year old per 1,000 live births. Excludes fetal deaths.

3. Per 100,000 resident population.   4. Per 10,000 persons 18 years old and over.

Source: U.S. Department of Commerce, Bureau of the Census, *Statistical Abstract of the United States, 1993*; 1990 Census of Population and Housing, *Summary Population and Housing Characteristics, United States*.

INDEX

M

MSA (See Metropolitan Statistical Area)
Machinery, 191
  Manufacturing statistics, 185, 187, 188, 194, 195, 196, 197, 198, 199, 200
  Pollution abatement, 189
Manufacturing
  Capital expenditures
    Cities, selected, 209
    Counties, 205
    MSA's, 193, 194, 195, 196, 197, 198, 199, 200
    New, by sector, 185
    Pollution abatement, 190
  Durable goods
    Hours and earnings, 188
  Earnings, 132, 185, 188, 192, 193, 194, 195, 196, 197, 198, 199, 200, 205, 209, 213, 214
  Employment, 132, 133, 140, 142, 146, 184, 186, 191, 215, 216
    By sector, 185, 187, 191
    Cities, selected, 209
    Counties, 201, 205
    Foreign investment, 767
    MSA's, 193, 194, 195, 196, 197, 198, 199, 200
    Southeastern states, 213, 215, 216, 764
  Establishments, 184
    By employment size, 187, 201
    By sector, 185, 187
    Cities, selected, 209
    Counties, 201, 205
    MSA's, 193, 194, 195, 196, 197, 198, 199, 200
    Southeastern states, 213
  Export statistics, 191, 216
  Gross state product, 58, 61
  Hours, 188, 192
  Income, personal, 64, 69, 72, 75, 78, 81, 84, 87
  Layoffs, 173
  Lumber and wood products, 450
  Nondurable goods
    Hours and earnings, 188
  Payroll
    By sector, 185
    Cities, selected, 209
    Counties, 201, 205
    MSA's, 193, 194, 195, 196, 197, 198, 199, 200
    Southeastern states, 213
  Pollution abatement expenditures, 189, 190
  Production workers, 184, 188
    By sector, 185

  Cities, selected, 209
  Counties, 205
  Earnings, 188, 192, 214
  Hours, 188, 192
  MSA's, 193, 194, 195, 196, 197, 198, 199, 200
  Southeastern states, 213, 214, 215, 216
  Unemployment insurance claimants, 173
  Union membership, 214
  Value added, 184
    By sector, 185, 186
    Cities, selected, 209
    Counties, 205
    MSA's, 193, 194, 195, 196, 197, 198, 199, 200
    Southeastern states, 213
  Value of shipments, 216
    By sector, 185, 191
    Cities, selected, 209
    Counties, 205
    MSA's, 193, 194, 195, 196, 197, 198, 199, 200
  Wages and salaries, 132, 133, 188
Map
  Birth rates, 688
  Congressional districts, 540
  Development districts, 528
  Education expenditures, 650
  Equalized tax rates, 582
  Farm products sold, value, 429
  Gas pipeline, 384
  Higher education institutions, 642
  Highways, 346
  Housing unit values, 244
  Judicial districts, 534
  MSA's, xii
  Mining, 219
  National parks, 476
  Newspapers, 333
  Physiographic, 455
  Population, 16
  Railroads, 375
  State parks, 476
  Telephone availability, 328
  Tennessee Valley Authority
    Generating plants, 390
  Transfer payments, 721
  Unemployment rates, 162
  Vocational technical institutions, 645
  Wages and salaries, 167
Marriages, 705
  Counties, 694
Media (See Communications)
Medicaid (See also Medical assistance
  or Public assistance and
    Social insurance), 728

INDEX

129664